Bernard Shaw: The Diaries, 1885–1897
Volume II

Bernard Shaw:
The Diaries
1885–1897

With early autobiographical notebooks
and diaries, and an abortive 1917 diary

Volume II

Edited & annotated by

Stanley Weintraub

*Transliterated by Stanley Rypins, with additional
transliterations & transcriptions by Blanche Patch,
Barbara Smoker, Louise Goldschmidt, John
Wardrop, Ray Weintraub, and Suzanne Wills*

The Pennsylvania State University Press
University Park and London

For my London sleuths,
Eileen and Alan Hanley-Browne

Bernard Shaw diaries and journals, and extracts in editorial notes from Shaw material Copyright © 1986 The Trustees of the British Museum, The Governors and Guardians of the National Gallery of Ireland and Royal Academy of Dramatic Art.

Introduction and editorial notes Copyright © 1986 Stanley Weintraub

Library of Congress Cataloging in Publication Data
Shaw, Bernard, 1856–1950.
Bernard Shaw : the diaries, 1885–1897 with early autobiographical notebooks and diaries, and an abortive 1917 diary.
Includes index.
1. Shaw, Bernard, 1856–1950—Diaries. 2. Dramatists, Irish—19th century—Diaries.
I. Weintraub, Stanley, 1929–   . II. Title.
PR5366.A33   1985   828′.91203 [B]   84–43065
ISBN 0–271–00386–3 (set)

Contents

Diary 1891

Notes

INTRODUCTIONS

Van Dyck (Belgian diplomat) at Fitzroy Square by Karl Armbruster. 17th May.

HEALTH

On the 7th June I caught the influenza. For a few days before I had noticed that my voice had lost its tone; but I was not ill. On this day I got a headache and what I thought was an attack of indigestion, to which, however, I am not subject. I had a very bad night—feverish and delirious. Next day I was weak and ill as if sickening from the fever—headache, pains in the back, weakness, nausea, etc. I did my day's work and forced myself to eat as usual. In the evening I got the inflammation in the eye. That night I slept well; and next day I was strong again, though the pain in the eye remained, with sore throat and local pain. Next day my head was stuffy and uneasy and I was the least bit in the world feverish, as if the affair were a cold in the head. Although it merely lasted for four days, yet it left a headache behind it which at last grew so unpleasant that on the 19th I went down for a couple of days to Broadstairs and baked myself on the sands there. This got rid of it, though it returned for a while the evening I came up to town. I suspect it had much to do with the following.

On the 25th July my right calf, in which there has been for a long time a slight tendency to varicoses, developed this tendency rather emphatically. After a few days it passed away. I took some of Mattei's anti-angiotico. On the 22nd August on coming up from Oxted, where I had been staying a few days with the Salts', I had an attack of looseness of the bowels, not bad enough to be called diarrhea, but still bad enough to disturb me once in the night. Next day as I had to deliver three addresses in the open air, I took out with me a tube of Mattei's antiscrofoloso giappone, and took it whenever I felt troubled. It kept it off; and I was well next day.

On the 9th September I caught what I thought was a slight cold; but next day it became a pretty bad cold in the head, and lasted until the 16th, though bad only for three days.

On the evening of the 11th November I caught—or became conscious of having caught—a cold. It was, I thought, a fairly bad one; but on the night of the 13th, when I thought it was mending, it became very troublesome, so that I could not sleep, but lay reading for the great part of the night. I slept well on the following night, after which matters began to mend. I got rid of it very slowly and incompletely.

On the evening of the 9th December, having been working late at nights and having no change or relaxation for a longish time, I got a bad attack, slept feverishly, and could do nothing next day; when, however, I mended in the evening.

> Mattei's anti-angiotico was a now obsolete remedy for varicoses, compounded and sold in "globules" (like the *scrofoloso giappone* mentioned several lines later) by the chemist (pharmacist) Mattei, of Pall Mall East, at 8/6 per dozen.

January

1   *Albert Hall.* The Messiah. *Newton Hall. Address, "The Positivists," by Frederic Harrison.*

Sang all morning. After dinner went to the Stores to get my watch. Went on to the Museum and there read *The New Review* which I had just purchased. Much exasperated to find that Grove had cut the reference to my atheism out of the article, in spite of his express agreement not to alter it. Continued reading the 1847 debates. Webb and Wallas were at Newton Hall. We walked together as far as Webb's door, stopping in Oxford St.—or rather in Holborn to get some supper. I walked back with Wallas to Tottenham Court Rd. and came back here. Wrote a letter or two before going to bed.

Star $\frac{1}{2}$d   Dinner 1/1$\frac{1}{2}$ New glass in Watch 6d   *New Review* 7d
Train to Farringdon 2d   Maccaroni &c at Romano's 1/–

"The Socialist Ideal. II: Politics," *New Review*, January 1891 (C771).

2 *Fabian Society. Bloomsbury Hall. Hart St. E. Harold Spender on "The Land Purchase and Land Nationalization in Ireland." 20.*

Still working my voice. After dinner went to the Museum. At 17 went to the Aerated Bread Shop in Oxford Circus and had tea there with F. Emery by appointment. Went back to the Museum and worked at the Eight Hours business until it was time to go to the Fabian, where I spoke. Webb walked back with me.

Star $\frac{1}{2}$d   Dinner 1/1$\frac{1}{2}$

E. Harold Spender (1864–1926), a journalist, was a Liberal and a Fabian. He would edit several papers, including the *PMG* and the *Daily Chronicle*.

3 *Go down to Bristol by the 11.5 train from Paddington. Stay with H. H. Gore.*

Wrote letters and sang before dinner. Read the old Fabian paper in the train. Watson met me at the station and we took a cab to Franklin Rd. Went to the Pantomime *Aladdin* in the evening with Gore's brother.

Star $\frac{1}{2}$d   Train to Paddington 1$\frac{1}{2}$d   Padd[ington] to Bristol 19/9
Ins[uran]ce 1d   Cab to Franklyn Rd 2/6

"I found myself one evening in Bristol with nothing better to do than to see whether pantomime is really moribund. I am bound to say that it seems to me to be as lively as it was twentyfive years ago. The fairy queen, singing In Old Madrid with reckless irrelevance at the entrance to the cave where Aladdin found the lamp, was listened to with deep respect . . . ; and in the cave itself The Bogie Man, in about fifty verses, took immensely." To G.B.S., writing in his 21 January 1891 column (C775), "the absurdity of the whole affair on the dramatic side was amusing enough from an indulgent holiday point of view. . . . I told Mr Macready Chute, the manager, that he should come to London to learn from our famous stage managers here how to spend ten times as much money on a pantomime for one-tenth of the artistic return."

4 SUNDAY *Lecture for the Bristol Sunday Society on "Ferdinand Lassalle." St. James's Hall. 19. Go down to Gore's schoolroom and talk to the men about [the] Eight Hours [Bill].*

Spent the afternoon reading up Lassalle for the lecture. Small audience—only about 120 people.

5 *°Grossmith's recital. St. James's Hall. 15. °Monday Pop Concert. Stavenhagen. Go up to Jacques' in the evening. 19.*

Read Morris and Magnusson's sagas in the train. May made me a present of a copy the other day. Spent the evening with Jacques. His wife went out to the Popular Concert and returned with Chester. Whilst they were out we played some duets and I sang a bit. JP came in before I went out to Jacques', whilst the rest were out at Georgina's.

Daily News 1d   Train Padd[ington] to Portl[and] Rd 1½d   *Star* ½d
Dinner 1/5½   Telegrams to Thomas &⁓ JP 1/3

> *The Saga Library*, edited by William Morris and Erík Magnússon, I (London, 1890). ▪
> C. Thomas was on the staff of Messrs. Robson &⁓ Son, printer of *The World*. Shaw was
> probably reporting that no G.B.S. music column would be forthcoming for the next issue.

6   *Fabian General Executive. 12 Millbank St. 17.*

Writing letters. Dircks called to borrow *Love Among the Artists*. After the Executive Wallas came with me to the restaurant in Buckingham St., where we had tea. Then he walked with me to Victoria, where I took the train for Shaftesbury Rd. and spent the rest of the evening with FE. Lost the last train back and had to walk home.

Star ½d   Dinner 11½d?   Bus to West[minster] 2d   Cocoa &⁓c at
Buck[in]g[ha]m St 1/–?   Train Ch[arin]g + to Shaft[e]sb[ur]y Rd
(Walked to Victoria) 6d

7   *Lecture at the United Democratic Club, 57 and 58 Chancery Lane, on "Alternatives to Social Democracy." (R. E. Dell) Call on Mrs. Noble at 16 Birchington Rd. W. Hampstead in the afternoon.*

Spent whole day writing a long letter to Janet Achurch in Australia. Went to Mrs. Noble's after dinner.

Star ½d   Dinner 1/1½d?   Train to Marlboro Rd &⁓ back 4d   Train to
Farringdon Rd 2d   Deposit on application for membership of U.D.C.
[United Democratic Club] 1/–

> Gertrude C. Noble was a Fabian.

8   °*Steinway Hall. 20. Hilda Abinger's concert.*

Got at the piano with Mother in the forenoon and spent a long time playing over a lot of oratorio music with her. After dinner went to Archer's to ask about the performance of Ibsen's *Doll's House* announced in *The Star*. Archer was not in but was expected in a few minutes, as was also the Nora of the announced performance, Miss Marie Fraser. She came in presently and turned out to be the young woman with whom I acted at the Novelty Theatre years ago in the performance to copyright Rose's play. When I got home I found JP here: she goes out to the East for the rest of the winter tomorrow. Long parting talk with her. Wrote a letter to the *PMG* complaining of the managers not allowing actors to play in the Ibsen matinees. When it was finished went over with it to Archer's, where I did not arrive until after 23. Left a little before 1.

Star ½d   Dinner 1/1½   Telegram to F. Emery 2/–

Marie Fraser would not display sufficient talent to survive on the commercial stage after 1891. ■ See 6 November 1886 for Rose's farce and Shaw's role in it. ■ JP would be away, largely in Egypt, until late in April, giving Shaw the opportunity to intensify his intimacy with FE. See 27 April 1891. ■ "Ibsen in Difficulties," *PMG* 9 January 1891 (C772).

9 *Press View. Charles Sarton's Sketches from a Caravan Window. Dow-deswell's.*

Up too late to do anything in the morning. After dinner went to the Museum to read a bit for the debate. Went up to Salts' in the evening.

Star ½d   Dinner 1/1½

Charles Sarton's sketches were unreviewed and probably unseen by Shaw.

10 °*Saturday Pop. Stavenhagen.*

Spent the whole day at the Museum reading for the debate with Foote. Wallas was there; and we dined at the Porridge Bowl together. Went to FE in the evening. Jackson came back with me as far as Baker St. in the train from Shepherd's Bush.

Dinner 1/3½ (at PB)   *Spectator* 6d   Train to Shepherd's Bush & back 1/–

11 SUNDAY *Lecture at the Hatcham Liberal Club on "Alternatives to Social Democracy." Supper with Magny.*

Darkness all day from a reddish brown fog. Up very late. Wrote letters. Fog terribly difficult at New Cross. Hardly expected any audience; but about 40 people turned up. Missed the last tram and walked home, the fog having cleared a little. Enjoyed the tramp better than I expected.

Train to Farringdon 2d   Bus to Elephant [and Castle] 1d   Tram El[ephant] to Magny's 2d

12 *Monday Pop. Ilona Eibenschütz.*

Preparing for debate at Museum. I have forgotten the details of the day, as I made this entry on the 21st.

Star ½d   Dinner 1/1½?

Ilona Eibenschütz: Shaw's sketchy and belated reference in the diary is misleading. This was the English debut of the brilliant Hungarian pianist (1873–1967), then seventeen—"a wild young woman" whom G.B.S. predicted in his 21 January 1890 column (C775) would do great things. "In spite of her not being yet at her best, she left the platform amidst such a storm of applause that . . . she dashed at the piano again and gave a brief but terrific sample of her powers of mechanical execution." Although one of the most highly respected performers of her day, her career tapered off after her marriage in 1902.

13 *Lecture at the National Liberal Club on "Politics, Tory, Liberal and Working Class." 20. Dine with Massingham there at 18. Fabian Literature Committee. 12 Millbank St. 17.*

Still preparing for the debate. At the Museum, if I recollect aright. Norman dined with Massingham and myself at the club.

Star $\frac{1}{2}$d   Dinner 1/1$\frac{1}{2}$?

14 *Debate. Eight Hours Question with G. W. Foote at the Hall of Science, 142 Old St., at 20. 1st night. I open. G. Standring in the chair.*

Webb called in the morning bringing me documents on the Eight Hours Question. Hard at the work of preparation all day. Walked back from the debate with Salt and Dryhurst.

Star $\frac{1}{2}$d   Dinner 1/1$\frac{1}{2}$?   Train to Aldersgate (ret[urn] not used) 6d

> G. W. Foote was an orator of the old-fashioned, effulgent school, long on quotations likely to receive applause. Shaw was more direct. Workers, he concluded, will continue to be oppressed by Property exercising itself as the State until they seize the power of the State "to emancipate themselves, and impose their will on the minority which now enslaves them. . . . I believe that they can, by concerted action, not merely in trade unions, but in a united democracy, get complete control of the State, and use its might for their own purposes . . . ; their emancipation will only be delayed until they have learned from experience the true conditions of social freedom."

15 *°3rd London Symphony Concert. St. James's Hall. 20. Debate. Eight Hours Question with G. W. Foote at the Hall of Science. 2nd night. 20. Foote to open.*

Working up material for the debate all day. Salt and I walked back from the debate to Wallas's rooms and went in with him for a while. Dryhurst went on, having to hurry home.

Star $\frac{1}{2}$d   Dinner 1/$\frac{1}{2}$?   Train to Aldersgate (ret[urn] not used) 6d

> Edward Pease presided over the second evening of the debate.

16 *Fabian Society. Sidney Webb on "The Relation between Co-operation, Trade Unionism and Socialism." 20.*

Began article for *The World*. After the Fabian went to Wallas's rooms, where we found the Carrs. Webb walked home with me.

Star $\frac{1}{2}$d   Dinner 1/$\frac{1}{2}$?

17 *Lecture at Nottingham on "Evolution of Socialism." Mechanics' Hall. 20. Stay at 4 Upper College St. Catch the 15 train (Midland) arriving at 17$\frac{1}{4}$.*

Finished and sent off *World* article. Dined here. Intensely cold weather. Read [M.A.] de Bovet's *Life of Gounod* in the train. Hamilton and [E. Lawrence] Manning met me at the station.

Train to Nott[ingham] & b[ac]k 20/6   Insurance 6d   Tip to porter 6d

G.B.S. would review Marie Anne de Bovet's biography of Gounod in his 1 April 1891 column (C788).

18 SUNDAY *Lecture at Nottingham on "Alternatives to Social Democracy." Mechanics' Hall. 19. Go to hear English debate with [A. W.] Slater at the Secular Hall. 15.*

Extremely cold. Went out for a turn after breakfast with Hamilton and Brown. Then sat reading Poe's *Arthur Gordon Pym* until dinner, after which Brown came with me to the debate.

English is unidentified. ▪ Brown was one of Hamilton's Nottingham housemates.

19 *°Lecture at South Place Institute (William Rawlings. 406 Mare St., Hackney). Altered to tomorrow, q.v.*

Reading the life of Gounod in the train. Still very cold. Archer and Wallas called in the afternoon. I had myself called on Archer on my way back from dinner; but he was out.

Star ½d   PMG 1d   Dinner 1/1½?   Bus Oxford O to Hart St 1d

20 *Lecture at South Place Institute on "Nationalization of Capital." (Conrad Thies. Royal Free Hospital. Gray's Inn Rd. W. C.) 20. Coit in the chair. Fabian Literature Committee. 12 Millbank St. 17.*

Writing letters all day. Mrs. Mallet, Wallas, D'Arcy Reeve etc. in the train with me after the lecture.

Dinner (at OG) 1/1   *Star* ½d   PMG 1d   Cocoa &c at Buckingham St 8d   Wash 1d   Train Ch[arin]g + to Mans[ion] Ho[use] 1½d   Moorgate to P[or]tl[an]d Rd 2½d

Dr. Stanton Coit (1857–1944), American expatriate, was president of the West London Ethical Society and a leader of the ethical culture movement. ▪ D'Arcy W. Reeve, 2 Thanet Place, Strand, W.C. and the National Liberal Club, was a well-to-do Fabian who furnished funds for the Society's Strand office to be established in 1891.

21 *Call on Archer after dinner. °Israel in Egypt at the Albert Hall. 20.*

Began *World* article. In great spirits—singing pleasantly etc. Stayed longer than I intended at Archer's, where I met Miss Robins who is to do Mrs. Linde in *The Doll's House*. Wrote up this diary when I got home. It had fallen into arrear for 10 days. In the evening went over to FE.

Star ½d   Dinner 1/½   PMG 1d   Bus to Holborn 1d   Train to Shepherds Bush & back 1/-   Toffee 1/-

Elizabeth Robins, dubbed "St. Elizabeth" by Shaw, would take an instant dislike to him which never abated. An American actress who moved to England after the suicide of her husband, George Richmond Parks, in 1887, she would become influential as actress and producer in establishing Ibsen on the English stage. Her suffragette play, *Votes for*

Women, would be produced by Barker at the Court Theatre in 1907; however, by that point she was turning from the theater to write novels as "C. E. Raimond." ▪ Mrs. Linde is Nora Helmer's confidante in the play, the subordinate female role.

22   °*Debate. Eight Hours Question with G. W. Irons at Chelsea Liberal Club, 237 Kings Rd. S. W. (Mrs. Bellot). Transferred to Webb. Stavenhagen's Orchestral Concert. St. James's Hall. 20.*

Wallas called whilst I was at breakfast. We walked round Regents Park to have a look at the skating. Then we went up to Hampstead, and called on Mrs. Wilson. We had lunch there. Pearson, the anarchist, was there. We walked home, calling on Salt on the way. He was not in; but we met him afterwards on our way back. I wrote a couple of pages of the *World* article, and did some correspondence.

The *World* article was probably the Stavenhagen concert, reviewed by G.B.S. on 28 January 1891 (C777). Stavenhagen played concertos by Beethoven and Liszt, and introduced his bride, a soprano who sang nervously. ▪ William C. Pearson was an anarchist active in Charlotte Wilson's "Freedom Group." He would drift away into the S.D.F., and would become a Dockers' Union activist by 1898, the year he was accidentally drowned while working at the London Docks.

23   °*Wind Instrument Society Concert. Royal Academy of Music. 20½. °Hallé Manchester Band. St. James's Hall. Press View. Anderson Hague's North Cambria. Dowdeswell's. Liberal and Radical Association. South St. Pancras. Executive meeting. 20. 195 Gray's Inn Rd. County Council election.*

Finished *World* article very slowly. Carte sent up a set of proofs of the vocal score of Sullivan's new opera *Ivanhoe*; and I spent some time over that. Met Mrs. Pennell at Dowdeswell's and went on with her to the Fine Art Society and to Vokins'. Sat up to finish the article—not very late. Owing to the thaw, I suppose, my teeth are tingling all over.

Star ½d   P.O. to pay In[come] Tax £1/5/6   Dinner 1/½   Train to Kings + & back 2d

Joshua Anderson Hague (1850–1916), a landscape painter and watercolorist from Lancashire. ▪ Richard D'Oyly Carte (1844–1901) was light opera impresario at the Savoy Theatre.

24   *Catch the 14.10 train to Liverpool from Euston. Stay with Joseph Edwards. 20 Moscow Drive.*

Wrote a few letters. Had *Ivanhoe* to read in the train. It whiled away the journey capitally. Dibdin, to whom I brought down a personal [message] from Archer, met me at Lime St. [John D.] Ford was with him. I drove off with Edwards and Reeves. A lot of people came in for the evening; and I had to do a tremendous lot of talking.

Train to Liverpool (return) 33/–   Insurance 6d   Newspapers 1½d

Joseph Edwards (1865–?) would become head of the Liverpool Fabian Society in 1892. From 1894 to 1901 he edited and published *The Reformers' Year Book* (afterwards *The Labour Annual*).

25 SUNDAY *Lecture to the Liverpool Socialist Society (Samuel Reeves, 50ᵇ Reading St., Kirkdale, Liverpool). "Evolution of Socialism." 15.30. "Alternatives to Social Democracy." 19.30. Rodney Hall. Mount Pleasant.*

In the morning four of us walked out through Earl Sefton's Park and back again. Between the two lectures we went to Chapman's restaurant, where we had tea and I corrected the *World* proof. Several fellows came back to supper with us, especially McHugh, the organizer of the dockers.

Expended (£1/15/0).   Lozenges 1½d   Tram back from Edwards's 2d

E. McHugh was one of the organizers of the National Union of Dock Labourers in 1889.
■ Shaw put in parentheses the amount he expected to be reimbursed by the Liverpool group.

26 °*National Concert. Albert Hall. 19.45. Private View. New Theatre, Royal English Opera, Cambridge Circus. 22 to 24. Catch the 9.45 from Lime St., due at Euston at 14.15.*

Ivanhoe again made the journey easy. I took a short turn through the town before the train left. After dinner I called on Archer; but he was out. I saw Mrs. Archer; and it was arranged that I should go with Archer to the Globe Theatre. I went home and corrected part of the MS of the report of the Foote debate and sent it to Standring. This kept me so late that though I took a cab to Archer's, he had gone; and I understood from what was told me that Mrs. Archer had gone with him in my place, though it afterwards turned out that she had gone to another theatre. I drove back and continued working over the debate report. At the Private View of the new opera house, I felt much out of sorts, and only waited a few minutes before going off with Archer, Norman, and Walkley to supper at Kettner's.

Tram into Liverpool 3d   Newspaper 1d   Dinner 1½d?   *Star* ½d
Cab to Queen Sq & back 2/6

The New English Opera House was quickly a commercial failure. By July 1892 (C875) G.B.S. was speculating as to "whether it will be pulled down, or turned into a music hall, or utilized as a carriage repository. . . ." It would become the Palace Theatre, and home for musical comedies and revues. ■ Kettner's refers to the fashionable Soho restaurant, much frequented by Oscar Wilde.

27 °*South Place. Graham Wallas on "The Co-operative Movement." 20. Fabian General Purposes Committee. 12 Millbank St. 17. The Doll's House at Terry's Theatre. 14¼. Marie Fraser. Albéniz's concert. St. James's Hall. 20.15. Arbos, the Spanish violinist.*

Did some letter writing. At least I think I did; but I do not recollect exactly. Barely squeezed into the pit of the *Doll's House* performance, which was very bad. Met FE coming out. We walked along the Embankment to Westminster where we had tea together in the Aerated Bread Shop at the corner of Parliament Square. I left her at Westminster Bridge station and went on to the Fabian Committee. Dined at home on a bit of bread.

Bus to Garrick St 1d   *Star* ½d   Theatre 2/6   Tea &c with FE at West[minster] 1/7   Her train to Shaftesb[ury] Rd 9d

> Violinist and conductor Enrique Fernandez Arbós (1863–1938), G.B.S. reported belatedly on 18 February 1891 (C780), played coldly at his first London appearance—"in a take it or leave it sort of manner that half provoked the audience to leave it."

28 Began *World* article. Made further progress with the correction of the debate MS. Wrote several letters and went over to FE in the evening, not arriving there until just past nine. Missed the last train back through her clock being wrong. Had to walk home.

Star ½d   Dinner 1½?   Train to Shepherd's Bush (ret[urn] not used) 1/–

29 *4th London Symphony Concert. St. James's Hall. 20. °The World dinner. The Albion. Aldersgate St. 19.15 or 19.30. °Society of Rhymesters. 20 Fitzroy St. (Century Guild). 20½. Dress rehearsal of* Ivanhoe *at Royal English Opera all day.*

Continued *World* article. Went to theatre after dinner.

Star ½d   Dinner 1½?   Cab M[other]–I to concert 1/6

> Not an admirer of George Henschel's conducting, Shaw said nothing in print about it after deprecating in advance (on 21 January 1891) the first concert in the series (C775).

30 *°Gerardy's cello recital. St. James's Hall. 15. Dress rehearsal* Ivanhoe *all day from 11.30. Meeting of the Committee of Liberal and Radical Association Executive to consider candidates for County Council at Bonnell's, 19 Euston Square (Endsleigh Gardens). 1st sitting.*

Went down to the theatre after breakfast. Left at about 16½. Continued *World* article. Sat up writing letters after Committee.

Star ½d   Dinner (at Orange Grove) 1/1   Stamped telegram form to FE 6d

31 *Opening of Royal English Opera with Sullivan's* Ivanhoe. *20. °Hammersmith Socialist Society annual meeting. Kelmscott House, 19.*

Out of sorts after troubled sleep. Spent the early part of the day writing letters and posting up this diary. Indeed the letters lasted the whole day. I did not go out to dinner and was quite addled when it was time to go to the theatre.

> Whether or not Shaw's condition had anything to do with it, his two notices of Sir Arthur Sullivan's attempt at grand opera in *Ivanhoe*, 4 February and 11 February 1891 (C778 & C779), were unenthusiastic. In the first, G.B.S. declared that *Ivanhoe* was "disqualified as a serious dramatic work by the composer's failure to reproduce in music the vivid characterization of Scott, which alone classes the novel among the masterpieces of fiction." The second saw the opera's initial success as a triumph of press agentry over music.

February

1 SUNDAY   *Lecture on "Alternatives to Social Democracy" for the Chelsea Branch S. D. F. (George McCarthy, 19 Stanford St. W.S.)*

Worked hard all day remodeling *World* article. After the lecture I was very tired. Mrs. Sandham walked with me as far as Keppel St.; Mrs. Ballard and her husband came to South Kensington station with me. But the last train had gone; so I walked home across the park.

Train to South Kensington (ret[urn] not used) 9d

> Adolphus Ballard, of Woodstock, Oxfordshire, was a Fabian.

2   °*Second inaugural performance of* Ivanhoe. *Royal English Opera. 20. Gave tickets to Norman and FE. Call on Strudwick any time after 16. Call on FE after Normans'. Normans in the afternoon. Bring score of* Ivanhoe.

Tried to take it easy—sang a little etc., but did not get much rest. Did not dine. Took a few bananas. Had tea with FE.

Bus to West[minster?] 2d   *Star* ½d   Train Victoria to Shaftesbury Rd 6d?   Sh[aftesbury] Rd to West Kensington for self and to Victoria for FE 1/4?   West Kensington to St Ja[me]s's Pk 3d?

3   °*South Place. De Mattos on "The New Trades Unionism." 20. Fabian Executive. 12 Millbank St. 17.* °*Winifred Parker's concert. St. James's Hall. 20. Levy (J. H.) on "The Method of Unreason," at National Liberal Club. 20¼.*

Began article on Strudwick for *Art Journal*—at least I think so; but I will not swear that it was not tomorrow that I began. After the Executive went with Wallas to the Club and had some grub. We went into Levy's lecture, which rather bored us. We saw Massingham and Burns for a moment. Wallas came home with me and we had a walk round Regents Park together.

Star ½d   Dinner 1/½?   Bus to West[minster] 2d

4   °*Dialectical Society. South Place Institute. Tea. Reed on "General Booth's Darkest England." 20. Third inaugural performance of* Ivanhoe. *Royal English Opera. 20.*

Working at Strudwick article. Went to *Ivanhoe* for a while. Lucy had the other seat. Came back and wrote letters.

Star ½d   Dinner 1/½?

> *In Darkest England and the Way Out*, by William Booth.

5   *Committee of the Liberal and Radical Association to elect County Council candidates. 2nd sitting. Dine with Beale and Davies and Burnell at the National Liberal Club at 18.* Maid Marian *at the Prince of Wales Theatre. 20.15.*

Began *World* article. In the afternoon wrote report for the Caucus committee. Dined at the National Liberal Club.

Star ½d   Dinner 1½?   Bus to Ch[arin]g + 1d

> John Burnell of 19 Glenavon Road, Clapton, N.E., was a Fabian. ▪ *Maid Marian* (known later as *Robin Hood*), with music by Reginald de Koven and libretto by H. B. Smith, was, to G.B.S., "a good deal better than anyone dared to expect. . . ." His 11 February 1891 notice (C779) compared it favorably to the more pretentious *Ivanhoe*, and credited it with "ease and vivacity, and sometimes with real feeling." "O, promise me . . . , " with lyrics by Clement Scott, G.B.S. noted, "goes on prettily."

6   *Fabian. David F. Schloss on "Profit Sharing and Co-operation." 20. Go over to FE at 15¼.*

Working at Strudwick article. Went over *Rosmersholm* (first few scenes) with FE. Found it hard to leave and indeed did not get to the Fabian until 20.45. Webb and Wallas walked home with me. Sat up until I was dead tired to finish and send off the *World* article and to write letters.

Dinner 1¼   *Star* ½d   Bus to Uxbridge Rd 4d   Train Shep[herds]
Bush to Gower St 6d

> David Frederick Schloss (1850–1912), assisted Charles Booth with surveys of London for Booth's *Life and Labour of the People in London*. In 1895 he was engaged by Webb as Hutchinson Lecturer for the Fabian Society. He would publish *Methods of Industrial Remuneration* in 1892 to promote concepts of profit sharing and in 1909 a study of unemployment insurance. Beatrice Webb would refer to him later as a "Cambridge Fabian."

7   °*Private View. 19th Century Gallery. 10. Go down to Yarmouth (10/– tickets) by the 15.20 train from Liverpool St. Stay at Mrs. [Ethel] Leach's. Stradbroke. Gorleston. Yarmouth. Call for the watch at the Stores.*

Went off to the Stores to get my watch. Worked at the Strudwick article in the train. Headley met me and put me into a tram, where we found Mrs. Leach.

Star ½d   Dinner (at Orange Grove) 1/1?   Train to Bishopsgate 3d
Train to Yarmouth (ret[ur]n) 10/–   Ins[uran]ce 6d   Tram to Gorleston (Mrs. L[each] paid)   *Black & White* 6d

8 SUNDAY   *Lecture at Yarmouth. Gladstone Hall at 11 and 19 on "Evolution of Socialism" and "The Landlord's Share" (J. Headley. Socialist Society. Row 56, Market Place, Yarmouth).*

Leach came in with me and took the chair at the morning lecture: his wife came in the evening. In the afternoon corrected proof for *The World*, wrote to FE and took a walk on the pier and along the strand, coming back along the cliffs.

Tram Gorleston to Yarmouth 2d   Back (L[each] paid)   Back at night
(L[each] paid)   *Commonweal* 1d   Copy of *Fabian Essays:* presented
to Mrs. Leach 1/–

9 *Last day to send in article on Strudwick to* Art Journal. *Catch the 9.25
train from Yarmouth, due at Liverpool St. at 10.45. Monday Pop Concert.
Joachim's first appearance this season.*

Got up before 6 and walked into Yarmouth. Worked at the Strudwick article
in the train. Rested after a couple of hours and looked over *The Irrational
Knot*. Got to work again when I got home. Slept in the afternoon. Finished
the article and sent it off. Revised it, wrote up this diary—a week in
arrear—and wrote a few letters before going to bed.

Tip to Mrs. Leach's servant 2/6   Train Bishopsgate to Portl[an]d Rd
3d   *Star* ½d   Dinner 10½d   Bus to St Ja[me]s's 1d   Telegrams to
Massingham & FE 1/11½

> "Joachim is back again in much better preservation than he was two years ago . . . , "
> G.B.S. observed (C780). But much of the time the veteran violinist played with "empty
> haste." ■ "J. M. Strudwick," *Art Journal*, April 1891 (C787). Shaw used Strudwick to
> make a statement—that technical skill in art, however prodigious, is barren when there is
> no creative thought behind it. "The conception of the Strudwick picture is as exhaustive
> as the execution."

10 *Bach Choir. St. James's Hall. 20*¼*.* °*South Place. Hubert Bland on "Eight
Hours." 20. Fabian Literature Committee. 12 Millbank St. 17. Stavenhagen's
recital. St. James's Hall. 15. Meet FE at Piccadilly entrance. 14.55.*

Revised Webb's tract for distribution among agricultural labourers. Webb
walked home from Committee with me.

Star ½d   Dinner 1/½   Tea &c at Aerated B[rea]d Shop, corner of Parliament St 1/7   FE's ticket West[minster] Br[idge] to Shaftesbury Rd 9d
Bus to St Ja[me]s's Hall 1d

> The Bach Choir was reviewed in mixed fashion on 18 February 1891 (C780). The cantata
> *Ich hatte viel Bekümmernis* was so sensitively performed that G.B.S. visualized "even the
> densest Philistine in the room" being moved; however, a motet which followed "was a
> mere exhibition of incompetence." The closing cantata, *O, Ewiges Feuer*, was too long and
> strained. ■ Stavenhagen, G.B.S. observed on 25 February 1891 (C782), "must not be
> judged by his performances this season. When he was last over here, though he was very
> ill on the day of his recital, he played at least six times as well as at his recital the other
> day, when there was nothing specially the matter with him." His critical philosophy
> (C747) was that "When people do less than their best, and do that less at once badly and
> self-complacently, I hate them, loathe them. . . ." ■ *Fabian Tract* No. 19, *What the
> Farm Labourer Wants* (BB11).

11 °*The Redemption at the Albert Hall. 20. FE's at 16.*

Revising Webb's Poor Law Tract. Hard work. Wallas called to ask me to
take a walk with him; but I thought it best to stick to the tract. So we met
at dinner at the Pine Apple, and afterwards he walked with me as far as

Marble Arch on my way to FE's. She gave up her intention of going out to dinner and I stayed all the evening. We were playing, singing, trying on *Rosmersholm* dresses, going over the part etc.

Star ½d   Dinner 1/2½   Bus to Uxbridge Rd from Marble Arch 3d
Train Shep[herds] Bush to Portl[an]d Rd 6d

> *Fabian Tract* No. 17, *Reform of the Poor Law* (BB10).

12   °*5th London Symphony Concert. St. James's Hall. 20. Reményi's matinée at Col. North's, Avery Hall, Eltham. 15. Special trains from Charing Cross at 14 and 14.30. °Albéniz's concert. St. James's Hall. 15.*

Up late. Resolved to put off work until evening. In the evening I found myself with a headache and slight indigestion; so I did nothing after all. I would have gone to the concert had I not lent my ticket to FE.

Dinner (at Buckingham St. [vegetarian restaurant]) 10d   Lav[a]t[or]y 1d   Gloves at Stores 2/6   Star ½d

> Col. John T. North was a millionaire who spent lavishly and showily, but charged a guinea per ticket to music-lovers interested in listening to the eminent violinist Eduard Reményi (1830–1898). North, wrote G.B.S. (C780), "wound up the concert by . . . remarking that this classical music was all very well, but that we wanted something that we knew something about, [and] he called upon Reményi to give us Home, Sweet Home, which was accordingly done with imperturbable complaisance. . . ."

13   *St. Anne's Church, Soho. Special Lenten service. Bach's St. John Passion. 20.*

Began *World* article; but Massingham came in and interrupted me. He stayed until it was time to go out to get something to eat. We went to Pagani's. In the afternoon I got along with the article. On my return from the Church I put in some more work which kept me up until past 1. Kate Gurly returned from Bognor. She has been staying at the convalescent home there.

Star ½d   Dinner (at Pagani's) 1/10   Collection in St. Anne's 1/–

> "Never since I was baptized have I felt less in harmony with consecrated walls than whilst listening, with my teeth on edge, to that execrable discord. . . . Have these clerical gentlemen ever noticed how the noblest music becomes ridiculous and noxious when uttered by the sort of amateur who is too self-satisfied or too slovenly to cultivate his powers carefully?" G.B.S., 18 February 1891 (C780).

14   *Crystal Palace Concert. Stavenhagen, Fanny Moody etc. 15. Dine at Mrs. Bateson's. 12^c Oxford and Cambridge Mansions. 19.45.*

Worked at *World* article. FE came down to the Palace with me. She walked to the top of St. James's St. with me from Victoria afterwards. Nobody at Mrs. Bateson's except Clarke, the Peases, Miss Brooke, Roberts, a Mrs. Sitwell, and a young fellow whose name I did not catch. Clarke walked home with me. Did not get to bed until after 1.

Star ½d   Train to Palace & back 2/–   *Review of Rev[iews]* 4½d   Train
to Edgware Rd 2d   Tea &c at Pal[ace] 1/1

Fanny Moody, soprano, sang arias from Meyerbeer and Gounod (C782). ■ Probably
Mrs. A. Bateson (see p. 615). ■ The only Mrs. Sitwell of any consequence in London
was Mrs. Frances ("Fanny") Sitwell (1839–1924), long-time companion of art and literary
critic Sir Sydney Colvin. After the death of her husband, the Rev. Albert Hurt Sitwell, in
1903, she married Colvin, with whom she had been intimate for thirty years (despite
separate addresses).

15 SUNDAY *Morris lectures at Kelmscott House on "Idiots and Idiocy."
20. Go down to Walker's as early as possible to get the light for photographing. Call on Strudwick after 17 to go over* Art Journal *proof and go
down to the lecture with him.*

Finished *World* article. Did not go down to Hammersmith until the 13.05
train. Wallas and his sisters were there. Also Lily Yeats. Walker took a
number of photographs of me before dinner. The Radfords and the Grants
came in after dinner; also another Miss Yeats. Wallas walked with me to
West Kensington at 17, calling at the Sparlings on the way. There were a lot
of people there, among them the [Gustav] Steffens. After I parted from
Wallas, and before I reached Strudwick's, I met Mrs. Jopling and we had a
long talk in the street. She turned up at the lecture afterwards. Spoke in the
discussion. Stayed to supper. Came home in the train with Blundell and his
wife. Sat up to send off *World* article after copying on the typewriter what I
had done in the train.

Train to Hammersmith & back 1/2   (took ticket to Shaftesbury Rd.)
1/2   Bus to St. Peter's Rd. 2d

W. B. Yeats's sister Susan Mary Yeats (1866–1949) was always known as "Lily." ■ S.
Maudson Grant, who had moved to London from Lincoln, was a member of Morris's
Hammersmith Branch. ■ W. B. Yeats's sister "Lollie"—Elizabeth Corbet Yeats (1868–
1940). ■ Louise Jopling-Rowe (1843–1933), painter in the Whistler school, had an
atelier and studio to which young women were especially welcomed.

16 *Liberal and Radical Union Council Meeting at National Liberal Club.
20. °Monday Pop. Call on FE after 16 to go over* Rosmersholm. *Bring down
the Ibsen article to Theodore Wright at Clifford Inn for Mrs. T. W.*

Corrected proof of the *Art Journal* article on Strudwick. Wrote letters etc.
After the meeting went down to the smoking room of the National Liberal
Club and sat for an hour with Webb, Costelloe, Dodd, Wallas, Bunting etc.
Webb and Wallas walked with me as far as the corner of Grafton St.

Star ½d   Bus to Chancery Lane 1d   Dinner (at St Mary[lebone]
St[ation]) 1/–?   Train Temple to Shaftesbury Rd & back to Ch[arin]g +
11d

17   *South Place. Oakeshott (Dell ill) on "Methods of Socialist Evolution."*
20. Fabian Literature Committee. 12 Millbank St. 17. °Group meeting. Cen-
tral Fabian Group. Wallas's rooms. 32 Great Ormond St. 20½. Playgoers'
Club. Mona Hotel. Covent Garden. 20½. Discussion of Ibsen's Ghosts.
°Florence May's concert. Royal Academy of Music. 20.

Began article on *Rosmersholm* for *PMG*. Worked at it until late in the
evening. After Committee walked about Trafalgar Square neighborhood
with Wallas and then had cocoa etc. at the Orange Grove. Went into Charing Cross station afterwards and wrote there at the *Rosmersholm* article
until it was time to go to the Playgoers' Club where I sat next to Mrs.
Armbruster. I spoke, attacking Clement Scott, the dramatic critic of *The
Daily Telegraph,* violently for his hostility to Ibsen. Went to Archer's for a
few moments afterwards to tell him about the meeting.

Star ½d   Memo book 1d   Dinner (at Orange Grove) 10d   Cocoa &c
(same place) 7d

> "The Story of *Rosmersholm*," unsigned, *PMG*, 21 February 1891 (C781). ▪ Probably
> actress Violet Armbruster, who would have a role in Ibsen's *The Lady from the Sea* (in the
> Eleanor Marx Aveling translation), which would play five matinees at Terry's Theatre in
> mid-May.

18   *Dialectical Society. J. Lyons on "Has Socialism any Economic Basis?"*
20. Max Pauer's recital. Prince's Hall. 15. °Miss D'Esterre Keeling's lecture
on Art and Letters at Mrs. Jopling's studio, 1 Clareville Grove Studios,
Gloucester Rd. 16 to 17.

Finished *Rosmersholm* article and sent it off to the *PMG*. Sat up to write
letters. Spoke in opposition to Lyons at the meeting, which contained 10
people all told.

Star ½d   Dinner 1/½   Train to Moorgate & back 6d

> J. Lyons was a Dialectical Society member delivering his first paper. ▪ Max Pauer's
> piano recital was briefly noted by G.B.S. on 18 March 1891 (C785).

19   *°Meeting of Fabian Group Secretaries at Carrs'. 28 Ashley Gardens. 20.*

Began *World* article. I do not very clearly remember the events of this day—
I think I did not go at the article until the afternoon. In the evening I went
to FE; but we were both in a most worried frame of mind.

Star ½d   Dinner 1/½?   Train to Shep[herds] Bush & back 1/–

> The opening of FE's production of *Rosmersholm* was then only four days away, account-
> ing for Shaw's concern.

20   *°Hallé Manchester Band. St. James's Hall. °Wind Instrument Society*
Concert. Royal Academy of Music. 20½. (Smoking). Fabian Society. "An Indi-
vidualist View of Capital and Interest." J. H. Levy. 20. South St. Pancras
Liberal and Radical Assn. Executive meeting. 195 Gray's Inn Road. 20.15.
Subcommittee 19½.

Working at *World* article. Again I cannot recall exactly what happened—I have left it over too long. I only looked in for a moment or two at Gray's Inn Rd. and then went on to the Fabian where I spoke. D'Arcy Reeve walked back with me, discussing his project of starting a new paper. Sat up writing.

Star ½d   Dinner 1½?   Train to Kings + 1d

21 *Crystal Palace Concert. 15. Ilona Eibenschütz (Chopin concert). Rosina Isidor. Call on [C. N.] Williamson, editor of* Black and White. °*Kirwan's recital. St. James's Hall. 15*¼.

In very low spirits. Up late. Went to the Palace alone and dinnerless. On my way out of the building I was overtaken by the Carrs, who came back with me. Dined with them. Mrs. Dryhurst was there. Picked up tremendously. Went to FE at 21 in high spirits. On my way to the Palace I had called on the editor of *Black and White* at his request and saw Braekstad there.

Train to Farringdon 2d   Temple to Victoria 1½d   *Star* ½d   PMG 5d   Train to C[rystal] P[alace] 2/-   Victoria to Hammersmith 6d Shep[herds] Bush to Portl[an]d Rd 6d

> Miss Eibenschütz played the Chopin F minor concerto—happily, to G.B.S. (C782). ▪ Rosina Isidor, soprano, sang a mediocre aria from *Lucrezia Borgia*—out of place, G.B.S. thought, in a program featuring Beethoven and Chopin (C782). ▪ C. N. Williamson (1859–1920), was the founding editor of *Black & White*, an illustrated weekly which began publication on 6 February 1891. It would publish R. L. Stevenson, Henry James, and Thomas Hardy. Almost certainly Shaw's talk with him concerned contributing to the magazine—which did not work out.

22 SUNDAY *Lecture at Hall of Science on "Freethinking, New and Old."*

Finished *World* article and prepared lecture. Robertson made an extraordinarily bitter attack on me after it. Went home with the Archers, Robertson coming as far as the door with us. Sat there until midnight. Sat up writing. Archer had called on me in the morning.

Train to Aldersgate 2d   Tram Old St to Bloomsbury 1d

> "I dealt," Shaw recalled in 1912 in his lay sermon "Modern Religion" (A116), "with the whole mass of superstition which [Secularists] called free thought: I went into their Darwinism and Haeckelism, and physical science, and the rest of it, and showed that it did not account even for bare consciousness. I warned them that if any of them fell into the hands of a moderately intelligent Jesuit—not that I ever met one—he could turn them inside out."

23 *Rosmersholm (first time in England) at Vaudeville Theatre (Florence Farr, F. R. Benson etc.), 15. Adjourned discussion on "Ghosts" (Aveling's paper) at the Playgoers' Club, Mona Hotel, Covent Garden. 20*¼.

Went down to Spottiswoode's, who now print *The World*, to correct proof of *World* article. After the play went to Gatti's with FE, and Berlyn and his wife to feed. Afterwards we strolled about the Embankment in the fog until it was time to go to the Playgoers' Club. I spoke in the discussion. Norman came in towards the end; and when it was over he and I and FE went to Rule's and had some supper. We then went with her on her way home as far as St. James's Park station, where we got out and went to Norman's rooms. I played a few songs for him and did not get home until $24\frac{1}{2}$. Wrote some letters and did not get to bed until past 3.

Star 1d   Train to Farringdon St 2d   Dinner (Rule's) 11d?   *PMG* 1d   Programme at Vaudeville 6d   Gatti's 7/–   Train Ch[arin]g + to St Ja[me]s's Pk, Norman & I 4d

> According to the *Illustrated Sporting and Dramatic News*, 7 March 1891, covering the opening matinee, "Never before at an entertainment for the mentally or physically inflicted, . . . at an asylum concert or hospital treat . . . [were there] so many deformed faces; so many men and women pale, sad-looking. . . . It was an assemblage of out-patients waiting for the doctor." Such was the conservative press's reaction to Ibsen.   ▪ Alfred Berlyn (1860–1936), was a minor playwright who specialized in adaptations of French comedies.   ▪   Rule's Restaurant, 35 Maiden Lane, stuffily British, is still at the same location. It was *the* fashionable place to dine in London.

24   °*South Place. Sidney Webb. "Reform of the Poor Laws." 20. Fabian Finance Committee. 12 Millbank St. 17. Go out to Lee with Bland afterwards. °Church and Stage Guild. 31 Upper Bedford Place. Selwyn Image on "Dancing, a Question of Dress."*

Not up until past 11. Worked at correcting the MS of the report on the Foote debate until near 17, when I started for the Fabian, stopping on my way to dine at the Orange Grove. After the meeting the fog was so bad that Bland and I and Miss Hoatson hesitated to go down to Lee; but at last we ventured and were only delayed half an hour. Nobody at Lee excepting us three. I came back by the 22.27, getting out at London Bridge to avoid the bad bit of the line. Sat up again until past 3.

Daily Telegraph 1d   *Star* $\frac{1}{2}$d   Dinner 1/3   Train Ch[arin]g + to Lee $7\frac{1}{2}$d   Lee to London Br[idge] 6d   Bishopsgate to P[or]tl[an]d Rd 3d

25   *Gerardy's recital. St. James's Hall. 15.*

Worked, I think, at the debate. Wrote letters. After the recital, FE and I went to the Orange Grove in St. Martin's Lane, where I dined and she had some tea. Then I went home and worked away at my letters until 20, when I went to Hammersmith.

Star $\frac{1}{2}$d   Dinner and tea (FE and myself) 2/–   Train to Shep[herds] Bush & back 1/–

> "Gerardy . . . shewed a melancholy falling-off at his last recital," G.B.S. wrote on 4 March 1891 (C783). His ornamental passages were "prettier than ever," but in the "lengths of straightforward work" his cello's tone became "common, careless, valueless."

26   *6th (last) London Symphony Concert. St. James's Hall. 20. Albéniz's concert. St. James's Hall. 15*

Did not get at the *World* article until the evening, being out of sorts except for fiddling about at letters etc. Only heard about half the concert.

Star $\frac{1}{2}$d   Dinner 1/$\frac{1}{2}$?

> "Henschel has just brought his six symphony concerts safely into port. . . . The orchestra has not improved during the season. . . . Altogether, the [final] performance would have done admirably in the Malay Peninsula" (C783).

27 *Fabian Private Meeting. 31 Upper Bedford Place, to pass Agricultural Labourers' Tract,* Facts for Bristol, *etc. 20.*

Finished and sent off *World* article. Hicks called here in the evening, and walked with me part of the way to the Fabian. Webb and Wallas walked home with me.

Star $\frac{1}{2}$d   Dinner 1/$\frac{1}{2}$?

28 *Crystal Palace Concert. 15. Joachim (Beethoven concert), Oxford Symphony etc.*

Correcting MS of Fabian debate. Worked at the last portion (which I did not send off until Saturday). FE came to the Crystal Palace, and I spent the rest of the evening with her.

Star $\frac{1}{2}$d   Train to C[rystal] Pal[ace] from Vict[oria] (FE & I) 4/–   Tea &c after concert 1/1   Another *Star* $\frac{1}{2}$d   *Speaker* 6d   *PMG* 1d Train Victoria to Ravenscourt Rd 6d   Shepherds Bush to Portl[an]d Rd 6d

> There was no G.B.S. review of the Crystal Palace concert.   ▪   The Fabian debate was *The Legal Eight Hours Question* (A11), between Shaw and G. W. Foote (see 14 January 1891), published as a pamphlet, at sixpence, by R. Forder, 28 Stonecutter Street. Both disputants had an opportunity to revise and correct the verbatim copy.

March

1 SUNDAY *Lecture at Kelmscott House, Hammersmith Socialist Society, on "The Upshot of Fabianism." Dinner at Sparlings'. 14. Tea at Radfords'. 19. Stay the night at Sparlings'.*

Finished with the MS of the Foote report. Prepared lecture in the afternoon at Sparlings'. Mrs. Holman Hunt and her daughter were there. Also Charlotte Roche, and others. Met several people at Radfords', notably Miss Dowie. After the lecture, at which Wallas took the chair, went to Lang's.

Train to Hammersmith 6d

> The former Edith Waugh, second wife of William Holman Hunt. Since she was his deceased wife's sister, the marriage had questionable validity in England, and she was often cut socially. Shaw would use that device in *Major Barbara* to give Adolphus Cusins

technical status as an "orphan," as he was described as offspring of such a marriage.   ∎
Ménie Muriel Dowie (1870–1945), who would shortly become Mrs. Henry Norman, was a
journalist and fiction writer who would be best remembered as a contributor to *The
Yellow book* and for *Gallia* (1895), a novel on the "sex question."

2   *Wallas on "Trade Union Movement"—one of his University Extension
Series. Essex Hall. 20. °Jeanne Douste's concert. Steinway Hall. 15.*

After breakfast called on Walker. We went together to Sussex House, where
Pennell took a couple of photographs of me. On my way from St. James's
Park to the Pine Apple restaurant I went into Dowdeswell's to see the
exhibition there. After dinner I went home, did some singing, and wrote
letters. In the evening I went to Wallas's lecture (University Extension) at
Essex Hall. We went with Geraldine Carr as far as the corner of Parliament
St. and then took a bus and went on it to the corner of High St. Bloomsbury.
Jacques got off at the corner of St. Martin's Lane. I went to Wallas's rooms;
and we talked there until after midnight.

Train Hammersmith to St Ja[me]s's Pk 6d   *Daily Chronicle* 1d   Dinner 1/–   *Star* ½d   Bus to St Martin's Ch[urch] 1d   Ch[arin]g + to
Essex St 1d   Whitehall to Bloomsbury 2d   (Wallas's fare 2d)

3   *°South Place. Nelson Palmer on "New Reform Bill." 20. Fabian Executive.
Miss Warley's. Westminster Palace Hotel. 17.*

Wrote a tremendous lot of letters. Did not get through them until near 17.
Walter came in about 13 and sat until past 15. One of the Nottingham men,
whose name I forget, came into the restaurant when I was dining. After the
Executive walked as far as Charing Cross with Bland and Miss Hoatson.
Then turned back to Westminster and had cocoa etc. in the Aerated Bread
Shop next to the railway station. Went to FE's and spent the rest of the
evening with her.

Dinner (at Orange Grove) 1/–   Cocoa &c (at Aerated Bread Shop) 1/–
      Telegrams to Archer and FE 1/1   Train West[minster] to Ravens-
c[our]t Rd 6d   Shep[herds] Bush to P[or]tl[an]d Rd 6d

4   *°Conference on Housing of the Poor at National Liberal Club. 20. Students' Concert. Guildhall School. Embankment. 18½. °Dialectical Society.
South Place. T. Atwood on "The Basis of Morality." 20. °Jeanne Douste's
second concert. Steinway Hall. 15. °Lyric Theatre. 100th performance of* La
Cigale *and production of* A Double Divorce, *operetta by Frank Latimer and
Ivan Caryll. Revival of* Charles I *at Lyceum. Go for Archer and write notice
for* Manchester Guardian.

Wrote a long letter to Fisher Unwin, pressing my suggestion about getting
Wallas to write a history of the century to be published in 1900. Also to
Mrs. Morgan Thomas about a song of hers, explaining her mistakes in
harmony etc. This took me, with some singing thrown in, until 17½, when I

hurried off to dine at the Central restaurant before going to the Guildhall Concert. Met Mme. Schack in the restaurant. After the play, where I had a talk with Slater and others, went to the *Manchester Guardian* office and wrote a notice. Did not get to bed until past 2, as I sat up to write some letters.

Train to Farringdon 2d   *PMG* 1d   Dinner (at Central [Restaurant]) 10½d

No notice discernibly by Shaw appeared in the *Manchester Guardian*; however, the material was reused in the 18 March 1891 (C785) G.B.S. music column: "I go to see Irving play Charles I; and my critical sense is highly gratified by his now consummately cultivated artistic sense and perfect certainty of execution. . . . But now comes the difficulty. *Charles I* interests me so little as a drama that the actor cannot, with all his art, make it affect me one tenth as strongly as a play of Ibsen's acted by novices who have not a twentieth part of Irving's skill." *Charles I*, by W. G. Wills, would run for twenty-eight performances. ▪ Wallas was then delivering a series of London University Extension lectures on the XIX Century (CL). ▪ Mrs. Alice Morgan Thomas of Beechwood Hall, Caterham Valley.

5   °*Tea at Pennells'*, 16¼. 6 *Barton St. Westminster. Second performance of* Rosmersholm *at the Vaudeville.* 14¼. *First Philharmonic Concert. St. James's Hall.* 20.

Writing letters, as well as I can remember. Left the concert early and went on to FE. Fisher Unwin came in the train with me as far as Earl's Court.

Star ½d?   Dinner 1/1½?   Vaudeville Theatre 2/–   prog[ram]me 2d   Train St Ja[me]s's Pk to Hammersmith 6d   Shep[herds] Bush to Portl[an]d Rd 6d

The Philharmonic was reviewed on 11 March 1891 (C784). As usual G.B.S. found it poorly rehearsed, suffering from a rapid turnover in conductors.

6   *Fabian Society. G. W. Foote on "The Case Against an Eight Hours Bill."* 20.

Worked at the *World* article, not getting along very fast. Did not speak in the debate.

Star ½d?   Dinner 1/1½?

7   *Crystal Palace Concert.* 15. *Ravenswood music. 3rd Act* Tannhäuser. *Berlioz's* La Mort d'Ophelie. *Dine at Carrs' in the evening at 21. 23 Ashley Gardens.*

Worked at *World* article. Mother came to the concert with me. We went back in the train with the Carrs. Miss Dowie and others were with them in the evening. Clarke and I walked home together as far as our roads allowed.

Star ½d   Train to C[rystal] Pal[ace] 2/–   Train to Victoria 6d   Cab [from] Victoria 1/6

"Were it not for the Crystal Palace band, it would be quite correct to say that we [Londoners] have no orchestra . . ." G.B.S. wrote (C784).

8 SUNDAY   *Lecture at the Woolwich Radical Club on "Alternatives to Social Democracy." 20. (William James Broad. Radical Club. William St.) °Go out to Blands' in the afternoon. Tea with Archer at 18.*

Finished *World* article. Had no time to do anything else. When I got to Woolwich I found that a mistake had been made about the lecture. It ended in my taking the chair for Dr. Moir instead of lecturing myself. Read Gosse's translation of *Hedda Gabler,* which I borrowed from Archer.

Train to Woolwich & back 1/8

> Dr. John Moir—a follower of Keir Hardie—was active in West Ham politics.

9   *Liberal and Radical Union Council Meeting. National Liberal Club. 20. Marriott's Land Nationalization Resolution. °Monday Pop. Call on Archer at 14 and go into the City typewriter hunting.*

Corrected proof of part of Foote debate and of the *World* article. Walter was here. Archer and I went about the City until about 18 when a snowstorm came on and we took a cab back to Queen Square. From that I went down to the National Liberal Club and spoke at the meeting. Webb walked home with me after we had seen Mrs. Sandham into Charing Cross station.

Dinner (at Porridge Bowl) 1/1½d   Cocoa, eggs &c (Char[ing] +) 1/1

> A. J. Marriott was author of *Song of Brotherhood between the English and Irish People* (London, 1888). As a boy he had been a rent collector from impoverished families, an experience which weighed heavily in his politics.

10   *St. James's Hall. Bach Choir. 20¼. °F. Gilbert Webb on "National Music, Race etc." at the Royal Academy of Music. 20. Fabian Literature Committee. 12 Millbank St. 17. °Mary Townsend's concert. Marlborough Rooms. 15. Jeanne Douste's Chopin recital. Steinway Hall. 15. °Lunch at Wedmore's. 13.45. 6 Thurlow Rd. N.W.*

Writing letters etc. all the morning (this correspondence is getting intolerable). Gave up idea of going to Wedmore's. Snow and general discomfort.

Star ½d   Dinner 1/½?   Cloakroom at St Ja[me]s's Hall 6d

> Reviewed on 18 March 1891 (C785). In addition to the Bach Choir portion of the program, Eibenschütz and Borwick played the Bach *Concerto for Two Pianos.*   ▪ The snow was, by London standards, a blizzard.

11   *°Albert Hall. St. Paul. 20. Call on Archer between 12 and 16. °Dress rehearsal of* Ghosts, *Royalty Theatre. 19¼.*

Writing letters etc., as well as I can remember. Stayed with Archer until 16, when Miss Robins and Miss Lea came, and I fled. I had intended to go to FE in the evening; but I now, having suddenly made up my mind to go to the rehearsal of *Ghosts,* resolved to go out to her in the afternoon and come back by 19. So I went straight from Archer's to Hammersmith, only stopping to dine at the Orange Grove on my way. But when the time came to return I hesitated and was lost. Was in desperately low spirits all the evening in consequence.

PMG 1d   Dinner (at OG) 1/–?   Train to Ravensc[our]t Pk from Ch[arin]g + 6d   Shep[herds] Bush to P[or]tl[an]d Rd 6d

> On Friday the 13th, J. T. Grein would inaugurate his Independent Theatre with Ibsen's controversial *Ghosts,* scandalizing the London press. Since the play was interdicted by the censorship—the Lord Chamberlain's Office—the device of an Independent Theatre Society would make the performances technically "private" (open only to members). The play would be execrated as "An open drain; a loathsome sore unbandaged; a dirty act done publicly . . ." (leading article, *Daily Telegraph*).

12   °*Agnes Zimmermann's recital. Prince's Hall.* 15½. *Council meeting (2.50) Liberal and Radical Association. South St. Pancras. Prospect Terrace Board School, Gray's Inn Rd. County Council candidates.* 20. °*Jeanne Douste's recital. Steinway Hall.* 15. *Miss Donkersley's concert, Kensington Town Hall.* 15.

Webb called before I got to work; and just as he was going Massingham came. He stayed until I went out to catch FE at the theatre. I went first to the Princess's by mistake, and had to drive to the Olympic post haste. Hurried down to the New Olympic Theatre to waylay FE on her way into the matinee. Did not see her. Went off to Kensington to the concert, returning in time to see the people come out of the Olympic after waiting half an hour in the street. Missed her again—it turned out afterwards that she was not there. Rushed home to get a letter off to her about the exchange of tickets with Vera C. for *Ghosts.* Spoke at the meeting. Sat up writing letters.

Cab Princess's Theatre to Olympic 1/6   Dinner (opposite St. Mary's) 1/–?   Train Temple to Kensington High St & back 8d?   Telegram to Archer 6d

> Miss Isabella Donkersley led a quintet of Royal College of Music instrumentalists in a program G.B.S. (C786) did not stay to hear to the end, not because of their playing but because he was in a rush to meet FE. ▪ Lady Colin Campbell disliked her given name, Gertrude, and was known to friends as Vera.

13   °*Janotha's concert. St. James's Hall.* 20. *Independent Theatre started at the Royalty with Ibsen's* Ghosts.

Began *World* article. Got a telegram from Lady Colin Campbell to say that she had not received the ticket for *Ghosts* from FE in exchange for her own. I got this just as I came in from dinner, and went off to Hammersmith to make inquiries. FE was out; so I went to Walker's and stayed about an hour there. There was a Mrs. Archibold presently—she had been in Roumania and knew Utley there. Returned to FE's and waited for her until she came in. Then got back there for tea and went off to the theatre. After the performance Massingham, Ashton, FE and I went in a cab to Norman's where we stayed until it was time for FE to catch the last train at St. James's Park at about 12.58. I went with her to the station and walked home alone.

National Review 2/2   *Star* ½d   Dinner 1½d?   Train to Shep[herds] Bush & back 8d?

14   *Crystal Palace Concert. 15. Marmaduke Barton. Private View. Diaz's pictures at Goupil Gallery. °St. James's Hall. Albéniz's concert. 20.15 Meet FE at Temple station at 13.50 and go to* Ben my Chree *at New Olympic. 14.*

Worked at *World* article. After the theatre we had some tea etc. in the Strand and then went off to Hammersmith together. We read *Hedda Gabler* etc.

Pall Mall Gaz[ette] 1d   *Telegraph* 1d   *Star* ½d   Programme at theatre 6d   Tea &c 1/6   Train to Ravenscourt Pk 6d   Shep[herds] Bush to Portland Rd 6d

> Narcisse Diaz de la Peña (1807–1876), genre painter, lived in France. ■ *Ben-My-Chree*, a melodrama by Hall Caine and Wilson Barrett based on Caine's novel *The Deemster*, had first been performed in 1888; it was now revived for three matinees.

15 SUNDAY   *Lecture at the Star Radical Club, 8 Mayall Rd., Herne Hill, S.E. (Sec. George G. Steele) on "Alternatives to Social Democracy." 20½. Three minutes' walk from Brixton station, from Victoria or Ludgate Hill.*

Finished and sent off *World* article.

Train to Brixton & back (to Viaduct) 1/–

16   *°Fabian At-Home, Hood Barrs'. 19¼ to 24. 1 Brainskill Gardens. Dartmouth Park Hill. Junction Rd. (Midland) or Gospel Oak (North London).*

Not up until near 12. Set to work at once getting the Ibsen paper which I read at the Fabian in July last year ready for publication, and stuck at it without a break, except to go out for dinner, until about 2 in the morning.

Dinner (at Orange Grove) 1/–

17   *Fabian Policy Committee. 12 Millbank St. 17. °Watts-Russell's concert. Prince's Hall. 15. °Irish National Concert. Albert Hall. 20. Haymarket Theatre.* The Dancing Girl. *FE's box. 20.*

Still at the Ibsen paper. After the Committee De Mattos came with me to the Orange Grove and we had tea together.

Dinner (at Orange Grove) 1/–   Cocoa &c (same place) 10d   Cab to Victoria from theatre 1/6

> *The Dancing Girl*, by Henry Arthur Jones, had opened on 15 January and would run 266 performances. Herbert Beerbohm Tree had the leading male role; the female lead alternated between Julia Neilson and Beatrice Lamb.

18 °*Dialectical Society. South Place. "Marriage." 20. Commune Celebration, Communist Club. 20. Speak.*

Was about to attack the Ibsen paper when Wallas called and we sat talking until 14, when we went out to dine and went on to Peases' afterwards, where Bruce Wallas presently came in and gave us an account of the American Co-operative communities which he had been visiting. He walked with us to Baker St. station when we left. I only had time to do a very short turn at the paper when it was time to go to the Commune Celebration, where I spoke, meeting Mendelsohn, the Polish refugee (to whom I was introduced), and Louise Michel for the first time. Came home and wrote a few letters before going to bed.

Dinner 1/½   Collection at Comm[unist] Cl[ub] 1/–

> J. Bruce Wallas, born in Gujarat, India, was a Congregational minister and Christian Socialist who founded the Brotherhood Church, Southgate Road, London.   ▪ Stanislas Mendelsohn was an émigré trade union organizer among Jewish immigrants in the East End. On May Day (actually Saturday, 3 May) he would address a Hyde Park rally in Polish. He would found the Polish Socialist Party in 1892.   ▪ Louise Michel (1830–1905) was a French anarchist associated with Peter Kropotkin, active in the Paris Commune of 1871. Released from prison, she established herself in London, where she was active in anarchist causes. Her play, *The Strike*, was published in *Commonweal* during 1891–92.

19 *Speak at the S. D. F. Commune Celebration at St. Andrew's Hall.* °*Students' Orchestral Concert. Trinity College.*

Worked at the Ibsen paper, not very successfully.

Dinner 1/1½?

20 °*Wind Instrument Society. Royal Academy of Music. 20½. Fabian Society. Dr. R. M. Pankhurst on "Radicalism and Socialism." 20.*

Began, finished and sent off *World* article. Spoke at Fabian. Wallas walked part of the way home with me and Webb the whole way.

Dinner 1/–

> R. M. Pankhurst (?–1898) was a radical Manchester barrister better known for having married (in 1879) militant suffragist Emmeline Goulden Pankhurst (1858–1928).

21 *Crystal Palace Concert. 15. Ysaye. Boat race day. Walker's. Go to Sparlings' afterwards. Wallas to call for me and walk over. Call for FE en route.*

Wallas did not call until after 10; and the result was that FE had gone when we called for her and the boat race was over before we reached Walkers'. I went on to Sparlings' and had a long chat with Geraldine [Spooner] Carr about the Executive election then went to Radfords'; but found that FE was gone. Followed her home but she was not there. Went to Victoria, and lost the 14.15 train there. Came back from concert with [Montague] Chester and was about to walk home with him when I found FE waiting for me at

Victoria. Got dinner at a café opposite the station and went home with her.
Lost the last train and had to walk.

Train Shaftesbury Rd to Victoria 6d   *Star* ½d   Train to Crystal Pal[ace]
& back 2/–   Vic[toria] to Ravenscourt Pk 6d   Macaroni &c at
rest[auran]t 2/–

> Eugene Ysaÿe (1858–1931), Belgian violist and composer who debuted in London in 1889,
> would not be noticed by G.B.S. in his current round of recitals until the review of 29 April
> 1891 (C792). ▪ Oxford won, but it was a close race.

22 SUNDAY *Lecture at Camberwell for the (John Hampton Davis. 147
Denmark Rd. Camberwell S.E.) North Camberwell Enterprise Radical Club.
36 Southampton St. Camberwell. Club is at New Church Rd. end of Southampton St. Bus to Camberwell Gate or Addington Square. Open air at the
Triangle, Southampton St. 11½. Go out to Blands' in the evening.*

Corrected *World* proof and wrote some letters. Had rather a vivid conversation with Mrs. Bland and Bland about the forthcoming Executive election at
the Fabian.

Train to Farringdon 2d   Bus to Elephant 1d   Tram to Camb[erwell]
Gate 1d   Tram Camb[erwell] Rd to Obelisk 2d   Train Ch[arin]g + to
Blackheath 6d   Lee to Ch[arin]g + 7½d

> A handbill announced Shaw's topic as "Labour Politics."

23   Wrote a long letter to Bland about the Executive election.

24   °*New Fellowship. William Morris on "Art for the People." Percy Hall.
Fabian General Purposes Committee. 12 Millbank St. 17. Meeting of the
Euston Fabian Group at Brunswick Rd. Co-operative Hall, Poplar, to hear
address by Tom Mann.*

Worked at the Ibsen paper. Had intended to spend the evening at Salts'; but
changed my mind (fortunately, as it happened; for Salt is out of town) and
went with Webb to Poplar after having grub with him at the National
Liberal Club. Spoke at the meeting.

Bus to Orange Grove 1d   Dinner there 1/–   Train Ch[arin]g + to
Mark Lane 1½d?   Fench[urch] St to Poplar 5d (return not used)   Poplar to Camden Town 3d

25   *Dine with Slater, [4] Courtfield Rd. 19¾.*

Worked all day, dining off a little brown bread. Ibsen paper chiefly, as well
as I can recollect. Barton and a fellow named Kemball—if I caught it
aright—the only conversable people at Slater's. Left in time to run into
Barton's (he had already vanished for a while). One of the guests came
home in the train with me—I forget his name.

Train to Gloster Rd & back 9d

26   *Dine with Magny at 19, to meet Standring.*

Feeling too tired for serious work, I set to to cut up a lot of old *Stars* to get the Bassetto columns out of them with a view to arranging them for republication by Unwin, who has just made me an offer for them. Did not go out to dine. Standring came back with me as far as Moorgate St[ation].

Train to Bishopsgate & back 5d   London Br[idge] to Old Kent Rd & back 4d?

> The proposal fizzled, Shaw was less than eager to reprint the columns, about which, after looking them over again, he wrote Unwin (*CL*), "Such sickening, vulgar, slovenly slosh never blasted my sight before. I cannot believe that there is enough good stuff sunk in this mud to be worth diving for."

27   Wrote *World* article. Went out to FE in the evening.

Train to Shep[herds] Bush & back 1/–

28   *Crystal Palace Concert. 15. Dora Bright (her own concerto).*

Wrote to V[era Colin] C[ampbell] about the objection raised by Yates to her arranging with me to do the picture criticism for *The World* during her Easter holidays. FE came to the Palace with me and I went home with her afterwards. After the concert we strolled about the grounds instead of going into the tea rooms as usual.

Train Victoria to C[rystal] Pal[ace] FE and I 4/–   Train Vict[oria] to Ravenscourt Pk 6d   Shep[herds] Bush to P[or]tl[an]d Rd 6d

> Dora Bright, G.B.S. wrote on 1 April 1891 (C788), in very faint praise, "is a pianist who writes her concertos better than she plays them."

29 SUNDAY   *Call for A. R. Dryhurst at 14¼ and go for a walk.*

Corrected *World* proof. Took a longish walk by Hendon and Mill Hill with Dryhurst. Spent the evening at Downshire Hill.

Tram to Hampstead 2d   Train West Hampstead to Hendon 1½d

30   30th to 3rd *April*. During all this Easter I was at home working furiously at the book on Ibsen. In the evenings I sometimes went up to Dryhursts' or elsewhere; but I forget the particulars, as I was too absorbed in my work to trouble about this diary. When I tried to make up arrears I found that I could not remember what had passed; so I had to leave the week blank.

31   [I can only describe *L'Enfant Prodigue*, at the Prince of Wales', as touching. I was touched when I laughed no less than when I retired in tears at the end of the third act. But my emotion was not caused by the music.

That is simply conventional French ballet music and *mélodrame*, elegantly fitted out with the latest harmonic refinements. . . . For the rest of this most entertaining dumb show I have nothing but praise. The service rendered by the music in making the drama intelligible is not great: there is only one point which would not be as intelligible to a deaf man as it was to me. That was the stipulation made by Phrynette that the Baron must marry her, a point which could easily be conveyed by pantomime, but which was more concisely and amusingly intimated by the introduction of the opening strain of Mendelssohn's wedding march. . . .]

> The musical play without words by Michel Carré *fils*, and André Wormser, opened on 31 March and is assigned to that date since G.B.S. as reviewer would probably have seen it at the first or second matinee. His notice was the first lengthy review in his 8 April 1891 column (C789). The 13 London matinees had been preceded by 223 performances in Paris.

April

1 *Dialectical Society. South Place. Dr. Alice Vickery on "Woman's Suffrage."*

2–3 [ ]

4 *Crystal Palace Concert. 15. Mackenzie's Dream of Jubal. Nordica etc.* FE came down to the Crystal Palace with me.

Train Ch[arin]g + to Vict[oria] 1½d   Vict[oria] to C[rystal] P[alace] & back 2/–   Vict[oria] to Ravenscourt Pk 6d   Shep[herds] Bush to P[or]tl[an]d Rd 6d   Sweets 1d   *PMG & Star* 1½d

> Alexander Campbell Mackenzie (1847–1935), composer and conductor, wrote oratorios and cantatas because, Shaw felt, they were the only kinds of music which were truly serious. To Shaw these efforts were only anachronistic and dull. "Like poor Jubal," G.B.S. wrote (C789), "I was bored beyond all description."

5 SUNDAY *Go out to Sparlings' in the afternoon.*

Finished *World* article and corrected the proof. Did not get to Sparlings' until late in the afternoon. Found Walker there. Spent the evening at [Andrew] Lang's. Lang was in bed and did not appear—laid up with neuralgia and gout. May came with me; but Sparling went to a lecture.

Train to Hammersmith & back 1/–

> Andrew Lang (1844–1912), Scottish poet, translator, and critic, was a friend of William Archer.

6   *Covent Garden. Opening night.* Orfeo. *Giulia Ravogli. 20½.*

[At Covent Garden there is nothing new before the curtain except a lining of mirror to the walls of the corridors; so that on diamond nights boxholders who are tired of being admired by the audience can go outside and admire themselves. (C790)]

> G.B.S. reviewed Gluck's *Orfeo ed Euridice* in his 15 April 1891 column (C790). Sofia Ravogli (?–1910), the lesser known sister of the great Giulia, was also in the cast, but G.B.S. found that even the pair could not bring the opera off this time.

7   *Fabian Executive. 12 Millbank St. 17. Covent Garden.* Faust. *Miss Eames. 20.*

Working all day at list of books for the use of the Fabian to give to inquirers into Socialism. Dined on my way down.

PMG 1d   Dinner (O[range] G[rove]) 1/–

> Emma Eames (1865–1952), American soprano, was making her London debut. She would become the chief rival at Covent Garden to Nellie Melba; however, G.B.S. (C790) found her "intelligent, ladylike, and somewhat cold and lifeless."

8   *Wallas to call after 10 to go over Fabian list of books.* °*Opening soirée of the Ballad Singers. Suffolk St. Galleries.*

Worked with Wallas at the list of books until it was time to go to dinner. Afterwards we went to the Museum and went through a collection of drawings in the White Wing. Came back here and did a little work. Then off to FE.

Dinner (at Orange Grove) 1/2   Train to Shep[herds] Bush & back 1/–

9   *Albéniz' concert. St. James's Hall. 15.* °*Press View. New English Art Club. 1st day. Egyptian Hall. Covent Garden.* Carmen. *Giulia Ravogli (first time in England).*

Began *World* article. Sat up to write letters after coming in from the Opera.

PMG 1d   Dinner 1/– (O[range] G[rove])

> The concerts by Isaac Albéniz, G.B.S. wrote (C790), "are deservedly growing in favor."
> ■ G.B.S. was 75 minutes late for *Carmen*, but what he saw (C790) "went off brilliantly," although Alberto Randegger (1832–1911) "conducts it worse than ever" and Sofia Ravogli "played Micaela exactly as she would have played Norma." Moreover, Giulia Ravogli's Carmen was "gloriously bad" and "made havoc with the flimsy and fanciful figment she was impersonating."

10   *Fabian Annual Meeting. Barnard's Inn. 20.* °*Fifth Annual Reading. Shakspere Reading Society. Royal Academy of Music. 20. Press View. New English Art Club. Egyptian Hall. 2nd day. Press View. H. P. Riviere's drawings. Rome and the Campagna. Burlington Gallery. Press View. Japanese drawings at Larkin's. 28 New Bond St.*

Gadding about most of the day. Finished and sent off *World* article.

PMG 1d   Dinner (O[range] G[rove]) 1/–   Bus—Shaftesbury O to Grafton St 1d   Grafton St to Oxford St 1d   Oxford St to Barnard's Inn 1d

Although Shaw visited the spring art exhibitions as of old, he would publish a review only of the Royal Academy show, that in *The Observer*, 3 May 1891 (C793). ▪ Henry Parsons Riviere (1811–1888), a watercolorist, had depicted mostly Italian landscapes and subjects, and came from a family of painters.

11 °*Crystal Palace Concert. 15. Frederic Lamond. Private View of several pictures at Lefevre's. 1ª King St. Willy Hess and Hugo Becker's 1st concert. St. James's Hall. 15. Private View. Continental Gallery.* Lohengrin. *Miss Eames. Covent Garden. 20. Private View. New English Art Club.*

Made a desperate onslaught on my letters and on this diary, which is 12 days in arrear. FE was at the concert with me and afterwards at the galleries.

Dinner (P[ine] Apple) 1/–?   Bus to Long Acre 1d

The first of three Saturday afternoon concerts by Willy Hess, pianist (and conductor), and Hugo Becker, cellist. G.B.S. (C790) called them "worth hearing." ▪ Shaw's review of the Wagner opera with Miss Eames appeared in *The World* on 22 April 1891 (C791). The "intellectual vacuity" of Édouard de Reszke (1855–1917) as the king in *Lohengrin*, to G.B.S., "baffles description."

12 SUNDAY   *Lecture at Leighton Hall on "The Iron Law of Wages." (Miss Margaretta Hicks, 46 Carlton Rd. Kentish Town, N.W.). Turn to the left out of Leighton Rd., which runs beside Kentish Town station (Midland).*

Correcting proof of *World* article and finishing it. Wrote notices of galleries. Magny was at my lecture and came back on the tram with me.

Tram to Kentish Town & back 4d

Shaw's gallery notices were not published.

13   *Covent Garden.* Faust. *The de Reszkes.*

Working at Ibsen essay.

Dinner (O[range] G[rove]) 1/–

Most of the G.B.S. column for 22 April 1891 (C791) was devoted to the de Reszke brothers, Edouard and Jean. Edouard "no longer sings," G.B.S. wrote; "he bawls, revelling in the stunning sound. . . . It is magnificent; but it is not Mephistopheles." Jean, a baritone who had an "anxiety to prove himself a real tenor," was able to create "very little dramatic illusion."

14   *Tea at Archer's.* °*Fabian. First meeting of new Executive. 12 Millbank St. 17.*

Still at the essay. After dinner called for Archer but found that he was out at the Museum where I went and brought him back. We sat reading Ibsen until about 21 when I came home and got to work again. Clean forgot the Fabian.

Dinner (O[range] G[rove]) 1/–   British Museum concert ticket 2/6

15   °*Dialectical Society. South Place. Miss Law "Land Question from Individual Standpoint." 20. Romeo et Juliette. Covent Garden. Miss Eames. 20.*

Still at Ibsen.

Dinner (at Orange Grove) 1/–

A brief mention of *Romeo and Juliet* referred only to Jean de Reszke's inability to act Romeo, and Edouard's "puzzleheaded air" as Friar Laurence.

16 °*Carmen. Giulia Ravogli. Covent Garden. 20. °Fabian Historic. 28 Ashley Gardens. H. W. Carr on Ricardo.*

Finished the Ibsen MS in great excitement. Sat working at it all the evening.

Buses to St Martin's Lane & back 2d? Dinner (O.G.) 1/1?

17 °*Wind Instrument Society. Royal Academy of Music. 20½ (smoking). Press View. Cotman's Devon drawings at Dunthorne's. Press View. Tooth's. Press View. Old Water Colour Society. Press View. Menpes' India, Burma and Kashmir at Dowdeswell's. Press View. Jubilee Garden Party at Graves's. °Press View. Ladies Exhibition. Egyptian Hall.*

Began *World* article but did not do much of it. After the galleries met FE by appointment at the Aerated Bread Shop at Oxford Circus and went home with her.

Dinner (OG) 1/1 Cocoa &c Oxford O 1/9 Bus FE and I Uxbr[idge] Rd 8d Train Shep[herds] B[ush] to P[or]tl[an]d Rd 6d Postage of Ibsen MS. to Scott 4½d? Insurance 2d Postage Yeats' drawings to Shorter 3d

No reviews of the exhibitions were published.

18 *Crystal Palace Concert. 15. Jean Gerardy.* Tannhauser *at Covent Garden. Perotti, Albani, Maurel. °Hess and Becker's 2nd concert. St. James's Hall. 15.*

Working at *World* article—did not do much. Walter called; also Butterfield. FE came to the Palace with me.

Bus to St Martin's Ch[urch] 1d Train Ch[arin]g + to Vict[oria] 1½d Train Vict[oria] to C[rystal] P[alace] (FE and I) 4/– Bus to Longacre 1d

Gerardy played "very well indeed" (C791). ■ To G.B.S. (C791) the performance was "a rather desperate business." Jules Perotti, the tenor, G.B.S. "propose[d] to leave to his own reflections," but he found fault with Emma Albani's "curious helplessness in using the middle [range] of her voice." Maurel's Wolfram stood out from the others "by its intelligent artistic quality."

19 SUNDAY *Lecture at the Pimlico Radical Club at 20 on "Socialism, Old and New." (Sid M. Peartree, 17 Marston Place, Belgrave Rd. S.W.)*

Working at *World* article. Salt called in the afternoon; and I went out for a walk with him and eventually went home with him and stayed to tea. This involved sitting up until past 2 to finish my work for *The World*.

Bus York & Alb[any] to Ptld [Portland] Rd 1d to Vict[oria] 2d back 2d

20 Hedda Gabler *at the Vaudeville Theatre at 15, first time in England. Miss Robins and Miss Lea. Meet Wallas and Salt at Orange Grove at 13.45 to dine and go together to the pit. Covent Garden.* Traviata. *Albani.*

Corrected proof of *World* article. Salt and Wallas came back with me from the theatre and Wallas came in to tea. Wrote a note to Miss Robins between the acts of the Opera and copied it out when I got home. Not in bed consequently until about 2. Neuralgic signs of the overwork of the past week.

Dinner (O[range] G[rove]) 10d   Theatre 2/–   Bus to opera 1d

> G.B.S.'s 29 April 1891 column (C792) observed ironically how unrealistic *La Traviata* was, and noted how little Albani's impersonation of Violetta contributed to tubercular illusion because she is "pleasingly plump": "it does away with the painful impression which the last act produces. . . . Even in the agonies of death Albani robs the sick bed and the medicine bottles of half their terrors. . . ." ■ Shaw's letter (CL), intended to improve the performance, noted such things as the inaudibility of much of the play "from the back of the pit." No one had considered "the effect on us of the law of nature by which the resonance of a human body is considerably reduced when it sits down." The intention of the letter was to convey cautious and informed encouragement—though Miss Robins did not take kindly to criticism, however sweetened.

21 *Fabian Executive. 12 Millbank St. 17.* °*Rev. Joseph Wood lectures on "Wealth and Commonwealth" at 307 Strand. 19½.* °*Conference of Liberal Associations on School Board Election, Marylebone Division. First meeting. Paddington Liberal Association. 59 Porchester Rd., opposite Royal Oak station.*

Loafed and wrote letters. Wallas called me and sat for a few minutes until Miss Mackenzie (Hector Mackenzie's sister) called on me. Still toothachey. Went to FE after the Executive.

Dinner (at the new Wheatsheaf, Rathbone Pl[ace]) 1/–   Bus to St Martin's Ch[urch] 1d   Wash and Brush up Villiers St 2d   Train Ch[arin]g + to Ravenscourt Pk 6d   Shep[herds] Bush to P[or]tl[an]d Rd 6d

> The Wheatsheaf was under new management. Shaw had taken his business elsewhere when the quality declined.

22 °*Birkbeck Institute. Henry Murray's lecture on "Economics of Literature and how to Abolish Them." 15.* °*Covent Garden.* Rigoletto. *Maurel, Albani.*

Rather giddy and out of sorts. Took things easy; sat at home writing letters to Unwin and FE, etc., and singing. In the evening I went up to Dryhursts'; but they were not at home; so I came back as far as Salts', where I stayed until 23.45. When I got back I found that a stall for the Opera had come during my absence, too late to be of any use. Wrote to Simpson about it.

Tram to Hampstead 2d

> Shaw wrote Fisher Unwin (CL) that he preferred, rather than to collect his music criticism, to "leave di Bassetto to rot peacefully in his grave." He also suggested that his Ibsen

book would be "better let . . . alone" by Unwin, as Scott had more invested in Ibsen via his translations of the plays. The letter to FE has not survived. ▪ E. T. Simpson was the subeditor who handled the business side of the critics' needs for *The World*.

23 *Wolverhampton. Catch the 14.45 train from Euston. "The Capitalist's Share." Stay with J. W. Buttery at Strafford.* °*Grosvenor Club. Ladies' Night.* 22½.

Wrote to Archer about his article (in MS) on *Hedda Gabler*. Read Reclus' *Primitive Folk* in the train.

Cab to Euston 1/6   Train to Wolverhampton 10/5   Ins[uran]ce 6d
Cocoa &c at Strafford 1/6   Cloakroom 2d   Train to Strafford 1/1½

> Shaw's lecture to the Wolverhampton Trades and Labour Council was the third of four lectures under the general title "The Distribution of Wealth." Harold Cox, William Clarke, and W. S. De Mattos were the other speakers. ▪ J. W. Buttery, 1 Myrick Road, Strafford, a Fabian, was a contributor to the *Workman's Times*. He would be Shaw's host again in September and then again in March 1892. ▪ Since Archer was Ibsen's translator, he had followed the custom of critics in being silent about his own work; however, the new Ibsen productions needed to be brought to un-hostile attention, and he had prepared a column for his usual space in *The World* for 29 April 1891. Shaw's letter (CL) worried about "the House of Lords unnaturalness" of the style, by which Archer attempted some distance from his own role; with that and a few minor reservations, however, he "approve[d] immensely of the article."

24 *Lecture at Hanley on "Distribution of Wealth—the Capitalist's Share." Temperance Hall. New Street (off Market St.). 19½. (R. A. Reeve, 5 Ash Tree Villas. Basford. Stoke upon Trent). Stay at North Strafford Station Hotel.* °*Albéniz' concert. St. James's Hall. 15¼.* °*Fabian. Barnard's Inn. Oakeshott brings forward a Socialist Budget.*

Began the day by trying to ride on Buttery's bicycle. Then we walked to the Castle and went through it. We got back to dinner at 14 and sat talking until about 15½. Then we went out for another walk. I went to Stoke by the train which left between 17 and 18. Reeve met me at the station and when I had taken a room at the hotel we went out to Hanley.

Tip to woman at Strafford castle 6d   Train Strafford to Stoke 1/4½
Daily Chron[icle] 1d   Cocoa &c at Hanley 1/3

> This was apparently Shaw's first experience with bicycling, which later in the 1890s would become a passion with him. See also 1 May 1893.

25 *Crystal Palace Concert. 15. Mann's benefit.* °*Hess and Becker's third concert. St. James's Hall. 15. Private View. Detaille's picture at the Goupil Gallery. Private View. Lessore's Plymouth drawings at Buck and Reid's. Catch the 9.35 train up from Stoke.*

Wrote *World* article in the train. Mother came to the Crystal Palace with me. Went over to FE in the evening.

Hotel bill 7/–   Tips 1/–   Train to London 12/1½   Ins[uran]ce 1d
Cab to Ch[arin]g + 1/6   Train Ch[arin]g + to Victoria 1/½   *Star* ½d

Train M[other] & I to C[rystal] Pal[a]ce 4/–   Train to Shep[herds] Bush & back 1/–

> The Crystal Palace review appeared on 29 April 1891 (C792). The major performer was Ysaÿe, who played "the eternal but never quite unwelcome Mendelssohn concerto." Shaw would not publish reviews of the art exhibitions.

26 SUNDAY   *Lecture for the Camberwell Branch National Secular Society. 61 New Church Rd. S.E. at 19¼ on "Freethought, Old and New." (R. G. Lees). Catch the 12.30 train from Charing Cross to Woolwich Arsenal and go down with Wallas to dine with Whale at Shooters Hill.*

Train Ch[arin]g + to Woolwich 8d   Woolwich to Deptford 4d   Tram to New Cross Gate 1d   N.C.G. to Camberwell 2d   Camberwell to Blackfriars 2d   Farringdon to Ptld [Portland] Rd (train) 2d   *National Reformer* 2d

27   *Gerardy's recital. St. James's Hall. 15.*

Taking it easy over letters, singing etc. I expected a stall for the Opera; but it was sent to Archer by mistake and did not arrive. Emery Walker called and sat with me until about 21½ when we walked over to Brompton together and I went in to JP's. Fearful scene about FE, this being our first meeting since her return from the East. Did not get home until about 3.

Dinner 1/–

> "Gerardy was himself again," G.B.S. wrote on 6 May 1891 (C794), recalling the disappointing previous concert. ". . . The sustained artistic quality of his performances would be· extraordinary in an adult." ▪ Shaw's amorous relationship with Florence Farr had not escaped the notice of Jenny Patterson's friends while she was away. Shaw would write FE (*CL*), "Not for forty thousand such relations [as that with JP] will I forego one forty thousandth part of my relation with you. . . . You must give me back my peace. . . . The hart pants for cooling streams."

28   *Ysaÿe's recital. St. James's Hall. 15. Fabian Executive. 276 Strand (1st meeting there). 17.*

Began short article on the Eight Hours Day for *The Labour World*; but JP came before I had got far with it and the scene of last night was resumed until Walter happened to come in. I went over to FE in the evening getting there about 18½.

[Dinner] 1/1½   Bus Ch[arin]g + to Fabian 1d   Train to Shep[herds] Bush & back 1/–

> To G.B.S. (C794), Ysaÿe's performance was "sensational" but at a price. He "destroyed" the Beethoven violin concerto by imposing his own cadenzas, which were "monstrous excrescences on the movements." ▪ Shaw's *Labour World* article never appeared, and probably was never completed; however, his picture would appear in the 3 May 1891 issue with a biographical sketch labeling him "the best platform logician in London."

29 °*Birkbeck Institute. Chancery Lane. H. Murray's 2nd lecture on "Economics of Literature." 15. Press View at the [Royal] Academy.*

Did not get the Academy ticket until midday, and not then until after some telegraphing.

Telegram to Cooke 1/–?   Dinner 1/$\frac{4}{2}$?

30 °*Jerome Hopkins' piano-lecture concert. 20$\frac{1}{4}$.*

I forget this day; but I must have been working at the Academy article.

> Shaw's unsigned review in *The Observer*, 3 May 1891 (C793), began with the irony that the 1891 exhibition may "safely be assumed . . . [to be], on the whole, as good as any former one, in spite of all appearances to the contrary. There is, as usual, a numerous contingent of pictures, each of which has been compounded, like a chemist's prescription, according to a formula of proved popularity."

May

1 *Henschels' vocal recital. St. James's Hall. 15. Private View at the Academy.*

Finished article on the Academy for *The Observer*, not getting it done until very late. JP was here to tea and I went over to see her afterwards; but did not arrive until about 23. There was a young P. and O. ship's doctor there. Wrote letters in train going and coming. Had not time to dine.

Train to South Kensington & back 9d

> "At the vocal recital given by the Henschels at St James's Hall on Friday last, my equanimity was upset by an outrage perpetrated on me by the concert agent, the same being nothing less than my eviction from the corner seat to which *The World* has a prescriptive immemorial right, and the sandwiching of me into a place which I could not reach or leave without pushing past a row of people and making a public disturbance. I denounce the proceeding as a revolutionary one, and demand of that agent how he would like it himself if he had to go to thirtythree concerts every afternoon from Easter to Midsummer, and could not possibly avoid either arriving late or leaving early at every one of them. How would he like to feel as I do when I see the eyes of those young ladies who have been told the secret of where the celebrated critic sits, turning with awe and curiosity upon some impostor thrust into the seat which is morally mine?" (C794). ▪ JP had probably traveled to Egypt on a Peninsular and Oriental vessel, plucking therefrom a candidate to replace Shaw.

2 °*Logrew Harrison's concert. Queens Gate Hall. 15$\frac{1}{2}$. Eugene Holliday's recital (pianoforte). Prince's Hall. 15. °Strolling Players Amateur Orchestral Society. 20$\frac{1}{4}$. Boïto's Mefistofele at Covent Garden. Albani, Montariol, de Reszke, etc.*

Began *World* article. FE was at Prince's Hall with me. After the recital, which we both enjoyed immensely, we went to the Aerated Bread Shop at Piccadilly Circus and had some tea and cocoa. Then we walked to St.

James's Park station and, as she had a lot of time to spare, from that to Victoria. We went by train together to Portland Rd., she coming merely to kill time. At High St., Mrs. Home (whose new name I cannot remember) and her new husband got in and we chatted as far as Baker St., where they got out. When we got out I walked back to Baker St. with FE and left her.

Dinner 1/2   Cloakroom at Prince's Hall 3d   Railway tickets 1/8
Tickets for Railway Porters [   ]   *Sports* 1d   Bus to Long Acre 1d

> Eugene Holliday, a pupil of the great Anton Rubinstein, according to G.B.S. (C794), perpetrated "occasional violence" upon his Broadwood piano, in "exaggerations of genuine executive power." ▪ Shaw missed the opera and noted (C794) only that it had been revived "with success." ▪ Mrs. Home's new husband was W. H. Wynne, of 14 Argyll Road, Kensington, W., a lawyer with chambers at 40 Chancery Lane, E.C.

3 SUNDAY   *Lecture for the S. D. F. Southwark and Lambeth Branch, New Nelson Hall, Lower Marsh, on "Alternatives to Social Democracy" (George Fleming, 41 Walnut Tree Walk, Kennington Rd.). Labour Day in Hyde Park. Eight Hours. Speak from No. 6 platform.*

Finished *World* article before going to the Park. Came away from the meeting with Wallas. Ugly crush at the Marble Arch. Wallas came here to tea. Hunter Watts and his wife and sister came as far as Westminster with me from the S. D. F. When I got the *World* article revised and ready for post it was too late to go to Lady Colin's; so I wrote an apology. Got to bed about 2.

Bus to Oxford St 1d   Oxford St to West[minster] Br[idge] 2d
West[minster] Br[idge] to Grafton St 2d   *Justice* (2 weeks) 2d
Common[wea]l 1d

4   °*Kensington Town Hall. Concert. 20. Fabian Central Group Meeting. 32 Great Ormond St. 20. Margaret Wild's recital. Prince's Hall. 15. °Oliviers' in the evening, if possible. Put off.* °*Liberal and Radical Union. National Liberal Club. 20. °Covent Garden.* Carmen. *Zelie de Lussan.*

Wrote to Scott about the Ibsen book and went at my letters etc. Busy all day in this way. Got away early from Fabian meeting. Mother went to the Opera. Went out to FE; but found the place in darkness. Wandered about disappointed for a time and then came home. Reading over the old "Refutation of Anarchism" to see whether it would do for republication by the Fabian.

Star ½d   Bus to Ch[arin]g + Rd 1d   Dinner (at OG) 1/–   Train
Gower St to Shep[herds] B[ush] [and] back to P[or]tl[an]d Rd 1/–

> Shaw returned from FE's darkened house to write to her—poetically, he thought—that, without her, "I have fallen in with my boyhood's mistress, Solitude, and wandered aimlessly with her once more, drifting like the unsatisfied moon" (CL). ▪ Margaret Wild's recital was neither attended nor reviewed by G.B.S. ▪ Shaw's dissection of Anarchism was published as *Fabian Tract* No. 45 (A21), *The Impossibilities of Anarchism*, in 1893.

5   *Waldemar Meyer's concert. St. James's Hall. 15. Meet Gordon at 10.30 at Walter Scott's, 10 Warwick Lane, to discuss Fabian Review etc. °Lawrence Kellie's vocal recital. Steinway Hall. 15. Fabian Executive. 276 Strand. 17. Beatrice Potter on "Co-operative Workshops." Essex Hall. 20. °Ernest King's concert. Prince's Hall. 20.*

Webb was at Scott's. Walked along the Embankment with him to Whitehall. When I got home wrote a letter to Kinloch-Cooke about the *Observer's* treatment of my Academy article. FE and I left Meyer concert when it was half over and sat in St. James's Park until it was time for me to go to the Fabian. After the Executive, Wallas, Webb and I had a meal together. Then we went to the Potter lecture. I went out at 21.20 and hurried out to the Mona Hotel to the rehearsal of the Independent Theatre play. Found no one there but Grein and Jarvis who told me how the play (Mrs. Edgren's) had been given up through Braekstad's obstinacy about his translation. I then, acting on a message left with them by FE, went off to Raleigh's rooms in Great Portland St. where I found her with him and Miss Kenward. I saw her home.

Telegram to FE 6½d   Omnibus to Newgate St 1½d   *Observer* 4d   Bus Longacre to Grafton St 1d   Dinner 1/⁴   Train St Ja[me]s's Pk to Temple 1½d   FE's ticket St Ja[me]s's Pk to High St 7d   Cocoa &c at Aerated B[rea]d Shop op[posite] St Clem[ent] Danes 1/–   Bus Essex St to Bedford St 1d   Train to Shep[herds] Bush & back, also FE's ticket 1/8

> Reviewed on 20 May 1891 (C797). Waldemar Meyer was an "easygoing *virtuoso*," playing everything "with apparent facility and satisfaction." ▪ Clement Kinloch-Cooke was "such an unspeakable greenhorn" as an editor, Shaw wrote Emery Walker (*CL*), that he permitted the propietor of *The Observer* to "mutilate" the Royal Academy review, "interpolate" into it "scraps of insufferable private view smalltalk," and "season it with obvious little puffs of his private friends." What remained were "broken fragments of Shaw sticking ridiculously in the proprietary mud." ▪ Mrs. Anne Charlotte Edgren (1849–1892) was author of *True Women* (1883); the English translation from the Swedish by H. L. Braekstad was published in 1890. ▪ Cecil Raleigh (1856–1914), melodramatist; Edith Kenward (?–1905), actress, then in a minor role in *Husband and Wife*, at the Criterion.

6   *°Birkbeck Institute. H. Murray's 3rd lecture on "Economics of Literature." 15. Edgar Haddock's 1st Musical Afternoon. 15. °Albert Hall. The Golden Legend. Nordica. Ben Davies etc. 20. °Gerardy's last recital. St. James's Hall. 15.*

Worked at the old essay "Refutation of Anarchism" which the Fabian is to re-issue as a tract. Went out to FE in the evening. Called on Archer in the afternoon and spent an hour with him.

Dinner 1/⁴   Bus Oxford O to Kingsgate St 1d   Gower St to Shepherd's Bush (ret[urn]) 1/–

> G.B.S. (C797) described Edgar Haddock, a violinist, as "an ambitious orchestral player from Leeds" with nothing "sufficiently exceptional" in "conception or quality of execution" to warrant exposure as a soloist.

7 *Mme A. de Swiatlowsky and Monsieur Max Reichel concert. Prince's Hall. 15. °Jules Hollander's recital (pianoforte). Steinway Hall. 20½. °South St. Pancras Liberal and Radical Association Executive Meeting. 195 Gray's Inn Rd. 20. Don Giovanni at Covent Garden. 20. Maurel. °Miss Horrock's concert. Prince's Hall. 15.*

Still at Anarchism paper. JP came in in the evening and made a scene about FE. I was just then beginning my *World* article. Opera rather spoilt in consequence. When I got back after midnight I found her wandering about the Square. Took her home in a hansom. Walked back and did not get to bed, very tired, until after 3. In the afternoon I went to Steinway Hall by mistake before going to Prince's Hall.

Dinner 1/1½?   Bus down Bond St 1d   Hansom to Brompton Sq 3/–

> Violinist Max Reichel proved not nearly so interesting as Mme. Swiatlowsky, "a very clever and original singer . . . with a certain variety and fire peculiar to herself, and with some charming *virtuoso* tricks of *mezza voce* . . ." (C797). ■ G.B.S.'s 13 May 1891 review (C795) was completely given over to *Don Giovanni*. He had been in search "of a satisfactory performance" of that masterpiece since boyhood, and had now concluded "that Mozart's turn will hardly be in my time." Even Maurel proved able to give only "a description" of the Don rather than "an impersonation of him." ■ The *her*—a faulty pronoun reference—is JP, not FE, and the Square is not Brompton Square, where JP lived, but Fitzroy Square, where she was spying on Shaw.

8 *Fabian. Barnard's Inn. W. S. DeMattos on "Co-operation." 20.*

Tried to write *World* article but could do nothing, I was so tired and out of sorts. Wallas called in the morning. Day wasted. Spoke briefly at the Fabian. Webb walked home with me—Wallas part of the way.

9 *°Dialectical Society. Business meeting at Miss Baines's. 38 Wellington St. Strand, W. C. 19. °Private View. 19th Century Gallery.*

Worked at *World* article. Bax called in the forenoon; and we went to lunch together at the new Wheatsheaf. Went out to FE in the evening. Let the time slip and lost my train back. Picked up a drunken old woman who was prowling in the Goldhawk Rd. and was delayed half an hour putting her into the way to get home. Out of sorts: revolted by everything. Not in bed until past 2.

Dinner (Wheatsheaf) 1/–?   Train to Shep[herds] Bush (ret[urn] not used) 1/–

10 SUNDAY *Lecture on "Freethinking, Old and New" for the Battersea Branch National Secular Society. Shed of Truth (A. Watkin, 32 Stanley St., Queens Rd. S. W.). JP's to tea before lecture.*

Finished article for *World.*

Train to S[ou]th Kensington 4d   Bus Knightsbridge to Battersea Pk Rd 1½d   Chelsea Br[idge] to Knightsbridge 1d

> The Battersea Secularists called their meeting hall "Shed of Truth."

11 *Terry's Theatre.* Lady from the Sea. *First time in England. 14¼. Rose Miller.* °*Mme. Burmeister-Peterson's pianoforte recital. Prince's Hall. 15.* °*Leonard Borwick's recital. St. James's Hall. 15. Sims Reeves's farewell concert. Albert Hall. 20.* °*Clara Myer's concert. 1 Belgrave Square. 15.*

When I was dressing a couple of musical people called, introduced by Dowdeswell. Set to work on correspondence, this after the *Lady from the Sea.* FE came with me to the Orange Grove; and after I had had something to eat I saw her to Charing Cross station.

Bus to Garrick St 1d   Programme at theatre 6d   Dinner (at Orange Grove, FE and me) 1/7   Bus Oxford O—Marble Arch 1d

The previous year, when Shaw first met Florence Farr, she asked him if he would be willing to play the Stranger in Ibsen's *The Lady from the Sea,* should she get a performance underwritten, since Shaw's red beard would create a striking effect when set off against a seaman's pea-jacket. Shaw "pleaded ineptitude and declined." Further, he turned her toward *Rosmersholm* instead, leaving the other play for Rose Miller. ▪ Shaw wrote two notices of the farewell concert of Sims Reeves (1818–1900), who was especially noted for his Handelian repertory. In *The Sunday World,* 17 May 1891 (C796), signed Corno di Bassetto, he declared Reeves "perhaps the greatest tenor in the world." In *The World,* 20 May 1891 (C797), he added that although at seventy-three Reeves had lost some "powers of endurance" and could not cope with a few "trying" songs, "he can still leave the next best tenor in England an immeasurable distance behind."

12 *Bach Choir. Prince's Hall 17 to 18¼.* °*Fabian Executive. 276 Strand W.C. Ysaÿe's recital. St. James's Hall. 15. Call at Jaeger's to try on new suit.* °*Winter and Van Lennops' concert. St. James's Banqueting Hall. 20.*

I think it was today that the first batch of Ibsen proofs came. If so I began to work on them. FE was at the Bach Choir concert. We went into the Aerated Bread Shop at Piccadilly Circus (parting from Mother at the door) and had some milk etc. Then I saw her to St. James's Park station.

"I can frankly and unreservedly say," G.B.S. wrote (C797) of the unaccompanied part singing, "that I would not desire to hear a more abominable noise than was offered to us under pretext of Bach's [motet] *Singet dem Herrn....*" ▪ This entry was written so long after the events that Shaw could not recollect his expenses for the day and made no attempt to reconstruct them.

13 *Meeting of Paddington Women's League at 58 Porchester Terrace (Queens Rd. station) to discuss Eight Hours. Evening (Mrs. Mallet). Mrs. Green's. 14 Kensington Square (High St. station) at 22½. To meet Haldane etc. Waldemar Meyer. 15. St. James's Hall.*

Working at Ibsen proofs. Spoke at Porchester Terrace. Walked home with Webb, Olivier coming as far as Park Lane.

Dinner 1/1   Train to Bayswater & return to High St. 4½d

Mrs. Alice Sophia Amelia Green (1847–1929), also known as Mrs. Stopford Green, historian of Irish birth and loyalties, was also an ardent radical on other political issues. She was the widow of historian J. R. Green.

14 °*Philharmonic Concert. St. James's Hall. 20. Mrs. Carr's At-Home. 28 Ashley Gardens. 20¼ to 24.*

Began *World* article. Massingham wrote to me for an article on Sims Reeves. Went to 276 Strand to see him about it after dinner. When I got back I began this article.

Dinner (at Orange Grove) 1/2   Bus thither 1d   Ch[arin]g + to 276 Strand 1d

> "The Man of the Week: Sims Reeves: The Last of the Great Tenors," *Sunday World*, 17 May 1891 (C795).

15 °*The Henschels' second recital. St. James's Hall. 15. °Covent Garden. Don Giovanni.*

Finished *World* article. Did not go to the Opera. JP was here and kept me a long time talking. At last, at about 21, I went up to Salts' to get some rest. Also finished the Sims Reeves article for *The Sunday World* and brought it down myself to 276 Strand where everybody was out.

Bus westward along Strand 1d   Dinner (at Orange Grove) 1/-   Bus home 1d   to Y[or]k & Alb[any] 1d

16 *Mme. de Pachmann's recital. St. James's Hall. 15. Call on Bax about 18.*

Working at Ibsen proofs. Went off to FE in the evening. She was at the concert with me (so was Kate Gurly: I had 3 tickets). After it we took a stroll in St. James's Park. I then left her to call on Bax; but he was not in. I went on to Archer's: he was out also; so I wrote a letter for him on his typewriter and went home to tea, getting wet in a heavy shower as I did so. Then I went off to FE for the rest of the evening.

Dinner 1/2   Train to Shepherds Bush 1/-

> The former Maggie Oakey, pianist Mme. de Pachmann was married to pianist and pantomimist Vladimir de Pachmann. G.B.S. admired her skills but on this occasion did not review her performance.

17 SUNDAY *Go up to Salts' to tea at 18 and go with H. S. to his paper on Shelley at the Anarchist place on Great College St. Camden Town at 20. Karl Armbruster and van Dyck to call at noon.*

Intended to do a lot of work; but did hardly anything except write a letter in French to van Dyck after he went away. When I got home about 22, I wrote a letter to the East Bradford people who had telegraphed to me asking me to contest the Parliamentary seat. Advised them to choose a working man.

Bus to York & Alb[any] 1d   Tram Britannia to Euston Rd 1d

> Ernest Marie-Hubert van Dyck (1861–1923) was a Belgian tenor who had sung at Bayreuth. He would debut in London on 19 May 1891.

18 Wet day. Sang a lot and read *Review of Reviews* etc. Did not get to work until 14 and then had to write up this diary—in arrear as usual—and to look up my frightfully neglected correspondence. Made out my Income Tax return. Did some work on the Ibsen proofs and brought them to Archer, who was going out with his wife to the Vaudeville Theatre. Went with them in the bus, they getting out at Covent Garden and I going on to St. Martin's Lane on my way to FE's. Only stayed about 45 minutes with her, as I had promised to go to JP. Got the 22.18 train from Ravenscourt Park to South Kensington. Did not leave JP's until past 1.

Bus South Row to St Martin's Lane 1d   Train Ch[arin]g + to Ravenscourt Pk 6d   R. P. to S[ou]th Kensington 6d

19 °*Fabian Executive. 276 Strand. 17. Archer lectures at Royal Institution at 15. Covent Garden.* Manon. *Debut of van Dyck.*

Up rather late. Found that the Fabian meeting had been put off and so lost my time.

Bus Albemarle St to St Martin's Lane 1d   *St Ja[me]s's Gazette* 1d
Dinner (O[range] G[rove]) 1/–   Bus to 276 Strand from Ch[arin]g + 1d   Bus to Opera 1d

> G.B.S.'s first positive review of van Dyck was in a notice of a concert, in the 17 June 1891 *World*, in which the tenor is reported to have been "recalled . . . three times to the platform." In *Manon* he sang the role of Des Grieux.

20 *Waldemar Meyer's recital. St. James's Hall. 15. Meeting of Free Russia People at Reynolds' in St. James's St. to arrange concert. 16. Covent Garden.* Les Huguenots. *Albani, Mravina (Russian soprano) (debut), the de Reszkes etc.*

Worked at appendix to Ibsen essay. Mrs. Pease was at the concert with me. Sat up after the Opera to finish a fable I was writing in reply to one written by FE. Archer came in whilst I was dining at the Pine Apple and walked down Regent St. with me.

Star ½d   Dinner 1/1   *Saturday Review* 6d   Bus to Oxford St 1d

> Reynolds & Co., printsellers, were located at St. James's Street, S.W. ▪ *Les Huguenots* was reviewed by G.B.S. on 27 May 1891 (C798). Eugenia Mravina (1864–1914) as Marguerite had "a voice of . . . exceptional range and flexibility." ▪ FE would publish a short novel, *The Dancing Faun*, in 1895. There is no way to identify her "fable" with any preliminary version of the novel. ▪ G.B.S. did not attend the Waldemar Meyer recital.

21 °*Royal Minuet and Concert party. Mrs. Vincent Glass's, 49 Baker St. W.* 15¼. °*Albéniz's concert. St. James's Hall. 20.15. L. Borwick's second recital. St. James's Hall. 15.* °*Lawrence Kellie's second recital. Steinway Hall. 15.*

Began *World* article and got along famously with it. JP was at the concert with me; she left me at Oxford Circus. Webb called whilst I was at tea. In the evening I went to FE's; but she was out; so I went on to the Sparlings'. Sparling was there alone; but we went off to Lang's (who was in bed with the influenza) and found May there.

Dinner 1/1?   Train to Hammersmith & back 1/—

> Leonard Borwick's piano recital was not reviewed by G.B.S.   ▪   Lang is Andrew Lang.

22   Fabian. Barnard's Inn. Hampstead Group to bring up Unemployed report. 20. °Steinway Hall. Mabel Senior's concert. 15. Wagner birthday concert at Earl Dysart's, Ham House, Richmond. 15.

Finished *World* article. The Carrs were at the concert. I did not see them until we reached Ham House. We came back together; and I dined with them after a little singing whilst the dinner was being prepared. Then I went on to the Fabian in a hansom with Geraldine, Carr following us later on. Webb and Wallas came back with me from the Fabian as far as Wallas's Rooms in Ormond St., where I left them.

Train to Richmond & back 1/3   Excess fare to Twinkenham 1½d
Twickenham ferry 1d   Tram along Vauxhall Br[idge] Rd ½d   Cab to
Barnard's Inn 2/—

> The 9th Earl of Dysart was a devoted Wagnerite and a patron of the Richter concerts. G.B.S.'s mixed but largely satisfied notice appeared in the 3 June 1891 *World* (C799).

23   °G. Grossmith's recital. St. James's Hall. 15. Rose Lyton's violin recital. Prince's Hall. 15. Die Meistersinger. Covent Garden. 19½. Call on Archer for the Ibsen proofs on the way to the Opera.

Still at the Ibsen paper.

Dinner 1/1?

> The performance, said G.B.S. (C798), was "the most deeply enjoyable of the season," with Jean de Reszke's robust tenor utilized, for once, "in earnest," in the *Meistersinger* leading role.

24 SUNDAY   Speak in the open air for the North Kensington Socialist Society (B. F. Dean, 7 Westwick Gardens, West Kensington W.). Wet weather. Go into the church or coffee house.

Correcting *World* proof. In the afternoon JP came here and made a terrific scene. The wet weather spoilt the meeting in the evening. We had to collect an audience from house to house and have a little meeting in the coffee tavern.

Train to Latimer Rd & back from Nott[ingham] Hill 1/—

25   First Richter Concert. St. James's Hall. 20½. °Poznanski and Eva Lonsdale. Historical and Musical Matinee. Steinway Hall. 15. °Miss Edith Greenoff's concert. Marlborough Rooms. 15. °Miss Mary Ditchburn's concert.

Steinway Hall 15. °Liberal and Radical Union Meeting. National Liberal Club. 20.

Worked at the proof of the Ibsen paper. FE was at the concert; I left her at Baker St. station at about 16.20. Went back to work at the proof after the Richter Concert.

Dinner 11d   Bus along Regent St 1d   *Star* ½d

> G.B.S. (C799) noted ironically the "thrilling novelty" of the program (by which he meant its opposite) and observed that the Richter orchestra "is by no means what it ought to be; and it has been getting worse instead of better for some years past."

26   Fabian Executive. 276 Strand. W.C. 16¼. Take the chair. °Blackburn's Black and White lecture at Mrs. Jopling's studio, Clareville Grove. 21. Archer's second lecture at the Royal Institution. 15.

Up rather late. Little time to do anything except write up this diary and write a line to JP. Walkley and Lowe were at the lecture. Walkley came with me as far as Piccadilly. After the Executive went with Wallas and Oakeshott to the Orange Grove and had cocoa etc; they left before me. As I was going out I found FE having tea at the table next to the door with a young fellow whose name I forget. Presently Mrs. Sheldon Amos, her daughter, and Miss Whitehead came in and sat at the same table. FE and I went to Hammersmith together, parting from her friend at Charing Cross.

Dinner 1/–?   Bus Picc[adilly] to Fabian 1d   Fab[ian] to Ch[arin]g + 1d   Cocoa &c at Orange Grove 1/–?   Train Ch[arin]g + to Ravenscourt Pk, FE and I 1/4   Shep[herds] B[ush] to Ptld Rd 6d

> A vocal advocate of women's suffrage, Mrs. Amos was the widow of Sheldon Amos (1835–1886), professor of Jurisprudence at University College, London, from 1869 to 1879. ▪ Catherine M. Whitehead, of 10 Montague St., W., first came to Shaw's notice as a Browning Society member on 27 April 1888. That she remained in his circle is evident from her handling arrangements for a Shavian music lecture on 31 October 1895.

27   °Marianne and Clara Eisslers' concert. Prince's Hall. 20¼. °Edgar Haddock's 2nd afternoon. Steinway Hall. 15. °Town Hall, Westminster. 20.

Working at Ibsen proofs. Went to the Museum after dinner and stayed there until closing time. Sat at home over them all the evening.

Dinner 1/–?   Bus to Musuem 1d

28   °Philharmonic Concert. St. James's Hall. 20. Ysaÿe's violin recital. St. James's Hall. 15.

Began *World* article. Went to the Museum after the concert and worked over the Ibsen proofs until closing time. Stayed in over them all the evening.

Dinner 1/–?

> Reviewed by G.B.S. on 10 June 1891 (C800). Ysaÿe "came triumphantly through the highest test a violinist can face—a Mozart sonata."

29 *Frank Howgrave's pianoforte recital. Prince's Hall. 15. Press View. Early English Masters at Dowdeswell's.*

Finished and sent off *World* article. Went to the Museum again after the recital and worked at the proofs there. Went up to Salt's late in the evening. Did not play.

Dinner 1/1½?   Bus Picc[adilly] O to Drury Lane 1d   Ptld Rd to Regents Pk Rd 1d

Frank Howgrave's "fluency of execution" as a pianist, said G.B.S. (C800), "is so prodigious that it produces an irresistible comic effect."

30 *Sarasate's first concert. St. James's Hall. 15. °Misses Albissers' concert. Portman Rooms. 20. °Patti concert. Albert Hall. 15. Faust at Covent Garden. van Dyck.*

Working at Ibsen book. JP was at the concert with me. Left her at the corner of Vigo St.

Dinner 1/–?   Bus Vigo St to Clipstone St 1d

Sarasate, although "an extraordinarily good violinist," was again handicapped, G.B.S. wrote (C800), by William Cusins, "an extraordinarily bad conductor." ▪ Van Dyck, G.B.S. noted with regret (C799), "was unlucky enough to have a baddish cold" when he appeared in the title role, and had to take the highest notes "in a curious falsetto." Still, he was "by far the best Faust" Shaw had seen, not the usual "sentimental walking gentleman."

31 SUNDAY *Lecture at Milton Hall on "Freethought, Old and New" (Miss Vance, 24 Caroline St., Camden Town. N.W.). 20. Call on FE in the afternoon to meet Grein. Tea at Salts'.*

Finished *World* article and corrected proof. Thompson called in the morning. We made a mistake about the hour the lecture commenced, and went down at 19. Had to return and go back at 20. Mrs. Salt and I played *Don Giovanni* afterwards until midnight. JP came in in the afternoon.

Train to Shep[herds] Bush 6d   Chiswick to Hampstead H[ea]th 8d

Possibly William Marcus Thompson, who knew Shaw and would have been interested in the subject.

June

1 *Richter Concert. 20⅘. St. James's Hall. °Irene and Rene Ortmans' concert. °Miss Isaacson's concert. Prince's Hall. 20. Cusins' concert. St. James's Hall. 15.*

Finished and sent off galley proofs of the Ibsen book.

Dinner 1/–   Bus to Richter concert 1d

> G.B.S.'s 10 June review (C800) found Richter, in conducting Mozart and Beethoven, far more "decisive, strenuous, full of serious business." ▪ Sir William George Cusins (1833–1893) was a conductor, composer, and professor of piano at the Guildhall School of Music. Master of the Music to Queen Victoria, he also conducted the London Philharmonic from 1867 to 1883.

2 *Paderewski's Orchestral Concert. St. James's Hall. 15. Fabian Executive. 276 Strand. 17.* °*Archer's 3rd lecture at the Royal Institution. 15.* °*Romeo et Juliette at Covent Garden. Re-entree of Melba.* °*Concert at Chelsea Town Hall. 20. Liberal and Radical Association, Endsleigh District Annual Meeting. 30 Fitzroy Square. Reform Club.*

Trying to do something at the appendix to the Ibsen paper, but not getting on much, as JP called in the morning. After the Executive went with Wallas and Massingham into Gatti and Rodesano's for a meal. Left Wallas at Charing Cross and went on to FE. Disillusion.

Dinner 1/3½   Bus Ch[arin]g + to Fab[ian] 1d   Grub at Rodesano's
2/2   Bus to Ch[arin]g + 1d   Train Ch[arin]g + to Rav[enscourt] Pk
6d   Shep[herds] B[ush] to P[or]tl[an]d Rd 6d   Gave boy in Villiers St
6d   Wash at Faulkner's 3d

> Paderewski, G.B.S. wrote (C800), "gave two concertos—one too many—Beethoven in E flat and Schumann. It was hard on us, and harder on Schumann." ▪ Shaw's "disillusion"—if with Florence and not a reference to something or someone earlier in the day—cannot have lasted more than overnight, as the next day's entry evidences.

3 *Sarasate's first recital. St. James's Hall. 20. Carl Fuchs's violincello recital. Prince's Hall. 15.*

Wrote up this diary—a week in arrear. Met Kropotkin at Prince's Hall. After the recital went to St. Martin's Lane for dinner and then to the Stores where I bought a nest of drawers to keep my tickets etc. in. Wrote to Hedwig Sonntag asking her to give me lessons in German. Actually wrote a few verses to FE, being more deeply moved than I could have imagined. JP was here for tea. She stayed after the others had gone out to the concert, which I did not reach until late.

Dinner (O[range] G[rove]) 1/5   Nest of drawers at Stores 2/6   Bus self to St Ja[me]s's Hall & JP to Brompton Sq 3d

> Sarasate's "miraculous technical feats," Shaw wrote (C800), included "a chromatic run in sixths . . . with a speed, a delicacy of touch, and an exquisite precision of intonation that would have astonished [Giuseppe] Tartini's devil." ▪ Carl Fuchs, a young Manchester cellist, was "an unpretentious but excellent player" (C800). ▪ Shaw's verses to FE have not survived among her correspondence, but his letters of this period to her show a tendency to wax poetic (and passionate). For a draft of verses to her which Shaw kept, see 30 August 1892.

4   *Leo de Silka's recital. St. James's Hall. 15. °Argosy meeting. 9 St. John's Wood Park. E. Bennett on Hedda Gabler. 20. Albéniz's concert. St. James's Hall. 20.15.*

Began *World* article. Went to JP to tea. She followed me to the concert and walked with me to Oxford Circus, where I put her into a bus.

Dinner 1/2½   Train to S[ou]th Kensington 6d   Bus Brompton Rd to St Ja[me]s's Hall 2d   JP (bus fare) 2d

> Leo de Silka was "not yet quite clear . . . of relapsing into a mere brilliant drawing room player," possessing "technical vigor" as a pianist rather than interpretative subtlety (C800). ▪ Probably Enoch Arnold Bennett. See also 1 July 1889 for an earlier Bennett presentation. ▪ G.B.S. "looked in" at the Albéniz concert "for a few minutes"—long enough to catch Albéniz "napping over the A flat polonaise of Chopin, which he really played shockingly" (C800).

5   *(6th) Press View. John Lavery's pictures. Goupil Gallery. 10 to 18. (6th) Moscheles' pictures at Stacey's Gallery. 28 Old Bond St.*

Finished and sent off *World* article.

Dinner (Wheatsheaf) 1/–?

> (Sir) John Lavery (1856–1941), Belfast-born portraitist, was a Whistler disciple. Among his canvases would be a Shaw, now in the National Gallery of Ireland, Dublin.

6   *Sarasate's second concert. St. James's Hall. 15. °Scottish Home Industries Concert. 6 Carlton House Terrace. 16. See yesterday. Call on Hedwig Sonntag in the evening to arrange about German lessons. 46 St. Petersburg Place W.*

Worked at the Ibsen appendix, with which I get on very slowly. JP was at Sarasate's concert, which I left early. Spent the evening at the Sonntags'. Went round by Torrington Square on my way there to call on Jacques and get the current number of *The Musical Times,* in which there is an attack on me.

Dinner 1/1?   Bus Tott[enham] Ct Rd corner to Bayswater 4d

> G.B.S. did not review the Sarasate concert. ▪ Shaw was attacked largely for his hostility to Brahms.

7 SUNDAY   *Lecture at the Deptford Liberal Club on "Alternatives to Social Democracy." 20. (J. Olivier. Broadway, Deptford).*

Troubled by what I first took for indigestion caused by eating a heap of cherries, but which afterwards turned out to be the influenza. Read a lot of *An Unsocial Socialist.* Corrected *World* proof. Did some work on the Ibsen book. Very bad night—delirious.

Train to New Cross &° back 1/4?   Sweets 1d   Sent H. Sonntag for German lessons in advance £5

8   *Richter Concert. St. James's Hall. 20½.* °*Poznanski and Eva Lonsdale. Steinway Hall. 15.* °*Liberal and Radical Union meeting at National Liberal Club. 20 H. Sonntag. 17.*

Regularly weak and ill, but managed to get through my work as usual. Worked at the Ibsen appendix and preface. When I got to Sonntag's I nearly gave up the idea of going in, I felt so weak; but on venturing I did two hours' study without noticing how long it was. At the concert I noticed a pain in the eyes for the first time. Walter [Gurly] called in the afternoon. Slept well.

Dinner (Orange Grove) 1/2   Train to Bayswater & back 8d

> "Richter was himself again on this occasion" was all G.B.S. could write, as tag to his review (C800), being ill with influenza.

9   *Archer's 4th lecture at the Royal Institution. 15. Fabian Executive. 276 Strand. 17. Committee on Autumn Course of lectures. 16.* °*Farley Sinkins' 1st Orchestral Concert. St. James's Hall. 15.*

Strength recovered. Finished and sent off MS of Ibsen appendix and preface with agreement executed. Spoke to old Mrs. Archer, and to Miss Robins at the Royal Institution. After the Executive went to the Orange Grove and had a meal there with Olivier, Massingham and Wallas. Then went to JP and stayed with her until about 1.

Dinner 1/-   Supper at Orange Grove 1/4   Train Ch[arin]g + to S[ou]th Kensington 4d

10   °*Edgar Haddock's 3rd Musical afternoon. Steinway Hall. 15. Royal College of Music Orchestral Concert. St. James's Hall. 15.* °*H. Sonntag's. 17. Mireille at Covent Garden. Miss Eames. 20.* °*John Thorman's concert. Portman Rooms. 20.* °*Great Liberal Demonstration. South St. Pancras Liberal and Radical Association. Holborn Town Hall. 20.*

Correspondence, diary etc. After the concert went to the Orange Grove and dined, and then on to David Nutt's, the booksellers, to ask about Glasenapp's new Wagner lexicon. There was a difficulty about getting to Bayswater because of the bus strike and eventually I got into a bus which only took me back to Charing Cross. So I gave up the idea of going to Sonntag's and telegraphed an apology. JP here to tea.

Dinner (at Orange Grove) 1/-   PMG 1d   Train Ch[arin]g + to Temple 1d   Bus Nutt's to Ch[arin]g + 2d   Telegram to H[edwig] Sonntag 9d   Libretto of *Mireille* 1/6

> With Henry Holmes (1839–1905) replacing Villiers Stanford as conductor, G.B.S. saw, in his 17 June 1891 review (C801), improved ensemble musicianship from the student instrumentalists, "who are probably individually better solo players than the members of the best professional orchestra Beethoven ever saw in his life." However, "the vocal department . . . seems as hopeless as ever." ■ The Gounod-Carré opera, to G.B.S., was a poor choice for Covent Garden and poorly cast, Emma Eames lacking conviction in the

crucial title role. ▪ The David Nutt publishing house was run by Alfred Trübner Nutt (1856–1910), a folklorist and son of the founder of the foreign bookselling and publishing firm. ▪ The "lexicon" was the *Wagner Encyklopädie*, by Carl Friedrich Glasenapp, 1891.

11   *H. Sonntag's at 18.*

Cold in the head very bad indeed. Began *World* article. Went into the City to buy ink-ribbon for typewriter. On my way back called at Pennells', thinking that this was the day of the At-Home. Found nobody in. Went on to Sonntag's, and worked there for more than an hour. Did not get there until past 18. Went to FE in the evening.

Train to Moorgate 4d?   Irish hose 4/–   Spanner 6d   Dinner (at Arcadian) 1/3?   Train Mansion Ho[use] to Westminster ?   West-[minster] to Notting Hill Gate ?   Bayswater to Ptld Rd ?   (I forget all these fares.)   Ptld Rd to Shep[herds] Bush & back 1/–

12   *Fabian. Barnard's Inn. 20. Graham Wallas on "National Workshops." Dine at Wallas's at 18. °Handel Society's concert. St. James's Hall. 20½. König Thamos (Mozart) and Allegro e Pensieroso. Mrs. Pennell's at 16¼ to meet Elizabeth Robins. Olga Vulliet's recital (pianoforte). Prince's Hall. 15.*

Cold suppressed, if not quite cured. Continued *World* article. Clarke and Olivier were at Wallas's. Spoke at the Fabian.

Dinner 1/–?

G.B.S. neither attended nor reviewed the piano recital, but noted only that he had missed the Handel concert.

13   *°Sarasate's concert. St. James's Hall. 15. Independent Theatre Society Members' Meeting. Mona Hotel. 16. °Jan Mulder's concert. St. James's Banqueting Hall. 15. Miscellaneous Operatic Concert at Albert Hall. 15.*

Writing letters. Walked away from the Independent Theatre meeting with [C. W.] Jarvis. In the evening went out to look for FE; but she was out and I went on first to Radfords' and then to Walkers'. Mrs. Walker, who leaves for Ireland tomorrow, was in bed; but Dolly came down to talk until Walker came in. He came with me to the station.

Dinner 1/–?   Train S[ou]th Kensington to Ch[arin]g + 4d   Prog[ram]me at concert 1/–

14 SUNDAY   *Speak in Battersea Park at 18½. Speak at the Demonstration of the General Railway Workers' Union, in Hyde Park, from No. 4 platform.*

Corrected proof of *World* article and finished it.

Bus Chelsea Br[idge] to Knigh[t]sbridge 1d   S.D.F. collection 1/–
Papers bought in park 3d   Acid drops 1d

15   *Richter Concert. 20½. Todhunter's* Poison Garden *and* Sicilian Idyll *at the Vaudeville Theatre. 14½.*

Writing letters.

Bus to Ch[arin]g + 1d   Dinner (Orange Grove after theatre) 1/–
Prog[ram]me at theatre 6d   Bus to Richter [concert] 1d

> Richter conducted, said G.B.S. on 24 June 1891 (C802), "a succulent treat" for Brahms devotees—the *German Requiem*. It communicated "mountainous tedium."   ▪ Dr. John Todhunter's *A Poison Flower* was his theatrical adaptation of Nathaniel Hawthorne's story, "Rappaccini's Daughter." Florence Farr played Beatrice Rappaccini and Brandon Thomas her father. *A Sicilian Idyll* was an original play by Todhunter, with Florence Farr as Amaryllis. There would be five matinees of the pairing.

16   *Paderewski's recital. St. James's Hall. 15. °Henry Phillips's concert. St. James's Banqueting Hall. 15½. °National Liberal Federation. Meeting of General Committee to consider Government proposals on Free Education. Westminster Palace Hotel. 14½. Fabian Executive. 17.*

Diary, letters, etc. Else Sonntag was at the concert with me. After the concert went to the Orange Grove with Olivier and Bland and had a meal. Then went on to FE's.

Dinner 1/–   Cocoa &c (at Orange Grove) 1/6   Wash etc at Faulkner's
3d   *Figaro* 2d   Train to Rav[en]s[cour]t Pk 6d   Shep[herds] Bush
to Ptld Rd 6d

> Although G.B.S. attended Paderewski's concert, he did not review it.

17   *°Sarasate concert. St. James's Hall. 20. °Ganny's concert. St. James's Hall. 15. Lilian Revell's matinee. Globe Theatre. 15. A Golden Sorrow. Call on R. P. B. Hutchinson at Langham Hotel. 17¼ to 18½.*

Corrected first proof of appendix to Ibsen book. In the evening went up to Dryhursts' and found Olivier there. Mrs. D. did not come in until late. Called on Archer after leaving Langham Hotel; but he was not in town.

Bus to Shaftesbury O 1d   Glass of milk 2d   Bus Bloomsbury to Oxford
O 1d   Oxford O to Kingsgate St 1d   Tram to Hampstead 2d

> The play by Albert E. Drinkwater (1852–1923), based on a novel of the same title by Shaw's cousin Fanny (Mrs. Cashel) Hoey, would have several scattered matinees through the year. Lilian Revell (Mrs. Drinkwater) played the role of Mary Bellamy.   ▪ R. H. Percy Hutchinson lived at Bosworth House, Husbands Bosworth, near Rugby.

18   *°Leo de Silka's recital. St. James's Hall. 15. Cancelled. Sgambatti's concert. Prince's Hall. 15. Annual meeting Land Nationalization Society. 19.45. National Liberal Club. Miss Sonntag in the late afternoon.*

Sang a little. Cant get rid of the influenza headache. JP came up from Broadstairs. The headache got so troublesome that at last I resolved to go down to Broadstairs tomorrow by the earliest train and stay until Sunday. Met Wheeler on way to the Sonntags'.

Dinner (at O[range] G[rove]) 1/6?   Bus St Martin's Lane house 1d
Train to Bayswater & back 5d?   Bus Ptld Rd to Ch[arin]g + 1d

> In his 24 June 1891 review (C802) G.B.S. called Sgambatti "the Brahms of Italy," adding, "But I mean to be complimentary."

19 °*Handel Festival rehearsal.* °*Madame Paprity Lineff's concert—Russian Friends of Liberty affair. Prince's Hall. 15.* °*Frederick Dawson's recital (pianoforte). Steinway Hall. 15. Catch the 8.30 train Victoria to Broadstairs.*

JP was in the train coming down with me. Spent the day writing the *World* article lying on the sands, in the forenoon halfway between Broadstairs and Ramsgate, and in the afternoon at Ramsgate.

Cab to Victoria 2/6   Train to Broadstairs 10/—   Tip to porter at Faversham 6d   *Tit Bits* 1d   Paper at Ramsgate 2d

> He was, G.B.S. wrote in the issue of 24 June 1891 (C802), "at this moment lying broiling on the sands at Broadstairs, at peace with all mankind, and indulgently disposed even towards Brahms."

20 °*Sarasate recital. 15.* °*Private View. Crane's works. Fine Art Society. 10 to 18.* °*Albert Hall. Patti concert. 15. Broadstairs.*

Again lying on the sands reading proofs of the Ibsen book, in the morning at the North Foreland and in the afternoon at Dumpton Gap.

21 SUNDAY *Lecture at the Progressive Association, 81 Pentonville Rd. Penton Hall, at 19, on "Progress and Morality." (George Margerison, 4 Titchfield Terrace N.W.). Come up from Broadstairs by the 9.37 train.*

Corrected proof of *World* article and finished it. Wrote some of it in the train, also some bits for the Ibsen appendix. Young Turner walked with me from the Progressive to Kings Cross.

Tips to serv[an]ts 5/—   Bus Viaduct to Bloomsbury 1d   Train to Kings + 1d   Bus Kings + to St Panc[ras] St[ation] (got into wrong bus) 1d

> "Young Turner" may be George Turner (1878–1926), son of George T. Turner. He would become a London County Council official. See 19 March 1894.

22 *Handel Festival. Crystal Palace. Messiah.* °*Richter Concert. 20½.* °*Poznanski and Eva Lonsdale. Steinway Hall. 15. Call on Archer after 11.*

Called on Archer about the Ibsen appendix and stayed there until it was time to go on to the Festival, which I reached during "O Thou that tellest." Mother was there with me. We had some lunch in the board room. In the evening I had intended to go to the Richter concert; but finding a letter in the *World* proofs from Vert, the agent, complaining of my criticism, I sent him back all his tickets and spent the evening at home writing letters. Wrote some bits on Ibsen appendix in the train.

Bus along Tott[enham] Ct Rd 1d   Glass of milk &c in Holborn 3½d
Train Viaduct to [Crystal] Pal[ace] & back 2/–   Excess fare on M[oth-
er]'s ticket back 7d   Train M[other] & I from Farringdon Rd home 7d

"My favorite oratorio," G.B.S. wrote on 1 July 1891 (C803), "is the Messiah, with which I
have spent many of the hours which others give to Shakespear, or Scott, or Dickens." The
3,500 choristers sang, however, not with spirit, but with "the insufferable lumbering
which is the curse of English Handelian choral singing." ▪ Nathaniel Vert managed the
Richter concerts (see also 17 July 1891). Shaw had experienced difficulties with Vert
earlier, complaining of being assigned "the most uncomfortable seat in St. James's Hall"
(C599) and about Vert's deceptive ticket prices and "scratch performance[s]" (C686).

23 *Paderewski's recital. St. James's Hall. 15. Fabian Executive. 17.*

Copied out the Ibsen bits I had written in the train. FE was at the recital,
but left before I did. After the Executive I went with the Blands and had tea
at the Aerated Bread Shop opposite St. Clement's Church. Then went to FE's
and spent the rest of the evening there.

Dinner 1/2½   Bus along Strand 1d   Glasenapp's *Wagner Encyclopaedia*
15/–   (Nutt's)   Cocoa &c at ABS 11d   Bus back along Strand
1d   Wash at Faulkner's 3d   Train to Ravenscourt Pk 6d   Train
from Shep[herds] B[ush] 6d

Paderewski's recitals, G.B.S. wrote on 15 July 1891 (C806), "have been crowded in spite of
the heat. He has shewn himself proof against hero worship, never relaxing the steadiest
concentration on his business as an artist. . . ."

24 *Handel recital. Selections. °First Annual General Meeting British Economic Association. 9 Adelphi Terrace. 17. °Louise Schumann's recital. Steinway Hall. 15. °Lucia—Melba—Covent Garden. Miss Sonntag's. 20.*

Writing up this diary. Did not work, feeling rather tired.

Bus to Shaftesbury O 1d   Train to Victoria 1½d   Train to Crystal
Pal[ace] 2/–   *Star* ½d   Tip to waiter 1/–   M[other]'s ticket to Holborn 1/3   Excess fares, myself to Aldersgate 3d   M[other] to Ptld Rd
8d   Train Aldersgate to Ptld Rd 2d   Train to Bayswater & back 5d

The Handel recital was reviewed, with the *Messiah* notice, on 1 July 1891 (C803), as a
mixed success.

25 *Schönberger's pianoforte recital. St. James's Hall. 15. °Welsh Ladies'
Choir. St. James's Hall. 20. °South St. Pancras Liberal and Radical Association Executive meeting. 195 Gray's Inn Rd. Tramways Purchase Question.*

Began *World* article. Had intended to go out in the evening, but changed
my mind and stayed at home working at article. Wrote to the Caucus
people instead of attending.

Dinner 1/–?

Benno Schönberger "avoided a stereotyped program" and played "with remarkable elegance and brilliancy; but in simple passages, where elegance and brilliancy are of little
use, he appears diffident and uneasy" (C806).

26 *Handel festival.* Israel. °*Fabian. H. Roberts on "Population." Barnard's Inn. 20.* °*Wieniawski's pianoforte recital. St. James's Hall. 15. Covent Garden.* Marta. *Mravina.*

Continued *World* article. Telegraphed to JP to come to the Festival; but she did not get the telegram in time and I went alone. Came back by the 16.55 train. JP here in the evening, made rather a scene.

Telegram to JP 8d   Train to Palace from Via[duct] & back 2/–   Tip to waiter at lunch 6d

> *Israel* was reviewed in the omnibus Handel notice (C803). "Mr. Manns was at his best on the last day. . . ." ▪ Eugenia Mravina, the Czech soprano, was featured in an opera by Friedrich von Flotow revived especially for her. The first two acts, G.B.S wrote on 15 July 1891 (C806), were "a capital piece of *naïve* storytelling, and the rest is . . . hopelessly dull and artificial." However, Mravina's "beautiful unspoiled voice" was "just the thing," and Giulia Ravogli and Edouard de Reszke were "at their ease."

27 °*Last Philharmonic concert. St. James's Hall. 15.* °*Covent Garden.* Othello—*changed to* Tannhauser. °*Operatic concert at the Albert Hall. 15. Miss Sonntag's. 17.*

JP called in the morning with my letter unopened. I did some work on the *World* article. She remained after the others had gone to the Albert Hall concert. When I got to the Opera I found that it was changed; so I went off to look for the Carrs to offer them the tickets. They were out of town. Came back home and worked.

Dinner 1/2?   Bus to Bayswater from Ox[ford] O 2d   Train back to Ptld Rd 2½d?   Bus to opera 1d   Bus Ch[arin]g + to Ashley Gardens 1d Back home 2d

28 SUNDAY *Speak on Clapham Common at 18½. Labor League.*

Corrected proof of *World* article. Completed and sent off the Ibsen proofs. Spoke for 1¼ hours at Clapham. Hard day's work. Went to JP very tired after Clapham. Walked home. JP was here in the forenoon before I went out. Lucy came up by a late train.

Train Victoria to Clapham 2d   Back 4d   Vict[oria] to S[ou]th Kensington 3½d

29 °*Richter Concert. 20½. Miss Sonntag's. 17.* °*Otta Bray's concert. Prince's Hall. 20½.*

Worked at the article on Anarchism to be converted into a Fabian tract. Did not go out to dinner but ate some bread and fruit here. I was tired and got up late. The Sonntags insisted on my staying to tea and for the rest of the evening. [James] Headlam (Else's fiance) was there, also his cousin and a man named Steven, with whom I at last got into a barren controversy about Socialism and the universities, which spoilt the whole evening.

Train to Bayswater & back (took ticket by mistake to Notting Hill and came back from Edgware Rd) 6d

Robert Steven was secretary of the North Islington Liberal Club.

30   *Paderewski's recital. St. James's Hall. 15. Press Day. Portrait painters, at the Institute. 10 to 18. °Mrs. Alice Shaw's concert. Prince's Hall. 21. First night Solomon and Dance's new Opera at the Savoy. 20½. °Louise Douste [de Fortis]'s concert. Steinway Hall. 20. Fabian Executive. 17.*

Writing up this diary etc. After the Fabian had tea at Orange Grove with Mrs. Sandham, Olivier and Lowerison. Lucy was at the Savoy with me. JP was here in the evening.

Dinner 1/–?   Bus to Fabian 1d   to Shaftesbury O 1d   From Savoy to Ch[arin]g + to Grafton St L[ucy?] & I 4d

The Nautch Girl, comic opera by George Dance, score by Edward Solomon; reviewed on 8 July 1891 (C804). "Solomon," said G.B.S., "has given me the worst headache I ever had in a theatre by an instrumental score which is more wearisome . . . and more noisy than the *melodrame* which accompanies the knockabout business in a music hall."

July

1   *Private View. Portrait Painters at the Institute. 10 to 18. Stojowski's pianoforte recital. Prince's Hall. 15.*

Wrote notice of the Portrait Painters for *The Star* (and I afterwards gave it to Bland to save him the trouble of going into town to see the show). May Sparling was at the recital with me. I had sent her the ticket, as she had arranged to meet my Mother at Broadwood's at 16 to choose a piano. Went out to FE in the evening. Worked on the Anarchism article. JP was at the Private View.

Dinner 1/–?   Train to Shep[herds] Bush & back 1/–

Sigismond Stojowski, G.B.S. wrote on 15 July 1891 (C806), "can play . . . very cleverly" but left the impression that his ability was not "irresistibly specialized for the pianoforte."

2   *Isidor de Lara. Steinway Hall. 15. Meet FE at the Temple station at 20 and go with her to the Lyceum to see* Nance Oldfield *and* The Corsican Brothers.

Began *World* article and sent off what I had written, as Thomas had asked me to do so this week. *The Corsican Brothers* proved so dull that we left after the first scene of the second act.

Dinner 1/–?   Bus to Shaftesbury O? 1d   Train Temple to Ravenscourt
Pk 6d   Shep[herds] B[ush] to Ptld Rd 6d   Telegram to Miss Sonntag
6d

> Ellen Terry was starring in the play by Charles Reade. Henry Irving was the lead in the
> Dion Boucicault play based on the novel by Alexandre Dumas. The roles were box-office
> stand-bys for the pair. ▪ C. Thomas and Son were *The World*'s printers.

3 *Simonetti's concert. Portman Rooms. 15. Miss Sonntag's. 17. Covent
Garden. Fidelio. Tavary.*

Continued *World* article. Only went to the concert for a few moments as I
could not get into the Rooms.

Dinner 1/–?   Train to Bayswater & back 5d   Bus to opera 1d

> Achille Simonetti (1858–1928) was a violinist and composer who performed with the
> London Trio. His concert was so crowded that G.B.S. "had to content myself with hearing
> a few bars through the doorway" (C806). ▪ Maria Basta Tavary had "earnestness" and
> "ability" going for her as Leonore, wrote G.B.S., but the role Beethoven wrote required
> "nothing less than genius" to carry it off (C806).

4 °*Students' concert. Academy Higher Development Pianoforte Players.
Marlborough Rooms. 15½. Covent Garden. Carmen. Jean de Reszke and de
Lussan.*

Working at the Anarchism article. JP was here in the day.

Dinner 1/–?   Telegram to Miss Sonntag 6d   Gloves, 2 pr 5/6   Bus to
opera 1d

> The strong Don José of the de Rezske in *Carmen* was "touching proof" of the recent
> "regrettable illness" alleged for his repeated postponements of *Otello* (C806), while Zélie
> de Lussan "has now been seen quite enough for one season."

5 SUNDAY *Speak at the Arsenal Gates, Woolwich. 18¼. (Banner)*

Corrected *World* proof. Took things easy afterwards. Spoke for an hour and
a half at Woolwich. Got out at Blackheath on my way back and went to Lee
to the Blands'. Found Grinling and his wife there, also Mark Barr. We all
went for a walk toward Woolwich; and Mark came back with me as far as
London Bridge. We took the 23.13 train.

Train to Woolich from Ch[arin]g + (ret[urn]) 1/8   Ticket from Blackheath to Chg + 6d

> C. H. Grinling, of 47 Woolwich Common, Kent, was a Fabian. Journalist Mark Barr lived
> in Kent.

6 °*Richter Concert. 20¼. Go down to Harrow and spend the afternoon with
Steffen. °Miss Valling's concert. Portman Rooms. 20.15.*

Did a little work at the proofs of the Ibsen book. Went down to Harrow by
the 14 train from Baker St. Steffen showed me his curves of wages etc. We

went for a walk through the fields and I came back to town by the 19.30 train. Had tea here, and went on to JP. Looked through Oakeshott's Fabian tract in the train.

Milk & biscuit 2d   Train to Harrow & back 1/6   Train to S[ou]th Kensington & back 9d

Fabian Tract no. 39. *A Democratic Budget*, 1892 (BB12).

7   *Fabian Executive. 17. °Madame de Pachmann's recital. St. James's Hall. 15.*

Writing up this diary etc. Prevented by extremely heavy and constant rain from going to the concert. Olivier came here with me from the Executive to tea. Whilst he was here Maggie Gardner came and I had to entertain them as well as I could in different rooms.

Dinner 1/6   Bus Oxf[ord] O to Holborn 1d

8   *°Visit of German Kaiser to the Opera. 20$\frac{1}{2}$. Miss Sonntag's. 20.*

Working at Ibsen paper. Archer called. I gave him the ticket for the State function at the Opera. Can't recollect very well what happened in the afternoon. In the evening I went to the Sonntags' and found Olivier there. He came back with me as far as Baker St.

Dinner 1/–?   Train to Bayswater & back 5d

The State visit of Kaiser Wilhelm II was physically snubbed, thus, by G.B.S., who then wrote (C806) of the defections from the performance of offended French singers.

9   *Miss Sonntag's. 17.*

Began *World* article. Forget what else happened. I think I sat at home during the evening writing letters.

Dinner 1/–   Train to Bayswater & back 5d?

10   *Fabian. Barnard's Inn. Oakeshott's Budget Tract, etc. Autumn Course committee at Aerated Bread Company at 18$\frac{1}{2}$. Miss Sonntag's. 17.*

Finished *World* article. After the Fabian, the Cohens came back with me in the train. Do not remember the afternoon very clearly—have left it over too long. Dined at home.

Train to Bayswater 5d (return not used)   Bus Bayswater to Barnard's Inn 3d   Eggs &c at A[erated] B[read] shop 9$\frac{1}{2}$d   Train Farringdon to Ptld Rd 2d

11   *Paderewski's last recital (Chopin only). St. James's Hall. 15. °Covent Garden. Les Huguenots. 20. Go out to Sparlings' and sleep there so as to be ready in the morning. Miss Sonntag's. 17.*

Revised appendix to Ibsen book. JP was at Paderewski's recital with me. Left her at Oxford Circus and went on to Bayswater. Went to FE on my way to Sparlings', where I did not arrive until near midnight.

Bus to St Ja[me]s's Hall 1d   Bus Oxford O to Bayswater 2d   Train from Bayswater 2d   Train to Shepherds Bush 6d

> The St. James's Hall recital was briefly mentioned by G.B.S. (C806), who observed that Chopin's B minor sonata "found out the limits of Paderewski's skill."

12 SUNDAY   *Speak in Battersea Park. Burns Demonstration at 18½. Meet the Hammersmith people at Richmond (Metropolitan and District Railway) at 11 and go up the river. Furnivall, all the Langs, the Sparlings, E. Walker, Cockerell and Miss Philpot.*

We carried out our programme successfully. Towed most of the way. Picnicked at Hampton Court. I left them in the building and caught the 18.11 train from Teddington to Battersea. After the Demonstration, went to JP's where I found a young artist named Bell, Stuart Glennie and Miss Garnett.

Train Shaftesbury Rd to Richmond 4d   Teddington to Battersea 1/2 Bus Chelsea Br[idge] to Knightsbridge 1d

> (Sir) Sydney Carlyle Cockerell (1867–1962) had just become secretary to Morris's Kelmscott Press. He would become a printing and engraving partner of Emery Walker, director of the Fitzwilliam Museum at Cambridge (1908–1937), and literary executor of the Morris and Hardy estates. ▪ Mr. and Mrs. H. S. Philpot of Fulmer House, West Worthing, were Fabians. Miss Philpot may have been a daughter. ▪ Robert Anning Bell (1863–1933) had begun exhibiting at the R.A. in 1885. He would be professor of Design at the Royal College of Art from 1918 to 1924, and would become an R.A. in 1922. Among his portraits was one of Mrs. Patterson. ▪ Miss Garnett is probably one of the three daughters of Richard Garnett, Keeper of Printed Books at the British Museum until 1899. Shaw knew his second son, Edward, who married Constance Black.

13   °*Richter Concert. 20½.* °*Ragglenanti's concert. 105 Piccadilly. Call on Parke in the afternoon at the* Star *office. Miss Sonntag's. 17.*

Sent off Ibsen proofs after giving them some last touches and wrote to Scott about them. Cleaned the typewriter. Found it was getting on to 16 o'clock when I was done. Called on Parke and found that he wanted me to write an article on the Jubilee of *Punch*. Went on to H. Sonntag and stayed there from 18.10 to 19. Walked to Paddington and took the train home. Sat up to write the article and did not get to bed until near 3.

Train to Farringdon 2d   Dinner (at Central) 1/–   Bus Holborn O to Bayswater 3d   PMG 1d   Train Padd[ing]t[o]n to P[or]tl[and] Rd 1½d

> On the occasion of the fiftieth anniversary of *Punch*, Shaw wrote a piece for *The Star*, 14 July 1891 (C805), on the magazine's "services to art" over half a century. So many artists "come to grief in their attempts . . . to be humorous," Shaw wrote (as Corno di Bassetto), that *Punch*'s rare success was a reason for celebration.

14   °*Frances Allitsen's concert. 8 Maida Vale. 20½. Covent Garden. Aida. Nordica etc.*

Webb, who returned from Norway yesterday, called whilst I was dressing. Wrote letters and posted up this diary. In the evening, as no one would go to the Opera, I gave the ticket to Else Sonntag and drove her down to Covent Garden in a hansom. When I got home I—I forget what I did— either played or wrote or both.

Dinner ?   Train to Bayswater (returned to house) 5d   Cab to Cov[ent] Garden 3/–

15 *Covent Garden. First night of* Otello *(Verdi). de Reszke, Maurel, Albani, etc. Miss Sonntag's. 17.*

Miss [Agnes] Henry also called to ask me to write something in the papers to help the anarchist Malatesta, whose extradition has been demanded by the Italian government from the Swiss. I forget what I did else. Sat up after the Opera to write article for *The Star* about Malatesta.

Dinner (Wheatsheaf) 1/–?   Train to Bayswater 5d   Bus to opera 1d

> Reviewed by G.B.S on 22 July 1891 (C808). Jean de Rezske's Otello "was about equally remarkable for its amateurish ineptitudes and for its manifestations of the natural histrionic powers which he has so studiously neglected." ▪ *The Star*, 16 July 1891, two unsigned subleaders (C807) on the Italian government's attempts to extradite the anarchist Enrico Malatesta.

16 °*School Board singing at Exeter Hall. 12¼. °Miss Sonntag's.*

Forgot all about School Board. Tired rather. Did nothing or next to nothing to *World* article. Wallas called whilst I was dressing and stayed for some time. Got to work tidying up my papers. This kept me all day practically. Started with the intention of going to H. Sonntag's after tea, but finding myself in a Hammersmith train went right on to FE. We went off for a walk, and strolled from Chiswick Mall to Kew Bridge, returning by tram. Pleasant evening.

Star ½d   Dinner (Wheatsheaf) 1/–?   Train to Shep[herds] Bush & back 9d   Tram New Br[idge] to Shaftesb[ur]y Rd 4d

17 *Miss Sonntag's. 17.*

Wrote *World* article. Sat up after it was done to write to Prange about the Richter Vert articles. Did not get to bed until about 3.

Dinner (Wheatsheaf) 1/–?

> See 22 June 1891 for background on Hans Richter and his manager Nathaniel Vert.

18 *Miss Sonntag's. 20. Go down to Sparlings' and sleep there.*

Ibsen proofs came. Did nothing on them. Was writing to JP when Massingham called about Bayreuth. Eventually he decided to come; and we went off in search of tickets. We tried Cook's and Gaze's; but there were none to be had. We parted at the Fabian office; and I went off to try to see Prange,

on chance of his knowing something about the ways of Bayreuth. He was
not at the Institute when I got there; so I went home and wrote to him and
to Armbruster, also to Chappell. Went to Sonntags' after tea and then on to
Sparlings' which I reached about 22.

Bus Tott[enham] Ct Rd to Chancery Lane (Mass[in]gh[a]m & I) 2d   Bus
Strand to Picc[adilly] O 1d   Foreign postcards 3d   Dinner 1/–?
Train to Bayswater 2d   Turkish delight for M.S. [May Sparling] 1/–
Train Westbourne Pk to Ravenscourt Pk 4d

19 SUNDAY °*Speak on Clapham Common for the S. D. F. at 15¼ (H. B.
Rogers, 6 Gwynne Rd., Battersea. S.W.). Too wet.*

Heavy showers all day. Gave up the idea of going to Clapham. In the
forenoon Walker was photographing me under difficulties, as the rain interrupted us. Went up to see Morris in the afternoon. Bruce Glasier was there
and Ellis, the ex-publisher. Came back to Sparlings' and found a lot of
people there, among them Wallas. He and I did not go to the lecture, but
stayed with May. We went into Ellis's over the garden wall for a while.

Train Hammersmith to Portland Rd 6d

> John Bruce Glasier (1859–1920) of Glasgow, compiler of *Socialist Songs*, journalist, and
> writer on Socialist issues. ▪ Frederick S. Ellis (1830–1901) of Hammersmith Terrace,
> retired publisher and bookseller, had published Dante Gabriel Rossetti's poems.

20 °*Richter Concert. 20¼. Ninth and last. Miss Sonntag's. 17.*

Read the proofs of the Ibsen appendix for the last time very carefully, and
wrote to Scott suggesting that he should take over *An Unsocial Socialist*.
After leaving Sonntags', which I reached at 17, I went across Kensington
Gardens to JP, who was very ill and very wretched. Trying evening. Did not
get home until near 2.

Dinner (Wheatsheaf) 1/3½   Bus Oxford O–Bayswater 2d

21 *Speak at meeting of National Union of Clerks at the Ceres Restaurant,
Amen Corner, Paternoster Row, at 19¼ (W. M. Sutherland, N.U.C., 63 Aldersgate St.). Fabian Executive. 17.*

Wrote to Hutchinson after reading his Fabian paper on Capital. Then wrote
up this diary, which was, as usual, in arrear for the week. After the Executive Wallas came with me to the meeting. He took the chair when Thompson left; and we both spoke.

Dinner 1/–? Wh[ea]ts[hea]f   Bus to Holborn? 1d   Bus Strand to Ludgate O 1d

22 °*Go down to Magny's in the afternoon. 16. Put off.* °*Chester Triennial
Festival. Bridges's* Rudel *in the Music Hall. Miss Sonntag's. 17.*

As well as I can remember I wrote letters today. In the evening I went down to Hammersmith to arrange with Walker about the Italian trip etc. He was not in, and neither were the Sparlings; but I met the latter on the Mall and went back with them. Played some duets on May's new piano. Walker came with me to the train.

Dinner 1/–? Wh[eat]s[hea]f   Train to Bayswater & back 5d   to Hammersmith & back 9d

> *Rudel* was a new cantata by Joseph Cox Bridges (1853–1929), who had revived the Chester Festival. The Middlesex Music Hall in Drury Lane was known for its low admission fees, which began at sixpence. Shaw did not attend.

23 *Orange Grove. 18.15. °Call on Standring at Finsbury St. at 16¼. Miss Sonntag's. 17. °Chester Musical Festival. Berlioz's* Faust. *Music Hall.*

Began *World* article; but I had not got very far when the typewriter broke down, and I spent the whole day trying to repair it. Finally I left it worse than ever. FE and I met as arranged and we went to the Naval Exhibition.

Dinner 1/–? Wh[ea]tsh[eaf]   Cocoa &c FE (at Naval Ex) 2/9?   Bus to Naval Ex[hibition] 6d   Bus Kings Rd to Hammersmith 6d   Train Shep[herds] Bush to P[or]tl[an]d Rd 6d

> The Naval Exhibition was at Earl's Court exhibition halls.

24 *Fabian. Barnard's Inn. Kentish Moore on "Nationalization of Railways." 20. Covent Garden. Debut of Teleky as Violetta in* Traviata. *20¼. Miss Sonntag's. 17.*

Tried some further unavailing botching at the typewriter, which only prevented me from getting on with my work. Added a little to the *World* article, but not much. Left the Opera after the second act. In the middle of the day the Salts called; and they had hardly gone when Aileen Bell, just over from America, came. She stayed until it was too late to get any dinner. JP came whilst she was here. Aileen came with me in the train as far as Edgware Rd. on the way to Bayswater. On my way back I met my Mother going to the Opera at the Islington Theatre with A. McKernon.

Train to Bayswater & back 5d   Bus to opera 1d

> Kentish Moore, 6 Lee Terrace, Blackheath, S.E., was a Fabian. ■ Emma Teleky, the German soprano, was "clever and attractive," G.B.S. wrote on 29 July 1891 (C809), but the performance was "hackneyed" and the rest of the cast "bad." ■ Mrs. Shaw's friend, A. McKernon, is unidentified.

25 *Miss Sonntag's. 17. Go down to Magny's in the evening.*

Finished *World* article. Magny is going to translate *An Unsocial Socialist* for *Le Courrier Français*. They are giving him £6 for the job. I agreed to forego all claim on this; but I recommended Magny to reserve the copyright of his translation.

Dinner 1/2½ Wh[eat]s[hea]f   Telegram to Magny 8½d?   Train to Bishopsgate & back 7d?   London Br[idge] to Old Kent Rd & back 5d?

26 SUNDAY *Speak in the Canning Town Branch of the S. D. F. at Beckton Rd. (open air) at 11½. In the afternoon go to E. Walker's to try again at the photographing. JP's in the evening.*

After Walker and I had finished our photographing we went to Sparlings'. An Irish journalist named Joyce was there. May only appeared as I was leaving. McKernon, Mother and Kate were at JP's. Gloomy evening. Sorry I left Hammersmith. Revised *World* article in the train going to Canning Town.

Train to Aldgate & back 9d?   Fenchurch St to Canning Town & back 10d   Ptld Rd to Hammersmith 6d   H[ammer]s[mi]th to South Kensington 4d?

    The unidentified Irish journalist cannot be James Joyce (1882–1941).

27   *Miss Sonntag's. 17.*

Wrote a couple of letters. Read a couple of Schopenhauer books which I bought to send to FE. JP was here in the evening. I refused to sentimentalize and read and played at my ease. Rather put out by development of varicosis in my left calf.

Dinner 1/2½ (Wh[ea]ts[hea]f)   Schopenhauer's *Aphorisms*, 2 vols 3/10
Train Farringdon Rd to Bayswater 3d   Bayswater to Ptld Rd 2d

28   *Fabian Executive. 17. Miss Sonntag's. 17. Stepniak on Nihilism at Mrs. Graham Tomson's At-Home. 20 St. John's Wood Rd. 17.*

Writing up this diary, sending off Schopenhauer books to FE, writing letters etc. After the Executive, at which I had to take the chair (by chance I went down to the office an hour beforehand), Wallas came with me to tea at the Orange Grove, and then on to Sonntags'.

Dinner (at Wheatsheaf) 1/-?   Bus to Holborn 1d   Supper at Orange Grove 1/9?   Wash &c. Wallas & I 5d   Bus Ch[arin]g + to Marble Arch, Wallas & I 4d   Train, Wallas to Gower St and I to Ptld Rd from Bayswater 4½d (Wallas got out at Ptld Rd)

    Mr. and Mrs. Arthur Graham Tomson were well-to-do Fabians.

29   *Miss Sonntag's. 17. Mrs. Sparling's in the evening.*

Writing letters, especially a longish one to a secularist in Camberwell about my lecture last April. In the afternoon played a good deal and did not get to Sonntags' until half past 18, nor to May's until past 20. Played duets—Grieg and Beethoven. Sat talking with her and Walker, who came in later on. Only it was too late for the last train. Slept at Walker's. Very wet weather.

Train to Bayswater $2\frac{1}{2}$d   Westbourne Pk to Ravenscourt Pk 4d   Dinner 1/3½ (Wh[eat]s[hea]f)

E. C. Chapman, who had heard Shaw speak on "Freethought, Old and New." The long letter (*CL*) ended with the suggestion that he had "dealt with the subject more carefully" in *The Quintessence of Ibsenism*, then in press.

30   *Concert at Collard's Rooms. Mr. Watts. The Seifferts to play. Miss Sonntag's. 17.*

Awake early chatting with Walker whilst he was dressing. Breakfast at May's and then to Sussex House with Walker, whom I left in the train at Charing Cross. Still very wet. Wrote letters in the evening, especially one to Seiffert about his wife's playing. Paid up a lot of debts. I am not quite sure whether I really went to Sonntags' or not, but I suppose I must have done so, as there was no reason to the contrary.

Train H[ammer]smith to Ch[arin]g + 6d   Bus Chg + to Grafton St 1d   Subs[criptio]n to Vegetarian Soc[iet]y (my 1st) 2/6   Subs[criptio]n, 2 yr[s] ending Oct [18]91 to *Quarterly J[ournal] of Economics* 18/– Subscr[iption] for [18]91 to Brit[ish] Ec[onomics] Asso[ciatio]n £1/1/0 & cost of order   Jaeger's bill £5/7/6.   Train to Bayswater (return) 5d

The unidentified Mr. Watts may be the singer Arthur Watts (see also 17 March 1891, where Shaw notes but does not attend a Watts-Russell concert, which may have been Arthur Watts with Ella Russell). ▪ Reviewed by G.B.S. on 5 August 1891 (C810). The cautiously diplomatic paragraph identified the "last concert of the season" as a benefit "to help a lady who has been unfortunately disabled." The audience was "feeble [in] numbers." ▪ Henry Seiffert had recently married a Mlle. de Llana, a pianist whose interpretation of Francis Thomé's "Sérénade d'Harlequin" in the benefit concert Shaw admired.

31   °*300th night of* La Cigale. *Lyric Theatre.*

Lucy here and her husband in the afternoon. Seiffert called as I was going out to dinner. As he was going a man called to put the typewriter in order. Went off to the Orange Grove to get my dinner and tea together and then came back and set to to write a *World* letter, as Thomas had just written to say that the paper would be short of copy unless I sent something. This kept me pretty late; but it was fortunate that the typewriter was ready for use. Left my Ollendorff behind me at the Post Office—shall have to buy another one.

Telegram to H[edwig] Sonntag 6d

The *World* "letter" was probably Shaw's weekly review (C810), published on 5 August 1891, and padded out with such boiler plate as a discussion of the implications (to G.B.S.) of impresario Augustus Harris's new knighthood. ▪ C. Thomas was an employee of Messrs. Robson & Son, printers of *The World*. When Shaw was late with copy, he would send a reminder.

August

1 *Miss Sonntag's. 17.*

Finished *World* article and brought down the remainder of it to the printing office in New Street Square, where I corrected the proof. Went on from the City to Sonntags' and from Sonntags' to FE's, where I passed the evening.

Train to Farringdon 2d   Dinner (at Central) 1/–?

2 SUNDAY *Speak for the Clapham Labour League at 11.30 at the Polygon, Old Town, Clapham (Fras. Connolly, 144 High St. Clapham). Spoke indoors, as it was wet.*

Missed the train at Victoria.

Bus Holborn O to Bayswater 3d   Bayswater to Brackenbury Rd 3d
Train Shep[herds] B[ush] to P[or]tl[an]d Rd 6d   Bus Victoria to Chelsea Br[idge] 1d   Tram to Cedars Rd 1d   Train Clapham to Victoria 4d

3 Began book *Technical Socialism* which I promised to write years ago for the University Series published by Sutton of Ludgate Hill under Gonner's editorship. Emery Walker called. We went off to the National Gallery and spent an hour or so there. Then we came back and dined here. In the evening I went to JP's, Walker coming with me as far as Gloucester Rd. station. Did not get home until pretty late.

Train to S[ou]th Kensington 4d

"Technical Socialism" would never be completed, Shaw losing interest in it.

4 °*Meeting of the Central Fabian Group at 22 Great Ormond St., 20, to appoint delegates to Westminster School Board Committee. Miss Sonntag's. 20.*

Worked at *Technical Socialism*. Archer, just come up from Nottingham, called; and we went off to dinner together, and then into the City, as he wanted to buy a new ribbon for his typewriter. I parted from him at the corner of Paternoster Row, as I wanted to return by the Strand to buy a new Ollendorff.

Dinner (Wheatsheaf) 1/–?   Bus to Mans[ion] Ho[use] 1d   Ollendorff's *German Method* 5/3   Morris's *News from Nowhere* 9d   3 Stone's World files at Stores 2/4   Bus Ch[arin]g + to Grafton St 1d   Train Bayswater & back 5d

5 *Miss Sonntag's. 17.*

Working at *Technical Socialism*. Got my Mother to get me some more of the books at the Stores for keeping papers in. Tried to continue writing in the evening; but was much interrupted by JP.

Dinner (Wh[ea]ts[hea]f) 10½d?   Bus to Lincolns Inn F[ie]lds 1d   Lessing's *Emilia Galotti* at Nutt's 1/–   [Palgrave's] *Golden Treasury & Pilgrim's Progress* 2/6   Bus Tott[enham] Ct Rd to Bayswater 2d   Train Bayswater to P[or]tl[an]d Rd 2d

6   *Miss Sonntag's 17.*

Writing letters, writing up this diary, and doing odd jobs. Walter here in the middle of the day. Dined at home.

7   Worked at the book, I suppose; but my memory fails me as to this day. No doubt there was also a reading of *Rosmersholm* with FE and a lesson in German from Miss Sonntag.

8   *FE's in the afternoon. JP's to tea. Miss Sonntag's. 20.*

Working at the book.

Dinner (Wheatsheaf) 1½?   Bus to Nott[ingham] Hill Gate from Oxford O 3d   Train Ravenscourt Pk to South Kensington 4d?   Train Bayswater to Portland Rd 2d

9 SUNDAY   *Speak at Demonstration of General Railway Workers' Union on Peckham Rye at 15. It was wet, and we held it in the Liberal Club (James Solly, 186 Lancaster Rd., North Kensington). 14.45 train from Victoria. Lecture at Kelmscott House, Hammersmith Socialist Society, on "Communism." 20.*

Still at the book. It was too wet to hold the demonstration on the Rye; so we adjourned to the [National] Liberal Club. I slept at May's.

Train Ch[arin]g + to Victoria 1½d   Victoria to Peckham Rye 4d   Peckham Rye to Ravenscourt Pk 8d?   Bought some doggrell at the Club for 1d

> The program (BL) gives the title of Shaw's speech as "Socialism and Scoundrelism." Shaw could obviously play variations on this more attractive title.

10   *Miss Sonntag's. 20. Barton's any time after 22.*

Working at the book when I got up from Hammersmith, which I accomplished so as to be here by 11. Went on to FE to work on her dramatic elocution after dinner and stayed for tea with her. Went from Sonntags' on to Barton.

Daily Chronicle 1d   Lavatory 1d   Train H[ammer]smith to Ptld Rd 4d   Dinner (Wheatsheaf) 1½   Bus to Uxbridge Rd 3d   Tram Brackenbury Rd to Uxbridge Rd 1d   Bus Uxbridge Rd to Bayswater 2d   Train Bayswater to Ptld Rd 3½d   Bayswater to Gloster Rd ret[urn] 5d?

11 *Special Fabian Executive, 17, to arrange lecturing tour. FE's in the afternoon—meet her at the Wheatsheaf at 14.*

Still at the book. Archer called before dinner, which we took together at the Wheatsheaf. I went off with FE to Hammersmith. We walked from the Marble Arch to Bayswater. After the Executive, Wallas and Olivier came with me to the Sonntags'. We had a meal at the Orange Grove on our way. Adolphe Smith was on the bus we took from Charing Cross to Marble Arch, whence we walked to Sonntags'. We did not stay much after 22. Wrote a few letters when I got home.

Dinner (F.E. & I at Wheatsheaf) 1/4½   Bus (2) to Marble Arch 2d
Bayswater Rd to Uxbridge Rd 6d   Train to Temple 6d   Supper at
Orange Grove 1/9

12 *Private View at Bruce Joy's studio, West Kensington. Afternoon. Miss Sonntag's. 17. °Call on Mrs. Wynne (Mrs. Horne) to see Aileen (Bell) in the afternoon. °Call at National Liberal Club in the evening to join Shorter and Burrows.*

Working at *Technical Socialism.* Found nobody in either at Argyll Rd. (Mrs. Wynne's) or at the National Liberal Club, which I did not reach until past nine. Met Massingham on the doorstep and had a few words with Anderson.

Dinner (Wh[eat]sh[ea]f) 1½   Bus Shaftesbury Road to West Kensington
3d   W.K. to Argyll Rd 1d   Train Bayswater to Ptld Rd 2d

  Probably G. Wherry Anderson.

13 Working at the book. Wrote several letters in the afternoon on my return from the City, where I failed to find Standring. Went to FE in the evening, and had a hard grind over the first half of the 3rd act of *Rosmersholm.* Wrote a letter to Shorter in the train, suggesting Bayreuth. I did not go to Sonntags', having written the day before to say that I was going to take a day off.

Dinner (Wh[eat]sh[ea]f) 1/–   Bus to Holborn O 1d   Train Moorgate
St[ation] to Ptld Rd 4½d   *St Ja[me]s's Gazette* 1d   Train to Shep[herds]
Bush (ret[urn]), but walked to Edgware Rd on the way out 9d

14 Got a telegram from Shorter offering to guarantee £15 of Bayreuth expenses. Went down at once to Chappell's to ask if there were any tickets left. There were none. Went on to Shorter at the *Illustrated London News* office and got him to telegraph to Bayreuth to ask were there any tickets there. Returned home to await the reply, dining and buying some traveling stores on the way. The reply was simply that it was impossible to obtain seats; so I went off to FE and we worked at *Rosmersholm* pretty hard.

Bus Regent St to Ch[arin]g + 1d   Chg + to *Ill[ustrated] London News* 2d
(the conductor gave me the wrong ticket & I stood the loss)   Housewife

at Stores 3/6   Dinner 1/4½   Telegram to FE 9d   American bank (toy) 6d   Train to Shep B 9d (walked to Edgware Rd on the way out)

Housewife: a small sewing kit for use when traveling.

15 *Miss Sonntag's. 17.*

Books which I ordered last week at the Stores came this morning; and I spent most of the day putting up my old MSS in them, labeling them etc. Mrs. Collier and Mabel called just as I was going out to dinner, which was not until past 16. Got to H. Sonntag's at about 17½. Scott sent me a copy of *The Quintessence of Ibsenism* today—probably one of the first made up. Had tea with FE, and then went off for a walk. We took the train to Richmond; walked along the towpath to Kew, and came back by tram. Read a number of anti-vivisection tracts sent to me by Miss Cobbe. Mother went up to the north to stay for a while with Lucy, leaving Kate here with me.

Dinner 1/3¼   Bus to Bayswater 2d   Bus Nott[ingham] Hill Gate to Uxbridge Rd St[atio]n 1d   Train Ravenscourt Pk to Richmond 1/2 (2) Tram Kew Br[idge] to Shaftesbury Rd (2) 4d   Train Shep[herds] Bush to Ptld Rd 6d

Miss Frances Power Cobbe (1822–1904), founder and secretary, 1875–1884, of the National Anti-Vivisection Society, and the author of books on Unitarianism, Darwin, and women's issues.

16 SUNDAY *Speak at Demonstration of General Railway Workers' Union in Finsbury Park at 15 (James Solly, see last Sunday). Blands' in the evening.*

Wrote up this diary for a day or two and wrote some letters. I had to speak twice at the Demonstration. De Mattos came back with me and had tea here, Solly coming with us as far as King's Cross. Wallas, Barrs, Marsh and Griffiths were at the Blands'. Wallas came back with me, Marsh coming as far as London Bridge.

Train Kings + to Finsbury Park & back ?   Bus Kings + to Tott[enham] Ct Rd (de M[attos] & I) 2d   Train Ch[arin]g + to Blackh[ea]th 6d

One letter (NIL), dated the next day and written to the editor of *The Star*, was published on 18 August 1891. *The Agnostic Journal*, Shaw observed, had announced that he had given up Socialism and become a convert to Individualism, an apostasy, said the journal, which would create dismay among "the cranks and frumps" of the Fabian Society. Shaw assured readers that his well-advertised "convictions remain as obstinate as ever." ▪ Dr. C. T. Marsh (?–1901), of 56 Fitzroy St., W. ▪ Probably Major Arthur Griffiths.

17 *Miss Sonntag's.*

Working at the book as far as I can remember. I think I went to FE's about half past 18; found that she was not at home; waited for her a long time; and when she came in, had tea with her; read the last act of *Rosmersholm* and then went off to Miss Sonntag's. She came with me a little way until I caught a bus.

Dinner 1/–? Wh[ea]ts[hea]f   Bus to Uxbridge Rd 3d   Bus Goldhawke Rd to Bayswater 3d   Train Bayswater to Ptld Rd 2d

> Reading *Rosmersholm* with FE had a special meaning: he was not only coaching her for a possible production but giving her voice and elocution lessons. It was also another reason for being together often.

18   *Fabian Executive. 17*

As well as I can recollect I did not work at the book today, but wrote letters etc. After dinner I went to FE and then went on to the Fabian. Afterwards Massingham and Wallas met me going to the Club and dined there with them. After dinner we went out and strolled about the Embankment gardens talking about Aristophanes etc. Then Wallas came home with me and sat a while.

Dinner (at Wh[ea]ts[hea]f) 1/–?   Bus to Uxbridge 3d?   Train Ravenscourt Pk to Temple 6d

19   *Meet the Salts at Victoria and go down to Oxted by the 14.35 train.*

When we got to Oxted Salt and I walked across Limpsfield Common to see the house Olivier is having altered for himself. On the way we stopped to talk to Miss Brooke at Pebble Hill. She promised to call in the evening to hear Mrs. Salt and I play duets. She did so. Olivier came in. Miss Brooke's nephew called for her; and when she was gone we went out with the Oliviers. Mrs. Olivier and Mrs. Salt soon went indoors; and Olivier, Salt and myself walked over to Oxted Village by moonlight. I slept very badly, partly because the bed was too short, partly from the effect of the change of air.

Dinner (Wh[ea]ts[hea]f) 1/–?   Train Ch[arin]g + to Victoria 1½d Victoria to Oxted 1/8

> The formidable Miss Emma Frances Brooke had apparently forgiven Shaw for the Grace Gilchrist affair. ■ In a letter to Florence Farr dated 20 August 1891 (*CL*), he estimated the bed as "about 5 ft 2 in. long." To FE he described himself in the sandpit as "grovelling among the thistles & bees. . . ."

20   In the morning I went out and lay down among the thistles on the brink of a sandpit, keeping off the rain with my mackintosh and writing letters to Standring etc. After dinner we all went out and joined Mrs. Olivier and her children, who were going off for a picnic with Miss Brooke and her nephews. We met Miss Brooke on the way to Limpsfield. Arriving there, we left them and made for the top of the ridge of the downs on the other side of Oxted. Eventually it began to rain and we were drenched. This rain lasted 24 hours. When we got back a telegram came from Edward Carpenter to say that he was coming at 20. He came, pretty wet.

Daily Chronicle 1d

21 Still raining. Carpenter went off at midday. In the afternoon we had fine weather enough to enable us to get a walk through Oxted Village and beyond it.

Daily Chronicle 1d   *Review of Reviews* 6d

22 *Come up from Oxted by the 6.46 train.*

I spent all the early part of the day cleaning my boots, playing and singing. In the afternoon we went for a walk to Limpsfield. Mrs. Olivier and her mother called for a while during the day. Salt and Olivier saw me off. The train was half an hour late and I changed at Croydon into a Charing Cross train and got out at Cannon St., where I took the Underground for Ravenscourt Park. FE and I did not do any reading, as I was tired and depressed by the change from the country. When I got home had a slight attack of looseness of the bowels.

Stamps 6d   Telegram to *World* 6d   *Daily Chronicle* 1d   Train Oxted to Cannon St (Victoria ticket) 1/8   Cannon St to Ravenscourt Pk 7d   Shep[herds] Bush to P[or]tl[an]d Rd 6d

23 SUNDAY *Speak for the S. D. F. on Clapham Common at 15.30 ([H. B.] Rogers), on "Communism." Speak for the S. D. F. at East Hill, Wandsworth. 19½. Speak for the Hammersmith Socialist Society at Hammersmith Bridge at 12.*

Dined at Sparlings'. Went to bed the moment I got home. My address on Clapham Common was cut rather short by the rain. Hentsch and some others then brought me as far as the Criterion Restaurant. I had a good deal of time to kill between 18 and 19½.

Train to Addison Rd 6d   Ravenscourt Pk to Vauxhall 6d   Tram Vauxhall to Swan, Stockwell 1d   Tram from Swan to Clapham Common 1d   Maccaroni &c at Crichton Rest[auran]t Wandsworth 1/6   Train Wandsworth to Waterloo 6d

> H. A. Hentsch of 8 Petworth St., Bridge St., Battersea, S.W., had been in charge of arrangements for Shaw's Clapham Common address. ▪ Swan, Stockwell, the printers. Shaw was using the firm only as a geographical landmark here.

24 At letters, diary etc. After dinner, which I took at home, went down to FE and went over the 2nd act of *Rosmersholm*. York Powell came in whilst we were at tea and gave us the particulars of the drowning of Helen Paget. I left at about 19.40 and went to Miss Sonntag's, but did not find her in. Went over then to JP, who had just returned from Boulogne. Young Sidney Drew was there. Did not get to bed until past 2.

Train to Shep[herds] Bush 6d   Bus Uxbridge Rd to Bayswater 2d

> Frederick York Powell (1850–1904), legal historian and literary scholar at Oxford, would become Regius Professor of Modern History in 1894. (A Socialist, he would help found Ruskin College, Oxford, in 1899.) Shaw then was planning a Fabian speaking tour of towns in the Oxford area. ▪ Helen Paget was the sister of Florence Farr's brother-in-law, H. M. Paget.

25 Much depressed. Did nothing but cut notices out of old *Stars*. After dinner went to the Strand to buy some books. Then back home, where I found JP and young Drew, who amused himself with the typewriter. Emery Walker called. I went out with him after we had had tea and we walked to Royal Oak and there took train for Shepherd's Bush. He left me at FE's door.

Dinner 1½ (Wh[ea]ts[hea]f)   Bax's *Outlooks from New Standpoint* 1/11   Robertson's *Modern Humanists* 1/11   Morris's *Odyssey* 4/11 Train Royal Oak to Shep[herds] B[ush] 3d   Sh[epherds] B[ush] to Ptld Rd 6d

26 *Lecture at the Central Reform Club. 38 Fitzroy Square (W. Johnson Smith). 20.45. "Liberalism and Socialism." [Edward J.] Beale in the chair. Miss Sonntag's. 17.*

Wrote a lot of letters. Began looking up the arrangements for the lecturing tour. Met FE by appointment at the Wheatsheaf. Walked to Portland Rd. and went out by train to Hammersmith.

Dinner (Wh[ea]ts[hea]f) 1/1½   Train to Shep[herds] B[ush] (2) 1/– Bus Uxbridge Rd to Bayswater 2d

27 Did a long spell of work at the book *[Technical Socialism]*. Did not give it up until near 18. Cut up some old *Stars*. Went to H. Sonntag's about 21. Wrote a letter to York Powell arranging about tomorrow and then went to bed just after 24.

Dinner (Wh[ea]ts[hea]f) 1/2½   Telegrams to FE & JP 1/–   Train to Bayswater & back 5d

28 *Speak at St. Mary's Butts, Reading, on "Programme of Social Democracy," 19.15 (A. J. Fears. 238 Southampton St. Reading). Paddington 18.20. Go to Oxford by the 22.5 train from Reading and put up with York Powell at Christ Church.*

> Shaw lists no expenses for his lecture trip, through 6 September 1891, apparently because various local committees and Henry Hutchinson's Fabian lecture fund were taking care of his bills.

29 *Speak in the market place, Bicester, at 19.45 (William Hines, 92 St. Clement's, Oxford).*

Wandered about Oxford in the morning. The rain kept me standing for some time under the trees at the other side of the bridge. Then I had a long walk through Magdalen College. In the afternoon JP came about a bit with me.

William Hines (?–1904), a former chimney sweep, was that rarity among the bourgeois Fabians, a member of the working class. He was now a trade union organizer. Hines would compile *Labour Songs for the Use of Working Men and Women*, for which York Powell composed a preface.

30 SUNDAY *Oxford. Speak in Dorchester (open air) at 14½. Speak at Great Milton at 18 (W. Hines for both meetings).*

We drove about with Hines's daughter in a trap. York Powell took the chair at the meetings. Glorious day.

31 *Speak at Walsall, Town's End Bank, at 19. (Anarch-Communist Club, 18 Goodall St., Walsall). Changed to indoors by rain.*

Left Oxford early in the afternoon. Meeting a failure through the rain. Wretched indoor meeting with only about 15 present. Slept at The George.

Judging by the interest in his talk, Shaw wrote Sidney Webb (CL) that the wild name of the Club "mean[s] absolutely nothing." In 1892, however, six Walsall anarchists were arrested for manufacturing bombs, and four were sentenced to prison terms.

September

1 *Speak on "The Labour Question" at Wolverhampton, on Waste Ground at the corner of Oldfield St. and Stafford St. at 19¼ (J. W. Buttery, 1 Meyrick Rd., Stafford). Leave Walsall by the 11.35 for Stafford, changing at Wolverhampton and stay with Buttery.*

Went on to Stafford in the morning, getting there about 13. Wrote letters etc. all the afternoon. Meeting good.

One letter Shaw wrote that afternoon, to Sidney Webb (CL), describes the lecture tour graphically.

2 *Speak in the Marsh St. lecture hall. Newcastle under Lyne on "Municipal Socialism." 20. (R.A. Reeve. Stonefield House. Stone. Stafford). John Gilliame, chairman. Leave Stafford by the 17.50 train for Newcastle under Lyne, and change at Stoke. Drive over to Church Eaton with Buttery to see Rev. Talbot.*

Fine day for the drive to Church Eaton, where we dined with Talbot, who turned out a very pleasant fellow. Put up at The Borough Arms at Newcastle by the advice of Nicklin, who met me at Stoke. Poor meeting.

The Rev. Edward Stuart Talbot (1844–1934), bishop of Rochester from to 1895 to 1905, afterwards bishop of Southark and bishop of Winchester, was a High Churchman who held liberal social views.   ▪   John Nicklin, of High St., Wolstanton, Staffs.

3   *Lecture on "The Programme of Social Democracy," in Lion School Room, Commerce St., Longton, at 20. Councillor Hawley in chair. Go over to Hanley and see the Museum; dine; and then to Stoke to see Minton's pottery.*

Called for Nicklin and carried out the programme with him. Goodish meeting in the evening—highly respectable—vote of thanks seconded by Mayor. Reeve and I walked from Stoke to Newcastle.

4   *Lecture on "Social Democracy" in the Temperance Hall, New St., Hanley. Rev. William Lansdell, Chairman. Go over to Alton Towers and spend the day there.*

Got away to Alton Towers alone and strolled about there all day.

5   *Go to Lichfield, see the Cathedral, etc., and then on to Northampton.*

Buttery met me at Stafford as I passed through. After seeing the Cathedral I got some dinner at a little refreshment house; bought some plums for dessert; and went along the water basin to St. Chad's. Put up at The Angel in Northampton. Went to the theatre in the evening, and saw *Jane*, the farcical comedy.

> *Jane*, by Harry Nicholls and William Lestocq, had opened on 18 December 1890, and would have several runs in the early 1890s, in London and the provinces, adding up to hundreds of performances.

6 SUNDAY   °*Lecture for North Kensington Branch S. D. F. on Wormwood Scrubbs (open air). R. A. Peddie, 29 Bracewell Rd., North Kensington, W. Put off to 13th. Lecture at Northampton (open air—market place) for S. D. F. 11¼. Lecture at Northampton (open air—market place) for S. D. F. 18¼. Come up to London by the 20.17 train.*

Both meetings very successful in spite of the rain in the evening. Dined with Purvis and went out with him in the afternoon to see the round church and strolled on the racecourse. We had tea at the house of one of the Fellows—I did not catch his name. [I . . . heard . . . a brass band of shoemakers, conducted by a compositor, playing for pure love of their art on the racecourse . . . , and playing very well indeed. They gave us a Gloria of Haydn's with a delicacy of execution and a solemn reverence for the old master which were extraordinarily refreshing after the stale professional routine playing of the London concert platforms. It was like seeing a withering flower put into water.]

> R. A. Peddie (1869–1951), a member of William Morris's Socialist branch, was a librarian and professional bibliographer.   ▪   Purvis may be the R. A. Purvis, Ll.D., who spoke on Home Rule for Ireland to the Bedford Debating Society on 13 January 1887.   ▪   G.B.S.

reported further on the impromptu racecourse concert in *The World*, 16 September 1891 (C814).

7 *Debut of Paulus at the Trocadero Music Hall.* °*Fabian Central Group meeting. 32 Great Ormond St. 20.*

Attending to letters, making out accounts and expenses for Fabian etc. JP called in the middle of the day. Met E. Walker at the Wheatsheaf. Called at Jaeger's and ordered boots. Met Archer as I came out of Trocadero. He walked with me half way down Piccadilly. I was on my way to JP's. When I got there the lights were out and everybody gone to bed; so I came home.

Dinner (Wh[ea]tsh[ea]f) 1/–?   Bus Hyde Pk corner to Brompton Sq 1d   back to Bond St 2d

> Jean Paulus, popular French music hall singer and comedian. "It may be said of him, as Marx said of Mill," Shaw wrote (C814), "that his eminence is due to the flatness of the surrounding country."

8 *Fabian Executive. 276 Strand. 17. "Budget" Committee. 16. Call on Parke at the* Star *office in the afternoon.*

Began *World* article. Olivier called in the morning. After the Executive went home with Wallas and had tea there. There was a young fellow named Kerney dining. I left at a little after 20 and went to FE's.

Train to Farringdon 2d   Dinner (at Central) 11d?   Bus to Strand 1d   "News from Nowhere" to send to Mrs. Atkinson at Hanley 1/1½ Train Gower St to Shep[herds] B[ush] & back 1/–

> The G.B.S. notice (C814) was mostly a lament over the writer's failure to secure tickets for Bayreuth; a review of the shoemakers and Paulus served as its tailpiece.

9 *Call at 14 Argyll Rd. (Mrs. Wynne's) in the evening to see Aileen Bell.*

Continued *World* article. Found myself towards evening with a slight cold, which afterwards developed into a very bad one. JP was here in the evening. I dined at 5 Oxford St. because FE telegraphed to me to meet her there; but she did not come to the same room as that in which I dined and we did not meet until I went on to the Museum. We walked through all the rooms there together.

PMG 1d   Dinner (at 5 Oxford St) 11d?   Train to High St & back 9d

10 *Go to the meeting of the Blavatsky Lodge of the Theosophical Society at 19 Avenue Rd. 20¼.*

Wrote review of LeGallienne's *Narcissus* for *The Star*. Also wrote a note on plays for Webb to put in his letter for *The Bradford Observer*. McKernon, returned from his continental trip, was here. At JP's there was a man named Smythe. Had a talk with Mabel Besant at the meeting in the evening. Cold bad. Met FE by appointment at the Wheatsheaf at $14\frac{1}{2}$; but she had no particular business.

Dinner (at Wh[ea]ts[hea]f) 1/–?   Bus to 447 Oxford St 1d   [Sent] Longden bal[anc]e of money for Italian trip £3/10/0   *Baedekers* for Switzerland & Northern Italy 10/6   Train to S[ou]th Kensington & back (to Baker St) 9d

> Shaw's review of *The Book Bills of Narcissus*, by Richard Le Gallienne (Derby, 1891), *The Star*, 12 September 1891 (C813), was signed "C. di B." ▪ Shaw's "note on plays" for insertion in Webb's regular column was a paragraph on *The Quintessence of Ibsenism*, *Bradford Observer*, 12 September 1891 (C812). ▪ Henry Longden (?–1920) of 447 Oxford St., W., a metalworker who was an early member of the Arts and Crafts Exhibition Society, was one of the organizers of the Art Workers Guild trip to Italy.

11   *Fabian Special Meeting. 31 Upper Bedford Place. 20. To press Questions for Candidates, County Council, School Board, Rural County Councils and Town Councillors.*

Spent the morning writing up this diary etc. Archer called. McKernon was here: he brought Mother off to the Crystal Palace. Went into the City to buy things after dinner.

Dinner 1/–? (Wh[ea]ts[hea]f)   Bus to City 1d   Umbrella 10/6 *Manual of [Italian] Conversation* (Baedeker) 1/11   Bus to Bedford St 1d   Insect powder $8\frac{1}{2}$d   Nail Brush 1/2   Sponge bag 1/7   Mirror 2/7   Soap Box $1/3\frac{1}{2}$ (all at Stores)   *PMG* & *Star* $\frac{1}{2}$d   Bus to Grafton St 1d

12   °*Promenade Concerts begin at Covent Garden. 20. Production of Yvette at the Avenue Theatre—Musical Pantomime play. 20.20. Meeting of the Art Workers Guild Italian trip at 29 Great George St. Westminster at 15 and visit to the National Gallery.*

Wrote article for the first number of *The Workers' Cry* in its new form as combined with *The Leader*. Archer was in the pit at the Avenue. I went and sat there with him during the 2nd act and we left at the end of the 3rd, the ballet being a hopeless failure. I did not stay long in the National Gallery. Walker and I left together.

Star $\frac{1}{2}$d   *PMG* 1d   Dinner (Wh[ea]ts[hea]f) $1/5\frac{1}{2}$?   Bus to Grafton St 1d

> Shaw would be one of 27 trippers on this, his first, visit to Italy. In charge of arrangements was Thomas Okey, scholar and translator (1852–1935), who would hold the chair in Italian Studies at Cambridge from 1919 to 1928. ▪ "Our Opportunity," *Leader and Workers' Advocate*, 19 September 1891 (C815). Shaw suggested backing Gladstone in order to get a new reform bill. ▪ The ballet, with music by André Gédalge, was "utterly void of interesting ideas," G.B.S. wrote (C814).

13 SUNDAY   *Speak on Wormwood Scrubbs for North Kensington Branch S. D. F. (see last Sunday). $18\frac{1}{2}$. Go to Emery Walker's in the morning with Archer (photographing Archer).*

Archer and I went to Hammersmith by the 10.36 train. The photographing took all the morning. Archer came in to Sparlings' for a while; but did not stay to dinner. Miss Ellis and the Langs came in afterwards. Also Cockerell. I did a little work at Sparling's typewriter on the article before I left. After speaking on the Scrubbs I went to FE's, a couple of members of the Branch walking the whole way with me; but she was not in. So I went back to the Terrace and tried to get into Walkers'—in vain. Then I went back to FE. When I got home I finished the *World* proof and sent it off with the *Workers' Cry* article.

Train to Ravenscourt Pk 7d   Tram to Broadway 2d   Train to Latimer Rd 1½d   Train Shep[herds] B[ush] home 6d   Bottle of Ginger Ale 2d

14 *Give Elliot and Fry a sitting for a photograph at 13.30. 55 Baker St. Manouili, Mme. Pogowski's Russian friend, to call in the morning.*

Manouili, to whom I delivered a long dissertation, took all the morning. On my way from the photographing I met Pardon, who walked with me to Rathbone Place. After dinner I wrote letters etc. Mother laid up with a cold—in bed all the morning.

Train to Baker St 1d   Dinner (Wh[ea]ts[hea]f) 1/1   PMG 1d   *Star* ½d

Elliot and Fry were among the best commercial portrait photographers in London and would have Shaw as a client more than once.

15 *Fabian Executive. 276 Strand. 15.*

Slippers 2/8   Bootlaces 4d   Studs 6d

Shaw was doing little else than prepare for his expedition to Italy.

16 *Italian Expedition with members of Art Workers Guild. Be at Holborn Viaduct well before the departure of the train at 9.55. Dover 12. Ostend 16. Leave 16.26. Brussels (Nord) 18.15.*

17 *Leave Brussels 7.27. Bettingen 11.37. Basle arrive 19.32. Hotel St. Gotthard.*

18 *°Fabian Society 1st meeting of Winter session. St. James's Restaurant Banqueting Hall. 20. Sidney Webb on "Wages of Working Women." Leave Basle at 7.10. Goschenen 13.10 Leave 13.35. Chiasso 17.25. Leave 18.14. Milan 19.35. Hotel Gran Bretagna.*

19 *Milan.*

[Go to Milan, and join the rush of tourists to its petrified christening-cake of a cathedral. . . . In Italy, . . . churches are used in such a way that priceless pictures become smeared with filthy tallow-soot. . . . But worse than this are the innumerable daily services which disturb the truly religious visitor. . . . The English tourist is often lectured for his inconsiderate behaviour in Italian churches, for walking about during service, talking loudly, thrusting himself rudely between a worshipper and an altar to examine a painting, even for stealing chips of stone and scrawling his name on statues. But as far as the mere disturbance of the services is concerned, . . . the priest and his congregation [are] troublesome intruders. . . . It is the sacristan who teaches you, when once you are committed to tipping him, not to waste your good manners on the kneeling worshippers who are snatching a moment from their daily round of drudgery and starvation to be comforted by the Blessed Virgin or one of the saints. . . .]

"On Going to Church," *The Savoy*, January 1896 (C1111). Much in this essay reflects Shaw's first experience of Italy.

20 SUNDAY   *Leave Milan 12.50. Verona 16. Hotel Cola.*

21   °*Fabian Central Group meeting. 32 Great Ormond St. 20. Leave Verona at 16.20. Venice. 18.35. Hotel Cappello Nero.*

[The only great church I saw in Milan was an old one called San Ambrogio, with the altar—made of gold, jewels, filigree, mosaic &c—shut up in Chubb safe doors, which they opened after energetic chaffering for 10 francs for the lot of us. This was a Romanesque church; and it and one at Verona called St Zeno are the only places I felt happy in. . . .]

Shaw's experience of Italian hotel food was catastrophic, as even the macaroni was doused with meat gravy. Finally, Thomas Okey hit upon the expedient of going to the head-waiter at each hotel (so he wrote in *A Basketful of Memories*, London, 1930) to explain that one of their number was "under a vow." This was immediately understood, and Shaw was fed "as a devout Catholic under a vow to abstain from flesh, wine, and tobacco." ■ Chubb's still makes quality English safes. ■ The Church of San Ambrogio report is in a letter from Shaw to William Morris from Venice, 23 September 1891 (CL).

22   °*Fabian Executive. 276 Strand. 17.*

22–28   *Venice.*

[The Venetian municipality has placed at our disposal a person supposed to be a young architect, whom I rather suspect of being a plain clothes policeman set to watch that we do not steal bits of mosaic, or cut our names in the monuments. . . . I have not put my nose inside St Marks yet; but the outside disappointed me: I expected above all things color, and it is *scraped clean.*]

Shaw to Morris. According to Sydney Cockerell's 1891 diary (BL 52628), on the 22nd they went up and down the canals, and on the 23rd, after touring the Ducal Palace in the morning and sitting out a thunderstorm in the early afternoon, he, Shaw, Walker, and Okey went to the Roman amphitheatre "and stayed at the top of it until the sun sank." Then they made their way back through the "Gothic streets" to their hotel. On the 24th they looked at pictures and sculpture in the Accademia; on the 25th they met at St. Mark's to spend the morning there, then took gondolas to San Giorgio Maggiore. On the 26th the party went to Torcello in a procession of four gondolas; on the 27th Cockerell, Shaw, and Emery Walker went to the Rialto, the Church of the Frari, and again to the Ducal Palace to look at the *Paradiso*, this time armed with Ruskin's description. On the 28th they bought photographs of art and architecture they had seen, listened to the band in the Piazza, strolled the "splendid" market place, and returned for a final look at Giotto's frescoes.

29 *Leave Venice 9 A.M. for Padua.*

30 *Leave Padua 5.38 A.M. Mantua 10.50.*

Cockerell's diary notes that they walked the "medieval streets" of Mantua until 10.30. Perhaps they were postponing as long as possible the ordeal of their hotel room (which Cockerell shared with Shaw and Walker): "We did battle with bugs most of the night and slew multitudes."

October

1 *Leave Mantua at 11.15. Pavia 16. Hotel Tre Re.*

2 *°Fabian. Syndey Olivier on "Socialist Individualism." St. James's Restaurant. French Chamber. 20. Leave Pavia at 16. Milan (Central) 18.50. Hotel Gran Bretagna. Certosa on the way.*

Cockerell reports that in the morning the party went to San Michele, "a glorious Lombardic church" which he felt rivaled the more famous San Ambrogio, and later wandered the "picturesque back streets."

3 *Leave Milan at 7.30. Chiasso 8.56. Leave at 9. Goschenen. 13.45. Leave at 14.10. Basle 19.10. Leave at 21.11. Travel all night.*

4 SUNDAY *Brussels 8.15. Leave at 9.20. Ostend 11.2. Leave at 11.10. Dover 15.20 and Holborn Viaduct 17.5.*

5 *Fabian Central Group meeting. 32 Great Ormond St. 20.*

Busy over letters, business etc.—at least I suppose so; I do not remember this day very well. I went to the Stores in the afternoon to buy some brushes.

Dinner 1/–?   Boot brushes 4/10   Nail brush 2/7   Bottle of Howell's Chameleon Ink 6d   Bus Garrick St to Grafton St 1d

6   °*Fabian Executive. 276 Strand. 17. Birmingham Musical Festival.* Elijah *at 11½. Mackenzie's* Veni Creator *and miscellaneous programme at 20. Go down to Birmingham by the 10.10 train and stop at Cobden Hotel.*

Got down to Birmingham so late I only heard the last 3 or 4 numbers of *Elijah.* Very wet miserable day. In the afternoon I went out to Girdlestones' and had tea there.

Cab to Euston 1/3   Train to Birmingham &^ back 18/10   Programme at evening concert 1/– [?]   Bus to Harborne 3d   Train Harborne to Birmingham 3d?   Dinner (at C[obden] H[otel]) 1/–?

> G.B.S. reviewed the Festival on 14 October 1891 (C816), finding Mackenzie's *Veni Creator* a "sham classic" and the performance of Bach the next day "stolid trudging" without sensitivity.

7   *Birmingham Musical Festival. Bach's* St. Matthew Passion *at 11¼. Stanford's* Eden *at 20.*

In the morning went down to St. Martin's Church in the Bullring, and spent some time looking at it inside and out. Then went into the Art Gallery to see the Loan Collection of pictures there. Much struck with Madox Brown's. Went out to Girdlestones' in the afternoon as before and had tea there. Some Bristol friends of theirs and their landlord came in and talked a bit.

Programmes 2/–   Dinner at Garden 1/2?

> Villiers Stanford's cantata was another "sham classic" (C816).

8   *Birmingham Musical Festival.* Messiah *at 11.30. Concert at 20.*

In the morning went to see St. Philip's Church and had another look at the pictures to which I returned after the concert with Sydney Pardon. In the afternoon I worked at the *World* article in the hotel. In the evening a sister of Mrs. Carr's introduced herself to me.

Dinner (CH) 1/–?   Programme at evening concert 1/–

9   *Second performance of the Independent Theatre at the Royalty. Zola's* Thérèse Raquin. *20. Come up from Birmingham by the 15 train. Birmingham Musical Festival. Dvorak's* Requiem. *11½.* °*Birmingham Musical Festival. Berlioz's* Faust. *20.*

Did not do anything particular in the morning. Worked on my article in the train.

Dinner 1/–?   Hotel Bill 16/10?   Newspapers 1½d   Programme at theatre 6d

> Zola's novel had been dramatized by Teixeira de Mattos with some help from George Moore. Mrs. Theodore Wright, who would later act for Shaw, was Mme. Raquin; Therese was Laura Johnson.

10 *First Crystal Palace Concert of the winter series. Popper (cellist). 15.*
FE came down to the Palace with me. Spent the evening at her place.

Dinner ?   Train Ch[arin]g + to Vict[oria] 1½d   Vict[oria] to [Crystal]
Pal[ace] 2/–   *Saturday Review* 6d   Newspapers 4d?

> David Popper "proved quite as fine a violoncellist as his great reputation had led us all to
> expect" (C430). ▪ Shaw had written FE a passionate letter (in the guise of a mock-pas-
> sionate one) from Birmingham (*CL*), declaring that she was his "best and dearest love" as
> well as his "secret glimpse of heaven."

11 SUNDAY *Lecture at the Star Radical Club, 8 Mayall Rd., Herne Hill, on
"Practical Communism." 20½. (G. G. Steele, Hon. Sec.). Brixton station L. C.
and D. Railway. Go down to Walkers' with Archer to remedy the photo-
graphic failures of the 13th September and catch the 19.45 train from
Richmond Park to Brixton.*

Dined at Walkers'. Afternoon at Sparlings'. Ellis and a friend of his came in
for tea. Very wet evening.

Train to Ravenscourt 4d?   R[ichmond] Pk to Brixton ?   B[r]ixton to
Victoria 2d?   (can't remember these fares)

12 *Go to see Ada Rehan in* The Last Word *at the Lyceum Theatre, Daly
Co., 20.15. Miss Sonntag's afternoon.*

Could get no work done as JP came in the morning and made terrible
scenes all day. I went out before dinner to the Museum and to Archer's to
avoid her; but she was there when I returned. Walked to Bayswater.

Dinner 1/–?   Train Bayswater to Ptld Rd 2d?   Lyceum Theatre 2/6

> Ada C. Rehan (1860–1916), who had been Ada Crehan until a typographical error altered
> her name, was playing in an Augustin Daly adaptation of a melodrama by Franz von
> Schönthan. G.B.S. would note on 4 November 1891 (C819) that her "exquisite" talents
> were being squandered in such a vehicle.

13 *Fabian Executive. 276 Strand. 17.*
Worked at Fabian paper for Friday. Forget all particulars.
Dinner 1/–?

14 Still at Fabian paper. Forget all particulars—I have left these few days
unwritten too long: it is now the 9th November. I have of course not left all
the subsequent days neglected like this.
Dinner 1/–?

15 *Graham Wallas's University Extension series of lectures on Constitu-
tional History ("The English Citizen") begins at the Town Hall, Chelsea.
20.15. °Grosvenor Club At-Home. 21½. Concert.*

Still at Fabian paper.

Dinner 1/–?   Train to S[ou]th Kensington & back 6d

16 *Read paper on "The Difficulties of Anarchism" at the Fabian. St. James's Restaurant Banqueting Hall. 20.*

Another desperate day finishing the paper amid intercourse and scenes from JP. Very tempestuous whilst I was at tea. At last pretended to throw her out of window. Went into Regents Park after dinner hoping that she would not be there when I came back.

Dinner 1/–?

17 *Crystal Palace Concert. 15. °Miss D'Esterre Keeling's pianoforte recital. 41 Holland Rd. W. 15½.*

At *World* article. FE came to the Palace with me. Spent the evening with her.

Dinner 1/–?   Train Ch[arin]g + to Victoria 1½d   Vict[oria] to C[rystal] P[alace] 2/–   Papers 1½d ?   Train Vict[oria] to Ravenscourt Pk 6d Shep[herds] Bush to Portl[an]d Rd 6d

> Reviewed on 21 October 1891 (C817). G.B.S. was impressed by the "brilliant" piano virtuosity of Adeline de Lara, featured performer at the Crystal Palace.

18 SUNDAY *°Lecture at the Deptford Liberal Club on "Communism." 20½? (Found Bland announced in my place; and took the chair for him.)*

Finished and set off *World* article.

Train to New Cross & back 1/–?

19 *°Fabian Central Group meeting. 32 Great Ormond St. 20. Go down to Halifax by the 13.30 train from King's Cross and lecture at the large hall of the Mechanics' Institute on "Labour Representation." 19½. Stay with Lister at Shibden Hall. Dentist's (W. J. Macdonald) at 10. 32 Weymouth St. W. °Opening night Lago's Opera enterprise at the Shaftesbury Theatre.*

Very wet morning. Had a front tooth stopped. Much more frightened than hurt by the operation. In the train wrote a letter to Miss Robins and read newspapers etc. About 400 people at the lecture.

Train to Kings + 1d   Kings + to Halifax 31/6   Insurance 1/–   Tip to porter at Halifax for getting my hat 6d

> John Lister, squire of Shibden Hall, near Halifax, Yorkshire, would become treasurer of the Independent Labour Party in 1893. ▪ The letter (CL) apologized for failing to respond to her letter about her production plans. Miss Robins was planning more Ibsen.

20 *°Fabian Executive. 276 Strand. 17. Come up from Halifax by the 14 train, reaching King's Cross at 18.50. °Opening night Opera at Covent Garden.*

Spent the morning in the neighborhood of Shibden Hall, chiefly in the fire brick works, looking at the processes. Came up to town expecting to have to go to the Opera, but found no tickets. Stayed at home and made a beginning at writing up this diary—untouched since my Italian trip—and attacking my vast arrears of correspondence.

David Copperfield to read in train 6d   Papers 2d   Train Kings + to Ptld Rd 1d

---

21 *Dentist. 32 Weymouth St. 16$\frac{1}{2}$. °Dialectical Society. South Place. Dr. Drysdale on Mrs. Besant's Objections to Neo-Malthusianism. 20. Go to hear Cavalleria Rusticana at the Shaftesbury Theatre. 20. Miss Sonntag's. 15.*

Writing letters. Macdonald stopped my right upper wisdom tooth, which I had supposed to be sound.

Dinner 1/3?   Bus to Queens Rd 2d   Train Bayswater to Portl[an]d Rd 1$\frac{1}{2}$d   Shaftesbury Theatre 2/6

> *Cavalleria Rusticana* was reviewed on 28 October 1891 (C818). Pietro Mascagni's short *verismo* opera was performed with the comic one-act *Crispino e la Comare*, by Luigi Ricci, incongruously "round its neck," but to G.B.S. it succeeded through its "passionate melody."

---

22 *Graham Wallas's second English Citizen lecture at the Co-opera-time Lecture Hall, 310 Kings Rd. Chelsea. 20.15. Mrs. Dryhurst to call at 16$\frac{1}{4}$.*

Began *World* article. Very wet day. After dinner went over to Wallas's to consult him about the invitation to stand for the County Council in Chelsea. Then went up to Webb's on the same business; but did not find him at home. Got back just in time to meet Mrs. Dryhurst.

Dinner 1/3   Tram Euston Rd to Park St 1d   Train to S[ou]th Kensington & back 6d

---

23 *Press View at Dowdeswell's. Thorne Waite's water colours. Press View. 19th Century Gallery. 9 Conduit St. Press View. British Artists. Suffolk St. Press View. Tooth's in the Haymarket. Webb to call in the morning. °Fabian At-Home at Mrs. Cotton's, 19 Burton St. W.*

Continued *World* article; but did not get on very much with it. After Webb's call I wrote a letter to L[ord] Monkswell about Chelsea; and then went off to the galleries. Finished the article in the evening.

Dinner 1/2?

> Robert Collier (1845–1909), the second Baron Monkswell, was a barrister and Liberal member for Chelsea of the London County Council. He and his wife, Mary, were friends of Mark Twain when he lived at Tedworth Square.

---

24 *Crystal Palace Concert. 15. Private and Press View. Hanover Gallery. Bierstadt's pictures etc.*

Hanover Gallery in the morning. FE with me at Palace. She came here with me afterwards, as I wanted to see whether there were any Opera tickets waiting for me. There were none; so we went off to Hammersmith together.

Dinner (Orange Grove) 9d   Train Ch[arin]g + to Victoria 1½d
Vict[oria] to C[rystal] Pal[ace], self & F. Emery 4/–   papers 1½d   Bus
Victoria to Grafton St (2) 4d   Telegram F. Em. 6d   Train to Hammersmith (Shep Bush) (2) 1/3

> The Crystal Palace concert was reviewed only in passing, on 4 November 1891 (C819).
> ■ Albert Bierstadt (1830–1902) was the great American landscape painter, particularly of the West. Shaw had gone to see his work rather than review it, having given up that trade. ■ Displeased with the G.B.S. treatment of its productions, the management at Covent Garden was ignoring Shaw. He would write in his 28 October 1891 notice as tailpiece, "I hear that a few operatic performances are given every week at Covent Garden; but I presume they are of no particular importance, as my attention has not been specifically called to them."

25 SUNDAY   *Lecture at Kelmscott House, Hammersmith, for the National Secular Society (Sparling) on "The Difficulties of Anarchism."*

Train to Hammersmith & back 1/–   Excess to Ravenscourt Pk 2d

26   *Write to Billson about next Sunday. Dentist. 32 Weymouth St. 9.30.*

> James Billson, who was in charge of arrangements for Shaw's lecture at Leicester.

27   *Fabian Executive. 276 Strand. 17. Dentist. 32 Weymouth St. 9.30. Paderewski's recital. St. James's Hall. 15. Production of* The Flying Dutchman *at the Shaftesbury Theatre. Lago's Company. (Miss) Macintyre and Blanchard.*

The [dental] appointment accounted for the whole day.

Dinner 1/5?

> G.B.S. noted that Paderewski had cut his hair, "but only a little," and that his playing was "positively better, technically, than when he last played in London" (C819). ■ Most of the G.B.S. 4 November 1891 notice (C819) was given over to *The Flying Dutchman*, which had "sorry makeshifts" for scenery and was underrehearsed. Margaret Macintyre and Robert Blanchard, in the principal roles, were excused as having been "in earnest."

28   [   ]

> Shaw was apparently under the weather in the aftermath of the long siege at the dentist the previous day. See also 4 November for his continuing dental problems.

29   *Wallas's 3rd lecture. 310 Kings Rd. S.W. 20.15.*

Began *World* article.

Dinner 1/4?   Train to Gloster Rd & back 6d

> Gloucester Rd. was one of his codes for a visit to Florence Farr, as were Dalling Road and Ravenscourt Park.

30 °*Meeting of Lyulph Stanley and Mrs. Maitland's School Board Committee at Percy Bunting's. 17. Meeting of Money and his friends re Eastbourne
riots, at 2 Museum Buildings, Bury St. (No. 12 flat) 17. Meeting of Fabian
Group Secretaries and Executive. 276 Strand. 20.*

Finished and sent off *World* article. Did not get down to the Fabian until
after 22. The Group Secretaries were all gone; but Wallas, Webb, Pease, and
Oakeshott were there discussing the "Pan-Fabian Conference" which we are
arranging. Webb and Wallas walked home with me.

Dinner 1/3?

> Edward Lyulph Stanley (1839–1925), Lord Stanley of Alderley, later Lord Sheffield, was
> M.P. for Oldham and a member of the London School Board. Mrs. Charlotte Maitland (?–
> 1931) was also on the board. ▪ (Sir) Leo Chiozza Money (1870–1944) would become
> M.P. for North Paddington and again for Northhamptonshire East. A Fabian, he often
> wrote on economic issues. ▪ The 21 October and 25 October riots at Eastbourne were
> apparently provoked by the town authorities against the local Salvationists, who, in
> defiance of a local ordinance, insisted on their right to play their instruments in public.
> The right would be sustained by Parliament in September 1892. ▪ The first Fabian
> delegate conference, to be held at Essex Hall, the Strand, in February 1892.

31 *Crystal Palace Concert. 15. Meeting of the 4 Fabian Groups interested
in Marylebone School Board election at 20 at the Liberal Association, 121
Marylebone Rd. N.W.*

Mother came with me to the Palace. I got away from the School Board
Committee meeting as soon as I could, and went off to see FE.

Dinner 1/–?   Train Ch[arin]g + to Vict[oria] 1½d   Victoria to [Crystal]
Palace 2/–   Vict[oria] to Ch[arin]g + 1½d   Zola's *Le Rêve* 2/6   Train
Edg[ware] Rd return to Shep[herds] B[ush] & single to Ptld Rd 8d?

> The concert—apparently unremarkable—occurred "between notices," and went unre-
> viewed. (Other Crystal Palace concerts would also go unnoticed.) ▪ See 19 November
> 1891 for Shaw's attendance at *Le Rêve*.

November

1 SUNDAY *Lecture at Leicester for the Leicester Secular Society (S. Gimson,
20 Glebe St., Leicester) on "Progress in Freethought." Stay with Billson at
Desford.*

Corrected *World* proof. Wrote letters. Prepared lecture in the train. Had tea
at Gimson's before lecture. Drove out to Desford with Billson and his sister
in a brougham.

Cab to St Pancras 1/3   Train to Leicester 8/0½   Insurance 1d

2 °*Fabian Central Group meeting. 32 Great Ormond St. 20. Lecture at Oxford for the University Russell Club on "Alternatives to Social Democracy." (G. W. Steevens. 31 Holywell. Oxford). Randolph Hotel. 20. Drive to the meet at Market Bosworth and thence to Hinckley station, where catch the 13.10 train for Nuneaton and take the 14.38 London and Northwestern train Nuneaton to Oxford, arrive 17.31. Stay with D. G. Ritchie, 39 Banbury Rd.*

Billson's sisters came with us in a trap to the meet. We drove on to Hinckley and went in for a moment into the house of one of Billson's relatives named Atkins, who walked from his house to the station with us. At Nuneaton I had an hour to wait, which I spent in walking down the town and looking at the old church and getting some lunch. When the train came in I found De Mattos in it and we traveled together as far as Northampton, where he got out. After the lecture I went with Hines to Powell's rooms, but he was out. Morse Stephens and another man were there. I stayed for a while on the chance of Powell's turning up; but he did not. A Mrs. Firth with us at Ritchies'; also a University man whose name I forget.

Train Hinckley to Oxford 5/7   Grub at Nuneaton 9d

> George W. Steevens (1869–1900), then an Oxford student, would publish the college satire *The Autobiography of a Boy*, then make his reputation as a journalist with controversial reporting of the Dreyfus case, and the Boer War. ▪ Henry Morse Stephens would later be professor of modern European history at Cornell University and chairman of History at the University of California, Berkeley. At the time Stephens was a fellow at Oxford. (See 8 February 1885.) ▪ Wife of Charles Harding Firth (1857–1936), then a lecturer in history at Pembroke College, Oxford.

3 *Fabian Executive. 276 Strand. 17. Meeting of the South St. Pancras Liberal and Radical Association Executive at 195 Gray's Inn Rd. 20. Paderewski's farewell recital. St. James's Hall. 15. °Stewart Macpherson's pianoforte recital. Prince's Hall. 20. Come up by the 9.7 Great Western train.*

Did nothing in the train but read the paper. Wrote several letters. Olivier came back from the Fabian with me and had tea here. JP ventured to come; but I did not see her, as she did not leave the next room. Walked back from Caucus meeting with Davis.

Train Oxford to Portland Rd 5/4   Papers 2d   Dinner 1/6?

> G.B.S. would sum up Paderewski's performance in a 2 December 1891 (C826) essay comparing him to his greatest contemporary rival, Stavenhagen. ▪ C. F. Davis of Kentish Town was an S.D.F. stalwart.

4 *Macdonald's (dentist). 32 Weymouth St. 11. Look in at the Institute in the afternoon. Go to La Basoche in the evening—English Opera House.*

Hardly any work done. After dinner (at which I saw Salt for a while) I went to the Stores to get some Condy's Fluid, and to leave some of the Venice photographs to be framed. The Condy I got because I wanted to rinse my mouth with it, being unable to get rid of the nuisance produced by having the old stuffing removed from the tooth I got done in Dublin 20 years ago, and the putrified inside broken up and let loose.

Dinner 1/2   Condy's Fluid 9d   Camphor 4 oz 7d

André Messager's light opera *The Basoche*, or *King of the Students*, was described by G.B.S. on 11 November 1891 (C820) as "an appealing combination of farce and fairy tale in an historical framework." Since the work was "high comedy," the music French, and the setting medieval, he predicted that English audiences would not take kindly to its delights. G.B.S. also predicted a great career in opera for the lead, David Bispham (1857–1921), an American-born baritone who would indeed make his Covent Garden debut the next year and become a star of the Metropolitan Opera in New York. ▪ "Condy Sanitat: the new disinfectant" (according to a contemporary advertisement) was an all-purpose product manufactured in Battersea and used in varying dilutions as mouthwash, hair bleach, floor cleaner, and general cleansing agent.

5   *Wallas's 4th lecture. 310 Kings Rd. 20.15. The Peases' At-Home to meet Podmore and his wife. 2 Hyde Park Mansions. 20½. °School Board Election Committee, Paddington Radical Club. 20½. °Playgoers' Club. W. Alison on "What is the Function of the Stage?" Mona Hotel. 20½.*

Began *World* article, and got on very badly at it. Pease called in the evening and told me that it was not worth while to go to the Paddington meeting, as our candidate (Mrs. Bateson) would probably not stand. So I went to the Wallas's lecture. Wallas's sister (Molly) came back with us as far as High St. Kensington. We got out at Edgware Rd. and went into Pease's, where we stayed until after midnight. Wallas, Utley and I walked home together.

Dinner 1/3?   Train to Gloster Rd & back 6d

6   *Fabian. Take the chair for Rev. Joseph Wood on "Municipal Socialism." 20. Banqueting Hall. Press View. Herbert Schmalz's Return from Calvary at Dowdeswell's.*

Still getting on very badly with the *World* article, which I did not succeed in finishing. Beginning to relapse into my old late rising—the benefit of the Italian trip is apparently already spent.

Dinner 1/4?   Bus Oxford O to Fabian 1d   *Justice* 1d

The Rev. Joseph Wood (1842–1931), then headmaster of the Tonbridge School, would become canon of Rochester Cathedral in 1919.

7   *Crystal Palace Concert. 15. Meeting of Borough of Marylebone Fabian Groups re School Board Election. 121 Marylebone Rd. 20. Meeting to promote candidature of Baum for School Board, 8 George St. Euston College. 20½.*

Wrote letters to Archer and to Harris of *The Fortnightly Review*, who asks me for an article on musical criticism. FE, who is staying down at Hayes, met me at the Palace. In the evening the meeting at Marylebone Rd. adjourned to Gower St., where we adopted Baum as our candidate.

Telegram to FE 6d   Dinner 1/2?   *Fortnightly Review* 2/6   *Star* $\frac{1}{2}$d
Train Ch[arin]g + to Victoria 1$\frac{1}{2}$, Victoria to [Crystal] Palace & back 2/–
Baker St to Gower St 1d

> F. C. Baum, a Fabian, would be elected to the London County Council in March 1892.
> ▪ Shaw's letter to Archer (*CL*) was mistakenly put in the Harris envelope, and Harris's in
> Archer's envelope. Shaw had to write to both to make amends. Archer had just published
> a negative review of *Quintessence of Ibsenism* (as "Shawpenhauerism") in the November
> *New Review* in the form of an open letter to Shaw. ▪ Frank Harris (1855–1931), then
> editor of the *Fortnightly Review*, had invited Shaw to contribute an essay. Harris would
> later edit the *Saturday Review*, where Shaw would take his initials to become drama critic
> in January 1895.

8 SUNDAY *Lecture at the Newington Reform Club on "Social Limits to Individual Liberty" (their subject) in the evening. (F. W. Clark. Political Secretary, N. R. D., Manor Place, Walworth S.E.)*

Finished the *World* article with great labour, working all day at it. JP went off to Ireland; but I did not see her. Constantine walked with me from Walworth as far as the hospital in Gower St.

Train to Farringdon 2d   Bus to Elephant & Castle 1d

9 °*Macdonald's (dentist) at 12. Put off to Thursday at 10.*

Set to at arrears of correspondence, diary etc. Interrupted by finding that I put Archer's and Harris's letters into the wrong envelopes on Saturday. Had to write and explain. Did a little work at the Fabian *Unemployed* tract sent me to report on. Corrected *World* proof. After dinner set to at my correspondence, and made a tremendous clearance, working up to midnight.

Dinner 1/1$\frac{1}{2}$

> Shaw's letter to Archer on the correspondence blunder is in *CL*. ▪ *The Unemployed*
> (BB16) would become *Fabian Tract* No. 47, not published until November 1893.

10 *Fabian Executive. 276 Strand. 17. Go down early and take the chair.*

In the morning worked at Fabian *Unemployed* draft. After it, went down to Fabian office and stayed there until the Executive began. Sat at home all the evening writing a long letter to Archer and some other letters.

Star $\frac{1}{2}$d   PMG 1d   Dinner 1/1$\frac{1}{2}$ "Life in Our Villages" Reprint from
Daily News 9d   Thompson's *Modern Cremation* 9d

> Shaw's fourth letter to Archer in six days was another airing of their deep philosophical
> differences on political, social, and dramatic matters, G.B.S. declaring on the 13th (*CL*),
> "Do not suppose that when I insist on my view of a question that I am reproaching you
> for not being a Shaw. The notion of two Shaws corresponding with one another is one
> which staggers even me."

11 °*Meeting of Shelley Society to discuss Centenary Celebration, University College. 20. Look through the Institute. Go to All Saints' Church, Ennismore Gardens, any time except between 13 and 15 to see Spence's Paradiso. Miss Sonntag's. 21. Handel Festival at Westminster Abbey. The Messiah. 19.*

Very wet day—missed to go out as I had intended. Tremendous gale blowing—saw an iron roof blown off in Charles St. Wrote some letters. Found I had rather overdone the letters and staying in the house for the past couple of days. Walked to and from Miss Sonntag's in the evening. Caught cold.

Dinner 1/2½   Papers 1½d

Thomas Ralph Spence (1850?–1903), painted historical and classical subjects in the manner of Alma-Tadema. He remains best known for his decorative paintings in Manchester Cathedral. ▪ The *Messiah* went unreviewed. Although not marked with an °, the concert was probably not attended by Shaw.

12 °*Wallas's 5th lecture. 310 Kings Rd. 20.15. London Symphony Concert. St. James's Hall. 20½. Macdonald's (dentist) at 10. °Il Matrimonio Segreto at the Shaftesbury Theatre. °W. Nicholl and Septimus Webbe 1st concert. Prince's Hall. 20½.*

Began *World* article. Cold a little troublesome.

Dinner 1/2½   Bus Oxford O to St Ja[me]s's Hall 1d   programme 6d

The Symphony concert was not reviewed by Shaw.

13 °*Sparlings' in the evening, to meet Stepniak, Max Hambourg, etc. 20. Special Fabian Members Meeting to discuss proposed amendment of Eight Hours Bill. Barnard's Inn. 20. Private View at Buck and Reid's. Water colours by W. W. May.*

Finished *World* article. Archer after dinner. Cold bad. Webb and Wallas walked with me as far as University College on the way back from the Fabian, Olivier leaving us at Russell Square. Very bad night with the cold, which suddenly became quite ferocious.

Petit Parisien 1d   *Petit Journal* 1d   *Star* ½d   *Justice* 1d   Dinner 1/2

Walter William May (1831–1895) was a marine painter in watercolors.

14 °*Crystal Palace Concert. 15. °Miss D'Esterre Keeling's pianoforte recital. 41 Holland Rd. W. 15¼. Meet Archer at the Wheatsheaf at 14 and go with him to the Alhambra at 15 to see Annie Abbott "the little Georgia Magnet." Go over in the morning to All Saints', Ennismore Gardens, to see Spence's Paradiso. Did not see it after all.*

Could not get into the church. After the Alhambra performance, went home (Archer leaving me at the corner of Montague Place) and wrote an account of it for the Webb-Massingham London letter to *The Bradford*

Observer. Jackson, Beatty's friend, met me at Shepherd's Bush station and came with me as far as Bishops Rd. Had a good night.

Bus Ennismore Gardens to Institute 1d   Dinner 1/2½   Train to Shep[herds] B[ush] & back (walked to Edgware Rd.) 1/–   *Star* ½d

> Annie May Abbott acquired the *magnet* from her act in American vaudeville, in which no one could lift her off the stage floor. The "young American lady, petite and rather pretty," Shaw wrote, ". . . was endowed with a strange psychical force, which . . . had no connection with muscular power" (C821). It was a nonsinging turn adopted by others, such as bantamweight champion Johnny Coulon and muscleman Victor McLaglen, who would dare anyone in the audience to lift them off the stage. ▪ Unsigned note (part of a two-column "From Our London Correspondent" potpourri, otherwise by Archer) on Annie Abbott, *Bradford Observer*, 16 November 1891 (C821).

15 SUNDAY   *Lecture on "Social Limits to Individual Liberty" at the Shed of Truth, Prince of Wales Rd., Battersea. National Secular Society. (A. Watkin. 54 Landseer St. Battersea S. W.)*

Wrote letters and found the whole day unexpectedly going that way. Corrected *World* proof. Prepared lecture in the train. [William] Saunders walked with me on the way back as far as Sloane Square station.

Train to Sloane Sq & back 1/–   Bus S. Sq to Albert Pal[ace] corner of Batt[ersea] Pk 1d

16   °*Fabian Central Group meeting. 32 Great Ormond St. 20. Macdonald's (teeth) at 15. 32 Weymouth St.* °*Monday Popular. Ysaÿe. 20. Production of Messager's* Fauvette *at the Royalty Theatre. 20.*

Spent the morning emptying out my old chest of drawers to transfer contents to the new wardrobe. Walter was here when I returned from dinner. Sat up until past 1 writing letters to JP and to *Daily Chronicle* about their article on Ibsen's *Brand*.

Dinner 1/1½   Programme at theatre 6d

> After his so-recent delight with *The Basoche*, Shaw failed to review *Fauvette*, which also had music by André Messager, suggesting his disappointment with the light opera, which would run only six performances. ▪ Shaw's letter to the *Daily Chronicle* defending Ibsen's play was published on 18 November (C822).

17   *Fabian Executive. 276 Strand. 17.*

Slept until 11. Read the papers, played and sang until 14.30. Busy in my mind; but could not settle down to work. In the evening sat here alone writing letters and reading Ibsen's *Brand*.

Dinner 1/1½   *Brand* 3/9   Newspapers 2d

18   °*Albert Hall. Stanford's Eden. 20. Royal Choral Society.* °*Costume reading of* Measure for Measure *by Shakspere Reading Society. Ladbroke Hall. 20½. Last performance of* Philemon et Baucis *at Covent Garden. 20½.*

Again up late. Find that I cannot shake off the cold—or at least its after effect. Still raining—has been for days past. Could not settle down to anything—wrote letters and muddled over old papers etc.

Dinner 1/½?   Opera 5/–

Reviewed by G.B.S. on 25 November 1891 (C824). Gounod's *Philemon et Baucis* was "a charming work, all pure play from beginning to end, but play of the most exquisite kind—a tranquilly happy recreation for really hard-worked and fine-strung men and women."

19 °*Wallas's 6th lecture. 310 King's Rd. 20.15. Macdonald's at 16.15. Go and see* Le Rêve *at Covent Garden. 20.*

Began *World* article. Front tooth filled—took nearly 3 hours.

Dinner 1/2¼   Opera 5/–   Libretto 1/6

Le Rêve (*The Dream*), a sentimental light opera by Alfred Bruneau based upon a poem of the same title by Émile Zola, had only two performances. According to G.B.S. (C824), the work "would have been ranked as a miracle fifty years ago. . . . The score is filled with the most delicate melody; and the harmonies and orchestral coloring are appropriately tender and imaginative." However, "at the end of the last scene but one, the band got up and went home, leaving the opera unfinished. . . . Sir Augustus Harris consequently owes me sevenpence-halfpenny. . . ."

20 *Fabian. Banqueting Hall. St. James's Restaurant. D. G. Ritchie on "Natural Rights." 20. Max Hambourg's pianoforte recital. Steinway Hall. 15. °Wind Instrument Concert. Royal Academy of Music. 20½. 1st of series.*

Was finishing *World* article when Wallas came in and stopped me. We dined together at Rathbone Place and went to Hambourg's recital. Then we went to Wallas's rooms and dined with Muirhead. Clarke came in for a moment. Wallas and Muirhead went off to the Fabian together, leaving me to follow when I had finished the *World* article, which I presently did. Spoke in the debate on Ritchie's paper, and walked with him and two young ladies to Manchester Square Mansions where I left them and came home.

Dinner 1/6¼   *Justice* 1d   *Star* ½d

As "Our London correspondent," Shaw wrote in the *Bradford Observer*, 30 November 1891 (C825), that Hambourg "has real genius as a player and has not merely been coached up for the prodigy market."

21 *Crystal Palace Concert. 15. °Mrs. Sandham At-Home. 7 Durham Place. Chelsea Hospital. 16½ to 18½. °Meeting of Baum's School Board Committee at 59 Porchester Rd. at 18.*

Had no time to do anything in the morning except write up next year's diary, which came home from the Stores before breakfast. FE was at the Palace with me; and I spent the evening with her.

Star ½d   *PMG* 1½d   Train Ch[arin]g + to Vict[oria] 1½d   Vict[oria]
to [Crystal] Pal[ace] (2) 4/–   Vict[oria] to Rav[enscourt] Pk 6d
Shep[herds] B[ush] to Ptld Rd 6d

> The Crystal Palace concert was reviewed by G.B.S. on 2 December 1891 (C826). Stavenhagen played the Beethoven fourth piano concerto muddily.

22 SUNDAY *Lecture for the Chelsea Branch S. D. F. on "Communism"*
(C. A. Smart. Bedford House. 20 Lots Rd. Chelsea S. W.). 20. Speak at the
East India Dock Gates at 11.30 (A. C. H. Grahame. 175 Abbott Rd. E.)

After dinner wrote a letter to Elkin Mathews about Joynes's poems, which
he has asked me to get published for him. Corrected *World* proof and wrote
a letter or two.

Train to Aldgate 3d   Tram to East India Dock 2d   Tram E. I. [Dock]
Road to Bloomsbury 4d

> Elkin Mathews (1851–1921) was a proprietor of the Bodley Head publishing firm, with partner John Lane. Shaw noted on the envelope containing Mathews's letter (BL), "Offers to publish on condition of omitting certain poems. Wrote decisively refusing [for J. L. Joynes] to suppress or alter anything and asking does he still care to publish." Matthews did not. *On Lonely Shores and Other Rhymes* would be privately printed in 1892.

23 *Speak at the St. Pancras Vestry Hall at 20 in support of Baum's School*
Board candidature. °Monday Popular Concert. St. James's Hall. 20.

Slept until 11.30. Resolved to have a holiday, and sat at home all day
reading Elinor Huddart's novel and doing no work until about 18, when I
wrote some letters before going to the meeting.

24 *Fabian Executive. 276 Strand. 17. Macdonald's at 10.30. Speak in sup-*
port of Mrs. Mallet's School Board candidature at Stamford St. Chapel. 20.
°Heckmann Quartet. Steinway Hall. 15. Postponed. Stavenhagen's recital. St.
James's Hall. 15.

No time to do anything but keep appointments and get tooth stopped.

Star ½d   Dinner 1/2½   Paid Pease for copy of *Essays* sent Macdonald
4/6

> Stavenhagen went at Chopin "like a thousand blacksmiths . . . in a fine Lisztian reading." But G.B.S. (C826) found that the virtuoso pianist played too many works "frivolously . . . because they are technically easy to him. . . ."

25 *Popper's Orchestral Concert. St. James's Hall. 20½. Kyrle Society Meet-*
ing. 24 Pearl Lane W. (Lord Brassey's) 16.45. Attend.

Began the stuff for Massingham—see tomorrow's diary. At least that is my
best recollection of how I was occupied in the morning. When I got to the
Kyrle Society meeting, I found the arrangements so bad and the affair so
dull that I came away at once without waiting to speak.

Dinner 1/2½   Papers 1½d?   Popper's Concert 1/–

The cellist played much of his own music, "which is elegant and fanciful in its lighter phases, and elegiac on its sentimental side" (C826).   ▪ Thomas Brassey, first Earl Brassey (1836–1918), was Liberal M.P. for Hastings from 1868–1886. Although known for his involvement in naval matters, he was also involved in wages and labor questions.

26   °*Wallas's 7th lecture. 310 Kings Rd. 20.15. °London Symphony Concert. 20½. St. James's Hall. The Prancing Girl and Miss Decima at the Prince of Wales Theatre. 19.40. School Board Election polling day. Station on Pancras St. Tottenham Court Rd.*

Wrote a long bit for Massingham's London letter to *The Bradford Observer* on the musical season. Archer was at the theatre in the pit, but left after the first piece. I called on him on my way back.

Dinner 1/2½?   Telegram to Massingham 6d   Papers 3d

The Prancing Girl, by Campbell Rae-Brown, with music by B. Brigata, was described as a travesty upon Henry Arthur Jones's *The Dancing Girl*. *Miss Decima* was a musical comedy by F. C. Burnand and Percy Reeve, with score by Edmond Audran, based on a French original, *Miss Hellyett*. The pair survived for twenty-one performances.   ▪ "The Music Season in London," by "Our London correspondent" (C825).

27   Wrote *World* article, which I did not finish until 22.20.

Dinner 1/2½d?

The *World* article over which G.B.S. took such pains was largely devoted to an analysis of the pianistic differences between Paderewski and Stavenhagen, but it also summed up other recent concerts. It appeared on 2 December 1891 (C826).

28   *Crystal Palace Concert. 15. Gerardy.*

Wallas called in the morning; and we went for a walk round Regents Park, afterwards dining together at the Wheatsheaf. FE at the Palace with me: we spent the evening together.

Dinner 1/2½   Train Ch[arin]g + to Vic[toria] 1½d   Papers 1d
Vic[toria] to [Crystal] Pal[ace] 2/–   Vic[toria] to Rav[enscourt] Pk 6d
Shep[herds] B[ush] to Ptld Rd 6d

"Gerardy, hugely petted by the public, needs a good deal of indulgence both for himself and his instrument after Popper" (C826).

29 SUNDAY   *Lecture on "Evolution of Socialism" at the Dulwich Working Men's Liberal and Radical Club, 108 Lordship Lane, Dulwich, at 19¾. (A. C. Kellett, Honorable Political Secretary). Call on Walkley.*

Lay asleep until near 12. Reading Statham's *Thoughts about Music* for review. Corrected *World* proof. Read Fabian tract etc. in the train. Had not time to see Walkley before the lecture; so called on my way to Victoria to say that I would look in before 23, which I did. Straughan walked with me from the Club to Peckham Rye station, from which I returned. Lucy came to stay for a week.

Train Victoria to Lordship Lane (ret[urn] from Peckham Rye) 1/6

> H. Heathcote Statham, *My Thoughts on Music and Musicians*, reviewed in the *Illustrated London News*, 20 February 1892 (C843). Statham, Shaw wrote, looked uncompromisingly backward. ▪ For J. W. Straughan, see 30 November 1891.

30   °*Carter's Scotch Festival. Albert Hall. 19.45. °Press View. Victorian exhibition (sent ticket to Pennell). Macdonald's (teeth). 32 Weymouth St. 10.30. Lecture instead of Bland at the Anerley Liberal and Debating Society on "Socialism" at the Lecture Hall, Jasmine Grove, Anerley. 20. (J. W. Straughan, 57 Kent House Rd., Sydenham S. E.). Brighton and South Coast train to Anerley.*

At the dentist all the morning. Writing letters in the afternoon. Working in the train at Fabian tract. Also spent some time hanging up pictures.

Star ½d   PMG 1d   Dinner 1/2½   Train Ptld Rd to Bishopsgate &
back 7d   London Br[idge] to Anerley [Park] & back 2/–

December

1   *Fabian Executive. 276 Strand. 17. °Woman's Franchise League Conference. 19½. °Miss [Louise] Douste's concert. Prince's Hall. 20.*

Began review of musical book for the *Illustrated London News*.

2   °*Woman's Franchise League Conference. 19½. °Annual Meeting South St. Pancras Liberal and Radical Association at Athenaeum Hall, Tottenham Court Rd. 20. °Friends of Russian Freedom Meeting in French Chamber, St. James's Restaurant. 16½. Max Heinrich's recital. Steinway Hall. 20½. °Trinity College Students' Orchestral Concert. Prince's Hall. 20. Miss Sonntag's in the afternoon.*

> Max Heinrich's "lyrical" singing was mentioned in passing in G.B.S.'s 16 December 1891 review (C829).

3   *Wallas's 8th lecture. 310 King's Rd. 20.15. °Woman's Franchise League Conference. 19½. °Nicholl and Webbe's 2nd concert. Prince's Hall. 20½.*

4   Writing Mozart article for *The World*. In the afternoon JP came. She came into this room and made a scene. I got out of the room by main force and went to the Museum, telegraphing on my way to Mother to get the house cleared before I came back. Wrote at the Museum until closing time

and then came back; found the coast clear; and finished the article, getting pretty late to bed. The scene upset me much.

Dinner 1/2½?   Telegram to M[other] 1/9½?

"Mozart's Finality," on the centenary of Mozart's death, 9 December 1891 (C827), incorporating reviews of the special Mozart concerts of the observance.

5 *Crystal Palace Concert. 15. Royal Choral Society. Mozart's Centenary programme.* Requiem *and* Jupiter Symphony. *20. Albert Hall.* °Mrs. Puty's *Fabian At-Home. 5 Stanley Gardens, England's Lane, Hampstead. 20 to 22½. Private View of Bronzes from Atelier of Susse Frères. Goupil Gallery.* °Resumption of La Basoche *at Royal English Opera.*

Up late, as well as I can remember. FE came with me to the Palace. Mother came with me to the Albert Hall: and we walked back across the park in the rain and got a bus to Oxford Circus at the Marble Arch. I gave the *Basoche* tickets to FE. Did not get to the Albert Hall until after the *Requiem.*

Dinner 11½d?   Train Ch[arin]g + to Victoria 1½d   Vict[oria] to C[rystal] P[alace] 2/-   Papers 1½d   Bus to Lanc[aster?] Gate 1d Bus M[other] & I Marble Arch to Oxford O 2d

The *Jupiter* was conducted by August Manns "in the true heroic spirit" (C827), but he and Mozart were both let down by the string section.

6 SUNDAY *Lecture at the Socialist Co-operative Federation. 7 Lamb's Conduit St. at 19½ (W. G. Killick, the Sec.) on "The Goal of Co-operation." Beerbohm Tree lectures at the Playgoers' Club. St. James's Restaurant Banqueting Hall. 20.*

Finishing *World* article and correcting proof. Reading Beatrice Potter's book to get up material for the lecture. Did not get to St. James's Hall until the discussion on Tree's [lecture] was nearly over. Archer walked back with me part of the way—as far as Montague Place—or rather I went with him that far.

Cab Holborn to St Ja[me]s's Rest[auran]t 2/-

Beatrice Potter (Webb), *The Co-Operative Movement of Great Britain* (London, 1891).

7 °Fabian Central Group meeting. 32 Great Ormond St. 20. °Liberal and Radical Union meeting. National Liberal Club. 20. Edmund Gosse lectures on Ibsen and his critics at the London Institution. 17. °Call on Miss Harkness at the Devonshire Hotel. 12 Bishopsgate St. Without at 16. Dropped; business settled by letter.

Wrote article on Mozart for *The Illustrated London News*, which I did not finish until 3 in the morning.

Train to Moorgate & back 6d   Papers 1½d   Dinner (at Arcadian) 11d?

A second Mozart centenary article, in the *Illustrated London News*, 11 December 1891 (C828), was more biographical than the *World* piece. Mozart's music, Shaw declared, was still "hardly known in England" except for a few works.

8   *Fabian Executive. 276 Strand. 17. Macdonald's at 16. Call at* Illustrated London News *office to correct proof.*

Up very late, not much done except look over the heap of music sent from the *World* office until it was time to go out. Massingham was at the *Illustrated London News* office. Macdonald cried off our appointment as he was very tired, and I was glad to get away to the Executive. Spent the evening mostly in writing a long letter of instruction to a Fabian who is to be examined before the Labour Commission. Did not get to bed until past 2.

Papers 1½d   Dinner 11½d?   Cab Strand to Weymouth St 2/–   Bus Ch[arin]g + to Fabian office 1d

9   *Royal College of Music performance of [Peter] Cornelius's* Barber of Bagdad *at the Savoy Theatre. 14½. Miss Sonntag's in the evening.*

Up late again, much the worse for sitting up. In the evening I got a bad headache and I slept feverishly.

Dinner 11½d   Papers 1½d   Train to Bayswater & back 5d

> *The Barber of Bagdad*, by Peter Cornelius, although first produced—to some furor—on the Continent in 1858, was receiving its first performances in England. It was "carefully prepared" by the principals and "enjoyed as a rare bit of fun by the chorus and band," G.B.S. wrote on 16 December 1891 (C829).

10   *Wallas's 9th lecture. 310 King's Rd. 20., 5. °Mrs. Charles Yates' concert, 6 Carlton House Terrace (Mrs. Mackay's). 15. °Davies's concert for the Poor of St. Pancras. Prince's Hall. 20. °Mlle. Yrac's concert. Prince's Hall. 15. (violinist). °Fred Dawson's concert. Steinway Hall. 15. Macdonald's. 16. (Put off) °Aveling lectures on "The Theatre and the Working Classes." Playgoers' Club. Mona Hotel. 20½.*

Found myself knocked up; I unable to do anything in the way of regular work, though I got through a good deal of letter writing. Very wet day. I started to go to the concert, but gave up the idea and called on Macdonald on the chance of his being disengaged and giving me the appointment which I had put off. Found him in the same condition as myself. Felt better in the evening, and went to Wallas's lecture. Wrote a letter to the meeting of the Playgoers' about the stage and the working classes.

Train to S[ou]th Kensington & back 6d

11   *Fabian. W. Clarke on "Party Politics of Socialism." 20. Banqueting Hall. Goupil Gallery. H. de Glazebrook's* C'est L'Empereur.

Wrote *World* article. After dinner walked up as far as Holborn Viaduct to ask whether the "Yost" typewriter would carry paper of a size I use. Did not speak at the Fabian, where we had a stormy meeting, Burns attacking Clarke with some vehemence. Several Fabians walked home with me. Walter was here in the middle of the day.

Dinner 1/2½?   *Star* ½d   *Justice* 1d   *PMG* 1d   Train Farringdon to Ptld Rd 2d

Hugh de Twenebrokes Glazebrook (1855–1937) was principally a portrait painter. He had four Goupil shows and exhibited twenty-eight portraits at the Royal Academy.

12 *Crystal Palace Concert. 15. °Miss D'Esterre Keeling's pianoforte recital. 41 Holland Rd. N. Macdonald's. 9½. °Annual dinner of the Playgoers' Club.*

At Macdonald's all the morning. FE was at the concert with me. Stupidly forgot my tickets for the Palace; but Grove passed us in. Spent the evening at Dalling Rd.

Dinner (at Pine Apple) 1/–?   *Star* ½d   *PMG* 1d   Train Vict[oria] to Pal[ace] 2/–   Vict[oria] to Rav[enscourt] Pk 6d   Shep[herds] Bush to Ptld Rd 6d

The Crystal Palace concert was reviewed on 16 December 1891 (C829). Frederic Cowen conducted his own "Scandinavian" symphony, which "is not quite so fresh as it was," while Clotilde Kleeberg played the Beethoven second piano concerto, "that charming early work."

13 SUNDAY *Lecture at the Hammersmith Club (S. Bullock, Hammersmith Club. Grove House. Hammersmith. Broadway). "County Council Politics." 20. °Playgoers' Club. St. James's Restaurant Banqueting Hall. Frank Linds reads* A Social Victim, *his play. 20.*

Busy day. Tried over a mass of music for review. I wrote notices of the presentable pieces for *The World.* Maggie Gardner was here in the evening.

Train to Hammersmith & back 1/–

Samuel Bullock, of 13 Wellesley Avenue, Hammersmith, W., an engineer, was a Fabian as well as a Morrisian Socialist. ■ No review of recent sheet music was published.

14 *°Charity Concert. Kensington Town Hall. 19¼. Bonetti's concert. Steinway Hall. 14½. Macdonald's. 16. Monday Pop Vocal Quartets—Brahms— first time. 20. Private View. Kenton and Co.'s Furniture. Barnard's Inn. 10 to 18. °Liberal and Radical Union. Adjourned meeting of Council. National Liberal Club. 20.*

Called on Webb in the morning and sat talking until it was time to go to dinner. No work done except getting teeth filled and going to concerts. After I came back from the Pop I wrote a letter to JP.

Dinner 1/2¼   *Star* ½d   Bus to St Ja[me]s's Hall 1d   Dropped in St Ja[me]s's Hall 6d

The Pop was reviewed on 23 December 1891 (C830), G.B.S. pleased by the "vivacious, positively romantic" side of Brahms, which he contrasted to the "heavy . . . German sentimentality" of the larger works.

15 *Fabian Executive. 276 Strand. 17. South St. Pancras Liberal and Radical Association. 195 Gray's Inn Rd. 20. Executive. °Louise Douste's Chamber*

Music Concert. Prince's Hall. 20$\frac{1}{2}$. °*Bach Choir Concert. Mozart's* Requiem *and end of Act I of* Parsifal.

Began article entitled "Home, Sweet Home." Met FE by appointment at the Wheatsheaf. Went to the Museum and sat there reading Böhm-Bawerk on Interest and Stainer on Harmony until it was time to go to the Executive. After it was over Bland came as far as Charing Cross with Olivier and myself, we two going on to the Orange Grove, where we had tea. Then I went on to the meeting in Gray's Inn Rd., at which I took the chair. Wrote some letters and postcards when I got home.

Dinner (FE & I) 2/$\frac{1}{2}$ "Tea" at Orange Grove 1/4   Bus St Martin's Lane to near Gray's Inn Rd 2d   Train Kings + [   ]

> Shaw considered the Brahms *Requiem* a "colossally stupid" bore (C830), and would not go, despite the attraction of Wagner. ▪ "Home, Sweet Home"—the title suggests the sheet music review Shaw had begun—was not published, perhaps never completed. ▪ Eugen von Böhm-Bawerk, *Capital and Interest. A critical history of economic theory*, trans. by William Smart (London, 1890). ▪ Sir John Stainer, *A Theory of Harmony, founded on the Tempered Scale* (3rd ed., London, 1876).

16   *2nd performance* Barber of Bagdad. *Savoy Theatre (Royal College of Music). 14$\frac{1}{2}$. Meet Salt at Wheatsheaf at 14 to discuss* Cenci *arrangements.* °*Dialectical Society. W. S. Crawshay on "The Criterion of Morality." 20.*

The paint downstairs—there are some men at work in the basement—made me a little ill: I had something like a faint attack of colic. I forgot what I was doing in the afternoon—writing letters, I suppose. FE was at the Savoy with me. After the performance we walked along the Embankment to Westminster and went to Dalling Rd. together. I spent the evening there. Had a terrific run for the train back, barely catching it.

Dinner 1/2$\frac{1}{2}$?   Star $\frac{1}{2}$d   Train West[minster] to Rav[enscourt] Pk 6d Shep[herds] B[ush] to Ptld Rd 6d

> G.B.S. "paid the Royal College students the very considerable compliment (from a critic)" of a return visit to their production, which he found vastly improved by "the elimination of stage fright" (C830).

17   *Wallas's 10th and last lecture. 310 Kings Rd. 20.15. Royal Academy of Music. Students' Concert. St. James's Hall. 15. Macdonald's at 11.*

Began *World* article. Salts were at the Wheatsheaf.

Star $\frac{1}{2}$d   Dinner 1/2$\frac{1}{4}$ Train to Gloster Rd & back 6d

> "Everything I heard," G.B.S. wrote (it was a very long program and he "held out until after the second concerto") was "well-prepared and creditably executed" (C830).

18   *Fabian. Hubert Bland on "Communism." 20. St. James's Restaurant Banqueting Hall.* °*2nd Wind Instrument Concert. Royal Academy of Music. 20$\frac{1}{2}$.* °*Art Workers' Guild meeting. Barnard's Inn. 20. Papers by Expeditioners. Carlo Ducci's concert. Prince's Hall. 15.*

Finished *World* article. Spoke at the Fabian meeting. Walked a bit with Wallas afterwards. Wrote to JP before going to bed.

Dinner 1/2½   *Star* ½d   Bus to Fabian from Oxford O 1d

Carlo Ducci was a pianist and piano accompanist whom Shaw had heard perform before and whom he had reviewed; however, there was no notice this time.

19   *Fabian Society Special Meeting to consider the Runciman affair. Barnard's Inn. 20. Move the resolution.*

Wrote letters and prepared the Fabian speech. Runciman having behaved handsomely, this is no longer a very delicate business.

Dinner 1/2½   *Star* ½d   Paid Jaeger £3/10/6 bill   Press Cuttings ann[ua]l subs[criptio]n 21/–   cost of order 2d   Train to Farringdon St 2d

According to *Fabian News*, January 1892, a private meeting was held "to consider conduct of J. F. Runciman in circulating an unfounded accusation against Sidney Webb. On motion of G. B. Shaw, on behalf of the Executive, it was unanimously resolved 'That this meeting approves of the action of Sidney Webb in the chair on Nov. 20, and is unable to find any justification for the resolution passed by the members of the Southern Group.' " Runciman thereupon apologized to Webb and withdrew his charges.

20 SUNDAY   *Lecture at the Fawcett Liberal Club, Blechynden St. North Kensington (Henry Lewis) on "Liberalism as a Working Class Policy." 20½. Opposite Latimer Rd. station. Go down to Massingham's for the day.*

Hard frost. Massingham had gone out by the time I got to his house. Went to Wandsworth Common in search of him; but did not find him and so had to walk by myself. Left with the Pennells by the 6.29 train. Parted from them at Victoria.

Bus Knightsbridge to Chelsea Br[idge] 1d   Train to Cedars Road 1d
Train Wandsworth Com[mon] to Vic[toria] 4d   Ptld Rd to Latimer Rd & back 6d

21   *°Fabian Central Group meeting. 32 Great Ormond St. 20. Macdonald at 10.30.*

Hard frost. Fog set in. FE telegraphed to me to meet her at Museum. I went there after dinner; but she did not come. I did not fulfill my intention of writing an article for young [Smedley] Yates—I only read some magazine articles. Went to FE after tea.

Dinner 1/2½?   Writing paper 3d

G. Smedley Yates, one of Edmund Yates's four sons, was editor of *The Players*.

22   *Fabian Executive. 276 Strand. 17. Macdonald's at 14. Go down to Sparlings' in the evening and stay there the night. Go to Besson's in the Euston Rd. to hear the new contrabasso clarinet. 15 to 18. °Production of* The Mountebanks *at Lyric Theatre. Postponed to 29th.*

The most abominable, skinning fog. Worked hard at *The Democratic Budget*, a Fabian tract which I had to revise. Wrote a new opening for it.

Dinner 1/2½   *Star* ½d   Train Gower St to Farringdon 1½d   Temple to Rav[ens] C[our]t Pk 6d

> Messrs. Besson, the instrumentmakers, who were demonstrating a "pedal clarinet" (C829). ■ Edited and rewritten by Shaw (BB12), the tract was *Fabian Tract* No. 39, *A Democratic Budget*, by J. F. Oakeshott (1892).

23   Stayed at Sparlings' until Walker called on his way into town to see whether I had left. We went as far as Charing Cross together. I took an early dinner on my way home. Mother went down to Broadstairs and I had to go with her to Holborn Viaduct to see her off. Met Cohen on my way back and walked with him to the Museum corner. Then went back to Holborn to buy a pair of skates. When I got home found they were too narrow, so went back and changed them. Sat at home writing letters etc., the fog being worse than ever.

Train Hammersmith to Ch[arin]g + 6d   Dinner 1/1   Train M[other] & I to Farringdon 7d   Skates 15/- (Acme)   Bus along Tott[enham] Ct Rd 1d   Present to Sparling's servant 5/-

24   *Macdonald's. 11.30.*

Began article for *Players* commissioned by Smedley Yates. Macdonald did not turn up until 12.30; and the fitting of the crown on to my tooth was not completed until past 14. Went right on to the Wheatsheaf, where I found Archer. Went home and worked at article. After tea I went out to see whether there was any skating to be had. I went to the Serpentine, making my way across from the Marble Arch in utter darkness, the fog being still bad, though not so bad as yesterday. The ice was not opened for skaters. I then went to St. James's Park, forgetting that every part of it except the bridge was closed at this hour. So I came home and resumed the article.

Present to Macdonald's servant 2/6   Dinner 1/4½   Xmas box to waitress 2/6   Train S[ou]th Kensington to St Ja[me]s's 2d

> "The Superiority of Musical to Dramatic Critics," *The Players*, 6 January 1892 (C831).

25   *Call for Webb before 11 and walk until 14. Dine with him.*

When I went out in the morning a light rain had frozen on the ground and it was hardly possible to walk without slipping. Webb and I walked up to Hampstead and back. Nobody had dinner with us except his mother and sister. Worked a bit at the article in the evening.

26   Went over the article ["The Superiority of Musical to Dramatic Critics"], cancelled the middle section and rewrote it. Cleared off several letters etc. Went to FE's in the evening.

Train to Shep[herds] Bush & back 6d

27 SUNDAY   *Dine with Barton. 14.*

Was out from 1 to 5 at Barton's, whose wife I met for the first time. All the rest of the day, until past midnight, I was working at the review of Walkley's book.

> *Playhouse Impressions*, by A. B. Walkley, review signed "C. di B." in *The Star*, 9 January 1892 (C833). "To say that 'Spectator' [i.e., Walkley] passes for a brilliant critic in England," Shaw wrote, "is to pay him a doubtful compliment; for it cannot be denied that the national genius does not lie in that direction; and in the kingdom of the blind, the one-eyed is king. Even I cut quite a figure here as a critic."

28   Finished the Walkley review; wrote several letters, including a long one to JP, and went to FE in the evening. In the afternoon I went to the Stores to look for a present to give to Miss Middleditch and met Mrs. Armbruster there, but could not get what I wanted. Went home by Regent St., inspecting the shop windows on the same errand, still unsuccessfully.

Star ½d   Dinner [   ]

> Miss Middleditch was Florence Farr's household factotum. See 11 January 1892.

29   °*Fabian Executive. 276 Strand. 17?. None. Macdonald's at 16. Call on Lady Colin Campbell between 17½ and 19. °Production of* The Mountebanks *at Lyric Theatre. Again postponed to Thursday.*

30   *Lecture on "The Working Day" at the Golborne Liberal Club, 363 Portobello Rd. North Kensington (James Pottle, Sec.). 20½. Notting Hill station. Tea with Gordon at 18 at 44 Fermoy Rd. Westbourne Park, meet Lowerison and Samuel. °Dress rehearsal of* The Mountebanks, *Lyric Theatre. 11½. Postponed to 2nd prox.*

In looking up my "Eight Hours" papers for the lecture I got arrang[ing] a lot of letters. Then I spent some time singing to get my voice into order. Then came a letter from Lady Colin Campbell enclosing a draft of a letter she was about to write to [Edmund] Yates. I had to redraft part of this; and this occupied me until it was time to hurry off to the lecture. As it was very wet I did not go out in the middle of the day, but dined at home on a couple of fried eggs. Corrected proof of article for *Players*.

Train to Westbourne Park & back 6d

31   °*First night of* The Mountebanks. *Lyric Theatre. Again postponed to 4th January. Macdonald's at 10.*

Got back from Macdonald's a little after 11 and sang for about an hour. Then set to at letters, diary etc.

Notes

[INCOME, 1891; EACH MONTH ON A SEPARATE PAGE]

January

14	*The World*	25/ 0/ 0

February

4	*Manchester Sunday Chronicle*	4/ 4/ 0
12	*The World*	20/ 0/ 0

March

11	*Pall Mall Gazette*	2/11/ 6
13	*The World*	20/ 0/ 0

April

7	Walter Scott, balance of Royalties on *Cashel Byron's Profession* from date of publication up to 31st March.	3/ 9/ 6
16	*The World*	20/ 0/ 0
	The first item above is included in the Income Tax return of 1890–91.	

May

13	*The World*	25/ 0/ 0

June

12	*The World* (including some arrears for picture notices).	21/12/ 6
18	*The Art Journal*	5/10/ 0

July

13	*The World*	20/ 0/ 0

August

10	*The Star*	2/ 2/ 0
14	*The World*	25/ 0/ 0

September

13	*The World*	20/ 0/ 0
30	Swan Sonnenschein & Co, royalties on *An Unsocial Socialist* for year ending 30th June	7/10

October

15th	*The World*	25/ 0/ 0

November

4	*The Star*	1/ 16/ 0
4	*The World*	20/ 0/ 0
	" future notice	3/ 6

December

15	*The World*	20/ 0/ 0

Diary 1892

Notes

INTRODUCTIONS

Auguste Couvreur and "Tasma," his wife, at 88 St. James's St. by R. W.
Reynolds.
F. H. Wilson [Editor, *Morning Leader*]. The Savoy Theatre, by Edward Rose.
H. Reece, 123 Dalling Rd. Mrs. Emery.

HEALTH

Caught a cold on the 10th March. It was not very bad, but it was a well
defined one and went through the easiest stages.

On the 13th July I caught a headache in the afternoon of the concert; and
in the evening, at the opera, I suffered so much from nausea that I had to
leave before the end. I was violently sick when I got home; and did not
quite recover for the few days after, though I got much better next day. My
knee joint (the right) also began to give [way] in its old fashion. There is
evidently some loose cartilage in it. It bothered me a good deal all through
the autumn months. At last the left knee showed the same symptoms in the
lighter degree.

On the 15th September I watched the sunset on Barnes Common, staring at the blinding light for nearly quarter of an hour. In the evening I found myself with a bad headache; and next day the headache continued all day.

On the 8th November I got another bad headache after going without any day off work for some time. Also the trouble in my knees was felt again. It is evident that I have been overtaxing myself by working continually for the last few years without having a day of rest every week, and taking no real holiday except for a fortnight at a time when I have gone abroad. All the autumn I vowed repeatedly to make a "Sunday" for myself—that is, a day set aside every week for rest; but I find I cannot carry it out. Circumstances are too strong for me. Also I want bodily exercise badly. I am, however, more than ever convinced of the value to me of my vegetarianism and my abstinence from tea, coffee and alcoholic stimulants. Although I was much more seriously overstrained this summer than ever before by the very active part which I took in the general election, which came in the busiest weeks of the musical season, and though I was disappointed in being prevented by the cholera from going to Italy, yet I found that I recuperated remarkably even without a change, by taking walks and dropping my musical work altogether.

> Auguste Couvreur, Belgian politician and journalist; editor and contributor, *Indépendance Belge*; Liberal representative for Brussels; in London a member of the Cobden Club. Jessie Catherine Couvreur, London-born and Tasmania-educated (hence "Tasma"), wrote short fiction occasionally for *The World* and published several novels. ■ R. W. Reynolds, of 88 St. James's Street, was a Fabian. ■ H. Reece, 10 Ladbroke Square, W., was associated with Kirkman's, the piano manufacturing and sales firm at 3 Soho Square, W.

MEMORANDA OF REFERENCE, &C.

Thomson & Sons. Woodhouse Mills, Huddersfield.
Mrs. Thornton Smith. 28 Townshend Road, St John's Wood N.W.

January

1 Messiah *at the Albert Hall.* 20.

> Shaw apparently went to the Albert Hall on New Year's Day but did not review the occasion. From Fitzroy Square this day he also wrote to publisher Fisher Unwin (*CL*).

2 *Dress rehearsal of* The Mountebanks, *Lyric Theatre, 11.30.*

Spent most of the day at the theatre and stayed in to write the *World* article in the evening—or at least to get it well under way.

Dinner 1/-?   *Players* 3d

> *The Mountebanks*, with libretto by W. S. Gilbert and music by Alfred Cellier, was reviewed on 6 January 1892 (C832). "It made me laugh heartily several times," G.B.S. wrote. The second tenor, "Cecil Burt," was Shaw's brother-in-law, Charles Butterfield.

3 SUNDAY *Lecture for North Kensington S. D. F. at the Clarendon Coffee Tavern, 20 (G. W. Spry. 31 Rackham Rd., North Kensington W.), "County Council Politics."*

Finished *World* article with much labour and waste of time, not being in the vein, or much interested in the subject.

Train to Latimer Rd & back 6d

4 *Lecture at the Hackney Radical Club. 20.40. "County Council Politics."* °*Fabian Central Group meeting. 32 Great Ormond St. 20. Get review of Walkley's book ready—must appear in* The Star *on the 8th.* °*First night of* The Mountebanks *at the Lyric Theatre. 20.*

Spirits reviving. Worked all day at article for *The Novel Review* on my own works of fiction. Lucy used my ticket for the Lyric as I could not get out of going to Hackney.

Dinner 11d   *Star* ½d   Train to Bishopsgate & back 7d   Broad St to Hackney & back 5d

> "Mr Bernard Shaw's Works of Fiction. Reviewed by Himself," *Novel Review*, February 1892 (C839). Shaw would write (in shorthand) next to his monthly summary of earnings at the end of the 1892 volume, "Cheque for £3. 13. 6 from *Novel Review* returned to Miss [Margaret] Harkness on the 13th. I did not care to take it from her, as she is presumably not making anything out of the review, which she has only just bought. . . ." For Miss Harkness see also 8 June 1888.

5 *Fabian Executive. 276 Strand. 17. South St. Pancras Liberal and Radical Association Executive meeting, 195 Gray's Inn Rd. 20.*

Working at article; but not getting along quite so brilliantly as I had hoped.

Dinner 1/3   Cocoa &c at Orange Grove with [Sydney] Olivier 1/3   Bus St Martin's Lane to Foundling Hospital 2d

6 °*South St. Pancras Liberal and Radical Association Soiree, Athenaeum, Tottenham Court Rd., 18 to 24.* °*Meet Salt at Wheatsheaf at 14. (Was late).* °*Dialectical Society. South Place Chapel. H. A. Jones on "Abolition of Post Office Monopoly." 20.*

Finished and sent off the article to Margaret Harkness. Wrote several letters. Did not go out in the evening. Played a lot of Schumann, having been seized with the fancy so strongly that I went out and bought a volume of his works.

Dinner 11d   Schumann's p[iano]f[or]te w[or]ks. Vol. III (Peters) 3/3

7 *Graham Wallas's 1st lecture of 11 on Chartism at South Place Chapel. "Origin of the Six Points." 20. Call on Miss Sonntag. 17. Call at Jaeger's to try on clothes.*

Found myself incapable of work and craving for exercise. Took a walk across Hyde Park and round Kensington Gardens. Went home for a while for dinner but only wrote one short letter and got rid of the pen, finding it still unbearable. Walked to Bayswater and found Miss Sonntag engaged with a pupil. Killed time for half an hour by strolling about and walking a bit with Tomson whom I happened to meet. Then went into Hedwig's and was introduced to the man who was finishing his lesson and his brother, who came after he had left to make arrangements for pianoforte lessons. Had some of Hedwig's dinner, and then went off to South Place. Went home with Wallas and sat with him until past midnight drawing up plan of the Fabian conference.

Dinner (at Pine Apple) 1/2?   Train Bayswater to Moorgate 3d?

Arthur Graham Tomson, a Fabian, of 20 St. John's Wood, N.W.

8 *Fabian Society. Essex Hall, Essex St., Strand. Stewart Headlam on "Christian Socialism." 20.*

Tried to begin *World* article, but it was no use. Set to at the Fabian conference agenda. After dinner brought it down to the Fabian office and sat with De Mattos finishing it for the press whilst the meeting of the "Friends of Russia" was proceeding in the other room. De Mattos and I went over to the Inns of Court Restaurant and had a meal, Pease joining us. Spoke in the discussion. Webb and Wallas walked home with me.

Dinner 1/2?   Meal at Inns of C[our]t Rest[aurant] 2/6

The "Friends of Russia" was the Friends of Russian Freedom, which issued anti-Czarist pamphlets from 1890.

9 *Sidney Webb lectures on "Some Problems of Trade Unionism" at the Working Men's College Economic Club. Great Ormond St. 19.45. St. James's Hall. 15. Second performance this season of Berlioz's* Faust *by the Manchester Band. Meeting of Fabian Group Secretaries to consider County Council election. 276 Strand. 17. Meet FE at Wheatsheaf. 13.30.*

Began *World* article. Webb and Wallas had a meal with me at the Inns of Court between the Fabian meeting and Webb's lecture. They walked home with me.

Dinner 1/–?   Concert 2/6   *Star* $\frac{1}{2}$d   Meal at Inns of C[our]t Rest[aurant] (Webb paid)

Reviewed by G.B.S. on 13 January 1892 (C834), with praise for the Hallé orchestra as the "only first-class" ensemble outside of London.

10 SUNDAY *Lecture at Brighton for the S. D. F. there. (B. Riley, 4 Agnes, Elm Grove, Brighton). "Program of Social Democracy," Athenaeum Hall, North St. 19$\frac{1}{2}$. Pullman trains 10.45 there and 20.40 back. Impossible to catch the latter.*

Went to Brighton by the 10.45 train. Massingham, who was to have joined me at Caterham Junction, missed the train. I finished the *World* article in the train going and coming. On arriving I went to Riley's and dined with him. After dinner we called on Grace Black. [Edwin] Human was there, and a couple of Grace's brothers. Then I went to Joynes's, parting at the door from Riley, and stayed there until it was time to go to the lecture. Returned to town by the 21.30 train and sat up very late correcting article and writing letters.

Train to Brighton & back 12/–

11 *Article for* Novel Review *to be ready on the 15th. Article for* Star *to be ready for publication on 18th. Lunch with Fisher Unwin and Graham Wallas at the National Liberal Club to discuss the question of History of the Century. 13.30 Conference with Sir Charles Russell on Free Speech difficulty at Chelsea, 10 New Court. 16. Meeting of Fabian lecturers to discuss County Council campaign. 276 Strand. 20.*

Up late. Nothing particular done until it was time to go to the club. Went on with Wallas to 276 Strand, and thence with Webb to Russell's, where Wallas and Massingham were waiting for us. After the conference, Massingham left us, and we went to Rodesano's to eat. I left the Fabian meeting at about 20½ and went to FE.

Chocolate & Maccaroni at Rodesano's 2/3   Train Temple to Ravenscourt Pk 7d?   Shep[herds] Bush to P[or]tl[an]d Rd 6d   FE to purchase a present for Miss Middleditch 10/–

> Shaw would not publish a *Star* article until August. ▪ On 1 January (*CL*) Shaw had proposed to Fisher Unwin that Graham Wallas be commissioned to write a history of the 1800s, to be released as the century ended.

12 *Fabian Executive. 17. Sir Charles Russell's. 86 Harley St. 20½.*

Spent most of the morning reading Shorter's edition of Meredith's *Tragic Comedians* for review, and in writing letters, diary etc. When I had just finished tea and was about to settle down to write the review of Meredith's book I got a telegram from Wallas summoning me to Russell's. I met him at Russell's door. The others did not come; so it was a conference of three. Russell had only to announce that the Home Office would see us tomorrow. I forget whether I began the review on my return or merely wrote letters. On consideration I am almost sure that I did begin it.

Dinner 1/2?   Papers 1½d

> "The Truth About 'The Tragic Comedians' " (unsigned review of the third, "revised and corrected," edition of George Meredith's novel), *Daily Chronicle*, 18 January 1892 (C835).

13 *Lecture at the Club Autonomie on "Difficulties of Anarchism." (W. Mac-Queen, 6 Windmill St. W). °Meet Salt at the Wheatsheaf at 14 and go on with him to see G. W. Foote about the proposed Shelley celebration. Post-*

poned. Go to the Home Office with Webb, Wallas and Massingham at 16¼ to confer with Lushington on the Free Speech affair.

Working at review.

Dinner 1/2?   Papers 1½d

> An Anarchist club at 6 Windmill Street, Tottenham Court Road, W., the Club Autonomie had a name which did not reflect its clientele. ▪ Sir Godfrey Lushington was permanent under-secretary at the Home Office.

14 °*London Symphony Concert. St. James's Hall. 20¼. (Postponed until 24th because of death of Duke of Clarence). South Place. Wallas's second Chartism lecture. "Radicals and Reform Bill." 20.*

Working at review. After dinner went down to St. James's Hall to see whether concert was postponed or not. Found that it was and telegraphed to Mother who had gone over to Brompton Square to that effect. After the lecture Wallas and I went together to Webb's where we found Beatrice Potter and the family. Webb did not come in until after 23.

Dinner 1/1?   Telegram to M[other] 6d   Train to Moorgate 2½d
Moorgate to Gower St 2½d

> The death from pneumonia of Prince "Eddy," the Duke of Clarence (1864–1892), heir to the throne after his father, the future Edward VII, was much mourned publicly if not privately. Known as "Collars-and-Cuffs" because of his languid love of pleasure, much gossip about his alleged dissipation and emotional instability swirled about him. His brother, to become George V, would marry the bereaved fiancée, Mary of Teck.

15 Novel Review. *See 11th. Meeting of Group Secretaries at the Fabian office, 276 Strand, to discuss the London County Council election. 20. Executive at 19 to discuss Free Speech business.*

Working at review. At the Executive meeting it was decided that Wallas should go to Bristol in my place, and that I should stay in town to attend the meeting on Sunday. On reflection I saw that this would involve my offering to speak at the World's End and get arrested. After dinner I spent some time in the British Museum library verifying my dates etc. in the review. Had a chat with Runciman there. Saw FE for a moment.

> Shaw entered no expenses although it is likely that he had some. ▪ The World's End (a pub gave its name to the location) was just off New King's Road, Chelsea. The police were threatening to arrest speakers there on the charge of obstruction of traffic, a device used before to break up demonstrations, in the Dod Street affair. Hunter Watts would actually be arrested at the World's End on the 17th.

16 Finished and sent off review to Massingham who is down with influenza. Wrote letters. Went to FE in the evening. Walked there.

Dinner 1/2?   Train Shep[herds] Bush to Ptld Rd 6d

17 SUNDAY °*Lecture at Bristol for the Sunday Society (F. G. Vellaway and T. Hulin, 125 Gloucester Rd., Bishopston, Bristol). Postponed. (Changed*

lectures with Wallas on account of Free Speech affair) Free Speech Commit-
tee, S. D. F. Hall in the Strand. 11½. Go with Lowerison as Fabian delegates
and move resolutions. Lecture at Kelmscott House for Wallas. Hammer-
smith Socialist Society. 20.

Drew up resolutions at breakfast. Moved them as amendments to Hunter
Watts's motion that the matter be not reopened. Was defeated by two votes
(29 to 27) and was relieved of the prospect of getting arrested. After dinner
wrote a report of my speech and brought it down to the *Chronicle* office.
[Robert R.] Steele came back with me from Sparlings' (where I went after
the lecture) as far as Shepherd's Bush.

Train Temple to Rav[enscourt] Park 7d   Ham[mersmi]th to Ptld Rd 6d

"The Socialists at Chelsea" (unsigned), *Daily Chronicle*, 18 January 1892 (C835). Rather
than hold mass meetings which would draw police retaliation, the leadership voted, on
Shaw's motion, that public meetings just within police limits in numbers be held, every
Sunday afternoon, with speakers "whose position will command public attention, and
upon whose behalf the committee may avail itself of the eminent legal assistance which
has been placed at its disposal." Without naming names, this suggested Sir Charles
Russell.

18   °*Fabian Central Group meeting. 32 Great Ormond St. 20.*

Wallas called on his way from Paddington; and I described to him the
proceedings of yesterday. We dined at the Wheatsheaf together. And we
hurried off from there to the Museum. I had intended to go to the picture
galleries to rest myself; but it was too late in the evening when I left the
Wheatsheaf. I cannot remember what I did then except that I spent some
time looking at the evening papers for accounts of yesterday. Now I went
out to FE in the evening—as often: I remember now. Louis Cohen called on
me at about 17 and stayed talking until past 20 when I went to Shepherd's
Bush, he coming as far as Baker St. on his way to Hampstead. His object
was to interview me for the paper called *The Pelican.*

Dinner 1/–?   Papers 2d or 3d   Train to Shep[herds] Bush & back 9d

"Pelican's Press-Men. V. George Bernard Shaw," *The Pelican*, 20 February 1892, was an
interview done in affectedly clipped journalese. "He wrote about pictures [in *The World*].
Later, he put art criticism into *Truth*. Revolutionary instincts too strong. He put truth into
art criticisms. Then he and *Truth* in the concrete parted. But he still clings to abstract
truth. . . . Is unmarried. Thinks he will continue so. Some changes are too revolutionary.
Even for him."

19   *Fabian Executive. 17.* °*Fabian Special Meeting to pass County Council*
tracts. 20. Dress rehearsal of Hamlet *at the Haymarket Theatre. 18¼. Hen-*
schel's music. Go to Old Masters at the Academy and to the Victorian
Exhibition at the New Gallery.

Spent the day at the picture galleries to get a relief from the grind of my
work. Paget was at the *Hamlet* rehearsal. It lasted from 19 to 2.30.

Dinner (at Orange Grove) 1/–?   Supper at same place in the evening 10d

G.B.S. wrote a cautiously complimentary interview-column about Henschel's incidental music for *Hamlet* on 27 January 1892 (C837). ▪ Henry Marriott Paget (1856–1936) of Bedford Park, Florence Farr's brother-in-law, was an artist and member of the Art Workers' Guild.

20 °*Sullivan's* Golden Legend. *Albert Hall. 20. Put off till 27 through the Duke of Clarence's death. °Dialectical Society. J. Blanchard on "Limitation of Hours of Labour." South Place. 20.*

Began *World* article and worked at it all day up to the time of my starting for Hammersmith, with the result that I was stale and hipped and conscious of being much in want of a walk. Went to FE and spent the evening there.

Dinner 1/2? Star ½d Train to Shep[herds] Bush & back 9d

21 *Karl Armbruster lectures on the Bayreuth Festival at the London Institution. 18. Lecture on "The Future of Working Classes" at Harpenden House, Phoenix St. N.W. 20½. °Wallas's 3rd Chartism lecture. South Place. 20. "Period of Apathy."*

Owing to dense fog overhead, leaving it clear underneath, the day was so like night, I did not realize what hour it was until past 11 when I got up. Continued *World* article, very nearly finishing it. Met Oakeshott at Armbruster lecture.

Train to Moorgate 2½d Eggs, cocoa &c at Arcadian 1/2 Train Moorgate to Kings + 1½d

Karl Armbruster's lecture "once or twice" was "more ornate than candid" about Bayreuth but was effective on the music (C840).

22 °*Wind Instrument Concert. Royal Academy of Music. 20½. Fabian Society. Essex Hall. De Mattos on "Present Position of the Labour Movement in the Provinces." 20.*

Finished and overhauled *World* article before dinner. Afterwards attacked correspondence which was appallingly in arrears, like this diary. Got through a good deal before going to the Fabian. Wet muddy day. Frost quite gone.

Star ½d Dinner 1/2

23 °*Hampstead Conservatoire. Bauer-Walenn concert. 20.15.*

Up late. Wrote several letters. Did not go out until evening, when I called on Archer who was not in. Walked to Oxford Circus and had some cocoa, etc. at the Pine Apple. Then started to walk to FE's; but as my heel was sore from a blister raised by a new boot I took bus from Bayswater to Uxbridge Rd. station.

Cocoa &c at Pine Apple 1/3 Star ½d Bus Queens Rd to Uxbridge Rd Station 2d Train from Shep[herds] Bush 6d

Harold Bauer, pianist, and Herbert Walenn, cellist and professor at the Royal Academy of Music. G.B.S. would refer to them at other times and places.

24 SUNDAY   *Lecture for Southwark and Lambeth Branch S. D. F. at Cashman's Coffee House, Borough Rd. S. E. (John Kent, 30 Holbeck Row, Kennington Chambers). 20. "County Council Politics." Call on Emil Behnke at 18 Earl's Court Square at 15 or after.*

Corrected *World* proof and wrote some notes for *The Star* about Seiffert. Did nothing in the afternoon except visit the Behnkes' and read Schopenhauer in the train. Archer called for a few minutes at about 14.

Train to High St Kensington & back 9d   To Boro' Road & back 1/3

Shaw was attempting to persuade Emil Behnke to take on a class in public speaking for about twenty Fabian political lecturers. The project would be delayed by Behnke's death later in the year. ▪ Two unsigned paragraphs about Seiffert appeared in the "Mainly about People" section of *The Star*, 25 January 1892 (NIL).

25   *Carter's concert at Albert Hall. H. Seiffert etc. 19.45. Burns' anniversary. °Monday Pop. Brahms' Vocal Quartets. 20. °Prince's Hall, 19½. Miss Larkcom's Royal Free Hospital Concert.*

By a heroic effort I finished the arrears of this diary, which went as far back as the 12th. Wrote several letters. Did not go out until about 17 and took dinner and tea together. FE was at the concert; and we left at the end of the first part. On my way to the train from her house I met [Alfred] Beasley, who came back with me as far as Notting Hill station.

Star ½d   Dinner 1/2   *Ill[ustrated] London News* 1/–   Libretto of *Mountebanks* for Mrs H 1/–   Bus Picc[adilly] O to Ptld Rd 1d   Hair cut & shampooed 1/–   Bus Albert Hall to Hammersmith (FE & I) 2d Train Shep[herds] B[ush] to Ptld Rd 6d

The Scottish part-songs offered by William Carter's choir, G.B.S. wrote on 3 February 1892 (C840), "were so primly British in their gentility as to suggest that the native heath of the singers must be Clapham Common at the very wildest." ▪ The Robert Burns centenary program at the Albert Hall drew only a "scanty and scattered" audience, probably, G.B.S. wrote (C840), because of "crofter emigration." ▪ "Mrs H" is probably Mrs. Hadkinson.

26   *Fabian Executive. 17. London Symphony Concert. Postponed from 14th. St. James's Hall. 20½. °Society of Arts. William Morris on "Woodcuts in Gothic Books." 20. John St. °Louise Douste's concert. Prince's Hall. 20½.*

Began *World* article, and wrote some postcards. Did not go out until past 17. A long delay was caused at the last moment by the discovery that I had lost my pocket case full of concert tickets. I had not time to dine before the Executive. Bland came down to the Orange Grove with me, and I had a good meal there; but my nerves were very highly strung all the rest of the evening. Had to write a letter or two when I got in; but managed to get to bed in decent time.

Dinner (at Orange Grove) 1/6

> The program included Henschel's *Hamlet* music, some of which had "dramatic force" to
> G.B.S. although "the pastorale, the march, and the dirge would probably have been better
> done by Sir Arthur Sullivan" (C840).

27 °The Golden Legend *at the Albert Hall. 20. Deferred from 20th.*

Finished the *World* article all but a few words, but did not revise it. Dined
at home. As well as I remember I stayed at home in the evening and began
the paper for the Fabian Conference on the 6th February.

Dinner 1/–   Star $\frac{1}{2}$d??

28 *South Place. Wallas's 4th Chartism lecture. "Publication of the Char-
ter." 20. Special Fabian Executive. 276 Strand. 22. To discuss politics. °Press
View. Wimperis's Rustic and Riverside Pictures at Dowdeswell's. Today and
tomorrow.*

Working at Fabian paper: "On the History and Present Attitude of the
Fabian Society." Wallas and I came together from South Place to the Executive. Webb and Wallas walked home with me.

Dinner 1/–?   Star $\frac{1}{2}$d   Train to Moorgate 2$\frac{1}{2}$d

> Shaw's address to the delegates from the suburbs and provinces, "The Fabian Society:
> What it has done; and How it has done it," would be a "virtuoso performance," published
> afterward as *Fabian Tract* No. 41 (A16).

29 The Vicar of Bray. *2nd night. Savoy Theatre.*

Working at paper. In the afternoon went out to FE. We came into town
together, she to Charing Cross and I to the Temple. Lucy was at the Savoy
with me; and we walked home.

Dinner 1/–?

> *The Vicar of Bray*, a comic opera by Sidney Grundy with music by Edward Solomon, had
> first been performed in 1881. The revival was to fill the gap made by the withdrawal of
> *The Nautch Girl*, which had been failing at the box office. "Mr Rutland Barrington is very
> funny as the Vicar; but in the work as a whole there is not life" (C840).

30 °Soiree of the Hammersmith Socialist Society. 20. Kelmscott House.
°Private View. 19th Century Art Society. Conduit St. 10.

Working, I think, all day at the paper. Went to FE in the evening, walking
as far as Royal Oak. Met Baum on the way. He explained his reasons for
withdrawing from the County Council contest in Southeast St. Pancras and
going to North Kensington.

Dinner 1/–?   Star $\frac{1}{2}$d   French Letters 10/–

31 SUNDAY °Lecture for the Mile End Branch S. D. F. (H. J. Benton, 69
Ernest St. Mile End E.). "County Council Politics." 20. Assembly Rooms.

Beaumont St. Mile End Rd. Cancelled. Branch evicted. Lecture at Woolwich Radical Club on "Municipal Anarchy." 20. Call on Bland en route. °Sunday Soc. Concert. British Artists. 18½.

Corrected and finished *World* proofs. I suppose I had a turn at the Fabian paper. Went down to Blackheath by the 16.45 train and from Blackheath to Woolwich by the 20.13. Mrs. Bland and Miss Hoatson are away in France. A few people came in, and we had a good deal of talk.

Train to Blackheath 6d   Bl[ackheath] to Woolwich 3d?   Woolwich to Chg + 1/–   Toffee 1d

February

1   I have clean forgotten what happened today, but I suppose I worked at the Fabian paper.

2   *Fabian Executive. 17. Conference Committee at 16. South St. Pancras Liberal and Radical Association Council meeting. Athenaeum Hall. Tottenham Court Rd. 20. Charity Concert, St. James's Hall. 15.*

Up too late to get much work done before it was time to go to dinner and to the concert. Very wet afternoon. Did not speak at the meeting in the evening except to second the vote of thanks to the chairman—two or three words. After the Executive Bland came with me to the Orange Grove where we had a meal.

Dinner 9d?   *Star* ½d   "Tea" at Orange Grove 1/6?   Bus to Russell Sq from St Martin's Lane 1d

> Reviewed on 10 February 1892 (C841). G.B.S. registered his impatience with charity concerts, which, however well intentioned (as was this one organized by singer Margaret Macintyre), were usually scrappy affairs that were ineffective in raising funds worth the effort expended. Still, "if a concert is musically important, I shall not be deterred from noticing it by the fact that the aims of the promoters are philanthropic."

3   *°Dialectical Society. W. H. Southran on "Biological Generalizations and Methods." South Place Chapel. 20. Open debate for the Lolesworth Working Man's Club. 34 Commercial St. Whitechapel (R. W. Kittle, Toynbee Hall, 28 Commercial St. E.). "Future of the Working Classes." 20. °Gompertz's concert. Prince's Hall. 20½.*

Began *World* article.

Dinner 1/–?   *Star* ½d   Train to Aldgate & back 6d

4 °*W. Nicholl and Septimus Webbe's concert. Prince's Hall. 20½. (3rd concert!) South Place Chapel. Wallas's 4th lecture on Chartism. "The First Convention." 20.*

Finished the *World* article. Walked home with Wallas after the lecture, which ended in his walking home with me.

Dinner 1/–?   Train to Moorgate 2½d   *Star* ½d

5 *Fabian. Essex Hall. 20. H. W. Massingham on "The Method of Fabianism."*

Archer called and went to dinner together at the Wheatsheaf. Working away at the paper. Spoke at the Fabian.

Dinner 1/–?   *Justice* 1d   *Star* ½d

6 °*Meeting of Projectors of Irish Literary Club at Barry O'Brien's, 3 New Square, Lincolns Inn. 14. °Goupil Gallery. Private View of de Back's drawings. Fabian Conference, first sitting, Essex Hall. 20. Read paper on "The History and Present Attitude of the Fabian Society."*

Heavy day's work revising the paper and completing it in detail for reading. Only got it finished just in time to go down and read it. Not equal to discussing it afterwards. Corrected the *World* proof when I got home.

Star ½d   Dinner 1/–?

> Shaw's audience was not up to discussing the long history either, Pease recalling afterwards that it "so exhausted the brains of delegates that, after a few feeble attempts at raising debate by questions, the chairman fell in with the evident wish of members and declared the sitting at an end."

7 SUNDAY *Pan-Fabian Conference. Essex Hall. 11 to 13¼. Dinner at Café Florian. 13¼ to 14¼. Essex Hall again 14½ to 17¼. Reports read in the morning, Politics for General Election in the afternoon. Soirée at Cavendish Rooms, Mortimer St. 20.*

Got a headache in the evening from too much Conference. Spoke twice, once in the morning and once in the afternoon. After the Soirée Wallas and I went home with Webb and sat there for a while. Wallas walked back here with me.

Dinner 1/2

8 *Liberal and Radical Association Executive Committee. Gray's Inn Rd. 20.*

Quite done up. Did not improve matters by singing rather violently from the second act of Verdi's *Otello*. Burt [Butterfield], who had spent the night here, lay in bed all day. Fred Fawcett came here in the afternoon. I lay down for an hour or so at 17 and got a bit of sleep, which refreshed me greatly. I went off to the Caucus meeting and got away in time to be with FE about 22. Reading for review a book on musical and dramatic copyright.

Star ½d   PMG 1d   Dinner 1/–?   Train Kings + to Shep[herds] Bush ret[ur]n 1/–

Fred Fawcett was a tenor described by G.B.S. (C959) as having "a distinguished presence and an unmistakable devotion to his art." ▪ Richard Winslow, *The Law of Artistic Copyright* (London, 1889); not reviewed.

9 *Fabian Executive. 17. Go down early—my turn in the chair. Musical Association. Royal Academy of Music. E. A. Baughan on "The Development of Opera." 20. °Church and Stage Guild. Phil. Howard on "The Stage as a Mirror of the Age." 31 Upper Bedford Place. 15.*

Did nothing but amuse myself at the piano. After the Executive Olivier came with me to the Orange Grove, where we had a meal. I went on to the Musical Association and spoke there in the discussion. Jacques and another man whose name I did not catch walked with me as far as the corner of Southampton St.

Star ½d   Dinner 1/–   "Tea" (at Orange Grove) 1/2?

Music and theatre critic Edward A. Baughan (1865–1938) wrote for the *Daily News*. Shaw would include him among the critics satirized (he would be "Mr. Vaughan") in *Fanny's First Play* (1911). Shaw's reply to Baughan in the Musical Association discussion appeared in the association's *Proceedings* for 1892–93 (B8) and was reprinted in *Shaw's Music*, II (A310). Shaw's comments were on Wagner and the attraction his operas held for people "with very little musical faculty," who "simply ignore the musical element altogether, and address themselves to the dramatic alone."

10 *°St. Paul at the Albert Hall. 20. Lecture on "County Council Politics" at the Central Reform Club, [38] Fitzroy Square, on "County Council Politics." Jan Mulder's concert, 97 Gloucester Place. Portman Square. 15¼. Shelley Committee (Cenci performance). University College. 20.*

Went into the City to buy an ink ribbon for the typewriter. FE came to Mulder's concert and we walked together across the park to Gloucester Rd. afterwards. Was commissioned by the Shelley Committee to take in hand business of getting a cast for the performance of *The Cenci*.

Train to Moorgate 2½d   Ink ribbon 4/6   Bus Holborn to Tott[enham] Ct Rd 1d   *Star* ½d   Train Gloster Rd to Ptld Rd 3d

Mulder's performance at Mrs. Jackson's was "more important than drawing-room concerts generally are, as it brought forward a capital cello sonata by the Rev. J. Ridsdale" (C842). ▪ Shaw began to cast *The Cenci* by trying to talk Alma Murray into repeating her 1885 role, this time opposite Beerbohm Tree.

11 *London Symphony Concert. St. James's Hall. 20¼. Wagner programme. °South Place. Wallas's 6th Chartism lecture. "The Newport Rising." 20. Lecture on "The County Council Election" at 2 Royal Avenue, Chelsea. 17. Call on Aveling at 65 Chancery Lane at 15.30 if possible in reply to his card.*

Found I could not begin *World* article with no prospect of doing it decently. Made an attempt to write up this diary, now exactly a fortnight in arrear— and now when I resume, it is 14 days in arrear. I am writing this on the 25th. I called on Aveling after dinner and found that he wanted me to contribute to a projected volume of outspoken essays under his editorship. When I got back from the concert in the evening I wrote him a letter about it.

Star ½d   Dinner 1/–?   Train Temple to Sloane Sq 1½d?   Sl[oane] Sq[uare] to Ptld Rd ?

> Reviewed on 17 February 1892 (C842). "The performance proved afresh that Mr. Hen-schel has now got hold of the art of orchestral conducting."

12   °*Wind Instrument Concert. Royal Academy of Music.* 20¼.

Wrote *World* article. Did not get it finished. Went to FE in the evening, if I remember aright—but am not sure about this.

Dinner 1/–?

13   °*Crystal Palace Concert, 1st of the year.* 15. °*Bauer and Walenn's concert, Hampstead Conservatoire.* 20.15. *Go down to Bristol by the 15 train from Paddington.*

Think I must have done some work on the *World* article. Lucy was here. Finished the *World* article in the train. Went to the big hotel in College Green. Revised and posted the article there before I went to bed. Spent the evening in vainly trying to get into the theatre, which was full, and then going off to the suspension bridge and wandering about in the moonlight.

Train to Paddington (Bayswater Road) 1½   Padd[in]gton to Bristol (return) 19/9   Insurance 1/–   PMG 1d   *Star* ½d   Tram to Suspension Br[idge] 1d

14 SUNDAY   °*Lecture for the Kentish Town Branch S. D. F. Phoenix Hall, Malden Rd. N.W.* 20. *(John Moore) Put off to 13th March. Lecture at Bristol (deferred lecture from 17th January) on "Social Limits of Individual Liberty." The Sunday Society. St. James's Hall.* 19¼.

Spent the day exploring the town. After the lecture went home with Paul Stacy and his sister and made the acquaintance of the family. Tremendous talkie-talkie. Paul Stacy walked back with me to the hotel.

> Paul Stacy and his sister Enid (Mrs. P. E. T. Widdrington) were Bristol S.D.F. members. Enid, also a Fabian, wrote on women's issues.

15   *Come up from Bristol by the 9.30 train. Cohen to call between 17 and 18 with proofs of* Pelican *sketch.*

I got a lift on my way to the station by the judge with whom Wallas stayed when he came down for me on the 17th January. In the evening Cohen came and stayed until it was too late to do anything. Opened all letters to be attended to. Could not get away from *A Tale of Two Cities* which I bought to read in the train.

Daily Chronicle 1d   *Tale of Two Cities* 1/6

16 *Fabian Executive. 17. South St. Pancras Liberal and Radical Association, Meeting of Council of 250. Percy Hall. 20.15. Miss Bertha Newcombe's, 1 Cheyne Walk, 10.30, to sit for portrait. °National Liberal Club discussion, "Co-operation vs. Socialism." G. J. Holyoake.*

Lunched at Miss Newcombe's. Had a meal with Wallas, Olivier and Pease at the Orange Grove after the Executive.

Train to South Kensington & back 6d

> Bertha Newcombe (@1860–@1947), was an artist then known for her work in the *English Illustrated Magazine.* Also a Fabian, she was one of many women in the organization who had fallen, vainly, in love with Shaw. To see more of him, she asked him to sit for a three-quarter-length portrait to be exhibited in April at the New English Art Club, known as *The Platform Spellbinder.* Shaw would insist that it was "the best vision" of himself at this period. In 1895 (17 July) Newcombe would publish in *The Sketch* a celebrated drawing of Sidney Webb, Beatrice Potter (Webb), Graham Wallas, and Bernard Shaw at ease in a field. Her pursuit of Shaw would be as obvious to him as it would be unsuccessful. ▪

17 *°Guildhall Concert. 18½. Embankment.*

As well as I can remember I spent the afternoon and the time before dinner in writing a long letter to Hutchinson about Fabian affairs to conciliate him, he being very indignant at his letters not being answered. I had arranged to go down to Wheatsheaf at about 14 to meet FE. Did not get there until nearly 15, when I found her talking to Archer. We walked out to Dalling Rd. together and I stayed there whilst she went to the theatre, drafting a letter asking Beerbohm Tree to play *The Cenci* for the Shelley Society and the Independent Theatre.

Dinner (FE & I) 2/–?   Train Shep[herds] Bush to Ptld Rd 6d

18 *°South Place. Wallas's 7th Chartism lecture. "The Second Convention."* *20. °Gompertz's concert. Prince's Hall. 20½. Stock Exchange Orchestral Society Concert. St. James's Hall. 20.*

Did not begin *World* article. Had to copy out letter to Tree and write other letters about *Cenci* performance. Reading Praeger's life of Wagner for review—much caught by it.

Dinner 1/–?   *Star* ½d

> The Stock Exchange concert was reviewed on 24 February 1892 (C845). G.B.S. attended at the urging of one of his stockbroker friends who played cornet in the amateur orchestra, and found that "the combination of professional steadiness and accuracy with the amateur freshness, excitement, and romance, produces a better result than an ordinary

routine performance by professional [musician]s alone." ▪ Ferdinand Praeger's *Wagner as I Knew Him* (London, 1892) was reviewed as part of a weekly column (C845). G.B.S. found it "vivid and convincing."

19   Fabian. Essex Hall. Mrs. J. G. Grenfell on "Socialism and Women," and Mrs. D. G. Ritchie on "Women under Socialism." 20.

Wrote *World* article, sitting up until near 3 to finish it. Spoke at the Fabian. Dinner 1/–?   *Justice* 1d   *Star* ½d

Mrs. J. G. Grenfell was a Fabian and suffragette. Ellen (Mrs. D. G.) Ritchie, whose outlook was similar, had married Oxford philosopher David George Ritchie in 1889 as his second wife.

20   °Crystal Palace Concert. 15. Go down to Oxford. 16.45 from Paddington. Private View. Nettleship's pastels at Dunthorne's. Spend the evening in Best's rooms, Magdalen College, and speak on "Socialism."

Writing letters—at least that is my recollection. I know I intended to take plenty of time to catch the train this time, and yet I ran it rather close after all. Spent the journey down trying to compose a few verses to put into a copy of *The Quintessence* for Mabel Besant. Hines met me at the station and came on to Powell's, where we had some grub. Then he brought me off to the affair at Magdalen. I expected a mere chat on things in general; but when I arrived there were about 15 or 16 undergraduates assembled; and I was called on for a lecture. An opposition party outside screwed us up and wrecked the adjoining room. It threatened to be a very serious business, but I got out at last with a whole skin. Could hardly get any sleep afterwards.

Train to Bishops Road 1½d   Paddington to Oxford 5/3   *Star* ½d

(Sir) Thomas A. V. Best (1870–1941) would take his B.A. from Magdalen in 1894. He would become a Colonial Office administrator who would govern the Falkland Islands, the Leeward Islands, Trinidad, and Malta. ▪ Shaw wrote about the incident, complete to his escape, minus hat, gloves, and umbrella, under a flood of dirty water poured from rooms above, from a Magdalen College lecture hall sealed from the outside and made unbearable inside by hot cayenne pepper blown into the room. His not-entirely-facetious account of the dangerous practical joke, "Revolutionary Progress at Oxford," appeared in *PMG*, 22 February 1892 (C844). "Three Oxford ladies who admire Mr. Shaw" (MS., BL) sent him a replacement hat. The head of Magdalen, (Sir) Thomas Herbert Warren (1853–1930), later Oxford vice-chancellor and Regius Professor of Poetry, sent Shaw a letter of half-hearted apology (BL), promising restitution which never came.

21 SUNDAY   °Lecture at Kelmscott House for Hammersmith Socialist Society. 20. Cancelled. Lecture at the Oxford Reform Club. Godfrey R. Benson in the chair. Dine with him in the Common Room at Balliol at 18.

Corrected proof of *World* article. Cooke, a Wadham man, came in—also Hines. At about midday Powell and I went to the fencing club. Cooke and Crackanthorpe fenced, and the instructor, Goudourville, gave me a lesson—to my great astonishment—at Powell's request. In the evening Powell brought me over to Balliol where I dined with Jowett and the rest of the dons. Sat up pretty late talking to Powell but slept very well. In the afternoon I wrote a letter to the *Pall Mall Gazette* ironically describing the affair of the night before.

Godfrey Rathbone Benson (1864–1945), the first Baron Charnwood, was the brother of actor-manager (Sir) Frank Benson (1858–1939), and a man of letters as well as a Liberal politician. He would become M.P. for Woodstock in 1892. His best-known book was his biography of Abraham Lincoln (1916). ▪ George Albert Cooke (1865–1939), professor of Hebrew and canon of Christ Church, Oxford, had been educated at Wadham College, Oxford. He would become Regius Professor of Hebrew in 1914. ▪ Dayrell (Cookson) Crackanthorpe (1871–1950)—the family name was changed in 1888 for reasons of inheritance—entered Merton College after preparation at Winchester, and would have a life-long Foreign Service career. His elder brother was Hubert Crackanthorpe (1870–1896), briefly editor of *The Albermarle* and a contributor to *The Yellow Book*. His mother, Blanche Crackanthorpe (1845–1928), was a writer-friend of Elizabeth Robins, Selwyn Image and Stopford Brooke; his father, Montague Cookson Crackanthorpe (1832–1913), a Queen's Counsel, would be Standing Counsel to Oxford University from 1893 to 1899. ▪ Benjamin R. Jowett (1817–1893), Regius Professor of Greek since 1855 and Master of Balliol College, was translator of Plato, Aristotle, and Thucydides. The year after his death Shaw wrote of him unkindly, "I remember conversing once with the late Master of Balliol, an amiable gentleman, stupendously ignorant probably, but with a certain flirtatious, old-maidish frivolity about him that had, and was meant to have, the charm of a condescension from so learned a man" (C999).

22 *Lecture in the Town Hall, Woodstock (Oxfordshire), 19½. Catch the 18.25 from Oxford and change at Kidlington. Drive back with Hines.*

Corrected *World* proof. Powell went up to town; and I wandered about looking into his books. Hines came and kept me in until after lunch. Cooke called and warned me that a second attempt would be made at Woodstock to "rag" me. After Hines went away I went out for a walk, spent some time in the Museum; and called on the Ritchies. Ritchie was out; and I had a chat with Mrs. Ritchie, who had lost her voice through a cold, until he came in. On the way to Woodstock I found that about half a dozen undergraduates or so were coming down in the same train, disguised as farmers and equipped with sticks for a disturbance. At the hotel, however, they were completely cowed by my supporters, and the meeting came off all the better for the fun of chaffing them. I drove back with Hines, three of his daughters, Miss Clifford and [George] Cotton. We had tea with [Adolphus] Ballard.

Train Oxford to Woodstock 1/3

A handbill announces Shaw's title as "The Progress of Social Democracy." ▪ Miss Clifford, unidentified, may have been a friend of one of Hines's daughters (all grown and all Fabians); George Cotton and Adolphus Ballard were Oxfordshire Fabians.

23 *Fabian Executive. 17. °National Liberal Club. "Work of a Woman's Liberal Association" by Miss Orme. 20. Come up from Oxford by the 10.57 train. Liberal and Radical Union Deputation to Home Secretary about Free*

Speech affair. Large Conference Chamber of House of Commons. 16.

Wallas and Massingham walked with me from the House of Commons to the Fabian along the Embankment. After the Executive some of us arranged to go to the Orange Grove, but I lost them on the way and had my meal by myself. Came home for a short time and then went to FE.

Tip to Heath, Y. Powell's scout 5/–   *Daily Chronicle* 1d   Train Oxford to Ptld Rd 5/4   Dinner 1/–?   Telegram to F.E. 6d   Train to Shep[herds] Bush & back 1/–

---

24   °W. Ashton Ellis's 1st lecture on "Wagner's Art Work of the Future." *Trinity College. 20. 2nd performance of L. E. Mitchell's* Deborah *at the Avenue Theatre. 14½. Miss Newcombe's to sit for portrait in the forenoon.*

Did no work except reading a little for review whilst Miss Newcombe was painting. FE was at the theatre; I met her when I came out and went back to Hammersmith with her. We had tea and came together again to town. I left her at the stage door of the theatre (the Comedy) and went home intending to work. But I only read *The Idler* and wrote a letter to Mitchell about his play.

Umbrella at Slater's 19/6   Train Ch[arin]g + to Sloane Sq 2d   Back 2d   Train FE and I Ch[arin]g + to Rav[enscourt] Pk & back 1/6   *Idler* 4½d   *Globe* 1d   *Star* ½d

> Langdon Mitchell's *Deborah* would have five matinee performances at the *Avenue*, Northumberland Avenue, Charing Cross. His wife, Marion Lea, would play the title role, while Elizabeth Robins would be the Prologue. ▪ Slater & Hicks, umbrella manufacturers, 22 Aldermanbury, 1st Floor.

---

25   London Symphony Concert. St. James's Hall. 20½. °Wallas's 8th Chartism lecture. South Place. "The Plug Riots." 20. °Women's Suffrage meeting at Prince's Hall. 20. Call on Shorter at Illustrated London News *about Rossini article. Press View. Dowdeswell's. Aubrey Hunt's Tangier sketches and C. E. Hern's London ones. Also J. V. Fisher's Stour Valley drawings and Monk's drypoint of Cardinal Manning.*

Up late. A man named O'Brien called to ask me to do something for him, as he was very hard up. Made an attempt to write up this diary, now 14 days in arrear. Also to clear off my letters. After dinner went to Shorter and looked in at the Fabian for a while. I did not get the diary fully up to date until 23.15 when there was not much time, without staying up, for answering the fearful accumulation of neglected letters.

O'Brien of Acton 10/–   Dinner 11d   *The Swordsman*, Hutton 3/6 Umbrella ring 1d   *Star* ½d

> Clement Shorter would commission an article from Shaw, "The Rossini Centenary," *Illustrated London News*, 5 March 1892 (C848). Unimpressed by the anniversary, Shaw wrote that Rossini "was one of the greatest masters of claptrap that ever lived. His moral deficiencies as an artist were quite extraordinary." ▪ J. V. Fisher (1859–1925?) was a Liverpool landscape painter. ▪ William Monk (1863–1937) was a Hampstead-based

painter and etcher who later worked in Venice and New York. ▪ J. W. O'Brien of 6 Artillery Row, Victoria St., Acton, was repeatedly successful in his begging letters to Shaw.

26 *Introduce a Local Government Bill for Rev. A. Leslie Lilley at his Parliament in Chelsea. Upper Chelsea Institute. 40 Sloane Square S. W.*

Began *World* article. Walked back from Sloane Square.

Star ½d   *Justice* 1d   Dinner 1/–?   Train to Sloane Sq & back (return not used) 6d?

The Chelsea Parliament was another of the popular mock-legislatures.

27 *Crystal Palace Concert. 15. Give Miss Newcombe a sitting on my return from Palace until 21.30. Dine there.*

Not much work done. Went down to Palace alone. Talked a good deal to Graves and Fuller Maitland in the carriage going down. Came back with Thomson and a man to whom he introduced me whose name I forget. Got the 16.55 train and was able to give Miss Newcombe some time before dinner. Went on to FE. Seiffert and his wife traveled with me from Victoria to Sloane Square.

Dinner 1/–?   Star ½d   Train Ch[arin]g + to Vic[toria] 1½d   Vic[toria] to [Crystal] Palace 2/–   PMG 1d   Train Vic[toria] to Sl[oane] Sq 1d   S[ou]th Ken[sington] to Ravenscourt Park 3d?   Shep[herds] Bush to Ptld Rd 6d

Charles Larcom Graves (1856–1944), a journalist, would be assistant editor of *Spectator* from 1899 to 1917. ▪ John Alexander Fuller Maitland (1856–1936) was music critic of *The Times.* ▪ "Thomson" was Sidney R. Thompson, who was Shaw's successor as *Star* music critic, signing his articles "Piccolo."

28 SUNDAY *Lecture for the S. D. F. at their Central Hall, 337 Strand (H. W., Sec.). "Fabian Tactics." Speak at County Council Demonstration held by Metropolitan Radical Federation in Victoria Park. 16. (S. D. Harris. 35 Grosvenor Rd. Canonbury).*

Finished *World* article and wrote a letter to *The Daily Chronicle* on the marriage question. Wallas walked back with me from Victoria Park here and we had tea together. He also walked with me to the meeting, but he did not come in. Had to sit up late to get article off.

Train to Bishopsgate 3d   Broad St to Victoria Pk (return not used) 6d
Gave loose coin to man at meeting ?

Shaw's letter was published in the *Daily Chronicle* on 1 March 1892 (C846) as "Economic Independence of Women."

29 °*Kropotkin's lecture on "Mutual Aid in the Struggle for Life." Portman Rooms. 16. Entrance in Dorset St. Article of 1000 words on Rossini must be*

posted to Illustrated London News *tonight. Rossini concert at Crystal Palace. 15. Train 13.55. °J. C. Ames's pianoforte recital on Janko keyboard. Hampstead Conservatoire. 20.*

Read up Rossini in Groves' *Dictionary*. FE came to the Palace with me. We had a meal at the Orange Grove together; and I left her at the stage door of the Comedy. When I got home I did not get to work very quickly at the article, of which I had only a few words already written. I even spent some time at the piano. It was 3 in the morning before I posted it, and half past 3 before I got into bed. [Robert] Buchanan wrote to say that he had offered a review of my *Quintessence of Ibsenism* to a leading review, and had been told that they would print nothing whatever concerning me.

Telegram to FE 6½d   *Star* ½d   Dinner 9d   Train Ch[arin]g + to Vic[toria] 1½d   Vic[toria] to C.P. &o back, FE &o I 4/–   Telephone room 6d   Grub at Orange Grove (2) 2/9

> Reviewed on 9 March 1892 (C849). G.B.S. "was astonished to find [the Rossini overtures] all still so fresh, so imposing, so clever, and even, in the few serious passages, so really fine." ▪ See 9 June 1892 for the Janko Keyboard.

March

1 *Fabian Executive. 17. °Theresa Benay's concert. Lyric Club. 20¼. °Miss Newcombe's in the morning.*

Up late after last night. Wrote up this diary; attended to correspondence etc. After dinner went to *Illustrated London News* office and corrected proof of article on Rossini. Wallas came to the Orange Grove. I then came home and wrote letters.

Star ½d   Dinner 10d   "Tea" at Orange Grove 1/9

> As Shaw noted in his code, he forgot the appointment. "I got to bed last night at half past three quite exhausted," he wrote to Bertha Newcombe, "and awoke at twenty minutes past eleven this morning. After struggling through a mass of business I suddenly (at about two o'clock) recollected that I had promised to be at Cheyne Walk. . . ." He signed the postcard "yours most guiltily, G. Bernard Shaw." (From Francis Edwards sale cat. 1023, 1979.) The diary corroborates his excuses.

2 *°Gounod's Redemption. Albert Hall. 20. °4th Independent Theatre performance. Royalty Theatre. 20. De Banville's Kiss. Symons' Minister's Call and Brandes' Visit (translated by Archer). Put off to Friday. Speak at County Council Election Meeting for Burns and Tims. Miss Newcombe's in the morning.*

Spent the whole day at Cheyne Walk [Bertha Newcombe's]. Before dinner I helped with the County Council circulars which the Home girls were sending out. Afterwards we got to the portrait; and I did not leave until it was time to go to Battersea. Webb turned up at the meeting and came back with me, Burns seeing us off at the station. In the afternoon we stopped the painting for afternoon tea. I sang a couple of songs for Bertha Newcombe.

Train to S[ou]th Kensington 3d   Battersea to Victoria 1d

> The play by Arthur Symons, based on a short story by Frank Harris, would open on 4 March. It would be Symons's only work for the theater, and would have only one performance. The same fate would occur to the Danish play by Edward Brandes.

3 °*Nichol and Webbe's concert. Prince's Hall. 20½. °Graham Wallas's 9th Chartism lecture. South Place. "The Chartists and the Anti-Corn Law League." 20. Postponed.*

Began *World* article. Went out to FE in the afternoon, walking all the way, in reply to a telegram saying that she had some news about the *Cenci* performance. We went back to town together, she getting out at Charing Cross for the theatre and I going on to the Mansion House for Wallas's lecture. When I got to South Place I found that the lecture was postponed on account of the County Council Election. So I hurried back to the Comedy Theatre and saw the first piece in which FE is acting, and also the first two acts of *The Gray Mare*. I left before the third so as to catch FE at Charing Cross, as she always goes by the 22.40 train. Went back with her.

Dinner 1/–?   Star ½d   Train Rav[ens] C[our]t Pk to Ch[arin]g + &° back for FE 9d   Single to Mansion Ho[use] for self 7d   Mans[ion] Ho[use] to Ch[arin]g + 3d   Ch[arin]g + to Rav[enscour]t Pk 6d Shep[herds] Bush to Ptld Rd 6d   Comedy Theatre 2/–   prog[ram]me 2d

> Florence Farr was playing the role of Mrs. Cunliffe at the Comedy Theatre in *Lady Fortune*, a comedy by Charles Thomas, which had opened on 18 February and would run fifty-two performances. • *The Grey Mare* was a comedy adapted from the German by George R. Sims and Cecil Raleigh. Several of Shaw's friends were in it. It would run eighty-seven performances.

4 °*Fabian. Graham Wallas on "The Nature of Government." Essex Hall. 20. °Otta Bronnum's and Alfred Christensen's concert. Steinway Hall. 20. Independent Theatre performance, [as] on Wednesday, Royalty Theatre. 30. °Bach St. John Passion at St. Anne's, Soho. 20.*

Finished *World* article.

Dinner 1/–?   Star ½d   Justice 1d

5 *Crystal Palace Concert. 15. °Go down to General Booth's farm at Benfleet. Train leaves Fenchurch St. at 12.15; returning 18½. County Council election polling day. Help Webb at Deptford. Albion St., Deptford. °Ludovici?*

Was not up in good time. When I got down to Deptford I was directed to Albion Rd., Rotherhithe, instead of Deptford. Canvassed Costerwood St., returned to office (of which Wallas was in charge), got something to eat there; went to Crystal Palace, catching the 15.57 train at New Cross (Joist traveled with me from Deptford Rd. to New Cross); heard the last half of the concert; returned to Deptford; canvassed Ada St., came back with Wallas and [H. W.] Just after the close of the poll to Charing Cross; got out with Wallas and went with him to the Club; had eggs and cocoa there with him, Llewellyn Smith and Harold Spender, with another man whose name I did not catch joining us at our table, went down to the smoking room for a few minutes, left and caught FE at her train; went to Ravenscourt Park with her; quarreled with her because she had tried to cure a headache by a spoonful of brandy; and came home.

Train P[or]tl[an]d Rd to Deptford Rd ?   *Pick me up* (comic paper) 1d
Deptford Rd to Crystal Pal[ace] 9d   Back 9d   Tram New Cross G.E. to
New Cross L.B. & S.C. 1d   *PMG* 1d   *Star* ½d   Train Deptford Rd to
Ch[arin]g + ?   Ch[arin]g + to Rav[enscourt] Pk 6d   Shep[herds]
Bush to Ptld Rd 6d

> G.B.S. was "unable to give any account" of the concert, he wrote on 16 March 1892
> (C850), "because the . . . performance was unreasonably fixed for the day of polling for
> the County Council. Municipal bands were at stake at that election, and I threw myself
> into it with ardor, my candidate having pledged himself not only to vote steadily for
> municipal music but to agitate for giving citizens a really effective power of moving street
> pianos out of earshot. . . ." ▪ *Pick-Me-Up* was a new comic paper to which Max
> Beerbohm (1872–1956) was contributing some of his earliest caricatures, and Phil May
> (1864–1903) his humorous sketches of London low life.

---

6 SUNDAY   *Lecture for the Battersea S. D. F. at Sydney Hall. (H. B. Rogers, 6 Gwynne Rd. Battersea S. W.). "The County Council Election and its Lessons." 20.*

Spent all the morning with Johan Castberg, who called with an introduction from Wallas, he being a young Norwegian sent over here to investigate the Factory Acts. He left at 14. After dinner Edward Rose called and left me tickets for his matinée Tuesday. I did not get to Sydney Hall, to which I walked from South Kensington, until half past 20, and did not get away until 23.40 having to walk all the way home.

Train to South Kensington 4d

> Rose's new play was *The Plowdens.* See 8 March 1892.

---

7   °*Fabian Central Group meeting. 32 Great Ormond St. W. C.*

Writing letters, writing up this diary, correcting proof of the Fabian tract called *A Democratic Budget,* etc. Archer was at the Wheatsheaf. Findon called in the afternoon and left me a play of his to read.

PMG 1d   Dinner 1/–

> B. W. Findon (1859–1943), the editor of *Play Pictorial,* apparently wanted Shaw to look
> over his one and only play to be produced in the 1890s, *The Primrose Path,* which would
> have a single matinee performance on 11 May 1892 at the Vaudeville.

8 *Fabian Executive. 17. Edward Rose's matinée at the Prince of Wales Theatre. 15. The Plowdens.*

I forget this day, but suppose I was busy in the morning with correspondence. FE was at the matinee with me.

Star ½d   Dinner 1/–?   programme at theatre 6d

The comedy by Danish playwright Otto Benzon (1856–1927) was adapted by Edward Rose. Although Ben Webster (1864–1948) had a leading role, the play did not survive beyond the opening matinee.

9 *Shelley Society. Cenci Committee. University College. 19½. Miss Burney to recite Beatrice [Cenci].*

Here again my memory fails me.

Estelle Burney, who was being considered for the lead in *The Cenci*, was a playwright as well as an actress. Her play *Settled Out of Court* was produced in 1897 and reviewed by G.B.S. (C1212) in *SR*.

10 °*Speak at Whitstable on "Programme of Social Democracy"—cancelled.* °*Wallas's 10th Chartism lecture. South Place. "O'Connor's Land Scheme." 20. Philharmonic Concert. St. James's Hall. 20.*

Began *World* article. Had to sit in a furious draught at the Philharmonic and caught a slight cold.

Star ½d   Dinner 1/–?   Bus to St John's Hall 1d

11 Finished *World* article. In the afternoon went over to FE and worked with her on the *Cenci*. When she went off to the theatre I went to Bedford Park and called on Todhunter. He was out; so I called on the Pagets next door and spent the evening there. Left in time to walk back to Ravenscourt Park station and met FE coming back from the theatre. Had to sit up very late correcting *World* article and writing letters.

Star ½d   *Justice* 1d   Dinner 1/–?

The *World* review, 16 March 1892 (C850), was largely on the Philharmonic's Mozart program.

12 *Crystal Palace Concert. 15. Miss Newcombe's after Palace for portrait sitting.*

Cannot remember what work if any, I did in the morning. Letters, I suppose. Did not leave Cheyne Walk until 23. Walked home. At least I think I did.

Telegram to Miss Newcombe 1/–   Dinner 1/–?   *Star, PMG,* 2 old *PMGs* for C.C. figures, and *P.M. Budget* 9½   Train Ch[arin]g + to Vic[toria] 1½d   Vic[toria] to [Crystal] Pal[ace] 2/–   Vic[toria] to Sloane Sq 1d

"Some alarm was created at the Crystal Palace . . . by the announcement that 'Professor Joseph Joachim' was to play Max Bruch's latest violin concerto. At a time when all the best friends of art are striving to turn our professors into artists, it seemed too bad to turn one of our greatest artists into a professor. However," G.B.S. wrote on 23 March 1892 (C851), "he did not play in the least like one."

13 SUNDAY   *Lecture for the Kentish Town Branch S. D. F. Phoenix Hall. Preston St., Malden Rd., N. W. 20. (John Moore) on "The London County Council Elections and their Lessons."*

Corrected *World* proofs and prepared fresh set of notes for my lecture, as I accidentally tore up the Battersea ones. After dinner went to FE and tried over some of *The Cenci*. Walked with her as far as Todhunter's, where she was to recite before Furnivall, Salt, Grein etc. Went to Sparlings' and had "tea" there. There were some people there whose names I forget. Very personal and persuasive debate.

Train to Shep[herds] B[ush] (return not used) 6d   Chiswick (North London) to Kentish Town 8d   Tram Britannia to Euston Rd 1d

14   *Miss Newcombe's for portrait sitting.*

Got to Cheyne Walk a little after 12 and remained until 16½. When I got home I set to writing letters and did not finish until past 2.

Train to South Kensington 3d   Sloane Sq to St Ja[me]s's Pk 1½d   *Star* ½d

15   *Fabian Executive. 17. Meeting to revise Tract 24 at 16. °National Liberal Club. Clement L. Bailhache on "Municipalization of Land." 20. Call on G. Standring, 7 Finsbury St., between 15 and 16, about the printing of the Fabian Conference paper.*

Wrote a long letter to the Newington Reform Club in answer to a string of questions about the policy of the Fabian at the next election. Wrote up this diary, now a week in arrear. Called on Standring after dinner. Abominable wet day. The change from the frost, which always agrees with me, put me so much out of sorts that I was as dull as possible with FE to whom I went in the evening. Olivier came to tea with me after the Executive.

Train to Moorgate 2½d   *Star* ½d   Dinner (at "Arcadian") 1/–?   Train to Shep[herds] Bush & back 9d

Questions for Parliamentary Candidates, by Sidney Webb (1891).

16   *Algernon Ashton's concert. St. James's Hall. 20*

Began *World* article, so as to leave tomorrow free for the portrait sitting. Wrote to her [Bertha Newcombe] about the design for the cover of the Fabian Conference paper.

Star ½d   Dinner 1/–?

Algernon Ashton, pianist, gave a concert of his own music with the assistance of a string quartet. G.B.S. (C851) found Ashton's most successful pieces "pretty and not lacking in appropriate feeling."

17 *Wallas's 11th and last Chartism lecture. South Place. 20. "The Year of Revolution." Miss Newcombe's all day if possible. °Patrick's Day Irish National Concert. Albert Hall. 20.*

Got to Cheyne Walk a little after 12. We gave up the painting towards 17 and went into the drawing room, where we sat playing and singing until we found that it was past 18, when we hurried off to the train, she coming with me on my way to the Mansion House as far as St. James's Park. I walked home with Wallas and went in and sat with him and Muirhead for a while. Reading article on "Trusts in America" in *The Economic Review*.

Train to Sloane Sq 4d?   Sl[oane] Sq to Mans[ion] Ho[use] ?   *Star* ½d

18 *°Wind Instrument Concert. Royal Academy of Music. 20½. Fabian. Gustav T. Steffen on "The Purchasing Power of Wages." Essex Hall. 20. Press View. Whistler Exhibition at Goupil Gallery.*

Finished *World* article. After dinner went to the Goupil Gallery. Then went on to FE. Returned to town with her and so got to the Fabian by 19.30. I looked in for a moment at the [Fabian] office, but found the women in, consulting there, and went on to Essex Hall. A number of us walked away from the Hall together; but at last we got separated; and I went as far as Francis St. with Steffen and then went home alone. Presently, however, Wallas and Webb called and sat until past midnight talking. In the afternoon I came out without sufficient money and had to leave my dinner unpaid for and to borrow something from FE.

Dinner—left owing (10d)   Bus to Uxbridge Rd 4d   Train FE & I Rav[enscourt] Pk to Ch[arin]g + –Temple 1/1   Her ticket of the day before which she had not paid for 9d (borrowed 3/6 from her for this expense, which I paid, as well as the dinner, on the following day)   *Star* ½d   *Justice* 1d

> The Goupil show was an artistic vindication and marked a complete turn-around in public feeling toward Whistler, whose work Shaw had long championed. Excited preview crowds thronged the exhibition galleries, but Whistler and his wife, Trixie, who arrived at five, remained in a curtained-off area, privately savoring the triumph.

19 *Crystal Palace Concert. 15. Private View. Whistler Exhibition. Miss Newcombe's in the evening.*

O'Brien called in the morning and I had to give him 5/– and a pair of trousers. Then a letter came from Herbert Burrows which I had to answer. This left me hardly five minutes for my dinner. Left the concert early and got back by the 16.10 train. Went to Whistler Exhibition and met FE there. We went to Gatti and Rodesano's in the Strand for a meal, all nearer places being either shut or overcrowded. I walked with her to the theatre and went on to Cheyne Walk. Did not leave until after 23.

Dinner 5d & 10d   *Star* ½d   *Pall Mall [Gazette]* 1d   *Pick-Me-Up* 1d   Cab Oxford St to Ch[arin]g + 1/6   Train Chg + to Vic[toria] 1½d   Vic[toria] to [Crystal] Pal[ace] ret[ur]n 2/–   Grub, FE & I at Gatti's & Rodesano's 3/–   Wash & brushup at Faulkner's 3d   Train Ch[arin]g + to Sloane Sq 1½d   Sl[oane] Sq to Ptld Rd 3½d

> A paragraph in the 23 March 1892 review (C851) praised a new piano concerto by "the veteran E[duard] Silas . . . the brilliancy and cleverness of which we would hear no end if the composer were forty years younger." Silas (1827–1909), an organist and teacher of harmony, played his own work, and was not up to its technical difficulties, which, G.B.S. thought, cooled its reception.

20 SUNDAY   °*Lecture for the Croydon Branch of the S. D. F., 11 Devonshire Rd., West Croydon (J. Cooper). Cancelled 1/2/92. Lecture at the Central Finsbury Radical Club. 241 Goswell Rd. 11.30, (Henry Mundy), on "The County Council Election and its Results."*

Got my umbrella run over and broken by a bicyclist in Goswell Rd. Looked over some Fabian proofs and corrected *World* proofs. Went for the afternoon and evening to FE arriving there a little after 16. We went for a walk across Wormwood Scrubbs before 20.

Bus Euston Sq to Angel 1d   Kings + to Tott[enham] Ct Rd 1d   Train to Shepherds Bush & back 1/–

21   °*Fabian Central Group meeting. 32 Great Ormond St. 20. Leave Wallas's spectacles at 32 Ormond St. for him and bring umbrella to Stores for mending.* °*Annual meeting Liberal and Radical Union. National Liberal Club. 20. Monday Pop. Joachim and Berwick.*

Up late. Wrote up this diary, which took quite a long time. Called on Wallas and at the Stores on my way to dinner. Wrote a few letters, notably one to Mrs. Pease about Pease's position as Secretary of the Fabian. Did not finish this until my return from the concert. Wet night—to my disgust, as I had calculated on a continuance of the fine cold weather when I left the umbrella at the Stores.

PMG 1d   *Star* ½d   Dinner 1/5   Bus to St Ja[me]s's Hall 1d   back 1d   Programme 6d

22   *Fabian Executive. 17.* °*National Liberal Club. Charles T. Gatty on "Village Politics." 20. Bach Choir. Mass in B. Minor. St. James's Hall. 20½. Miss Newcombe's as early as possible.*

Spent the day at Miss Newcombe's until it was time to go to the concert.

Train to South Kensington 3d   Sloane Sq to St Ja[me]s's Pk 1½d Concert 1/–   programme 1/–

Reviewed on 30 March 1892 (C852). G.B.S. felt that he might "most mercifully leave the Bach Choristers to their own consciences. . . ."

23 *Dvorak's* Requiem, *Albert Hall. 20.* °Mrs. *Lee's Musical At-Home, 21 to 23, 21 Campden Hill Rd. Miss Newcombe's in the afternoon.*

Began *World* article. Went to Miss Newcombe's in the afternoon, dined there; and went on to the Albert Hall.

Dinner 1/–?   *Star* ½d   Train Ch[arin]g + to Sloane Sq 2d   Concert programme 1/–

> "I gave Dvorak's *Requiem* one more chance on Wednesday last, when it was performed— and very well performed too—for the first time in London, . . . under Mr. Barnby. And I am more amazed than ever that any critic should mistake this paltry piece of orchestral and harmonic confectionery for a serious composition" (C852).

24 *Philharmonic Concert. St. James's Hall. 20.* °Shakspere Reading *Society.* Two Gentlemen of Verona. *St. James's Hall, Banqueting Room. 20. Call at Stores for umbrella. Miss Newcombe's in the afternoon.*

Finished *World* article. Went to Miss Newcombe's in the afternoon and stayed until it was time to go to the concert.

Dinner 1/–?   *Star* ½d   Repairs to umbrella 2/6   Train Ch[arin]g + to Sloane Sq 2d   Sl[oane] Sq to St Ja[me]s's Pk 1½d

> "At the Philharmonic . . . Sapellnikoff, who was received coldly, like a forgotten man, had his revenge after the concert in a series of recalls and an *encore* which were, for a Philharmonic audience, quite frantic" (C852).

25 *Lecture for the Leek Trades Council on "Socialism." 20. (Harry Roberts, Westwood Lane, Leek). Euston to Stafford 10.30; break journey and call on Buttery; go on to Leek at 16.45.* °Col. *Shaw-Hillier's lecture on Military Bands at United Service Institute. 15. Banqueting House, Whitehall.* °Dr. *Sandford's lecture on "Necessity of Voice Training for Public Speakers" at Medical Society. 11 Chandos St. W. Discussion, about 16¼.*

Read for review in the train: J. H. Levy's *Individualism*. Had a meal with Buttery at Stafford. Made the acquaintance of Kineton Parkes and Sugdon at Leek, also of Roberts' wife, whom I had not met before.

Train to Stafford 11/1½   Stafford to Leek 2/3?   Biscuits & apples at Rugby 6d

> *The Outcome of Individualism*, 3d ed., unsigned review in the *Daily Chronicle*, 5 April 1892 (C853).

26 °Crystal *Palace Concert. 15. Stepniak's in the evening, 31 Blandford Rd. Bedford Park. Supper 19½. Miss Newcombe's to dinner and to sit until past 21. Come up from Leek by the 11.30. Go over to the London Institution after breakfast.* °Miss Edith Clay's *concert, 97 Gloucester Place West. 15¼.*

Wrote review of Levy's *Outcome of Individualism* in the train coming up. Came up from Stepniak's in the evening with Mrs. Pease and a number of other guests.

Train Leek to Euston 12/9½   Dinner at refreshment room, Stoke 1/6 Lavatory 2d   Train Ptld Rd to S[ou]th Kensington 3d   S[ou]th Kensington to Turnham G[ree]n?   Turnham G[ree]n to P[or]tl[an]d Rd?

27 SUNDAY   *Lecture at the Pioneer Reform Association, 102 Brompton Rd. on "Socialism and Human Nature" (G. E. Odell). 20. °Call on the Peases in the afternoon. °Mrs. Jopling's Academy pictures. 3 Pembroke Rd., Kensington S. W. 15 to 18.*

Corrected *World* proofs and finished and sent off review of Levy's book to the *Chronicle*.

Train to South Kensington 3d

28   *°Jeanne Douste's 2nd Rubenstein concert. Steinway Hall. 15. Miss Newcombe's.*

Nearly all of this week was devoted to the portrait, as the day for sending it in to the New English Art Club is Friday. I do not recollect this day very clearly. I left Cheyne Walk in time to go to FE and catch her on her return from the theatre by the 22 train.

Train to South Kensington 3d

29   *Fabian Executive. 17. Miss Newcombe's. Adjourned debate at Playgoers' Club on Archer's attack on the Censorship. Adelphi Restaurant. 20.*

Portrait up to Fabian Executive hour. Spoke [at] the Playgoers' Club.

Train to South Kensington 3d   *Star* ½d   Sloane Sq to Temple 2½d Grub with Massingham after Exec[utive] at Gatti & Rodesano's 2/6

30   *°W. Ashton Ellis's 2nd lecture on "Wagner's Art Work of the Future." Trinity College. Mandeville Place W. 20. Annual meeting of Fabian East London Groups at the Town Hall, Poplar, 20. Walsh in the chair. Go down and speak. Miss Newcombe's.*

Portrait. Reading *A Plea for Liberty* for review during sitting. A large party of us came from Poplar to Broad St. together from the meeting, but Webb, Wallas and I walked home by ourselves from Broad St.

Train to South Kensington 3d   Sloane Sq to Aldgate ?   Tram Aldgate to Poplar 2d   Train Poplar to Broad St 2d

According to the *Daily Chronicle*, 31 March 1892, Shaw noted that there was "extraordinary difficulty in getting Progressive candidates. . . . He knew of one case in which a . . . candidate, . . . when he was asked to address his constituents, all he could tell them was how he had fought with a tiger in India. (Laughter) A man might fight fifty tigers without knowing much. . . . It has been said that the Fabian policy was a policy of permeation, and it was to a certain extent but they did not intend to try and permeate Sir William Harcourt or Mr. [John] Morley any more than they meant to try to permeate the tigers at the zoo with vegetarianism." ■ "A Derelict Plea" (unsigned review of *A Plea for Liberty: An Argument against Socialism and Socialist Legislation*, ed. Thomas Mackay), *Daily Chronicle*, 29 April 1892 (C859).

31 *Miss Newcombe's all day.* °*Press View at Dowdeswell's. Early English Masters.*

Sitting all day, before luncheon and after dinner, as this was the last day, the portrait having to be sent in tomorrow. Still reading *Plea for Liberty* during the sitting, which was not over until about 23.

Train to South Kensington 3d   *Star* ½d   Back 3d

April

1 *Go to the Empire in the evening to see the Ballet.*

Began *World* article, but gave it up after a few lines and went out. Called on Emery Walker at Cliffords Inn about Miss Newcombe's drawing and stayed with him until we went off together to Broad St. for dinner. Parted from him at Ludgate Circus and went to FE, with whom I stayed until it was time for her to go to the theatre. She got out of the train at Charing Cross and I went on to the Temple, intending to go to the performance of *Henry VII* at the Lyceum. On finding, however, that Ellen Terry was not to play I changed my mind and went to the Empire instead. Met Image and Horne on my way back.

Dinner (at Central) 1/–?   *Star & PMG* 1d   Train Blackfriars to Ravenscourt Pk 7d   Rav[enscourt] Pk to Ch[arin]g + ret[urn] for FE 9d   to Temple for me 6d

Reviewed on 6 April 1892 (C854). "The last place a musical critic ordinarily thinks of going," G.B.S. wrote, "is to a music hall." But the Empire had been including ballet—"the most abstract of the arts"—in its program, translating it into a "mixed *genre*" suggesting entertainment of a "seaside" humor as well as artistic dance. ■ Selwyn Image and Herbert Horne were regulars at the Empire. Shaw apparently met them as they left. Image and Horne were magnetized by the Empire's promenade, where refreshments were available, and which prostitutes used as their beat. In 1894 a group of outraged ladies would attempt to get the theatre's license rescinded because of the promenade's attractions, and a partition was erected to protect the eyes of the virtuous. Soon, however, young swells tore it down.

2 °*Crystal Palace Concert. 15. Go down to the Booth Colony at Benfleet with Miss Harkness, Tom Mann, the Stepniaks, etc. by the 23.15 train from Fenchurch St.*

Began *World* article in the train. Did not join the others until I got out of the train at Benfleet. Found Massingham and Fletcher, the editor of *The Daily Chronicle*, with them. Massingham was going down to stay with Fletcher; but came with us to the Colony. He, I, and Tom Mann dined at Fletchers', leaving the others to dine at the inn.

Train to Mark Lane 3d   Biscuits for journey back from Benfleet 1/2
Mark Lane to Portland Rd 3d   Train to Shepherds Bush & back 1/−

> A farm colony, "Hadleigh," established on 800 acres in Essex by "General" William Booth of the Salvation Army as a model attempt to cure urban misery. The experiment, begun the year before, was attracting much press attention.

3 SUNDAY °*Lecture for Hammersmith Socialist Society at Kelmscott House. 20. Postponed. Take the chair at J. T. Grein's lecture "Are Actors Puppets?" at the Playgoers' Club, Adelphi Restaurant. 19½.*

Finished *World* article, copying out what I wrote yesterday.

4 *Call on Miss Newcombe in the afternoon to explain about the drawing for the cover of the Fabian Tract. °Central Group Fabian meeting, 32 Great Ormond St. 20.*

Polished off a good deal of correspondence before going down to Spottiswoode's to correct the *World* proofs. Yeats was there. Emery Walker dropped into the Central Restaurant when I was dining there. I met Heinemann as I got out of the train at Sloane Square. He walked with me to the Newcombes' and talked for a long time. I did not get home until 19½, when I set to again at this diary and at my correspondence etc.

Train to Farringdon 2½d   Dinner (at Central) 1/−   PMG & Star 1½d
Train Blackfriars to Ch[arin]g + 1d   PMG of Thursday & Saturday
2d   Train Ch[arin]g + to Sloane Sq 2d   South Kensington to Ptld Rd
3d   Postcards 1/−

> William Heinemann (1863–1920) had founded his publishing firm in 1890, and one of his first books was Whistler's *The Gentle Art of Making Enemies*.

5 *Fabian Executive. 276 Strand. 17. Last meeting of 91–2 Executive. National Liberal Club. J. M. Robertson on "Payment of Parliamentary Representatives." 20. °Nellie Hartson's concert. Prince's Hall. 20½.*

6 *Speak on "The Woman Suffrage Question" at Battersea (Louise Ortner, 71 Gowrie Rd., Lavender Hill S. W.). 20. Sydney Hall. 36 York Rd. Meet FE at the Orange Grove at 14 and go to see* Lady Windermere's Fan *at the St. James's Theatre at 15. °Wind Chamber Concert, G. A. Clinton's, Steinway Hall. 20. °Miss Mackenzie's At-Home, 27 Torrington Square W.C. 16½.*

> Wilde's play had opened on 20 February and would run 197 performances. Later as drama critic (C1071) G.B.S. would observe—in a musical metaphor—that Wilde had "written scenes in which there is hardly a speech which could conceivably be uttered by

one real person at a real at-home; but the deflection from common sense is so subtle that it is evidently produced as a tuner tunes a piano; that is, he first tunes a fifth perfectly, then flattens a shade."

7 *Philharmonic Concert, St. James's Hall. 20. Call on Miss Newcombe in the afternoon to see the amended drawing. °Clapham High School Prize Distribution. 15.*

Reviewed on 13 April 1892 (C855). The poorly rehearsed program proved to G.B.S. "why the Philharmonic is the worst band of its class in London."

8 *°Wind Instrument Concert. Royal Academy of Music. 20½. Annual Meeting Fabian, Election of Executive, etc. 20. Barnard's Inn. Take the chair. °Edgar Hulland's concert. Steinway Hall. 20¼. °Bach's* St. John Passion *at St. Anne's, Soho. 20*

9 *Crystal Palace Concert. 15. Boat Race. 12. Sparlings'. New English Art Club. Private View. 10 to 18. °Kirwan's recital of* Othello. *Prince's Hall. W. 1.*

Got down with great difficulty to Hammersmith, 18 in the carriage. Met Macdonald (the dentist) on the platform. Talked mostly to Barnes at the Race. Went down to the Palace with Graves. Intended to catch an early train back; but my watch stopped and I did not get away until the 16.55; so that I did not get to the New English Art Club until 17.45. Bertha Newcombe was there and I saw her home. When I got back I had such a bad headache (probably from my haste and the egg salad I took at the Race) that I could do nothing but play a bit and go to bed.

Train to Hammersmith 9d   H[ammersmi]th to Victoria 2½d?   Victoria to [Crystal] Pal[ace] & back 2/–   Star ½d   PMG 1d   St Ja[me]s's Pk to Sloane Sq 1½d   S[ou]th Kensington to Ptld Rd 3d

G.B.S. "heard a new note in the orchestra, and traced it to the [new] first flute, Mr. [Albert] Fransella" (C855), who "shewed himself a fine artist." ▪ Although the Sparlings were Shaw's hosts, their house was across Hammersmith Terrace from the Radford and Walker houses, the back lawns of which looked out on the Thames, where, as Shaw put it (C854), "sixteen gentlemen" were "going to row from Putney to Mortlake" in the annual Oxford-Cambridge competition.

10 SUNDAY Finished *World* article. Did not get free until about 16, when I went off to spend the evening with FE. I met her going out for a walk, she having given me up. We took a walk together towards Acton.

Train to Shep[herds] Bush & back 1/–   Bus Acton to Shep[herds] Bush (2) 4d

11 *Monday Popular. Last of the season. 20.*

[Joachim and Neruda played Bach's concerto in D minor, and were so applauded that they at last returned to play again with a new accompanist in the person of Hallé, who was received with three times three, but who probably retained his own opinion as to the way his Manchester enterprise was treated by the London amateurs. (C857)]

> Reviewed on 20 April 1892 (C857). The concert was a star-studded success from which the instrumentalists, singers, orchestra, and conductor left covered with glory.

12   *Fabian Executive, first meeting of new Council. 17.*

Finally revised and sent off *Pickwick* review. After the Executive went to the Orange Grove and had a meal with Olivier, Wallas and Sparling. Went on to Hammersmith with Sparling and played duets with May until past 22, when I went off to FE.

Dinner 1/–?   PMG 1d   Star $\frac{1}{2}$d   Orange Grove 1/6?   Train to
Ravenscourt Pk from Ch[arin]g + 4$\frac{1}{2}$d   Shep[herds] Bush to Ptld Rd 4d

> "The Pickwick Pantomime," unsigned review of a reprint of Dickens's *The Posthumous Papers of the Pickwick Club, Daily Chronicle*, 14 April 1892 (C856).

13   Wrote *World* article. Also one or two letters.

Dinner 1/3?   Star $\frac{1}{2}$d   PMG 1d

14   *Go down to Arundel with Webb, Wallas and Beatrice Potter. Catch the 10.30 train, London, Brighton and South Coast at Victoria. Put up at Bridge Hotel.*

After lunch at Arundel we went off for a walk through the park. Miss Potter and Webb presently left Wallas and myself to extend our walk by ourselves.

Train Ptld Rd to Victoria 4$\frac{1}{2}$d   Victoria to Arundel 4/10$\frac{1}{2}$

15   °The Messiah *at the Albert Hall. 20.*

We walked off through the park and Wallas and I dropped the other two, as before, and walked off to Amberley and round the country. We did not get back until nearly 17. Then Emery Walker called having walked over from Worthing. Wallas and I saw him some way along the road. After dinner we sat chatting. The weather suddenly changed, and there was a heavy snowstorm. Corrected *World* proofs in the morning.

Bread & Cheese at Amberley 9d

16   °Crystal Palace Concert. 15. Go over to Three Bridges by 11.52 train *with party; and spend afternoon with Bertha Newcombe at Balcombe. Return 5.55 train from Three Bridges.*

Spent the morning answering letters and writing up this diary. Beatrice Potter did not come with us to Balcombe. Bertha Newcombe did not meet us at Three Bridges as arranged, as the heavy snowfall had made her give us up. We therefore overshot our mark by about a mile and a half, going to Balcombe instead of to "High St.," where she lodges. However, we found her at last and she walked with us back to Three Bridges, where we parted, returning by train in opposite directions.

17 SUNDAY   Worked at the review of Robertson's *Fallacy of Saving* all the morning at the hotel. In the afternoon Wallas and I walked over to Little Hampton and came back by train after strolling about the beach for a couple of hours.

"A Gospel for Spendthrifts," unsigned review of John Robertson's *The Fallacy of Saving*, *Daily Chronicle*, 23 April 1892 (C858).

18 [   ]

19   *Come up from Arundel by the 11.52 train. Dine at Albemarle Club, 13 Albemarle St., with Beatrice Potter, Webb and Wallas, and go on with them to the opening night of* A Doll's House *(the Charringtons) at the Avenue Theatre. 20½.*

Janet Achurch played Nora while her husband alternated between Torvald Helmer and Dr. Rank. The production would survive thirty performances despite vicious critical onslaughts from conservative critics. Shaw would write a long letter to "Mrs. Charrington" (*CL*) on the 21st detailing the acting shortcomings of the principals. Some of it was "painful," he wrote; "and I go to the theatre to be *moved*, not pained."

20   °*Speak at the meeting of the National Union of Warehouse Assistants at St. Agatha's Schoolrooms, Finsbury Avenue. (G. W. Patterson, N. U. W. A., 63 Aldersgate St. E.C.).*

21   ["... scribbling a letter in a train; it is my only opportunity. ...."]

From the opening of Shaw's letter to Janet Achurch Charrington (above).

22   *Fabian. Essex Hall. J. Watson Grice on "Pensions for the People." 20. Committee to Prepare Eight Hour Demonstration. 276 Strand. 16.*

James Watson Grice, a Fabian, would be author of *National and Local Finances* (1910) and *The Resources of the Empire* (1917).

23   *Crystal Palace Concert. Manns' benefit. 15.*
[... a huge success, and would have been made so by the unassailable popularity of the beneficiary if it had been the worst concert ever known. Its only fault was that there was too much of it. (C860)]

Reviewed on 4 May 1892 (C860). The concert included an overture, a concerto, and several operatic scenes in concert form.

24 SUNDAY   *Speak at the Labour League Eight Hour Demonstration, Clapham Common. 15½. (G. J. Symonds, 451 Battersea Park Rd., S. W., Labour League).*

25   *Fabian Executive. 276 Strand. 17.30. Sub-committee 16¼. °Stock Exchange Orchestral Society Concert. St. James's Hall. 20.*

26   *°Debate with J. H. Levy at the National Liberal Club on "The Legislative Enforcement of an Eight Hours' Day." Take the Affirmative. Put off on account of next item. Women's Suffrage Movement, St. James's Hall. J. H. Levy in the chair. Heinrich Lutters' pianoforte recital. St. James's Hall. 15.*

> Levy was the author of the book on Individualism which Shaw had just reviewed. ▪ Lutters, G.B.S. wrote (C860), was "accurate and businesslike, reasonably tasteful and intelligent, and altogether the sort of artist you praise when you want to disparage the other sort." He played Beethoven and Schumann.

27   *Philharmonic Concert. St. James's Hall. 20.*

[The Philharmonic concert . . . was better than the previous one. The worst of this admission is that the Philharmonic is certain to presume on it by so neglecting its next program that it will be necessary to invent some exceptionally poignant form of insult to flog it up to the mark again. (C860)]

> Seldom content with the quality of Philharmonic playing, G.B.S. (C850) nevertheless found the orchestra lifted this time by the energy of pianist Sophie Menter. "I have seen her leave Weber and Schumann for dead on the platform. . . . In the [Emperor] concerto, however, Beethoven, though somewhat put out of countenance at first, finally rose to the occasion, and gave her all she could manage of the softly brilliant, impetuous revelry which suits her Austrian temperament and her Lisztian style."

28   *Mme. Frickenhaus's matinee. St. James's Hall. 15.*

[I retired disheartened at the end of the first part, which concluded with those heavy and barren variations by Saint-Saëns for two pianos, on a theme of Beethoven's. (C860)]

> Fanny Frickenhaus, pianist (wife of singer Norman Salmond), was "not in the vein for Beethoven" and "rattled through" that part of her program (C860).

29   [   ]

30   *First night of* The Fringe of Society (Le Demi-monde). 20¼.

> Alexandre Dumas, *fils'* melodrama *Demi-Monde*, in an adaptation by Charles Wyndham and John Moore, starred Lillie Langtry as Mrs. Josephine Eve-Allen and would have eighty performances.

May

1 SUNDAY   *Labour Day in Hyde Park. Eight Hours Demonstration. I take the chair at the Fabian Platform, No. 16. Begin speaking 15½. Put resolution 17.*

2 °*Musical Artists' Society. Prince's Hall. 20. Fabian Executive. 276 Strand.*
17½. Sub-committee 16½. Call on Standring about type of Fabian Tract.

3 °*Charles Phillips's matinee. 32 Cadogan Gardens. 15¼. G. Clinton's 3rd*
Wind Chamber Concert. Steinway Hall. 20.

> G.B.S. on 11 May 1892 (C862) found the clarinet quintet by Brahms ("the Leviathan
> Maunderer") "a verbosity which outfaces its own commonplaceness by dint of sheer
> magnitude."

4 Elijah *at Albert Hall. 20.* Cenci Committee. Aerated Bread Shop. Rathbone Place. 17.

> G.B.S.'s verdict (C862) on the performance of "our pet oratorio" was "remarkable excel-
> lence," although he saw in Mendelssohn's music only "exquisite prettiness" rather than
> "true religious sentiment."

5 *Ernest Kiver's conert. Prince's Hall. 20. Florence Shee's concert. Steinway*
Hall. 20½.

> Ernest Kiver's string quartet played a new quartet by Carl Heinrich Reinecke, which
> G.B.S. (C862) found "full of all the composer's engaging qualities." ▪ Miss Shee shared
> the singing with Mr. Plunket Greene. G.B.S. (C862) thought her "a pretty talent" in need
> of further cultivation.

6 *Go out to Magny's in the evening.*

> "I am Laocoon in the coils," Shaw wrote (CL) to Janet Achurch in response to her letter
> which had followed his on the Charringtons' inadequate acting. Between his engagements
> the next day he wanted to see her, he wrote.

7 *Sparlings' in the evening. Elsie Lincoln's concert. Prince's Hall. 15. Call*
on Janet Achurch in the afternoon.
Gloves 5/6

> Shaw did not review Elsie Lincoln's concert, and apparently did not get to it, overstaying
> his visit with Mrs. Charrington.

8 SUNDAY [   ]

9 °*Otto Hegner. 15. Fabian Executive. 17½. Sub-committee 16¼.*

10 °*Harold and Ethel Bauers' concert. Prince's Hall. 20¼. Vaudeville The-*
atre. Matinee. Karin. °*Lawrence Kellie's vocal recital. Steinway Hall. 15.*
°*Heinrich Lutters' 2nd recital. St. James's Hall. 15.*

> *Karin*, by Alfhild Agrell, in a translation from the Swedish by Mrs. Hugh Bell, would have
> two matinees. Kate Bateman and Ben Greet had major roles, while Elizabeth Robins
> played the lady of the title.

11 °*Philharmonic Concert. St. James's Hall. 20. °Raddie and Taylor's concert. Prince's Hall. 20. Dinner of the Political-Economic Circle. National Liberal Club. 19. E. B. Bax on "The Theory of Value." 20. Evangeline Florence and Marguerite Hall's concert. St. James's Hall. 15.*

Vinolia Cream at Stores 1/7

> G.B.S.'s 18 May 1892 notice (C863) described Evangeline Florence as "an American soprano with the extraordinary range of three octaves from the B natural below the treble stave upward (the same, allowing for the rise of pitch, as recorded by Mozart of Lucrezia Agujari)." Marguerite Hall was "that clever and cultivated singer. . . ."

12 Nydia, *G. Fox's new opera at the Crystal Palace. 14.45.*

Writing letters about the *Cenci* affair all the morning. Mother was at the Palace with me, though she did not come down with me and left before I did. I sat out the opera and returned by the 17.48 train to St. Paul's where I took the Underground to Ravenscourt Park.

Dinner 7d?   Train Ch[arin]g + to Vict[oria] 1½d   Vict[oria] to [Crystal] Palace with admission 2/6   Blackfriars to Ravenscourt Park 6d? Shep[herds] Bush to Portl[an]d Rd 6d

> *Nydia*, an opera by George Fox, singer and composer, based upon Edward Bulwer-Lytton's *The Last Days of Pompeii*, was described by one-time art critic G.B.S. (C863) as "*a la* Gérome." The conclusion: "I find that the point of view from which he regards operatic composition is so far remote from mine that I shall continue to esteem him rather as a singer than as a composer."

13 *Fabian. Private meeting to receive report of committee appointed to prepare "Trade Exemption." Eight Hours Bill. 20. Barnard's Inn. °Behnkes' At-Home. 18 Earl's Court Square. 22. Hallé's 2nd Schubert recital. St. James's Hall. 15. °Demonstration of Gouin's method of teaching languages, by Howard Swan and Victor Bétis. Latin Hall. 34 John St. Gray's Inn. 11½.*

Wrote *World* article. FE was at the Wheatsheaf; she came to the Hallé recital, where I left her. Webb and Wallas and Pease walked home with me.

Papers 1½d?   Dinner 1/—   Train to Farringdon St 2d

> Hallé's Schubert recital was briefly mentioned in Shaw's *World* column (C683). Sir Charles Hallé, pianist as well as conductor, performed with the young Dutch violinist Elkan Kosman.

14 °*Viol concert, Arnold Dolmetsch. 20 Fitzroy St. 20½. °Private View. 19th Century Art Society. 9 Conduit St. 10. Go down to Oxted and stay with the Salts until Monday.*

Wrote letters etc. and worked at the Fabian Manifesto in the train. I missed the 17 train and waited for the 17.52, by which I went down.

Star ½d

> *Fabian Tract No. 40, Fabian Election Manifesto, 1892 (A14).*

15 SUNDAY   *Oxted. Oliviers' in the afternoon.*

We went for a short walk through the fields in the morning. Mrs. Salt did not come to the Oliviers'. After tea there we all visited Maurice Adams. Then it began to rain and we hastily broke up, Salt and I going back to Oxted. The Adamses came in for an hour later in the evening. Mrs. Salt and I played duets.

> Maurice Adams, a pioneer member of the Fellowship of the New Life, conducted a printing business at Thornton Heath.

16   *Fabian Executive. 17½. Sub-committee. 16½. °Aguilar's pianoforte recital of his own works, St. James's Hall. 15½. °Opening night of the Opera.*

Working at the Fabian Manifesto. Sat up to finish copying out and piecing together what I have done in trains etc. Sent it off to Webb. Wallas and Webb walked back as far as the corner of Grafton St. with me from the Executive, at which I took the chair. No tickets sent for the Opera.

Star ½d   Dinner 10d   *Chronicle* at Oxted 1d   *Ill[ustrated] London News Jubilee No.* 6d   Train Oxted to Victoria 1/8   Vict[oria] to Ch[arin]g + 1½d   Bus St. Martin's Ch[urch] to Grafton St 1d

17   *°Meeting at Headlam's to consider the programme of the Women's Franchise League. 15¼. Slivinski's pianoforte recital. St. James's Hall. 15. Winifred Robinson's Chamber Music concert. Prince's Hall. 15. °Compleat Angler at Dulwich College.*

My diary keeping has broken down at last—I am actually a month in arrear; and it is of course impossible for me to remember what I have been doing each day. Spent all the day and up to past midnight writing letters etc.

Star ½d   *PMG* 1d   Dinner 1/–?

> Reviewed by G.B.S. on 25 May 1892 (C864). Joseph von Slivinski (1865–1930) was, as pianist, a gymnast as well as artist: "His steely finger is always elastic: it leaves the piano ringing unhurt—indeed, you feel no more pity for the instrument than you do for a sword that has parried a brilliant thrust." ▪ The Chamber Music concert was briefly mentioned (C684): "I only got in for a scrap of a trio by Dvořák, which was not going smoothly enough to make me regret having missed the rest of it."

18   *°Otto Hegner. 15. Carl Fuchs' and H. S. Welsing's violoncello and pianoforte recital. Prince's Hall. 15. Meet Salt at 14 at the Wheatsheaf to discuss Cenci with Furnivall and Todhunter. [Eugenio] Pini, the Italian fencer, at St. Martin's Town Hall. 21. Call on H. Sonntag at 16¼.*

Still bothered about neglected business; but not making as much progress as yesterday.

Star ½d   *PMG* 1d?   Dinner 1/–   Assault at Arms [with Eugenio Pini] 5/–

The recital was briefly mentioned (C864): Beethoven required "a more contemplative and less impetuous temperament than Mr. Welsing's," while "As to Herr Carl Fuchs, I can only say that if his right hand were as skilful as his left, he would rank as a first-rate player."

19 °*Zangwill At-Home. 20. 24 Oxford Rd. Kilburn N. W. Sauret's first violin recital. St. James's Hall. 15. °Miss Lascelles' concert. Kensington Town Hall. 20¼. Go to the Trocadero to see Celia Patti dance (Headlam).*

Began *World* article.

Star ½d   *Justice* 1d   Dinner 1/–?   Trocadero 2/–   Programme 3d

Shaw would get to know Israel Zangwill (1864–1926) well, although he missed this occasion. Zangwill had made a sensation in 1892 with his novel *Children of the Ghetto*. A playwright as well as a novelist, he would use his literary fame to help promote Zionism, in which he was a pioneer. ▪ Émile Sauret, violinist, performed with a string quartet as well as with a piano accompanist. G.B.S. (C864) observed of Sauret that "violin playing is with him an accomplishment carried to the most brilliant degree, but not a calling." See 25 October 1890. ▪ Headlam's Church and Stage Society was promoting dance as art, and therefore as "moral" as the other performing arts. Celia Patti was a dancer apparently unrelated to the famous diva.

20 *Gaston de Merindol's pianoforte recital. Prince's Hall. 15. Fabian Central Group meeting at 32 Great Ormond St. Paper by Wallas on "The Unemployed." 20. John Farmer's concert, at Grosvenor House, in aid of Maria Grey College. 15¼. °Press View. Madame Ronner's Cats and Kittens at the Goupil Gallery.*

Condensed *World* article. Miss O'Connor, from Clapham, came here to tea after Farmer's concert. I went to University College at 18½, thinking that there was a Shelley Committee there; but no one came until 19½, when Furnivall turned up and told me I had made a mistake. Went off then to Wallas's. He walked home with me, George Turner coming part of the way also.

Star ½d   Dinner 1/–?

To G.B.S. (C864), Gaston de Merindol was "hardly more than a cultivated amateur." ▪ G.B.S. (C864) left de Merindol's recital "to go to Grosvenor House, where Mr. John Farmer was shewing what could be done with a choir of young ladies selected from the pupils of the Public Day Schools. . . . [T]o provide the opportunity—to carry the musical idea so far into the dense jungle of English middle-class Philistinism as to make such a concert possible—this has meant, in Mr. Farmer's case, a lifelong struggle with the powers of darkness."

21 *Bonawitz's Historical Recital, with lecture by [Edgar] Jacques. Prince's Hall. 15. Go to the Comedy Theatre to see the burlesque* Poet and Puppets.

Added a paragraph to the *World* article. Went down to Clifford's Inn to leave Miss Newcombe's drawing for the Fabian Tract to be processed. Had a chat there with Boutall, Walker being out. Dined at Orange Grove and went into the National Gallery for half an hour before going to the recital.

After tea I went out vaguely intending to go to some theatre. At last I went into St. James's Park and sat there until closing time writing some additions for the Fabian Manifesto. Then to Comedy Theatre.

Bus Tott[enham] Ct Rd to Chancery Lane 1d   Dinner (at Orange Grove) 1/3   Comedy Theatre 2/–   programme 2d

> "I had to leave after the sixteenth piece," G.B.S. noted with reluctance (C864), "and there were eleven, including the Appassionata Sonata, yet to come." ▪ *The Poet and the Puppets*, by Charles H. E. Brookfield, was a Gilbertian burlesque of Wilde's *Lady Windermere's Fan*, starring Charles Hawtrey (1858–1923) as "A Poet." In the cast in the very minor role of "3rd Young Man" was Harley Granville Barker (1877–1946), then fourteen and in his first stage role. Almost certainly he went unnoticed by G.B.S., in whose life he would play such a major role from 1900 to 1920. ▪ Had Shaw forgotten *Forget-Me-Not?* Given his passionate interest in Janet Achurch, who opened that night, with her husband, in Herman Merivale's and F. C. Grove's revival at the Avenue, one would assume that Shaw would have been at the performance. First-night tickets from the Charringtons would have assured his presence. For whatever reasons, however, he is not recorded at *any* performance. The play would close on 28 May 1892.

22 SUNDAY *Lecture at Kelmscott House for Hammersmith Socialist Society. (Sparling) Dine with Sparlings at 14.*

Corrected and finished *World* proofs. Spent the afternoon at Sparlings'. Nobody called.

Train to Hammersmith & back 1/–

23 °*Mme. Isabel George's concert. Portman Rooms. 15. Fabian Executive. 17¾. Sub-committee 16¼. Production of Mascagni's* L'Amico Fritz *at Covent Garden. 20¼.*

Wrote up this diary—nearly a week in arrear again in spite of all good resolutions. Webb called and we discussed Fabian matters, our conclusion being that the Manifesto was most urgent. Wrote some additional paragraphs for it.

Dinner 1/–   *Star* ½d   Opera Stall 21/–

> Reviewed on 1 June 1892 (C865). "Some of it," G.B.S. wrote, "is fresh, freehanded, bouncing, rather obstreperous, like *Cavalleria* [*Rusticana*]—was composed before it, perhaps. The rest is more artificial without being in any way better."

24 *Slivinski's 2nd recital. St. James's Hall. 15. FE at Wheatsheaf at 14¼. Lunch with Archer at 13.30. Go to Standring and put the Fabian Manifesto in hand.*

Went over the Manifesto and brought it down to the City. Standring was not there. On my way to Archer's I met Philip Webb. We had a long chat. I spent the evening at home and wrote a finish to the Manifesto, which I sent off to Standring; also sang for a couple of hours, as I have had no practice of late and my voice wants work.

Train to Moorgate 2½d   Moorgate to Farringdon 1d   *Star & PMG*
1½d   Dinner (FE & I) 1/7

> Slivinski's second concert at St. James's Hall was not reviewed, other than collectively, 8
> June 1892 (C866), with Slivinski's third concert on the 31st. "It was amazing to see the
> smallness of . . . his audience, considering the extraordinary quality of the perfor-
> mance. . . . If Slivinski meets [Anton] Rubinstein now, Rubinstein will not ask him
> whether he has succeeded in England, but simply whether the English have failed, as
> usual, to appreciate him."

25 °*Operatic concert. St. James's Hall. 15.* °*Westminster Orchestral Society
Concert. Westminster Town Hall. 20. Charles Lunn's lecture on Voice Production. Prince's Hall. 15. Call on Miss Sonntag. 17.*

Went in for a nearly idle day. Sang for more than two hours in the morning.
Lucy was here. Sang again in the evening and wrote some letters, notably
one to Miss Robins about a notice of [Clement] Scott's which she sent me.

Star ½d   *Morning Leader* (3rd number issued) [   ]d   Dinner 10d

> "It is now thirty years since I first met a singing-master [Vandeleur Lee, in Dublin] who
> was having a discussion with Mr. Lunn. . . . A more hot-headed, pugnacious, intolerant,
> impossible controversialist than Mr. Lunn does not exist" (C865). ▪ The visit to Hedwig
> Sonntag was for a German lesson. ▪ Scott's vicious review of the *Doll's House* produc-
> tion in the *Daily Telegraph* was the subject of the Robins-Shaw exchange.

26 *Janotha's recital. St. James's Hall. 15.* °*Handel Society's Concert. St.
James's Hall. 20½. Look in at Christie's to see the Leyland pictures etc. Spend
the evening with Bax in the Temple. 20.*

Began *World* article. FE was with me at the concert. We left early and went
into Christie's. Then we went off to go to Dalling Rd., as FE wished to get
some things there. She is staying with a friend in Cavendish Square for the
present. We came back together at about 19 and I went on to Bax's, where I
found Wherry Anderson and a man named MacIntosh. I did not leave until
past midnight; and it rained tremendously on my way home.

Dinner 1/–?   *Star* ½d   PMG 1d   Train St Ja[me]s's Pk to Ravenscourt Pk (2) 1/—   Shep[herds] Bush to Ptld Rd (2) 1/–

> Nathalie Janotha, G.B.S. wrote sadly (C866), was no longer the exquisite performer of
> yore. "I found her idly displaying her rare dexterity of hand and her capricious individual-
> ity of style without a ray of thought or feeling; so that I left sorrowfully after sitting out
> two or three barren numbers." ▪ Frederick Leyland, the wealthy shipowner, had
> continued to buy pictures, especially works by Burne-Jones. On 4 January 1892 he died
> suddenly in an Underground train between Blackfriars and Mansion House stations.
> When the Goupil sale of his collection opened, his estate—it would amount to more than
> £700,000—was in process of settlement.

27 *Fabian. George Turner on "A Practical Land Policy," Essex Hall. 20.*
°*Hallé's 3rd Schubert recital, St. James's Hall. 15. Clotilde Kleeberg's 1st
recital. Prince's Hall. 15.*

Continued *World* article but did not quite finish it. At the Wheatsheaf I met Dibdin, a Liverpool friend, and the artist Fowler. FE was there also; she came on with me to the concert, which we sat out. Then I went alone to the Fabian office, where I collected the *World* article and also the proofs of the Fabian Manifesto, a job which I had to finish at home after the meeting. Morison, back from Australia, turned up and spoke. Wallas and Webb walked home with me.

Star ½d   *Justice* 1d   Dinner 1/–?

> Robert Fowler (1853–1926), a Liverpool painter in the Albert Moore and Alma Tadema pale, neoclassic style, was a friend of Edward Dibdin. ▪ "Sat out" suggests some discomfort with the performance, which G.B.S. would not review. On other occasions he classified Mme. Kleeberg's technique as "dainty," lacking in verve. ▪ (Sir) Theodore Morison (1863–1936), Cambridge-educated educational administrator, would be widely traveled, heading a college in India and directing the British Institute in Paris.

28   °*Sarasate. 15. Call on the Newcombes in the afternoon.*

Finished the *World* article. Spent the afternoon with Bertha Newcombe, who was alone at Cheyne Walk. In the evening worked a good deal on the proof of the *World* article and sang a bit.

Star ½d   Paper 2d   Dinner 1/–?   Train St Ja[me]s's Pk to Sloane Sq 1½d   S[ou]th Kensington to Ptld Rd 3d

29 SUNDAY   °*Speak at Women's Suffrage Demonstration in Hyde Park (Mary Cogens, 38 Erdlay Crescent, S.W.). Altered. Speak in Battersea Park for the Labour League (G. J. Symonds, 13 Totteridge Rd. Battersea S.W.).*

Spent the whole morning writing a long letter to [August] Bebel, protesting against his contemptuous attitude to the Fabian as reported in the *PMG*. Also wrote to E. Huddart. Burns turned up at the meeting and spoke. Afterwards I went over to Morris's; but was too late for the lecture. Bax was there. He and I and Touzeau Parris went to supper with May. Sparling was not at home. Bax and I walked to the Broadway together.

Train to S[ou]th Kensington 3d   Bus Kings Rd to Hammersmith 3d Train Ham[mersmi]th to Ptld Rd 3d

> August Bebel (1840–1913), a leading German Social Democrat, was editor of *Vorwärts*.

30   °*Otto Hegner. 15.* °*First Richter Concert. Fabian Executive. 17½. Subcommittee. 16¼.* °*Isidor Colins' pianoforte recital. Prince's Hall. 15.* °*Lawson and Marzials' concert. Mrs. Jopling's studio. Logan Place. Earl's Court Rd. 15¼.*

Wrote up this diary and answered some letters. Searched out the old numbers of *Our Corner* containing *The Irrational Knot*, and tore the leaves out with a view to sending them to Chatto and Windus. Did not do so, as I thought it best to attempt some sort of revision first. Wallas came home to tea with me after the Executive, Webb and Olivier coming as far as University Hospital with us. Wallas stayed until 21½ and I did some singing and wrote a longish letter to Bertha Newcombe which kept me out of bed until past two.

Star ½d   Dinner 10d

31   °*Bach Choir Concert. Prince's Hall. 17 to 18¼.* °*Alice Roselli's concert. Chelsea Town Hall. 20.* °*Mary Phillip's concert. St. James's Banqueting Hall. 15. Else Sonntag's first recital. Steinway Hall. 15. Slivinski's 3rd recital. St. James's Hall. 15.* °*Miss Florence Christie's concert. Prince's Hall. 20.15. Clara Eissler's harp recital. Erard's, 18 Great Marlborough St. 15.* °*W. H. Brereton's concert. Collard's. 15. Lazarus's [farewell] concert. St. James's Hall. 20.*

Made out my Income Tax return for the year 91–92. [I found myself with tickets for nine concerts and a speech by Mr. Gladstone. At this I lost my temper, and declared that I would not stir out of the house all day. But I have never been a man of my word; and at three I began my round as usual.]

Star ½d   Dinner 1/ ?

> G.B.S. did more than prepare his tax form, reporting in *The World* (C866) that he found Miss Eissler playing the harp "as if she appreciated it, instead of pinching it to make it speak in the professional manner." Also, he noted that Miss Sonntag (although a friend) was "not at her best," but that Slivinski demonstrated "the most astonishing power of making the pianoforte sing," and that Henry Lazarus ("twelve years ago . . . the best clarinet player in England"), had, at seventy-seven, "fingers that trembled a little, but . . . something of his old habit of assured competence, . . . his old fineness of tone."

June

1   *Philharmonic Concert. St. James's Hall. 20*

Began *World* article.

Star ½d   Dinner 1/–?

> The Philharmonic "was good only in the accompaniments to the Beethoven concerto" (C866).

2   °*Lawrence Kellie's 2nd Vocal recital. Steinway Hall. 15.* °*Sauret's 2nd recital. St. James's Hall. 15.* °*Edith Higgs' concert. Prince's Hall. 20.*

Finished and sent off *World* article. Spent the evening at home over it.

Star ½d   Dinner 10d?

3   *Look in at the Guildhall to see the Loan Collection of Pictures. Fabian Special Private Meeting to pass the Election Manifesto. Essex Hall. 20. Conduct the Salès election business and pilot the Manifesto.*

Took things easy. I do not quite clearly remember what I did—I suppose I wrote letters and practised singing for a bit. After dinner I went into the City and met Theo Marzials, who has lately returned to London after an absence of nine years. We had a long chat. Then I walked along the Embankment to the Fabian office where I found Miss Brooke, Lorraine and Oakeshott. We went to Gatti and Rodesano's together for a meal. After the meeting I went to Wallas's. Found him walking up and down outside the house. He walked home with me.

Star ½d   Justice 1d   Dinner 10d?   Bus to city 1d   Maccaroni &c at Gatti & Rodesano's 1/8

Mme. de Salès, proposed for membership by W. S. De Mattos and Miriam Williams, was rejected, 55 votes to 14, according to the *Fabian News* for July 1892. ▪ J. C. Lorraine, of Norfolk House, W.C., was secretary of the Chiswick Radical Club.

4 °*Richter Concert. St. James's Hall. 15. Go down to Oxted and stay with the Salts.*

Went carefully over all the letters sent up to the Fabian about the Manifesto and noted their corrections. Went down to Oxted by the 17 train. The Oliviers' and Hilda Cox were coming down; and we traveled together. I found the Salts expected Carpenter and Adams; and I had to sleep at the station master's post instead of in the usual room.

Star ½d   Dinner 10d?   Train to Victoria 4½d   Victoria to Oxted 1/8

5 SUNDAY   Worked at the proofs of the Manifesto. The day was very rainy; but in the evening it cleared up and we went over to the Oliviers' and had some music there.

6   Finished revising and correcting Manifesto proof in the morning. After dinner went to Croydon and walked to Hayes; where I found at August Manns' house, FE with William Caldecott and Miss Bennett. When I got back to Oxted I found that Carpenter and Adams had arrived. In the evening we went over the common and Carpenter and Adams and Salt called on Maurice Adams whilst I and Mrs. Salt called on the Oliviers. We met them just going out for a walk and strolled about with them for some time.

Train Oxted to Croydon & back 1/7

Possibly Miss Harriet M. Bennett, a London painter and illustrator.

7   FE. °*Miss Douste's concert. Prince's Hall. 20.* °*Madame da Veiga's harp recital. St. James's Hall. 15.*

Went for a walk in the morning with Carpenter, Salt and Adams. On the way we met Maurice Adams. After dinner I played a bit. I came up by the 16.12 train. Went to FE in the evening.

Train Oxted to Victoria 1/8   *PMG* 1d   *Star* ½d   Train Vict[oria] to
Ch[arin]g + 1½d   Bus Chg+ to Portl[an]d St 2d   Train Ptld Rd to
Shep[herds] Bush & back 1/–

8 Siegfried *at Covent Garden. Alvary, Sucher, etc. °Ernest Moss's Chamber
Concert. Brixton Hall. 20. °Nettie Atkinson's violin recital. Prince's Hall. 20.
°Clotilde Kleeberg's recital. Prince's Hall. 15. °Opera Concert. St. James's
Hall. 15.*

Wrote several letters to the Fabians who had written up about the Manifesto.
Called at the Fabian office late in the afternoon and found Reynolds and Utley
there. Archer called at about 14, and read me an article he is writing about
the drama. We went to the Wheatsheaf together; and we afterwards met
Marion Lea (Mrs. Mitchell) in Wardour St. where I left them.

Star ½d   Dinner 11d?   Stall for *Siegfried* 21/–   MacDonald's a/c
£16/16/10   Cost of postal orders 2d   Bus to Shaftesbury O 1d

> Shaw's review was published on 15 June 1892 (C867). "The performance was vigorous,
> complete, earnest—in short, all that was needed to make *Siegfried* enormously interesting
> to operatic starvelings like the Covent Garden frequenters." Max Alvary (1856–1898), a
> Wagnerian tenor, was the first Siegfried at the Metropolitan Opera in New York. Rosa
> Sucher (1849–1927) came to London from Germany in 1882, singing the first Isolde there
> as well as the first Eva in *Meistersinger.*

9 *°Portman Orchestral Society. Portman Rooms. 20. Farley Sinkins' Orchestral Concert. St. James's Hall. 15. (Janko keyboard). Fabian Meeting of
Executive and Group Secretaries at office. 20.*

I remained all day under the impression that this was Wednesday and so
did not begin my *World* article. Magny called in the evening bringing me
tickets for the concert tomorrow. Wallas came home with me after the
Fabian and sat for some time. In the morning I spent most of the time
singing to get my voice into condition. Lucy has been staying here for some
days past.

Star ½d   Dinner 11d   Bus along Tott[enham] Ct Rd ½d   To Lincoln's
Inn corner Holborn 1d

> Shaw did not attend the concert arranged by Farley Sinkins, whom he would later (14
> June 1893) describe as "an enterprising concert agent." Sinkins was then promoting a
> new piano keyboard invented by Paul von Janko (1856–1919).

10 *Fabian. Private meeting. Adjourned Eight Hours discussion. Barnard's
Inn. 20. °Hallé's 4th Schubert recital. St. James's Hall. 15. Press View.
Menpes' Venice pictures at Dowdeswell's. Albert Hall concert for Distressed
Foreign Artists. Bernhardt, Coquelin, Sarasate, Albani etc. 15.*

Wrote *World* article; but did not finish it to sending off point. Mother came
to the Concert with me. The Fabian meeting was a short one. I went to
Muirhead's rooms with Wallas and we sat there for some time.

Star ½d   Dinner 11d   Bus Tott[enham] Ct Rd corner to Marble Arch
1d   Jaegers bill £12/17/3   Train to Farringdon 2d

Shaw did not attend the Albert Hall gala.

11 °*Sarasate. 15. Speak at the Labour League Demonstration in Battersea Park. 16¾. (A. Gaiger, John Burns Election Committee. 451 Battersea Park Rd. W. S.)* °*Norman Salmond's concert. 17 Grosvenor Place. 15¼.* °*Marie Wurm's concert. Prince's Hall. 15. Private View. [Mortimer] Menpes' Venice pictures at Dowdeswell's.* °*Maud Lancaster's concert. Portman Rooms. 20¼. Production of de Lara's* Light of Asia *at Covent Garden. 20½.*

Finished *World* article. Sang a good deal. Met Fitzgerald, the Australian delegate, at the meeting in the park.

Dinner 11d?   *Star* ½d   Stall for Cov[en]t Garden £1/1/0   Train Temple to Victoria 2d   Vict[oria] to Batt[ersea] Pk 1d   S[ou]th Kensington to Ptld Rd 3d   Bus to Endell St 1d

Reviewed on 22 June 1892 (C868). An opera with a Buddhist background and imaginative suggestions of Oriental music, *Light of Asia* was labeled by G.B.S. "sincere and original" but lack "intellectual vivacity," a "symphonic grip" of the music and "variety of mood." It would survive only three performances, but de Lara would go on to other operas.

12 SUNDAY *Speak for the North West Fabian Group at Willesden. Take the 10.47 train to Willesden Green. (J. Henderson. 1 Burns Rd., Harlesden).*

The meeting in Willesden ended in a heavy downpour of rain, though not until I had spoken for more than an hour. After dinner I went to FE. Met Cecil Sharp on my way there. I had not seen him since he used to be at Barton's on Saturday evenings years ago. FE told me a lot of odd and interesting things about herself. Revised and sent off *World* article.

Train Baker St to Willesden G[ree]n 4d   Willesden Gr[een] to Ptld Rd 4d   Portland Rd to Shepherds Bush & back 1/–   Sweets 1d

Cecil James Sharp (1859–1924), musician and writer, is best known as a collector of English folk songs and country dances. His *Book of British Song* (1902) led a resurgence of interest in research on traditional English music and dance.

13 °*Richter. Fabian Executive. 17¼. Sub-committee. 16¼. Leo Stern's (violoncello) orchestral concert. St. James's Hall. 15.* °*Macdonald's (dentist) at 10.*

Not up until 11—forgot all about Macdonald. Diary, letters, etc. Webb walked home with me from the Executive, Wallas leaving us at Holborn. I do not quite remember the evening; but I think I stayed at home and wrote letters. On reflection I am almost certain that I began work on the proof of the Fabian paper which I read at the Conference in February and which is to be printed as Tract 41.

Star ½d   Dinner 11d

Leo Stern's concert was mentioned in passing on 6 July 1892 (C871). The performance also included Stern's wife, Nettie Carpenter, in Bruch's first violin concerto.

14 Worked away on the proof of the Fabian paper. After dinner I went to the museum to get some dates etc. for it. Wallas proposed that I should go out with him to West Kensington and dine with his sisters. I did go; but I first went down to the Fabian office to get some further particulars. Utley, who has just been appointed Secretary *pro tem* in consequence of Pease's illness, was in command there. I returned to the Museum and Wallas and I went for a little walk before 19. We walked back together. Muirhead, Hale, his wife and all the Wallas sisters were there.

Star ½d   Dinner 11d   Bus Tott[enham] Ct Rd corner to Marble Arch 2d

15 *Last Philharmonic Concert. St. James's Hall. 15. Max Schwarz's recital. Steinway Hall. 15. °Tristan at Covent Garden.*

Finished and sent off the proofs. Left the Philharmonic early thinking that this was the day for the Press View of Ludovici's pictures. Found my mistake and went off to Covent Garden to make a last effort to get tickets for *Tristan*. Failed. Spent the evening at home writing letters, as well as I can remember.

Star ½d   Dinner 11d

"Max Schwarz, . . . a professor of the piano, reminded me a little of Heinrich Lutters. He is Director of the Raff Conservatoire at Frankfurt" (C871). ▪ Shaw's memory—he was filling in his daily arrears—was inaccurate. A poster (BL) announces him as speaker at a Labour League meeting chaired by Clementina Black this date at 8 P.M., at Landseer St. Schools, Battersea Park Road, on "The Interests of Women."

16 *Queen Vocal Quartet. Collard's Rooms. 15. Else Sonntag's 2nd recital. Steinway Hall. 15. South St. Pancras Liberal and Radical Association. Meeting of Council of 240. Athenaeum. Tottenham Court Rd. 20¼. Press View. Ludovici's pictures at Larkins's.*

Made a bad beginning on the *World* article—hardly able to get along. FE was at the Wheatsheaf. When I got home from Steinway Hall I found JP here. I had not seen her since before her trip to Australia. Spoke at the meeting.

Star ½d   Dinner 1/1   Bus to Portman Sq 2d

17 *°Edgar Hulland and Alison Phillips's concert. Prince's Hall. 15. Go to see* La Statue du Commandeur. *Prince of Wales Theatre. 15.*

Still stumbling wretchedly over my *World* article. At last I gave it up and went out. Could not even bring myself to go to the concert, and went into the Prince of Wales Theatre instead. Then on to Ravenscourt Park. Recovered myself later in the evening.

Justice 1d   *Star* ½d   Dinner 11d (at Pine Apple)   Theatre 2/6
Train St Ja[me]s's Pk to Ravenscourt Pk 6d   Shep[herds] Bush to Ptld Rd 6d   French Letters 20/–

La Statue du Commandeur, a French pantomime with music based upon the Don Juan legend, would become one of the influences which would converge into the "Don Juan in Hell" episode of *Man and Superman*, written 1901–02. "The piece needs to be visited twice," G.B.S. wrote (C871), "because on the first occasion one sees hardly anything but the petrified personality, or rather colossality, of [Abel] Tarride as the Commendatore. You lose all sorts of good things whilst you are gaping at the huge white marble man." Tarride, a Parisian actor-manager, was also a prolific creator of pantomimes and a collaborator/adapter on plays and musicals. He would co-author for his own theater in December a *Madame Pygmalion*.

18 °*Sarasate. 15.*

Worked hard all day up to 24, finishing the *World* article, and writing a long letter in the evening to the young woman in the Post Office who writes for information about the question of women's wages, etc. Maggie Gardner was here in the evening.

Star ½d   Dinner 1/1

19 SUNDAY *Speak for the Labour League on Clapham Common at 18. (F. V. Connolly. 64 Crescent Rd., Clapham S.W.). Wet—no meeting.*

Writing paragraph for Ellen Terry about the concert she is to recite at. Also letters, diary etc. Began article on "Value" for *Personal Rights Journal* in the train on my way back from Clapham, where I did not speak as the Common was deserted and the rain coming down in torrents. Met Cunninghame Graham in East James St. JP came in late with Mother; and I saw her to a cab.

Train Victoria to Clapham 2½d   back 2½d   Vict[oria] to Ptld Rd 6d

(Dame) Ellen Terry was still Henry Irving's leading lady at the Lyceum. Edmund Yates had passed on to Shaw her request that *The World*'s music critic attend the concert to be given by her young friend Elvira Gambogi (1870?–1940), at which Miss Terry (to promote attendance) would offer a recitation. Shaw also provided her with a publicity paragraph. ■ "A Symposium on Value: III," *Personal Rights Journal*, July 1892 (C870). E. Belfort Bax and Wordsworth Donisthorpe had written the first two parts.

20 °*Richter. Fabian Executive. 17¾. Sub-committee. 16¼. °Miss Allitoon's concert. Steinway Hall. 20. °Prince's Concert Society. 21.15 to 24. °Nettie Atkinson's 2nd violin recital. Prince's Hall. 20. °Contessa san Carola's concert. Prince's Hall. 15. Speak for Benjamin Jones at Plumstead Railway Bridge, 19¼, and at Abbey Wood, 20½.*

Wrote letters hard and corrected *World* proof.

Dinner 11d   *Star* ½d   Opera stalls at Chapppells £3/3/0   Cocoa & eggs at V[ictoria] Rest[auran]t in Strand 11d   Train to Plumstead & back 2/–   Abbey Wood to Wool[wi]ch Ars[ena]l (should have taken ticket to Pl[umstead] only) 2d

Shaw went to none of the concerts scheduled, giving that period up to politics.

21 °*Mlle Douste de Fortis's concert. Prince's Hall. 20½. Mlle. Szumowska's recital (pianoforte). St. James's Hall. 15. °Frank Boor's concert. Prince's Hall. 15.*

Took things easy. Looked over the proof of the Fabian History tract and sent it on to Wallas. Wrote a few letters, sang a bit, etc. Went out to FE after the concert; intended to go to the Douste concert, but changed my mind on looking at the program.

Star ½d   Dinner 1/1?   Train to Shep[herds] Bush & back 1/– (I forget how I went—possibly down by District and up by Metropolitan)

To remember this day is a bad job. It is now the 18th July.

> Miss Szumowska "played so beautifully and intelligently that I think Paderewski would have admitted that she gave his interpretations of the works in her program better than he, in his coarser and more headstrong moods, has often given them himself" (C871).

22 °*W. G. Cusins's concert. St. James's Hall. 15. °Max Schwarz's 2nd recital. Steinway Hall. 15. Das Rheingold at Covent Garden.*

I am afraid I must give up trying to remember this day as a bad job. It is now the 18th July. [I am frightfully pressed for electioneering speeches just now. . . .]

> The performance, G.B.S. wrote, was "none of the liveliest." The "wonderful water music prelude suggested that the Rhine must be a river of treacle—and rather lumpy treacle at that; the gold music was arrant pinchbeck; and the rainbow music . . . might have been pleasant deck music during a steamboat excursion to Hampton Court." ▪ The comment on electioneering speeches is from Shaw to Emery Walker, *CL*. The 1892 General Election would be in July, and Shaw was both writing and delivering political exhortations, one reason for the lacunae in his diary—he was filling in the gaps on 18 July—and his failure to attend many scheduled concerts.

23 °*Braxton Smith's concert. Portman Rooms. 15. Speak for Keir Hardie. 2 meetings (Keir Hardie Committee rooms. 161 Barking Rd. E.). Beckton Rd. 20. Henriette Markens and Arthur Lestrange's concert. Steinway Hall. 15.*

I suppose I began the *World* article. I spoke at two meetings for Keir Hardie.

Star ½d   Dinner 1/1   Train to Mark Lane & back ?   Fenchurch St to Canning Town & back 10d   Excess fare for going back via Liverpool St 1d

> James Keir Hardie (1856–1915), Lanarkshire coal miner who founded the Scottish Miners' Federation in 1886, would be elected Independent Labour Party M.P. for West Ham in the general election. In 1893 he would become chairman of the newly formed Independent Labour Party.

24 *Fabian. John Trevor on "The Labour Church in Relation to Life." Essex Hall. 20. °Hallé's 5th Schubert recital. St. James's Hall. 15. °Constance Howard's 1st Meistersinger lecture (1st act). Steinway Hall. 15. Elvira Gam-*

bogi's concert. Lyric Club. 15. Ellen Terry, etc. °Maude V. White's concert. Prince's Hall. 15¼. °Jan Mulder's concert. Steinway Hall. 20½.

I was awakened in the morning by Hutchinson who called at 9. We talked for a long time. This disposed of much of the morning. I did not speak at the Fabian in the evening.

Star ½d   *Justice* 1d   Dinner 1/1

Shaw would utilize the Rev. John Trevor's concept in the last act of *Major Barbara.* ▪ Miss Gambogi would receive some extremely cautious praise (C871), Miss Terry having, G.B.S. claimed, "projected herself into a recitation with such superb artistic power that I was quite unable to face the feeble superficiality of ordinary concert business after it. . . ."

25 *°Sarasate. 15. Shelley Commemoration dinner. Wheatsheaf Restaurant. Rathbone Place. 18. Crystal Palace Festival Performance of Judas Maccabeus. 15. Trevor to call in the morning. Open air meeting to support Beale. Crescent Place. Burton Crescent. 20. °Domonici's concert. Prince's Hall. 15.*

Trevor spent a whole morning here. Lucy was at the Palace with me. We came back by the 17.30 train. I did not go to the Wheatsheaf until 19. Spoke after the "Banquet." Then hurried off to the meeting at Burton Crescent and spoke there.

Dinner ?   Train Ch[arin]g + to Victoria 1½d   Vict[oria] to C[rystal] Pal[ace] 2/–   Gave Lucy, who had lost her purse 10/1½   Papers 1½d Train Vict[oria] to Ch[arin]g + 1½d

Since the audience, G.B.S. wrote (C869), "was the usual festival crowd, big and extremely barbarous," the soloists improvised "unscrupulous alterations of the [Handel] text in order to finish with the most absurd high notes . . . ; and the more outrageous they were, the better the audience liked them." ▪ "A Feast for Faddists," *PMG*, 27 June 1892. "Mr. Bernard Shaw regretted that Shelley's artistic excellence, now beyond question, overshadowed his importance as a leader of thought."

26 SUNDAY *Speak in the Arsenal Square, Woolwich, at 18½ on the Election. (Banner).*

Finished *World* article. I calculate this rather than remember it. Wrote paragraphs about [Eight-Hours] Bill for the *Star* and *Chronicle*.

Train to Woolwich & back 1/8

Shaw's political paragraphs were apparently not published.

27 *Richter. Fabian Executive 17½. Sub Com[mit]tee 16½. °Concert for Society Prevention Cruelty to Children. St. James's Hall. 15. Sims Reeves &c. Miss Palliser's concert. Prince's Hall. 15¼. Prince of Wales Theatre. Did you Ring? and La Statue du Commandeur.*

I forget what happened today; but I think I must have gone down to Beale's committee rooms to see Slack about getting boards to hang out of the window here. It was either today or tomorrow; and the chances seem in favour of today; though at this distance of time (18th July) I cannot be certain.

Star ½d　　Dinner 1/1

A miscellaneous program arranged by Esther Palliser, reviewed at length by G.B.S. (C871). "Miss Palliser produced a child fiddler, Arthur Hartmann, small enough to be Gerardy's younger brother, but grave, self-possessed, and capable to a degree which four times his years have not enabled me to attain. . . . I was [also] much struck by the singing of Mr. David Bispham, who seems to me fully qualified to take his place on the stage as an operatic artist of considerable distinction." ▪ This was Shaw's second visit to *La Statue* (which he "enjoyed . . . more than I had done before"), to which had now been added a curtain-raiser by John W. Houghton and J. W. Mabson, with music by Landon Ronald, *Did you Ring?*—a "tom-foolery," wrote G.B.S. (C871), "which at first moved me to majestic scorn, and afterwards brought me down off my pedestal (like Le Commandeur), and made me laugh with undignified heartiness." (Sir) Landon Ronald (1873–1938), at the age of seventeen, had played the piano solos in *L'Enfant Prodigue*. He would become a distinguished conductor—literally Hans Richter's successor in England—and in 1910 principal of the Guildhall School of Music. ▪ Shaw was campaigning for Liberal parliamentary candidate Edward J. Beale (who would lose). Slack was managing Beale's campaign.

28　*Go down to Dover and speak for Major Edwards at the Town Hall. 20. Alfred Reisenauer's recital. St. James's Hall. 15. Lunch at Reynolds's, 88 St. James's St., at 13.15 to meet Auguste Couvreur et sa femme "Tasma."*

Forget what I did in the morning—letters, I suppose. Spoke at the Town Hall in Dover. Edwards and a friend of his then saw me to my hotel. I walked a little way back with them along the sea front; but it suddenly began to rain as well as lighten; and I had to run back between the showers, sheltering from time to time in the seats. Did not get to sleep for a long time, being somewhat excited by my speech, which I delivered with great force—very unnecessarily.

Papers 1½d?　　Train to Dover (return) 10/6　　Insurance 1/–

Major Eustace G. Edwards of Willesley Park Avenue, Dover, a Canadian-born Fabian, and another candidate in the General Election. ▪ G.B.S. (C871) described Reisenauer as "a most Boanergetic disciple of Liszt, who has acquired a huge superfluity of technical power, which . . . he has resolved to take out in speed rather than thought." ▪ For "Tasma" see the introductory notes to 1892.

29　*Operatic Concert (Wagner program). St. James's Hall. 15.* Die Walküre *at Covent Garden. Come up by the 9.30 train from Dover.*

A Battersea man, an employee of Taylor's Repository, came up in the train with me; and we had a good deal of chat. Met Wicksteed on the bus.

Hotel Bill [　]　　Tip 1/–　　Lavatory at Richmond 2d　　*Chronicle* 1d　　Dover paper 1d　　Train Victoria to Chg + 1½d　　Bus to Grafton St 1d

G.B.S. (C871) praised the first act of *Walküre*, but thought the rest "not so good."

30　*Speak for Frank Smith at Hammersmith.*

Began *World* article, I presume. After dinner I called on Janet Achurch, who was alone; and we had a long conversation, interrupted only by her doctor, until some visitors came, when I left. I met Edward Rose outside; and we went off together in the train from Sloane Square. He got out at Hammersmith and I went on to Ravenscourt Park. I had intended to go to Clapham and speak for McKenna there; but finding that I could get no train I changed my mind and went off and spoke for Smith, returning to FE afterwards. She was ill, having fainted at the *Cenci* rehearsal.

Star ½d   Dinner 1/1?   Bus Picc[adilly] to Sloane St 1d   Sloane Sq to Rav[enscourt] Pk, train 3d?   Shep[herds] Bush to Ptld Rd 6d

Frank Smith would not win a parliamentary seat. ■ Reginald McKenna (1863–1943), Liberal candidate, would not win a seat until 1895. He would later serve in several cabinets and become an influential banker.

July

1 °*Hallé's 6th Schubert recital. St. James's Hall. 15.* °*Emil Sauret's Orchestral Concert. St. James's Hall. 20½.* °*Independent Theatre. Nouhuys' Goldfish. Opera Comique. 20½. Wrong date. Speak for Beale at open air meeting in Fitzroy Square. 10.*

Finished the *World* article. When I was speaking at the meeting in the evening, my voice broke down and became hoarse. This, in view of Bradford, alarmed me greatly; but, as it turned out, it did not disable me.

Star ½d   *Justice* 1d   Dinner 1/1?

2 *Go down to Bradford and campaign for Tillett (speak at 2 meetings).*

Went out in the morning to buy books to read on journey and lozenges. Whiled away the journey reading. Was met at the station by Tillett, whose wife was in the train though I did not know it, and Drew, Miss Conway etc. We drove off at once to the Committee rooms; and I spoke at two meetings after having had some warm milk and bread and butter at the house of one of the men. Then I went into another friend's house for supper; and I went off soon to the Royal Hotel, where I slept. I went there because Edwards of Liverpool, who had turned up at Bradford, was staying there too. I was much afraid that my voice would give out; but it was all right; and I spoke all the better for having to take it quietly.

Stevenson's *Wreckers* 4/6   Wicksteed's *Ibsen* 1/10½   Throat pastillis 1/–
Star ½d   Dinner 1/1   Train to Kings + 1d   Train Kings + to Bradford 15/10½

Benjamin (Ben) Tillett (1860–1943), founder of the Dockers' Union in 1887 and a power in the later Transport and General Workers' Union, would not win a parliamentary seat until elected from North Salford in 1917. ▪ W. P. Drew, chairman of the Bradford Labour Union, had led the Manningham Mills strike in Bradford. ▪ Katherine St. John Conway (Mrs. John Bruce Glasier in 1893), a Newnham graduate, was a Fabian who lived in Walthamstow, Essex, and contributed to a number of radical and labor papers, including *The Workman's Times*, *The Clarion*, and *Labour Leader*. ▪ *The Wreckers*, by R. L. Stevenson and Lloyd Osbourne (London, 1892). ▪ The Rev. Philip H. Wicksteed, not only a political economist but a translator and literary scholar, was one of the earliest proponents of Ibsen in England.

3 SUNDAY   °*Lecture in Victoria Park at 15¼ for the Hackney Group of the Fabian Society (Oswald H. Stephenson. 272 Richmond Rd. Hackney N.E.). Put off. Bradford. (Speak at 5 meetings).*

After breakfast went down to Salem St. committee rooms and corrected *World* proof, then drove off with Drew and set to work. Addressed five meetings. Had dinner and tea at the house of workmen friends of course. During tea there was one of the most tremendous showers of hail with a thunderstorm that I ever saw. After the last meeting I got away from the politicians and went off to call on Byles, whose house I had some difficulty in finding. When I did find it there was nobody at home. Shortly after that I met Edwards strolling about; and we went back to the hotel together.

4   °*Last Richter Concert. Fabian Executive. 17½. Subcommittee. 16½. Come up from Bradford by the 9.45 train. °Otto Peiniger's pupils' concert. Portman Rooms. 15.*

Reading *Wreckers* in the train. Edwards came down to the station with me. The train was delayed for nearly an hour by an engine off the line at Hatfield. After the Fabian I went to tea at the Orange Grove, where I met Olivier and his wife (he had not been at the Executive). I parted from them at the corner of Trafalgar Square and went on to Charringtons'. They were both at home and I sat there until 22½. Walked home.

Train Bradford to Kings + 15/10½   Hotel Bill (Royal) 11/– [?]   Tips
2/–   Papers 3d   Dinner 1/1?   Bus Picc[adilly] to Sloane Sq 1d

5   °*Speak for John Burns (A. Gaiger, John Burns Election Committee. 451 Battersea Park Rd. S. W.). Holden St. Board School. Shaftesbury Estate. Off Lavender Hill. Constance Howard's 2nd Meistersinger lecture (2nd act). Steinway Hall. 15.*

Wrote a longish letter to Ellen Terry sending her a copy of *Quintessence of Ibsenism*. The Salts called in the afternoon and Mrs. Salt came with me to the lecture at Steinway Hall. It rained furiously. JP was here in the evening. I wrote a long letter to Blatchford of *The Clarion*, asking him whether he had taken up Hyndman's line of attacking the Fabian. Did not get to bed until past 2. I was up very late this morning, as I awoke at 6, read *Wreckers* until 8.10, and then slept until past 11—a quite unusual thing for me to do.

Cab Steinway Hall to Chappells, Ch[arin]g + & Underground (with Mrs. Salt) and the Orange Grove 3/–   Dinner 1/1

> Reviewed on 20 July 1892 (C874), when Miss Howard's series of three lecture-demonstrations, with piano, concluded. ▪ Shaw's letter to Robert Blatchford was not published in *The Clarion*.

6 °*Opera Concert. St. James's Hall. 15. (7th) Call at Jaeger's and try on new evening suit.*

I forget what I did this morning—not much in the way of work. The McKernons have been much about the house this week. Stop—I believe I wrote a long letter to Ellen Terry and sent her a copy of *The Quintessence of Ibsenism.*

Star ½d   Dinner 1/1   [Jules] Michelet paper at Lechertier's 10d Train to Shep[herds] Bush & back 1/–   Postage "Ibsenism" to Ellen Terry 3d

7 Wrote the greater part of the *World* article and sent it off, the printers having a vacation on Saturday. Did not get much done in the morning; but in the afternoon a book on the history of the Leeds musical festivals came in; and I read it and wrote my article about it.

Star ½d   Dinner 1/1?

> *History of the Leeds Music Festival*, by Joseph Bennett and Frederick Spark, reviewed by G.B.S. on 13 July 1892 (C872).

8 °*Fabian. Private meeting. Tracts etc. Barnard's Inn. 20. Given up. Independent Theatre. Production of Nouhuys' Goldfish. Opera Comique. 20½.* °*Elaine at Covent Garden. Put off. Call on Archer in the afternoon.*

Can't for the life of me remember what I did in the morning. In the evening JP was here and the McKernons. I went to the Independent Theatre. Coming out I was talking to Miss Robins when Miss Newcombe asked me to get her a cab, which I did. Then I walked with Miss Robins along the Strand to Somerset House, where we got a cab. I got in to drive her home; but in Brook St. she remembered some forgotten appointment and we turned back. I got out at Trafalgar Square and left her to go on alone. JP was still here when I returned and I saw her to a bus. I now remember that I was occupied in reading Archer's translation of *Peer Gynt.*

Star ½d   Dinner 1/1   Bus along Tott[enham] Ct Rd 1d   Bus to Lincolns Inn Fields 1d

> *The Goldfish*, a comedy by W. G. van Nouhuys, had been translated by Shaw's friend A. Teixiera de Mattos. It would have only one performance. Alexander Teixiera de Mattos (1865–1921) was secretary of the Independent Theatre.

9 *Reisenauer's recital. St. James's Hall. 15. Spend the evening with the Normans. The Homestead. Barnes. Dinner at 19.*

Finished *World* article. Barnes and Massingham were at Normans'. He took a flashlight photograph of the three of us after dinner.

Star ½d　　Dinner 1/5　　Bus to St. Martins Ch[urch] 1d　　Waterloo to Barnes & back 1/–

10 SUNDAY *Dine with the Normans. Catch the 13.10 train from Waterloo.*

Revised end of *World* article and corrected proof of printed part. Massingham was at Normans'. We spent the afternoon photographing. Fisher Unwin and his wife [Jane Cobden] came in late in the afternoon. A little after 18 I went off to FE.

Bus to St. Martin's Ch[urch] 1d　　Train Waterloo to Barnes 6d　　Bus Barnes to Hammersmith 2d　　Train Shep[herds] Bush to Ptld Rd 6d

11 *Fabian Executive. 17½. Sub-committee. 16½. °Royal College Orchestral Concert. St. James's Hall. 20. Royal English Opera House. Sarah Bernhardt in* Frou Frou. *Call for Archer at 19½.*

Wrote a long letter to Yates about the [Frank] Harris affair and corrected *World* proof. Wallas came with me to Archer's from the Executive. On the way we had a meal at Gatti and Rodesano's. After dinner I called at Clifford's Inn and had a chat with Boutall. I left the Michelet paper to have some proofs of the design pulled for Bertha Newcombe.

Star ½d　　PMG 1d　　Dinner 1/1　　Grub at Gatti & Rodesano's 2/– Soda Water at theatre 3d

> *Frou Frou* was a comedy by Henri Meilhac and Ludovic Halévy. Sarah Bernhardt was well past her prime, and relied on paint and cleverness, but Shaw would go to see her several times more as drama critic. ■ Frank Harris had claimed that *The World* had libeled him as having "jumped from Father Damien's shoulders through the window of Marlborough House"—an alleged reference to his increasing intimacy with the Prince of Wales arising from Royal support of leprosy research through creation of a fund-raising Father Damien Committee.

12 *°Constance Howard's 3rd* Meistersinger *lecture (3rd act). Steinway Hall. 15. Maurel's lecture on "The Application of Science to the Arts of Speech and Song." Lyceum stage. 15. °Percy Pinkerton's concert. Collard's Rooms. 15.*

Rather preoccupied in the morning with the *World* affair—the upshot of the threat of a libel action made by Harris. I do not remember exactly whether it was today or Wednesday on which I wrote a long letter to Stacy of Bristol about Fabian matters there; but I had a lot of correspondence this week of this kind. Now that I think over it, it must have been this evening after tea. The O'Briens called just as I was going out to Maurel's lecture, and prevented me from dining until after it was over. Wet day.

Bus to Endell St 1d　　Dinner (at Orange Grove) 1/6?

Maurel's new lecture on singing, G.B.S. wrote on 20 July 1892 (C874), "was a much more businesslike affair than the crowded and fashionable reception of 1891." ▪ Probably the J. W. O'Brien who had begun cadging money from Shaw in February.

13 *Goring-Thomas Memorial Concert. St. James's Hall. 15.* Götterdämmerung *at Covent Garden.*

Writing letters in the morning, etc. In the afternoon, at the concert, I got a bad headache. At the opera I got horrible nausea, and after holding out desperately until just before the death of Siegfried I had to leave hastily. I was very sick when I got home and had a bad night.

Star ½d   Dinner 1/1   Bus to Opera 1d   Libretto 2/–

G.B.S. (C874) called the memorial to *Nadeshda* composer Arthur Goring Thomas "the smoothest of successes," and regretted that, despite his gifts, Thomas had been too "Frenchified" to have become "really original and powerful." Injured in a fall in the autumn of 1891, Thomas had not recovered either physically or psychologically, and on 20 March 1892 had committed suicide by throwing himself under a train at the West Hampstead Station of the Metropolitan Railway. ▪ *Götterdämmerung* had been reviewed in a summary of the *Ring* performances (C874), G.B.S. confessing, "After contemplating *Götterdämmerung* for over three mortal hours exactly as I usually contemplate the Calais light during the last half of a rough crossing from Dover, I fled in disorder, leaving Siegfried with about a hundred bars still to live."

14 Cenci *scenes, Bedford Park Club. 16.* °Elaine *at Covent Garden.* °Miss *Frances Simpson's concert. Portman Rooms. 20*¼. °Miss Violet Defries's *concert. Steinway Hall. 15.*

Began *World* article. Still very ill. Got better as the day went on. Met Archer by appointment at Charing Cross and went to Bedford Park with him. After the performance went to Todhunter's to tea. Left with FE and went home with her. Saw her off to the theatre and went back to Bedford Park and spent the evening until 21.50 with York Powell. Then returned to FE. I had purchased a stall for the opera, but did not feel well enough to go; so left it for Lucy.

Telegram to Archer 1/2½   Train Ch[arin]g + to Turnham G[ree]n 6d Rav[ens] C[our]t Pk to Ch[arin]g + & back for FE 9d   Same to Turnham Green for self 1d   Shep[herds] Bush to Ptld Rd 6d

15 *Fabian. Graham Wallas on "Origins of English Local Government." Essex Hall. 20.*

Continued *World* article and wrote notice of *The Cenci* for *The Chronicle.* Took the chair for Wallas at the Fabian.

Star ½d   *Justice* 1d   Dinner 1/1?   Train to Farringdon St 2d

"A Shelley Celebration," *Daily Chronicle*, 16 July 1892 (C873).

16 Finished the *World* article and wrote several letters. Also wrote a postscript to Fabian Tract 41, made some corrections in the proof, and sent it

off to Standring. Did not get out all day except to dinner. Played a little in
the evening.

Star ½d   PMG 1d   Dinner 1/1

17 SUNDAY *Lecture in Victoria Park at 15¼ for the Hackney Fabian
Group. (Oswald H. Stephenson, 272 Richmond Rd. Hackney N.E.).*

Corrected *World* article and wrote several letters. It was too wet for the
meeting in the Park though I went there to see what could be done. Spent
the evening with FE.

Train to Bishopsgate 3d   Broad St to Vict[oria] Pk 4d   Vict[oria] Pk to
Hammersmith 1/–   Shep[herds] Bush to Ptld Rd 6d

18 *Fabian Executive 17¼. Sub-committee. 16½. °Miss Fredeswide Slater and
Miss Martin Harts' concert. Portman Rooms. 15.*

Copied out a letter to the Brighton Fabian which I drafted in the train
yesterday about the election. Wrote up this diary. Went into the City to get
the Blue Book which I ordered at Spottiswoode's for [Johan] Castberg and to
buy an ink ribbon for the typewriter. Met E. Muirhead at the Central
Restaurant. Met Dell in Queen Victoria St. Bruce Glasier and [Samuel]
Bullock called on me at the Fabian. I walked home from the Executive with
Webb. It was raining heavily; and I did not go out again.

Train to Farringdon 2d   Dinner (Central) 10½d   Ink ribbon for typewriter 4/–

19 Wrote a longish letter to Castberg giving him the information he asked
for, and sending him the Blue Book. Mrs. Hewitt, our charwoman, gave me
particulars as to the prices of provisions. When I finished it was raining so
heavily that I did not go out. JP came here and went off to the theatre, leaving
Georgie here. I intended to go out in the evening; but the rain was still bad.

The World, repayment for Opera stalls, £7/7/0   Postage blue book &
letter to Castberg 4d   Postage Hunt's *Memoirs* back to York Powell 4½d

> *The Autobiography of Leigh Hunt, a new edition, revised by the author, with Introduction
> by his Eldest Son* (London, 1860). James Henry Leigh Hunt (1784–1859) was essayist,
> critic, and poet.

20 I forget what I did today. In the afternoon I went out to avoid some
visitors at about 18 and had some macaroni and chocolate round the corner
at an Italian café. Then I went off to Olympia (*Venice in London*) and sat
there until about 21.20, when I went off to FE, thinking that she would be
back from the theatre at about 22. But she did not come until near 23. I
read for review Ellis's *Vindication* of Wagner's part in the rising of 1849.

Star ½d   Dinner 1/1?   Maccaroni at café 1/2   Train to Shep[herds]
Bush & back 9d   *Venice in London* 2/–   Glass furnace 6d

The spectacle *Venice in London*, produced by Imre Kiralfy, was advertised as an "aquatic pageant and reproduction of the modern city." ▪ Part of G.B.S.'s music column for 3 August (C877) would be a review of William Ashton Ellis's *Wagner-Sketches. 1848: A Vindication.* "To me Wagner's conduct needs no apology, since it is plain that every man who is not a Pangloss is bound to be in a state of incessant revolutionary activity all his life long if he wants to leave things better than he finds them."

21   *Meet FE at the Wheatsheaf at 14.30–15. and go for a walk.*

Began *World* article. Had hardly done so when Wallas came in, wanting me to go for a walk. Eventually we went together to the Wheatsheaf and waited for FE. Bax came in, much to our dismay. When he left we joined FE, who had come in meanwhile, and we three went off for a walk across Regents Park and up to Hampstead Heath, where we sat on the grass for a long time. We crossed Parliament Hill to Highgate and came back by bus and tram to St. Martin's Lane, where we had a meal. FE then left us to go to the theatre and we came back here. I went on with my *World* article; and Wallas read the Blue Book on *Town Holdings* until 22, when he went off.

Star ½d   Dinner 1/5   Tram Highgate to Kentish Town (3) 6d   Bus Kentish Town to St. Martin's Lane (2) 6d   Grub at Orange Grove (2) 2/6?

22   Finished *World* article. After dinner went into the City to buy a gold pen; and found in the shop that I had left my money at home. Came back and spent some time oiling and cleaning the typewriter. JP and Georgie came. I sat playing until 21, when I took a tram to Hampstead, and after trying unsuccessfully to get into Dryhursts' walked off across the Heath to Highgate Rd. station, where I took the train back.

Dinner 1/1?   Bus to Cheapside 1d   Bottle of machine oil 6d   Train Farringdon to Ptld Rd 2d   Papers 1½d   Bus Euston Rd to Hampstead 2d   Highgate Road to Kings + (train) 3d   Bus Kings + to corner 1d

23   °*Speak at Hungerford to the farm labourers. (Miss C. E. Skerritt, Wokingham). 20. Hungerford Branch Berkshire and Wiltshire Agricultural and General Workers' Union. Put off to 30th. Elaine at Covent Garden.*

Went into the City in the morning. First to the Stores and then to Cheapside to get the gold pen. Began article for *Manchester Sunday Chronicle* on the elections. Miss Brema sent me a stall for the opera and begged me to go to see her play Guinevere. I went, and chatted a good deal with Sutherland Edwards, who sat next to me, and also a bit with Mapleson.

Ream of Blue MS paper 4/9   Ream of Typewriter paper 2/10   Isobath inkstand 2/–   Bottle of ink (Blackwood's Old English Record) 8d   Gold pen and handle 17/–   Dinner 1/1   Bus to Opera 1d   Star ½d

Elaine, by Hermann Bemberg (1859–1931), based upon Tennyson's version of the Arthurian saga, had opened on 5 July 1892 and would manage five performances. Nellie Melba sang the lead. G.B.S. wrote (C877) that Bemberg was not a composer "but rather a music-weaver who, having served an apprenticeship to Gounod . . . now sets up in business for himself. In Elaine we have the well-known Gounod fabric turned out in lengths like the best sort of imitation Persian Carpet. . . ." ▪ Marie Brema (1856–1925), English contralto who would sing at Bayreuth and at the Metropolitan, had the role of Guinevere. G.B.S.—perhaps out of kindness—made no reference to it. His other notices of her in 1892 would be positive. ▪ Henry Sutherland Edwards (1828–1906), journalist with *The Times*, later music critic for *PMG* and the *St. James's Gazette*. ▪ James Henry Mapleson. See 19 September 1888.

24 SUNDAY   °*Speak on Wormwood Scrubbs for the North Kensington S. D. F. at 18½ (G. W. Spry, 31 Rackham St., North Kensington). Fallen through. Speak at Grays, Essex, for the S. D. F.. (W. E. Monroe. 16 Oak Rd., Grays, Essex). Go down by the 10.28 from Fenchurch St. or the 10.15 from Liverpool St.*

Corrected proof of *World* article and finished and sent off the article to the *Sunday Chronicle*. Went to FE in the evening, not leaving there until 20½.

Train to Aldgate East 3d   Fenchurch St to Grays [Inn] & back 2/6
Bus City to Tott[enham] Ct Rd 1d   Train to Shep[herds] Bush & back 1/−

25   *Fabian Executive. 17¼. Sub-committee. 16½. South Kensington Museum Students' pictures. Meet FE at 15. Eight Hours Committee. Fabian office. 19¼.*

Wrote a few letters in the morning. Griffiths, Oakeshott and Wallas came to "tea" with me at Gatti and Rodesano's between the Executive and the Eight Hours Committee. Wallas left the Committee early and I walked home alone.

Star ½d   *PMG* 1d   Dinner 1/1?   Testing sight at St Ja[me]s's Station 1d   Train to S[ou]th Kensington from St Ja[me]s's Pk 2d   S[ou]th K[ensington] to Temple [   ]

26   Spent the whole day writing a long letter to Janet Achurch to amuse her at Clacton on Sea, where she is convalescing. Too restless to do anything else. In the evening went off to the Sparlings'. They were in [Frederick] Ellis's garden next door with Morris. The party presently broke up; and I went indoors with May and Sparling, who told me about their holiday in France. After dinner I started off with a vague intention of going for a walk somewhere; but when I got to Regent St. a passing bus tempted [me] to get on it and come back here. I am still much out of sorts.

Star ½d   *PMG* 1d   Dinner 1/3   Bus Regent St to Clipstone St 1d
Train Edgware Rd to Hammersmith 3d   H[ammersmi]th to Portl[an]d Rd 6d

27   Began *World* article. Was up rather late; so did not go out to dinner in the middle of the day, but had a meal at the Orange Grove in the evening. FE met me there by appointment. We strolled about St. James's Park until it was time for her to go to the theatre, when I went off to JP—the first visit I have paid her since she returned from Australia. Left at 21½ and went on to FE.

Telegram to FE 7½d   Letter cards 9d   Pears for Kate 4d   Omelette, cocoa &c at Orange Grove, FE & I 2/8   Bus Albert Gate to Brompton Sq 1d   Train S[ou]th Kensington to Ravenscourt Pk 4½d   Shep[herds] Bush to Ptld Rd 6d

28 *Eight Hours Committee. Fabian Office. 20. Call for FE at Museum after dinner and go for a walk.*

Working at *World* article in the morning. Wrote up this diary since Monday. At the Museum I met Mrs. Havelock Ellis—Miss Lees that was. Also Miss Cameron. FE and I went off by train to Kentish Town and walked through Waterloo Park and from Highgate to Hampstead by the Spaniards Rd. We rested on the Heath for an hour or so. Wallas and I walked back together. I sent off the *World* article.

Star ½d   Dinner 1/1?   Train Kings + to Kentish Town (2) 10d Cherries at Highgate 6d   Bus Hampstead to St. Martin's Lane (2) 8d Archer's *Masks or Faces* at Dobell's 2/–   Grub at Orange Grove 2/–?

Mary Cameron, a Fabian, would be on the Executive during 1893–94.

29 Began to set papers in order, and came across the comedy which I began in 1885 and left aside after finishing two acts. In the evening JP was here; and she urged me to get her the old numbers of *The World* and to cut out my articles so that she might paste them up for me. Set to work at them and got through the whole lot. Cut out Archer's also and packed them up to send off to him.

Star ½d   *Justice* 1d   Dinner 1/1

The "comedy" ("Rhinegold") was to become *Widowers' Houses*. Shaw's rediscovery of it in this fashion (and subsequent completion of the play) sets to rest any theories that he dug it up and finished it because he had specific revolutionary directions for the theater in mind; rather, finding it again was the impetus. See 25 August 1885. ▪ The *World* articles would become BL MS. 50961.

30 *Speak to the farm labourers at Hungerford under the Railway Bridge. See entry on 23rd. Leave Paddington at 17.15—Reading 18.10—Hungerford 18.51.*

Set to work to finish the comedy. After speaking at Hungerford we all went to Quelch's house for a while. Miss Skerritt and her sister came in the train with me as far as Reading.

Star ½d   Dinner 1/1?   Train to Padd[ingto]n & back 3d Padd[ingto]n to Hungerford & back 10/3

Miss C. E. Skerritt, of Markham House, Wokingham, was a Fabian.

31 SUNDAY *Speak on Streatham Common on "The Lesson of the General Election," at 18.30 (J. F. McAndrews, 51 Natal Rd., Streatham S.W.). 17.45 from Victoria to Streatham Common.*

Still amusing myself finishing the comedy. At Streatham it rained; as the audience would not go away I got rather wet. However, Crickmay turned up; and after the address he brought me to his house and gave me a dry coat and some supper. Malvin came in. Have not seen Crickmay or Malvin for several years. Came back from Streatham Hill.

Train to Streatham Com[mon] & back (from St[reatham] Hill) 1/6

> Crickmay and Malvin are otherwise unidentified Streatham Socialists.

August

1   °*Go to Dryhursts' in the evening.*

Rather knocked up after the speaking yesterday and the day before. I am still not at all recovered from the overstrain of the season and the election. Finished the third act of the comedy. It was too wet to go up to Hampstead. Wallas called at about 20½; and as the rain had stopped we went over to see the Sonntags in their new house in Grove Gardens.

> The "comedy" was "Rhinegold," which Shaw had gone back to with great dispatch; not until October, however, would he give it the revisions it still needed—and a definitive title.

2   *Meet FE at Cannon St. at 14 and go down to Hayes.*

Began to revise the comedy. FE and I found that we had made a mistake about the train at Cannon St. and we had to wait in the City from 14 to 15.7. We spent the time going through the Guildhall. At Hayes it was too cloudy to be very pretty; but it was warm and did not rain; so we were able to rest well on the Heath. I went home after she went off to the theatre; and then rejoined her at her house at 22.

Star ½d   PMG 1d   *Pick Me Up* 1d   Dinner 1/1?   Return tickets Ch[arin]g + to Hayes (2) 4/6   Ch[arin]g + underground to Can[non] St 1½d   Tea &c at Orange Grove 2/6?   Train P[or]tl[an]d Rd to Shep[herds] B[ush] & back 9d

> FE was then playing in Ernest Cosham's comedy *The Homecoming*, which had opened on 4 July and would run through 4 November.

3   *Meet Archer at Wheatsheaf at 13. Go down to Cobham with Archer by the 17.25 train and stay the night.*

Wrote puffs of Shelley affair and sent them off to *Star* and *Chronicle*. After dinner, met Nettleship in Oxford St. and went off with him to his studio to see his *Crie*. Then went to Jaeger's and got a new pair of boots. Archer and I, down at Cobham, went for a walk after tea, and called on Walkley. I slept at Hill's farmhouse, there being no room for me in Walden (Archer's cottage).

Star ½d   PMG 1d   Dinner 1/1?   Train Waterloo to Effingham Junction 1/9

Only *The Star* printed his piece, as "Shelley's Birthday," 4 August 1892 (C878).

4 *Speak at Shelley Celebration at the Hall of Science. Shelley Celebration at Horsham. 16¼. School in Albion St. °Fabian Eight Hours Committee. 276 Strand. 20.*

Archer and I walked over to Guildford by way of Hewlett's Corner and got the 14.5 train on to Horsham. We dined at the King's Head, and then went on to the celebration, where I found Miss Newcombe and Mr. Sandham. They came back to town by the 17.15 train with Salt, Archer and myself. Archer left us at Victoria. The rest of us went to the Orange Grove. Salt and I went on to the Hall of Science. Foote walked back with us half way up the Gray's Inn Rd. Salt came on to Tottenham Court Rd. Sat up until past 1 attending to correspondence.

Ginger Beer on the road 2d   Train Guildford to Horsham 1/7½   Dinner at the King's Head 3/3   Train Horsham to Victoria 3/1½   PMG 1d
Bus Vict[oria] to St Martin's Ch[urch] 1d   Cocoa &c at Orange Grove 1/–
Lavatory at Bloomsbury 1d   Tram Theobald's Rd to Hall of Science 1d

The meeting at the Hall of Science, 42 Old Street, City Road, was an evening event, separate from the suburban affair at Horsham. In London, G. W. Foote presided, and Shaw (according to Henry Salt's memoirs) "convulsed the audience by his description of the Horsham apologetics [of local dignitaries trying to whitewash Shelley's character]."
■ The Shelley "celebration" was ironically described in "Shaming the Devil about Shelley," *The Albermarle*, September 1892 (C884), reprinted in *Pen Portraits and Reviews* (1931).

5 *Go up to Dryhursts' in the evening.*

Did some correspondence and wrote up this diary since last Thursday.

Star ½d   Dinner 1/1?   Tram to Hampstead 2d

6 *Go down to Marple by the 10 train (Midland) and stay with John Trevor. Sleep at the Devonshire Arms, Marple.*

Worked so hard at the article on Shelley for *The Albemarle* in the train that I felt quite sick during the last 15 minutes of the journey. Trevor met me at Marple; and we went straight off for a walk over the hills, only stopping in the village for some bread and cheese. I was very tired when I went to bed;

but the walk over the hilltops in the wind did me good. In the course of our walk we went into a tea garden to get some refreshment and found ourselves with a party of mill girls out for a holiday. They were very respectable; sang the usual grace to the tune of the Old Hundredth; and took nearly a glassful of neat rum in their tea, every girl of them. Slept at the inn, as arranged.

Expenses entered opposite by mistake. Bus to St Pancras 1d   Train to Marple 14/7½   *Nat[iona]l Observer* 6d   *Daily Graphic* "Parl[iament]" number 1d

The "Old Hundredth": "Praise God from whom all blessings flow."

7 SUNDAY *Labour Church, Manchester. Speech in the afternoon (open air) on "Lesson of the Election" at Ordsall Fair Ground and on "Socialism and Human Nature" in the People's Concert Hall at 19.*

I lost my way from the inn to Trevor's and was nearly late for breakfast. When we got into Manchester we spent the day at his house, getting our meals next door. A little after we started for the afternoon lecture it began to rain, and it did not stop until I left Manchester. I held my umbrella up whilst speaking in the Fair Ground. We took cabs to the evening meeting and back. A young fellow whose name I forget had supper with us.

8 *Come up to town by 10 train. Great Northern. Call at Fabian office and go on to Magny's to get his corrections to the questions sent by La Justice.*

As I was looking for a place in the train George Standring called me and showed me that G. W. Foote was coming up to town. I got in with him; and we (Foote and I) traveled up together and had a good deal of chat about his imprisonment and one thing and another. I went to the Fabian office in the afternoon. Had supper at Magny's. Took a bus home from the station. The driver was bilious and very miserable—disposed to quarrel badly with his 15½ hours a day.

"Answers" 1d   Cab to station 2/–   Train Manchester to London 15/5½   Train Kings + to Ptld Rd 1d   Dinner 1/–? (I think this was at Orange Grove)   Bus to Holborn 1d   Train Temple to Monument 1d   London Bridge to Old Kent Rd & back 4d?   Bus London Bridge to Bloomsbury 3d

The editor of *La Justice*, B. Guinandeau, had sent him twenty-eight questions about British socialism.

9 *Lecture on "Socialism" to the Post Office Savings Bank Employees at the Memorial Hall, Farringdon St., Committee Room No. 16. 18. (Miss Amy Lawrence, 64 Guildford St., W.C.).*

I think I must have worked today on the Shelley article. I know I did not get away until it was time to hurry off to the lecture. After it I telegraphed to

FE to say I was coming and then went by train from Waterloo to Putney and walked along the towpath to Hammersmith.

Train to Farringdon 2d   Papers 1½d   Dinner (at Central) 10d? Telegram to FE 7d   Train Waterloo to Putney 7d   Shep[herds] Bush to Ptld Rd 6d

> Shaw added a postscript to his 12 August letter to Webb (*CL*): "On Tuesday about 40 female clerks in the G.P.O. took a room in the Memorial Hall & got me to lecture to them on Socialism. They were bored by the subject but fascinated by the lecturer."

10   *Call on Edward Rose in the evening. 95 Brook Green.*

Copied out the answers to the *La Justice* catechism as revised by Magny, and sent him the typewritten fair copy with the draft of my reply to the letter written me. After dinner went off to Wimbledon Common and sat there for a while, returning by Roehampton Lane to Hammersmith. Got to Rose's about 20. Spent the rest of the evening there. I am not quite clear about the day's work. The copying out of the French matter and the completion and sending of the article on Shelley certainly came in on these three days—Tuesday, Wednesday and Thursday; and I think I have placed them rightly; but I am not absolutely sure.

Papers 1½d   Dinner at O[range] G[rove] 1/4?   Train Waterloo to Putney 7d   Ham[mersmi]th to Ptld Rd 6d

> Shaw's reply, which took him a great deal of time, was never published. The letter, in French, is in the BL as Add. MS. 50677A. A facsimile is in *CL*.

11   °*Eight Hours Committee. 276 Strand. 20. Put off. Sparlings' in the evening—JP's en route. °Call at Fabian office to arrange about Scotch tour. 16¼.*

Copied out the reply to *La Justice* as revised by Magny and sent all off. I was too late for the Fabian. Wilbur Gunn, an American professional singer, was at JP's; but we had no conversation and were not even introduced. Mother was there. Got to Sparlings' about 21.

Dinner (at O[range] G[rove]) 1/6?   Bus Hyde Pk corner to Brompton Rd 1d   Train S[ou]th Kensington to Rav[enscour]t Pk 4d?   Hammersmith to Ptld Rd 6d   Papers 1½d?

> G.B.S. did not review any concert in which Gunn appeared.

12   *Call on FE in the afternoon and go for a walk to Kew. Fabian office. See yesterday.*

Went to the Fabian office as soon as I could get away, only waiting to write a few letters—I to do no regular work. When we got to Kew Gardens we found John Burns and his wife there; and I stopped talking to him so long that FE was left to stroll about alone during all the time we had at our disposal. This quite spoiled the expedition.

Bus to Holborn 1d   Swan's *German for Travellers* 1/2   Dinner (at Orange Grove) 1/4?   Train Ch[arin]g + to Ravenscourt Pk 6d   FE & I tram to Kew 4d   back 4d   Train Rav[enscourt] Pk to St Ja[me]s's Pk 1/−

13   *Press View. Pictures at People's Palace. 10 to 14. Call on Archer in the morning.*

Called on Archer on my way to the People's Palace. Spent most of the day at the Palace. Sat at home in the evening and finished the Shelley article for *The Albemarle* ready for sending off.

Bus Holborn to Bank 1d   Tram Aldgate to People's Pal[ace] 2d   Milk, scones &c 4d   Train Whitechapel (Mile End) to Portland Rd 6d *Justice* 1d   *Players* 2d   *PMG* 1d   *Star* ½d

14 SUNDAY   *Lecture in Victoria Park at 15½ for the Hackney Fabian Group. (Samuel).*

Was very unlucky in the morning. Attempted to walk to Liverpool St.; but found myself too late and took a ticket at Farringdon St. for Bishopsgate. Found that the booking clerk had misled me about the train; so got my money back and walked on, missing my train. Had endless trouble in finding out Bishop, the man I was to dine with. Did not get there until it was too late for dinner. Got some plum tart and bread and cheese before starting to the park with Bishop and Samuel. After the lecture Fay (the "Bounder" of *The Clarion*) interviewed me and came as far as Dalston Junction with me, Samuel getting out at Hackney. Went on to FE, with whom I spent the rest of the evening.

Train Liverpool St to Hackney Downs 4d   Victoria Pk to Hammersmith 1/−?   Shep[herds] Bush to Ptld Rd 6d   Sweets 1d

Edward Francis Fay (1853–1896) had written for the *Sunday Chronicle* until 1891, when he left with Robert Blatchford to write for the new *Clarion*.

15   *Call at the Fabian office.*

Felt rather tired after yesterday. Muddled over some letters; and then went off to Longdon's in Oxford St. to pay my instalment of the Italian trip expenses. Went on from that to the Fabian, dining at the Orange Grove on the way and calling at the Stores to get a photograph of Cunninghame Graham's bust which I left there to be framed. On my way back I was overtaken by Florence O'Driscoll and finding that he has just been returned to Parliament as Member for [South] Monaghan, I went into his rooms with him; and we had a long discussion about John Morley's position at Newcastle. When I came home I wrote a long letter to Webb.

1st instalment Italian trip exp[en]ses pd to H. W. Longden £10   *Star* ½d   *PMG* 1d   Dinner (at O. G.) 1/3?   Framing photo of Cunninghame Graham's bust at Stores 1/4

16 *Call on FE in the afternoon and go for a walk.*

Wrote longish article for *The Star* on picture exhibition at People's Palace. Then dined at the restaurant opposite Parliament Rd. station; and went off to Hammersmith to FE. We walked to Barnes Common and sat there for a while; then walked up Roehampton Lane to Wimbledon Common and back to Putney Heath, where we got the 19.4 train to Waterloo and had a meal at the Orange Grove, where she left me. I came home and wrote up this diary (ten days in arrear) besides answering a few letters.

Dinner (at Italian cafe) 1/6   *Star & PMG* 2d   Train to Shep[herds] Bush 6d   Train Putney to Waterloo (2) 1/2   Sweets 2d   Soup &c at Orange Grove (2) 1/5

"Pictures at the People's Palace," unsigned, *The Star,* 18 August 1892 (C880). The pictures, to the "Star man," were Bond St. mediocrities, including "work which every true connoisseur would go a long way to avoid seeing."

17 Wrote up this diary and polished off a lot of correspondence—no: I am mixing up today with last night. I believe I am right about the correspondence. After a hard day's business I went off to the Fabian office, dining on the way, and not getting there until close to 17. On leaving met Sparling, who told me that if I wished to call on Morris I would find May and Walker there. I did so at about 21, spending the nightfall in lying on my back on Wimbledon Common. When I got tired of that I began to scribble at the letter about the Newcastle election; and I kept on working at it from lamp to lamp as I walked along Roehampton Lane to Barnes.

Star & PMG 1½d   Dinner 1/1?   Bus to Chancery Lane (overshot my mark) 1d   Train Waterloo to Putney 7d   Chocolate & lemonade at Putney 8d   Train Hammersmith to Portl[an]d Rd 6d

The subject was John Morley's campaign in Newcastle. The Newcastle by-election was necessary because Morley had been appointed to the Cabinet and needed a parliamentary seat, which—despite Shaw—he would win easily, via Irish voters in the largely working-class constituency.

18 °*Last day for sending in Vote Claim to Bennell. Go down to Balcombe and spend the afternoon with Miss Newcombe. Train from London Bridge at 14.45 or Victoria 14.3. Frampton and Bell to spend the evening here.*

Wrote letters and worked at the letter about Newcastle in the train. Bertha Newcombe met me at the station. It was raining heavily; but it cleared up whilst we walked for about two hours and a half. I had cocoa and eggs at Mrs. Model's and then hurried off to catch the 19.3 train back. It just began to rain heavily as I approached the station. The adventure was a very pleasant one. Slept in the train mostly. JP, Lucy and Georgie were here entertaining Bell and Frampton. All left before 24.

Star ½d   *Freethinker* 1d   *Nat[iona]l Reformer* 2d   *PMG* 1d   Dinner 1/1   Tram Ch[arin]g + to Vict[oria] 1½d   Vict[oria] to Balcombe & back 5/4 (came back by London Bridge)   Moorgate St. to Portld Rd 2½d

(Sir) George James Frampton (1860–1928) would be the sculptor of Peter Pan in Kensington Gardens (1912), of Edith Cavell near Trafalgar Square, and other commemorative works. Bell was painter Robert Anning Bell.

19   °*Call for Rose at 95 Brook Green and go for a walk. Too wet.*

The weather was too threatening for a walk; so I telegraphed to put Rose off and worked away at the letter to the *Chronicle* about Morley, which I did not get finished to my satisfaction until it was going on to 17. Went off to FE, where I found York Powell dining with her. We saw her to a bus at Broadway; and I strolled back with York Powell to Bedford Park and took a train there for South Kensington. Spent a couple of hours with JP. Got home a little after 23. Dined at home as it was too wet to go out. At least it was too threatening. Fine sunset—hopeful for tomorrow.

Telegram to Rose 7½d   *Star & PMG* 2d   Train to Shep[herds] Bush 6d   Turnham G[ree]n to South Kens[in]gt[o]n 4d   S[ou]th K[ensington] to Portl[an]d Rd 4d

"Mr. John Morley's Seat," *Daily Chronicle*, 20 August 1892 (C881).

20   *Change [Harry B.] Samuels' address to 64 Cricketfield Rd., Lower Clapham E. Spend the day with the Havelock Ellis's at Haslemere. Go down by the 11.25 train from Waterloo.*

Went up to the top of Hindhead and lay on my back in the sun all day talking to Ellis. His sister turned up afterwards. Came back by the 20.13 train.

Cab Oxford St to Hungerford foot bridge 1/6   Train Waterloo to Haslemere & back 6/4

21 SUNDAY   *Go over to Massingham's after breakfast.*

Copied out letter to Blatchford which I wrote yesterday in the train. Caught the 13 train to Massingham's. Burns came in in the afternoon. We all three walked to Clapham Junction, where I caught the 18.35 train to Addison Rd.

People 1d   *Sunday Times* 1d   Train Victoria to Wandsworth Com[mon] 6d   Clapham Junct[ion] to Ravensc[our]t Pk (got out at Add[ison] Rd) 6d   Shep[herds] Bush to Ptld Rd 6d   Sweets 1d

The letter to Blatchford of *The Clarion*, like the last, would not be published.

22   *Call on Parke at the* Star *office in the forenoon.*

Called on Parke and went with him to the Central Restaurant, where we dined together. He wants me to write an article on "What London Wants" for *The Morning Leader*. Went on to the Fabian office. Came home and wrote letters etc., besides drafting a Fabian circular and a paragraph for *Fabian News*. This took me until near midnight.

Star 1d   Train to Farringdon 2d   Dinner (at Central Rest[aurant]) 9½d

> The circular was directed to trades councils and concerned the November elections of town councils. It is listed as A17 in the Laurence *Bibliography* from descriptions of it, as no copy has been located. ▪ The paragraph for *Fabian News* was unsigned, concerned the town council elections, and appeared in the September 1892 issue (C885).

23 *Call for Rose before 12 if possible and go for a walk.*

Did not go to the Roses' until 13. Found that he had forgotten all about the appointment and had gone out. As he was expected back to lunch at 14, I sat on the ground outside and began review of Engels' *Utopian and Scientific Socialism* for *The Chronicle*. Then went in and had some lunch. We took train to Richmond and walked through the park and through Kingston (where we had a swim in the floating bath) to Hampton Court, which was of course closed at that late hour. I had supper with the Roses when we returned.

Train to Hammersmith 4d   Ham[mersmi]th to Richmond ?   Ginger beer 1d   Bath at Kingston & tip 7d   Ferry 1d   Tram Hampton Ct to Addison Rd ?   Hammersmith to Ptld Rd 6d

> "Socialism, Utopian and Scientific," review of Frederick Engels' *Utopian and Scientific Socialism, Daily Chronicle*, 1 September 1892 (C886).

24 *Call on FE in the afternoon and go for a walk.*

Worked at the Engels' review as well as I recollect. FE and I walked along the towpath from Hammersmith to Putney and then went up and sat for a while on Putney Heath. I suppose I wrote letters etc. in the evening.

Paper 1½d?   Dinner (at Avalon Restaurant opposite Portland Rd. station) 1/6?   Train Putney to Waterloo (2) 1/2   Soup &c at Orange Grove (2)?   Sweets 2d

25 °*Call on Seifferts at 16 or half past. Cancelled.*

Seiffert called in the morning to put me off; and I did not get any work done early in the day. I quite forget what I did in the afternoon. In the evening I went to FE. On consideration I believe I worked at the Engels' review; for I now remember traveling first class to Hammersmith so as to work comfortably at it.

Papers 1½d?   Dinner ?   Train to Shepherds Bush & back 1/–

26 *Go down to Abinger to the Dryhursts'. Catch the 10.43 train from Victoria. Sleep at Dryhursts'.*

Corrected proof of article on Shelley for *The Albemarle* in the train and sent it back from Holmwood by railway post. Dryhurst met me at the station. In the afternoon two young brothers of Carr's came over; and we played cricket for a long time. Afterwards I played tennis with Dryhurst—at least as far as knocking the ball from one to the other can be called tennis. This violent exercise, coming after many years of London life, wrenched and strained every muscle in my body external and internal; and I was unable to move without pain afterwards. I shared a bed with Dryhurst and got hardly any sleep until about an hour before rising.

Train Ch[arin]g + to Victoria 1½d   Victoria to Holmwood 2/6   Railway postage letter to London 2d

27 *Go over to the Carrs' at Leith Hill in the morning; and get over somehow to Oxted to sleep.*

Desperately stiff after my exertions yesterday. Yet we did some cricketing at Carrs' until the rain came down in torrents and forced us to stop and go indoors. We had a meal and passed away the time for a while with Carr's microscope. Then Mrs. Carr drove me over to Holmwood station in spite of the torrents of rain. Carr came part of the way with us on foot, probably because he wanted to get out of the way of the Dryhurst children. In the train I amused myself by writing a lot of verses about the drive in the rain. When I got to Salts' I found Olivier there. In the evening Mrs. Salt and I played duets as usual.

Train Holmwood to Dorking 5d   Box Hill to East Croydon [ ]   East Croydon to Oxted 10d

> The shorthand verses are in BL Add. MS. 50725; the holograph transliteration is in the HRC. An eight-line extract appears as #564 in *Shaw: An Exhibit* (A304).

28 SUNDAY *Oxted.*

In the morning I wrote a little more doggerel and played a bit, as it rained horribly. In the afternoon we went up on the Common. Mrs. Salt went home then and Salt and I went on to Oliviers'. Shore, the innkeeper, and his wife were having tea there. In the evening, more duets. I read some of Herman Melville's story "The Whale"—enough to get a complete notion of his style and calibre.

> *Moby Dick or the Whale*, first published in 1851. Herman Melville's masterpiece was out of print both in the United States and abroad.

29 *Come up from Oxted with FE by the 17.31 train.*

FE came down and spent the day at Oxted. Salt and I took a walk with her up to the village before dinner; afterwards we all went up to the Common and sat there until it was time to come back to catch the train and get some tea. I spent the evening at home over the letters which had accumulated during my absence. Before Mrs. Emery came in the morning I copied out and finished the verses for Mrs. Carr.

Star ½d   *Chronicle* 1d   Train Oxted to Victoria 1/8   Bus Vict[oria] to Ch[arin]g + (2) 2d   Meal at Orange Grove (2) 1/6

30 *Lecture for the Fabian Poplar Group at the Co-operative Hall on "The Political Situation of the Labour Party." (A. C. H. Grahame. 175 Abbott Rd.)*

Finished and sent off the review of Engels to *The Chronicle*. A heavy job. Walter was here. Did not get out until past 17. Met Pease on the Embankment. Other Fabians came with me from South Bromley to Bow in the train. During the rest of the journey I scribbled verses to amuse FE.

PMG 1d   Dinner (at Orange Grove) 1/5   Train Temple to Mark Lane 1½d   Fenchurch St to Poplar 4d   Sweets 1d   Train South Bromley to Camden Town 3d   Camden Town to Euston Rd 1d

> The verses are quoted from item #565 in *Shaw: An Exhibit*, an HRC shorthand manuscript with autograph transcription on the reverse side. Cautioning FE not to assume that his wandering affections for other women meant any less love for her, he wrote:
>
> > Then grudge me not this overplus
> > That elsewhere I let fall
> > For if you were ubiquitous
> > You should, I swear, have all.

31 *If Wallas does not call, dine at the Wheatsheaf at 14 and meet him there.*

Corrected proof of review for *Chronicle*. Wallas called; and we dined together. We came back here to escape a bad shower of rain and found JP and Georgie here with their traps for their journey to Ireland. Wallas and I then called on the Sonntags. Jim Headlam was there. When we came back Wallas parted from me at the door. JP was still here. She and Georgie went over by the Irish Mail. Wrote up this diary.

Star ½d   *PMG* 1d   Dinner 1/1   Train to St John's Wood 1d

September

1 *Meeting of South St. Pancras Executive Committee. 195 Gray's Inn Rd. 20.15.*

Worked at the revision of *The Irrational Knot* for republication. Butterfield, Lucy's husband, called here to say goodbye. He leaves for India tomorrow. In the morning I wrote a letter to *The Chronicle* about some blundering criticisms of "Bad English" which have been appearing in it.

Star ½d   *Nat[ional] Ref[ormer]* 2d   *Freethinker* 1d   Dinner 1/2 Train to Kings Cross 1d

> "And Which, Etcetera," signed letter, *Daily Chronicle*, 2 September 1892 (C887).

2 Still at *The Irrational Knot*. In the evening I walked to the Royal Oak on my way to Hammersmith, where I called on the Sparlings and played duets with May. Walker came in; but he and Sparling had to go off to a meeting. I missed the last train back, and had to walk home—a heavy job, but one which did me good, I think. In the morning I wrote a couple of letters to provincial papers contradicting statements that I had gone down to Newcastle to oppose Morley at the recent election.

Justice 1d   *Star* ½d   *PMG* 1d   Dinner 1/2?   Train Royal Oak to H[ammersmi]th 3d

3   Felt the effects of yesterday's work too much to go at the *Knot* again. Wrote a long letter to Miss Churchill giving her the advice she asked for concerning her position at the Margate Theatre. After dinner went down to Barnes and spent the evening with the Normans. We passed the time first in rifle shooting in the garden—then singing, chatting etc.

Star ½d   *PMG* 1d   Dinner 10d   Train Waterloo to Barnes 7d Barnes to Waterloo 7d

   Kate Churchill, of 21 Woburn Place, W.C., apparently an actress.

4 SUNDAY   Wrote fresh matter for the *Knot*. After dinner brought *The Albemarle* down to the *Chronicle* office for Norman. Then went to FE. We walked to Kew and came back by tram.

Train to Farringdon Rd 2d   Blackfriars to Ravenscourt Park 7d   Tram Kew to Dalling Rd (2) 6d

5   °*Tea at 18¼ with Philip Webb. 1 Raymond Buildings, Gray's Inn. Special meeting of the Art Workers Guild Italian Expedition to consider the cholera. 29 Great George St. Westminster. 20½. Fabian Executive. 276 Strand. 17. °Fabian Eight Hours Committee. 276 Strand. 20.*

Still working at the *Knot*. Met William Thompson at the Wheatsheaf and had a chat with him. After the Executive went to the Orange Grove with Olivier for a meal. Stole down to the National Liberal Club with him, then, leaving him, went back to the lavatory at Trafalgar Square and had a wash; then to the meeting at Westminster, where it was decided to give up the Italian Expedition. Lang (the oculist) asked me to go home with him to see his new house (22 Cavendish Square). Cockerell came also. He tested our eyes and declared that my sight is perfectly normal, as Borden declared it to be years ago. Am relieved to find that I do not need glasses yet. I waited a while after Cockerell left to have my field of vision explored. McKernon was here in the afternoon.

Star ½d   *PMG* 1d   Dinner 1/1   Chocolate &c at Orange Grove 1/–? Lavatory 2d

6   *Tea with Philip Webb put off from yesterday. 18¼. Meet FE at Earl's Court station in the covered bridge leading to the Horticultural Hall at 14.30 and go to see Buffalo Bill's show.*

Was up so late that there was hardly time to do anything before starting.
Star & PMG 1½d   Dinner (at Orange Grove) 11d   Train Ch[arin]g +
to Earls Court & back, with admission to Horticultural Ex[hibition] 1/6
F.E. admission 1/–   Programmes &c 8d   Seats at Wild West show 6/–
Floral Maze 1/–   Tea & Cocoa 10d   *Pick Me Up* (comic paper) 1d
Excess fare Ch[arin]g + to Temple 1d

> William Frederick ("Buffalo Bill") Cody (1846–1917), one-time Buffalo hunter and Indian
> fighter, organized in 1883 his first Wild West exhibition, a traveling show which eventually
> starred crack shot Annie Oakley and Chief Sitting Bull and became an American institu-
> tion. The tours earned Cody a fortune, which he then lost through mismanagement.

7   *Lyric Theatre. Production of* Cigarette. *20.15.*

Working at the *Knot*. It got very wet in the afternoon. I had arranged to
meet FE on the Duke of York's steps at 16.45; but I telegraphed to appoint
the Orange Grove instead. We met and traipsed about—first to Oxford [St.],
where I bought a couple of Italian photographs; then to Museum St. on a
false rumour of a photograph shot there. Then she walked along Gower St.
with me and got into a bus for Tottenham Court Rd. I came home and
dried my clothes. I came away after the second act of the opera, which was
very silly, and wrote some letters and this diary.

Telegram to FE 10½d   Dinner (at Orange Grove) 2/6   Photograph of
Donatello's Gattamelata statue at Padua 2/6   Horse's head from Naples
Museum 1/–

> G.B.S. on 28 September 1892 (C888) called *Cigarette* "a work of uncertain *genre*, melodra-
> matic and farcical in alternate episodes," some of its light-opera moments "intended to
> be comic but void to a stupefying degree of any passable nonsense or fun, not to say sense
> of humor." Its music was by J. Haydn Parry, libretto by W. E. St. Leger and Barry
> Montour. It would have eighty-eight performances. • The *Gattamelata* of Donatello
> (Donato di Niccolo di Betto Bardi, 1386?–1466) stands before the Basilica di Sant' Antonio
> in Padua.

8   In the morning Mrs. Stanley, the landlady, called in great agitation
about the house. Wrote a long affair for *The Daily Chronicle* purporting to
be an account of a Trade Congress. Sent it off just in time for the 19 post;
and then walked over to FE's. Walter was here in the afternoon; McKernon
in the morning.

Nat[iona]l Reformer 2d   *Freethinker* 1d   *PMG* 1d   *Star* ½d   Dinner 1/4   Train from Shep[herds] Bush 6d   Sweets 1d

> Not accepted by the *Chronicle*, "Another Trade Congress" (signed "From a Correspon-
> dent") was published in *Workman's Times*, 1 October 1892 (C889).

9   *Go down to Leith Hill to the Carrs' in the evening by 16.55 from Victoria
to Holmwood.*

Worked, as well as I remember, at the *Knot*. Was nearly late for the train—
had to run all the way from Rathbone Place to Charing Cross. Mrs. Carr

met us at the station (Carr had come down in the London Bridge portion of the train) and drove us over, Carr walking most of the way. Spent the evening talking.

Papers 8½d (*PM Budget, P[all] M[all] Gazette, Star & Pick Me Up*) Dinner 1/1?   Train Ch[arin]g + to Victoria 1½d

10 °*Opening of the new theatre (the Trafalgar Square) in St. Martin's Lane with Toulmouche's* Wedding Eve.

We walked to Abinger Hutch where we lunched, and back. In the evening Carr read Thucydides aloud to us.

> Shaw would see the play on the 15th and declare it "homogeneous in its triviality" (C888). *The Wedding Eve*, a comic opera with music by F. Toulmouche and Ernest Ford, and libretto by William Yardley, adapted from *La Veilée de Noces* by Alexandre Bisson and Bureau Jattiot, would have sixty-two performances. The Trafalgar Square is now the Duke of York's Theatre.

11 SUNDAY   We walked over to Shore, where we lunched. Back across the hills. Evening same as yesterday.

12 °*Fabian Executive. 17¼.*

We walked over to Ockley to get Carr's business telegram and from that to Capel where he lunched. On the way back we helped to pull a horse out of a pond into which it had fallen. Thucydides and Plato in the evening.

13 *Come up from Leith Hill by the 9.20 train from Holmwood to London Bridge.*

Mrs. Carr drove us over from Oakeshott Farm to the station. I parted from Carr at the corner of the Bank of England. Wrote up diary, answered letters, etc. Worked at the *Knot* after dinner. Archer called, having just come back from a tour in Ireland. We went to the Wheatsheaf together, I went to the Stores and left some photographs there to be framed. JP and Georgie were here in the evening. I walked to Hammersmith to see FE.

Tip to servant at Oakeshott farm 3/6   Train Holmwood to London Bridge 2/6   Moorgate to Portland Road 2½d   *Star & PMG* 1½d   Dinner 1/1   Bus St. Martin's Lane to Grafton St 1d   Train Shep[herds] Bush to Ptld Rd 6d   Dinner (I think this was at Wheatsheaf) 1/–?   Telegram to FE 6d

14 *Art Workers Guild Italian Expedition starts. Abandoned because of the cholera. Take the 14.45 train Waterloo to Wandsworth and go for a walk with [John F.] Runciman.*

Worked at *The Irrational Knot*. Runciman and I walked from Wandsworth across Wimbledon Common and into Richmond Park, where we lay on the grass for a while, and then went on to Richmond, where we had a meal. We then walked along the towpath to Kew and then by road to Shaftesbury Rd., where we took train, and I went to Sparlings' and spent the rest of the evening there. Walker came in and walked with me to the station. I came back by the 23.34 train.

Star ½d   PMG 1d   Train Waterloo to Wandsworth 4d   Maccaroni &c at Richmond 1/7   Train Ham[mersmi]th to Portland Road 6d

15 Worked at the *Knot* in the morning. FE got into the train with me at Ravenscourt Park by appointment; and we went together to Richmond and walked to the Park, where we lay down for a while, and then went out at Sheen Gate and walked to Barnes, where we took train to Waterloo at 18.19 after watching the sunset. She left me at the Orange Grove. I went into the new Trafalgar Theatre and saw the first act of *The Wedding Eve*. Then came home and wrote up this diary, besides writing to Sonnenschein to ask for my final account of sales of *An Unsocial Socialist*, and adding a short stroke at the *Knot*. Went to bed with a headache.

Star ½d   *Freethinker* 1d   *Nat[iona]l Reformer* 2d   *PM Budget* 6d PMG 1d   Dinner 1/1   Train to Richmond 1/2   Barnes to Waterloo (2) 1/2   Grub at Orange Grove 2/9   Trafalgar Theatre 2/6   programme 2d   Telegram to FE 7½d

16 Found the headache still bad. It may be the result of watching the sun on Barnes Common last evening. At any rate I did nothing but read desultorily the translation of *Peer Gynt* just published, and Emmonds' essays on architecture which Philip Webb lent me. Instead of going out to dinner I ate some bread, apples, etc. Went out feeling rather indisposed, and wandering to the British Museum, where I had a talk with Wallas and read Tom Paine's letter to Washington. Besides looking through a large volume of reproductions of Martin Schongauer's engravings. Left the Museum at about 19½. Played a bit and wrote a letter or two when I got back.

Justice 1d   *Star* ½d

Alexander Hamann Emmonds (1816–?), architect. ▪ Martin Schongauer (1440?–1491), engraver.

17 *Go down to Oxted and stay with Salts.*

Wallas called whilst I was dressing. We went to his rooms at Ormond St. for a moment and then to Victoria, where I left my bag in the cloak room. Then we went to Richmond and walked through the Park to Putney, where Wallas left me and I took train to Clapham Junction for Oxted, giving up the idea of fetching my bag at Victoria. Olivier was at Salts' when I arrived—he only stayed a few minutes. In the evening Mrs. Salt and I played duets.

PMG 1d   Train Temple to Victoria 2d   Cloak room fee 2d   Victoria
to Richmond 1/–   Dinner at Ferrari's rest[auran]t at Richmond 1/9
Train Putney to Vauxhall (got out at Clapham Junction) 4d   Clapham
J[unction] to Oxted 1/5½   *Rev[iew] of Reviews* 6d

18 SUNDAY   *Oxted.*

In the morning Salt and I walked to Oxted village. In the afternoon we all three
went over to Oliviers' and afterwards called on Hartley. In the evening Mrs. Salt
and I played duets a good deal. Later on we tried spiritualism; and Salt and I
cheated Mrs. Salt outrageously by an exhibition of table turning.

> Eustace D. Hartley (?–1897), a Fabian, also had a London residence, at 15 Museum
> Mansions, Great Russell Street, W.C.

19   °*Fabian Central Group Meeting. 32 Great Ormond St. W. C. 20. Fabian
Executive. 276 Strand. 17½. Preliminary Committee. 16¼. °Eight Hours Committee. 276 Strand. 20. Come up from Oxted by the 10.43 train.*

Olivier came up in the train with me. Wrote letters etc. when I got home.
Went on to Fabian office after dinner, and was there from 16¼ to about 19. I
went to Hammersmith with Sparling, his wife being away at Kelmscott. We
called at Morris's as we passed and stayed there chatting with him for a
long time. Walker came in.

Train Oxted to Victoria 1/8   *Daily Chronicle* 1d   Bus St Martin's
Ch[urch] to Grafton St 1d   Dinner 1/6   Chocolate &c at Gatti &
Rodesano's with Sparling & Utley 1/10   Bus Strand to Hammersmith 3d

20   *H. Longden, return of my deposit on account of the expenses of the
Italian Expedition now abandoned. £9/19/0.*

Sparling and I looked in at the Kelmscott Press and found Morris there. We
went back with him to his house and were there until 11, when we left and
walked into town together. Spent the whole day writing letters. At about 19
I took a turn at the *Knot*, which is beginning to worry me by its unfinished
state. JP was here in the evening. She left early and I went over to her house
shortly after. Found her on the point of going out to a music hall. It was
arranged that she should return at 22; and I, meanwhile, went and had
something to eat and then went into the South Kensington Museum until
22. I left the Square a little after 23 and walked home.

PMG 1d   *Star* ½d   Dinner 10d   Train to S[ou]th Kensington 6d
Macaroni &c at café close to S[ou]th K[ensington] station 1/6?

21   [   ]

22   Worked at the *Knot*. In the afternoon went out to FE, bringing her the
translation of *Peer Gynt*, which I read to her for a long time. We came in to
town together. Spent the rest of the evening at home.

Papers 1½d   Dinner 1/1?   Train to Shep[herds] Bush 4d   Rav[ens-
cour]t Park to St Ja[me]s's Pk 1/–

23 *Fabian Members' Meeting at Barnard's Inn. 20. Elect new Executive
member* vice *[Robert] Banner and consider Trafalgar Square etc.*

Began *World* article. Was at work all day, except for a while after dinner
when I lay down and read. Wallas walked home with me after the Executive; and we took a stroll along Regents Park.

Justice 1d   *Star* ½d   Dinner 1/1?

24 *[Sir Arthur] Sullivan's* Haddon Hall *at the Savoy—first night.*

Worked at the *Knot* in the afternoon. After dinner went to South Kensington
Museum and spent the whole afternoon there. Bought a few photographs.
May came to the Savoy with me.

PMG 1d   *Star* ½d   Dinner 1/1?   Photographs of South Kensington
3/1   Bus down Tott[enham] Ct Rd 1d   Cab rest of the way to Savoy
1/6

> *Haddon Hall*, a comic opera by Sydney Grundy, with music by Sir Arthur Sullivan, would
> have 204 performances.

25 SUNDAY °*Labour Demonstration at Hammersmith. 16. Ravenscourt
Park. Dine with Archer.* 14¼.

Wrote notes of *Haddon Hall* for *The World*. When I got to Hammersmith I
found that I had forgotten to bring the letter explaining where the demonstration was to be held. I tried Brook Green and the [Hammersmith] bridge
in vain. The police could not tell me. At last I gave it up as a bad job and went
to Walkers', where I found Mrs. Walker in bed. I stayed until past 19 talking
to her and to the nurse, who was a pleasant intelligent woman. Then went on
to FE. Archer called for me at 14 and we went to Queen Square together.
Calmour traveled with me from South Kensington to Hammersmith.

Train Temple to Hammersmith 6d   Shep[herds] Bush to Ptld Rd 6d

> "I contend," G.B.S.—no admirer of W. S. Gilbert—wrote on 28 September 1892 (C888),
> "that Savoy opera is a *genre* in itself; and that Haddon Hall is the highest and most
> consistent expression it has yet attained. The result is due to the critical insight of Mr.
> Grundy." Still, G.B.S. concluded, not suggesting that this was necessarily bad, "Haddon
> Hall, in history, costume, logic and everything else of the kind, is perfectly impossible."

26 *Fabian Executive.* 17¼.

Revised a chapter of the *Knot.* Wrote up this diary and attacked my correspondence, which has again accumulated. Corrected *World* proof. After the
Executive meeting Sparling and I went out to Hammersmith together,
Oakeshott and Wallas dining with us on the way at the Orange Grove and
leaving us at Charing Cross.

Star ½d   *PMG* 1d   Dinner 1/1   Bus Tott[enham] Ct Rd to Lincoln's Inn 1d   Ch[arin]g Cross to Hammersmith 3d   Supper at Orange Grove 1/4

27 °*Distribution of Prizes at Trinity College, Mandeville Place. Address by E. H. Turpin on "Talent and Temperament, Their Power and Influence in Music." 17.*

Worked at the *Knot*. After dinner went to the Musuem to look for Wallas intending to call on Archer afterwards. Found Archer there; also Miss Brooke, with whom I had a conversation. Then Wallas, I and Archer went off to Queen Square. Then we went to the Fabian office, where Archer left us, and where I left Wallas after I had done some Fabian business there. I called at the Stores for my photographs of the equestrian statues at Padua and Venice (Gattamelata and Colleoni) and of the horse's head from the Naples Museum. Came home and hung them up. Whilst I was doing so I received a call from Drabig, the German whom Swan recommended to me as able to teach German on the Gouin system. Played for a long time—then wrote up this diary, wrote a letter or two, and to bed after a brief turn at the *Knot*. My object in calling for Wallas today was to see whether he would join Archer and myself in our trip to Winchester tomorrow.

Star ½d   *PMG* 1d   Dinner 10d   Framing photographs at Stores 11/4   picture wire 1/6

> The *General Bartolomeo Colleoni* sculpted by Andrea del Verrocchio (1435–1488), stands in the Piazza dei SS. Giovanni e Paolo, in Venice. ■ See 26 October 1892 and 15–16 July 1894 for the Gouin system.

28 *Go down to Winchester with Archer by the 11.15 train from Waterloo.*

Went down to Winchester with Archer. We went to the Cathedral and to the Church of St. Cross. In the evening we went to see Benson's Company play *The Merchant of Venice*. We put up at the Royal Hotel.

Train Waterloo to Winchester 5/6   Papers 3d   Lunch at Winchester 1/6   Cathedral donation 6d   Tip to Verger 2/–   Tip & ticket to St Cross 1/–   Theatre 3/–   program 2d

29 *Catch the 9.32 train Winchester to Alton and walk to Farnham by way of Selborne.*

We walked from Alton to Selborne; lunched there; and walked to Farnham, where we just caught the 17.45 train to town. It was a windy, showery day, not bad for walking until the last half hour when it began to rain steadily. I parted from Archer at the corner of Bow St. and came home and changed all my clothes. Then answered my letters—plenty of them already.

Bill, Royal Hotel, Winchester 10/–   Papers 2d   Train to Alton 1/6
Lunch at Selbourne 2/6   Ginger Beer at ? 2d   Train Farnham to Waterloo 3/0½

30 *Call at Jaeger's to re-fit suit.*

Worked at *World* article. After dinner went to Jaeger's and then to Museum to look for Wallas. Did not find him. Took a turn through the building. Came home; rested a bit; and then finished and sent off the article. In the evening I went up to Dryhursts' where I found an anarchist violinist named—I think—Graves. Also another man whose name I forget.

Justice 1d   *Star* ½d   Dinner 10d   Bus Vore St to Bloomsbury 2d

> G.B.S.'s 5 October 1892 column (C890), on the deaths of Emil Behnke and mezzo-soprano Zelia Trebelli (1838–1892).

October

1 *Concert 32 pianos. Musical Exhibition at the Aquarium. 16.15.*

Worked at the *Knot* in the forenoon. In the afternoon went to the Aquarium. Came back in the evening and played a good deal.

Star & PMG 1½d   Dinner 10d   Aquarium 1/–   Testing "personal error" 1/–   Bus Picc[adilly] O to Ptld Rd 1d

> The multi-piano concert was not reviewed by G.B.S. ■ "Personal error" was apparently a coin machine.

2 SUNDAY °*Italian Expedition returns.* °*Lecture at the Whitechapel and Spitalfields Liberal and Radical Club. Buxton St. Brick Lane E. on "Labour Politics and Labour Parties." 12. (J. S. Vander Hout). Attend the Trafalgar Square Demonstration Committee at the S. D. F., 237 Strand, as Fabian delegate with Wallas, at 12.*

The lecture at Buxton St. fell through owing to a misunderstanding about the hour. Wallas came back with me from the Trafalgar Square Committee and dined here. Then I corrected the *World* proof and set off at about 16 for Hammersmith. Spent the rest of the evening with FE. It was too wet to walk.

Train Royal Oak to Shep[herds] Bush 4d   Shep[herds] Bush to Ptld Rd 6d

3 *Fabian Executive. 17¼. Go on to Hammersmith with Sparling and stay the night.* °*Royalty Theatre. Cotsford Dick's* The Baroness. *First night. Postponed to 5th.* °*Central Group Fabian Society. 32 Great Ormond St. 20.*

Wrote a long letter to *The Workman's Times* about the attitude of the Fabian Society to "The Independent Labour Party," so-called. This took up the whole day. Dined at home on some bread and fruit etc. I quite forgot the opera at the Royalty, having omitted to enter it here. As far as I can ascertain, the performance, for some reason, did not come off.

Star ½d   PMG 2d   Train to Farringdon Road 3½d   Maccaroni &c at Gatti & Rodesano's 2/5   Train Victoria to Ravenscourt Park (return) 4d

Letter in *Workman's Times*, 8 October 1892 (C892).

4   *Call at Jaeger's in the afternoon to try on evening coat (5th). Take the train to Richmond about 14.30 and pick up FE at Ravenscourt Park.*

Walked in from Hammersmith with Sparling, calling at Morris's for a moment and found Walker there with him. Wrote off a dozen postcards when I got home. The walk was not a success as far as weather was concerned, as it began to rain when we reached Richmond, and came down more and more heavily as we walked through the park to Wimbledon and then to Putney, where we took the train. We did not get so wet as we should have done if there had been any wind. Fortunately, there was none. When I got home I was tired enough to want to take things easy; and after playing a bit and writing up this diary, I read a little and went to bed.

Star ½d   PMG 1d   Dinner 1/–   Train to Richmond 1/3   Putney to Waterloo (2) 1/2   Sweets 2d   Waterloo to Ch[arin]g + (2) 6d   Met at Orange Grove (2) 2/7   Builder 4d   *Pick-Me-Up* (comic paper) 1d

5   *Royalty Theatre. First night. Cotsford Dick's* Baroness. *20. See yesterday—Jaeger's.*

Wrote review of Le Gallienne's *English Poems* for *The Star*. Did not go out until late. Did not get to bed until past 2. [Cecil] Raleigh walked to the theatre with me and walked with me as far as Oxford St.

PMG 1d   *Star* ½d   "Tea" & dinner combined at Orange Grove 1/9

Cotsford Dick (1847–1911) had begun his comedy, G.B.S. wrote on 12 October 1892 (C893), "as a burlesque of *King Lear*," and continued it "on the lines of the Who's who? pattern of farce," which was "funny enough, especially in the Turkish-bath scene, until the third act, in which the tangled threads of the plot are unravelled in a rather butter-fingered way." Shaw would put a portable Turkish bath into his own play *Misalliance* (1910).   • "Bassetto on Logroller," review of Richard le Gallienne's *English Poems*, *The Star*, 27 October 1892 (C898). "Logroller" was Le Gallienne's pseudonym as *Star* book reviewer. C. di B. dismissed the verses as dainty, commonplace, and banal. The poet responded with verses "To C. di B." in which he mourned "the bludgeoning of my little song bird," now "bruised and broken in the mud":

> A nightingale within Minotaur's paw—
> So seemed my little book within the grasp of Shaw.

6   *Savoy Theatre. 15. J. W. Boulding's* Dorothy Vernon. °*Eight Hours Committee. 276 Strand. 20. Lyric Theatre, [Alexandre Charles] Lecocq's* Incognita. *20. First night.*

Up late and not in much trim for working. Nothing very particular done before it was time to go out. After leaving the Savoy, FE (to whom I had sent the spare ticket) walked with me along the Embankment to Scotland Yard and then back along Whitehall to the office of *The Manchester Guar-*

dian where I left a few lines about the play *vice* Archer, who had gone to Brighton to see the performances of *Hedda Gabler* and *The Doll's House* by Janet Achurch and Elizabeth Robins.

Star, Freethinker & National Reformer 3½d   PMG 1d   Dinner 1/2
Soup &c at Orange Grove (2) 2/–?

> *Dorothy Vernon* was reviewed, unsigned, for William Archer, *Manchester Guardian,* 7 October 1892 (C891). James Wimsett Boulding had earlier written a number of verse dramas and historical plays. ▪ *Incognita,* with Lecocq's music, libretto by Burnand and lyrics by Harry Greenbank (1866–1899), would run 101 performances. G.B.S. (C893) noted that "the more you see of it the less you like it," as each act was progressively worse than the preceding one.

7 Fabian Society. Essex Hall. 20. Gustav Steffen on "The Industrial Revolution."

Began *World* article. Took a light lunch of fruit and then walked to Hammersmith to FE. Spoke at the Fabian, where Webb and his wife appeared for the first time since their marriage. Came home alone, Wallas and the Webbs having left the meeting before Steffen's reply. Wrote up this diary and sent off a couple of postcards when I got back.

Train Ravenscourt Park to Ch[arin]g + (FE) 6d   self to Temple 7d
PMG & Star 2d   Justice 1d

> Sidney Webb had married Beatrice Potter on 23 July 1892 in the St. Pancras Vestry Hall. See 26 October 1892 for Shaw's wedding present to them.

8 Spend the evening at the Democratic Club, Essex St., with the Sparlings. 19½. Call on Florence O'Driscoll, 18 Gower St., at 16.

Worked at *World* article. Met a singer named Caprili at O'Driscoll's. Came home for a few minutes before going to the Democratic Club. It was a very stupid affair. I left with the Sparlings at 22.30 and walked with them along the Embankment to Charing Cross station.

Star ½d   PMG 1d   Dinner 1/–

9 SUNDAY Lecture for the Kentish Town Branch S. D. F. at Phoenix Hall, Preston St., Malden Rd., N.W. on "Superstitions of Socialism." (C. A. Gibson). Tea with the Dryhursts.

Finished and sent off the *World* article. After dinner walked to Hampstead and by way of the Spaniards Rd. to the Highgate Ponds where I turned back across Parliament Hill to Dryhursts'. Dryhurst came with me to the lecture. Tom Walker walked home with me.

> Tom Walker was listed in the 1890 Fabian directory of members at 15 Delaney Street, Regents Park, N.W.

10 Fabian Executive. 17½. °Eight Hours Committee. 276 Strand. 20. No. On Thursday. Tea at Sparlings' and stay the night.

Wrote a letter to *The Daily Chronicle* about the scene in *Incognita* licensed by the censor of plays, comparing it with the suppressed scenes in the plays done by the Independent Theatre. Wrote a few letters.

PMG 1d   *Star* ½d   Train Ch[arin]g + to Ham[mersm]ith 5d   *Idler* 6d

The letter to the *Daily Chronicle* about *Incognita* was not published. Shaw had already written in his review of *Incognita* (C893), part of a notice of five musical comedies, that the Lord Chamberlain, by licensing "vulgar business" in both plays, had "cleared himself of all suspicion of Puritanical intolerance. . . . I could not help feeling how vast an advance we had made since last year, when all London was supposed to have shuddered with horror at the wickedness of that scene in Ibsen's *Ghosts*, where the mother in the drawing room overhears her son kissing the housemaid in the dining room.

11   *Dine with Fred M. Wilson at Members Mansions, Victoria St., at 19.*

Walked in from Hammersmith with Sparling, May coming with us as far as the corner of Earl's Court Rd. Attended to my letters when I got in. After dinner went to the Stores to make some purchases. Came home and played a good deal and wrote some more letters. Left Wilson's at half past 22. His niece dined with us but left us when we rose from table.

Star ½d   *PMG* 1d   Dinner 1/1   Note paper 5 quires 2/6   Envelopes (100) 1/3   Condy's Fluid 1/6   Gayetty paper 1/4

Fred M. Wilson was editor of *The Morning Leader*.

12   *Lunch with Archer. 13.30.*

Worked at the *Knot* both morning and evening, composing new matter. After lunch went out to FE. We came into town together, walking part of the way. I left her at the theatre.

PMG 1d   *Star* 1d   Train Gower St to Shep[herds] Bush 6d   Bus Shep[herds] Bush to Bayswater (2) 6d   Bus Knightsbridge to Picc[adilly] O (2) 2d

13   °*Eight Hours Committee. 276 Strand. 20. Empire Music Hall— (Señorita C. de Otero: dancer and singer).*

Began *World* article. After dinner came back here to get Janet Achurch's reply to my telegram suggesting an interview for publication about her trip to Brighton with *A Doll's House*, etc. JP and Maggie Gardner were here. Then went off to Archer's to see whether he would come to the Empire with me. He had to go to Hampstead. I had tea with him; and we walked together as far as the corner of Tottenham Court Rd. Wrote up this diary when I got home.

Railway tickets for Crystal Pal[ace] Concerts 21/–   Cost orders 2d Telegram to Janet Achurch 1/11½   *PMG* 1d   *Star* ½d   *Freethinker* 1d   *Nat[iona]l Reformer* 2d   Dinner 1/1   Empire Music Hall 5/– Programme 3d

Caroline (actually Augusta Otero Iglesias) de Otero (1868–1965), a dancer, was later mistress to Leopold II of Belgium, Edward VII of Great Britain, Prince Albert of Monaco, Nicholas I of Montenegro, and others. Of her performance at the Empire, which shocked her Victorian audience, G.B.S. wrote on 19 October 1892 (C894):

> One performance at the Empire exhibited the audience to pitiful disadvantage. A certain Señorita C. de Otero, described as a Spanish dancer and singer, danced a dance which has ennobled the adjective "suggestive" for me forever. It was a simple affair enough, none of your cruel Herodias dances, or cleverly calculated tomboyish Tararas, but a poignant, most meaning dance, so intensely felt that a mere walk across the stage in it quite dragged at one's heartstrings. This Otero is really a great artist. But do you suppose the house rose at her? Not a bit of it: they stared vacantly, . . . and finally grumbled out a little disappointed applause. Two men actually hissed—if they will forward me their names and addresses I will publish them with pleasure, lest England should burst in ignorance of its greatest monsters.
> Take notice, oh Señorita C. de Otero, Spanish dancer and singer, that I wash my hands of the national crime of failing to appreciate you. You were a perfect success: the audience was a dismal failure. I really cannot conceive a man being such a dull dog as to hold out against that dance. . . .

"La Belle Otero" would return to London in 1898, where, at the Alhambra, she finally had her big English success.

14 Continued *World* article. Dined here off some fruit. At about 16 went out and called on Miss Robins. Then went to the Orange Grove and had a meal. Then to the St. Martin's Free Library (which I had never been in before), where I waited until about 20, when I went and waited near the stage door of the Comedy Theatre to see FE. We agreed that I should wait for her until 21 and that we should then go out to Hammersmith together. I went back to the library and read there for an hour. Then back according to the arrangement.

Star & PMG 1½d   Dinner &c (at Orange Grove) 1/4   Telegram to FE 8d   Bus Bayswater to Uxbridge Road first Shep[herds] B[ush] (2) 6d Train Shep[herds] B[ush] to Ptld Rd 6d   Sweets 1d

15 °*Lecture at Wheatsheaf Hall, Clapham, on "Social Democracy." Cancelled. First Crystal Palace Saturday Concert of season. 15. Pachmann. New works by Lidgey and Wormser.*

Worked at *World* article. FE came to the Palace with me. When I got home in the evening I felt very tired; but I lay down and read for a while, and presently felt so much revived that I went off to FE in time for her return from the theatre at 22. On the way I met Lilian Revell, who came along as far as Westbourne Park.

Review of Reviews 6d   *Star* ½d   *PMG* 1d   Meal at Orange Grove (2) 2/8   Train to Shep[herds] Bush & back 1/–   Sweets 1d

Reviewed by G.B.S. on 19 October 1892 (C894). Vladimir de Pachmann played the Beethoven Third Piano Concerto and two new works were premiered, the *Ballade for Orchestra* by C. A. Lidgey, which had "no special originality or distinction," and a "symphonic poem" by André Wormser, the composer of *L'Enfant Prodigue*, which was "second-hand" Offenbach.

16 SUNDAY *Lecture at the Dulwich Working Men's Liberal and Radical Club. 108 Lordship Lane. Dulwich. S. E. (Frederick Rubic, Sec.). "Liberalism and Labour." 20. Train to Rye Lane and bus to club, or train to Rye Lane. Trafalgar Square Committee. 337 Strand. 11.30. Speak with O'Driscoll at Irish National League meeting. Catholic Schools, near London Bridge station. 16. Call for him at 15½ at Gower St.*

Finished and sent off *World* article. In spite of all my resolutions to cut my public speaking short and never go beyond half an hour or 40 minutes in a lecture, I spoke five separate times, the lecture running to an hour and a quarter.

Bus Holborn to Bank 1d   Bank of London Bridge 1d   Eggs, cocoa &c at London Br[idge] 1–   Train L[ondon] B[ridge] to Peckham 3d

17 *Fabian Executive. 17¼. °Fabian Central Group Meeting. 32 Great Ormond St. 20. D. McEwen on "Co-operation in Home Life." Elect secretary. Production of Tchaikowsky's* Eugene Onegin. *Olympic Theatre. 20.*

Quite clear that I ought to have kept my good resolutions about speaking yesterday. Tried to take things easy—read the paper at full length and read the libretto of *Eugene Onegin*. Corrected *World* proof. Wrote several letters then and did not get down to the Executive until near 18. Went with Massingham to the National Liberal Club and dined there with him. Norman joined us.

Star ½d

> Reviewed by G.B.S. on 26 October 1892 (C897), with regrets that there was not more originality in Tchaikovsky, who, nevertheless, "composes with the seriousness of a man who knows how to value himself and his work too well to be capable of padding his opera with the [usual] claptrap that does duty for dramatic music. . . ."

18 *Slivinski's recital. St. James's Hall. 15. First night of Rose's new play,* Agatha Tylden. *Haymarket Theatre. 20½. Mrs. Langtry.*

Up very late—breakfast at 12.20. Cold weather and late hours making me hibernate as usual. Spent all the time I could spare hunting for Loewe's autobiography to return to H. W. Just. Found it on my return from the theatre and sent it off by book post. Wrote a few postcards and this diary before going to bed, which I did not accomplish until past 1. After leaving the Haymarket, walked with FE to Victoria. Dined at the Orange Grove after the concert, and then went to Jaeger's to buy some warm underclothing to wear with my evening suit, which is very light.

Bus to St Ja[me]s's Hall 1d   Dinner (at Orange Grove) 1/4   PMG 1d   Star ½d

> Slivinski, who had filled in for the ailing Paderewski, seemed to have his "edge very perceptibly taken off by . . . too much drawing room playing" (C897). ■ *Agatha Tylden, Merchant and Shipowner*, with Lillie Langtry in the title role, would run for fifty-two performances. Mrs. Langtry was not much of an actress, but her first nights were each a social event. ■ Loewe may be Karl Loewe (1796–1869), Westphalian

composer of ballad-like songs. Shaw's review of a concert of Loewe's songs on 22 June 1893 (C957) would reveal solid knowledge of the composer's life and work, familiar to many only via "The Erl King."

19 *Sparlings' in the evening to meet Mme. Pappajannople, etc.*

Wrote a long letter to *The Star* about vivisection, attacking it. In the afternoon went to FE, and left her at Ravenscourt Park station, she going into town by train and I going to Sparlings', where I slept. Stepniak, the Ellises etc. were there.

Macaroni &c at café opposite Portland Rd 1/2?   *Star* ½d   Train to Shep[herds] Bush 6d   FE's train Rav[enscourt] Pk to Ch[arin]g + 6d

> Mme. Pappajannople, obviously a Greek socialist, is not identified. ▪ Shaw would publish two letters on vivisection in *The Star*, "For Humanity's Sake," 20 October 1892 (C895), and "The Live Controversy," 24 October 1892 (C896).

20 In the morning Sparling went to town by train, having to go to Hull. May and I went off for a walk along the towpath to Richmond, where we dined at Ferrari's Restaurant. We came back by train to Ravenscourt Park, where we parted, and I went to FE. She was out; and I went in and waited, working at the play, which I decided to call *Widowers' Houses*. I wrote in a new scene near the end of the second act. FE did not come in until past 17.

Chiswick Ferry 4d   Lunch at Richmond 2/4?   Train Richmond to Ravenscourt Pk (2) 10d?   Rav[enscourt] Pk to Ch[arin]g + (we got out at St. James's Pk) (2) 1/–   *Star* ½d

21 *Fabian Society. Essex Hall. Stepniak on "Anarchism, Social-Democracy and the English Labour Parties."*

Tried to begin *World* article, but could not get the play off my mind and at last set to work and finished revising it. Sent it off and then walked along the Marylebone Rd. to the Victoria Gate of Hyde Park, from which I went to Brompton Square and spent half an hour with JP. Then to the Orange Grove and on to the Fabian. Got to bed before midnight.

Bus Brompton to Picc[adilly] O 1d   Meal at Orange Grove 2/–   *Justice, Freedom &* "Anarchist Morality" 3d

22 *Crystal Palace Concert. 15. New overture by Barclay Jones. Second part of programme in honour of anniversary of Liszt's birthday. [David] Popper. °Tea with JP. Lohengrin at the New Olympic Theatre. Albani. 19¼.*

Began *World* article and worked at it in the train. Left the opera before the end of the second act. Did some work when I got home. FE came to the Palace with me.

Star ½d   Dinner 1/–?   Train Ch[arin]g + to Victoria 1½d   Supper at
Orange Grove (2) 2/6?   Ch[arin]g + lavatory 2d   Hair cut &c 1/–

Such work as that of Barclay Jones was only suggested by the opening line of G.B.S.'s 2
November 1892 column (C899), "The young English composer is having a good time of it
just now, with his overtures and symphonies resounding at the Crystal Palace. . . ." ∎
Shaw "saw an act and a half of Lohengrin," and ventured to "certify that the pit got
handsome value for its money, although they would do it differently at Bayreuth" (C897).

23 SUNDAY   *Dine with the Sidney Webbs at 10 Netherhall Gardens. 14.*
Lecture at the Co-operative Hall, Chelsea, on "Labour Politics and Labour
Parties." (S. Masterson, 57 Dartray Rd., Chelsea, S.W.). 20. Tea with Mrs.
Sandham, 7 Durham Place, at 18. Trafalgar Square Committee. 337 Strand.
11.30.

Bertha Newcombe was at Mrs. Sandham's. Had to sit up until about 3 in
the morning to send off my *World* article and a letter to *The Star* about
vivisection. Worked at article also in the bus and train.

Bus Picc[adilly] to Oxford Circus 1d   Oxford O to Baker St Station 2d
Baker St train to Finchley Rd 3d   Finchley Rd to Sloane Sq 5d   S[ou]th
Kensington to Portl[an]d Rd 5d   Sweets 2d

24   *Fabian Executive. 17¼. First Monday Popular Concert of the season. St.*
James's Hall. 20. Arbos and Szumowska. °Eight Hours Committee, 276
Strand, for final version of report. 20.

Steffen called whilst I was dressing (about 11); and he stayed here until we
went out together to dinner at the Wheatsheaf at 14. I parted from him at
Holborn and went on to the Fabian, where I remained until the Executive,
at which I took the chair. Afterwards Webb walked with me to Charing
Cross Rd. I left the concert at the end of the first part, having had a chat
with the Normans and with Pardon. Came home to write up this diary and
make an attempt to answer some letters.

Star ½d   Dinner 1/–   Meal (at Orange Grove) 1/10   Program at
Monday Pop 6d   *Star & PMG* 1½d

"I have to . . . congratulate Señor Arbós on his playing in the adagio of Beethoven's
quartet in E flat (Op. 74) . . . and Mlle. Szumowska on her neat handling of the last three
movements of the Pastoral Sonata" (C899).

25   *Independent Theatre performance of* The Duchess of Malfi *at the Opera*
Comique. 15. (Second performance, the first having been last Friday.) Caed-
mar and L'Impresario at the New Olympic Theatre—Lago Opera—also the
coronation scene from Ernani. 20. °Decorated pianoforte on view at Broad-
wood's. 11 to 16.

Running about all day. After *The Duchess of Malfi* FE and I went to the
Orange Grove and had a meal. Then we walked about St. James's Park until
19.30, when she went off to the theatre and I went into the lavatory at
Charing Cross to clean myself up for the Opera.

Star ½d   Dinner 10d (also paid for yesterday)   Meal at Orange Grove
(2) 3/7   Lavatory Ch[arin]g + 2d   Bus to Olympic 1d   Bootblack
6d

John Webster's 1619 play had been adapted by William Poel. It would star Mary Rorke (1858–1938) as the Duchess and have two matinee performances. ■ G.B.S. found *Caedmar*, by Granville Bantock (1868–1946), "an enthusiastic and ingenious piece of work" (C899), and heavily redolent of Wagner. *The Impresario* was an English version of Mozart's 1786 light opera *Der Schauspieldirektor*. "Every number in it," said G.B.S., "is a masterpiece." The scene from *Ernani* completed the evening.

26 *Demonstration of Gouin's method of teaching languages at 70 Cornhill, Linguistic Agency, at 18.*

Intended to make a holiday of it; but found myself hard at my letters, which I did not clear off until 16, eating some bread and fruit instead of going out to dinner. Played and sang for half an hour and then went to the City to see the demonstration and to buy a couple of gold pens to present to Sidney and Beatrice Webb. Podmore was in the train with me from Broad St. to Hampstead. Webb's brother (Charles) and his sister-in-law were there. I caught the 21.50 train to Chiswick and got to FE at 22.30

Star ½d   Train to Moorgate 3d   Cocoa, eggs in Poultry [?] 1/–
Train Broad St to Hampstead Heath 5d   Finchley Road to Chiswick
8d   Shep[herds] Bush to Portland Rd 6d   Telegram to FE 6d

F. Gouin's *The Art of Teaching and Studying Languages*, translated by Howard Swan and Victor Bétis, had just been published in London.

27 °*Social "Browning" at Mrs. Revell's. 58 Oxford Gardens W. 19. °Personal Rights Association Soiree and Discussion on "Free Trade and Individualism" opened by Alfred Milnes. St. Martin's Town Hall. 20. °Willeby to call between 12 and 1. Put off to Saturday. Go up to Grein's at 20½ to discuss the cast for the play* [Widowers' Houses].

Began *World* article. Archer called and we went to dinner at the Wheatsheaf together. Very wet day.

2 *Stars* 1d   Dinner 1/–?

Charles Willeby was a writer on music whose new book, *Frédéric François Chopin*, a biography, would be included in Shaw's 7 December 1892 review (C910). See 9 November 1892.

28 *Press View. Henri's paintings at the Goupil Gallery. Reece to call for me at 14.30 to go over Kirkman's factory. Fabian Special Committee. 276 Strand. 20. To discuss Hammill's resolution "That a Committee be formed to consider whether it is desirable that the Fabian Society should take steps to form a united Socialist party."*

Finished and sent off *World* article. Very wet day. After going over the factory I went on to FE; and we came into town together, I going on to the

Fabian Committee. On leaving it I tried to overtake Webb and Wallas, but missed them and walked home alone. At the Committee the project mentioned in the resolution was negatived.

Star ½d   Dinner 1/–   Train to Hammersmith 9d   Train FE to Ch[arin]g + from Rav[enscourt] Pk 6d   & self to Temple 7d   *Justice* 1d

> Robert Henri (1865–1929) was an American landscape and genre painter. ▪ Jacob and Joseph Kirkman were piano manufacturers at 3 Soho Square, W. ▪ Fred Hammill (1856–1901) was an engineer, an early Fabian, and an I.L.P. member.

29 *Crystal Palace Concert. 15. Szumowska. Cliffe's new symphony and Moskowski's Boabdil excerpt. Private View. 19th Century Gallery. Willeby to call between 12 and 13.*

Willeby called. Got to work on *The Irrational Knot* again. When I got back for a couple of hours in the evening I found JP here. Worked again at the *Knot*. After the concert FE and I strolled about the grounds of the Palace, as we had been almost stifled by the stuffiness of the concert room.

Cream & wheatcake at shop in Buck[ingha]m Pal[ace] Rd 5½d   Meal at Orange Grove (2) 2/5   Train to Shep[herds] Bush & back 1/–

> Szumowska is noted 9 November 1892 (C901) as playing Weber's *Konzertstück*; G.B.S. delayed commenting upon the Frederick Cliffe (1857–1931) Symphony in E minor until 30 November 1892 (C908) because he was unsure how to confess his dislike for it. "The general mood of the work," he explained, finally, "is too sentimental for me; and the orchestration, to my taste, is particularly cloying. Mr. Cliffe seems to have no respect for the instruments: instead of giving them real parts, or at least firm virile touches to lay in, he uses them only to rouge his themes up to the eyes, and to hang rings on their fingers and bells on their toes, so to speak." Cliffe was professor of pianoforte at the Royal Academy of Music.

30 SUNDAY *Lecture at Canning Town at 20.15. (Percy Alden, Mansfield House, 165–7 Barking Rd., Canning Town E). Mansfield Hall, 143–5 Barking Rd. Trafalgar Square. 337 Strand. 11.30.*

Wrote an additional paragraph for *World* article. Sang a little in the afternoon. Then lay down and read, finishing Gogol's *Revizor*. I fell asleep and did not awake until 19. After the lecture I went into Mansfield House, a "university settlement," and had some supper. When I changed carriages at Farringdon St. on my way back I met Mrs. Thornton Smith, and we traveled together to Portland Rd., where I left her in the train. I hoped to copy out the addition to the *World* article. Got to bed at one.

Train to Bishopsgate (from Mark Lane) 3½d   Train Fenchurch St to Canning Town & back 1/–   Mark Lane to P[or]tl[an]d Rd 5d   Sweets 2d

> *Revisor: The Inspector General (The Government Inspector)*, a comedy first produced in 1836.

31 *Fabian Executive. 17¼. Monday Popular Concert. St. James's Hall. 20. Wietrowetz and Szumowska.*

Hard at work clearing off correspondence until 17. Then went off to Executive. Dined at home. By mistake I dated all the letters the 30th instead of the 31st. I altered the postcards; but the letters were closed before I found out the error. Did not go down to the Executive until about 18. Olivier came with me to the Orange Grove. I left the concert after the first part. Posted up this diary when I got back and got to bed before 23.

Subs[criptio]n for 1892 to British Ec[onomic] Ass[ociatio]n (John B. Martin, Treas[urer]) 21/–   Cost of order 2d   Cocoa &c at Orange Grove 1/3   Concert program 6d

> Gabrielle Wietrowetz, violinist, a pupil of Joachim, made her London debut on 23 April 1892, G.B.S. writing then (C860) that she "bounded into immediate popularity on the back of Mendelssohn's concerto." Shaw did not review the 31 October concert.

November

1   *Meet Wallas at Euston at 13.45 and go down with him to Watford to see the St. Pancras Pauper Schools at Leavesden. Sparlings' for the night.*

Still at the letters; but did not do much before it was time to go to Euston. One of the Vestry officials, whose name I did not catch, came down with us. We went through the place and had tea with the Rules, the master and matron. I got out at Willesden and went to Hammersmith to ask the Sparlings to put me up for a few nights, the smell of paint at Fitzroy Square, where they are doing up the house, being unbearable. I played duets with May and then ran over to see FE at 22. Got back just before midnight.

Star ½d   Train Euston to Watford & back (to Willesden) 2/4   Grub at Watford 1/9   Tip to collector at Willesden 6d   Train Willesden to Hammersmith 5d

> George Rule had been superintendent of the schools at Leavesden and his wife, Rhoda, had been matron since October 1883.

2   *°Dvorak's Requiem. Albert Hall. 20. °Harold Bauer's pianoforte recital. Erard's. 15. Matinée.* The Wedding Eve. *Trafalgar Square Theatre. 15.*

Walked into town. Sparling left me at the Broadway, as he was in too great a hurry not to take the train. On our way thither we called on Morris and found Cockerell there. When I got to the Square I corrected the typewriter copy of the third act of the play and sent it back to Teixeira de Mattos to be copied properly. After leaving the theatre I went back to the Square and packed up some traps. Then back to the Sparlings, taking FE on my way. I did not get there until close to 19; so that I was only with her for a few minutes when she had to start for the theatre. It was very wet just then, and when I got to the Terrace I had to borrow a change of clothes from Sparling. May and I played duets until near 23, when I wrote a few cards before going to bed.

Star $\frac{1}{2}$d   *PMG* 1d   Dinner (at Pine Apple) 1/2   Train Portl[an]d Rd to Shep[herds] Bush 6d   FE, I [to] Ch[arin]g + & back 9d

3   *London Symphony Concert. St. James's Hall. 20$\frac{1}{2}$. °Webbe and Nicholl's subscription concert, first of the season, Steinway Hall. 20$\frac{1}{2}$. Pennells', 2 Buckingham St., after the concert.*

Began *World* article. I had intended to go into town in the middle of the day; but the weather was so fine that May and I went off to Richmond, where I got some lunch, after which we took a walk through the park to Roehampton, losing ourselves in the most complicated way in some private grounds through which we tried to make a short cut. At Putney station we parted, May returning home via Richmond and I going to Waterloo. I went home before the concert, taking a meal at the Orange Grove on the way. I left Pennells' at midnight; got to Sparlings' at about 1; and did not get to bed until 2, as I had to answer all the letters I had brought out from the Square.

Train Ravenscourt Pk to Richmond (2) 1/2?   Maccaroni &c at Ferrari's 1/9   Train Putney to Waterloo 7d   M[ay], Putney to Richmond 5d   Toffee 1d   Grub at Orange Grove 1/4?   Train Ch[arin]g + to Rav[enscourt] Pk 6d

> The London Symphony concert was reviewed by G.B.S. on 9 November 1892 (C901). "The band was very rough . . . it made a great noise and gave no sort of satisfaction."

4   *Fabian. Graham Wallas on "Working Class Economics." Essex Hall. 20. Call on Mrs. Mallet, 13 Torrington Square, at 18 and go to the Fabian together. Call on Kate Phillips, Exeter Mansions, Shaftesbury Ave., at 17, about the part of Annie [the parlormaid] in the play.*

Continued *World* article and wrote a letter to *The Chronicle* in answer to the manifesto of Bax's and seven other Socialists about Marx and Jevons. Then I went over to FE, who gave me a plate of porridge (I was horribly hungry) after which I went into town. After supper at Mrs. Mallet's I called at the Square for my letters. JP was there. After the Fabian, O'Driscoll walked with me along the Embankment to Charing Cross, where I took [the] train. Sent off the *World* article when I got back and was in bed before 1.

Train Ravenscourt Park to Temple & back (fr. Ch[arin]g +) 11d   *Star* $\frac{1}{2}$d   Wash at Faulkner's 3d [?]   Telegram to Mrs. Mallet 6d   *Justice* 1d   Bus along Tott[enham] Ct Rd 1d   Bus to Lincolns Inn corner 1d

> Kate Phillips refused the role of Blanche's abused parlormaid, and Shaw enlisted instead "N. de Silva" (according to the program)—Angelita Helena de Silva (1869–1949), the wife of (Sir) John Martin-Harvey (1863–1944). ■ "English Socialism," *Daily Chronicle*, 7 November 1892 (C900). English Socialism, Shaw insisted, "is *not* Marxism." Shaw's seven "other" Socialists were actually six. Bax was the seventh.

5 *Crystal Palace Concert. 15. Sullivan's* Martyr of Antioch.

Wrote some letters etc. and posted up this diary. Had to go to the Square before the concert to get a supply of railway tickets. May came with me to the Palace. I left the concert early and came back by the 16.4 train. Then I went to JP and had tea with her. She made rather a scene and was very disagreeable. Went on to FE. Left her at about 22, and went to bed when I got back to the Terrace.

Star ½d   Train Ham[mersmi]th [?] to Portl[an]d Rd 6d   Dinner 1/–
Train Ch[arin]g + to Victoria 1½d   *Idler* 6d   *Freethinker* 1d   Train
South Kensington to Ravenscourt Park 5d

The Sir Arthur Sullivan cantata *The Martyr of Antioch* (1880) was received generally with hostility, but "Margarita's immolation," based upon the fourth-act finale of Rossini's *William Tell,* may have interested Shaw. However, he did not review the performance, nor did he stay for the conclusion.

6 SUNDAY   °*Lecture at Central Finsbury Radical Club. 241–3 Goswell Rd. E.C. (Henry Mundy). 11.45. "Labour Politics and Labour Parties." Lecture at the Washington Music Hall for the Battersea Labour League on "The History of Socialism" (W. Sanders), York Rd. Trafalgar Square Committee. 337 Strand. 11.30.*

Wrote a few letters and a bit of the *World* article at Fitzroy Square. Lay down for an hour before going off to a lecture. Corrected and sent off proof of *World* article when I got back.

Bus Hammersmith to Picc[adilly] O 3d   Train Ch[arin]g + to Victoria
1½d   Vict[oria] to Battersea Pk 1d   Battersea to Ravenscourt Park 4d

7 *Fabian Executive. 17⁴⁄₂. °Shelley Celebration at South Place Chapel. Paper by H. S. Salt. °Countess Castelvecchio's 2nd dramatic and musical recital. St. James's Banqueting Hall. 15. Central Group Meeting (Fabian). 32 Great Ormond St. 20. Mrs. Carr on "Women's Guild of Co-operators." °Monday Pop. Norman-Neruda and Adeline de Lara. 20.*

Wrote letters before starting to walk into town with Sparling. We met Wallas and Walker in Piccadilly. I met Aveling afterwards in Greek St. This was odd after the letter in *The Chronicle* this morning. Ernest Williams and Salt were at the Wheatsheaf. Salt walked back with me and left me at the corner of the Square. When I got in I was kept so long writing in the engagements into next year's diary, answering letters, correcting the *World* proof, and talking to Walter, who called, that I had to give up my intention of going to the concert and go straight to the Fabian, Walter walking with me as far as Holborn by way of Gower St. After the Executive I went with Olivier to Gatti and Rodesano's for something to eat and then to the Group Meeting, where I took the chair. I went to Gray's Inn with Mrs. Carr and sat with her until it was time to catch the 23.38 train at the Temple. Carr came in a few minutes before I left.

Star $\frac{1}{2}$d   Diary for next year at Stores 6/–   Dinner 1/2   Macaroni &c
at G[atti] a[nd] R[odesano]'s 1/4   Train Temple to Ravenscourt Park 7d

> Ernest Williams, author of *Made in Germany*, was an exponent of tariff reform. He was
> on the Fabian Executive in 1893–94, from which he resigned after a quarrel. ▪ On the
> order form for next year's *Lett's Diary* No. 11D (at 5/–), loosely inserted at this date, Shaw
> has written, "This time I changed to a larger diary—3B."

8 °*Cecil Sharp's first Tuesday afternoon lecture on Bach and Beethoven. 5
Langham Chambers. W. All Souls Place. 15. °Meeting of the Humanitarian
League at the Wheatsheaf, Rathbone Place. 20. Rev. J. Stratton on "Stag
Hunting" and Col. Coulson on "Rabbit Coursing." °Katherine Fisk's concert.
St. James's Hall. 20. Sauret. Meeting of Writers of Plays to discuss formation
of Society of British Dramatic Authors at Terry's. 3 Bedford St. Strand. W.C.
at 16. °Deutscher Sangerbund Concert, Holborn Town Hall. 20*$\frac{1}{2}$*. Seiffert.*

Spent the early part of the day drawing up a scheme of lectures for the
spring and summer session at the Fabian. May had gone into town; but
Sparling was working here (at 8 Hammersmith Terrace). After dinner I
went over to FE, and stayed with her until it was time to catch the 16.55
train to Charing Cross. I went to the meeting of playwrights, which lasted
until near 18.30. Resolved very emphatically to have nothing to do with it.
Rose was there. He walked with me to the Orange Grove, looking in for a
moment at the Green Room Club for letters. I had a bad headache and
quite gave up the idea of going to either of the concerts in consequence. I
played and sang a bit at the Square and then walked to St. James's Park and
got back here at about 23.30.

Star $\frac{1}{2}$d   Train Rav[enscourt] Pk to Ch[arin]g + and back 9d   Orange
Grove 1/10

> Shaw would join the Society of Authors in 1897, was elected to its council and to the
> Committee of Management in 1905, and served on the dramatic subcommittee from 1906
> to 1915. ▪ The Society of British Dramatic Authors, which Shaw resolved to ignore,
> never came into being.

9 *Lecture at Democratic Club. 36 Essex St. W.C. on "Labour Politics." 20.
(Shaw Maxwell). "Evolution of Socialism" announced by mistake.*

Resolved to take things easy. Spent the morning reading Willeby's *Chopin* for
review. After dinner dawdled a bit, reading *The Personal Rights Journal* and
posted up this diary. Walked into town. Animated debate at the club. I came
back in the train with the Sparlings, Touzeau Parris, Bullock and Grant.

Stars 1$\frac{1}{2}$d   Train Portland Road to Farringdon St 2d   Temple to Ravenscourt Park 6d

10 °*Bauer-Walenn concert. Hampstead Conservatoire. 20.15.*

Began *World* article. After dinner took things easy, sitting before the fire to
finish Mark Twain's *Tom Sawyer*. Went in to the Square to get my letters
and returned at about 20$\frac{1}{2}$. Bad fog. Played duets with May.

Star ½d   Train H[ammersmi]th to Portland Rd & back 9d

11 °*Meeting at Beeton's to discuss a paper by Wicksteed on "The Co-ordination of the Laws of Distribution." 9 Maresfield Gardens, N.W. 20. Gorski's Orchestral Concert. St. James's Hall. 20. Henschel conducts.*

Finished *World* article, working at it here until 17. Went in to the Square to get my letters. Wrote to Grein. Dined at the Orange Grove on my way to the concert. I met C. Dowdeswell in Piccadilly and walked with him to Victoria. Got back here about 20.

Star ½d   Train H[ammersmi]th to Portland Rd 4d   Dinner (at Orange Grove) 1/10   Train Victoria to Ham[mersmi]th 6d

12 *Crystal Palace Concert. 15. Heermann.*

Went over to FE in the morning and arranged to call in the evening to go over her part in the play. Lucy came to the Palace with me. Left Dalling Rd. about 22. Corrected *World* proofs when I got back.

Star ½d   Train Ravenscourt Pk to Victoria & back 9d   PMG 1d
Wash &c at Victoria 4d   *Pick-Me-Up* (com[ic] paper) 1d

> Hugo Heermann (1844–1935), German violinist, was also professor of violin at the Hoch Conservatory, Frankfurt, and leader of the Frankfurt String Quartet. Shaw and his sister attended the concert in which Heermann was soloist, but there would be no G.B.S. review. ▪ FE would have the leading role of Blanche Sartorius. Rehearsals of *Widowers' Houses* would begin two days later at the Mona Hotel, Covent Garden, often used by companies as a low-cost space close to the theaters.

13 SUNDAY   *Lecture at the Hammersmith Club. "Labour Politics and Labour Parties." 20. (A. Beasley). Demonstration in Trafalgar Square. 15. First since 13th November 1887. Speak from balustrade (East). No. 5.*

Went in to town in the morning to get my letters. Came back from the Square with Mrs. Sparling. Barnes was here when we got back. Began Fabian Notes for *Workman's Times*, which I undertook to do for Sparling this week.

Bus Uxbridge Rd to Holles St 4d   Programme of Demonstration 1d
Train St Ja[me]s's Pk to Rav[enscourt] Pk 6d   Excess fare for M[ay Morris Sparling] 1d

> Resolutions that were adopted at the unsuppressed demonstration asserted the unrestricted right to public meeting in the Square, urged the transfer from police to L.C.C. control of public open spaces, and demanded that unemployment be eased through a program of public works.

14   *Fabian Executive. 17¼. °Countess Castelvecchio's 3d dramatic and musical recital. St. James's Banqueting Hall. 15. °Liberal and Radical Union Council Meeting. National Liberal Club. 20. First rehearsal of* Widowers' Houses *at the Mona Hotel. 14. Call at the old office of* The Novel Review, *18 Tavistock St., to be interviewed by Miss Wilson. 15.*

Spent the morning finishing Fabian Notes for *The Workman's Times*. The rehearsal did not come to anything, as there were not enough present to get to work. I went on to *The Novel Review*, though I had telegraphed to put the inconvenience off. After the Fabian I went home and wrote some letters and changed my clothes. Did not get back here until past midnight. One of the letters I wrote was to the *PMG* about the right of public meeting.

Train Hammersmith to Ch[arin]g + (return not used) 9d   Dinner (at Orange Grove) 10d   *Star* ½d   Train Portland Rd to Ham[mersmi]th 6d

"Mr. Bernard Shaw's Play," interview by "R.Y.P." (presumably Miss Wilson), *Novel Review*, December 1892 (C909). ▪ "Differences and Divisions among Socialists," *Workman's Times*, 26 November 1892 (C906). ▪ Letter-to-the-editor, *PMG*, 16 November 1892 (C902), under the title, "Mr. Bernard Shaw and Trafalgar-square."

15   °*Cecil Sharp's 2nd lecture. 15. °Podmore's, 32 Well Walk, Hampstead, at 20½, to meet Geddes. Rehearsal. Mona Hotel. 20½.*

Wasted the whole day fooling indoors (it being very wet) over a reply to Bax's letter in *The Chronicle*, which I finally tore up. It was raining desperately when I went out to the rehearsal. At 17 May dismissed her work people so as to allow us to get to the piano and play Mendelssohn's Scotch Symphony, which she had just bought as a duet. FE and I came back together. I saw her home and sat with her until a little after midnight. We walked from the Mona Hotel to St. James's Park.

Train to Ch[arin]g + & back 9d   Papers–PMG & *Star* 1½d   Train St Ja[me]s's Pk to Rav[enscourt] Pk for F. E. 6d

16   *Rehearsal, Mona Hotel.*

Working at cutting the first and second acts of the play for performance. Called on FE and went through the part with her. Found Todhunter there. Went home after leaving the Orange Grove and got my letters. Got back here about 22 and wrote some letters.

Train Rav[enscourt] Pk to Ch[arin]g + single, self, 6d, return FE 9d   Papers 1½d   Orange Grove, table d'hote &c (2) 3/10   Train Portl[an]d Rd to H[ammersmi]th 7d

17   °*London Symphony Concert. St. James's Hall. 20½. Lart and Boosey's Operas, Globe Theatre. Ma Mie Rosette. 20½. Sleep at Fitzroy Square.*

Began *World* article—or rather read Santley's *Reminiscences* with a view to writing about them. Called for FE. We went into town together after dinner. Went home after rehearsal.

Train Rav[enscourt] Pk to Ch[arin]g + (2) 1/–   Pocket Book 6d   Program at Globe 6d

Reviewed on 23 November 1892 (C905). The light opera by Paul Lacome, with English libretto by George Dance and Ivan Caryll (from the French of Jules Prével and Armand Liorat), set in the period of Henry IV of France, would run ninety-four performances. G.B.S. found it "refreshingly free" from the "stale vulgarities" of its genre, but distractingly over-lighted by the new "electric candles." ▪ Sir Charles Santley's *Reminiscences* of his singing career were reviewed in G.B.S.'s 23 November 1892 column.

18 *Fabian. Sidney Webb on "The New Parliament." Essex Hall. 20. Press View. New English Art Club. Dudley Gallery. Look in at Ribot's pictures at Bernheim's Gallery, 186 Piccadilly. Rehearsal, Mona Hotel. 11.30. Sleep at Fitzroy Square. °Royal Society of Musicians. Elijah, at St. James's Hall. 20.*

Started for Press View immediately after breakfast. FE and I dined at Orange Grove after the rehearsal. We parted in St. Martin's Lane. I did some work on the *World* article in the afternoon. Intended to do more in the evening and after the Fabian; but Wallas came home with me and stayed until 24.

Star ½d   Dinner (at O[range] G[rove]) FE & I 3/10

"The Dudley Gallery," unsigned, *Daily Chronicle*, 21 November 1892 (C904). Shaw singled out for special praise two portraits by J. S. Sargent, a portrait by George Sauter, a study by J. J. Shannon, and a picture by Jacques-Émile Blanche "executed with a feeling akin to that of the old Dutch masters." ▪ Shaw published nothing about the paintings of Theodore Augustin Ribot (1823–1891).

19 *Crystal Palace Concert. 15. Rehearsal, Mona Hotel. 12. Private View. New English Art Club. Egyptian Hall.*

Worked at *World* article. Left rehearsal with de Lange at 13.30, parting from him in St. Martin's Lane. Was joined by FE at the Orange Grove. Rushed off to catch train at Charing Cross, leaving her to pay. Left concert by 16.3 train, Kate Gurly and Mother having come down with me. Went to Private View of New English Art Club to look for FE; but she was gone; but I found Bertha Newcombe instead, and walked with her to the South Kensington Museum, where Mrs. Sandham had asked a party of Fabians to meet her. I did not stay with them, as I was very hungry; so I returned here to Hammersmith to spend the evening singing to May. Shouted away until past midnight.

Orange Grove tips 2d   *Star* ½d   Train Ch[arin]g + to Victoria 1½d
S[ou]th Kensington to Rav[enscourt] Pk 5d   *PMG* 1d

The Crystal Palace concert went unnoticed by G.B.S. ▪ Herman De Lange (1851–1929), producer of *Widowers' Houses*, would play the role of Giuseppe in Shaw's *Man of Destiny* in the 1901 and 1907 productions.

20 SUNDAY *Lecture for the S. D. F. Mile End Branch on "Liberalism and Socialism" (R. J. Benton. 69 Ernest St. Mile End), 461 Commercial Rd., 20½. Unemployed Committee (late Trafalgar Square Committee). 337 Strand, W. C. 11.30.*

Sparling came to the Committee with me. I moved and carried a resolution condemning violent language. In the afternoon Mme. Stepniak, Joseph Lane, Steffen called; and I had great difficulty finishing my *World* article and the picture gallery notes, which I got posted on the stroke of midnight.

Train Rav[enscourt] Pk to Temple & back 9d   Rav[enscour]t Pk to Aldgate East & back 1/5   Tram Aldgate to Com[mercial] Rd 2d

> Joseph Lane had been a member of the S.D.F. Executive Council and was still active in
> Morris's Socialist League.

21 *Fabian Executive. 17$\frac{1}{2}$. Fabian Central Group Meeting. 32 Great Ormond St. F. Galton on "The Place of Trade Unionism in Social Reconstruc-
tion." 20. Rehearsal, Mona Hotel. 12.30. Call on Williamson of* Black and
White *in the afternoon. Sleep at Fitzroy Square.*

Murray Carson came to the rehearsal to read the part of Trench. After
dinner at the Orange Grove I went to *Black and White* and arranged with
Williamson to send him an article on the music of the month at the end of
December. Then to the Executive, where I took the chair. Got something to
eat alone at Gatti's and then went to the Fabian Group Meeting, where I
took the chair. Then home.

Train to Ch[arin]g + 6d   Dinner (at Orange Grove) 1/–?   Macaroni
&c at Gatti & Rodesano's 1/4   Pinero's *Magistrate* 1/1$\frac{1}{2}$

> There is no evidence of byline or payment that Shaw contributed to *Black and White*.

22 °*Cecil Sharp's 3rd lecture. 15. School Board Vocal Music Competition.
Exeter Hall. 14. Rehearsal, Mona Hotel. 12.30.*

No rehearsal, the part of Trench being still rejected by all; Murray Carson
came in; and we had a long discussion of acting. Finally we all went off to
get something to eat. Spent three hours at Exeter Hall. Went out to FE's;
and stayed there until 22. Read over her part with her. On my way out from
town got into the train with Charley Burkinyoung. Got out with him at
Earl's Court and walked with him to the corner of Philbeach Gardens,
where we parted, I walking on to FE's.

Train to Ch[arin]g + 6d   Dinner (at Orange Grove) 1/4?   Papers
1$\frac{1}{2}$d?   Train Ch[arin]g + to Earls Court 5d?

23 °*Royal Choral Society. Berlioz's* Faust. *Albert Hall. 20. Rehearsal,
Mona Hotel. 12.30.*

Worked at the *Knot* before starting for town by the 11.55 train. Again no
rehearsal. Went home and wrote several letters, notably one to Webb about
public speaking. FE was not at rehearsal, as she was busy at The Comedy;
so I called on her on my way back to Hammersmith. Spent the evening on
the *World* article. The Sparlings went out for a while to a party at the Ellis's
next door.

Train Rav[enscourt] Pk to Ch[arin]g + 6d   *Pick-Me-Up* 1d   Dinner (at
Orange Grove) 10d   *Star* $\frac{1}{2}$d   *PMG* 1d   Train Royal Oak to
Shep[herds] Bush 3d

24 *Rehearsal, Mona Hotel. 12.30.*

Worked at the *Knot*. Went in to town with FE. We had something like a real rehearsal at last, though we were unable to finish the second act and had no Lickcheese. Afterwards I went to the Square to get my letters. I got back here before 18. Finished and sent off a large instalment of the *World* article, and played a lot with May.

Train to Ch[arin]g + 6d   Dinner 11d   Train P[or]tl[an]d Rd to Rav[enscourt] Pk 7d

> Lickcheese is the Dickensian rent-collector in *Widowers' Houses*, a craven employee of Blanche's father, Mr. Sartorius.

25 *Fabian Members' Meeting. Barnard's Inn. 20. Eight Hours Committee Report, Appointment of Auditors, and Miss Brooke's resolution re framing new Constitution. Press View. Troubetskoy's portraits and studies in oils. Dowdeswell's. Press View. Miniatures at the Fine Art Society. Press View. Old Water Colour Society. 5 Pall Mall East. Press View. Stephen Coleridge's oil studies,* Water Ways of England, *at Dowdeswell's. Rehearsal, Mona Hotel. 12.30.*

Went in to town by the 10.17 train and did the Bond St. Galleries before rehearsal. Welch turned up to play Lickcheese; and we rehearsed the first two acts for the first time with the full cast. Afterwards I dined with FE at the Orange Grove and then went to the Old Water Colour Society. Then home, where I found Mrs. Sparling visiting my mother. JP and Georgie came in later on. I had to speak several times at the Fabian. Came home with Sparling.

Train Ravenscourt Park to St Ja[me]s's Pk 6d   Dinner (at O. G.) (2) 2/2   *Justice* 1d   *Star* ½d   Train Ptld Rd to Far[r]ingdon 2d Temple to Rav[enscourt] Pk 6d

> Prince Paul Troubetskoy (1867–1938), Russian émigré, artist, and sculptor, would eventually have Shaw as one of his most famous subjects. ▪ Stephen Coleridge (1854–1934), London landscape painter, travel writer, and memoirist. ▪ James Welch (1865–1917) would later play Major Paul Petkoff in *Arms and the Man* (1894) and William the Waiter in *You Never Can Tell* (1899).

26 *Crystal Palace Concert. 15. W. Wallace's orchestral ballads,* The Passing of Beatrice. *Ravogli and Adeline de Lara. Call with Sparling on Mrs. Larkom Jacobs, 53 Westbourne Park Villas, Royal Oak W., at 20, to see about a Fabian speaking class. Rehearsal, Mona Hotel. 12.30.*

Came back from the Palace with Thompson, who walked with me as far as the corner of Holles St.

Train Rav[enscourt] Pk to Ch[arin]g + 6d   Ch[arin]g + to Victoria 1½d   Dinner (at Orange Grove) 1/–?   Papers 1½d?   Portland Road to Royal Oak 2d?   Royal Oak to Ham[mersm]ith 2d?

> Adeline de Lara (1872–1961) had been the piano child prodigy Adeline Tilbury; she first performed publicly in London in 1891. Although G.B.S. did not notice her performance,

in his 30 November 1892 column (C908) he wrote of "a new symphonic poem, *The Passing of Beatrice*, by Mr. William Wallace, a young Scotch composer with a very tender and sympathetic talent." He found, however, that the piece "needed to be cut down by about nine-tenths." Wallace (1860–1940) was not related to William Vincent Wallace (1812–1865), an Irishman and the composer of the opera *Maritana*.

27 SUNDAY   *Off—Club evicted. Lecture on "Practical Communism" at the Workpeople's Educational Club. 40 Berners St. Commercial Rd. E. 20. (C. W. Mowbray, 25 Little Alie St., Leman St. E.). Unemployed Committee. 337 Strand. 11.30. Crane lectures on his American trip at Kelmscott House. 20.*

We did not get back from the Committee until 14½. I met Mowbray there and learned that the lecture was off. Bax and another man whose name I forget came in in the evening. We all went to Crane's lecture. Had a few words with Mrs. Jopling afterwards. Very busy writing interview for the *Star*. Up late over it. I did not go in to supper at Morris's in order to get back to work.

Train Rav[enscourt] Pk to Temple & back 1/–

> Shaw's spoofing self-interview, publicizing *Widowers' Houses*, would appear in *The Star* 29 November 1892 (C907). He toyed with the title, which the "interviewer" misunderstands as *Wendover's Horses*, and described the setting—his own room at Fitzroy Square—apparently only too accurately. "The table was untidy beyond belief: dusty heaps of letters and papers in utter disorder were mixed up with stationery, inkstands, *Stars*, *Chronicles*, butter, sugar, stray apples, knives and spoons, a full breakfast cup of cocoa, and a plate upon which Mr. Shaw, as I entered, was dumping down a helping of porridge which he had just extracted from a saucepan on the hob."

28   *Fabian Executive. 17¼. Rehearsal, Mona Hotel. 12.*

Was rather addled after yesterday's work, and went in by the 10.55 train instead of the 11.55. Found, however, that the hour of our rehearsal had been changed to 12; so had only half an hour to wait instead of an hour. Revised part of Miss Wilson's interview with me for the *Novel Review* and brought it down to the office myself. Found nobody there except a manager (presumably) who told me where to find the printers, with whom I left the proof. When I got back to Hammersmith after the Executive I found the *Star* proof waiting for me. Revised it and sent it off. After the Executive Sparling, Olivier and I had some grub at the Orange Grove. Then Sparling and I walked across St. James's Park to the station and so home together.

Train Rav[enscourt] Pk to Ch[arin]g + 5d   Dinner (Orange Grove) 1/6?   Papers 1½d?   Meal at O[range] G[rove] after Exec[utive] 1/6? Train St Ja[me]s's Pk to Rav[enscourt] Pk 5d?

29   °*Cecil Sharp's 4th lecture. 15. Rehearsal, Mona Hotel. 12.30.*

Worked at the revision of *The Irrational Knot*, now very nearly finished. Great fun over the interview in the *Star*. Went to Dalling Rd. with FE and worked over her part with her. She went back to town by a train about 19.15. I went to the Terrace and did some work and played some duets with May. I called at the Square after dinner, and changed my clothes. Walker came in whilst I was here; but as I had just parted from FE and had agreed to meet her in quarter of an hour at Portland Rd. station, I had to hurry off at once.

Train Rav[enscourt] Pk to Ch[arin]g + 6d   13 *Stars* 6½d   Dinner at Orange Grove (2) 2/6?   Train Portland Rd to Shep[herds] B[ush] (2) 1/–

30   *Albert Hall. Scotch National Concert. 19.45. Rehearsal, Mona Hotel. 12.30.*

Busy and exhausted after the *Widowers' Houses* rehearsals, Shaw did not review the Scotch National concert. It is very likely he did not attend it.

December

1   *London Symphony Concert. St. James's Hall. 20½. Rehearsal (first on stage), Royalty Theatre. 14½.*

Began *World* article. Slept at the Square. Very wet day.

Train Rav[enscourt] Pk to Ch[arin]g + 6d   Dinner (Orange Grove) 1/–? *Star* ½d

G.B.S. reviewed the London Symphony on 7 December 1892 (C910). Henschel conducted Raff's "Lenore" symphony, a Shaw favorite.

2   *Fabian. B. F. C. Costelloe on "The Incidence of Taxation." Essex Hall. 20. Rehearsal, Royalty Theatre. 14½.*

Finished the *World* article all except a couple of sentences. Wallas came back with me from the Fabian and came in for a while. O'Driscoll walked with us as far as Queen Square. Spoke in the debate. On my way to the Fabian left Lucy's spectacles at the Trafalgar Theatre.

Dinner (at Wheatsheaf) 1/1?   *Star* ½d

Lucy Shaw Butterfield was playing in yet another revival of *Dorothy*, this one to survive only nineteen performances.

3   °*Crystal Palace Concert. 15. Rehearsal, Royalty Theatre. 14½. Look in at Unwin's exhibition of Vierge's Quevedo drawings at Barnard's Inn.*

Met Robertson and Mrs. Reid at the Vierge exhibition before dinner. Saw Georgina at the restaurant. After the rehearsal went with FE to Dalling Rd. and went over her part with her. Saw her off by the 21.15 train to town. Went to the Terrace and corrected and sent off the proofs to the *World*. The

Sparlings did not come in until midnight from the dinner to [A. E.] Fletcher at the Democratic Club.

Train to Farringdon 2d   Dinner (at corner of Ch[arin]g + Rd) 1/1
Train St Ja[me]s's Pk to Rav[enscourt] Pk (2) 1/–   *Star* ½d   *PMG* 1d

> Daniel Urrbieta Vierge had illustrated works by the great Spanish poet and satirist Francisco Gómez de Quevedo y Villegas (1580–1645), producing the first line-block drawings of artistic importance.

4 SUNDAY *Lecture on "The Working Day" at the West Norwood Reform Club, Auckland Hill, West Norwood, S.E., at 20½ (James Attfield). Webbs' (Sidney) in the afternoon.*

After the Committee went home. Wrote several letters after dinner. Then went up to Webbs' where I found Wallas. He left before I did. The Webbs and I then came in to town together and went to the Albemarle Club, where we had a meal. I caught the 19.29 train from Victoria to West Norwood and came back by the 22.35. It was too late to get a train to Hammersmith; so I walked home. Felt so unusually tired and hungry that I took some gruel and a lot of fruit.

Train Rav[enscourt] Pk to St Ja[me]s's Pk 6d   Baker St to Finchley Rd &
back 4d   Bus Baker St to Bond St 2d   Train Victoria to West Norwood
& back 1/3

5 *Fabian Executive. 17½. °Monday Pop. Brahms's Clarinet Quintet. Muhlfeld. 20. Also next Saturday. °Jeanne Douste's recital. Prince's Hall. 20½. °Rehearsal. 14½.*

Was not down to breakfast until 11. Wrote letters, and tried to write up this diary for the past week. Did not attend the rehearsal, as I promised to keep away so as to leave them to get their words. Came back with Sparling from Executive.

Train to Ptld Rd 7d   Dinner 1/1?   Macaroni &c at Gatti & Rodesano's 1/8

6 *°Cecil Sharp's 5th lecture. 15. °Stock Exchange Concert. St. James's Hall. 20. Rehearsal. 14½.*

Began revising my old paper against Anarchism for the press, to reissue as a Fabian tract. After the rehearsal went with FE to the Aerated Bread Shop in Rathbone Place. Parted from her at the corner and went to Archer's. George Moore came in. I stayed until past 20, and then went back to the Square, where I was busy sending off tickets for the dress rehearsal tomorrow until 20. Then went off to Hammersmith.

Train to Ptld Rd & back 1/–   Dinner 1/1   *Star* ½d

7 *°Royal Choral Society. Sullivan's Golden Legend. Albert Hall. 20. °Carli's Guitar and Vocal recital. Steinway Hall. 20. Dress rehearsal, Royalty Theatre. 18.*

Finished revising the tract on Anarchism for the Fabian. Came in to town by the 16.9 train with May. Benson (the coppersmith) traveled with us as far as Edgware Rd. May got out at Baker St. The rehearsal was so atrociously bad that I could think of nothing else all the rest of the evening. Wrote to Grein and FE about it. Played a Mozart quartet with May (duet) to quiet myself. Rose came back from the theatre with us (May and I) as far as Hammersmith. We walked to St. James's Park.

Train Rav[enscourt] Pk to Ptld Rd, M[ay] & I 1/2   "Answers" 1d
PMG 1d   Train St Ja[me]s's Pk to Hammersmith (May paid)

8 *Special Fabian Executive on Unemployed Question. 17$\frac{1}{4}$. Last rehearsal. 14$\frac{1}{4}$.*

Wrote a couple of letters and then walked into town. Left the theatre with FE at 18.15; and went with her to the door of the Orange Grove, where I left her and hurried on to the Executive. They were all gone except Miss Priestley and Sparling. Miss Priestley gave me her opinion of the play. Came back with Sparling. Got home a little after 20 or thereabouts. Wrote some letters, etc.

Bus Marble Arch to Halles St 1d   *Star* $\frac{1}{2}$d   Dinner 10d   Chas. Hoppe, for pit tickets for Mrs. Hewlett 5/–   Train Temple to Rav[enscourt] Pk 6d

> Isobel E. Priestley (later Mrs. Bart Kennedy) was assistant secretary of the Fabian Society. ▪ Charles Hoppe was the acting manager of the theater.

9 *Production of* Widowers' Houses *by the Independent Theatre at the Royalty. 20$\frac{1}{2}$.* °*Wind Instrument Chamber Music Society 1st concert. Prince's Hall. 20$\frac{1}{2}$.*

I forget what I did today, except—Oh, I remember. I went over to FE at about noon and stayed there for some hours. Then I walked into town. Made a speech at the end of the play. Spent the night at Fitzroy Square.

Watchkey 3d

> Shaw assured his audience that had his play been "received lightly," he would have been disappointed. What he had dramatized was going on in actual life, but he "heartily hope[d] the time would come when the play . . . would be both utterly impossible and utterly unintelligible." He hoped that the critics—who he assumed would castigate the play—would "carefully discriminate" between the writer and the actors who had so zealously carried out his intentions. His play, he insisted, "was in all particulars the faithful reflex of a sordid and unpitying age." (Archibald Henderson, in his 1911 *George Bernard Shaw*, credits the quotations from Shaw's remarks at the curtain to an unidentified informant who had been in the opening audience.)

10 °*Crystal Palace Concert. 15. Gerardy. Mackenzie conducts.* °*Fisher Unwin's At-Home. Barnard's Inn. 21. Royal College of Music performance of Gluck's* Orfeo. *Lyceum Theatre. 14$\frac{1}{2}$.*

Busy reading criticisms. Wallas came in; and we went for a turn in Regents Park after I had finished a letter to Grein to read at the meeting of the cast, which I could not attend. FE was at the Lyceum with me. I sent back to Hammersmith with her, calling at the Square on the way to look for letters. I left her about 19 and came on to the Terrace, where I found Gilbert Ellis. I went out again to Hammersmith Broadway and back. On my return Ellis took his leave; and I got to work on the *World* article. Did not carry it very far but took to reading Dumas's *Balsamo* and went to bed early.

Papers 1/–?   Dinner 10d?   Train Ptld Rd to Shep[herds] Bush (2) 1/–

Orfeo received a G.B.S. review despite his overwhelming involvement with the first play he had completed and committed to the stage. In *World*, 14 December 1892 (C912), he wrote that Gluck's opera "was admirably put on. . . . The principal performer, Miss Clara Butt, a comparatively raw recruit from Bristol, far surpassed the utmost expectations that one could have reasonably entertained." G.B.S. predicted "a considerable career" for her. (Dame) Clara Butt (1872–1936), contralto, would make her professional debut later in Arthur Sullivan's cantata *The Golden Legend*. Her stage career would be one of performances in ballads, song cycles, and oratorios. ∎ Few critics approved of Shaw's play. The London Correspondent of the Glasgow *Herald* observed. "The characters are treated naturally, and not in the glorified form so common upon the conventional stage. . . . It was a treat for once to see a hero (like one of Thackeray's) no better than one of his fellow-men. . . ." On the other hand, *The Times* complained that "There can hardly be said to be a single estimable personage in the whole play." The *Daily Telegraph* called the characters "entirely selfish and despicable." According to the *Athenaeum*, "Mr. Shaw's [seamy] world has not rags enough to cover its nudity," and was depicted with "Zolaesque exactitude." *The World* (in the person of William Archer) saw everyone in the play as "ill-conditioned, quarrelsome, fractious, apt to behave . . . like a badly brought-up child." The *Sunday Sun* saw "a distorted and myopic outlook on society." *The Speaker* (where A. B. Walkley now held forth) attacked Shaw's allegedly warped vision, saying, "The mere word 'mortgage' suffices to turn hero into rascal. Mr. Shaw will say that it is his point—scratch a middle-class hero and you find a rascal." ∎ Gilbert Ellis, nephew of Frederick Startbridge Ellis (the Sparlings' Hammersmith Terrace neighbor), had succeeded to the directorship of the publishing firm founded by his uncle. ∎ *Joseph Balsamo* (1846), by Alexandre Dumas, *père*, set in the eighteenth century.

11 SUNDAY *Lecture at the Lewisham and Lee Liberal and Radical Club, 170 High St., Lewisham, at 20½. (Marshall Steele, Sunbury, Grove Park, Lee). °Grein on "The Effect of the Drama on the Emotions" at the Playgoers' Club. Adelphi Restaurant. 20. Archer in the chair.*

Finished and sent off *World* article. Went to Blackheath by the 17.15 train and spent a couple of hours at Blands'. Morris, Griffiths, Miss Doran, Bellingham Smith, Marshall Steele were there; I had a hard run for the train after the lecture and was up late getting the article off. Slept at Fitzroy Square.

Train Rav[enscourt] Pk to Ch[arin]g + 6d   Ch[arin]g + to Blackheath & back (from Lewisham Junction) 1/4   Toffee 1d

12 *Fabian Executive. 17¾. Rehearsal, Royalty Theatre (in the saloon). 14¼. °Special Fabian Preliminary Executive. 13.*

Read criticisms; wrote letters; and corrected *World* proof. Made certain alterations in the play for tomorrow's performance. Went on to the Fabian after the rehearsal. Came back to the Terrace with Sparling. Wrote draft circular on the unemployed question for the Fabian Groups, and a letter to *The Workman's Times* in reply to Scheu. Also several letters. Did not get to bed until about 2.

Star ½d   Dinner 10d   *Speaker* 6d   *Pick-Me-Up* (comic paper) 1d Train to Rav[enscourt] Pk 6d

> "Differences and Divisions among Socialists," *Workman's Times*, 17 December 1892 (C913). ▪ Like his circular to trades councils (A17), the circular on the Unemployed Question (A18) seems to have been distributed but not one copy survives.

13 *Ashton Ellis at the Musical Association on "Wagner's Prose Writings." Royal Academy of Music. 20.15. °Cecil Sharp's 6th and last lecture. 15. Matinee of* Widowers' Houses, *Royalty Theatre. 15. °Press View. Early English pictures at Dowdeswell's.*

Up late. Wrote up this diary. Walked in to town. Went straight on to the theatre after dining. Made a little speech before the curtain. JP, Georgie, Lucy and May Sparling came to the Square to tea. After the meeting at the Royal Academy of Music, at which I spoke, I went to Barnard's Inn (Ellis walking with me as far as Holborn to pick up May at the Arts and Crafts meeting; but they were all gone). So I took the train from Farringdon to Hammersmith and amused myself during the journey by writing a letter to Archer which I afterwards tore up. Sparling was away lecturing in Leicester.

Star ½d   *PMG* 1d   Dinner (O[range] G[rove]) 1/–   Train Farringdon to Ham[mersm]ith 7d

> According to G.B.S., 21 December 1892 (C915), "When Mr. [Ashton] Ellis sat down, I asked myself was there no man left to get up [to complain in the old anti-Wagner clichés of yesteryear]." Since "the enemy" was "speechless," those in Ellis's "party"—including Shaw—"had the discussion to themselves." The discussion, including Shaw's comments on Wagner's views of Mendelssohn and Brahms, appeared in the *Proceedings of the Musical Association 1892–93* (B11) and were reprinted in *Shaw's Music*, II (A310).

14 [The drains are up at Fitzroy Square, thanks to our friend the sanitary inspector; and I am staying out here (at Sparlings' in Hammersmith) in consequence.]

> Shaw to A. J. Marriott, 14 December 1892, in *CL*.

15 *Call on the Charringtons in the evening. Charity Concert. (St. Mary's Nursing Home, Plaistow). St. James's Hall. 15.*

> Shaw had written to Charles Charrington the day before (*CL*), deploring the fact that he and Janet had not gone to see *Widowers' Houses*. "I have got a blue book across the footlights," he crowed. ▪ The Charity Concert was reviewed by G.B.S. on 21 December 1892 (C915). Among the well-known singers was the famed American contralto Katherine Fiske, whose singing G.B.S. found "mechanical." "The concert," he explained, ". . . was varied by the appearance from time to time of a cheerful clergyman, who made the most sinister announcements without blenching, and retired each time smiling blandly at the horror-stricken audience."

16   *Fabian. David F. Schloss on "Industrial Peace." Essex Hall. 20. Fabian Executive. 276 Strand. 17½.*

17   *°Crystal Palace Concert. 15. Tchaikovsky's Violin Concerto. Sauret. °Crane's At-Home at his new house, 13 Holland St., Kensington W. 21. Meeting of Fabian Group Secretaries and Executive to discuss Unemployed Question, 276 Strand, 15¼.*

18 SUNDAY   *Lecture at Kelmscott House for the Hammersmith Socialist Society. 20. (Sparling).*

Revised proof of letter to the *Star* in reply to critics of the play. Also *World* proof. This involved finishing the *World* article. After dinner I went out intending to go over to Clapham to see Massingham; but I mistook the hour of the train and missed it. I went to Bedford Park and visited the Pagets. On my return I found Blomfield, Pinker, and Miss Dalbshoff here. Pinker stayed until long after 18. I had "tea" and then lay down and slept for more than half an hour. After the lecture I went into Morris's to supper. Bax, who had taken the chair for me, was there; also Catterson Smith, Touzeau Parris, Beesly, Walker and Bullock. Bertha Newcombe was one of the afternoon callers.

> "Bernard Shaw Replies to Critics of 'Widowers' Houses,'" *The Star*, 19 December 1892 (C914). "The evidence of the notices," Shaw wrote, ". . . is irresistible. With hardly an exception the men who find my sociology wrong are also the men who find my dramatic worksmanship bad. . . . Even the criticism of the acting is biassed in the same way. The effect on me, of course, is to reassure me completely as to my own competence as a playwright." ■ (Sir) Reginald Blomfield (1856–1942) was the architect who would restore the official prime minister's residence, Chequers, and design the Menin Gate at Ypres; James Brand Pinker (1863–1922) was a literary agent; Miss Dalbshoff may have been one of Mrs. Shaw's voice students.

19   *°Fabian Executive. 17¼. °Time to be thinking about article for* Black and White. *Monday Pop. Muhlfield.*

Wrote up this diary. Went into the City to get a new gold pen, having broken the point of the old one.

New gold pen 11/–   −5/6 = 5/6 (deduction for the old pen)

> Richard Muhlfield, clarinetist. Shaw would not publish a review of this concert.

20   Found that the new gold pen was too hard, so went into the City again and changed it.

21   *Go down to Kelmscott by the 13.25 train from Paddington.*

Went up to the Square for my bag; packed it; and got to Paddington in good time. Miss Allen saw us off. We had an hour's wait at Oxford and walked through the town to within a few hundred yards of Magdalen Bridge. The party at Kelmscott consisted of the Sparlings, myself, Morris, Jennie [Morris] and Mary De Morgan.

X'mas boxes to May [Morris Sparling] & servants & May's parents 20/–
Train to Portl[an]d Rd from Rav[enscourt] Pk 7d   Train Ptld Rd to
Paddington 1½d   Paddington to Lechlade (return) 15/11   Paste (at
Oxford) 6d   Buns & milk 6d

There are two Miss Allens in Shaw's addressbook at this time, both Fabians.

22   (at Kelmscott)

Set to work making an album of all the press notices of the play. Cold
weather, very muddy underfoot. Sparling and I went for a walk before
dinner. The routine here is that Sparling and I work all day in the green
room, the others visiting us occasionally, but using the tapestry room.
Breakfast at 9; dinner at 13; afternoon tea at about 17; and supper at 19½.
Then we all go up to the tapestry room and play at "20 Questions." All
except Morris and myself go to bed at about 22½ or 23. We sit up and jaw a
bit longer. Tonight Morris talked a lot about Iceland. This evening we had
the mummers in.

The album of press notices of *Widowers' Houses* is now at Cornell.   • On their first
evening at Kelmscott, G.B.S. wrote on 4 January 1893 (C917), they were "invaded" by
farm laborers dressed as mummers, "overgrown with strips of colored paper as a rock is
overgrown with seaweed; and they went through an operatic performance. . . . I gathered
that one of them was King Alfred, and another St. George. A third, equipped with a stale
tall hat, was announced as 'the doctor.' He drew a tooth from the *prima donna*, whom I
did not succeed in identifying; revived the other characters when they were slain in single
combat; and sang a ballad expressive of his aspiration to live and die 'a varmer's b'woy.'
This he delivered with such a concentrated lack of conviction that I at once concluded
that he actually was a farmer's boy. . . ."

23   Still at the pasting. Hard frost set in. We all (except May, who followed
us and met us on the way back) walked over to Buscot, where we saw the
little church and went through the garden of Birchall, the parson. Morris
and I had a long talk about the proposal to form a Socialist alliance.

The Rev. Oswald Birchall (1843–?), a B.A. from Brasenose College, Oxford, in 1867,
became Rector of Buscot, near Lechlade, in the diocese of Oxford, in 1884.

24   Frost harder than before. Still pasting. Took a walk through the fields
with Sparling before dinner. Took a walk by myself along the Langford
road before supper. Finished the pasting. Serenades, etc. by the villagers
outside. Talked to Morris about Durer, etc. before we went to bed.

"On Christmas Eve there was more music, performed by the school children, the carol
singers, and finally by an orchestra consisting of a violin, a tambourine, a toy instrument
with a compass of one wrong note, which it played steadily on the second and third beats in
the bar, and anything else that would make a noise *ripieno, ad lib.* The singers sang traditional—*i.e.* inaccurate—versions of old airs and modern music hall songs . . ." (C917).

25   Pasting done—took to answering my letters. We all went for a walk
along the Langford road before dinner. Reading and letter writing in the
afternoon. Talked about printing in the evening.

26 Wrote up this diary, leaving large gaps. Wrote some letters. Frost harder than ever.

> To J. L. Joynes, on 27 December 1892, Morris wrote, "Shaw is happy because (as he sleeps with his window wide open) his water-jug is frozen deeper than anyone else's."

27 The Birchalls came to dinner. In the morning May, Sparling and I took a walk down the river and back. I worked at copying bits out of press notices for quotation in the preface to *Widowers' Houses.* Wrote a letter to *The Speaker* in reply to an article on the play.

> The letter, a response to A. B. Walkley's derogatory review, was published as "Unconscious Villainy and *Widowers' Houses,*" *The Speaker,* 31 December 1892 (C916).

28 Worked at picking out press notices for quotation in preface to the play. Sparling went up to town. May and I walked over to Buscot Wood in the afternoon.

29 *Come up from Kelmscott by the 14.42 train.*
Packing, writing letters, etc. in the morning. Went for a short stroll along the river—trees covered with hoar frost to the very tops, bright sunshine, very pretty. After dinner May and I walked over to the station through the fields, our lunch going on in the trap. At Oxford we went for a short walk as far as the water to see the skating.

Tips to servants 10/–   Milk &c at Oxford 1/2   Train Bishops Rd to Rav[enscourt] Pk (2) 1/2

30 *Fabian Executive. 17¼. Preliminary Committee. 16½. Go to* King Lear *at the Lyceum. 20.*
Worked at preface to play. After dinner went up to town. Slept at the Square.

Train to Portl[an]d Rd 7d   Papers 1½d   Lyceum Theatre 2/6   Book of play 1/–

> Shaw's *World* column on 4 January 1893 (C917) found Hamilton Clark's incidental music "graceful" and "sensitive to the tenderer emotions of the drama," but "far too civilized" for the "powerful and barbaric" element of *Lear.*

31 *Private View. Old Masters at the Academy.*
Wrote some letters. Called at Jaeger's to buy gloves on my way to the Academy. May joined me there. We parted outside and I went back to the Square. In the evening I intended to call on FE, but as there was no light in her window I concluded that she had gone off to the theatre and so went straight on to the [Sparlings' at Hammersmith] Terrace, where I began my *World* article.

Dinner at Orange Grove 1/–   *Speaker* 6d   *Star* ½d   *Justice* 1d
Train to Shep[herds] Bush 6d   Remitted Lambert for sheets 9/–   Cost
of orders 1½d

> Shaw's *World* musical column, 4 January 1893 (C917), leaned heavily upon his Christmas
> in the country. ■ Brooke Lambert (1834–1901), a Christian Socialist, was vicar of
> Greenwich and a social and educational reformer in the East End. It is possible that Shaw
> was reimbursing Lambert for unbound sheets of an unspecified publication with the
> purchase of a postal order (as he had no checking account).

Notes

[INCOME, BY MONTH; FOLLOWING 1892 ENTRIES]

January

15	*The World*	25/ 0/ 0
16	*Illustrated London News*	3/12/ 0

February

9	*[The] Star*	2/ 7/ 0
10	*The Players*	3/ 3/ 0
15	*The World*	20/ 0/ 0

Cheque for £ 3/13/6 from *Novel Review*
    returned to Miss Harkness on the 13th.
    I did not care to take it from her,
    as she is presumably not making anything
    out of the review, which she has only
    just bought. The nature of the article,
    too, made me averse to making a commercial
    transaction of the affair.

March

12	*The World*	20/ 0/ 0
11	*Illustrated London News*	1/16/ 0

April

15	*The World*	25/ 0/ 0
"	*The Illustrated London News*	3/ 3/ 0

May

12	*The World*	20/ 0/ 0
23	*The Daily Chronicle*	19/ 8/ 6
25	"	3/ 1/ 6
		22/10/ 0

[On lower part of page:] The second item above
    (£ 22/10/0) is included in the
    Income Tax return for 1891–92.

June

	Walter Scott, royalties on *Cashel Byron's* *Profession* from 31st March 91 to 25 May 92	2/18/ 6
	Quintessence of Ibsensism	24/ 3/ 9
14	*The World*	20/ 0/ 0
	The first two items above are included in the Income Tax return for 1891–92.	

July

12	*The World*	25/ 6/ 0

August

16	*The World*	20/ 0/ 0

September

9	*Manchester Sunday Chronicle*	5/ 0/ 0
13	*The Star*	1/ 4/ 6
9	*The Pall Mall Gazette*	7/ 6
14	W. Swan Sonnenschein & Co, royalties on *An Unsocial Socialist* for year ending 30th June	1/2
16	*The World*	25/ 0/ 0
	W. Swan Sonnenschein, royalties on *An Unsocial Socialist* from 30th June as above up to date, this being a final settlement, as the agreement has expired and the last copy been sold.	4/10

October

14	*The World*	20/ 0 0

November

10	*The Star*	3/ 3/ 0
15	*The World*	20/ 0/ 0

December

10	*The Star*	3/ 3/ 0
16	*The World*	26/ 6/ 6

REMINDERS FOR NEXT YEAR

January:

Lecture on the 29th at Croydon (J. T. Dunlop, 24 Stroud Road, Woodside, S. Norwood).

London Symphony Concert. St Ja[me]s's Hall. 20½. 19th.

Lecture at the Chiswick Rad[ical] Club. 20. Evolution of Socialism. (J.A. Lorrain. Norfolk Ho[use]. Strand W.C.) 22nd.

Albert Hall. Messiah. 2nd.—E. M. Smyth's Requiem + Mass of the Creation on the 18th Jan.

Lecture in Lincoln on the 15th.—Go down on the Saturday?—Cathedral not to be seen after 16. (S. Maudson Grant, 22 Trentercroft St.).

February:
London Symphony Concerts. 2nd & 16th.
First Crystal Palace Concert. 18th.
Albert Hall. Redemption [?]. 15th.
Lecture for Chelsea Labor League on last Sunday. (C.A. Smart).
Lecture for Battersea Labor League on the 19th at the Washington Music
　Hall on History of Liberalism.

March:
London Symphony Concert. 2nd.
Albert Hall. Israel in Egypt. 20. 8th.
Albert Hall. Messiah. 31st.

April:
Albert Hall. St. Paul. 19th.
Lecture on the 30th on Progress in Free Thought to the Bethnal Green
　Br[anch] N. L. S., Libra Hall, 78 Libra Rd. Roman Rd E (Ja[me]s Neate.
　385 Beth[nal] G[ree]n Rd E.) 19.

May:
Albert Hall. Elijah. 10th.

Diary 1893

Notes

BOOKS FOR REVIEW

Title & Author	Paper	[Received]	[Posted]	[Published]
Wagner's Prose Works, Vol. I, W. Ashton Ellis (translator)	*The Daily Chronicle*	19/1/–	15/2/–	18/2/–
Mediæval Lore, Bart[holomew] Anglicus, ed. [by] Rob[ert] Steele; pref. [by] W[illia]m Morris	"	20/1/–	1/2/–	13/2/–
Land Nationalisation, Harold Cox	"	[@28/1]	2/2/–	4/4/–
Essays on Vegetarianism, A. J. Hills	"	3/2/–?		
Form & Design in Music. H. Heathcote Statham.	"	10/5/–		[31/5]
The Beethoven—Cramer Studies, J. S. Shedlock, ed.	*The World*	27/2/–?		
Voice Training Primer, Mrs. Behuke & D.C.W. Pearce.	"	13/6/–		

Shaw also reviewed Charles Willeby's *Masters of Contemporary Music*, in *The World* for 16 August 1893 (C969), and Mariam Tenger's *Recollections of Countess Theresa Brunswick* and Richard Wagner's *Opera and Drama*, both in *The World* for 1 November 1893 (C980).

INTRODUCTIONS

To Miss Erichsen by Bertha Newcombe at Joubert's Studio. 24th April.
To [Henry J. W.] Dam by Ernest Parke, Express Dairy, Fleet St. 3 June.
Mrs. Francis Adams, [by] the Salts, Hygeian Restaurant. 20th September.

See under dates noted for each individual.

HEALTH

On the 21st January I got a headache in the afternoon that was almost a sick headache. Had the remains of it in the morning; but it passed off.
On the 23rd April had a slight headache in the evening.
During the week ending the 14th May I had a cold of a tolerably pronounced sort. It left me with a nervous cough; but when I spoke in the open air on the Sunday evening I thought I was rid of it. On the night of Monday the 15th, however, I was very feverish and the next night was almost as bad. I interpreted my condition as due to the return of the influenza.
On the 5th June I felt very much out of sorts, as if I had caught cold in my inside. For the first time in my life I found although I could pass urine without any difficulty, yet at the end of the operation came a severe pang. This frightened and disconcerted me a good deal. Evidently a cystitis. It lasted about a fortnight. All through this period I was extremely weak physically, well as far as appearance went, but very easily fatigued and not very far above prostration point. I attributed all this to the fact of the influenza. About the last week of June I began to recover a good deal.
In August and September I got some change and holiday at Zurich and with the Webbs in the Valley of the Wye. I came home to town in rougher and coarser health than I have enjoyed for a long time. But on the 28th September I caught cold by sitting in FE's rooms with no fire and the window open at the top behind me, producing the sort of draught which always gives me colds.

January

1 SUNDAY *Dine at Kelmscott House.* $13\frac{1}{2}$.

Worked at *World* article. Emery Walker called at about 12 and I went for a walk with him along Chiswick Mall before going to Morris's. Cormell Price was there—I had not met him before. In the evening I went to hear Sparling lecture at the Hammersmith Socialist Society's meeting.

Herbert Cormell Price of 13 Douglas Road, Canonbury, N., was a Fabian, a friend of William Morris, and headmaster of United Services College in Devonshire.

2   °The Messiah *at the Albert Hall. 20.*

Began article for the *Fortnightly Review*, "What Mr. Gladstone Ought to Do." Had to leave early so as to get into town at about 1, to correct my *World* proof, which did not come until nearly 15 after all. Waited for it and then went out and dined before going on to FE, with whom I stayed until past 21. Saw her off by the 21.15 train to the theatre. Went at the article again when I got back. Brought my skates from the Square and spent some time preparing them for action.

Train Ravenscourt Park to Portland Road 7d   Xmas box to Spottis-woode's messengers 2/6   Dinner (top of Ch[arin]g + Road) 1/–   Train St Ja[me]s's Pk to Ravenscourt Pk 6d   *Star* $\frac{1}{2}$d   Miss Middleditch, Xmas box 10/–

"What Mr. Gladstone Ought to Do," part 4 of a series, signed, *Fortnightly Review*, February 1893 (C923).

3   *Hipkins's lecture on the harpsichord, clavichord, etc. at the Midland Grand Hotel. 15.30. One of the meetings of the annual conference of the Independent Society of Musicians.*

Finished the *Fortnightly* article. Went in to the concert with May after dining here. Went to the Square after the concert, leaving May in Totten-ham Court Rd. She called for me afterwards and had some tea with Lucy and Kate. Then we came back here together. After I had had a meal I took the skates I bought last Christmas and went off to Grove Park to skate. I arrived a little after 21 and found only a few people there; so that my awkwardness was not observed in the dark. I had not tried for many years. Sat up pasting notices of the play and writing up this diary. Not in bed until past 1.

Train Hammersmith to Kings + return & excess coming back to Ra-v[enscourt] Pk 10$\frac{1}{2}$ *Star* $\frac{1}{2}$d   Admission to Grove Park skating pond 6d

Both the lectures by A. J. Hipkins and Arnold Dolmetsch (1858–1940) were reviewed warmly by G.B.S. in his 11 January 1893 column (C918). Dolmetsch (see 4 January) both made and performed upon facsimiles of pre-pianoforte instruments. ■ Shaw would publish extracts from the press's reaction to *Widowers' Houses* as an appendix to the preface to the first (1893) edition of the play (A20), much as William Archer (ironically, now one of his critics) had published a compendium of negative criticism to Ibsen's *Ghosts*. In many ways the rhetoric of one parallels the other.

4   *Be at Downey's the photographers, Ebury St., at 12 to sit for portrait for Cassell's Cabinet Portrait Gallery. Put off to Saturday by the fog. Call on Sidney Webb in the afternoon and bring him MS of* Fortnightly *article. Arnold Dolmetsch's lecture on Viol and Lute music, with concert, at the Midland Grand Hotel. 15$\frac{1}{2}$.*

When I got into town I found a fog there. It was impossible for Downey to photograph me; so I arranged to go again on Saturday. I walked home and got my letters. Wrote a couple of letters, especially one to Beatty. At the Webbs' I met a man named Ball. Massingham was there also. I came back by the 19.22 train and called on FE, returning her volume of Browning. Then back to the Terrace where I had something to eat and immediately started off to the skating ground, which I did not reach until 21.50. I skated until 22½, having the lake to myself most of the time. When I got back I wrote a few postcards and pasted a notice or two into the *Widowers' Houses* scrapbook, besides writing up this diary.

Train Rav[enscourt] Pk to Victoria 6d   *Star* ½d   Dinner at the café opposite Portland Rd 1/8   Train Kings + to Finchley Rd 7d   Finchley Rd to Hammersmith (L. & N. W.) 8d   Skating, Grove Park, 6d

> Shaw, photographed three-quarter length, in tweeds, fingering his watch chain, is one of thirty-six celebrities in the 1893 volume of *Cassell's Portrait Gallery*, which also included his friends John Burns, Marion Lea, Elizabeth Robins, Lady Colin Campbell, Justin McCarthy, and Sidney Webb. ■ Sidney Ball (1857–1918), Fellow of St. John's College, Oxford, became chairman of the Oxford Fabian Society in 1895. Later he would be on the London Executive. He would be author of *Fabian Tract* No. 72, *The Moral Basis of Socialism* (1896).

5   Stayed at Hammersmith all day working at the appendix to *Widowers' Houses*. Got the draft finished at about 16 in the afternoon. Went up to the workroom and played for an hour and a half or so; and then went off and had tea with FE, who brought me to the skating ground at Grove Park—not the one I have hitherto gone to. She left me after five minutes walk of it and turned back to go to the theatre. I skated from 20½ to 22 and came back here. Wrote up this diary and read over the appendix.

Skating—Tappington's pond 6d

6   *Fabian Executive. 276 Strand. 17½. Preliminary Committee. 16¼. Fabian Public Lectures. Essex Hall, Essex St. W.C. Harold Cox on "Socialism Applied to Land."*
Began *World* article. After dinner went off with May to the skating pond at Grove Park. We skated for about two hours and a quarter. Then we walked to Turnham Green station and I went on to the Temple, May getting out at Ravenscourt Park and taking the skates home. I spoke at the Fabian meeting, and instead of going to the Square as I had intended came back here to Hammersmith, being a bit tired after the skating. Miss Newcombe and Miss Cameron came with me as far as Sloane Square station.

Skating, M[ay Sparling] & I 1/—   Train Turnham Green to Temple (return) & to Rav[enscourt] Pk, (single) 1/3   *Star* ½d   *Brotherhood* 1d
Miss Newcombe & Miss Cameron train Temple to Sloane Sq. 8d? barley-sugar 1d

Beatrice Cameron (1868–1940), actress, would be married to Richard Mansfield (1854–1907), who performed with her in Shaw's own *Arms and the Man*, in 1894. Shaw had first met her at the Charringtons' production of *A Doll's House*, where she was William Archer's guest.

7   *Downey's at 12. See Wednesday last.*

Up rather later than usual. Had not time to do anything particular before going into town. Bertha Newcombe met me at Victoria. I had written to her telling her about the glove I found in the train last night; and she came to get it from me. She came with me to Downey's, where the light was almost too bad for even an attempt at a photograph. We tried, however. Then Bertha and I went to the Strand and dined there and then to the Stores and to Russell St., where I left her. When I got back to Hammersmith I went on to join May at the skating ground. Skated until 19, but was too tired to enjoy it much. [Robert R.] Steele, from [the] Bedford [Debating Society], spent the evening here; so I did not get to work at the *World* article as I had intended.

Train Ravenscourt Park to Victoria 6d   Dinner at Buckingham St (2) 2/–
Bottle of ink at Stores 8d   Train Portland Rd to Ham[mersm]ith 7d
Skating at Grove Park 6d

8 SUNDAY   Finished and sent off *World* article. In the evening went over to FE to tea. Returned at about 22½ and sat up until near 2 correcting the first act of *Widowers' Houses*.

9   *Fabian Central Group Meeting. 32 Great Ormond St. Mrs. Fagan on "Women and Fabianism." 20. Wallas to call at Fitzroy Square at 13.*

Went into town by the 12.5 train, having worked a little on the revision of the play for the printer. When I got into town I set to work on the *Fortnightly* article, cutting out the middle according to the suggestion of the Webbs and altering the end—or rather adding to it. Wallas called. I corrected the *World* proof and went off to dinner at the Wheatsheaf with Wallas. When I got back I went at the play, as being lighter after dinner work than the article, which I finished and sent off on my return from the Fabian meeting.

Train Rav[enscour]t Park to Portland Road 7d   *Star* ½d   Dinner (Wheatsheaf) 1/–?

Mrs. Fagan, of 56 Russell Square, was a Fabian.

10   Finished the revision of the play. Quite forgot to dine in the middle of the day. Wallas called in the afternoon. Went into the City to buy some woolen things and to arrange about exchanging my typewriter for a new one. Went back for a while to the Square and wrote to Henry and Co. about the terms of agreement for the play. Then went to FE and stayed there until near midnight. Came back to Hammersmith Terrace to sleep. Began reading Buchanan's *Wandering Jew*, a copy of which arrived from him in the evening.

Telegram to Lincoln 6d   Train to Moorgate (return not used) 5d   Paid Barlock Co for new typewriter to exchange against my old one £8/17/6 Shirt & pants at Lutz's 13/4   Train Mansion Ho[use] to Ch[arin]g + 2½d   Dinner at Orange Grove 2/-   *Star* ½d   *Pick Me Up* 1d   Train Portl[an]d Rd to Shep[herds] Bush 6d

> J. T. Grein of the Independent Theatre had an interest in the Henry & Company publishing firm. ▪ Shaw did not review Robert Buchanan's book. ▪ Lutz and Co., hygienic woolen underwear manufacturers, 9 Trump Street, Lawrence Lane, E.C., had the striking cable address, "Ramfleece, London."

11 °*Call on Beatty at Ealing in the afternoon. Put off.*

Up rather late. Did not get to work until 11, and then only at this diary, though I was anxious to get at the *World* article and clear it out of the way of Bradford. Went into town in the evening, walking most of the way, as I had to buy some collars at Jaeger's. Worked at the *World* article. JP was at the Square.

Income Tax remitted W. G. Burrows £3/13/6   Bus Hammersmith to Prince's Gate 2d

> "The Bradford Conference. From the Fabian Point of View," *Workman's Times*, 28 January 1893 (C922).

12 *Go down to Bradford by the 13.30 train from Kings Cross; and stay with the Byles's. Look out for Buttery at Doncaster. Meeting of Fabian delegates to the Conference at Bradford. 20.*

Finished *World* article and got off at the last moment, all but late, as usual. Finished Buchanan's *Wandering Jew* in the train and began Defoe's *Moll Flanders*. Buttery got in at Doncaster. Aveling, Naylor and several other delegates were in the train; but they wanted to smoke; so I did not travel in their carriage. After dinner at Byles's I went back into Bradford to the Fabian meeting. I forgot to note that in the morning my time was rather cut into by J. W. O'Brien, who called on his usual errand.

Lent O'Brien 2/6   Train Kings + from Ptld Rd 1d   "Answers" 1d *Star* ½d   Tip for footwarmer 6d   Train Kings + to Bradford 15/10½ Telegram to Toothill (from Peterboro) 1/-   Tram to Park Gates 1d Steam tram back into town (Byles paid)   Return 2d

> The Bradford meeting was the founding conference of the Independent Labour Party. Fabian delegates were Shaw and W. S. De Mattos. ▪ John Naylor, 86 Fairfax Road, Hornsey N., was a Fabian although not a Fabian delegate.

13 *Bradford Conference. First day. 10, at the Labour Institute, Peckover St. Speak at Great Hotton in the evening—Cross Lane Schools. 20½ (meeting begins 19½). °Fabian Private meeting, Barnard's Inn, 20. Resolution about*

Woman tract, Mrs. Fagan and Oakeshott; Farm Labour and Anarchism tracts; Guardians' Election Committee. °Fabian Executive. 17¼. Preliminary Committee. 16¼.

The Conference sat all day except from 13 to 14, rising at about 17½. Keir Hardie came out with me to dine at Byles's. After dinner we went out together as far as the cab yard, where I took cab for Great Horton, and Byles and Hardie went off to another meeting.

Tram into town 2d　　Dinner at café 1/2　　Tram to Park Gates 2d　Cab to Great Horton 3/–　　Tram back from town 2d　　"Tea" at the Institute 9d　　cab (Hardie & self) 6d

14 *Bradford Conference. Second day. °Tea, music, dancing, etc. in the evening at the Labour Institute.*

Conference as before. In the evening I hurried off to Byles's and had a meal alone. Then I went to the theatre; but the house was full and I had to come back and set to work letters and correcting the *Fortnightly* proof. Later on the Byles's came in and soon after J. H. Wilson, M.P. (of the Sailors and Firemens Union) came to stay, he having to lecture next day at a Sunday Society. He had a good many stories to tell us about the Middlesbrough election and the Union; so that it was nearly 2 when we went to bed.

Tram into town 1d　　Dinner at café 1/5　　Steam tram back 2d　Tram back from theatre 1d　　*Bradford Observer & D[aily] Chronicle* 2d　　Delegate's share of conference expenses 6/–

Joseph Havelock Wilson (1858–1929), founder of the National Union of Seamen, had been elected Liberal M. P. from Middlesbrough after first seeking his seat from Deptford.

15 SUNDAY　°*Lecture in Lincoln (S. Maudson Grant, 22 Trentercroft St. Lincoln). Put off for Bradford. Speak at the Labour Club, Keighley, after Utley's lecture there. Speak in St. George's Hall for the Labour Church at 15.*

We were all up rather late. Wilson and Byles went out. I stayed at home working on the proof of the *Fortnightly* article. Then I took a turn in the park just before dinner and was waylaid by an ardent labour politician. We walked into town after dinner. There were 4000 people in the Labour Church. After it was over I went to the Institute and joined the tea there.

Tea at Institute (Utley & self) 1/6　　Collection in Lab[our] Ch[urch] 2/–　(Utley paid the 2 fares to Keighley)

16 *Come up by the 9.45 train—Great Northern. °Monday Pop.*

Wilson came up with me; and we got through the journey very pleasantly between talking and reading the papers. In the afternoon I began an article on the Congress for *The Workman's Times*. At about 21 I left the Square and came out to Hammersmith to spend the night.

Tip to cabman 6d   Train Bradford to King's + 15/10½   *Bradford Observer & D[aily] Chronicle* 2d   Tip for footwarmer 4d   ditto for luggage 6d   Train Kings + to Portland Rd 1d   Dinner at Wheatsheaf 1/6   Train Portland Rd to Hammersmith 6d   Tips to servants at Oakfield 5/−

"The Bradford Conference. From the Fabian Point of View," *Workman's Times*, 28 January 1893 (C922).

17   *Shaftesbury Theatre.* La Rosiere. *(last Saturday the first night). 20.*

Still a little tired and headachy after the Conference, though picking up rapidly as the day goes on. Spent the morning writing up this diary, and making out accounts of expenses for Fabian etc. etc. Dined here at Hammersmith. Went into town after dinner, working at the article for *The Workman's Times* on the way. When I got home there were a lot of letters to be answered at once; they took until past 18.

Train Rav[enscourt] Pk to Ptld Rd 7d   Refunded Fabian Soc[iet]y balance left out of £3   advanced by it for my expenses to Bradford 8/7   Cost of orders 1½d

G.B.S., 25 January 1893 (C921), described Harry Monkhouse's *La Rosière* as a "hotchpotch of points, situations, *contretemps.*" The music by Edward Jakobowski "saved the piece" as it was "more generous and vigorous than the French work to which we are accustomed." It would run forty-one performances.

18   *E. M. Smyth's* Requiem *and Parts I and II of* The Creation *at the Albert Hall. 20. Miss Muirhead to call at 11.30 and interview me for Cassell's Cabinet Portrait Gallery.*

Wrote a longish letter to the *Newcastle Daily Leader* in reply to an article of theirs about the Bradford Conference. This, and the business of being interviewed by Miss Muirhead, took up all the forenoon and most of the afternoon. On my way to dinner met Blathwayt. Went on to the Stores to buy a pocket diary so as not to be always forgetting the matters to be entered here. Wrote some letters when I got back. Went over to JP to tea and brought her with me to the Albert Hall—or rather gave her a ticket and left [her] to come on after and join me. I walked home after spending a short time in Brompton Square.

Star ½d   Dinner at Hygeian 1/5   Paste 7½d   Red pencil 1½d   Account book for Fabian travelling expenses 1/1   Small pocket diary, Walker's No. 3 1/6   Train to South Kensington (return ticket but walked back) 6d

G.B.S. (C921) found Miss Smyth's mass as belonging "to the light literature of Church music" in its quality of briskness. It evidenced, too, "a genuine feeling for the instruments." ■ Annie Muirhead, of Leighton Crescent, Kentish Town, N.W., who wrote for Cassell's. Her interview essay (B9) would describe Shaw as "one of the most versatile actors on the stage of London Life." ■ "The Independent Labour Party," signed letter correcting the paper's account of the Bradford conference, *Newcastle Daily Leader*, 20 January 1893

(C920). ▪ The pocket diary habit, with interruptions, would continue the remainder of Shaw's life; however, he would soon limit his entries largely to appointments.

19 *London Symphony Concert. St. James's Hall. 20½. Lyric Theatre, first night of* The Magic Opal.

Began *World* article and made a large hole in it. After dinner went to the Stores to make some further purchases. Just after coming out met Archer and turned back with him to Waterloo, where he was going to catch the 17.25 train. I walked back and corrected and sent off the *Fortnightly* proof, besides writing to Frank Harris about it. Sent off MS of *Widowers' Houses* to Henry and Co. Got to the theatre rather late. After the first act I went over to St. James's Hall and heard Brahms's Symphony in F and Mrs. Fiske's solo. Then returned to the theatre. Wrote up this diary on my return, and wrote a couple of postcards, but did not go out to post them.

Star ½d   Dinner at Hygeian 1/8   12 inch rule 5d   Condy's Fluid 1/6   Postage of MS to Henry & Co 3d   Registration 2d

> G.B.S. noted (C921) of the London Symphony only that Henschel demonstrated "ingratitude" at the critic's appearance "by striking up Brahms." ▪ The comic opera with libretto by Arthur Law and score by Isaac Albéniz would run forty-five performances. The music was "pretty" and "shapely" (C921) but wasted on a weak book. Shaw missed the dance, he noted, by Mlle. Candida because he left to cover a concert; he did not, however, forget her name. ▪ Since G.B.S. had found so little to praise about Mrs. Katherine Fisk's contralto in *The World* of 21 December 1892, he must have remained impressed enough by her American reputation to try her again; however, he did not comment upon her performance.

20 *Fabian Executive. 17½. °Committee. 16½. Fabian Public Meeting, H. M. Hyndman on "Socialism and Foreign Policy." Essex Hall. 20.*

Finished *World* article. Met Theodore Wright at the Orange Grove. After the Fabian, where I reported to the meeting on the Bradford Conference, I went with Wallas to the National Liberal Club, where he had some business, but I did not go in, waiting outside under the lamppost, reading *Justice*. He walked back with me to the door. Read over the *World* article and sent it off. Wrote a card or two. I was not at the Fabian Committee, as I did not get to the Executive until about 17.45. After the meeting, at which I gave a report on the Bradford Conference, but did [not] speak in the Hyndman discussion, I went with Wallas along the Embankment to the National Liberal Club and waited outside whilst he went in for a moment. He then walked with me as far as the door here. I wrote a few postcards before going to bed.

Bus Tott[enham] Ct Rd to Orange Grove 1d   Dinner there 1/-   *Star* ½d   Bus along Strand 1d   Macaroni &c at Gatti & Rodesano's 1/4 *Justice* 1d   Gave Bradford out-of-work man 2/6

21 *°Lecture for the Hammersmith Progressist League on "Labour and the Liberal" (F. W. Hayes, 12 Westcroft Square W.). Cancelled—no hall avail-*

able. Go up to the New Gallery to see the Burne-Jones exhibition. Call on the Charringtons in the evening. 21 Elm Park Rd. S.W.

After I left the New Gallery I went to the Wheatsheaf and dined. Found myself with a headache—almost a sick headache. Wrote some letters and lay down for a bit and had a sleep. JP was here. At Charringtons' I found George Moore, who was reading his play *The Strike at Arlingford* to them. Heard the 3rd act. Stayed after he left and returned by last train before midnight from Gloucester Rd. Out of sorts—bungled over a letter to Hyndman which I had to tear up.

New Gallery 1/–   catalogue 6d   Dinner 1/6   Train to Gloster Rd &
back 9d

Shaw would see the play on 21 February 1893 and review it in *The Star*. See 26 June 1893.

22 SUNDAY *Lecture at the Chiswick Radical Club. "Evolution of Socialism." 20. (J. C. Lorraine Norfolk House, W.C.). Dine with the Sidney Webbs. Wallas to call for me—take 17.40 train Finchley Rd. to Hammersmith and tea with Lorraine. Sleep at 8 Hammersmith Terrace.*

Remains of headache. Wrote to Beale about Fabian resolutions before Wallas came. We walked to Webbs'. After dinner we all went for a walk on the Heath from 15.30 to 16.30.

Train Finchley Rd to Hammersmith 8d

23 °*Fabian Central Group Meeting. 32 Great Ormond St. R.W. Reynolds on "Rousseau's Ghost in Modern Politics." 20. Meeting at 276 Strand between 7 Fabian delegates and the "Olive Branch" Committee of the Hammersmith Socialist Society, to discuss possibility of a Socialist Alliance. °Tobias Matthay's pianoforte recital (his own compositions). Royal Academy of Music. 20.*

Suddenly remembered that I had forgotten to correct the *World* proof; so started for town early, but called on FE on the way and so did not get here until 13. Corrected proof and sent it off by express postal messenger. After dinner met [Eduard] Bernstein in Oxford St. and walked about Bloomsbury with him for a long time arguing about Bebel and Singer's treatment of the Fabian, and about Marx. Walter [Gurly] called a little after I got home but did not stay long. I worked at the postscript to *Widowers' Houses* until 19½, when I went off to the Fabian.

Papers 1½d   Train Shep[herds] Bush to Portl[an]d Rd 6d   Express postal messenger for *World* proof 6d   Dinner at Hygeian 1/–   Telegram to Bertha Newcombe 6d

Eduard Bernstein (1850–1932) of Zurich was then London correspondent of *Vorwärts*.
■ Paul Singer (1844–1911), an associate of August Bebel in the German Social Democratic Party, had been a member of the Reichstag since 1884.

24 °*Arnold Dolmetsch's Viol concert. Barnard's Inn. 20¼. First of the Plowitz concerts. Prince's Hall. 20. Call on Bertha Newcombe in the afternoon.*

Began preface for *Widowers' Houses* and worked at it until 15. Met Glover on my way to dinner. He asked me to go to see his ballet and I promised to do so tomorrow. I sat with Bertha Newcombe until near 19 when Mrs. Newcombe joined us. Parted from them outside the studio. Went to Baker St. by mistake thinking that the concert was at Steinway Hall instead of in Piccadilly.

Star ½d   Dinner at Orange Grove 1/2   Train St Ja[me]s's Park to Sloane Sq 1½d   Cocoa, eggs &c in Aerated Bread Shop in Kings Rd 10d   Train Sloane Sq to Baker St 6d

> Signed note in the "What the World Says" column, *The World*, 1 February 1893 (C924) on Theodor Plowitz's "string quartet of remarkable merit." ▪ James M. Glover's ballet was *London to Paris*, which Shaw did see the next day. Several paragraphs about it appeared in Shaw's *World* column on 8 February 1893 (C925), where it was called "a really amusing entertainment." More a pantomime (with some spoken dialogue) with music than a ballet, it was concocted with the collaboration of Cecil Raleigh and Augustus Harris, who provided the narrative for Glover's music. Originally a longer notice intended for publication on 1 February 1893, it was trimmed by C. Thomas of *The World*, who thought that portions referring to Harris were potentially libelous.

25 °*Scotch National Concert. Albert Hall. 19.45. Go to the Palace Theatre to hear Glover's ballet* London to Paris. *19.50.*

Worked away at the preface and at last sent it off and got out at about 16. Salt called; also Walter [Gurly]. Got some dinner opposite Portland Rd. and walked to the Royal Oak, where I took train for Shepherd's Bush. FE was out when I arrived; but she came in presently; and we went together to the Palace Theatre. As we came out we met Reece. Put FE into a bus and then parted from Reece in Shaftesbury Ave. Wrote some letters when I got home.

Maccaroni &c at café Portland Rd 1/5   Royal Oak to Shep[herds] Bush train 3d   Train Ravenscourt Pk to St Ja[me]s's Pk (2) 1/–   Program at Palace Theatre 6d

26 *Performance of André Raffalovich's* Roses of Shadow *and Ibsen's* Ghosts *at the Athenaeum, 72 Tottenham Court Rd.—Private At-Home of J. T. Grein of the Independent Theatre. 14.30.*

Began *World* article and wrote to Beatty. JP called; but I had to hurry off. After *Ghosts* I came back here with May Sparling. There was no one here and no fire to make tea; so she was going away when my Mother met her at the door and she turned back. I left her here and went on to FE. We read a lot of Walt Whitman and were very happy. I had a desperate run to catch the train on my return.

Star ½d   *Freethinker* 1d   *National Reformer* 2d   Dinner (Wheatsheaf) 9d   Train to Shepherd's Bush & back 9d

> André Raffalovitch (1864–1934), Russian-born and French-educated poet and long-time companion of poet John Gray (1866–1934). *Roses of Shadow* was more dramatic dialogue than drama, and poked fun, with Wildean dialogue, at affectation in contemporary

society. Raffalovitch would be better known for his study of homosexuality, *Uranisme et Unisexualité* (1896).

27   *Fabian Executive. 17½. Committee. 16½. Fabian Group Secretaries Meeting at office. 20.*

Began *World* article—or rather attempted to continue it, but made very little progress. [Francis V.] Connolly of Clapham called, ostensibly to book me for a lecture, but really, as it turned out, to borrow fifteen shillings. Not getting on well with my work I sang for a while. I have sung so little of late that my voice is getting quite weak. Did not go out until about 16. Met Parke and Le Gallienne in the street. Between two Fabian meetings had a meal with Oakeshott, Olivier, Wallas and Miss Brooke. After the Group Secretaries meeting, Wallas walked home with me; and we took a turn along Regents Park before parting. Then sat up until past 1 to write several postcards.

Lent Connolly 15/–   *Star & Chronicle* 1½d   Dinner (at Orange Grove) 1/–   Omelette &c at Gatti & Rodesano's 1/6   Lamb's Registration pamphlet 2d

28   °*Private concert at Mrs. Lee's, 21 Campden Hill Rd. W. at 21.* °*Private View. Ayerst Ingram's pictures at Dowdeswell's. Bertha Newcombe's studio in the afternoon—1 Joubert's Studios, Jubilee Place, King's Rd., Chelsea.* °*Private View. 19th Century Gallery. 9 Conduit St. 10—Wrong—not until next Saturday.*

Answered Jacques' letters about sight reading. Sang and amused myself until about 14½. Then went off to Bertha Newcombe's, taking over in my bag the summer suit in which she painted me. Gave her a sitting. When I got back I should have finished the *World* article; but instead I began to write a long and foolish letter in reply to Johnson of Manchester, which I tore up afterwards after sitting up late over it when I should have gone to bed.

Dinner at Orange Grove 1/–   *Star* ½d   Train Ch[arin]g + to Sloane Sq 2d   South Kensington to Portland Rd 4d

> William P. Johnson (1866–1923), secretary of the National Union of Shop Assistants and a delegate to the Bradford conference. Shaw's substitute letter (*CL*), written the next day, blasts Johnson's political naiveté: "I blush for you. . . . I apologise to the British nation for associating Socialism with men who set about making the millenium as children set about making a mud pie."

29 SUNDAY   *Lecture in Croydon (J. T. Dunlop, 24 Strand Rd. Woodside, South Norwood) in Gladstone Hall, Manor Rd., for the South Norwood Liberal and Radical Club. "Liberalism and Socialism." 19.45. Norwood Junction station on London Brighton and South Coast from London Bridge—18.45.*

Ground out the rest of the *World* article much against the grain, finishing about 17, when there was barely time to lie down before starting for the train. Took Cox's book on *Land Nationalisation* to read in the train.

Train Portland Rd to Monument & back 1/–   London Bridge to Norwood Junction (main line) 8½d

30 *Go up to Philip Webb in the evening and bring him back Emonds' essays.*

Felt good for nothing. Set to work pasting up the scrap book containing notices etc. of *Widowers' Houses.* Wrote to Johnson of Manchester and to Lady Colin Campbell. Did not go out to dinner, but played and sang a bit and dawdled irresolutely. Went out at about 17 and took a meal at the Wheatsheaf, after which I called on Archer. Went on after that to Webb, with whom I spent the rest of the evening very pleasantly. Talking about art, as usual, and about the proposed Socialist Alliance. Was much disturbed at night by noises in the Square. Could not get to sleep for a long time.

Soup & eggs at Wheatsheaf 1/2

Shaw had borrowed Alexander Emmonds' essays on architecture on 16 September 1892.

31 *Lecture in Balham on "The Liberal Party and Labour Politics." (G. W. Johnson, Lensfield, Balham). 18.30 train Victoria to Balham—sup with Johnson. Lecture at 20½ in Balham Baths.*

Up very late, still unable to settle down to work. Wrote another letter to Jacques about our dispute as to musical sight reading. Polished off a lot of correspondence and wrote up this diary, which was rather in arrear, but which was rescued by my new plan of keeping a pocket diary from the forgetfulness which interfered with those of former years. Archer called with his boy Tom. After dinner looked into the St. Martin's Free Library to see whether I could get the *Contemporary Review* to read Clarke's article, but did not succeed. Waited half an hour at Victoria for the train.

Telegram to FE 6d   Dinner at Orange Grove 1/5   *Westminster Gazette* first number 1d   Train Victoria to Balham & back 9d

William Clarke, "The Limits of Collectivism," *Contemporary Review*, February 1893.

February

1 °*Lunch at Archer's at 13, to meet Charles Archer (clean forgotten).*

The new typewriter came whilst I was at breakfast. Began, finished and sent off review of *Medieval Lore.* Walter [Gurly] called in the afternoon. I did not go out until past 17 when I dined at the Wheatsheaf. After that I started to walk to Hammersmith. As I was looking into the windows of Bumpus's Shop in Oxford St. I was accosted by a man who introduced himself as the librarian of Trinity College [of Music]. He walked to the Marble Arch with me. I walked on past Notting Hill Gate and then turned down Ladbroke Grove and took train at Notting Hill station. May was alone when I reached Hammersmith Terrace; but Walker came in just as we were going to play some duets after tea. He left before Sparling came in. We played a lot of the *Zauberflöte*. I came back by the last train.

West[minster] Gazette & Star 1½d   Dinner at Wheatsheaf 1/3   Train Notting Hill to Hammersmith 3d   H[ammersmi]th back to Portland Road 6d

"Mr. William Morris and the Middle Ages," unsigned review of *Medieval Lore ... being ... gleanings from the Encyclopedia of Bartholomew Anglicus on the Properties of Things*, edited by Robert Steele, with preface by William Morris, *Daily Chronicle*, 13 February 1893 (C927).

2 *London Symphony Concert. St. James's Hall. 20½.* °*Joint Committee Fabian, Hammersmith Socialist Society and Social-Democratic Federation, 7 delegates each, "Olive Branch," at 276 Strand. 20½.* °*Pennells' in the evening. 14 Buckingham St. (forgotten).* °*Call on Miss Newcombe in the afternoon, if possible, at her studio. Write to Jim Connell giving him the date he wants.*

Wrote several letters. At about 13 began review of Harold Cox's book on *Land Nationalisation* and worked away at it until 17.30 when it was ready to send off. Went down to St. Martin's Lane and dined; then walked along Pall Mall and through the Green Park to Hyde Park Corner and up into Oxford St. until it was time to go to the concert. It was muddy and drenching rain; but I trudged about for the sake of the exercise. After the concert I went home with Jacques and sat with him and his wife until near 1.

Star ½d   *Justice* 1d   *West[minster] Gaz[e]tte* 1d   Dinner at Orange Grove 1/10   Lent the Bradford man in Cockspur St 2/–

To G.B.S. (C925), on the evidence of the Beethoven *Pastoral* symphony, George Henschel seemed to be succeeding in creating a "first-rate orchestra" from the London Symphony players. ▪ "Nationalisation, Restoration, Taxation," unsigned review of Harold Cox's book, *Land Nationalisation* (London, 1892), *Daily Chronicle*, 4 April 1893 (C939).

3 *Fabian Executive. 17¼. Committee. 16½. Fabian Public Meeting. Rev. Percy Dearmer on "Socialism and Disestablishment." Essex Hall. 20.*

Began *World* article. After dinner went into the City to get my new combinations at Lutz's, but found the place shut as it was past 17. Spoke in the debate and drafted a letter to be written to Tillett. Dark walked back with me, Pease coming as far as the corner of Grafton St. Got to bed at midnight. Olivier and Oakeshott were at Gatti's with me after the Executive. I was precipitated into saying that I got to bed by midnight. I had to stay up until near 1 after all to write some postcards.

Star ½d   *West[minster] Gaz[ette]* 1d   Dinner at O[range] G[rove]
11d   Train Ch[arin]g + to Mansion [House] & back (to Temple) 3d
Musical News 1d   *Musical Opinion* 2d   Omelette &c at Gatti & Rodesano's 1/8   Note book 3d   Pamphlet "Labor Robbery" from Harrigan
1d

> Rev. Percy Dearmer (1867–1936) would be on the Fabian Executive from 1895 to 1898,
> and would author *Fabian Tract* No. 133, *Socialism and Christianity* (1907). He was best
> known for his *Parson's Handbook*, which was inspired by medieval English Catholic
> liturgy. At the time he was secretary of the London Christian Social Union, but he would
> become vicar of St. Mary's, Primrose Hill, in 1901. ▪ Sidney E. Dark, a Christian
> Socialist, was a Fabian and the editor of the *Church Times*. Later he would be a *Daily
> Mail* journalist under the pen name of "Phoebus," and a minor playwright.

4 °*Private View. 19th Century Gallery. 9 Conduit St. 10. Call on Elizabeth
Robins at 17—28 Manchester Square Mansions. (6th) Revise Massingham's
Halifax Manifesto.*

Tried to finish *World* article but was interrupted by Home. Slipped away
whilst he was talking to my Mother inside. Miss Robins got rather alarmed
about the interview and swore she would shoot me if I said anything she
did not approve of. In the evening I went to FE; and JP burst in on us very
late in the evening. There was a most shocking scene, JP being violent and
using atrocious language. At last I sent FE out of the room, having to
restrain JP by force from attacking her. I was two hours getting her out of
the house and I did not get her home to Brompton Square until near 1, nor
could I get away myself until 3. I was horribly tired and shocked and upset;
but I kept patience and did not behave badly nor urgently. Did not get to
bed until 4; and had but a disturbed night of it. I made JP write a letter to
me expressing her regret and promising not to annoy FE again. This was to
send to FE to reassure her.

Star & *West[minster] Gaz[ette]* 1½d   Dinner 11d   Train Baker St to
Shep[herds] Bush (return not used) 9d   Cab Ham[mersmi]th Broadway
to Brompton Sq 4/–

> Elizabeth Robins had moved from 41 Marlborough Rd., St. John's Wood, N.W., to Dorset
> St., W. Unable to relate to Shaw's brand of blarney, she would turn hostile to him at every
> encounter as would happen again this time. Shaw published no interview with her. ▪
> "To the Workers of Halifax," a Fabian manifesto urging workers to vote Labour in a
> Parliamentary contest, *Workman's Times*, 11 February 1893 (C926). ▪ Shaw would
> utilize the episode with the two women in writing the altercation between Grace and Julia
> over Leonard Charteris into a scene of his next play, *The Philanderer*, begun on 14 March.

5 SUNDAY *Lecture on "Program of Social Democracy" at the Acton Liberal
Club, Horn Land, W. (C. A. Bolscher, Pol. Sec.). 23 minutes' walk from Great
Western station; 8 from North London, 5 from red Bayswater bus. 20.*

Corrected proof of *World* article (first half) and finished and sent off second
half. Wrote to FE. Went out to Hammersmith Terrace and found them at
dinner. Furnivall was there. After dinner May and I went out for a walk;

and she delivered the letter to FE for me. Miss [Elsie] Hall came in in the evening and played [piano] for us a bit. Wrote to E. Robins after my lecture. Began to pick up spirits towards the afternoon and passed the night at the Terrace.

Train to Hammersmith 6d   H[ammersm]ith to Acton & back 3d
Toffee 1d

> Shaw sent (*CL*) a "rough sketch" of his interview to Elizabeth Robins. She refused to permit publication in any form. ▪ Hammersmith Terrace, "the Terrace," and similar designations inevitably mean (unless otherwise noted) the Sparlings—May (Morris) in particular.

6 °*Monday Pop. Ilona Eibenschutz. See Saturday—Halifax Manifesto. Call on the Charringtons in the evening.*

Got up rather late from Hammersmith. Walked into town, or rather into the City, stopping at Rathbone Place to dine. The fine weather is delightful. Corrected and sent off the Halifax Manifesto. Then began a letter to JP which was interrupted by the appearance of Home, who, as it now appears, wants me to try to get a little money out of Mrs. Wynne (formerly Mrs. Home) for him. On consideration I promised to write to Wynne, not to Mrs. W. When he was gone I went off to the Charringtons, Janet having called here in the morning to see me. Got there at 22 and found that they wanted me to set about the interview which is to introduce their scheme at the Royalty to the public. Came back by the 23.55 train from Gloucester Rd. My business in the city was to get the woollen combinations I ordered at Lutz's. I had some chat with Mrs. Reid and Ernest Williams at the Wheatsheaf. Began drafting letter to Wynne in the train in the evening.

West[minster] Gazette 1d   Dinner (Wheatsheaf) 1/1   Train Moorgate to Portland Rd 4d   *Star* $\frac{1}{2}$d   Portland Rd to Gloster Rd & back 6d Telegram to Olivier about Woman's Tract meeting $7\frac{1}{2}$d

> "A New Theatrical Enterprise. An Interview with Mr. and Mrs. Charrington," unsigned, *Daily Chronicle*, 27 February 1893 (C932).

7 *Fabian Publishing Committee. 276 Strand. 16$\frac{1}{4}$. (8th) Call on Wallas, ill.*

Copied out the letter to Wynne on the typewriter. Then went at my correspondence etc. Got a letter from Oakeshott, to say that Wallas is ill and that I should call on him. Found it impossible to do so owing to want of time. After the Fabian Committee went out to Ravenscourt Park with Sparling, but left him at the station and went to FE. She walked with me to the top of St. Peter's Park at about 22, when I went to Sparlings'. May and I played for a while and then had some conversation about old times—rather an emotional one. Stayed the night at the Terrace.

West[minster] Gaz[ette] & Star 1$\frac{1}{2}$d   Dinner 1/1   Bus Tottenham Ct Rd to Holborn 1d   Train Temple to Rav[enscour]t Park 6d

Despite Shaw's intimacy with Florence Farr, which was no secret among their acquaintances, Shaw had been seeing her in recent months often while staying at the home of yet another young woman, May, who was openly in love with him. (May had even delivered a letter to Florence for him about the JP affair a few days earlier.) May's marriage, contracted only on the rebound from Shaw's declared aversion to matrimony, was now being eroded by his continuing presence. His attempted break here would come too late to rescue Henry Halliday Sparling's marriage. May would continue to see much of Shaw throughout the year, often accompanying him when Florence was otherwise occupied.

8   *Meeting of the Fabian Committee to draw up a tract on the Woman question at Mrs. Fagan's, 56 Russell Square W. C. at 20¼. Call on Morgan-Browne en route at 46 Ridgmount Gardens at 19½. Press View. Exhibition of Signorelli's work at the Burlington Fine Arts Club. See yesterday—Wallas.*

Left the Terrace with Sparling pretty early. Looked in at Morris's for a few minutes and found Cockerell and Janie there with him. Parted from Sparling at the Broadway and came up to town by Metropolitan line. Read Hills on Vegetarianism for review in the train. When I got home was rather put out by finding my last letter returned by JP, with a denial that she had read it. Returned her letter and sent back mine with it. Began review of Wagner's prose works vol. 1, for the *Chronicle*. Called on Wallas after dinner—found him in bed and rather bad. Went home after telegraphing for his sister and wrote a letter about the *Westminster Gazette* to [Edward Tyas] Cook. When I got back from the Committee, leaving [Morgan-]Browne at his door, I found a letter from May referring to our last night's conversation. Answered it.

West[minster] Gaz[ette] 1d   Dinner 10d   Telegram to Mrs. Muirhead about [Graham] Wallas 1/1½

Hubert Morgan-Browne, who lived just off Gower St., W., was a Fabian who would be elected in 1897 to the London School Board.   ▪   About 1490 the Umbrian painter Luca Signorelli began painting sinewy nudes that had a plastic, three-dimensional force heretofore lacking in the drawings and frescoes of his time. He would have a great influence on his Florentine contemporaries.   ▪   "The legal husband," Shaw explained in his 1936 essay "William Morris as I Knew Him," "was a friend whose conduct towards me had always been irreproachable. To be welcomed in his house and then steal his wife was revolting to my sense of honor and socially inexcusable. . . . I knew that a scandal would damage both of us. . . . It seems easy in view of my later position to have sat down as three friends and arranged a divorce; but at that time I could not afford to marry and I was by no means sure that he could afford to be divorced. Besides, I hated the idea of a prosaic and even mercenary marriage." Further, Shaw did *not* add, he was still much involved with Florence Farr, continued to encourage Bertha Newcombe, was still smitten by (the married) Janet Achurch, and was keeping his eyes open for still other possibilities.   ▪   No review of Arnold Frank Hills's pamphlets for the London Vegetarian Society was published.   ▪   "Wagner—At Last!"—unsigned review of the first volume of Wagner's *Prose Works* (London, 1892), ed. and trans. by William Ashton Ellis, *Daily Chronicle*, 18 February 1893 (C929).

9   *Miss May Joseph's concert. Steinway Hall. 20. °Meeting of Holburn and St. Pancras Branch of the London Reform Union at Stapley's, 33 Bloomsbury Square. 20. Wallas on "Local Elections" and Turner on "Local Government."*

Wrote a card to Home and another to Wynne, who has refused to help Home. Did not get to work, being fidgety and out of sorts. Went to the piano and sang a good deal—Handel, Verdi's *Otello*, etc. Wet day. After dinner went to see how Wallas was. Found two of his sisters there. I waited a long time for the upshot of the consultation between the two doctors. Verdict: severe cold, with bronchitis and probably a touch of influenza. Went to Bertha Newcombe and sat with her in her studio until near 20. She gave me some cocoa and eggs. Looked into the concert for a while and then came home and wrote a few letters, besides making a draft letter to defaulting members for the Fabian.

Star ½d   *West[minster] Gaz[ette]* 1d   *Freethinker* 1d   *Nat[iona]l Reformer* 2d   Train Temple to Sloane Sq 4d   S[ou]th Kensington to Baker St 4d

The Fabian Executive minutes for 10 February note approval of Shaw's circular to defaulting members (A19), but no copy has been located.

10 *Fabian Executive. 17¼. Committee. 16¼. Fabian. Private meeting of the Society. Barnard's Inn. 20. Report to the meeting on the Unemployed Agitation.*

Wrote *World* article. Dined here. When I got back in the evening I sat up late to finish and send off the article, but chiefly and most disagreeably to write to Home refusing to lend him money. Mrs. Sandham, Olivier, Utley and Bland were with me at Gatti's.

The Contemporary Review 2/–   Maccaroni &c at Gatti & Rodesano's 1/8   *West[minster] Gaz[ette]* 1d

His G.B.S. column, *The World*, 15 February 1893 (C928), a miscellany reporting few visits to concert halls, as "music is dying out in London."

11 °*Miss Loidore's concert. Studio, 31 Tite St. Chelsea. 15.* °*Soirée of the Hammersmith Socialist Society. Kelmscott House. 20.*

Wrote an article for the *Workman's Times* and sent it off to Burgess. Maudson Grant called and booked me for a lecture in Lincoln on the 19th. Wrote some letters. After dinner felt restless and began sorting my books with the idea of getting rid of those I do not want. But I soon gave it up and resolved to spend the evening quietly at home. I sang a good deal and finished my *World* proof. Also began correcting proof of Miss Muirhead's biographical notice of me for *Cassell's Cabinet Portrait Gallery*.

Star ½d   Dinner 1/1

"Cry-Baby Stalwarts," *Workman's Times*, 18 February 1893 (C930), on the reaction to the I.L.P. ▪ Joseph Burgess (1853–1934) was the London manager of *Workman's Times* and a member of the original Council of the I.L.P., and would be the biographer of John Burns.

12 SUNDAY *Lecture at the North Camberwell Hall, New Church Rd., Camberwell, at 11½ (W. M. Vogl, 9 Vaughan Rd., Camberwell).* "*Liberalism*

and Labour." Lecture at the Washington Music Hall, Battersea, on *"History of Liberalism"* in place of John Burns whose voice is unfit for speaking. Night changed for next week.

Read *All's Well That Ends Well* in the train—found more charm in it than I had expected. Played and sang in the afternoon. Read *Twelfth Night*. Kate [Gurly] was in one of her stupors when I got back from Battersea; I had to help Mother to get her on a sofa and wake her. Put in a little work on Miss Muirhead's proof in the afternoon.

Train Portl[an]d Rd to Farringdon & back 5d   Bus to Elephant & back 2d   Train Camb[erwe]ll to Elephant 1d   Train Victoria to Battersea & back 2d   Victoria to Portland Rd 8d   Toffee 1d

> Kate Gurly, hunchbacked since childhood after a fall from a horse, found solace only in drink, which made the Shaw household, where she spent most of her time, long for the opportunities to pack her off ("like a parcel," Shaw once said) to Ireland.

13 °*Monday Pop. Joachim.* °*Fabian Central Group Meeting. 32 Great Ormond St. J. F. Oakeshott on "Why Do We Want Socialism?" 20. Changed to 15 Museum Mansion, Russell Square, through Wallas's illness.* °*St. Pancras Vestry Hall. Meeting on behalf of the Unemployed. 20.*

Spent all the working part of the day drafting agreement for the publication of *Widowers' Houses,* and sent it off to Henry and Co. Wrote to Burns and Webb about the Trade Union clause in it. Took a nap before tea. Then discovered that I had not posted the *World* proof on Saturday night. Rushed off with it to New Street Square—too late to be of any use. Walked back and wrote several letters, especially one to Miss Priestley about her friend who wants to go on the stage.

Dinner 10d   *Star* ½d   *Justice* 1d   Train to Farringdon 2d

14 °*Honor Brooke and Valleria At-Home. 40 Abbey Rd. N.W. 21. Music and Acting. Arnold Dolmetsch's 2nd Viol concert. Barnard's Inn. 20½.*

Worked away at the review of Wagner. After dinner sang for a while, chiefly *Dinorah,* which I have not touched for a long time and which now seems very mechanical stuff in spite of its cleverness and charm. Wrote to Henry and Co. offering a new version of the Trade Union clause, Burns's letter having shown me that my first draft will not do. Lady Colin Campbell was at Dolmetsch's concert. Gilbert Webb walked from it with me to the Bloomsbury corner. When I got back I found a letter from Henry and Co. which made me write to them and to Grein crying off the publication scheme.

Dinner 1/3   Train to Farringdon 2d   Papers 2½d

> Barnard's Inn, Holborn, one of the few remaining Inns of Chancery, possessed a fine panelled chamber with an open-timbered roof, an ideal space for performance of English music of the sixteenth and seventeenth centuries. G.B.S., 22 February 1893 (C931), noted that at Arnold Dolmetsch's viol concert there, "I enjoyed the unexpected sensation of

having one of my criticisms read aloud to the audience. . . . The precedent appears to me an excellent one. I am confident that the Philharmonic concerts and those of the Bach choir, nay, the very Opera itself, could be most agreeably enlivened by a judicious selection from my articles." ■ Shaw was negotiating a contract for publication of *Widowers' Houses*. Henry & Co. wanted to delete a union-labor clause Shaw had inserted. The publisher wrote Shaw on 14 February (BL 50513) that "we do not think such an elaborate agreement [is] necessary, especially as we do not expect the sale to be sufficient to recoup us for our outlay, and as we are publishing your work chiefly to oblige our Mr. Grein." Only 162 copies would be sold in the next three years.

15 The Redemption *at the Albert Hall. 20. Fabian Publishing Committee. 276 Strand. 17$\frac{1}{2}$.*

Finished and sent off review of the first volume of Ellis's translation of Wagner's prose works. After the Fabian Committee went with Olivier to the Orange Grove. We parted at the corner of Trafalgar Square. Bertha Newcombe came and sat beside me during the interval and part of the second part of the concert, and we had almost a scene, as far as that was possible in so public a place, about our recent correspondence. I walked home and wrote up this diary besides sending off a letter or two.

Musical Times 3d   *School Music Review* 2$\frac{1}{2}$d   Dinner 9d   "Tea" Olivier & myself at Orange Grove 2/11   Train St Ja[me]s's Park to S[ou]th Kensington 2d   Subway 1d

> Gounod's "wearisome" oratorio, G.B.S. wrote (C931), was akin to "going through five miles of pictures by Fra Angelico."

16 *London Symphony Concert. St. James's Hall. 20$\frac{1}{2}$.*

Began *World* article. Corrected proof of Wagner review. Rested after dinner, reading papers and playing. But the piano was so abominably out of tune that I had to give it up after a while. Wrote a couple of letters—to Bertha Newcombe and Miss Muirhead before the concert. Mother came there with me; and we walked home together from it.

Papers 1$\frac{1}{2}$d   Dinner 1/1

> The Wagner program drew Shaw as well as a "large audience," G.B.S. (C931) again observing the new "artistic maturity of Mr. Henschel's enterprise."

17 *Fabian Executive. 17$\frac{1}{2}$. Committee. 16$\frac{1}{2}$. Take the chair. Fabian meeting at Essex Hall. 20. W. S. Caine on "Socialism and the Drink Trade."*

Finished and sent off *World* article. Miss Muirhead called. Spoke at the Fabian meeting. Walked home with Miss Priestley.

Dinner at Hygeian 1/1$\frac{1}{2}$ Omelette &c with Oakeshott at Gatti's & Ro[desano's] 1/6

> William Sproston Caine (1842–1903), was lay pastor of a mission church in Stockwell, S.W., known as the Wheatsheaf. President of the British Temperance League, he was briefly (1880) an M.P. via a by-election at Scarborough.

18   *Crystal Palace Concert. 15. (first this year). Hegner, Mme. Duma, Nicodé's* Faschingsbilder.

Began writing interview with the Charringtons. Added a little. Interview in the evening. Also wrote some letters and played. Fine concert—band in great form.

Train Ch[arin]g + to Victoria 1½d   *Star & West[minster] Gaz[e]tte*
1½d   Dinner 10d

> Reviewed on 1 March 1893 (C933). August Manns "unexpectedly" managed to press his orchestra, G.B.S. wrote, to meet the occasion of a Beethoven symphony, even to "beauty of tone" in the wind section. ▪ Otto Hegner (1876–1907) was a young pianist; Marie Duma, a strong-lunged soprano, went unmentioned; Jean Louis Nicodé (1853–1919) was a pianist and composer whose programmatic *Faschingsbilder* was (C933) "charming dance music."

19 SUNDAY   °*Lecture in the Washington Music Hall, York Rd. Battersea. "History of Liberalism." 20. Altered to last Sunday, q.v. Lecture in Lincoln (go down by the 9.50 from Liverpool St.) to the Lincoln Liberal Club on "Labour Politics." 20.*

Very pleasant journey down to Lincoln. Sunshiny morning; nobody in the carriage except between Cambridge and Ely; and they did not object to the windows being open. Stayed with Grant. After dinner we walked up to the Cathedral; and I attended the 16 service there to get a better look at it. Grant went home and left me to myself. I strolled about until 18, when I went back to tea and found Belcher and Howells—local politicians—there. Read a novel of Du Boisgobey's in the train. I never read anything of his before.

Train Portland Rd to Bishopsgate 3d   Liverpool St to Lincoln 10/9
Papers 3d

> Fortuné Du Boisgobey had already published eleven novels; the most recent was *Un Cadet de Normandie* (1891).

20   °*Dress rehearsal of Moore's play at 15. Opera Comique. Performance of Ibsen's* Master Builder Solness *at the Trafalgar Theatre. 14½, first time in England. Come up from Lincoln by the 10 train to King's Cross.*

Read the papers and Du Boisgobey in the train. Wet day and dull journey. After the play went with Archer to the Stores and then home with him to tea. His brother Charles was there, and Mrs. Archer. Came home about 20, Archer coming out with me and taking me to the Southampton St. post office and back again before we parted. Worked at the Charrington interview and wrote some letters. Dined here.

Received: Maudson Grant, Lincoln expenses, £1/1/6
Lavatory at Lincoln 2d   Papers 2½d   Train Lincoln to Kings + 10/9
Kings + to Portl[an]d Rd 1d   Condy's Fluid 1/6   Gayetty paper 1/4

The Master Builder featured Elizabeth Robins as Hilde Wangel. After the performance Shaw praised her portrayal of the young woman whose re-entry into Solness's life spells his doom, but his letter (*CL*) failed to melt Robins's coolness toward him. The production would have twenty-one performances, a good run for Ibsen at that time.

21   *George Moore's* Strike at Arlingford *at the Opera Comique. 20½. Independent Theatre Society.*

Corrected and sent off Charrington's review to the Charringtons—or rather to Janet, for their approval. In the afternoon went out to Morris's to submit to him the proof of the page of *Widowers' Houses* just sent by the printer. He could not suggest anything better. Janie was there; and Cockerell; and Mrs. Norman called whilst I was there. After the play got a cab for Bertha Newcombe and Miss McCarthy. Home in the rain and sent off the page to Henry and Co.

Express messenger with the interview to Janet Achurch 3d   Papers 1½d   Train to Hammersmith 4d   Back 4d   Program at I[ndependent] T[heatre] 6d

> Although Shaw's review of *Strike*, cast in the form of an interview with him, would not be published until June (C956), he would write William Archer on 23 February (*CL*) that Moore's "strikology" was defective, confusing classes and interests and political persuasions. "I have written to him," Shaw added, "to warn that his sociology is not what it might be. . . ." ■ Janie was Mrs. William Morris. ■ Miss McCarthy may be Maud McCarthy (see 16 May 1894).

22   °*Annual meeting of the Hammersmith District Labour Council at The Ship, Hammersmith Bridge Rd., at 20. (C. F. Brown, 21 Alexandra Rd., West Kensington Park W.). °Fabian Publishing Committee. 276 Strand. 17¼. °Hallé's Concert. St. James's Hall. 20. The Manchester Band.*

Miserably wet day. Got a letter from JP, which I burnt at the first glance. Wrote to tell her so, feeling the uselessness of doing anything else. Wrote a scrap of further preface for *Widowers' Houses;* but soon gave it up, feeling out of sorts. My impression is that I am getting out of health for want of exercise. I dined here on my macaroni and then put on my mackintosh and walked up to Hampstead to Sidney Webb to consult him about Sophie Bryant's complaints of the Technical Education Committee. But he was not there, nor his wife, both having gone out to dine. I forgot about the Publishing Committee. When I went down to the Hallé Concert, half an hour late in consequence of having been delayed by an inopportune call from Blanchard, I could not get in—at least there was only standing room; so I came away, rather out of temper at their not having sent me a seat. When I got home I wrote up this diary and wrote a few cards. Was rather interested in the papers because of the criticisms of Moore's play.

Papers 5½d   Train Finchley Rd to Portland Rd 4d

> J. T. Blanchard, of Winchester House, Old Broad St., E.C. ■ G.B.S. wrote (C933) that when he arrived at St. James's Hall he was informed that there was only standing room

remaining. The public, he was happy to note, "has found out what a mistake it made last year in neglecting the Manchester band."

23 *"Olive Branch" Committee at the S. D. F. Hall. 337 Strand. 20½. Five Fabians, five S. D. F., five Hammersmith Socialist Society delegates.*

Began *World* article. After dinner called at Archer's, but he was not in. Walked around Regents Park, having found that the walk to Hampstead yesterday did me good. When I got home I made a sketch of a manifesto for the "Olive Branch" Committee.

Papers 1½d   Dinner 1/–

24 *Fabian Executive. 17¾. Committee 16¼. °Terry's Bijou Theatre, Bedford St. W.C. J. T. Grein's At-Home. Performance of Ibsen's Ghosts. 14½. See 26th January—arrangements changed. Be at the Wheatsheaf at 14¼ to meet M. B. Williams (just back from Topolobampo). Call on the Charringtons in the evening.*

Finished and sent off *World* article. Wallas came with me to the Fabian. After tea went to Orange Grove and then to lavatory. Walked out to Charringtons'.

> Topolobampo was a socialist utopian colony in Mexico, on the Gulf of California. ▪
> Shaw's activities, omitted from his diary, are supplied, 24–28 February, from his pocket diary.

25 *Crystal Palace Concert. 15. Santley, Mary Cardew (violinist), Dvorak's Symphony in G. °Miss Helen Hulme's concert. Steinway Hall. 15.*

Corrected and sent off Charrington review to the *Chronicle*. Met Ernest Williams at the Wheatsheaf and brought him down to the Palace with me. Met Jacques at Victoria. He walked with me to the Orange Grove where we had some grub and walked back together. Only looked in for a wash and then off to Sophie Bryant's. Then to Webbs'. Laura [Warley] there. Walked back. Not in bed until after 1.30.

> Mary Cardew, G.B.S. wrote (C933), was "a remarkable violinist of the Joachim school"; Charles Santley sang French arias with "an unspoiled . . . voice, skilfully produced, and guided by a tender and upright artistic conscience." Dvořák's Symphony in G (No. 8) was mere "promenade music."

26 SUNDAY *Lecture at the Co-operative Hall, Chelsea, for the Chelsea Labour League. 20. (S. Masterson, 57 Dartrey Rd., Chelsea S.W.). Cancelled—hall not available. Speak at the Dock Gates, Poplar, at 11.30. Paper on "The Need of the British Academy" by Fanny Brough at the Playgoers' Club, 409 Strand W.C. 20.*

Chelsea off. Went down to the Docks but it was too wet for the meeting. Took a walk round the Dock with [H. B.] Samuels and then went home, leaving him at the corner of Portland Rd. Walked home. Dined on some fruit and revised *World* proof. Also some paper of agreement ready for giving out to copy. Went to Playgoers' Club and spoke there. A. Lewis walked back with me to the corner of Grafton Street in Tottenham Court Rd.

Fanny Brough (1854–1914) would play Mrs. Warren in the 1902 Stage Society "private" production and the remarkable Mrs. Collins (the Mayoress) in *Getting Married* (1908).

27 *Fabian Central Group Meeting. 32 Gt. Ormond St. G. Turner on "Some Parliamentary Reforms." 20.*

Spent the morning reading the paper and writing letters. Very wet. Called on Archer and Wallas after dinner on my return from Chancery Lane to get agreement *re Widowers' Houses* copied. They were out, and I called on Clarke and met a young Irishman there named Weakes. Left after 18 and spent the evening here writing letters and revising Fabian leaflet about Poor Law.

Copies of agreement 4/–

28 *Sub-committee of the "Olive Branch," Hyndman, Morris and myself, at Kelmscott House. 20½.*

Morris' 20 to 20½. Writing to Walter, etc. Revised Poor Law leaflet at office.

One of Shaw's letters this date (*CL*), to Oscar Wilde, acknowledged receipt of a presentation copy of *Salome*, "in purple raiment." The Poor Law leaflet was *A Plea for Poor Law Reform* (BB13), *Fabian Tract* No. 44, published in April 1893. It was originally drafted by Frederick Whelen.

March

1 *Meeting of the Executive Committee, South St. Pancras Liberal and Radical Association, at Percy Bunting's, 11 Endsleigh Gardens, 20. Fabian Publishing Committee. 276 Strand, 17½. °Anglo-Russian Gathering at Barnard's Inn Hall. 20 to 22½.*

Day a little wasted. At least I am not convinced that I was doing much good by writing a long minute about the projected manifesto of the "Olive Branch" Committee and sending it to Hyndman for transmission in due course to Morris. This took up the morning chiefly. After dinner I walked into the City to buy some supplies for the typewriter ("Supplies" is the trade term for paper, ink ribbon, etc.) and back to the Fabian office, where I found only Dark and Miss Priestley, who told me that there was to be no committee. I walked home and found Olivier waiting for me. He came to borrow the first volume of Wagner's prose works. He had tea with me and then I went off to the Caucus. When I got back I wrote a couple of cards and wrote up this diary partly.

Papers—*Star & West[minster] Gazette* 1½d   Dinner 1/1   Half ream typewriter paper No. 1 quarto 2/6   A dozen sheets carbon transfer paper 2/–

2   *London Symphony Concert. St. James's Hall. 20¼.*

In all day until 17. Worked on proofs of *Widowers' Houses*. Drafted letter *re* Hammill when I got back from concert.

> Reviewed on 8 March 1893 (C934). Henschel conducted the Beethoven Ninth, "which was quite enough for one evening," although he began the program with the Schubert "Unfinished Symphony." ▪ Fred Hammill was actively supporting the right of public meeting in Trafalgar Square. See 14 April 1893.

3   *Fabian Executive. 17½. Committee. 16¼. Fabian Meeting at Essex Hall. 20. S. Olivier on "Socialism and Rights of Civil Servants." Altered to Wilshire's lecture, see 17th inst.* Get *Widowers' Houses agreement stamped. Wind Instrument Society Concert. St. James's Banqueting Hall. 20¼. (Smoking concert).*

Began *World* article but did not get along with it. Played Kistler's opera. Milk and cake at Orange Grove with H. Sonntag 3d. Supper at Gatti and Rodesano 1/8. Walked home with Morgan-Browne along the embankment.

> Shaw did not review the Smoking Concert and apparently did not attend it. ▪ *Baldur's Tod*, by Cyrill Kistler (1848–1907), had just been produced at Würzburg. Shaw would discuss it in his *World* column on 15 March 1893 (C936), calling him "one of the coming men in Germany."

4   *Crystal Palace Concert. 15. Belle Cole, Slivinski, Marshall Hall's Overture. Opening night at the Royalty Theatre under the management of the Charringtons. Production of Dr. Richard Voss's* Alexandra.

Worked on *World* article. FE with me. We went together to the Orange Grove for tea. 2/3. Then she, having to go to her occult society, came with me as far as the corner of Howland St. Royalty in the evening.

> Marshall Hall's concert overture was too derivative to retain G.B.S.'s attention. "I cannot say how it ended," he confessed (C934). Slivinski played "one of those concertos of Chopin's which never should have been written by a man of genius after Beethoven's fourth and fifth concertos. . . ." Belle Cole, contralto, went unremarked. ▪ More and more active in the Order of the Golden Dawn, Florence Farr was beginning to drift away from Shaw, even from acting, but the drift would be a slow, almost imperceptible one until both parties suddenly recognized it late in 1894. ▪ The play at the Royalty, starring Janet Achurch in the title role, would fold after seven performances. Nothing further would be heard from the playwright.

5 SUNDAY   *Lecture at Ferndale Club, Bedford Rd., Clapham, for the Clapham Labour League, on "An Independent Labour Party." (F. V. Conolly, 64 Crescent Rd., Clapham SW.) Train to Clapham Rd.*

Finished and sent off *World* article. Longish day's work. Lay down and read Hugo's *Miserables* for a while between 17 and 18. Went down to Clapham by 19.42 train.

6 Worked all day at *Widowers' Houses* proofs. Feel very tired after Sunday's work. Dinner 11d. After it took a walk round by Lisson Grove, etc. Wrote several letters; sang a bit; and went at the proofs again in the evening. Lay down for a while after the walk and read *Les Mis[erables]*.

7 *Mrs. Besant lectures at the National Liberal Club on "What can be done by Politics and what cannot." 20. Samuel Butler lectures at the Somerville Club, 231 Oxford St., on "Was* The *Odyssey Written by a Woman?" 20. Dolmetsch's 3rd Viol concert. Barnard's Inn. 20½.*

Up very late. Pay for yesterday's *Chronicle.* Proofs again. Went to Grafton Gallery. Came home. Hyndman and Hobson walked with me to the Broadway. Read act III between 17 and 19¼.

> Samuel Butler would publish his speculation, *The Authoress of the Odyssey*, in 1897. See also 24 April 1893. ■ Dolmetsch's concert went unreviewed.

8 *Israel in Egypt at the Albert Hall. Royal Choral Society.*

Corrected proofs of *Widowers' Houses.* As it was a very fine day I went off to FE, who got some purchase and came off with me to Kew and then on the water to Richmond. We called for [C. Duncan] Lewis but he was out. We had a meal at Ferrari's and then took a walk in the park. Then back to Dalling Rd. I came back by the 22.37 train.

> Out at Kew and Richmond, Shaw was not in his reviewer's seat at Albert Hall.

9 *Go up to Dryhursts' in the evening. 20. First Philharmonic Concert of the season. St. James's Hall. 20. Slivinski.*

Began *World* article, and worked a little at *Widowers' Houses.* Walked in Regents Park and worked at manifesto. *Widowers' Houses* again in the evening. Philharmonic. Lucy came back from Ireland.

> Reviewed on 15 March 1893 (C936). G.B.S. found the orchestra—and program—uneven, while Slivinski performed the Schumann concerto "brilliantly" but without feeling.

10 *Fabian Executive. 17½. Committee. 16¼. Meeting of the General Committee of the National Liberal Federation at the Conference, National Liberal Club. 15. Attend as one of the three delegates of the South St. Pancras Liberal and Radical Association.*

National Liberal Club. 15. General Committee National Liberal Federation. Signed name on entering library. Nearly finished *World* article. Left the meeting when I discovered that it was to be nothing but twaddle. Went to Somerset House and got agreement stamped. Wallas walked home with me.

> Somerset House, in the Strand overlooking Waterloo Bridge, was then the General Register Office for British birth, marriage, and death certificates as well as legal documents of other kinds.

11   *Crystal Palace Concert. 15. Dvorak's* Mass in D. *Production of Goring Thomas's* Golden Web *at the Lyric Theatre. 20. Gluck's* Orfeo *at the Lyceum. Royal College of Music. 15$\frac{1}{2}$.*

Wrote some letters. Went down to the *World* office to see the Spitzer catalogue. Got back by early train. Lyric in the evening.

> Reviewed on 22 March 1893 (C937). The first performance in England of Dvořák's *Mass* left G.B.S. unimpressed. ▪ The posthumous production of *The Golden Web* demonstrated Thomas's musical gifts, G.B.S. thought (C937), but the composer had been defeated by the "wretched" libretto of B. C. Stephenson and Frederick Corder, "void as it is of a single passage which calls for musical expression." The light opera would last twenty-eight performances. ▪ Having seen the *Orfeo* production earlier, Shaw went instead to *The Golden Web.* ▪ Frederic Spitzer (1815–1890) was a Viennese-born Parisian art collector whose huge collection, which Shaw described as a "South Kensington Museum ready made," would be sold in Paris from Spitzer's mansion in the Rue de Villejust from 17 April through 16 June. Shaw's two unsigned paragraphs in *The World,* 15 March 1893 (C935), were based upon the sumptuous catalogue—two folio volumes and accompanying portfolio of photogravures.

12 SUNDAY   *Lecture on "The Evolution of Socialism" at the Tottenham Radical Club (H. Bond Holding, 7 Lynwood Villas, Wood Green N.). Train Liverpool St to Bruce Grove. 19.25; return 21.57.*

[Went to] Tottenham. Finished and sent off appendix to *Widowers' Houses*—last of the copy. Wrote notes for *World* on Spitzer catalogue and finished *World* article. Went to the Gro[svenor] with Morgan-Browne in the evening.

13   *(10th) Last day to get agreement stamped, with Henry and Co. for* Widowers' Houses. *Central Group (Fabian) meeting at 32 Gt. Ormond St. H. Morgan-Browne on "Inequalities of Taxation." 20. Fabian Publishing Committee. 276 Strand. 17$\frac{1}{4}$.*

Drafted letter for Cox. Wrote long letter to a singer who wrote to me for advice. After dinner left here out of sorts and strolled about the Embankment. Tried to work a bit on the Socialist manifesto without success until it was time to go to the Fabian. Corrected proof of Poor Law leaflet. Grub at Gatti's with Wallas. Group meeting in the evening. Wallas came home with me.

14   *Wagner Concert. London Symphony Band. St. James's Hall. 20$\frac{1}{4}$.*

Read the revises of *Widowers' Houses* except the last few pages of proofs. Went out into the park in the morning to work but found it too cold and came back. Called on FE but she was not at home.

Notebook to begin new play in 1/−.

> Shaw did not review the London Symphony concert. ▪ The notebook would be used to begin *The Philanderer* (BL Add. MS. 50596A).

15 *Strolling Players' Amateur Orchestral Society Smoking Concert. St. Andrew's Hall. 21½. James Brown's concert. Steinway Hall. 20½. Ilona Eibenschutz's recital. St. James's Hall. 15. Westminster Orchestral Society. Westminster Town Hall. 20.*

Revised proofs of *Widowers' Houses.*

Shaw reviewed no concerts this date, being too intent on his play proofs.

16 *"Olive Branch" Committee (now Joint Committee of Socialist Societies) at 337 Strand. 20.*

Began *World* article. The Salts were at the Wheatsheaf. Called for Archer: he had just gone to *World*; so I sent him down proofs of *Widowers' Houses* (dialogue only). Went to Fabian office. When I got back from Committee I copied out certain scraps of my draft manifesto (out of my notes for once) and sent them to Morris.

17 *Fabian Executive. 17½. Committee. 16½. 23rd the last day for nominations for Executive 1893–4. Fabian meeting at Essex Hall. 20. H. G. Wilshire on "Socialism and Free Trade." Altered to Olivier's lecture above. See 3rd inst. °Irish National Concert. Albert Hall. 20. Press View. British Artists, McLean's, Tooth's, Fine Art Society's and Bernheim's (186 Piccadilly).*

Got a lot of picture books from Lady Colin Campbell, who is ill, with request that I should go at them for her. Had to drop my *World* article and rush off to the galleries. Met M. B. Williams (at Orange Grove). Large party there—Olivier, Dix, Mrs. O., Mrs. Sandham, Oakeshott, and Bertha Newcombe. Spoke in debate. Little scene with Bertha afterwards.

Henry Gaylord Wilshire (1861–1927), well-to-do writer on Socialism and future candidate for office in Canada, California, and New York. In 1894 he would run for a seat from Manchester. ▪ Whatever Shaw wrote on art for Lady Colin Campbell would appear under her initials, "Q.E.D."

18 *Crystal Palace Concert. 15. Mary Harris and Joachim. Ridley Art Club. Exhibition at 9 Conduit St. Also on the 20th, 21st and 22nd.*

Worked at *World* article. Wallas called at about 12. I went out with him and we took a turn in Regents Park and then went to the Crystal Palace together.

Reviewed on 22 March 1893 (C937). Joachim's "finest qualities seem to improve," G.B.S. wrote. Mary Harris "touched up" her arias with additional high notes, eliciting a warning from G.B.S. "that she must not do that again if she wishes to be respected as an artist as well as admired as a young lady with a pretty voice. . . ."

21 *Fabian Publishing Committee. 276 Strand. 17½. Sub-Committee Joint Socialist, at Morris's, at 20½. °Trinity College. Mandeville Place. Students' Chamber Concert and Conversazione. 20½ to 23.*

Slept by snatches, disturbed by the hammering of the workmen at the drains, until past 11; so that I was abominably late. Again read over the preface to *Widowers' Houses*—fortunately, as I found one or two stupid oversights in it. After dinner called for Archer, but he was in the country. I then, having an hour to kill before the Publishing Committee, called on the Carrs' and found Geraldine there. She has taken to painting at the Slade School. Carr came in afterwards. After the Committee I went out to Hammersmith with Sparling and had "tea" at the Terrace. Before dinner I had to go to Bloomsbury to the lavatory there, as the one at Portland Rd. was out of order.

Lav[a]t[or]y, Bloomsbury 1d   Papers 1½d   Dinner 1/1   Train
Temple to Rav[enscour]t Pk 6d   Hammersmith to Portland Rd 6d

22   °*Mrs. Morgan-Browne's At-Home. 46 Ridgmount Gardens. 16–19. Boat Race. 15¼. Sparlings'. Meet Oakeshott at the Wheatsheaf at 14 and walk out together. °Ridley Art Club; see Saturday last.*

Drafted advert of Independent Theatre for *Widowers' Houses*. Played through some of Verdi's *Falstaff*. The Salts were at the Wheatsheaf; and Mrs. Salt walked with me to the Circus, Salt coming behind with Oakeshott. They left us at the Circus. Oakeshott and I walked out to Hammersmith. We met Bertha and Mabel Newcombe on the way and put them into a cab. After the Race I went into Walkers' for a while. Then I returned to Sparlings' where there were still a good many people. Eventually all left except the Steffens and Miss Priestley, who made an elaborate examination of my hand and described my character. We did some playing later in the evening. I came back with Miss Priestley by the 23.5 train, and saw her home to Woburn Place.

Papers 1½d   Lav[a]t[or]y 1d   Dinner 1/3   Tip to cab tout 6d
Train Rav[enscour]t Park to Gower St 9d

> G.B.S. would use an image from the competition in his weekly music column, referring to playing an instrument with the kind of "impetuosity" that results in "retiring finally amid the sort of enthusiasm that follows a pluckily rowed boat race" (C938).

23   *Last day for nominations for Fabian Executive. Philharmonic Concert. St. James's Hall. 20. Fabian Publishing Committee. 276 Strand. 17¼. Meet Miss Leeds (Miss Priestley's friend) at the Fabian office at 16.45.*

Began *World* article. Returned here after dinner to change my clothes and wash. After the Committee Olivier came with me to the Orange Grove. I left the concert at the end of the first part. When I got home I read the last proofs of *Widowers' Houses* and sent them off. Also began reading Archer's article "The Mausoleum of Ibsen" in proof and MS.

Lav[ator]y 1d   Hair cut &c 1/–   Papers 1½d   Dinner 3d   "Tea"
at Orange Grove 1/6

Gabriele Wietrowetz gave "a very remarkable performance" of the Brahms violin concerto (C938)—"powerful, impatient, and . . . not by any means musically satisfactory." The orchestra was in such fine form that the conductor, Alexander Mackenzie, earned G.B.S.'s special compliments. ▪ The Archer essay would appear in the *Fortnightly Review*, July 1893.

24   *Fabian Executive. 17½. Committee. 16¼. °Wind Instrument Chamber Music Society's Concert. St. James's Banqueting Hall. 22¼. Press View. Wetherbee's drawings. Fine Art Society. New Operetta,* Mr. Jericho *at the Savoy Theatre. 19.45. Words by Harry Greenbank, music by Ernest Ford.*

Finished and sent off *World* article. After dinner called on Archer; and as he was not in, wrote a letter on his typewriter and left it for him with his article and proofs of *Widowers' Houses*. Oakeshott came with me to the Savoy. We were together at Gatti's; but we did not go to the theatre together, he having to go to Hartley's first.

Papers 1½d   Dinner 1/1   Omelette &c at G[atti] & R[odesano]'s 1/6

George Faulkner Wetherbee (1851–1920), born in Cincinnati, settled in London in the 1870s after studying art in Antwerp. He was a painter of landscapes and genre subjects as well as of mythological themes. ▪ *Mr. Jericho* was "funnily absurd and wittily funny" (C938). G.B.S. thought that the libretto he enjoyed, by Harry Greenbank (1866–1899), was by a better-known writer appearing here under a pseudonym, but young Greenbank was genuine. The music was "passably upholstered" by Ernest Ford. ▪ Archer's article was "The Theatres," *English Illustrated Magazine*, May 1893. ▪ Probably Eustace D. Hartley (see 18 September 1892).

25   *Crystal Palace Concert. 15. Klengel (cellist) and Mlle. Landi. Dine with Wilshire at Glenmore, Elmbourne Rd. Balham. (dinner at 19).*

Worked at the advertisement sheet for *Widowers' Houses*. There was nobody at Balham except Wilshire.

Dinner 10d   Papers 2½d   Train Ch[arin]g + to Victoria 1½d
Vict[oria] to [Crystal] Palace 1/–   Palace to Balham 4d   Balham to Vict[oria] 4d

Shaw attended the concert but did not refer to it in his column. Julius Klengel and Camilla Landi (a soprano) were only briefly noticed in other columns. ▪ Henry Gaylord Wilshire lived at "Glenmore" in Upper Tooting with his sister Norah. Shaw's designation of the address as Balham (which is contiguous with Upper Tooting) was an error.

26 SUNDAY   *Lecture for the Kentish Town Branch S. D. F. at Phoenix Hall, Malden Rd. on "Entire Social Democracy." (C. F. Davis, Lec. Sec.). Dine with R. G. Beresford at 57 Lillie Rd. and get photographed in the afternoon.*

Did a little work on the advertisement and then walked over to Lillie Rd. Barron was also there. I left at about 16.40 and walked to Hammersmith and had a meal with FE. Went to Kentish Town by the 18.45 train.

Train Ham[mersm]ith to Kentish Town 8d   Bus Chalk Farm Rd to Euston Rd 2d   *Justice* 1d

George Charles Beresford was given the wrong initials by Shaw. He then worked for Collier Gwyn, a photographer with premises in Fulham at Lillie Road. ▪ Both Arthur C. Barron of Blackheath and Oswald Barron of Wandsworth Common were Fabians listed in Shaw's addressbook; it is unclear which this is.

27   °*Fabian Central Group. 32 Great Ormond St. Mary Belcher on "Socialism and Sanitation." 20. Tea at Archer's. 18. Liberal and Radical Union Council meeting. National Liberal Club. 20.*

Wrote some letters and sent off the last revises of *Widowers' Houses* marked "press." Also finished and sent the advertisement sheets to Henry and Co. By that time it was nearly four o'clock. I dined at the café opposite Portland Rd. station and went to see FE; but she was out. I walked back to Queens Rd. Bayswater and took bus to Holborn. Had tea alone with Archer who walked with me as far as Waterloo Place on my way to the National Liberal Club. I did not speak there, except to ask a question. Wrote a few letters.

Dinner at Menegallo's 2/–   Papers 1½d   Lav[ator]y 1d   Train to Shep[herds] Bush & back 9d   Bus Queen's Rd to Oxford O 2d   Oxford St to Holborn 1d

28   °*Dolmetsch's 4th Viol concert. Barnard's Inn. 20½. Go down to Oxted by the 17 train. Stay with the Salts.*

Worked at [Noel L.] Griffiths' proposed Fabian manifesto on the Labour Party with a view to making it good enough to enable me to support it; but at its best it does not come to anything definite. Olivier came down with me in the train and came into Salts for a while. I read a bit of a play which he has begun and of which he is very full. In the evening we did not get to duet playing as usual, Mrs. Salt having a great deal to say, chiefly about May Sparling.

Lavatory 1d   Dinner 1/1   Papers 2½d   Train Ch[arin]g Cross to Victoria 1½d   Victoria to Oxted 1/8

Noel L. Griffiths was on the Fabian Executive from 1892 to 1895. ▪ Olivier's unpublished play, *A Freedom in Fetters*, for which a license was denied by the Lord Chamberlain's censor in 1894. It would be privately produced, as *Mrs. Maxwell's Marriage*, by the Stage Society.

29   *Oxted.*

After breakfast went up to the Common by Rickfield Rd. and selected a spot on the West Heath, near the orphanage, where I lay down and got to work on the new play which I have resolved to call *The Philanderer*. After dinner I went up on the downs with Mrs. Salt, who was still very full of May. In the evening we played duets.

By "full of May" Shaw means full of gossip about May Morris Sparling—possibly references to his closeness to May and what friends might be saying.

30   *Oxted.*

Morning as before. After dinner we went up to the West Heath and I sat there for a while. Called on Rix and exchanged a few words with him in the street, his wife joining us presently. On our way back we met Olivier, who turned back with us. Evening as usual.

> Herbert Rix, a member of the Fellowship of the New Life, would become assistant secretary of the Royal Society.

31   °The Messiah *at Albert Hall.* °Fabian Executive. 17½. Committee. 16¼. *Not this week. Oxted.*

Morning as before. After dinner played and sang *Die Zauberflöte* until the arrival of Ernest Williams and a musical friend of his whose name I forget. We all walked over to Olivier's. The two visitors returned with us and had tea before they continued their walk to Godstone. Olivier came back with us and sat for a while whilst Williams's friend played some pages from *Götterdämmerung.* Evening as usual.

April

1   °*Crystal Palace Concert. 15. Mrs. Hutchinson, L. Borwick. German's* Marche Solennelle.

Morning as before, except that I was earlier than usual and did three hours hard work on the play, which tired me enough to induce me to take a nap after dinner until M. B. Williams came. We all went over to Rix's half built new house and picnicked there, the Adamses joining us. We parted from them near Pebble Hill and brought M. B. Williams back to tea. After he left, evening as usual.

> Francis William Lauderdale Adams (1862–1893) and his strikingly attractive second wife (his first wife had died), Edith Goldstone Adams, an Australian and a former actress. A novelist and poet best known for his politically radical *Songs of the Army of the Night* (1888, 1890), Adams would commit suicide on 4 September 1893, shooting himself when despondent over his worsening tuberculosis.

2 SUNDAY   Morning as usual, except that I came back rather early to write some letters before dinner, and did not return by Rickfield Rd. as usual. Mrs. Salt went up on the downs alone and left us to dine without her. After dinner we joined her. Back by the lime quarry and evening as usual.

> Easter Sunday was no different from other Sundays for Shaw's friends, although the very reason he was holidaying in the country was the Easter hiatus in his professional activities.

3   *Oxted.*

Morning as before. It was much colder and when we went out in the afternoon we lay down in a sheltered spot near Pebble Hill instead of braving the east wind on the Common. Then we walked through the park to the downs, Mrs. Salt leaving us on the way and returning home. Salt and I went on to the top of the ridge and returned by the lime quarry. Evening as usual. After dinner Mrs. Salt and I played some Mozart.

Gave a tramp on my way to the Common 1/–

4   *Come up from Oxted by the 10.43 train.*

Came up from Oxted by the 10.43 train with the Oliviers, from whom I parted at Victoria. Before I started I read over the Fabian report, reported myself on Griffith's manifesto, and wrote a letter to the Halifax Fabians in answer to a letter of theirs asking for an explanation of a passage in *Fabian Essays*. Busy before and after dinner with correspondence, etc. Wrote a letter to the *Chronicle*—a joke. Went out to FE in the evening.

Carriage of umbrella mislaid in train & porter 10d   Train Oxted to Victoria 1/8   *Daily Chronicle* 1d   Dinner 1/1

> Shaw's "joke" was not published.

5   Did not feel inclined to work hard; so did some pasting into scrap book to begin; and then drafted a circular letter to be sent by Henry and Co. about *Widowers' Houses* to several press correspondents, of whom I made a list of 50. Then walked to the Strand to buy a *Fortnightly Review*. Then off to FE. We took a walk and discovered Perivale Church and heard an extraordinary performance by a nightingale close to Ealing on our way back. Wrote to Henry and Co. a second time when I got back in reply to their objection to mention other publishers in their advertisements of my other works in *Widowers' Houses*.

Fortnightly Review 2/–   Dinner at Orange Grove 1/3   Train Ch[arin]g + to Ravenscourt Pk 6d   Rav[enscourt] Pk to Ealing Com[mon] (2) 1/4   *West[minster] Gaz[ette]* 1d   Almonds 3½d   Ealing to Ealing Common (2) 4d   Shep[herds] Bush to Portl[an]d Rd 6d

> Perivale St. Andrews, in the London suburbs, would be the name of Undershaft's utopian factory town in Shaw's *Major Barbara*.

6   *Else Sonntag's and Jim Headlam's wedding, Marylebone Parish Church. 14½. Clever Alice at the Royalty. First night. 20.*

Began *World* article. In the afternoon went out to FE to go over Mrs. Linde with her. Salt was at the Wheatsheaf. Wrote to Charrington when I got back from the theatre. In the morning Teixeira de Mattos called about the circular *re Widowers' Houses.*

National Reformer 2d   *Star* ½d   *West[minster] Gazette* 1d   Bus Oxford Circus to Goldhawk Rd 4d   Queens Rd Bayswater to Oxford O
2d   Program at theatre 6d

> *Clever Alice*, an adaptation by Brandon Thomas of *Die Maler*, by Adolf Willebrandt, with
> Janet Achurch in the title role and Charles Charrington playing another lead as well as
> managing the production. There would be fourteen performances. ▪ Mrs. Linde was
> the confidante in Ibsen's *A Doll's House*.

7 *Press View. Menpes' paintings in France, Spain and Morocco. Dowdes-
well's. Fabian meeting at Essex Hall. Touzeau Parris on "Socialism and
Individual Liberty." 20. Fabian Executive. 276 Strand. 17¼. Preliminary
Committee. 16¼. Private View. New English Art Club. Egyptian Hall.*

Worked at *World* article. Bertha Newcombe walked with me from the New
England Art Club to Piccadilly Circus. Spoke at the Fabian and walked
home afterwards, Runciman coming as far as Holborn and Wallas to the
door, rather savage with me for my speech.

Papers 1½d   Dinner 1/1   Omelette &c at Gatti's and Rodesano's 1/6

8 *Crystal Palace Concert. 15. Braxton Smith, Fanny Davies, Raff's Im
Walde Symphony.*

Finished writing *World* article. Looked over *Falstaff* a bit. Worked at the play
in the evening here, and in the train; but had a headache and did not get on
very well. FE came with me as far as London St. from the Wheatsheaf.

Lent O'Brien 4/−   Telegram to FE 6d   Papers 2½d   Dinner 1/1
Bus Ch[arin]g + Rd 1d   Train Ch[arin]g + to Vict[oria] 1½d
Vic[toria] to [Crystal] Pal[a]ce (2) 4/−   Grub at Orange Grove (2) 2/4

> A paragraph in G.B.S.'s 19 April 1893 column (C941) noted the "fine performance" of
> Raff's symphony, about which he asked, "[W]hy don't they cut away all that repeti-
> tion . . . in the *finale?*" Singer Braxton Smith, whom Shaw did not admire, went unnot-
> iced, whereas Fanny Davies' "triumph" in the Chopin F minor concerto (No. 2) was
> characterized as her "most successful feat of interpretation and execution." ▪ "Easter
> has afforded me," G.B.S. began his 12 April 1893 (C940) column, "an opportunity for a
> look through the vocal score of Verdi's *Falstaff...* "

9 SUNDAY *Dine with Sidney Webbs, Charringtons in the evening.*

Revised proof of *World* article. Walked out to Hampstead. After dinner we
went to Pinner, arriving ·there about 16 and returning by the 19.21 train.
The Webbs got out at St. John's Wood; and I went on to Gloucester Rd. S.W.,
and on to Charringtons'. I read them as much of the new play as I have
written. Finished and sent off *World* article on my return.

Train Finchley Rd to Pinner & back 1/1   Tea at Pinner (Webb paid)
Excess fare Finchley Rd to Baker St 2d   Baker St to Gloster Rd & back
9d   Excess to Portl[an]d Rd 1d   Chocolate &c 3d

10   *See next Monday. Strudwick.* °*Fabian Central Group. 32 Great Ormond St. Miss Foley on "Fashion." Speak at Southwold for the Liberal Association. Train at 12 from Liverpool St. (Laurence Debney). Meeting at 19½. Speak on "The Political Situation" with Mrs. Morgan-Browne.*

Worked at the new play in the train for a couple of hours, getting along famously. Then ate some apples and biscuits and went to sleep until we came to Halesworth, the junction for Southwold. At the Debneys' I found Mrs. Morgan-Browne, whom, by the bye, I had never met before; but before going there Debney brought me into the house of Herrington next door, a pilot and local radical, at whose house I am to sleep. After the meeting I sat up a while with Debney and then went into Herringtons' where they kept me up until near 1, talking to my host, his wife, and a local character named Harry Smith. Beautiful weather.

Remitted Condy & Mitchell for disinfector 2/6   Cost of order 1d
Telegram to Debney 6½d   Train to Bishopsgate 3d   *Star* ½d   *Penny Illustrated Paper* (insurance) 1d   Train Liverpool St to Southwold (return) 15/–

Laura Morgan-Browne, wife of Hubert Morgan-Browne.

11   *Lecture on Kistler's* Kunihild *by W. Ashton Ellis at Trinity College, Mandeville Place, 20¼. Come up from Southwold by the 14.20 train.*

Weather changed deplorably for the worse—atrocious northeast wind. All my plans of lying on the beach and having a quiet morning's work upset. Debney brought me for a walk over to Walberswick to see the church there. We first had a look at Southwold church. Then I took a turn in the town by myself. We dined at 1. In the train I slept a bit at first and then worked for nearly 2 hours at the play, getting on, as before, very well. Lucy was here when I got back from the lecture.

Bootlaces at Southwold 1d   Tip to Herrington's servant 1/–   Papers 1½d   Train Bishopsgate to Portl[an]d Rd 7d

12   *Dora Bright's concert. Prince's Hall. 20.*

In the morning the proof of the Joint Socialist Manifesto arrived; and I spent most of the working end of the day in correcting it and writing to Morris an explanation of my alterations; so that he may send them to Hyndman and obtain his consent to bring them before the Committee on Thursday as suggestions from the sub-committee. I also wrote to Henry and Co. about the specimen cases for binding *Widowers' Houses*, sending them back with instructions as to getting them right. Then I walked to Edgware Rd. and took train there to FE, who came with me to the concert. I put her into a bus outside the hall and came home before ten to write up this diary a bit and send off a few cards. Walter [Gurly] was here in the afternoon.

Dinner at Menegallo's 1/9   Papers 1½d   Train Edgware Road to Shepherds Bush 6d   Rav[enscourt] Pk to St Ja[me]s's Pk (2) 1/–

Pianist Dora Bright and her instrumental colleagues, playing Mozart ("there is nothing better in art than Mozart's best"), wasted "a very good program on a very bad audience" (C941).

13 *Call on Braekstad at* Black and White *office at 15. Go to* The Magic Ring *(Magic Opal revised), Prince of Wales Theatre. 20.15. 3rd night. °Joint Socialist Committee. 20.*

Began *World* article. Sang a little of *Falstaff.* After dinner called on Braekstad in reply to his invitation. He wanted to arrange for some articles on art from me for *Black and White.* Then I took the 16.10 train to Richmond and worked at the play on the Terrace. Took a short turn in the park. Lucy was at the theatre with me.

National Reformer 2d   *West[minster] Gaz[ette]* & *Star* 1½d   Dinner 1/3   Bus to Holborn 1d   Train Waterloo to Richmond & back 1/6 Omelette &c at Ferrari's 1/8   Programme at theatre 6d

> *The Magic Opal,* now retitled, was an "attempt to rescue Señor Albeniz's score . . . from sinking under the weight of its libretto." The labor, claimed G.B.S. (C941), was wasted, but the opera would survive, nevertheless, for seventy-seven performances.

14 *°Independent Theatre Society performance of* Set Free *by Anon. Elizabeth Robins. Postponed. Fabian Executive. 276 Strand. 17½. Committee. 16¼. Fabian Private meeting at Barnard's Inn. 20. Joint Socialist Manifesto and Griffith's and Hammill's Labour Party Tract.*

Worked at *World* article. Spoke at the Fabian meeting on the Labour Tract, and introduced and read the Manifesto. Wallas walked home with me.

Dinner at Orange Grove 1/7   Papers 1½d   Bus along Strand 1d Omelette &c at Gatti's 1/6

15 *°Crystal Palace Concert. 15. Berlioz's* Faust. *°Private View. Society of Lady Artists. Maddox St. Galleries. 10 to 18. (17th) Strudwick—last chance. Sauret's first violin recital. St. James's Hall. 15.*

Began article for the *Workman's Times* to replace Sparling's Fabian Notes. FE was at the concert. After it we went to the Orange Grove, where I met Jessie Newcombe. We then went from Waterloo to Putney and walked across the Heath and Common to Richmond Park and across that to Richmond.

Dinner 11d   Papers 1½d   Tea &c at Orange Grove 1/4 (2)   Train Waterloo to Putney (2) 1/2   (Waiting room) 1d   Supper at Ferrari's (2) 3/10   Train Richmond to Ravenscourt Park (2) 1/2   Shep[herds] Bush to Portland Rd 6d

> The St. James's Hall concert was reviewed on 26 April 1893 (C943). Émile Sauret left G.B.S. impatient because he continued to "rasp" through violin pieces famous in his youth although now passé. ▪ "Fabian Notes," *Workman's Times,* 22 April 1893 (C942). ▪ Jessie Newcombe was a sister of Bertha Newcombe.

16 SUNDAY   Slaved all day, before and after dinner, at the Fabian Notes for *The Workman's Times*. After tea walked to Hampstead and called on the Webbs, but they were out. Went to Hammersmith and found Steele at Sparlings' alone with May. He left presently; and I read May some of the play.

Train Finchley Rd to Hammersmith (Chis[wick]) 8d   H[ammersmi]th Broadway to Portland Rd 6d

> The play referred to was apparently the beginnings of *The Philanderer*, which Shaw read in a philandering setting—an evening alone with a friend's wife.

17   *Last day to see Strudwick's pictures at his house, 14 Edith Villas. Go down to Blackheath by the 15.32 train from Charing Cross and meet Scheu there.*

Corrected proof of *World* article and finished it. Then went to Strudwick's. Scheu read his play to me.

Express Messenger with proof to *World* 6d   Train to Addison Rd 4d West Kensington to Ch[arin]g + 4½d   Papers 1½d   Dinner at Orange Grove 1/1   Train Ch[arin]g + to Blackheath & back 1/4

> The tradition in London was to pay calls on one's artist friends to see their new works in the private studio before these were shipped off to the Royal Academy to be seen by the Hanging Committee for the Spring Exhibition.

18   °*Marie Elba's concert. Steinway Hall. 20. Richmond Orchestral Society's Concert. Star and Garter. 20.*

Did a little business—letters, diary, etc. Called at the *World* office to see C. D. Yates, who had written to say that he wanted to speak to me about the opera; but he was not in. I went into the Embankment Gardens and worked at the play until it was time to go to the Wheatsheaf, where FE had agreed to meet me at 15. A false alarm of rain induced us to hurry off to Portland Rd. station, I calling for my umbrella on the way. When we got to Ravenscourt Park it was quite fine; so we sat for a while, she looking at the peacocks and I working at the play. Then we went in and had something to eat. Finally I went off to Richmond to the concert.

Papers 1½d   Dinner (2) 1/8   Train Portl[an]d Rd to Ravenscourt Pk (2) 1/2   Rav[enscourt] Pk to Richmond return 10d   Excess fare to Ptld Rd 7d   Chocolate & roll at Richmond after concert 7d

> The terrace of the Star and Garter would be the setting of Act II of Shaw's *The Doctor's Dilemma* (1906). The ambitious program arranged by conductor James Brown "was of the usual amateur kind: that is to say, it would have taxed the finest qualities of the best band in the world," G.B.S. wrote (C943).

19   St. Paul *at the Albert Hall. Royal Choral Society. 20. Dora Bright's second concert. Prince's Hall. 20. Mme [Fanny] Frickenhaus's matinee. St. James's Hall. 15. Fabian Publishing Committee. 276 Strand. 17¾. Bring "Administrative Reforms" and "Eight Hours."*

Fabian Publishing Committee. 17½. Loafed rather. Played the Volume of Irish airs (Stanford and Grove) that Jacques sent me. Met Walker in Rathbone Place and went with him to the Orange Grove. After Committee Sparling and Olivier came with me to the Orange Grove. 1/7. Olivier paid as he owed me 2/6 and gave me 1/–. Came home and played a bit—then worked at *Widowers' Houses*.

Shaw's daily *activities* through 22 April are taken from his pocket diary. He appears to have attended none of the events on his 19 April calendar.

20 *Philharmonic Concert. St. James's Hall. 20.*

Began *World* article. Met FE in Rathbone Place. I went to the Orange Grove whilst she went to do some business in Covent Garden. We met Reece and he came to Dalling Rd and had a cup of tea. Lucy was at the concert.

The Philharmonic concert was "half an hour too long, and crowded to the doors." The orchestra played a Mendelssohn symphony, and with Sapellnikoff a Chopin concerto. Marie Brema, "happening to be tremendously in the dramatic vein," carried away the crowd (C943).

21 *Fabian Annual Meeting. Essex Hall. 20. Fabian Executive. 276 Strand. 17¼. Preliminary Committee. 16½.*

[John] Trevor called whilst I was dressing and stayed for nearly an hour to talk about the Starnthwaite affair and other matters. Called on C. D. Yates and then went on to Fabian and corrected Olivier's draft letter to *Kendal Times*. After supper at Gatti's (1/8) went by myself with Mrs. Webb to the Embankment Gardens and sat for a while, the rest smoking. Mattos and Olivier walked home with me. Sat up acknowledging letters [of] Enid Stacy.

The Home Colonisation Society organized by Herbert V. Mills had founded the 130-acre Starnthwaite Colony in Westmorland, with thirty-odd colonists, intending to be self-supporting. Enid Stacy would complain to Shaw about being ejected from Starnthwaite.

22 *Crystal Palace Concert. 15. Liza Lehmann and Wietrowetz. Agnes Jansen's concert. St. James's Hall. 15. Private View. Calvert drawings. Goupil Gallery (new). 5 Regent St., Pall Mall.*

Worked all the morning at letter to Enid Stacy about the Starnthwaite affair. Olivier called whilst I was dressing and stayed until after 10.

23 SUNDAY *Lecture at the Lotus Club, 41 Henry St., Avenue Rd., N.W., on "Socialism and Human Nature." (M. A. Moore, 17 Avenue Rd., N.W.). 20½. Mrs. Besant in the chair.*

Was all the morning reading the papers and correcting the *World* proof. After dinner lay down upstairs and finished V. Hugo's *Les Misérables*, which I have been reading in scraps for a long time. Was quite affected by the end. Sang for a while. The lecture was rather a ghastly affair. Bertha Newcombe was there, and the Webbs. When it was over I went to Avenue

Rd. with Mrs. Besant and Mrs. Thornton Smith and sat at their supper. Walked home. Headache—not very bad.

24 *Fabian Central Group. 32 Great Ormond St. Samuel Butler on "The Odyssey and the Woman Question." 20. Bertha Newcombe's At-Home. Joubert's Studios. 16¼.*

Spent the morning writing letters. Got rid of some old correspondence in this way. Took things easy. After dinner went to Jaeger's and ordered a suit of clothes. Then went to Hyde Park and lay down on the grass working at the play. At 16.45 got up and went to Bertha Newcombe's, where I found Wallas and a Miss Erichsen, who attracted me considerably. They went presently and I was left with Bertha, to whom I read a bit of my play. We went to the Central Group Meeting together, stopping at the Wheatsheaf on the way to get something to eat. After the meeting Wallas and I put Bertha into a bus and took a walk together by the side of Regents Park.

Dinner at Menegallo's 1/6   Bus to Marble Arch 1d   Train Sloane Sq to Ch[arin]g + (2) Bertha paid   Omelette &c at Orange Grove (2) 1/7 Bus St Martin's Lane to Russell Sq. 6d

> It is unclear from Shaw's diary whether he attended Samuel Butler's lecture on the same subject on 7 March 1893. Apparently he did, for he later wrote (for Pease's *History of the Fabian Society*) that since he realized that the Fabians "would have no notion of how great a man they were entertaining, I dashed down to the meeting; took the chair; gave the audience (about five strong including Butler and myself) to understand that the occasion was a great one; and when we had listened gravely to Samuel's demonstration that the *Odyssey* was written by Nausicaa, carried a general expression of enthusiastic agreement with Butler, who thanked us with old-fashioned gravity. . . ." ▪ Nellie Erichsen (@1860–1918), an artist and illustrator, lived at 6 Trafalgar Studios, Manresa Road, Chelsea, S.W. and also had a cottage in Upper Tooting. She created accompanying pictures for stories in *English Illustrated Magazine* and illustrated Thomas Okey's *Venice and Its Story* as well as several volumes in the *Highways and Byways* series. With Edwin Björkman she also translated several of Strindberg's plays.

25 °*The Sisters Nunn's concert. Steinway Hall. 20.*

Read the papers, wrote a letter, and sang a bit in the morning, taking things rather easy. Went off to Richmond by the 14.10 train from Waterloo, meeting Verinder on the way. Went up into the Park and lay on the grass in the sun until near 18, working at the play. Then went down into the town and had something to eat at Ferrari's. Took train to Ravenscourt Park and called for FE; but she was out, as there is a dress rehearsal of *Adrienne Lecouvreur* tonight, of which I did not know. So I went to Sparlings' and played a couple of duets with May, coming back by the last train but one.

Star ½d   Dinner 10d   *Chronicle & West[minster] Gaz[ette]* 2d   Train Waterloo to Richmond 1/–   Maccaroni &c at Ferrari's 1/10   Train Richmond to Ravenscourt Pk 4d   Hammersmith B[roa]dw[a]y to Portland Rd 6d

Adrienne Lecouvreur, an 1880 adaptation by Henry Herman of the 1849 play by Eugène Scribe and Ernest Legouvé, with both Florence Farr and Janet Achurch, would run only three performances at the Royalty after its revival on 26 April 1893.

26   *Dora Bright's concert. British composers. Prince's Hall. 20. Fabian Publishing Committee. 276 Strand. 17$\frac{1}{2}$. Get clothes fitted at Jaeger's. Middlesex Choral Society's Concert. St. James's Hall. Parry's Job. 20. F[red] Fawcett to call after 12 and sing.*

Got a few scraps of work at the play done. Fawcett stayed until after 14$\frac{1}{4}$. [Uncle] Walter called as I was going out. Wrote several letters, arranging lectures, etc. when I got home from the two concerts.

West[minster] Gaz[ette] 1d   Dinner at Orange Grove 1/3   Omelette &c there 1/3   *The Communism of Ruskin* at Fab[ian] Of[fice] 1/6   Bus along Strand 1d   Concert St Ja[me]s's Hall 2/–   prog[ram]me 6d

> Dora Bright, impresario, presented as the star attraction Willy Hess, who gave, said G.B.S. (C941), "a remarkable performance of Brahms's violin sonata in G, in spite of the parching, freezing northeast wind which was making even me conscious of having a liver." ∎ Reviewed on 3 May 1893 (C945). "I take *Job* to be," G.B.S. concluded, "on the whole, the most utter failure ever achieved by a thoroughly respectworthy musician. There is not one bar in it that comes within fifty thousand miles of the tamest line in the poem." ∎ John M. Robertson, *Modern Humanists. Sociological Studies of . . . Ruskin, etc.*

27   *Go see* Adrienne Lecouvreur *at the Royalty. 20.*

Began *World* article. Wrote to Enid Stacy, 28 Theobald's Rd. Did not get out to dinner until past 16. Went out to FE, who had to leave for the theatre half an hour after I arrived. Sat up after I came home to write to FE about the performance and to Katherine Conway about the Starnthwaite affair. Findon sat next to me at the theatre.

Paper 1d   Dinner at Menegallo's 1/8   Train to Shep[herds] Bush 6d   Bus (2) Goldhawk Rd to Holles St 8d

> Shaw told Florence frankly (CL) that the "unspeakable absurdity" of the performance was only surpassed by the badness of the play. Janet Achurch was "transcendently bad," and in the first scene FE herself was "insufferable," although "you rather score off it."

28   *First meeting of the new Fabian Executive. 276 Strand. 17$\frac{1}{2}$. Preliminary Committee. 16$\frac{1}{2}$. Take the chair. Independent Theatre. Arthur Benham's* Theory and Practice *and* Alan's Wife *(Anon.), at Terry's Theatre. 20.15.* °Wind Instrument Chamber Music Concert. St. James's Banqueting Hall. *20$\frac{1}{2}$. Private View at the Royal Academy.*

Finished *World* article. Had not time to dine—hurried to Jaeger's to get a pair of gloves; then to the Academy to just walk through; and finally to the Fabian, stopping for five minutes to get a glass of milk and a cake. Olivier, Oakeshott and Wallas came with me to Gatti's afterwards. We then went to Terry's Theatre, where I found May Sparling waiting for the doors to open. We took a turn around by Waterloo Bridge whilst we were waiting. On my way home I overtook the Hartleys, Oakeshott, and Olivier. We all went to Hartleys' together. At 23½ Wallas came away with me and walked home with me. I wrote a few cards and posted up this diary before going to bed.

Bus along Strand 1d   Milk & cake at A[erated] B[read] S[hop] [   ]
Maccaroni &c at Gatti & R[odesano]'s 1/8   Papers 2d   Program at theatre 6d

> *Theory and Practice* was a duologue curtain-raiser by Arthur Benham (1872–1895), who had co-authored an earlier piece, *The County*, in June 1892, when he was only twenty. *Alan's Wife*, produced anonymously (even J. T. Grein, who ran the Independent Theatre, did not know the author's identity), was an adaptation from the Swedish by Florence (Mrs. Hugh) Bell (1852–1930), with some help from Elizabeth Robins—who Shaw guessed might be the playwright. The two plays had only two matinee performances.

29   *Crystal Palace. Manns' benefit concert. 15. Private View. New Gallery. 10 to 19.*

Read the paper and worked a little at the play. Then went to the New Gallery, where I stayed from about 12.45 to 13.15. Met Elizabeth Robins there. Had a few words with her about *Alan's Wife*. Lucy was at the concert. Went out to FE in the morning. Have caught a regular cold.

West[minster] Gaz[ette] & *Star* 1½d   Dinner at Orange Grove 1/–
Train Ch[arin]g + to Victoria 1½d   Vic[toria] to [Crystal] Palace & back 2/–   Chocolate, eggs &c at A[erated] B[read] S[hop] in Buck[ingha]m Pal[ace] Rd 1/1   Bus Sloane Sq to the Salisbury, Fulham 2d   Train Shep[herds] Bush to Portl[an]d Rd 6d

> Shaw would write Miss Robins (*CL*) about the authorship of the play, suggesting as another possibility Lucy (Mrs. W. K.) Clifford (@1855–1929), a fashionable novelist.   ∎ There was no G.B.S. review of the Crystal Palace concert.

30 SUNDAY   *Lecture in Libra Hall, 78 Libra Road, Roman Rd. E., on "Progress in Freethought." 19¼. Bethnal Green Branch National Secular Society (James Neate, 385 Bethnal Green Rd. E.). Speak at Deptford for the Independent Labour Party (F. Green). Broadway. 11½.*

Met Cecil Sharp on my way to lecture at Deptford. He introduced me to his fiancée. After speaking on the Broadway went home with the Greens. After dinner we walked over to Sydenham and had tea with Mrs. Green's people, the Binns.

Train to New Cross (ret[urn]) 1/–   Cough drops 1d   Train Sydenham to London Bridge 6d   Bus Liv[erpool] St to Libra Rd 2d   Train Coborn Rd to Liverpool St 3d

May

1   Spent the early part of the day reading the papers, writing letters, and

going through the Fabian Eight Hours Bill Tract as drafted by Macrosty. Also in writing to Henry and Co. about press copies of *Widowers' Houses.* Then I went out to dine at the café opposite Portland Rd. station—I have hitherto described it as Avalon Restaurant though I now find that this name was a flight of fancy on my part. Then I went into Regents Park and sat for a longish time near the lake writing a play under my umbrella, as it was spitting rain. Then I went to Praed St. and carried out a resolution which has been half formed for some time, by taking a lesson in bicycle riding at Goya's school. It was a most humiliating experience, but I paid for a dozen lessons, feeling that I must not retreat a beaten man. Then I got my hair cut, got something to eat; and went off to Hammersmith, where I found May alone, Sparling being in the country. We played Mendelssohn's *Scotch Symphony;* and I caught the last train home.

MS book for play 5d   Dinner at Portland Rd Café 1/6   Paid for 10 bicycle lessons at Goya's 10/−   Hair cut & washed 1/−   Omelette &c at the University Rest[aurant] near Edgware Rd 1/8   Train Royal Oak to Hammersmith 4d   H[ammersm]ith Broadway to Portland Road 6d

Henry W. Macrosty (1865–?) was a civil servant at Somerset House, director of the first government Census of Production, Fabian Executive from 1895 to 1907, and author of eight *Fabian Tracts*, including No. 47, *Eight Hours by Law.* ▪ *The Philanderer* would occupy seven notebooks, now BL Add. MS. 50596A–F, plus "G," an envelope of loose leaves derived from notebooks A to F. These are reproduced in facsimile in the Garland Edition of Shaw play facsimiles (1981), *Early Texts* (A309).

2 °*Browning meeting. Mrs. Hall Griffin's, Oneota, 11 Netherhall Gardens, N.W. Kathleen Walton's concert. Steinway Hall. 15. °Miss Trask's Choir, Portman Rooms. 20.*

Rather wasted the earlier part of the day—at least I got no regular work done. Had a search for a lost Fabian document, sang for a while with a view to keeping my voice in condition for next Sunday in the park, etc. Miss Elsie Mackenzie called to ask me to go to her concert. Met Emery Walker at the Wheatsheaf. Left the concert after the second item and went out to Richmond, picking up FE by arrangement at Ravenscourt Park station. We strolled about the Park and the riverside until the light began to fail. I sat up until 1 writing letters, etc.

Papers 2½d   Dinner 1/1   Bus Oxford O to Orchard St 1d   Train Baker St to Richmond ret[urn] 1/9   Supper at Richmond (2) 2/7 Train Shep[herds] Bush to Portland Rd 6d

Reviewed on 17 May 1893 (C949). Kathleen Walton was "a contralto whose powers I could not fully judge in the only song I was fortunate enough to hear during my brief visit to her concert." ▪ Elsie Mackenzie, G.B.S. predicted (C949), "is sure to be at least a favorite ballad singer by the time she is personally as mature as her talent already seems to be." (See also 18 August 1890.)

3 *Essipoff's recital. St. James's Hall. 15. Lennart Lundberg's recital (pianoforte). Steinway Hall. 15. Westminster Orchestral Society's Concert. 20. Westminster Town Hall. Fabian Publishing Committee. 276 Strand. 17¾.*

Set to work to clear up the table, on which a terrific heap of papers had collected. I was forced to the job by the necessity for finding some papers for the Fabian Publishing Committee. Dryhurst was at the Wheatsheaf. Olivier came to the Orange Grove with me. I had some more work at the papers when I got home.

Dinner 11d   Bus to Orchard St 1d   Bus along Strand 1d   Omelette &c at Orange Grove 1/7   Papers 1½d   *Labo[u]r Elector* 1d

> Annette Essipoff (in three recitals G.B.S. covered in three weeks) was "sometimes . . . interested and interesting, sometimes cold and absent, always amazing. . . . Leschetitsky's wife is undeniably one of the greatest exponents of his technique. If it were possible to believe that she cares two straws about what she plays, she would also be one of the greatest executive musicians in Europe" (C949). • The Danish Lundberg's Parisian training left him, G.B.S. wrote (C949), with "a French grace . . . that is fifty years behind the time." • The Westminster Town Hall concert was neither attended nor reviewed by G.B.S.

4 *Philharmonic Concert. St. James's Hall. 20. Isidor Cohn's recital. St. James's Hall. 15.*

Intended to begin my article; but I had so much to write to one person and another, chiefly about the Starnthwaite affair and to people to whom I sent copies of *Widowers' Houses*, that I gave up the idea of beginning today. After the concert I took a walk with Findon in St. James's Park; and we then got up on a West Kensington bus. He went home when we got there; and I took train to Ravenscourt Park and called on FE; but she was not in. So I went to Charing Cross and had a meal before going to the concert. Left Pennells about midnight and walked home. Wrote a card to Grein when I got in.

Papers 5½d   Dinner 11d   Bus St Ja[me]s's St to West Kensington 3d Train West K[ensington] to Ravenscourt Park 1½d   Train Rav[enscourt] Pk to Ch[arin]g + 6d   Omelette &c at Orange Grove 1/11

> Reviewed on 10 May 1893 (C947). The premiere of Villiers Stanford's Irish Symphony was a popular success although G.B.S. found the work disabled by internal contradictions: "the . . . feeling, the fire, the distinction, the passion . . . flash out occasionally through much artifice and much trifling." • Isidor Cohn, German pianist, was to G.B.S. (C949) "an artist who has unquestionably made the most of his natural talent."

5 *Fabian meeting at Essex Hall. 20. W. H. Utley on "Socialism and the Suffrage." Fabian Executive. 276 Strand. 17½. Preliminary Committee. 14½. Charles Phillips's concert. Steinway Hall. 15. Press View. Arthur Croft's drawings of Switzerland, America and Nile, at Dowdeswell's. Margarethe Eussert's recital. Prince's Hall. 15.*

Began *World* article. Spoke at the Fabian. Olivier and Webb were at Gatti's with me; Wallas walked home with me.

Papers 2½d   Dinner 1/1   Bus Sackville Pl[ace] to Holborn 2d   Supper at Gatti & Rodesano's 1/6

Charles Phillips, "a robust baritone" (C943), led a vocal quartet in five "Spanish" songs by William Wallace, which were "pretty and fluent" but left G.B.S. unimpressed (C949). ■ Arthur Croft (1828–1895?), a much-traveled London landscape and topographical painter, exhibited scenes not only of England and Wales but also of the United States, New Zealand, Switzerland, and Algeria. ■ Margarethe Eussert, a young German pianist, in dress and manner "proved . . . her artistic instincts . . . before she struck a note." Although her playing was "still girlish," it was "vigorous and promising" (C949).

6 *Dine with James Brown at Richmond at 17. Go down by the 15 train from Waterloo.*

Worked at *World* article. Dryhurst at Wheatsheaf. Brown met me at Richmond station; and we had a turn in the Park before we went in to dinner. Nobody there except a brother of his who played the viola. Brown and I played the *Egmont* Overture on the piano. I left after 20 and took train to Gunnersbury, Brown going with me to the station. Walked from Gunnersbury to FE's.

Papers 1½d   Dinner 11d   Train Waterloo to Richmond 1/–
Rich[mon]d to Gunnersbury 4½d   Train Shep[herds] B[ush] to Ptld Rd 6d

James Brown was the conductor of the Richmond Orchestral Society, about which part of a G.B.S. column had been devoted in April (C943).

7 SUNDAY *Labour Day in Hyde Park. Speak from Fabian platform. 15¼.*

Worked at *World* article until it was time to go to the Park. Left it with the Sparlings. Sparling took the train at South Kensington; but May and I walked on to Earl's Court. I came back, after playing all the evening with May, by the last train from Ravenscourt Park. Sent off *World* article when I got home.

Train Earls Court to Rav[enscourt] Park 3d   Rav[enscourt] Pk to Port-l[an]d Rd 7d

8 °*Sauret's concert. St. James's Hall. 20¼.* °*Fabian Central Group. 32 Great Ormond St. W. S. De Mattos on "Reasons for Depression in Trade." Liberal and Radical Union Council Meeting. National Liberal Club. 20. Resolution about the Budget.* °*Musical Artists Society's Concert. St. Martin's Hall. 20.*

Worked a little at the play; wrote to Kate Conway; corrected *World* proof, etc. After dinner went out to FE. Intended to speak at the Liberal and Radical Union; but did not, except to move a trifling amendment. Wallas walked home with me; and we sat here until midnight revising Pease's draft of the Manifesto about the Vestry Elections. FE and I spent an hour or so strolling about Ravenscourt Park.

West[minster] Gazette 1d   Dinner 11d   Bus Oxford O to Uxbridge Rd Station 4d   Train Rav[enscourt] Pk to Ch[arin]g + 6d

London local government then resided largely with local vestries elected within parishes. In 1899 a municipal consolidation would create borough and county council structures. ■ Pease's manifesto (BB15), in MS., is in the Fabian Society archives at Nuffield College, Oxford.

9   *Arnold Dolmetsch's Italian Viol concert. Barnard's Inn. 20.40. °Concert by Stock Exchange Orchestral Society in aid of the Chelsea Hospital for Women. St. James's Hall. 20. °Alice Roselli's concert. Chelsea Town Hall. 20. °Lawrence Kellie's vocal recital. Steinway Hall. 15. Essipoff's second recital. St. James's Hall. 15. Mme. Grimaldi's pianoforte recital. Prince's Hall. 20½.*

Began reading proof of Fabian Tract on Anarchism. After the Essipoff recital I went to Hyde Park and lay on the grass working at the play until between 17 and 18. Edith Shaw was here to tea. I left the Grimaldi concert to go to Dolmetsch's. Jacques and Runciman came away from Barnard's Inn with me, and after walking about a bit they eventually parted from me at the corner of Grafton St. I was troubled all day with a bad cold.

Papers 1½d   Dinner 11d   Bus Picc[adilly] to Hyde P[ar]k corner 1d
Marble Arch to Holles St 1d   Portl[an]d St to Vigo St 1d   Oxford O to
Barnard's Inn 1d

> Dolmetsch's "unique viol concerts" (erroneously assigned to Clifford's Inn in G.B.S.'s review) were "gems of musical entertainment in their way" (C949). ▪ Maria Louisa Grimaldi was "tastefully superficial." G.B.S. (C949) suspected that the pieces she played were "extraordinarily mannered and transmogrified, apparently by a long course of repetition without occasional careful verification by the score." ▪ Tract No. 45, *The Impossibilities of Anarchism* (A21).

10   Elijah *at the Albert Hall. Royal Choral Society. 20.* Stanford's East and West. *Opening of the Imperial Institute. Report ceremony for* Star. *Be in hall before 11.45. Fabian Publishing Committee. 17¾.*

Walked over to Institution. On my way back to *Star* office I got into the carriage with Champion, who was friendly. Whilst they were setting up my report I went round to the Central Restaurant and dined, then went back to the office to correct the proof. Walked home, calling on Archer on the way, but not finding him at home. Sat at home reading until it was time to go to the Publishing Committee. Did not wait for the *Elijah*, but went for a while into the Institute; then walked home, getting here at 21.40.

Train S[ou]th Kensington subway to Blackfriars 7d   Cab Blackfriars to *Star* Office 1/–   Dinner at Central 10½d   Papers 2d   Bus along Tott[enham] Ct Rd 1d   Supper at Orange Grove 1/8   Train S[ou]th Kensington from Ch[arin]g + 6d   Subway 1d   Program at Imperial Institute 2d

> Villiers Stanford's setting of Algernon Swinburne's verses (more accurately, *East to West*) composed for the World Columbian Exhibition in Chicago was not "great art" but had "the two qualities needed for a good Chicago ode"—"tunefulness and bounce" (C949).
> ▪ Shaw wrote "The Inside Ceremony" (C946), part of an unsigned, three-reporter account of the Royal Progress and festivities, including the musical critic's observation, "The air is pulsating with the music of military bands, playing respectable tunes, not the low 'Monte Carlo' and 'Seventh Fusiliers' to which the democracy marches when it takes the floor in Hyde Park." The account was published the same day.

11   *Elsie Mackenzie's concert. Steinway Hall. 20. Nellie Kauffmann's pianoforte recital. St. James's Hall. 15.*

Began *World* article. Was too late to dine before the concert. FE was there. She came to the Orange Grove with me whilst I dined and we then walked to Holborn and took bus out to Shepherd's Bush. She read me a story she has been writing. I left the concert early and wrote a few cards, etc. when I got home. Was rather headachey.

Bus to St Ja[me]s's Hall 1d   Dinner at Orange Grove with tea for F.E. 1/8   Papers 1½d   Bus Bloomsbury to Marble Arch (2) 4d   Bus Marble Arch to Uxbridge Rd station (2) 6d   Train Shep[herds] B[ush] to Baker St 6d

Elsie Mackenzie (see also 2 May 1893) was mentioned briefly but favorably in G.B.S.'s 17 May 1893 *World* column (C949). ▪ Young Nellie Kauffmann was "goodlooking, confident, and not without some natural talent and dexterity; so she will be able without much trouble to persuade some first-rate teacher to take her in hand and shew her how to begin her apprenticeship" (C949). ▪ *The Dancing Faun,* a short dialogue novel, parodied the Aesthetic fiction and drama of its period, and in Mr. Travers, its leading figure, who speaks in epigrams, it would satirize Oscar Wilde. John Lane would publish it early in 1894, with a cover design by Aubrey Beardsley mocking the epigram-happy artist James A. McNeill Whistler (as the faun), whom Beardsley disliked.

12 *Fabian Executive. 17¼. Committee. 16½. Fabian Group Secretaries Meeting. 276 Strand. 20. Open discussion on proposed Electoral Policy tract. °Wind Chamber Music Concert. St. James's Banqueting Hall. 20¼. °Lundberg's recital. Steinway Hall. 15. Meet Archer at 13½ at the restaurant at the top of Charing Cross Rd.*

Finished *World* article. Charles Archer was with William Archer at the restaurant. W. A. walked with me along Oxford St. as far as the corner of Duke St. I sat in the Embankment Gardens near the Temple station for a while before going into the Fabian Office. Wallas, however, looked in just as we were breaking up, and walked home with me. He came in for a while. I sat up to read over the *World* article.

Papers 1½d   *Nat[ional] Ref[ormer]* 2d   Dinner (Rest[aurant] top of Ch[aring]g + Rd) say 1/–   Bus Portman Sq to Ch[arin]g + 2d   Supper at Gatti & Rodesano's 1/8

Fabian Tract No. 43, *A Plan of Campaign for Labour* (1894) (A22).

13 *Balcombe. Go down by the 10.45 train from Victoria with Wallas and Miss Erichsen. Return 16.30 from Three Bridges. °Concert of Girls' Friendly Choral Society. St. Andrew's Hall. 20. (Fawcett to sing). Production of new opera by Ernest Ford and J. M. Barrie and Conan Doyle at the Savoy.* Jane Annie. 20.15.

I walked over to Victoria. Bertha Newcombe and Miss McCausland met us at the station. We drove to Miss McCausland's lodging to pick up some things and then walked to Sherlock's cottage and dined. Then we went out and sat under a tree for a time. Finally we started for Three Bridges. We soon left Wallas and Miss McCausland behind; and soon after Miss Erichsen sat down and said she would wait for Bertha's return. Bertha came on with me and put me into [the] high road for the station. I had a run at the end to catch the train. Returned alone, sleeping most of the way. Lucy was at the Savoy with me.

Train Victoria to Balcombe & back 5/4   Papers 2½d   Bus Vict[oria] to Grafton St 2d   Grafton St to Garrick St 1d

> Reviewed on 24 May 1893 (C950). *Jane Annie* was "the most unblushing outburst of tomfoolery that two responsible citizens could conceivably indulge in publicly." (Sir) James M. Barrie (1860–1937) was at the beginning of a distinguished career as a playwright. (Sir) Arthur Conan Doyle (1859–1930), physician and novelist, was already acclaimed for his Sherlock Holmes stories. *Jane Annie* would have fifty performances. ▪ Charlotte Katherine McCausland was a painter of portraits and figurative subjects who exhibited at the R.A. annuals seven times between 1886 and 1904.

14 SUNDAY   *Speak at 18½ for the Woolwich and District Labour Representation League (T. White, 175 Maxsy Rd., Plumstead). Beresford Square as usual. Train from Charing Cross to 17¼.*

Corrected *World* proof. Wrote letters to James Welch and Henry and Co.; and pasted a lot of press cuttings into a scrap book. Morgan-Browne called and we went to the zoo for a while. I called here on my way back to Charing Cross to get a bite and sup. Returned by 20.40 train and did a bit of work at the play before going to bed.

Train Ch[arin]g + to Woolwich 1/–   Back 1/–   *War Cry* 1d

---

15   *Essipoff's third recital. St. James's Hall. 15.*

Wrote a letter to Kate Conway that took up the best part of the morning, and it was time to go out before I had done more than one sheet of the proof of the tract about Anarchism. After the concert FE and I walked across the Park to Bayswater, and took a bus at Notting Hill Gate to Shepherd's Bush. I went into the Park [Ravenscourt] for half an hour by arrangement, as she was expecting a visit from Mrs. Hamilton, and wished to receive her alone. At a little after 18 I went in and found Mrs. Hamilton still there. She left presently. I came back by the 12.40 train. I had a very bad night—fever and dreams almost amounting to delirium.

Star ½d   Dinner 9d   Bus Nott[ingham] Hill Gate to Wyngate Rd (2) 4d   Ginger ale 2d   Train Shep[herds] B[ush] to Portl[an]d Rd 6d

> Mrs. Hamilton was a member (with FE and W. B. Yeats) of the Council of the Adepts of the Order of the Golden Dawn, which met at premises in Clipstone Street, just east of Great Portland Street. This was a dimension of FE's life that Shaw could neither reduce nor penetrate.

16   °*M. B. Williams lectures on Topolobampo at 20 at Rix's, Burlington House. Laistner Choir's Orchestral Concert. Prince's Hall. 20½. °Clotilde Kleeberg's concert. St. James's Hall. 20½. °Reginald Somerville's vocal recital. Grafton Gallery. 15.*

Corrected proofs of the Anarchism tract and sent them off to Standring. Dined off some gruel and a bit of bread and jam. Then went out to Hampstead, dozing on the top of the tram on my way there. On the Lower Heath I found Dryhurst playing cricket. I went to the Upper Heath and lay on my mackintosh for two hours, refusing to play. In the evening I could not make up my mind to go to the concerts. At last went out to hear the tag end of one of them, having meanwhile done some more work at the play. Met Runciman on my way home. He walked with me as far as London St.

Postage "Wid[owers] H[ouses]" to Walkley 3d   Tram to Hampstead 2d   *Labor Gazette, Star & West[minster] Gaz[ette]* 2½d   Train Hampstead to Camden T[own] 1½d   Tram Camd[en] T[own] station to Euston Rd 1d   Bus to Vigo St from Oxford O 1d

> Hearing only "the tag end" of the Prince's Hall concert, G.B.S. nevertheless recorded "a favorable opinion" on the basis of the choir's interpretation of the "expressive harmony" in Schumann's *Pilgrimage of the Rose* (C950).

17 °*Concert of the Westminster Orchestral and Streatham Choral Societies. 20. [Louis] Diemer's pianoforte recital. St. James's Hall. 15. Fabian Publishing Committee. 17⅔. °Fabian Open Air Meetings Committee. 17.*

Not up until past 11, having slept heavily after a disturbed night. Worked a bit over the play. Went from the Publishing Committee to Sparlings', where I spent the evening. I was rather dull with the influenza; but I slept well and rose early.

Bus to St Ja[me]s's Hall 1d   Dinner at Orange Grove (after recital) 1/3 Train Temple to Ravenscourt Pk 6d   Rav[enscourt] Pk to Ptld Rd 7d

> Louis Diemer (C950) was "a remarkably clever, self-reliant, and brilliant pianist, [but] artistically rather stale."

18 *Fifth Philharmonic Concert. St. James's Hall. 20. °Rigby Smith's meeting. "Experiments in Debating Procedure." British Artists Rooms. 20.*

Began *World* article. After dinner took a bus to Mornington Crescent and went into Regents Park to work at the play. H. A. Jones hailed me as I sat writing; and I walked with him to his doorstep. I left the concert at about 21½ and wrote some letters when I got home. In the afternoon I had a call from Powell's friend Gueraut, on whose behalf I wrote to Beatty and also to Powell.

Star ½d   *Nat[iona]l Ref[ormer]* 2d   Dinner Ch[arin]g + Rd 1/1½ Bus Tott[enham] Ct Rd to Mornington Crescent 2d   Bus to St Ja[me]s's Hall 1d

> Reviewed on 31 May 1893 (C951). The conductor, Alexander Mackenzie, was "beginning to take advantage of his great opportunities." ▪ Robert Gueraut, a Belgian living then at 454a Fulham Road, S.W., claimed to have developed a method of mounting pictures which he had carried out for the private galleries of wealthy collectors. He was after a commission to mount the Christ Church (Oxford) collection, which he would indeed receive through the intervention of York Powell.

19 *Fabian Meeting at Essex Hall. 20. Fabian Executive. 276 Strand. 17¼. Preliminary Committee. 16½.*

Finished *World* article. We had a large party at Gatti's after the Executive, including May. Spoke at the Fabian. Wallas walked home with me and came in for a while. Read over *World* article and sent it off. Got to bed about 1 pretty well tired out, having been busy all day.

Dinner at Ch[arin]g + Rd 1/–?   Papers 1½d   Supper at Gatti's before meeting 1/6

20 Wrote several letters, notably one to Welch about his proposals to get *Widowers' Houses* played at the East End. Corrected proof of *World* article. Then went out to Ealing and spent the rest of the day with the Beattys. Came back by the 22.20 train, getting out at Gloucester Rd. and walking home across the Park.

Papers 1½d   Dinner at Orange Grove 1/3   Train Ch[arin]g + to Ealing (ret[urn]) 1/2

21 Wrote some letters, especially one to Walkley about his *Star* notice of *Widowers' Houses*. Then rushed off to Hammersmith, not getting there until past 14. May was at the Terrace alone, Sparling being in France. Spooner called in the afternoon whilst we were sitting out in the garden. He stayed until after 17, when May and I walked to Richmond by way of Strand on the Green, Kew Gardens and the towpath. We came back by train and I played *Die Walküre* to her after tea. I slept at the Terrace.

Train to Hammersmith (ret[urn] not used) 10d   Richmond to Rav[enscourt] Pk (2) 1/2

> Walkley had written an initialed notice in the *Speaker*, 17 December 1892, describing the play as a "singularly bad piece of work," as well as a pseudonymous notice in the *Star* a week earlier, on 10 December 1892, calling Shaw "a detestable dramatist." Shaw had sent the published play to Walkley on 16 May. ▪ Spooner is unknown—possibly a brother or other relative of Geraldine Spooner Carr.

22 May and I went off after breakfast and walked over Hammersmith Bridge across Barnes Common and into Richmond Park by the Sheen Gate. We lay down in the grass and fell off to sleep, getting frightfully sunburnt. We came out by the Star and Garter Gate and had dinner at Ferrari's. Then we parted, I coming back to Waterloo and home, she going back to Hammersmith from the other station. When I got home I wrote a letter or two. Went out to FE for the evening; found her not very well.

Dinner at Ferrari's (2) 2/7   Train Richmond to Waterloo 1/–   to Rav[enscourt] Park–May 7d   Train P[o]rtl[an]d Rd to Shep[herds] Bush & back 9d

23 The working part of the day slipped away in writing letters to Mrs. Beatty and others, which rather put me out of temper with the waste of time this letter writing involves. After dinner I went out to Putney and walked by way of Roehampton to Richmond Park, where I tried to get to work at the third act of the play, but could not think of a subject for it. Whilst I was in the Park it began to rain lightly. So I went off to Hammersmith Terrace, but found nobody in. Annie persuaded me to wait; and May came in after a while, Sparling being still in Paris. We played Beethoven's Second Symphony as a duet, as she had been hearing it at the Philharmonic. Emery Walker came in whilst we were playing; but he did not stay long; and after he was gone May and I had a long and rather confidential conversation.

Papers 1½d   Dinner at Orange Grove 11d?   Train Waterloo to Putney 7d   Richmond to Rav[enscourt] Pk 4d   Ham[mersm]ith to Ptld Rd 6d

Annie was May Sparling's maid.

24 *Olivier to read his play at Archer's at 15½. °Muriel Elliott's recital. St. James's Hall. 15.*

Read proof of tract on Anarchism right through to pass it for press. Wallas was at Archer's for the reading of the play. He and Olivier went off together afterwards; and I stayed to tea with Archer. He went off presently to see the first performance of the Italian actress Duse; and I parted from him in Oxford St., where I took a bus to Shepherds Bush. During the journey I hit on the third act of my new play. FE was just coming out to post some letters as I came to the door. We took a short walk together before going in.

Star ½d   Dinner at Ch[arin]g + Rd 11½d   Bus to Southampton Row 1d   Bus Tott[enham] Ct Rd corner to Shep[herds] Bush 4d   Train Sh[epherds] B[ush] to Ptld Rd 6d

For Sydney Olivier's play see 28 March 1893. ■ Eleanora Duse (1858–1924) was opening in Alexandre Dumas *fils' Camille*. Shaw as drama critic would become one of her outspoken admirers.

24 *°Elsie Hall's pianoforte recital. Clapham Hall, Old Town, 20. Martha Moller's concert. Prince's Hall. 15. Hans Wessely's Orchestral Concert. St. James's Hall. 20½.*

Began *World* article. On leaving the concert in the afternoon I walked along Piccadilly as far as Bond St. with Fuller Maitland, and then walked through Mayfair to Oxford St., where I took a bus to Baker St., and went into Regents Park and worked at the play until 18. Wrote a couple of cards when I got back from Wessely's.

Nat[iona]l Ref[ormer] & Star 2½d   Dinner, Ch[arin]g + Rd 11½d   Bus Oxford St to Baker St 2d

Soprano Martha Möller seemed "forced and uneasy" in attempting "the richer, stronger, more sympathetic tone natural to some contraltos" (C951). ■ Hans Wessely, a professor of violin at the Royal Academy of Music, was "sincere and unreserved" in the Brahms and Mendelssohn concertos, performed as part of a "casual orchestral concert" (C951). Pianist Isidor Cohn added the Beethoven *Emperor* concerto.

26   *Fabian Executive. 17½. Committee. 16¼. °C. P. More's recital (dramatic and humorous), Portman Rooms, 15.*

Finished and sent off *World* article. After dinner went into Regents Park and worked there at the play. After the Executive there was the usual meal at Gatti's, with Miss Brooke, Miss Dix, Olivier, Wallas and Oakeshott. After it Wallas and I took a turn on the Embankment and then made up our minds to go to the Haymarket Theatre to see Wilde's play. But it was closed, as Tree was lecturing at the Royal Institution; so we went on to the Lyceum. However, we were too late to get good seats; so we finally went off to the Court Theatre and saw Pinero's *Amazons*. We walked back.

Papers 1½d   Dinner at Portl[an]d Rd Café 1/6   Bus along Tott[enham] Ct Rd 1d   T[ottenham] C[ourt] R[oad] to Lincoln's Inn corner 1d Meal at Gatti & R[odensano]'s 2/–   Train Ch[arin]g + to Sloane Sq 2d   Court Theatre 2/6

> Gertrude Dix, a Fabian and a novelist, would write *The Image Breakers* (1900), with British Socialism as background. ▪ Wilde's *A Woman of No Importance* had opened on 19 April and would run 113 performances. ▪ Pinero's *The Amazons* had opened on 7 March 1893 and would run 114 performances.

27   *Address meeting to inaugurate Northampton Fabian Society (Alexander Ellis Anderson, 36 Victoria Rd., Northampton). Catch the 16.30 to Northampton from Euston. °Private View. 19th Century Art Society. 9 Conduit St. 10. °Bonawitz's pianoforte recital. Prince's Hall. 15.*

Worked a little at the play; played *Parsifal* etc. until I was interrupted by a visit from Fred Fawcett who stayed for some time and sang. In the train to Northampton there was an altercation in the carriage about the windows— ventilation *versus* non-ventilation. I did not take part in it; but it spoilt the journey. I had tea with Anderson, he met me at the station. In the evening made the acquaintance of a curious fellow named Cohen, a phrenological lecturer and dealer in electrical machines, with long black hair—rather like the Christ in Hunt's picture *The Shadow of the Cross*. I put up at the Angel.

Star ½d   Dinner Ch[arin]g + Rd 1/4½   Bus along Tott[enham] Ct Rd 1d   Train to Northampton (ret[urn]) 10/7

> *The Shadow of the Cross* (1871), painted by William Holman Hunt (1827–1910), one of the original Pre-Raphaelites, shows Jesus in the carpenter's shop (echoing an earlier depiction by his associate John Millais), with raised arms foreshadowing the Crucifixion.

28 SUNDAY   *Speak at Northampton for the S. D. F. (J. W. G. Smith, 8 Junction Rd., Kingsley Park, Northampton) in the Market Square. 11 and 18½. Come up to town by the 20.19 train.*

Nobody at the hotel except an elderly commercial traveler. Watched the Corporation going to church in state. After dinner (at the hotel) brought my bag down to the station. My knee got badly out of order for the first time this year. Tea at Ernest Wright's: Cohen in great form. He electrified me with his machine.

29 °*Diemer's second recital (pianoforte). St. James's Hall. 15.*

Spent the morning writing letters. After dinner took train from Waterloo to Barnes. But it turned out a wet afternoon; and I spent the time walking under the trees in the Richmond lanes, working at the play. Then I took train from Barnes to Richmond and after getting something to eat, strolled about the river and in the Terrace gardens still working at the play. At last I went to Hammersmith and called on FE. She was not at home when I arrived; but she came presently; and I went through the whole part of the play of Rebecca West in *Rosmersholm* with her—a long job. She is getting it up again because Elizabeth Robins was afraid of getting ill at the Opera Comique, and has asked her to be ready to go on with Rebecca in case she breaks down.

Papers 1½d   Dinner at Orange Grove 1/3   Train Waterloo to Barnes 7d   Barnes to Richmond 2½d   Omelette at Richmond 1/4   Train Richmond to Rav[enscourt] Pk 4d   Shep[herds] B[ush] to Portland Rd 6d

30 °*Reginald Somerville's second recital. Grafton Gallery. 15. Benno Schönberger's Orchestral Concert. St. James's Hall. 15. °The Walenn Quartet, Athenaeum, Camden Rd. 20. Miss Emmott-Herbert's matinee*—Captain Thérèse *at the Criterion Theatre. Duse in* Cavelleria Rusticana *and Goldoni's* Locandiera *at the Lyric Theatre 20½.*

In the morning Parke sent me a note from *The Star* asking me whether I could call on him. Gave up working at the play and went off to see him. He wants me to write articles in *The Star*. In the evening went to see Duse.

Train to Farringdon St 2d   Lunch at Express Dairy Co. 1/1   Lyric Theatre 4/−   Book & bill 1/2

Reviewed on 7 June 1893 (C953). Schönberger played the Beethoven fourth piano concerto as well as the Saint-Saëns concerto in G minor, each with "clockwork" precision. ▪ Miss Emmott-Herbert's production of the light opera by F. C. Burnand, Gilbert Beckett (libretto), and Robert Planquette (music) had a single matinee. G.B.S. (C953) left the Beethoven concerto to see the "specimen of the work she has been doing in the provinces." The habit of playing to "the provincial gallery" resulted, he thought, in a less "jaded" performance. ▪ Duse was continuing her repertory of Italian staples. *La Locandiera* was a comedy by Carlo Goldoni first performed in 1753. Shaw knew Giovanni Verga's melodramatic *Cavalleria Rusticana* (1884) from the Mascagni operatic version.

31 *Fabian Publishing Committee. 276 Strand. 17½. Be at the Fabian office at 17 to met Mrs. Brownlow.* °*Ernest Kiver's concert. Prince's Hall. 20.* °*Margarethe Eussert's second recital. Prince's Hall. 15.*

Wrote interview with Lady Colin Campbell and sent it off to her. It was past 15 when I got out. Wallas called. In the evening I felt too headachey to go to the concert; so I went off to Hammersmith with Sparling and Miss Priestley. I came back with Miss Priestley also.

Papers 1½d   Dinner at Orange Grove 10d   Express letter to Lady C[olin] C[ampbell] 6d   Bus along Strand 6d   Train Temple to

Rav[enscourt] Pk 6d   Rav[enscourt] Pk to Portland Rd (2–Miss P to Gower St) 1/6

> Mrs. Jane M. E. Brownlow of 30 Theobalds Rd., W.C., taught elementary economics in university extension courses. ▪ " 'Bud and Blossom': A 'Star' Man's Unconventional Interview with Lady Colin Campbell" (unsigned), *The Star*, 2 June 1893 (C952). The piece was publicity concocted for the Charrington/Achurch production of Lady Colin's playlet.

June

1 *Sixth Philharmonic Concert. St. James's Hall. 20. T. A. Wallworth's lecture on "Wagner's Influence on Singing," Trinity College, Mandeville Place, 15.*

Disturbed by a violent knock and ring from the postman before 8. Got up to answer him, but he was gone before I got down. Polished off a lot of correspondence and business. Then went off for a walk to the top of Primrose Hill and back. At the Hygeian I found May Sparling and brought her to the lecture at Trinity College. She came on here to tea and at last came to the concert with me and walked with me afterwards as far as Portland Rd., where she took the train home. We called at the shop in Oxford St. [Morris and Company, 449 Oxford St., W.] before the lecture.

Telegram to Norman 1½   *Nat[iona]l Ref[ormer]* & *Star* 2½d   Dinner at Hygeian 1/3½   Bus Tott[enham] Ct Rd to Morris & Co's (2) 2d

> G.B.S. (C953) congratulated the Philharmonic on "having at last made a resolute and fairly successful effort to give a concert of nearly reasonable length. Instead of the usual two or three concertos, five or six symphonies. . . ." ▪ Reviewed on 14 June 1893 (C954). To G.B.S. it was "a very remarkable lecture." Wallworth, a singer as well as a musicologist, illustrated his points vocally. ▪ May displayed and sold her embroidery work at the Morris and Company shop.

2 °*Fabian meeting at Essex Hall. 20. J. Bruce Wallas on "Socialism and Social Experiments." Fabian Executive. 17¼. Committee. 16½. Edith Blyth and Mabel Wood's concert, Steinway Hall. 15. °Press View at Dowdeswell's. Early British Masters. Independent Theatre Society performance at the Comedy Theatre. H. M. Paull's At a Health Resort and Josine Holland's Leida. 20.15.*

Began *World* article.

Star ½d   Dinner at Hygeian 1/3½   Bus to Portman Sq 2d   Bus Marylebone Lane to Lincoln's Inn corner 2d   Macaroni &c at Gatti & Rodesano's 1/8

> Edith Blyth, although "very nervous," sang soprano arias creditably, while Mabel Wood sang ballads "with good sense and feeling" (C953). The concert included cello and piano pieces as well. ▪ *Leida* was an adaptation from the Dutch by Teixeira de Mattos. *At a*

Health Resort was a one-act comedy by H. M. Paull (1854–1934). There would be only one performance.

3 *The Charringtons re-open at Terry's Theatre. Program of five new pieces. Patti concert at the Albert Hall. 15. °Private View. André Sinet's pictures. Goupil Gallery. 10 to 18.*

Worked at *World* article. Lunched with Parke, Geard, and Dam at the Express Diary in Fleet St. Took a turn in Regents Park before I went into the City. Left the theatre promptly when the curtain came down to avoid meeting anybody, and picked up Archer and his wife on the opposite side of the Strand. Walked with them as far as the top of Bow St.

Train to Farringdon 2d   Papers 1¼d   Lunch (Parke paid)   Train Temple to S[ou]th Kensington 6d   Bus Marble Arch to Holles St 1d Grafton St to Coventry St 1d

> The five playlets, each to receive six performances, were *An Interlude* by Walter H. Pollock and Lucy Clifford, *The Three Wayfarers* by Thomas Hardy, *Becky Sharp* by James M. Barrie, *Bud and Blossom* by Lady Colin Campbell, and *Foreign Policy* by Arthur Conan Doyle. All pieces featured Janet Achurch. ▪ "Time," wrote G.B.S. (C953), "has transposed Patti a minor third down; but the middle of her voice is still even and beautiful." Her cantabile singing remained captivating. ▪ Charles Geard was a photo-engraver at 27 Bouverie Street. ▪ Henry J. W. Dam (1858–1906) was author of *Lyrics for a Shop Girl* and a writer of minor plays, including *The Silver Shell*, which opened at the Avenue Theatre on 15 April 1893 and closed this date in June after forty-four performances.

4 SUNDAY Finished *World* article after a good deal of work, interrupted by visits from Wallas and Seiffert. Then walked out to Hammersmith. Called for FE, but found that she had just gone out. Went on to the Terrace and found May there alone. We took a walk; and I played *Die Meistersinger* a bit after tea. On my way to the station I met Emery Walker who turned back and came to the train with me.

Train Hammersmith to Portland Rd 6d

5 Hedda Gabler. *Opera Comique. Tivadar Nachez's concert. St. James's Hall. 15.*

Telegraphed to FE to come to the concert. Wrote letters—had far better have gone out, as my health is unsatisfactory. Left the concert soon and went off with FE to Regents Park, where we sat until it was time for me to go home. May was at the theatre with me. I went with her to the Temple station and walked home alone. Wrote a letter to Elizabeth Robins about the play before going to bed.

Dinner at Hygeian (since Wheatsheaf now closed) 1/2½   Bus to Picc[adilly] O 1d   Train Temple to Rav[enscourt] Park for May 9d

> *Hedda Gabler* was in a series of twelve subscription performances of Ibsen by Miss Robins. Shaw did not endear himself to her by writing that evening after the peformance (CL) to suggest improvements in direction and acting; nor did he when he added that,

despite her rejection of him, "I cannot help being in love with you in a poetic and not in the least ignoble way." He was interested in her as a forceful missionary of the New Drama, but she preferred to find her own paths. ▪ Tivadar Nachéz, G.B.S. wrote (C954), played his violin "with a certain forcing of his inclination." Nachéz (1859–1930) was an Hungarian protégé of Joseph Joachim.

6   °*Arnold Dolmetsch's French Viol concert. Barnard's Inn. 20.40. Frieda Simonson's (8 year old pianist) recital at St. James's Hall. 15. (Ticket came late).*

Very much out of sorts. Took a walk to the top of Regents Park and Primrose Hill, where I sat for a while and did a scrap of work on the play. At the restaurant I found May Sparling, with whom I went to Gloucester Rd. station. I then called at the Charringtons'. Found Janet alone and talked to her for a long time about the play and one thing or another. Charrington came in at 18 for dinner, and I went off and had a meal and a wash at South Kensington. Then I went to FE with whom I spent the rest of the evening.

Star ½d   Dinner (Hygeian) 1/–   Bus to Marble Arch (2) 2d (May paid for this)   Maccaroni at Veglio's (S[ou]th Kens[ing]t[o]n) 1/6   Lavatory opp[osite] the Oratory 3d   Train South Kensington to Ravenscourt Park 6d   Shep[herds] Bush to Portland Road 6d

Shaw had written to Miss Robins that *The Philanderer* was finished, but he was still toying with the third act, which he sensed was unsatisfactory.

7   °*Rosmersholm. Opera Comique (tickets changed for tomorrow). Prince's Hall. Dora Barrington's concert, (Seiffert). 20½. Handel Society's concert. St. James's Hall. 20½. Mme. Swiatlowsky's concert. Grafton Gallery. 15. °Fabian Publishing Committee. 17½.*

Again went up to the top of Primrose Hill and did no work except writing a scrap of the play. After leaving the concert at the Grafton Gallery I had a look at the pictures and then went back to Regents Park, taking Jaeger's on my way to get some things. In the park I lay on the grass and looked at the cricketing. Got back from the evening concert before 23 and wrote a letter or two.

Star ½d   Bus along Tott[enham] Ct Rd 1d   Dinner (Hygeian understood henceforth) 1/3   Gave boy on Primrose Hill 1d   Bus to Vigo St 1d

G.B.S. (C954) felt like "a caged bird . . . between two perches and a ring, . . . caged in London in June hopping restlessly from St. James's to Prince's Hall, and from that again to Steinway Hall. The Grafton Gallery is an extra perch for me. . . ." Mme. A. de Swiatlowsky had "the merit of inventing her own way of singing a song." August Manns led the Handel Society orchestra (a "Mahometan paradise of lady violinists") and chorus, in performances of Cherubini, Haydn, and Beethoven that G.B.S. deemed "creditable" and "admirable." Dora Barrington and others sang a miscellaneous program of uneven quality.

8 °*Albert Visetta's At-Home to receive Boito. 14. Trebovir Rd., Earl's Court. 21. Marie Roberts' concert. Steinway Hall. 15½. Rosmersholm at the Opera Comique. 20.15. °London Male Voice Clubs Concert. St. Martin's Hall. 20.*

Began *World* article. Had a turn in the park and up to Primrose Hill before dinner. Also after the concert. May and I walked along the Embankment from the Temple to Charing Cross on leaving the theatre. Met the Salts at the Hygeian; Mrs. Salt rather mad about May.

Star ½d   *Nat[iona]l Reformer* 2d   Dinner 1/–?   Bus to Orchard St
1d   M[ay]'s ticket to Rav[enscour]t Pk 9d?

> Marie Roberts (C954) was "one of those artists who sit down at the piano and play their own accompaniments at their ease . . . , not an orthodox feat of concert singing . . . but an entertainment to be judged on its own merits." ▪ *Rosmersholm* was performed as part of the Elizabeth Robins series. She played Rebecca West, with Lewis Waller as Rosmer. ▪ "Rather mad about May" defies easy translation. Since Kate Salt was a lesbian, Shaw's meaning is equivocal.

9 *Fabian Executive. 276 Strand. 17½. Committee. 16¼. °Speak in St. James's Hall at the annual meeting of the Central National Society for Women's Suffrage (Edith Clinton, Asst. Sec., 29 Parliament St., Westminster). Changed to June 16th. °Frida Scotta's concert. St. James's Hall. 20¼. Edgar Hulland's recital. Prince's Hall. 15. °Agnes Giglie and Edith Nott Bowers' concert. Grafton Gallery. 15. Go up to 70 Cornhill at 18.15 to enquire about the German (Gouin) class. Fabian Private Meeting. Barnard's Inn. 20. Make the Executive report on the proposed Electoral Policy tract.*

Worked at World article. Sent a telegram to FE to come to St. James's Hall thinking there was a concert on there. I met her there and found that I had mistaken the date of the concert; so we went over to Prince's Hall. Then we walked to Charing Cross together and I went on to the Fabian. I left a little before 18 to go to a German class. When I got there only two others turned up; and it was agreed to put the class off until next Wednesday to see whether more people could not be recruited. I returned to the Temple and had a meal at Gatti and Rodesano's with Olivier before going on to the Fabian, where I made a statement about the Policy tract. Met Foulger on my way home.

Bus along Tott[enham] Ct Rd 1d   *Star* ½d   Dinner 1/–?   Bus along
Shaftesbury Av[e] 1d   along Strand 1d   Train Temple to Man[sion]
Ho[use] 1d   Back 1d   Omelette &c at Gatti & Rodesano's 1/6

> Edgar Hulland's piano recital including his joining violinist Émile Sauret in work for both instruments. Either the pieces, or the playing, seemed so "diffuse" to G.B.S. (C954) that "I thought over my past life exhaustively, and elaborated several plans for the future. Finally I had a long and delicious sleep, from which I woke to find by the change in the light that the afternoon was now far advanced."

10 °*"Friends of Russian Freedom"* At-Home at Barnard's Inn to meet *George Kennan. 20 to 22½.* Go to The Master Builder *at the Opera Comique. 20.15.*

Master Builder 9d

> George Kennan (1845–1924), an American diplomat, a historian, and the author of *Siberia and the Exile System* (New York, 1891) and *Tent Life in Siberia* (New York, 1902). ■ The production at the Opera Comique was another in Elizabeth Robins' Ibsen series, in which she played Hilde Wangel to Lewis Waller's Master Builder Solness.

11 SUNDAY   *Go up the river with Furnivall, Walker, etc., etc. Richmond (Redknapp's) at 11.30.*

Corrected proof of *World* article and finished it before starting. Was too late to catch the party at Richmond; so I walked across Richmond Park to Kingston and by the river ferry to Hampton Court, where I found them picnicking on the opposite bank. I hailed them; and Furnivall came and ferried me over. After our meal we loafed for a while, then sculled back to Richmond, stopping at the island for tea. We took train at Richmond and the whole party got out at Ravenscourt Park except Furnivall, who had left us and gone by the North London line, and Miss Buckland, whom I left at Shepherd's Bush, where I got out and went to FE with whom I passed the rest of the evening.

Train to R[ic]hmond 1/2   R[avenscourt Pk] to Sh[epherds] Bush 6d
Sh[epherds] B[ush] to Ptld Rd 6d   River collection for Burlington Cottage Hospital 1/–

> The composition of the group suggests that Miss Buckland may have been an artistic sister of Arthur Herbert Buckland (1870–1930?), a London painter and illustrator.

12 °*Winifred Robinson's concert. Prince's Hall. 20. St. James's Theatre. 15. Mrs. Oscar Beringer's Bess.*

I find myself getting up late again. Spent the early part of the day writing letters. Met Archer at the restaurant, also Drabig. On my way back from the theatre I overtook Beatrice Webb and Mrs. [W. P.] Byles in Albermarle St. and walked on with them. Mrs. Byles left us in Harley St., where she had to make a call. Beatrice and I walked together across Primrose Hill beyond which I had to turn back as it was late and I intended to go to the concert. We had a long discussion about the Woman Question, started before we parted from Mrs. Byles, but greatly intensified by our meeting Ada Webb in Regents Park, wheeling her mother about in a bath chair, a striking example of the sacrifice of a young woman to domestic duty. After all, I did not go to the concert but to Hedwig Sonntag's. I read her the play and was horrified to find that it is far too long: it took me three hours to read it. Did not get to bed until 1.

Star ½d   Dinner (Hygeian, which will henceforth be taken for granted) 1/–

> *Bess*, a romantic play by Mrs. Oscar Beringer (1856–?), had one matinee performance.

13 °*Reginald Somerville's 3rd Vocal recital. Grafton Gallery. 15. Ernest Fowles' Brahms recital. Prince's Hall. 15. Opera Comique. 14½. His Highness, opera by Auscal Tate (composer) and J. W. Houghton.*

Up rather late. Had a turn in the park in the morning but not a very long one. Worked at the cutting and revision of the play. Left the theatre at the end of the first act, and walked right away (after a conversation with Teixeira [de Mattos] on the steps of the Opera Comique) to the top of Primrose Hill, where I sat for a time working at the play in a high wind.

Star ½d   Bus along Tott[enham] Ct Rd 1d   Dinner 1/4   Bus to Holborn Rest[aurant] corner 1d   *The Master Builder* 9d   Bus to Vigo St 1d   Back 1d

> Reviewed on 21 June 1893 (C955). Ernest Fowles, pianist, proved to G.B.S.'s satisfaction that Brahms was a "sentimental voluptuary" with an ear for harmonies. ■ *His Highness; or Exchange No Robbery* was not reviewed. This comic opera with music by Auscal Tate and Neil O'Donovan, and libretto by John W. Houghton, did not survive its opening matinee.

14 *Annual Meeting of the British Economic Association. Address on "Ethics and Economics" by [George] Goschen. 20. Prince's Hall.* °*Liebich's pianoforte recital. Steinway Hall. 15.* °*Annual meeting of Anti-Vivisection Society. St. James's Banqueting Hall. 15.* °*Sir W. Cusins' Concert. St. James's Hall. 15.* °*Fabian Publishing Committee. 17¼. German Class (Gouin system). 70 Cornhill. 18.15 to 20.15. Production of Ibsen's* Enemy of the People *at the Haymarket Theatre. 14.15.*

Working away at the cutting of the play. Went into the park and lay down near the cricket pavilion for a while. May was with me at the Haymarket; indeed, it was she who gave me the seat. We left the theatre together and went to the Orange Grove, Bond Holding and another man walking with us from the corner of Suffolk St. to the corner of St. Martin's Lane. From the Orange Grove we went to the German class. I left her in the train on her way back to Hammersmith, getting out at Charing Cross to go to hear Goschen speak at Prince's Hall. When I got home I wrote up this diary; sent off a card or two; glanced at the play and got to bed.

Star ½d   Dinner 11d   Bus along Shaftesbury Av[e] to Trocadero 1d Meal at Orange Grove (2) 1/9   Bus Ch[arin]g + to city (2) 2d   Set of German lessons, one quarter 63/-   Train May to Rav[enscourt] Pk from Mans[ion] Ho[use] 7d   myself to Ch[arin]g + 3½d (took ticket to St James's Park)

> The production of *An Enemy of the People* was by Herbert Beerbohm Tree, who played the title role of Dr. Stockmann. ■ George Joachim Goschen (1831–1907), first Viscount Goschen, a brilliant economist, became a director of the Bank of England at 27. A long-time Liberal cabinet minister, his last post was a return to the Admiralty from 1895 to 1900.

15 *Seventh (last of the season) Philharmonic Concert. St. James's Hall. 20.*

Began *World* article and wrote to a man who picked a hole in the first Fabian Essay. After dinner walked out to Hammersmith Terrace, intending to read the last act of the play to May; but she was not in. Sparling was there and I sat with him until it was time to go back for the concert.

Nat[ional] Reformer 2d   Dinner 1/2   Bus to Oxford O 1d   *West-[minster] Gaz[ette]* & *Star* 1½d   Train Ravenscourt Pk to Ptld Rd 7d Bus Oxford O to St Ja[me]s's Hall 1d   Bun & gingerbeer in Rav[enscour]t Park 3d

> A "tremendous crush" (C955) materialized to hear Paderewski "fly up and down the keyboard, playing the piccolo and the cymbals and the big drum and every instrument except the pianoforte on it. . . ." The program was "horribly long," with a second concerto, a symphony, an overture, and incidental music.

16 *Fabian meeting at Essex Hall. 20. B. T. Hall on "Socialism and Seamen." Fabian Executive. 17¼. Committee. 16½. Speak at the meeting of the Central National Society for Women's Suffrage at St. James's Banqueting Hall. 15¼. (Miss Edith Clinton, C. N. S. W. S., 29 Parliament St. S. W.). Support Resolution II. °Royal College of Music, Orchestral Concert. St. James's Hall. 20. Stojowski's recital. St. James's Hall. 15. Gouin German class, 70 Cornhill. 18.15 to 20.15.*

Up before 8. Finished the *World* article as far as possible and sent it off. Took a turn in the park and did a stroke of work on the play at the top of Primrose Hill. Left the Women's meeting with Bertha Newcombe, who came with me as far as Charing Cross. Wallas and Webb walked home with me from the Fabian.

Telegram to Williams (M. B.) 7½d   Bus along Tott Ct Rd 1d   Dinner 1/4   Papers 2d   Milk & cake 2½d   Sainsbury drink 3d   Train Temple to Mansion Ho[use] & back 3d   Bus along Strand after C.N.S.W.S. meeting [   ]

> Benjamin T. Hall (1864–1931), Fabian and one-time carpenter, was chairman of the Labour Party branch in Deptford and general secretary of the Workmen's Club and Institute. See also 14 July 1893.

17 *Poor Jonathan, opera by [Karl] Millöcker and Albéniz, at Prince of Wales Theatre (3rd night). °Dine with G. Wherry Anderson at National Liberal Club. 19.15. 67 Carlisle Mansions at 15½ to read play to Lady Colin Campbell.*

Weather terribly hot. Spent all the forenoon on the top of Primrose Hill, working at the play. In the afternoon read it all to Lady Colin, who pointed out to me that the third act at which I have been working ought to be put into the fire. This opened my eyes for the first time to the fact that I have started on quite a new trail and must reserve this act for the beginning of a new play.

Star ½d   Dinner 1/5   Bus to Victoria 2d   back 2d

Poor Jonathan, a musical comedy by Charles H. E. Brookfield and Harry Greenbank, and music by Karl Millöcker and Isaac Albéniz, would manage only fourteen performances. "What is wanted," said G.B.S. (C955), ". . .is a vigorous blue pencil." ▪ Rather than put the third act in the fire, Shaw wrote on the forty-sixth folio of notebook F, "Cancel all the foregoing." Act 3, never used or staged, begins—in Dr. Paramore's house—on the evening of the third (or fourth) anniversary of his marriage to Julia Craven, one of the philandering Leonard Charteris's two mistresses in the earlier acts. Paramore is now more interested in the other woman, Grace Tranfield, and wants a divorce. The relevant characters gather in the dining room to discuss the matter. Shaw would begin a replacement act on 22 June.

18 SUNDAY   *Lecture for the Battersea Branch National Secular Society. Battersea Secular Hall, Prince of Wales Rd. (office address 48 Park Grove, Battersea Park Rd.) on "Socialism and Human Nature." (A. Watkin, 22 Standen Rd., Southfields S.W.). 20.*

Revised proof of *World* article and finished it. Went out to Hammersmith Terrace by the 13.28 train from Baker St., where I met Fitzgerald Molloy, who came on as far as Edgware Rd. with me. Miss Duncan was at Sparlings': she stayed the night. O'Donoghue and Rose called. I stayed the night at the Terrace.

Train to Hammersmith 6d   Rav[enscourt] Pk to Queen's Rd, Battersea 4d   back 6d

Possibly Emily Duncan, a London painter of flowers, figure subjects, and scenes of the Thames. ▪ David J. O'Donoghue (1866–1917), journalist with the *Dublin Evening Standard* and later (1909–17) librarian of University College, Dublin, was then editing *The Humour of Ireland* (1894), for which he would extract from Corno di Bassetto's columns (B12).

19   °*Fabian Special Committee to draw up tract on Woman Question. 56 Russell Square. 20¼. Duse in* Antony and Cleopatra. *Lyric Theatre. 20½. Call on M. B. Williams at 5 Barnes Terrace as early as possible for a turn on the river. Strelitski's Orchestral Concert. Portman Rooms. 15.*

May and I took a turn on the river with Williams from Barnes to Isleworth and back. I tried my hand at sculling, and got abominably blistered. We dropped Williams at Barnes and walked back to the Terrace, where we snatched some lunch and went into town to the concert, after which May came on here to tea. After the theatre I walked with Archer to the *Manchester Guardian* office, and he came with me to the corner of Russell St. on my way home. Got some long letters about the play, notably one from Karl Pearson.

Chiswick ferry both ways (2) 1/−   Train Ravenscourt Park to Baker St (2) 1/2   Theatre 4/−   prog[ra]m 2d

Eleonora Duse was playing a repertory season in London with her own Italian company, doing Shakespeare and all else in Italian. ▪ Louis Strelitski, impresario, flutist, and violinist, played only the flute, G.B.S. reported on 28 June 1893 (C957); however, he trotted out "a bright, nimble, sure-fingered boy pupil of his"—unnamed in the review to avoid encouraging the exploitation of further "infant phenomena."

20   °*Lawrence Kellie's recital. Steinway Hall. 20. Edie Reynolds' concert (violin). Erard's. 15. Paderewski's recital. St. James's Hall. 15.*

Wrote several letters, especially one in reply to Pearson. This took all the morning and left me no time for a walk before dinner. I was late at the concert. [Wallace] Crowdy, who was there, asked me why I was not at the Paderewski recital. I told him no ticket had been sent to *The World*. He gave me his own, protesting that the omission was a mistake; and I went on to St. James's Hall. When I got home I felt exceedingly tired and took some arrowroot and fruit to eat. I did not go out again, but played for a while, and then made out my Income Tax return and disposed of some petty business. On my return from St. James's Hall I started to go for a walk in the park, but turned back, overcome by a feeling of fatigue. I found a drop of thirty or forty pounds in my income.

Star ½d   Dinner 1/6   Bus to Marlboro St 1d   Bus from St Ja[me]s's Hall 1d

> The Edie Reynolds violin recital went unreviewed. ▪ "I did not hear the whole recital," G.B.S. wrote of Paderewski (C957), "but what I did hear was, humanly speaking, faultless. . . . I simply mean that all the work he did was exhaustively studied, and the reading founded on the study was in no case trivial, cheap, or unworthy of a great artist." ▪ By not continuing to write concurrent art notices, Shaw saw his major source of income reduced to his music columns. His book earning were negligible. On the 14th he had received from Walter Scott £4.9.7 in royalties for *The Quintessence of Ibsenism* and on the 17th £4.17.5 for *Cashel Byron's Profession*.

21   *German class. 70 Cornhill. 18.15 to 20.15.* °*Walter Wadham's recital, vocal and dramatic. Steinway Hall. 15. Fabian Publishing Committee.*

Began article on Moore's *Strike at Arlingford* for *The Star*. This would have prevented my getting a walk before dinner if I had not dined at Isotta's opposite Portland Rd. station and taken a short turn in the park beforehand. I met Macdonald (the dentist) there, and found that he has been suffering from weakness after influenza much as I have been. When I got to the concert I asked for a program and it was refused, whereupon I left and wrote to Steinway's about it. In the evening I went to work again on *Star* article, but I did not get on very well with it.

Dinner at Isotta's 1/6   P[all] M[all] *Gazette* 1d   Bus Tott[enham] Ct Rd corner to Lincoln's Inn 1d   Milk & cake at A[erated] B[read] S[hop] St Clemence Dane's 3½d   Train Temple to Mans[ion] H[ouse] 1d   Bus Mans[ion] Ho[use] to Tott[enham] Ct Rd 1d   Train to Marble Arch 2d

> "Playwright Cut Playwright. Bernard Shaw on George Moore" (mock-interview), *The Star*, 27 June 1893 (C956). ▪ Shaw thought that, on principle, programs should be free, a practice still alien to most London theaters; he was particularly incensed that a critic with a complimentary ticket did not receive a program as well.

22   °*Socialist Joint Committee. 276 Strand. 20¼. Elsie Hall's recital. Lady Stanley Alderley's, 40 Dover St., at 15½. Albert Bach's Loewe recital. Steinway Hall. 20. (24 Grosvenor St., Edinburgh).* °*Operatic concert. St. James's Hall. 15.*

Began *World* article, but it did not get on very well. I went up to the top of Primrose Hill and there wrote a new scene for the beginning of the new third act of the play, as suggested by Lady Colin. After the concert I went back again to the hill and finished this scene. I also got something done in the readjustment of the scenes after my return from the Bach concert.

Papers 1½d   Bus along Tott[enham] Ct Rd 1d   Dinner 1/1   Bus along Ch[arin]g + Rd & Shaftesbury Av[e] 1d

> Miss Elsie Hall, once an infant phenomenon, was "still in short frocks" and still needed, said G.B.S. (C957), some disciplined training for her "undeniable talent." ∎ Basso Albert Bach's program of songs by Karl Loewe was accompanied on the piano by Madame Bach, whose "Erl King" Shaw found insufficiently "galloping." Although Bach himself was forceful and dramatic, his bass singing lacked the lyricism to carry off a full evening alone (C957).

23   *Fabian Executive. 17¼. Committee. 16¼. German class. 70 Cornhill. 18.15 to 20.15. Mrs. Henschel's recital. St. James's Hall. 20¼.*

Worked at *World* article. Went up to the top of Primrose Hill as usual and had a turn at the play. Today and yesterday I began to feel some appetite and interest in life at last, as if I were recovering a bit.

Nat[iona]l Reformer 2d   *Star* ½d   Dinner at Orange Grove 1/1   Bus along Strand 1d   Train Temple to Cannon St (got off at Mansion House) 1½d   Mansion House to Charring + 2½d   Milk & cake before class 3½d

> Lillian Bailey Henschel sang Irish and Scottish songs as well as music by Mendelssohn, Liszt, Schubert, and Beethoven, with her conductor husband ("an incomparable accompanist") and his choir in support (C957). Some songs were projected with "exquisite feeling," and G.B.S. wondered why others elicited a "hardhearted" approach.

24   *Sullivan's* Golden Legend *on Handel Festival scale at Crystal Palace. 15.*

Finished *World* article, working at it morning and evening. Went into the City in the morning to buy an umbrella. Lucy was at the Palace with me.

Umbrella 24/–   Dinner at Arcadian 11d   *West[minster] Gaz[ette]*, *PMG & Petit Journal* 3d   Train Blackfriars to Victoria 3½d   Vict[oria] to C[rystal] P[alace] (2) 4/–   Omelette &c at Orange Grove 1/8

> G.B.S. (C957) deplored "the liberal allowance of blissful but indeterminate meandering for mere love of musical sound." The men's chorus was particularly effective, not having to sing Sullivan's "sentimental prettiness."

25 SUNDAY   *Speak on the Embankment opposite Old Chelsea Church. 19. (S. Masterson, 57 Dartrey Rd., Chelsea S. W.), for the Chelsea District Labour League. Call on Charringtons, 16, and on Bertha Newcombe for tea before the meeting.*

Read over *World* article. Took a turn in the park and on the hill before dinner, meeting Reynolds on his way back from the Fabian meeting. Found Janet alone. Flemming came in later on. Miss McCausland called whilst I was at Bertha's. Bertha walked with me to the meeting on the Embankment, where I spoke for nearly an hour and a half. Samuel turned up. I returned to Charringtons on my way back and found Brookfield there with Flemming and Charrington and Janet.

Train to Gloster Rd & back 9d   Sweets 1d

Herbert Flemming (1856–1908), an actor, had appeared in the Charringtons' *A Doll's House* as the villain Krogstad. ▪ Actor and playwright Charles H. E. Brookfield (1857–1913), whom Shaw would see (and review) in *An Ideal Husband* and *The Home Secretary*, would later become Shaw's bane as Examiner of Plays for the Lord Chamberlain's office.

26   Revised, finished and sent off the interview about Moore's play to *The Star*. After dinner called on Archer and stayed with him all the afternoon and evening until he went off to the theatre and I went off to the Dryhursts' to read the play to them, I having met Dryhurst at dinner and promised to go up if I could. There was a Mlle. Nicole there. On my way from Archer's to Hampstead I called here for a wash and a couple of eggs.

Dinner 1/–   Star ½d

27   *Hirwen Jones's matinee, Meistersingers' Club Room, 63 St. James's St. 15. Fabian Publishing Committee. 17½. Ruy Blas at Drury Lane. Comedie Française. 20. °Mabel Elliot and Olga Reuter's concert. Prince's Hall. 15. Tickets late. °Schonberger's recital. St. James's Hall. 15.*

Worked at the play, taking it up to the top of Primrose Hill after sticking at it here all the morning. On the hill it began to rain and kept at it—the first wet day we have had for a very long time. After the concert I went to the Fabian office and sat there for an hour before the committee meeting.

Star ½d   First number of *The Sun* ½d   PMG 1d   Another *Star* ½d
Bus along Tott[enham] Ct Rd 1d   Dinner 1/3   Bus to St Ja[me]s's St
2d   Bus Picc[adilly] O to Fabian Office 1d   Omelette &c at Orange
Grove 1/8?   Bus Grafton St to Long Acre 1d   Program at Drury Lane
6d

Reviewed on 5 July 1893 (C959). G.B.S. also heard the American minstrel-show virtuoso, C. P. Shortis, "playing the banjo with a delicacy and conscientiousness that ought to have been devoted to some musical instrument." The featured artist, tenor Hirwen Jones, was barely mentioned. ▪ The Comédie Française was doing a series of plays at Drury Lane. In *Ruy Blas*, the Victor Hugo drama, the title role was played by Mounet-Sully.

28   *Mrs. Pennell At-Home. 16¼. 14 Buckingham St. German class. 70 Cornhill. 20.15. Call on the Charringtons at 21, and read the entire play to them.*

Began account of Ibsen's *Master Builder* for new edition of *The Quintessence of Ibsenism*. Had a turn to the top of Primrose Hill. Met Sidney Dark in the park, where he was taking part in a cricket match. I went to Primrose Hill, not before dinner, but after it, having spent an hour before in singing. I have got almost out of the habit of singing for a year past; and for the sake of my lungs, if for nothing else, I must try to give a little time to it.

Star & Sun 1d   Dinner at Isotta's 1/6   Bus to St Martin's Lane 1d
Orange Grove 1/–   Train Ch[arin]g + to Mansion Ho[use] 1½d   Mansion Ho[use] to S[ou]th Kensington for self & to Rav[enscour]t Park for May 1/3   Gloster Rd to Portland Rd 4d   Toffee 2d

29   *The Begum Ahmadee's concert. Grosvenor Club. 15. Alfred Gallrein's concert. Steinway Hall. 20. Operatic concert. St. James's Hall. 15.*

Began *World* article. Went up to Primrose Hill before dinner. I came away early from Gallrein's concert and spent the rest of the evening pasting press notices into a scrap book. Walked with C. L. Graves from the Grosvenor Club to Piccadilly, and with Runciman from St. James's Hall to Oxford Circus.

Nat[ional] Reformer, Star & Sun 3d   Dinner 1/3   Bus to Oxford O 1d

> The Begum Ahmadee sang Indian songs in a mezzo-soprano of "agreeable quality" (C959), but her Irish accompanist, unable to follow her Eastern scale, made it a "disastrous" duet. ▪ Alfred Gallrein, cellist, gave a suite by Corelli "a rather commonplace treatment" (C959).

30   *Fabian Executive. 276 Strand. 17¼. Committee. 16¼. Crament's concert. Kensington Town Hall. 15. Estrella Belinfante's concert. St. James's Hall. 15. German class. 20.15.*

Working at *World* article. After the German class I went to the Terrace with May and slept there. Took a turn in the park as usual before dinner.

Bus along Tott[enham] Ct Rd 1d   *Star* ½d   *Sun* ½d   Dinner 1/2?
Bus to Picc[adilly] O 1d   Bus St Ja[me]s's Hall to Hyde Pk corner 1d
On to Kensington Church 1d   Train High St to Temple 5d?   Ginger
Lemonade 3d   Temple to Mans[ion] Ho[use] 1½d (Took ticket to Cannon Street)   Bus Mansion House to Charing + (May paid)   Train St Ja[me]s's Pk to Ravenscourt Park (2) 1/–

> John Maude Crament's performance of early and unfamiliar organ music was "more refreshing" than the "forty thousandth repetition" of a warhorse (C959). ▪ Signora Belinfante appeared to G.B.S. (C959), on the basis of a brief exposure to her "force and charm," less a concert singer than "a stage singer who has to resort to the concert platform as a means of introducing herself to the London public."

July

1   *Art and Literature Dinner at the Mansion House. 19 for 19¼. °Patti concert. Albert Hall. 15. Mrs. Charles Yates's concert. 1 Palace Gate. 15. °Jan Mulder's concert. Meistersinger's Club Room. 15.*

Spent time before dinner in beginning a report on the English Socialist Movement for the Zurich Conference. Left the Mansion House with Norman, with whom I walked to Blackfriars. [I could not eat; my feelings as a musician and vegetarian were too much for me; and save for some two or three pounds of ice pudding I came away empty, unless I take account of the great feast of chin music afterwards. . . . (C959)]

Train Rav[enscourt] Pk to Gloster Rd 4d?   White ties 2/9   Train to Moorgate 4d   Tip [to porter] at Mans[ion] Ho[use] 1/–

> There were, G.B.S. wrote (C959), "about three hundred and forty representatives of Art and Literature. Music, the art for which England was once famous throughout Europe, was represented by the police band, Mr. [Wilhelm] Ganz, Mr. [William] Kuhe, Sir Joseph Barnby, and myself. . . . [T]he City . . . has not yet discovered that music is an art." ▪ Mrs. Charles Yates (later Mrs. Dutton Cook) was supported in her piano recital by an array of musical friends, and G.B.S. himself implied (C959) that he had attended more because her husband was on the *World*'s editorial staff than because of her virtuosity. Once she played Grieg's "rococo suite" (Holberg Suite), he confessed, he left. ▪ Shaw's "Report for Zurich Conference on Political Position of the Working Class in England" fills seventy-three notebook pages in BL Add. MS. 50681. The International Socialist Workers Congress was to be held in Zurich, 6–13 August 1893. Shaw would be a delegate.

2 SUNDAY   *Mrs. Morgan-Browne's. 46 Ridgmount Gardens. 15 to 18.*

Took a stroll to the top of Primrose Hill before dinner, and called on the Morgan-Brownes in the afternoon. Except for this I was busy all day finishing and sending off the *World* article, and writing an article for *The Star* at Parke's request on the Mansion House banquet.

> "Moderates" (unsigned leader), *The Star*, 3 July 1893 (C958). The event, Shaw wrote—not in his "G.B.S." tone—was not a success. "Either some of our greatest artists and writers must have flatly refused to have anything to do with Mansion House, or else the Lord Mayor invited the wrong people. . . ."

3   °*Fabian Lecture Committee at Miss Cameron's. Put off to tomorrow. Mme. Inverni's concert. St. James's Hall. 15. Bertha Newcombe's studio at 16½, to meet Vernon Lee.*

Worked at report for Zurich and did some business correspondence etc. Had not time to dine before concert, and in fact did not dine at all. Bertha came with me to Charing Cross where we met Edward Rose; and as he was coming to the Comedie Française and she was going there too, I introduced them to one another and came home to work at the report. What kept me so late for the concert was that I had to return here from Primrose Hill and correct the *World* proof. I did not get to Chelsea until past 17.

Telegram to B[ertha] N[ewcombe] 7½d   Bus Portland Rd to St Ja[me]s's Hall 1d   Milk & cake at A[erated] B[read] shop Picc[adilly] O 7d   Train St Ja[me]s's Pk to Sloane Square 1½d   Sloane Sq to Ch[arin]g + (2) 7d

> Reviewed on 12 July 1893 (C961). Elise Inverni sang love songs with Isidore de Lara. "Although English is evidently her native language she has acquired a diction so artificial that I have no doubt that many of her hearers took her for a foreigner who had made a very close and conscientious study of English for artistic purposes." ▪ Vernon Lee was the pen name of Violet Paget (1856–1935), eccentric author of philosophical musings and novels who spent much of her life in Italy.

4 °*Dolmetsch's Bach Viol concert. Barnard's Inn. 20.40. Fabian Publishing Committee. 17½. 276 Strand. Fabian Autumn Course Committee. Miss Cameron's. 90 Holbein Buildings. Chelsea. 20. °Guild of St. Matthew at Headlam's. 19½ to 23½.*

Still hammering away at the report for Zurich. Primrose Hill as usual. Came back here after dinner and lay down for a while—played a little etc. My strength has returned to a great extent; but I am so restless that I almost regret the weakness. Olivier and Pease came with me to Miss Cameron's. I left alone at about 20½ and walked to Gloucester Rd.

Bus along Tott[enham] Ct Rd 1d   *Sun & Star* 1d   Dinner 1/7   Bus back to Grafton St 1d   Buses to Lincoln's Inn corner 2d   Maccaroni &c at Gatti & R[odesano]'s 1/4   Train Temple to Sloane Square 2½d Gloster Rd to Ptld Rd 4d

5 °*Mrs. Johnson's At-Home. Balham. 16 to 18¼. German class. 19¼. National Liberal Club at 21 to consult with Olivier, Bax, etc. about Zurich.*

Set to and polished off a lot of correspondence. This kept me busy up to dinner time. At the restaurant I met May [Sparling]. We left together and just outside I met Wallas. We went together on the bus to Oxford Circus and then May left us, arranging to meet me here later on and go to the German class with me. Wallas came with me to Jaeger's, where I had to get a few things; and then we walked back together to Bedford Square, where I left him going to the Museum and went to Primrose Hill for an airing. I did nothing there but read the papers. I returned to the Square and went off with May to the City, stopping on the way for "tea" at the Aerated Bread Shop at the corner of Grafton St. Wallas walked back with me from the club and came in for a while.

Papers 1d   Dinner 1/3?   Bus to Oxford O (3) 3d   Tram Euston Rd to Mornington Cres[cent] 1d   Cocoa &c at A[erated] B[read] Shop (2) 1/4   Bus along Tott[enham] Ct Rd (2) 2d   Bus Oxford St to St Martin's Ch[urch] (2) 2d   Train Ch[arin]g + to Mans[ion] Ho[use] (2) 5d? Mans[ion] Ho[use] to Temple, May paid.

6 *Wedding of the Duke of York. Be at the South Gate of Buckingham Palace before 10.30.*

Saw the wedding start. Very hot day—warm work writing in the sun and rushing of full speed afterwards to the office. Handed a column of description to the printer at Stonecutter St. 25 minutes after the Queen's carriage passed out of the gate of the palace. I do not find that this sort of thing gives me great trouble at the moment. Whilst it was being set up Parke and I went off to Fleet St. and had some lunch, for which he paid. Dam, who had been on the same duty outside St. James's Palace, joined us there. I returned to the office and corrected the proof. Then I went home, intending to work on the *World* article; but I found that I had done enough for the day and went off to kill the afternoon, which I did by calling on the Charringtons. Flemming was there with Janet. He had some dinner and left. Soon after Charrington came in. We chatted a good deal about their pecuniary difficulties, which are very present just now. At about 19 I went on to Hammersmith, to the Terrace, where I found May alone. Sparling was off at the Illuminations.

Train St Ja[mes]s Pk to Blackfriars 4d?   Cab Blackfriars to *Star* 1/–
Train Farringdon to Portland Rd 3½d   Ptld Rd to Gloster Rd 4d   Earls
Court to Ravenscourt Park 3d?   Rav[enscourt] Pk to Ptld Rd 7d

> "The Wedding . . . Departure from Buckingham Palace," unsigned second section of a
> report of the marriage of the Duke of York, the future George V, to Princess May of Teck,
> later Queen Mary, *The Star*, 6 July 1893 (C960).

7   *Fabian Executive. 17½. Committee. 16½. German class. 18¼.*

Began *World* article. Took a turn up to Primrose Hill. It was terribly hot and I had a light headache, as if the sun had been a little too much for me yesterday at Buckingham Palace. Got to the Fabian office pretty early, and took the chair at the preliminary committee. May came back with me from Cornhill as far as the door here, as she was going to see the [Andrew] Langs. She produced ten pounds and asked me to lend it to the Charringtons for her. I sent it off to Janet and posted what I had done of the *World* article.

Papers 1d   Bus to Orange Grove 1d   Dinner there 1/6?   Cake, milk,
iced drink 9d   Train Temple to Mansion Ho[use] 1½d   Train Farringdon to Portl[an]d Rd (2), May paid.

> Shaw (*CL*) explained the matter to the Charringtons as a necessary "indelicacy."

8   Finished *World* article and wrote a long letter to old [Henry] Hutchinson about Fabian affairs. The heat and thunderstorms and heavy showers made it impossible to go out; but at 20½ I went up to St. John's Wood and called for the first time on Arthur and Mrs. Graham Tomson. [Arthur] Studd, the caricaturist and artist, was there. It appears I met him in Paris; but I had forgotten it, though he is a man I should have expected to remember.

Papers 5d   Dinner 1/3

> Arthur Haythorne Studd (1863–1919), landscape and figure painter, was influenced by
> Paul Gauguin, whom he met in Brittany in 1890. Later he would even work in Tahiti.

9 SUNDAY   *Speak in Battersea Park at 18½ for the Labour League (W. F. Champion, 451 Battersea Park Rd., S.W.). "Labour Politics at Home and Abroad."*

Dawdled, read the papers, and corrected the *World* proof. Then went to the piano, where to my great surprise I had a fit of composing and actually produced some bars of a very amateurish minuet. Burns was in the park and we spoke for about an hour apiece. On the way there I met [Alfred] Moul at the Marble Arch. Burns walked with me as far as Kings Rd.

Bus Knightsbridge to Batt[ersea] Pk 1d   Train Sloane Sq to Portland Rd 8d   Butterscotch 1d

10 *Independent Theatre. Grein's At-Home at St. George's Hall. 14½. The Cradle by Emiel van Goethen, Dante by G. H. R. Dabbs and Edward Righton, and The Jerry Builder (parody of Ibsen's Master Builder) by Mrs. Hugh Bell. °Fabian Committee to draw up tract on Woman Question. 56 Russell Square. 20.15.*

Working at the Zurich report. Went up to Primrose Hill. Met [George] Alexander at Isotta's Café, where I dined. He walked with me to St. George's Hall, where I sat next to Theodore Watts. He left before it was over, and then I sat with Beringer. Was introduced to Mrs. [Frida] Strindberg, who wants to translate my new play. May came back with me. After tea she and I went off for a walk over Primrose Hill where we sat for a while looking at the beautiful sunset. Then to Hampstead Heath all round by the Highgate Ponds. I slept at the Terrace.

Papers 1d   Dinner at Portl[an]d Rd 1/6   Expressing proof to World 6d   Brown bread 2d   Train Finchley Rd to Chiswick (2) 1/4

All of the one-act plays were by prolific minor dramatists. The event was for supporters of the Independent Theatre enterprise, and for publicity. ▪ (Sir) George Alexander (1858–1918), stage name of George Alexander Gibb Samson, actor-manager who learned his trade with Henry Irving and managed the St. James's Theatre from 1891 to 1911. ▪ Beringer is possibly the husband of the playwright Mrs. Oscar Beringer. ▪ Frida Uhl Strindberg (1872–1943), an Austrian writer and translator, was the Swedish playwright's second wife. They married in Paris early in 1893; had a daughter, Kerstin, in 1894; and separated in 1895. A feminist who even insisted on maintaining her own flat after her marriage, she may very well have traveled to London alone. Shaw did not offer her his play. (Some years later Frida Strindberg would open a night spot in London, the Cabaret Theatre Club, also known as the Cave of the Golden Calf.)

11 *Fabian Publishing Committee. 17½.*

Came from Hammersmith by 11.20 train, North London. Sat on the top of Primrose Hill working at Zurich report. Called here for letters on my way to dinner after which I bought some chessmen to work out the stage positions in my play and went on to the Fabian office, where I found an old school master of Pease's and Miss Priestley. Whilst I was at the Orange Grove it began to rain furiously and when I left at closing time I took shelter in Peter's Court opposite to 4 men, who, to my great surprise, presently began to sing in parts very prettily. Got home at about 20½ and worked at the report and this diary, etc. for the rest of the evening.

Train Hammersmith (L. & N.W.R.) to Finchley Road 8d   Dinner at Orange Grove 1/2   Chess board & men at Stores (for staging play) 3/11   Lemonade at Sainsbury's 3d   Omelette &c at Orange Grove 1/5   Papers 1d

Peter's Court, off of St. Martin's Lane, no longer exists. The episode of the impromptu concert in the rain would be described in the G.B.S. column of 31 January 1894 (C998), where Shaw remembered only three men singing, "*sotto voce*, . . . raising their voices a little when they found that the passers-by were too preoccupied by the deluge to notice them."

12   *German class. 18¼. Mrs. Aylmer Jones's concert. 16 Stanhope Gardens, Queen's Gate. 15. Go to Sidney Webbs' in the evening and read draft report for Zurich.*

Corrected Zurich report and made up my mind to read it to the Webbs in the evening, which I did with the result of convincing myself that the time is not right for it yet. I must wait until I have looked about me at the Congress, and then elaborate the report as a paper on Internationalism to be read to the Fabian Society.

Star ½d   Dinner 1/4   Bus to Bayswater 2d   Bus Oxford O to Clipstone St 1d   Portl[an]d Rd to Moorgate 4d   Broad St to Finchley Rd. May paid.   Finchley Rd to Portland Rd 4d?

Reviewed on 19 July 1893 (C963). Mrs. Aylmer Jones had "a soprano voice of nice quality, a sensitive ear, a refined style, and an intelligent delivery." G.B.S. did not recommend that she take to the stage to "play Carmen: she is too ladylike for that. . . ."

13   Began *World* article. Went to Primrose Hill after dinner and began scribbling a letter to [John M.] Robertson about his notice of *Widowers' Houses* in *The National Reformer.* Came back and had cocoa etc. here between 17 and 18; then went off to FE who returned today from the country where she has been for more than a month past. Willy Yeats came in at about 21 and stayed a long time chatting.

Reformer, Star & Sun 3d   Dinner 1/6   Ellis's *Speech in Song* at Novello's 2/–   Train to Shep[herds] B[ush] & back 9d

All the reviews of *Widowers' Houses* by Shaw's Socialist so-called friends were hostile, on alleged grounds of art as well as doctrine. Robertson's notice appeared in the issue dated 16 July 1893, which apparently became available, like many journals, slightly in advance of the published date. ▪ W. B. Yeats, who visualized himself as possible successor to Florence Farr's affections, was seeing much of her in the occultist circles in which they both moved, especially the Golden Dawn. ▪ Alexander John Ellis (1814–1890), *Speech in Song, being the singer's pronouncing primer of the principal European languages for which vocal music is usually composed* (London, 1887). Ellis had been a Cambridge philologist. Shaw was preparing for a lecture he was to give on the 15th.

14   *Fabian Executive. 17½. 276 Strand. Committee. 16¼. Fabian Private Meeting. Barnard's Inn. 20. "Socialism and Sailors" tract, School Board, etc. German class. 18¼.*

Worked at *World* article. Took a turn on Primrose Hill after dinner. May came with me from Cornhill to the Fabian. Wallas walked home with me and came up for a while.

Papers 1d   Dinner at Portland Rd 1/6   Bus Euston Rd to St Martin's
Lane (Ch[arin]g + Rd) 1d   Omelette &c at Orange Grove 1/8?   Train
Temple to Mans[ion] Ho[use] (Can[non] St ticket) 1½d   Bus Mans[ion]
Ho[use] to Barnard's Inn (2) 2d

Fabian Tract No. 46, by Benjamin T. Hall. See 16 June 1893.

15 °*Trinity College Students' Orchestral Concert. Prince's Hall. 20. Lecture
on "Elocution" to the class of the Poplar Fabian at Leven Rd. Mission Hall.
17.*

Worked a bit at the *World* article, but was very full of the lecture on
Elocution, my first attempt at anything of the kind. Took Ellis's book to the
top of Primrose Hill and studied it before dinner. Only half a dozen fellows
turned up, but the lecture was a success. I spoke so long that I was too late
back to go to the concert. I played a couple of pianoforte duets with Lucy
for the first time for many years.

Dinner at Orange Grove 1/8?   Train Ch[arin]g + to Aldgate 2½d
Tram to Poplar 2d   Train Poplar to Camden Town 8d   Tram to
Euston Rd 1d

16 SUNDAY *Speak for the Independent Labour Party at the Triangle,
Limehouse, at 11½ (F. C. Calvin, 92 Locksley St., Limehouse).*

Finished and sent off *World* article and wrote a couple of cards. Called on
the Charringtons in the evening. Found Janet alone: Charrington came in
later on.

Sun 1d   Train to Aldgate & back 8d   Aldgate to Limehouse Ch[urch]
& back by tram 4d   Train to Gloster Rd to Ptld Rd 4d

17 *Meeting of delegates to Zurich International Conference at Central Hall
S. D. F. 337 Strand, 20½.*

Wrote some letters, corrected *World* proof; and, if I remember aright, did
some scribbling of some sort or another. At the restaurant I met May, who
came for a walk with me in Regent's Park after coming with me also to
Jaeger's where I paid my bill. She came back here and had tea. I wrote a
letter to *The Star* about the case of the Policeman Cooke sentenced to death
for killing a woman on Wormwood Scrubbs. Sat up to finish this after I
came back from the committee. Olivier walked back with me as far as the
Gower St. corner of Grafton St.

Papers 1d   Dinner 1/6?   Jaeger's bill £11/18/0   Bus along Tot-
t[enham] Ct Rd to Endell St 1d g3

"The Wormwood Scrubbs Murder," *The Star*, 18 July 1893 (C962). Constable George
Samuel Cooke had murdered his nagging mistress and would be hanged for it. Shaw's
letter was precipitated by one he had just read, in which E. Belfort Bax (*Star*, 17 July)
pleaded that the condemned man had been provoked to violence. Shaw saw a larger
issue, describing the murder as "lynch law produced by anarchy." Neither party, he

wrote, had a legal remedy. She had no claims as a wife; he was unable to free himself of a connection she continued to press and which put his constable's job in jeopardy. "[T]he difficulty will recur tomorrow or the next day with some other pair. We shall never be rid of these butcheries until we make up our minds as to what a woman's claims exactly are upon a man who, having formerly loved her, now wishes to get free from her society. If we find that she has some claims, let us enforce them and protect the man from any molestation that goes beyond them. If she has no claims, do not let us have men going in fear of being discharged from public employment for action on that assumption."

18   *Debate on Anarchism* vs *Social-Democracy. H[arry B.] Samuels and Herbert Burrows. Grafton Hall. 20.*

Found that I could not work; so resolved on a holiday. Called for FE, but she was out; so I went off to Richmond, and from there telegraphed to her that I was going to Hampton Court. On my way thither I traveled from Richmond to Twickenham with Gordon Hogg, who is now Middlesex Coroner, on his way to Shepperton to hold an inquest on an old woman who had broken her neck. Spent the afternoon looking at the pictures. Came back by the 18.26 train from Teddington.

Papers 8½d   Train to Shep[herds] Bush 6d   Rav[enscourt] Pk to Richmond 7d   Dinner at Richmond 1/6   Telegram to FE 6½d   Train Richmond to Teddington 8d?   Teddington to Waterloo 1/6   Ginger Beer at Ted[dington] 2d   Supper at Orange Grove 1/5   Bus to Grafton St from Tott[enham] Ct Rd corner 1d

19   *Fabian Literature Committee. 17¼. German class. 18½.*

Wrote letters, especially one to [Uncle] Walter about the Carlow property. advising him to sell it and buy an annuity. I might as well have saved myself the trouble, for he called at about 14, just as I was going out, and delayed me for some time. I got no airing today. Went to the Fabian office an hour before the committee and found Miss Brooke there with Miss Priestley, Pease being away for his holiday. Wrote up this diary and had a late meal when I got back from the City. In the morning I pasted some reviews of *Widowers' Houses* into the scrap book to relieve the monotony of writing, which is beginning to worry me again.

Bus to Orange Grove 1d   Dinner there 1/3   Bus along Strand 1d Ginger lemonade at Sainsbury's 3d   Train to Cannon St 1½d   Moorgate to Portland Rd 4d   Papers 2d

20   *Meeting of Socialist Joint Committee. 276 Strand. 20.*

Working at the preparation of old essays of mine for the proposed "Fabian Library" book. In the afternoon I went out to FE. Came back into town by the 18.35 train and joined Olivier at the Orange Grove. Lively scenes at the

Committee. Hyndman and I squabbled all the time. This was the last meeting of the Joint Committee whilst the Fabian Society belonged to it. A Miss Van Elten, from America, came in whilst it was going on and introduced herself to us. When I went home I wrote to Webb and Wallas about the Committee. I am making this entry on the 3rd January 1894 from the pocket diary of last year.

Train Rav[enscourt] Pk to Ch[arin]g + 6d   Meal at Orange Grove 1/8 (as to dinner & how I got out to Hammersmith, the little diary says nothing about them)

> "The Fabian Library" was abandoned, although subscription funds in excess of projected needs were quickly guaranteed for the initial volume.

21 *Fabian Executive. 17$\frac{1}{2}$. Committee. 16$\frac{1}{2}$. German class. 18$\frac{1}{4}$. Cornhill.*

Spent all the early part of the day hunting up stuff for the Fabian Library. From the German lesson I went out to Hammersmith with May. In the train we met Philip Webb, with whom I had a vehement talk about the Joint Committee, which I denounced with great energy, he listening very patiently considering that he did not in the least agree with me.

Dinner 1/3   Milk & cake 3$\frac{1}{2}$d   Tram to Mansion Ho[use] 1d Mans[ion] Ho[use] to Rav[enscourt] Pk 1/2 (2)

22 *Revival of* La Fille de Madame Angot *at the Criterion Theatre.*

I suppose I must have begun *World* article today. There is no entry in the little diary from which I am now filling in the blanks in this big one (on the 3rd January 1894).

> La Fille de Madame Angot was a comic opera originally produced in 1873, with a score by Alexandre Charles Lecocq, and English libretto by H. J. Byron. It would have eighty-five performances. G.B.S.'s review, 26 July 1893 (C965), judged that the work in most respects "stood the test of revival very well," particularly because of the "triumphant" performance as Clairette by Decima Moore (1871–1964), although she remained "hopelessly British."

23 SUNDAY *Speak in Regent's Park for the Fabian. 11.30.*

The Chatteris's turned up in the park to hear me speak. It was a tiresome business—lively orators bawling in all directions. I spoke very long and was rather dried up, nervously speaking, afterwards. I had a nightmare in consequence, as I suppose. In the afternoon worked at the *World* article.

24 Working at the essay on "Socialism and Human Nature" for the first volume of "The Fabian Library." After dinner went off to FE. We went out to Gunnersbury by train and then walked to Richmond. When I got home I wrote a letter to *The Star* in reply to one written by JP about the murder case in reply to my own former letter. All these letters were published.

Dinner 1/3   Bus to Uxbridge Rd 4d   Train Rav[enscour]t Pk to Gunnersbury (2) 6d   Richmond to Rav[enscourt] Pk (2) 1/2   Sweets 3d   Shep[herds] Bush to Portl[an]d Rd 6d

> A letter signed "E" (almost certainly Jenny Patterson) had appeared in *The Star* 21 July 1883, identifying the writer as being in a "similar position" to Constable Cooke's rejected (and then murdered) Maud Merton. Mrs. Patterson apparently used the affair to vent her wrath at Shaw. "I know too well the feeling when a girl knows she is no more loved by the one she has given her all to, but is only a thing to be cast aside like a toy which has been tired of." Shaw's signed response (he must have known from his mother or sister that he was really answering Jenny) was headed in *The Star*, 25 July 1893 (C964), "Bernard Shaw's Reply. Shows That, Spite of All His Critics Have Said, He is No Hater of Women." What is surprising is that it appeared in a Victorian family newspaper. "At the bottom of all the unreason," he wrote, ". . . will be found the old theory that an act of sexual intercourse gives the parties a lifelong claim on one another for better or worse. . . . I do not mind committing myself so far as to say that I cannot for the life of me see what claim the woman had. . . ."

25 Still working at Essay. Went out to Dalling Rd. and called for FE, but she was out. Went to the Terrace and found May, with whom I paid a visit to Mrs. Walker. We then walked to Kew Bridge through Strand on the Green and came back on the tram. We played duets in the evening. Came back by the 23.10 train.

Dinner 1/3   Bus to Uxbridge Rd 4d   Tram Kew Bridge to St Peter's Park (2) 4d   Train Rav[enscour]t Pk to Ptld Rd 7d

26 Wrote enough stuff for *The World* to make up an article with what was left over from last week. Went for a stroll to the top of Primrose Hill. I take this one record from the little diary, which contains nothing further.

> No activities were entered by Shaw after this date except his expenses 31 July 1893, through 14 August, when he was returning from Switzerland. English appointments on his calendar were obviously not kept. Shaw's reports from Zurich on the International Socialist Congress were published (as "From a Special Correspondent") in *The Star*, 8–12 and 14 August (C967), and also in minor pieces in *Freedom* (C972) and *Workman's Times* (C971).

27 [   ]

28 *Fabian Executive. 17½. Committee. 16¼.*

29 [   ]

30 SUNDAY *Speak at 11.30 (F. J. Osborne, 50 Westmoreland Rd. S.E.).*

31 Whisk 1/–   Nailbrush 1/2   Keating 8d   Camphor 1/2   Copying leads 6d   5 quires Ammunition note 10½

> *Keating:* a powder used as a specific against ants.

August

1–3   [   ]

4   *Zurich*

5–12   [   ]

13   [After a fortnight of Swiss art, musical and pictorial, anything would have . . . sounded wonderfully distinguished . . . so I had better reserve my opinion until I have recovered my critical balance. (C973)]

14   *Basle. Join the return party at 9.25—train from Brussels, Ostend, Dover and Holborn.*

15   *Dover. Holborn Viaduct 6. Promenade Concert. Covent Garden. Slivinski—Tchaikowsky's Concerto.*

When I got home I found the door chained and had to knock up Kate to let me in. My mother was not here: she is staying with JP at Pangbourne. As I was changing my clothes after the journey, I lay down for a few minutes, and before I knew where I was, I had slept for five hours soundly. I read papers and muddled about arrears of correspondence—Walter coming in for a while in the meantime—until 17, when I went off to the Orange Grove and then to the Embankment Gardens, where I read the *Review of Reviews* until it was time to go to the concert. I met Bernhard Sickert there. I got back here at about 22, and found Wallas at the door. He sat with me for a while and we took a stroll together before midnight.

Train Farringdon to Ptld Rd 5d   *Chronicle* 1d   Dinner at Orange Grove 2/2   Note Book 3d   Drink at Sainsbury's 3d   *Review of Reviews* 4½d   Program at concert 2d

The Promenade Concert was reviewed by G.B.S. in *The World*, 23 August 1893 (C970). Slivinski played with "refined strength and feathery swiftness."

16   *Meet Archer at the Hygeian at 13½. Promenade Concert. Ysaÿe—Bruch's Scottish Fantasia. German class. 18½.*

The morning was rather wasted writing letters in a desultory way. I took a turn in the park before going to meet Archer, with whom I went home after we had called at the Fabian office to get [Sidney] Ball's address for him (he wants the water of a well analyzed). The weather is terribly hot.

Bus along Tott[enham] Ct Rd 1d   Dinner 1/6   Drink at Sainsbury's 4d   Bus Holborn to City 1d   Supper at the Arcadian 1/7   Train Mans[ion] Ho[use] to Temple 1d   Program at concert 2d

Ysaÿe played Bruch "better than one could have supposed it capable of being played, and set a rather diffident audience cheering at the end" (C970). ▪ It is unclear how Sidney Ball could have helped other than through using his good offices at St. John's, Oxford, to locate an appropriate scientist.

17 Wrote *World* article and sent it off. McKernon called. After dinner went out to Barnes and walked to the Richmond Gate and into Richmond Park, where I lay under the trees and wrote a letter to Archer about Pinero's play, *The Second Mrs. Tanqueray*, a copy of which, printed for private circulation, Archer lent me yesterday.

Papers 1d   Dinner 1/6?   Train Waterloo to Richmond (got out at Barnes) 9d   Macaroni &c at Ferrari's 2/–   Train Richmond to Rav[enscourt] Pk 4½d   Grapes 6d   Bus Uxbridge Rd to Holles St 4d

Shaw would see the play on 11 December 1893.

18 *Meet FE at the Orange Grove at 17 and go to Earl's Court Exhibition.*

Went off for a turn into the park with a notion of getting to work on a new play. However, no ideas came; and after sitting for a while on the top of Primrose Hill I went off to Finchley Rd. to look for a swimming bath. Opposite Swiss Cottage station I met Nettleship and walked with him to a livery stable in Belsize Crescent where he was going to get a horse for some exercise. I left him there and returned to Finchley Rd., meeting Larkin, the Japanese art dealer, on the way. He walked with me as far as the station. I had a swim and then got some milk and bought some nuts and a pair of nutcrackers, with which I went up to the Upper Heath, where I lay idling and sleeping until 15½, when I went back to town to keep my appointment with FE. We spent the evening at the Exhibition, and ended by coming down "the water shoot." I went home with her and came back here by the last train but one.

Hampstead Swimming Bath, 10 tickets 5/–   Milk 4d   Nuts 6d Nutcrackers 1/3   Ginger beer 3d   Bus Adelaide to Euston Rd 2d Grafton St to Ch[arin]g + Rd 1d   Orange Grove (2) 2/7   St Ja[me]s's Pk to Earls Court Exhibition with adm[ission] (2) 2/6   Guide, program &c 4d   Seats at Water Show & chute (2) 8/– (3)   Up light house (2) 1/–   Iced drinks (2) 1/–   Train West Kensington to Rav[enscour]t P[ar]k (2) 6d   Train Shep[herds] Bush to Portland Rd 6d

The exhibition, advertised as featuring "Gardening and Forestry," also had a water show. ▪ Thomas Joseph Larkin, 28 New Bond Street.

19 *Be at Finchley Rd. station at 15.17.*

Did no work all day. Strolled off across the park to Hampstead and bathed. Then had some lunch and met FE. We went up to the Heath and bought some fruit, with which we sat down on the ferns not very far from "The Spaniards," in the same place where I sat yesterday. I went there because I had left my pencil there. I found it all safe. We read the papers, talked, and dozed. Finally I went asleep, and when I awoke the sun was setting and there was a bank of clouds on the horizon which were so extremely like mountains with sun on them that I was astonished, and thought for a moment that I was dreaming, and mixing up Switzerland with Hampstead in my dream. I went home with FE by the 19.40 train.

Lunch at St John's Parade 1/1   Fruit 1/–   Milk (2) 3d   Excess fare on FE's ticket to Ham[mersm]ith 3½d   Finchley Rd to Ham[mersm]ith (Chiswick) 8d   Shep[herds] B[ush] to Portl[an]d Rd 6d

20 SUNDAY   Felt very giddy all day; I imagine the sun must have affected me yesterday a little. Spent the day in desultory reading mostly—notably *The Pilgrim's Progress*, which still retains its fascination for me. In the evening I resolved to overcome the giddyness; so I walked over to the Charringtons', where I found them with Flemming. I came back in the train, and at last succeeded in beginning a new play.

Train Gloster Rd to P[or]tl[an]d Rd 6d

> The new play would become *Mrs Warren's Profession*, in notebook BL Add. MS. 50598A (followed by B and C).

21   Wrote a letter to *The Chronicle* on the suicide question. Felt more headachey and giddy than yesterday. After dinner went off to Barnes and spent a long time in Richmond Park, but only did a little at the play. Walked to Kew Bridge and took tram for Hammersmith. On second thoughts I got off and called at the Terrace; but there was no light in the house, so I went on and called on Morris, whom I found alone. I also wrote in the morning a longish letter to Archer, pressing him to try his hand at a play.

Papers (in Cleveland St) 2½d   Dinner at Orange Grove 1/6?   Train Waterloo to Barnes 6d   Supper at Ferrari's 1/8   Tram Kew Bridge to St Peter's Park 2d   Train Ham[mersm]ith Broadway to P[or]tl[an]d Rd 6d

> No letter apparently by Shaw was published in *The Daily Chronicle*.

22   Felt rather better. Got to work fairly at last on the Fabian Eight Hour pamphlet—Macrosty's draft—which I have to supply with a framework. Stuck at it until past 14 and finished the introduction. After dinner went to the Fabian office and stayed there with Pease until near 19 when I went back to the Orange Grove for a meal. I had thought of going over to the Charringtons to get from Janet the scenario of the play she wants me to write; but I changed my mind and came home. Wrote to Archer in reply to his reply to my letter of yesterday.

Papers 1d   Dinner at Orange Grove 1/3   Bus along Strand 1d Supper at Orange Grove 1/6?   Bus Picc[adilly] O to Clipstone St 1d

> *Fabian Tract* No. 48, *Eight Hours by Law* (1894).   ■   For Janet Achurch's scenario, see 4 September 1893.

23   *German class.* $18\frac{1}{4}$.

24   *Lady Colin Campbell.*

> Shaw may have planned to read his revision of *The Philanderer* to Lady Colin, who had convinced him that the original last act was useless.

25   *German class.* $18\frac{1}{4}$. *Podmore's in the evening. 32 Well Walk.*

Finished going over the Eight Hours tract. Went out to FE early at her request—got there about 1. We went out to Kew, walking to Richmond. I came back all the way into the City. May came with me by the North London on my way to Podmore's. He wanted to know all about the Zurich Conference. The Dryhursts were there and I walked with them as far as their gate when we left. Mrs. Podmore was not there.

Telegram from FE to Martin, reply paid 1/2   Tram to Kew (2) 4d
Fruit 10d   Train Richmond to Rav[enscourt] P[ar]k for FE 7d   to
Bishopsgate for me 1/3   Eggs &c at A[erated] B[read] shop, Bishopsgate
St $11\frac{1}{2}$d   Lavatory at Broad St 6d   Train Broad St to Hampstead
H[ea]th. May paid.

26   *Go down to the Webbs' at Monmouth. 10.20 train from Paddington.*

Worked at the play in the train until I was tired. Wallas and Webb met me at the station; and a man carried my bag up the hill for me. After lunch we all four—Mrs. Webb and the three of us—walked to Trellech Common. After dinner ($19\frac{1}{2}$) Webb read us a chapter of his book on Trade Unions.

Train to Paddington $1\frac{1}{2}$d   Padd[ington] to Redbrook 12/$4\frac{1}{2}$ Milk &
buns at Swindon 4d   Ferry at Redbrook 1d

> Beatrice Webb called The Argoed her "old Monmouthshire home; still in the hands of my father's executors." ▪ The Webbs' book was *The History of Trade Unionism* (London, 1894); Beatrice Webb recalled that Shaw worked "almost every morning on our book" (BB19).

27 SUNDAY   At the Argoed. In the morning I walked about a mile along the Monmouth road and turned to the left over a stile in the fields. After crossing a stile or two I came upon some broken ground, the remains of a quarry. Here I lay down on a bank and got to work from 11 to 13 on a new play *Mrs Warren's Profession*. Lunch was at 13.30. In the afternoon we all went out and called on some people named Pelham at their house Moorcroft. They both took a walk with us, leaving us at the Argoed gate. After dinner ($19\frac{1}{2}$) Webb read another chapter of his Trade Union book.

> He would write Archer on 30 August (*CL*) that he had "skilfully blended the plot of *The Second Mrs Tanqueray* with that of *The Cenci*." ▪ Arthur Pelham was the younger son of the Earl of Chichester. He and his wife Evelyne had settled at the neighboring property of Moorcroft in the early 1880s.

28   *The Argoed.*

Spent the morning just as I spent yesterday morning. After lunch we all went to Raglan to Beaufort Castle, taking the two women servants with us. We did not get back until after 20, when we found Mrs. Dyson Williams ("Rosie"), Mrs. Webb's sister, whose little boy has been here all along, waiting for us. She had come on a visit. After dinner we small-talked, the Trade Union book being supposed to be too much for Mrs. Williams. Wallas and I sat up to read some of it after the others were gone.

Train Troy to Raglan & back 1/1   Castle 6d

> Beaufort Castle would enter Shaw's play early in Act 2, when Frank Gardner explains the architect Praed's social position facetiously to Rev. Samuel Gardner: "He built that place down in Monmouthshire for the Duke of Beaufort—Tintern Abbey, they call it. You must have heard of it." Later he would alter the line to "He built that place in Wales for the Duke. Caernarvon Castle they call it. You must have heard of it." Shaw would visit Tintern Abbey the next day, suggesting the rest of the original dialogue.

29   *The Argoed.*

Did the usual morning's work at the play, finishing the first act. Wallas went back to town by the 15.51 train. Webb and I went with him as far as Tintern, where we got out of the train and walked to the Abbey and thence back to the Argoed. It was a lovely walk.

Ferry 1d   Train to Tintern 7d   Abbey 6d   Refreshments at Tintern Abbey ?

30   *The Argoed.*

Read over and corrected the first act of the play. May [Sparling] sent a bundle of numbers of *Les Temps* containing reports of the Zurich Conference. Read the first act of the play to the Webbs after lunch whilst Mrs. Williams was at the other end of the lawn playing with the boy. We made a lazy day of it; but after tea in the afternoon we walked to Wyebrook. Mrs. Dyson Williams never came with us on these walks. In the evening I began reading the Trade Union book, correcting it and suggesting what improvements I could in it.

31   *At the Argoed.*

Did nothing in the morning but hold a Fabian Council with Webb; go down to the post with some letters and play all the old glees in the bound volume in the next room. We three went off by the 12.30 train to Chepstow, where we visited the Castle; lunched there al fresco, and walked to Tintern by way of the Windcliff.

Train Redbrook to Chepstow 1/1   Grapes & apple 8d   Castle 6d
Gingerbeer there 2d   Moes Cottage at the Wyndcliff 6d   Lemonade at Tintern (Webb paid)   Drive to station 6d   Train Tintern to Redbrook 7d   Ferry 1d

September

1   °*Fabian Executive. 17¼. Committee. 16¼. At the Argoed.*

Did not go out in the morning, but sat within and worked on a long letter to *The Workman's Times* re the Zurich Conference. We did nothing in the afternoon on the pretext of being tired by yesterday's excursion. I took a stroll by myself before dinner. Worked at the revise of the Trade Union book before going to bed.

> "The Zurich Congress. The 'Star' Man, George Bernard Shaw, Replies to Dr. and Mrs. Aveling," *Workman's Times*, 9 September 1893 (C971).

2   *At the Argoed.*

Corrected the Zurich letter, which took a long time. Went down to the field which commands a view of the Wye and did about an hour's work at a play. In the afternoon, Webb and I walked to the Raglan station. The Dowager Mrs. Webb arrived in the evening. Did a little work on the play. New book before bedtime.

3 SUNDAY   *At the Argoed.*

Went down to the same field as yesterday; but found the insects annoying and the place somehow not a good one to work in; so I shifted my quarters to the arboretum where I continued work on the play and watched the squirrel that was playing in the tree above me. In the afternoon I lay on the lawn and finished reading [Dickens's *The Mystery of*] *Edwin Drood.* Pelhams called. They, the Webbs and I walked to the Bigges hillock and back. To my surprise found myself with a headache which stopped me after trying to do a few pages of the Trade Union book.

4   *Look out for article for* Justice, *due next Monday (q.v.).*

Very fine day. In good spirits and blooming after the depression of yesterday. Went to the old place and worked at the play for nearly three hours; varying it by watching a terrific spider. After lunch we went to Lydney Junction (train Redbrook to L. J. 7½). Apples and ginger ale there 3d. Train Lydney Junction to Redbrook 7½.

> "The play progresses bravely; but it has left the original lines," Shaw wrote to Janet Achurch on this date (CL). "I have made the daughter the heroine, and the mother a most deplorable old rip. . . . The great scene will be the crushing of the mother by the daughter. . . . The second act is half finished and wholly planned." His version of De Maupassant's novel *Yvette*—the basis of the scenario she had urged on him—was now diverging significantly from its source. Her own play based upon the same novel would be called *Mrs. Daintree's Daughter.*

5   Not quite so full of go as yesterday; but did three hours good work on the second act of the play in the usual place. After lunch read the first act

of *The Philanderer* to the company. Afterwards we three went out for a walk through the fields—not very far.

6   Gave up the play for the present and set to work in earnest to read over and revise the Webb's Trade Union book. After lunch read second act of *The Philanderer*. Then the Webbs and I went out for a walk to the old church in the rain.

7   Working at the Trade Union book. After dinner we three went for a walk to Trellech Common. Webb and I left Mrs. Webb to walk home alone from there; and we went off together to Trellech and back through the Cledden Woods. Read the third act of *The Philanderer* after lunch.

8   °*Fabian Executive. 17½. Committee. 16¼.*
Work at Trade Union book. The two Mrs. Webbs went away with the boy by a forenoon train. In the afternoon we all three walked to Trellech Common.

   "The boy" was the son of Mrs. Dyson ("Rosie") Williams. See 28 August 1893.

9   Still at the book. Webb got a bad headache and Mrs. Webb and I went out for a walk after lunch. I wrote letters to Wallas and Sparling about Fabian Manifesto. Just before, I walked down to Wyebrook and back by myself.

10 SUNDAY   Morning as usual. After lunch we all walked over to New-lands and back through the tin works—a beautiful walk.

11   °*Send an article to* Justice *as per their letter (Socialist Joint Committee) of 30th June.*
Morning as usual. In the afternoon Webb and I walked into Monmouth and back.

12   Morning as usual. In the afternoon we three walked down into the Wyebrook valley and back by the Trellech road. In the evening we had a long discussion about Roman Catholicism.

13   Work at the Trade Union book. Wrote letters after lunch, which was at one today. At 3.30 Webb and I walked to St. Brigvel's and back, not getting home until 19.45.

14   Still at the book. We must have taken a short walk all three together this evening, unless we took the walk put down for tomorrow.

   Shaw was still reconstructing from his pocket engagement book.

15   °*Fabian Executive. 17½. Committee. 16¼.*

Still at the book. Webb and I went off for what we intended to make a short walk; but we really took rather a long [walk] across a valley between Trellech and Monmouth way, going through a valley called Cumgarven. I will not swear that this was not yesterday; but I think not.

16   Still at the book. Webb and I took a walk round by the Wyebrook valley and got back at 17. Did a stroke more work before dinner.

17 SUNDAY   Still at book. All three a short walk in the afternoon.

18   Up by 9.30 train. Walked from the Argoed.

19   Began drafting political manifesto for the Fabian. Dined off some nuts and pears. Mrs. Wynne and Aileen Bell called. Then I went out, called for Archer, who was not in; left word that I would call back; went to the Fabian office and had a talk with Pease; returned to Archer's and sat there until he came in; made up my mind to go to the theatre with him, but changed my mind; and finally came back here and sat up until past 24 answering letters asking for lectures.

> "To Your Tents O Israel!" (signed "By the Fabian Society" but drafted by Shaw and revised by the Webbs), *Fortnightly Review*, November 1893 (C979); further revised and augmented by Shaw as *Fabian Tract* No. 49, *A Plan of Campaign for Labour* (A22).

20   *Fabian Literature (Publishing) Committee. 276 Strand. 17¼. German class. 18¼. Meet the Salts and Mrs. Francis Adams at the Hygeian Restaurant at 1.30.*

Up early again. Worked at manifesto until past 11, when O'Brien called for some money. He kept me for some time. I was dressing to go out for a stroll in the park when Webb called to discuss the manifesto. We walked to the top of Primrose Hill together, and I left him near his mother's house and took a bus back to meet the Salts. After dinner I went to the Stores, parting from the Salts and Mrs. Adams at Shaftesbury [Cambridge] Circus. Then I went into the National Gallery and spent more than an hour over the Turner drawings in the basement with deep pleasure in them. After the German class May and I walked along the Embankment to Charing Cross, when she proposed to go to the Democratic Club, where Fletcher, of *The Chronicle*, was delivering a lecture on Christianity. We were too late to hear anything but the close of the discussion. Stayed talking to Foote, W. Johnson and others, and did not get home until near midnight.

Bus Britannia to Oxford St 2d   Dinner 1/3   Eagle pencil 9d   Lent O'Brien 2/6   Omelette &c at Orange Grove after National Gallery 1/6 Train Temple to Cannon St 1½d

21   *Call on the Wynnes in the evening. 14 Argyll Rd. to meet Aileen.*

Up early. Worked at the manifesto until past 11, and then wrote several business letters. The day being too wet for much outing I set to work upstairs to go through my books and set aside those which I do not want to keep. I got to the Wynnes' about 20½, having dined at the Orange Grove on my way there. Aileen [Bell] was there, and Mrs. Wynne, also Wynne and his two sons. We played poker—my first attempt at that game. I also saw for the first time young Douglas Home, Mrs. Wynne's second son, whom I have never seen before.

Dinner at Orange Grove 1/10   *Star & Sun* 1d   Train St Ja[me]s's P[ar]k to High St 3½d   Bayswater to Portland Rd 2½d

22   *Fabian Executive. 17¾. Committee. 16½. °German class. 18¼. No—the set of lessons ended on Wednesday.*

Still at the manifesto. At about 11 or 12 gave it up for the day and went off for a walk over Primrose Hill and up Fitzjohn's Ave., working at the play as I went along and occasionally sitting down on the wayside seats to work out a few speeches. Took a bus from the Adelaide to the Orange Grove, where I had a meal before going on to the Executive. Wallas and I had supper at Gatti and Rodesano's afterwards and then went to Daly's Theatre, where we were much bored by *Dollars and Sense*.

Bus from Adelaide to Orange Grove 2d   Dinner 1/3   Maccaroni &c at Gatti & Rodesano's 1/8   Daly's theatre 2/6

> Revival of the comedy by Augustin Daly (adapted from the German) first performed in New York in 1883. It survived fourteen performances.

23   *"Junta" dinner at Webbs' at 41 Grosvenor Rd. (the first). 19¼.*

Worked away at the manifesto, chiefly revising, but largely writing, until after 1. After dinner went into the park and was caught in a thunderstorm on Primrose Hill. Saw it sweep over London from the top—a sight worth seeing. Returned here for a while before going to Webbs', where I found Beatrice alone in Costelloe's house (No. 40) where they are staying until their own (No. 41) is ready to go into. We went into the new house together and looked at wallpapers etc. Wallas walked home with me. I read the manifesto to them, as far as it has gone, and found it very long and sleepy.

Sun ½d   Dinner 1/3   Bus Grafton St to West[minster] 2d

> The "Junta" was Beatrice Webb's name for the Fabian brain trust of Wallas, Webb, and Shaw.

24 SUNDAY   Went out for a walk in Regents Park in the forenoon and stayed until it was time to go back to dinner at 14. Chatted with a lot of fellows at the meetings. Did some work on the play. Morgan-Browne called

in the afternoon. In the evening I went over to the Charringtons. Flemming was there. Walked back.

Train Edgware Rd to Gloster Rd 4d

25   °*Go down to Salts at Oxted. No—tomorrow. Saint-Saens'* Samson et Dalila *at the Promenade Concerts. Covent Garden. 17.45.*

Work at the manifesto. Resolved to stay in town for a Promenade Concert instead of going to Oxted. Took a turn in the afternoon on Primrose Hill and worked at the play. Mother came with me to Covent Garden—or rather she met me there.

Dinner 1/1   Bus Oxford St to Mornington Crescent 2d   Orange Grove table d'hote (ordinary fare) 1/10   Program at Cov[en]t G[arden] 3d

> The Promenade Concert was reviewed on 4 October 1893 (C793) in G.B.S.'s first music column since 23 August 1893. He was bored, calling the opera the French equivalent to a contemporary English oratorio.

26   °*Trinity College inaugural address by E. H. Turpin, Mandeville Place. 16. "The Study of Music as a Science and as an Art." See yesterday. Salts'. 11.15 train from Victoria.*

Made a fresh start at the Fabian manifesto, as I have come to the conclusion that the stuff already done is of little or no use. Went down to Oxted by the 11.15 train. Read the two acts of the new play (I finished the second act in the train) to the Salts and Mrs. Adams after dinner. Then we went out for a walk, the two women going only part of the way and Salt and I going on across the Common to visit Mrs. Pease. When we got back Jupp was having tea at the cottage. Later on Olivier came and then Mrs. Olivier and Hilda Cox, with whom Salt and I walked part of the way home. We had some playing.

Train Victoria to Oxted (return) 3/2   *Chronicle* 1d

> William Jesse Jupp, a Fabian who continued as a member of the Fellowship of the New Life, wrote religious books.

27   *Fabian Publishing Committee.* 17½.

Came up from Oxted with Olivier by the 9.47 train. Wrote letters until far into the afternoon. Walter [Gurly] called. After the Executive, went with Olivier, to whom I had given the two acts of the play to read, to Gatti's. Then I took a bus out to the Queen's Elm and called on the Charringtons. Janet was not in; so I read the stuff to Charrington alone. Met Touzeau Parris and young Holyoake in the train on my way from the Orange Grove to the Fabian.

Dinner at Orange Grove 1/1   Paid Pease for copy of *The Times* containing description of Coal Trust 3d   Omelette &c at Gatti & Rodesano's 1/6
Bus Strand to Queen's Elm 3d

28 Began *World* article and wrote some letters. Went out at half past 12 to British Museum to look at the collection of old newspapers exhibited there. Did not succeed in finding them. Met Steffen and brought him off to lunch at the restaurant at the corner of Charing Cross Rd. Then went out to FE. It was rather a wet afternoon; so I sat indoors with her and read her the two acts of the play. At about 17 we went out and walked to Acton. Getting out of the train on the way back I came upon Cobden-Sanderson. Came home by the 22.36 train. Caught cold from a draft at FE's. She read me part of a novel she is writing.

Dinner (self & Steffen) 3/–   Bus corner of Ch[arin]g + Rd to Uxbridge Rd station 4d   Train Acton to Ham[mersm]ith (Chis[wic]k) (2) 4d
Sweets 4d   Train Shep[herds] Bush to Portland Rd 6d

> Florence Farr had now nearly completed *The Dancing Faun.*

29 *Fabian Executive. 17¼. Committee. 16½. My turn in the chair.*

Finished and sent off *World* article. I was rather late in getting it done as I did not wake until nine, thereby breaking a succession of early risings I have kept up since my return from the country. Also wrote some letters and then went straight to the Orange Grove, where I dined and sat reading the papers until it was time to go to the Executive. When I got to the office [G. C.] Beresford was there, arranging his photographs and taking leave of us going to Edinburgh. After the Executive I went with Olivier and Wallas to the National Liberal Club, Webb coming with us as far as the door. Norman joined us at table in the grill room. Wallas walked with me for a turn to Westminster and through the Green Park. I parted from him at Charing Cross and walked home. Wrote a note to Olive Schreiner to remind her of my existence before she leaves England. My cold is troublesome.

Papers 2d   Dinner at Orange Grove 1/6

30 *Private View. Arts and Crafts Exhibition. New Gallery. 10 to 18.*

Worked at Fabian *Fortnightly* article [the manifesto]. Went for a turn in the park, calling at Isidor's on the way to get my hair cut, but leaving untended sooner than wait my turn. When I got into the park I felt so hungry that I had to get some bread and cheese and milk at the refreshment pavilion. Went to the top of Primrose Hill, where, at two o'clock, I suddenly remembered that Jaeger closes early on Saturday and that I wanted a pair of decent gloves. So I hurried off there. Then dined at the Hygeian. Came home for a wash, and went to the Private View, where I met a great many people. Left at 18 with Phene Spiers, from whom I parted at Piccadilly Circus. We had a word with [Harry] Furniss in Regent St. Went to the Orange Grove and had a meal there. Then off to Webbs', where I read what I had done of the manifesto. Wallas left a little before nine, and I then read to the Webbs part of the second act of the play, which we discussed. Walked home.

Bread & cheese in Regents Pk 3d   Dinner 1/2   Omelette &c at Orange
Grove 1/2   Bus to New Gallery 1d

> Isidor Levald, Shaw's barber, Albany Street, N.W.

October

1 SUNDAY *Speak at Highbury Corner (bottom of Highbury fields) on*
"Labour at the Next General Election" at 11.30 (W. Aug. Steward, 75 Bon-
well Rd. Dayton Park N.). Cancelled.

I worked until past 23 at manifesto. Then dined and went off to Oxted by
the 15 train after calling on FE and finding her busy with somebody over
the papers of her Occult Society. She arranged to meet me at the Comedy
Theatre tomorrow. Took a walk with Salt in the afternoon to Tandridge.

Train to Shep[herds] Bush 6d   Rav[enscourt] Pk to Victoria 6d   Victoria to Oxted (ret[urn]) 3/2   *Weekly Sun* 1d

2 *Comedy Theatre. 20.10. Sowing the Wind. Grundy.*

In the morning went up to the West Hill and worked at the manifesto. After
dinner took a walk with Mrs. Francis Adams, who told me a good deal
about herself. I came up to town by the 16.12 train and walked home. It
was a wet night. Cold very troublesome.

Daily Chronicle 1d   Program at theatre 6d   Cab theatre to Ch[arin]g
+ underground 1/3

> *Sowing the Wind*, a comedy by Sydney Grundy, would run for 120 performances.

3 *First German lesson of the 2nd course at Mrs. Edwards's, 55 Buckland*
Crescent N.W. 11.30 to 13.30.

Worked at Manifesto. May walked with me from Hampstead to the restaurant. I parted from her when we left it and came back here. Lay down for a
while looking over some of my old notes of the German lessons. Then went
out and got my hair cut. Morgan-Browne called to ask me to write to *The*
Chronicle introducing him as a possible Indian correspondent. Put in some
more work on the manifesto and then went to see H. Sonntag. I arrived
there about 21. I read her the first two acts of the new play. Horace
Headlam came in for a while.

Bus along Tott[enham] C[our]t Rd (2) 2d   Dinner 1/2   Hair cut &
washed 1/–

> The German lessons were actually taught by P. Drabig. ▪ Horace Headlam was
> brother-in-law of Else Sonntag, who had married James Headlam.

4 *Fabian Publishing Committee. 17.30. Call on Brocklehurst at Demo-cratic Club after Committee—he lectures on the Labour Church with Tillett in the chair.*

Still struggling with the manifesto. Went into the park after dinner with the play in my pocket; but I finished reading the first volume of Buckle and did no writing. Heavy shower, which I stood out under a tree. After the Com-mittee, went to Gatti's with Olivier. Then on to see Brocklehurst at the Democratic Club. I stayed for the lecture and spoke.

Chronicle 1d   Dinner 1/3?   Bus to Mornington Crescent 2d   Bus Grafton St to Endell St corner 1d   Omelette &c at Gatti & Rodesano's 1/6   Bound set of Fabian tracts 3/6   Collection for miners at Dem-[ocratic] Club 2/–

Fred Brocklehurst of Manchester was secretary of the Labour Church Union and financial secretary of the National Independent Labour Party. ■ H. T. Buckle, *History of Civilisation in England* (London, 1837–61).

5 Got up early as usual, and did a long morning's work at the manifesto, which I at last got together in the form I proposed for the *Fortnightly* article. I took a turn on Primrose Hill and did a wee bit of work on the play. After dinner I went out to FE. We took a walk from Kew Bridge through Brentford, where we met Beatty. We walked by way of Isleworth and St. Margaret's to Richmond, where we sat on the Terrace for a while before catching the 19.40 train to Ravenscourt Park.

Bus along Tott[enham] C[our]t Rd 1d   Dinner 1/3?   Bus to Uxbridge Rd station 4d   Tram to Kew Bridge (2) 4d   Caramels 3½d   Train Richmond to Ravenscourt Park 1/2   Shep[herds] Bush to Portland Rd 6d

6 *Fabian Executive. 17½. Committee. 16½. German lesson at Buckland Cres-cent. 11.15.*

Got up early as usual, but did not get any work done before going off to Hampstead. May walked back with me to the Hygeian, Drabig coming with us as far as the corner of Great Russell St. Came home after dinner for a while, and read a lot of letters that had come, notably one from JP. After the Executive, Olivier and Miss Cameron and I went to Gatti's to eat. I then went off to call on the Charringtons, amusing myself on the way by com-posing a rhyme to put into a copy of *The Quintessence of Ibsenism* which I was bringing to Janet. But they were out; so I left the book and came home.

Dinner 1/4   Bus to Grafton St 1d   to Endell St 1d   Omelette &c at Gatti's 1/6   Bus to Queen's Elm 2d   Train Gloster Rd to Portl[an]d Rd 4d

The lines for Janet Achurch's copy of *Quintessence*, unusually sentimental for Shaw, are in *CL*. The book was written, he suggested, "To keep me in your mind."

7 *New Gilbert-Sullivan Opera at the Savoy. Utopia. 20.15. Webbs'. 17½, to read manifesto in its* Fortnightly *form.*

Made a beginning for the *World* article. After dinner, which I took early, went to Primrose Hill, where I was accosted by—I cannot remember his name—and went with him to the top of the hill, where we sat talking under our umbrellas during a heavy shower. When I came back I changed my clothes and stayed at home until it was time to dress for the theatre.

Dinner 1/3?   Bus to Britannia 2d   Cab to Webb's 2/–   Tip at theatre to a man who called me a cab for Mrs. J[ustin] H. McCarthy 6d

> Reviewed on 11 October 1893 (C974). *Utopia (Limited); or, The Flowers of Progress* marked the return of the partners, and G.B.S. gave it a warm welcome, with such words as "unhackneyed," "charmingly humorous," and "exquisite." The comic opera about the Anglicization of Utopia would run for 245 performances.

8 SUNDAY *Lecture at the Hatcham Liberal Club on "The Next General Election." 20.15. (J. Matthews, Hatcham Liberal Club, Portland House, New Cross Rd. S.E.). Tea at Archer's, 18, to meet Robertson and his wife.*

Bungled a good deal over the *World* article and eventually did not get it finished. Archer called, and I went for a walk in the park with him. We met Wallas and Bradlaugh on the way. Worked a little at the play in the train on my way to the lecture.

Train Ch[arin]g + to New + & back 9d

> This was possibly the actor Ian Robertson, brother of Johnston Forbes Robertson, for whom the dual name was always used. Ian Robertson's wife, Gertrude, was the daughter of critic Joseph Knight.

9 Finished the *World* article. Disturbed by calls from Tocchatti, who is going to start another Socialist paper and wants an article, and from one of *The Star* men, who wanted to know where he could see the picture of Doré's which I had suggested might be applied to the case of Tom Mann. At last I got it finished though not until about 1, and went off for a walk through the park (after dining at the café) to the Primrose Hill. I returned home before going to the *World* printers to correct the proof. From Spottiswoode's I went on to London Bridge, where I took the 17.8 train to Oxted to see the Salts. Mrs. Adams was there. I came back by the 21.22 train.

Expressing *World* article to Spottiswoode's 6d   Telegram to Leeds 7d
Papers 1d   Dinner at Isotta's 1/7   Train to Farringdon 3½d   Train London Bridge to Oxted & back 3/2   Moorgate to P[or]tl[an]d Rd 4d

> Tochatti's paper would be called *Liberty*. See 29 November 1893. ▪ The Doré drawing appears unidentifiable.

10 *New comic opera. Little Christopher Columbus by Caryll, Sims and Raleigh at the Lyric Theatre. 20. German lessons, 55 Buckland Crescent, 11.15.*

Worked at the play in the morning before starting for Hampstead. May walked back with me and left me after dining with me at the Hygeian. I then took a bus out to Shepherd's Bush where I found FE unwell and sat with her for some time—until past 17 I think.

Bus along Tott[enham] C[ourt] Rd 1d   Dinner 1/8   Bus to Oxbridge
Rd 4d   Train Shep[herds] B[ush] to Portland Rd 6d

> Reviewed on 18 October 1893 (C975). G.B.S. found the work "utterly beneath serious criticism." It ran, however, for 356 performances.

11 °*Fabian Publishing Committee. 17¼. Fabian Special Executive. 20. To consider manifesto. Charringtons at 15, to read* Mrs. Warren's Profession *to Mrs. Charrington.*

Found myself with a certain sense of having my lungs congested, possibly the effect of standing in my evening clothes talking to Thompson on Shaftesbury Ave. last night. I began the *World* article and then, as the day was wet, sang for more than an hour, chiefly *Tannhauser* and *The Flying Dutchman.* I have an idea that the way in which I have been compelled to discontinue singing for the past year or so by the pressure on my time is making my lungs less robust than they were. So I shall try and sing a little every day if I can. Then wrote up this diary. The day became very wet: it rained steadily and heavily all the afternoon and evening. I read the two acts of the play to Janet.

Dinner at Isotta's 1/6   German lessons, remitted Drabig 63/–   cost of orders 5½d   *PMG & Sun* 1½d   Train to Gloster Rd 4d   Gloster Rd to Temple 4½d

12 Added a little to the *World* article and wrote some letters, especially one to Mrs. Theodore Wright asking her to let me read her the play with a view of her taking one of the parts. After dinner went off to FE, but she was not at home; so I went on to Richmond and walked across the park to the Roehampton Gate, and thence to Barnes station, where I took train to Waterloo. Spent the evening at home writing a tremendous lot of letters.

> Slivinski "threw away an opportunity by playing the Saint-Saëns concerto in G Minor. . . . He made an attempt to treat it seriously, with the result that it became very dull . . ." (C975). ■ William Wallace (1860–1940) wrote the orchestral prelude to *The Eumenides* of Aeschylus, to be performed at the next Crystal Palace concert, about which G.B.S. would write on 25 October 1893 (C976), "it shewed that Mr. Wallace knows how to use every instrument except the scissors."

13 *Fabian Private Business Meeting. Barnard's Inn. 20. To pass manifesto (*Fortnightly *article), Burns's "Unemployed" article, and Eight Hours Tract (Macrosty). Also Williams's Resolution re Joint Committee. German lesson at Mrs. Edwards's. 11.15.*

Worked at revise of manifesto proof before going to Hampstead and after dinner. Mamie O'Byrne called with her daughter en route to Blois, where the daughter is going to school. Wallas walked home from the Fabian, where I read the manifesto to the meeting.

Bus along Tott[enham] C[our]t Rd 1d   Dinner 1/6?   Bus to Grafton St
1d   Cab to Fabian 2/–   Omelette &c at G[atti] & R[odesano]'s 1/6
Paid Pease for copies of Costello's tract for myself & Leonard Hall 7d

For the fate of Ernest E. Williams's resolution, see 10 November 1893.

14   *Crystal Palace Concert, first of the season, 15. Slivinski. Opening of the
Princess's Theatre by [John] Hollingshead at reduced prices. Opera—Mi-
ami. Put off.* °A *Gaiety Girl at the Prince of Wales Theatre. 20½. Return of
Hayden Coffin. Transferred to Archer. Webbs' at 19½.*

Worked at the *World* article and wrote a letter to Archer, besides writing up
this diary. Wallace, the musician (not Graham), introduced himself to me
at Victoria, and we sat out the concert together. It gave me a headache.
Came back by the 16.55 train, too soon to go to Webbs'. Dawdled in a
confectioner's for a while over some chocolate. Rather wet unpleasant evening. Olivier was at Grosvenor Rd. Wallas walked home with me.

Dinner 1/1   Bus to St Martin's Ch[urch] 1d   Train Ch[arin]g + to
Victoria 2½d?   Victoria to C[rystal] Pal[ace] 2/–   Papers 3d   Chocolate & cake in Victoria St[ation] 6d   Tram along Vauxhall B[ri]dge Rd ½d

15 SUNDAY   *Lecture at the Lee and Lewisham Liberal and Radical Club,
170 High St., Lewisham S.E., "Political Organization of Labour." 20. Tea at
Blands' en route. Speak in Hyde Park, Platform 12. Demonstration in behalf of the coal miners on strike. 16.*

Finished *World* article. Did a bit of work at the play. Left the park before
17. Steele called at the Blands' for me and took me to the Club. The party at
Blands' was Kentish Moore, Adkin and his wife, and the household as usual.

Train Ch[arin]g + to Blackheath & back (from Lewisham) 1/4   *Sketch*
6d   Taffy 1d

16   *Go to* The Mascotte *at the Criterion. 20.15.*

Corrected proof of Fabian manifesto for *Fortnightly*—5 hours' work. Intended to go to the Museum to get a quotation for it; but I did not get there
until about 16; so I did not go in; concluding that the newspaper room
would be closed at 16. I went to the office of *The [Fortnightly] Review* and
had an interview with Frank Harris, whom I had not met before. Then
went to the Fabian office and from that to the Orange Grove to get my first
meal since breakfast, meeting Mrs. Adams on the way. In the morning I
had been delayed in getting to work by having to answer a letter from
Walter [Gurly] about her. I sat at the Orange Grove a pretty long time
reading the papers; then had a wash and strolled about the Mall writing a
play under the lamps until it was time to go to the theatre.

Sun & Star 1d   *Life of Barry Sullivan* by Lawrence 1/–   Dinner at
Orange Grove 1/10

The revival of Edmond Audran's light opera had just transferred from the Gaiety to the Criterion, where it continued its run of fifty-six performances. Florence St. John (1855–1912) as leading lady "still keeps it going with ease, though from the middle of the last act onwards it is as crazy a piece of dramatic botchwork as . . . human intelligence could desire" (C976). ▪ Uncle Walter was intensely curious about the young, beautiful, and recently widowed Mrs. Francis Adams, who seemed to turn up in Shaw's path with some frequency. ▪ The play written in Monmouthshire fields and London streets was *Mrs Warren's Profession*. He was still two weeks from completion of a draft of the third act. ▪ (Thomas) Barry Sullivan (1821–1891) was the first major actor Shaw had seen as a boy in Dublin. He was often seen in Shakespeare, and had made his last stage appearance in 1887 as Richard III in Liverpool.

17 °*Mrs. Jopling-Rowe's, 3 Pembrook Rd., Kensington, at 15, to sit for portrait. Put off to Thursday. German lesson. 11.15.*

Worked at the play in the morning. In the afternoon it became very wet and May and I came back from Hampstead by train and dined together at the café at Portland Rd. Then she left me to go into the City and I came back here and sang a little before going to Hammersmith—also wrote up this diary. It was so very wet that we could not go out. I read a poem out of *The Earthly Paradise* to her—that about the king who had to spend the day as a beggar.

Review of Reviews 6d   Train Swiss Cott[age] to P[or]tl[an]d Rd 4d
Dinner at Gatti's 1/8

18 *Fabian Publishing Committee. 17¼. Fabian "Bee" for sorting papers, pamphlets, etc. 20.*

Began *World* article; then went out into the park and sat on Primrose Hill for some time working at the play but not getting on as well as I had expected to. Came back here after dinner and amused myself for a while by touching up a scrap of music I had composed and which I found by accident. Wrote a letter or two and went off to the Fabian, late—did not get there until 18. Left with Wallas and parted from him at Charing Cross. I went to the Orange Grove and found Olivier and his wife there. We were joined presently by Hilda Cox. I went back to the Fabian. While we were there an angry letter came from Massingham resigning membership on account of the Manifesto. I went home to write to him and found another letter of the same sort waiting for me. Wrote him a letter.

Papers 1d   Bus along Tott[enham] C[our]t Rd 1d   Dinner 1/1   Bus
to Endell St 1d   Omelette &c at Orange Grove 1/8

19 *See last Tuesday—Mrs. Jop. Go to* Miami *at the Princess's Theatre.*

Revised proof—or rather revise—of the Manifesto. This took me until past 12. Very sick of it. Wrote to Webb about it. In the afternoon went to Kensington for the portrait—a pastel head—carrying the clothes Mrs. Jopling-Rowe asked me to wear in my portmanteau.

Dinner 1/3?   Bus to Grafton St 1d   Papers 1d?   Train to High St &
back 9d   Cab High St to Pembroke Rd 1/3   Princess' Theatre 3/–

> G.B.S. (C976) hoped there was room in London for the "Volkstheater" concept of ticket
> prices launched by playwright-manager John Hollingshead (1827–1904) with his melo-
> dramatic musical play *Miami*. The "opera," with music by J. Haydn Parry, adapted from
> the creaky melodrama *The Green Bushes* of J. B. Buckstone (1802–1879), would, however,
> run only twelve performances, as it represented the "extraordinary freak of combining the
> most advanced arrangements before the curtain with an attempt to revive the Crummles
> repertory behind it."

20 *Take the chair for Mrs. Mallet at the Humanitarian League, 32 Sackville St. W., 20. "Dangerous Trades." °Fabian Executive. 17½. Committee.
16½. German lesson. 11.15.*

Worked at *World* article. May walked back from Hampstead with me.
Came back here after dinner and, after reading a bit and taking a nap,
went at the *World* article again, to such purpose that I quite forgot the
Executive. Made a speech in the chair at Mrs. Mallet's meeting. The Salts
were there. I walked with them as far as the corner of Regents Park Rd.,
[Leo Chiozza] Money coming with us a little way up the side of the park.

Dinner 1/3?   Bus to Grafton St 1d   Papers ? 1d   Bus to Vigo St 1d

21 *Crystal Palace Concert. 15. Frida Scotta, Emma Juch, Bispham.*

Worked at *World* article. Went to the Fabian office to see what had been
done yesterday. The Sonntags came down to the concert. FE was with me;
but I traveled 2d class with the Sonntags and left her by herself on the
journey down. On our way back we walked from Victoria to South Kensington, where we had a meal, and then to Earl's Court.

Dinner at Orange Grove 1/1?   Papers 3d   Train Ch[arin]g + to
Vict[oria] 1½d   Vict[oria] to Palace (2) ret[ur]n 4/–   Grub at South
Kensington (2) 3/4   Train Earls Court to Rav[enscour]t P[ar]k (2) 6d
Train Shep[herds] B[ush] to P[or]tl[an]d Rd 6d

> Frida Scotta, violinist, "failed to interest" G.B.S. (C976) despite her technical skill, because
> she played the highly derivative Saint-Saëns violin concerto in B minor. Emma Juch was
> "a highly cultivated singer," while David Bispham "was completely victorious." Manns
> and his orchestra "covered themselves with glory in Schumann's first symphony."

22 SUNDAY *Lecture at the Washington Music Hall, Battersea, on "Labour
at the Next General Election." (W. F. Champion, 39 Kingsley St., Battersea,
S. W.).*

Finished the *World* article. It was too wet to go out; though it stopped
raining in the evening. After dinner I read the papers and dozed. The
lecture came off rather well. My chairman traveled back with me as far as
[ ]. I met Johnson & the family of Massingham in the train from Charing
Cross to Victoria.

Train Ch[arin]g + to Vict[oria] 1½d   Vict[oria] to Battersea 1d   back
1d

23 *Mrs. Jopling's 14.45.*

Worked at the 3rd act of the play. I went out before 1 to Jaeger's where they
had nothing that I wanted to get. I strolled about the west end of Oxford St.
looking for a vegetarian restaurant, and at last found one after going to the
Marble Arch and returning on a bus in my search. I walked across to Mrs.
Jopling's and back except for brief bus rides. In the evening I worked here at
the play alone. Maggie Gardner called for a few minutes, but went away on
finding my mother not here.

Bus back along Oxford St 1d   Dinner at "Grosvenor" 1/2   Bus along
High St to Earls C[our]t Rd 1d   Bus Marble Arch to [Oxford] O 1d
Papers 2d

24 *German lesson. 11.15. Hampstead.*

Had to go by train to Hampstead as the copying out of an exercise kept me
until it was too late to walk. In the afternoon stayed at home and worked at
the play. Got the third act finished and brought it over to Charringtons' to
read to them.

Train to Swiss Cottage 2d   Bus along Tott[enham] C[our]t Rd & back
2d   Dinner 1/7   Train to Gloster Rd 3d   High St to P[or]tl[an]d
3d   Papers 2d

25 *Fabian Publishing Committee. 17¼. Leave MS of F[rancis] Adams's Ti-*
berius at the Democratic Club for Mrs. Adams. Dress rehearsal, A Question
of Memory at the Opera Comique, Independent Theatre. 14.

I forget what I did in the morning. As JP was coming here I had to keep out
of the way all the evening. Pease took the MS to the Democratic Club for
me. I was at the Opera Comique for a long time, the rehearsal being very
tedious. After a meal at the Orange Grove I was quite at a loss what to do
with myself. Finally I went to Terry's Theatre to see a play called *The*
American Bride with Miss Janet Steer, Jimmy Welch, etc. Came away at the
end of the second act.

Dinner ?   Orange Grove ?   Terry's Theatre 2/6   program 3d

Mrs. Adams was seeking someone to edit for publication her late husband's verse
drama. Eventually the task would be undertaken by William Michael Rossetti. Perhaps
one aspect of the future *Doctor's Dilemma* was already beginning to incubate here: the
personable, tubercular artist (here a poet) whose work—questionable in value—will be
posthumously promoted by a beautiful, loyal young widow in whose matrimonial
prospects the professional men around her dying husband are interested. (Shaw had
already visited the setting-to-be—the Star and Garter in Richmond.) A dozen years

would pass before the conscious impetus to the play would come through Shaw's friendship with research physician Almroth Wright, who was working on a possible cure for tuberculosis. ▪ *A Question of Memory*, by "Michael Field" (Katherine Harris Bradley and Edith Emma Cooper), would have only one performance. ▪ *The American Bride*, by "Lawrence Olde" (Sir William Young) and Maurice Noel, had opened on 11 October and would have twenty-four performances. James Welch had played for Shaw in *Widowers' Houses*. Janet(te) Steer was in the role of Stella Durand, the "American bride."

26 *Mrs. Jopling-Rowe's. 14.45.*

Began *World* article. Went into the park and worked a little at the play. Dined at Hampstead, where I met Drabig, who came into the restaurant as I was eating. Went to Earl's Court by train from Finchley Rd. Spent the evening here, singing and writing letters.

Eggs &c at Hampstead 1/1?   Train Finchley Rd to Earls Court 6d?
Pall Mall Budget & Gazette 7d   Train Bayswater to P[or]tl[an]d Rd 3½d

27 *Fabian Members' Meeting at Barnard's Inn. Introductory lecture to series "Implications of Collectivism" by Hubert Bland. 20. Fabian Executive. 17¼. Committee. 16½. German lesson. 11.15. °Press View. Dowdeswell's. Max Lundley's Thames water colours.*

Got nothing done in the morning except a scrap of *World* article and sending off the *Quintessence* to Mrs. Jop[ling]. Was so late that I had to go to Hampstead by train. Walked back alone by way of Avenue Rd. I found May at the restaurant; she came here on her way to Macdonald's. I dawdled about over some photographs before going to the Executive. Wallas walked home with me remonstrating with me as to my intention of pitching hard into Massingham for his desertion of us over the Manifesto, as I conceived it necessary to do as a matter of policy.

Postage "Quintessence" to Mrs. [Louise] Jop[ling-Rowe] 3d   Train to Swiss Cott[age] 2d

28 *°Crystal Palace Concert. Meisslinger. Janotha. Hiles's concert. Overture of Youth. 15. Webbs's in the evening. 19½. Saturday Popular Concert. 15. St. James's Hall.*

Worked at *World* article. Managed to get a little more done on my return from the concert before going to Webbs'. Wallas, very tired, came back with me, but got off the bus at Great Russell St. I also was tired—how much, I didn't realize until after Sunday's work.

Dinner 1/6?   Papers 2d?   Bus to Picc[adilly] O 1d   Concert & program 1/6   Bus to West[minster] 2d   Back 2d

Saturday Pop reviewed on 1 November 1893 (C980). G.B.S. was pleased with the Brahms quartet in G minor, Op. 25, being always happier with Brahms's chamber music than his large-scale compositions.

29 SUNDAY *Go down to Crays and speak for the S. D. F. (J. Collingwood, 8 Broadway, Crays) at 11.30 and again at 19. Subjects "The Government and the Workers" and "Socialism, Old and New." Open air.*

Dined at the house of Gardiner. Finished and sent off *World* article after dinner. Then took a walk with the local men who kept me talking all the time. I was utterly exhausted when I got home.

Train to Aldgate 3d *Weekly Sun* 1d Train Fenchurch St to Crays & back 2/6 Moorgate to P[or]tl[an]d Rd 6d

> By "Crays" Shaw is referring to the communities south of Greenwich and along the River Cray, known as North Cray, Foots Cray, St. Mary Cray, and St. Paul's Cray.

30 *Mrs. W. K. Clifford's, 26 Colville Rd. W., at 16, to hear a light opera. Catarina by Ben-Tayoux.*

Still suffering from yesterday's excessive nervous work. Spent the morning reading the attacks in the papers on the Fabian Manifesto. As I was going out for a turn in the park a *Pall Mall* interviewer called and I dictated a longish interview to him. Then I walked up to the top of Primrose Hill, rather revived by this piece of fighting. At Mrs. Clifford's I made the acquaintance of the *PMG* musical critic, and was interviewed on the Manifesto in the hall by the editor of the *St. James Gazette*. I also had a long talk with Elizabeth Robins. On leaving at 18½ I went out to Shepherd's Bush to see FE but she was not at home; so after getting a meal at Hammersmith and coming back past her windows to see if by chance she had returned in the meantime, I came home and wrote a few cards before going to bed early.

Papers 5d Dinner 1/9 (Isotta's) Train to Westbourne P[ar]k 4d Westb[ourne] P[ar]k to Shep[herds] B[ush] 3d Omelette &c at Hammersmith 1/8 Train Shep[herds] B[ush] to P[or]tl[an]d Rd 6d

> The private concert at Lucy Clifford's home was not reviewed by G.B.S. Louis André Frédéric Ben-Tayoux, French composer of chamber pieces and songs, was often performed from 1872 through 1903, then faded from notice. ▪ "The Revolt of the Fabians: Interview with Mr. Bernard Shaw," *PMG*, 31 October 1893 (C977), on the small storm raised by the *Fortnightly* article ("To Your Tents, O Israel!") just published. ▪ "The Revolt of the Socialists: An Interview with Mr. Bernard Shaw," *St. James's Gazette*, 31 October 1893 (C977a).

31 °*Conference of Metropolitan MPs and others on the Unemployed, Mansion House, 15. German lesson. 11.15.*

Did a scrap of work on the play before going to Hampstead. May walked back with me. When I came back here after dinner I was captured by a *Pall Mall* artist to whom I had to sit for a sketch for *The Pall Mall Budget*. When he was gone I played for a while; then had tea and wrote up this diary.

Bus along Tott[enham] C[our]t Rd & back 1d Dinner 1/6?

> "Interview with Mr. Bernard Shaw" (with sketch of Shaw, seated), *Pall Mall Budget*, 2 November 1892 (NIL).

November

1 *Fabian Publishing Committee. 17$\frac{1}{2}$.*

I am writing this on the 13th November and can't be sure of what I did in the morning; but I think I must have worked at the play. After dinner I went into the British Museum and sat there beside Ashton Ellis, reading Molière until it was time to go to the Fabian. Olivier and Hilda Cox were at the Orange Grove afterwards. I think it likely that I spent this evening and last at home; but I have no exact recollection.

Dinner 1/6?   Orange Grove, omelette &c 1/6?

2 *Mrs. Jopling's. 14.30. Royal Choral Society. Berlioz's Faust. Albert Hall. 20.*

Finished the play. Mrs. Jopling's brother turned up at the Albert Hall—I gave her the spare ticket.

Dinner at Isotta's 1/6?   Train to Earl's Court & back ?   *Pall Mall Budget* 6d   Train to High St?

> Reviewed on 8 November 1893 (C981). The performance of the "sulphurous" work, by Sir Joseph Barnby's chorus, was "dull and suburban." ■ The dated conclusion to Mrs Warren's Profession is followed in the manuscript notebook by four undated pages labeled "New Ending to the third act from Crofts' exit."

3 *Fabian Executive. 17$\frac{1}{2}$. Committee. 16$\frac{1}{4}$. °Fabian School Board Committee Meeting. 276 Strand. 20. °Westminster Orchestral Society, Phonograph lecture on Brass etc. by Blaikley, Westminster Town Hall. 20. German lesson. 11$\frac{1}{2}$ to 1$\frac{1}{2}$.*

Worked at *World* article morning and afternoon if I recollect aright. Went to Charringtons in the evening and read then the last act of the play. Miss [Beatrice] Cameron and her sister [Mary] were at Gatti's after the Executive with us.

Train to Swiss Cottage 2d   Bus along Tott[enham] C[our]t Rd & back 2d   Dinner 1/6?   Buses to [Fabian] Exec. ? say 1d   Omelette &c at Gatti's and R's 1/6   Bus Ch[arin]g + to Beaufort St 2d   Train Gloster Rd to P[or]tl[an]d Rd 4d

4 *Crystal Palace Concert. Cowen's* Water Lily *15. Webbs'. 19$\frac{1}{2}$.*

Working at *World* article. Missed the 14.18 train to the Palace—went on by the next. After the concert went into the Reading Room and killed time there. Came back by the 18.10 train. Wallas walked most of the way home with me from Webbs'.

Dinner 1/6?   Papers 2d?   Train Ch[arin]g + to Vict[oria] 1d Vict[oria] to Pal[ace] 2/–   Reading room 2d   Chocolate at A[erated] B[read] shop at Victoria 5d   Tram along Vauxhall B[rid]ge Rd $\frac{1}{2}$d

Frederic Cowen's Norwich Festival cantata had a libretto of "Christmas card" vapidity (C981) by Joseph Bennett and "little harmonic sweetmeats" by the composer, who had produced "a hopelessly obsolete thing."

5 SUNDAY *Dine with Massingham at 14. °Lecture at the Tottenham Liberal and Radical Club, Bruce Grove, on "The Evolution of Labour Politics." (George Brown). Put off. Clement Scott lectures for The Playgoers' Club on "Dramatic Free Trade in England and America" at St. James's Restaurant Banqueting Room. 20.*

Finished *World* article. Spoke at the Playgoers' Club.

Train Victoria to Wandsworth Common & back from Clapham Junction 9d   *Weekly Sun* 1d

6 *London Liberal and Radical Union Council Meeting. National Liberal Club. 20.*

As far as I remember I spent the morning writing letters. In the afternoon I called on Archer, who had, I found, already called on me. We sat talking and finally I read him an act and a half of the play at his request. After tea I went off to the meeting, where I spoke recklessly, without tact or temper, and probably did more harm than good.

Dinner 1/6?   Papers 2d?   Bus Russell Sq to St Martin's Lane 1d

7 *°G. Spiller on "Shawism or Ibsenism" at Youen's Assembly Rooms, Cottage Grove, Grove Rd., Mile End Rd., at 20. East London Ethical Society. German lesson. Hampstead. 11.15.*

Did not attempt to do any work. FE had written to me to say that she had been offered £500 to produce Ibsen's *Wild Duck*, so I went over to her from Hampstead, May coming with me as far as Young's Corner. We forgot to get out of the train at South Action and went on to Gunnersbury. At about 18 FE and I went out for a short walk.

Train Baker St to Swiss Cott[age] 1d   Restaurant at Hampstead, lunch (2) 1/9   Train Finchley Rd to Hammersmith (2) 1/4   Excess fares at Gunnersbury (2) 4d   Tram to Young's Corner (2) May paid.   Train Shep[herds] Bush to P[or]tl[and] Rd 6d

8 *London Symphony Concert. St. James's Hall 20½. Parsifal Garden Music, etc. °Fabian Publishing Committee. 17¼.*

Worked all the morning revising proof of Fabian Eight Hours Tract. After a light lunch of fruit etc. I set to work on an unpremeditated reply to the critics of the Fabian Manifesto in the form of an "open letter" to T. P. O'Connor. This took so long that I did not succeed in getting to the Publishing Committee. The Webbs were at the concert. I went with them to their bus at Piccadilly Circus afterwards. The concert began at 20. I did not know this, and spent some time between 20 and 20½ strolling on the Mall in St. James's Park putting in little bits of work at the play.

Table d'hote at Orange Grove 1/10   Papers 2d?

> The London Symphony concert, except for the opening, which Shaw missed, was re-
> viewed on 15 November 1893 (C983). George Henschel conducted; Frida Scotta and
> Plunket Greene were soloists. The major work was the vigorously played Brahms first
> symphony, "magnificent lumps . . . of absolute music," smothered with "mere slag." ▪
> "The Fabian Manifesto" (open letter to T. P. O'Connor) appeared in *The Sun* on 13
> November 1893 (C982). ▪ G.B.S. would make a point in his review that the London
> Symphony tickets had 8:30 printed on them, causing many to miss the opening.

9   Madame Favart *at the Criterion. Tea with Archer. 18.*

Began *World* article, and got along well enough to be able to send off two-thirds of it. Did not go out in the middle of the day but ate some fruit etc. here. Went out between 16 and 17 and had a meal at the Hygeian before going to Archer, to whom I read the 2nd act of the play and the 3rd act. When I got back from the theatre I found a proof of the *Sun* "open letter" waiting for me; and I sat up until past midnight revising it.

Dinner 1/1?   Bus Russell Sq to Criterion 2d

> *Madame Favart*, a Jacques Offenbach opera first performed in Paris in 1878, had lost its
> effervescence in Charles Wyndham's limp revival (C983).

10   Fabian Executive. *17½. Committee. 16½. Fabian Private Meeting. Barnard's Inn. 20. Williams's Resolution* re *Joint Committee. Move Amendment.
Eight Hours Tract (Macrosty). German lesson 11½. Hampstead.*

Walked over to Hampstead. No time to get anything done before I went out as I was up rather late after last night. May walked back with me. After dinner worked at Fabian business—amending circular *re* Manifesto, prepar-ing speech for tonight, etc. Also wrote several letters, notably to Cunning-hame Graham about last Monday's meeting. Did not get to the Executive until 17.30. When it was over I went off to the Orange Grove and had a meal by myself. All the old gang spoke in the debate on Williams's Resolu-tion and we won by 42 votes to 14. Walked home alone.

Paper ½d   Bus along Tott[enham] C[our]t Rd 1d   Dinner 1/1   Bus
to Endell St 1d   Omelette &c at Orange Grove 1/8

> Shaw's amendment, carried overwhelmingly, would end Fabian participation in the Joint
> Committee of Socialist Bodies, in which the Fabians represented the most conservative
> end of the political spectrum.

11   Crystal Palace Concert. *15. Granville Bantock's* Fire Worshippers *Overture. Beatrice Langley (violinist). Webbs' (Junta dinner). 19½.* °*Private View.
Arthur Tonson's cat pictures at Van Wisselingh's, 14 Brook St. W.*

Finished *World* article. Came back from Palace by the 18.10 train and walked to Webbs'. Wallas walked home with me from Grosvenor Rd. We did not work in the evening.

Dinner 1/1   Bus along Ch[arin]g + Rd 1d   Papers 2d   Railway
Tickets at Palace 16/–   Ch[arin]g + to Vict[oria] 1½d   Train Vict[oria]
to Pal[ace] & back 2/–   Reading Room at Pal[a]ce 2d   Burnt almonds
3d

> Reviewed on 22 November 1893 (C984). Beatrice Langley's "quick and delicate musical feeling" in the Bruch violin concerto won G.B.S.'s praise, but he wondered whether youthful female violinists were current sex symbols receiving concert precedence over males of equal or superior technical endowment. The overture of (Sir) Granville Bantock (1868–1946), then a young composer and conductor, was "pure Mendelssohn." To G.B.S. the gem of the program was the underrated symphony by Hermann Goetz, "the only real symphony that has been composed since Beethoven died."

12 SUNDAY *Lecture for the S. D. F. at the Clarendon Coffee House, North Kensington, on "Old and New Socialism" (G. W. Spry, 31 Rackham Rd., North Kensington). 20. Dine with the Theodore Wrights at Clapham at 14. Read Mrs. Warren's Profession to them. 13.20 from Victoria. L. C. and D.*

Corrected *World* proof. Only got as far as the middle of the 3rd act of the play at the Wrights', as some people called and interrupted us. I rushed home and got something to eat before going to the lecture. Did not get to bed until after 1, as I had to sit up and write a few letters.

Train Victoria to Clapham & back 4d   *Weekly Sun* (2) 2d   Train
Vic[toria] to Portland Rd 6d   P[or]tl[an]d Rd to Latimer Rd & back
(from Nott[ing] Hill) 6d

> The L. C. and D. was the London, Chatham & Dover Railway to the south of England.

13 *"Second edition" of* Morocco Bound, *Shaftesbury Theatre.* °Leighton *and Hall concert. Prince's Hall. 20.* °Liberal and Radical Union, adjourned Council Meeting. 20.*

Not up until 10 in consequence of late going to bed last night. Set to work to write up this diary, which has fallen frightfully into arrear. Got through it and through a heap of correspondence about 15½, when I went off and had dinner. Then I went on to Archer. I had tea with him and read him the 3rd act of the play.

Dinner 1/6   Papers 2d   Program at theatre 6d

> The very successful *Morocco Bound*, a musical comedy by F. Osmond Carr (1858–1916), with libretto by Arthur Branscombe (?–1924) and lyrics by Adrian Ross (1859–1933), would transfer to the Trafalgar Theatre and run for 295 performances. G.B.S. (C984) found it "not bad fun" despite a "tedious, inept, unpardonable" plot.

14 *German lesson. 11.*

Very nasty day—dreadful fog. Walked to Hampstead and back, alone both ways. After dinner came and read and dozed for a while over the piano. At 16½ got to work at my letters which are still unfinished. But I did very little, wasting a lot of time in drafting a letter to T. P. O'Connor which I at last thought better of, and spending some time at the piano. It was a very wet night; but I went off to FE's at 21. She was not at home when I arrived, but came in within ten minutes.

Papers 1d   Dinner 1/6   Train to Shep[herds] B[ush] & back 1/–

15 *Lecture at the Chelsea Town Hall for the London Reform Union on "How to make London Businesslike." (Frederick Whelen, 59 Rossetti Mansions, Chelsea S.W.). Fabian Publishing Committee. 17$\frac{1}{2}$.*

Wrote an article on barrel organs for *The Morning Leader*, which has been pressing me to do something for their double number. Ulrich Just called on me. I stayed working at the article and at some Fabian matters until past 16. I walked straight down to the office except that I went into the Aerated Bread Shop close by in the Strand to get a glass of milk and a cake before going in. After the lecture I walked to Cheyne Walk with Bertha Newcombe.

Milk & cake 3$\frac{1}{2}$d   *Speaker* 6d   *Rev[iew] of Reviews* 6d   Papers 1d   Omelette &c at Orange Grove 1/8   Train St Ja[me]s's Pk to Sloane Sq 1$\frac{1}{2}$d   S[ou]th Kensington to P[or]tl[an]d Rd 4d   Sweets 1d

Frederick Whelen (1867–1955), who became a Fabian in 1892, was a political lecturer and writer who in 1898 would found the Incorporated Stage Society. ▪ "The Barrel-Organ Question," *The Morning Leader*, 27 November 1893 (C985), signed Corno di Bassetto. A reminiscence on street musicians, deploring their decline in quality. ▪ The Fabian Ulrich Just, brother of Colonial Office civil servant Hartmann W. Just, lived at 46 St. Michael's Hill, Bristol.

16 °*Lecture for the London Reform Union, Chelsea, on "How to Make London Businesslike" (F. Whelen, 59 Rossetti Mansions, S.W.). Changed to 15th.*

Began *World* article. After dinner went out to FE. We went for a short walk before tea. She read me some of her novel.

Papers 1d?   Dinner 1/6?   Train Ch[arin]g + to Rav[enscourt] P[ar]k 6d   Sh[epherds] B[ush] to P[or]tl[an]d Rd 6d

17 *Fabian Public Meeting at Essex Hall. Mrs. Sidney Webb on "Trade Unionism: its Past and Future." 20. German lesson. 11. Fabian Executive. 17$\frac{1}{2}$. °Fabian Preliminary Committee. 16$\frac{1}{2}$.*

Up too late to do any work before going out. Had to take train to Hampstead. May walked back with me. After dinner I corrected and sent off what I did yesterday of *World* article, but did not add to it. Was late at the Executive. Wrote some letters. Tillett took the chair at the Fabian. After the Executive I went to Reeves to buy *The Labour Elector* and *The Free Review*, and then went to Gatti and Rodesano's to join Bland. Mrs. Bland joined her later on, with another lady whose name I forget. [Arthur] Griffiths also came afterwards. Wallas walked home with me.

Train to Swiss Cottage 2d   Paper $\frac{1}{2}$d   Bus along Tott[enham] C[our]t Rd May paid.   Dinner 1/6   Bus to Endell St 1d   *Free Review* 10d   *Labour Elector* (2) 2d   Omelette &c at Gatti's 1/6   *Justice* 1d

18 *Crystal Palace Concert. 15. C. H. Couldery's* Candle Song for Orchestra. *Soloti (pianist). Berlioz's* Harold.

Finished *World* article. Came back from Palace by the 17.30 train, and got to Webb's at 18.30. Vile weather—snowstorm. Walked home alone, sending cab from Westminster for Wallas.

Papers 1d   *Today* 2d   Dinner 1/2   Train Ch[arin]g + to Vict[oria] 1½d   Wash at Palace 2d   Tram along Vauxhall Br[idge] Rd ½d

> Although Shaw attended, he published no review. He found the music of C. H. Couldery lacking in originality; and on the one occasion that he noticed a Couldery composition (14 February 1890), he pointedly omitted the composer's name. ▪ Alexander Soloti (1863–1945), Russian pianist, until 1890 had been a professor at the Moscow Conservatory of Music.

19 SUNDAY *Lecture at the West Norwood Reform Club, Auckland Hill, S. D. F. on "Socialism, Old and New" (F. Elliott), West Norwood station. London, Brighton and South Coast. 20½.*

Corrected and sent off *World* article. Worked at the Fabian Manifesto—the draft for its re-issue as a tract. Read a good deal of Wagner's *Opera and Drama*. Benjamin Jones took the chair for me. Very bad weather.

Train to Victoria & back 1/–   Vict[oria] to West Norwood & back 1/3   Sweets 1d

20 *Sit for photograph* (Review of Reviews *portrait) at the Stereoscopic Co., 110 Regent St., 11. Monday Popular Concert. Neruda, etc. 20.*

After the photographing business came back here and worked away at the Fabian Manifesto all day. I do not distinctly recollect the afternoon; but I conclude that I went to the Orange Grove for a meal before I went to the concert.

Orange Grove 1/6?   Papers 1d?

> Shaw's and Webb's portraits appeared on the same page in the *Review of Reviews*, 1 December 1893. ▪ Reviewed on 6 December 1893 (C988). David Bispham was accompanied by Henry Bird, and was "tremendously applauded." Lady Hallé (Norman-Neruda) gave "an astonishingly able performance. . . ."

21 *Recital-lecture on Chopin, Mrs. Liebich, at 17 Stanley Crescent, Notting Hill. 15. German lesson. Hampstead. 11. Noel Home to call in the morning.*

Home called and walked across the park with me. He is full of the idea of syndicating a set of newspaper "London Letters," as I suggested to him. I did not get to Mrs. Edwards's until 10.30. After dinner, where I found May, though she did not walk back from the lesson with me, I went out to Notting Hill, and from that went on to FE's. I came back by the train about 18 and did a couple of hours work here on the Manifesto. Then I went to Charrington's for an hour, and talked over with him their scheme of doing a professional tour with FE on the strength of the money that has been promised to her for theatrical purposes. Before I went out in the morning I wrote some German for Drabig. Copied out a lot of German exercises in the train.

Papers 1d   Dinner 1/6   Bus to Nott[ing] Hill Gate 3d   Train Shep[herds] B[ush] to P[or]tl[an]d Rd 6d   P[or]tl[an]d Rd to Gloster Rd &c back 6d

> Louise (Mrs. Franz) Liebich delivered the lecture while her husband played the "illustra-tions." G.B.S. (C988) found the combination less than compelling.

22   *London Symphony Concert. St. James's Hall. 15. Fabian Publishing Committee. 17½.*

Worked at the Manifesto all day until it was time to go to the Fabian Committee. Lunched off some nuts etc. here. [Uncle] Walter came in for a while. Olivier went with me to the Orange Grove, where we found Mrs. Olivier and Hilda Cox.

Orange Grove 1/5   Papers 2d

> Reviewed on 29 November 1893 (C986). Paderewski was Henschel's featured artist, intro-ducing his own *Polish Fantasia* for piano and orchestra. Although he wrote for the orchestra "with excellent judgment, [he] shews the deafest partiality when he comes to write for the pianoforte. He cannot deny it a lion's share in all the good things, whether they suit it or not; and the result is that in most of the big climaxes he is making such a thundering noise that the audience cannot hear him and can only gaze raptly at the inspiring spectacle of his fists flying in the air as he trounces the keyboard."

23   *Armbruster lectures on "Two Remarkable Song Writers" at the London Institution. 17. Royal Choral Society—Israel in Egypt. Albert Hall. 20.*

Not up until 10. Began *World* article. Did not go out between 15 and 16. Walked to the London Institution. FE was at the Albert Hall. We left after "The Lord is a Man of War" and I put her into a bus and walked home. I wrote a letter to Janet Achurch about [Ibsen's] *The Vikings* before going to bed.

Milk, wheaten cake &c at Moorgate 4½d   Train Mansion Ho to Ch[arin]g + 2½d?   Papers 2d?   Orange Grove 1/6   Train St Ja[me]s's Park to South Kensington subway 4½d

> Armbruster, said G.B.S. (C988), "does for Bayreuth what our University Extension lectur-ers do for Oxford and Cambridge." On this occasion, however, assisted by soprano Pauline Cramer, he was lecturing on Karl Loewe and a contemporary German composer of songs, Hans Sommer. ▪ The Royal Choral Society of Sir Joseph Barnby "was much more at home with Handel that it had been at the previous concert with Berlioz" (C986). ▪ The letter to Janet Achurch dealt with her interest, and that of Florence Farr, in playing the lead in Ibsen's play. Shaw thought that FE had the greater claim.

24   *Fabian Executive. 17½. °Fabian Committee. 16½. Fabian Semi-Public Committee. Bernard's Inn. 20. Macrosty on "Limits of Collectivism in Pro-duction." German lesson. 11.*

As I was about to go out D. J. Nicoll, the Anarchist, called to ask could I get any work for him. He walked to Hampstead with me, telling me about his 18 months' imprisonment and his delusions about hearing voices, which he believes to be real. Walked back alone; but found May at the restaurant. I then went out to see FE and returned in time for the Executive. Wallas walked with me from the Fabian to Museum Chambers, where he went in to see the Hartleys.

Papers 1d   Train Ch[arin]g + to Rav[enscourt] Pk & back 9d   Excess to Temple 1½d   Omelette &c at G[atti] & R[odesano]'s 2/–

25 °*Crystal Palace Concert. 15. Klengel. Webbs', 19¼, to meet Sellicks.* °*Saturday Pop. Private View. New concert hall (Queen's Hall), Langham Place. 20 to 24.*

Finished and sent off *World* article. Then went to the Orange Grove and had something to eat. Then to Charringtons'. Charrington read me part of the first act of his play. As it was raining heavily I took a cab to the Webbs'. Mother in bed with a cold.

Papers 1½d   Dinner at Orange Gr[ove] 1/6   Train St Ja[me]s's Pk to Sloane Sq 2½d?   Bus to Beaufort St 1d   Cab Elm Pk to Webb's 2/6

> Alfred Sellicks (1845–1902) of Woolwich, a Socialist, was a member of the Amalgamated Society of Engineers; the Webbs were studying the spectrum of labor unions. ▪ Charrington's play was probably his *Sister Helen*.

26 SUNDAY *Lecture at the Hall of Science, Old St., at 11.15, on "Individualist Socialism" (Miss E. M. Vance, 28 Stonecutter St. E.C.).*

Had a long chat with Miss Vance in the Green Room about the stage. In the afternoon JP called ostensibly to cheer up Mother, who is still in bed with influenza. I went out to avoid her and called on Archer and on the Carrs, but they were both out. So I came back here and spent the evening in playing and in beginning a new play—a romantic one—for FE.

Train to Aldersgate 4d   Tracts at Hall of Science 6d   Tram Old St to Bloomsbury 1d (where we both ate. Then I came back and spent the evening playing and beginning a new play.)

> The play for FE, *Arms and the Man*, was begun without title or any firm idea of place for the action; the first words of the first act are "November 1885. Scene—a lady's bedchamber. . . ." The holograph notebook is BL Add. MS. 50601A. The romantic lead conceived for Florence bore little resemblance to her personality. ▪ Shaw's repetition is retained at the end of the day's expense listings.

27 *Monday Pop. Stanford's quartet. 20.* °*Amateur Orchestral Society, Smoking Concert, Queen's Hall. 21.*

Did a long day's work at the Manifesto and at a letter to *The Workman's Times* in reply to Burgess's attack. Did not go out until evening when I found myself rather out of sorts. I felt as if I had caught the influenza from

Mother. I had a bad night—delirious, rather. Between dinner and my evening meal I went out to Hammersmith and looked for FE, but as her windows were dark I did not go in.

Papers 2d?   Dinner 1/6?   Bus to Queen's Rd, Bayswater 2d   Train Rav[enscour]t Pk to Ch[arin]g + 6d   Omelette &c at Orange Grove 1/6?

Villiers Stanford's string quartet was "exceedingly clever: this I say in praise; for if I am to have scientific music, I had rather have it cleverly scientific than stupidly so." Further, said G.B.S. (C988), in a reference to Professor Stanford's origins, it could hardly have been "more creditable to the Irish intellect." ■ "The Fabian Panic," letter, signed, replying to the attack by "Autolycus" (Joseph Burgess) on the "To Your Tents" Fabian manifesto, *Workman's Times*, 2 December 1893 (C987). Fabians admitted to being clever people, said Shaw, and would not act stupidly merely to "make the donkeys in the [Socialist] movement more at home with us. . . ."

28   °*Ernest Fowles's pupils' concert. St. James's Banqueting Hall. 20.* °*Royal Society of Musicians. Elijah. St. James's Hall. 20. German lesson. Hampstead. 11.*

I find that the excellent early rising habits I established at the Argoed have by this time broken down. I was late to Hampstead. I lunched there and went right across to Hammersmith to FE's. Got to her house at 15, but she was not expected in for an hour; so I went into the park and sat there working at the new play until past 16, when I called again and found her at home. I stayed the rest of the evening. The attack of influenza, if it really was one, passed off.

Train to Swiss Cottage 2d   Dinner at Hampstead 1/1   Train Finchley Rd to Chiswick 8d   Papers 1d   Shep[herds] B[ush] to P[or]tl[an]d Rd 6d

29   *Fabian Publishing Committee. 17½. Go to Daly's Theatre in the evening. School for Scandal. Ada Rehan etc.*

Went at the Manifesto again and did as much as I thought there was any use in doing before the others have had a turn at it. Wrote an article for Tocchatti for his new paper *Liberty* which I promised him a long time ago, of which he has just reminded me by sending me a copy of the design for the front page. Did not go out until it was time for the Committee. In the evening went to Daly's Theatre to see the *School for Scandal*. Worked at the new play between the acts. On my way to the Committee I went round by Judd St. and left a copy of the *Fortnightly* article with Marriott.

Bus along Euston Rd to Judd St 1d   Dinner at Orange Grove 1/10 Papers 2d   Daly's theatre 2/6

The revival of Richard Brinsley Sheridan's 1777 play, "arranged" for performance by Augustin Daly, had opened on 13 November and would run until 30 December. ■ "Why I Am a Social-Democrat," *Liberty*, January 1894 (C993). Shaw admitted to not believing that Socialism would quickly bring any kind of millenium. Rather, it would have "for many a long day its prisons, its armies, its gallows, its humbugs, its intriguers, its selfishness and sloth . . . and its big talk and enthusiasm . . . , its helpless dependence upon a minority of able men, and its mass of people, capable of nothing but their immediate concerns, taking advantage of the higher wages, shorter hours and better education obtainable . . . without in the least understanding it."

30 *Mrs. Jopling's at 14½. Scotch National Concert. Albert Hall. 19.45.*

Began *World* article. From Mrs. Jopling's I went on to FE. We came into town together at about 20, she having to go to her Occult Society. I then came back here and worked further at the *World* article. On my way from Earl's Court to Hammersmith I called on Tocchatti and had a longish chat with him.

Dinner at Isotta's 1/8   Papers 2d   Train to Earls C[our]t, ret[urn], 9d   Train Shep[herds] B[ush] to Latimer Rd 2d   to P[or]tl[an]d Rd & back for FE 9d

Shaw's massive disinterest in Scottish music, predicated on what he had already been exposed to as a musical critic, again kept him from the Albert Hall. ▪ Tocchatti had just begun publishing *Liberty*, to which Shaw had contributed his far from starry-eyed picture of the growing pains of Socialism.

December

1 *Fabian Executive. 17¼. °Fabian Preliminary Committee. 16¼. Dinner at Webbs', 19½, to discuss re-issue draft of Manifesto. German lesson. °Fabian School Board Election Committee. 276 Strand. 20.*

Late at German lesson. Walked back alone. After dinner came back here and corrected *World* article etc. We got into rather an ardent discussion at Webbs', and did not leave until past 23. Wallas walked nearly but not quite home with me. His conscience is jibbing sorely at the rascalities, from the ideal point of view, of our practical politics.

Papers 2d   Dinner 1/6?

Feeling less and less comfortable with the Webbs and their ways, Wallas would finally resign from the Fabian Society in 1903. Basically a skeptic, he could not believe that improving social institutions would or could improve people as long as the irrational elements in human consciousness dominated them.

2 *Crystal Palace Concerts. 15. Wagner program. Lady Colin Campbell's at 17.30—read Mrs. Warren's Profession. °Private View. D. S. MacColl's drawings at Goupil's. 10 to 18.*

Up late; a little business done in the way of answering letters and entering concerts etc. in this diary, but no work. FE came to the Palace with me. When I left Lady Colin's I had a meal and a wash and then went to the Charringtons'. Janet read me as much as she has written of her play—the original Mrs. Warren—which she has recommenced and is going to finish in collaboration with Lady Colin. Charrington came in later. He read part of the 2nd act of his play, and I read the existing fragment of mine—an orgy of play-reading over which we all made merry. On my way to Charing Cross in the afternoon I met Walkley.

Papers 2d   Dinner 1/6?   Train Ch[arin]g + to Victoria 2½d   Milk & cake at A[erated] B[read] Shop Vict[oria] 3d   Omelette &c at Mone-galli's café 2/1   Wash, brush &c at Victoria lav[a]t[or]y 6d   Bus Vict[oria] to Kings Rd 2d   Train Gloster Rd to P[or]tl[an]d Rd 4d

> Janet Achurch's play was *Mrs. Daintree's Daughter* (performed in 1903 in Manchester), about mother-daughter conflict, ending with the mother's suicide. No commercial theater manager would take to it.

3 SUNDAY   *Lecture on "How We Become Atheists" at the Pioneer Reform Association, 102 Brompton Rd. S. W., 20 (G. E. Odell, Sec.).*

Spent the morning reading, and writing up this diary.

4   °*Monday Pop. Bazzini's Quartet in G.* °*Royal Female Philanthropic Society Concert. St. James's Banqueting Hall. 15. Read* Mrs. Warren's Profession *to Partridge (Bernard Gould) at 11 Marlborough Rd., St. John's Wood., 20.*

Made a resolute attack on my neglected correspondence, and on the job of collating all the suggested amendments and corrections to the Eight Hours tract. Worked away up to 17 o'clock, when Mrs. [Alice Lockett] Sharpe called and, being pretty tired, I went into the next room and sat chatting with her until it was time to post the letters.

Papers 2d   Dinner 1/6   Train to Marlboro Rd 1½d

> Alice Lockett had married Dr. William Salisbury Sharpe, a former house surgeon at St. Mary's Hospital, where she had been a nurse, in 1890.

5   °*Plunkett Greene and Leonard Borwick recital. St. James's Hall. 15. Special Fabian Executive. 276 Strand, at 20, to discuss reissue of Manifesto.*

I was late at the German lesson; but Drabig was late too; he got into my train at Baker St. May walked back with me as far as the corner of Soho Square, where I left her and went down to Charing Cross, as I wanted to buy a scrap book in Leicester Square for the press notices of the Manifesto. In the afternoon I quite forgot the Plunket Greene concert and worked complacently at the Manifesto. Nobody turned up at the Executive except Bland, Standring, Miss Cameron and Pease.

Papers 1½d   Dinner at Orange Grove 1/3   Scrap Book 2/–

> The second line of the entry ("... Manifesto.") was inadvertently written twice. The repetition is omitted here.

6 *London Symphony Concert. St. James's Hall. 20½. Fabian Publishing Committee. 17¼. Royal College of Music performance of Schumann's* Geno-veva *at Drury Lane. 13.30.*

Wrote some letters which I had no time for on Monday before going to Drury Lane. FE was there with me. We went to the Orange Grove afterwards and then I went to the Fabian and afterwards to the Orange Grove again with Olivier. Hilda Cox was there. FE came to the concert in the evening.

Dinner at Orange Grove (2) 2/3?   Omelette &c there 1/3?

> The London Symphony concert was reviewed on 20 December 1893 (C991). Anton Rubinstein's "Ramsgate Symphony" was revived—a "drenchingly copious" work. Beatrice Langley played the ninth piano concerto of Ludwig (Louis) Spohr (1784–1859), which made "a brilliant impression." ▪ *Genoveva* was reviewed on 13 December 1893 (C989). The first London production of Robert Schumann's commercially unsuccessful opera was "never absolutely vulgar and trivial except in the witch music. . . . I cannot blame the world for dropping its acquaintance."

7 *Independent Theatre dress rehearsal of* The Black Cat. °*Royal Choral Society. Albert Hall. 20.* Jephtha.

Began *World* article. At dinner met Emery Walker, with whom I had a long discussion about the withdrawal of the Fabian from the Joint Committee of Socialist Bodies, of which he strongly disapproves. He walked with me to Oxford Circus talking about it. Then I went on alone to the Bayswater Rd., where I took a bus and went out to FE. Did not get there until near 18. Found a young fellow named Percy Andrews there. He came with us as far as Ravenscourt Park station. We went into the restaurant in Buckingham St. before going to the theatre. FE left with Todhunter when his play was over. I waited for the other little piece.

Dinner 1/5   Papers 2d   Bus Bayswater Rd to Uxbridge Rd (beyond Sh[epherds] B[ush]) 3d   Train Rav[enscourt] Pk to Ch[arin]g + (2) 1/–
Omelette &c at Buckingham St (2) 1/10

> The Black Cat, by FE's friend Dr. John Todhunter, would have a single performance the next day. ▪ The "other little piece" to complete the evening with the Todhunter play was *The Debutante*, a two-character play by James D. Vyner, otherwise unknown to the stage. ▪ Percy Andrews was an actor who would move to films in the early 1900s, performing minor roles into the 1920s.

8 *Fabian Executive. 17½. Take the chair. Fabian Preliminary Committee. 16½. Fabian Semi-Public Meeting. Barnard's Inn. George Samuel on "Limits of Collectivism in Distribution." 20.* °*Independent Theatre. 20¼. Opera Comique.* Todhunter's Black Cat *and James D. Vyner's* Debutante. *Press Views. McLean's (water colours), Dickinson's (S. J. Barnes's oil landscapes), Continental (Lucien Besolie's* Amor et Vita *), and Fine Art Society (H. W. Wendon's drawings). German lesson. 11.*

Busy all day fulfilling engagements. After the Fabian, where I spoke (I was the only member of the Executive present except Standring), I went with

Miss Priestley to the Austrian Café and then saw her home. She was also at Gatti's with myself, Olivier, Oakeshott, Podmore after the Executive. When I got home after leaving Miss Priestley I sat up late correcting and sending off the *World* article. Did not get to bed until about 3. The result was, of course, that I slept late in the morning and lost more time than I gained.

Train to Swiss Cottage 2d   Back 2d   Bus Holborn corner to O[range] G[rove] 1d   Dinner at Orange Grove 1/6?   Bus Ch[arin]g + to Fabian 1d   Maccaroni &c at Gatti's 1/8   Chocolate at the Austrian café (2) 1/4

> Shaw reviewed all three shows in an unsigned paragraph in *The World*, 13 December 1893 (C990), McLean's receiving only a sentence as its pictures were "mostly by the old guard."

9   *Crystal Palace Concerts. 15. Paderewski. Mackenzie's "On the Waters"* (*Jason*) *Dine at Webbs'. 19½.*

Slept so late that I was only able to get about an hour's work at *World* article before it was time to go off to the Palace. Telegraphed to FE to come; but she did not. Came back by the 17½ train (Graves in the carriage with me) and, being very hungry and having time to kill, called at Bertha Newcombe's studio, but found nobody there. Walked to Webbs'. Mrs. Webb was away at Newcastle; only Wallas there. Read them the prologue to my new play. Wallas walked home with me—we had a long conversation about his father. I walked to Victoria in the early part of the day and checked the corrections in the Fabian Eight Hours tract on the way down to the Palace.

Papers 2d   Train Victoria to Sloane Sq 1d

> *Jason* was a cantata by Alexander Mackenzie first performed in 1885. The "great crowd" (C989), however, came to hear Paderewski.

10 SUNDAY   *Lecture for the Peckham S. D. F. on "Old and New Socialism"* (*John Falkner, 24 Sylvester Rd., East Dulwich*). *Pioneer Hall, 40ª Peckham Rye. 20. Peckham Rye station or tram to Rye Lane. Call at Headlam's afterwards, to meet Miss Belinfante.*

Finished *World* article and wrote notes on the picture galleries for *The World*, Lady Colin being away in Paris. I stayed at Headlam's until near 3 in the morning. Lionel Johnson, whom I had not met before, walked back with me. Not in bed until about 4.

Train Farringdon to Moorgate (ret[urn] not used) 6d   Bus to London Br[idge] 1d   London Br[idge] to Peckham Rye & back 8d   Bus Mans[ion] Ho to South[amp]ton Row 2d

> Shaw had favorably reviewed Estrella Belinfante's concert appearance in June (C959).
> ▪ Unsigned review in the "What the World Says" section on the three exhibitions he had seen on 8 December (C990). ▪ Lionel Johnson (1867–1902), poet and critic, was in the "Rhymers' Club" circle with Yeats, Symons, and Dowson.

11 °*Trinity College Orchestral Concert. Prince's Hall. 20. Massingham's friend [Arthur] Lestrange to play. Wrong date (see December 18). °Liberal and Radical Union Council Meeting. National Liberal Club. 20.*

Up pretty late after last night. Wrote letters, corrected *World* proof etc. After dinner went out to FE feeling thoroughly tired. When I got to Prince's Hall about 20½ I found that I had mistaken the night of the concert; and though my ticket was accepted without question, I found when I got inside that the concert about to begin was another one at which I had no business. So I went to the St. James's Theatre and saw Pinero's *Second Mrs. Tanqueray.*

Dinner, Orange Grove 1/5   Train St Ja[me]s's Pk to Rav[enscour]t Pk & back 9d   Papers 1d   St Ja[me]s's Theatre 2/6

> G.B.S. (C991) applied himself as music critic to Stella (Mrs. Patrick) Campbell's performance as Paula Tanqueray:
>> I was late, and only saw a scrap of the first act; but when the curtain rose on the second it revealed a pianoforte, at which the chief lady in the piece—a very attractive person—presently sat down and began to play. To my surprise, she played not only with sufficient skill, but with such convincingly right expression and feeling and so sympathetic a hand that I immediately forgot all about the comedy, and prepared to enjoy Schubert.
>> Will it be believed that the wretched people on the stage interrupted her after a few bars? The same thing happened at a subsequent and equally promising attempt. After that she never succeeded in even sitting down to the piano; and at last, worn out by repeated interruptions, she left the stage abruptly, and we were presently given to understand that she had committed suicide. No wonder!

12 °*Lecture on "Socialism" to the Social Club of the London and Westminster Bank at The Swan's Nest, Moorgate St., at 19½. (Frank Plowright, London and Westminster Bank, 41 Lothbury E.C.). Put off. °Arnold Dolmetsch's music room, etc. Dowland, West Dulwich. 20.40. °Mlle. Douste de Fortis and René Ortman's concert. Prince's Hall. 20½. °Church and Stage Guild. G. Lupino on Pantomime. 31 Upper Bedford Place. 16¼. Fred Fawcett's concert. St. James's Hall. 20. German lesson. 20.*

In the middle of the day it began to rain heavily, and in the afternoon it blew quite a hurricane. I sat at home and wrote letters, went over some of the German exercises, etc. The rain stopped in the evening. I left Fawcett's concert early and came home and played and sang for a while. Walked back from Hampstead alone, but found May at the restaurant afterwards.

Train to Swiss Cott[age] 2d   Dinner 1/1

> G.B.S. (C991) succinctly labeled the Fred Fawcett program a "miscellaneous concert of considerable pretension."

13 *Fabian Publishing Committee. 17¼. Fabian School Board Committee. 276 Strand. 20. Noel Home to call at 10.*

Busy finally revising the Fabian Eight Hours Tract for press and looking through the proof of the Manifesto. Walter [Gurly] came in the afternoon. I did not go out until about 17, eating a little fruit here instead of going to dinner. After the Executive I went to the Orange Grove, where I found the Salts, Hilda Cox and Mrs. Olivier, also Olivier. From that I went to the Charringtons'. Janet read some of the play she is writing.

Lent Walter 2/–   Orange Grove 2/–?   Train St Ja[me]s's Pk to Sloane Sq 1½d   Bus along King's Rd 1d   Train Gloster Rd to P[or]t[lan]d Rd 4d

14 Finished and sent off *World* article, working at it morning and evening. Went out to Hammersmith and called on FE after dinner; but she was out. I got a walk by going across the park to Hampstead and from there by London and North Western North London line to Chiswick.

Dinner at Finchley Rd rest[auran]t 1/8   Train F[inchley] R[oad] to Chiswick 8d   Shep[herds] B[ush] to P[or]tl[an]d Rd 6d

15 *Fabian Executive. 17¼. Fabian Committee. 16½. Fabian Members' Meeting at the L. S. Compositors' Board Room, 7 and 9 Bride St., Ludgate Circus (3rd floor), to pass Manifesto tract. 20. German lesson. 11.*

May walked back from Hampstead with me. In the afternoon I worked at the Manifesto, not to much purpose.

Train to Swiss Cott[age] 2d   Dinner 1/6?   Papers 2d   Omelette &c at Gatti's 2/1

16 *Crystal Palace Concerts. 15. German's Norwich Festival Symphony. Junta dinner at Webbs'. 19¼.*

Did some scraps of work at Manifesto. I am heartily sick of it. After the concert stayed at the Palace until the 18.10 train looking up a file of *The Times* in the Reading Room for Manifesto purposes. Wallas was not at Webbs'. I read the prologue of the new play to Beatrice.

Papers 2d   Dinner 1/1?   Train Ch[arin]g + to Vict[oria] 2½d   Reading Room at Palace 2d

> Reviewed on 27 December 1893 (C992). The *Norwich Symphony* of (Sir) Edward German (1862–1936) was "dramatic music without any subject, emotional music without any mood, formal music without conspicuous beauty and symmetry of design." "Symphony," said G.B.S., "is no more Mr. German's business than epic poetry is mine."

17 SUNDAY *Lecture at the Eleusis Club. 180 King's Rd., Chelsea, at 20 (George Templeman Jr., Pol. Sec.), on "The Political Situation." Tea at Bertha Newcombe's studio before the lecture, with Wallas.*

Rather tired out. Did nothing but read and correct *World* proof, besides preparing my lecture, which was a bad one, much too long, the invariable result of not being fresh. I had tea beforehand at Bertha Newcombe's studio with Wallas.

Train to S[ou]th Kensington & back 9d

18 *Trinity College Orchestral Concert. Prince's Hall. 20. Massingham's friend [Arthur] Lestrange to play.* °*Monday Pop. 20.*

Writing letters. In the afternoon went to FE by way of Hampstead. Came back for the concert. Left it early and found that Archer had been here twice looking for me. So as it was only 21.45 I went over to Queen Square and found Mrs. Archer there. Archer came in later and I read them the prologue of the new play.

Train Baker St to Finchley Rd 2d   *Sun* ½d   Dinner at Finchley Rd rest[auran]t 1/1?   Train to Chiswick 8d   Rav[enscour]t Pk to St Ja[me]s's Pk 6d

> The orchestra was faculty conducted, and some of the desks were also faculty occupied, but, said G.B.S. (C992) of the students, "so far as their share went, it was creditably discharged." ▪ Lestrange—"a feverish player"—was "the wrong man" to perform a piano concerto in F minor by Ferdinand Hiller (1811–1885), "which is very difficult, very able, very handsome, and quite heartless, [and] requires a certain serene elegance" (C992).

19 *German lesson. 11.*

After dinner I sat for a couple of hours in an easy chair before the fire in the next room reading Thackeray's *Barry Lyndon*. Then I began the *World* article and worked at it until past 19, when I went off to FE's. On the way I met Crowdy, who traveled with me as far as Edgware Rd. Sent off what I had done of the *World* article when I got home. Atterbury (I think that is his name) traveled with me from Shepherds Bush to Portland Rd. Did not get to bed until past 1.

Train to Swiss Cottage from Baker St 1½   Papers 2d   Dinner 1/6
Train to Shep[herds] B[ush] & back 9d

20 °*Fabian Publishing Committee. 17*¼*. Comedy Theatre.* **The Piper of Hamelin** *by F. W. Allwood and Robert Buchanan, and* **Sandford and Merton** *by Ed Solomon and F. C. Burnand. 15.* °*Westminster Orchestral Society's Concert. Westminster Town Hall. 20.*

Wrote letters and paid bills by post in the morning. After the opera I went to the Orange Grove and thence home to finish and send off the *World* article. I broke off work for a while to go and play the piano for a while, and the result was that I did not get to bed until 2.

Subscription to British Economic Association 1893–4, 2 years, £2/2/0
Press cuttings, 1 year, £1/1/0   Cost of postal orders 6d   Bus to Picc[adilly] O 1d   Milk & cake at A[erated] B[read] Shop Picc[adilly] O 3d   Dinner at Orange Grove 2/2

> *The Piper of Hamelin*, a light opera based on Robert Browning's poem, with book by Robert Buchanan and music by Fred W. Allwood, would have thirty-five matinee performances

paired with *The Masters Sandford and Merton*. G.B.S. found the *Piper* "a happy thought" (C992) made tedious by an imitative score. The burlesque of the once-popular *Sandford and Merton* was "not, as far as I can judge, worse than other burlesques of its kind."

21 Wrote letters, especially one to Beerbohm Tree. After dinner went to the Stores to buy a diary (a big one) and then called on Ashton Ellis, the translator of Wagner's prose works, and borrowed from him [Georges] Noufflard's book to read down in Wales and write a *World* article about. Then came home, finished reading *Barry Lyndon*, and completed my preparations for tomorrow's journey. At the Orange Grove I met M. B. Williams, and had a long talk with him about his return to Topolobampo. He was about to call on Lady Martin [Mrs. Victoria Claflin Woodhull] and wanted some information about her.

Star ½d   Dinner 1/5   Pocket diary 1/6   Bus Picc[adilly] O to Oxford O 1d   Jaeger's bill £3/1/3   Couple of scarfs 3/6

> Georges Noufflard's *Richard Wagner d'après lui-même* (Paris, 1893), reviewed on 17 January 1894 (C995) to fill a G.B.S. music column, most of which had to be written while the critic was on holiday. ■ Victoria Claflin Woodhull (1838–1927), born in Ohio, had become a New York stockbroker in 1870, and ran for president of the United States as nominee of the feminist Equal Rights Party in 1872. Her combination of enthusiasms— Socialism, spiritualism, and feminism—earned her more enemies than friends. Once she and her sister, Tennessee Claflin, had arrived in England in 1877 on a lecture tour they decided to stay. Mrs. Woodhull—already married twice, the first time at 15—met the wealthy English banker John Biddulph Martin, who wed her in 1883 after overcoming family objections. (Her sister would marry the merchant Francis Cook two years later, and become Lady Cook.) From 1892 to 1910 she published *The Humanitarian*, a journal emphasizing eugenics.

22 *Fabian Executive. 17¼. Cancelled. Fabian Committee. 16¼. Go down with the Webbs to the Argoed by the 10.20 train from Paddington. German lesson at 11.*

It rained very heavily during the last half hour of our journey; but stopped just as we got to our station (Monmouth-Troy). Wallas and I walked up to the Argoed, Webb and Beatrice going in the fly. Felt very comfortable when we arrived—back home in fact.

Train Portland Rd to Paddington (Bishops [Bridge] Rd) 1½d   Padd[ing]t[o]n to Monmouth (Troy) 12/1   Milk & biscuit at Swindon 3d

23 [Wales is on the other side of the Wye . . . —a land of quietly beautiful hills, enchanting valleys, and an indescribable sober richness of winter coloring. This being so, need I add that the natives are flying from it as from the plague? . . . I cannot walk far without coming upon the ruins of a deserted cottage or farmhouse. The frequency of these, and the prevalence of loosely piled stone walls instead of hedges, gives me a sensation of being in Ireland which is only dispelled by the appearance of children with whole garments and fresh faces acquainted with soap.]

"Music," *The World*, 10 January 1894 (C994).

24   [   ]

25   Wallas and I went off before 10 for a walk. We crossed the ferry at Redbrook and walked along the Wye to Bigsweir, where we crossed the bridge and climbed straight up the hill before us, walking back to the Argoed by way of Trellech Common. Got a smart dash of rain. Got fairly to work reading over and revising the Webbs' trade union book.

Ferryman at Redbrook 1/–

> They were awakened by "Two little cornets, four baritone saxhorns, and a euphonium" (C994), whose "strains burst expectedly on my ear." G.B.S. "went cautiously to the window to reconnoitre."

26   Wet day. Did not take a walk until late in the evening, when I went down the road skirting the Wyebrook Valley, and stood a long time at the top of the road going down to the mill looking at the stars, which were very brilliant. Behaved rather extravagantly about them. In the afternoon Mrs. Goldney, the parson's wife, called. I worked at the trade union book.

27   Working away at the trade union book. Took a walk before dinner with Wallas and Webb to Trellech Common and back by the Monmouth road. Read a bit of Mirabeau's *Memoirs*.

28   Finished my work on Webb's book. Wallas and I walked round Wyebrook Valley before lunch, and to Trellech Common and back at four o'clock. In the evening I read Noufflard on Wagner. Before going to bed I wrote up this diary, which was sent down to me by parcel post yesterday. This was the day on which Wallas and I met the hounds on our way back from Wyebrook.

29   °*Fabian Executive. 17¼. °Fabian Committee. 16¼. Concert of the Penallt Musical Society at the Schoolroom. 20.*

Began work on the Fabian Manifesto. We did not go out before lunch; but after it we all four sallied out. Wallas and I soon left Webb and Beatrice to themselves and took a long turn following up the course of the stream that wandered through the fields between the Monmouth and Trellech roads. Wallas did not come to the concert.

> The concert was "not only refreshingly different from the ordinary London miscellaneous article, but much better. The difference began with the adventurousness of the attempt to get there [in the darkness]. Fortunately, I have a delicate sense of touch in my bootsoles, and this enabled me to discriminate between road and common in the intervals of dashing myself against the gates which I knew I had to pass. At last I saw a glow in the darkness. . . ." The program itself convinced G.B.S. (C994) "that here, on the Welsh border, we were among a naturally musical and artistic folk."

30   Wallas went up to London by the 9.5 train and I walked with him down to the Ferry. Worked away at the Manifesto, having now overcome my disgust over it, and getting along pretty well. Before lunch we three took a tolerably long walk on the wild land over Trellech way. In the afternoon I read Wallas's Poor Law article and Webb's paper of suggestions to Hammill for the London Trades Council as to their action at the next election. Then I worked at the Manifesto until 19, when I played and sang a bit, the piano having come back from the schoolhouse none the worse for having been tuned. After dinner I read Noufflard.

> The Argoed piano had been borrowed for the Christmas concert.

31 SUNDAY   Working away at the Fabian Manifesto. Misty morning. We three went for a short walk before lunch. After lunch the Webbs went out leaving me to work; but I presently gave up and took a turn through the fields after playing for a bit. The Galtons and Shepherds came in for afternoon tea.

> Frank W. Galton (1867–1952), once an engraver, a student of Webb's at the Workingmen's College. In January 1892 Beatrice and Sidney Webb had appointed him as their assistant at £100/year plus traveling expenses. He would be secretary of the Fabian Society from 1920 to 1939. ▪ The Shepherds were Monmouthshire neighbors.

Notes

January:	11	*The Star*		2	12	6
	17	*The World*		20	0	0
				22	12	6
February:	15	*The Fortnightly Review*		5	0	0
	16	*The World*		20	0	0
				22	12	6
				47	12	6
March:	16	*The World*		20	4	0
				47	12	6
				67	16	6
April:	15	*The World*		26	9	6
				67	16	6
				94	5	6
May:	16	*The World*		20	0	0
				94	5	6
				114	5	6
June:	13	*The Star*		1	10	0
	15	*The World*		25	0	0

		£	s	d
19	Walter Scott, royalties on *Cashel Byron* for yr ending 31st May		19	10
"	(Walter Scott, royalties on) *Quintessence of Ibsenism* for yr ending 31st May	4	9	7
21	*The Daily Chronicle*	12	10	0
		114	5	6
		158	14	5

The Royalty items above are included in the Income Tax return for 1892–3

			£	s	d
July:	5	*The Star*	3	12	2
	"	*World*	20	4	0
			158	14	5
			182	10	7
August:	4	*The Star*	5	15	6
	15	*The World*	20	0	0
			182	10	7
			208	6	1
September:	6	*The Star*	10	10	0
	15	*The World*	25	0	0
			208	6	1
			243	16	1
October:	17	*The World*	20	0	0
			243	16	1
			263	16	1
November:	15	*The World*	20	0	0
			263	16	1
			283	16	1
December:	11	*The Morning Leader*	2	2	0
	15	*The World*	25	0	0
			283	16	1
			310	18	1

Reminders for Next Year

January: Democratic Club lecture "The Limitations of Soc. Dem." 17th. 20. Lecture at Washington Music Hall on the 28th. W. F. Champion, 451 B. P. Rd.

June: Handel Festival, Rehearsal 22nd Friday, Messiah 25th Monday, Selection 27th Wednesday, Israel 29th Friday.

Diary 1894

Notes

This year, after three months' effort to keep a note of my daily movements and expenditures in the same way as I have done since 1885, I finally gave up the attempt and rid my mind of it. The years during which a record has been kept are a sufficient sample of the way I live.

This year Edmund Yates died and the editorship of *The World* passed into other hands. As the production of *Arms and the Man* for the moment put me in possession of some spare money (I opened a bank account for the 1st time in my life on the 6th November with a lodgement of £187 American royalties) I was able to venture on the step of giving up my position as musical critic. I have said all I want to say on that subject for the present (next year I got into harness again as dramatic critic for *The Saturday Review* under the editorship of Frank Harris).

I still reside at 29 Fitzroy Square.

The household still consists of my mother and Kate Gurly (her half sister).

It is perhaps worth noting here that when I dropped musical criticism, the same thing happened as in the case of my picture criticism: that is, I immediately gave up going to musical performances. The few exceptions I made to this on special occasions, when asked to write musical articles by

The Pall Mall Budget and *The Daily Chronicle,* tired me a good deal—in fact I had not before realized the severity of the strain on the attention involved by musical criticism, especially after the first half hour of our absurdly long concerts. I began writing musical criticism for *The World* in May 1890 after a couple of years at the same work at *The Star* ("Corno di Bassetto"). This makes seven years of musical criticism without a break—enough for a lifetime if done as I did it.

> Shaw actually opened an account on 5 November (see his accounts at the end of the 1894 portion of the diary).

January

1 *At the Argoed.*

Worked furiously at the Manifesto so as to get it ready for the 16 post. Webb set to with me as the hour approached and we raced together down the avenue to catch the postman. In the evening, after dinner, we did a great deal of talking about my personal history.

> Shaw and Webb may have been attempting to sort out Shaw's woman (women?) problems. The Florence Farr relationship was souring, although neither admitted it to the other, and some of the other women in Shaw's life (May Sparling, Janet Charrington) had husbands to whom he professed loyalty. And Mrs. Patterson still claimed him.

2 *At the Argoed.*

Began *World* article. We three took a good walk before lunch by the Green Pond and the Green Lake and the old church. The weather has set in very cold, with slight snow and hard frost. In the evening I read Noufflard and wrote a scrap of the play, as to which my conscience has been aroused by a letter from FE. I intended to go to bed early, but sat up to read some tempting pages from M'Clintock's account of his expedition in search of Franklin, and Prescott's *Conquest of Peru.*

> Sir Francis Leopold M'Clintock, *The Voyages of the "Fox" in the Arctic Seas: a narrative of the discovery of the fate of Sir John Franklin and his companions* (London, 1859). Shaw was exploring the Potter library at the Argoed for reading matter. ▪ William Hickling Prescott, *A History of the Conquest of Peru* (Boston, 1847).

3 *At the Argoed. °Fabian Publishing Committee. 276 Strand. 17¼.*

Finished and sent off *World* article. Did not go out before lunch. After lunch Webb and I walked to Monmouth and back, Beatrice seeing us on our way as far as the first stile. We called at the post office and came back by the Welsh bank of the Wye and across the ferry at Redbrook.

Post cards & letter cards 1/3

4   *At the Argoed.*

Began an article on the pianoforte for *The Fortnightly Review*, ordered by Harris last month, but put off by the Fabian Manifesto. Weather intensely cold—ripping east wind and snow, which was blown away before it could settle. We all went out for a short turn before lunch and called at Moorcroft (the Pelhams being away in Italy) to borrow some books from the library. In the evening I read Noufflard. Played and sang as usual for a while before dinner.

> "The Religion of the Pianoforte," *Fortnightly Review*, February 1894 (C999). "The day will come," Shaw concluded, "when every citizen will find within his reach and means adequate artistic representations to recreate him whenever he feels disposed for them. Until then the pianoforte will be the savior of society." ■ Shaw's pocket diary reads "after lunch"—an error corrected here when he wrote the entries from his pocket diary into this diary (see 9 January).

5   *At the Argoed.*

Worked all day at the article, before and after lunch. Before lunch we went for a walk on the waste land towards Trellech. Up on the heights the wind was bitingly cold. We stayed in the house the rest of the day. In the evening, after dinner, I read Noufflard and *The World*. Got to bed just a little earlier than usual.

6   *At the Argoed.*

Working at the *Fortnightly* article. We all went for a short walk before lunch. Young Shepherd came to skate. He lunched with us and sat for a while afterwards, calling back for afternoon tea. I worked at the article off and on all the evening.

7 SUNDAY   *At the Argoed.*

Worked away at the article. Did not get out before lunch. Read the article to the Webbs afterwards. We all went for a walk between 15 and 16. On our return I began reading Nasmyth's autobiography, which interested me, though I dozed over it for ten minutes once. After dinner, I intended to finish the article, but got into a long chat with Beatrice instead.

> *James Nasmyth, An Autobiography*, ed. Samuel Smiles (London, 1883). Edinburgh-born Nasmyth (1808–1890) was a Manchester engineer and industrialist who invented the steam-hammer and other hydraulic tools. In later years he turned to astronomy, and with a telescope and other devices of his own design became one of the leading experts of his time on comets and the moon.

8   *At the Argoed.*

Finished the article, revised it, and enclosed it for sending off tomorrow. Did not go out before lunch. Mrs. Galton called after lunch; and when she left we all went out with her as far as the parsonage. From there we took a short walk. The weather very cheerless. It began to rain just after we got home and kept at it all night.

9 *At the Argoed.*

Letter from FE, reproaching me vigorously for not having worked at the play for her. So I set to and wrote 12 pages of it, working up to lunch time, although the Webbs went out for a walk. After lunch I felt rather unwell, although I had begun the day in brilliant condition. I played for a while and then took a walk through the fields by myself for nearly an hour. When I got back I felt weak and out of sorts; so I lay down on my bed for a while and slept. Then I came down and set to work writing up this diary and last year's, which still lacks several entries to be copied from the little pocket diary which I use.

10 *Come up to London by the 9.5 train from Redbrook. Fabian Publishing Committee. 276 Strand. 17¼. Fabian School Board Committee. 276 Strand. 20.*

11 *London Symphony Concert (4th). St. James's Hall. 20¼.*

Began *World* article. Took some lunch at home—fruit etc. Walked to the top of Primrose Hill and worked at the play there. Came home and chatted with Mother and Lucy until about 18, when I went to the Orange Grove and had a meal 1/6 *Westminster Gazette* 1d. Runciman walked home from the concert with me.

> Reviewed on 17 January 1894 (C995). The Schubert "unfinished" and arrangements from Wagner were supplemented by the appearance of a new violinist, César Thomson, who played a concerto by Karl Goldmark and Niccoló Paganini's Rossini variations—neither, according to G.B.S., tests of artistry.

12 *Fabian Semi-Public Meeting. H. H. Sparling on "Persistence of Classes under Collectivism," 20, at Barnard's Inn. Fabian Executive. 276 Strand. 17½. Fabian Executive Preliminary Committee. 16¼. °Press View. Edwin and Claude Hayes pictures at Dowdeswell's.*

Finished the *World* article, going out into the park to do some of it. (I was driven out by the fact that the water pipe here has burst and put the closet out of order). Dined at Isotta's 1/8. After dinner worked still at the article. Got to Executive about 17.15. Gatti's 2/–. Went from there to Fabian with Miss Priestley. Spoke in the debate. Miss Priestley made me walk home with her. Was up until near 2 finishing and sending off the article.

13 *Address the Economic Club, Borough Rd. Polytechnic Institute, S. E. on "The Study of Economics." (W. A. Andrews, Hon. Sec.)*

Runciman [called]. I got up late and was unable to do any work. I thought that the Polytechnic lecture was at 16, and got down there that hour, but I found to my disgust that it was really at 20. Went back and called on Runciman. He was out; so I left a card. Also called at Archer's; but he was out. So I went home.

Dinner O.G. 1/–   Bus to O 1d   Bus to Holley Town Hall 2d   Train to Farringdon & back 5d   Bus 1d

14 SUNDAY   *FE. Portland Rd. 17.20.*

I intended to work today; but the *World* proof took me a long time; and when it was done Wallas came in. He went out to get some meat to eat, and came back afterwards. Only got a look at the Manifesto. To my great annoyance I bungled the meeting with FE. Chimney fire next door.

Train to Ship St. & back 9d

15   Called to see Massingham's typewriter. Called on Parke in the morning at the *Star* office. Had to call several times before I caught him. Worked at the play all day. [D'Arcy] Morell called in the evening. Went out with him for a turn in the rain. Went to Charringtons' in the evening to read a bit of the play to them. Janet read her play to me.

Train to Farringdon 2d   Dinner (Gatti's) 1/3½   Train Farringdon to Old Rd. 2d   Express *World* proof 6d   Train to Gloster Road & back 6d

16   *German lessons recommence at Mrs. Edwards's, 55 Buckland Crescent, Hampstead N.W.*

Train to Swiss Cottage from Baker St. 1½d. Walked back alone. Began correcting Manifesto revises. In the evening went to *Twelfth Night* at Daly's 2/6.

Bus along Tott. Court Road 1d   Paper 1d   Dinner 1/7

> Reviewed on 24 January 1894 (C996), an occasion for G.B.S. to protest "the theatrical tradition that any song written by Shakespear is appropriate to any play written by him, except, perhaps, the play in which it occurs."

17   *Lecture at the Democratic Club on "The Limitations of Social-Democracy." 20. °Concert in aid of Home for Consumptive Women, Queen's Hall. 15.*

Spent the whole day finishing the Manifesto proof. Went out at 16 to call on Foote by appointment. Hilda Cox was at the Orange Grove. We talked about Bayreuth. After the lecture Runciman brought me to his rooms and we played some duets and he gave me some of his songs to look over.

Train to Kings Cross 1d   Bus to Peacock's Arms 1d   Tram Caledonian Road to Holborn 2d   Bus to Charing Cross 1d   O.G. 1/5   Bus back along Strand 1d

> Shaw continued to use Hilda Cox's former husband's name, despite the fact that the sister-in-law of Sydney Olivier was now married to Dr. George Frederick McCleary, an authority on population and public health, and the treasurer of the Fabian Society in 1894–95.

18 *Lecture for the Christian Social Reform League, Rectory Road Church, Stoke Newington, on "Labour in Parliament." (F. W. King, 33 Dunlace Rd., Clapton Park, N.E.). Rectory Rd. station. Great Eastern Railway. 20.*

Worked all day at the final proof. Played *Cavalleria* for a while before 18, when I went out.

O.G. Dinner 1/8   Train Charing Cross to Mansion House 2½d   Liverpool St. to Rect. Rd. & back 7d   Bishopsgate to Ptld Road 4¼d

19 *Fabian Executive. 17¾. Fabian Executive Preliminary Committee. 16¾.*

Did not do any literary work in the afternoon. I forget exactly what happened. After the Executive I went with Wallas to the Orange Grove, Webb leaving us at Charing Cross. Having nothing to write my *World* article about, I went to the Alhambra and caught an abominable headache, besides being bored.

Train to Swiss Cottage from Baker Street 1½d   Dinner O.G. 1/3?   Omelette &c. 1/6   Alhambra 4/6

"The other evening," G.B.S. began his review (C996), "feeling rather in want of a headache, I bethought me that I had not been to a music hall for a long time."

20 Train Finchley Road to Victoria 8d. Began *World* article. Headache still bad; had to give up work in the afternoon. Lucy gave [me] two antipyrene lozenges, which I swallowed thoughtlessly. They had the usual poisonous effect of drugs on me. I walked across the park to Finchley Rd. and took train to Victoria, and read the final revise of the Manifesto in the train. At Webb's I could eat nothing and was rather knocked up. Finished the proof and left it with Webb. Walked home, Wallas and Olivier (who was going to Manchester) coming as far as the corner of St. Martin's Lane, where they took a bus to St. Pancras.

Train Finchley Road to Victoria 8d

21 SUNDAY *Lecture at the Tottenham Liberal and Radical Club on "Progress in Socialistic Ideas" (J. W. Greenaway). Train from Liverpool St. to Bruce Grove 19.25.*

Worked all day at *World* article. Samuels was at the lecture. Had some talk with him in the train coming back.

Train Bishopsgate and back 8d?   Liv. St. to Bruce Grove and back 10d

22 *Monday Popular Concert—Eibenschütz. Beethoven septet, etc.*

Wrote letters all day until 18.30. Went to the Pop in the evening and could not listen to anything. Sat and sketched Norman, who was downstairs. Pardon walked to the Circus with me.

Dinner at O.G. 1/2   Papers 1d

Reviewed on January 1894 (C998). Miss Eibenshütz played piano pieces by Brahms in which the composer was "at his best, overflowing with purely musical impulses and letting them run into their own shapes and not into any academic mold."

23 °*London Liberal and Radical Union. National Liberal Club. 20. School Board resolutions.*

I was so truly tired that I resolved to have two full days' rest. Did not go to Hampstead until after 11. Then train to Swiss Cottage 1½d from Baker Street. On leaving I first took a turn with May in the neighborhood, discussing Mrs. Adams with her. I got my hair cut and washed 1/–. Then I came by train to Uxbridge Rd. 6d and called on FE, with whom I found Yeats. We presently went out and called on the Pagets. We played with Paget's toy cannons and soldiers for a while and then went down to tea. I read the prologue of first act of the play. Then we left; Yeats took the train and left us; and I stayed with FE until after 22, when I walked home.

> Apparently the matrimonial future of the pretty Australian widow was a regular subject of discussion until, in a church in Hampstead in 1897, Edith Adams married Frank Dean (1865–?), a London landscape painter. William Michael Rossetti gave the bride away.

24 Called on Ashton Ellis on my way to the Publishing Committee. He was out. Read the papers, sang, played, loafed and did odds and ends. Got to the Fabian at 17 and drafted letter for Pease *re* Fabian Manifesto. Then went back to the Orange Grove, where I found Olivier and Hilda Cox. They gave me the Salts' address at Lafone St.; and I went there and found Miss Joynes and Carpenter there. I read the prologue of my play to them. They received it very well. We then walked along the Embankment with Carpenter to Parliament Square and I left them and came home by train.

Dinner O.G. 1/2   Omelette &c 1/2   Papers 1½d

> The cyclostyled letter for Pease (A23) was to accompany copies of *Fabian Tract* No. 49, *A Plan of Campaign for Labour*, sent to the press.

25 °*Albert Hall. Scotch National Concert. 19.45.* °*Mrs. Mattieson on Browning's "James Lee's Wife" at Miss Whitehead's, 117 Gower St., 19¼.*

Worked at *World* article. It was very wet. I came back after dinner and presently set to work on an answer to [George] Lansbury's letter in *The Star*. After that I had intended to finish the *World* article, but I was too tired or rather too restless. I gave up the idea of going to the Albert Hall on getting a letter from Ashton Ellis telling me I might review his translation of *Oper und Drame* just received in next week's *World*.

Dinner 1/1   Drabig for German lessons £3/3/0   Papers 5½d

> "Burns and the S.D.F.," on the S.D.F.'s position on the Eight Hours Question, *The Star*, 27 January 1894 (C997). ■ A review of Richard Wagner's *Opera and Drama* in the Ellis translation appeared as part of the 14 February 1894 G.B.S. column, *The World* (C1001).

26 *Fabian Public Meeting at Essex Hall. S. Webb on "The Progress of Collectivism." 20. Fabian Executive. 17½. Fabian Preliminary Committee. 16¼.*

> The title of the paper, read at the tenth-anniversary meeting of the Fabian Society, is given by Beatrice Webb in *Our Partnership* (London, 1948), as "Socialism: True and False."

27 *Rehearsal of Arnold Dolmetsch's Viol concert (Henry VIII's pieces) at his house "Dowland," West Dulwich, at 17. Train from Victoria at 16.24. Private View. Joe Pennell's* Devils of Notre Dame *at Dunthorne's.*

> Reviewed on 7 February 1894 (C1000). Shaw found the quality of the music and the performances "surprisingly good, considering the strangeness of the instruments." The pieces by Henry VIII "did more to rehabilitate that monarch in my estimation than all the arguments of Mr. Froude." ∎ Joseph Pennell, influenced by Charles Meryon's etching *Le Stryge* (1853), had clambered about the Gothic towers of the Cathedral of Notre Dame in Paris to sketch the gargoyles and other grotesques.

28 SUNDAY *Lecture at the Washington Music Hall, Battersea, 20. (W. F. Champion, 451 Battersea Park Rd., S.W.) on "Social-Democracy and the Labour Program."*

29 *Monday Pop. St. James's Hall. 20.*

[When there is no music—for there is nothing beyond the barest routine going on—I diligently attend the Popular Concerts and saturate myself with Brahms. (C1000)]

> G.B.S. (C1000) found the chamber music of Brahms as "feeling his way from one sensuous moment to another, . . . [with] no more form than a mountain brook has. . . ."

30 *Supper at Podmore's at 19½ (32 Well Walk) to meet Miss Borchardt. Put off to tomorrow. German lesson. 10.*

31 *Podmore's, see yesterday. Fabian Publishing Committee. 17½.*

[I first heard the name of Nietzsche from a German mathematician, Miss Borchardt, who had read my *Quintessence of Ibsenism*, and told me that she saw what I had been reading: namely, Nietzsche's *Jenseits von Gut und Böse*. Which I protest I had never seen, and could not have read with any comfort, for want of the necessary German, if I had seen it.]

> Miss Sophie Borchardt, of The Ferns, 153 Finchley New Road, N.W. ∎ The bracketed supplement is from the preface to *Major Barbara* (1907).

February

1 *Fabian South Western Group. Social Meeting at Mrs. Sandham's, 40 Cheyne Court.*

[I was able to hear only a couple of acts of Mr Harold Moore's *Magic Fountain*, produced . . . at St. George's Hall. It is practically a ballad opera with the connecting links of dialogue treated as fully accompanied recitative. . . . The book is a boyish affair—an enchanted fountain, a maiden, a sorcerer, an absent lover, and so forth: one can conceive Scott writing it at eight years old.]

Shaw expected to meet Frederick Whelen there at Mrs. Sandham's (*CL*), to further insist that a Shavian candidacy for Parliament from Chelsea was a "forlorn hope" and a "waste of resources." ▪ The ballad opera *The Magic Fountain* apparently did not survive beyond the single performance, which G.B.S. (C1000) did not see through in order to go to Mrs. Sandham's.

2   *Fabian Executive. 17½. Take the chair. Fabian Preliminary Committee. 14¼. Take the chair. German lesson. Hampstead. 10.*

3   *Saturday Pop. Stanford's Irish pieces for violin. Lady Hallé. Dinner at Webbs'. 17¼.*

Began article for *Fortnightly Review* in reply to Mallock's "Fabian Economics." Still lame but getting better. Come back here after the concert. Wallas came back with me.

Dinner 1/6?   Bus to Piccadilly O from Tott[enham] C[our]t Rd corner 1d   Bus to Parliament St 2d   Back 2d

The new pieces by "the distinguished principal of the Royal Academy of Music," Sir Charles Villiers Stanford, were received "with deep veneration." To G.B.S. (C1000), however, they were merely "elegant musical sentences put together with a practised hand." ▪ "On Mr. Mallock's Proposed Trumpet Performance," *Fortnightly Review*, April 1894 (C1009), revised and augmented (1909) as *Socialism and Superior Brains*, Fabian Tract No. 146 (A102). "Fabian Economics," by William Hurrell Mallock (1849–1923), had appeared in the *Fortnightly Review* in February 1894.

4 SUNDAY   *Lecture for the North Camberwell Branch S. D. F., 208 Camberwell Rd. S.E. on "Progress in Socialistic Ideas." (J. C. Gordon).*

Working at the article. My watch stopped while I was lecturing and I lost the last train back. Had to walk from Waterloo.

Train Portland Rd to Camberwell (return half not used) 1/6   Bus Camb[erwell] to Elephant ½d   Elephant to Waterloo ½d

5   *Monday Pop. Joachim. 20.*

Worked at the *Fortnightly* article. Got nothing to eat except a biscuit and an apple or two. Very wet day. My watch stopped and I made a mistake of an hour in setting it; so that when I went down to the Orange Grove intending to make up for my abstinence by a good meal before the concert found that it was 20 o'clock instead of 19, and had to rush off empty to St. James's Hall, where I had arranged to meet FE. After the first two movements of the quartet I could stand it no longer, as the playing was not very good, and went off to the Café Monico to get something to eat. Then I returned to the concert. I walked to the Marble Arch with FE. Then returned home and went to bed after writing a card or two.

Café Monico 1/10   Papers 1d

> G.B.S. wrote frankly on 21 February 1894 (C1002), "I said with my usual irreverence 'Joachim is flat; and the quartet is not going to be good: I will go and recapture the missing dinner: next week probably he will play splendidly.'"

6 *Society of British Dramatic Art. Royalty Theatre. 14½. Aveling's Judith* Shakespere, *etc. German lesson. Hampstead. 10. Yeats to read his play* The Land of Heart's Desire *at 123 Dalling Rd. 20.*

May walked back with me from Hampstead. I killed as much time as possible over dinner and then called on Archer, expecting that he would go to the theatre with me; but he was out. However, he had the stall next to me and I went back to his house after the performance (he did not wait for the last piece) and walked to Waterloo with him. Miss Herbert turned up at the theatre. After leaving Archer I came back across Charing Cross Bridge and had a meal at the Orange Grove then went on to Dalling Rd. Came back by the 23.36 train from Shepherd's Bush.

Train to Swiss Cottage 2d   Bus along Tott[enham] C[our]t Rd (2) 2d
Papers 1d   Dinner 1/6   Bus to Kingsgate St 1d   Program at theatre
6d   Bus Dean St to Kingsgate St 1d   Omelette &c at Orange Grove
1/6?   Train Ch[arin]g + to Rav[enscour]t Pk 6d   Sweets 1d   Train
Shep[herds] Bush to P[or]tl[an]d Rd 6d

> The play was advertised as by Alec Nelson, Edward Aveling's pen name. There would be only one matinee performance. ∎ Yeats's one-act fantasy had been written at Florence Farr's request as a vehicle for her niece Dorothy Paget, who was eleven. FE was to use it as curtain-raiser for a new John Todhunter play, A *Comedy of Sighs*, to be produced in her new season at the Avenue Theatre.

7 °The Redemption *at the Albert Hall. 20. Fabian Publishing Committee.* 17½.

Read Hammill's article and wrote letters, wrote up this diary—fearfully in arrear—etc. Took some dinner at the café opposite Portland Rd. station and walked to Primrose Hill and back. Then on to the Fabian, calling here for a moment to see whether a telegram had come from FE in reply to mine. Pease walked with me from the Fabian to the corner of St. Martin's Lane. Met Parkin at the Orange Grove. Worked a little at the play on my way out to Ravenscourt Park. Spent the rest of the evening with FE. I have not been sleeping very well lately—at least not well for me. Before going to bed I ate something, contrary to my usual custom.

Dinner at Isotta's 1/6   Papers 1d   Bus to Endell St 1d   Porridge &c
at Orange Grove 10d   Train Ch[arin]g + to Rav[enscour]t Pk 6d
Cayenne jujubes 1d   Train Shep[herds] Bush to P[or]tl[an]d Rd 6d

"Labour Representation," by Fred Hammill, *Fortnightly Review*, April 1894, which Shaw was revising prior to submission. ▪ Thomas Parkin was a Radford relative who would become secretary of the I.L.P. See also 23 June 1886.

8 *London Symphony Concert. St. James's Hall.* $20\frac{1}{2}$.

Began *World* article.

Dinner 1/6?   Papers 1d   Bus to concert 1d

George Henschel had programmed a Wagner Memorial Concert, which crammed the hall with enthusiasts. G.B.S. (C1001) declared him "fully equal" to the occasion, especially in the Good Friday music from *Parsifal*.

9 *Fabian Executive.* $17\frac{1}{2}$. *Fabian Committee.* $14\frac{1}{2}$. *Fabian Members' Meeting in Clifford's Inn Hall (first meeting in this hall) to pass Sweating Tract, etc. 20. °Bach's St. John Passion music at St. Anne's, Soho. 20.*

Worked at *World* article in afternoon, and again when I got home from the Fabian. Did not get to bed until very late. Wallas walked home with me from the Fabian. Bertha Newcombe, Miss Cameron, Oakeshott came to Gatti's after the Executive. Regular cold coming on.

Train to Swiss Cottage 2d   Papers 1d   Dinner 1/6?   Cayenne jujubes 3d   Macaroni &c at Gatti & Rodesano's 2/6

Fabian Tract No. 50, *Sweating: Its Cause and Remedy*, by H. M. Macrosty.

10 *Rehearsal at Dolmetsch's, "Dowland," West Dulwich. Concert of the music of Henry and William Lawes. 17. Train from Victoria at 16.24. Dinner at Webbs'.* $19\frac{1}{2}$.

I forget exactly what work I did in the morning—probably odds and ends. I walked from Herne Hill to Dulwich.

Dinner at Orange Grove 1/6?   Papers 1d   Train Victoria to Dulwich & back 10d   Tram to Vauxhall Br $\frac{1}{2}$d

11 SUNDAY Worked from 10 in the morning until 10 in the evening at Hammill's article, except about 1 hour after dinner when I played a little. I then went off to the Charringtons' and stayed with them until near 12, when I walked home. Flemming was there.

Train to S[ou]th Kensington (ret[urn] not used) 6d

12 *°Fabian Central Group Meeting at 32 Great Ormond St. to appoint secretary. °Mrs. Clarinda Webster's Mendelssohn lecture and concert. Gresham Hall. Brighton. 20. °Liberal and Radical Union Council Meeting. National Liberal Club. 20. House of Lords.*

Worked at article for *Fortnightly Review* in reply to Mallock. Stayed at home in the evening to go on with it. After dinner at the Orange Grove I went to the New Gallery to see the exhibition of early Italian painting there. This took up the whole afternoon.

Dinner at Orange Grove 1/3?   New Gallery 1/–   Catalogue 1/–

13 *German lesson. 10. Gompertz's Chamber Music Concert. Prince's Hall. 20.15. Stanford's Quartet in A. Beethoven's posthumous C# minor. °Abdy-Williams on "The Revival of Ancient Gregorian Music" at Mrs. Hullah's. 20½.*

Still at the article. Cold on the mend. Jacques walked home with me from the concert.

Train to Swiss Cottage 2d   Dinner 1/6?   Bus to Grafton St 1d   Bus to concert 1d

> Richard Gompertz's ensemble played a quartet in A minor by Villiers Stanford, which G.B.S. (C1002) found "a genuine piece of absolute music, alive with feeling from beginning to end," and Beethoven's posthumous quartet in C sharp minor (No. 14, *Op.* 131), a "beautiful, simple, straightforward, unpretentious" work, usually "avoided because the professors once pronounced [it] obscure and impossible."

14 *Fabian Publishing Committee. 16¼. Copyrighting performance of Janet Achurch's play,* Mrs. Daintry's Daughter *at Ladbroke Hall. 14.45. Go and help.*

As I have now relapsed comfortably into my old habits of getting up between 10 and 11 in the morning, I had not much time for work before going off to the performance, at which I read 3 parts. Lady Colin Campbell came back in the train with me as far as Edgware Rd. Came home after the Committee and worked at the article.

Papers 1d   Train to Notting Hill & back 6d?   Dinner at Orange Grove 8d   Subscription to Hammill's election fund 21/–

> The title of Janet Achurch's play varies in spelling from *Daintry's* to *Daintree's* in Shaw's references. *Daintree's* is the correct spelling.

15 I had intended to get to work at the *World* article today, thinking that the *Fortnightly* article was all but finished, but, as it happened, I was all day getting the latter sent off. Butterfield, Lucy's husband, was here in the evening.

Papers 1d   Dinner 1/6?

16 *Fabian Executive. 17¼. Fabian Committee. 14½. German lesson. 10. Press View. Dowdeswell's. Lely, Morland, etc.*

Finished all of the *World* article that was possible before the opera tomorrow. Came back here after the Executive to do it. Olivier and Wallas came with me to the Orange Grove. Wallas went off to see *Twelfth Night* at Daly's Theatre.

Train to Swiss Cottage 2d   Dinner 1/6   Papers 1d   Table d'hote at O[range] G[rove] 1/8

Peter Lely (1618–1680), Baroque portrait painter of the Flemish school, went to England in 1641 and became Court Painter; George Morland (1763–1804), London rustic genre, animal, and landscape painter, despite his successes, ended his life in debtors' prison, a victim of his extravagances.

17 *Crystal Palace Concert, first of the year. 15. [R.] Burmeister's* Chase after Fortune (*Symphonic Fantasy*). *Lady Hallé. Production of* Wapping Old Stairs *at the Vaudeville Theatre. 20.20.*

Richard Burmeister's symphonic fantasy had been suggested by a picture by Rudolf Henneberg (1826–1876) in the Berlin State Museum. G.B.S. (C1002) found the music "utterly commonplace": "Henneberg has certainly much to answer for." ▪ G.B.S.'s "mirth" at the new comic opera, with music by Howard Talbot (1865–1928) and book by Stuart Robertson, became "hollower and hollower" as the evening wore on (C1002). But he conceded that if it were not "very clever," it was at least "not deliberately base."

18 SUNDAY °*Playgoers' Club. St. James's Banqueting Hall. D. Christie Murray on "Trade or Art." 20. Go over to Webbs' in the afternoon to read the last chapter of the Trade Union book.*

Finished *World* article and began one for Keir Hardie on the Fabian Society, but did not persevere beyond a few sentences. Went over to Webbs' in the afternoon, meeting old Wheelhouse on the way. He treated me to a vehement discourse on the land question. I passed through a demonstration in Trafalgar Square and got to Webbs' between 16 and 17. The Webbs went out at 20, leaving me still at work reading their last chapter. Webb came in at about 21. I then took myself off to the Charringtons where I found Flemming and Janet. Charrington came in later.

Train S[ou]th Kensington to P[or]tl[an]d Rd 4d

David Christie Murray (1847–1907), journalist and novelist, was correspondent for *The Times* in the Russo-Turkish wars of 1878–1888, and a novelist. Shaw would read some of his old dispatches for background when researching an historical context for his play in progress. ▪ Only two Wheelhouses appear in the post office directories for London and suburbs: William Wheelhouse of 4 Town End Villas, Town Road, Edmonton, and Joseph Wheelhouse of 4 Park Place, Greenwich, S.E.

19 *Monday Pop. Joachim. 20.*

Spent the early part of the day writing letters, writing up this diary since the 8th, etc. It was past 16 when I went out. After dining at the Orange Grove I called on Ashton Ellis and borrowed Wagner's *Eine Kapitulation* from him. Left him at $18\frac{1}{2}$ and came back here to tea. FE was at the concert with me. I left her at the Marble Arch, where she got into a bus. Wrote two letters when I got home, one to Norman suggesting that *The Daily Chronicle* should get Houston Chamberlain to write on Wagner subjects, and the other to Webb proposing that he should get Burns and Massingham together next Saturday evening and try to get them to undertake the political work which the Fabian Manifesto paved the way for.

Papers 1d   Dinner at Orange Grove 1/3

Reviewed on 28 February 1894 (C1004). This time G.B.S. appreciated Joachim's "excellences as an artist," as he played "in his finest vein." ▪ *Eine Kapitulation*—written in the winter of 1870–71, during the Prussian siege of Paris, but not published until 1873— was a satirical play by Wagner with such characters in it as Victor Hugo, Jacques Offenbach, and members of the government of the republic that had displaced Napoleon III. They offer the Germans their restaurants and their opera, and suggest that to unmilitant tourists everything in Paris will be open without violence. ▪ Houston Stewart Chamberlain (1855–1927), English expatriate writer who lived most of his life in Vienna, was a passionate Wagner disciple, his son-in-law (via Wagner's stepdaughter), and the author of *Die Grundlagen des neunzehnten Jahrhunderts* (1889)—translated in 1911 as *Foundations of the Nineteenth Century*. Much of the philosophical basis of Nazi racial theories and sense of destiny came via Chamberlain's book, praised in Hitler's *Mein Kampf.*

20 °*Stock Exchange Orchestral Society. St. James's Hall. 20. London Trades Council Conference on the Unemployed Question, Club and Institute Union, close to Holborn Town Hall. 18. German lesson. 10.*

I do not quite clearly remember what I was working at in the afternoon. Wallas walked home with me.

Train to Swiss Cottage 2d   Papers 2d   Dinner 1/3   Bus to Grafton St 1d   Orange Grove 1/6   Bus to St Martin's Lane to Theobald's Rd 1d

21 *Unemployed Conference continued from yesterday. 18.* °*Fabian Publishing Committee. 16½.*

Worked at *World* article. After dinner I went to the top of Primrose Hill, forgetting all about the Publishing Committee, my mind being occupied with the Unemployed Conference. It was a hopeless affair—the Social Democrats of the Federation more perverse and absurd than ever.

Dinner 1/6?   Bus to Mornington Crescent 2d   Orange Grove 1/6 Bus to Theobald's Rd 1d

22 *London Symphony Concert. St. James's Hall. 20½. Dress rehearsal* Heirs of Rabourdin. *Opera Comique (Independent Theatre). 14½.*

Worked at an article on the Fabian Society for Keir Hardie's *Labour Leader;* but did not finish it—found it rather tedious. Looked in at the Fabian office for a few minutes between the 2nd and 3rd acts of the rehearsal.

Dinner at Orange Grove 1/–?   Papers 1d   Bus to concert 1d

The Heirs of Rabourdin, by Émile Zola, in a translation by Teixiera de Mattos, had only a single performance in an Independent Theatre Society production. ▪ Ilona Eibenschütz played the Beethoven Emperor concerto "as fast as possible" (C1004). Brahms's setting of Goethe's *Harzreise im Winter* for contralto and chorus "sounded godlike" after an unimpressive Schumann symphony (No. 4) in D minor. ▪ Although the *Labour Leader* article most likely appeared on 24 February or 3 March 1894 (C1003), no copy of either date survives.

23 *Fabian Semi-Public Meeting. Harriet Stanton Blatch on "Collectivism and the Economic Freedom of Women." 20. Clifford's Inn Hall. Fabian*

Executive. 17¼. Fabian Committee. 16½. °Independent Theatre. Zola's Heirs of Rabourdin. Opera Comique. 20.15. °German lesson. 10. Press View. Wilson Steer's pictures at the Goupil Gallery.

When I got over to Hampstead I found that the lesson was postponed, a telegram having come from Drabig to say that he was ill. So I walked back and finished the *World* article at my ease. There was a great crowd in the Square, attracted by the funeral of Bourdin, the Anarchist, which, as it happened, passed another way after all. Salts called. Wallas, Oakeshott, Olivier, Miss Brooke and Miss Newcombe were at the café after the Executive, at which I took the chair. I spoke in the debate after Mrs. Blatch's paper. Wallas walked home with me.

Train to Swiss Cottage 2d   Dinner at Orange Grove 1/–   Macaroni &c at G[atti] & R[odesano]'s 2/4   *Justice* 1d   Papers 1d

> Mrs. Harriet Stanton Blatch (1856–1940), of 44 Woodstock Rd., Bedford Park, was on the Fabian Executive 1894–95. ■ Philip Wilson Steer, Gloucestershire-born landscape painter, absorbed French nineteenth-century painting techniques into the tradition of Constable and Turner. ■ Martial Bourdin had blown himself up unintentionally while trying to set the fuse of a bomb at the Royal Observatory, Greenwich Park. Joseph Conrad would utilize the attempted anarchist "outrage" as the central incident of his novel *The Secret Agent.*

24   *Crystal Palace Concert. Hoffman's flute concerto. [Albert] Fransella and Eibenschütz. 15. °Hammersmith Socialist Society's evening. Kelmscott House 20. °Saturday Pop. Concert. 15. Cherubini's quartet in D minor. 15. Webbs', 19½, to meet Burns.*

Wrote up this diary. FE came to the Palace with me. On our return I had to go home for the list of proposed Labour candidates and seats for the next election, which I had forgotten. Wallas was not at Webbs' but Burns was.

Papers 1d   Dinner at O[range] G[rove]?   Train Ch[arin]g + to Vict[oria] 2½d   Bus to West[minster] 2d

> Reviewed on 7 March 1894 (C1005). Albert Fransella was an "excellent artist" in Hoffman's concerto for flute. Miss Eibenschütz went unnoticed. Ernst Theodor Wilhelm Hoffman (1766–1822), the writer of the famous *Tales*, was also a composer, altering his initials to E. T. A. after the *Amadeus* in Mozart.

25 SUNDAY   *Lecture for the Kensal Town Branch S. D. F. on "Progress in Socialistic Ideas" at Levell's Coffee Rooms, No. 4 Carlton Terrace near Westbourne Park station W. (C. T. Hondin, 41 Woodfield Rd., Harrow Rd. W.)*

26   *Monday Pop. 20. Mozart's G major quartet. Joachim, etc.*

> The Pop concert went unreviewed.

27   *Dolmetsch's Viol concert at West Dulwich. 20.45. [John] Jenkins and Christopher Sympson's music. German lesson. 10.*

The Dolmetsch concert was reviewed jointly with his next program in G.B.S.'s 14 March 1894 column (C1006); however, there were no references to music by John Jenkins (1592–1678) or Christopher Sympson (?–1669).

28 *Philharmonic Concert, first of the season, Queen's Hall. 20. °Political Economic dinner at the National Liberal Club. Hyndman on "The Final Futility of Final Utility." 19.*

The concert was notable for its English premiere of Tchaikovsky's "Pathetique" symphony (No. 6), "which was very interesting, and far too novel and difficult to leave the band any middle course between playing it well and not playing it at all." To G.B.S. (C1005) it was a Gothic novel in mood, "a veritable Castle of Otranto."

March

1 [   ]

It is possible that Shaw went to the special matinee (and only) performance of *Liberty Hall*, a comedy by R. C. Carton (1856–1928), as friends of his were involved in the revival at the St. James's Theatre. However, there was no musical excuse for a review.

2 *German lesson. 10. Fabian Executive. 17½. Fabian Committee. 16½.*

3 *Crystal Palace Concert. 15. [Walter] Wesche's Orchestral ballad* Excalibur. *[Hugo] Becker. Rose Olitska. Miss Borchardt's in the evening, 153 Finchley Rd.*

The concert at the palace was not reviewed by G.B.S.

4 SUNDAY *Lecture at Penton Hall, 81 Pentonville Hill, for the Progressive Association (F. T. Ormerod) on "Growth of Social-Democracy." 19.*

5 *°Liberal and Radical Union Council Meeting. Annual meeting. National Liberal Club. 20.*

6 *Dolmetsch's Locke and Purcell Viol concert. West Dulwich. 20.45. German lesson. 10.*

Reviewed on 14 March 1894 (C1006), the entire column devoted to Dolmetsch and old music. G.B.S. was especially interested in Matthew Locke, "the last English musician who composed for the viols, and the founder of my school of musical criticism. His denunciation of the academic professors of his day is quite in my best manner."

7 *°Algernon Ashton's concert—own compositions. Prince's Hall. 20. Open a debate on "Certain Aspects of the Theatre" for Grein's "Sunday Popular Debates" at the Opera Comique. 20. Fabian Publishing Committee. 20. Call* *at the* Idler *office, Talbot House, Arundel St., on G. B. Burgin. 15¼ (interview).* °*Westminster Orchestral Society's Concert. Westminster Town Hall. 20.*

> G.B. Burgin (1856–1944) journalist and short-story writer, was then subeditor of *The Idler* and was interested in publishing Shaw. The only result in 1894 would be a contribution in Burgin's "Some Literary Critics," *The Idler*, June 1894 (C1023).

8 °*London Symphony Concert. St. James's Hall. 20½.*
Began *World* article.

9 *Fabian Semi-Public Meeting. Sydney Olivier on "Collectivism and the Family." 20. Clifford's Inn Hall. Fabian Executive. 17¼. German lesson. 11.*

10 *Crystal Palace Concert. 15. Joachim. Miss Monteith. Raff's Lenore Symphony. Webbs'. 19¼.*

> Again, the Palace concert was not reviewed. Involved with his new play and with Fabian activities, Shaw was writing his musical columns on issues often remote from performance. In effect, he was sliding out of his six-year career as musical critic.

11 SUNDAY *Lecture for the Hammersmith Socialist Society, Kelmscott House, on "Progress in Socialist Ideas." 20.*
Worked vigorously at the play in the morning and sang an act of *Falstaff.* Finished and sent off *World* article. Took a walk to the top of Primrose Hill between 16 and 17. Just as I was starting for the lecture—at which I was half an hour late—Alice [Lockett] arrived, bringing her husband, Salisbury Sharpe, who carefully examined my lungs, but could find nothing but a spot which he said might be "consolidation" and might be nothing but an artery a little out of its normal position. After the lecture I walked home with Walker, who lent me *King Florus and the Fair Jehane* to read in the train, and he walked with me to Broadway.
Train to Hammersmith & back 9d

> *The Tale of King Florus and the Fair Jehane*, translated by William Morris from the thirteenth-century French for his Kelmscott Press and first issued in December 1893 in a limited edition of 350 copies. *Floris and Blaunchfloure*, a medieval romance in a Saracen setting (but intended for Christian audiences), also exists in a southeast Midlands dialect, which may antedate the French version.

12 °*Fabian Central Group. Miss A. A. Brown on "Poor Relief." 32 Great Ormond St. 20.*

13 *Miscellaneous concert. Queen's Hall. 15.*
[I looked in at a charity concert . . . and found the band of the Coldstream Guards desperately playing one selection after another to keep the audience amused until the arrival of the artists who were first on the program, which had at last to be taken anyhow . . . until the missing philanthropists turned up.]

G.B.S. in *The World*, 21 March 1894 (C1008). "If you are an artist," he wrote in exasperation, "and [you] have promised to sing at a charity concert for nothing, then keep your engagement in all respects as if it were an ordinary professional one."

14 °*Philharmonic Concert. Queen's Hall. 20. Preliminary Meeting, St. Pancras Public Library Committee. H. W. Eve's, 37 Gordon Square. 20½. Fabian Publishing Committee. 16½.*

15 *Bach Choir Concert. Queen's Hall. 20. St. Matthew Passion.*

G.B.S.'s highly unfavorable review of the Bach Choir would be suppressed. See 20 March.

16 *Fabian Public Meeting at Essex Hall. 20. Graham Wallas on "The Coming School Board Election." Fabian Executive. 17½. Fabian Committee, 16½; also to meet Drew of Bradford.*

On this date Shaw signed his Institute of Journalists membership form, on the nomination of H. W. Massingham. He would retain his membership until his death fifty-six years later.

17 °*Crystal Palace Concert. 15. The Redemption. °Boat Race. Cobden-Sanderson's "Doves" Bindery. 8¼ to 12. °Irish National Concert. St. James's Hall. 20. °Irish National Concert. Albert Hall. 20. Lunch with Stepniak at 13.30 and read the play to him. Dine with the Webbs, as usual.*

Did not get down to the river until the race was over. Went first to the Doves and had a chat with Mrs. Dryhurst there. Then went on to Walkers', where there was a great crowd. Among others Radford turned up, wonderfully restored. On leaving Walkers' I went over to FE and stayed with her until it was time to go to Stepniak's. A Russian who commanded the Bulgarian fleet during the war was present: I did not catch his name. At about 18 I left and walked to Ravenscourt Park, where I took train for Victoria. Dined with the Webbs.

Train P[or]tl[an]d Rd to Turnham Green & back (used it to Rav[enscourt] Pk only) 1/6   Rav[enscour]t Pk to Victoria 6d   Tram to Vauxhall Br[idge] ½d

Via Sergius Stepniak and the former Russian admiral Esper Aleksandrovich Serebryekov (he had fled to England on learning he was suspected, accurately, of Nihilist sympathies), Shaw secured the Balkan background he needed in order to set his play in a war-torn, "underdeveloped" (in later terms) country. Choosing Bulgaria meant revising his characters' names, and one of the two male leads—the pompous Sergius Saranoff—would be given Stepniak's.

The efficient Swiss Captain Bluntschli, whose surname is unchanged and who is never given a Christian name, suggests Shaw's earlier work in the library, as Johann Kaspar Bluntschli (1808–1881), whose book *Das moderne Kriegsrecht* (1866; *The Modern Law of War*) was to be the basis of the codification of the laws of war at the Hague conferences of 1899 and 1907, was Zurich-born.

In an apparently self-drafted interview, "Ten Minutes with Bernard Shaw," published in *To-Day*, 28 April 1894 (C1017), Shaw went into detail corroborated by the manuscript of the play as to how he transformed *Arms and the Man* into a Bulgarian setting, after first trying a Servian one, filling in details from the *Annual Register* and "a modern railway map of the Balkan peninsula."

Stepniak and Admiral Serebryekov would be Shaw's guests at opening night.

18 SUNDAY   *Trade Union Demonstration* vs *House of Lords in Hyde Park.*
15.

Corrected *World* proof; finished article. Rewrote the first few pages of the preface to the Webbs' Trade Union book. Spent the afternoon in the park, listening to the talk there. Came home and worked in the evening.

The demonstration was against legislation deceptively entitled "Employers' Liability Bill."

19   *Free Library Committee, University Hall, 19.45 (R. M. Montgomery's rooms).*

Worked at the play in the morning, going over the prologue and making the necessary corrections on points of local colour, etc. After dinner called on Archer and met him coming out of his house. Went with him to the Museum where I sat until near 19 reading up the account of the Servo-Bulgarian War in the *Annual Register,* and studying the maps of the Balkan Peninsula. When I got home I found that I had mistaken the hour of the Library Meeting and that I should have gone there earlier. However, I got there at about 20 and found myself in time enough to hear most of the work. Young George Turner strolled about with me a bit before I came home. Sat up until about 1 writing letters, etc.

Papers 1d   Dinner at O[range] G[rove] 1/1   Bus to Theobald's Rd
1d   Paid subscription to Library Com[mit]tee 21/–   Income Tax sent
W. G. Burrows £6/3/8, cost orders 1½d

20   *German lesson. 10. Go down to Oxted by the 17.52 train. Meet Vernon Blackburn at Swiss Cottage station at 12.15. Meet Archer at the Hygeian at 13.*

Blackburn walked back from Hampstead across the park with me and asked me to support him in the contest which has arisen in the *Pall Mall Gazette* over his criticism of the Bach Choir. I showed him the proof of my own criticism, publication of which has been delayed in order to submit the technically libelous parts to Yates; and on my return home after dinner I wrote a letter to the *PMG* on the subject. This prevented me from catching the 17 train, as I had originally intended; and I went down to Oxted by the 17.52. Olivier traveled with me. In the evening I played several of Mozart's sonatas.

Train to Swiss Cottage 2d   Dinner 1/4   Expressing a letter to *PMG*
3d   Train P[or]tl[an]d Rd to Victoria 6d   Vict[oria] to Oxted 1/8

Vernon Blackburn (1867–1907), composer and *PMG* music critic, had been attacked in a 20 March *PMG* letter to the editor for his Bach Choir review, the signers including such people respected by Shaw as Grove and Parry. Shaw's response, published on 21 March 1894 (C1007), observed, "I knew that Sir George and Dr. Parry loved [Choir conductor] Mr. Villiers Stanford well, but I thought they loved Bach more." Shaw's own derogatory review remained suppressed by *The World*, a factor in his burgeoning disenchantment with music criticism. The galley proof of the suppressed notice survives at Cornell (Burgunder Collection).

21 °*Fabian Publishing Committee. 16¼. Not this week.*

As Salt was coming up to town and there was some housecleaning in hand I came up to town too, traveling with Olivier, Salt and Mrs. Pease and her boy. I went to Fitzroy Square for a while and then to the Orange Grove to dinner. Then I went out to Battersea and called on the Charringtons. They were out; so I went into Battersea Park for a while. Met Nora and her nurse there. Sat on the Embankment for a while reading Parry's book and then tried again at Charringtons; but they were still out. I went in and left a note for C. On my way back I was joined by Flemming, who said I had passed him and Janet without noticing them. I came to Oxted by the 17 train with Salt. Wrote some letters in the evening.

Train Oxted to Victoria & back 2/–   Papers 3d   Bus St Martin's Ch[urch] to Victoria 1d   Bus & tram Vict[oria] to P[rince] of W[ales] Road, Battersea 1d   Bus Chelsea Br[idge] to Vict[oria] 1d   [Parry's book 12/–]

The Charringtons' daughter was named Nora after their *Doll's House* success. ▪ *The Art of Music*, by C. H. H. Parry, reviewed in a G.B.S. column 4 April 1894 (C1011), concluded, "I must acknowledge my deep obligation to him for having written a book from which I have learned much. No critic can afford to leave it unread." ▪ The purchase price of Parry's book is added to Shaw's daily expenses from the evidence of Shaw's review, where he mentions buying it.

22 I have kept no account of my movements at Oxted, my diary keeping having broken down decisively at last; for I am writing this on the 30th April, after having made no record all this time. I did much as I usually do at Oxted: that is, after breakfast I went up to the West Heath, and worked until about 1 o'clock, when I returned to dinner. In the afternoon we would go out for a walk, or I would play a duet with Mrs. Salt, or the like. My work was on the play, afterwards called *Arms and the Man*, but at this time still nameless. Sometimes we went up to Olivier's. He read his new play to us one evening. Jupp called one day and stayed to tea. Another day the executor of Francis Adams, whose name I just now forget, came with a friend of his.

The "decisive" breakdown in the diary would be the failure to note expenses further; recording of incident suffered a more gradual breakdown. ▪ Shaw appeared to be forgetting Mrs. Adams as well as the name of her late husband's executor. Florence Farr and Bertha Newcombe were occupying his hours.

23 °The Messiah *at the Albert Hall.*

24 *Crystal Palace Concert. 15. Elkan Kosman, Lucille Hill. Dvorak's new symphony.*

Mrs. Salt and I went over to the Crystal Palace Concert via East Croydon and Sydenham—back by West Croydon, from which we walked to East Croydon.

> G.B.S. published no review of the Crystal Palace concert.

25 SUNDAY [   ]

26 In the afternoon I went up to Peases' and found a party there— Oakeshott, Miss Belcher, Miss Wallace (daughter of Alfred Russel Wallace), Mrs. Hartley, Miss Dix, little Brynhild Olivier, etc.

> Alfred Russel Wallace (1823–1913), naturalist, was coordinate originator, with Charles Darwin, of evolutionary theory.

27 *Go over to Balcombe. Train Oxted to East Grinstead 11.27. Change to high level there and leave at 11.50 for Three Bridges 12.17. Return from Three Bridges 20½. East Grinstead 20.50. Depart 21. Oxted 21.22.*

Bertha [Newcombe] met me at the crossroads near Three Bridges, and we walked to Balcombe through the woods. After dinner we went out and sat on a bank all the afternoon, I reading the play, which she did not like at all.

28 °*Fabian Publishing Committee, 16¼.*

29 *Opening of the Avenue Theatre under FE's management with Todhunter's* Comedy of Sighs *and Yeats'* Land of Heart's Desire. *20.* °The Flying Dutchman *at the Crystal Palace. Turner's English Opera Co. 15. Come up to town from Oxted in the afternoon.*

Began *World* article—a review of Parry's *Art of Music*. Mrs. Salt went off alone to the Crystal Palace. In the afternoon her father and Hermann Joynes called, to our great astonishment. They had had to break their journey to Brighton, the Rev. James [Joynes] being unwell. I came back to town by a train which left somewhere about 16. The play at the Avenue Theatre failed rather badly, owing to a lot of unlucky circumstances.

> The production capital for the Avenue Theatre venture was quietly furnished by Annie E. F. Horniman (1860–1937), a member, with FE and Yeats, of the Order of the Golden Dawn, and the possessor of some private income from the W. H. and J. Horniman, Ltd., tea company. (Later she would back Yeats's efforts to establish an Irish theater in Dublin.) Shaw would not learn until 1905 where the money came from. ▪ The failed play was not Yeats's modest curtain-raiser, but Todhunter's *A Comedy of Sighs* (privately Shaw called it a "fiasco"), which would limp along for sixteen performances for lack of a replacement.

30 *Fabian Executive. 17½. Fabian Committee. 16¼. German lesson. 10.* °*Mrs. Norman's At-Home. 27 Grosvenor Rd. S. W. 21½. Avenue Theatre. 14.*

Found telegram waiting for me on my return from Hampstead, summoning me to Theatre. Went down and found FE and Helmsley (the acting manager) with *Widowers' Houses* open before them, contemplating its production in despair. I dissuaded them from that and after some discussion took my new play out on to the Embankment Gardens and there and then put the last touches to it before leaving it to be typewritten. Stayed at home in the evening and worked at the *World* article.

> Charles T. H. Helmsley (1866–1940) would impress Shaw with his efficiency in handling theater business. He would later take over as manager at the St. James's for (Sir) George Alexander. ■ Shaw also wrote a letter (*CL*) to Alma Murray coaxing her to play the title role written for FE, as theater economics dictated a "name" actress. The other leading female role, that of the servant, Louka, had sufficient importance, he suggested, "for a leading lady to play her without any sacrifice of dignity."

31 *Crystal Palace Concert. 15. Stanford's* Becket *music. Kleeberg.* °*François Flameng's Napoleon pictures at the Goupil Gallery. Dine at Webbs'.* 19½.

FE came to the Palace with me.

> The Crystal Palace concert was reviewed on 11 April 1894 (C1012). "Stanford and the rest" had to return to absolute music, said G.B.S., and leave the "theatrical exploitation" of music to "the brood of young lions" who could do that better. The incidental music had been composed for Henry Irving's production of Tennyson's verse drama *Becket.* ■ Perhaps in kindness, Shaw left unmentioned in his review the piano concerto performed by Mlle. Clotilde Kleeberg. ■ Although Shaw did not get to the press view of Napoleonic canvases by François Flameng, he clearly got to the pictures sometime. His play *The Man of Destiny*, written between May and August 1895, opens revealing Napoleon immersed at his work, seated at a table littered with writing materials and dishes. Flameng's work (@1880) portrays a youthful Napoleon in similar pose. His discarded boots lie in a heap on the floor, and his jacket hangs behind him.

April

1 SUNDAY Working all day at *World* article. Went to FE in the evening. Did not get there until quite late, the article having turned out a heavy job.

2 *Spend the evening with Jules Magny. Arrive between 18 and 20.*

3 °*Miss Violet Delna's concert. Steinway Hall. 20½.*

4 *Fabian Publishing Committee. 16½.*

5 *London Symphony Concert, last of the season. St. James's Hall. 20½.*

Reviewed in passing on 25 April 1894 (C1016). Henschel's concert of Wagner "was not up to his own standard."

6 [   ]

7 *Crystal Palace Concert. 15. Choral Symphony and Dunkley's* Wreck of the Hesperus. *°J. H. Bonawitz's "Invisible Musical Performance." 17 Chesterfield Gardens, Mayfair W. °Bristol Orphans Glee Society's Concert. St. James's Hall. 15. °Private View. New English Art Club. 10 to 18. Dudley Gallery.*

The Crystal Palace concert went unmentioned until 9 May 1894 (C1019), when G.B.S. observed that "an hour and three-quarters should be fixed as the extreme outside limit for a concert of high-class music, and that the addition of any item whatsoever to a program containing the Ninth Symphony should be punished by imprisonment without option." As it was, he added, "with the honorable exception of Miss [Marie] Fillunger" (1850–1930), the Viennese concert soprano, the additions to the program were "abominably sung."

8 SUNDAY *Lecture for the Kilburn Branch of the Independent Labour Party, Phoenix Hall, Peel Rd., Canterbury Rd., on "Labour in Parliament" (J. Seager Wilder, 75 Netherwood St., Brondesbury). °Organ recital. Queen's Hall. 15.*

9 *°St. Pancras Free Library Committee, University Hall. 20.*

10 [   ]

11 *Rehearsal [of* Arms and the Man, *Avenue Theatre], 11. Fabian Publishing Committee. 16½.*

12 *Royal Choral Society. Mackenzie's* Bethlehem, *first performance, Albert Hall. 20.*

Reviewed on 18 April 1894 (C1014). The oratorio, with impossible libretto by the ubiquitous Joseph Bennett, "suggests a morally reformed Offenbach." It was G.B.S.'s feeling that the academic composer's compulsion to put large musical works into the form of the obsolescent oratorio was the cause of the musical "impotence" of Britain on the world scene.

13 *Fabian Semi-Public Meeting. Clifford's Inn. J. W. Martin on "State Education at Home and Abroad." 20. Fabian Executive. 17½. Take the chair. Fabian Committee. 16½. Take the chair. °Press View. Wyllie's drawings. Dowdeswell's.*

John W. Martin, a member of the Fabian Executive from 1894 to 1899, was author of Tract No. 52, *State Education at Home and Abroad*. After his marriage to an American, he would settle in New York, where he edited the short-lived *American Fabian* and became an authority on educational matters.

14   °*Crystal Palace Concert. 15. Wagner concert. Rehearsal. Avenue. 11.*

> Appearing this date in *The Star*, credited to "The extra special *Star* man who is retained for the sole purpose of interviewing Mr. Bernard Shaw on great occasions," was a humorous, self-drafted "interview" (C1013), " 'Arms and the Man.' Terrible Scenes at the Avenue Theatre."

15 SUNDAY   [   ]

16   °*Reginald Clarke's pianoforte recital and concert. Victoria Hall in Queen's Hall. 20.15. Rehearsals, Avenue Theatre, 11 and 19. Meet Olivier at Orange Grove 18.40.*

> Shaw's letter to Alma Murray (*CL*) later in the day, after the rehearsals, observed that the third act had gone "capitally."

17   *Wagner concert conducted by Mottl at Queen's Hall. 19.58.* °*Bijou Theatre. Albert Hall. John Gray's* Sour Grapes, *etc. 14½. Frederick Dawson's pianoforte recital. St. James's Hall. 15.*

> The Wagner concert was reviewed by G.B.S. on 25 April 1894 (C1016). It was the first appearance of Felix Mottl (1856–1911), Austrian conductor, in England. He had conducted the first season of *Ring* performances at Bayreuth. G.B.S. applauded his skills. ■ Dawson was a young pianist "with a technique which enables him to rattle off Beethoven's sonatas quite [too] cheerfully" (C1016).

18   °*Richard Mackway's concert. Steinway Hall. 20. Meet the Salts at the Orange Grove at 18. Fabian Publishing Committee. 16¼.*

19   °*Philharmonic Concert. Queen's Hall. 20. Dress rehearsal. Avenue Theatre. 18½.*

> Sapelnikoff played, but Shaw was busy with *Arms and the Man*.

20   *Fabian Executive. 17¼. Fabian Committee. 15¼. 2nd dress rehearsal, private. 19. Rehearsal, words only, 11.*

21   *Crystal Palace Concert. 15. Sophie Menter. First night of* Arms and the Man *at the Avenue Theatre.* °*Golden Legend. Queen's Hall. 15.*

[I had the curious experience of witnessing an apparently insane success, with the actors and actresses almost losing their heads with the intoxication of laugh after laugh, and of going before the curtain to tremendous applause, the only person in the theatre who knew that the whole affair was a ghastly failure.]

> Madame Menter was "still irresistible; but there were signs of wear and tear on her playing of . . . Schubert" (C1016). With Liszt "there was more of her old power and audacity." ■ Taking a curtain call at the close of the play, Shaw was booed amid the cheers by a solitary voice from the gallery. "I quite agree with you," said Shaw; "but what can two do against so many?" The voice was that of Reginald Golding Bright (1874–

1941), a young man eager to become a drama critic. (Eventually he would become Shaw's London theatrical agent.) The retort is repeated in slightly variant form by W. B. Yeats in *The Trembling of the Veil*. Press reaction ranged from an anonymous "Enormously amusing, if slightly perplexing" in *The Star* to predictably negative responses from Archer ("bright, clever, superficially cynical extravaganza") and Walkley ("second-handed Gilbertism"). ▪ Shaw to Henry Arthur Jones, 22 December 1894 (misdated 2nd December in *CL*). The "failure" Shaw read into the performance was that his play would be misperceived by his audiences, whatever their sense of fun.

22 SUNDAY   *Open a debate at the Playgoers' Club (Percy House, Playgoers' Club, Strand W. C.) on "Criticism, Corruption, and the Remedy."*

23   °*St. Pancras Public Library Committee. University Hall. 21. St. George's Day National Concert. Queen's Hall. 20.*

24   °*Dolmetsch's Viol concert at "Dowland." 24.45. French music.*

25   *London Reform Union Poor Law Conference. Club and Institute Union. 19½. Fabian Publishing Committee. 16½.*

The result would be J. F. Oakeshott's *Fabian Tract* No. 54, *Humanizing the Poor Law* (1894).

26   *Poor Law Conference continued from yesterday. 19½—move resolutions.* °*Simonetti's concert. St. James's Hall.*

27   *First meeting of new Fabian Executive. 276 Strand. 17½. Preliminary Committee. 16½. Fabian Public Meeting. Essex Hall. 20. William Clarke on "Social and Labour Movements in the United States."*

28   °*Crystal Palace Concert. 15. Manns' benefit. Wagner selections and 3rd act of* Lohengrin *at Queen's Hall. 15.*

Reviewed on 9 May 1894 (C1019). G.B.S. was impressed by the music from *Lohengrin* when performed "without the usual opera house butchery."

29 SUNDAY   *Lecture at the Hall of Science, Old Street, at 11.15, on "The Price of Brains under Socialism" (Miss Edith E. M. Vance, 28 Stonecutter St. E.C.).*

30   *Scuderi's concert. Steinway Hall. 15.*

G.B.S. (C1019) was particularly indebted to Salvatore Scuderi "for letting me hear the *obbligato* to the serenade in Don Giovanni played on the instrument for which it was written, that is, the mandolin." In Signor Scuderi G.B.S. admired "vigorous individuality and irrepressible musical talent."

May

1 °*Marie Wurm's concert. 22^b Ebury St. 15—her own compositions.* °*Public Libraries Committee, St. Pancras. 20.15. University Hall. Janet Achurch to call at 12.30 to try the typewriter.*

2 *Philharmonic Concert. Queen's Hall. 20. Call at the Avenue Theatre at 14. Fabian Publishing Committee. 16½.*

> Paderewski again played his Polish Fantasia, impelling G.B.S. to cry (C1019), "Hold, enough!" Since the pianist "can play better music than he has composed . . . , it offends all my notions of artistic economy to see Paderewski the first-rate player thrown away on Paderewski the second-rate composer."

3 *Lunch at the Orange Grove at 14 to meet the Salts.*

4 *Production of Ibsen's* Wild Duck *(first time in England) by the Independent Theatre Society at the Royalty Theatre. 20. Fabian Executive. 17½. Fabian Committee. 17.*

> The J. T. Grein production would have three performances.

5 *3rd act of* Tannhauser *and Wagner selections. Queen's Hall. 15.* °*Dolmetsch rehearsal. 17.*

> Tenor Edward Lloyd, known for recital and oratorio appearances rather than the operatic stage, sang in the concert version of *Tannhäuser,* "playing a little to the gallery." As conductor of Wagner, G.B.S. observed (C1019), Frederic Cowen was failing to "insist on accurate reading of the notes and nuances."

6 SUNDAY *Eight Hour Demonstration (Labour Day) in Hyde Park. Speak from Fabian Platform No. 12.*

7 *Fabian Central Group. 32 Great Ormond St. Cotterell-Tupp on "The Silver Question as it Affects the Workers." 20.* °*National British Women's Temperance Association. Lady Henry Somerset's At-Home. St. Martin's Town Hall. 18¼.*
Meet Archer at the Strand corner of Wellington Sq. at 15½ and go with him to the Savoy Hotel to hear Yvette Guilbert.

> The economist Alfred Cotterell-Tupp (1840–1914) published books on money and on the Civil Service in India and Indo-China. ▪ Yvette Guilbert (1867–1944), Parisian chanteuse, would make her London debut at the Empire on 9 May 1894. G.B.S. found her "a highly accomplished artist. She makes all her effects in the simplest way, and with perfect judgment." Reviewed on 16 May 1894 (C1020).

8 *Handel concert at Dolmetsch's. W. Dulwich. 20.45.* °*Elsie Mackenzie's concert. Queen's (Small) Hall. 20.* °*Frances Allitsen's concert. Steinway Hall.*

15. °*London Reform Union Poor Law Conference—adjourned meeting. Club Union Hall. 19½.* °*Miss Kate Woolf's concert. 12 Portman Square W., 15¼.*

No review of the Handel concert was published.

9 °*Ward meeting No. 7, Public Libraries for St. Pancras, University Hall. 20.15. Fabian Publishing Committee. 16¼.* °*Miss Emily Shinner's concert. Prince's Hall. 20. Max Laistner's Orchestral Concert. St. James's Hall. 20¼.*

The Max Laistner Choir "distinguished itself . . . by an excellent performance of Max Bruch's setting of Schiller's Lay of the Bell. . . . Bruch's work, passionate and grandiose at best, and lively and interesting at worst, is so very superior to the sort of thing we turn out here. . . . It might well be heard oftener" (C1020).

10 *Mrs. Clarinda Webster's Mendelssohn concert. Queen's Hall (small hall). 15.*

[In the evening I repaired to the same place . . . to hear Mr. Charles Fry recite *Eugene Aram* to an accompaniment composed by Dr. Mackenzie. I arrived just in time to have the door closed in my face, under the very proper rule which forbids people to come in during the performance of a piece. (C1020)]

When Mrs. Webster, as impresario of the event, began reading at length not only a biography of Mendelssohn but "a letter from the composer descriptive of his reception at Buckingham Palace, I regret to say that my loyalty broke down under the strain. I stole out as quietly as I could" (C1020). ▪ "Eugene Aram" was the poem by Thomas Hood about the 18th-century schoolmaster and murderer.

11 *Fabian Annual Meeting. Clifford's Inn. 20. Fabian Executive. 17½. Fabian Committee. 17. Professional matinee of* Arms and the Man. *Avenue Theatre. 15. Call on Yates at the* World *office between 11 and 1.*

Shaw would write to Alma Murray (*CL*) that her performance as Raina "lacerate[d] every fibre in my being" in lacking "the sincerity of the noble attitude and the thrilling voice." He wondered whether she had "turned cynic" and was playing instead the newspapers' misreading of the play as a spoof for laughs. Miss Murray would reply with apologies: "I have altered one or two points I confess and generally find them go[ing] better with the audience. I suppose it is these comedy touches you object to. I will do my best to take them all out. . . ." ▪ Edmund Yates's son, C. D. Yates, was running *The World*. His father, then very ill, would die on 14 May. Shaw was still unhappy over the handling of the Bach Choir affair, and was contemplating resignation.

12 *Call on Yates at 12.30.*

13 SUNDAY [   ]

Shaw was then busy writing his response to critics of his military references in *Arms and the Man*, an essay due that week at the *New Review*. "A Dramatic Realist to his Critics," to be published in the July 1894 issue (C1028), would reveal in detail the extent of his military homework. It would also net him £18.

14   *Opening night at Covent Garden. Production of Puccini's* Manon Lescaut. *20½.*

Reviewed on 23 May 1894 (C1020). G.B.S.'s first experience of the new realism of Giacomo Puccini (1858–1924) found the "ground so transformed that you could almost think yourself in a new country." The "domain of Italian opera is enlarged" and was "also unmistakably symphonic in its treatment."

15   °*Miss Minny Cortese's concert. Prince's Hall. 15¼. Daniel de Lange's Amsterdam Choir. St. Martin's Town Hall. 20¼. Opera.* Faust. *20.*

Promoting the Amsterdam Choir, G.B.S. reminded his readers (C1020) that he would "never forget the effect produced on me [by their visit in July 1885], or the stupendous insensibility of most of the other droppers-in to the fact that they were listening to one of the finest and rarest performances they had ever heard in their lives." His expectations of the revisit, he wrote afterwards (C1021), were "far surpassed. . . . I wish I had space to do justice to the extraordinary excellence of their execution and the surpassing interest and beauty of the music, sacred and secular, of Josquin, Orlando, Sweelinck, and the rest . . . of the old Netherlandish school." ▪ *Faust*, unattended, was only briefly mentioned in his omnibus opera column (C1021).

16   °*Fabian Publishing Committee. 16¼. Not held this week.* °*Miss Agnes Bartlett's concert. Queen's Hall (small). 20¼.* °*Miss Maud McCarthy's concert. Prince's Hall. 15¼. Opera.* Orfeo *and* Cavalleria. *20.*

Orfeo was "immortal" (C1021); *Cavalleria Rusticana* derived "exceptional dramatic force" from the acting of tenor Fernando De Lucia.

17   *Opera.* Philemon *and* Pagliacci. *20.*

Gounod's *Philémon et Baucis* was highlighted by basso Pol Plançon (1845–1914), who was "splendid" as Jupiter (C1021); in *Pagliacci*, tenor Mario Ancona was strong in the leading role.

18   *Fabian Executive. 17¼. Fabian Committee. 17.* °*Fabian School Board Election Committee. 20. Opera* Carmen *(Calvé). 20. Meeting at the* Review of Reviews *office, Norfolk St., to discuss Stead's proposal of a National Council to Federate the Moral Forces making for Social Progress. 15.*

"I *hate* performers who debase great works of art," G.B.S. wrote on 30 May 1894 (C1022). " . . . but I am necessarily no less extreme in my admiration of artists who realize the full value of great works for me, or who transfigure ordinary ones. Calvé is such an artist. . . . But I have no eulogies for her Carmen, which shocked me. . . ." The role was so brutally realistic as drama that French soprano Emma Calvé (1858–1942) was "incapable of paying the smallest attention to the score." Yet her Santuzza in *Cavalleria* had been "irresistibly moving and beautiful."

19   *Opera. Production of Verdi's* Falstaff. *20½.* °*English Ladies' Orchestral Society's Concert. Sheldonian Theatre. Oxford. 14.15. Concert at the Crystal Palace. 15¼. Arthur Argiewicz, boy fiddler. Patti concert. Albert Hall. 15. Fisher Unwin's affair at Clifford's Inn Hall. Bookseller's, Conway's Himalayan book and McCormick's pictures.*

The opera, G.B.S. thought (C1021), suffered from the phenomenon that the play had outlasted "the freshness of the subject, a fate which invariably overtakes *The Merry Wives of Windsor*, except when the actor who plays Falstaff has an extraordinary power of inventing humorous and varied character traits." ■ Shaw's 30 May 1894 review (C1021) of the Palace program, on principle, ignored the infant phenomenon. G.B.S. praised Patti's artistry with a song, even one by Wagner, not "regretting that Time has stolen some of the five or six notes above the B flat which she once possessed, and has made the rest hardly safe for everyday use." ■ (Sir) William Martin Conway (1856–1897), mountaineer, explorer, and archeologist, had published *Climbing and Exploration in the Karakoram-Himalayas* (London, 1894), with 300 illustrations by Arthur David McCormick (1860–1943), the Irish-born landscape painter who specialized in African and Asian scenes and would publish his own *An Artist in the Himalayas* in 1895.

20 SUNDAY   *Speak in Battersea Park at 18.30 in place of John Burns.*

21   °*Reception at the Netherlands Ministry, 5 Queen's Gate Place S.W. 22. Amsterdam Choir.* °*Miss Grainger Kerr's concert. Queen's Hall (small hall). 15¼. Dine with the Webbs on their return from Venice. 19½.* °*St. Pancras Free Libraries Committee. University Hall. 20½.*

22   *2nd Mottl Concert. Queen's Hall. 19.58. [J. H.] Bonawitz's Invisible Musical Performance. Queen's Hall (small hall). 15.* °*Mathilde Verne's and Ethel Barnes's pianoforte and violin recital. St. James's Hall. 15.* °*Charles Phillips' concert. Steinway Hall. 15. (Wallace's songs).* °*Dolmetsch's last concert—Bach. "Dowland" at 20.45.* °*Fritz Masbach's recital. St. James's Hall. 15. Pianoforte. German lesson. 11 to 1.*

Shaw blamed a sudden "desolating Arctic wind" (C1022) that chilled London for blighting Mottl's ranks of instrumentalists and producing a "slack" performance. ■ The "Invisible Musical Performance" was referred to in advance on 16 May 1894 (C1020). G.B.S. did not go. "I do not at all object to seeing the performers at a concert: it is hearing them that upsets me. If Mr. Bonawitz will try an inaudible concert, he may rely on my eager support."

23   *Fabian Publishing Committee. 16¼. Lunch with the Harold Cox's at 1 Field Court, Gray's Inn, at 13½. Address School Board Election Meeting at Willesden for John Cash, Regency Hall, High Rd., Willesden Green. 20. Call on Heinemann between 11 and 12 at 21 Bedford St. Mathilde Verne's and Ethel Barnes' concert. St. James's Hall. 15.*

John Cash was a Labour candidate who lived in Hampstead. His wife was a Fabian.

24   *Philharmonic Concert. Queen's Hall. 20.* °*Meeting at Chelsea Town Hall to protest vs British Institute of Preventive Medicine. 20½. Sevadjian's pianoforte recital. St. James's Hall. 15.*

The Philharmonic was reviewed on 13 June 1894 (C1025). The guest conductor was Edvard Grieg, who was "so successful in getting fine work out of the band that if the directors were wise they would make him a handsome offer to take it in hand permanently." ■ Jean Sevadjian, G.B.S. wrote on 6 June 1894 (C1024), "though an accurate player, has a peculiar way of scrutinizing the keyboard as if he did not quite know where he would find the note he wanted, which gives him an old resemblance to a person trying to write a word on a typewriter for the first time. These peculiarities of manner perhaps handicapped him a little unfairly with the audience."

25   *Fabian Semi-Public Meeting at Clifford's Inn. 20. Stewart Headlam on "What the Present School Board has done." Fabian Executive.* 17½. *Fabian Committee. 17. German lesson. 11 to 1.*

26   °*Miss Muirhead's Mozart lecture. 60 Belsize Park Gardens. 15.* °*Frederick Frederiksen's concert. Queen's Hall (small). 20.* °*Tivadar Nachéz's violin recital. St. James's Hall. 15. Go down to Oxted by the 17.52 train from Victoria.* °*Evelun Carlton's concert. 8 Beaufort Gardens, South Kensington.* 15¼. *Postponed to 9th June.*

27   SUNDAY   °*Speak in Battersea Park for the Labour League.* 18½ *(W. F. Champion, 451 Battersea Park Rd. S. W.). Last week.* °*Mrs. Graham Tomson's in the evening. 20 St. John's Wood Rd. 19. Oxted.*

28   *Grafton Hall. Performance of Otto Wichers v. Gogh's* Die Soziale Frage. *20.* °*Arthur Argiewicz's concert. Prince's Hall. 20. Clotilde Kleeberg's recital. St. James's Hall. 15.* °*Florence Shee's concert. Queen's Hall (small). 20. Come up from Oxted by the 11.21 train to London Bridge.*

"Miss Kleeberg . . . , if not so neat and even-handed as she used to be, has gained in freedom of expression" (C1024).

29   °*Olivier lectures on "Economic Science" to the New Fellowship, 337 Strand.* 19½. °*Public Libraries for St. Pancras, Executive Committee, University Hall.* 20½. *German lesson. 11 to 1.*

30   °*Scuderi's 2nd concert. Steinway Hall. 15. Fabian Publishing Committee.* 16¼.

Shaw's major business of the day was to write to C. D. Yates (*CL*) to suggest moving up Major Arthur Griffiths in the aftermath of the death of Edmund Yates, and to ask whether it would be "a serious inconvenience" if he gave up his music critic assignment. "I shall, of course," he promised, "keep my department going until fresh arrangements are made, if the editor desires it." Griffiths, who was indeed moved up to editor, asked Shaw to stay to the end of the season.

31   °*Charles Lunn on Voice Training. St. Martin's Town Hall.* 20½. °*Handel Society's concert. Queen's Hall.* 20¼. Les Huguenots *at Covent Garden. [Ada] Adiny.* °*Concert at Dudley House for St. Matthew's, Lisson Grove.* 15¾.

G.B.S. was discouraged by the "staleness" of *Les Huguenots*, which remained reinforced by the obsolescent mutilations of the score and the antiquated stage business (C1024). The role of Valentine was sung by Madame Ada Adiny, "a tall, powerfully built lady with a serviceable high C, . . . but without invention as an actress. . . ."

June

1 *Fabian Executive. 17½. Take the chair. Fabian Committee. 17.
°Hope-Jones Electric Organ. 19 Hyde Park Terrace. 15 to 17. German lesson.
11 to 1.*

2 Faust *at Covent Garden. Melba. Ada Wray's concert. Prince's Hall. 15.*
[We had *Faust,* with Melba as Margaret. De Lucia accosted her in the
second act in Italian; she snubbed him in French; Bauermeister kept her in
countenance by conversing with her in French in the garden; and Mephistopheles, at home in all countries, tempted Faust in Italian and Marta in
French. And, to give the devil his due, his French was the best in the
collection: Margaret's, in particular, being occasionally rather like mine.]

> Shaw skipped Ada Wray's recital for *Faust.* ▪ Despite the dramatic absurdity of the
> babel of languages, Mario Ancona's Valentin was "the best we have had for a long time"
> (C1024). The other principals were Mathilde Bauermeister and Fernando de Lucia.

3 SUNDAY *Call on Richard Mansfield at the Langham Hotel at 11.*

> Richard Mansfield had come to London on theater business. As actor-manager he special-
> ized in romantic melodrama. He was interested in producing *Arms and the Man* in the
> United States. Shaw would draft a contract.

4 *Leonard Kane's demonstration of his "Perfect Natural Voice System."
French Room. St. James's Restaurant. 15. °Royal Academy of Music Students' Concert. Tenterden St. 15.*

5 *Josef Ludvig's Orchestral Concert. St. James's Hall. 20. °Call on Charles
Wyndham at the Criterion Theatre at 14. Put off to tomorrow. °Conference
of the National Reform Union, Westminster Town Hall. 20½. German lesson.
11 to 1.*

> Ludvig's concert went unreviewed. ▪ Charles Wyndham was actor-manager at the
> Criterion Theatre. See also 11 July 1888.

6 *Last day to send in Income Tax return. Fabian Publishing Committee.
16½. Call on Wyndham, see yesterday.*

7 *Philharmonic Concert. Queen's Hall. 20. Leonard Kane's "Perfect Natural Voice System" concert. St. James's Hall. 20¼. °Lawrence Kellie's second
recital. Steinway Hall. 15.*

> Saint-Saëns was guest conductor, performing his own symphony (No. 3) for organ, two
> pianos, and orchestra, "a model of elegant instrumentation. . . . It is a pity that this
> particular work . . . degenerates so frightfully at the end. All that barren *coda* stuff . . .
> should be ruthlessly excised" (C1025). ▪ Kane's recital, despite Shaw's interest in the
> subject, went unreviewed.

8 *Fabian Semi-Public Meeting at Clifford's Inn. 20. H. Lowerison on "Our School Board Program and How to Carry It." Bispham's Schumann recital. St. James's Hall. 15. Fabian Executive. 17¼. °Fabian Committee. 17. °Executive Committee South St. Pancras Liberal and Radical Association Meeting at 11 Endsleigh Gardens. 20. °German lesson. 11. Put off.*

> David Bispham, with Marguerite Hall and Lillian Henschel, and Henry Bird as accompanist, produced a "prodigiously successful" concert (C1025).

9 Rigoletto *at Covent Garden (Melba, Ancona). °Evelun Carlton's concert. Postponed from 26th ult.*

> Reviewed on 20 June 1894 (C1026). Ancona was a "disappointment" while Melba was "as beautiful as ever" and Ravogli as "clever" as Maurel was "painful."

10 SUNDAY *Lunch with the Webbs at 13¼.*

Corrected *World* proof. Morse Stephens was at the Webbs'. We all sat talking until 17, when he went away, and we four, Wallas, the Webbs and myself, walked to Battersea Park, where I left them and went into Charringtons. Flemming was there. I stayed until past 21 and then made for FE, but I did not get to Hammersmith until 22.30; so I changed into a Metropolitan train and came home, it being too late to call on her.

11 *Covent Garden. Production of Massenet's* Werther—*Jean de Rezske. °Fabian Central Group. 32 Great Ormond St. Reports from delegates to School Board Committees.*

> Jean de Rezske, said G.B.S. (C1026), was "masterly" as Werther, while Emma Eames as Charlotte furnished only a passionless "cold radiance."

12 *Leonard Borwick's recital. St. James's Hall. 15. °Wagner Society's Conversazione. 160 New Bond St. German lesson. 11 to 1.*

> Although Borwick "cannot play Beethoven" (C1026), his playing of Chopin was "really worth hearing."

13 *Isidor Cohn's recital. St. James's Hall. 20. Covent Garden. Romeo. °Miss Trask's Choir. Prince's Hall. 20. Bruch's Lay of the Bell. 20. °Miss Goodwin and Mme. Griffith's concert. Queen's Hall (small hall). 20. Fabian Publishing Committee. 16¼.*

> A trio by Dvořák was "mere rhapsody" with little sonata form about it (C1026); in addition to the Cohn chamber group, Lydia Müller "sang some German songs very competently." ■ What G.B.S. saw of Jean de Reszke in Gounod's *Roméo et Juliette* (apparently after sampling Borwick's program) was happy. His "impersonation" was not only "unflaggingly interesting, but exquisitely attractive" (C1026).

14 *°Schubert, Schumann and Brahms recitals. Queen's Hall (small hall). 20. (Schubert) Last night of Duse—Dame aux Camellias. °Bernoff on his*

Russian travels. Savoy Hotel. 15¼. Foreign Press Association. °Sydney Brook's concert. Steinway Hall. 20. °Hirwen Jones's concert. Steinway Hall. 15.

G.B.S. had earlier compared the acting of Duse to Calvé, giving the former higher marks for sensitivity of portrayal (C1022).

15   *°Verne and Barnes's piano and violin recital. St. James's Hall. 15. Committee to prepare Fabian tract on "Women." 276 Strand. 20. Press View. Paintings by Troyon. Goupil Gallery. 5 Regent St. 10 to 18. °Harvey Lohr's concert. Prince's Hall. 20¼. Fabian Executive. 17½. Fabian Committee. 17. German lesson. 2 to 4 instead of 11 to 1. °Private View. Menpes' Egyptian pictures. Dowdeswell's. Miss Mary Symons' concert. Steinway Hall. 15.*

The result would be *Fabian Tract* No. 67, *Women and the Factory Acts* (1896), by Beatrice Webb. Fabian committees were extraordinarily energetic and peopled with well-organized talents.   ▪   Constant Troyon (1810–1865), French landscape and animal painter. Shaw was still receiving press tickets, and often used them.   ▪   An unusual failure by Shaw to use a 24-hour clock. He was probably repeating the times on a message received changing the lesson schedule.   ▪   Miss Symons's concert went unreviewed.

16   *Sidney Dark's vocal and dramatic recital. Brinsmead Galleries, Wigmore St. 15. °A. E. Dawson's concert. Prince's Hall. 15. Call on Major Griffiths at the World office at 12.30. °Antonietta Palloni's concert. Lady Jeune's, 79 Harley St. 14½. Lunch with H. A. Jones. 14.*

Dark, G.B.S. would write on 25 July 1894 (C1033), alternated songs for bass voice with recitations from "standard authors, from Marlowe to Rudyard Kipling," and "acquitted himself, both as elocutionist and singer, very handsomely, and with a certain personal ability not too common in his profession."   ▪   The call on Major Griffiths was to continue negotiations on ending G.B.S.'s assignments as music critic. Shaw, weary of the regimen, was willing to chance his earnings now from plays and freelance journalism.

17 SUNDAY   *Speak at Croydon at 15¼ (Edgar E. Bottle, 17 St. Peter's Rd., Croydon). 15 train Victoria to East Croydon. Lowenfeld to call at 12.*

Theater manager Henry Lowenfeld (1858–1931) would move in 1901 from the Prince of Wales's Theatre to the Apollo Theatre. An Austrian from a wealthy brewing family, he would ask Shaw, unsuccessfully, several years later (1897) for rights to make a Viennese-style light opera out of *Arms and the Man.* (CL).

18   *°Mme Caravoglia's concert. St. James's Banqueting Hall. 15. Miss d'Esterre Keeling's pianoforte lecture recital. Queen's Hall. 15¼. °London Liberal and Radical Union Council meeting. National Liberal Club. 20. Covent Garden.*

"As a rule," G.B.S. confessed (C1033), "I detest lady-lecturers on music, because they never even pretend to say what they think; but Miss d'Esterre Keeling relied on her mother-wit, and made it go as far as a ton of clergy. . . . I was not bored; and the playing was adequate."

19 °*Ernest Fowles' pianoforte recital. Prince's Hall. 20.* °*Robert Hensler's concert. Steinway Hall. 20.* °*Chaplin Trio's concert. Queen's Hall (small). 20. Drury Lane. German opera, first night.*

> Reviewed on 27 June 1894 (C1027), G.B.S. protesting "against the way in which *Die Walküre* was shoveled on at Drury Lane" by Sir Augustus Harris.

20 *Fabian Publishing Committee. 16½.* °*Annual General Meeting Economic Association, Museum of Geology, 28 Jermyn St. 20. J. S. Nicholson on "Political Economy and Journalism." Covent Garden.* Orfeo *and* La Navarraise *(first performance).*

> *La Navarraise*, by Jules Massenet, starred Pol Plançon and Emma Calvé. G.B.S. (C1027) saw it as frankly modeled upon *Cavalleria:* "He has not composed an opera: he has made up a prescription." Nevertheless, it was "simple and powerful, . . . credible and touching."

21 *Philharmonic Concert. Queen's Hall. 20. Last of the season. Take the 1.55 train (Metropolitan) to Richmond.* °*Brinsmead Galleries. Bernhardt's lecture on "Vocal Methods." 20.* °*Clerici's pianoforte and vocal recital. Steinway Hall. 15½.*

> The Philharmonic concert was not reviewed.

22 °*Handel Festival rehearsal. Fabian Public Meeting at Essex Hall. 20. G. W. Foote on "A Secularist's View of Social Progress." Fabian Executive. 17½. Fabian Committee. 17.* °*Society of British Dramatic Art, performance of Cumberland's* Box Lobby Challenge *at the Royalty Theatre. 14½. Meet Bertha Newcombe at the Orange Grove between 14 and 15 and go to the Burlington Fine Arts Club with her to see the exhibition of Ferrara— Bologna pictures.* °*German lesson. 11. Put off.*

23 °*Opera concert. Queen's Hall. 15. Recital of* Faust. *Nuovina, etc. Drury Lane.* Siegfried. *19½.*

I finished the *World* article in the morning. After dinner I went out to Hammersmith; called for FE; found she was not at home; took train from Chiswick to Finchley Rd.; got my hair cut there, and walked back across the park.

24 SUNDAY   *Go down to Carrs's cottage at Dunsfold—10.15 train from Waterloo to Godalming.* °*Committee of Foote Testimonial Fund, Hall of Science. 21.*

25 °*Handel Festival.* The Messiah. *Crystal Palace.* °*Concert of Ancient Greek Music. Queen's Hall (small room). 17. Come up from Carrs's by the 20.22 train from Whitley.*

26 *German lesson. 11. Dolmetsch exhibits the new clavichords he has made at West Dulwich. 20.45.* °Tannhauser *at Drury Lane (tickets miscarried).*

Reviewed on 4 July 1894 (C1029). The Royal College of Music had commissioned a clavichord—"a little masterpiece, excellent as a musical instrument and pleasant to look at, which seems to me likely to begin a revolution in domestic musical instruments as William Morris's work made in domestic furniture. . . ."

27   *Handel Festival. Selection. °Fabian Publishing Committee. 16$\frac{1}{2}$. Council Meeting, Progressive School Board Election Council; Memorial Hall. 20.*

G.B.S. called the Handel Festival (C1029) a "national institution . . . applauded for its nonsense much more than for its sense." "Bigness" was no merit: "you cannot get artistic magnitude by the multiplication of nobodies." Its social function was its only redeeming feature: "If the sole useful function of a choral performance were the perfect execution of the masterpieces of choral music, then I should unhesitatingly recommend the dispersion of the Handel choir by armed force. . . ."

28   *Schubert, Schumann and Brahms recital. Queen's Hall. 20. (Schumann). Go down to Effingham Junction by the 14.40 train from Waterloo to Archer's to meet Miss [Annie Payson] Call. Miss Margaret Carter's recital. Brinsmead's. 20. (Mrs. Brownlow). °Martha Möller's concert. St. James's Banqueting Hall. 20.*

In the country at Archer's cottage, Shaw covered none of the musical events of the day for review.

29   *°Handel Festival.* Israel in Egypt. *Fabian Private Meeting at Clifford's Inn to consider Education tract. 20. Go early to meet Rose (say 19.40). Fabian Executive. 17$\frac{1}{2}$. °Fabian Committee. 17. German lesson. 14$\frac{1}{2}$. °Countess of Radnor's concert. St. James's Hall. 21.*

30   *Production of [Sir Frederic] Cowen's* Signa *at Covent Garden.* Tristan and Isolde *at Drury Lane. °Operatic concert. Queen's Hall. 15. Lunch at Archer's at 13$\frac{1}{4}$. Drawings by the Sickerts and Steer at Robert Sickert's, 38 Wilton Place W.*

Signa was reviewed on 11 July 1894 (C1030). "When a four-act opera is cut down to two acts, the composer is entitled to claim suspension of judgment as to the merit of his work as a whole. I have seldom been so taken aback as when the three leading persons in the opera, whose acquaintance we had barely made . . . , suddenly pulled out daggers and ended one another's existences on no discernible provocation." ▪ *Tristan and Isolde* was reviewed on 18 July 1894 (C1031). Katharina Klafsky, despite her vocal and dramatic gifts, "completely perverted the music by making it express the most poignant grief for the loss of Tristan—the very sort of stage commonplace to which Isolde's sacred joy in the death towards which the whole work is an aspiration, ought to be the most complete rebuke." ▪ Robert Sickert (1861?–1922) was one of the Munich-born literary and artistic Sickert brothers, all of whom found some measure of success in England. More of a misfit than his brothers, and a semi-invalid because of a kidney ailment, Robert Sickert first opened his own gallery and finally became secretary of the Carfax Gallery.

July

1 SUNDAY   *Call for [Edward] Carpenter at 38 Gloucester Rd. N.W. at about 15.*

2   *Call on Miss [Elizabeth] Marbury at the Royal Palace Hotel, High Street, Kensington, at 11.45. Call on John R. Rogers, Cecil House, Savoy, at 14.30, to meet Howard Talbot.* °*Miss D'Esterre Keeling's pianoforte lecture recital. Queen's Hall (small). 15¼.*

> John R. Rogers (1842–1903), soon to be a baronet, was chairman of the London County Council from 1892 to 1895, and deputy lieutenant of the County of London. He lived at Cecil House, Savoy, W.C. ▪ Howard Talbot, composer and conductor, wrote the music for *Wapping Old Stairs*, which G.B.S. had seen on 17 February 1894.

3   °*Lohengrin at Drury Lane. 19½.* °*Mme Pheroze Langrana's concert. Queen's Hall (small). 15.* °*Jan Mulder's concert. Brinsmead Galleries. 20. Production of Messager's* Mirette. *Savoy Theatre. 20.10. German Lesson. 11.*

> *Mirette* had music by André Messager, whose *Basoche* G.B.S. had admired. Michel Carré and Harry Greenbank wrote the libretto and Frederick E. Weatherly the lyrics. A talented assemblage, G.B.S. concluded (C1030), had produced a pointless and tedious sentimental opera, staged with great professionalism by the Savoy management. It would have a run of 101 performances.

4   *Miss Amina Goodwin and Mme Lilian Griffiths' second concert. Queen's Hall. 15.* °*Fabian Publishing Committee. 16¼.*

> Briefly noted (C1033) as one of a series of concerts of "good chamber music . . . well worth the subscription."

5   *Chelsea Town Hall. Lady Ramsay's* Blessed Damozel. *15¼.* °*Marie Geselschap's recital (pianoforte). Steinway Hall. 20¼. Wrong date. Last week.* °*Go up to Frampton's, 32 Queen's Rd., St. John's Wood, at 21½.*

> "I found Sir John Stainer gravely conducting a setting of Rossetti's Blessed Damozel by Lady Ramsay of Banff. It was very pretty; and it was . . . composed by Lady Ramsay entirely and sincerely on her own impulse and in her own way." But, G.B.S. concluded (C1033), she hardly knew enough of composition "to write a barcarolle."

6   *Fabian Executive. 17¼.* °*Fabian Committee. 17.* °*Press View. Roussel's drawings at Dowdeswell's.*

7   *Patti concert. Albert Hall. 15. Mr. A. J. Bates to call between 12 and 13.* Fidelio *at Drury Lane. Elaine at Covent Garden (the de Reszkes).* °*Last night of* Arms and the Man *at the Avenue Theatre.*

> "Patti continued her new departure into Wagnerland by singing Elisabeth's prayer from Tannhäuser" (C1031). ▪ Arthur J. Bates, a well-to-do Fabian, lived at 20 St. Stephen's Rd., Bayswater. ▪ The artistry of the principal singers—Klafsky, Alvary, and Wie-

gand—made *Fidelio* "live again" (C1031), the singers demonstrating an "affectionate intimacy" with the work. ▪ G.B.S. (C1031) felt that Jean de Reszke was wasting his time in the "inanely pretty" *Elaine* of Henri Bemberg. ▪ Shaw's critic duties kept him from the 75th and last performance of *Arms and the Man*. Although he had written Henry Arthur Jones on 11 June (*CL*) that the play "only twice [had] drawn as much as half the cost of sending up the curtain" and had also been hurt in box office take by a cab strike, the date of closing had been set long in advance by the expiration of the manager's theater lease that date. Shaw would write C. T. H. Helmsley, Florence Farr's manager, on 12 July (*CL*) that out of the production "I have made £90 and your acquaintance. This is handsome payment, thanks to the latter item, which will, I hope, outlast the former."

8 SUNDAY   *Lunch at Webbs'. 13½.*

9   *Zeldenrust's recital (pianoforte). Queen's Hall. 21.*

Eduard Zeldenrust proved (C1033) to be "gifted with a high degree of musical intelligence; but he failed to convince me that his evident enjoyment of his skill in playing was accompanied by much love of what he played."

10   °*Mlle. Caroline de Radio's pianoforte recital. Steinway Hall. 15.* °*Clément's concert. St. James's Hall. 15. German Opera, Drury Lane, Der Freischütz. 19½.* °*De Lara's At-Home. 4 Portman Mansions West. German lesson. 11.*

The "freshness and charm" of *Der Freischütz* still delighted G.B.S. (C1031).

11   °*"Inauguration" of Érard's new premises—Paderewski. 16 to 18. 18 Great Marlborough St.*

Although he recorded missing the opening, G.B.S. was able to write soon after (C1033)— since he visited on the 12th—that the *Salle Érard* in Great Marlborough Street "is by a very great deal the best-looking room of the kind our great pianoforte houses have yet given us."

12   *Lecture at the Pioneer Club, 22 Barton St. W., on "Art" (Mrs. Stanton Blatch). 20.* °*Schubert-Schumann and Brahms recitals, Queen's Hall. 20. (Brahms).* °*Miscellaneous concert. St. James's Hall. 15. E. de Reszke, etc. Clément and Delafosse's concert. Érard Rooms. 16. Miss D'Esterre Keeling's third lecture. Queen's Hall (small). 15⅔.*

According to Vernon Lee, who was reporting this meeting of the Pioneer Club for Women, Shaw was "very personal and caddish, but delightfully suggestive." ▪ Pianist Léon Delafosse accompanied Edmond Clément, a tenor from the Opéra Comique. He also played, on his own, the Beethoven "Moonlight Sonata"—"and left it for dead in the shortest time on record." Clément sent G.B.S. "flying into the street . . . with one of those strident notes of which he is so proud" (C1033). ▪ G.B.S.'s survey of Keeling's lectures on great composers (C1033) appeared as a note to the 2d lecture, 18 June 1894.

13   °*Miss Mary Barton's matinée musicale 15. Queen's Hall. Fabian Executive. 17½. Fabian Committee. 17.* °*Call on George Moore at 20 and read* Mrs. Warren's Profession *to him. Put off. German lesson. 14½.* °*Clara Daniel's concert. 97 Gloucester Rd. W. 15.*

14 *Miss [Edith] Nalborough's matinée. Brinsmead Galleries. 15. Liza Lehmann's concert. St. James's Hall. 15.*

G.B.S. gleaned little about Miss Nalborough's piano technique, writing (C1033) of the venue that "Messrs. Brinsmead . . . have set apart a room in 'cellar cool,' outside which the belated critic can sit cosily on the warm stairs and enjoy an excellent view of the platform through the bannisters." ▪ Liza Lehmann's farewell concert (so advertised) resulted in the comment from G.B.S. (C1033): "As Miss Lehmann's only reason for retiring is that she is getting married, I question whether her renunciation of the lucrative activity of public singing will be permanent. Though a bachelor, I venture to doubt whether matrimony is so absorbing a pursuit as she thinks at present. . . ." In any event, she sang "with freshness and charm."

15 SUNDAY *°Mrs. Theodore Wright's At-Home. Fairbourne. "Merry Piper of Nuremberg." Call on Drabig at Richmond and go over his German translation of* Arms and the Man. *Put off.*

16 *Call on Drabig at the Institute of Languages. 14 to 16. Start for Bayreuth, leaving Holborn Viaduct at 17.40. Go straight through to Darmstadt.*

[By Dover, Ostend (four hours' sea), Brussels, Cologne, and Nuremberg, which is on the whole the most expeditious route, the price of a return ticket, second-class, with first-class on the boat, is £6.11s.6d. (C1035)]

17 *Spend the afternoon at Darmstadt and make for Wurzburg to spend the night. °Isidore de Lara's Conférence and Recital (Paul Milliet, conférencier). 67 Lancaster Gate. 16.*

[It is just the sort of afternoon to spend in a second class foreign town—too sultry to make even the lightest mackintosh bearable, and raining like mad every ten minutes. . . . Baedeker suggested going to the top of the Duke of York's column, for the sake of the view. I should have expected more sense from Baedeker on a wet day.]

From a fragment of an unpublished travel essay intended as a "Corno di Bassetto" column in *The Star*, Humanities Research Center, University of Texas at Austin. Quoted from the pocket notebook in *Shaw. An Exhibit* (1977). While in Darmstadt Shaw also visited the *Madonna* of Hans Holbein (1497?–1543), which contributed to his concept of *Candida*, soon to be begun.

18 *°Trinity College Conversazione. Royal Institute Galleries. 20¼ to 11 [23]. See Wurzburg and go on to Nuremberg between 14 and 15 arriving between 17 and 18.*

19 *Go on to Bayreuth by the 10.33 train. Lodge with Kapper, 1 Hintere Damenallee. Parsifal 16.*

[I am strongly tempted to insert here a picture of one of the wicked flower maidens in *Parsifal*, whose dresses, made of huge dock-leaves, come down very little below the knees. . . . What makes it worse is that these flower maidens really do make downright bold advances to Parsifal, who very properly gives them no encouragement. (C1035)]

20   Lohengrin. *16, first performance at Bayreuth.*

[I nearly killed myself yesterday in trying to get an account of the first performance off to the *Star* by the 8.45 post, the last act beginning at 8.30.]

> Shaw would write a number of pieces on Bayreuth, summing up his mixed feelings about the Bayreuth experience. Two were G.B.S. "Music" columns in *The World*, 1 August 1894 (C1034) and 8 August 1894 (C1036). Also there was "The Bayreuth Festival," *Pall Mall Budget*, 2, 9 and 16 August 1894 (C1035); and " 'Bassetto' at the Wagner Festival," *The Star* 21, 23–26 July 1894 (C1032).

21   *Go out to the Fantasie Hotel to meet the Oliviers, the Thornycrofts, Miss Warley and Mrs. Henderson at 13. No performance today.*

[If you wish to make an impression of the most unexampled singularity and eccentricity in Germany, you only have to reply to the universal inquiry "Pilsener or Münchener?" with a statement that you do not drink beer at all. (C1035)]

22 SUNDAY   Tannhäuser. *16.*

[The Venusberg ballet . . . of the Three Graces . . . has been quite defeated by draping these three excellent young ladies so copiously that, but for that ravishing glimpse of their alabaster shoulders . . . they only require veils and gloves to be totally invisible. And as to their dancing, . . . a minuet would have appeared quite bacchanalian in contrast (C1035).]

23   Parsifal. *16. Leave for Nuremberg after the performance by the 23 train.*

[I have never found it worth my while to see any work performed more than once at Bayreuth except *Parsifal*, which cannot be seen elsewhere. (C1035)]

24   *Leave Nuremberg at 7.12 and travel right through to Ostend, arriving 23.15.*

[Theatre tickets £4, traveling expenses £6.11s.6d., other expenses, including lodging at Bayreuth £5. . . . (C1035)]

25   *Spend the day at Ostend.*

26   *Cross to Dover by the 10.53 boat and come home.*

27   *Lunch with Grant Allen at the Saville Club at 13$\frac{1}{2}$.*

Before Bayreuth Shaw had written an indignant letter (*CL*) to Grant Allen asking him to pay his back Fabian dues. At Allen's request they were meeting now to restore friendly relations. "Can they feed a vegetarian?" Shaw asked Allen (*CL*) about his club.

28 [I am so busy this week . . .]

A comment in Shaw's letter of 28 July 1894 (*CL*) to Joseph Edwards, a Liverpool Fabian. Shaw was rushing to complete his musical articles.

29 SUNDAY Miss Barton called in the morning. I finished stencilling the drawings of the costumes for *Arms and the Man.*

Miss Barton is probably the Mary Barton mentioned on 13 July 1894, whose Queen's Hall concert Shaw missed. ▪ Shaw does not explain why new drawings of *Arms and the Man* costumes were needed four months after the London opening. Probably these were intended for the provincial tour (see 21 August 1894).

30 [ ]

31 [For months I have held the whole subject of musical art in an intense grip, which never slackened even when I was asleep; but now the natural periodicity of my function asserts itself, and compels me to drop the subject in August and September. . . . (C1036)]

Shaw would not write any further musical criticism for *The World* on a regular basis after the Bayreuth series. After the early autumn hiatus in performances, his place would be taken by Robert Smythe Hichens (1864–1950), who had studied music but had just found himself as a novelist with *The Green Carnation*, a satire on Oscar Wilde. Hichens's greatest success in fiction would be *The Garden of Allah*, in 1905.

August

1–20 [Sitting, as I am today, in a Surrey farmhouse with the sky overcast, and a big fire burning to keep me from shivering, it seems to me that it must be at least four or five months since I was breathing balmy airs in the scented pine-woods on the hills round Bayreuth. If I could only see the sun for five minutes I could better recall what I have to write about. (C1036)]

21 *First rehearsal of* Arms and the Man *for provinces. Mona Hotel. 12. Come up from Milford by the 10.10 train.*

Shaw had been staying with the Salts in Surrey, at their farmhouse at Tilford. The nearest rail junction to London was to the east, at Milford.

22 *Rehearsal. Mona Hotel. 11. Go down to Milford by the 17.5 train.* °*Fabian Publishing Committee. 16½.*

23   Very wet day. The Connors did not come after all.

The Connors were unidentified friends of the Salts.

24   *Come up from Milford by the 10.10 train. Rehearsal. Mona Hotel. 12.*

25   *Rehearsal. Elephant and Castle Theatre. 11. Charringtons' in the evening.*

The Elephant and Castle Theatre, no longer extant, was in the New Kent Road, S.E., and was home to touring companies.

26 SUNDAY   *Rehearsal. Drinkwater's rooms. 1 Ladbroke Crescent. 19.*

A. E. Drinkwater (1852–1923) would play Bluntschli in provincial tours of *Arms and the Man*; in 1895 he would play Marchbanks in his touring company of *Candida*.

27   *Rehearsal. Elephant and Castle Theatre. 11 ? Mona ?*

28   *Rehearsal. Elephant and Castle. 11.*

29   *Rehearsal. Elephant and Castle Theatre. 11. Private rehearsal. Drinkwater's rooms. 1 Ladbroke Crescent. 19$\frac{1}{2}$.*

30   *Rehearsal. Mona Hotel. 11. Miss Verne to call in the evening after 19$\frac{1}{2}$ to rehearse Raina.*

Ethel Verne, who had played Portia in an 1893 production of *The Merchant of Venice*, and had a minor role in a February–April 1894 melodrama, *The World*, would play Raina in the South Shields *Arms and the Man*, and Proserpine in *Candida*.

31   *Rehearsal. Mona Hotel. 11. Go down to Milford by the 17.5 train from Waterloo. °Fabian Executive. 17.*

September

1   [   ]

2   [   ]

3   [   ]

4   *Come up from Milford by the 10.10 train.*

5 *Start from Holborn Viaduct (Art Workers' Guild Italian Expedition) at 19.55 for Dover en route for Brussels via Ostend (Hotel Central).*

This was Shaw's second visit to Italy with this group; the first was in September 1891.

6 *Start from Brussels (Nord) at 7.10 for Basle (Hotel St. Gotthard).*

7 *Leave Basle at 7.30 for Pallanza. Boat from Luino (Hotel Eden).*

Pallanza is on the western shore of Lago Maggiore.

8 [ ]

According to the MS. diary of Sydney Cockerell (BL 52631) for the date, "A restful day. Cruised the Lake in a little boat with Walker, Shaw, . . . Okey . . . & others to the chapel of St. Catterina del Sasso, which was restored & rather a sell. Then for a walk over the glorious hills, among the vines. . . . There was a fête in the evening & the peasants were dancing in the covered market place. This was very pretty & we stayed for an hour or so watching them."

9 SUNDAY *Leave Pallanza at 6.30 for Milan. Boat to Laveno (Hotel Bellini).*

Laveno is on the eastern shore of Lago Maggiore, where the party would entrain for Milan.

10 *Leave Milan at 11.30 for Florence (Hotel Anglo-American).*

"I remember," Shaw wrote in a theater review in 1897 (C1183), "losing myself once in Milan, and wandering into a big garden where a crowd of people were consuming the usual light refreshments at small tables before a Punch and Judy stage large enough to accommodate human actors. I sat down with the rest, and, at the cost of a bottle of the Milanese equivalent for Apollinaris, witnessed a musical farce. Now that farce filled me with appreciation and even gratitude. But if I had had to leave my fireside (or anybody else's) on a winter night in London, and pay half a guinea to witness three acts of it, I should have felt myself the most pitiable of gulls at the fall of the curtain."

According to Cockerell's diary, before leaving Milan he, Shaw, Walker, and Okey went to the Ambrosian Library, where they saw a "very fine" Botticelli Virgin and Child. They were in Florence by 18.30, and in the evening light walked along the Lung Arno to the Ponte Vecchio and then to Giotto's Tower, which was "more wonderful than I could have imagined."

11 *Florence (11 through 18).*

On this day the party went to the Duomo and were disappointed by the bare interior. On the 12th they visited the Uffizi Gallery and Pitti Palace, and their collections. On the 13th the highlight was the church of Santa Croce and the Bargello; on the 14th it was the Church of Santa Maria Novella, and back to the Bargello collections. On the 15th they went into the hills near Settigiano to get a view of Florence from above. On Sunday they returned to the Uffizi and to Santa Maria del Carmine, with its frescoes by Masolino, Masaccio, and Filippino Lippi. One evening some in the party—it is not clear whether Shaw was included—saw the last act of *Charley's Aunt* in Italian. Shaw never saw it in English.

19   *Leave Florence at 7.22 for Pisa. Arrive 8.56. Leave Pisa at 2.45 for Genoa. Arrive 6.35 (Hotel Smith).* °*Fabian Publishing Committee. 17.*

"At Genoa," Thomas Okey remembered, "Mr. Shaw asked me to get him entrance to the great Carlo Felice theatre. Much of the time there he spent in examining the construction, arrangements, and measurements of the stage. . . . Among the sculpture at Genoa we came upon a realistic representation in marble, by a famous Italian artist, of [William] Jenner vaccinating a girl's arm. As Shaw's eyes met the figure a thrill of horror and indignation shook his frame. . . ."

20   *Leave Genoa at 18.58 for Como (Hotel Volta).*

21   *Como.*

22   *Leave Como at 8.47 for London via Basle, Brussels and Ostend.*

23 SUNDAY   *Arrive at Holborn Viaduct at 16.30.*

24   [   ]

25   [   ]

26   °*Fabian Publishing Committee. 17.*

27   [Louis Weighton, royalties on *Arms and the Man* from beginning of tour on 3rd Sept. to 15th Sept. . . . £5.9.9. . . .]

From Shaw's accounts at the end of the 1894 diary. Louis Weighton (see 18 October 1894) was a theatrical business manager involved in touring *Arms and the Man* with A. E. Drinkwater's company.

28   °*Fabian Women's Tract Committee. 276 Strand. 20.*

29   Odette *at the Princess's Theatre. Anna Ruppert. 20.*

Odette, the melodrama (1882) by Victorien Sardou in an English adaptation by Clement Scott, would have twelve performances. Mrs. Anna Ruppert played the title role. A wealthy socialite amateur, she had essayed *Camille* four months earlier in her debut.

30 SUNDAY   *Dine at Emery Walker's. Charringtons' in the evening.*

October

1   *Go down to Milford by the 17.5 train.*

2   [*Candida*—A Domestic Play. . . . Begun 2nd Oct . . . .]

Title page of BL Add. MS. 50603A.

3   °*Fabian Publishing Committee. 16½.*

4   [R. Mansfield for Miss Marbury, royalties on *Arms and the Man* for week ending 22nd Sept. in New York (1st performance on 17th), net £80.16.6.]

From Shaw's accounts at close of 1894 diary.

5   *Fabian Executive. 17½.* °*Fabian Committee. 17. Come up from Milford by the 13.28 train. Women's Tract Committee (Fabian) at Pioneer Club, 22 Bruton St. 20.*

6   *Go down to Milford by the 16. ? train.*

7 SUNDAY   [   ]

8   °*Ethel Bauer's pianoforte recital. Broadwood's. 15¼.*

9   *German lesson. 55 Buckland Crescent. 11.*

10   *Fabian Publishing Committee. 16½.*

11   *Come up from Milford by the 16.20 train.*

12   *Fabian Executive. 17¼. Fabian Committee. 16¼. Fabian meeting at Clifford's Inn. Harold Cox on Population. 20. Call on Grein at 34 Craven St. at 18.15.* °*German lesson. 55 Buckland Crescent. 11.*

13   *Lecture at the Westbourne Park Literary and Debating Society at 20 in the Westbourne Park Institute, Porchester Rd. W. (opposite Royal Oak). W. J. Black, 29 Upper George St. W.*

14 SUNDAY   *Dine at Webbs'. 13½. No—dine at Massingham's instead at 13¼. No. Put off.*

15   °*London Liberal and Radical Union. National Liberal Club. 20. Council meeting.*

Act 1 of *Candida* completed this date.

16   *Lecture at the Church and Stage Guild on "Parsifal" at Headlam's, 31 Upper Bedford Place, at 16. German lesson. 55 Buckland Crescent, N.W. 11.*

17   *Go to Richmond by the 1.55 train from Portland Rd. °Royal College of Music. College Concert. 16.*

18   *Weighton to call before 14. Meetings at Percy Bunting's, 11 Endsleigh Gardens, Executive of Liberal Association at 20 to consider School Board election, and School Board Election Committee at 20½.*

19   *German lesson. 55 Buckland Crescent N.W. 11. Fabian Executive. 17¼. Fabian Committee. 17. Fabian Public Meeting at Essex Hall. B. F. C. Costelloe on "The Tenification of London." 20.*

> Tenification was a PMG coinage to describe a plan to make London more governable by separating the metropolis into ten smaller cities.

20   [   ]

21 SUNDAY   *Lecture at St. Thomas's Square Chapel at 20.15 (Rev. John H. Belcher. Penprys. St. Thomas's Square N.E.).*

22   *Princess's Theatre. 19½.* Robbery under Arms. *19½.*

> The melodrama about Australian bushrangers by Alfred Dampier and Garnet Walch included in the cast Shavian friends Bernard Gould, Herbert Flemming, and Charles Charrington. Since the female lead was being played by Mrs. Anna Ruppert, there is the possibility that she was financing the venture. It would last seventeen performances. Archer, reviewing both her autumn efforts and her bony frame, decided that she was better as horsewoman than as adulteress.

23   *German lesson. 11. (the last). Call on [Herbert P.] Horne at 4 King's Bench Walk at 19.*

24   *°Irish Literary Society's housewarming. 8 Adelphi Terrace. Fabian Publishing Committee. 17.*

25   *Go up to Overstrand Mansions in the evening.*

> Overstrand Mansions was the Charringtons' new flat, Prince of Wales Road, Battersea.

26   *Speak at the Inaugural Public Meeting of the London Reform Union (East St. Pancras Branch) at People's Hall, Somers Town, Charlton St., Euston Rd. 20. (J. Timewell, 141 Gower St. W.C.). Fabian Executive. 17½ (chair). Fabian Committee. 17.*

27   *Dine with the Webbs. 19½.*

28 SUNDAY   *Stead's Conference, "If Christ Came to London," at Queen's Hall. 15 and 19.*

I went to the Conference but was so disgusted by Stead's opening with an hysterical prayer that I left the hall and went over to Charringtons', where I found Flemming and Janet. Later on Charrington came in, and Flemming left. I spent the rest of the evening there.

29 *Speak at Demonstration in Newcastle in support of Fred Hammill's candidature. Town Hall. 20. (R. P. Chaloner, 1 Loraine Terrace, Low Fell, Gateshead on Tyne). Catch the 10 train from King's Cross to Newcastle. Grand Hotel.*

30 *Lecture on "Labour Politics" for the Newcastle Fabian Society at the Central Halls, Nelson St., at 19½. Rev. W. E. Moll in the chair. Go to Durham to see the Cathedral.*

31 *Lecture on "Social-Democracy" to the S. D. F. at Burnley. St. James's Hall. 19½. See Spence's church (St. George's) and the Bewicks in the museum, and catch the 12.45 train to Burnley via York and Normanton—Bull Hotel.*

Thomas Bewick (1753–1828), Newcastle, the illustrator who revised wood engraving as a printmaking technique for books on birds and animals. Many of his watercolor studies are in the Hancock Museum, Newcastle-upon-Tyne.

November

1 *Lecture on "Socialism in Parliament" to the Northampton Boot and Shoe Operatives Club and Institute, 111 Overstone Rd. 20. Leave Burnley for Manchester at 9.3 and catch the 11.15 train from Manchester (Exch.) to Northampton via Stockport and Rugby. George Hotel.*

2 *Catch the 10.40 train Northampton to Euston.*

3 [   ]

4 SUNDAY *Lecture at the Limehouse, Ratcliff and Shadwell Independent Labour Club, at 19½ (20 really) (F. C. Calvin, 92 Locksley St., Limehouse). "The Socialist's Place in Labour Politics." 663 Commercial Rd. E. opposite Stepney station.*

5 *Look out for the article on "How to Become a Man of Genius" for* Town Topics—*must reach them on the 20th—2500 to 4000 words. Speak at the Ealing Debating Society on "The Twentieth Century." Victoria Hall. 20.15.*

Call on Lady Colin Campbell at the Realm *office, Norfolk St., between 15 and 17.*

[Lodged in London & County Bank, Bills of Exchge . . . .]

"How to Become a Man of Genius," *Town Topics* (New York), 6 December 1894 (C1042). Without regular income from music criticism, and unsure of playwriting income with only one play of four completed seemingly actable, Shaw was resorting to freelance writing. He would be paid $40 for the article. ▪ Bracketed banking data is from Shaw's accounts at the end of the 1894 diary. With his first American royalties from *Arms and the Man,* he suddenly discovered that he had a real need, for the first time in his life, to open a bank account. Now, for the first time, he was able to write his own checks.

6   *Orchestral Concert. Queen's Hall. Debut of Siegfried Wagner as conductor. 20. Last day to send article to* Pall Mall Budget, *Monday. Must arrive at Spottiswoode's by first post and proof must be returned by last. Weighton to call between 13 and 14. No: call on him at Actors' Association at 16.*

"His Father's Ghost," Shaw's piece on Siegfried Wagner as conductor, *Pall Mall Budget,* 15 November 1894 (C1040). He was paid four guineas. ▪ Shaw was also busy writing *Candida,* completing Act 2 this date.

7   *Fabian Publishing Committee. 17.* °*Meeting at Cleveland Hall to form organizing committee for local elections. 20. Evening at home.*

8   *Dalling [Road to visit FE]. 20. Trennung.*

Shaw's only use of German in the diaries (other than names and titles) to this point is the single word meaning *parting,* or *separation.* Another visit to Florence is listed for the 24th, a meeting which Shaw kept, at which they discussed the forthcoming production of Ibsen's *Little Eyolf.* However, they had not been seeing each other regularly since the close of *Arms and the Man.* They would continue to meet desultorily, but the fire was out.

Trennung was probably a reference to a *Lied* of that title by Brahms (Op. 97, 1886), which seems to summarize Shaw's feelings about Florence:

> Down there in the valley
> The waters are troubled,
> And I can't tell you
> How much I love you.
>
> You talk always of love,
> And of being true to me;
> But I think there is
> A little bit of falsehood in it.
>
> If I tell you ten times over
> That I love you and want you,
> And you still won't understand,
> Then I must go away.
>
> For the time when you loved me,
> I thank you from the heart,
> And I hope it will
> Go better for you elsewhere.

9   *Meet Olivier at the Orange Grove at 18.45 and walk with him to Salts', 133 Cheyne Walk.*

10   *Call on M. Levenston at Daly's Theatre between 15 and 16. Call on the editor of* The Sunday Times *at 46 Fleet St. Call on the Charringtons in the evening.*

> Michael Levenston (1856–1904) managed several theaters in London in the 1890s. ■ Shaw would not publish anything in the *Sunday Times*, but he was clearly exploring possibilities.

11 SUNDAY   *Lecture at the Washington Music Hall, Battersea, at 20 (W. F. Champion, 451 Battersea Park Rd. S.W.) on "Compromise." Lunch with the Webbs. 13½.*

12   *Look out for article "How to Become a Musical Critic" for* The *Scottish Musical Monthly (J. Cuthbert Hadden, 2 St. Fillan's Terrace, Morningside, Edinburgh)—must be in by the 20th. Hughes of Manchester (Independent Theatre) expected in town until the 16th. South St. Pancras Progressive Local Election Committee meeting, Cleveland Hall, 20.*

> "How to Become a Musical Critic" would be published in the December 1894 issue (C1041). It would be posted to Edinburgh on the 15th.

13   *Lecture at the Reform Club, Oxford, on "Twentieth Century Forecasts" (Percy E. T. Widdrington, St. Edmund's Hall. Oxford). Train from Paddington 16.45. Stay with the Peters's, 12 St. Margaret's Rd.*

> Percy E. T. Widdrington, St. Edmund's Hall, Oxford, who would marry Enid Stacy in 1898, became vicar of St. Peter's, Coventry, and canon of Chelmsford.

14   *Drabig lectures on Goethe and Schiller at Howard House, Arundel St., at 19¼. °Progressive School Board Demonstration at Shoreditch Town Hall. 20.*

15   *Presentation of address to E. J. Beale at Sir John Hutton's, 10 Cumberland Terrace, Regents Park. 20.*

> Edward J. Beale was making a run for a school board seat, and Shaw as usual was encouraging the candidacy.

16   *Speak for C. A. Gibson (School Board Candidate, Marylebone) at Brondesbury Hall, Iverson Rd., West Hampstead, at 20. (Frank Durrant, 4 Springfield Gardens, Kilburn N.W.).*

17   *Lecture at the Harlesden Radical Club, 4 Manor Villas (top of Station Rd.), Acton Lane, Harlesden, on "Rent and Interest" (F. R. Coulson). 20. Three minutes from Willesden. Graham Wallas's School Board Open Air meetings. Be at his committee room, 293 Old St. E. C., at 15.20. Speak at Eagle Wharf at 16, at Rosemary Bridge or at overflow meeting at 17 and at Old St. at 18.*

18 SUNDAY   *Lecture at the Dulwich Working Men's Liberal and Radical Club, 108 Lordship Lane, on "Communism" (Fred Rubic).*

19   [   ]

20   *Orchestral Concert. Queen's Hall. Felix Mottl. 20. Be at the Orange Grove between 14 and 15 to meet Bertha Newcombe.*

21   *Speak for Mrs. Bridges Adams (School Board, Greenwich) at [   ]. (John Elliott, 3 Queen's Cottage, Blackheath Rd., S.E.). °Meeting of South St. Pancras Local Election Committee at 101 Gower St. at 20½. Call on [Henry] Lazarus at 38 Tavistock Square between 16 and 18 about the Vestry candidates' address.*

> Mary Daltry (Mrs. Walter) Bridges-Adams (1856–1939) would serve on the London School Board from 1897 to 1902. ■ Henry J. Lazarus (1874–1946) would become an LCC member and, in 1929, mayor of Stepney. He then lived at Tavistock Square.

22   *School Board Election. Work for Wallas at 4 Ivy St., St. John's Rd., Hoxton. Take charge of the Committee Room.*

23   *Fabian Executive. 17¼. Take the chair. Fabian Committee. 17. Take the chair. Fabian meeting at Clifford's Inn. P. H. Wicksteed on "The Law of Distribution."*

24   *Dalling [Road to visit FE].*

> Shaw would write to William Archer on 27 November 1894 (unpubl., Fales Coll., NYU), "I saw Mrs. Emery the other day. . . ."

25 SUNDAY   *Lecture at the Lee and Lewisham Liberal Club at 20.15 (Walter Slater, Lee and Lewisham Liberal Club, 170 High St., Lewisham). "Liberalism between Two Stools." Lunch at Webbs'. 13¼.*

26   *Address Oxford's circle of parsons on "The Natural History of the Parson" (Rev. A. W. Oxford, 8 Henrietta St. Cavendish Square W.) at 80 Eccleston Square, at 18.45. Liberal and Radical Union Council meeting. 20. House of Lords resolution.*

> The Rev. A. W. Oxford, a Fabian, was vestryman for Marylebone. Shaw had visited his Sunday School on 23 October 1889.

27   *Second Mottl concert. Queen's Hall. 20.*

28   *Fabian Publishing Committee. 16¼. Charringtons' in the evening.*

29   *Meeting South St. Pancras Local Elections Committee at 101 Gower St. at 20½.*

30   *Fabian Executive. 17¼. Committee. 17. Fabian Private Meeting at Clifford's Inn. Oakeshott on Tract 5 and Webb's statement as to the Hutchinson Trust.*

> The Hutchinson Trust originated with the death of Henry Hunt Hutchinson in 1894. A Derby solicitor, he had donated £100 in 1890 to underwrite a Fabian lecture campaign in the provinces. On 26 July 1894 he had killed himself. His will assigned half of his £13,000 estate to be used for "the propaganda and other purposes" of the Fabian Society "in any way" that Sidney Webb and such other trustees assigned by the society should "deem advisable." The Webbs, to whom the bequest was a surprise, were determined not to let the money be frittered away by futile political campaigns or impractical propagandizing. In time it would enable the Webbs to divert much of the money to their dream of founding a School of Economics in London. But they had to conceal this from Fabians who suspected that the Hutchinson Trust was being manipulated (as indeed it was) for non-Fabian purposes even though these advanced Fabian objectives.

December

1   *Speak at Havelock Hall, Gough St., Gray's Inn Rd. (Ward VIII South St. Pancras) at the Vestry and Guardians Election. 20. Miss Dietrick lectures on "Nerve Training" at Mrs. [George] Henschel's, 45 Bedford Gardens, Campden Hill, at 15¼.*

> Miss Dietrick was associated with the Women's Trades Union League, 9 Fitzroy Square.

2 SUNDAY   *Lecture at Milton Hall, Kentish Town (C. R. Linden, 40 Queen's Crescent N.W.). "Limits of Social-Democracy." 19½. Dine with Massingham at 13.45.*

> Shaw wrote Golding Bright afterwards (*CL*), "I have been blazing away on the platform this evening for an hour and a half, and ought to be in bed instead of clattering at this machine."

3   *Speak at Athenaeum Hall, Tottenham Court Rd., and at the Wesleyan Chapel, Camden St. (Ward III) on local elections. Meet Massingham at Archer's (Queen Square) at 15, to hear* Little Eyolf *read.*

[I really am giddy & headachy & livery with rushing about from one place to another; and I had this afternoon to attend a private & confidential reading of Ibsen's new play for the purposes of reviewing it red hot of publication. I then had to address 2 vestry election meetings.]

> H. W. Massingham had asked for a review for the *Daily Chronicle*; however, he would spurn it in favor of one of his own, which he published on 12 December 1894. • The bracketed supplement is from a letter this date to Pakenham Beatty in *CL*.

4 °*Speak at the Bedford Congregational Chapel, Charrington St. (E. St. Pancras) on the Local Elections. 20. (M. King, 142 Ossulston St., Somers Town). Wrong date. Should be tomorrow. Call on Frank Harris at the* Saturday Review *office between 17 and 18.*

> Shaw called his meeting with Harris "bread and butter business." He was asked—and accepted the offer—to be the *Saturday Review*'s drama critic at £6/week, beginning the following month.

5 *Fabian Publishing Committee. 16½. Go out to Beatty's in the evening.*

> Shaw had written Beatty on the 3rd about his Wednesday dinner there, "I must have beans, ginger beer, and the latest scandal about [Morell] Johns and the rest to soothe me."

6 *Lecture at the Kingston Debating Society on "The Twentieth Century" (J. Rencarrow, Public Schools, Kingston on Thames).* °*Dolmetsch's Bach concert at Clifford's Inn. 20½. Cantata Burlesque, etc.*

7 [   ]

> Shaw noted on the *Candida* manuscript that he completed the play on this day.

8 [   ]

9 SUNDAY *Lecture at the Hammersmith Socialist Society, Kelmscott House, at 20 (R. A. Muncey, 97 Sulgrave Rd., Hammersmith W). "The Twentieth Century."*

10 °*Speak on the Local Elections at Stepney. Cancelled. Meeting of Local Elections Committee at 19 at Grafton St. Committee Room.*

11 *Speak on the local elections at the Fulham Town Hall (Mrs. [Grace] Goodall). 20½.*

12 °*Speak on the local elections at Woolwich. No—Coffee Tavern—against the Act.*

Went over to Charringtons' in the evening.

> The meeting was sponsored by the London Reform Union and the Woolwich Trades Council. Shaw at the last minute discovered that "refreshments"—although "against the Act"—were being sold on the premises, and absented himself.

13 [   ]

14 *Public Meeting Vestry and Guardian Candidates at Athenaeum, Tottenham Court Rd. 20½. Fabian Executive. 17½. Committee. 17. Fabian meeting at Clifford's Inn. Miss McKillop on "Socialism and Science." 20.*

Margaret McKillop would be co-author, with Mabel Atkinson, of *Economics: Descriptive and Theoretical* (London, 1911).

15 Read **Candida** *at Normans', 27 Grosvenor Rd., at 20. Vestry Elections.*

Shaw would begin a round of readings of *Candida* to interested friends, a means of trying out the impact of his lines. According to Henry Salt in *Company I have Kept*, at one of these readings, unrecorded in the diaries but held "on a winter evening in 1894," Shaw read the play to a group in Salt's London rooms, with Edward Carpenter expostulating unprophetically at the close, "No, Shaw. It won't do." ▪ Shaw had run for a St. Pancras Vestry seat, and was (he said) "most ignominiously defeated."

16 SUNDAY *Lecture at the Richmond Liberal and Radical Club, "Old Friars," The Green (James P. Napier) on "The Natural History of Monopoly." Dine at Webbs'. 13½.*

17 *[Poor Law] Guardians Election*

18 *Fabian Women's Tract Committee, 276 Strand, at 20.*

19 *Call on George Alexander at 6 Park Row, Knightsbridge, at 16, and read* Candida *to him. Charringtons' in the evening. Fabian Publishing Committee. 16¼.*

Alexander was looking for new vehicles for the St. James's Theatre, which he was managing. Henry Arthur Jones's *The Masqueraders* was now near the end of its 139-performance run, and Alexander was about to stage Henry James's *Guy Domville*. Alexander "instantly perceived," Shaw wrote to Archer (*CL*) on the 28th, "that it was Marchbanks' & Candida's play . . . and not his. He said he would produce it if he could get down to the poet's age; but he would not play Morell."

20 *Settling-up meeting of Local Elections Committee at Dr. Williams' Library. 20¼.*

Not a person, but the venerable library in Bloomsbury. See 18 September 1885.

21 *Meet Wallas at Charing Cross at 16¼ to catch the 16.30 train to Folkestone. Put up at the West Cliff Hotel at Dover.*

22 *Folkstone (22nd through 28th).*

Walked to Hythe. [Here I am, taking the sea air with Wallas. The sea air travels at the rate of 120 miles an hour and goes through clothes, flesh, bone, spirit and all, so that one walks against it like a naked soul, exhilarated, but teeming at the nose. We are in an immense hotel, with 180 rooms and a few guests, who have nothing to do, and are miserable exceedingly having come down expressly to be happy.]

Shaw describes Hythe to Janet Achurch on this date in *CL*.

23 SUNDAY Walked to Dover.

24 Wet day.

25 Wet day.

26 [   ]

27 Walked inland to Caesar's Common and on to Pluckley.

28 Spent the day in Folkestone itself, Wallas being lame and unable to walk far. Met Fitzgerald Molloy. [I return to town tomorrow afternoon to take up the duties, fairly forced on me by Harris, of dramatic critic. . . . It is questionable whether it is quite decent for a dramatic author to be also a dramatic critic; but my extreme reluctance to make myself dependent for my bread and butter on the acceptance of my plays by managers tempts me to hold to the position that my real profession is that by which I can earn my bread in security. Anyhow, I am prepared to do anything which will enable me to keep my plays for twenty years with perfect tranquillity if it takes that time to educate the public into wanting them.]

> Shaw describes his holiday to William Archer on this date in *CL*.

29 *Come up from Folkestone by the 12.20 from Radnor Park.* °*First night at the Garrick. [Sydney] Grundy's* Slaves of the Ring.

> Shaw (as G.B.S.) would review *Slaves of the Ring*—which he would finally see on 1 January 1895—as his first *SR* column, 5 January 1895 (C1044). Impatient with the play, he would call it "a mere contrivance for filling a theatre bill."

30 SUNDAY *Lunch at the Webbs' at 13½—on to Charringtons' in the evening. Wallas came with me to the Charringtons'.*

31 *Go down to Tonbridge by the 17.35 from Charing Cross and read* Candida *at Marlfield House to the Oliviers, Thornycrofts, etc. Stay the night.*

Notes

		£	s	d
January				
16	*The World*	20	9	6
February				
7	*The Star*	1	10	0
15	*The Fortnightly Review* ("The Religion of the Pianoforte")	12	0	0
"	*The World*	25	0	0
March				
15	*The World*	20	0	0
April				
11	Henry & Co, royalties on *Widowers' Houses* from Ap[ri]l 1893 (date of publication) to 31st Dec. 1893—156 copies at 6d	3	18	0
16	*The World*	20	0	0
25	*Fortnightly Review* (Mallock article)	23	0	0
30	Royalties on *Arms & the Man* (Avenue Theatre) from 1st night, 21st, to the 28th, inclusive. 5% on £177.4.3.	8	17	2½

The first item above (£3.18.0) is included in the income tax return for 1893–94.

		£	s	d
May				
9	Walter Scott, royalties on *Quintessence of Ibsenism* from the 1st June 1893 to 31st March 1894	£3	2	2
"	" on *Cashel Byron's Profession* to 30th Ap[ri]l (edition sold out)	5	12	5
		5		
10	*The Star*	8	14	7
11	*Arms & the Man* royalties to 5th May on £161	2	10	0
		8	1	0
15	*The World*	20	0	0

The first item above (£8.14.7) is included in the income tax return for 1893–94.

June

1	Arms & the Man, royalties to 26th May on £492.7.6 (should be £491.3.6)		24	12	5
5	The World		25	0	0
	Arms & the Man " 2nd June on £178.3.6	8	18	2	
	" 9th " 212.10.0	10	12	6	
	16th " 177.3.3	8	17	2	
	[Royalties] on Crystal Pal[a]ce mat[in]ee share 31.15.0	1	11	9	
	£599.11.9	£29	19	7	29	19	7

July

6	The New Review		18	0	0
2	Arms & the Man, royalties to 20th June on £166.1.6	8	6	1	
	" " 30th " 93.12.0	4	13	7	
	" " 7th July 110.17.6	5	10	11	18	10	7
6	The World		20	0	0

August

3	The Star (Bayreuth articles)	12	12	0
5	The World	20	0	0

September

4	Pall Mall Budget	12	12	0
"	The World	10	0	0
27	Louis Weighton, royalties on Arms & the Man from beginning of tour on 3rd Sept. to 15th Sep. (cheque actually for £5.9.9 only) (the 6d was paid up on the 6th Oct.)	5	10	3

October

4	R. Mansfield for Miss Marbury, royalties on Arms & the Man for week ending 22nd Sept. in New York (1st performance on 17th), net	80	16	6
11	The Same, week ending 29th Sept.	64	13	6

Date		Description	£	s	d
10		L. Weighton, on a/c	1	0	0
19		R. Mansfield, as above, royalties for week end[ing] 6th Oct. (3 performances)	25	10	6
31	"	" performances on 9th & 10th Oct.	14	8	7
November					
5		Lodged in London & County Bank, Bills of Exch[an]ge	80	16	6
		"	64	13	6
		"	25	10	6
		"	14	8	7
		Postal order "	1	0	0
		" 10/– (2)1		0	0
			£187	9	1
14		Cheque. (School Board election) 40251 £ 1 . 1 . 0	161	8	1
29		(Charrington) 2 25 . 0 . 0	26	1	0
December					
1		*Great Thoughts*	2	2	0
8		*Pall Mall Budget*	4	4	0
12		R. Mansfield for Elisabeth Marbury, royalties of performances of *Arms & the Man* at Boston on the 19th & 20th.	24	1	3
		Philadelphia 26th, 27th, & 29th Nov.	32	1	2
			5	0	0
20		Louis Weighton, on a/c			
27	"	for A. E. Drinkwater, royalties for week ending 22nd inst at Leicester (first payment from the Drinkwater management).	4	11	8
27			8	4	3
31		Town Topics, New York ("How to Become a Man of Genius") $40 coming on order	161	8	1
		London & County Bank, bal[an]ce	161	8	1
5		Cheque—house 40253 £25 0 0			
"		Vestry Election (exp[en]ses) 4 2 0			

Date	Item			
6	" Independent Theatre shares	5	20 0 0	47 2 0
12	Lodged			114 6 1
20	"			24 1 3
				32 1 2
				178 8 6
21	Cheque, self, Folkestone 40256		5 0 0	10 0 0
25	Lodged			160 8 6
30	"		5 1 8	10 1 8
				170 10 2
"	Cheque 40257			1 1 0
				169 9 2

REMINDERS FOR NEXT YEAR

January: Lecture at the Hatcham Lib[eral] Club on the 27th. (J. Matthews 20 Edric Rd. New + S.E.).
Lecture to the Camberwell Nat(iona)l Sec[ular] Soc[iety] 61 New Ch[urch] Rd S.E. on "The Religion of the 19th Century" 19½ (Ralph S. Hose 18 Claribel Rd Holland Rd Brixton S.E.)

February: Lecture on the 14th to the Wimbledon Debating Soc[iety] (J. N. McDonald). Lecture on the 3rd at the Ideal Club (Mr. H. Otto Thomas Ideal Club 185 Tott[enham] C[our]t Rd W.C.)
Lecture on the 10th at the Boro of Bethnal Green Rad[ical] Cl[ub] & Inst[itute] 29 Abbey St. B[ethnal] G[reen] Rd E on Labor Politics 11.45 T. J. Farrell 31 Viaduct St. B[ethnal] G[reen] E.

March: Deliver an address to the Womens' Progressive Soc[iet]y Ideal Club, Tott[enham] C[our]t Rd. at 17 (Mrs. Brownlow 30 Theobalds Rd W.C.) on the 30th.
Lecture on the same economics subject at the Boro Rd Polytechnic on the 16th (G. F. Comford.)

Diary 1895

Notes

Still living at 29 Fitzroy Square.

I began the year by taking the post of dramatic critic to *The Saturday Review*, under the editorship of Frank Harris. This was the first regular appointment I ever held as a critic of the theatres. Salary £6 a week.

During my stay with the Webbs at the Argoed in August and September I wrote a play in one act about Napoleon entitled *The Man of Destiny*. At the end of December I began another play title as yet unknown to me. During the Easter holidays with the Webbs, Trevelyan, etc, at Beachy Head. I learnt to ride the bicycle and got much more exercise during the year than usual, with advantage to my health so far. I kept up the habit of going to the Webbs for lunch every Sunday.

It was agreed between myself and Richard Mansfield that he should produce my play *Candida* in New York; and he actually engaged Janet Achurch for the part. She went out; but Mansfield then changed his mind; so I withdrew the play.

In November Janet, when playing *The New Magdalen* for the week at the Metropole Theatre in Camberwell, caught typhoid fever, and her illness occupied me a good deal during the last two months of the year, partly because of its bearing on all possible plans for the production of *Candida*, and partly because I have come into relations of intimate friendship with the Charringtons during the past two years or so.

Frank Harris tried to establish a regular lunch every Monday for choosing members of the *Saturday Review* staff at the Café Royale. I attended them for some time. Harold Frederic, Mrs. Devereux, Marriott Watson and others used to come. Oscar Wilde came once, immediately before the Queensberry trial, with young Douglas. They left in some indignation because Harris refused to appear as a witness—a literary expert witness—to the high artistic character of Wilde's book *Dorian Gray*. These lunches wasted my time and were rather apt to degenerate into bawdy talk. When a play called *The Home Secretary* was produced at the Criterion Theatre, I took the opportunity to protest against the attempt in the play to trade on the Anarchism bogey, my object being to call attention to some hard features in the case of Charles, "the Walsall Anarchist." Harris alarmed by this, cut the passage out of the article. This incident brought my growing impatience with the brag and bawdry of the lunches to a head; and I never went again. They seem to have fallen through afterwards.

> *The Man of Destiny*, begun in May, was *completed* in Monmouthshire in September. ▪ The untitled new play was *You Never Can Tell*, finally referred to by its title on 19 February 1897. ▪ (Sir) Charles Trevelyan (1870–1958), then a wealthy young Liberal who would be elected to the London School Board in 1896, and who would be a Liberal M.P. from 1899 to 1918, and a Labour member from 1922 to 1931, serving in two Labour cabinets. ▪ Harold Frederic (1856–1898), journalist and novelist, represented *The New York Times* in London. Mrs. Devereux Pember, who wrote as "Roy Devereux," lived in Paris at 3 rue Hamelin and wrote travel articles. H. B. Marriott Watson was known for his short stories which flirted with sexual innuendo. ▪ Lord Alfred Douglas (1871–1945), youngest son of the Marquess of Queensberry, whom Wilde unsuccessfully sued for libel when characterized as a sodomite, precipitating his downfall. ▪ "Charles" was Fred Charles Slaughter, one of six Staffordshire anarchists convicted in the alleged bomb plot. ▪ *The Home Secretary*, by R. C. Carton, opened on 7 May 1895 at the Criterion. The G.B.S. review (as censored) appeared in *SR* (*Saturday Review*) 18 May 1895 (C1074).

January

1 *Read* Candida *at Webbs'. 17*$\frac{4}{2}$*. Go to the Garrick Theatre to see Grundy's* Slaves of the Ring*. 20. Come up from Tonbridge with Olivier by the 9.45— missed, caught 10.25.*

> G.B.S. (C1044) labeled the limp predictability of the play "mathematic lifelessness."

2 *London Liberal and Radical Union Council Meeting. Memorial Hall, Farringdon St. Harold Rose on "The Making of New London." 20.15. Send article on Garrick play to* Saturday Review *by 14. Fabian Publishing Com-*

mittee. 276 Strand. 16¼. Call at SR *office at 18 to correct proof and arrange terms with F.H.*

Gimson called with a friend named Porter.

3 *First night of Oscar Wilde's* Ideal Husband *at the Haymarket.*

[The performance is very amusing. The audience laughs conscientiously: each person comes to the theatre prepared, like a special artist, with the background of a laugh already sketched in on his or her features. Some of the performers labor intensely at being epigrammatic. (C1045)]

> Reviewed by G.B.S. on 12 January 1895 (C1045). "In a certain sense Mr Wilde is to me our only thorough playwright. He plays with everything: with wit, with philosophy, with drama, with actors and audience, with the whole theatre." The play would run 124 performances.

4 *Independent Theatre production of Miss Dorothy Leighton's* Thyrza Fleming *at Terry's Theatre. 20.15. Fabian Executive and Committee. 17 and 17¼.*

> Reviewed by G.B.S. on 26 January 1895 (C1047). A counterblast to feminist drama, it portrayed "a heroine who leaves her husband on their wedding day, and presently returns repentant to confess that she was wrong, that her husband is really a blameless gentleman with no past at all." There would be seven performances.

5 *First night of Henry James's* Guy Domville *at the St. James's Theatre.*

[I am not myself in Mr James's camp. . . . And yet when some unmannerly playgoer . . . chooses to send a derisive howl from the gallery . . . , we are to sorrowfully admit, if you please, that Mr James is no dramatist, on the general ground that "the drama's laws the drama's patrons give." Pray, which of its patrons? —the cultivated majority who like myself and all the ablest of my colleagues, applauded Mr James . . . , or the handful of rowdies who brawled at him? (C1045)].

> James was the victim of boos and catcalls on opening night. "The truth about Mr. James's play," G.B.S. began (C1045), "is no worse than that it is out of fashion." Shaw thought that it would be "a deplorable misfortune" if the play did not "hold the stage long enough to justify Mr Alexander's enterprise in producing it." However, it would survive only thirty-two performances.

6 SUNDAY *Speak at the East India Dock Gates for the Poplar Labour Electoral League (Alfred Graham, 175 Abbott Rd., Poplar E.). 11.45. "Labour Prospects for the New Year."*

7 *Dine with the Salisbury Sharpes at 20 and read* Candida *to them.*

> Shaw intended to read *Candida* to Alice Lockett Sharpe and her husband, but apparently that entertainment did not materialize, and the last five words of the entry were then crossed out.

8   °*Call on Miss Robins at 20½ and read* Candida. *Cancelled.*

9   *Fabian Publishing Committee. 16¼.*

10   [   ]

11   *Fabian Executive. 276 Strand. 17½. Committee. 17.*

12   *Production of Comyns Carr's* King Arthur *at the Lyceum. 20.*

Reviewed on 19 January 1895 (C1046). J. W. Comyns Carr (1849–1916), a veteran playwright and theater manager, had concocted a spectacle for Henry Irving. "But how am I to praise this deed," asked G.B.S., "when my own art, the art of literature, is left shabby and ashamed amid the triumph of the arts of the [scene] painter and the actor?"

13 SUNDAY   *Lecture to the Camberwell Branch National Secular Society, 61 New Church Rd. S. E., at 19½ on "The Religion of the Twentieth Century" (Ralph S. Hose, 18 Claribel Rd., Holland Rd., Brixton S.E.). Bertha Newcombe's At-Home. Joubert's Studios. 16¼ to 19.*

14   [   ]

15   *Read* Candida *at Miss Brooke's, 19.55, to the Wilsons, the Dryhursts and the Cobden-Sandersons.* °*Arnold Dolmetsch's concert at the Salle Érard, 20¼. English 16th and 17th century music.*

16   *Terry's Theatre.* An Innocent Abroad. *3rd night. 20.20.* High Life Below Stairs. *22.15. Meet Mrs. Bridges Adams at Fabian office at 16. Fabian Publishing Committee. 16¼.*

An Innocent Abroad, part of a double bill, was W. Stokes Craven's staging of Mark Twain's book. The farce *High Life Below Stairs*, by James Townley, completed the evening. The pair would have sixty-four performances. There would be no G.B.S. review.

17   [   ]

18   °*Sidney Thompson lectures on "Musical Criticism" at the Society of Arts, 21 John St., to the Society of Women Journalists at 20¼. Take the chair. Fabian Society. Keir Hardie on "Socialism and Politics." 20. Essex Hall. Fabian Executive and Committee. 17 and 17½.*

19   *Read* Candida *at Massingham's, 18¼ (the Pennells, Drabig, Hood, Barrs and Walkley were there).*

Basil Hood (1864–1917), producer and playwright, whose new play Shaw would see on 2 March 1895.

20 SUNDAY *Lunch with the Webbs. 13½.*

21 *°Meeting of London Liberal and Radical Union, Memorial Hall. Address by Acland. 20.*

22 *Dine at Webbs', 19½, to meet Independent Labour Party men, Keir Hardie, Tom Mann, Frank Smith, and J. R. MacDonald.*

James Ramsay MacDonald (1866–1937), a member of the Fabian Executive from 1894 to 1900, would be the first Labour prime minister, in 1924.

23 *Fabian Publishing Committee. 16½.*

[Just as I thought I had cleared away all work for the moment I got a letter from the publishers of Archer's annual volume of criticisms republished from the *World*, to which I had promised to supply a preface. They implored me not to delay the manuscript any longer; and as the transaction was not a business one but a personal one between myself & Archer, I had to set to work. . . .]

Shaw to Mrs. Felix Moscheles, 24 January 1895; he had apparently missed a gathering at her home the evening before.

24 *Performance of* All's Well that Ends Well *at St. George's Hall, 20, by the Irving Amateur Dramatic Club (the second performance: the first was on 22 January).*

Reviewed by G.B.S. on 2 February 1895 (C1048), with praise for the lyricism of the spoken language.

25 *Women's Tract Committee. Fabian office. 20. Fabian Executive. 17½. °Fabian Committee. 17. °Meeting at Dr. Williams Library, Gordon Square, to consider lectures at Vestry Hall under University Extension and Technical Education Board auspices.*

26 *Lecture to the Fulham Branch of the Independent Labour Party on "The Fabian Society" (A. C. Burn, 14 Fabian Rd., Fulham). °J. A. Hobson lectures on "Quantity and Quality in Life" at the Women's Progressive Society, Ideal Club, 185 Tottenham Court Rd. 16 to 19.*

27 SUNDAY *Lecture at the Hatcham Liberal Club. "The County Council Election" (J. Matthews, 20 Edric Rd., New Cross), 20.15. Look up Magny beforehand.*

28 *County Council Election meeting at Bunting's, 11 Endsleigh Gardens. 20 to 21. °The Immortals at Mrs. Jopling's studio. Shuttleworth on "D. G. Rossetti." 21. Read* Candida *to Lewis Waller at 16.*

Shaw had written Janet Achurch on the 25th (*CL*) of his date with actor-manager Lewis Waller (1850–1915), adding, "I shall read Eugene for all he is worth, as to sacrifice him would be to sacrifice the play. The only chance is . . . that Waller . . . may play for a managerial and financial success at the cost of playing Morell."

29   °*Toynbee Economic Club. Conference on "Conciliation and Arbitration in Industrial Disputes," opened by F. Maddison. Gorst in the chair. 20. Toynbee Hall.* °*Arnold Dolmetsch's concert at the Salle Érard. 20½. Italian composers, 16th 17th and 18th centuries. Charringtons' in the evening. Met John Burns on the way.*

(Sir) John Eldon Gorst (1860–1911), Liberal M.P., was then vice-president of the Privy Council Committee on Education.   ▪   Shaw wrote to Dolmetsch on 31 January (*CL*), when he was unable to attend the concert, "My chief regret at the discontinuance of my musical work is that I lose the power to help you to make your work known quickly."

30   °*Fabian Publishing Committee. 16½.*

31   [Now that I have taken to dramatic criticism I find that the theatre keeps me away from concerts almost as completely as the concerts used to keep me away from the theatre.]

Shaw to Dolmetsch, 31 January 1895 (*CL*).

February

1   *Fabian Executive. 17¾.* °*Fabian Committee. 17. Press Day at exhibition of blue and white Oriental porcelain, Burlington Fine Arts Club. Fabian meeting at Essex Hall. Graham Wallas on "The Issues of the County Council Election." 20.*

2   *Call at 28 Theobald's Rd. at 19½—Miss Cox—Mrs. Olivier.*

3 SUNDAY   *Lecture at the Ideal Club, 185 Tottenham Court Rd. (H. Otto Thomas) "The Twentieth Century." 20½. Webbs' as usual. 13½.*

4   °*Meeting of Fabian Central Group at 32 Great Ormond St. to discuss County Council Election. 20.*

[I am hopelessly overdone—no less than ten evenings this month are already booked for public orations alone, without counting theatrical & private-public engagements.]

Shaw to Edward Pease in *CL*.

5 *Call on Wyndham at the Criterion at 12.30.*

6 *Dinner to Stewart Headlam, Holborn Restaurant. 18½. Second the toast.* °*Read Mrs. Warren's Profession to Grein and others at Hartley's. Postponed to 13th.* °*Fabian Publishing Committee. 16¼.* °*Debate on "Is Socialism Necessary, or will Land Nationalization solve the Social Problem?" opened by T. F. Walker of Birmingham. Memorial Hall. 20. Go down to Dolmetsch's with Runciman by the 2.20 train from Victoria.*

7 *County Council Election Meeting. Storr Street Hall. Liberal and Radical Union. Attend and speak. 20.*

8 *Fabian Executive. 17½.* °*Fabian Committee. 17. Fabian Members Meeting at Clifford's Inn, Tracts and resolutions re canvassing for Executive Committee. 20. Macdonald's, 32 Weymouth St., at 11 (my teeth).*

9 *First night of* A Leader of Men *at the Comedy Theatre by C. E. D. Ward (Mallet). 20.15.*

> The play by Charles E. D. Ward (a pseudonym) was reviewed on 16 February 1895 (C1050). The play was a thinly disguised version of the Parnell real-life drama, watered down by fears of the Censor. "Mr Ward . . . has had to choose between infanticide and abortion; and he has chosen abortion." There would be twenty-six performances.

10 SUNDAY *Lecture at the Borough of Bethnal Green Radical Club and Institute, 29 Abbey St., Bethnal Green Rd., on "Labour Politics" at 11.45 (T. J. Farrell, 31 Viaduct St., Bethnal Green E.). Supper at Haldane's, 3 Whitehall Court, 20½ (morning dress). Lunch at Webbs'. 13½.*

11 *Charringtons' in the evening.*

12 *Arnold Dolmetsch's concert. Queen's Hall. 20½. German 17th and 18th century music.*

> In a Shakespeare review on 6 July 1895 (C1081), G.B.S. would manage to squeeze in an observation that it was "only very lately that Mr Arnold Dolmetsch, by playing fifteenth-century music on fifteenth-century instruments, has shewn us that the age of beauty was true to itself in music as in pictures and armor and costumes."

13 *Read Mrs. Warren's Profession at Hartley's to Grein and others.* °*Fabian Publishing Committee. 14½.*

14 *Lecture to the Wimbledon Debating Society on "Great Men: Are They Real?" (William C. Sutherland, Kings College, Wimbledon) St. George's Hall, St. George's Rd. 20. Dine with Octavius Beatty at 11 Darlaston Rd. at 19. Drury Lane pantomime. 13.15.*

15 °*Fabian Executive. 17½—cancelled—no Executive.* °*Fabian Committee.*
*17. Cancelled. Fabian meeting at Essex Hall. Andrew Reid on "The New
Party." 20. Macdonald's at 11. Mrs. Charrington to call at 12½.*

She came in the afternoon late.

> Andrew Reid of Slough was editor of the pro-Fabian *New Party.*

16 *Production of* An M. P.'s Wife *at the Opera Comique. 20.15. Meet
Whelen at the Orange Grove between 14½ and 15.*

[Taking advantage of the second interval to stroll into the Strand for a little
exercise, I unfortunately forgot all about my business, and actually reached
home before it occurred to me that I had not seen the end of the play.
(C1050)]

> Reviewed on 23 February 1895 (C1051). The drama column heading used a question
> mark in place of title and author, G.B.S. observing, "For some reason I was not supplied
> with a program; so I never learned the name of the play." In any case, he walked out. The
> play closed after one performance.

17 SUNDAY *Lecture on "Twentieth Century Politics" at the Reformers
Club, 7 St. Agnes Place, Kennington Park, near the New Street station of the
Electric Railway, at 20½ (Thomas A. Gilbert). First turn to the right out of
South Place, train from Blackfriars to South Place.*

18 *Go to Oscar Wilde's* Importance of Being Earnest *at St. James's Theatre, 4th night.*

[I cannot say that I greatly cared for *The Importance of Being Earnest.* It
amused me, of course; but unless comedy touches me as well as amuses
me, it leaves me with a sense of having wasted my evening. (C1051)]

> G.B.S. (C1051) was disappointed by what he perceived as the one-dimensional nature of
> the farce. The incidents, he felt, "could only have been raised from the farcical plane by
> making them occur to characters who had, like Don Quixote, convinced us of their reality
> and obtained some hold on our sympathy." The play, nevertheless, would have run longer
> than its eighty-three performances if the Wilde scandal had not led to its abrupt closing.

19 *Lecture in the afternoon to Miss Newcombe's club. 16½. Charringtons'
in the evening.*

Went up to Charrington's in the evening.

20 *Fabian Publishing Committee. 16½. Lantern lecture at Town Hall Chelsea. 20.15.*

21 *Speak in support of John Burns's County Council candidature at St.
Saviour's Hall, Battersea.*

22 *Fabian Executive. 17¼. Take the chair. Fabian Committee. 17. Macdon-ald's at 11.*

Shaw also this date wrote a long letter to Richard Mansfield (*CL*) urging him to import Janet Achurch to New York to play opposite him in *Candida*.

23 [   ]

24 SUNDAY °*Speak at the Central Hall, High St., Peckham, for the People's League (Jno. Nisbet), morning. Cancelled.*

After lunch at Webbs', Wallas, Mrs. Webb and I went to see the Leonard Courtneys. Lubbock, Roby and others were there. Lecture at the Limehouse Independent Labour Club, 663 Commercial Rd. E., on "Liberalism and Progressivism." 20 (F. C. Calvin, 92 Locksley St., Limehouse). Lunch at Webbs' as usual.

Leonard Henry Courtney (1832–1918), later Baron Courtney of Penwith, long-time leader-writer for *The Times*, Liberal Unionist M.P., and member of several Liberal cabi-nets, was a brother-in-law of Beatrice Webb. ▪ Sir John Lubbock (1834–1913), later Lord Avebury, had been vice-chancellor of the University of London from 1872 to 1882, and would be M.P. for the University of London from 1886 to 1900. He had been L.C.C. chairman from 1890 to 1892, and principal of the Working Men's College. ▪ Henry John Roby (1830–1915), Fellow of St. John's College, Cambridge, and a Classical scholar and educational reformer, was then Liberal M.P. for the Eccles division of Manchester.

25 *Call on Archer in the afternoon to discuss the death of the Censor.*

E. Smyth Pigott (1824–1895), for twenty years the Lord Chamberlain's Licenser of Stage Plays, would receive a scathing obituary from G.B.S. in the 2 March 1895 *SR* (C1053) as "a walking compendium of vulgar insular prejudice, who, after wallowing all his life in the cheapest theatrical sentiment . . . had at last brought himself to a pitch of incompe-tence . . . in which the only thing definitely discernible in a welter of intellectual confu-sion was his conception of the English people rushing toward an abyss of national degeneration in morals and manners, and only held back on the edge of the precipice by the grasp of his strong hand."

26 °*Arnold Dolmetsch's concert. Queen's Hall. 20½. French 17th and 18th century music. Speak at Wimbledon in support of Octavius Beatty. 20.15. Dine with him at 19.*

Beatty was a candidate for the Surrey County Council.

27 °*Fabian Publishing Committee. 16¼. Send off prompt copy of* The Phi-landerer *to Mansfield.*

28 *Humanitarian League Conference. St. Martin's Hall. Afternoon 15 to 17, Evening 19. The Criminal Code and Public Control of Hospitals.*

[I went and delivered speeches at the Humanitarian Conference; partook of a dinner with the Humanitarians, made another speech; went home with Olivier and a violent headache; got sick. . . .]

Shaw to Charles Charrington, 1 March 1895, in *CL*.

March

1 *Humanitarian League Conference. Afternoon, Slaughter House Reform, 15 to 17; Evening, °Cruel Sports, 19. °Fabian Executive. 17¼. Cancelled. °Fabian Committee. 17. Cancelled. Macdonald's at 11.*

[To sit in an easy chair, hypnotised by keeping my mouth open, and soothed by the buzzing of the drill as it flies round inside my tooth, all the time watching another man working hard, is extraordinarily restful to me. I think it is because the yielding up of oneself utterly to be operated on by another instead of operating on the minds of others produces such a complete change of attitude and suspension of the overworked faculty. . . .]

> Shaw to Charrington, *CL.*

2 *County Council Election. Take charge of Webbs' Committee Room, New Cross Rd., Wards 2 and 3.*

[In a dismantled shop without a fire, and with the light of heaven obscured by election bills, you would have found me shivering in charge of one of Webb's committee rooms.]

> Shaw to Janet Achurch, 3 March 1895, in *CL.* Apparently he found enough time that evening to see *Gentleman Joe,* a farce by Basil Hood with music by Walter Slaughter, at the Prince of Wales' Theatre. A review would appear on 9 March 1895 (C1055), in which G.B.S. wondered at seeing the audience "in the wildest ecstasies at nothing." There would be 391 performances.

3 SUNDAY *Lecture at the North Camberwell Branch of the S. D. F., 208 Camberwell Rd., on "The Fabian Society" (J. C. Gordon, Social Democratic Club, 208 Camberwell Rd. S.E. Ted Watkins, Lecture Secretary). 20. Lunch at Webbs'.*

[I have just done the wretched hour of lecturing & arguing in a little den full of tobacco smoke in Camberwell; and I have to lecture tomorrow in polite society in Hampstead. . . .]

> Shaw to Janet Achurch, *CL.*

4 *Lecture to The Argosy on "The Theatre" (Ed. Bennett, 8 St. Stephens Mansions, Church St., Westminster, S. W.) at Mrs. Katherine St. Osyth Eustace Smith's, 16 Upper Park Rd., Haverstock Hill N. W.*

5 [   ]

6 *°Fabian Publishing Committee. 16½.*

7 [   ]

8 *Fabian meeting at Clifford's Inn. F. W. Hayes on "The Possibilities of the Poor Rate,"* 20. *Fabian Executive.* 17½. °*Fabian Committee.* 17. °*Private View. Denovan Adam's pictures illustrating the months in Scotland.*

Frederick William Hayes, of 7 Westcroft Square, W.

9 *Production of* That Terrible Girl *at the Royalty—Miss Hope Booth.* 20.45. *Revival of* Sowing the Wind, *at the Comedy.* 20¼.

That Terrible Girl, by the otherwise unidentified J. Stephens, featured Hope Booth (1872–1933), whose only earlier appearance had been the year before in *Little Miss Cute*, which had one performance, also at the Royalty. The new play would have twelve performances; on 23 March 1895 G.B.S. would characterize (C1058) its star as "a young lady who cannot sing, dance, act or speak, but whose appearance suggests that she might profitably spend three or four years in learning these arts...." ▪ *Sowing the Wind*, a revival of the Sydney Grundy play, starred Evelyn Millard (1869–1941), who "freshened the piece wonderfully.... Miss Millard is clearly a young lady with a future" (C1058).

10 SUNDAY *Lecture to the Leicester Secular Society on "Religion in the Twentieth Century" (Sydney A. Gimson, 20 Glebe St., Leicester). Go down by the 15.15 train from St. Pancras; and stay at Gimson's.*

11 *Come up from Leicester by the 19½ train.*

12 *Call at Miss Dickens's office for 2 copies of the* Candida *script.* 17. *Production of F. W. Sidney's* Loving Legacy *at the Strand Theatre.* 21.

Miss Ethel Dickens (1864–1936), proprietress of a "Type Writing Office" patronized by Shaw, at 6 Tavistock Street, off Wellington Street, Strand, was a granddaughter of Charles Dickens. ▪ *A Loving Legacy*, by Fred W. Sidney, was not reviewed by G.B.S. It survived for thirty-nine performances.

13 *Fabian Publishing Committee.* 16¼. *First night of Pinero's* Notorious Mrs. Ebbsmith *at the Garrick.* 20. *Call at Miss Dickens's office for the other* 4 *copies of* Candida, *the parts, and Wickers'* Die Ehre.

Reviewed on 16 March 1895 (C1056). The melodrama, with Johnston Forbes-Robertson and Mrs. Patrick Campbell, would have eighty-six performances. G.B.S. thought the play was "a piece of claptrap so gross that it absolves me from all obligation to treat Mr. Pinero's art as anything higher than the barest art of theatrical sensation." But Mrs. Campbell was "a wonderful woman." ▪ Apparently Shaw was having a copy made of a script by Hermann Sudermann (1857–1928), *Die Ehre* (1889), owned by Otto van Wickers, listed in Shaw's addressbook at 47 Wandsworth Bridge Road, Fulham, S.E. There would be four performances in London (in German) in June and July. (*Honor*—the English equivalent to the title—was the first play by the earliest major German proponent of Ibsenite naturalism. His more famous *Heimat*—*Magda* in English—would also have four performances in June and July.)

14 *Call at Charringtons' in the evening.*

Did not get there until 22. Was so tired that I took a hansom all the way—an unheard of extravagance for me. °Olivier to read his new play at Charrington's at 17½. °Fabian soiree at Headlam's, to meet Glasse. 20.

15   *Fabian Meeting at Essex Hall. Rev. John Glasse on "The Relation of Socialism to Christianity." 20. °Fabian Executive. 17½. °Fabian Committee. 17. Janet Achurch to call at 15 and go through her part.*

> The Rev. John Glasse, of Old Grey Friars, Edinburgh, was a Christian Socialist as well as a corresponding member of William Morris's Socialist League. Since this was Janet Achurch's last night in London for some time—Richard Mansfield had offered her $250/week plus travel expenses to play Candida opposite him in New York—Shaw was spending as much time with her as he could. As a result he missed the opening night of a double bill at the Independent Theatre (using the Opera Comique). Very likely he went the following night. The plays were A Man's Love, adapted from the Dutch of J. C. de Vos, and Salvé, by Mrs. Oscar Beringer, both reviewed by G.B.S. on 23 March 1895 (C1058), neither with much enthusiasm.

16   *Lecture at the Borough Rd. Polytechnic (Institute Economic Club) (G. F. Comfort) on "The Educational Value of Economics." See Felix Mansfield, Albert Gran and Janet Achurch off to New York by the 9.40 train from Waterloo, and hand F. M. the script and parts of* Candida.

[I have seen them off; and . . . on my return here I tumbled on my bed and slept like an exhausted dog for an hour. . . .]

> George Fisk Comfort was author of The Land Troubles in Ireland. A historical, political and economical study (1881).   ▪ Felix Mansfield (1852–?), Richard Mansfield's brother and business agent, was escorting Janet Achurch to New York. Albert Gran (1852–?), a Scandinavian actor who played much Ibsen, was a Felix Mansfield crony. Both may have been as shocked, as was Shaw, when Janet turned up with her hair in a frizzy wave and dyed an un-Candidalike "refulgent yellow." It was an augury of difficulties to come. Shaw's indulgence was nearly endless, but not Richard Mansfield's.   ▪ Shaw to Richard Mansfield, CL.

17 SUNDAY   *Lecture at the Tottenham Liberal and Radical Club on "The Twentieth Century" (A. Axford, Liberal and Radical Club, Warwick House, 604 High Rd., Tottenham). Lunch at Webbs'. 13½.*

18   *Meet Bertha Newcombe at the Burlington Fine Arts Club at 12.*

19   *°Annual Meeting of London Liberal and Radical Union. National Liberal Club. 20.*

20   *°Fabian Publishing Committee.*

21   *Go down to Richmond by the 15.5 from Waterloo.*

[I went down to Richmond and met there by appointment, F(lorence Farr), who had written at last rather bitterly of my apparent avoidance of her. We strolled about the park all afternoon, from seat to seat . . . ; and I chatted and chatted and she laughed and laughed in her obliging way and we had something to eat at the Swiss café and went to her sister's in Bedford Park by tramtop and I told her all the news and she told me all the news. . . .]

Shaw to Janet Achurch, 23 March 1895 (CL), on events of the 21st. "Pleasanter company one could not desire," Shaw went on to Janet (one must understand the audience in this case). ". . . Why, then, the frightful vacuity, the levity, the shallowness, the vulgarity, the pointlessness . . . ? It must be that she has no religion." The problem may well have been that Florence indeed had one—her occult one, which had contributed crucially to the gulf between them.

22   °*Fabian Executive. 17½. °Fabian Committee. 17.*

23   *Olivier to read his new play at Wallas's at 15. Van Marcke exhibition at the Goupil Gallery. Private View. Meet Bertha Newcombe there at 13.*

Originally Shaw was to go to Miss Emma Brooke's in Hampstead on the 27th for the play reading, but he was alerted by Olivier to the earlier opportunity. ▪ Emile van Marcke (1827–1890), born in France of Dutch parents, was an animal painter, a landscape painter, and an engraver.

24 SUNDAY   *Lecture at Folk's Hall, Dalston Lane, opposite German Hospital, at 20, on "Social-Democracy and Practical Politics" (Thomas Jarvis, 169 Brooke Rd., Upper Clapton).*

25   °*Reception to Maeterlinck and Lugné-Poe (of L'OEuvre) at the Hotel Victoria. 15 to 18. Opera Comique. Performance of* Rosmersholm *by L'OEuvre, 20, followed by Maeterlinck's* L'Intruse.

[The first act of *Rosmersholm* had hardly begun . . . when I recognized, with something like excitement, the true atmosphere of this most enthralling of all Ibsen's works rising like an enchanted mist for the first time on an English stage. (C1059)]

Maurice Maeterlinck (1862–1949), Belgian playwright, was considered by Shaw to be "a man of genius." Aurélien Lugné-Poe (1869–1940), actor-manager of the Theatre de L'OEuvre in Paris, was the leading experimentalist in French dramatic circles. G.B.S. would review the L'OEuvre productions in his 30 March column (C1059), finding the settings shabby and the costuming and make-up incredible, but the acting powerful and evocative.

26   °*Mrs. Corrie Grant lectures on "Woman" at Miss Pearse's studio, 2 New Court, Lincoln's Inn, 19½, for the New Fellowship. Performance of Maeterlinck's* Pelléas et Mélisande *by L'OEuvre. Opera Comique. 20. Lunch at National Liberal Club at 12.30 to meet Maeterlinck. Frampton to call for me at 12.*

27   °*Fabian Publishing Committee. 16¼. Performance of* Solness (The Master Builder) *by L'OEuvre, Opera Comique. 20.*

[At first it seemed as if M. Lugné-Poe's elaborate and completely realized study of a self-made man breaking up, was going to carry all before it. . . . The last act, with a subjugated Hilda, and a Mrs. Solness who was visibly struggling with a natural propensity to cheerful common sense, all but failed. . . . (C1059)]

28 [   ]

29 *Fabian Executive. 17¼. Fabian Committee. 17. °Shakespere Reading Society,* Romeo and Juliet, *Steinway Hall. 20½.*

30 *Deliver an address to the Women's Progressive Society, Ideal Club, Tottenham Court Rd., at 17 (Mrs. Brownlow, 30 Theobald's Rd. W. C.). "Feminine Meanness."*

31 SUNDAY *Lecture at Milton Hall for the North London Progressive Society on "Great Men: Are They Real?" 19¼. (C. R. Linden).*

April

1 *Speak for half an hour on "The Theatre" at a soiree at South Place at 20. (Mrs. Dixon, 69 Tollington Park N.).*

2 [I went to Onslow Square to see Charrington. . . . He seems very comfortable. . . .]

> Shaw to Janet Achurch, 3 April 1895, referring to the previous night (*CL*). It was becoming clear from her messages to London that Mansfield was preparing to abandon *Candida* as the wrong vehicle for him (too much talk, insufficient action), and jettison Janet (whom he could not visualize as any sort of heroine) in the process. Charrington had moved from Battersea since her departure.

3 *°Annual Meeting, Friends of Russian Freedom, St. Martin's Town Hall. 20¼. Speak.*

4 [I was to have met the McKennals at Onslow Square . . . but I had to interview Massingham at the *Chronicle* office, and so did not arrive until they had departed.]

> Shaw to Janet Achurch, 5 April 1895, referring to the previous night (*CL*). Bertram McKennal (1863–1931), a London sculptor, later designed the George V coinage and the tomb of Edward VII at St. George's Chapel, Windsor. The same day, keeping up his pressure on Richard Mansfield—he understood the damage Janet would do when he saw

her off at the dock—Shaw published "Mr. Bernard Shaw and His New Play," a self-drafted interview about *Candida*, in *The New Budget* (C1062). "Come to New York and see it," Shaw told the interviewer, "and you won't find it dull."

5 *Fabian Meeting at Essex Hall. Geoffrey Drage on "Some of the Administrative Difficulties of Socialism." 20. Cancelled—Sidney Webb on "Democracy." °Poel's lecture on Shakespere and the Modern Stage, Burlington Hall, Savile Row, 20½.*

Geoffrey Drage, Conservative M.P. for Derby, 1895, was secretary to the Labour Commission.

6 [I have been to see the Living Pictures at the Palace Theatre. The moment Lady Henry Somerset called public attention to the fact that they were obnoxious to the National Vigilance Association, I resolved to try whether they would offend me . . . and incidentally brought five shillings into the till . . . , not because I wanted to wallow in indecency—no man in his senses would go to a public theatre with that object even in the most abandoned condition of public taste, privacy being a necessary condition of thorough-going indecency—but because, as a critic, I perceived at once that Mr. Coote had placed before the public an issue of considerable moment . . . in artistic matters. . . .]

Lady Isabella Caroline—Lady Henry Somerset (1851–1921), daughter of the last Earl Somers—married Lord Henry Somerset in 1872 and thereafter devoted herself to temperance promotion and other "good works," serving as president of the World W.C.T.U. from 1898 to 1906. ▪ William A. Coote (1842–1919) was secretary of the National Vigilance Association. Shaw called him a "monomaniac" on sexual questions, while "in artistic matters" he was "an intensely stupid man." ▪ "The Living Pictures," G.B.S.'s column on the posed reproductions of art works at the Palace Theatre, was published in SR on this date (C1063). It is unclear when he actually visited the *poses plastiques.*

7 SUNDAY *Lecture at the Oddfellows' Hall, London Rd., Sevenoaks, at 15½, on "What the Twentieth Century will be like." Pleasant Sunday Afternoons, etc. (Fred Hooker, 4 Argyle, Sevenoaks, Secretary Municipal Labour Election Committee). Train leaves Charing Cross at 11.15.*

8 [   ]

9 [   ]

10 *Go down to Beachy Head with the Webbs, Wallas, Trevelyan, Miss Newcombe. 15.27 from Victoria.*

Shaw was spending the Easter holidays with the Webbs, who were still attempting to pair him up with Bertha Newcombe.

11 [   ]

12 [At Beachy Head I have been trying to learn the bicycle; and after a desperate struggle, renewed on two successive days, I will do twenty yards and a destructive fall against any professional in England. My God, the stiffness, the blisters, the bruises, the pains in every twisted muscle, the crashes against the chalk road that I have endured—and at my age too. But . . . I will not be beaten by that hellish machine.]

> Shaw to Janet Achurch, written on 13 April 1895 (*CL*), referring to the previous two days.

13 *First night of* The Girl I Left Behind Me *at the Adelphi. 20. Come up from Eastbourne by the 14.15 train.*

[My frequent allusions to Adelphi melodrama were all founded on a knowledge so perfect that there was no need to verify it experimentally; and now that the experiment has been imposed on me in the course of my professional duty, it has confirmed my deductions to the minutest particular.]

> G.B.S.'s review of *The Girl I Left Behind Me*, by Franklin Fyles (1847–1911) and David Belasco (1853–1931), appeared on 20 April 1895 (C1066). He did not object to "a simple and sincere drama of action and feeling"—his definition of melodrama—but the new Adelphi example was merely a bad play.

14 SUNDAY   *Go down to Eastbourne by the 11 train from Victoria.*

15 *Excursion to Alfriston.*

> Alfriston, a tiny village on the southeast coast between Brighton and Eastbourne, was once a rendezvous for smugglers, who hid their loot in secret rooms of the timbered houses and in the still-active Star Inn.

16 [Telegram just received from Mansfield "Am opening Garrick with Arms Man will produce Candida if I need not appear." The benevolent object here is to produce the play with a bad cast, and by making it a failure, at one stroke prevent any other manager from getting it and prevent Janet from making a success in New York.]

> Shaw to Charrington, 16 April 1895 (*CL*). At the same time that he sent his telegram, Mansfield wrote a long letter to Shaw (dated 14 April) explaining why both *Candida* and Janet Achurch were "of the impossible." The play was a "sermon"—and he required "a strong, hearty—earnest—noble—genuine play," which he urged Shaw to write. "To be frank and go further—I am not in sympathy with a young, delicate, morbid and altogether exceptional young man who falls in love with a massive middle-aged lady who peels onions." (Shaw had described Candida Morell as an attractive young mother of 33.) "I couldn't have made love to your Candida (Miss Janet Achurch) if I had taken ether—I never fall in love with fuzzy-haired persons who purr and are business-like and take a drop when they feel disposed and have weak feminine voices—my ideal is quite different. I detest an aroma of stale tobacco and gin. . . . I don't like women who sit on the floor—or kneel by your side and have designs on your shirt-bosom—I don't like women who comb their tawny locks with their fingers, and claw their necks and scratch the air with their chins."

17 *Come up from Eastbourne by the 14.15 train. First night of Sardou's* Delia Harding *at the Comedy Theatre. 20.15.*

[*Delia Harding* is the worst play I ever saw. . . . The whole business was so stale, so obviously factitious, so barrenly inept, that at last the gallery broke out in open derision. . . . As for me, I felt ashamed and remorseful. . . .]

> *Delia Harding*—a melodrama which would survive for twenty-eight performances—was an adaptation from the French of Victorien Sardou by J. W. Comyns Carr, who took a curtain call to a chorus of boos (C1066).

18 *First night of* The Ladies' Idol *at the Vaudeville. 21.*

> Reviewed on 27 April 1895 (C1067). G.B.S. found it "not bad fun," especially because "The audience, convinced that Mr. [Weedon] Grossmith is one of the funniest of men, laughs whenever he opens his mouth." Arthur Law (1844–1913) was a prolific writer of farces.

19 *[Eduard] Bernstein to call between 12 and 13. Fabian Executive. 17¼.* °*Fabian Committee. 17.*

Went to Pagets' in the evening.

> Going to the Pagets may also have meant an evening with Mrs. Paget's sister, Florence Farr.

20 *Go down to Basingstoke (Mrs. Stanton Blatch's) by the 11 train from Waterloo.*

21 SUNDAY *Lunch at Webbs'. 13½.*

22 *Meet the Webbs at Battersea Park Gates at 15—bicycling.*

[I went to Battersea Park . . . to bicycle; and Nora (Charrington) came to see me fall. Florence Farr was there, caracoling on her machine with surpassing elegance, to the admiration of all the park. The Webbs also struggled with their new machines.]

> Shaw to Janet Achurch, 23 April 1895 (*CL*), referring to the previous day.

23 [Charrington has just been here. . . .]

> Shaw to Janet Achurch, 23 April 1895. The opening words of the long letter in which Shaw explains patiently to Janet how to lecture in America on Ibsen, her solution to having been shorn of her *Candida* role. Charrington had just told him "the dire news" of her intentions.

24 *Miss Herford's recital, Salle Érard. 15¼.* °*Fabian Publishing Committee. 16¼.*

> Miss Herford, a pianist, is otherwise unidentified.

25 *Speak at Annual Meeting of the Humanitarian League, 32 Sackville St. 15.* °*Production of* The Passport, *by B. C. Stephenson and W. Yardley, at*

Terry's Theatre. 20$\frac{1}{2}$. Ticket changed to 29th. Concert at Queen's Hall, Levi's first appearance in England.

> The symposium, to which Shaw contributed, concerned the question, "Should social problems be freely dealt with in the Drama?" His contribution was published in "The Problem Play: A Symposium," *The Humanitarian*, May 1895 (C1070). Shaw's response was that "when a play depends entirely on a social question—when the struggle in it is between man and a purely legal institution—nothing can prolong its life beyond that of the institution. . . . But every drama does not involve a social question, because human feeling may be in conflict with circumstances which are not institutions, which raise no question at all, which are part of human destiny." ▪ Hermann Levi (1839–1900) was a protegé of Wagner who conducted at Bayreuth. His devotion to the master was complete, despite the open antisemitism of both Cosima and Richard Wagner; his reward had been to preside over the premiere of *Parsifal*. Shaw wrote an unsigned leader for the *Daily Chronicle*, 29 April 1895 (C1069), on "the famous Munich orchestral conductor."

26 *Fabian meeting at Clifford's Inn. Edwin Goadby on "Municipalization of Drink Traffic." 20. °Private View. "Connoisseur's Treasures," Goupil Gallery.*

> Edwin Goadby, editor of the *York Herald*, had just published a book on governmental control of the alcohol trade, *The Gothenburg Licensing System* (London, 1895).

27 *Dine with [Henry Arthur] Jones. 19$\frac{1}{2}$.*

[I . . . dashed out and sent a copy of the interview (with Janet Achurch, in the New York *Evening Sun*, received in the evening) by express messenger to the *Weekly Sun* at the eleventh hour with the vulgar but satisfactory result that the interview was reprinted at full length the next day. . . . It was altogether too good to be lost. . . .]

> Shaw to Janet Achurch, 30 April 1895 (*CL*), referring to the previous Saturday evening. The interview with Miss Achurch had been in the 17 April *Evening Sun* under the byline of Acton Davies. With a small editorial note by Shaw (C1068) it appeared in the London *Weekly Sun* on 28 April 1895. Apparently Shaw's new skirmish in the war against Mansfield over Janet occurred after his return from dinner with Jones. Following Miss Achurch's quoting Richard Mansfield as rejecting her with "You're a new woman. You play Ibsen. I detest new women who play Ibsen," Shaw had added, maliciously, "Mrs. Mansfield has played Nora in 'A Doll's House' in New York."

28 SUNDAY *Lecture for the Hammersmith Socialist Society at Kelmscott House on "Great Men: Are They Real?" 20. (E. Walker). Lunch at Webbs'.*

29 *Terry's Theatre. See 25th—last Thursday. Call on Miss Marbury at the Kensington Palace Hotel at 16.*

Felix Mansfield called in the morning. He has just returned from America. [Mrs. Harris (our domestic assistant) came in and . . . wanted to know whether I would see him. As the usual course is for him to come up without misgiving, the proceeding was eloquent of his unhappy position. I received him with boisterous good humour; and he wrung my hand with the fervency of a man whose mind is relieved of a ton of lead. There were no explanations. I assumed remorselessly that I knew all about it and he did not force a discussion on me. In the afternoon I had an interview with Miss Marbury, who is quite a foot broader than she was before, and Daniel Frohman. She had nothing to tell me I did not know. . . .]

> *The Passport*, by B. C. Stephenson and William Yardley, reviewed by G.B.S. on 4 May 1895 (C1071). It was "an amusing piece, with thirteen parts, of which no less than eight are very well acted . . . ; the scenes and circumstances, both in the frontier railway station and in the London house, are fully imagined and realized." There were 122 performances. ▪ Bracketed supplement: Shaw to Janet Achurch, 30 April 1895, referring to the previous Monday morning. Elizabeth Marbury was handling Shaw's theater business in New York; Daniel Frohman (1851–1941)—the extra *e* was Shaw's—was a New York theater manager who had already produced Pinero and Jones in the United States. His brother Charles (1860–1915) would become better known in England, where he would lease the Duke of York's Theatre, later producing Barrie's *Peter Pan* (1905).

30   *Court Theatre. Production of Godfrey's* Vanity Fair *(3rd night). 20¼.*
[Mr. Arthur Cecil was . . . so unequal to the mere taskwork of remembering long strings of sentences which were about as characteristic and human as the instructions on the back of a telegraph form, that he had to be spoon-fed by the prompter all the evening.]

> *Vanity Fair*, by George W. Godfrey (1844–1897), a series of satiric vignettes built around the style of Oscar Wilde and the attractive personality of Mrs. John Wood (1831–1915). Arthur Cecil (1844–1896) played opposite her. To G.B.S. (C1071) the pseudo-Wildean wit failed because Godfrey "tries to say the absurd thing without precisely knowing the sensible thing [to be inverted]."

May

1   °*Fabian Publishing Committee. 16¼.* °*"First Socialist Carnival," Independent Labour Party, Holborn Town Hall. 19. Austin Fryers' A Human Sport at the Actors' Benevolent Fund Matinee. Globe Theatre.* °*Meeting at Clayden's, 13 Tavistock Square, to reorganize Liberal Party.*

> "Austin Fryers" was the playwright W. E. Cleary. To G.B.S. (C1071) the one-act piece was "hardly a drama at all: it is rather the exhibition of an incident which does not develop in any way."

2   [   ]

3   *Fabian Meeting at Essex Hall. Liebknecht on "The Development of Social-Democracy in Germany." 20. Changed to Gertrude Tuckwell on "Women and the Factory Bill." Fabian Executive. 17¼. Fabian Committee. 17.*

Wilhelm Liebknecht (1826–1900) was editor of the German Socialist newspaper *Vorwärts*. ▪ Gertrude Tuckwell (1861–1951), a former London teacher and one of the first women magistrates, was author of *The State and Its Children* (London, 1894). She had recently been elected president of the Women's Trade Union League, and would become a recognized authority on industrial employment matters, health insurance, and local administration of justice.

4   *Lyceum Theatre. Conan Doyle's* [A] Story of Waterloo *and W. G. Wills's* [A Chapter From] Don Quixote.

Reviewed on 11 May 1895 (C1072). For G.B.S. it was an occasion to pan the acting of Henry Irving, who played Corporal Gregory Brewster, age 86, a veteran of Waterloo, who "dodders across the stage." The other two short plays on the bill (the diary mentions two rather than three pieces) were a vignette about the author of *Don Quixote* by the late W. G. Wills (1828–1891), and an early Pinero one-act work, *Bygones*, in which Sydney Valentine (1865–1919) played the foreign-accented Professor Mazzoni "with notable skill and judgment."

5 SUNDAY   *Morris lectures at Kelmscott House on "The Middle Ages." Postponed to 24th November. Labour Day in Hyde Park. Speak from Platform 2.*

Walked to Hammersmith afterwards with Walker, Charrington coming part of the way with us.

6   *Call on Yorke Stephens in the afternoon. Bax's in the evening, call for him at the National Liberal Club at 20.*

Called for him but could not find him.

Yorke Stephens (1862–1937) had played Captain Bluntschli in the Avenue production of *Arms and the Man,* and would play the dentist Valentine in the 1899 Stage Society production of *You Never Can Tell.*

7   °*Newspaper Society Soirée. Royal Institute Gallery. 21. Fabian Publishing Committee. 17 (new day and hour). Production of R. C. Carton's* [The] Home Secretary *at the Criterion Theatre. 20.10.*

Reviewed on 18 May 1895 (C1074). According to Shaw's preface to the 1895 diary, Frank Harris cut a passage about Anarchism out of the article, ending any chance that their professional association would lead to a warmer relationship. R. C. Carton's *The Home Secretary,* according to G.B.S., was "a well-acted, well-staged, occasionally entertaining, and hopelessly slovenly play."

8   [ ]

9   *Performance of* Macbeth *by the Shakespere Reading Society and Glossop Such in aid of Siddons's Memorial Fund. St. George's Hall. 20.*

Reviewed on 25 May 1895 (C1075). "From the ordinary professional standpoint," G.B.S. wrote, the performance was "a very bad one." But a young actress was "thrilling" as Lady Macbeth. "I should like to see Miss Lillah McCarthy again." Lillah McCarthy (1875–1960) in later years would become almost surrogate daughter to G.B.S. She would work closely with Granville Barker and become his first wife, in the process creating many of Shaw's leading roles, including that of Anne Whitefield in *Man and Superman*. ▪ On Glossop Such, who played the title role, Shaw was mercifully silent.

10 *Fabian Annual Meeting. Clifford's Inn. 20. Resolution about Webb and Elliott—Important. Fabian Executive. 17$\frac{1}{2}$. (Took the chair). Fabian Committee. 17.*

The text of the resolution by disgruntled Fabian J. Kent, which was circulated prior to the meeting, was that Sidney Webb be censured "for not publicly associating himself with John Elliott [of the Deptford branch of the S.D.F.] in the recent L.C.C. Election; and also for supporting Progressive [rather than Radical] candidates in those divisions where S.D.F. or I.L.P. candidates were running; and records its disapproval of the action of those Fabians who ran as Progressives or supported Progressives during the campaign." The resolution was defeated, sustaining Fabian policy of supporting candidates, regardless of party, who supported its positions. ▪ Shaw began *The Man of Destiny* this morning, in Regent's Park. The manuscript (Add. MS. 50604) is mistakenly dated 10/5/96. Whether the catalyst in getting the play about Napoleon going was his dissatisfaction on 4 May with Henry Irving's playing a doddering veteran of Waterloo is unknown; ironically, he would even consider Irving for the role of the young Napoleon, but the later negotiations with Irving came to nothing. The personality of the swaggering young general, Shaw would confide, would be drawn from his recent memories of Richard Mansfield.

11 *Production of H. A. Jones's* Triumph of the Philistines *at the St. James's Theatre. 20$\frac{1}{2}$.*

[When Mr. Jones appeared before the curtain several persons howled piteously, like dogs who had been purposely run over. Every play which is a criticism of contemporary life, must, if it is an honest play, involve a certain struggle with the public.]

G.B.S., 18 May 1895 (C1074). "There is a sense," he added, "in which Mr. Jones's plays are far more faulty than those of most of his competitors, exactly as a row of men is more faulty than a row of lampposts turned out by a first-rate firm." The comedy about the "narrowness and hypocrisy" of the town of Market Pewbury, with George Alexander in the lead role, would have thirty-nine performances.

12 SUNDAY *Lunch at Webbs'. 13$\frac{1}{2}$. Catch 15.5 at Vauxhall for Richmond to walk through the Park with Bax and finish up at Haldane's lecture at Kelmscott House. Mrs. Webb in the country. Webb came to Richmond with us.*

13 [ ]

14 *Speak at meeting of the London Vegetarian Society at the Memorial Hall (Miss F. I. Nicholson, Memorial Hall). 20. °Fabian Publishing Committee. 17. Battersea Park. 15$\frac{1}{2}$. Cycle.*

15 *(18th)* Notorious Mrs. Ebbsmith *at Garrick Theatre recommenced with Olga Nethersole. Performance by County Council Bands at Drury Lane Theatre. 14¼.*

[Saturday evening found me lurking, an uninvited guest, in an obscure corner of the Garrick Theatre, giving Mrs. Ebbsmith another trial in the person of Miss Olga Nethersole. This time I carefully regulated the dose, coming late for the preliminary explanations, and hurrying home at the end of the second act, when Mrs. Ebbsmith had put her fine dress on, and was beginning to work up towards the stove. I cannot say I enjoyed myself very much; for the play bored me more than ever. . . .]

> Olga Nethersole (1863–1951) had replaced Mrs. Campbell in the title role of the lady who is no lady, but who on second thought reaches into the stove to retrieve the Bible she had scornfully consigned to the flames. G.B.S. took the opportunity of the cast change to reconsider the play he had castigated earlier (C1075).

16 *Go out to Blands' and read* Candida. *Train Charing Cross to Grove Park. 19.25.*

17 *Fabian Annual Meeting. Clifford's Inn. 20. Changed to 10th. Fabian Executive. 17½. Fabian Committee. 17.*

18 [Cheque No. 40 287 (bicycle) 23. 10. 0]

> On 14 May Shaw had noted going to cycle in Battersea Park. He may have been trying out a bicycle he now formally purchased by personal check, as noted in his accounting at the close of the 1895 diary.

19 SUNDAY *Lunch at Webbs'.*

20 °*Put off. Supper at Max Hecht's, 35 Belsize Park Gardens, at 20½, to meet Felix Mottl (gemuthlicher Abend).*

21 *Fabian Publishing Committee. 17.*

22 °*Mottl Concert. Queen's Hall. 20.15.* The Prude's Progress *at the Comedy Theatre. Eden Phillpotts and Jerome K. Jerome.*

> Eden Phillpotts (1862–1960) would be well known as a novelist as well as a playwright. Most of his plays were collaborations. Jerome K. Jerome (1859–1927) wrote humorous fiction as well as plays. On 1 June 1895 G.B.S. (C1076) found The Prude's Progress a "shrewd, goodnatured, clever cockney play."

23 [I was bicycling in Battersea Park . . . with Trevelyan when Charlie (Charrington) came along. He had been toting Nora to Redcliffe Square, Miss Dickens (the governess) having incurred the displeasure of that establishment by some indiscretion or other. . . . He seemed in excellent spirits, the day being pleasant. He is going to lecture . . . at the Hackney Radical Club and at the Hammersmith Socialist Society; and this I think a good thing on the whole, as he ought to make an above-the-average public speaker, although among the Fabians he will probably be an Impossibilist of the Impossibilists.]

Shaw to Janet Achurch, 24 May 1895, referring to the afternoon of 23 May (*CL*).

24   *Fabian meeting at Clifford's Inn. H. Samuel on "The Problem of Unemployment." 20. Fabian Executive. 17½. Fabian Committee. 17.*

Although he was not a Fabian, Herbert Louis Samuel (1870–1963)—later Viscount Samuel—had written *Fabian Tract* No. 53, *The Parish Council Act: What it is and How to Work it* (1894), and three other tracts on rural government problems.

25   [Up to this day . . . I had preserved my innocence as a playgoer sufficiently never to have seen *Fedora*. Of course I was not altogether new to it, since I had seen *Diplomacy Dora*, and *Theodora*, and *La Toscadora*, and other machine dolls from the same firm. And yet the thing took me aback. To see that curtain go up again and again only to disclose a bewildering profusion of everything that has no business in a play, was an experience for which nothing could quite prepare me.]

Sardou's *Fedora* (1883) opened on 25 May 1895 for a run of fifty-five performances under Beerbohm Tree's management at the Haymarket. Mrs. Campbell was Princess Fedora Romazoff. Shaw's review appeared in *SR* on 1 June 1895 (C1076).

26 SUNDAY   *Speak at East India Dock Gates at 11.30 for Popular Labour Election Association. Lunch at Webbs'.*

Shaw wrote Pease (*CL*), who was handling arrangements, that he would speak on "Practical Socialism or what they please."

27   °*Liberal and Radical Union Council Meeting. National Liberal Club. 20.*

28   *Fabian Publishing Committee. 17.*

29   *Speak at the meeting of the Independent Anti Vivisection League. St. Martin's Hall. 20. (Mrs. Mona Caird, 7 Kensington Court Gardens W.).*

30   [   ]

31   °*Fabian Executive. 17½. Cancelled. °Fabian Committee. 17. Cancelled.*

June

1 [   ]

2 SUNDAY   *Lunch at Webbs'—be in good time, as they start for Huddersfield in the afternoon.*

3   *Sarah Bernhardt in* Gismonda *(Sardou) at Daly's Theatre.* 20½.

[Sardou's latest edition of the Kiralfian entertainment which Madame Bernhardt has for years dragged from sea to sea . . . is surpassingly dreary, although it is happily relieved four times by very long waits between the acts. . . .]

> Victorien Sardou's *Gismonda* would have twelve performances, in French. G.B.S. (C1076) considered Sarah Bernhardt an "ex-artist" who now only bothered "to posture in a travelling show."

4   [   ]

5   [The appearance of Duse at Drury Lane . . . in *La Femme de Claude*, is too recent for my judgment to have recovered from the emotional disturbance produced by such an appeal as she made to my passion for very fine acting . . . the best modern acting I have ever seen. . . .]

> G.B.S., 8 June 1895 (C1077), had little to say about the play by Alexandre Dumas, *fils*, preferring to probe the sources of Eleonora Duse's acting genius. Both Duse and Bernhardt were then competing in brief London seasons. Translated into French and read to Duse by Laurence Alma Tadema, daughter of the artist, the G.B.S. review gave her "very sincere delight"—so Tadema wrote Shaw on 14 June (BL Add. MS. 50513).

6   *Siegfried Wagner Concert. Queen's Hall.* 20.15.

> This, Siegfried Wagner's second London visit, was less rapturously received. Shaw would write, in an unsigned subleader in the *Daily Chronicle*, 6 November 1895 (C1099), "unhappily this time the band was in a bad temper; and the youthful conductor, staggering under the weight of a great name, yet had the hardihood to introduce himself as a composer by a symphonic poem. . . . The result was that . . . the press turned and rent poor Siegfried. . . ."

7   °*Fabian Executive.* °*Fabian Committee.* °*Fabian meeting at London Reform Union offices, Helen Dendy "Errors of Socialism."* 20. *Duse in* Cavalleria *and* La Locandiera *at Drury Lane.* 20½.

> Helen Dendy (1848–1923), the wife of Professor Bernard Bosanquet, was active in the Charity Organisation Society.   ▪   In "Duse and Bernhardt," 15 June 1895 (C1078), G.B.S. compared the competing tragediennes, having experienced a second week of their performances.

8   *Duse in* La Dame aux Camellias *at Drury Lane.* 14.

Duse's interpretation was "unspeakably touching because it is exquisitely considerate," and "immeasurably dwarfs the poor little octave and a half on which Sarah Bernhardt plays such pretty canzonets and stirring marches" (C1078).

9 SUNDAY *Bicycle down to H. A. Jones's at Blackheath, near Chilworth and stay the night.*

10 *Ride up from Blackheath (Surrey). Sarah Bernhardt as Magda at Daly's Theatre (Sudermann's* Heimat*).*

[Sarah was very charming. . . . And she did not trouble us with any fuss about the main theme of Sudermann's play, the revolt of the modern woman which exacts the sacrifice of her whole life to its care. . . . (C1078)]

11 °*Speak on "Dress" for "The Healthy and Artistic Dress Union" at the Cavendish Rooms, Mortimer St., at 20 (Mrs. C. E. Kelsey, 13 Berkeley Rd., Crouch End N.). Read* Candida *to the Carrs at 19 Park Village West. 20.*

> G.B.S. would write about the Healthy and Artistic Dress Union in his *SR* column, "The Tailor and the Stage," 15 February 1896 (C1120). All he knew about the organization, he would own, was gleaned from its illustrated journal, *Aglaia*.

12 *Duse as Magda at Drury Lane. 20$\frac{1}{2}$.*

[On the whole, I come off best at the theatre in such a case as that of *Magda*, where I began by reading the synopsis, then picked up a little of the play in French at Daly's Theatre, then a little more in Italian at Drury Lane, then a little more in German from the book, and finally looked at Duse and was illuminated beyond all the powers of all the books and languages on earth. (C1078)]

13 [   ]

14 *Fabian meeting at Essex Hall. Herbert Burrows on "Socialism and Women." 20. Fabian Executive. 17$\frac{1}{2}$. Fabian Committee. 17. Call on Mrs. St. Hill at 4 Park Row, Knightsbridge, to allow her to take casts of my hands.*

> Mrs. Katherine St. Hill published a photograph of the cast in *The Palmist and Chirological Review* (which she edited), July 1895. Shaw would write Janet Achurch (31 August 1895, *CL*), "The palmist, working from a cast of my hand, is struck by a 'curious extension of the mount of Saturn in the direction of the line of the heart' (I quote from memory) and draws conclusions therefrom. The said curious extension is really a sort of broad flabby corn or callosity which you may have noticed on my right hand. The palmist, I regret to say, accuses me, as you do, of atrocious cruelty."

15 The Girl I Left Behind Me *at the Adelphi—Harry Nicholls and Nanette Comstock for the first time. 20.*

> G.B.S. would not review the new cast. Harry Nicholls (1852–1926) was a songwriter as well as an actor. Nanette Comstock (1873–1942) would have a long career in popular comedy.

16 SUNDAY   *Lunch with the Trevelyans at 13½. 8 Grosvenor Crescent.*

17   *Sarah Bernhardt in* Princesse Lointaine *at Daly's Theatre. 20¼.* °Ex-*ecutive meeting reorganized South St. Pancras Liberal and Radical Associa-tion at Clayden's, 13 Tavistock Square. 20¼.* °A Modern Hypatia *at Terry's Theatre—matinee.*

> Reviewed on 22 June 1895 (C1079). Edmond Rostand (1868–1918) had written only one previous play, not produced in London. G.B.S. found the play's medievalism overly pre-cious, and sympathized with Madame Bernhardt that it was "not humanly possible for an actress to do much with a play in which, when the other characters are not describing what a peerlessly beautiful and wonderful creature she is, she is on the stage accepting that ridiculous position."

18   Die Ehre *at Drury Lane, Saxe-Coburg and Gotha Grand Ducal Com-pany. 20.*

> G.B.S. (C1079) promised a review of Sudermann's *Die Ehre* the next week, but none was forthcoming.

19   °*Arnold Dolmetsch's, 34 Queen Square, 20¼ to 22, clavichord and early English music.*

20   °*Mottl Concert. Queen's Hall. 20.15.* The Strange Adventures of Miss Brown *by [Robert] Buchanan and Charles Marlowe, at the Vaudeville. Postponed. 20.45.* °South St. Pancras Liberal and Radical Association Pub-*lic Meeting at the Mission Hall, Compton St., Judd St. 20¼. T. P. Whittaker on "The Local Veto and Compensation."*

> G.B.S. would see the play on the 26th. "Charles Marlowe" was Harriett Jay (1853–1932), actress and manager, who would collaborate further with Buchanan on comedies. ▪ (Sir) Thomas Palmer Whittaker (1850–1919) was a Liberal M.P. also active in the tem-perance movement. In October 1900 he would second Shaw's nomination for the St. Pancras Borough Council.

21   *Elizabethan Stage Society's performance of* Twelfth Night *at Burlington Hall, Saville Row. 20¼ for 21.*

> Reviewed on 20 July 1895 (C1083). The performance brought out "the immense advan-tage of the platform stage to the actor. It places him in so intimate a relation to the spectators that the difficulty of getting a delicate play 'across the footlights,' and of making vehement play forcible enough to overcome the remoteness of the 'living picture' stage, all but vanishes."

22   *St. James's Theatre. Revival of* The Second Mrs. Tanqueray *(3rd night).* [At the end of the second act I silently melted away and resolved to say nothing until the twelve nights were almost fulfilled. (C1080)]

> The revival to G.B.S. was "too heavy a joke for the hot weather," and indeed it folded quickly. His 29 June 1895 review (C1080) even found the "admirable" Evelyn Millard "wildly impossible" as Paula Tanqueray.

23 SUNDAY   °*Charrington lectures on "A People's Theatre" to the Battersea S. D. F. Sydney Hall. Ride down (on bicycle) to Limpsfield to Oliviers' with [John W.] Martin (he will call at 10), return the same evening.*

24   [Life just now is impossible: there is some confounded performance every night in all sorts of languages.]

> Shaw to Sydney C. Cockerell, 24 June 1895 (CL).

25   °*Personal Rights Association Conference on Lunacy Laws at National Liberal Club. 19½. Opening night, Daly Company, Daly's Theatre,* The Railroad of Love. *20.15.*

[Yet another foreign language—that of Amurrica! (C1080)]

> The comedy by American playwright Augustin Daly, said G.B.S. (C1080), belonged "with Mr. Vincent Crummles at Portsmouth in the early Dickens days. . . ." It was a fossil just short of being "an absolute outrage on the public." Shaw saw the German original of Daly's adaptation, *Goldfische*, 23 May 1888.

26   [*The Strange Adventures of Miss Brown*, at the Vaudeville, is said to resemble a piece called *Charley's Aunt* (which I have not seen) in point of introducing a man disguised as a woman. Such disguises are usually more or less disagreeable; but this is not so in the present case. The piece . . . offers itself unashamedly as pure fun and pastime for a couple of hours; and it succeeds perfectly. (C1080)]

> Shaw was busy as a music critic when *Charley's Aunt*, by Brandon Thomas (1856–1914), opened at the Royalty on 21 December 1892; however, it would have 1,469 performances in London through 19 December 1896, giving him ample time to see it had he wanted to.

27   [   ]

28   [   ]

29   *Prize Opera at Covent Garden.* Petruccio *and* Cavalleria. *14.* °*South St. Pancras Executive Liberal and Radical Association. 13 Tavistock Square. 20¼.*

> *Petruccio*, a new one-act opera by Alexander MacLean (1872–1936) was given a single matinee. He would become better known as a conductor of theater music.

30 SUNDAY   *Ride down to Oliviers'.*

> Shaw's usual Sunday dinner at 41 Grosvenor Road with the Webbs was again not possible because they were in Derbyshire. Shaw would write Sidney the next day (Passfield Papers, L.S.E.) of the Fabian Executive's suspicions about his intentions regarding the Hutchinson bequest—that Sidney was planning to establish his London School of Economics and Political Science regardless of opposition, buying off as many Fabians as possible "by subsidies for country lectures and the like." Webb would go ahead anyway, setting up a faculty of moderate Socialist views (to gain confidence) and acknowledged academic repute. The first session in the fall would enroll 291 students, including 87 women.

July

1 [How shall I excuse myself for having enjoyed *Ma Cousine?* It is a masterpiece of levity, and to say that Réjane plays it unscrupulously is to convey but a faint idea of the unconscionable allurements which she brings to the aid of her drollest and cleverest comedy. . . . Even I understood a quarter of the dialogue. . . .]

> *Ma Cousine,* a farce by Henri Meilhac (1831–1897) opened on 1 July 1895 at the Garrick Theatre for a limited run, performed in French. It starred Réjane [Gabrielle-Charlotte Réju] (1856–1920). G.B.S.'s review appeared on 6 July 1895 (C1081).

2 Two Gentlemen of Verona *at Daly's Theatre. 20.15. Fabian Publishing Committee. 17. °Fabian Special Private Meeting to pass election literature. 20. Clifford's Inn.*

> G.B.S. (C1081) called Augustin Daly's version of Shakespeare's play "a vaudeville. And let me hasten to admit that it makes a very pleasant entertainment for those who know better. . . . Mr. Daly has proceeded on the usual principles, altering, transposing, omitting, improving, correcting, and transferring speeches from one character to another."

3 °South St. Pancras Liberal and Radical Association Executive Meeting. *13 Tavistock Square. 20½.*

4 °Mottl Concert. Queen's Hall. 20.15. The Idler *at the St. James's Theatre. (Revival). 20¼.*

> G.B.S. thought (1081) that George Alexander's revival of the 1891 play by Haddon Chambers (1859–1921) would be a success, and noted that "the house received the play with enthusiasm"; it survived, however, only eight performances.

5 °Liberal Demonstration at the Albert Hall. 20. Fabian Executive and Committee. 17.

6 [ ]

7 SUNDAY *Speak in Battersea Park at 18½ on "The Twentieth Century" (C. Clifford, 27 Stormont Rd., Lavender Hill S.W.).*

8 *Garrick Theatre.* Madame Sans-Gêne. *Réjane. 20.15.*

[Before *Madame Sans-Gêne* I think it best to retire in good order without committing myself. I have never seen a French play of which I understood less; and that, for me, is saying a great deal.]

> G.B.S. reviewed the revival of Victorien Sardou's *Madame Sans-Gêne*, again starring Réjane, on 13 July 1895 (C1082). In *SR* he called it "idle chatter with a minimum of drama."

9 *Daly's Theatre.* Midsummer Night's Dream. *20.15.*

Revised Miss Belloc's interview with Janet Achurch; and rode over to Onslow Square on the bicycle after the theatre to submit my version.

> Daly's newest tampering with Shakespeare was reviewed even more negatively (C1082) than the last. The "magic spell" of the play did not survive the "slaughterings of the text." ▪ Marie Belloc [Mrs. Belloc-Lowndes] (1868–1947), sister of Hilaire Belloc, was a journalist, then on the staff of W. T. Stead's *Review of Reviews*, and later a novelist.

10 [   ]

11 *Speak in support of Harris, Liberal candidate South St. Pancras, at the Prospect Terrace Board School. 20½.*

> George Montagu Harris (1868–1951), a writer on local government issues, contested South St. Pancras unsuccessfully in both 1895 and 1896.

12 *Speak in support of Steadman at Askew Rd., Starch Green. 20.*

> W. C. Steadman, secretary of the Barge-Builders' Union, would become an L.C.C. member for Stepney, and later an M.P. for Tower Hamlets (1898–1900) and Central Finsbury (1906–1910). He would be the author of *Fabian Tract* No. 103, *Overcrowding in London and its Remedy* (1900).

13 *Speak at Demonstration at the corner of Beckton Rd., Canning Town, in support of Keir Hardie. 18. Speak at Demonstration in Canterbury Music Hall in support of C. P. Trevelyan. 15.*

14 SUNDAY *Call on Miss Robb at 16. 48 Sydney St., S. W. Lunch at Lady Carlisle's at 13. 1 Palace Green, Kensington W. Speak in Beresford Square, Woolwich, in support of Ben Jones, in the evening.*

> The house in Chelsea to which Shaw went to call on Miss Robb was listed in the Post Office Directory under a Mrs. Ponsonby, suggesting that Miss Robb lived in lodgings. ▪ Rosalind Frances Howard, Countess of Carlisle (1845–1921), temperance advocate, and suffragist, was president of the Women's Liberal Federation from 1891 to 1901. She would be Shaw's model for Lady Britomart in *Major Barbara*.

15 °*Annual Meeting International Arbitration and Peace Association. St. Martin's Town Hall. 15. Go down to Southampton to support J. R. Macdonald. 11.15 train. Speak at Demonstration. 20.*

16 *Come up from Southampton by 8.46 train from West Station. Archer's at 14¼ to meet Murray and discuss his play.*

> Gilbert Murray (1866–1957), then a professor of Greek at Glasgow University, would become Regius Professor of Greek at Oxford in 1908. He had written a play, *Carlyon Sahib*, in 1893. Reading the manuscript in 1895, William Archer found it "curiously grim and powerful, though unskilful," and asked Shaw's opinion. In 1899 Mrs. Patrick Campbell would produce the melodrama in London (Kennington), playing the role of Vera, the

heroine and daughter of the imperious (and evil) Sir David Carlyon. Shaw's own friendship with Murray—who would advise him on historical sources for *Caesar and Cleopatra* (1898)—would lead to Murray's becoming the model for Professor Adolphus Cusins in *Major Barbara*. (Murray's wife, Mary, was the daughter of the Countess of Carlisle.)

17   °*Pennells' in the evening. 20½. 14 Buckingham St.*

An interview with Shaw on "The Political Situation," possibly self-drafted, appeared in *The Sketch*, 17 July 1895 (NIL).

18–30   [   ]

There are no entries in Shaw's diary through the 30th. However, sometime early in this period he saw music hall comedienne Cissie Loftus (1868–1943) at the Palace. Loftus's imitations of popular actors G.B.S. "studied with much interest," as reported in *SR* on 27 July 1895 (C1087), in a review of the season's theater.

In the same period Shaw saw published his influential—and caustic—review of Max Nordau's *Degeneration*, "A Degenerate's View of Nordau," in the form of letter to the editor, in Benjamin Tucker's New York magazine *Liberty*, on 27 July 1895 (C1086). (It would be revised and augmented as *The Sanity of Art*, 1908.) He would also publish "Plutocrats and Local Veto," a letter on the general election which was occupying his time almost exclusively in the *Daily Chronicle*, 22 July 1895 (C1086), and "Bassetto on the Bicycle," *The Star*, 24 July 1895 (C1085), a humorous piece on learning the techniques of cycling.

31   *Go down to The Argoed, Monmouth, with the Webbs. At The Argoed until the 21st September.*

[I now propose to banish the theatre from my mind for a couple of months at least. (C1087)]

August

1–7   [I find that the new play is not coming. Instead, I keep fiddling at the little one-act thing I began that morning in Regent's Park, with Napoleon in it. . . . I will finish it anyhow, as I want to see whether I can write a good curtain-raiser.]

Shaw to Janet Achurch, 8 August 1895 (*CL*, where it is dated 8 July 1895), referring to his ongoing work on *The Man of Destiny* and his abortive efforts to find a way into a new full-length play which would get going, finally, in December and become *You Never Can Tell*.

8   [After 24 hours perfect weather, it is raining again like March and December rolled into one. . . . It is a vile country for bicycling: yesterday morning I was charging down a ruinously steep lane when a heap of stones capsized me and I razed twelve feet of hedge from the face of the map with my left temple & shoulder.]

Shaw to Janet Achurch, 8 August 1895.

9–13 [   ]

14 [I have just written like a father to the provincial Bluntschli, who is deep in my debt over "Arms & the Man," to tell him that he must either pay up or else shew me some reasonable prospect of his doing something more with it than making all the provincial managers resolve privately to book no more dates for plays of mine.]

A. E. Drinkwater was touring *Arms and the Man*, and playing Capt. Bluntschli. Shaw to Janet Achurch, 16 August 1895 (*CL*).

15 [   ]

16 [The weather has changed. Fierce sunshine and a heavy heat are upon the land; there has been a multitudinous birth of insects. . . .

My little Napoleon play progresses very slowly, and grows more ridiculous from page to page. The fun of it to me is that the character is not Napoleon at all, but Mansfield.]

Shaw to Charles Charrington, 14 August 1895 (*CL*).

17–22 [   ]

23 Wallas returned to London [from the Argoed] today.

24 [I have just finished the first draft of "The Man of Destiny," as I provisionally—perhaps permanently—call my one-act play. It is not exactly a burlesque: it is more harlequinade, in which Napoleon and a strange lady play harlequin and columbine, and a chuckle headed, asinine young sub lieutenant . . . and an innkeeper . . . play clown and pantaloon. The dialogue is all pure Shaw. . . .

Great heavens, I have just rescued it from a terrible fate. I am lying in a field, writing in any old notebook with a fountain pen. A foal came up behind me . . . & was just stretching out for a mouthful of the little book with the play in it when I became aware of him. And now he won't go away. I must move into the next field. . . .]

Shaw to Janet Achurch, 24 August 1895 (*CL*).

25–28 [   ]

29 [The hills are so bad that it sometimes takes an hour & a half to go five miles; and each ride ends by shoving the thing up 800 feet through impossible lanes to this Argoed-Ararat. The other evening, after riding over

thirty miles up hill & down dale, and finishing by fifteen miles at full speed to escape being overtaken by darkness (I had left my lamp at home), I was so abominably tired after pushing the thing up the lane that when I mounted to try and ride a level bit, I tumbled off. I thought I was alighting on a grass strip by the wayside; but it was a briar bush which let me gracefully down to the bottom of a deep ditch. The bicycle fell over me across the top of the ditch, and as I lay there looking up peacefully at the moon through the spokes of the wheel and the laced thorntwigs of the briar, I felt blessedly happy and at rest. It required the strongest exertion of my common sense to get up and force myself on to the house.]

Shaw to Janet Achurch, 31 August 1895 (*CL*), referring to the previous Thursday.

30 [ ]

31 [Tomorrow morning . . . I ride to Cardiff on bikeback. . . . Trade Union Congress, special correspondence for *The Star.* . . .]

Shaw to Janet Achurch, 31 August 1895. The ride to Cardiff was thirty-five miles by bicycle. Shaw would publish unsigned articles in *The Star* on the Congress on 3, 4, and 6 September 1895 (C1089–91).

September

1 SUNDAY   *Ride to Cardiff. Park Hotel.*

2   *Trade Union Congress at Cardiff opens. Do special correspondence for The Star.*

3   *Trade Union Congress, September 3 through 5.*

4–5 [ ]

6   °*Fabian Executive. 17¼. °Fabian Committee. 17. Leave Cardiff in the afternoon; ride through Pontypridd to Merthyr; take train to Abergavenny and sleep there at The Angel.*

7   *Ride back to The Argoed. Mr. and Mrs. Byles to arrive in the evening and stay until Monday.*

William Pollard Byles and his wife were arriving from Bradford to be guests of the Webbs.

8–11 [   ]

12 [I have had a most awful bicycle smash—the quintessence of ten railway collisions—brother of Earl Russell . . . dashed into at full speed flying down a hill—£3.10.0 damage to machine—got up within the prescribed ten seconds, but had subsequently to admit knock-out—Russell bereft of his knickerbockers but otherwise unhurt—lay flat on my back for ten minutes, but then rose and rode 16 miles back on a wheel the shape of an hourglass . . . .]

> Shaw to Pakenham Beatty, 17 September 1895 (*CL*), referring to 12 September. More dramatic details were offered on 16 September 1896 (*CL*) to Janet Achurch. Bertrand Russell (1872–1970), third Earl Russell (from 1931), had just been elected a Fellow of Trinity College, Cambridge, on the strength of a philosophical dissertation he would publish in 1897 as *An Essay on the Foundations of Geometry.*

13–20 [   ]

21 *Leave The Argoed for London. Ride to Chepstow; take train across Severn to Bath, and ride on to Warminster. Sleep there at The Bath Arms.*

22 SUNDAY *Ride across Salisbury Plain, via Stonehenge, to Amesbury; leave the Webbs behind there; and ride on to Hartley Row via Andover and Basingstoke.*

23 *Ride up to London from Harley Row. Go to* Romeo and Juliet *at the Lyceum (2nd night). Forbes Robertson and Mrs. Pat Campbell.*
["Mrs. Campbell's dresses," says the program, "have been carried out by Mrs. Mason, of New Burlington Street." I can only say that I wish they had been carried out and buried. They belong to Mrs. Mason, and are her triumph, instead of to Mrs. Campbell.]

> Reviewed on 28 September 1895 (C1092). In judging a performance of *Romeo and Juliet*, G.B.S. wrote, "It should never be forgotten . . . that the parts are made almost impossible, except to actors of positive genius, skilled to the last degree in metrical declamation. . . ." (Sir) Johnston Forbes-Robertson (1853–1937) possessed "gentlemanly limits."; Mrs. Campbell remained "a wonderful person" and could do no wrong although there was "not a touch of tragedy" in her performance.

24 *Go to* Cheer, Boys, Cheer *at Drury Lane Theatre (3rd night).*
[Do what I will, I cannot acquire a taste for these morbid, realistic-didactic plays on which Sir Augustus Harris lavishes his huge resources. They make me long inexpressibly for a breath of honest, wholesome, simple, straightforward Ibsen.]

> *Cheer, Boys, Cheer!* a "morbid, realistic-didactic play" by Augustus Harris, Cecil Raleigh, and Henry Hamilton, would run 177 performances. G.B.S., 5 October 1895 (C1094), deplored the stage villain, the stage Jew, the stage hero, and everything else about what he declared was a non-play.

25   [   ]

26   *Production of* Her Advocate *by Walter Frith at the Duke of York's (late Trafalgar) Theatre. Cartwright, etc.*

[Mr. Frith . . . represents a lady as insisting, because she comes from the country, on opening the windows of a London room for the sake of ventilation. This suggests to me that Mr. Frith has not yet been out of London. If he has ever met a human being in the country with any notion of the value of fresh air—if he has ever been in a country-house which did not still contain most of the air which was bottled up in the rooms on the day when the builders locked the door and handed over the key to the first occupier, he may regard himself as an exceptionally fortunate man.]

> Walter Frith (?—1941), playwright and novelist, had written a stage trial which G.B.S. (C1094) found "passed the evening pleasantly enough" with realism "quite genuine as far as it goes." Charles Cartwright (1855–1916) played the lawyer who defended a hospital nurse (Lena Ashwell, 1872–1957) wrongfully charged with murder, and who naturally falls in love with his client.

27   *No [Fabian] Executive.*

28–30   [   ]

October

1–3   [   ]

4   *Read a paper to the Fabian Society on "The Political Situation" at Essex Hall. 20. Fabian Executive. 17$\frac{1}{2}$. Fabian Committee. 17.*

> Miss Dickens' 57-page typescript of Shaw's lecture, and his 111-page manuscript draft, are BL Add. MS. 50684. Shaw concluded: "I no longer address my appeal to the working classes, in whose political initiative I no longer believe. I appeal to the rising parliamentary generation, whatever their class or party. And I believe that only by responding to this appeal will any party in future gain the force, the conviction, the power of interesting and persuading which will be necessary to impose Progress on the tremendous Conservatism of the newly enfranchised working classes." Shaw would deliver this lecture several more times, including to laboring audiences.

5   [   ]

6 SUNDAY   *Lecture to the Hammersmith Socialist Society, Kelmscott House, on "The Political Situation." 20. Lunch at 13$\frac{1}{2}$ with the Jopling-Rowes.*

7 [On paying a somewhat belated visit to *The Chili Widow* . . . I was astonished to find that Mr. Bourchier has not only taken the Royalty Theatre . . . but has actually founded there, with apparent success, a new school of stage art. At least it is new to the regular professional stage. . . . It is the school of the romping, gleeful amateur, . . . the facetious undergraduate who dresses up for a lark. . . .]

> *The Chili Widow*, by actor-playwright Arthur Bourchier (1863–1927) and Alfred Sutro (1863–1933), was an adaptation of *M. le Directeur* by Alexandre Bisson and Fabrice Carré. It had opened for a run of 223 performances on 7 September, and starred Bourchier, Kate Phillips (1849–1931), and Irene Vanbrugh (1872–1949). (It is arbitrarily placed here because Shaw published his review on 12 October 1895 [C1095] and would have needed a free evening within his *SR* deadline.) Although he found the play amusing, he also objected to it: "I sorrowfully profess my conviction . . . that the performers have not only been encouraged, but positively ordered, to clown as much as possible so as to keep the fun going and make the [otherwise weak] play lively."

8   *Speak at "Socialist Scouts" meeting at Club and Institute Union (Harold Creswell, 1 Silver St., Bloomsbury W.C.). 20.*

9   [   ]

10   *Vaudeville Theatre. 21.* Poor Mr. Potton.

[I am obliged to make the strange confession that I do not enjoy this sort of stage effect; though I admit that the guffaws which it invariably elicits shew that London audiences do not agree with me.]

> Reviewed on 19 October 1895 (C1096). The farce by Clarence Hamlyn and H. M. Paull was "tolerably good fun of its kind, childish fun. . . ." The saga of an aging fat lady and a puny young suitor (played by Weedon Grossmith) would have 58 performances.

11   °*No [Fabian] Executive.*

12   *Chelsea Bridge. 10.15. Cycle down to Leatherhead, etc. with the Webbs and Trevelyan.*

13 SUNDAY   *Lecture to the S. D. F. Bow and Bromley Branch (E. E. Metivia, 193 Bow Rd.), "The Political Situation." 2 minutes walk from Bow station, North London Railway. 20.15. Dine with Massingham at 14.*

14–15   [   ]

16   [This time Mr. Pinero has succeeded. *The Benefit of the Doubt* is worth *The Profligate*, *Mrs. Tanqueray*, and *Mrs. Ebbsmith* rolled into one and multipled by ten. It is melancholy to have to add that it has broken the back of our London stage, and may even fail through the sniffling monotony and dreary ugliness of the acting.]

Pinero, said G.B.S. on 19 October 1895 (C1096), "has not exactly been born again—but at least there are no intercepted letters, or sendings of one set of people to France and another to India to enable a lady to arrive unexpectedly or a gentleman to walk in by night at the drawing room window." Unfortunately, "the acting is almost too painful to face." Nevertheless, the play would have seventy-four performances.

17–18   [   ]

19   [With every possible disposition to tolerate all views of life on the stage, I cannot quite keep my patience with . . . your maudlin pessimist who, like Mr. Jerome K. Jerome, says, "We are all hopeless scoundrels; so let us be kind and gentle to one another": him I find hard to bear. Mr. Jerome's hero Dick Halward . . . cannot deny himself a dram of sympathy at the price of leaving everybody disgusted, ashamed, and miserably uncomfortable.]

> G.B.S. excoriated *The Rise of Dick Halward*, by Jerome Klapka Jerome (1858–1927), in his 26 October 1895 *SR* column (C1097). He refused to believe that the dramatist's aim was other than "to make money in the cheapest possible way." If so, Jerome failed. The play had only twenty-four performances.

20 SUNDAY   *Lecture at St. Thomas's Square Chapel, Hackney, at 20.15 (J. H. Belcher, Penprys, St. Thomas Square N.E.)*

21   [In order to fully realize how bad a popular play can be, it is necessary to see it twice. Messrs. Morell and Waller gave me that opportunity by reopening the Shaftesbury with Mr Carton's *Home Secretary*. . . . At the Criterion there was an atmosphere of conviction about the piece: here, it seemed to me, there was an atmosphere of incredulity. At all events, at the end of the second act I tried the atmosphere outside, and did not change it again. . . .]

> The play was no better than when G.B.S. had first reviewed it on 18 May 1895 (C1074). Now (C1097) he found the performance "perfunctory," and the home secretary himself, Lewis Waller, disabled by "a devastating cold." H. H. Morell (?–1916) was co-manager with Waller.

22   [   ]

23   *Fabian Publishing Committee. 16½. Call on Grein at 34 Craven St. 18¼.*

24   *(Next week) °Lecture on "Music" at the Pioneer Club (Miss C. M. White-head, 10 Montague St., Montague Square W.)*

25   *Fabian Meeting at Clifford's Inn. J. R. MacDonald on "Electoral Reform." 20.*

26   *Shareholders' meeting, Independent Theatre Company, 34 Craven St. 15 (Sec. Henry E. McCardle, 60 Haymarket S.W.)*

The Independent Theatre Company, co-founded by Dorothy Leighton (Mrs. G. C. Ashton-Jonson) and J. T. Grein, had been forced to reorganize because Grein, a Dutchman, had taken a new job as London representative of the Dutch East India merchants Wellenstein, Krause & Co., and his new employers would not permit him to retain the I.T. management (although he continued to write theatrical journalism). Shaw promoted Charles Charrington for managing director.

27 SUNDAY   *Lecture to the Kensal Town S.D.F. at Levell's Coffee Tavern, Westbourne Park, on "Socialism in Practical Politics." 20 (James Bramwell, 35 Hiley Rd., Kensal Rise, N.W.).*

28   *Revival of* The New Magdalen *at the Metropole Theatre. Janet Achurch as Mercy Myrick. 20½.*

[Until this week, I had never been invited by a suburban manager to a first night, because the suburban manager has usually nothing to shew except a piece already produced and criticized at a west end theatre. Now, however, Mr. Mulholland, the manager of the Metropole, has taken a step forward by producing a play on his own account. . . .]

> Reviewed on 28 October 1895 (C1098). The revival of the Wilkie Collins melodrama, with Janet Achurch, could only find a home in a suburban theater in Camberwell, S.E. Shaw gave it as kind—and as long—a review as he could, declaring that Miss Achurch as Mercy Myrick "preserved the heroic element in Mercy's character." The revival lasted a week, during which Shaw loyally saw it twice. J. B. Mulholland (1858–1925) would move to the West End in 1898.

29   [   ]

30   [*Trilby* is the very thing for the English stage at present. No need to act or create character: nothing to do but make up after Mr. du Maurier's familiar and largely popular drawings, and be applauded before uttering a word as dear old Taffy, or the Laird, or darling Trilby, or horrid Svengali.]

> Reviewed on 9 November 1895 (C1101). Paul Potter (1853–1921) in dramatizing artist George du Maurier's best-selling novel *Trilby* had "done his business with considerable knowlege of what was wanted of him. . . . Nearly all the favorite pictures and passages from the book are worked in, without violence, if possible, but at all events worked in. . . ." The play opened at the Haymarket on 30 October 1895. Its 254 performances were followed by numerous revivals.

31   *Lecture on "Music" at the Pioneer Club (Miss C. M. Whitehead, 10 Montague St., W.).*

November

1   *Go to see* The New Magdalen *again.*

2   [   ]

3 SUNDAY   *Lecture at the Reformers' Club, 7 St. Agnes's Place, Kennington Park, at 20½, on "The Political Situation." (Thomas A. Gilbert).*

4   [   ]

5   [At the Criterion Mr. Wyndham . . . has a tolerably good part—that of De Ryons in *L'Ami des Femmes*, transmuted by Mr. Carton into Mr. Kilroy in *The Squire of Dames.* . . .]

> *L'Ami* was characterized by G.B.S. (C1101) as "a bad play with good material in it," with acting "a good deal better than most theatres provide at present."

6   [   ]

> Although Shaw continued ("full up") his writing and his political activities, he was now distracted by Janet Achurch's illness, which materialized just as her play was closing. What was first thought to be pleurisy was clearly something worse, and Shaw's time became almost completely taken up by the situation.

7   [The revival of *Liberty Hall* at the St. James's was chiefly remarkable for the happy termination of an absurd incident by Mr. Alexander's reception, which attained the proportions of a public demonstration, and was so tremendously enthusiastic that he must have felt almost glad that the occasion of it, intensely disagreeable as it must have been, had happened to him.]

> R. C. Carton's *Liberty Hall* had been revived for sixteen performances, with George Alexander back in his leading role. A few days earlier he had been arrested by a London constable on the accusation of "intercourse with a prostitute in the ordinary pursuit of her trade." Shaw rushed to his defense in a letter implicitly evoking public awareness of former prime minister W. E. Gladstone's known predilections. In "The Charge against Mr. George Alexander," in the *Daily Chronicle*, 7 November 1895 (C1100)—the opening day for *Liberty Hall*—Shaw observed that the circumstances of being accosted by a streetwalker and offering her charity until "the intervention of the policeman" had also occurred to him "more than once." The G.B.S. note about the incident appeared as the tailpiece to his 16 November 1895 notice (C1103).

8   [The devil, the devil, the devil! Everything is going to hell—uncle drunk, paralytic, collapsing and threatening to leave me his cursed property and debts—sister declared by my mother to be going mad—Kate Gurly a wreck—all, damn them. . . .]

> Shaw to Charles Charrington, 8 November 1895, CL. His worry about Janet's condition was intense. His concern over the family holdings in Ireland was valid but premature. Shaw would indeed inherit some useless parcels of debt-riden Carlow property from his Uncle Walter in 1899, turning over in 1919 the eighteenth-century Assembly Rooms, nearly derelict, to the diocese for conversion into a technical school. In 1944 he made over the rest, a special act of the Irish parliament being necessary for the transfer.

9   [   ]

10 SUNDAY   *Lecture at Bremerton Hall, 2 Bremerton St., Copenhagen St., Caledonian Rd., to the West Islington Branch S.D.F. on "Social-Democracy and Practical Politics" (A. Blackwell).*

Miserable wet day. [J. Kingston] Barton, called in to consult about Janet [Achurch], declares that she has typhoid fever.

> Barton, Shaw told Charrington (*CL*), was not "Such a swell" that he was likely to be overwhelmed with patients, "but he is not a bloody fool." According to a memoir by Bertha Newcombe (*BL*), Charrington, on hearing the news, broke down. She wrote that Shaw, who spent as much time as he could spare at the Charringtons', "would tell me of the wretchedness of the household, the want of proper nursing, and how he himself sat for hours holding Janet up in his arms on her pillow. . . . Then came a day when he came to tell me that he had been forbidden in her room and that her death was possible. . . . He said to me, 'Should Janet die, I should *never* forget her.' He then characteristically spent a quite cheerful evening with me & even told me that he had had a delightful time & enjoyed himself."

11   [Of *The Rivals* at the Court Theatre, I can only say that Mrs. John Wood's Mrs. Malaprop is so good that it almost atones for the atrocity of the rest of the performance.]

> Reviewed on 23 November 1895 (C1104). Shaw saw the opening performance.

12   [   ]

13   [The seventh annual musical display by the London Board Schools, at Queen's Hall, would have been altogether commendable but for the element of competition introduced by the Challenge Medallion. Only six school choirs had been selected to compete; but a glance at the dress and physique of the children was sufficient to shew that nothing but an elaborate and odious system of handicapping could have made the competition even approximately fair. . . . *Poor Mr. Potton*, at the Vaudeville, is now preceded by a little play by Mr. H. V. Paull, entitled, *Merrifield's Ghost*, which I cannot honestly pretend to have enjoyed. . . . Merrifield's ghost . . . does not interest me; and I do not see why I should be put to a great deal of trouble simply to form a low opinion of him.]

> "A State Concert—New Style," *Daily Chronicle*, 14 November 1895 (C1102).   ▪   The curtain raiser, *Merrifield's Ghost*, by H. M. Paull (1854–1934), was noted on 16 November 1895 (C1103), Shaw giving the playwright the wrong middle initial.

14–16   [   ]

17 SUNDAY   *Lecture at the Ideal Club, 185 Tottenham Court Rd. (C. J. Melrose). Off.*

18   [Whether the speeches in *The Manxman* are interpolated Wilson Barrett or aboriginal Hall Caine I cannot say, as I have not read the celebrated

novel, and am prepared to go to the stake rather than face the least chapter
of it. . . . Even when I put my personal distaste . . . as far as possible on one
side, I cannot persuade myself that it is likely to live very long, although no
device is spared to move the audience, from a cascade of real water to a
poor little baby, which is exploited as shamelessly as if it had been let out
on hire to an organ-grinder or a beggar.]

> *The Manxman* was actor-manager Wilson Barrett's adaptation of the melodramatic novel
> by (Sir) Hall Caine (1853–1931). There would be twenty-eight performances. Shaw's *SR*
> review appeared on 23 November 1895 (C1104).

19–22   [   ]

> At a Fabian meeting on the 22nd (unnoticed in the diary—Shaw was still distracted by
> Janet Achurch's illness) at which Henry Macrosty was the speaker, Shaw moved "That the
> Fabian Society desires to assure Herr Wilhelm Liebknecht of its entire sympathy with him
> in his recent conflict with the Imperial power, and to express its astonishment that it
> should be possible nowadays in Germany to imprison a Member of Parliament for an
> expression of opinion which would be free to any English citizen." The resolution (C1106)
> was adopted unanimously.

23   ["At last a charming play," I was able to exclaim at the St. James's, . . .

after weeks of splenetic denunciation of the theatre and everything connected with it. . . . That the author, Mr. Esmond, is youthful in appearance,
we all know. Whether he is a young man really, I have no idea.]

> H. V. Esmond (1869–1922), actor and playwright, was in his mid-twenties. His play, a
> romantic drama with an unhappy ending, concerned a woman who married the brother
> of her fiancé when she thought the man she really loved was dead; when he materializes
> she risks social opprobrium to go off with him. Despite G.B.S., *The Divided Way* would
> survive for only twenty performances. Shaw's *SR* notice appeared on 30 November 1895
> (C1105).

24 SUNDAY   °*Lecture for the Christian Socialist Union Sunday Afternoons at Chelsea (Rev. Percy Dearmer, 59 South Lambeth Rd., S.W.). Off.*

25–27   [   ]

28   [I am in the thick of this Beardsley business, the post of fighting man in chief having been conceded to me with unanimity by the scandalised contributors.]

> For the inaugural issue of *The Savoy* (January 1896), for which Shaw had contributed the
> lead article, "On Going to Church" (C1111), art editor Aubrey Beardsley (1872–1898),
> had prepared an announcement illustrated by a John Bull holding up a poster labeled
> "No. 1, December 1895." More significantly, his breeches showed that he was in a state of
> sexual excitement. The malicious prank was quickly noticed, and contributors and pro-
> spective contributors, led in outrage by George Moore, gathered to fashion a protest to the
> indecency to Leonard Smithers (1861–1907), the publisher. Beardsley had also drawn a
> cover for the first number which showed a cherub, naked under his open coat, poised to
> urinate upon a copy of *The Yellow Book*—the quarterly which had fired Beardsley as art

editor earlier in the year when Oscar Wilde was arrested (although Beardsley was no friend of Wilde's and had only the professional connection of having illustrated Wilde's play *Salome*). Cleansing the cover postponed the first issue to January. Shaw deplored Beardsley's "puerile mischievousness" in the matter. Cleansing the prospectus was a moot matter: all 80,000 copies had been distributed. Shaw's comment about the "Beardley business" this date was to Charles Charrington (*CL*).

29 *Fabian Private Members' Meeting to discuss Halliday's resolution* re *Watt. Clifford's Inn. 20.*

A motion by A. Halliday assured Dr. Watt of the Society's "hearty sympathy in his gallant struggle for the rights of tenants. . . ."

30 [ ]

December

1 SUNDAY *Lecture at the Battersea Baths for the Labour League (C. Clifford, 27 Stormont Rd., Lavender Hill S.W.). "The Political Situation."*

2 *Read* Candida *to Charles Wyndham at 11.30—Criterion [Theatre].*

3 *Vaudeville Theatre. Revival of* The New Boy.
[The effectiveness of this piece of buffoonery appears to be undiminished. . . .]

Reviewed on 7 December 1895 (C1107). *The New Boy*, by Arthur Law (1844–1913), was a "genuine appeal to our sense of fun," but its revival, G.B.S. noted, seemed to evoke little audience interest, suggesting "that the public have had enough. . . ."

4 *Go to see* Mrs. Ponderbury's Past *and W. D. Howells'* Dangerous Ruffian *at the Avenue. 20.15.*
[I have discovered, quite by accident, an amusing farcical comedy. Somebody told me that there was a farce by Mr. W. D. Howells at the Avenue Theatre. I looked in the daily paper, but could find no mention of the name of Mr. Howells. However . . . I went, and duly found the name "Howels" on the program. The little piece shewed, as might have been expected, that with three weeks practice the American novelist could write the heads off the poor bunglers to whom our managers generally appeal when they want a small bit of work to amuse the people who come at eight. (C1107)]

Mrs. *Ponderbury's Past*, adapted by F. C. Burnand from the French farce *Madame Mongodin*, had opened 2 November 1895. G.B.S. called it "harmlessly naughty" (C1107). On 30 November it was joined by a curtain-raiser, *A Dangerous Ruffian*, by the American writer William Dean Howells (1837–1920), better known as a novelist.

5 [I have had all my spare time taken up by an article on Churches for the *Savoy*, one on Socialism for Millionaires (not yet finished) for the *Contemporary*, a circular for the I. Theatre, and a heavy pile of dawdling.]

> Shaw to Frederick H. Evans, 5 December 1895 (*CL*). "Socialism for Millionaires" would appear in the *Contemporary Review* for February 1896 (C1116), and would be revised as *Fabian Tract* No. 107. ■ The circular was the *Short Summary of the Position and Prospects of the Independent Theatre*, issued gratis later in the month (A24).

6 *Women's Vegetarian Union at the Pioneer Club. 4.30 to 6.30.* °*Farrell and Bax's supper. 1 The Cloisters, Temple. 20.*

7 °*Address "It" at 3 Hare Court, Temple, on "Great Men: Are They Real?" Elizabethan Stage Society's performance of* Comedy of Errors *in Gray's Inn Hall. 21.* °*Orange Grove, 14.30, meet Bertha Newcombe and go with her to Private View of Whistler lithographs.*

[Usually I enjoy a first night as a surgeon enjoys an operation: this time I enjoyed it as a playgoer enjoys a pleasant performance.]

> G.B.S.'s review of *The Comedy of Errors*, performed at Gray's Inn Hall by the Elizabethan Stage Society (C1108), an evening which "wound up with a Dolmetsch concert of lute and viol, virginal and voice, a delectable entertainment which defies all description by the pen."

8 SUNDAY [   ]

9 *H. A. Jones's at 17, to hear him read his new play,* Michael and His Lost Angel *and to dine. Call on Mrs. Dashwood, 13 James St. Mansion, Buckingham Gate. 16.*

> Shaw would shortly see the new Jones play in production, reviewing it on 18 January 1896 (C1114). ■ Mrs. Rose Dashwood was an actress who had appeared in a Sydney Grundy play the year before.

10 °*Humanitarian League lecture on "Rights of Man and Animals." "The Church's View" by Rev. A. L. Lilley. Canon Wilberforce in the chair. Bispham's concert—classical popular music (Dolmetsch). St. James's Hall. 15½. Lecture on "Music" in the Church and Stage Guild at 31 Upper Bedford Place at 16. (16¼ will do).*

> Ernest Roland Wilberforce (1840–1907), canon of Winchester from 1878 to 1882, bishop of Newcastle from 1882 to 1895, and bishop of Chichester from 1895 to 1907, would be chairman of the Church of England Temperance Society in 1896.

11 °*Fabian Publishing Committee. 17.*

12 [   ]

13 *Fabian Meeting at Clifford's Inn. E. R. Pease on "Municipal Drink Traffic." 20.*

> Pease would be author of *Fabian Tracts* Nos. 85 and 86, *Liquor Licensing at Home and Abroad* and *Municipal Drink Traffic* (both 1896).

14 [ ]

15 SUNDAY *Lecture to the St. George and Wapping Branch of the S. D. F., Sutton Hall, 50 Sutton St. E., on "Social Democracy and Practical Politics." 20. Sutton St. is off the Commercial Rd. (C. W. Ellis).*

[I expect to weather Xmas without sinking within ten pounds of bottom. . . .]

> Shaw to Charles Charrington, 15 December 1895 (*CL*), in sending him a check for £10 to cover expenses caused by Janet's illness. He had discovered that Charrington had pawned his wedding ring.

16 [ ]

17 [ ]

18 *Fabian Publishing Committee. 17.*

19 [ ]

20 *Purcell concert by Dolmetsch at Portman Rooms. 20.*

21 *Production of* One of the Best *at the Adelphi. 20. Seymour Hicks and George Edwardes.*

> Reviewed on 28 December 1895 (C1110). Seymour Hicks (1871–1949) and George Edwardes (1852–1915), both actor-playwrights (Edwardes was also a theater manager), had written a play which G.B.S. saw as "the reproduction on the stage of the dramatic effect of the military ceremony of degradation undergone not long ago in France by Captain Dreyfus." However, the punning title, "One of the Worst," conveyed his feeling—that, "even judged by melodramatic standards," the play "is a bad one." It ran, with William Terriss in the lead role, for 163 performances.

22 SUNDAY [ ]

23 [The new drama is shaping itself slowly—at least the people are coming to life.]

> Shaw to Janet Achurch, 23 December 1895 (*CL*). Shaw's aside on his play *You Never Can Tell*, with which he was having difficulty, appeared in a letter otherwise devoted to concerns about Janet's increasing addiction to brandy as she recovered from her bout with typhoid. "Save your body and soul alive," he concluded, "and don't turn me into granite."

24–25   [   ]

26   *Call on Mrs. Vivanti Chartres at Pool's Pension, 20 Bedford St.*

Anita Vivanti Chartres (1870–1942), a novelist, had asked Shaw for advice about her writing.

27   **A Woman's Reason,** *Shaftesbury Theatre, 20$\frac{1}{2}$, by F. C. Philips and Charles H. E. Brookfield.*

[It was such pleasure to see Mr. Lewis Waller and his company divested of the trappings of Manxmanity and in their right minds again, that we all received *A Woman's Reason* with more gaiety and enthusiasm than can easily be justified in cold blood. (C1112)]

A Woman's Reason was reviewed on 4 January 1896 (C1112). For co-author Charles Brookfield, see 25 June 1893. His collaborator, F. C. Philips (1849–1921) is listed with some of his many plays as Phillips. Their purpose in the play, said G.B.S., was "the same purpose as that of *Daniel Deronda*. All the Jews in it are heroes and heroines, and all the Christians the meanest and feeblest wretches conceivable. Serve them right!" It would have eighty performances.

28   **The Late Mr. Castello** *at the Comedy Theatre. 20.40. Sydney Grundy.*

Sydney Grundy's newest play was mentioned almost without comment (C1112), as if beneath comment. The comedy would have fifty-five performances.

29 SUNDAY   *123 Dalling Rd. in the evening.*

W. B. Yeats was at Dalling Rd. The Pagets are staying there at present.

W. B. Yeats would gradually become Shaw's replacement in Florence Farr's life, but his tenure would be brief.

30   *Call on [William] Rothenstein at 53 Glebe Place, Chelsea, and give him a sitting for a portrait.*

Miss Kingsley (the actress) was at Rothenstein's, also a friend of his whose name I forget. I went to the Orange Grove for dinner and then returned to Chelsea and spent the afternoon with Bertha [Newcombe] in her studio. In the evening read latest installment of *Life of Napoleon* by W. Sloane in *The Century Magazine*. I ordered all the back numbers of this in September to read for my play, and have continued it since. Afterwards I played several games of "Halma" with my mother, a most unusual thing for me; but the game amused me. I learnt to play it at Pagets' the night I read *The Man of Destiny* to them.

(Sir) William Rothenstein (1872–1945), painter and printmaker, would be best known as a portraitist. He would be principal of the Royal College of Art from 1920 to 1935.   ▪
Alice Kingsley was the stage name of Alice Knewstub (1870–1958), daughter of the painter Walter Knewstub (1831–1906), once Rossetti's assistant. She would marry William Rothenstein in 1899, taking two weeks' leave from Herbert Beerbohm Tree's production of *The Three Musketeers*.   ▪   William Milligan Sloane's biography had completed its

serialization in the October issue. Shaw had long ago finished *The Man of Destiny*, which dealt with the young Napoleon. He was catching up on back issues now because of his interest in the subject rather than for research.

31 *Call on Mrs. Charrington at 16$\frac{1}{2}$. Call on Mrs. Vivanti Chartres between 20 and 21 at Bedford Row. Did not get there until 21.5 and just missed her.*

In the morning began my *Saturday Review* article. Bicycled to the Orange Grove and then on to Onslow Square, where I found Janet alone. Worked again at the *Saturday* article in the evening.

Notes

January

2   Louis Weighton for A. E. Drinkwater, royalties on *Arms & the Man* for week ending 29th Dec. at Harrogate ... 1 10 11

10   *Pall Mall Budget* ... 2 12 0

12   *Saturday Review* (review of Ibsen) ... 4 0 0

19   Richard Mansfield for Miss Marbury, royalty on performance of
Arms & the Man at Brooklyn on the 17th Dec. ... 8 10 2

21   "   "   at Baltimore on the 24th Dec. ... 7 5 5 ... 15 15 7

31   "   "   at Washington   "   31st   "   ... 18 6 5

Walter Scott, royalties on sales of *The Quintessence of Ibsenism* from the
1st April to the 31st Dec. 1894. ... 2 17 0

Arms & the Man.   £ 1–10–11
                        15–15– 7
                        18– 6– 5
                        35–12–11

London & County Bank. Bal[an]ce.

2   Lodged ... 169 9 2 ... 169 9 2

19   "   ... 9 15 2

21   "   ... 15 15 7
          18 6 5
          213 6 4

3   Cheque No 40257 (already entered, mistake corrected
in March account)

      £ 1 1 0
         4 2 8
         3 11 6
         1 0 0
        25 0 0

"   "   40258

"   "   9

"   "   60

5   "   (house) 1 ... 34 15 2 ... 178 11 2

178 11 2

February

2   Richard Mansfield for Miss Marbury, royalty on performance of
    Arms & the Man on the 11th Jan @ Atlanta   20 9 10
    "   15th "   New Orleans   15 18 10
                                                                    36 8 8
                                                                    24 0 0

13 *The Saturday Review*
    Louis Weighton for A. E. Drinkwater, royalties on *Arms & the Man*
    at Oxford 4th–6th Feb. 7½%   4 9 0
    at Banbury 7th & 8th, 5%   3 3 11
                                                                     4 12 11
                                                                        10 0
                                                                     5 2 11

    Over-remitted in error   1 2 10
    " Yarmouth, 11th–16th Feb.   10 0
20 Less over-remittance as above

21 Richard Mansfield for Miss Marbury, royalties on performances of *Arms
    & the Man* at Memphis on the 29th Jan[uar]ly & Louisville on the 2nd Feb.   31 0 0

28 Louis Weighton for A. E. D., as above, Cambridge 18–20th inst 7½   1 16 6
                                           Doncaster 20–23rd " 5   1 2 0
                                                                               2 18 6
    Over-remitted through error in return 19th   1 0
                                                                               2 19 6

Arms & the Man   £ 35 12 11
                       36 8 8
                        5 2 11
6–12   31 . .
24–0   108 4 6

London & County Bank Bal[an]ce   178 11 2   178 11 2

2   Cheque 40262   5 0 0

    173 11 2

"   Lodged   36 8 8

    209 19 10

13   "   29 2 11

    £ 239 2 9

6   Cheque 40263   £ 20 0 0

18   "   4   5 0 0

"   "   5   6 6 0

    31 6 0

    207 16 9

21   Lodged   31 12 10

    239 9 7   239 9 7

March

4   R. Mansfield for Miss Marbury, royalties on performance of *Arms & the Man* at Chicago on the 5th ult.   7 16 5

6   Louis Weighton for A. E. Drinkwater, royalties Paisley, week ending 2nd inst   1 12 4

7   R. Mansfield as above, royalties, Chicago, 11th & 16th ult.   33 12 8

13   Louis Weighton as above, Belfast, week ending 9th inst. 7½%   5 9 4

19   R. Mansfield as above, Milwaukee, 19th ult: St Louis, 26th ult: St Louis 2nd inst.   36 14 2

25   " Cincinnati, 5th & 9th   23 4 5

    108 9 4

Arms & the Man.   £ 108 4 6

   108 9 6

   216 13 10

£ 30–12

London & County Bank, bal[an]ce

Date	Description	No.	£ s. d.		
	London & County Bank, bal[an]ce			239	9	7
4	Cheque	40266	£ 10 . 0 . 0		
"	" house	7	15 . 0 . 0	25	0	7
				214	9	7
7	Lodged			10	15	11
				225	5	6
"	" (this should be £ 35.5.0, see correction in Dec.)			33	5	0
				258	10	6
8	Cheque	40268	£ 20 . 0 . 0		
13	"	9	6 . 10 . 2		
"	"	70	50 . 0 . 0	76	10	2
				182	0	4
20	Lodged			42	3	6
				224	3	10
24	Cheque	40271		5	0	0
				219	3	10
"	Lodged			23	4	5
				242	8	3
25	Cheque No 40272		£ 2 . 2 . 0		
27	3		5 . 0 . 0		
"	4 (home)		25 . 0 . 0		
"	5		1 . 2 . 6		
29	6		5 . 0 . 0		
30	7		25 . 0 . 0		
"	8		5 . 0 . 0	68	4	6
				174	3	9
				1	1	0
				175	4	9

Cheque No 40257 entered a second time by mistake in Jan.

April

3   The *Saturday Review* (for Feb.) including 2 pol[itica]l art[icles] [?] @ £2.5.0 & £2.15.0 .... 29 0 0

22 R. Mansfield for Miss Marbury, royalties on performances of *Arms & the Man* at Columbus on 13th Mar, Pittsburgh on 19th, & Harlem on 30th. 19 13 4

25 The *Saturday Review* (for March) including 2 pol[itical] art[ic]l[e]s [?] @ £3.10.0 & £2.5.0 & 1 note 6/- 36 1 0

Arms & the Man   £ 216–13–10
                        19–13– 4
                       236 7 2

The first and third items above are included in the Income Tax return 1894–5

£ 30–12–0
  29– .–.
  36– 1–0
  95 13 0   175 4 9   175 4 9

                £ 10 . 0 . 0
                  31 . 9 . 5   41 9 5
                                  216 14 2

London & County Bank, balance

1   Lodged   175 4 9
4   "
6   Cheque No 40279   £ 1 . 1 . 0
9   "   80   5 . 10 . 0
17 "   81   3 . 13 . 2
22 "   82   25 . 0 . 0   35 4 2
                                          181 10 0
"   Lodged   25 3 4
25 "   £ 206 13 4
                                           36 1 0
                                          242 14 4
                                            5 10 0
                                          237 4 4
                                            1 1 0
26 Lodgment returned "no account" (Palmer)

"   Cheque No. 40283   236 3 4

May

		£	s	d
1	The Humanitarian	5	0	0
"	R. Mansfield for Miss Marbury, royalties on performance of *Arms & the Man* at Washington, 9th Ap[ri]l.	9	17 ·	10
23	*Henry & Co, royalties on sales of *Widowers' Houses* from 31st Dec 1893 to 30th Ap 1895 (6 copies)		3	0
29	The Saturday Review	24	0	0

Arms & the Man   £ 236– 7– 2
                        9–17–10
                      246– 5– 0

*This item is included in the Income Tax return 1894–5

£ 95–13
  5– 0–0
 24–
124–13–0

London & County Bank

1	Lodged	236	3	4
		14	17	10
		251	1	2

13	Cheque No 40284	£ 5 . 5 . 0
17	" "	25 . 0 . 0
"	" "	5 . 0 . 0
18	" " 7 (bicycle)	23 .10 . 0
30	" " 8	25 . 0 . 0

"	Lodged	83	15	0
		167	6	2
		24	0	0
		£ 191	6	2

Date	Description	Amount			
June	London & County Bank			£ 191 6 2	191 6 2
24	Cheque No. 40289	£ 10 . 0 . 0			
27	" " 90	2 . 0 . 0		37 0 0	154 6 2
29	" " 91	25 . 0 . 0			24 6 0
					124 13
					148 19
July					
13	*The Saturday Review* (for May)				154 6 2
	London & County Bank			154 6 2	154 6 2
5	Cheque No. 40292	£ 17 . 6 . 0			
6	" " 93	2 . 11 . 0		21 17 0	
8	" " 94	2 . 0 . 0		132 9 2	
				29 6 0	
18	Lodged			161 15 2	
22	"			10 0 0	
	"			151 15 2	
"	Cheque No. 40295	£ 10 . 0 . 0			
23	" " 6	5 . 0 . 0			
28	" " 7	1 . 1 . 0		41 1 0	110 14 2
31	" " 8	25 . 0 . 0			

August

Date	Item	Draft	£ s d	£ s d
8	The Star			3 3 0
16	The Saturday Review (for June)			31 5 0
				148 19
				183 7 0
1	London & County Bank		110 14 2	110 14 2
	Dft No. 40299	£ 12 . 12 . 0	12 12 0	
			98 2 2	
10	Lodged		34 8 0	
			£ 132 10 2	132 10 2

September

Date	Item	Draft	£ s d	£ s d
13	The Saturday Review (for July)			24 0 0
26	The Star (Cardiff)			12 12 0
				183 7 0
				219 19 0
3	London & County Bank		132 10 2	132 10 2
	Dft No. P. 40300	10 . 0 . 0	35 0 0	
9	" Q 99652 (51)	25 . 0 . 0	97 10 2	
13	Lodged		24 0 0	
			121 10 2	
17	Dft No. 99652 (52)		3 16 6	
			117 13 8	
26	Lodged		12 12 0	
			130 5 8	

October

London & County Bank

Date	Description	£	s	d	£	s	d
3	Dft No Q 99653 (53)	1	15	10	130	5	8
11	" 54	10	0	0			
14	" 55	4	0	0			
"	" 56	25	0	0			
"	" 57	6	10	0			
17	" 58	2	4	11	49	10	9
					80	14	11

November

Date	Description	£	s	d	£	s	d
6	The Star	2	2	0	80	14	11
21	*The Saturday Review* (remitted as "for September")	24	0	0			
23	" (August & October)	54	0	0			
		219	19				
		299	19				

London & County Bank

Date	Description	£	s	d	£	s	d
4	Dft No Q 99659 (59)	80	14	11	125	6	11
		25	0	0			
18	" (60)	55	14	11			
		5	0	0			
21	Lodged	50	14	11			
22	Dft No (61)	26	2	0			
		76	16	11			
		5	0	0			
23	Lodged	71	16	11			
		54	0	0			
		£ 125	16	11			

December

London & County Bank

			125	6	11
			125	6	11
4	Dft Q99662 (62)	25 . 0 . 0	125	6	11
15	" (63)	10 . 0 . 0	35	0	0
			90	6	11
24	" (64)	4 . 0 . 0			
28	" (65)	7 . 1 . 0			
29	" (66)	1 . 1 . 0			
"	" (67)	12 .13 . 1	24	15	1
			£ 65	11	10
	Cheque Books	8 . 4			
	Charge on 2 Carlow cheques	1 . 0	10	10
	Stamps on American bills of exchange	1 . 6	65	1	0
			2	0	0
	To Correct error in entry of 7th March		67	1	0
			67	1	0

REMINDERS FOR NEXT YEAR

January: 26th Lecture at the Gladstone Club, Harrow Green, Leytonstone, on "Socialism & Practical Politics". (John Hattersley) Maryland Point station & tram to Club.
5th Lecture at the Woolwich Rad[ical] Cl[ub] William St (H. W. Oliver) on "The Political Situation".
12th Lecture at the Lee & Lewisham Lib[eral] & Rad[ical] Cl[ub] 170 High St (off) Lewisham. "Democracy". (Walter Slater)
19th Lecture at the Plumstead Rad[ical] Cl[ub] "Socialism & Practical Politics" 64 Walmer Rd Pld. S. E. opp[osite] station (J. A. Turnbull) 20.15

February: 1st Sunday. Walthamstow Br. S. D. F. Workmen's Hall, High St. (Geo. Cunnew 60 Linford Rd, Wood St. Walth[amsto]w).

July: Bayreuth—19, 20, 21 & 22.

Diary 1896

January

1 [ ]

2 [ ]

3 *Give Rothenstein a sitting at 11, and lunch with Bertha Newcombe at 14.*

4 [ ]

5 SUNDAY *Lecture at the Woolwich Radical Club on "The Political Situation" (H. W. Oliver). 11.45.*

In consequence of the news from the Transvaal I devoted my whole time at the Club to foreign policy, the first lecture I ever delivered on that subject. In the evening I went out to Walkers' and supped at Morris's. Morris lectures on "One Socialist Party" at Kelmscott House. 20.

> Having failed in his unauthorized attempt to raid the Boer arsenal at Pretoria, Dr. Leander Starr Jameson (1853–1917) surrendered with his men and was imprisoned on 2 January. He would be handed over to the British and sent to England for trial. His almost

immediate release would further increase hostility between the Boers and the British in South Africa.

6   I did a good day's work on the new play [*You Never Can Tell*] today. Went over to Bertha's studio after dinner but hurried back expecting to have to go to the theatre. But the expected tickets did not come; so I resumed my work at the play; wrote several postcards making appointments, etc.: and played a game of "Halma" with Georgina. My mother of late has given up playing Patience and has taken to Bezique and Halma. The Bezique has led to a custom of Georgina coming in in the evenings.

7   *St. James's Theatre.* The Prisoner of Zenda, *adaptation by Edward Rose from Anthony Hope. 19.45. Fabian Publishing Committee, 276 Strand. 17.*

> Reviewed on 11 January 1896 (C1113). G.B.S. found the novel had been better, because the visual element had to jar awake "our common sense, which, if aroused, must immediately put a summary stop to the somewhat silly Ruritanian gambols of our imagination." It would have 255 performances.

8   *Go to [Wilson Barrett's]* The Sign of the Cross *at the Lyric Theatre. 20. (4th night)*

> G.B.S. (C1113) was impressed by the professionalism of the Roman melodrama. "The mounting is handsome, and the stage management good and unselfish, all the parts being played with quite extraordinary spirit, and in no way sacrificed to the actor-manager's. I have never seen better work got out of a company. Mr. Wilson Barrett has honestly sunk the actor in the author, and done his best for the play, instead of for himself personally." It would run 438 performances.

9   Did not get to bed until 4 in the morning. Spent the small hours at the *Saturday Review* office discussing the affair of Runciman's article of last week and the terms of the apology. Spent the earlier part of the evening at Dalling Rd. with the Pagets, FF and Miss Horniman. Wallas called in the middle of the day and came to the Orange Grove with me.

> John Runciman was now the music critic of *SR*. In its 4 January 1896 issue he had the bad manners to call the Royal Academy of Music "a cesspool of academic musical life." As editor, Frank Harris had to arrange for a retraction.   ▪   Florence Farr Emery, at Shaw's urging, had got a divorce, which he recognized in the changed initials. However, if she expected her legal availability to be followed by Shaw's proposal of marriage, she had been disappointed.

10   *Fabian Meeting at Clifford's Inn. 20½. Mrs. Sidney Webb on "Woman and Factory Legislation." Fabian Executive. 17¼. 276 Strand. Fabian Committee Preliminary to Executive. 17. °Executive Meeting South St. Pancras Liberal and Radical Association at Clayden's, 13 Tavistock Square. 20½.*

11   *Read* Candida *at Emery Walker's. 20.*

12 [   ]

13 [   ]

14 *Executive Meeting South St. Pancras Liberal and Radical Association, Clayden's, 13 Tavistock Square, to select candidate. 20½.*

[Today I went to get my hair cut. The man asked whether I wanted it short. I said "Yes," and was about to add certain reservations when he suddenly produced an instrument like a lawnmower, and in an instant my golden locks fell like withered grass to the floor and left my head like the back of a Japanese pug dog. Nothing escaped except a little wiglike oasis on the top.]

Shaw to Janet Achurch, 14 January 1896 (*CL*).

15 *Production of Jones's* Michael and His Lost Angel *at the Lyceum Theatre.*

[The performance at the Lyceum has taken all the heart out of my hopes of gaining general assent to my high estimate of *Michael and his Lost Angel.* The public sees the play as it is acted, not as it ought to be acted.]

Reviewed on 18 January 1896 (C1114). To G.B.S. it was "a genuinely sincere and moving play, feelingly imagined." But it was inadequately produced, and would fail after ten performances.

16 [   ]

17 *Fabian Executive and Committee. 17. No Executive this week. Council of Liberal and Radical Association meets at Bunting's, 20½, to select candidate.*

18 *[°Address "It" on "Great Men: Are They Real?" (Mrs. Bland, 3 Gables, Grove Park, Kent). Changed to 18th.]*

Moved from 25 January; otherwise unaltered.

19 SUNDAY   *Lecture at the Plumstead Radical Club, 64 Walmer Rd. S.E. (opposite railway station) "Socialism and Practical Politics" (J. A. Turnbull). Dine at Emery Walker's to meet Lethaby.*

William Richard Lethaby (1857–1933), architect and art critic, and surveyor of Westminster Abbey, would become a professor of design at the Royal College of Art.

20 *Stepniak Memorial Committee. 3 Arundel St. (London Reform Union). 17. °London Liberal and Radical Union Council Meeting. National Liberal Club. 20.*

Sergius Stepniak had been struck by a railway engine as he was crossing the tracks at Chiswick, and killed instantly, on 23 December 1895. Shaw was helping to create a fund for his widow, who was without resources.

21   *Read* Candida *to H. A. Jones and Edward Rose at Rose's, 36 Upper Addison Gardens. 20. Call on Mrs. Vivanti Chartres at the Victoria Hotel in the afternoon.*

22   *Stepniak Memorial Executive Committee, 276 Strand. 16½. Speak at election meeting, Cleveland Hall, in support of G. M. Harris, 20½.*

> George Montagu Harris had contested South St. Pancras unsuccessfully the year before, and would fail again.

23   °*Miss Stronach to call at 12.30 about the article on "Leading Socialists." Put off to tomorrow.*

> Miss A. L. Stronach had published *A Simple History of English Literature* in 1889.

24   *Fabian Meeting at Clifford's Inn. 20½. Graham Wallas on "Board Schools and Free Meals." Fabian Executive and Committee. 17½ and 17. See yesterday—Miss Stronach.*

25   *Revival of [Dion Boucicault's]* The Colleen Bawn, *at the Princess's Theatre.* °*Walter Crane's At-Home. 21 to 24. 13 Holland St. W.*

[I have lived to see *The Colleen Bawn* with real water in it; and perhaps I shall live to see it some day with real Irishmen in it, though I doubt if that will heighten its popularity much.]

> Reviewed on 1 February 1896 (C1118). "I regret to say," G.B.S. added, "that the patrons of the gallery at the Princess's, being admitted at half the usual west end price, devote the saving to the purchase of sausages to throw at the critics. I appeal to the gentleman or lady who successfully aimed one at me to throw a cabbage next time, as I am a vegetarian, and sausages are wasted on me."

26 SUNDAY   *Lecture at the Gladstone Club, Harrow Green, Leytonstone, on "Socialism and Practical Politics" (John Hattersley). To Maryland Point station and tram to club.*

27   °*Miss [Nellie] Erichsen's studio. 15.45. Read* Arms and the Man, *6 Trafalgar Studios, Manresa Rd., Chelsea; see 4th. Stepniak Memorial Committee. 276 Strand. 16½.*

28   [I had rare scenes with the poetess-dramatist before she left for France. . . . Florence, once callous, has strange awakenings and cries over me—positively cries. . . . The result, though, is alarming—desiring nothing further, I have become sort of sublime monster. . . .]

> Shaw to Janet Achurch, 29 January 1895 (*CL*), assigned to the previous day since Shaw seems not to be referring to the day of writing. Florence Farr, it is clear, was miserable about Shaw's altered relations with her, and although he may not have behaved as callously as he suggests to Janet, he was increasingly unresponsive to a woman he had once called (*CL*) his "best and dearest love" and his "secret glimpse of heaven."

29   [   ]

30   The Fool of the Family *at the Duke of York's Theatre. 20.15*

[About a dozen people laughed; the rest of the audience stared with stony disfavor. What they felt I do not know: as for myself, I was disgusted. . . .]

> Reviewed on 8 February 1896 (C1119). The play by Fergus Hume (1859–1932) failed after four performances. G.B.S. was "disgusted" by scenes which "exhibited a foolish middle-aged spinster making love to a handsome young man, who submitted to her caresses with many wry faces, and finally consented to marry her for her money."

31   *Fabian Executive and Committee. 17.*

February

1   *Dine at the Socialist Club, 17 St. Andrew St., Holborn E. C.*

2 SUNDAY   *Lecture at the Walthamstow Branch S. D. F., Manor Hall, Workmen's Club and Institute, High St. (George Cunnew, 60 Linford Rd., Wood St., Walthamstow). 19½. "Practical Socialism."*

3   *Read* Candida *to the Pagets at Dalling Rd. in the evening.*

Called there but [H. M.] Paget was busy making a drawing of [Sir Frederick] Leighton's funeral and there were a couple of young fellows who had dropped in to pay a visit. So I did not go upstairs, but stayed with F. below; and the reading of the play did not come off.

> Florence Farr had been away in France only briefly since she was already back visiting her sister. Shaw's earlier comment to Janet Achurch about FF's departure scene had suggested a lengthy stay.

4   *Read* Arms and the Man *to Miss Erichsen and Miss Fanny Johnson, 6 Trafalgar Studios.*

[I have finished the first act of the play—with another extraction, this time under gas.]

> "Read" here is past tense rather than the notation of an appointment reminder, for Shaw would write Bertha Newcombe the same day (*CL*) that he was surprised to find that Nellie Erichsen was not alone, and in effect had a chaperon in the person of an artist friend "who was drawing N. on millboard." Apparently the play-reading still took place, although Shaw did not mention the fact to Miss Newcombe, only noting that (presumably afterward) the other young woman "hurried up the tea; and then . . . nodded at us in an 'I know you want to get rid of me' way; snatched up her things; and deserted her hostess, leaving us in the most miserable confusion & [self-]consciousness." For a further

hour and a half they "clung to Wagner, Shakespere & other topics" until parting "on fair terms" with an open invitation to Shaw for future Monday afternoons. ▪ The first act of "the [new] play" (Shaw to Bertha Newcombe, 4 February 1896 ([*CL*]), *You Never Can Tell*, is set in a dentist's office, the result of Shaw's many visits to Dr. Macdonald.

5 *Dine with [R. B.] Haldane at 19, to meet [H. H.] Asquith and Arthur Balfour. 3 Whitehall Court.*

Shaw did not use *meet* to mean a first acquaintance with someone, but only in the sense of a meeting. He had met Asquith years before, then a new M.P. who had not yet become Parnell's junior counsel before the Parnell Commission. At the time Asquith was publicly hostile to the coercive policies of Arthur Balfour (1848–1930), then chief secretary for Ireland. By 1896, Balfour who would be prime minister from 1902 to 1905, had become First Lord of the Treasury. Asquith, who had been home secretary from 1892 to 1895, was, with the Liberals out of power, out of office but considered likely to be a future prime minister—as indeed he would be from 1908 through 1916.

6 *Call on the [Comyns] Carrs in the evening. 20. 19 Park Village. Read* The Man of Destiny.

7 *°Fabian Executive and Committee. 17. °Else Sonntag's pianoforte recital. Queen's Hall. 15.*

8 [ ]

9 SUNDAY *°Lecture for the West Islington Independent Labour Party (J. F. Schillaker, 25 Liverpool Buildings, Station Rd., Highbury). Lecture at St. Saviour's Schools, Hyde Rd.; Hoxton, at 16, on "Socialism" (Rev. Ernest Kilburn, Clergy House, 60 Hyde Rd., N.).*

10 *Call on the Ashton Jonsons at 19 and go on with them to the debate on* The Rights of Animals *at the Sesame Club to oppose the opener.*

G. C. Ashton Jonson was the husband of Dorothy Leighton, who had taken over from Grein the direction of the Independent Theatre.

11 [ ]

12 [ ]

13 *London School of Economics, 9 John St., Adelphi. First lecture of Bertrand Russell's course on German Social Democracy. 20.*

The L.S.E. was in its first year of operation, in rented quarters just below the Savoy Hotel in the Strand.

14 *Fabian Meeting at Clifford's Inn. 20½. Honorable Bertrand Russell on "Lessons from Germany in Independent Labour Politics." Fabian Executive and Committee. 17.*

15   *Revival of* On Change *at the Strand Theatre. First night.*

[*On 'Change,* a revived play, was new to me, as far as a piece made up of such stale material could be new. At all events, I had not seen it before, and I was duly captivated by Mr. Felix Morris's impersonation of the Scotch professor.]

> Reviewed on 22 February 1896 (C1122). *On 'Change* was an adaptation by Eweretta Lawrence from Gustav von Moser's *Ultimo,* first performed in London in 1885. The revival would survive for twenty-seven performances. Felix Morris (1845–1900) played Professor Peckering Peck.

16 SUNDAY   *Wallas lectures on "Democracy" to the Ethical Society, Essex Hall. 19.*

17   *Go to* Jedbury Junior *at Terry's Theatre (third night).*

[*Jedbury Junior* is a flimsy, almost schoolgirlish, work. . . .]

> G.B.S. (C1122) found *Jedbury Junior,* by Madeleine Lucette Ryley (1865–1934), "a flippant, stuck-together-anyhow little play" vivified by a pervasive sense of ridicule.

18   [   ]

> Glued over this date is an invitation card ("Admit three" written in) to a lecture scheduled for the next evening. (See 19 February.) Three performances that Shaw attended in mid-February cannot be dated later than this week, as they were referred to in a tailpiece to his 22 February *SR* review (C1122). At the Strand, opening on 15 February, was a revival of *The Man in the Street,* by Louis N. Parker (1852–1944), which G.B.S. thought "should not be missed" because of James Welch's characterization of the "old vagabond Jabez Gover." At Terry's, having opened on 11 December (although Shaw could not then get to it) was a curtain-raiser, *The Old Garden,* by Hill Davies, which was "a very ordinary sentimentality" acted "with conscientious sincerity and force." And "on the concert platform" he had seen Beatrice Herford (1868–1952) in a one-woman show with only a chair as prop. Impressed by her comedy skills, G.B.S. urged her to go "on the stage," not knowing that she would open in a play by Mrs. Hugh Bell on 12 March.

19   *Read* Candida *to the Ashton Jonsons. 20. 28 St. Ermyn's Mansions.*

> Shaw cancelled his *Candida* reading to attend Capt. Stuart's lecture, the evening with the Ashton Jonsons being rescheduled for the 23rd. The invitation this date, for 8:00 in the evening, St. Martin's Town Hall, was to a lecture "by Donald Stuart (Late Captain 86th Royal Regiment) when he will (1) point out the unsatisfactory state of the Criminal Law, by a brief reference to his unjust conviction and sentence to 3 Years Penal Servitude, by the Common Serjeant, for a trumpery County Court affair, and invite any one to point to one act of his, verbal, documentary or circumstantial, that can be construed into fraud. (2) Urge the necessity for a Court of Criminal Appeal, and show the ignorance that prevails in regard to the true state of Convict Prisons as evinced by the late Parliamentary Committee . . . , and the farce of such evidence as that of Prison Warders and Prison Commissioners. And conclude with Specially Designed Coloured Illustrations 15 feet by 15 feet of horrors that would disgrace Siberia. . . ." Shaw's copy of the invitation remains between the pages of his diary (LSE).

20   *London School of Economics. Russell's second lecture.*

21 °*Fabian Executive and Committee. 17. Put off. Ashton Jonson lectures on Wagner at St. Ermyn's Mansions. 20½. Go to Salts' in the afternoon to meet Dalmas—and take him to the Wagner meeting.*

Philip Dalmas, of 22 Stanley Gardens, Kensington Park, W., was an American dilettante in music—he sang, composed, and played the piano—who lived mostly in Paris on remittances from home and had Whitmanite and Socialist friends in England, chief among them Henry Salt.

22 °*Charrington lectures to "It" on "Sport, Stage and Church" at Miss [Helen] Coombe's studio, 27 Southampton St., Fitzroy Square. 20. Production of* Gossip *at the Comedy Theatre. Call on Lady Colin at 12. Speak at Peace Society meeting at Moscheles's studio, 80 Elm Park Rd., at 15.*

Reviewed on 29 February 1896 (C1123). *Gossip*, by American playwrights Clyde Fitch (1865–1909) and Leo Dietrichstein, was a "third-rate . . . composite plagiarism" of twenty-year-old farces, based on a French novel by Jules Clairette. It managed twenty-seven performances.

23 SUNDAY

[I am going to read *Candida* at Mrs. Ashton Jonson's (Dorothy Leighton's). . . .]

Shaw to Henry Arthur Jones, 20 February 1896 (*CL*), referring to the following "Sunday evening."

24 [ ]

25 [ ]

26 *First night of* The Shopwalker *at the Vaudeville Theatre. 21. Annual Meeting Liberty and Property Defense League (the thirteenth) at Westminster Palace Hotel. 15. Address by Mallock.*

In the afternoon I met the Charringtons at the Orange Grove and showed them my letter to Heinemann about *Little Eyolf.* We went on to the Ashton Jonsons', but they were not at home; and we presently found them at the Sesame Club.

The play by Robert Buchanan and "Charles Marlowe" (Harriett Jay) would have only thirty-four performances. "I got on very well" with *The Romance of the Shopwalker*, wrote G.B.S. (C1123), who was a fan of its featured actor, Weedon Grossmith, and enjoyed, besides, the situation of the shopwalker electioneering as a parliamentary candidate. ▪ Shaw's chastising letter, dated 24 February 1896, concerned Heinemann's refusal to publish a translation of *Little Eyolf.*

27 *London School of Economics. Russell's 3rd lecture. Production of Davidson's* For the Crown *(Coppée's* La Couronne*) at the Lyceum. 20.15.*

Reviewed at length on 7 March 1896 (C1124). The romantic *Pour la Couronne*, written by François Coppée (1842–1908), adapted into English blank verse by John Davidson (1857–

1909), and starring Forbes-Robertson and Mrs. Campbell (both of whom Shaw admired), would have ninety-four performances. The opening night was for both actors a personal success, however the play itself was "an alexandrine wilderness, windy, barren, and platitudinous to the last degree," redeemed only by "several moving and effective situations" (C1123).

28   *Fabian Meeting at Clifford's Inn. 20½. J. W. Martin on "The State in Relation to Education." Fabian Executive and Committee. 17.*

29   *Walter Crane, At-Home. 21 to 24.*

March

1 SUNDAY   *Lecture on "Are We All Socialists Now?" at the Mechanics' Institute, Dudley Rd., Tunbridge Wells, at 15 (F. Lawson Dodd, Grosvenor Lodge, Tunbridge Wells and 41 Wimpole St. W).*

> F. Lawson Dodd (1868–1964), on the Fabian Executive from 1900 to 1916, and treasurer of the Society from 1911 to 1916, would be author of the Fabian tracts Nos. 122, *Municipal Milk and Public Health* (1906), and 160, *A National Medical Service* (1911).

2   *Miss Erichsen's. 16½. °Annual Meeting Liberal and Radical Union. National Liberal Club. 20.*

3   *Fabian "Women's Tract" Committee. 276 Strand. 17. Fabian Publishing Committee, 276 Strand, after the other.*

4   *Stepniak Memorial Fund Committee. 276 Strand. 17. °Dine with the Webbs to meet Olivier after his return from West Indies. I forgot this.*

5   *London School of Economics. 4th lecture. Meet FE at the Orange Grove restaurant at 15—Richmond.*

6   *Fabian Executive and Committee. 17. Not this week. °Charrington to be at the Orange Grove. 15½ to 16.*

7   *Dine with the Bertrand Russells at 90 Ashley Gardens. Call on Terriss at the Adelphi Theatre at 13.*

> William Terriss (1847–1897) was actor-manager at the Adelphi, to which he gave a reputation for stirring melodrama. He was interested in having a Shaw play constructed about his talents and needs, and *The Devil's Disciple* (1897) would be the result. Terriss, however, would be murdered by a frustrated job-seeking actor before he could produce the play.

8 SUNDAY [ ]

9 Wrote to Ellen Terry and to Terriss. After dinner went to the Salts; and spent the rest of the afternoon there playing piano duets and singing. Abominably wet weather.

> Shaw's letter is in *CL*. He was trying to blarney Ellen Terry into playing *The Man of Destiny* with Henry Irving, her acting partner. Shaw would write many further letters to her, but none would be noted in the diary.

10 *Call on Mrs. Archer at 9 Fitzroy Square at 12.*

[Mrs. Archer has been relaxing me joint by joint; but I am still hardly safe without a chain and muzzle.]

> Shaw to Janet Achurch, 24 March 1896 (*CL*). Mrs. Archer was proficient in the Annie Payson Call method of relaxing the joints and muscles, described in *Power through Repose* (1891).

11 [ ]

12 *London School of Economics. 5th lecture.* °*Production of* True Blue *at the Olympic Theatre. 19½. Postponed to next week.*

> Instead, Shaw went to the matinée opening of a variety bill at the Comedy Theatre, he wrote in his G.B.S. column for 21 March 1896 (C1126), consisting of "one of Miss Beatrice Herford's monologues, a couple of Mrs. Hugh Bell's drawing room pieces, trivial but amusing enough on their scale; and a one-act piece of hardly greater pretension, but much more serious merit, by Mrs. [W. K.] Clifford." The *SR* notice did not furnish the titles, which were *Blue or Green?* and *The Bicycle* by Mrs. Bell, and *A Honeymoon Tragedy*, by Mrs. Clifford. There would be ninety-six matinees—all, apparently, patronized by ladies in "huge towering hats, piled up, for more effectual obstruction of the view, with every conceivable futility, vulgarity and brutality (in the dead-bird line). . . ."

13 *Fabian Meeting at Clifford's Inn. 20¼. J. F. Oakeshott on "Revenue Reform and Old Age Pensions." Fabian Executive and Committee. 17.*

Very bad night. Fever, headache, weakness—what they call an attack of influenza.

14 Weak and good for nothing all day.

15 SUNDAY *Read* Candida *to Esmond at Charringtons. 20.*

> Shaw was industriously pursuing ways to get *Candida* commercially staged, and Henry V. Esmond, an actor as well as a playwright, sought vehicles as well for his wife, Eva Moore (1870–1955), an actress in light comedy who would later be signed for a role in an abortive production of *You Never Can Tell*, but who would not do *Candida*.

16 [ ]

17   °*Council Meeting South St. Pancras Liberal and Radical Association, meeting to elect officers, etc. Compton St. Mission Hall. 20½.*

18   [   ]

19   *London School of Economics. 6th lecture.* True Blue. *Olympic. See last week.*

[*True Blue* . . . is funnier by a good deal than *H.M.S. Pinafore* in the absurd parts, and not bad, as melodramas go, in the presentable parts.]

> Reviewed on 28 March 1896 (C1128). The melodrama about the Royal Navy by Leonard Outram and Stuart Gordon, Lieut., R.N., G.B.S. wrote, was full of "unspeakable fatuities." It would have thirty-four performances.

20   °*No Executive.*

21   °*Miss Payne Townshend At-Home to the London School of Economics lectures. Meet Archer in British Museum Reading Room at 12 and go to see bicycle. Look in at the Technical Education Board's art exhibition at Bolt Court.*

> Shaw's first reference to Charlotte Payne-Townshend (1857–1943), whom he would marry on 1 June 1898, is frustratingly abortive. She was a wealthy Irishwoman who, Beatrice Webb would note in her diary (16 September 1896), had "drifted about." The Webbs had been encouraging her to assist the L.S.E. (she gave £1,000 for its library), and at their house on 29 January she had already met Shaw. After the at-home in her rooms in Adelphi Terrace above the School of Economics—the rent of which she was, in effect, paying through her own—she would go to Rome for the spring, returning in June. This would be the last occasion in the diary when Shaw would remember to note an unkept engagement by the superscript circle.   ▪   Archer was contemplating the purchase of a bicycle, and Shaw wanted him to see the Elswick model, at 19 Great Portland St., and the Osmond, at 3 Holborn Viaduct.

22 SUNDAY   *Read* Man of Destiny *at the Russells', 90 Ashley Gardens.*

> Bertrand Russell had married Alys Pearsall Smith (1867–1951) in December 1894, at the Quaker meeting house in St. Martin's Lane. They were living in London while Russell lectured at the L.S.E.

23   [I called on the Salts and played a duet or two. Mrs. Salt complained considerably of me: she said she believed I had been practising scales (an unheard-of accusation); said I was in a destructively electrical condition and . . . that if I undressed in the dark when going to bed, sparks would come out of me; and generally made me conscious of a grinding, destroying energy. . . .]

> Shaw to Janet Achurch, 24 March 1896, referring to the previous night (*CL*).

24   *Lecture to the Willesden Independent Labour Party on "Socialism and Education" at the Willesden Assembly Rooms, 233 High Rd., Willesden Green. 20 (G. T. Monson, 21 Chaplin Rd., Willesden Green N.W.).*

25 *Article Club dinner at the Midland Hotel. 19. Mrs. Dryhurst's, 19½, to meet Mrs. Cash.*

Shaw apparently did meet Mrs. Cash, as a menu card survives in BL Add. MS. 50701 for the Article Club dinner at the Midland Grand Hotel, 20 Gambolt Rd., Putney Hill, W. The subject of the evening's debate is described as "The Settlement of Disputes between Capital and Labour."

26 [I have an idea for a little play about King Pippin and his wife, with a lovely medieval French court for a stage setting.. . .]

Shaw to Ellen Terry, 26 March 1896 (*CL*). He would never, more's the pity, write a *Pippin*.

27 *Fabian Meeting at Clifford's Inn. Ronald M. Burrows on "Socialism and Foreign Politics." 20. Fabian Executive and Committee. 17 and 17½.*

Ronald Montagu Burrows (1867–1920), author of articles on social and educational reform and on Greek culture, taught at the Universities of Glasgow and London, becoming principal of King's College, London, in 1913.

28 *University Boat Race. Emery Walker's, 13 to 19. Ashton Jonson reads paper on "The Theory of Wagnerian Musical Drama" at Hartley's, 5 Gray's Inn Square. W. C.*

The Putney to Mortlake boat race was won by Oxford—by half a length—in a gale accompanied by showers of rain and bursts of hail.

29 SUNDAY [   ]

30 *Go down to Stocks Cottage, Aldbury, Tring, to stay with Wallas.*

Mary Augusta (Mrs. Humphry) Ward (1851–1920), popular novelist and opponent of woman suffrage, had lent her country place to Wallas for the Easter holidays.

31 [Here I am in a lonely cottage on a remote hillside. . . . Wallas (to whom Mrs. Humphry Ward lent this place for Easter) has gone up to town to look after the education bill and will not be back until tomorrow. I arrived yesterday night; this I rode to the railway station for newspapers on my bike; then worked on my drama until lunch; after that meal went for a walk with Wallas; after his departure . . . tired myself by hard riding enough to greatly enjoy the fire within and the immense darkness, silence & solitude without. I could find no book here fit to read except "The Last Chronicle of Barset" which I had not read these 25 years past; and I have begun renewing my acquaintance. . . .]

Shaw to Bertha Newcombe, 31 March 1896 (*CL*).

April

1–3   [   ]

4   [Here I am drafting stacks of letters in reply to a sackful of the un-answered communications of the last six months. I send them up to Fitzroy Square to be typewritten and dispatched. . . . I spent the morning bicycling through the park. . . .]

> Shaw to Janet Achurch, 4 April 1896 (*CL*).   ▪   Although Shaw sent his drafts home, they were for Kate Salt, who checked regularly at Fitzroy Square to do typing for Shaw.

5–7   [   ]

8   *Come up from Stocks Cottage, 16.51 train, for the first night of* A Mother of Three *at the Comedy. 20.*

[I am bound to say that there is not much philosophy in Miss Clo Graves's play. However there is plenty of fun in it, and in that fun there lurks occasionally a certain sense of the humor of indecency which drives me to conclude that Miss Clo Graves is an Irish lady.]

> Reviewed on 11 April 1896 (C1131). Clotilde Graves (1863–1932)—a popular novelist using the pseudonym Richard Dehan—had succeeded, in 1890, in having one matinee performance at the Haymarket of her monologue, *Rachel*. Her new comedy lasted for sixty-one performances.

9   *Production of G. Stuart Ogilvie's* The Sin of St. Hulda *at the Shaftesbury. 20.*

[The nearest Salvation Army barrack or London Mission will supply half a dozen saints of infinitely greater sanctity and heroism than the waxwork angel whom Miss Kate Rorke impersonates at the Shaftesbury.]

> Reviewed on 18 April 1896 (C1132). G. Stuart Ogilvie (1858–1932) had successfully adapted Charles Kingsley's novel *Hypatia* to the stage in 1893. Shaw's experience of the play as seen in his notice anticipates his writing of *Major Barbara*, toward which many subtle influences were already directing him.

10   [   ]

11   *Production of* Biarritz *at the Prince of Wales's Theatre. 20.*

[I have rarely seen an audience so unanimous as that which crowded to witness the first representation of *Biarritz*. . . . *Biarritz* is sure to run triumphantly for several years, since nothing but the substitution of "special features" for every five minutes of the original work, and their frequent renewal, including the conversion of the whole into a variety entertainment, could possibly keep it in existence for a fortnight.]

"Two minutes of *Biarritz*," G.B.S. concluded (C1132) about Jerome K. Jerome's farce, "would reconcile a Trappist to his monastery for life." It would have seventy-one performances.

12 SUNDAY [   ]

On this date, from Stocks Cottage (to which he had returned after his reviewing assignment the day before), Shaw wrote to Ellen Terry (*CL*) offering to read *Candida* to her, but still insisting it was reserved for Janet Achurch.

13 [I have finished the second act of the play—finished it triumphantly on Sunday morning. . . . And now, if I had the very *faintest* idea of the next act, I should be happy. . . .]

Shaw to Janet Achurch, 14 April 1896 (*CL*). The play that had reached the end of the 2nd act was *You Never Can Tell*.

14 [Instead of inventing that next act I have jumped over its head on to the melodrama for Terriss. . . . I have completed the scenario of not only that act, but the second and third. . . . I have no longer any doubt of my being able to carry out that project with considerable force.]

Shaw to Janet Achurch, 14 April 1896 (*CL*). The new play would become *The Devil's Disciple*. Shaw's three-page shorthand scenario (BL), dated the 14th, was not set in New England during the American Revolution, but only "on the [nameless] border during warfare." As with *Arms and the Man*, he would do his homework and find a proper war in which to set his concept.

15–16 [   ]

17 *Fabian Meeting at Clifford's Inn. Sidney Webb on "Chartered Companies." 20.*

Shaw had returned the same day from his long holiday at Tring.

18–20 [   ]

21 [A safe rule for the dramatist is, "When in doubt, revive Punch and Judy." Mr. Henry Arthur Jones . . . has fallen back on Punch and Judy, the eternal rogue's comedy. . . .]

"Punch and Judy Again," review, 25 April 1896 (C1133), of *The Rogue's Comedy*, which opened on 21 April at the Garrick. The play would survive for forty-one performances.

22 [I am greatly obliged to whoever sent me a belated ticket for an afternoon performance at the Court Theatre. . . . I did manage to arrive in time for the last act of something; but as the playbills were all gone before I arrived, I know not what, or by whom, it was. . . . I think it must have been a burlesque of *The Corsican Brothers*; but I am not sure.]

The play, opening that afternoon, was *My Astral Body*, by actor-playwright Charles Hudson (?–1897) and Nicholas Colthurst, whose only recorded drama this was. It would run for ninety-six matinees.

23   [I have long ceased to celebrate my own birthday; and I do not see why I should celebrate Shakespear's. . . . I went to Camberwell . . . because, on the whole, I thought it my business to be there. . . . The hour appointed was half-past two; and though I spared neither energy nor expense in my journey, making no less than three separate embarkations in train, bus, and tram, at a total cost of fourpence, it was three o'clock before the Métropole was sighted. This had two grave consequences. First, Camberwell had rallied round the Bard so multitudinously that the offer of untold gold could procure me nothing better than a mere skylight of a box, from which my view of the legitimate drama was considerably foreshortened. Second, I was late for Miss Dorothy Dene's Juliet. . . .]

G.B.S. in *SR*, 2 May 1896 (C1134), on the celebrations at the Metropole Theatre, Camberwell. The Dorothy Dene reference was tongue-in-cheek, as Miss Dene (1830?–1899) had been too old to play Juliet even in her heyday.

24   *Fabian Members' Meeting, Council Room at Essex Hall. 20. Plenty of business.*

25–27   [   ]

28   [The Royalty piece, *The New Baby*, is . . . so far beneath contempt that it never once rises to the point of even suggesting the disgust which its story would rouse in anyone who took it seriously. . . .]

The New Baby was an English adaptation by actor-manager Arthur Bourchier (1863–1927) of the apparently crude German farce *Der Rabenwater*, which, G.B.S. wrote on 9 May 1896 (C1135), "includes incest among its bewilderments." It lasted nineteen performances, along with its curtain-raiser, *Monsieur de Paris*, by Alicia Ramsey (?–1933) and Rudolph de Cordova (1860–1941), which Shaw found "of exceptional merit."

29   [*A Night Out*, at the Vaudeville, . . . is not in the main badly acted. In . . . the unnecessary noisiness of some of the scenes, one sees the chief fault of the production—puerility of stage management.]

A Night Out, a farce by Georges Feydeau (1863–1921) and Maurice Desvallières (1857–1926), originally titled *Hôtel du Libre Échange*, had been adapted by Seymour Hicks (1871–1949). G.B.S. (C1135) thought it "a masterpiece of ingenuity and urbanity" in comparison to the sleazy farce at the Royalty. It would run for 525 performances.

30   [   ]

May

1 [I went to the Hotel Cecil . . . to shake hands with Mr. Wyndham, and never succeeded in getting within a dozen yards of him. . . . There we were in our thousands—players and authors and critics—geniuses and beauties—lost sheep strayed from the Philistine fold of respectability— . . . the mighty *cabotinage* of London in all its fascination, and all its unlimited capacity for flattery, champagne, and asparagus. Nine out of every ten guests were players by profession; and fully one out of every two hundred and fifty could really act—first among these, beyond all challenge, Wyndham himself, whose health was proposed by that tragic comedian the Lord Chief Justice.]

> Charles Wyndham was celebrating twenty years as manager of the Criterion. After an afternoon-and-evening of performances—the evening merely two short pieces, with proceeds going to the Actors' Benevolent Fund—he and his dutiful wife (Wyndham's mistress and actress-business partner was Mary Moore, whom he could not marry until Mrs. Wyndham died in 1916) entertained 1,500 guests at the new Hotel Cecil in the Strand, which was not yet open to the public. Mary Moore insisted that the affair be a sit-down supper, which it was. The Lord Chief Justice, who proposed Wyndham's health, was Lord Russell of Killowen. Shaw described the scene in a tailpiece to his *SR* column 9 May 1896 (C1135).

2–7 [   ]

8 *Fabian Meeting at Clifford's Inn. W. A. S. Hewins on "A Legal Minimum Wage."*

> W. A. S. Hewins (1865–1931), economist and historian, was the first director of the London School of Economics, serving from 1895 to 1903. He would become secretary of the Tariff Commission (from 1903 to 1917), and would be its chairman from 1920 to 1922. From 1912 through 1918 he would also be Conservative M.P. for Hereford City. • Shaw apparently also attended a Beerbohm Tree production of *Henry IV. Part I* at the Haymarket on 8 May, reviewing it on 16 May (C1136) and finding it "bad."

9 [*The Matchmaker* at the Shaftesbury . . . is thoroughly characteristic of the phase of social development represented by the two ladies—a London actress and a London journalist respectively—to whose pens we owe it.]

> *A Matchmaker*, by Clotilde Graves and Gertrude Kingston (1866–1937), would close (after twelve performances) before the G.B.S. notice appeared on 23 May 1896 (C1137). The comedy was "tacked together anyhow, and built on the sandiest of foundations. . . ."

10–15 [   ]

16 *Production of* Rosemary *at the Criterion Theatre (Parker and Murray Carson). 20.15.*

[I will not pretend I found it tedious; indeed, Mr. Wyndham entertained me better than I expected, considering that the art of senile make-up . . . is to me the most transparent and futile of impostures. (C1137)]

> *Rosemary*, a romantic melodrama by Louis N. Parker (1852–1944), a prolific-but-now-forgotten playwright, and Murray Carson, was sold outright to Wyndham for one thousand pounds. After its run of 195 performances in London, it was a comparable success in the provinces and in America, and netted many thousands for Wyndham. G.B.S. (C1137) found it little more than "a pleasant piece of storytelling," with a "nonagenarian monologue."

17 SUNDAY. *Speak for Hampstead and Kilburn Branch of the Independent Labour Party at 11.30 at the street corner opposite the Heath St. Fire Brigade Station.*

18 *Go to Jo at Drury Lane (4th night). Meet Olivier at Orange Grove at 19.*
[. . . the unnamed four-act comedy just finished. . . .]

> *Jo* was an adaptation of *Bleak House*, replete with the traditional "stage sentimentalities" that were once "the height of melodramatic fashion." It was never, said G.B.S. (C1137), "anything more than third-rate work at any period of our stage history." ■ Shaw's manuscript of *You Never Can Tell* concludes, on p. 121 (BL), "Regent's Park, 18th May 1896." His comment about its completion appears in a letter to R. Golding Bright, on 10 June 1896 (*CL*).

19 *Fabian Publishing Committee. 16½.*

20 *Reception meeting at Queen's Hall for Liebknecht. 20. Call on Mrs. T. P. O'Connor in the afternoon to see her son's studio.*

21 [   ]

22 *Fabian Annual Meeting. Clifford's Inn. 20.*

23–29 [   ]

30 *Walter Crane's At-Home. 21 to 24.*

31 SUNDAY [   ]

June

1 [Miss May Yohe might, I think, have given us something fresher at the Court Theatre than a revival of *Mam'zelle Nitouche*.... She will only waste her time and money if she tries to back cast-off favorites.]

Mam'zelle Nitouche, a musical comedy by Henri Meilhac, Albert Millaud, and Florimond Hervé, would have fifty-five performances. G.B.S. noticed it on 20 June 1896 (C1142).

2 [Herman Merivale's adaptation of *Divorçons* began by putting me out of temper. . . . At the end of the first act I was in the worst possible temper with the whole performance. . . . But I was unable to maintain this unfavorable attitude.]

> Herman Merivale's *The Queen's Proctor*, his adaptation of Sardou's comedy, had at first little to recommend it to G.B.S. (C1140) because he found Sardou's formula-plays exasperatingly impossible; but the acting of Irene Vanbrugh and Arthur Bourchier made it, finally, to him, "the most amusing play in London." It would have fifty-seven performances.

3 [*Magda* . . . will not run long: human nature will not endure such a spectacle for many weeks. That is not the fault of the play. . . .]

> *Magda*, with Mrs. Patrick Campbell and Forbes-Robertson, would have fifteen performances. The G.B.S. reveiw of the new Louis Parker translation appeared on 6 June 1896 (C1140), and observed that as actress, Mrs. Campbell "did nothing."

4 [   ]

5 *Fabian Meeting at Essex Hall. Address by Liebknecht. 20.*

6 [I fear I must ask the responsible parties, whoever they are, what they mean by this *Carmen* business at the Gaiety Theatre? . . . The execution of this tedious, inept, absurd, and at its most characteristic moments positively asinine play only emphasized its defects.]

> The dramatic version of Prosper Merimée's novel, better known from the opera, was by Henry Hamilton. G.B.S. on 13 June 1896 (C1141) found it "cheap, tawdry business." It would survive for fifteen performances.

7 SUNDAY   [   ]

8 [*The Wanderer from Venus; or, Twenty-Four Hours with an Angel* . . . was produced at the new theatre in Croydon. . . . I paid three shillings for a stall, and twopence for a program. Add to this the price of a first-class return to London, three and sixpence. . . . And as Miss Kate Rorke not only plays the part of an angel in her most touching manner, but flies bodily up to heaven at the end of the play, to the intense astonishment of the most hardened playgoers, there is something sensational to talk about afterwards.]

> The fantasy by Robert Buchanan and "Charles Marlowe"—possibly a foreshadowing of Barrie's *Peter Pan* (1904)—was described by G.B.S. (C1141) as "a variation on the Pygmalion and Galatea theme."

9 [   ]

10 [At the Garrick . . . Mrs. Kendal, forgetting that London playgoers have been starved for years in the matter of acting, inconsiderately gave them more in the first ten minutes than they have had in the last five years, with the result that the poor wretches became hysterical, and vented their applause in sobs and shrieks. . . . *The Greatest of These*—is dramatic up to the brief but unbearable fourth act. . . .]

> Sydney Grundy's new play would have thirty-nine performances. G.B.S. (C1141) dismissed the last act as pure preaching and discussion, an objection which would be lodged against him as playwright more than once.

11 [   ]

12 *Fabian Meeting at Clifford's Inn. Olivier on "Land." 20.*

13–19 [   ]

20 [It is impossible to see *The School for Scandal* without beginning to moralize. . . . That the play is well acted goes without saying. Sheridan wrote for the actor as Handel wrote for the singer.]

> *The School for Scandal* was reviewed on 27 June 1896 (C1143). G.B.S. thought Sheridan's play had not dated after more than a century on the boards.

21 [   ]

22 [*On the March*, at the Prince of Wales's Theatre (now in the hands of Miss Cissy Grahame) . . . is a variety entertainment of no particular pretensions to smartness; . . . still, there is no incompetence, no parading of the unskilled, flashy girls who get engaged in theatres solely because their ineptitudes would not be tolerated for a moment in a music-hall. . . .]

> *On the March*, a music-hall entertainment disguised as a "musical comedy," would have seventy-seven performances. G.B.S. (C1143) declared it "good of its simple kind."

23–26 [   ]

27 *Walter Crane's At-Home. 21 to 24.*

28 SUNDAY *Speak on Wandsworth Common on "Suburban Politics" at 18½ for the Clapham Labour League, near the footbridge (E. W. B. Hutt, 68 Bramfield Rd., New Wandsworth, S.W.).*

29–30 [   ]

July

1 [ ]

2 [*The Mummy* is ingenious enough to have a narrow miss of being a successful play. . . . What is wrong with it is the perfunctory flimsiness of the figures who surround the mummy.

Kit Marlowe, however, did not bore me at St. George's Hall as he has always bored me when I have tried to read him without skipping. The more I see of these performances by the Elizabethan Stage Society, the more I am convinced that their method of presenting an Elizabethan play is not only the right method for that particular sort of play but that any play performed on a platform amidst the audience gets closer home to its hearers than when presented as a picture framed by a proscenium. . . . The E.S.S. made very free with *Doctor Faustus*.]

> Reviewed on 11 July 1896 (C1146). The farce about an Egyptian mummy who walks about in a modern household, by George D. Day and Alan Reed, survived for only a single matinee at the Comedy Theatre. ▪ "All the new problem plays, with their intense intimacies," G.B.S. suggested (C1146), should be thrust into the audience in something like the old Elizabethan staging.

3 [Miss Elizabeth Tyree, late of Mr. Daniel Frohman's company at the Lyceum Theatre, New York, invited London to see what she could do as Juliet, Fedora, and the Country Girl. . . . The work she can do so far can be done in any country without sending to America for assistance.]

> G.B.S. was unconvinced that the young American actress had "the power that crosses frontiers" (C1146), but thought she had shown, in the sequence from *Romeo and Juliet*, "that the Balcony scene makes a capital one-act comedietta."

4 [*Behind the Scenes*. A farcical comedy, adapted from *The First Night* . . . is really too much. . . .]

> *Behind the Scenes* had been adapted by comedian Felix Morris (who also had its leading role) and George P. Hawtrey (1846–1910) from *Le Père de la Débutante*. There was one matinee at the Comedy.

5 SUNDAY   *If in town, speak at Demonstration of National Union of Shop Assistants, Warehousemen and Clerks in Hyde Park at 15½.*

6–8 [ ]

9 [Mr. Bourchier's revival of *The Liar* produced an effect out of all proportion to the merits of the play by the contrast between Foote's clever dialogue and the witlessness of our contemporary drama.]

Reviewed on 18 July 1896 (C1147). Samuel Foote (1720–1777) was a dramatist whose heyday preceded that of Goldsmith and Sheridan. The revival at the Royalty had three matinees.

10   [   ]

11   [We are actually assured that *The Countess Gucki* was received with delight in America! . . . In London, at the end of a season of undistracted gaiety, it is about as interesting as a second-hand ball dress of the last season but ten. . . .]

The Countess Gucki was adapted by the indefatigable Augustin Daly from the German of Franz von Schonthan. G.B.S. (C1147) found it "insufferably tiresome." It would last eighteen performances at the Comedy.

12 SUNDAY   *Lecture at Kelmscott House for the Hammersmith Socialist Society on "What Will Socialism Be Like?" 20.*

13   [After lunch, as I was coming to the foot of the Haymarket after passing the National Gallery, a railway van came out of the Haymarket and made for Cockspur St. Suddenly the horse shied and plunged up towards the Nat. Gallery on his wrong side. I was going pretty fast and I hit him with the nicest accuracy in the middle of the breastbone. I went down in a forest of horse's legs, van wheels and whirling bicycle machinery; but with a nimbleness surprising in one of my years I made a twist, a roll, a bound and a spring all in one. As I did it, crack, smash, split, snap went all the bones of the bike, and as I shot on my feet the tail of the van rushed past me, and from underneath it came an amazing iron spider with twisted legs and umbrella-blown-inside-out wings which had once been my bike. Then crowd, police, frantic enquiries, names and addresses exchanged, driver of van too unspeakably relieved at finding that the smashed thing under his van was not me to deny that he was in the wrong: finally a certain indignation at my heartless composure. The van took the ruins of the bike away; and I walked off—to realise, presently, that my right knee and leg, on which I had come down, was beginning to stiffen. So I drove to the Charringtons' (having reasons for avoiding Fitzroy Sq.) and was stuped and nursed by Janet. . . .

I am a little shaken, I suppose, but not such as by the smash last year in Wales. If I rest my leg, I shall, I hope, be all right in time for Bayreuth.]

"So I drove . . .": Shaw hailed a cab. ■ Shaw's "reasons for avoiding Fitzroy Sq." were simply that Mrs. Patterson was visiting. ■ Letter to Florence Farr (*CL*), undated but established as 13 July 1896 in a letter dated 14 July 1896 to Max Hecht, in which Shaw describes the bicycling accident as occurring the previous afternoon.

14–15   [   ]

16 [*The Honorable Member,* produced at a matinee at the Court . . . , is a remarkable play; not because the author, Mr. Gattie, is either a great dramatic poet or even, so far, a finished playwright; but because he seems conversant with ethical, social, and political ideas which have been fermenting for the last fifteen years. . . .]

> Shaw's review, which appeared in SR on 18 July 1896 (C1147), needed time to make its way into publication, and is assigned the last probable date on which the limping play critic could have managed the assignment. Alfred Gattie (1856–1925), philosopher, inventor, and sometime dramatist, would provide the inspiration later for the "Breakages, Ltd." aspect of Shaw's late play *The Apple Cart* (1929); he is written about in its preface.

17–18 [   ]

19 SUNDAY *Bayreuth. Opening performance of* Das Rheingold.

[We all know . . . the moment near the close of *Das Rheingold,* when . . . Donner, mounting the rock, calls the clouds to him, and, when their black legions, crowding about him, have hidden him in their mists, swings his hammer, splits them with a thousand blinding ribbons of lightning, and reveals the skiey towers of Valhall, with Froh's rainbow bridge spanning the valley to the gate of the wonderful castle—the home of the gods. The effect of this on the stage of the Wagner Theatre is magnificent, but the management, not content to wait for this, took advantage of the Bayreuth custom of summoning the audience by sound of trumpet, to blare out Donner's call to the real heavens before the performance began. What was the result? No sooner was the call sent echoing from hill to hill than the cloudless sky darkened, and the trumpets were answered by a distant roll of thunder. I was up in the pine woods at the time, . . . and we sprang up from our carpet of scented pine needles and made for the theatre precipitately. Just as we reached it the rain came down in torrents. Consequently the entry of the audience to the first performance, usually a gay, busy, eager, hopeful function, was this time a damp scuttle.]

> "We sprang up . . .": Shaw had gone to Bayreuth with H. W. Massingham, editor of *The Daily Chronicle.* ▪ "Bassetto at Bayreuth," *The Star,* 22 July 1896 (C1148).

20 *Bayreuth.* **Die Walküre.**

[*Die Walküre* at full length, beginning at four and ending at half-past nine, and involving three hours and a half of concentrated attention, is hard work for a critic, and a considerable test of the endurance of an amateur.]

> " 'Siegfried' Fails at Bayreuth," *The Star,* 24 July 1896 (C1150).

21 *Bayreuth.* **Siegfried.**

[The first act of *Siegfried* has been the worst disappointment so far.]

> "Bayreuth: 'Die Gotterdammerung,' " *The Star,* 25 July 1896 (C1151).

22   *Bayreuth.* Die Götterdammerung.

[We are all somewhat exhausted after a first act lasting two hours, yet most of us are ready to go through it again. . . . I shall start for London after the performance (unless it kills me).]

23–25   [   ]

25   *Call on Miss Penfield, 6 Nottingham Terrace, at 16.*

Miss Mary Penfield, apparently an American journalist, failed to keep the appointment, yet asked for another. Although Shaw informed her several days later that she was one of the most audaciously irresponsible young women he had encountered, his listing her in his addressbook at two later addresses in 1897 suggests continued contacts.

26 SUNDAY   [   ]

27   *International Socialist Congress, Queen's Hall. International Socialist Congress, British Section, in the morning at St. Martin's Hall.*

28   [I have rushed from the thick of Bayreuth into the thick of this confounded Congress, doing a long article in *The Star* every day on both. . . .]

Shaw to Edward Carpenter (*CL*), 29 July 1896. His pieces on the Congress would appear 27–31 July 1896 (C1152–56).

29–31   [   ]

August

1   *Go down for six weeks with the Webbs and Miss Payne Townshend to Stratford St. Andrew Rectory, near Saxmundham.*

The Webbs, with Beatrice's income, had rented a large, uncomfortable house in Suffolk, which would suggest two names to Shaw for his future *Major Barbara*. (A Lord Saxmundham, a distiller, would precede Andrew Undershaft—his name also from the Church of St. Andrew Undershaft in East London—as a benefactor of the Salvation Army.) Other guests were to be Graham Wallas, Charles Trevelyan, and Charlotte Perkins Stetson. All three left after brief stays, and Shaw was thrown together more intimately with Charlotte Payne-Townshend.

2–18   [   ]

Because of his departure for a holiday with Charlotte and the Webbs, Shaw apparently did not attend an "International Demonstration . . . to demand a complete Amnesty for all political prisoners—especially for Charles, Cailes, and Battola. . . ," held in Trafalgar Square on 2 August. However, the broadside announcing the public meeting (B18) includes, on the verso, a Shaw statement under the heading, "The Opinions of Public Men on the Walsall Case."

19 [Since I came here on the first I have had exactly one idle day—a long bicycling excursion. I have had to toil over my play to get it ready for the stage & to write an article for *Cosmopolis* on the Congress.]

> The play was *You Never Can Tell*, for which he thought he had a producer. Shaw's practice was to pen in the stage business after completing the dialogue. The article was "Socialism at the International Congress," for the September 1896 issue of *Cosmopolis* (C1159).

20–31 [We . . . can only afford a country house for our holidays because one of us has a wife with a thousand a year. This time we have been joined by an Irish millionairess who has had cleverness and character enough to decline the station in life—"great catch for somebody"—to which it pleased God to call her, and whom we have incorporated into our Fabian family with great success. I am going to refresh my heart by falling in love with her—I love falling in love—but, mind, only with her, not with the million; so someone else must marry her if she can stand him after me.

What a holiday this has been! I never worked so hard before in my life. Four hours writing in the morning; four hours bicycling in the afternoon every day.]

> Shaw to Ellen Terry, probably sometime in the second half of August (*CL*).

September

1–16 [ ]

> While at the Rectory, on 10 September, Shaw finally began his play *The Devil's Disciple*, the scenario of which he had penned in Regent's Park in mid-May. Beatrice Webb would note about Charlotte Payne-Townshend in her diary on the 16th (*The Diary of Beatrice Webb*, II),

> > It was on account of her generosity to our projects and "for the good of the cause" that I first made friends with her. To bring her more directly into our little set of comrades, I suggested that we should take a house together in the country and entertain our friends. To me she seemed at that time a pleasant, well-dressed, well-intentioned woman—I thought she should do very well for Graham Wallas! Now she turns out to be an "original," with considerable personal charm and certain volcanic tendencies. Graham Wallas bored her with his morality and learning. In a few days she and Bernard Shaw were constant companions. For the last fortnight, when the party has been reduced to ourselves and Shaw, and we have been occupied with our work and each other, they have been scouring the country together and sitting up late at night. To all seeming, she is in love with the brilliant philanderer and he is taken, in his cold sort of way, with her. They are, I gather from him, on very confidential terms and have "explained" their relative positions. Though inter-

ested I am somewhat uneasy. These warm-hearted unmarried women of a certain age are audacious and are almost childishly reckless of consequences. I doubt whether Bernard Shaw would be induced to marry: I doubt whether she will be happy without it. It is harder for a woman to remain celibate than a man.

17 *Start from Stratford to bicycle to London with the Webbs and Miss Townshend. Sleep at Felixstowe.*

18 *Day at Felixstowe.*

19 *Start from Felixstowe and ride via Harwich and Colchester to Braintree.*

20 SUNDAY *Braintree to Hertford via Bishops Stortford.*

21 *Hertford to London via St. Albans.*
[I reached Fitzroy Sq an hour or so ago, sopping . . . What with changing & bathing & getting the mud off the bicycle & unpacking & hastily opening my accumulated letters I have had no time to sit down . . . but . . . scrawl this in the hideous underground train on my way to the theatre at Camberwell, where they have a real first night. . . .]

> Shaw to Ellen Terry, 21 September 1896 (*CL*). The first night was that of G. W. Appleton's *The Co-Respondent* (afterwards called *Our Kate*), at the suburban Metropole, Camberwell, reviewed in *SR* on 3 October 1896 (C1162). "The house laughed a good deal," G.B.S. wrote; but he thought the play unlikely to survive transfer to the West End. It was not transferred.

22 [I do not defend *Cymbeline*. It is for the most part stagey trash. . . . But Irving's Iachimo is a very different affair. It is a new and independent creation. . . .]

> "Blaming the Bard," review of *Cymbeline* in Henry Irving's Lyceum production, 26 September 1896 (C1161). It would have eighty-eight performances.

23 [The cast of *Two Little Vagabonds* . . . is quite up to the west end standard, and is, in fact, rather thrown away on the play. . . .]

> *Two Little Vagabonds*—by George R. Sims (1847–1922) and Arthur Shirley (1853–1925), both prolific minor playwrights—had opened at the Princess's on the 23rd. Labeled on the bill "an original melodrama," it was an adaptation of Pierre Decourcelle's *Les Deux Gosses*. The play, which Shaw thought was trashy but "quite likely to be successful" (C1162), would have 276 performances.

24 [There is at present running at Drury Lane an entertainment called *The Duchess of Coolgardie*, which is not a play at all in any serious technical sense of the word. . . . As an Irishman, I have, of course, noticed that the ceremony of drinking the health of my native land never palls on a true British audience.]

The Duchess of Coolgardie. A romance of the Australian goldfields, by Euston Leigh and Cyril Clare (pseudonymous, G.B.S. suggested—and they do not reappear on theater bills), had opened on 19 September, and is assigned here to the first possible date when Shaw could have seen it for review (C1162). It would have sixty-seven performances.

25 [Sir H.I. does not see why Sardou's Napoleon should exclude mine. He summons me to conference tomorrow (Saturday) at midday. I shall see him with the *Saturday* article (which he will get up at five in the morning to read) up to the hilt in his heart.]

Shaw to Ellen Terry, 25 September 1896 (*CL*). ▪ "Sir H. I." refers to Henry Irving. ▪ By "Sardou's Napoleon" Shaw implies *Madame Sans-Gêne*, which Irving would again produce at the Lyceum on 17 April 1897. Irving had claimed interest in doing *The Man of Destiny*. ▪ This *Saturday* article was the G.B.S. review of *Cymbeline*, with its transparently ironic praise of Irving's Shakespearean acting.

26 [I demagnetized him (quite unintentionally) and made him feel uncomfortable. . . . But I was much too conceited to be unfriendly. . . .]

Shaw to Laurence Irving, 25 October 1905 (*CL*). Reluctant to refuse the play outright, Irving convinced Shaw that he was interested in doing both Napoleons; but he would never attempt Shaw's, and only delayed its appearance onstage.

27–30 [   ]

October

1–2 [   ]

3 [*The White Silk Dress* at the Prince of Wales' shews that . . . repentant sinners are seldom happy in their first unaccustomed attempts at virtue; and . . . the house yelled with rage, and called for the author in a manner that decided him not to accept the invitation.]

H. H. W. Dam's *The White Silk Dress* was better, G.B.S. wrote on 17 October 1896 (C1165), than the opening night audience reaction suggested. And, indeed, it would have 132 performances at the Prince of Wales's Theatre.

4 SUNDAY *Lecture on "The Respectability of Socialism" to the Hornsey Socialist Society. 20. Felix House. Crouch End. Miss Cowrie's.*

[I had to orate at Hornsey; and a young lady got up afterwards and said, "I don't think what I have to ask belongs to the subject of the lecture; but will Mr. Shaw tell us when his play will be produced at the Lyceum?"]

Shaw to Ellen Terry, 5 October 1896 (*CL*). Shaw had unwisely rushed out with the news that Irving was still committed to *The Man of Destiny*.

5   [I am at my wit's end—telegrams every five minutes asking for articles about Morris, and a million other worries.]

> William Morris, long ailing, had died on 3 October. Shaw's obituary of Morris appeared in *The Daily Chronicle* on 6 October 1896 (C1163). He would also devote an *SR* column, entitled "Morris as Actor and Dramatist" (he was really neither, but G.B.S. needed a theatrical springboard), to his mentor on 10 October 1896 (C1164).

6   [As comedies go nowadays, *Mr. Martin* may almost be called a masterpiece of observation.]

> Charles Hawtrey's *Mr. Martin* had opened on the same evening as Dam's *The White Silk Dress*; Shaw obviously went to the Dam opening. To G.B.S. (C1165) *Mr. Martin* was hardly up to Wilde, but Wilde was not available. The comedy would survive for forty-one performances. Shaw's attendance is assigned to the first evening he is likely to have been available.

7–8   [   ]

9   [Fabian meeting at Clifford's Inn. The motion . . . "that Tract 70 be withdrawn from publication" is nothing more or less than a motion that the whole Fabian policy which it has taken us so many years to build up shall be publicly disavowed and recanted by the society.]

> Shaw to Jules Magny, 6 October 1896 [*CL*]. The motion had been made by J. Ramsay MacDonald, who was never comfortable as a Fabian.

10   [At the Fabian I have had a heroic victory. I rashly boasted beforehand that my side would be victorious. . . . And it all came off. *They were.* I made a tearing speech, and was insufferably pleased with myself. . . .]

> Shaw to Ellen Terry, 12 October 1896 (*CL*).

11–15   [   ]

> Between 12 and 14 October, Shaw wrote (*CL*) three letters to Florence Farr (in response to her letters) in which he effectively cut any remaining emotional bonds. A small volume she had just published, *Egyptian Magic*, emphasized their divergence in interests, which Shaw seized upon. "What *is* the 'true relation' between us?" he asked, obviously quoting her question. "The relation of the North Pole to the South." But he did not sever relations, suggesting instead future bicycle rides and other contacts.

16   [The play progresses—the new one—the melodrama. . . . I sit in a little hole of a room off Euston Road on a corner of a table with an easel propped before me so that I can write and be painted at the same time. This keeps me at work; and the portrait, for which I have to pay the artist's top price for millionaires (£5), is to make her fortune when exhibited.]

> Shaw to Ellen Terry, 16 October 1896 (*CL*). The young artist painting Shaw was Nellie Heath, who had studied under Walter Sickert. Her picture was not accepted for exhibition.)

17 [I . . . approach *The Red Robe* full of prejudice against it. The very name . . . suggests a companion piece to *The White Silk Dress*. . . . I thought it puerile to the uttermost publishable extreme of jejuniority. . . . Mr. Edward Rose, in dramatizing such a novel, had to dramatize situation without character. . . . Altogether a silly piece of business. Probably it will run for two seasons at least.]

> *Under the Red Robe*, based upon a novel by Stanley Weyman, would run at the Haymarket for 253 performances. G.B.S.'s notice appeared on 24 October (C1168).

18 [ ]

19 [*The Prisoner of Zenda* . . . is now a permanent institution, like Madame Tussaud's. I saw it again the other night, and after *The Red Robe* I do not hesitate to pronounce it a perfectly delectable play.]

> Anthony Hope's novel, also dramatized by Edward Rose, had opened at the St. James's on 7 January 1896 and would run nearly to the end of 1896—255 performances in all. It is assigned a rough date here, based upon Shaw's reviewing deadlines (C1168).

20 [Hyndman attacks me furiously in the *St. James's Gazette* for my "squirting my acidulous mendacity in the face of the dead."]

> Hyndman's spiteful remark appeared on 20 October 1896. Shaw responded in a letter to the editor the next day (C1167).

21 [In *Love in Idleness* . . . the acting success of the play is Mr. De Lange's fire-eating French Colonel, a perfectly original, absolutely convincing and extremely funny version of a part which, in any other hands, would have come out the most hackneyed stuff in the world.]

> *Love in Idleness*, by Louis N. Parker and Edward J. Goodman, would have sixty-five performances at Terry's. A G.B.S. review appeared on 31 October 1896 (C1169).

22–23 [ ]

24 [*His Little Dodge* is . . . a piece of farcical clockwork. . . .]

> Justin H. McCarthy first wanted to title his comedy, adapted from a Feydeau farce, *The Philanderer*, until he heard about Shaw's unproduced play. G.B.S. found it nothing but "sham" (C1169).

25–30 [ ]

31 [I have been up until 3 every morning for a fortnight, and am a miserable spectacle in consequence.]

> Shaw to Charlotte Payne-Townshend, 1 November 1896 (*CL*). He was busy campaigning for Keir Hardie, who was contesting a parliamentary seat in East Bradford. Hardie would be defeated.

November

1–3   [   ]

4   [I came up from Bradford by a slow train after the evening's meeting, starting before 10 & not arriving at Kings + until half past three. . . . I spoke badly & did no good, except by getting the editor of the *Bradford Observer* to promise to insert a letter from me on the election.]

> Shaw to Charlotte Payne-Townshend, 4 November 1896 ((*CL*). ▪ At one in the afternoon Shaw attended a matinee revival of *Donna Diana*, a comedy adapted from the German—itself taken from a Spanish original—by Westland Marston (1820–1890). It would have only two matinees at the Prince of Wales's. G.B.S.'s review, on 7 November 1896 (C1171), found the verse-play "sedately literary."

5   [The reading tonight (of *You Never Can Tell*) was an appalling failure. The play's no use: I looked for my gold and found withered leaves. I must try again & again. I always said I should have to write twenty bad plays before I could write one good one; and yet I'm taken aback to find that number seven is a phantom.]

> Shaw to Ellen Terry, 5 November 1896 (*CL*). ▪ Shaw read the play to Ellen Terry's actress daughter Edy Craig (1869–1947) and her American friend Sally (Satty or Sattie) Fairchild—another practitioner of the Annie Payson Call relaxation system, who was to work on him after the reading.

6–8   [   ]

9   [I shall start on Wednesday morning, and arrive at the Gare du Nord at seven. . . . Return on Friday.]

> Shaw to Bertha Newcombe, 9 November 1896 (*CL*). Miss Newcombe was arranging to stay at Miss Finlayson's English lodging house in Paris, and Shaw would remain there also, although their proximity did nothing to advance her fortunes with Shaw.

10   [   ]

> Charlotte returned from Ireland on this day, and thereafter would take up much of Shaw's time, going with him to plays and other events. This evening they were together at her Adelphi Terrace flat until late.

11   *Start for Paris at 11 from Victoria. Stay at Miss Finlayson's, 9 rue Galilée.*

12   Peer Gynt *at the Nouveaute Theatre, rue Blanche, Paris. 20.15. (Theatre de L'OEuvre)*
[Well, I have been to Paris, and seen "Peer Gynt" done in the sentimentallest French style with tenpenceworth of scenery, and the actor manager in

two nameless minor parts. . . . The scene where Solveig joins Peer in the mountains touched everybody to the marrow. The scene of the mother's death (with the lights going wrong, and everything as ridiculous as possible) was . . . enormously effective. . . .]

Shaw reviewed the Lugné-Poe production in *SR* 21 November 1896 (C1174), in which allowances were made for all the apparent defects in the production, which were seen as overshadowed by the history-making fact of performance. M. Lugné-Poe could not help presenting the play "sentimentally and sublimely" in the French manner, "but the universality of Ibsen makes his plays come home to all nations; and Peer Gynt is as good a Frenchman as a Norwegian. . . ." ▪ Shaw to Ellen Terry, 16 November 1896 (*CL*), is the source of "I have been to Paris."

13 *Fabian Executive and Committee. 17. Fabian Meeting at Clifford's Inn. Sidney Webb on [Trade-Union Democracy]. Start from the Gare du Nord at 9.*

Sidney Webb's talk would be published in abbreviated form in the *Political Science Quarterly* of December 1896.

14 [ ]

15 SUNDAY *Lecture on "Repairs and Alterations in Socialism" at Kelmscott House, Hammersmith Socialist Society. 20. Lunch at Webbs' as usual. Call for Miss Payne Townshend at 10 Adelphi Terrace at 19.*

16 [Cold much worse. . . .]

Shaw to Charlotte Payne-Townshend, 16 November 1896 (*CL*).

17 [ ]

18 [I have to go to the Lamoureux concert. . . .]

Shaw to Charlotte Payne-Townshend, 17 November 1896, referring to the following night (*CL*). The Concerts Nouveaux of Charles Lamoureux (1834–1899) were called by Shaw (to Charlotte, 18 Nov 96, *CL*) as "worth hearing as a French piece of musical machinery." In *SR* (C1174) he observed that M. Lamoureux could not help conducting the overture to *Tannhäuser* "as if it were the *Marseillaise*."

19 [*A White Elephant* at the Comedy is as pleasant as Mr. Carton's plays usually are, but has their easy-going defect of not making the most either of itself or the cast.]

R. C. Carton's farce was reviewed on 5 December 1896 (C1176). With veteran Charles Brookfield in the lead, it would have ninety-nine performances.

20–22 [ ]

23 [*Little Eyolf* . . . began at the Avenue Theatre. . . . that dress circle was odiously stuffy.]

> From the *SR* notice, 12 December 1896 (C1177). ▪ Shaw to Charlotte Payne-Townshend, 23 November 1896 (*CL*). It was not only the atmosphere that was bad: by the time of publication—28 November—of Shaw's initial review, predictably praising Janet Achurch in the lead (C1175), she had been replaced by the more commercial Mrs. Patrick Campbell, at whom Shaw then slashed (C1177) on the grounds of pandering to the box office. However, Miss Achurch, Shaw knew, was at least as wrong for the role as Mrs. Pat. There were only thirty further performances, a disappointing run for someone of Mrs. Campbell's audience appeal.

24–26 [   ]

27 [At Drury Lane we have had another drama, ostensibly by George Grant and James Lisle, but really, I suppose, by Mr. John Coleman. . . . Altogether a horribly bad play.]

> *The Kiss of Delilah* managed only two performances. John Coleman (1832–1904), man-ager of the Drury Lane, was known as a hack playwright who used pseudonyms, and the alleged co-authors of *Delilah* were names that had not appeared before and would not appear afterwards. An unpublished letter to Charles Charrington, 26 November 1896, establishes Shaw's attendance at the Drury Lane as the evening of 27 November.

28–29 [   ]

30 [I finished my play today. . . . Three acts, six scenes, a masterpiece completed in a few weeks, with a trip to Paris and those Ibsen articles thrown in—articles which were so overwritten that I cut out & threw away columns. Not to mention the Bradford election.

. . . The play only exists as a tiny scrawl in my note books—things I carry about in my pockets. I shall have to revise it & work out all the stage business, besides reading up the history of the American War of Independence before I can send it to the typist to be readably copied. Meanwhile, I can read it to Terriss, and to other people. . . .]

> Shaw to Ellen Terry, 30 November 1896 (*CL*). Shaw's four stenographic notebooks con-taining *The Devil's Disciple* are BL Add. MS. 50606–A–D.

December

1 [   ]

2 *Lecture on "The Jevonian Theory of Value" at the Economics Club, Bor-ough Rd. Polytechnic, at 20. Room 9 (D. J. Dorcey, sec.).*

[Mr. George Alexander . . . gives us *As You Like It* at full four hours' length. . . . This production . . . , though the longest, is infinitely the least tedious, and, in those parts which depend on the management, the most delightful I have seen.]

Reviewed on 5 December 1896 (C1174).

3–4 [ ]

5 [I am going straight back to Fitzroy Sq to work on Webb's chapter.]

The Webbs were still working on the book *Industrial Democracy*, which would be completed in the first months of 1897.

6–7 [ ]

8 [*Little Eyolf,* . . . at the Avenue Theatre . . . has been promoted into a full-blown fashionable theatrical speculation, with a *Morocco Bound* syndicate in the background. . . . Mrs. Patrick Campbell has entered thoroughly into the spirit of the alterations.]

Janet Achurch was dropped from the cast after the performance of 6 December. Mrs. Campbell had been eager to move to the lead role after playing a minor one, the Rat Wife, and the new backers of the play, the syndicate producing the long-running musical *Morocco Bound*, knew Mrs. Pat was more reliable and more popular at the box office. Rushing in under-rehearsed as Rita Allmers, she had to play the third act with her playbook hanging from a ribbon around her waist. G.B.S.'s review of her version of the play, "Ibsen without Tears," appeared on 12 December 1896 (C1177).

9 [I have been working for twelve hours, with no variety except lunch and the publishing committee. Theatre last night, and after it a frightful altercation with Archer until about 2 o'clock. . . .]

Shaw to Charlotte Payne-Townshend, 9 December 1896 (*CL*). Shaw's argument with Archer (who thoroughly disliked Janet Achurch) was over Mrs. Campbell's playing of the lead in *Little Eyolf* as compared to Mrs. Charrington's earlier version.

10 [The Lyceum. . . . My stall is F.18.]

Shaw to Charlotte Payne-Townshend, 9 December 1896 (*CL*). On the 10th Shaw took Charlotte to see Ellen Terry play Imogen in *Cymbeline*.

11–13 [ ]

14 [The latest exploit of the Elizabethan Stage Society—its performance of *The Two Gentlemen of Verona* in a City Company's hall in Threadneedle Street. It seems to me that Mr. Poel has now abandoned himself wholly to his fancy in dresses and equipments and stage business.]

The date of Shaw's attendance is unclear but very likely the 14th or 15th. His brief notice appeared on 19 December 1896 (C1178).

15   [There is a publishing committee meeting tomorrow at 4.30.]

Shaw to Charlotte Payne-Townshend, 15 December 1896 (*CL*), on his regular commitment to the Fabian Publishing Committee, which reviewed the development of *Tracts*.

16–18   [   ]

19   [*Richard III* ... was—well, it was Lyceum Shakespear.]

Reviewed on 26 December 1896 (C1180). Shaw thought Irving's production was his usual fustian, emphasized further by textual cuts.

20   [   ]

21   [*The Eider Down Quilt*, at Terry's, a somewhat artlessly amusing piece, owes a good deal to the genius of Miss Fanny Brough as a lady who has, as she believes, sat on a man and smothered him. . . .]

Reviewed on 2 January 1897 (C1182). The farce by Tom S. Wotton would have ninety-nine performances. Fanny Brough (1854–1914) would play Mrs. Warren in the "private" Stage Society production of Shaw's play in 1902.

22   [   ]

23   [The new bill at the Adelphi should not be missed. . . . *All that Glitters is not Gold* is a most fearful specimen of obsolete pinchbeck. . . . But what one goes for is *Black-Ey'd Susan*, . . . the real original. . . .]

The 1829 *Black-Ey'd Susan*, by Douglas Jerrold (1803–1857), remained to G.B.S. (C1182) "an excellent play." It was teamed with an 1851 drama by the author of the famous *Box and Cox*—J. Maddison Morton. Because of special matinees, *Black-Ey'd Susan* would run 118 performances, eight more than *All that Glitters is not Gold*.

24   [When I saw a stage version of *The Pilgrim's Progress* announced for production, I shook my head, knowing that Bunyan is far too great a dramatist for our theatre. . . . The Anglo-American Theatrical Syndicate, Limited, . . . has introduced the entertainment at the Olympic described as *The Pilgrim's Progress*, a mystery play. . . . Three of the scenes are called Vanity Fair, The Valley of the Shadow of Death, and Doubting Castle, from which Christian escapes with the key called Promise. I fancied, too, I detected a paraphrase of a Bunyan passage. . . . But these points apart, it would not have occurred to me that Mr. Collingham or anyone else connected with the Olympic production had ever read or heard of Bunyan.]

The drama founded upon *The Pilgrim's Progress*, attributed to George G. Collingham, was actually written by a wealthy dilettante, Mary Helen White (?–1923). It would survive for twelve performances. G.B.S.'s notice (C1182) mentioned "a lady of private means."

25–27   [   ]

28 [The afternoon performances of *Love in Idleness* at Terry's now begin with Mrs. Oscar Beringer's adaptation of *Boots at the Holly Tree Inn*. . . . It is very prettily done. . . .]

> The dramatization of Charles Dickens' story received two lines from G.B.S. (C1182). It survived for thirty matinees.

29 [*Betsy* has been revived at the Criterion to give Mr. Wyndham a holiday. . . . I enjoyed *Betsy*, which, though funny, is somewhat too pre-Ibsenite for my taste.]

> F. C. Burnand's *Betsy* received two polite lines from G.B.S. (C1182). The adaptation of the French *Bébé* would run for forty-seven performances.

30 [   ]

31 [I have been frightfully rushed by the theatres and by Peterborough Cathedral unfortunately, or I would not be in this helpless state of arrear.]

> Shaw to Frederick Whelen, 1 January 1897 (*CL*), referring to a heavy Christmas season of plays, and to Shaw's involvement with a protest campaign about the plans of the dean of Peterborough to "restore" the west front of the cathedral and rebuild the central tower. In the final days of the year, Shaw drafted the article with the assistance of architect Philip Webb (1831–1915), an old friend of William Morris's. It was published in *SR* on 2 January 1897 as "Must Peterborough Perish?" (C1181) and was credited to "Architect."

Notes

January

Date		£ s d			
1	*The Saturday Review* (November)	£ 1 . 0 . 0			30 0 0
4	London & County Bank		67 1 0		67 1 0
	Lodged		30 0 0		
			97 1 0		
	Dft Q 99668 (68) dated 31st Dec.	1 . 1 . 0			
1	" 9 (69)	5 . 5 . 0	7 6 0		
"	" 70 (70)		89 15 0		
7	" 71 (71)	£ 10 . 0 . 0			
8	" 72 (72)	13 . 3 . 4			
16	" 73 (73)	20 . 0 . 0			
21	" 74 (74)	3 . 0 . 0	46 3 4		43 11 8

February

Date		£ s d			
3	*The Melbourne Argus*				12 0 0
12	" *Contemporary Review*				21 0 0
18	" *Saturday Review* (December)				24 0 0
3	London & County Bank		43 11 8		43 11 8
	Lodged		12 0 0		
			55 11 8		
12	Dft No Q 99675 (75)		25 0 0		
			30 11 8		
13	Lodged	£ 21 . 0 . 0	45 0 0		75 11 8
19	"	24 . 0 . 0			

Date	Item	Ref	£ s d (col 1)	£ s d (col 2)	£ s d (col 3)
March					
10	*The Savoy*				18 12 0
14	Miss Elis. Marbury, royalties on performance of *Arms & The Man* at Kansas City on 21st Feb. (Richard Mansfield).				9 3 7
					5 0 0
21	*The Daily Chronicle*				75 11 8
5	London & County Bank			75 11 8	
	Dft Q 99676 (76)			10 0 0	
				65 11 8	
6	" (77)		£ 1 . 1 . 0		
	" (78)		2 . 2 . 0		
	" (79)		25 . 0 . 0	28 3 0	
				37 8 8	
10	Lodged			18 12 0	
				56 0 8	
12	Dft (80)			2 2 0	
				53 18 8	
16	Lodged			9 3 7	
				63 2 3	
30	Dft (81)			25 0 0	
				38 2 3	
April					
4	Miss Marbury (for R. Mansfield) royalties on performances of *Arms & The Man* at Chicago, 9th March $866.25 & 14th March $1067.75				38 2 3
17	*The Saturday Review* for January				36 5 6
21	" " February (including review)				24 0 0
	All the above items are included in the Income Tax return for 1895–6				35 0 0

		£	s	d	£	s	d
9	London & County Bank						
	Lodged	38	2	3	38	2	3
		41	5	6			
		79	7	9			
10	Dft N. Q. 99682 (82) £ 1 . 1 . 0						
17	" 3 . 8 . 6	4	9	6			
		74	18	3			
"	Lodged	24	0	0			
		98	18	3			
21	"	35	0	0			
		133	18	3	133	18	3

May

4	R. Mansfield for Miss Marbury, 1st instalment of $500 due for performances of *Arms & The Man* last year, the returns for which are missing	18	14	9	18	14	9
21	Walter Scott, royalties on *Quintessence of Ibsenism* to 3rd March	1	10	6	1	10	6

All the above items are included in the Income Tax return 1895–6

9	London & County Bank	£ 133	18	3	133	18	3
	Dft Q99684 (84)	25	0	0			
		108	18	3			
14	Lodged	18	14	9			
		127	13	0	127	13	0

June

4	*The Star*	127	13	0	3	3	0
					127	13	0
5	London & County Bank						
	Dft Q. 99685 (85) 25 . 0 . 0						
	" (86) 5 . 0 . 0						
	" (87) 1 . 17 . 0						
	" (88) 5 . 0 . 0	36	17	3	90	15	9

Date	Description	Detail		
July				
15	*The Saturday Review* (March & April)			48 0 0
16	" (May & June)			54 0 0
	(Half the first item above is included in the 1895–6 In Tax return)			
	London & County Bank		90 15 9	90 15 9
5	Dft No. Q 99689 (89)	£ 6 . 13 . 4		
6	" (90)	25 . 0 . 0		
16	" (91)	4 . 0 . 0		
25	" (92)	25 . 0 . 0		
	" (93)	25 . 0 . 0	83 13 4	
			5 2	
5	Lodged	£ 9 . 16 . 4		
15	"	58 . 0 . 0		
16	"	54 . 0 . 0	121 16 4	126 18 9
August				
6	*The Star* (Bayreuth & the International Soc[ia]l[i]st Congress)			37 18 6
	London & County Bank		£ 126 18 9	129 18 9
1	Dft Q 99694 (94)		21 0 0	
			105 18 9	
8	Lodged		37 18 6	
			143 17 3	
11	Dft " 95 (95)	7 . 18 . 1		
27	" " 96 (96)	7 . 1 . 6	14 19 7	128 17 8

Date	Particulars	£ . s . d			
September					
4	*The Star*				4 4 0
	London & County Bank		128	17	8	128 17 8
11	Lodged		4	4	0	
			133	1	8	
11	Dft No Q 99697 (97)	6 . 0 . 0			
	" 98 (98)	5 . 0 . 0			
	" 99 (99)	25 . 0 . 0	36	0	0	97 1 8
October					
4	*Cosmopolis*				20 0 0
14	*The Saturday Review* (July & Aug.)				54 0 0
	London & County Bank		97	1	8	97 1 8
8	Lodged		24	7	7	
			121	9	3	
15	"		54	0	0	
			175	9	3	
16	Dft No Q 99700 (100)		5	0	0	
	" S.88101 (101)	£ 2 . 0 . 0	170	9	3	170 9 3
	" 2 (102)	25 . 0 . 0	27	0	0	143 9 3
November					
5	*The Saturday Review* (Sept.)				24 0 0
24	*Die Zeit* (Vienna)				3 6 7
6	London & County Bank		143	9	3	143 9 3
	Lodged		24	0	0	
			167	9	3	
9	Dft No. S.88153 (103)	10 . 0 . 0			
	" (104)	25 . 0 . 0	35	0	0	132 9 3

December

		£	s	d
18	*The Saturday Review* (for Oct.)	30	0	0
21	Richard Mansfield for Miss Marbury, balance of $500 agreed on as the equivalent for the royalties on *Arms & The Man*, season 1894–5, the returns for which were lost.	75	6	8

7   London & County Bank
    Dft S88105 (105) 132 9 3

```
            132   9   3
              1   1   0
            131   8   3
            105   6   8
            236  14  11
             15   9   9
            252   0   9
```

21 Lodged

				£	s	d			
22	"			£					
"	Dft	"	(106)	25	. 9 . 0				
"	"	"	(107)	15	. 0 . 0				
31	"	"	(108)	2	.10 . 9				
"	"	"	(109)	1	. 1 . 0				

```
             44   0   9     208   3   2
```

Diary 1897

January

1 [Tomorrow is a first night at the Avenue.]

> Shaw to Charlotte Payne-Townshend, 1 January 1897 (*CL*). The play was the musical farce by Huan Mee (an obvious pseudonym), *A Man about Town*, about which G.B.S. wrote on 9 January 1897 (C1183), "There is nothing left to judge [the plotless farce] by, except the players." The music was by Alfred Carpenter, a veteran conductor and composer of theater music. There would be twenty-two performances.

2 [I am . . . to occupy myself with the American war and other follies. . . .]

> Shaw to Charlotte Payne-Townshend, 1 January 1897 (*CL*), about plans for the next day. Shaw was researching the American Revolution for background detail for *The Devil's Disciple*, and Charlotte was locating books for him.

3–6 [   ]

7 [I have worked continuously since I came down to breakfast, save only during my lunch at six.]

Shaw to Charlotte Payne-Townshend, 7 January 1897 (*CL*). He was busy with journalism and criticism, including a review for *The Academy* (16 January 1897) of William Archer's translation of Ibsen's *John Gabriel Borkman* (C1184).

8 [There is a play without words at the Prince of Wales's Theatre, entitled *A Pierrot's Dream*, . . . a very delectable entertainment.]

Reviewed as the tailpiece to G.B.S.'s 16 January 1897 *SR* column (C1185). The wordless pierrot play, with music by Michael Costa, had ninety-one performances, mostly matinees.

9 *Go down to Manchester by the 14.10 train from Euston and stay at Charles Hughes's.*

Charles Hughes, a Fabian, had formed a Manchester branch of the Independent Theatre, which was then presenting Janet Achurch in *Antony and Cleopatra*.

10 SUNDAY *Lecture on "Repairs and Alterations in Socialism" at the New Islington Hall, Ancoats, Manchester, at 18 (Charles Hughes, Kersal, Manchester).*

11 *Come up from Manchester by the 10 train.*

12 [*The Sorrows of Satan* . . . has not called forth any great display of acting at the Shaftesbury.]

Marie Corelli's novel, turned into a four-act melodrama by Herbert Woodgate and Paul Berton, would have fifty performances.

13–14 [ ]

15 [The executive agenda is ten miles long, and the usual retirement to Gatti & Rodesano's will be part of it—possibly the most important part, after . . . Charrington's . . . Municipal Theatre lecture.]

Shaw to Charlotte Payne-Townshend, 15 January 1897 (*CL*), referring to the same day's activities. Charles Charrington's talk was the formal program after the Executive session.

16 [ ]

"What It Feels Like to be Successful," signed by "Corno di Bassetto," was published in *The Star* this date (C1186).

17–18 [ ]

19 [Being no pantomime goer, I never saw one of Mr. Oscar Barrett's pantomimes until I went to *Aladdin*; so I am perhaps unwittingly disparaging his former achievements when I say it is the best modern Christmas pantomime I have seen.]

SR, 23 January 1897 (C1187). The pantomime with music by Oscar Barrett (1846–1941) had opened on 26 December 1896 and would run 138 performances. Decima Moore was the leading lady.

20–23   [   ]

24 SUNDAY   *Lecture at Croydon, Theatre Royal, Crown Hill, at 19 on "Confessions of a Socialist." (G. Tarry, 122 North End, Croydon).*

25–26   [   ]

27   [K . . . goes anon to the west of Ireland.]

The alcoholic Kate Gurly was the despair of 29 Fitzroy Square. Shaw's relief was registered in a letter to Ellen Terry, 27 January 1897 (*CL*). To Charlotte on 4 February 1897 (*CL*) Shaw noted that Kate had been "sent off like a parcel" in a state of "inclination."

28   [*The Free Pardon* . . . at the Olympic is one of those melodramas which produce no illusion, but which, played with well-known incidents and situations according to certain rules, are now watched by adept playgoers with the same interest that a football match creates.]

Reviewed on 6 February 1897 (C1189). The play, by F. C. Philips (1848–1921) and Leonard Merrick (1864–1939), survived only fifteen performances.

29   [   ]

30   [I have two stalls for the Lyceum . . . (first night of "Olivia") . . .]

Shaw to Charlotte Payne-Townshend, 28 January 1897 (*CL*). Charlotte, however, did not attend with G.B.S. who reviewed the revival of the stage version of Goldsmith's *The Vicar of Wakefield*, starring Ellen Terry, on 6 February 1897 (C1189).

31 SUNDAY   *Read* Devil's Disciple *at Pagets', 76 Park Rd., Haverstock Hill, N.W. 18¼.*

Presumably Florence Farr was at her sister's new home for the reading; Shaw cautiously mentioned (*CL*) only York Powell as guest in writing to Charlotte on 28 January 1897.

February

1   [*The Prodigal Father*, at the Strand, is a lively piece, without any other particular merit.]

The play, by Glen MacDonough (1867–1924), had a strong cast that G.B.S. described (C1189) as "more or less underparted." There would be fifty-eight performances.

2 [   ]

3 *Dine with [Richard Burdon] Haldane, 3 Whitehall Court, at 20.*

4 [   ]

5 *Address the National Individualist Club, Palace Chambers, on "The Extreme Desirability of Socialism from the Individualist Point of View" at 20. (Fred Millar, Sec.)*

6 [Mr. Wilson Barrett has found that he can always bring down the house with a hymn: the first act of *The Daughters of Babylon*, after driving the audience nearly to melancholy madness by its dulness, is triumphantly saved in that way.]

> The melodrama, reviewed in G.B.S.'s column as "Mr. Barrett as the Messiah," on 13 February 1897 (C1192), would have seventy-four performances. It was greeted by audience hooting at the alleged sacrilege.

7 [   ]

8 [A good deal of *Sweet Nancy* is highly diverting; Miss Hughes's personal success is unquestionable; and the little play by Mrs. Oscar Beringer, called *A Bit of Old Chelsea*, must well be worth seeing if it is all as good as the last five minutes of it. I arrived too late to be able to answer for the earlier passages.]

> *Sweet Nancy* was Robert Buchanan's dramatization of a novel by Rhoda Broughton. The double-bill, with the curtain-raiser sometimes not played, had ninety-two performances. G.B.S.'s review was on 20 February 1897 (C1194).

9–10 [   ]

11 [*Nelson's Enchantress* . . . is a mere waxwork. . . . Mrs. Patrick Campbell, in a wig so carefully modelled on that head of hair which is one of Elizabeth Robins's most notable graces that for a moment I could hardly decide whether I was looking at Miss Robins made up like Mrs. Campbell or Mrs. Campbell made up like Miss Robins, is a charming Lady Hamilton.]

> The play about Nelson, by Risden Home—whose only play this was, although Shaw (C1194) saw promise in his work—had forty performances at the Avenue.

12 [   ]

13 [*My Friend the Prince*, at the Garrick, is a farce in three acts—just two acts too long for a farce.]

Justin Huntly McCarthy's play was based on an American farce, *My Friend from India*. It would run most of the year—175 performances. G.B.S., however, thought that McCarthy was wasting his talent (C1194).

14 SUNDAY *Lecture for the S.D.F., Bow and Bromley Branch, 193 Bow Rd., E., at 20, on "Confessions of a Socialist."*

15 [ ]

16 *Lecture at Murphy Memorial Hall, Gurney St., New Kent Rd., at 20.15, on "Modern Socialism."*

17 [ ]

18 *Call at Mrs. Patrick Campbell's, 10 Mandeville Place, at 15, and read* The Devil's Disciple *to her and Forbes Robertson.*

19 *Haymarket Theatre at 11 to settle agreement for* You Never Can Tell. *Society of Women Journalists. Augustine Birrell on "Book Reviewing." 20½.*

Shaw's agreement with Cyril Maude (1862–1951), actor-manager at the Haymarket, resulted in rehearsals but no performance. Maude concluded from Maude's inability to cope with Shavian comedy that cancellation was the prudent course.

20 [Finished the stage business.]

Shaw's note on completing his newest play is from the last page—folio 66—of the fourth notebook of *The Devil's Disciple*, inscribed with this date (Add. MS. 50606D).

21 [ ]

22 [It is now nearly two years since I pointed out . . . that *Mariana* was pre-eminently a play for an actress-manageress to snap up. The only person who appreciated the opportunity in this country was Miss Elizabeth Robins. . . . The performance . . . began unhappily. In the first act everybody seemed afraid to do more than hurry half-heartedly over an exposition which required ease, leisure, confidence, and brightness of comedy style to make it acceptable.]

Mariana, by José Echegaray (1832–1916), was performed in a translation by James Graham. There would be five matinees at the Court Theatre. G.B.S.'s review was dated 27 February 1897 (C1195).

23–24 [ ]

25 [*The Mac Haggis*, at the Globe Theatre, is a wild tale of a prim young London gentleman who suddenly succeeds to the chieftainship of a Highland clan—such a clan as Mr. Jerome K. Jerome might have conceived in a nightmare after reading *Rob Roy*. . . . Although there were no dissentients to the applause at the end of *The Mac Haggis*, the authors did not appear to make the customary acknowledgments. For some time past the gods have been making themselves a more and more insufferable nuisance. The worry of attending first nights has been mercilessly intensified by the horrible noises they offer. . . .]

> The "gods of the gallery" had been disrupting performances at least since the performance of Henry James's *Guy Domville* on 5 January 1895, and cries of "Author!" at the close of first performances were seldom now being responded to by wary playwrights. G.B.S. would take up much of his 6 March 1897 column (C1196), "Gallery Rowdyism," to describe and deplore the phenomenon. The occasion was his review of *The Mac Haggis*, a play by Jerome K. Jerome and Eden Phillpotts (1862–1960), which would have fifty-seven performances.

26–27 [   ]

28 SUNDAY *Lecture at the Town Hall, Poplar, at 16. (F. Butler, Poplar Union Offices, Upper North St., Poplar E.) "Misunderstandings of Socialism."*

March

1–3 [   ]

4 *Lunch with Frank Harris at Willis's Rooms at 13 to meet Sir Charles Dilke.*

> Shaw had met Dilke as early as 1885. He did not lunch with Harris eagerly or often, feeling uncomfortable with Harris's booming voice as well as with Harris's conversation.

5 [I have simply stopped working, except for the inevitable Saturday article. I have been clearing up my table—*such* a job—two long days' work; but the green cloth has been reached at last. Even my bedroom table is clear. Whilst I am dressing & undressing I do all my reading. The book lies open on the table. I never shut it, but put the next book on top of it long before it's finished. After some months there is a mountain of buried books, all wide open; so that all my library is distinguished by a page with the stain of a quarter's dust and soot on it . . . ; for my window is always wide open, winter and summer. . . . A few days ago I met Florence Farr. She was horrified; said I looked my age; pointed out that my moustache and two great tufts of my beard were grey. . . .]

> Shaw to Ellen Terry, 5 March 1897 (CL).

6 [ ]

7 SUNDAY   *Lecture at Stanley Hall, Junction Rd. (Archway or Boston bus) at 19, on "Modern Socialism" (H. J. Masters, 160 High St., Camden Town, N.W.).*

8 [I am in a ridiculous difficulty with Miss P.T. She insists on coming to my lectures on Sundays in all sorts of holes & corners—dock gates next Sunday morning.]

> Shaw to Ellen Terry, 8 March 1897 (*CL*). Shaw noted further to Ellen Terry that his "demagogic denunciations of the idle rich" must "lacerate" Charlotte's conscience. Beatrice Webb would write in her diary the next day about returning a copy of Shaw's novel *An Unsocial Socialist* to Bertha Newcombe, "a sad soul full of bitterness and loneliness" because of Shaw's loss of interest in her. She told Beatrice of her "five years of devoted love, his cold philandering, her hopes aroused . . . , and then her feeling of misery and resentment against me when she discovered that I was encouraging him 'to marry Miss Townshend.' Finally, he had written a month ago to break it off entirely.. . ." That Bertha had ignored Shaw's other female interests, including his long intimacy with Florence Farr and his devotion to Janet Achurch, seems an exercise in self-deception. "You are well out of it," said Beatrice. "If you had married Shaw he would not have remained faithful to you." And she described him as a friend and colleague for whom she had a "warm" affection while recognizing that with women he was guilty of "a vulgarity that includes cruelty and springs from vanity." As she left, her eye caught Bertha's "platform spellbinder" portrait of Shaw, "full-length, with his red-gold hair and laughing blue eyes and his mouth slightly open as if scoffing at us both, a powerful picture in which the love of the woman had given genius to the artist." She escaped down the stairs.

9 [*The Mariners of England*, the new Nelson play at the Olympic, is a frankly cynical exploitation of cant, claptrap, and playgoers' folly by Mr. Robert Buchanan, in collaboration with "Charles Marlowe."]

> *The Mariners of England*, reviewed on 13 March (C1197), would survive for twenty-four performances.

10 [*Saucy Sally*, a farce in three acts, by F. C. Burnand . . . is a farcical comedy of the well-worn kind, about a gentleman who keeps two establishments. . . . It is always amusing to see Mr. Hawtrey lying his way in and out of domestic complications. His cleverness, tact, and humor are in constant play, . . . but he needs them all to play up to Mrs. Charles Calvert, whose performance as the mother-in-law is a triumph from the first look to the last word. I had not the advantage of seeing Mrs. Calvert's Cleopatra thirty years ago; but if she was as incomparably the first actress in her line then as she is now, I deeply regret my loss.]

> *Saucy Sally*, an adaptation of Maurice Hennequin's *La Flamboyante*, would have 110 performances at the Comedy. G.B.S.'s praise (C1197) of Mrs. Charles Calvert (1847–1921) suggested that he had not seen her act before, although she had played Mrs. Catherine Petkoff (Raina's mother) in *Arms and the Man* in 1894.

11 [ ]

12 *Early to Fabian Executive—take the chair.*

13 [I have . . . to go to the Haymarket to see the scene models for that wretched comedy.]

You Never Can Tell, which was already giving Cyril Maude second thoughts.

14 SUNDAY *Speak at the Dock Gates, 11.45, on "The Use of Political Power," for the Poplar Labour League (Alf. Graham, 175 Abbott Rd., E.).*

15 [I shall travel down to Manchester . . . tomorrow by the 10.10 from Euston. . . .]

Shaw apparently was the guest of Charles Hughes for several days in Manchester, and saw the play Tuesday the 16th, as his review of the Louis Calvert production appeared in SR on 20 March 1897 (C1198).

16 [Janet Achurch, now playing Cleopatra in Manchester, . . . carries out her original and often audacious conception of Shakespearean music. . . . The lacerating discord of her wailings is in my tormented ears as I write, reconciling me to the grave.]

He found Janet's performance "thoroughly wrong from beginning to end" and would continue to find her onstage and offstage behavior perversely self-destructive.

17–24 [ ]

25 [Half Mr. Jones's play—the women's half—is obliterated in performance.]

H. A. Jones's The Physician had opened at the Criterion Theatre, where it would run for seventy-eight performances. The lead was played by Mary Moore, a light comedienne too light for the role; G.B.S. wrote on 3 April (C1200): "My friend Jones, who would have made an excellent Dissenting clergyman, has a vulgar habit of bringing persons indiscriminately to the bar of his convictions as to what is needful for the life and welfare of the real world."

26–28 [ ]

29 [Mr. Pinero gets to business at about ten o'clock, and the play begins in the middle of the third act—a good, old-fashioned, well-seasoned bit of sentimental drawing-room fiction. . . . So, though it is true that the man who goes to the St. James's Theatre at 7.45 will wish he had never been born, none the less will the man who goes at 9.30 spend a very pleasant evening.]

Pinero's *The Princess and the Butterfly* dealt with the flight of youth and the onset of age forty, which G.B.S. saw as far from decrepitude. "Well, my own opinion," he wrote (C1200), as he approached his 41st birthday, "is that sixty is the prime of life for a man."

30–31   [   ]

April

1   [*The Yashmak* is an exceedingly copious musical hotchpotch in two acts, lasting two hours each. . . . I have seen much worse entertainments. . . . A Miss Aileen d'Orme had the happy idea of singing a song in French, which is evidently by no means her native tongue. The gallery, immensely flattered by the implied compliment to its high-class taste and linguistic accomplishments, applauded chivalrously. . . . I shall not be surprised if it makes its way with less exacting playgoers.]

> *The Yashmak*, by Cecil Raleigh and Seymour Hicks, with music by composer-conductor Napoleon Lambelet (1864–1932), would have 121 performances at the Shaftesbury. G.B.S.'s review appeared on 10 April 1897 (C1201).

2   *Conference of Fabian Society, Independent Labour Party and Social Democratic Federation, at 276 Strand, at 20.*

3   [Mr. Bruckman's galanty show at the reception given by the Dutch Club at Steinway Hall . . . was not dramatic. It is a series of historical illustrations . . . and is distinguished from the old galanty shows only by the decorative grace of the silhouettes, and not by any mechanical ingenuity, it being destitute even of an efficient contrivance for passing the profiles steadily across the screen. I confess I had a childish hope the figures would "work" and perform a little play . . . ; but it was not to be; and pretty as some of the silhouettes were, I cannot deny that I had had enough of them by the time the curtain fell.]

> A galanty show was a shadow play. W. L. Bruckman was one of its dwindling group of practitioners. G.B.S. (C1201) gave the title as *The Sphinx and the Chimney Pot*.

4 SUNDAY   *Lecture at the Town Hall, Turnbridge Wells, at 15, on "The Respectability of Socialism."*

In the weeks that followed, Shaw would be elected to the St. Pancras Vestry and begin spending many hours each frenetic week in municipal affairs, from politics to public lavatories. He would continue (for another year) his rounds of London theaters for the Saturday Review. *He would experience the foundering of hopes to produce* The Man of Destiny *and* You Never Can Tell, *but would permit a provincial tour of* Candida *for Janet Achurch, for whom he had written it; and he would begin writing* Caesar and Cleopatra *for Forbes-Robertson, who had valiantly played Antony to Janet's disastrous Cleopatra in Manchester. He would continue his myriad Fabian involvements, from publishing to proselytizing on spare evenings and Sundays. And he would persist in his cautious courtship of Charlotte, who had now taken over his secretarial work and even typed his plays. (They would be married the next year.) There would be much potential material for a diary, but the discipline of keeping one had disappeared.*

Notes

January

16   The Saturday Review (November)   24 . 0 . 0

18   R. Mansfield for Elisabeth Marbury, royalties on three
     performances of "Arms & The Man" in New York, 7, 11, 12 Ec.   24 . 19 . 0

London & County Bank   208 . 3 . 2

5   Dft S 88160 (110)   £ 2 . 0 . 0
9   "   1 (111)   18 . 14 . 8   20 . 14 . 8
                                                187 . 8 . 6
18 Lodged   48 . 19 . 0
                                               £236 . 7 . 6
22 Dft S 88162 (112)   25 . 0 . 0
     "   (113)   20 . 0 . 0   45 . 0 . 0

February

10   The Saturday Review (December 96)   24 . 0 . 0
"   Grant Richards, for article in "Politics in 1896".   24 . 0 . 0
4   The Academy ("Borkman" review)   5 . 0 . 0

London & County Bank   191 . 7 . 6

6   Dft No S 88164 (114)   £ 3 . 0 . 6
13   "   (115)   10 . 0 . 0
23   "   (116)   20 . 0 . 0   33 . 0 . 6
                                                158 . 7 . 0
11 Lodged   48 . 0 . 0

                                                                        191 . 7 . 6
                                                                        206 . 7 . 0

     Lodgment of £5 on 25th omitted: see March.

March
   The Saturday Review (Jan & on a/c Feb)

   London & County Bank   206 . 7 . 0   33 . 3 . 0
 1   Dft No S 88167 (117)   £ 3 . 14 . 11   206 . 7 . 0
13   "   (118)   3 . 0 . 6
20   "   (119)   10 . 0 . 0
27   "   (120)   20 . 0 . 0   36 . 15 . 5
                                                     169 . 11 . 7
                                                       5 . 0 . 0   174 . 11 . 7

   Lodgment on 25th Feb, omitted by mistake £5 . 0 . 0

April
22 Henry & Co, royalties on sales of "Widowers' Houses" for year ending
        31st Dec. 1896. (6 copies)   2

26 R. Mansfield (direct) royalties on "Arms & The Man" at Chicago on the 5th & 10th
        April & at St Louis on the 14th, less £2 . 12 . 5 com[missio]n to Miss Marbury   32 . 3 . 1
    The Saturday Review, balance for Feb.   20 . 17 . 0
        The 1st & 3rd items above are included in Income Tax Return—1896–7.

                                                                      174 . 11 . 7   174 . 11 . 7

   London & County Bank
 5   Dft No S 88171 (121)   £ 3 . 0 . 6
 "   "   (122)   2 . 2 . 0
 4   "   (123)   3 . 0 . 0
19   "   (124)   1 . 0 . 0
22   "   (125)   5 . 0 . 0
26   "   (126)   2 . 12 . 5   16 . 14 . 11
                                                     157 . 16 . 8

12 Lodged   £ 33 . 3 . 0   65 . 18 . 6   223 . 15 . 2
26   "   32 . 15 . 6

Date	Description	Amount	Subtotal	Total
May				
1	The Daily Mail			2 . 2 . 0
11	The Saturday Review (March)*			24 . 0 . 0
31	Miss Marbury, royalties on "Arms & The Man", Philadelphia, 3 May			10 . 14 . 5
	*Included in In. Tax return for 1896–7			
3	London & County Bank Dft No S 88177 (127)	£ 3 . 15 . 6		223 . 15 . 2
10	" (128)	1 . 2 . 1		
15	" (129)	25 . 0 . 0		
17	" (130)	5 . 0 . 0		
		34 . 17 . 7		
		188 . 17 . 7		
7	Lodged	£ 22 . 17 . 0	46 . 17 . 0	235 . 14 . 7
15	"	24 . 0 . 0		
June				
15	The Saturday Review (April)			24 . 0 . 0
21	R. Mansfield for Miss Marbury, royalties on "Arms & The Man," Pittsburgh, Ap. 21, Cleveland, Ap. 27, Philadelphia May 3			21 . 15 . 4
8?	Boston, 19th May 97			8 . 17 . 11
2	London & County Bank Dft No S 88181 (131)	£ 15 . 0 . 0		235 . 14 . 7
17	" (132)	10 . 0 . 0		
17	" (133)	5 . 0 . 0		
30	" (134)	2 . 15 . 0		
		32 . 15 . 0		
		202 . 19 . 7		
2	Lodged	£ 25 . 18 . 10	71 . 14 . 2	274 . 13 . 9
30	"	45 . 15 . 4		

July
16   The Saturday Review (May)   30 . 0 . 0
                                                         274 . 13 . 9

     London & County Bank
  2   Dft No S 88185 (135)   £25 . 0 . 0
  8   "   (136)   20 . 0 . 0
 13   "   (137)   5 . 0 . 0
 19   "   (138)   24 . 0 . 7
 29   "   (139)   25 . 0 . 0
 30   "   (140)   9 . 11 . 0
                               108 . 11 . 7
                               166 . 2 . 2

  8   Lodged   £20 . 0 . 0   116 . 2 . 2
 16   "   30 . 0 . 0   50 . 0 . 0

August
27   The Saturday Review (June)   24 . 0 . 2
                                                         116 . 2 . 2

     London & County Bank
  1   Dft No S 88191 (141)   £ 1 . 1 . 0   116 . 2 . 2
 11   "   (142)   11 . 1 . 6   14 . 4 . 6
 31   "   (143)   2 . 2 . 0   101 . 17 . 6
                                               44 . 0 . 2

  2   Lodged   £20 . 0 . 2   145 . 17 . 10
 28   "   24 . 0 . 0

September
17   The Saturday Review (July)   30 . 0 . 0
                                                         145 . 17 . 10

     London & County Bank
 14   Dft No S 88194 (144)   £ 5 . 0 . 0   145 . 17 . 10
 17   "   (145)   9 . 0 . 0   14 . 0 . 0
                                              131 . 17 . 10

Date		Description	£ s d (detail)	£ s d	£ s d
17		Lodged	£ 35 . 0 . 0	35 0 0	166 17 10
	October				
25		The Saturday Review (August)			24 0 0
		London & County Bank			
2		Dft No S 88196 (146)	£ 10 . 0 . 0	166 17 10	166 17 10
"		" (147)	10 . 0 . 0		
5		" (148)	10 . 0 . 0		
19		" (149)	1 .10 . 0		
20		" (150)	25 . 0 . 0	56 10 0	
				110 7 10	
25		Lodged	£34 . 0 . 0	34 0 0	144 7 10
	November				
3		Miss Marbury, royalties on performances of "The Devil's Disciple" at Albany on the 1st Oct (first performance) and in New York (5th Av. Theatre) for the week ending 9th Oct—7 performances, including Saturday matinee			168 16 4
4		The Star			2 2 0
10		Miss Marbury, as above, performances for week ending 16th Oct (incl. Sat. mat[in]ee)			147 5 2
17		" " " 23rd Oct ")			134 8 10
24		" " " 30 " ")			111 15 0
29		" " " 6 Nov. ")			112 2 1
2		Henry & Co, royalties on sales of "Widowers' Houses" to date. (This payment I accepted as closing our accounts on their retirement from business, taking their surrender of the agreement as an equivalent for royalties on the remainder (194 copies in sheets) handed over by them to Southeran & Co, and valued at £2.)			

Date	Description	£ s d	Draft (£ . s . d)	
4	London & County Bank Dft No U 84451 (151)	144 7 10		144 7 10
4	Lodged	10 0 0		
4	"	134 7 10		
"	"	178 16 4		
"		313 4 2		
"	Dft " (152)	2 2 0		
		315 4 2		
10		1 1 0		
		314 3 2		
17	" " (153)	147 5 2		
		461 8 4		
"	Lodged	25 0 0		
		436 8 4		
18	Dft " (154)	134 8 10	£ 13 . 10 . 0	
19	" " (155)	570 17 2	5 . 0 . 0	
23	" " (156)		25 . 0 . 0	
25	" " (157)		1 . 1 . 0	
"	" " (158)		1 . 0 . 0	
"	Lodged	45 11 0	£111 . 15 . 0	
29		525 6 2		
		225 17 11	114 . 2 . 11	751 4 1

December				
7	The Saturday Review (Sep. & Oct.)			54 0 0
16	Miss Marbury (for R. Mansfield) royalties on performances of "The Devil's Disciple" at the 5th Avenue Theatre, New York, for the week ending 13 Nov., including Sat mat.			83 7 2
22	" 20 "			89 12 1

		London & County Bank					
3	Lodged	£– . 6 . 6			751	4	1
8	"	64 . 0 . 0					
16	"	83 . 7 . 2	147	13	8	751	4	1
			898	17	9			
4	Dft No U 84459 (159)	£ 10 . 0 . 0					
6	" (160)	5 . 0 . 0					
14	" (161)	25 . 0 . 0					
15	" (162)	5 . 0 . 0					
17	" (163)	21 . 0 . 0					
22	" (164)	10 . 0 . 0					
24	" (165)	1 . 5 . 0					
"	" (166)	1 . 1 . 0	78	6	10			
			820	10	11			
26	Lodged	£113 . 15 . 5	123	15	5	944	6	4
28	"	10 . 0 . 0					

G.B.S. Confesses. A Day in the Life of the Busy Critic, Novelist, Playwright, and Socialist

Shaw's unsigned spoof diary entry of a "typical day" appeared in the Daily Mail *on 2 April 1901 (C1361), complete with an illustration showing "once round the clock with Mr. George Bernard Shaw, the well-known novelist, playwright, critic, and socialist." As the daily log suggests, beneath the levity, Shaw was then a hard-working St. Pancras Borough Councillor.*

Mr. Bernard Shaw, critic, novelist, playwright, and Socialist, is nothing if not normal.

He is a vegetarian, teetotaler, and non-smoker. He clothes himself in Jaeger from boots to hat, and his views on things in general are different from other people's.

Incidentally he is an Irishman and a member of the St. Pancras Borough

Council; while it was recently announced that he proposed adding to the calls upon his time by taking up market gardening.

Before his marriage Mr. Shaw used to lie in bed all the morning writing humorous letters on a typewriter balanced on his knees. He has reformed, however, for this is how, he confessed to a "Daily Mail" reporter, he now spends his day, and it will be seen that little time remains for market gardening or anything else.

8 o'clock.—Called. Resolve to get up.

8.1.—Go to sleep again.

8.30—Awakened by remorse. Am convinced that I have slept two hours. Try to look at my watch. Fall asleep again in the act.

9.0—Awakened as before. Reproach myself for laziness. Make plans for early rising in future. Interrupted by breakfast bell.

9.01—Dash out of bed. Air bath. Exercise. Cold-water bath. Looking-glass (twenty minutes). Down to breakfast.

9.30—Breakfast. Porridge, Apple, Cocoa. Newspapers. Resolve to give up newspapers as they deprave the freshness of my morning mind. Read letters and mislay them. Repeat this at every post during the day.

10.30—To literary work (except when there is a play to rehearse until luncheon 1.30) with the following interruptions:—

11.30—"Daily Mail" interviewer. Trade Union question. What are my views?

11.45—American interviewer. Local Government of America; wants to know what I meant last time.

12.0—Another Yankee interviewer. Shakespeare wants to know whether I think "As You Like It" or "The School for Scandal" his best play.

12.15—Another American interviewer. Will I give him a few thousand words on my private opinion of Edward VII?

12.30—Local politician. Will I contest the parliamentary seat in his district at the next election? Working Classes, Trade Unionists, Co-operators, Socialists, and Liberals unanimous in my favour. Victory certain with a really good candidate like myself. Liberal Whip promises party support and special letter from Campbell-Bannerman. Figures at last election: Conservative, 7,452; Liberal 323, two Independents 37 between them, Labour man 102, rival Labour man 7, Socialist (S.D.F.) 150, Socialist I.L.P. 134, Socialist (Freedom Group) 22, Temperance 6. Defeat attributed by Liberals to split vote—really a moral victory for forces of Progress.

12:45—Another "Daily Mail" interviewer. Trade Union question again. Retires with clenched teeth on being informed that he has been anticipated by a colleague.

1.0—Boy-messenger with note from Strand Liberal and Radical Association. Will I consent to receive a deputation to request me to be their candidate for etc., etc. Magnanimously suggest somebody else.

1.15—Another American interviewer. Will I say just what I please to him? I do.

1.30—Luncheon (during which interviewers accumulate in drawing-room and study). Really my dinner, but called luncheon in deference to social prejudices. Vegetarian, of course: that is, ordinary dinner, but without either meat, fish, soup, or vegetables.

2.15—Decline interviewing as the borough council meets at three. American reporter will not be denied—wants to know is it true that Sir Henry Irving is going to produce my well-known play, "A Doll's House." Tell him that it is not the "Doll's House," but a new one called "She Stoops to Conquer." He notes the name, thanks me, and retires.

3.0 to midnight.—St. Pancras Borough Council. Great strain on my tact. Have to convince my fellow-councillors that I never waste time, speak but seldom, and then very briefly and to the point. In order to do this I have to get up and address them, on an average, eight times per hour.

3.30—"Daily Mail" interviewer sends in his card. Wants to see me in my new robes. Explain to him that I have no robes; that the aldermanic proposal to robe me has been overwhelmingly defeated on the ground that I am conceited enough already; that the unfounded reports to the contrary are the work of a former interviewer. He says he has come a long way, and will I at least explain the housing question to him. I plead an urgent division and escape.

4.—American interviewer's card brought in by beadle. Will I give him my frank opinion as to the merits or demerits of Monarchy and Republicanism, with a few anecdotes told in my own inimitable style as to the private morals of the British aristocracy. I persuade him to go into the rate-payers' gallery and do a descriptive report of the proceedings of the council. He goes, and has the whole gallery to himself, with the exception of a single ratepayer, who occasionally leans over the clock and moves his finger rapidly round the dial in derision of what he considers our waste of time.

4.30—(On days when the council does not sit.) Committee of the Fabian Society.

5.30—Another committee of the Fabian Society.

6.0—Parliamentary committee of the borough council.

7.0—Dinner

8.0—Public meeting

10.30—Utter exhaustion.

11.30—Bed. Broken slumbers and whitening hair.

And yet there are people who are constantly pestering me with inquiries as to what I am working on at the present time, when my next production will appear, and what form it will take.

Shaw's next major play, in which he would place "all my intellectual goods in the shop window under the sign of *Man and Superman*," was in progress, to be completed the next year.

The 1917 Diary Fragment

The abortive 1917 diary, intended to run a year "as a sample slice of my life," broke off after ten days. It is BL Add. MS. 50711B. Shaw typed the entries himself. The shorthand draft is Add. MS. 63181.

*Ironically, the last fragments of the Shavian diaries return to his memory of Florence Farr, the love of Shaw's life in the early 1890s. Shaw still had some of his greatest plays to complete—*Heartbreak House *and* Saint Joan, *and a Nobel Prize was still nearly a decade into the future; but the "FE" of the diaries was dying, nearly forgotten, in a far-away country to which she had been attracted by the mystic predilections that had drawn her away from the stage, and Shaw.*

AYOT. MON. 1ST JAN. 1917.   Finished the draft of a manifesto declaring for a republican solution of the territorial problems raised by the war, and calling for the establishment of a republican party. Wrote a long letter to Pease (the Fabian secretary) enclosing the draft. Lunch at 13.30 as usual (I note the hours Italian fashion, one to twenty-four, all round the clock). Then a rest and then we go out into the garden, and Charlotte (my wife) saws logs whilst I split them with a beetle and wedges. At 16.30 I drink chocolate and she takes tea. Then I write until dinner at 19.30—mostly correspondence. After dinner I read for a while and then go to the piano and sing or play, with or without the aid of the pianola. This is the Ayot routine. Tonight I played the second half of *Die Meistersinger*, having read Madelin's *French Revolution*. The history of the Directory, which is the part I have just come to, seems to me much more instructive than the earlier ground covered by Carlyle and the stock XIX century writers. The directors were the most infernal blackguards of the revolutionary governments; and the helplessness of the French people under them impresses me more than ever (the same thing is occurring here and now through the war) with the need for educating people in citizenship, including political selfdefence.

> Shaw's manifesto called for republics to replace the discredited European monarchies, and suggested a new republican party in Great Britain. His proposal took the form of a motion at a Fabian Society meeting (the reason it was sent to Edward Pease), and was reported on in *Fabian News*, March 1917 (C2112). ▪ *La révolution* (1911), by Louis Madelin (1871–1956).

2ND JANUARY, TUES. Among my letters was one from Robert Bell, the vegetarian surgeon who protests against operation in cases of cancer, imposing his pamphlet on the subject.

In the morning I began the article entitled "What is to be done with the Doctors?" written for *The English Review*. I have now had Christopher Wheeler's comments and can correct the technical part accordingly. In the evening I wrote to Fred Gorle, who is amazed because I wrote to him that the German deportation of Belgian workmen was an inevitable application of industrial conscription. He thinks this a monstrous display of callousness on my part. I also wrote to Sidney Webb sending him a copy of the draft Fabian manifesto. We are to meet at Phillimore's on Sunday and can discuss it then.

Splitting logs as usual in the afternoon. After dinner read more of Madelin's *French Revolution*, and tried over the earlier scenes in *Electra* (Strauss-Hofmannstahl).

> Robert Bell (1845–1926), Scottish surgeon and contributor to medical journals, especially on vegetarian dietary approaches to diabetes and cancer. ▪ "What is to be Done with the Doctors?" *English Review*, December 1917–March 1918 (C2154). ▪ Charles ("Christopher") E. Wheeler, M.D., M.R.C.S., L.R.C.P., 82 Wimpole St., W., senior physician at London Homaeopathic Hospital. Shaw had known him since the 1890s. ▪ Frederick H. Gorle was a leader in the pro-war faction of the badly split British Socialist Party, which had been largely pacifist in 1914. ▪ Robert Phillimore (1871–1919), a well-to-do Fabian who had served on the St. Pancras Vestry with Shaw. Phillimore and his wife Lucy ("Lion") had a home in Kensington and a farm in Hertfordshire. ▪ *Elektra* (1909), score by Richard Strauss (1864–1949) and libretto by Hugo von Hofmannstahl (1874–1929).

AYOT. WED. JANUARY 3. Revising the article on the medical profession. Received a letter from Florence Farr dated the seventh December saying that she is in the General Hospital in Colombo, awaiting an operation for cancer of the breast. Odd, that this news should have come so close upon Bell's pamphlet yesterday. I began a letter to her, but broke off, resolving to cable for the latest news of her.

I began writing up this diary today, as the book did not arrive from the stationers until this morning. I am going to try to keep it for a year, as a sample slice of my life. After dinner I finished Madelin's book, and played Strauss's *Tod & Verklärung*, also sang a lot of songs by Gounod, reminded of him, no doubt, by the references to Lamartine in Madelin.

> Florence Farr had gone to Ceylon several years before the war (perhaps a logical outcome of her interest in Eastern thought), becoming principal of Ramanathan College, a Hindu school for girls. When she heard of the death from cancer of Aubrey Beardsley's sister Mabel, she responded, "I am always glad to hear of someone making a good end. I came here to make mine brave." To Shaw she now wrote that although she was not going to inform her family, she wanted to confide in him. "I shall like to get a letter from you someday. . . . Goodbye. Remember me to your people." She died on 27 April 1917. ▪ *Death and Transfiguration*, tone poem (1890) by Richard Strauss.

AYOT. THURS. JAN. 4TH.   As it was a very fine, bright, cold day, and I have been writing every day without a break for some time past, I resolved to make a Sunday of it and wrote only some letters. Before lunch I plied the beetle and wedges in the garden. After it I rode 13 miles on the motor bicycle, sending a reply paid cablegram for news of Florence Farr to Ceylon, and visiting Kilsby on the way back.

I am now reading *Essays in War-Time* by Havelock Ellis, and am much pleased by the one on War and Democracy, especially as to the relations between Germany and either Russia or England after the war—practically what I have said myself, except that there is no mention of the United States.

After dinner I pounded away at Beethoven's ninth symphony (Liszt's transcription). It did not seem so very difficult after Strauss; but it requires much more attention.

Note. Cable to Ceylon, reply paid £1–12–6.

> Albert J. Kilsby, Shaw's chauffeur, who was ill. ▪ *Essays in War-Time* (London, 1917). Ellis saw war as a devastating tragedy for the human race since it tends to wipe out those most worth preserving as genetic material.

AYOT. FRI. JAN. 5TH.   By the midday post I was busy answering the morning's letters, sent on to me as usual from London by my secretary Ann Elder. It is one of my troubles that I have so much business to do in connection with my former work that I have less and less time to work seriously in the present. As I grow old, I find for some reason that I attend to business the first thing in the morning, whereas formerly I always devoted the morning to my creative work, and attended to my business at long intervals, and sometimes not at all. Today when I posted my letters the day was as fine as yesterday. I stayed out splitting logs for more than half an hour; then came in and began a new section for my medical essay; but it was lunch time before I had done anything like a full morning's work on it. After lunch I went into the garage, and tried to tighten up the front wheel of my motor bicycle. As the nuts were very difficult of access, and I had no special spanners for them, it was a most tedious and worrying job. After tea I worked at the medical article. After dinner I finished Ellis's essays, and played and sang a lot of Mozart's *Idomeneo*.

AYOT. SAT. JAN. 6TH. 1917.   Today I have one of my headaches. The last one was on the 29th November last. This is not a very disabling one: it only kept me from working after tea. I dozed in my chair at the fire instead. In the morning I was, as yesterday, full of business until post time, when I went for a little walk with Charlotte. Then I finished the new section of the medical article.

In the morning my letters included an invitation from the Commander-in-Chief to visit the Front (at the war), the last thing I felt inclined to do with a headache. Charlotte said I must go, as I ought to see this terrible thing for myself. I grumbled that I should see nothing except a conventional round on which all the journalists are sent; but I suppose it will end in my going: my interest increased as the day went on, though the headache became rather worse.

After dinner the headache went away and I became happy and had a good night. But when I went to the piano I resorted to the pianola and played Strauss's *Don Juan*, MacDowell's *Celtic Sonata*, and a *Musical Moment* by Rachmaninoff.

> The letter suggesting a tour of the front as a correspondent came from Lt. Col. R. H. Hutton Wilson, press chief for the B.E.F., extending an invitation in the name of Sir Douglas Haig, British commander in France. Shaw's articles, "Joy-Riding at the Front," would appear in the *Daily Chronicle*, 5, 7, and 8 March 1917. ▪ Shaw's piano pieces were *Don Juan* (1889), *Keltic Sonata* (1901), and *Six Moments Musicaux* (1896).

AYOT. SUN. JAN. 7TH.   Wrote to De Smet, the Belgian painter, about getting his portrait of me, which hangs down here, up to town to his exhibition at the Leicester Gallery. Took a walk round the garden to warm my feet before driving the car over to the Phillimores' at Kendals, Elstree. The Sidney Webbs were spending the weekend there. Mrs. Phillimore's sister Kathleen and Phillimore's nurse (he is still an invalid with his heart trouble) made up the party. At lunch the Webbs and I disputed about republicanism with our customary violence, so astonishing to people who are not used to it. Phillimore did not appear: when we left at 15.30 he had gone out.

After tea a letter to Austin Spare criticizing the new art periodical called *Form*.

As to reading, the weekend brings a heap of weekly papers which one has to look through more or less thoroughly. The rage for devouring successive editions of daily papers which prevailed at the beginning of the war (from August 1914) has long since passed away; but still we read more papers and read them more carefully than in time of peace.

> The Belgian painter Leon de Smet (1881–1966) was portraitist of Shaw, Galsworthy, and Conrad. ▪ Austin Spare (1886–1956) first exhibited at the Royal Academy at sixteen. As editor he produced the journal *Form*, then, with Clifford Bax, the sumptuous quarterly *Golden Hind* (1922–1924), to which he contributed his finest drawings.

AYOT. MON. JAN. 8TH.   Wretched weather: the sky dribbling in wet that is neither snow nor rain. Worked all day at the Medical article, except for an hour after lunch, when I read *Augustus Does His Bit* to Edward Lane

Claypon (the Rector) and his brother Joe the soldier, who lunched with us. I got in some log splitting before tea for exercise. Except for this I spent the day indoors. After dinner I read the papers and explored MacDowell's *Sonatas* with the pianola.

> *Augustus Does His Bit*, about an eager but inept elderly volunteer for civilian home-front duty, was a one-act farce first produced on 21 January 1917 at the Court Theatre, London. It was first published in 1919 in *Heartbreak House, Great Catherine, and Playlets of the War* (A149). ▪ The Rev. Edward Lane-Claypon (Shaw did not use the hyphen) was rector at Ayot St. Lawrence from 1911 to 1921.

AYOT. TUES. JAN. 9TH. 1917.   Still disabling weather. Very difficult to get about. I worked at the Medical article, which I have at last got into what will be, I think, its final shape. I grudge the time it has cost. I have been tired of the controversy for years. I could have written a play in the time this article has cost me.

In the afternoon I took a walk with Kim, the West Highland terrier with a vile temper, the first dog I have ever had who was an untameable growler and fighter. Yet we spoil him.

After tea I tackled my correspondence. After dinner I corrected the proof of my review of Dixon Scott's book for *The Nation*, and played for awhile with the pianola: Elgar's *Carillon*, the Marche au Supplice from Berlioz's *Fantastic Symphony*, Schumann's *Traumerei* etc.

When I went into Charlotte's room to bid her goodnight, and manipulate her damaged knee for her, we fell to talking about a matrimonial scandal in musical circles in the provinces, of which I have just heard. As Charlotte has no charity for the polygamists of the artistic temperament, and attributes the fact that I not only tolerate them as inevitable, but even accord to them a certain degree of respect and sympathy, to a deplorable looseness in my own character, the subject is a dangerous one; and discussions of it have to be stopped when they threaten to produce personal recriminations. So we stopped just in time, and I went to bed and read Pigou's article in the *Economic Journal* on the export of capital after the war.

> Dixon Scott (1881–1915) was a brilliant young critic who had already become a war casualty. His literary journalism, including a still-shrewd analysis of Shaw's prose style, had been posthumously collected as *Men of Letters*, which Shaw reviewed in *The Nation* on 17 February as "The Artstruck Englishman." ▪ Sir Edward Elgar, *Carillon* (Op. 75, 1914); Hector Berlioz, *Fantastic Symphony* (1830); Robert Schumann, "Traumerei" (from *Kinderscenen*, 1839). ▪ A. C. Pigou, "Interest after the War and the Export of Capital," *Economic Journal*, December 1916.

AYOT AND LONDON. WED. JAN. 10TH.   Charlotte went up to London by the 12.17 train from Hatfield; and I had to drive her there and come back here because Higgs cannot drive the car. I shall send him up to have some driving lessons.

Last entry

> Henry Higgs was Shaw's gardener and houseman. ▪ "Last entry" was typed on the same typewriter as the earlier entries but apparently was added later.

Acknowledgments

Many friends and colleagues have helped with their expertise, their sleuthing, their suggestions for transliterations, and their good offices in other ways. Just as my thanks go to those identified below, my apologies go to those I have inadvertently missed in this roll-call:

Jean-Claude Amalric

Diane Atkinson

Erica Weintraub Austin

Joyce Bellamy

Roelina and Charles Berst

Olive and Sydney Checkland

Harry P. Clark

Bernard F. Dukore

Ellen Dunlap

Jenny and Kenyon Emrys-Roberts

T. F. Evans

Richard Finneran

Mary Fitzgerald

Janet Foster

Patrick Garland

Louise Goldschmidt

Agnes Hagan

Connie Hamburger-Planken

Eileen and Alan Hanley-Browne

Michael Holroyd

Leon Hugo

Sheila Johnston

Evelyn Rypins Kaplan

John Kelly

Dan H. Laurence

Norman Mackenzie

Charles Mann

Roland Marx

Barbara Nield

Martin Quinn

Shirley Rader

Angela Raspin

Susan Rusinko

Barbara Smoker

Robert Trehy   Ray Weintraub
Wendy and John Trewin   Rodelle Weintraub
James Tyler   Suzanne Wills
John Wardrop   Roma Woodnutt
David Weintraub   Daniel Zager

In addition to the British Library of Political and Economic Science of the London School of Economics, where the 1885–1897 diaries and the later appointment books are housed, the British Library, which includes the fragmentary diaries in its collections, the Society of Authors, representing the Bernard Shaw Estate, and other institutions and organizations have been of immense help in this project.

I would like to record my gratitude here also to the following: British Rail Public Affairs; the Burgunder Collection of Shaw, the Cornell University Library; Dictionary of Labour Biography project, The University of Hull; the Education Department of the Museum of London; Gemeentelijke Dienst van de Stadsschouwburg (Amsterdam); The Guildhall Library of the City of London; the Humanities Research Center of The University of Texas at Austin; Jaeger Company Shops Limited; the Manuscript Division of the Library of Congress; the Pattee Library of The Pennsylvania State University; and St. Bartholomew's Hospital (London).

Index

Out on a Limb

Books by Shirley MacLaine

Don't Fall Off the Mountain

You Can Get There From Here

Out
on a Limb
by
Shirley
MacLaine

Bantam Books
Toronto · New York · London · Sydney

OUT ON A LIMB
A Bantam Book / July 1983

All rights reserved.
Copyright © 1983 by Shirley MacLaine.

Book design by Renée Gelman.

This book may not be reproduced in whole or in
part, by mimeograph or any other means, without permission.
For information address: Bantam Books, Inc.

Library of Congress Cataloging in Publication Data
MacLaine, Shirley, 1934–
Out on a limb.

1. MacLaine, Shirley, 1934–   . 2. Entertainers—
United States—Biography. 3. Spiritualists—United
States—Biography. I. Title.
PN2287.M18A33 1983   791.43'028'0924 [B]   82-45955
ISBN 0-553-05035-4

Published simultaneously in the United States and Canada

Bantam Books are published by Bantam Books, Inc.
Its trademark, consisting of the words "Bantam Books" and
the portrayal of a rooster, is Registered in U.S. Patent
and Trademark Office and in other countries.
Marca Registrada. Bantam Books, Inc., 666 Fifth
Avenue, New York, New York 10103.

PRINTED IN THE UNITED STATES OF AMERICA
FG 0 9 8 7 6 5 4 3 2 1

Some of the people who appear in this book are presented as composite characters in order to protect their privacy, and the sequence of some of the events is adapted accordingly. But all the events are real.

To my Mother and my Father

"Never utter these words: 'I do not know this, therefore it is false.' One must study to know; know to understand; understand to judge."

—Apothegm of Narada

"There are more things in heaven and earth, Horatio, than are dreamt of in your philosophy."

—Hamlet

Chapter 1

"The dreams of ancient and modern man are written in the same language as the myths whose authors lived in the dawn of history. . . . I believe that symbolic language is the one foreign language that each of us must learn. Its understanding brings us in touch with one of the most significant sources of wisdom. . . . Indeed, both dreams and myths are important communications from ourselves to ourselves."

—Erich Fromm
The Forgotten Language

The sand was cold and soft as I jogged along the beach. The tide came in steadily and by sundown it would reach the pilings that supported the houses along Malibu Road. I loved to jog just before the sun set because watching the magenta clouds above the surf helped divert my attention from how much my legs hurt. Some health instructor had once told me that jogging three miles in soft sand was the same as jogging six miles on a hard surface. And I wanted to stay healthy no matter how painful it was. When I wasn't dancing, running kept me in shape.

But what was the story I had heard the day before—about the two brothers? One was a health nut who jogged along the boulevard five miles early every morning of his life regardless of how he felt. The other never did any exercise. One morning the health nut brother was out jogging along the road and turned around to shake a finger at his lazy brother when—bam! He just didn't see the truck . . .

Maybe it didn't really matter what we did to preserve ourselves. There was always some truck somewhere. The thing was not to let that stop you, not to let it direct your life.

I remembered sitting at the dinner table with my mother and father in Virginia, where I grew up. I was about twelve and the thought struck me that regardless of how much happiness I might feel at any given moment, I was *aware* of the struggle underneath. The "trouble" I called it then . . . everything had some brand of trouble attached to it. I remembered my Dad had said I had inadvertently struck on an old Greek principle—Pythagorean, I think he said. Dad was a kind of country philosopher and had almost gotten his degree in philosophy at Johns Hopkins University. He loved to speculate on philosophical meaning. I guess I inherited the same trait. I remembered he said my thought had a deep and principled meaning which was true of all life. No matter how good something might seem to be, there was always the negative compensating factor to consider. Vice versa was true too, of course— he said—but Dad seemed to focus on the negative. For me, it made me aware of the duality in life. In a blinding flash over the Birdseye peas, I had felt I understood *some*thing, without knowing quite what I understood.

❋   The wind came up sloshing the waves into whitecaps further out to sea. Sandpipers scurried in and out of the ripples, savoring what food might be washed up with the tide while their graceful wide-winged pelican brothers swooped and then dove, like mad kamikaze pilots, headlong into schools of fish swimming further out in deeper water.

I wondered what it would feel like to be a bird with nothing on my mind but flying and eating. I remembered reading that the smallest bird could travel thousands of miles across the Pacific unencumbered and alone, needing only one piece of baggage; one possession . . . a twig. He could carry the twig in his beak and when he got tired he simply descended to the sea and floated on it until he was ready to move on again. He fished from the twig, ate

from the twig, and slept on the twig. Who needed the *Queen Mary*? He flapped his wings, clamped his life raft in his mouth and set out to see more of the world.

What a life. I wondered if that bird ever got lonely. But even if he was alone he seemed to perceive the proper direction for his life. Birds seemed to have innate compasses that guided them wherever they wanted to go. They seemed to know just exactly what they were, how to live, why they were alive. But did they have feelings? Did they fall in love? Did they cocoon themselves off with only one other bird as though it was the two of them against everything? Birds seemed *part* of everything. Space, time, air. No, how could they shut out the world if they wanted to fly over it?

I remembered an experience I had had once. I call it an experience and not a dream, even though it happened when I was asleep, because it felt more real than a dream. I felt I was suspended over the Earth and I dipped and flowed with the air currents just like the birds. I floated over countries and mountains and streams and trees. As I drifted, the tops of trees brushed gently across me. I was careful not to pluck even one loose leaf from the branch to which it belonged because I, too, belonged to everything there was. I wanted to go further and faster and higher and wider—and the higher I went the more I became connected, my being concentrated and expanded at the same time. I had the sensation that this was actually happening, that my body was irrelevant and that *that* was part of the experience. The real me was floating free and clear, filled with the peace of connection to everything that was.

It was not the usual sexually oriented flying dream which psychologists describe. This was more. There was another dimension to it. The word I'm looking for, I thought to myself as I ran, is "extra." That was why I had remembered it so vividly, and whenever I felt displeased or lonely or out of sorts or strung up and nervous, I thought of that experience and of how peaceful I had

felt when I floated outside of my physical body feeling *involved* with all there was above and below me.

That feeling of belonging to "everything" gave me more pleasure than anything. More pleasure than working, than simply making love, than being successful or any of the other human endeavors people devoted themselves to in order to achieve happiness. I loved to *think*. I loved to concentrate. I loved to be *involved* with concerns outside myself because, to be honest, I believed that was actually my path to understanding myself. Somewhere way underneath *me* were the answers to everything that caused anxiety and confusion in the *world*. What an arrogant thought! But, if I could touch *me*, really touch *me*, I could touch the world . . . maybe even the universe. That was why I was a political activist, a feminist, a traveler, a kind of curious human reporter; and probably it was why I was an actress and performer. I needed to reach inside and touch me if I was going to understand the world and also if I was going to be any good in my work. That was probably why I began my life as a dancer. When I moved, I was in touch with who I was. Whatever . . . to me the journey most worthwhile taking was the journey through myself.

A chill wind scattered sand around my legs as I ran. I slowed down to a walk, remembering that after hard exercise it's good to ease off gradually so the lactic acid in the muscles doesn't congeal. "That's what makes your muscles sore," the gym instructor had said. "Never stop cold after hard exercise. Come down slowly. You'll hurt less later."

I listened with attentiveness to anything to do with physical culture because I understood that it put me more in touch with myself. I respected my body because it was the only one I had. I wanted to make it last. But, my God, it could be painful, especially when I had let fifteen years pass with no exercise at all to speak of. That was really dumb, I thought as I walked. All those years of acting, I thought my body wasn't that important. I had had good formal training as a dancer when I was young; that would be

enough, I thought. I was wrong. People have to take care of their bodies every day or they can wake up one morning and find it won't do what they want it to. Then they'll say they are old. I always felt old when I was not in touch with my body. And the process of connecting with my body put me more in touch with the real me inside of that body. And what was the real me? What was it that made me question and search and think and feel? Was it just the physical brain, the little gray cells, or was it the mind which was something more than brain? Did "mind," or perhaps "personality," include what people called the "soul"? Were they all separate, or was being human a recognition that one was the sum of all these parts, and if so, how did they fit together?

That is what this book is about . . . it's about the experience of getting in touch with myself when I was in my early forties; it's about what the experience did to my mind, to my forbearance, to my spirit, and *for* my patience and belief. It's about the connection between mind, body, and spirit. And what I learned as a result has enabled me to get on with the rest of my life as an almost transformed human being.

So this book is about a quest for my self—a quest which took me on a long journey that was gradually revealing and at all times simply amazing. I tried to keep an open mind as I went because I found myself gently but firmly exposed to dimensions of time and space that heretofore, for me, belonged in science fiction or what I would describe as the occult. But it happened to me. It happened slowly. It happened at a pace that apparently was peculiarly my own, as I believe all people experience such events. People progress according to what they're ready for. I must have been ready for what I learned because it was the right time.

❊ I had made about thirty-five movies—some good, some bad, and from each I think I learned, although, not surprisingly, more

from the bad ones than the good ones. I had traveled all over the world, sometimes as a private person, usually unrecognizable (because I wanted it that way), and sometimes as an entertainer (where I wanted to be recognized), either publicizing one of my films, shooting a television special, or touring with my live show. I loved performing live because it enabled me to *feel* the audiences; what they were thinking, where their interests lay, their differing senses of humor. But mostly I loved meeting new people and crashing head-on into foreign cultures until I learned to meld into them comfortably.

I developed a kind of home-away-from-home circle of friends. They were people in the arts—performers, movie people from every country that made films, writers (I had written two books myself about my travels and adventures in life and they had been translated nearly everywhere), heads of state, prime ministers, kings and queens (my political activism had been duly reported, pro and con, all over the world too). I was a privileged person, there was no doubt about that. I had worked hard for my success but still I felt lucky and as I said, *privileged* to be able to meet and converse with anyone I wanted to, from Castro, the Pope, the Queen of England, and other dignitaries, to India's sick and dying, or revolutionary peasants in the barrios of the Philippines, or Sherpas in the Himalayas, just to name a few.

And the more I traveled and met people, the more my social and political conscience became activated. And the more it became activated, the more I found myself identifying with the "underdogs" as my father defined them. But as I pointed out to him, most of the world could be classified as underdogs. Anyway, I found myself thinking a great deal about what was going wrong in the world. You can't avoid it when you actually *see* the destitution, the starvation, the hatred. I began traveling when I was nineteen, and now, at mid-forty, I could objectively say things had steadily progressed downhill. To me, democratic idealism seemed to be no longer possible because people who were part of the democratic

way of life were apparently more concerned with serving their own interests and were therefore abusing their basic philosophy of the well-being of the majority. Not many people were addressing themselves to international ethics. "Political thinking" in the world seemed to be based on the dual fields of power politics and material economics, with solutions expressed in terms of graphs, charts, polls, and industrial programs that ignored the individual human being.

Somewhere on the planet at all times there was war, violence, crime, oppression, dictatorship, starvation, genocide—a global spectacle of human desperation and misery. Meanwhile, leaders worldwide continued to examine the problems solely in terms of the *problems themselves* without recognizing their true relationship to a larger and more universal necessity—the deep-seated need to achieve an enduringly peaceful state of mind on an individual basis, with all the broad implications that that would entail. They had temporary solutions for permanent problems. Or, as Dad would say, "they are putting Band-Aids on cancer."

I found myself in endless discussions all over the world about whether mankind was fundamentally selfish, self-serving, and concerned primarily with the attainment of more luxurious creature comforts and personal gain. I found myself saying that maybe personal selfishness and competition were detrimental not only to happiness but even to personal success. It seemed to me that even though the world powers recognized the need for a unity of human interest, they always recommended more highly competitive economic policies to achieve that end, which could only lead to human conflict, discord, and inevitably larger wars. Something was surely missing.

Then, as I continued to travel, I noticed that something was changing. People I talked to began to speculate on what it was that was missing. The tone of our conversations shifted from dismay and confusion to a consideration that the answers might lie within ourselves, as though the self-created plight of mankind had noth-

ing whatever to do with economic solutions. We began to speculate on the inner search for what we as humans really meant. What
were we here for? Did we have a purpose or were we simply a
passing accident? That we were *physical* was obvious. Our physical needs were, in theory at least, the priority concern of governments and leaders. That we were *mental* creatures was clear too.
The world of the mind, the mental dimension, was attended to by
education, arts, sciences and the halls of learning.

But were we all not also *spiritual*? I found that more and more
people were focusing on the question of our inner spirituality which
had for so long been starved for recognition. Did confusion stem
from the fact that spirituality was not only obvious, but invisible?
The religions of the world didn't seem to explain or satisfy our
spiritual needs. In fact, the Church seemed to divide people more
than it unified them, whether one followed Christianity, Islam,
Judaism, or Buddhism. Indeed, the world seemed to be moving
into an era of Holy Conflict, what with the violent rise of Islamic
pride in the Arab world, of self-righteous Christian fundamental-
ism among the so-called moral majority in America, and of militant Zionism in Israel.

I found myself in touch with a network of friends all over the
world who were involved with their own spiritual search. We asked
questions about human purpose and meaning in relation not only
to our physical perspective of life on earth, but also to our metaphysical perspective in relation to time and space. It began to seem
possible that this life was not all there was. Perhaps the physical
plane of existence was not the only plane of existence. The marvellous possibility existed that the *real* reality was much more.

In other words, perhaps Buckminster Fuller was right when he
claimed that ninety-nine percent of reality was *invisible,* and our
inability to acknowledge that invisible reality was due to what was
now commonly being referred to as our low conscious awareness.

When I began to ask myself these questions and found a real
kinship with others who were also involved in the same inner

search, my life changed and so did my perspective. It was thrilling, at times frightening, and always mind-boggling because it caused me to reevaluate what being alive was all about. Perhaps we, as human beings, were actually part of an ongoing experience that continued long after we thought we died. Perhaps there was no such thing as death.

But I'm getting ahead of myself.

❋ The sun was setting chilled and shimmering beyond the hills of Point Dume. I remembered standing on those hills looking into the crashing waves of the Pacific below, wondering if the human race really did get its start in the sea. The Pacific always reminded me of my friend David. Or perhaps he was much on my mind these days simply because I seemed to be arriving at some kind of turning point in my life and he was easy to talk to. What was it he had said? Something about the spiritual need for respecting both the positive and the negative in life equally.

"It's impossible to have one without the other," he said. "Life is the *combustion* of the two. You just try to *overwhelm* the negative with the positive and you'll be much happier."

"Sure," I had said, "you don't have to be a rocket scientist to know that . . . but living it is something else."

David was an interesting man. About thirty-five years old, he was a sweet, very gentle person, with chiseled cheekbones and a kind of soft, sad smile. I had met him at an art gallery in the Village in New York. We struck up a friendship because I found it comfortable being with him. He was a painter and a poet and very much at home anywhere because he was an observer of life. In Manhattan we'd walk for hours watching people and wondering what they thought. When he was in California, which was often, we'd walk the beach in Malibu. David loved to travel too, and he'd done a lot of it, from Africa and India to the Far East and back

again to Europe and South America. He painted and wrote along the way. It didn't cost him much because he worked his way around the world doing all sorts of odd jobs. He had been married once. He didn't talk about it but he did volunteer one day that he used to be a "fast liver." When I asked him what that meant he just waved his hand and said, "That's in the past. I'm finished with the fast cars, high living—kid stuff. Now I'm alone, and happy." I didn't talk much about my personal life either. That was not the nature of our relationship. He was also into a whole lot of stuff I had no time for—reincarnation, past life recall, cosmic justice, vibrational frequencies, food-combining, spiritual enlightenment, meditation, self-realization, and God knows what else. He talked seriously about all that and seemingly with deep knowledge. But most of it went right by me because I was caught up in my movie scripts, my television specials, new numbers for my club act, losing weight, and Gerry. I wanted to talk to David about Gerry, but because of the circumstances, I couldn't talk to anyone, not even David, about Gerry.

❊ Now, in the chill breeze, I felt perspiration dripping down the back of my hair onto my neck. My legs hurt, but it was a good feeling. I had jogged hard. It was a satisfied kind of hurt. Maybe, as David said, that was the price for everything in life. And when you reached the proper place after struggle it wouldn't hurt anymore.

I took a last look at the setting sun and made my way up the wooden stairs that led to the beach. I loved those wooden stairs, scarred and broken from high tides and storms. For twenty years I had used those stairs, since I built the apartment building with the paycheck I had received from my first picture, *The Trouble with Harry*, for Alfred Hitchcock. The first thing I did was get a loan so I could put up a building where I could rent out apart-

ments and live rent-free myself . . . just in case I got hit by a truck and couldn't work. My middle-class upbringing, I guess. Always protect against the future. You never know.

I washed the sand from my feet under a shower at the top of the wooden stairs . . . mustn't track sand into the apartment. It lodges in the carpet that the builder told me I shouldn't install in a beach place anyway.

I climbed the last set of stairs leading to the patio, where I stopped and looked at the Japanese garden I had landscaped myself, complete with a bonsai tree from Kyoto and a trickling stream of water that flowed constantly up and over itself. The years I had traveled in the Far East, particularly Japan, had influenced me deeply. Their Spartan sense of respect for nature moved me. Since the Japanese were so buffeted by nature, they had no choice but to harmonize with it. They didn't believe in conquering it as we did in the West. They used it and became part of it . . . that is, until they forfeited their respect for nature in favor of their respect for business and profit. And when Japan became polluted, I stopped going there. I wondered how long it would be before the whole world would industrialize nature just so it could make more money. Simplistic, I suppose, but that's how it seemed to me.

I heard the phone ring in my apartment. I nearly tripped over myself in a lurching jolt to get there before it stopped. Phones did that to me. I'd answer someone else's phone if it rang when I was there. Something about being efficient and prompt and tidy. I was annoyed by people who let a phone ring four times before they picked it up. Sloppy it was to me—just plain lazy and sloppy.

I bolted through the door into the living room and dove for the phone on the floor. I had to laugh at myself. Who the hell could be that important? And if they were, they'd call back.

"Hello," I said breathlessly, wondering what the person on the other end would think I'd been doing.

"Hellooo . . ." It was Gerry. "How are you?"

I could hear the long-distance operator in the background.

Gerry's face, tumbling hair on his forehead, soft black eyes, swept through my mind.

"I'm great," I said, glad he couldn't see how happy I was to hear his voice. "How's it going with Her Majesty?"

"We are declining in England with grace," he joked with a twinge of serious concern I had learned to detect.

"Well," I cleared my throat, "grace is a quality everyone admires."

"Yes. Well, I'm doing what I can to prevent the ship from sinking completely."

I could feel him reach for a cigarette and inhale with a soft whistling sound.

"Gerry?"

"Yes."

"How's your campaign going? Are you making headway?"

"Oh, fine," he said. But there was a slight depression in his voice. "It's a long slow process. People need to be taught and educated with velvet-firm strokes. The balance isn't easy. But we'll talk about that when we're together."

"Oh?" I said. "Will that be soon?"

"Yes, I hope so. Can you meet me this weekend in Honolulu? I have a conference on North-South Economics."

"Oh, Jesus. Yes," I said. "Will there be many journalists?"

"Yes."

"Is that all right?"

"Yes."

"You are willing to take that risk?"

"Yes."

"Okay. I'll be there. When?"

"Friday."

"Where?"

"Kahala Hilton. I have to go now. I have a meeting with my Deputy Secretary. He's waiting."

"Okay. Great. See you this weekend."

"Goodbye." He hung up. There were never prolonged telephonic goodbyes with Gerry. His professional demeanor and habit precluded that kind of sloppiness. His personal life was another matter.

I hung up, took a shower and drove, more slowly than usual, to my big house in Encino.

I loved to sit behind the wheel in a California car, mosey along the wide open highways, and think. I loved to think in California. New York was so live-wired there was time only to act on instinct and for survival, which I found creative and exciting, but in California I could reflect. Of course, California wasn't called the Big Orange for nothing. You could turn into one if you weren't careful. So the Big Apple, for me, was a place where I could act on things that I had thought through in the Big Orange. Gerry had not been able to come to California since I'd known him.

I remembered our first night in New York together. Actually, I had been introduced to him several times before, when I was in London and once again when he had come to an anti-Vietnam rally in New York. I had been impressed by his self-assured soft-spokenness, and his mind of quick brilliance. He was in Parliament, a Socialist, and he believed he could make England work again.

He wasn't pompous like so many well-educated English people I knew. In fact, he was the opposite: a big man, well over six feet, with such shoulders and arms that he reminded me of a bear who needed to hug the world. Loose and freewheeling. His body moved in a careless way and his shirt fell open when his tie was slung around his neck. When he was excited about something a thick shock of hair tumbled into his eyes. And when he paced with long strides across a room, searching for the best way to make a point, one had the impression that the room tilted with his weight. He seemed unaware of how imposing he was. Often he had a hole in his sock. His eyes were moist and black. They made me think of olives.

When I had first been introduced to him in London I was play-

ing the Palladium. He came backstage and I liked him. I didn't know much about English politics but he seemed open, penetratingly intelligent, and involuntarily funny. When he left my dressing room he walked so deliberately that he fell over a chair, but not until he had first walked into my closet.

So when he happened to be in New York a year later and called me I said yes, I'd love to have dinner.

We went to an Indian restaurant on Fifty-eighth Street. He didn't eat much. He was hardly aware the food was there. And he had a habit of resting his eyes on my mouth when he needed to think through a point he was making. I thought he liked my lips but he was really only thinking about what he was going to say next.

After dinner we walked all the way to Elaine's on Eighty-eighth and Second. He wanted to see where my crowd hung out. I was wearing spike heels, felt uncomfortable, and couldn't keep up with his long strides. I had a blister.

When we walked into Elaine's people looked up. But I wasn't the only one they noticed despite Gerry's rumpled suit and scuffed shoes. Anyway, no one bothered us. We had squid salad and a few drinks. We talked about New York and London and when we were ready to leave I told him I was coming to London in a week to talk about a new script and I'd call him.

A limousine was supposed to pick him up and drive him to some political conference upstate, but the car never came. So there he was in my apartment looking at my shelves full of books on China, show business, American politics, Marxist theory, and ballet dancers. He was rattling on about the need for freedom in a Socialist society, towering over my low coffee table when his thick shock of hair fell into his eyes. And that's how it all started. I reached up to touch his hair. I needed to know how it felt, and as simply and easily as though we had known each other for a lifetime he looked away from the biography of Marx he was holding, stared into my

eyes and pulled me close to him. We held each other for a moment and I was lost. That had never happened to me before, at least not the same way. I didn't understand it then but it was part of the puzzle I would put together later.

❀ When we got up in the morning I fixed him some tea and biscuits. We were sitting in my sunny kitchen. From the window you can see the Fifty-ninth Street Bridge.

"You're coming to London next week?" he asked. I said yes.

"Can I see you there?" I said yes.

"Will you be able to come with me to Paris the week after?" I said yes again. With great determination he got up, headed for what he thought was my front door. It wasn't. He ended up back in the bedroom. Then he pointed himself in the right direction and was gone. He hadn't said goodbye or even looked back.

I arranged to have the script conferences in London and meet with Gerry at the same time. In the film business, a great deal of time is spent poring over scripts that never develop into pictures. Such was the case with this one. I was glad to have Gerry, so the time in London wasn't a complete waste. Sometimes I wonder if the script wouldn't have been better if I hadn't had Gerry to divert my attention. Anyway, all of London seemed to be on strike when I arrived. Gerry was right. The ship was sinking, but I wasn't sure it was gracefully, flowered cups at tea time and the misty morning walks in Hyde Park notwithstanding. But all that really mattered to me was the smell of his tweed jacket and his thick hair falling across my face: the softness of his fingers on my cheeks and the way he swayed me in his huge arms seemed to close out the reality that not only England, and my script, but also the world was in big trouble.

We were careful not to be seen when we were together (I stayed

in the apartment of a friend), and anyway Gerry was known for enjoying his privacy while walking the streets of the city he grew up in.

Then, after a few days, I went on to Paris and he met me there a day later. We watched the rooftops of St. Germain from my hotel room, and after we made love we never talked about our relationship or what we meant to each other. Gerry and I never discussed his wife or my personal life. It wasn't necessary or anything we needed to get into . . . not, that is, until the night he took me to dinner and a table full of English journalists recognized us. They smiled and waved. Gerry froze and couldn't eat. He talked of how this would hurt his wife—how she couldn't accept it and how we should progress more slowly. I said of course, but hadn't he thought of all this when we began? He was so terrified that my heart turned over. That night he couldn't sleep. His mind, he said, was tumbling in confusion. I offered to leave so he could collect himself. We stayed away from each other for a day while he attended conferences and meetings. I planned to leave anyway, when, in lonely desperation, he called me.

He said he couldn't bear to see me go. He had a terrible longing for me and could we be together again.

We met outside of Paris in St. Germain en Laye. He fell on me, showering me with kisses and touches, holding me so tightly I felt *he* couldn't breathe. He seemed abandoned and considerate, pleading and demanding all at the same time. It was rare and real and open and direct and a little bit frightening.

He said he had never done anything like this before in his life. He said he was confused and terribly guilty. He talked about the state of the world and how he wanted to make a contribution to improve it. He talked about Democratic-Socialist principles and how it was possible to have them both at the same time, if the rich would only share their wealth more.

He was soft and whispering and challengingly loud and hard driving, almost as though he was experimenting with the many

facets of his personality. He never asked me about myself or whether there were other men I might know or be involved with.

It seemed to be an emotional purge for him. And when the time came to leave each other, he was economical and not at all sentimental.

He wondered if I'd be all right getting back to America. I said I had found my way back from wilder places than the French countryside. He apologized for his behavior in Paris and said he'd call me soon. With no superfluous motions, he simply said goodbye in his Spartan English manner, opened the door and walked through it. The trouble was—he was in the closet. He laughed and, saying nothing, he walked out the right way.

The room we had brought to life for two days came to a silent halt. The walls closed in on me. And neither one of us had mentioned the word "love." I felt I had somehow been compelled to involve myself in this relationship that I knew could offer little more than irreconcilable obstacles. The question was, *why?* ❊

Chapter 2

"Pure logical thinking cannot yield us any knowledge of the empirical world; all knowledge of reality starts from experience and ends in it. Propositions arrived at by purely logical means are completely empty of reality."

—Albert Einstein
Albert Einstein:
Philosopher-Scientist

I drove through Malibu Canyon and onto the Ventura Freeway. There wasn't much traffic. The San Fernando Valley stretched out in front of me, household lights beginning to twinkle, like a giant jewel box in the night. I remembered how they had taken Khrushchev to the Valley when he came to California. It was America in progress, they said. It *was* beautiful if you looked at it from the right perspective. But otherwise everybody made jokes about the Valley—like saying a person was so bad off, the only thing he had going for him was he didn't live in the Valley.

I turned off the freeway to my street. Climbing my long driveway I felt the low-hanging cherry trees brush the top of my car. I loved those trees. They reminded me of the cherry trees my former husband Steve and I had had in his house in Japan before our divorce. Steve had planted them there when he lived in a residential section of Tokyo called Shibuya. He wanted to stay and live and work in and around Asia. I wanted to live and work in America, not because I grew up there, but because my work was there. We discussed the dilemma and decided to try to make the globe a golf ball and do both.

For a while it worked. But gradually we each developed separate lives. We remained friends as we raised our daughter Sachi,

who spent the first seven years of her life with me in America, the next six in an international school in Japan, and her remaining school years in Switzerland and England. She learned to speak and read and write fluent Japanese (which meant she could read most any Oriental language) and she began to *think* and *perceive* like an Oriental, which was sometimes amusing because Sachi is a freckle-faced blonde with the map of Ireland written on her face and the loping arms and legs of a Westerner, which she somehow manages to orchestrate as though she's wearing a restrictive kimono and obi when she walks and sits. She still kneels in a living room and looks up adoringly at whoever is speaking, and her Alice-in-Wonderland countenance can be quite confusing even when I think I understand her. What I'm really getting is a combination of straightforward, direct Western thinking tempered with circuitous Asian ambiguity usually employed to rescue what might be an embarrassing, impolite or insensitive remark.

I learned a lot about Asia from Sachi, which she didn't even mean to teach me. She is one of that new breed of people whose blood and ancestry is Western, but whose psychology and thought processes are half Asian. With Sachi this was a result of the "golf ball" belief that Steve and I had had in the beginning. As with everything, it has its duality—its drawbacks and its assets. In the long run, though, I would say the assets outweigh the liabilities, if for no other reason than the fact that Sachi is a combination of two worlds—and if she can handle it, she will help each understand the other. She has lived and studied French in Paris, where she says it was most difficult for her to make the sociological and cultural adjustment. Apropos of Parisian rudeness and cynicism, she said, "Mom, it's really hard to bow with Japanese politeness and say 'up your ass' at the same time!"

My house sat warm and homey at the top of the hill. "MacLaine Mountain" one of my friends called it, and wondered if I ever fell off it. If they only knew how often I had wondered the same thing.

My friend David had joked that the tallest mountain I was climbing was myself. He didn't have much time for small talk, yet he could make the smallest moment seem important. Like the time he peeled an orange into a flower and the juice of the luscious fruit gently dribbled down his chin as he ate it. He said there were no accidents in life and we all basically meant something important to each other if we'd just open our hearts and our feelings and not be afraid of the consequences. When he was in California we took walks on the beach and had lunch in a health food restaurant after yoga class. So many times he had suggested that I stop "climbing" myself and journey "into" myself instead.

"That's where all you are searching for resides," he said. "What's the matter with you? Why don't you take the time to look?" He hadn't said it angrily, really, but more impatiently.

He gave me books about spiritual teachings to read. He told me I should get more in touch with my true identity. I really didn't understand what he meant. I had always thought that was what I'd been doing, but apparently he was talking on a different level. When I asked him, he would never elaborate. He said I should just think about it and it would come. I thought about what he said, skimmed through the books, but continued to happily approach everything from a head-on, open-minded point of view. Not totally satisfying, really, but certainly functional.

I was not an unhappy person—not at all. And I always thought I had a pretty good sense of my identity. That's what everybody said about me. "She knows who she is," they'd say. In fact, it was sometimes difficult for me to relate to the complaint of the women's movement that they had been colonized away from their female identities. I had never really had that experience in my life. I sometimes felt to the contrary. I seemed to be so sure of what I felt and what I wanted that some others complained I was *too* liberated, that I didn't *need* anyone.

But I wasn't so sure of that anymore. Maybe David was right. Possibly he was seeing something much deeper in me that I was

missing *because* I was already so liberated. Maybe *because* of that I should realize that I had a long way to go. It's hard to know something really deep is missing inside yourself when you feel successful and busy and responsible and creative.

I could smell Marie's good French cooking waft across the driveway. Mine was the best restaurant in town, only I hardly ever invited anyone to eat. I liked being alone and I was uncomfortable entertaining anyway, especially when I could be spending the time reading or writing.

Slamming the front door shut so Marie would know I was home, I yelled that I was going to take a bath and relax a little before dinner.

Two steps at a time when there was no need to rush, I broke a nail as I opened my bedroom door. Damn, I thought, that will take a repair job. But there was the bedroom I loved—spread out, blue and cool and refreshing—waiting for me.

I loved my ice-blue colored bedroom and its adjacent sitting room-office, as much as a person could love a room. I spent hours there alone. I knew I could lock the door and without seeming impolite or unsociable I could shut out the world. I could have lived in those rooms and never wanted anything more. I never felt detached or abstract in those rooms. I designed the bedroom myself. The blue was pale enough yet vibrant enough to keep both the morning and the evening alive. The drapes were filmy and flowing and stretched across a solid glass sliding wall which overlooked a view of the San Fernando Valley and the mountains beyond— mountains which always took me by surprise on a clear evening. The furniture was covered in crushed blue velvet and the bed with a band-brocaded blue satin spread.

I remembered hearing about a movie star once who slid out of bed because she slept on satin sheets. I liked being stuck to my regular sheets because I usually read in bed and wrote in bed whenever I didn't want to feel professional. I had books and note-books strewn all around me, and whenever I was stuck on a transi-

tion or a story point, I would turn the electric blanket up very warm, take a little nap underneath all my research, and by the time I woke, usually had figured out whatever was bothering me. I loved to feel alone in my beautiful bedroom, with nothing but me and whatever I wanted to think about. It was such a fulfilling feeling to know I had concentrated on something deeply and had forgotten all about myself. Maybe David was right. Maybe I should actually learn to meditate . . . to meditate deeply. Maybe what I would find was what he was talking about.

I walked into my dressing room and changed. It was a room of mirrors. Mirrors on all four walls and the ceiling . . . a monument to vanity, I thought—which embarrassed me, because unless I was working on a film I didn't much care about how I looked.

I opened one of the mirrored closet doors to change into a robe. I wondered what Gerry would think of my movie star's closet indulgently crammed with clothes left over from pictures I had made or that I had bought in nearly every big city in the world. I wondered what he'd think if I told him that I loved the feeling of beautiful pearls around my neck at the same time that I felt ostentatious and out of place wearing them. I wondered what he'd think if I told him I loved to snuggle into the deep fur of a soft sable coat, but hardly ever wore it, even though I did get it just for posing for an ad. I wondered how he'd feel about how I loved to travel on the Concorde even though he had campaigned against it.

I wanted to talk to him about how I had made a lot of money and that it made me feel elite in a world that was broke to know I could buy just about anything I wished for. I wanted to ask him what he would do if he could demand large sums for his services. I had seen him eye my expensive luggage in the hotel room in Paris. Did he think physical manifestations of earned wealth violated socialist principles? Did being born poor automatically make one a good guy? I had wanted to talk to him about it all, but couldn't because once I had asked him if his wife had nice clothes

and luggage that would last a lifetime. "No," he had said, "my wife is a Marxist. She doesn't even like it if I wear fur gloves in the winter."

I took out a robe and looked around. One of the mirrored walls was a sliding door which led to a terrace with a tumbling rock waterfall and tropical plants and flowers. They were cared for by a Japanese gardener who loved them like children and believed that Peter Tomkins was correct, that plants had emotions. I remembered how silly Gerry thought I was when I first mentioned such a concept to him.

"Plants can feel?" he laughed. "Well, I'm just glad they can't talk back." I had wanted to pursue the conversation but his sardonic laughter nipped it in the bud, so to speak. So often I had longed to pursue some crazy metaphysical idea that might just be a recognized scientific fact in twenty years, but Gerry was the kind of man who dealt only with what he had proof of, what he could see, and what he could therefore parody or comment on sociologically in his occasional fits of black humor. It left out so many possibilities.

The bathroom was my favorite room. It was just adjacent to the dressing room on the other side of the terrace garden. A sunken square marble tub overlooked the rock waterfall where indirect light now played on the falling, dancing water in the evening light. There were two toilets and two sinks in pink marble and a shower head above the tub in brass. I loved the fact that the sunken tub was so large I didn't need a shower curtain to protect the carpeting from the spray of the shower.

I leaned over and turned on the tub faucet. Warm water always made me feel better. Often, no matter where I was in the world, a tub of warm water could change my spirits into happiness.

Now as I simply held my hands under the warm flow I began to feel more relaxed.

I sighed to myself, climbing into the hot VitaBath soap suds. I thought of my mother. She loved hot baths too. I remembered how

she'd sit in the tub and just think. I always wondered if she might be thinking about how to get out . . . how to get out of her life. It seemed as though everything Mother did, she did for Dad. And after him, for her children. It was the same story with everyone else's mother, I guess. Her cooking was punctuated by deep sighs. Often she would manage to burn something, and then she would have to wring her hands. Her lovely hands were the most expressive part of her. I always knew how she felt by watching her long, slim fingers, for they never stopped twisting or being busy with something around her neck or wrists. She was either fiddling with a high-necked sweater (wool against her skin bothered her) or toying with her silver chains. I understood that she enjoyed the sensuality of the chains slipping through her fingers. But there was a contradiction because I sometimes felt she would choke herself out of frustration. I wanted to understand the contradiction, scream for her to clarify what she was feeling—but when she reached a certain pitch of desperation, before I could sort out my own thinking, she'd launch into another project like peeling potatoes or making scotch cakes.

Dad knew that Mother had wanted to be an actress, so he said that most of what she was doing was a performance. The two of them, in fact, were like a pair of vaudevillians. I thought I remembered Dad saying something about wanting to run away with a circus when he was fourteen. He loved railway cars and traveling and said that he felt he wouldn't even have needed make-up to play a clown. And he had a way of commanding attention like no one I've seen before or since. He usually did it with his pipe. Regardless of where he sat in a room, it became the center. His chair would become a stage and his friends or family, the audience. He'd crook one leg over the other, pick up his pipe and knock it against the heel of his shoe, as though he were bringing a meeting to order. A tiny hunk of ash would spill from the bowl of his pipe onto the carpet beneath him.

The roomful of people would by now be uneasily watchful.

Then he'd sigh deeply, uncrook his leg, grunt a little and proceed to bend over to determine what to do about the ash. This was the master attention-getter. Would he pick it up? Would he gently squeeze the hunk of ash between his fingers so he wouldn't crush it into powder? Or would he rifle for a matchbook cover in the top drawer of his little pipe stand beside his chair and scoop it up? It never occurred to anyone watching to go to his rescue. This was a scientifically manipulated exercise of such commanding expertise that it would have been like rushing to the stage to help Laurence Olivier recover a prop he had purposely dropped.

Usually Dad picked the ash up with the matchbook cover. However, in mid-bend, out of the corner of his eye, he would spot a piece of lint on the shoulder of his jacket. With the pipe in one hand, matchbook cover in the other, the focus of attention on the ashes, he would slowly but surely proceed to flick any discernible flecks of lint he could find while everyone in the room waited on the fate of the ashes. His complete capture of attention accomplished, he was a happy man. If, however, no one paid any attention, Dad would get unmercifully drunk.

Mother would usually get up and go to the bathroom, returning after she sensed that Dad's act had run its course, to suggest a nice hot piece of apple pie that she had baked herself. In striding toward the kitchen maybe she'd bump into a piece of furniture which would produce a startled gesture of sympathy from whoever was closest. Meanwhile Dad would suck on his pipe, drink slowly from a glass of scotch and milk, not moving, knowing that Mother had successfully stolen his thunder, trying to understand that every play must have more than one central character. No wonder Warren and I became actors: we learned from the best.

Mother had done a Little Theater play once, all about a mother who went slowly bananas. Rehearsals took her away from the house at least four nights a week. So Dad began to complain that he never had hot meals waiting for him anymore and that there was dust on the mantelpiece. He teased Mother, said that she was

becoming a replica of that "bitch" she was playing in that "damn fool play" and warned her that conditions at home were slowly deteriorating. Little by little Mother began to succumb to his pressure. Her gracefully chiseled nose pinched up when she tried to express herself and her speech patterns became erratic. Soon she agreed that she *had* become the character and therefore it wasn't worth it. So she quit the play. She had bought Dad's propaganda, and came back home to tend her family.

Growing up, I too did what was expected of me. I wore standard white blouses, unscuffed saddle oxford shoes, bobby sox rolled down over nylon stockings, and pleated skirts that I neatly tucked under me when I sat down. I brushed my hair one hundred strokes every night and I finished my homework and I might have been Football Queen if my boyfriend hadn't gotten sick the day the team made their nominations and screwed up my chances. I had a bright-new-penny smile for everyone and never allowed myself to get overtly angry at anybody, because you could never tell where the crucial popularity vote might come from during the next election for Prom Queen. I went on hayrides but wouldn't do more than kiss. I was a good student but only because I learned how to cheat well. I had real "school spirit," wore the school colors at all times and when I heard the roll of the school drums before a ballgame my heart would pop with pride. I spent a lot of time after school smoking and carousing in cars with boys . . . always teasing but never going all the way because Mother had said I should be a virgin when I got married, since my husband would know if I wasn't. Still, I had to sneak around, because Mom and Dad were more worried about my reputation than about what I might actually be doing.

I laughed a lot, mostly out of tenseness, as a kind of outlet for suppressed feelings that often bordered on hysteria. Laughter was a life saver to me. But apparently it upset people too. My friends took to calling me "Silly Squirrely" because I laughed at most anything. They thought I was happy-go-lucky and my "carefree-

ness" was a topic of conversation. They said I was "such a nut" which I accepted as a compliment at first until I began to realize there was really something wrong. One day in the hallway I was holding hands with Dick McNulty. He told me a joke and I began to laugh. But I couldn't stop and with a kind of theatrical glee that I didn't want to control I began to scream with laughter. I laughed and laughed until the principal came and ordered the nurse to take me home. Dad and Mom only wanted to know why I had been holding hands in the hall. They didn't seem to be interested in why I was laughing so hard.

Dick McNulty was the first boy I ever loved. Three years later he was killed in Korea.

❋ I sat in the tub until the water was lukewarm. What clothes would I take to Honolulu? I had met Gerry in so many places in the world . . . in snow and in the tropics. I would go anywhere and at any time he suggested it . . . but oh, the clandestine trips to London! It had become so suffocating for me.

It wasn't easy to find an apartment for a week at a time. And it was doubly difficult to stay unrecognized by the press. But the most difficult emotional conflict was our being together in his home territory.

Once I found a place that was two or three tube stops from his office and another ten minutes walk from there.

So when I arrived we began a ten-day sojourn, he making subway trips, and I waiting in the dark apartment for him to visit me whenever he could. Why were all the apartments dark?

I would stand at the front window watching him amble up the road. Now and then he was stopped by well-wishers who wondered what he was doing in that part of London.

He walked in. I hugged him.

"I used to live in this area when I was first married," he said, as

he released me and walked around the apartment surveying the bookshelves and the pottery on the tables. He didn't say much about the books or the prints on the walls but he spotted a magazine that had arrived in the mail. It was *Penthouse*.

"How can people subscribe to junk like that?" he said as he led me into the bedroom.

"I don't know; pornography is only a question of geography or upbringing, isn't it?" I said. "A lot of people would think we were pornographic with what we're doing with each other."

He looked at me for a moment and smiled. His glasses looked incongruous perched on the bridge of such a proud nose.

We made love, but he was preoccupied. We lay together for a while and then he said he had to get back to work. A chill scribbled through me. But I let it pass. When he left I called a writer friend and was gone for the rest of the day and out to dinner at night.

The next day Gerry was freer and seemed more abandoned. He told me that he carried the joy of our meeting with him so intensely that he had not been able to sleep all night. He said it was an exquisite way to feel exhausted. He said he had feelings he had never had in his life before.

Around about the fourth day he walked in and sat down with a sheepish smile on his face.

"What's wrong?" I asked.

He breathed deeply. "My daughter went into my closet looking for something in my coat and asked why my clothes smelled of perfume. It caught me so off guard that I acted guilty. I rushed to the closet instead of brushing it off. My wife noticed and I could feel her eyeing me. I said I couldn't smell any perfume and then she came to the closet. She said she smelled it too. I said I didn't know what they were talking about and I walked away. I didn't handle it well. I was as bad as I was in Paris."

He walked into the kitchen, tripped over a waste bin and made himself some tea.

"Well, how was it left?" I asked.

"Oh. It's all right, I guess. Everybody forgot about it. I just hate this hypocrisy. I don't like to lie."

From that day on I never wore perfume. I didn't even wear it when I wasn't with him. I was afraid it would cling to my clothes. But whenever we had been together he took a shower and washed his hair too. And he always smiled shyly and shrugged at the absurdity of it.

✳ I put on glasses, a scarf, a hat over the scarf, and went to the English Parliament where Gerry was participating along with the Prime Minister and various opposition leaders in a debate on the economy. I sat in the last row of the balcony. It was the first time I had seen Gerry at work.

He paced aggressively around the floor as if he were the Prime Minister already. He was so sure of himself that he mingled challenging and aggressive jokes into his speeches and rebuttals. He seemed to toy with what he believed to be the inferior intelligence of his colleagues and his political superiors.

He didn't sit in his seat when it was another member's turn to speak, and when he did sit, he crossed one leg over the other and bounced his foot, his blue socks creeping down over his ankles. He leapt up impatiently, energetically calling for attention. Then he strode the floor of Parliament as though the place belonged to him. He spread his legs apart, stuffed his hands in his pockets and counted the house as though the number of people watching him from the gallery was more important than what anybody else might have to say. And when he asked for time to speak himself, he called one of his opponents half a man, said he was a hypocrite unable to follow through on an unpopular point of view, whether it dealt with the trade unions, nuclear energy, or tax revision. He took his glasses on and off to make his points. He never used notes.

He jabbed at the air. But beneath the podium his feet curled over and under each other like the feet of a school boy. As I sat there I wondered whether he would ever lead his party to victory. He was aggressive, and brilliant. But if the voters ever saw his feet moving and stepping on each other, they'd also know why he knocked all the contents of his briefcase to the floor with his elbow when he finally sat down. It was a good thing he knew the exits in the House of Commons.

That night he walked into the apartment and asked me what I thought. With my glasses, hat and scarf I didn't think he'd known I was there that afternoon.

"You knew I was there from the beginning?"

"Yes," he said, "certainly, for me you would be hard to miss."

I hesitated. Maybe he had been performing for me then. Maybe he didn't always act that way.

"Well," he said, "what did you think?"

"Were you performing for me or do you always act like that?"

He looked surprised. "Like what?"

"Well, aside from a little Jacques Tati number you acted as though *you* were the Prime Minister, like you owned the place."

He laughed and put down his coffee and leaned forward. "Yes?" he said with an interested gleam.

"Well, you just seemed so insensitive to your colleagues . . . calling them half a man and stuff. Is that how you're supposed to do it over here?"

He brushed his hair out of his eyes.

"Well, it's a game you see? That's half the fun of it for me. In fact that's half of politics for me. I love to make them squirm at their own inconsistencies. It's part of the game. Otherwise why am I in it?"

I saw a flicker of doubt cross his face but it disappeared quickly.

"Would you," I asked, "have acted that way if you knew television cameras were recording you?"

He blanched slightly but went immediately to the point that interested him.

"Why? Do you think I'm too intense for television? Do you think I should soften my approach from that point of view?"

I couldn't believe he was discussing technique. I thought it was clear I wanted to know *why* he acted the way he did.

"Why were you so combative with the people you were trying to change?"

"I told you," he said. "I hate their hypocrisy. I hate how they pussyfoot around. And they are liars. Besides, I represent working people who never have an opportunity to talk out strongly like that and this kind of approach appeals to them."

I listened carefully, trying to understand. Perhaps he wasn't really interested in changing the minds of the Parliamentarians he was addressing. I asked if he was combative so that his working class constituency could identify with what they wished to be like, or did he himself really mean it?

"Both," he said. "Anyway they are consistent with one another."

As he talked he seemed to be aware that he could be outsmarting himself. I wondered if I should press my criticism, or even if my feelings were accurate. His smile had that same sheepish quality to it. I couldn't figure out why. He was open-minded about the criticism while defending his strong approach, but there was something else underneath it that eluded me. Something like shame almost, as though he was aggressive because he was ashamed.

"You know," he said, "no one else will tell me these things. I mean they tell me not to move around so much. They tell me not to pace when others are speaking. But they don't talk to me about what you're talking about."

"I'm not even sure *what* I'm talking about. I only know your smile and something you're feeling right now doesn't jibe with how you defend yourself."

"Yes. I see what you mean."

"I wonder what it is."

"I don't know." He was uncomfortable but he didn't back away. I was uncomfortable discussing his political attitudes so candidly. I had known many politicians and they were rarely capable of such self-scrutiny. But I had introduced the discussion and felt it should go further.

"Maybe, you know, you could be too smart for your own good," I said. "Maybe you sense that that's what people sense about you. And whether it's true or whether it could translate into no votes, it's the same thing, isn't it?"

"No," he said. "I don't know. Maybe."

"Maybe you're so aggressive about other people's inconsistencies because you have them yourself."

"What do you mean? I'm consistent with my political beliefs. I'll tell the truth even if it's damaging to me."

I thought a moment. I believed him but that's not what I meant. I didn't know whether to go further. "I know you are consistent politically but you were attacking them on a personal level and on that level I'm not so sure you are as pure as you come on."

He got up and as he paced around the room he ran his hands through his hair.

"You mean," he said, "that I accuse others of personal hypocrisy *because* I recognize the same thing in myself?"

"Well, we all do that, don't we? In fact we usually accuse others of the things we're most apt to be guilty of in ourselves."

"So what am I guilty about?"

"Probably me."

"Well, we both know that, don't we? What has that got to do with politics?"

"What about all those phone calls you make to me?"

He stopped pacing. "What about them?"

"Well, don't you make those calls from your office?"

"Yes," he said. "Of course."

"So who pays for the calls?"

"It's a government phone."

"And who pays for the government?"

He stared at me.

"You're making about seven long-distance calls a week on the taxpayers' tab. That must have added up by now."

"What are you trying to do?" he said.

"I'm trying to see the truth. You called somebody half a man today and expect to get away with it. What if that guy looks up your telephone log and discovers your phone calls to Reno and Las Vegas are to me?" Gerry's face froze.

He quickly looked at his watch.

"Christ," he said, "I'm late for my party meeting. I'll call you later."

He went toward the door, hair falling in his eyes, put on the trench coat that I hoped would have a lining for the winter and as usual left without saying goodbye. His glasses were on the table.

I sipped the rest of his coffee. Self-confrontation was not one of Gerry's strong points. And diplomacy was not one of mine.

That night I went out with friends and stayed out until five in the morning.

Gerry called early the next day. "I thought you came to London to see me," he said.

I was taken aback. "Yes," I said, "I did."

"Where were you last night?"

"Oh. I went out."

"What was so interesting about what you did all night?" he said. "Couldn't you find better things to do with your time?"

"What do you mean?"

"Where did you go?" he asked.

"I went to dinner at the White Elephant with some friends and we talked for a long time. Then we stopped at Annabelle's and danced."

"And whom did you dance with?"

"Gerry. Wait a minute, what's going on?"

"Nothing," he said. "I'll be over later."

"I can hardly wait." I hoped he would hear the sarcasm.

❀ When he walked in I didn't hug him and he noticed it. He took off his trench coat and headed for the bedroom where he lay on the bed staring up at the ceiling. I made him a scotch and soda. He put it on the night table and I sat on the bed next to him. I didn't say anything.

"I'm not a deceptive man, you know."

"No," I said. "I know."

"But I'm acting like one. *I am being deceitful.*"

"So what else is new?"

He sighed. "I don't know. But it's tearing me up."

"Then tell your wife."

"I can't."

"Then don't tell her about me. Leave me out of it. Talk about what's wrong with the two of you."

He stared at my face. "There's nothing wrong with the two of us."

"Nothing wrong with the two of *you*? How can you say that?"

"There isn't. We don't have a stormy or passionate love but it's satisfactory."

I wondered what I'd feel like if someone said that about me. I wondered what his wife would say if someone asked *her* the same question.

"Does she ever complain about feeling lonely?"

"Oh, yes. Well, she used to. I'm gone so much, you know. But she got used to that a long time ago."

"Are you sure she's used to it?"

"I don't know," he said.

"Are you *sure* she's not lonely?"

"She's never said so."

He sipped his scotch for a while.

"Okay," I said, "we know you're lonely, right?"

"Yes." He put his arm under his head and said, "But I had gotten used to it."

"What do you mean *had*?"

"Just what I said. I *had* become used to it until you came along. I'm not as lonely now."

"Then why don't you see if you can't help her not to be so lonely . . . not so unhappy."

"What do you mean? I'd be lying to her. How could that possibly make her happy?"

"Well, you're lying to her because telling her the truth would be worse, right?"

"Yes."

"So, we're back to hypocrisy again. Maybe sometimes it's necessary. Maybe it's the price you pay."

He looked at me strangely. He concentrated on the ice in his drink as though he didn't want to talk anymore.

"Will you tell me something? Honestly?" I asked.

"Yes."

"Do you feel as though you are living alone? I mean deep down where you *really* live, are you living there alone?"

The question seemed to be new to him; as though he had never thought about it.

"Yes," he said, "I do."

"Then she must feel that way too."

He turned over on his side.

"Maybe she needs another relationship just like you did."

He stared out the window. "No," he said, "she's happy raising the children. She knows what my work requires." He put his arm over his face.

I put a blanket over him and lay under it beside him.

"You know," he said, "I sound like one of your male chauvinist pigs, don't I?"

I didn't say anything. Then he said, ". . . and besides, if I told her she wouldn't believe me."

"Oh, Gerry," I said, and soon we fell asleep together.

A while later he woke up and said, "I'm very clear about what you are to me."

"And what is that?" I asked.

Gerry didn't say anything.

"Gerry?"

"Yes?"

"Come on. Don't freeze up on me. What do you mean, you're very clear about what I am to you? Tell me, so I'll know too."

He cleared his throat and said, "Well, I've told one of my aides that we met. I've told him you are in town. I asked him to take over my speech for tonight so I could be with you."

"Oh? And what did he say?"

"Well, he asked if there was anything else he should know, and I said she's in town and I want to be with her and that's that."

I sat up in the bed. "I see," I said. "And that's what you mean by being clear about me?"

"Look," he said, "I have to go now. The speech would be over by now. I must go for the questions and answers."

The familiar chill went through me.

He took a shower, washed his hair and dressed.

"You didn't need a shower tonight, you know. Not tonight."

"No," he said, placing his glass on the sink in the kitchen. "I didn't, did I?"

He put on his coat and walked out of the door. For his sake I was glad it was the right one.

The next day I went back to California. ❊

Chapter 3

"What happens after death is so unspeakably glorious that our imagination and our feelings do not suffice to form even an approximate conception of it. . . . The dissolution of our time-bound form in eternity brings no loss of meaning."

—Carl G. Jung
Letters, Vol. 1

I got up from the tub, dried my prune-wrinkled skin, put on a pair of fuchsia colored slacks and an orange sweater and went down to see Marie and have dinner.

I walked into my kitchen. It was modern, fully equipped, and not really mine. Marie, being French and a cuisinière of exquisite ability, ruled her domain with possessive authority and wouldn't let me fix even a glass of Tab for myself. She was tiny and fragile, with legs the circumference of most people's wrists. Her fingers were twisted from arthritis and her hands and arms shook when she served. She wore slippers with toes cut out because her feet were deformed as a result of injuries sustained during World War Two running guns for the Free French against the Nazis. Her sister Louise, who had been in America twenty years and spoke not one word of English, was Marie's shadow, taking orders from her and clucking in desperation that nothing much ever went right.

Some six years before, about three in the morning, Marie had awakened me, excitedly knocking at my bedroom door and exclaiming that something was wrong with her husband John. I went downstairs to their room and saw he was stretched out on his bed. He was the color of oatmeal. His eyes were closed and he shuddered as though he was gagging for breath. I didn't know what to do. I was truly horrified and didn't want to touch him. I lifted his

head to apply mouth-to-mouth resuscitation. An awful sound came out of him, a deep guttural rattle. It sounded like an animal I didn't recognize. It frightened me deeply. At first I didn't know it was a death rattle and Marie didn't understand either. She kept insisting that he had just collapsed. I shook him, afraid that the rattle sound would come louder. It did. And finally it stopped. He died abruptly in my arms.

It was the first time I had ever seen a dead person. I wondered at what exact moment he had died, and I think it was at that moment that I began to seriously consider if there was such a thing as a soul. It seemed so impossible that what I held in my arms was all there could be that was left of a man. Did something that was John—his "soul"—live on? Did death hurt? If the soul survived the body, where did it go? To what purpose?

I couldn't sleep the rest of that night or for three nights after that, and I was working hard on shooting *Sweet Charity*. I seemed to be groping with the actual metaphysical meaning of death. I say metaphysical because it wasn't anything I could see, or touch, or hear, or smell, or taste. All I knew was that John, as I knew him, was gone. Or was he? I had been fond of him, but aside from the initial shock, I felt no great grief, no desperate gap. Yet I couldn't seem to accept his death as simply the end of his life. I knew somehow that there was more to it, and I knew I couldn't stop thinking about it. Every time I walked into the kitchen I thought about it and now was no different.

Marie and Louise and I talked awhile in broken French and English. I told her I was leaving for a long weekend, and she served me dinner in front of the television set in the living room. I watched the news and with the wine and a kind of exhaustion that I didn't understand, I went back upstairs and lay down on my bed. I was depressed and didn't know why.

What a world; we all seemed to be sleepwalking like cruel, friendly strangers—bumping into each other but never really mak-

ing contact with what was true . . . talking past and over and around each other . . . afraid of our own words as much as we were of those we might hear from others. There was such a communication breakdown that we were starving for trust, groping for handles and lifeboats and touching and niceness. We focused so much on big desperations and disciplined, quiet patience so as not to rock anybody's boat—much less our own. Always hoping maybe things would get better, always wondering what we could do—on and on until our futility became institutionalized, almost as though it had become safer not to know what our lives really meant.

I tried to feel sleepy. The glass in my hand dripped sweat from the warmth of my holding it. Little things, I thought. I should focus on the pleasure of little things. The soft green of the palm tree leaves just outside my window, the squashed black olives fallen on the cement driveway from the companion tree I had planted myself, wondering if I could actually be responsible for something growing . . . warm water and soap bubbles, the jog I would take tomorrow morning that would make me feel good all day because I had worked hard for it—small, but strung together, small stuff made me feel better.

✳ I remembered sitting on Clifford Odets' bed just before he died. I had loved and respected his plays very much. He could really write about human hope and triumph over adversity . . . especially in people with small and unrecognized lives. The cancer had made his head look like that of a shriveled bird. His massive mane of hair had fallen out; his stomach was swollen with the disease and tubes hung from his nose. He sipped milk from a plastic container and asked me to open the windows so cool air would blow across the chilled container.

"I want to live," he said, "so that I can write for large bunches of people about how much pleasure there is in things no bigger than a fly's eye."

❃ About two o'clock I felt sleepy. In London it was ten in the morning.

Images of my life drifted in and out of my mind . . . a long stretch of the Sahara Desert I wished I had crossed once just to see if I could do it . . . dancing with a handkerchief and a Russian peasant in a restaurant in Leningrad while the patrons clapped . . . a Masai mother in Africa dying of syphilis while giving birth . . . a squadron of birds flying as one, on a film location in Mexico, while I wondered how they kept together . . . wide, vast spaces through the countryside of China where I took the first American women's delegation, dressed in the same unisex Chinese clothing . . . Gerry's face when I told him I loved to travel alone . . . a big but compact trunk with drawers and closets that I wished could be my mobile home so I would never have to live anywhere permanently . . . dancers, choreographers, flying sweat, tinny pianos, flashbulbs, standing ovations, hot television lights, quiet movie sets, press conferences, difficult questions, political campaigns, bumbling but well-meaning candidates . . . George McGovern's crumpled face the night Richard Nixon won by a landslide . . . Academy Awards and my anxiety that I would *win* one for *Irma La Douce* when I thought my performance didn't deserve it . . . my disappointment when I *didn't* win one for *The Apartment* because that was the year Elizabeth Taylor had almost died with her tracheotomy . . . the four other times I was nominated and really didn't care . . . long rehearsals, professional arguments, painful muscles and stage fright, dumb studio executives, disciplined hours of writing which revolved around the personal and ever-present feeling of a long search for who I really was.

What was it that was missing? And was I, like so many other women, continually searching for the shape of my own identity in a relationship with a man? Did I believe the other half of me was to be found in loving someone, regardless of the frustration and futility involved?

Hong Kong and Gerry flooded my mind. I had met him there on another of his conferences. Another hope that this time it would be different, more fulfilling.

"It's wonderful how you love to pick up and go on a moment's notice," he had said. "How do you do that? How can you be so flexible? And you see so much. I never have time."

He never noticed that I didn't answer . . . that I wasn't sure whether I was running *toward* something or *away* from myself. I wondered if Gerry would really have taken the time if he had it. I didn't think he would see what he looked at . . . not really. He had traveled through Africa as a young man. But when he spoke of it, I suddenly realized that he never once mentioned what he ate, what he touched, what he saw, what he smelled, how he felt. He spoke mainly about Africa as a sociological trip, not as a human trip. He spoke of how the "masses" were exploited and poor and colonized, but never how they really lived and felt about it.

He had never been to Hong Kong before, and when we sat in his hotel room I had to interpret the surroundings for him. He didn't seem to feel the milling paradisiacal mess that was Hong Kong— the rickshaw coolies mingled with taxis; the teeming millions (5,500,000) swollen and spilling into the bay; the shoppers' paradise of Chinese silks, Japanese brocades, Indian cottons, and Swiss laces; goods and watches, and food and jewelry and dope and perfume and designs and jade and ivory and trinkets from all over the world brought to this free port for profit—none of it seemed to dazzle Gerry or cause his mouth to drop open. In fact, he said he hadn't even had a Chinese meal since he'd arrived.

He was concerned that the guards patrolling his floor would recognize us and think ill of him. I told him that in Asia everyone

always knows everything we foreigners do anyway and it doesn't matter to them. They just need to know.

He listened as though I were telling him a fairy tale when I described how I had walked to the bottom of Kowloon; past the silk shops, the jade factories, the watches from Switzerland and the residential district where his countrymen, the British, lived. I told him about the Star Ferry and the Bay itself where the crimson-sailed Chinese junks glided from the mainland. I told him about Cat's Street where shopping stalls spilled over with anything your imagination could conjure up. I told him how I had climbed to the top of Victoria Peak and watched the boats below in the harbor. He sat entranced at my dizzying description of diamonds, pearls, antiques, luxurious food, hand-woven materials, and intricate artistry done by children as young as twelve who were doing grown-up business before they realized what it was doing to them. I described the throngs of tourists . . . European, African, Japanese, Malay, Indian, American . . . on and on, all looking for bargains.

I described to Gerry how the spices hung in the air, how rock and roll music mingled with Chinese opera. How hawkers of plastic necklaces stooped and squatted to shovel rice into their mouths from delicate china bowls with hand carved ivory chopsticks. Tourists rushed, merchants rushed, children rushed, buses rushed, coolies rushed . . . a rush to cram as much buying and selling into the smallest amount of time.

And somehow it all worked. Everybody there was dedicated to making money, with no illusions, no pretensions about why Hong Kong existed. It was like Las Vegas. No self-righteousness about it. It was what it was. If you got taken it was part of the game. And somehow you expected it because all anybody wanted was a bargain anyway. Hong Kong was a place where you went broke saving money.

Gerry's eyes sparkled and gleamed as I talked every night of what I had done during the day while he was attending meetings.

It was true that he didn't get out as much as he wanted, but when he did it was as though he had never left his room.

And on our last day I had arranged for a small boat to take us to the New Territories where I knew a spot for a picnic. I packed lemon squash and sandwiches and tarts.

But on the boat he talked again of the squalid conditions he saw the Chinese living in. He spoke again of the disparity between rich and poor. He talked of how the wealthy must find a way to willingly share their profits with those who were less fortunate. It never occurred to him that the poverty stricken might have a richness of spirit the wealthy would envy if they knew of it. It never occurred to him that a rich person might be miserable in another more isolated and alienated way. He never thought "a rich person." It was "the rich," "the poor," an amorphous whole.

I remembered how a dear friend of mine had caught me in my sometimes knee-jerk liberalism by accusing me of having absolutely no compassion for the wealthy while I lavished my bleeding heart completely on only the poor. The truth of it had shocked me deeply.

"Gerry?" I stopped him. "What about those hills over there that look like jade that even the poor can enjoy?"

He looked up.

"And look at those sampans gliding by with the crimson sails. How about the way those people are waving at us?"

He stood up. "I guess I sound like the *Sunday Observer*, don't I?" Gerry smiled shyly. "I'm sorry," he said, "I can get tedious, can't I?"

We put into port at an inlet in the New Territories and went ashore. The crew remained aboard. Gerry carried the picnic boxes and I carried the thermos and a blanket.

Overhanging trees rustled in the sea breeze at the edge of the water as we began to walk into the lush hills above. We breathed the fragrant air. He took off his shoes and sank his feet into the earth. He sighed and spread out his arms into the warm sun. He

stopped at every tree and wild flower. He stuck a daisy behind his ear.

We came to a stream sparkling in the sun with birds swooping through the flowering bushes on either side. No one was around. He took off his shirt and trousers and with a movement like liquid he sprawled on his back in the gushing water. He reached up for me. I took off my summer dress and waded in and lay next to him. We felt the slippery rocks under us and didn't care when the stream began to gently glide us downstream. Birds chirped at us above from the trees. We locked arms and stood up at the same time dripping sparkling drops from our hair. Gerry circled his arm around my head and rolled me into his chest. Silently we walked back to our clothes.

I stood beside him.

"Oh shit," he said, resting his arms on my shoulders and looking into my eyes. "How am I going to reconcile you with the rest of my life?"

"I don't know," I said. "I don't know."

He unfolded the blanket and spread it out on the ground. We lay on it and looked up through the big tree at the sky.

About an hour later we walked back to the boat. I wondered how he would reconcile *himself* with the rest of his life.

❋ The next morning Marie fixed me breakfast as I sat on the patio. I wasn't sure what I was thinking—my thoughts were too jumbled, clanking against one another. Certainly I was frustrated with Gerry, but it was much more than that. I was in between pictures, but my work was going fine. And I had another date to play Vegas and Tahoe soon which I knew I'd be prepared for. So I can only say that I was a reasonably happy person by all comparative standards but I was not particularly peaceful.

David called. He had just gotten into town and asked if I was going to yoga class. I said I'd meet him there.

I loved hatha yoga because it was physical, not meditational, although it did require concentration and a sense of relaxation. But with the sun streaming through the window and the sound of the instructor's voice acting as accompaniment, I loved it as I strained every muscle and sinew in my body to feel activated. The physical struggle cleared my brain.

"Have respect for your body and it will be nice to you," said my teacher (he was Hindu), "and go slow. Yoga requires common sense. Don't take your body by surprise. You must warm up before you stretch. Don't ambush your muscles. Muscles are like people; they need preparation, otherwise they get frightened and tighten up. You must have respect for their pace. Think of it like an explorer going into new territory. A wise explorer goes slow, for he never knows what may be around the bend. Only when you go slow can you feel it before you reach it. You see, yoga gives you self-esteem because it puts you in touch with yourself. It is very peaceful inside yourself. Learn to live there. You will like it."

I listened to his words in between postures.

"Yoga achievement requires four attitudes," he said, "faith, determination, patience, and love. It is like life. And if you are good and faithful in your struggle in this life, the next one will be easier."

My leotard was damp with sweat. "Struggle in this life and the next one will be easier?" I guessed he really believed that stuff. He was, after all, a Hindu. I put on a skirt and T-shirt, and David and I left class.

Walking out into the drenching California sunshine, David said, "I'm going over to the Bodhi Tree bookstore. Want to come?"

"The Bodhi Tree?" I asked. "Isn't that the tree Buddha meditated under for forty days or something?"

"That's right," he said.

"So what kind of a bookshop is it—Indian?"

"Oh, a little," he answered. "They have all sorts of occult and metaphysical stuff there. Haven't you ever heard of it?"

I felt shy but admitted I hadn't.

"Well, I think you'll like it," he said gently. "If you relate so well to your yoga, you'll love some of the writing of the ancient mystics. I'm surprised you spent so much time in India without getting into the spiritualization of the place. Anyway, it's on Melrose near La Cienega. I'll meet you there."

"Sure, why not," I said. Looking back, I can say that making that simple, lazy-afternoon decision to visit an unusual bookstore was one of the most important decisions of my life. And again, I am reminded that we make important small moves when we are prepared. Earlier in my life such a suggestion would have seemed a waste of an afternoon when I had so many scripts to read and so many phone calls to answer. I was too busy being successful to understand that there were other dimensions to life.

David was already at the Bodhi Tree when I arrived, waiting for me outside, leaning against a tree. He smiled as I fitted my big Lincoln into a parking space meant for a Volkswagen.

"I rent this car," I said. "I don't own one. They're a pain in the ass and I don't understand them. As long as I have four wheels and some gas I'm satisfied. Do you know what I mean?"

"Yes," he answered. "Probably better than you realize." He took me by the arm and led me inside. As we walked in, I smelled sandalwood incense filtering faintly through the rooms of the cluttered bookstore. I looked around. Posters of Buddha and of yogis I had never heard of smiled down from the walls. Customers with books in their hands stood about drinking herb teas and talking in soft voices. I began to study the bookshelves. Lined up along the walls were books and books on subjects ranging from life after death to how to eat on Earth while alive. I smiled faintly at David. I felt out of place and a little silly.

"This is fascinating," I said, wishing that I hadn't found it necessary to say anything at all.

A young woman in sandals and a gauze skirt came over to us handing us tea.

"Can I help you?" she asked in a voice that was calm and peaceful. She matched the atmosphere in the shop—or maybe I was being theatrical. When I turned to look at her, she recognized me and suggested that she introduce me to the owner who was in his office having tea. David smiled and we followed.

The office was creaking with books. The owner was young, in his mid-thirties, and wore a beard. He was pleased to see me and said he was honored. He said he had read my books and was especially interested in what I had to say about my time in the Himalayas.

"How deeply are you into meditational technique?" he asked. "Do you use Kampalbhati breathing? It's difficult but effective, don't you think?"

I didn't know what he was talking about and just at that moment a young man with a crew cut and a football T-shirt sauntered in. He looked at me, at David, at the owner (whose name was John) and had a kind of smirk on his face.

"Listen, man," he said, "what's all this shit about if you think right you get happy? I mean, man, how *can* a dude be happy in this world and why are you people conning folks into thinking they can?"

David touched my arm when he felt how startled I was. John asked if he could help the guy, but he went right on. "I mean, what is this?" he said, "with the incense and the herb teas and the flashy posters—you guys are full of shit."

John gently took David and me by the arm and led us out of the office and back into the shop.

"I'm sorry," he said.

"No problem," said David. "He's got to find his own way like we all do." I nodded that it didn't matter, and David suggested we could find what we wanted by ourselves—not to be concerned.

"Jesus," I said, "why does he find this place so threatening?"

"I don't know," said David. "Maybe he's got a big emotional investment in hostility. It's hard to believe that peace is possible."

Then he led me over to a huge bookshelf marked "Reincarnation and Immortality." On it were books from the Bhagavad Gita to the Egyptian Books of the Dead to interpretations of the Holy Bible and the Kabala. I didn't know what I was looking at.

I looked at David closely. "Do you believe all this?" I asked.

"All what?" he asked.

"I don't know," I said. "Do you really believe in reincarnation?"

"Well," he said, "when you've studied the occult as long as I have you learn that it's not a question of whether it's true but more a question of how it works."

"You mean you believe it's that firmly established as a fact?"

He shrugged his shoulders and said, "Why yeah, I do. It's the only thing that makes sense. If we don't each have a soul—then why are we alive? Who knows if it's true? It's true if you believe it and that goes for anything, right? Besides, there must be something to the fact that the belief in the soul is the one thing *all* religions have in common."

"Yes," I said. "But maybe all religions are phony too."

He went on looking through the books not as though the conversation was uninteresting to him, but more as though he was simply and directly looking for a book.

I hadn't thought much about religion since I was twelve years old and played tic-tac-toe in Sunday school class.

David reached up for a book. "You should read some of the works not only on this shelf but also of Pythagoras, Plato, Ralph Waldo Emerson, Walt Whitman, Goethe, and Voltaire."

"Did those guys believe in reincarnation?"

"Sure, and they wrote extensively about it. But it always ends up on the occult bookshelf like it's black magic or something."

"Voltaire believed in reincarnation?"

"Sure," said David, "he said he didn't find it any more surprising

to be born lots of times than to be born once. I feel the same way."

I looked at him. His blue eyes were steady and clear.

"Listen," he said. "Do you know what the definition of occult means?"

"No," I answered.

"Well, it means 'hidden.' So just because something is hidden doesn't mean it's not there."

I looked more closely at David's bony-cheeked, sad face. He spoke in a peaceful tone, with no hesitancy except when he realized I was trying to comprehend what he was saying.

"Do you want me to compile a kind of reading list for you?" he asked with down-to-earth practicality.

I hesitated slightly, remembering five scripts I had to read and also wondering what Gerry would think if he saw me reading books like these.

"Sure," I said. "Why not? People thought the world was flat too until someone proved otherwise. I guess I should be curious about all kinds of 'hidden' possibilities. Whoever thought there were bugs crawling all over our skin until someone came up with the microscope?"

"Great," said David. "For me, real intelligence is open-mindedness. If you feel you're looking for something, why not give it a shot?"

"Okay." I found myself smiling.

David said, "Make yourself comfortable browsing around and I'll get you a bunch of stuff to read." He wiped the corners of his mouth and with an intense squint he began to survey the bookshelves. I thumbed through books on food-combining, yoga exercises, meditation and other healthful subjects I understood.

After about half an hour, David had an armful of books and I wondered as I thanked him and we walked out into the California sunlight if I'd ever crack one of them.

I was leaving for Honolulu the next day so I said goodbye to David and went home to think, rest, pack, and if I had time, to read.

❋ That night I found myself looking up reincarnation in the encyclopedia.

Let me say that I was not brought up to be a religious person. My parents sent me to church and Sunday school, but it was because it was the accepted place to be on Sundays. I wore crinoline petticoats and tried not to glance too often at the lyrics in the hymnal I was supposed to have memorized. I wondered where the money went after the collection plate was passed, but I really never had any feeling one way or the other whether there was a God or not.

Jesus Christ seemed like a smart, wise, and certainly a good man, but I viewed what I learned about him in the Bible as philosophical, mythological, and somehow detached. What he preached and did didn't really touch *me*, *so* I didn't believe or disbelieve. He just happened . . . like all of us . . . and he did some good things a long time ago. I took his being the Son of God with a grain of salt and, in fact, by the time I was in my late teens, had decided for myself that God and religion were definitely mythological and if people needed to believe in it that was okay with me, but I couldn't.

I couldn't believe in anything that had no proof and besides, I wasn't all that agonized by the need for a purpose in life or something to believe in besides myself. In short, where religion, faith in God, or the immortality of the soul were concerned, I didn't think much about them. No one insisted and I found the subject boring—not nearly so stimulating as something real and humorous like people. Every now and then as I grew older I would engage in a bemused argument over the pitfalls of such mythological beliefs and how they detracted from the real plight of the human

race. I didn't much like the authoritarianism of the church—any church—and I considered it dangerous because it made people afraid they would burn in hell if they didn't believe in heaven.

But as much as I was disinterested in God and religion and the hereafter, there was something I was extremely interested in. From the time I was very young I *was* interested in identity. My identity and that of everyone I met. Identity seemed real to me. Who was I? Who was anyone? Why did I do the things I did? Why did they? Why did I care about some people and not others? The analysis of relationships became a favorite subject of mine—the relationship I had with myself as well as with others.

So maybe because I was interested in the origin of my own identity it intrigued me that there might be more to me than what I was aware of in my conscious mind. Perhaps there were other identities buried deep in my subconscious that I only needed to search for and find. Indeed many times in my work with self-expression, whether dancing, writing, or acting, I would be amazed at myself, baffled as to where a feeling or a memory or an inspiration had come from. I had put it down to a hazy concept called the creative process, as did most of my fellow artists, but I have to admit that at the bottom of whoever I was I felt a flame that I was not able to understand, to touch. What was the origin of that flame? Where did it come from? And what had come before it?

I was always more interested in what went *before* than what might come after. So for that reason, I suppose I wasn't so interested in what would happen to me after I died as I was in what made me the way I was. Therefore when the notion of *life before birth* first struck me I guess you might say I was curious to explore it.

The encyclopedia said that the doctrine of reincarnation went back as far as recorded history. It consisted of belief in the connection of all living things and the gradual purification of the soul, or spirit, of man until it returned to the common source and

origin of all life which was God. It was the belief that the soul was immortal and embodied itself time and time again until it morally worked out the purification of itself. It said that the companion subjects of karma—that is, working out one's inner burdens—and reincarnation—the physical opportunity to live through one's karma—were two of the oldest beliefs in the history of mankind and more widely accepted than almost any religious concepts on earth. This was news to me—I had always vaguely connected reincarnation with disembodied spirits, hence ghosts, the occult and things that go bump in the night. I had never connected it with any major, serious religion.

Then I looked up religion. Although it was impossible to give a conclusive definition, several characteristics were common to most religions. One was belief in the existence of the soul, another the acceptance of supernatural revelation, and finally, among others, the repeated quest for salvation of the soul. From the Egyptians to the Greeks, to the Buddhists and Hindus, the soul was considered a pre-existent entity which took up residence in a succession of bodies, becoming incarnate for a period, then spending time in the astral form as a disembodied entity, but reincarnating time and time again. Each religion had its own belief for the origin of the soul, but no religion was without the belief that the soul existed as a part of man and was immortal. And somewhere between Judaism and Christianity, the West had lost the ancient concept of reincarnation.

I closed the encyclopedias and thought for a while.

Hundreds of millions of people believed in the theory of reincarnation (or whatever the term might be) but I, coming from a Christian background, hadn't even known what it actually meant.

I prepared to leave to meet Gerry wondering what else might be going on in this world that I had never thought about before. ✼

Chapter 4

"It is the secret of the world that all things subsist and do not die, but only retire a little from sight and afterward return again. . . . Jesus is not dead: he is very well alive; nor John, nor Paul, nor Mahomet, nor Aristotle; at times we believe we have seen them all, and could easily tell the names under which they go."

—Ralph Waldo Emerson
Nominalist and Realist

The flight from L.A. to Hawaii was blue and smooth. I slept and thought of Gerry most of the way. I thought of my friendship with David and wondered how many other people I had walked and eaten and hung out with and had never *really* known. I checked into the Kahala Hilton under another name. No one noticed. Then I went to my room to wait.

There I was . . . standing out on the balcony of yet another hotel room, overlooking the lilting, lulling Pacific, the red sun nestling on the water . . . waiting. Waiting for a man. Waiting for a man I loved or thought I loved, whatever that meant. I knew that what I felt for him was powerful and I knew that I'd go anywhere I had to to be with him. We were both busy and had creative work to fill our lives, but I guess we needed more. I know I did. As long as I could remember, I needed to be in love. A man seemed the most obvious object of such a feeling and desire. But maybe not, maybe I just needed to *feel love,* and a deeper objective was what seemed to be eluding me. I don't know.

Honolulu is one of my favorite places, especially at sunset, even though now it was crammed with muumuu-clad, camera-toting tourists on conventions. And the Kahala Hilton is one of the pret-

tiest hotels in the world, with its indoor-outdoor landscaping, the underwater bar, and the dolphins that leap playfully in the seawater pool below. I listened quietly to the lull of the water slapping the beach. I heard the coconut pines rustle. Then I heard a thud. A coconut had fallen ripe and ready to crack. I looked at my watch. Gerry said he would arrive by six-thirty. It was already seventhirty. The weather was good so there were no planes delayed. And airport control had said there was no weather problem out of London. So he must have taken off on time. Well, the world was only a golf ball. He'd be here soon. But I resented the tardiness because I knew we'd only have thirty-six hours. Jesus, how time seemed to be my enemy. No matter what I was involved with I never had enough of it. So much did I want to use and enjoy whatever there was of it that I was continually frustrated at the time I didn't have, and somehow the past and the future were always getting in the way; the past with its consequences, the future with its mystery. I wanted the present to be all there was.

I breathed the soft twilight air, walked inside the room and turned on the television set.

Carter was upset with Begin. Teddy Kennedy was upset with Carter. The dollar was still falling. Pierre Trudeau had called someone a dirty name in the Canadian Parliament. The world was funny or falling apart, depending on how you looked at it. Nobody had it together.

I looked around the hotel room. I hadn't wanted to attract attention so I had asked for a room, not a suite. But it was plenty for the time Gerry and I would have together. I knew he would love Honolulu. He had never been here. I hoped he would be able to *feel* it. The first thing he would do would be to walk out on the balcony and survey what surrounded him. He needed to do that. He would look out at Diamond Head and he would talk about the palm trees. He calmed down when he was surrounded by nature. His mind could actually idle in neutral over a rain-drenched tree with a bird quivering its wings in the wet. He could actually stop

fretting over the state of the world and the prospects of his reelection when the sun rose flamingo-pink. His spirit seemed soothed by the idea that nature was beautiful, more powerful than anything else. But then he had grown up in the English countryside, endured the English winters. He had walked in English meadows and swum in the cold water of the English Channel. City life got him down. He needed space and natural challenge. I was glad we were meeting in Honolulu. He would enjoy the swaying peace of it. There I was thinking of Gerry again as though I were he.

Another fifteen minutes had gone by. Fifteen minutes we'd never get back. The carpet in the room was deep maroon, tufted. The bedspread was olive green with maroon flowers. Why did the draperies always have to match the spread? I wondered if Hilton would hack a hotel into the side of a mountain in China. How silly the Chinese looked dancing to "Staying Alive" from *Saturday Night Fever* at the Chinese-American reception. And how were one billion Chinese going to turn on a dime yet another time in their long struggle toward modernization? Was it really worth it? I didn't know what was worth anything anymore.

I lit another cigarette. Gerry had tried giving up smoking a year ago and now continually scolded me for not even trying. He said he smoked because he was always walking into rooms where someone else was smoking. I knew what he meant. I could give it up too. And had—lots of times. But whenever I had big decisions to make I needed a silent companion; anything that would sit there and smolder but not interfere. I didn't inhale so it never bothered me when I sang and danced, but it did hurt my throat and make me feel like coughing. Okay, so I'd give it up when Gerry arrived and see if he would too.

The moon was coming up over Waikiki now. Diamond Head was a black hulk in the reflection of the sea. Maybe he missed the plane from London. The meeting to discuss North-South problems could take place without him, I supposed. But I couldn't.

The phone rang beside the bed. It was nearly eight o'clock.

"Hi," said Gerry, as though we hadn't been apart for weeks.

I melted at his quiet voice. He talked differently when he was away from his office.

"We've been at the airport in a reception hall," he said. "We were there for an hour. Somebody was supposed to be attending to the luggage while they told us to wait. But nobody was. I finally collected it myself. When did you arrive?"

"A few hours ago," I said, not wanting to say how I'd counted each wasted minute.

"I have to get rid of some worthy women who want to have a drink with our delegation."

"Worthy women?" I asked.

"Yes, worthy women. They're silly but they mean well. So I'll take care of that and be down as fast as I can. I'm longing to see you."

I hung up, looked in the mirror again, swallowed my irritation at his chauvinistic remark about the worthy women and decided to change into my favorite green wool sweater.

I opened my door so Gerry wouldn't have to knock and wait for me to answer. The hallway was alive with Secret Service and visiting politicians from all over the world. I wondered how he'd get through without being recognized.

I had my sweater over my head when I heard him open the door and come into the room. I knew he was there but I couldn't see him because the wool got stuck on my earring. I felt his arms around my waist. My eyes were full of green wool. He kissed my neck. I could feel myself gasp both at the warmth of his mouth and also because the sweater was tearing at my pierced ear. I couldn't move. He ducked his hand under the sweater and through the wool found my face. "Don't ever move," he said. "I like you just like this. Let me help you," he offered. He released my earring, then kissed my ear.

He backed away from me, looked me over. "I like that color,"

he said. "It's nice." Then he walked around the room and said it was just like his. As I thought he would, he walked immediately onto the balcony and looked out toward Diamond Head.

"Look at those palm trees," he said. "They seem unreal, almost painted against that sky. Is that Diamond Head?"

"Yes," I answered. "It looks like a backdrop, but it's real."

"It's a paradise, isn't it?" He took my arm and wrapped it around his waist. "Are you hungry?" he said. "You must be. You always are."

"Yes."

"So am I. Let's eat."

So I went to the phone and ordered two Mai-Tais and some dinner. Gerry didn't know what Mai-Tais were. He was amused by my asking for extra pineapple and went to the bathroom to soak in the tub.

He was in there when the waiter arrived. I covered the dinner plates and took the Mai-Tais into the bathroom. I sat on the toilet seat while he soaked.

He sipped his Mai-Tai through a floating cherry in the glass. He swished the hot sudsy water around his legs. They were too long for the tub.

"So," I said, "how's it going? How've you been?"

"Fine," he said.

"What else? That's what you always say."

"Well, we've been having our problems in London. You've read about it. Never mind about me. How is your life?"

I told him about the new choreography for my show, about the exercise I did every day to keep in shape, about the health-food diets I was experimenting with, and about how hard it was to find good movie scripts for women. He asked why, and I said it must have something to do with a backlash reaction from militant feminism. Nobody seemed to know how to write women's roles anymore because they didn't know what women really wanted. At least, the men writers didn't know. And the women writers wrote

about how unhappy and unfulfilled women were. So who cared? When it came to entertainment, who would pay to see that?

"I don't know," said Gerry. "I'm having enough trouble trying to decipher what *people* want . . . not what women want. I don't mean to sound arrogant," he said, "but we have an economy that's failing for everyone and I'm not sure we are going to be able to keep our chins up."

I said I could see what he meant, and then he questioned me about what was going on in America. I hesitated, then told him I wasn't sure. The American people were hard to figure out. Then I questioned him about what was going on in the world. We bantered back and forth, loving to savor one another as we talked and smiled and listened even if we were talking past each other. It wasn't *what* we were saying, it was *how* we were saying it. That's what we liked. We watched each other with a double fascination. We got something special from how our hands moved, our expressions, the way one would hold a head in a hand when trying to concentrate: one performer mesmerized by another.

We talked about Carter, inflation, the dollar, even about Idi Amin and solar energy, and as we talked it was like making love with our minds on a double level, each word setting off tiny sparks and explosions in our heads. It didn't matter whether the conversation was a new tax proposal or OPEC price hikes or women's roles in movies. Some kind of sensual dynamic was operating. A dynamic that was hard for me to explain, but we were both familiar with it. I would say something about the oil fields in Iran and the need for the workers to be unionized and behind Gerry's eyes he would melt over me like hot drawn butter. He was listening and heard my words, but I could feel a volcano slowly erupting inside of him spilling through his eyes. I didn't want to reach over and touch him or kiss him or even climb into the tub with him. I liked the feeling of holding back and communicating on the double level. I liked the feeling of using words to control what was under-

neath, because I felt it was almost too explosive. I wasn't sure why.

I gazed at his body in the warm water. VitaBath suds bubbled around the outline of his skin. I watched how his penis floated. I wondered what that felt like, yet in some way I felt I knew.

Gerry lay back in the tub and closed his eyes.

After a few moments, I said, "Gerry?"

He opened his eyes. "What?" he asked.

"Do you believe in reincarnation?"

"*Reincarnation?*" He was astonished. "My God," he said, "why do you ask that? Of course not."

"Why do you say, 'Of course not'?" I asked.

"Well, because," he laughed, "it's a fantasy. People who can't accept life as it is *here* and *now* on its own terms feel the need to believe such imaginings."

"Well, maybe," I said feeling somehow hurt that he would ridicule such a theory so resoundingly. "Maybe you're right, but more than a few million people do believe in it. Maybe they have a point."

"They *have* to," he said. "Those poor buggers don't have anything else in their lives. I can't blame them, of course, but if they believed a little more in the here and now it would make jobs like mine a great deal easier."

"What do you mean?" I asked.

"I mean, they don't tend to their lives as though they could improve them. I mean, they just exist as though it will be better the next time around, and this time isn't all that important. No, Shirl," he went on, his tone very determined, "I want to do something about the desperation of people's lives *now*. This is all we've got, and I respect that. Why? Do you believe in that gibberish?"

I felt put off by his put-down. I wished he would have been open-minded enough to discuss it at least.

"I don't know," I said. "Not really. But not Reilly either."

"Not Reilly?" he said. "What does that mean?"

"Just an Irish joke, Gerry. Just an Irish joke to an Englishman, if you get my meaning."

He flipped one hand over in the water and closed his eyes again.

Jesus, I thought, this metaphysical stuff certainly could get people upset. I wondered why. I didn't feel threatened by it at all. It seemed like a good dimension to explore. What harm could it do? I could see his point about people not taking responsibility for their own destinies here and now, but how *did* you reconcile the injustice of the accident of birth into poverty and deprivation when others were born into comfort? Was life really that cruel? Was life simply an accident? Accepting that seemed suddenly too easy, even lazy.

"This feels so good," said Gerry, lolling in the soapy tub. "This is a nice bathroom. This tub's too short, but it's nice. In fact this hotel is lovely, but especially this bathroom. It's just a bathroom, but it's nice because you're sitting here."

"Yes," I said, shifting my mind away from my thoughts. "Bathrooms are private places, aren't they? If you feel comfortable with somebody in a bathroom you've really got something important going with them."

Gerry smiled and nodded.

A bathroom *was* a private, primitive place, a place for basics. I thought of the time years ago a lover of mine had smashed up the bathroom in a hotel room in Washington. He had swept his arms violently through the drinking glasses on the sink and thrown my hair dryer into the mirror, shattering its pieces clear into the tub. We had been arguing in the bedroom about his jealousy but it was the bathroom where he went to be violent.

Then I thought of an incident in my childhood. I had lost the starring part in a school ballet I had dreamed for five years of doing. I remembered looking at myself in the mirror above the sink wondering what was wrong with me and before I realized what was happening I threw up in the sink.

I thought of the first dinner party I had given in California. I was so nervous and unable to cope as a hostess that I sat in my bathroom until dinner was over.

I thought of the bitter cold winter day that Warren and I had played in icy mud puddles. I was six and he was three. Mother was angry. She plunged Warren into the tub to wash him and I could hear his anguished cries coming from the bathroom. I remembered the day he fell on a broken milk bottle and Dad had rushed him to the bathroom to hold his gushing bleeding arm over the tub. I remembered his pleading face looking up at Dad's as he said, "Daddy, don't let it hurt."

I remembered a housekeeper I had had who retired to the bathroom every afternoon at six and lit a candle in the tub and prayed.

And I remembered how the most important, private, comfortable, relaxed and necessary place *I* could ever have wherever I was in the world was a well-lit room with a clean sparkling tub of warm, soft-flowing water. It helped me make transitions from depression, confusion and hard work. It helped me get in touch with myself. It put me to sleep. It soothed my aching legs. It woke me up. It coordinated my body and mind, gave me a burst of new ideas and hopes and wit. And whenever I was out during a day if I knew I had a nice bathtub that I could fill with liquid warmth in a nice bathroom to come home to I was happy.

Gerry finished his Mai-Tai and handed me the glass. He washed himself and asked me to wash his back.

"You know," he said, out of the tub and drying himself, "I'm glad there is such a thing as a telephone, taxpayers or not. By the way, you were quite right about that. I *am* paying the bills myself. It would have been difficult for me if I hadn't been able to talk to you all these weeks."

"Yes, I know," I said. "For me too," watching him swing the towel behind his back.

"But you know," he said, "I've been obsessed with your voice and I don't like feeling obsessed."

"What do you mean?" I asked, shivering a bit.

"Well, I find that my whole day revolves around the time when I can find the private time to talk to you. It just depletes my energy, that's all, and I don't like the feeling."

I stared at him. What was he saying? It made me apprehensive.

"Are you going to eat your cherry?" Standing there in his towel he looked at my empty glass.

"No, it's too sweet for me."

"May I have it?"

I handed it to him and took his hand as he led me into the bedroom. We sat down to the now cold seafood Newburg on the room service tray. The waiter had brought only one fork. I gave it to Gerry. He didn't notice that I was eating with a knife. I put my trench coat over him so he wouldn't be chilled and he looked like a clean, overgrown, rugged cherub as he began to eat.

"You know those scuffed shoes that you loved to see me wear all the time?" he asked. I nodded. "Well, my daughter threw them away into the dustbin. She thought I should have new shoes so she just threw them away."

"Your daughter threw away my favorite shoes?"

"Yes." He leaned forward in anticipation of what I would say with an almost lost smile on his face. I didn't know what he expected me to say. So I said, "Well, maybe they smelled of perfume."

He leapt up, throwing my coat from his shoulders. He lifted me above his shoulders and hugged me to him laughing, and tumbled me onto the bed. His soft warm hands were everywhere on me. His hair brushed against my face. His nose collided with mine and squashed it. His skin was creamy and warm, smelling of VitaBath. He trembled slightly and hugged me close to him.

I opened my eyes and looked at his face. It was astonished, ecstatic and abandoned all at the same time. I sat up and held his hair in my hands and tugged at it.

"How do you keep your nails so long?" he said.

"Do you think they're too long?"

"No. I think they're beautiful. But they must be very strong."

He lifted his left hand in the air wiggling the little finger from which almost all the top joint was missing, lost in a freakish accident when he was very small. The damage had healed so well that one seldom noticed the finger, except when he himself drew attention to it. Now he said, "I have arthritis in this finger and it hurts. It's only developed recently. I wonder why."

"Probably not enough vitamin C," I said. "And no exercise."

We lay together watching him work his finger up and down.

"You know," he said, "I think I have this arthritis because I'm depleting my energy. I'm too obsessed with you. Yes," he went on, "you know how life is made up of small but blinding insights?"

"Yes," I said, "I know what you mean."

"I think I have to cool my feelings. I have to get back on an even keel."

"All right," I said. "Make it easy for yourself." I could feel my heart stop, frozen.

"You know," he said, "I've never had this kind of experience. Nothing anywhere near it. I don't know what I think about it. And I don't know why I feel so drawn to you. In spite of myself, I can't stop it."

I stared at my long fingernails. "Maybe we've had another life together," I said. I turned my head quickly toward him to see his reaction. "Maybe we left things unresolved between us and need to work them out in this lifetime."

A flush of confusion swept across his face. For one brief instant he didn't ridicule my notion. Then his expression cleared and he smiled at me.

"Sure," he said. "But seriously, I don't know what I want to do about us. I want you to know that."

"I know," I said. "I know what you're saying. I don't know what to do either. So, why don't we do nothing and for the time being just enjoy what we have?"

"But I want to be fair with you," he said. "I want to be fair with everybody. I've always put my work first. And if I dissipate my energy now, I'll lose what I've been working for. I have so much to do in the next eleven months and I'm reluctant to fragment myself."

I turned over and looked at him and sighed. "Yes, Gerry, I know all that. So have you considered giving us up? Just walking away from it?"

He answered immediately and with certainty. "No." And with genuine anxiety in his face he said, "Have you?"

"No," I lied. "Never. And I won't."

He took a deep breath and went on. "But you see I'm terribly bothered by the idea that I might be disappointing you. That is a real problem for me. I don't want to disappoint you."

"The way you don't want to disappoint the voters?" I asked.

"I have to ask you," he said. "What do you want from me?"

He caught me off guard. I thought a moment and said as if I had known it all along, "I want us to be happy when we're together. I don't understand why we are together either. But I don't want you to have to choose between me and anyone or anything else. I think you can have everything you already have and me, too. You can have it all, can't you? So you add one more dimension to your life. What's wrong with that? Maybe life should include all kinds of dimensions we haven't had the courage to embrace yet. I don't need a commitment of any kind from you. I don't even want one. I just want to know that you're happy when you're with me, and somehow we'll figure out what it's all about."

"But the more I have of you the more I want."

"Then take more of me. What's wrong with that?"

"That would mean giving up something else."

"Why?"

"Because I haven't got the time for you and for the rest of my life too."

"Maybe if you gave more time to feeling you deserved happiness it would not take so much."

"I can't. I think of what else I should be doing."

"Why don't you just think of what you *are* doing?"

"Because I always feel I should be doing something else."

"But what about yourself? What about enjoying yourself more when you can? What's wrong with enjoying yourself? Why do you think you don't deserve a good time?"

"Because I've got better things to do with my life than having a good time. I can't think of myself first."

"Maybe you should. Maybe if you figured out more of who you are you'd be able to help more people."

I remembered a reporter who interviewed me when I first returned from China. He was cynical about the enthusiasm I had for how the Chinese had struggled to win their new self-identity. Like most of the others, he thought I had been naive to be as moved as I was by the Chinese revolution. I explained how the Chinese had improved themselves compared to the recent past, and I said that the thing that moved me most was how they seemed to believe so deeply in themselves. That really angered the reporter.

"What do you mean, they believe in themselves? That's only propaganda and you bought it."

I asked, even if it was just propaganda, why was he so upset by the idea of believing you can do and have anything? And to my astonishment the anger turned to tears. He said nobody had the right to believe he could do or have anything—because in the end he'd be crushed. I realized he was talking about himself. *He* felt unworthy, couldn't trust himself. He left my apartment in New York and five hours later he called me.

"I've been driving around all night," he said. "What you said is exactly why my marriage is falling apart. My wife tells me the same thing. She says we'll never make a go of it unless I believe in myself more, unless I *believe* I can be happy. That's why I got so

upset with you. I'm afraid I can't do it, not strong enough. In fact I've set up a set of eloquently cynical standards as a journalist so that I ridicule anyone who hopes or dreams or dares to be what they want. Myself included. And that's because I don't believe in myself. So how can I take seriously anyone else who does?"

I said I hoped he'd write a good article anyway and wished him well.

Suddenly I thought I understood why people had been so upset with the success of the Chinese revolution. Whatever their system was they had dared to believe in themselves alone, without the help of the rest of the world.

Gerry fell asleep holding me. In sleep he looked so vulnerable. My thoughts worried at the inner uncertainty of this otherwise very strong man. Did he somehow hold himself responsible for the tragedy of his first brief marriage because his wife had died in childbirth? Certainly the second marriage had been expedient for him and personally convenient in providing a mother for the baby. But did he now feel guilty because he sensed he had cheated *himself*? I thought of a conversation I had had recently with my father. With all his forceful command he had never believed in himself either. And he was one of the most talented people I had ever known. Aside from being a superb real-life performer he was an accomplished violinist, a good teacher, and a perceptive thinker.

Now he was reaching the end of his life—or so he thought. And he had always drunk too much. Lately my mother had been ill with a major hip operation. Dad was faced with what he would do without her, and began to drink so heavily from early in the morning that Mother called me, more deeply concerned than she had ever been that this time he was really killing himself. Dad was with her as she spoke to me openly and honestly on the phone. Neither of them minded. For years we had all been frightened of where his drinking was leading and the fear was culminating in this one phone call.

"I'm so worried about him, Shirl," she said, "and I can't help him. You know what a talented good man he is but he doesn't believe that he is."

I asked her to let me speak to him.

"Hi, Monkey," he said, calling me by my nickname. I could see him sitting in that favorite chair of his, pipe rack beside him, the telephone tucked into his shoulder. I could feel him reach for his pipe and light it with the old antique lighter I had brought him from England.

"Daddy, let me be to the point, okay?"

"Okay," he said.

"Why are you drinking so much now?"

I had never asked him that question. I could never bring myself to ask him, I suppose because I was afraid he would tell me.

He began to cry. This was what I had been afraid of. I had never wanted to see Dad openly crack. Then he said, "Because I've wasted my life. I may have acted strong but that was because I never believed I could do anything. My mother taught me too well to be afraid and whenever I think about how afraid I am I can't stand it. So I have to drink." I could see his hands shaking as they used to whenever he wanted to detract from any emotion he might be displaying.

"I love you, Daddy," I said. And I started to cry too. I felt somehow that I had never really said that to him before. "Look what you did. You raised Warren and me. Doesn't that mean anything?"

"No, but I know you two didn't want to be like me. That's why you turned out like you did. You didn't want to be nothing. Like me." We were both crying and trying to talk through our tears. I wondered if any ashes had fallen to the floor.

"That's not altogether true," I said. "We just did more with the help you gave us than you did with the help *you* never got."

"But I feel so worthless when I realize what I haven't done with what I've got."

"Okay," I said. "But there's still time, you know."

"How?" he said. "What do you mean?" He tried to clear his throat. I wondered if Mother was watching him.

"Why don't you get out a pen and paper and every time you feel worthless put those feelings down on a piece of paper? I'll bet you could come up with some great notions on the feeling of feeling worthless."

He was really sobbing now. "Sometimes I think I can't stand it and if I just drink enough I won't have to bother waking up in the morning."

I swallowed. "Daddy," I said, "I've never asked you to promise me anything in my life, have I?"

"No, Monkey, you haven't."

"Well, will you promise me something now?"

"Yes, anything. What?"

"Will you promise me that instead of drinking, that every day you'll write at least one page of something you're feeling?"

"Me write? Christ, I'd be so ashamed if anybody read it."

"Okay, then don't let anybody read it. Just do it for yourself."

"But I don't have anything to say."

"How do you know if you haven't tried?" I could see him brush the lint from his left shoulder. I heard him cough.

"I can't write about myself. I can't even think about myself."

"Then write about me or Mother or Warren."

"You and Warren?"

"Sure."

"Lots of people would want to read that, wouldn't they?" he said sarcastically. I knew he was smiling.

"Well, only because it's from your point of view."

"You think so?"

"Yes, I do," I said. I could see him begin to rock in the chair.

"You know old Mrs. Hannah, my sophomore teacher, once told me I should write. In fact she told me I should talk less and write more."

"Really?" I remembered how he spoke of Mrs. Hannah when I was little. She had a broken-down car he loved to fix.

"Old Mrs. Hannah had the goddamdest car. She'd have been better off with a horse and buggy. That damned car was like another person to her. Do you know that one day out in the hayfield. . . ."

"Hey, Daddy," I said, "why don't you start by writing about Mrs. Hannah's car out in the hayfield? Don't waste it by talking about it."

"Is that how it works?" he asked, clearing his throat and sounding funny and mischievous. "You mean all the times I've held court could have been a book?"

"Sure. Didn't Mrs. Hannah always say you talked too long and too much with nothing to show for it afterwards?"

"Yep," he said, "she sure did. She was a pisser. She burned down her barn to get the insurance money and then ran off with the guy who sold it to her."

"Well, she sounds like a good character to write about."

"Would you read something if I wrote it?"

"Sure. I can't wait. Send it to New York. It'll get to me wherever I am."

"You mean you really think I have something to say?"

"Well, I've been listening to you for over forty years and I think you're funny and touching. Why don't you write about your pipe?"

We had both stopped crying now.

"Will you do it? Will you try?"

"Well, Monkey, I guess I have to, don't I?"

"Yep."

"I promise then. I promise."

"I love you, Daddy."

"I love you, Monkey."

We hung up. I walked around the house crying for another hour. Then I went to the phone and called a florist. I ordered a

rose a day for a month with a note attached. "A rose for a page. I love you."

Dad has been writing on and off ever since. I'm not sure if he's completely on the wagon. But then no writer I know is! But I do wish old Mrs. Hannah had mentioned his talent and her belief in him a little more often.

The notes that he sends me are short and each one tells a story, a story from the life of a man who influenced me deeply, because he inadvertently taught me to love brilliant and complicated men who needed someone to help unlock them. ❈

Chapter 5

"I very much doubt if anyone of us has the faintest idea of what is meant by the reality of existence of anything but our own egos."

—A. Eddington
The Nature of the
Physical World

G erry and I slept. Whenever we moved we adjusted ourselves to fit, leaving no space between us. At some point he murmured something about a wake-up call so his delegation wouldn't wonder where he was in the morning. I called the operator and waited for dawn when he would have to leave. I felt forlorn as I watched him sleep. He went away. His eyes were shut. He was lost in his own unconscious. I watched his sleep until I finally did the same. As I slept, double images of my father and Gerry tumbled over each other in my dreams.

When the wake-up call came, Gerry sat straight up in bed as though a bugle had called him to duty. Quickly he kissed me, dressed, and said he'd be back after he got rid of his press aide and reporters.

"I'll probably have breakfast with them," he said, "so why don't you eat now? I'll tell everyone in the delegation I have jet lag and we can spend the day together."

He left, gone before I noticed he had forgotten one of his socks. I ordered some papaya and toast and ate on the balcony. Below me an attendant was feeding the dolphins. I remembered how Sachi used to ride the dolphins when she was a kid and we'd meet Steve in Hawaii as a halfway point to Japan. She used to say she understood the dolphins and they were her playmates.

Somewhere below me I could hear journalists talking about what would make good stories out of Hawaii. Interspersed in their professional kidding was speculation about Dr. Lilly's experiments with dolphins. I wondered if dolphins really were as highly intelligent as scientists said, or if they really could have their own evolved language. I remembered someone telling me once that residing in the great brains of the dolphins were all the secrets of some immense lost civilization called Lemuria. I had heard about Atlantis, but Lemuria was unknown to me.

I watched the Secret Service men and the journalists watching the dolphins. I wondered how Gerry and I would get through the day without being recognized.

About an hour later he called. "Look," he said, "meet me on the beach to the left of the hotel. Most everyone will be keeping close to these premises. I'll be there in fifteen minutes."

I dressed in jeans and a shirt and underneath I wore a bathing suit. I tied a scarf around my head and put on black-rimmed sunglasses.

Walking through the lobby and out the back entrance nobody noticed me, but I was afraid to stop and watch the dolphins because of the journalists. I walked quickly past the pool and out onto the warm sand where tourists were already lying on the beach with radios blaring rock and roll. The smell of coconut suntan oil hung in the air.

I walked along the edge of the beach where the clear blue waves lapped the shore, heading left. No one was swimming yet. The palm trees bent in a soft trade wind. I did a few bends in the shallow waves, not having done my exercises in the morning. My show seemed half a life away.

A few hundred yards up the empty beach I stopped, sat on the sand, lifted my head to the sun and waited for Gerry. It felt almost regular, almost human. More than anything, I hated the secrecy. I didn't like feeling furtive, clandestine, dishonest; it hurt. I hoped

that Gerry didn't get a dangerous kick out of it like some people did.

He was wearing khaki slacks and a white, loose shirt as I watched him amble up the beach through the edge of the surf. His arms swung out from his body and he carried a pair of sandals in his hand. He didn't wave when he saw me. I got up and met him in the water so we could continue to walk.

"So I see you *do* have another pair of shoes," I said.

"My vacation shoes," he laughed and touched my face.

"Did your delegation buy your story about jet lag?"

"Oh sure. They will do a little of the same themselves. Having a conference in Honolulu is too tempting anyway."

He buckled his sandals together, slung them over his shoulder and took my hand when we were well out of range of the hotel. I leaned my head against his shoulder and we began to walk.

We found a coral reef that led way out into the ocean and felt as though we were walking on water. Gerry teased that everyone thought that's what he claimed to be able to do anyway. The coral was sharp. We stopped and looked out at the big surf breaking further out to sea.

"Can you ride the waves?" he asked.

"I used to when I was in my twenties," I said. "Before I got old enough to be afraid of it."

I remembered how carefree I used to be with my body. It never occurred to me that I might break something or that anything could go wrong at all. Now I had to think ahead even when I got out of a taxicab. If I turned an ankle or banged my knee it would interfere with my dancing. When I was younger I had danced more recklessly. In fact, I guess I had done most everything without thinking very much. And I had had a wonderful time at it too. With adulthood, I had become more and more aware of the consequences of everything I did, whether it was leaping into the waves or having a love affair.

Awareness didn't lessen the fun or the wonder. On the contrary, now I wanted to learn to live totally in the *now*—in the present, with a confirmed completeness that that was all there really was anyway. If I had in fact lived other lives in the past and would possibly live other lives in the future, belief in that would only serve to intensify my commitment with all my heart and soul to the *present*.

Reincarnation was a new concept to me, of course, but I found that each time I thought about it I derived great pleasure from its implications. Were time and space so overwhelmingly infinite that they served to make one realize the preciousness of each and every moment on Earth? Did my mind need to take quantum leaps of imagination into other possible realities in order to appreciate the joy of reality now? Or, were real joy and happiness the *inclusion* of all those other realities that in effect expanded one's awareness of the reality of now?

Expanded consciousness. That was the phrase so many people were using more and more. One needn't trade in an old consciousness for a new one. One could simply expand and raise the consciousness one already had—an expanded consciousness simply recognized the existence of previously unrecognized dimensions . . . dimensions of space, time, color, sound, taste, joy, and on and on. Was the conflict between Gerry and me simply a difference in movement toward expanded consciousness? Perhaps I was trying to force him to move at a pace that was mine instead of his. His pace wasn't to be judged either. It was just different. I knew I could be demandingly insistent, a result in part of intense curiosity and in part of impatience. I was impatient with others who didn't indulge in the same search. My life seemed to be devoted to a series of questions. Gerry's seemed to be devoted to answers.

We headed away from Diamond Head, Waikiki and Kahala, walking toward the thick underbrush of the deserted side of the island. The further away we got from people, the more Gerry touched me. Soon we were walking with our bodies joined to-

gether. It was too lovely to talk. The sun fell behind the clouds and the coconut palms began to bend in the wind. It started to rain. We ran from the water into a grove of trees where ripe coconuts lay strewn on the ground. We stood under a tree and watched the rain fall on the fuchsia-colored azaleas around us. A blue bird shook its wings and flew further into the underbrush. Gerry put his arms around me and looked out to sea.

"This is so beautiful," he said.

He hugged me closer.

The rain fell harder now—one of those thick tropical rains that looked like a sparkling beaded sheet.

"Do you want to go swimming in this rain?" I asked.

Without answering Gerry pulled off his shirt and trousers. He too had a bathing suit underneath. He rolled his clothes into a ball, placed them under his sandals beneath the tree and ran into the ocean.

I took off my jeans and shirt and followed him.

The waves were higher now and whitecapped. We dove under them, feeling the salt spray mingle with the fresh rain. We laughed and splashed each other. I wiped the salt from my eyes, glad I hadn't worn mascara. Gerry swam out further, waving me to come with him. I was afraid to go, so floating in the rainy waves I watched him. He stopped and lay on his back past where the waves were breaking. Then he turned over on his stomach and waited for the right wave. It came, and he rode the crest of it until it subsided close to where I waited. He swam toward me and swept me up in his arms. I kissed his salty face and he smothered me in his big shoulder. We swam back to shore and lay together in the shallow breaking waves looking up at the rain, water soaking our faces.

"That . . . just then was the happiest I've ever been," he said, breathing hard and shouting slightly above the surf. "You know I've never done this before? That was the first wave I ever rode. I've missed a great deal, haven't I?"

I didn't say anything. I just turned over in the water and thought

it was the happiest I had been in a long time too—only I wished I had had the abandonment to ride that wave with him.

We lay in the water until the sun came out. Then on our backs we inched our way out of the sea and onto the wet sand where we lay until we could feel the sun drying us off.

"Gerry?" I asked, "when you look back at your life, when were you happiest?"

He thought awhile and then with a kind of startled look said, "You know, now that you've asked me, I would have to say all my happiness has been connected with nature—sometimes with people—but never with my work. That's astonishing to me. *My happiest moments have never been connected to my work.* My God, why is that?"

"I don't know. Maybe because you felt work was duty."

"But even when I win I'm depressed. For example, the last time I was elected I fell into a depression for days." He looked up into the sky. "I must think about that, mustn't I?"

I got up to get dressed.

"It seems a shame that you should feel depressed when you win. What do you feel when you lose?"

He got up and walked to the tree where we had left our clothes. "When I lose I feel challenged. I feel a sense of struggle and that makes everything worth it. I think I need to spit against the wind."

❀ We walked further around the island and soon found a small food stand by the sea that sold pineapples and papayas. We squeezed lemon over the papayas and sat on the sand. The Hawaiian who owned the place was reading a Raymond Chandler novel and intermittently looking at the sea. Gerry and I talked about Asia, the Middle East, and the time I had spent in Japan. He didn't ask me any personal questions and I didn't volunteer any information.

We continued walking until we found the directions to Sea World. We went in to see the dolphins and killer whales. It was feeding time. One of the dolphins got more to eat than the others. Gerry didn't think it was fair. He said survival of the fittest was cruel and there ought to be a way for man to restructure that basic fact of nature. He said that was what civilization was for . . . to make the world a kinder place. He felt sorry for those who couldn't fend for themselves.

At the large tank a killer whale was being fed. Seagulls circled overhead waiting for the whale to miss one of the fish that the attendant, who wore a wet suit, was dropping into the gigantic mouth. Then he missed one. A gull swooped down, scooped up the fish, and flew to the other side of the tank. The whale saw him and with a great lunge went after him. The gull sat on the rim where the whale couldn't get at him. The gull blinked at him. And the whale interrupted his feeding to glare at the gull for a full three minutes. Gerry laughed out loud, and the whale went back to his feeding.

We left the aquarium and walked into the hills above the sea. Birds of every color flitted and squawked through the lush tropical trees. We tried to open a dried coconut but we needed a machete. I told Gerry about the time I had gone to the big island of Hawaii once to be alone. I rented a little house on the Kona Coast and sat on the volcanic rocks for days thinking about competition, among other things.

I had been in Hollywood for five years and the way good friends would fight each other for good parts was getting me down. I had just been nominated for another Academy Award and I didn't like the false pressure that the nomination seemed to burden me with either. I didn't like the feeling that winning a little brass statue should be more rewarding than doing good work. It had confused me because everyone else thought it was what Hollywood was all about. But I didn't see why anybody should win or lose. I didn't like how crestfallen people felt when they lost. And I hated how

much money was spent trying to influence votes by giving parties and taking ads in the trade papers. Gerry seemed interested in what I was saying but couldn't understand that I had genuinely not cared whether I won or not.

"Why didn't you care?" he asked.

"I don't know," I said, "but I didn't. And I don't care now. I think I didn't want to be embarrassed to win something that had no business being a contest in the first place. I wouldn't be depressed the way you say you are when you win—I would be embarrassed. You *need* to win because that's how democracy and majority rule work and there's no other way to be a successful politician. But artists shouldn't be involved with that kind of competition. I think we should only be concerned with competing against the best we have in ourselves."

He asked me if I really had gone there alone. I told him yes, I had; that I had done a lot of that in my life. I needed to be alone. I needed time to reflect. He said he had gathered that from my first book, *Don't Fall Off The Mountain*. He said that book was one of his daughter's favorite books.

He asked me if I ever got lonely. I said being alone was different from being lonely but that I believed I was a basically lonely person in any case. He never asked me about my divorce, or my relationships with other men. If it was going to come up it would have come up then. I assumed he wasn't ready to know.

We stopped, sat, and watched sand crabs dig their holes as late afternoon began to fall. One of them fell over on its back. With a twig Gerry turned it upright and smiled gently. I told him how I had watched a colony of ants outside that little house on Kona. They diligently spent their days carrying a stale bun, crumb by crumb, from one rock to a hiding place under another rock. They were so organized and determined. There were no individuals. No way to be one. They seemed selfless. I wondered if that was a good way to be, to submit your own interests to the good of the species. Was that what Gerry thought he was doing? Gerry asked me about

China. Though he had never been there he knew a lot about it. We talked about the Chinese revolution and he said he wished there had been time when we were in Hong Kong to go across the border, if only for a few days.

We fell asleep in the afternoon sun, and when we woke a cool breeze had come up. We ran together on the edge of the surf laughing and pummeling each other. Gerry stopped to skim flat stones over the surf. Then we walked, holding hands, until we came in sight of the hotel, where we separated. Gerry walked ahead of me and disappeared into the throng at the pool area. I stood watching the sun set for a while. Then it struck me how free Gerry had seemed all day being outside and how inept he could be inside, with four walls around him. He was really a different person when he was unconstrained. I was sure that he'd be better at his work if he'd let himself go more, better at his marriage too probably, better with me.

Entering the hotel, Gerry was waylaid in the lobby by his delegation. "Where have you been? Are you feeling better?" I heard snatches of conversation as I walked unnoticed by him and everyone else. I felt like background music.

I got into the elevator, glad that I was alone in it, except for a porter.

I was taking a hot shower, washing the salt from my hair when the phone rang. Gerry said, "Why have you been away from me for so long?"

In five minutes he was in my room sitting on the floor. There was a TV special on from Las Vegas starring Sinatra, Sammy Davis, Jr., Paul Anka and Ann-Margret. He sat with his legs crossed, leaning forward, and asked me about musical comedy shows. Were the singers really singing or did they mouth to a playback? Did they have to memorize the lyrics or did they have cue cards? How much rehearsal did they have before they actually performed?

As we talked we decided to have dinner at an out-of-the-way

Japanese restaurant I knew on the other side of Waikiki. If we could successfully negotiate getting a cab there would be no problem from then on.

I left the hotel room first. The down elevator took so long that he found himself going up just to avoid arriving in the lobby with me.

The lobby was full of journalists and Secret Service men. I put my head in a magazine and kept it there until I got outside. A cab was waiting in line. Photographers popped flashbulbs as famous delegates entered and left. I got in the cab and asked the driver to wait for just a moment. He said he couldn't wait long. I looked nervously into the lobby. Gerry was there but he had been stopped by a visiting delegation. I counted the seconds.

"My friend is coming," I said. "Hang on just a moment." The driver waited.

A few minutes later Gerry extricated himself, smiled into a camera that popped a bulb in his face and saw me wave to him. Nonchalantly he walked toward the cab and got in. No one noticed anything.

We drove to the Japanese restaurant. I knew the manager but she wasn't interested in whom I was with. I asked her in Japanese for a private tatami room and she showed us in, brought us some hot saki and went to prepare our sushi. Gerry wasn't sure about the raw fish but he ate it anyway.

The candle on the table flickered under his face.

"Oh, how I loved today," he said.

I smiled.

"And oh, how I love talking to you."

I smiled again.

"And, oh, how I love being with you."

I smiled and rolled my eyes in mock disgust. He knew what I meant.

"And oh, how I love you."

I began to cry.

He reached over and took my hand. I couldn't talk.

"I'm sorry that makes you unhappy," he said.

I pulled out a Kleenex and blew my nose.

"Oh, Gerry," I said finally. "Why is it so hard for you to say?"

His face went solemn. "Because I say it in ways other than words. I say it with my hands, with my body."

"Why?"

"I don't know. I think it's because I have to manipulate words all day long in my work and I don't want to feel that I'm manipulating words with you."

"You mean that's playing fair with me?"

"Yes."

"Well, I need to manipulate words to express my feelings. Is that *un*fair?"

"I don't know how it is for you."

"I'm not sure that love is fair anyway."

"I don't think I know anything about love," he said. "This is all new to me. I only know I feel comfortable expressing myself physically because I've never done that before and I use words all the time."

I tried to grasp what he was saying. Did he mean he couldn't really be trusted? Or did he mean he didn't want to commit himself in so many words because he didn't want the responsibility later?

"How," I asked, "will you express yourself when we're apart then?"

He shrugged. "I don't know. It's a contradiction, isn't it? I'll have to think about it."

We ate dinner talking about Japan and how it was sacrificing its culture for the sake of industrial development. After dinner we walked awhile before we took separate cabs back to the hotel.

There was a convention banquet in the hotel dining room. I went to my room and waited. The dolphins leapt gently in the aquarium below and the palm trees rustled drily in the trade winds.

Half an hour later we were in bed. Gerry said his work had piled up for the next two days and he needed to be up early in the morning. I was leaving in the late morning.

We turned out the light and tried to sleep.

Suddenly he got up and with that determined walk he crashed into a chair. I laughed. He went to the bathroom and came back and paced up and down at the foot of the bed.

"What's wrong?" I asked.

"I don't know what I'm thinking," he said. "I don't know what to do. And I'm not even ready to think about what I'm thinking."

I watched him quietly. He got an apple out of the fruit basket. He paced with the apple in his hand. Then he came back to bed and began to eat it. Deliberately and with great concentration he chewed each bite thoroughly without saying a word. It was as though he didn't know I was there. He didn't eat the apple like most people, leaving the two ends. He ate the apple from the top down and finally he devoured the whole thing, seeds, core and all.

I laughed and it startled him.

"I don't eat much," he said, "but once I do I eat it all." He leaned over on his elbow. "Remember that."

❋ I tried to sleep. I didn't know when I'd see him again. I thought of what it would be like in the morning when he'd walk out the door and shut it behind him. I couldn't make myself comfortable. I turned from one side to the other. Each time I turned he touched me. On and off all night I tossed and slept, tossed and slept. Each time I moved he touched me. Soon daylight filtered through the curtains. He sat up, pulled the covers around me, and lifted my face.

"Listen," he said, "we've had thirty-six hours of something too extraordinary to describe. Most people never have that. Look at

the positive side. I always assume I begin at zero . . . so anything above that is a plus."

I swallowed hard. "I don't. I assume I start wherever I want and I can go anywhere I want after that. I feel I can make anything happen if I want and I'm not *grateful* for our thirty-six hours. I want more. I want all I can get."

He laughed and threw up his hands. He got out of bed and I could feel him prepare himself for a day of work. He had had his time with me, considered himself lucky, and now had to contend with his English sense of obligation. It was simple for him. He had made a career out of denial.

"Gerry," I said, "wait a minute. Could you live without this now?"

He thought for a moment and his face was grave. "Life would be bleak, gray, empty. Now give me a nice long kiss," he said, taking my face in his hands. I reached up and held his hair, letting it fall through my fingers. Quickly he dressed, and before I knew it he was at the door.

"I'll call you when I get back to London."

He didn't say goodbye. He didn't turn around. He walked straight to the door, opened it and left.

The room changed. It was the moment I was so afraid of. The silence made my ears ring. I felt sick. I sat up and threw my legs over the side of the bed. I looked around for something he might have forgotten. No, I thought. This is ridiculous. I'm not going to allow myself to wallow around like this. I got up and took a cold shower, ordered breakfast, and packed. Then I sat down and wrote him a letter about how right he was that half a glass of water was half full, not half empty.

I slept restlessly on the plane back over the Pacific.

"What do you want from *me*?" I could hear him saying it again. He was right. Did I want him to shatter his personal life, risk his political work and in general give up everything he had dedicated his life to for me? Now *I* didn't want to think about it.

"I have to finish the job I started in my work a long time ago," he had said. Did I want to risk that for this? And what, anyway, was *this*? Was it really love? Was it what people gave up everything for? Would he ever do that? Would I? Could I live in London? What would the English voters do if they knew? Would it really ruin him? He claimed with absolute certainty that his wife wouldn't be able to take it, but what would the people think?

So he had said, "I have to calm down. I need to cool myself out. I've been too obsessed with you. I need to be objective now. I don't want to think about what I'm thinking about." He had said all these things to me and when I tried to be helpful by assuming a cooler attitude myself he had said, "You're not going to get rid of me that easily." So I too was confused. . . . Bleak, empty, and gray, he had said. Would it be bleak, empty, and gray for me, too? Could I do without him? What was I really doing *with* him? What was I doing with myself? ❊

Chapter 6

"It is very difficult to explain this feeling to anyone who is entirely without it, especially as there is no anthropomorphic conception of God corresponding to it. The individual feels the nothingness of human desires and aims and the sublimity and marvellous order which reveal themselves both in nature and in the world of thought. He looks upon individual existence as a sort of prison and wants to experience the universe as a single significant whole."

—Albert Einstein
The World As I See It

W hen I got home I was irritated, frustrated, upset with myself, and more bugged than ever by something I couldn't touch. Yes, I was bothered by all the obvious problems relating to Gerry. But it was more than that.

I called David. He was still in California. He sensed immediately that something was wrong. He asked how my weekend had gone, knowing that I wouldn't say much but endeavoring to be my friend and lend support if he could. I asked him to meet me in Malibu.

He came right out with a bag of fresh peaches. We took them down to the beach. The peaches were juicy and sticky and sweet.

"What's wrong?" asked David, knowing that he could come right to the point because I had invited him.

I swallowed a huge bite of juicy peach sweetness and didn't know how to begin to tell him what I was feeling. "I don't know," I said. "I'm hung up . . . well, not exactly hung up. I just feel that there's something about why I'm alive that I'm not getting. I'm a happy person and getting plenty out of life—I don't mean I'm

hung up with all that middle-aged crisis stuff. It's something I can't explain. In fact age has nothing to do with it except maybe that after awhile you finally get around to asking the right questions." I hesitated, hoping David would say something that would trigger me into more clarity. He didn't. He just waited for me to say more. I went on. "I mean, maybe I'm not even talking about me. I mean, well . . . maybe it's the world. Why doesn't the world work? And why should that get to me? I mean, how come *you* never seem bugged? Do you know something I don't know?"

"You mean, like why are we alive and what is our purpose?"

"Yeah," I said. "I guess that's about it. I mean, when you have as much as I do and have lived as much as I have you finally have to ask yourself very seriously, 'What's it all about?' And I'm not asking out of any unhappiness. I'm successful, I think, personally and professionally, and I'm certainly happy with it. I'm not into drugs or booze. I love my work and I love my friends. I have a great personal life even with some complicated problems. No—that's not what I mean. I mean, I think there must be more going on about our real purpose in life than I'm able to see."

David wiped peach juice from his chin. It was fascinating to me that I had even felt comfortable asking him such a question, almost as though he could answer it. It was a question I wouldn't even have asked Einstein had I known him well enough to sit on the beach slurping peaches with him.

David brushed sand from his sticky fingers. "Well," he said, "I think happiness is in our own back yard, to quote Al Jolson."

"You're a big help," I laughed. "Look at my back yard—it's the Pacific Ocean. Sooo?"

"Sooo, I mean, *you*. I mean, happiness and purpose and meaning is *you*."

"Look," I said, "you're really a nice polite person, but could you be a little less nice and polite and instead be a little more specific?"

"Okay," he went on undaunted by my irritability. "*You* are

everything. Everything you want to know is inside of you. You are the universe."

Jesus, I thought, hippy-dippy jargon. He's going to use phrases that are simply not part of my realistic vocabulary. And as much as I might feel drawn to what he is saying, it is going to put me off because it's not part of my philosophic or intellectual lexicon of understanding. But then, I thought, my words and phrases and ideas have been limited to my own conceptions, my own frames of reference. Don't get bugged by words. Keep the mind open.

"David," I said, "please tell me what you mean. What you said then sounds so big and ponderous and hokey. I have enough trouble understanding what I'm doing day by day. Now I'm supposed to understand that *I* am the universe?"

"Okay," he said chuckling gently at my frustrated honesty. "Let's go at it another way. When you were in India and Bhutan, did you think much about the spiritual aspect of your own life? I mean, did it occur to you that your body and your mind might not be the only dimensions there were in your life?"

I thought for a moment. Yes, of course I had. I remembered how fascinated I had been when I saw a Bhutanese lama levitate in the lotus position (with his knees crossed under each other) three feet off the ground. Or to be possibly more accurate, I *thought* I had seen him levitate. It was explained to me that he had accomplished such a feat by reversing his polarities (whatever that was) and thereby had defied gravity. To me, it had made some kind of scientific sense, and also appealed to the metaphysical side of my nature. So I left it at that. For some reason, I had no trouble accepting that it had happened, but I really couldn't honestly say that I understood why. As another lama told me later, "You wouldn't have seen the levitation if you hadn't been prepared to see it." That's when I began to think maybe I just *thought* I had seen it. I remembered how, when living with the Masai in Kenya and traveling to Tanzania, I was met by other Masai who knew my name and the fact that I had been made a Masai blood sister

without anyone telling them. I accepted the safari white hunters' explanations that they believed the Masai had perfected thought transference. They said that the Masai had no other form of communication with each other throughout Africa so, out of necessity and also because they were communal thinkers, they could do what the white and civilized world was too competitive to do— communicate through clear mental telepathy and thought transference to their brothers.

Again, I had accepted what the white hunters told me. First, they had had a great deal of experience and years of observing the Masai and their habits and behavior patterns and second, it just made sense to me. I had no problem understanding that the energy of human thought could live and travel outside of the human brain. It didn't seem outlandish or preposterous to me at all. Nor to the white hunters, for that matter, and they were certainly practical students with down-to-earth experience of primitive tribes.

I thought of many moments in my life when I *knew* something was going to happen, and it did. When I *knew* someone was in trouble, and they were. When I *knew* someone was trying to reach me, and they did. I had often had such flashes about people I knew well. I would, for example, *know* that a close friend had just checked into the International Hotel in Seoul, Korea. I would call on a lark and he'd be there; wondering himself how I knew he was there. Those flashes happened to me often. And if common or garden stories are to be believed, these were experiences many, many people had had, and almost all had heard about.

As for me, I never really questioned such things. They just *were*. That was all. But no, I never really related to any of that stuff spiritually. Yes, I was interested in mind over matter, in metaphysical phenomena, in meditational isolation, and certainly in expanded consciousness. But how could I find it for myself? Or was I already aware without recognizing it?

For instance, I met a lama in the Himalayas who had been

meditating in near isolation for twenty years. I climbed 14,000 feet to his mountainside cave and when I arrived, he gave me some tea and a piece of saffron scarf that he had blessed to protect me, which he said would be necessary because I was soon going to run into trouble. He was right. On the way down the mountain, a man-eating leopard stalked me and my Sherpa guide. And one day later I found myself caught in a bizarre Himalayan coup d'état; I was arrested and held at bayonet point for two days while my captors tried to take away my guide and throw him in the *dzong* (a Himalayan dungeon where people usually died). The experience was like a bad grade-B movie—unbelievable to anyone who hadn't been there. To me, it was real—and the meditating lama had been right. About the danger, anyway. Even if the scarf only provided moral support.

But was his premonition or foreknowledge spiritual? I hadn't ever really thought in those terms. I was more of a pragmatist. I had respect for things I didn't understand, but I was more comfortable relating to those things on an intellectual or scientific level, which seemed more *real* to me.

"Yes," I said to David. "I'm thinking more and more about the spiritual aspect of myself or the world or whatever you want to call it."

David shifted his position around the bag of peaches and the sandy peach pits which were piling up between us.

"You mean," he said, "that the spiritual aspect of your life seems real to you?"

"Yeah," I answered, "I guess you could say that. But it doesn't seem to be a *real* part of the realistic life we lead. Maybe because I can't see it. I guess I'm saying that I believe what I have proof of."

"Sure," he said, "most Westerners feel that way. In fact, that's probably the basic difference between East and West—and never the twain shall meet."

"So what about you?" I asked. "How come you seem to have

this spiritual understanding in such a pragmatic world? You're a Westerner. How did you come by your beliefs?"

He cleared his throat almost as though he wanted to avoid answering me, but knew he couldn't. "I've just traveled and wandered around a lot," he said. "I wasn't always like this. But something happened to me once. I'll tell you about it some time. But believe me, I used to be a regular Charlie Crass with fast cars, fast girls—just living in the fast lane. It wasn't getting me anywhere but I have to admit I dug it while it lasted." David's eyes had grown misty as he talked, remembering. I wondered what it was that had happened but didn't want to press it since he'd said he would tell me in his own time.

"So," I said. "You traveled around a lot?"

"Yeah."

"So have I. And I love it. I love flying to new places, seeing new faces. I don't think I could ever stay still in one spot."

David looked at me sidewise.

"I hitchhiked," he said, "and worked my way across the oceans on tramp steamers. I don't think it matters *how* we do those things, but instead *why* is what counts. We were probably both looking for the same thing, but from different vantage points."

"Yeah," I said, "but I've always thought I was looking for myself whenever I traveled. Like a journey anywhere was really a journey through myself."

"Sure," he said, "so was I. That's what I meant a few minutes. ago when I said the answers are in *you. You* are the universe."

"Jesus," I said, "we both could have saved a lot of plane fares if we had known that in the beginning, couldn't we? We could have just sat in the back yard and meditated."

"You're joking, but I think it's true. That's why everyone is essentially equal. *Everyone* has *themselves* regardless of what station of life they're born into. Actually a person considered stupid might be a lot more spiritual than someone who is a genius in Earth terms. The village idiot might be closer to God than Einstein

although even Einstein said he believed there was a greater force at work than he could prove."

"But being a genius and being spiritual—whatever that means —are not mutually exclusive?"

"No."

I remembered a story someone at Princeton had told me. Einstein had been attempting to prove the theory of why those little mechanical birds you put on the edge of a glass would fill up with water and when they became unbalanced, would spill all the water out and begin again. He couldn't seem to explain how the little mechanical bird worked in mathematical terms and out of frustration, one day he went into town for a double dip strawberry ice cream cone. Strawberry was apparently Einstein's favorite flavor. He was licking the ice cream cone and walking along a curb in the road thinking about the mechanical bird when he tripped slightly and the top dip of the ice cream toppled off into the gutter. Einstein was so crushed he broke down and cried. . . . Here was one of the great geniuses of the world, but he couldn't handle his anxiety over what he didn't understand any better than the next guy.

I remembered reading that Einstein was an avid reader of the Bible. I never knew what he really thought of it other than the fact that he respected it. I wondered what he would have thought of the supposed imprint of Christ left on the Shroud of Turin. Some scientists said the imprint was caused by high-level radio-active energy, which spiritualists explained was an expression of the high level of spiritual energy Christ had acquired.

"So what about Christ?" I found myself asking David. "Who do you think he really was?"

"Okay," he said, straightening his posture as though he had finally found a thread to unravel. "Christ was the most advanced human ever to walk this planet. He was a highly evolved spiritual soul whose purpose on Earth was to impart the teachings of a Higher Order."

"What do you mean, 'A Higher Order'?" I asked.

"A higher spiritual order," said David. "He obviously knew more than the rest of us about life and death and God. I think his resurrection proved that."

"But how do we know it really happened?"

David shrugged his shoulders. "First of all," he said, "a lot of people saw it, and reported that they were awestruck and even terrified. And second, the remains of his body were never found, and third, a legend of that magnitude would be hard to make up. Besides, how do we *know* anything in history ever happened if we weren't witnesses to it ourselves? So, somewhere along the line education and knowledge of history require an act of faith that events are true, or we shouldn't bother learning anything about the past at all."

"In other words," I said, "why *not* believe it?"

"Sure," said David, "but first, take a hard look, *listen*, really listen, to what the man said. Everything Christ taught had to do with understanding the knowledge of mind, body *and spirit*. In fact, the First Commandment given to Moses, even long before Christ, was the recognition of the Divine Unity: Mind, Body, and Spirit. Christ said the First Commandment was the chief commandment and to misunderstand it would be to misunderstand all the other universal laws following it. But, he said to understand it fully we had to understand that the soul and spirit of man had everlasting life and the soul's quest was to rise higher and higher toward perfection until we were free."

I looked at David, trying to absorb what he was saying. A few years before I think I would have called him a Jesus freak, and launched into a dialogue accusing him of espousing beliefs that diverted attention from what was really wrong with the world.

"So how does all of this square with this world we're living in?" I asked instead. "I mean, how can belief in the soul and keeping the First Commandment and all that clean up the mess we've made of this world?" I didn't want to get upset, but it wouldn't have been difficult.

"Well," said David, "all our 'isms' and self-righteous wars and industrial technology and intellectual masturbation and socially compassionate programs have only made it worse, it seems to me. And the longer we disregard the spiritual aspect of life, the worse it will get. . . ." He folded his legs under him and used his hands to make points in the air. "See," he went on, "Christ and the Bible and spiritual teachings don't concern themselves with social or political questions. Instead, spirituality goes right to the *root* of the question—the individual. If each of us set ourselves right individually, we would be on the right path socially and politically. See what I mean?"

"Yes," I said, "I guess so."

"In other words, if we understood our own *individual purpose* and meaning in relation to God, or even to mankind and leave God out of it for the moment, it would automatically lead to social harmony and peace. There'd be no need for war and conflict and poverty and stuff, because we'd all know there was no need to be greedy or competitive or afraid and violent."

Well, it wasn't a new idea. Ultimate responsibility of the individual was basic to Quaker thought, for one thing, and—leaving God out of it as David suggested—the concept was also basic to Kropotkin's political philosophy of anarchism.

"Why are you saying we need to understand our individual purpose and meaning in relation to God?" I asked. "Why couldn't we just understand it in relation to our fellow men?"

David smiled and nodded. "You could," he said. "That would be a good beginning because in fact, in caring about mankind you *are* relating to God, to the divine spark in all of us." He paused. "But it's easier," he said, "if you first learn who *you* are. Because that's where cosmic justice comes in. We can't just relate to our lives here and now as though this has been the only life we've lived. All our previous lives are what have molded us. We are the product of all the lives we have led."

I thought of Gerry and his politics. Had such spiritual concepts

in a political context ever occurred to him? Or to any politician for that matter? The voters would think our political leaders crazy if they voiced such ideas. Jimmy Carter came as close as anyone but most of the "smart" people I knew liked to think he was doing a "media-grope with God" and didn't really mean it. They didn't know what to make of him if he *really* meant all that stuff about being born again, and in fact, they just laughed, let him have his idiosyncrasies but wished he'd get the hell on with being a better administrator and a stronger leader. In fact, they were pissed off at his God talk while the economy was falling apart. And as far as reincarnation was concerned, any born-again Christian would freak out at the idea. And, where Gerry was concerned, if he believed in either God or reincarnation I could just see the English cartoons. . . . The British Isles sinking slowly into the sea while God smiled down from above, with a caption saying, "Cheer up! Next time around you'll do it right!" Guaranteed to lose Gerry the election—even if our affair didn't.

My mind began to tumble with the ideas implicit in our conversation. I wasn't sure I liked them. On the one hand, it sounded plausible in an idealistic sort of way. On the other, it just sounded outrageously impossible and flat flaky.

"Cosmic justice?" I questioned sarcastically, dripping peach juice from my chin in the ocean breeze. "Is this where your reincarnation comes in?"

"Sure," he answered.

"You mean, you believe our souls keep coming back physically until we finally get it right?"

"Well, it makes sense, doesn't it?" he asked. "It certainly makes as much sense as anything else going."

"I don't know. Maybe."

"Big truths are hidden, but that doesn't mean they're not true."

"But if I really let myself believe that every one of my actions has a consequence, I'd be paralyzed."

"But that's already happening," he said. "You just aren't aware

of it. That's what Christ was trying to tell us. Everything we do or
say in our lives every day has a consequence and where we find
ourselves today is the result of what we've done before. If everyone
felt that, understood it in their gut, the world would be a better
place. We shall reap what we sow, bad *or good*, and we should be
aware of it."

"And you believe if we took our actions more seriously in this
cosmic sense, we'd be kinder and more responsible people?"

"Sure. That's the point. We are all part of a universal truth and
plan. Like I said before, it's really very simple. And you *should* be
more aware of it because you will ultimately then reduce how
much you hurt yourself."

"You mean you really believe we all create our own karma like
the hippy-dippies say?"

"Sure. That's not so hard to understand. The Indians said that
thousands of years ago. They knew it long before your hippy-
dippies. It's *how* we lead our lives that counts. And when we
live by that, we will all be kinder to one another. And if we
don't, each of us pays the consequences in terms of the universal plan. We don't live by accident—you know there are no accidents. There is a higher purpose going on."

"Well, maybe you believe that, but I'm just asking. I wonder
how six million dead Jews feel about being part of a higher conscious cosmic design."

"Why stop at six million Jews? What about twenty-five million
Russians? Or the kids in the Children's Crusade? Or God knows
how many so-called heretics burned at the stake? If you're asking
me to answer for every apparent injustice and horror the world has
seen, I'll tell you flatly—I can't. And I doubt very much that you'll
ever be able to either."

"Then what the hell is all this about for Christ's sake?"

"Shirley, I can only tell you what I believe." He paused. "Cause
and effect . . ."

"Oh, come *on!*"

"Now wait! Science believes in cause and effect. Most reasonable people believe in cause and effect, right? Say to the average
person, 'You reap what you sow,' and they won't give you an
argument. But *think that through*—if you *don't* reap in this life,
then *when*? In heaven? In hell? Even religion believes in cause and
effect—that's why, when they threw out reincarnation, they dreamt
up heaven and hell to take care of all the unfulfilled effects. But
why, for God's sake, are a hypothetical heaven or hell easier to
believe in than the justice of reincarnation on Earth? I mean, on
the face of it, what seems more reasonable to you?"

"Oh, God," I said. Then I thought a moment. "Maybe I don't
happen to believe in either. It could be life is just a meaningless
accident."

"Then nobody's responsible for anything. And as far as I'm
concerned, that's a dead end. I can't live with a dead end, and I
don't think you can. But it's up to you. It all comes back to the
individual, the person. Shirley, *that's* what karma means. Whatever action one takes will ultimately return to that person—good
and bad—maybe not in this life embodiment, but sometime in the
future. And no one is exempt."

I stood up and stretched. I needed to move. Maybe I'd think
better. I felt like a person caught in a real life version of *The
Twilight Zone*. I had been conditioned to believe in only what I
could see . . . not what I could *sense* or *feel*. What David was
saying made a kind of sense, at least in terms of individual responsibility. But I had always needed proof—something I could see,
touch, or hear. It certainly was the Western way. We were trained
to respect the physical and psychological sciences. But then even
we in the Western World were learning that just because something didn't fit our concepts didn't mean it wasn't to be respected.
Suppose the spiritual dimension of mankind *was* recognized as a
possibility? Would it act as a kind of connective glue to bind together the purpose of each of our other sciences from chemistry to

medicine to mathematics to politics? Weren't all of our sciences part of the search for harmony and understanding of the meaning and purpose of life? Maybe the science of the spirit was what was missing.

"Anyway," said David, "even Western scientists agree that matter never dies. It just changes form. That's all physical death means."

"I don't understand," I said. "What's the connection?"

"I mean," said David, "that when we die only our bodies die. Our souls simply leave them and take up residence in the astral form. Our souls, regardless of what form they assume, are what is permanent. Our bodies are only temporary houses for our souls. But what we've done with ourselves while we're alive is what counts. And it doesn't matter *who* we are. If we hurt someone in this life, we'll be hurt the next time around. Or the time after that. And it's like Pythagoras said, 'It's all necessary for the development of the soul.' He also said, 'Whoever fathomed *that* truth fathomed *the* very heart of the Great Mystery!' "

"Pythagoras, the great mathematician?"

"Yes," said David.

"You mean, *he* believed in all this stuff?"

"Sure," said David. "And he wrote a lot about it. So did Plato and a whole mess of other Westerners."

He smiled at me and gathered up the sandy peach pits. He put them into the bag, placed them under the house, and we slowly began to walk.

Jesus, I thought. I wished I could talk about this stuff with Gerry. But when you are *involved* with someone, you settle. You settle for whatever there is . . . because you are afraid of jeopardizing the blind illusion of love. And the blind illusion is sometimes so necessary, we can even allow it to obfuscate our real identities. I put Gerry firmly out of my mind. My personal search right now was more important.

Suppose humanity (and this human in particular) *could* solve the riddle of its identity?—its origin? . . . and end? Would such knowledge lead to greater moral responsibility? What if I could bring myself to understand that I was not merely a body with a mind, but that body and mind were inhabited by a soul, and furthermore, that my soul existed before my birth in this life and would continue to exist after the death of this body. Suppose for a moment that the behavior of a soul would determine not only what was inherited in this life, but also explain our fortunes or misfortunes? Would I, in that case, have an attitude of deeper responsibility and a feeling for justice and participation in whatever I did? If I understood that my "actions" would require dues to be paid, both good and bad, would I finally understand that my life had a reason beyond what I could see?

Would I act more responsibly or more kindly toward myself, and toward others, recognizing that if I didn't I would prolong the struggle in the fundamental quest for perfection which I was apparently compelled to achieve one way or another because that was the real meaning and purpose of life? And was all this true whether one was an Arab sheik increasing oil prices, or a Jew who had been marched to the gas chamber? Whether one was a mafia godfather or a PLO terrorist or simply a beggar on the streets of Calcutta?

My mind spun and tumbled and recoiled and boggled at the possibilities of what I was thinking. Again, I wasn't sure whether I liked it or not. It was too new—too preposterous and, finally, maybe too simple.

"Belief in reincarnation would make the world a more moral place?" I said. "Not necessarily. I could imagine plenty of people who would manipulate that belief to aggrandize their own lives, acquire power, enhance their lifestyle—whatever."

"Sure," said David. "But this life is not the only one to be reckoned with. That's the whole point!"

"Okay, suppose for a minute the whole thing *is* that honest and simple? Suppose life, like nature, is simply a question of getting back what we put into it, and suppose with every instant and every second of each of our days we are creating and dictating the terms of our futures by our own positive and negative actions?" I took a deep breath as I began to realize the implications. "Well, my God," I went on, "how long would it take to be a 'good' person in relation to your cosmic justice?"

"Time doesn't really matter," said David calmly, "not when you're speaking in an overall sense, with the knowledge that you already have lived and will continue to lead many lives. Remember, all of the great religions speak of patience being the great virtue. That means patience with ourselves as well as our fellow humans."

"You mean we should just be patient with the Hitlers of this world?"

"I mean that six million Jews did not really die. Only their bodies died."

"Beautiful," I said. "That's really great. Tell the families of those six million lucky people that only their bodies died."

David winced as though I had hit him. Sadness bathed his face as he looked out across the ocean.

After a long while he finally said, very quietly, "I know it's hard to fathom. But so is turning the other cheek."

"Well," I said, "if I could have, I would have nailed Hitler to the cross!"

David turned and looked deep into my eyes. "Yes," he said. "I see."

Then I realized what I had said. "Well hell, what would you have done with Hitler?" I asked, hearing the defensiveness in my own voice. "Shit, there are a lot of people who believe that if the British had not disarmed, had developed weapons instead, Hitler could have been stopped before he really got started. Was it *wrong*

to disarm? I mean you can really get into a can of worms this way."

"I know," said David. "That's why you have to start just with yourself. Think a minute—if Hitler had felt moral responsibility as a person, he would have stopped himself, wouldn't he? You have to make it personal. I don't believe in killing anyone. That's where your question about God and the grand design comes in because only God can judge in that context. An individual can only judge of his *own* behavior. Ultimately no one can judge another. Besides you know, Hitler is not the only monster that ever lived. What about Idi Amin or the guys in the Khmer Rouge, or Stalin? Genocide is an old human problem. Or how about the pilots who dropped bombs on hospitals in North Vietnam with no feeling that humans were under there?"

"So what are you saying? That humans are cruel to each other?"

"Right. And if they understood the consequences of their actions *for themselves* they would think twice."

"That would make reincarnation a form of deterrent."

"Of course. But an individual, a self-deterrent if you like. And that's only the negative aspect, remember. There are also positive consequences."

"How can you be so sure there are consequences? What proof do you have?"

"None. What proof do you have that there aren't?"

"None."

"Well, then. Why not give what I'm saying a shot? You might as well. What's going on in the world now certainly isn't working too well."

"Give what a shot? How?"

"I don't know," he said. "Just think about it, I guess. You're saying nothing has any meaningful purpose and I'm saying everything does. You say you're not peaceful and you want to know why I am. Well, this is why. I believe in that phrase you hate—Cosmic Justice. I believe that what we put in, good or bad, bal-

ances out somewhere, sometime. That's why I'm peaceful. Maybe you have a better idea."

David kissed me on the cheek and said he'd call me.

I stared out at the waves. I had a headache. On the whole, I thought, maybe I'd rather be a fish. ❈

Chapter 7

"I lived in Judea eighteen hundred years ago, but I never knew that there was such a one as Christ among my contemporaries."

—Henry David Thoreau
Letters

When I woke up the next morning, I found myself wondering whether my daughter was some other reincarnated adult. Who might be living in the body of a person I thought of as my daughter?

There had been so many moments during our mother–daughter relationship when I had had the feeling that she knew me better than I knew her. And, of course, every mother feels she *learns* from her children. That was the miracle of child-rearing. But, if I let my mind wander and then focus on the possibility of reincarnation, I looked at Sachi with a totally different perspective. When the doctor brought her to me in the hospital bed on that afternoon in 1956, had she already lived many many times before, with other mothers? Had she, in fact, been one herself? Had she, in fact, ever been *my* mother? Was her one-hour-old face housing a soul perhaps millions of years old? And as she grew, did she gradually forget her spiritual dimension in an attempt to adjust to the physical world she found herself living in? Was *that* what they called the "veil of forgetfulness"? Was that what happened to all of us as we found ourselves encased in physical bodies?

When she went to live with her father in Japan, maybe she had actually planned it before she was born, and her talent for languages was based on having actually spoken them in previous lives. Perhaps she *became* Japanese when she spoke Japanese because she had actually *been* Japanese in another lifetime. And

when, later on in her adult life, she argued with us to allow her more independence and self-identity, was she responding to a legitimate inner voice that murmured that she already knew who she was? Maybe parents were merely ancient friends, rather than authority figures who felt they knew better than their children. And too, maybe the unresolved conflicts of previous lifetimes contributed to the all-too-frequent antagonisms that erupted between parents and children today.

❁ I had some breakfast and drove into town and back to the Bodhi Tree bookstore.

John, the owner, was in his office having his herb tea and reading.

"Oh, hello," he said formally but sweetly. "Did you get some good reading in?"

Jesus, I thought, so many of these people into metaphysics were formal . . . formal and sort of awesomely patient. I mean, almost irritatingly patient.

I said I had been reading and thinking and talking to David, and now I'd like to talk to him for a few minutes.

"Certainly," he said, "along what lines?"

"Well," I said, "about reincarnation I guess, about reincarnation in relation to our children. I mean, who are our children if every soul has already lived many lives?"

John smiled and took off his glasses.

"Well," he began in a gentle tone, "from the teachings it says that we shouldn't treat our children as our possessions anyway. They are, as you say, just small bodies inhabited by souls that have already had many experiences. So, reincarnation principles help explain some of the crazy contradictions in parent-child relationships."

I thought of the news documentary I had seen on grown-up

children beating and abusing their parents. Were these children doing that because *they* had been beaten in some previous life? Or because the parent had beaten someone else in a previous life? Who was working out whose karma? But John was continuing, "I can tell you," he said, from some of my past-life recall, that I'm sure that my eight-year-old son was once my father."

I laughed out loud because of what I had been thinking about Sachi that morning. John put his fingers to his lips and smiled.

"I'm sorry," I said. "Did you ever tell your son that?"

"Sure. He laughed and said I should watch myself! See how Cosmic Justice works?"

Here we go again, I thought. The only way I'll get to hear about this is to listen to the "astral" jargon. Well, okay. The occult has as much right to its own verbiage as any science, or religion, or philosophy.

I sat down on a bench. "I'm not sure," I said, "if I see how anything works. How does a person find out who they were in a past life?"

"You go to the right person."

"Like who?"

"Like a psychic. That's what they're into."

"You mean fortune tellers?"

"Well, there's lots of cranks, but there have been some very well respected psychics, like Edgar Cayce. Have you ever read any of Edgar Cayce's stuff?"

"I've heard of him, but I've never read him," I said, knowing that, really, I had never heard of him either.

"Okay, that's what you'll read next."

John reached up on the bookshelf and pulled down some of Edgar Cayce's books.

"He was an uneducated man, essentially—in fact most psychics are. Cayce was actually a trance medium. But they are all very spiritually and psychically attuned to the Akashic Records. Do you know what the Akashic Records are?"

I bent over and cracked my back into place.

"Listen," I said under my breath, "I'm really in over my head."

"You what?" asked John.

"What kind of records?" I asked, not even able to remember the name he had just mentioned.

"Oh," he answered. "The Akashic Records?"

"Yes. What are they?"

"Oh, okay," he said, "okay, it's hard to find much written about the Akashic Records, but let me try to explain. They are referred to as 'The Universe Memory of Nature,' or 'The Book of Life.' Akasha is a Sanskrit word meaning 'fundamental etheric substance of the universe.' Okay?"

"Jesus," I said, "I guess so. What's etheric?"

"Okay, all the universe is supposedly composed of ethers—that is, gaseous energies which have varying electromagnetic vibrational properties. As you know, everything we do, see, think, say, react to—everything we are—emits, or creates, energy charges. These energy charges are called 'vibrations.' So every sound, thought, light, movement, or action vibrationally reacts in those electromagnetic ethers. They are a kind of magnetic plate that attracts all vibrations. In fact, *everything* is electromagnetic vibrations. So the Akashic Records are a kind of panoramic record of everything that's ever been thought or felt or done. And if you are really sensitively attuned physically, you can plug in to those vibrations and, in fact, 'see' the past in the cosmic sense. So a good psychic can tell you what your previous lives were like."

"God," I said, "do you believe all that?"

"Oh sure," he said simply, "and furthermore, I think, and all the books say, that the inherent ability to see these records is in all of us. It's just a question of developing the ability, which really means getting more in tune with ourselves first. If our spiritual and mental powers are developed enough, we can. It's nothing more than developing our ESP, which now even science regards as a fact pretty much. See?"

"You mean," I said, "that it's just a question of expanding our consciousness?" I was grateful that I understood what I said.

"Sure," said John.

"And if we become more consciously aware of these other dimensions, we'll know more about who we are and what our lives are about?"

"Look," he said, "it's no more fantastic than sound waves or light waves, only these are thought waves. Science certainly knows they are there because no energy ever dies. So, if you are sensitive enough to get on the right thought wave lengths which plug into the Akashic vibrational waves, you can see lots of stuff that's already happened. And, if you are aware of what pain you've suffered in the past and also what pain you might have caused someone else to suffer, it all acts as an educative process. See what I mean?"

"Yeah, sure," I lied.

"You've read the ancient psychics, haven't you?"

"The ancient psychics?" I asked. "Like who?"

"Well," said John, feeling, I'm sure, that he was in *under* his head, "like Plato, Pythagoras, Buddha, Moses."

"Oh, they were psychics, too?" I said as impartially as possible.

"Why sure," said John. "How do you think they could write all that stuff they wrote? For example, how do you think Moses wrote of the creation of the world if he hadn't been plugged in psychically? And the same with Christ. I mean, those guys were highly developed spiritual people who felt their mission in life was to impart their knowledge. That's why the Bible is so valuable. It's a storehouse of knowledge. And most all of their writings jibe too. There's hardly any discrepancy in what any of them was saying."

"Did they talk about reincarnation?"

"Well, not all of them used that word. But they all spoke at length about the relationship between the *eternal* soul of man and the Divine. They *all* spoke of the universal laws of morality. They

didn't always use the words karma or reincarnation, but the meaning was the same. Am I talking too much?"

I shook my head and coughed and smiled and cleared my throat.

"Well," I asked, "what did they say about *not* remembering your previous lives?"

"They talk about a kind of 'veil of forgetfulness' that exists in the conscious mind so that we aren't continually traumatized by what might have occurred before. They all say that the *present* lifetime is the important one, only sparked now and then by those déjà-vu feelings that you have experienced something before or know someone that you know you've never consciously met before in this lifetime. You know those feelings you sometimes get that you've been somewhere before only you know you haven't?"

"Yes, I know what you mean." It was a great relief to know what he was talking about. I was remembering how I had felt in the Himalayas when I was there—as though I had lived there alone for a long time. As a matter of fact, I remembered feeling *familiar* when I reached the top-of-the-mountain cave of the monk who gave me the saffron scarf. The familiar feeling was the reason I took his warnings seriously and why I have the scarf to this day. I always felt it meant something more than what the lama said, but I wasn't sure why I felt it.

John asked one of his assistants for some tea and then he sat down on the bench with me just below the bookshelf.

"I know I'm talking too much," he said, "but when I get into this stuff, I just can't quit. It's so important . . . see, for people like Pythagoras or Plato or any of those guys, all the misfortunes in life like disease, deformities, injustices, and all that, were explained by the fact that each life embodiment was a reward or punishment of a preceding life embodiment, and as each soul progressed, that person was rewarded with more choices of how to reincarnate, all with the moral purpose, of course, to work out his or her own individual karma. A really superior soul, for example, would

choose to work out his karma through choosing a life embodiment of self-sacrifice, but each identity has his own thing. And apparently the older and higher in spiritual accomplishment the soul, the more it can remember of past life embodiments."

"But," I asked, "what if a soul doesn't want to progress? What if a soul wants to forget the whole thing and say screw it?"

"Well, there's a lot written about that too. A soul can choose to advance or regress. If it chooses to continually regress, it will eventually lose its humanity and become animal-like with no choices for advancement or moral atonement left to it. That is what was spoken of as Hell. If you don't choose spiritual evolution, you don't get the chance after a while, and that's Hell."

"So that's what they meant when they said, if you didn't believe in God you'd go to Hell—a kind of never-never land of nonexistence?"

"Sure. And the reverse, of course—God, meaning the everlasting eternalness of the soul and the attainment of moral atonement. Do you know what atonement means?"

"I don't think so."

"Just analyze it. It means at-one-ment. At-one-ment with the original creator or with original creation. We are both creators and, unhappily, destroyers. But when we identify most strongly with creation, we are closest to at-one-ment. You know, when you begin to unravel a little bit of it, the whole tapestry begins to make sense."

"So this business of reincarnating souls makes even the worst kind of evil and suffering have meaning?"

"Of course, everything happens for a reason. All physical suffering, all happiness, all despair, and all joy happens in relation to the Karmic Laws of Justice. That's why life has meaning."

John stopped and began to lift his arm to make another point. Then, perhaps seeing the look on my face, he stopped and said, "Let's go have our tea."

We walked into his office and sat at a window shaded by a tree outside.

"How come you got interested in all this *after* you were in India?" he asked.

I sipped the hot ginger tea. "Maybe I was a Himalayan monk in another life who knew all the mysteries of life and I'm going back to relearn what I already know."

He laughed.

"Do many people around here believe in reincarnation and Karmic Justice and all that?"

"Sure. You know that. There are lots of us weirdos around." He winked and got up. "Okay, so you have your books on psychic readings. See what happens after the next week or so. I'll be here if you want to talk some more."

We finished our tea.

I thanked him, paid for my books, and walked out into the traffic on Melrose Avenue. Whatever John needed to believe was his affair, but at least I had listened, and now I would read.

I went home to Encino. Marie fixed me some tea and hot French bread with Brie cheese. She always kept the Brie in good French fashion, at room temperature until it melted to the edge of the Limoge china plate she always placed it on. I loved her sense of detail. It didn't matter that she didn't like me in her kitchen.

I knew I shouldn't be eating cheese and bread, but I didn't care. I took it upstairs with me, sat down with my new books, and began to read about Edgar Cayce.

❋   Edgar Cayce was born in 1877 near Hopkinsville, Kentucky. He was a simple and devoutly religious man (a Christian) who was essentially uneducated, having had to cut high school to go to work.

He had suffered from chronic asthma and went to a well-trained and highly respected hypnotist to seek relief when no traditional doctors were able to help him.

While under hypnosis a strange thing happened to Cayce. He began to speak in the third person and with a voice that had no resemblance to his own. He used the word "we" and began to prescribe a treatment for himself in great detail. When the session was over, the hypnotist reported what had happened and suggested that Cayce follow the instructions. Out of desperation Cayce tried it. The asthma soon disappeared. But when the hypnotist described the "voice" that was apparently speaking through him, Cayce was horrified. He considered it blasphemous. The Bible had instructed man never "to suffer any spiritual entity other than God." And Cayce was a man who believed in the Bible.

But Cayce also had great compassion for people. Since the Voice seemed to be one that served to help people, he decided to go along with it for awhile. Cayce soon learned to put himself into trance in order to help others. The Voice (which described itself as "we") always used medical terminology and prescribed from what was obviously a thorough knowledge of medicine, a subject about which Cayce knew nothing. If the prescribed treatments were followed accurately, they always worked. Cayce began to trust the process as much as those who came for help trusted him.

Word of Cayce's strange power spread. People from all over his community and finally the country began to contact him. He didn't need to see or meet the patients who sought help. The "we" seemed to be able to enter their minds and bodies, explore the condition in question, and prescribe treatments which if followed exactly, continued to always work.

The New York Times did an extensive investigative story on Cayce and pronounced that it had no explanation. There was no evidence that Cayce was speaking from his own subconscious (he knew nothing of the medical profession) and as far as "spiritual" entities were concerned, the *Times* couldn't comment.

Cayce became famous all over the world.

Soon people began to question Cayce's "Voice" about more cosmic issues. "What is the purpose of life?" "Is there such a thing as life after death?" "Is reincarnation of the soul accurate?"

The Voice answered in the affirmative and began to speak of the past lives of the people who inquired. It connected past-life experiences with certain maladies that an individual might be suffering now.

Again Cayce became flabbergasted and confused. Such cosmic connections had never occurred to him. Medical treatment had become acceptable to him but he considered past life information anti-religious. The Bible said nothing about such things. For awhile, he refused to accept the information in the readings. It was too outlandish. But soon, with continuing examples of confirmation of past-life identities, he began to wonder. Too many people returned to him with proof that there had been a Mr. or Mrs. So-and-so living in the identical conditions in the past that he had described. Of course, they had no proof that *they* had been those people, but whenever they investigated in detail, *they* all reported they had indeed felt strangely yet extremely familiar with what he described.

The morality of karma and reincarnation was heavily emphasized in each reading. For example:

A thirty-eight-year-old woman had complained of being unable to commit herself to marriage because of a deep-seated mistrust of men. It turned out that a husband in a previous incarnation had deserted her, immediately after their marriage, to join the Crusades.

A girl of eighteen had a terrible overweight problem which she couldn't control. Other than her obesity, she was extremely attractive. The readings submitted that two lifetimes ago she had been an athlete in Rome with both beauty and athletic prowess, but she frequently ridiculed others who were heavy and couldn't move well.

A young man, twenty-one, complained of being an unhappy homosexual. The readings reported that in the French Royal Court he had taken great delight in baiting and exposing homosexuals. The readings submitted: "Condemn not then. What you condemn in another, you will become in yourself."

The files and records compiled by Cayce were among the most extensive in medical history. The fourteen thousand readings produced examples of health karma, psychological karma, retributive karma, family karma, mental abnormality karma, vocational karma . . . on and on.

But what came through in the readings more strongly than anything else was the need for the assertion of free will. The Voice said that the basic error that man makes is his belief that his life is predetermined and therefore he is powerless to change it. It said that the lives we lead *now* hold the higher priority and the assertion of our free will in relation to our karma is our most important task. It was up to us to get in touch with ourselves spiritually so that we might achieve some insight as to what our purposes in life are. For every act, for every indifference, for every misuse of life, we are finally held accountable. And it is up to us to understand what those accounts might be.

❊ As I read about Cayce and the "readings" of other psychics and trance mediums, I found myself fascinated with the idea that they might be true. Wherever the information came from didn't matter as much to me as the sense it made. Maybe it *was* a psychic's subconscious talking; maybe they *were* just good actors.

But even if that were true, the morality of their message was unmistakable. And a good set of values to live by.

"All the answers are within yourself," they said. "Only look." ❊

Chapter 8

"If we could see ourselves and other objects as *they really are*, we should see ourselves in a world of spiritual natures, our community with which neither began at our birth nor will end with the death of the body."

—Immanuel Kant
Critique of Pure Reason

I read far into the night, and the next morning I got up early and walked into the Calabasas mountains to think. The mountains are craggy and steep with an eye-caressing view of the Pacific. Nestled in the high hills was "The Ashram," a kind of rough-and-ready, spiritually involved health camp ("spa" to those who had a lot of money). I loved the activities at The Ashram and often went there to get in shape for a television special, or whenever I knew I would be doing two shows a night in Vegas or Tahoe. I'd eat pure, raw food, take the long, ten-mile-straight-up-mountain walks, exercise in the open air, and get in touch with what the Swedes who ran the place called the "prana" in the air. The Swedes were Anne Marie Bennstrom (who founded The Ashram) and her assistant, Katerina Hedwig. They seemed to know just about everything there was to know about health. I trusted them anyway, because I always felt terrific when they got through with me.

Now, climbing the fire trail, I ran into Katerina, whom I adored. I called her Cat for short. She was leading a group of "inmates" on one of the torturous climbs. I only had to look at Cat in order to feel better. She *was* joy. Bubbly, funny, and light-heartedly intelligent, she and Anne Marie were also deep into spiritual exploration and were devotees of Sai Baba, an avatar in India.

Cat was a big woman and as strong as the mountains she climbed. She was also gentle but forceful, and her infectious personality had led me through a particularly arduous workout period when I first returned from the political campaign trail for George McGovern and finally from China—twenty pounds overweight. She made the pain and the discipline possible to endure. I also teased her that her nickname was Cat because she became a "cat"-alyst for events that followed which were responsible for completely changing my life.

We trudged up the fire trail together. For a while I didn't say anything. Neither did she. I was glad, because when you're climbing straight up you haven't enough breath to talk anyway. At the crest we stretched and looked out over the Pacific. Cat seemed to sense that I wanted to talk but didn't know how.

"Well, fickle lady of fame, how are you?"

'Fickle lady of fame?' It was such an odd way to refer to me.

"Hey," I said, "are you saying that you think I'm fickle?" I laughed, not really sure why I felt the need to do so.

"Yes, about fame you're fickle. You're not really sure you want it, are you?"

Cat had the damndest way of immediately zeroing in on the conflict a person might be feeling.

"Fame?" I said, "I don't think I've ever cared all that much about recognition, only about the quality of the work. And right now I care more about what I'm looking for."

"You mean yourself."

"Myself? I care more about myself?"

"I mean you seem to care more about finding out who you are than you do about fame. Isn't that true, Shirley?"

"Yes. . . . Yes," I said, "and it's a struggle. Because suddenly now I'm into a dimension of myself that I didn't know existed, much less ever explored before."

"You're talking about your spiritual dimension?"

God, it sounded so banal to hear another person put it into

words. But then no words were safe havens anymore. I remembered how often I had been judgmental about the words people chose to use when describing a deeply moving experience relating to some abstract occurrence in their lives.

"Yes," I said, "I guess you could say I'm really curious about this spiritual stuff. I don't know what's going on but the more I hear about it the more I want to hear?" I felt myself make the statement as though I were asking a question.

"Oh, Shirley, that's wonderful!" Cat said, her gay laughter enveloping every word. "It's so satisfying to be drawn to the spirit, isn't it?"

I shoved my hands into the pockets of my jogging jacket. "Drawn to the spirit?" I asked. "Is that what I'm experiencing?"

"Why sure, Shirley," Cat smiled. "God and spiritual recognition are everything. That's why we're here. It's the whole explanation of life and purpose. For me it's all I live for. I don't care if I never have another man, and you *know* how lusty I used to be. Well, forget about it. I feel my own spiritual light and I'm in love with that and I don't need anything else."

Jesus, I thought, if I could be in love with my own spiritual light it would save me a lot of plane trips and a lot of grief, too.

"Yeah, well," I said, "I guess I should plunge on ahead but I'm not sure I quite know how."

"Oh, Shirley," Cat went on, "I know a wonderful entity you must meet. Anne Marie is with him now in Sweden. But she's talking about bringing him over here."

"Wait a minute, Cat," I said, interrupting her all-out enthusiasm, "an entity in Sweden? What kind of entity?"

"A spiritual entity. His name is Ambres and he comes through a man named Sturé Johanssen."

"Comes through? Are you talking about trance channeling?"

"Oh," she said, surprised that I didn't understand, "oh yes. Sturé is a very simple carpenter who lives in Stockholm, and a spiritual entity called Ambres uses him as an instrument to speak through.

His readings are incredibly beautiful, Shirley. You should hear him. Of course he only speaks Swedish and an ancient Swedish at that but either Anne Marie or I will translate for you. He is such a strong, powerful, benevolent entity, Shirley. Oh my, you would love him."

"Stockholm?" I asked. "Jesus, that's a long way to go to talk to a spirit."

Cat laughed. "Well, maybe sometime next year Anne Marie will bring Sturé and his wife here to the States. Then you can have a session."

"Does his stuff work the same way that Edgar Cayce's stuff worked?" I asked, remembering what I had just read on Cayce.

"Yes," said Cat. "They both worked as trance channelers for entities on the other side to come through."

We walked on for a moment, Cat excitedly animated at the prospect of my being exposed to a dimension of life that she had long ago accepted. But I wanted to double-check her feelings.

"Cat?" I asked. "Do you honestly believe there is an 'other side' and that disembodied spiritual entities can talk to us and teach us and stuff like that?"

Cat turned and looked at me in astonishment. "Do I *believe* it?" she asked.

I nodded.

"No," she answered, shocking me into stopping dead in my tracks. "No. Not at all," she reiterated. "I don't believe it. I *know* it."

I realized that, because this was Cat, I had just heard a powerful statement of faith. And she said it with such love. Any other suspicious question I might ask her from then on would be a reflection of my own inability to accept Cat's fundamental value system. I would be judging or questioning the very depths of what made up her character and personality. I might fancy myself as a kind of adventurous human reporter, but I certainly wasn't going to ridi-

cule another human being's belief system or "knowingness" as Cat apparently defined it.

"Well," I said, "this Ambres seems like an interesting entity to get to know." I felt like an imposter as I heard the word "entity" come out of my mouth.

"Oh, Shirley, when Anne Marie and Sturé and his wife come to the States we'll give you a call. Too bad you have no reason to go to Stockholm. Don't you need to buy a pair of skis or something?" We laughed as we continued to walk, segueing into a conversation about food-combining and the latest info on what dairy products do to the digestive system. Soon we embraced and said goodbye, promising to follow up on our newly initiated spiritual exploration.

I went immediately home, feeling a strong urge to call Gerry in London. I just needed to speak to him. In fact, I felt I needed to see him. I guess I wanted to hear him and touch him and experience him as my other *real* world. I didn't feel much like seeing any other friends, and I had some time to myself before rehearsals for the new show began.

As I called him I was reminded of how conditioned I had been to checking out my feelings with the man I was involved with. Somehow my own feelings, my own questions, my own searching, my own new interests seemed partially inadequate and only half realized without including *the man*. I couldn't talk to Gerry about what I was into, but it would help me to check out my own perceptions just to be with him. It was hard to admit that I needed to ratify my own identity in relation to the man in my life, but there it was.

I reached him at his office in London.

"Hello," he said, not at all surprised to hear from me so soon after our Honolulu meeting.

"Gerry," I said, sensing that he was rushed, "I know you're busy, but I want to come to London to see you. I have a few weeks and I want to spend them with you."

I could hear him hesitate on the other end of the Atlantic cable. "Oh," he said finally, "but I'm going to Stockholm."

"In Sweden?" I said idiotically, stunned. I had just agreed with Cat it was too bad I didn't have a reason for going there.

As I think about it today, I would have to say that this was the beginning of a series of events which, as they unfolded, gave me a definite sense of pattern. Of course one could say most anything in life is simply coincidental, but after awhile, when coincidence becomes multiple, a redefinition of "accidental" is necessary.

In any case Gerry went on about his trip to Stockholm.

"Yes," he said, "I have a Socialist economic meeting and I'll be there for a week."

"Oh," I said, "so why don't I come to Stockholm? I love snow."

He didn't say anything. I heard him excuse someone from his office politely and shuffle some papers.

"Gerry?" I said.

"Yes, yes," he said. "Hello."

"Gerry. I need to talk to you. I need to be with you. I miss you. I mean, I really do. And I guess I need to know how you really feel."

I felt I was acting like a school girl pursuing her hero. I waited for him to say something. Every moment seemed to have some horribly anxious meaning. Finally he said, "Yes. Yes, I miss you too."

He was so uncomfortable, but I pressed on.

"So is it all right? Would it be convenient if I met you in Stockholm? I'll make all my own arrangements."

"What did you mean, you want to know how I really feel?"

He sounded frightened.

"What's wrong, Gerry?"

"I'm upset."

"I know. Why? Upset at what?"

"I'm upset at pleasure."

"What pleasure? What do you mean?"

"I'm upset at the pleasure it gives me to know what I mean to you."

"Why? Why would you be upset by that?"

"Because," he said, "I can't understand *why* I'm so important to you. And it makes me feel inadequate."

I didn't know what to say. I didn't know what he was really saying.

"Do you want to see me, Gerry?" I asked.

"I'm longing to see you, but I'm afraid I'll disappoint you. I hate that," he said. "I hate feeling that I'll disappoint you."

"Well," I said, "maybe the important thing is not to disappoint yourself. Can we talk?"

"Come to Stockholm in two days," he said. "I'll be at the Grand. You arrange accommodations somewhere else." He hesitated a few more moments. Then he whispered, "Goodbye," and hung up.

I sat there thinking about what it must feel like to feel inadequate to another person. It was a feeling I had never really experienced as far as I could remember. I had felt *dependent* on others, especially regarding the "man" syndrome, but the *inadequacies* I usually felt were to myself and that could be just as bad. The standards and goals I set for myself were sometimes impossible to live up to and made me too self-demanding. Maybe Dad was right. Maybe I didn't want to disappoint myself. I didn't want to do what he had done.

But Gerry wasn't the only man who had complained of feeling inadequate with me. I remembered several important relationships I had had which ultimately ended because the men simply became afraid they couldn't live up to my expectations of them, and because of it weren't comfortable with themselves. I wondered where the burden of responsibility for such breakdowns lay. Was it with me for demanding too much? Or did it lie with a feeling of low self-esteem the men had in themselves?

I remembered going to several psychologist friends about the

question, and they pointed out that behind every woman that a man found himself involved with was the haunting image of his own mother. And their mothers were the figures they couldn't live up to. Very few men saw their own women clearly. Instead they perceived them through the haunting screens of their mothers. And thinking of going to Sweden to meet Gerry, I remembered a very well documented research report I had read studying the problem of Swedish suicide. The high suicide rate was not caused by socialism or the weather or any of the popular cocktail-conversation myths. Instead, they found that most of the Swedish suicides were caused by the high standards and expectations that Swedish mothers placed upon their children who in turn felt they simply couldn't "live up to it." And out of intense depression and frustration, they felt so inadequate they resorted to suicide.

Maybe men everywhere were suffering a less intense but still disturbing sense of double imagery where women were concerned.

And in this age of female liberation, where women complained about feeling addicted to having to have a man, men might be suffering from these childhood pressures that exposed a basic lack of belief in themselves, which was just as devastating for them. In both cases, the problem lay in *self* identity. Gerry said he couldn't understand *why* he was important to me, as though he, with all his intelligence and talents and accomplishments, wasn't worth my attention. He was obviously and publicly a very successful man. So his sense of inadequacy had to come from something deep inside. And just by my acknowledging that he *was* very important to me in a very personal sense, I was bringing his own personal insecurities to the surface.

So female liberation was certainly important, but it seemed to me that male liberation was just as important. In fact, if men were freer about who they really were, it wouldn't be so necessary for them to colonize the women in their lives to such an extent. Maybe, in my case, because I was so personally *un*colonizable, it made them examine the real meaning of equality. And if there was

resistance to true equality in the relationship, it would inevitably dissolve. And how *could* a man feel equal if he didn't believe he was worth loving?

I didn't know anything about Gerry's mother, but in the long run it didn't matter. The real question was what he now thought of himself. It seemed to be *the* question for all of us.

I began to realize, from a new perspective, that *self* realization was the most painful but important search of all. None of us felt whole and self-loving enough to understand that our own self-identity was the answer to a fulfilled happiness. What we really needed most was a complete relationship within ourselves. Maybe that very problem—either in human or cosmic terms—was what Moses and Christ and Buddha and Pythagoras and Plato and all the religious and philosophical sages down through the ages had been trying to tell us . . . know thyself and that truth will set you free.

Suppose one of the paths to understanding who each of us really was lay in having knowledge of who we might have been in lifetimes previous? There were many examples where psychiatry just didn't seem able to go deep enough to get to the root of an individual disturbance. Maybe past-life understanding could. If mothers and fathers and childhood experiences in our present lifetimes molded and conditioned how we related to life and reality today, why couldn't experiences that went even further back affect us in the same way?

I remembered speaking to Paddy Chayevsky, before he died, about the novel he was writing, *Altered States*. He had done extensive scientific research on it and was saying that every human being carries, locked in his or her cellular memory, the entire experience of the human race from the beginning of creation. I guess my mind was following along the same lines. What was the difference between cellular memory recall from the beginning of time and past-life recall? Surely one form of memory was at least as miraculous as the other.

I wondered if I might in fact have known Gerry in another life,

and if I had, what our karma was that we were going through such an obstacle course in our relationship now. And I wondered if we were going about working it out in the right way.

I called Cat and said I was going to Stockholm. She wasn't surprised. She gave me the address and telephone number of the trance medium and I said I would look him up. ❀

Chapter 9

"A lifetime may be needed merely to gain the virtues which annul the errors of man's preceding life. . . . The virtues we acquire, which develop slowly within us, are the invisible links that bind each one of our existences to the others—existences which the spirit alone remembers, for Matter has no memory for spiritual things."

—Honoré de Balzac
Seraphita

I had been to Stockholm several times on tour and it was a place that intrigued me. The city lay under wall-to-wall snow when I arrived, looking like a picture postcard from a Nordic fantasy.

A friend I called met me at the airport.

It was seven o'clock in the evening. A veil of snow filtered down and I wondered how soon it got dark every day during the famous Swedish winters. I had been to Sweden once before during the winter and when my nose ran it froze on my face. During those days in the late fifties Sweden was something of a social and physical mystery to those of us who had heard only a little about the small country that had *voted* for socialism. I remember feeling chilled stirrings when I sat in the hall where the Nobel Peace Prizes were given and heard that there was no preferred seating or class distinction in Sweden. I had heard it was a country of free love and if a wife or husband wanted to sleep with somebody else, no one cared. But I had come to learn that that image was not accurate, and that many Swedes found such an image difficult to live with; particularly the Swedish women. They were basically as conservative as everyone else in the world, even though government policy allowed more legalized personal freedom than anywhere on earth.

I had been in Sweden during the Festival of Lights called Santa Lucia which commemorated the end of the long dark days and the beginning of the slow trek toward another summer. Swedes lived for the sun and seemed to hibernate in their minds until it came. A kind of institutionalized depression came over the Swedish people during the winter months—which was most of the year. "Summer came on a Tuesday last year" was a favorite Swedish joke. The winter in Sweden certainly wasn't going to lighten my relationship with Gerry.

My friend took me to dinner and after some oysters and herring, I went to the hotel where he had made a reservation for me in a small suite overlooking the harbor. The living room had bay windows and the bedroom a double bed. I knew I would be happy there. I fell into bed and about four hours later woke up with the urge to vomit, which I did for the rest of the night. It was one of the oysters.

The sun came out about nine the next morning to a day that was overcast from then on and slightly misty. A sheet of ice in the bay across the street was broken up every hour by a tugboat that circled around and around while lines of dump trucks piled all the snow they had scraped from the streets that morning into the bay. Sightseeing boats lay clutched in the ice in the surrounding frozen water waiting for spring to come.

I had breakfast and went for a short walk. I wanted to be in when Gerry called so I hurried back. Slick ice packed the city streets but the Swedes had no trouble at all negotiating corners and curbs. I felt as though I'd fall down at every juncture.

When I returned to the hotel, the woman manager came to see me asking if I had any requests. After asking for a hair dryer with Swedish current and an extra blanket, I was sure I'd be very comfortable.

There was a private entrance to the hotel where anyone leaving or entering could do so unnoticed and she promised that the telephone operators would protect my identity from the journalists.

I waited in my room for the rest of the day. Around six o'clock he called.

"Hi."

"Hi."

"How are you?"

"Fine."

"When did you get in?"

"Yesterday evening."

"Yesterday evening? I thought you'd be coming in around five o'clock today."

"No," I said, "I told you I was coming on the 16th."

"Oh. Can I come over?"

"Sure. Have you had anything to eat?"

"No, I'll stop along the way."

"Come now. I'll have something here for you. That way you'll get here sooner."

"All right. Goodbye."

His voice sounded more authoritative, as if he was in command of himself.

I left the room door open so he wouldn't have to wait after he knocked. And in about half an hour, there he was.

He came in wearing big fur gloves, the ones I imagined his wife disapproved of, looking very white and drawn.

I crossed the room to embrace him, but he went straight to the window and looked out, getting his bearings on where my hotel was in relation to his.

He wore his trench coat with no fur lining, a tweed suit that I had seen in the fall, and a pair of leather shoes with big rubber soles.

"My grandmother became very famous," he said, "for skating on thin ice in a bay like that wearing a skirt that was only a few inches below the knees."

"Well," I said, "maybe you'll become famous for skating on thin ice wearing trousers."

He smiled.

He walked to the other window. "And see the string of lights that look like a penis at the top? Just beyond that is my hotel."

A rising string of lights looked like a penis to him? Interesting . . .

I stood next to him at the window. He turned from the window and cupped one of my breasts in his hand.

I invited him to sit down with me. I had ordered two double decker club sandwiches that had turned out to be lettuce and tomato salad on toast.

He sat on the sofa and began to cut into one of the sandwiches. He talked of upcoming budget cuts, the problems of having to raise taxes in an election year, and an American journalist whom he had been talking to all day. He asked me how my rehearsals were going. I said I would be starting soon. While I talked, his eyes sopped me up—my hair, my movements, my clothes, my body . . . but he didn't touch me. I, in turn, felt too intimidated to touch him. We continued to talk . . . about the boat people from Vietnam and how much happier they would be in France if Europe was where they wanted to go, Sihanouk at the United Nations and the fact that the English Left was split down the middle on the Vietnamese invasion of Cambodia. We avoided the subject of us until we both got our bearings.

He lay back on the sofa. I could feel he was exhausted, and that he had been that way for some time. And I could feel that he knew it was all right for me to know. I sat close to him and touched his hair. He didn't object. He leaned his head against the back of the sofa. His arms rested in his lap. He didn't reach for me at all. I laid my head on his chest and looking up at him I kissed him gently on the lips. They were still slightly cold from the weather outside. Lifting his head, he turned away from me and slowly reached for more of his sandwich. I waited for him to finish.

He lay back again and sighed.

"Listen," I said, "why don't you let me give you a massage? You don't have to do anything but lie there. Okay?"

Immediately he got up and headed for the bedroom. He turned around and waited for me to take off his coat and shirt and tie. I tried but I couldn't get his tie undone. He laughed.

"I thought you said I wouldn't have to do anything."

He untied it himself and stood with his arms beside him. I didn't make any move to take off his trousers. I turned him around, gently pushing him face down on the bed. I reached for some Albolene cream and began to rub his back. He sighed with pleasure and curled his arms under him. I took off my slacks and sweater so I could straddle him around the waist and use the massage technique I had learned in Japan with more strength.

My nails were a problem so I used the base of my hands. His shoulders and arms were so muscular, my hands felt ineffective, but he sighed deeply.

"You know," he said, "this is the first massage I've ever had in my whole life."

I knew he was telling me the truth, regardless of how unbelievable it sounded. But then with Gerry there was so much he didn't know about self-pleasure. His skin was cold. I knew how warm my hands must feel to him. I massaged his neck until I felt him relax. I put more Albolene cream on my hands and moved down to his back and waist. He began to undulate under me and I playfully smacked him.

I continued to knead his back and waist. He reached around and put his arm around my waist. I knew he was too tired. But he wouldn't stop. He wound the other arm around me too.

This whole scene was unreal. We were perfectly free to make love together but somehow he wanted it to be as if it really wasn't happening.

I tried to squirm away from his hands, still massaging his back. He reached around and pushed me toward him until I fell on him pressing myself against his back and squeezing him with my legs. He turned over.

Before I knew what was happening, he clasped me to him and

we were making love. His arms held me so tightly I could hardly breathe. He held me tighter. Over and over I whispered that I loved him. His only reply was to breathe as though he were home again.

Afterward he rested. Neither of us said anything.

He stayed still as though he never wanted to move.

Suddenly I felt afraid. I stirred under him.

"Gerry," I said.

"Yes?"

"I'm afraid. I need to talk." I stammered when I said it and lay beside him.

He stared at the ceiling for awhile and then leaning on his arm looked deeply into my eyes.

"I have thought very hard every day," he said. "I'm going to state the problem. I'm not stating any solution because I haven't reached one."

I could feel my stomach turn over.

"I love you," he said. "I love you deeply, but half of me resists it. I hold myself back subconsciously because I know that I'm not strong enough to tolerate the consequences of our relationship either in a political or a personal sense. I feel that I have been in a kind of mental and physical hole with this relationship and what became so clear to me is that I am not strong enough. I have been confronting myself up 'til now, but now I see it clearly and I want to be fair with you."

He patted my hair and smiled shyly almost as a child would smile, guiltily at the truth of what he was saying.

"Please don't pat my hair and smile shyly," I said. "Just treat me seriously and tell me the truth."

His face went solemn. He understood that although he hadn't known me very long, I was more serious than I had ever been in my life.

He looked deeper into my eyes. "Without you I can push my feelings under, but when I see you, I love your face, your hair; I

love listening to the things you tell me. I love touching you. I love you and I love loving you. All those feelings come back and I can't cope with them."

I wanted to cry.

He took a long beat.

"I don't understand why you love me. Subjectively, I suppose I do, but objectively, I don't." He waited for me to say something.

"You don't understand *why* I love you or *that* I do?"

"I don't understand either. So now, I've stated the problem," he went on, "let's not talk about it anymore."

I didn't say anything. He seemed afraid that he might have given me the cue to walk away.

"Let's get under the covers," I said.

We did. I still didn't say anything. He decided to continue.

"The world is a crazy place right now. I want to help my party and my country into a better period, and politically our relationship could lose me the election. I know that is a terrible thing to say, but it's the truth, and I can't do that to my party. They depend on me to win again, nor do I want to lose my seat in Parliament. But personally acknowledging our love would make it three times harder for me. My wife and children have been so patient in putting up with me. There is no stormy loving passion in my relationship with her, but she and they have been a stabilizing force in my life. Morally, I can't do anything to hurt them. I have worked most of my life, usually to the point of exhaustion, and they have tolerated it. You see how this is morally unacceptable to me? And even if I leave out everyone else's feelings, I know I'm not strong enough to tolerate my own feelings if I hurt them or my party. And even as I say this to you I feel that I am speaking from a hole, but from this hole I see things clearly."

I turned over inside the covers and rested on my arm and looked into his face.

"Gerry, tell me something."

"Yes?"

"I feel that along with your own loneliness, that you feel that your family has held you back. Is that true?"

"Yes," he said, "that's true too, but we have a very intricate relationship with each other and maybe it was good that they held me back. Otherwise I might have grown into a weed."

"A weed?" The self-image was so inappropriate. Did he mean that if he was free of them he would strangle all other growth around him? That was what weeds did. Or did he think he'd just grow wild and unruly without the discipline of a family? I was turning the imagery over and over in my mind. I remembered how it struck me when I had read once that there was no such thing as a weed but only a plant in the wrong place.

"My wife is very harsh and judgmental of others," he said. "That's why I know she would never accept our relationship. I've never been able to understand that streak in her, but it's very strongly there. She's monopolistic. She rules the family with an iron hand."

"An iron hand?"

"Yes. And I think that's been good. But she would be very harsh in understanding my need for you."

The pangs of conscience I had been feeling rapidly vanished.

"But if you are unwilling to be what you'd call immoral to her, why do you accept her being immoral to you?"

"I don't think she's being immoral."

"Well, what's immorality anyway? Isn't it immoral to be harshly judgmental of someone you love?"

"But they have all been so sweet and patient. I can't hurt them now."

I tried to grasp what he was saying, particularly when I wasn't asking for any commitment from him.

"Well, listen darling, no one is suggesting you do anything. I'm certainly not. Please understand that. I'm more concerned with what you think you're doing."

"What do you mean?" he said.

"Well, has it occurred to you that you are afraid of bursting out with a new freedom?"

"How do you mean?"

"Well, bursting out with freedom carries a lot of pain and responsibility with it. Maybe you were ready to do that when you met me, but only up to a point. And maybe you are legitimately retreating back into your hole so you can avoid it for a little while longer. A new freedom for you can mean a better relationship with your family too."

He blanched. "I don't know."

"Well, maybe you're in your hole because your own potential might frighten you too much. I feel as though I fell in love with your potential and you're afraid of it."

He didn't say anything.

Then I said, "I guess I have to ask you, don't I?"

"Ask me what?"

"Could you do without me? Do you want to do without me?"

His face looked pained and drawn. I waited for him to answer, churning inside because he was taking so long and also because he was making a superhuman effort to be fair.

"I don't know," he said. "I suppose I would have to say yes. I could give up my feelings and go back to the loneliness you recognized. Yes, I think I could."

I could feel myself shaking inside. It seemed to be up to me now to make it easier for him and walk away *because* he loved me.

I stifled the tears. "What should I do?" I asked. "I don't know if I could stand how lonely I'd make you by leaving, to say nothing of myself."

"Yes," he said, "it would make me desolate if you left me."

"And if you can't understand that I love you that much, then how can you understand how you love me? If you loved yourself more, you'd be freer to love me and others too."

His face went quizzical. "I can't understand that," he said.

"What I mean is, you have to love yourself before you can really love anyone else."

"I still don't understand," he said.

"It's as though you've dedicated your entire life to helping others unaware completely that you were doing nothing to help yourself."

He got out of bed.

"Does this mean you don't want to discuss it any further?" I asked.

He laughed and fell on top of me sheepishly. "But there is a limit to how much I can take," he said. "You are very strong."

"Relentless is the word. But you are ready for relentlessness or you wouldn't be here."

He sat up beside me and said, "All right, there are three solutions as I see it. One—to continue this deception politically and personally. Two—to effect your solution . . . and . . ."

"Wait a minute. What's my solution?"

"The solution you suggested a moment ago. You know . . ."

He couldn't even say the words, "Leave me and walk away."

"And three—to reflect a while longer."

"We're reflecting right now, aren't we?"

He laughed.

"Well, at least we're *really* talking about it," I said.

He looked out the window.

"You know," he said, "this is the longest personal talk I have ever had."

"I think you're wrong," I said. "I think it's the *only* personal talk you've ever had. Is that true?"

"Yes."

We looked at each other.

"Look," I said, "I don't want to mess up your marriage and I don't want to mess up your political career. But I also don't like

participating in deception of any kind whether it's personal or political on any level."

"I know," he said.

"As far as a solution is concerned, I would be happy if you would be more free when you're with me, that's all. And in that respect, we can buy some more time."

"Okay," he said, "I understand. I'll try to be more free if you'll continue the deception awhile longer."

"Okay, it's a deal," I said, "but one more thing. You're right that there is a limit to how relentless I should be, but there is also a limit to how 'fair' you should be. Please stop being so fair and just enjoy yourself with me and I'll stop being so relentless."

"All right," he laughed.

He rolled his eyes and shook his head in mock despair. He was wonderful to talk to: no hostility, no giving up, no arguing; just a deep and desperate desire to understand what was going on between us.

He dressed and so did I. He said he had a youth meeting in some other city and wouldn't be back in Stockholm until the day after tomorrow. But we would see each other as soon as he returned.

I had agreed to more deception, but I didn't want to mention the true and real immorality he was committing by keeping this from his wife for what would be a whole year. And I didn't mention that I suspected what worried him the most was that if she knew about us, she would be harshly judgmental of him *in public*, which would not only lose him the election, but also shatter all the illusions he had as to how *moral* she really was . . . or wasn't.

I walked him to the private entrance, showed him how the key worked, and watched him walk away in the snow muttering about the night watchman who might recognize him.

Then I remembered something he had said that was too complicated for me to understand.

"I like to be admired," he had said, "but not by those people who really mean something to me."

I thought about that all night while I tried to sleep.

To be admired by people you care about carried with it a responsibility to live up to that admiration. It was more than public relations; it required substantial qualities which could stand the test of scrutiny and continued observation over a period of time.

Most people didn't seem to allow themselves close personal contact. It aroused too much anxiety, was too difficult to sustain . . . for a few days maybe, but on a long-term basis it became too threatening. The irony was that all of us looked for love. We spend our lives searching for another to share it with. And when we find someone with the potential for fulfilling that need, we back away. ❁

Chapter 10

"I think immortality is the passing of a soul through many lives or experiences, and such as are truly lived, used, and learned, help on to the next, each growing richer, happier and higher, carrying with it only the real memories of what has gone before . . ."

—Louisa May Alcott
Letters

I didn't see Gerry again for three days. During that time I sat in my hotel room and thought. I slept about four hours a night. I left to take frozen walks in the snow, but I was unaware of the cold. I turned over my whole life in my mind. I read some of the books I had bought at the Bodhi Tree, especially on Edgar Cayce. And then I pulled out the address and telephone number for the Swedish trance medium who channeled Ambres.

I called my friend who had met me at the airport. Lars and his wife were in advertising; they were upper-middle class, although the Swedes didn't like to think they still had a class society. I had met them when I was on tour in Stockholm a few years before.

They had been very discreet in meeting me at the airport and refrained from asking me why I was in Stockholm now. We chatted for awhile on the telephone and in that context I mentioned that I had been reading some metaphysical books, particularly on the psychic readings of Edgar Cayce.

"Oh yes," said Lars. "Edgar Cayce. I know quite a bit about his work. He was very astute."

I was slightly taken aback that in Sweden Edgar Cayce was known when I in America had only recently heard of him.

"It's strange and coincidental you should mention him," Lars went on, "because just tonight we are going to a psychic session

with a Swedish trance medium. Would you like to come along and meet the spiritual entity?"

"A trance medium?" I said. "Lars, *you* are seeing a spiritual entity?"

"Yes," he said simply.

"What's his name?" I asked.

"Ambres," he said.

Well, to put it mildly, the "coincidence" was not lost on me. I had been flipping through the Cayce book as we talked. Now I closed it firmly and said yes, I'd love to come. I was definitely in Sweden for reasons other than Gerry. Things were really getting interesting.

I was ready when Lars and Birgitta picked me up a few hours later. They didn't ask what I had been doing since I arrived, so I volunteered that I had an idea for a new book and was spending time away from my hectic life in America and needed peace and quiet in the Swedish winter. They seemed to accept my explanation, but then Swedes rarely expose their feelings.

They drove me toward the outskirts of Stockholm where the trance medium and his wife lived. They told me the trance medium's name was Sturé Johanssen and his wife's was Turid. The spiritual entity that Sturé channeled was becoming famous all over Sweden.

"Many people are coming to the teaching sessions of Ambres," said Lars, "because he helps so many with medical diagnoses."

"How do you mean?" I asked, remembering that Cayce had channeled what sounded like much the same thing.

"Oh," said Lars, "people come from all over Sweden with needs of every description. Some are suffering from chronic problems of health, some with terminal diseases, some with psychological confusion, some just with questions about where mankind came from and where we are going."

"And this Ambres can provide answers for all of that stuff?"

"Well," said Lars, "if people follow his holistic directions per-

fectly, they usually find some relief, and most of his instructions have to do with understanding the power each of us has within ourselves to know everything if we'd only recognize it and believe in it."

"What if someone is suffering with terminal cancer? Ambres can put it in remission?"

"No," he said, "Ambres doesn't put it in remission. He helps put each person on the right course mentally and spiritually so that they can attempt to do it themselves, or at least to deal with the emotional problems involved. It's basically a holistic and spiritual approach."

"Does it work?" I asked.

"Well," Lars replied, "the basis of Ambres' teachings is educating us that we have the power and the knowledge to become anything we want to become. That *we* have dimensions and understanding that we are not aware of. He teaches that our positive energy is awesome, just as his is, only *he*, as a spiritual being without a body at the present, knows it, and we don't."

"Well, what is a spiritual being really? I don't quite understand."

"We are all spiritual beings," said Lars. "We just don't acknowledge it. We are spiritual beings of energy who happen to be in the physical body at the present time and Ambres is a spiritual being of energy who does not happen to be in the body right now. Of course, he is highly evolved, but then so are we. The difference is that we don't believe it."

Shades of what David had said to me ran in and out of my mind. Snippets and phrases from articles and books I had read played around in my head. Sai Baba in India had said what sounded like the same thing. Likewise, the spiritual master Krishnamurti. "We are capable of everything there is," they had said, "and the acknowledgement of our seemingly invisible spiritual power would hasten our improvement."

"So," I said to Lars, "you and Birgitta really believe an actual spiritual entity is speaking through Sturé Johanssen?"

"Oh certainly," said Birgitta. "First of all, if he isn't an actual spiritual entity of a highly evolved nature, then Sturé Johanssen is not only a magnificent actor, but he has within himself information and remedies that have saved lots of lives, both physically and mentally. He has also told people things that were so deeply personal that it would be hard to comprehend how Sturé would know. Nor does anybody know where he would, from himself, get the medical information he uses in diagnosis. But each person must have the faith in themselves. Ambres also provides past life information that checks out to be so familiar to people that it has a great bearing on the lives they lead today."

I opened the car window and breathed deeply.

"You mean, past-life information relating to present-day relationships is possible to ascertain?"

"Yes," said Lars, "but Ambres emphasizes heavily that *this* lifetime is the most important because otherwise we'll get obsessed with the past rather than concentrating on the present."

"Does he always answer past-life inquiries then?"

"No," Birgitta answered, "not always. Many times he assesses the questioner and concludes that present-day evaluation is much more necessary. With others he will give quite extensive past-life readings. It depends on the individual."

I sat awhile in silence as I listened to Birgitta and Lars itemize how helpful Ambres had been in solving questions and issues that had plagued some of the people who had come to him for help. And others who had been simply curious to see how the phenomenon of spiritual channeling worked.

"Listen," I said finally, "would you say there is much of this sort of thing going on?"

"You mean elsewhere in the world?" asked Lars. "Or just here in Sweden?"

"I don't know," I said. "Anywhere, I guess."

"Well, we have lots of friends in America and Europe who are interested in spiritual metaphysics. And yes, trance channeling

of spiritual entities is becoming more and more common. It's almost as though the closer we come to the end of the millennium, the more spiritual help we are getting if we'd just take advantage of it."

"Well, are some of these trance mediums phony or frauds? I mean, how can you tell the difference between one who is only acting and one who is really in trance?" I asked.

Lars thought about what I asked as though he had never considered the possibility. He looked at Birgitta. They both shrugged.

"We don't know," he answered. "I suppose you'd sort of know it when it was happening if it was phony. The material coming through is usually too complicated, or too personal, for the medium to be putting on an act. In any case you would certainly be able to distinguish the difference by the results you yourself got. We've never experienced a fake, so we don't really know."

"Are many of your co-workers in your advertising firm into this stuff?" I asked.

"Only a few," answered Lars simply, "those who are interested in spiritual growth. We tend to shy away from people who aren't willing to be open-minded at least, but there are many, like us, with whom we have become close friends. People who are searching for their own spiritual understanding become those whom we can really communicate with. The others are only acquaintances. They seem to be living on the surface of life rather than in it."

I took another breath of the pristine Swedish winter air. "What about Sturé Johanssen? What is he like as a person when he's not channeling?" I asked.

"Sturé is a carpenter," Lars explained, "and not at all interested in the spiritual world."

"So does he mind being an instrument when he could be spending his time building bookshelves or something?" I asked.

Lars laughed as the car plodded through the icy streets of Stockholm. "No," he answered. "He says if it helps people, then he's all for it. He's a good man at heart. Simple, but really a good man."

"And what does Ambres sound like compared to how Sturé sounds?"

"Sometimes it's quite difficult to understand Ambres' language," said Lars, "because it's such ancient Swedish, something like what it would be for you to listen to biblical English. His phrasing is entirely different from Sturé's, and even different from the Swedish of today. Ambres says there is *no* language to express some of the knowledge he would like to give us."

"What do you mean?"

"Well," he said, "when he's trying to teach us about dimensions or concepts we've never even thought about, he says any language itself is a limitation."

"I'm sorry," I said genuinely, but I must have sounded doubtful, "can you be more specific?"

Lars nodded. "Our spoken and written languages," he said, "only really describe those dimensions which relate to our five senses. Our physical world. We are only just beginning, through the advancement of astrophysics and psychodynamics, to know that we need to develop language which relates to the worlds that are invisible to us. Little by little, we are beginning to perceive the exciting dimensions of what we simply and sometimes sarcastically refer to as the metaphysical world. That is why Ambres sometimes has a difficult time helping us to understand life from a non-physical plane point of view."

I shut my eyes as we drove, wondering what it would be like not to be "physical." I found that the minute I got into discussions of the metaphysical and heard people using words like "occult," "astral plane," "cosmic vibrations," "etheric memory," "soul," "God"—the standard vocabulary of a study as old as time—I reacted with nervous derision, sarcastic laughter, suspicion, or outright contempt. This time was no exception. Yet I wanted to know more. I wanted to "experience" a medium myself.

Lars continued as I held my eyes shut. "All sciences have their own vocabularies," he said, "usually incomprehensible to laymen,

to say nothing of their mysteries and marvels and miracles that we take on faith. And the same for all religions. We accept scientific marvels without really understanding them, and we accept religious miracles on faith. I wonder why we, in the Western world, have so much difficulty with the whole concept of experience and thinking that is popularly known as the 'occult.' "

I opened my eyes. "Because," I said, "when you think of 'occult' you think of dark forces and *Rosemary's Baby* and stuff. It's scary. Spirits from the dead and all that aren't very mirth-making, are they?"

Lars chuckled. "Well," he said, "many people have exploited the occult to focus on the dark side of the metaphysical world. But the light side is inevitably beautiful. You can take anything in nature and focus on the negative, but the positive beauty of it can change your life."

I rolled up my eyes into my head. Sure, I was sitting in a car in Stockholm with a man and his wife who sounded just like David in Manhattan and Cat in Calabasas, California. Was this stuff going on all over the world?

As though Lars heard my thoughts, he said, "Millions of people all over the world are so interested in this stuff that they support an entire industry of books, teachings, schools, individuals, and literature of all kinds devoted to the metaphysical dimensions of life. I wouldn't call it the occult anyway. I would call it an interest in the spiritual dimension of life."

Lars and Birgitta began to speak at the same time. Again they emphasized how "gloriously involving" their spiritual interests had become. They said it had made them happier and more loving people. Through their many sessions with Ambres, they had made lots of new friends who also found themselves believing in the same things. And there seemed to be no question in anyone's mind that Ambres was a genuine spiritual entity speaking from the astral plane.

I didn't want to be disrespectful, but I asked one more time,

"And you *honestly* believe that Ambres is a real spiritual entity?"

Birgitta turned to me as Lars smiled patiently. "It's almost impossible to explain to anyone who hasn't the open-mindedness to at least consider it possible," she said.

I peered out at the Stockholm countryside, pondering. I wondered how many other Swedes in their postcard-perfect houses were into spiritual exploration. Every corner, every house, every tree was a snow-covered postcard. The leather interior upholstery of Lars's Volvo gave off a faint fresh smell. It was comfortable, modern, austerely luxurious. The Swedish houses were modern and clean, nothing opulent, but individualistic in their personalities, I thought. Sweden had its problems, but somehow seemed to be moving into the twenty-first century with a studied balance of socialism and democracy. I wondered if they would make it as time went on. I wondered how prevalent or deep their spiritual interests went. It was remarkable to me that a successful, high-powered advertising man would be driving me to a spiritual reading with a trance medium.

About ten miles outside of Stockholm we pulled into what looked like a quiet residential community. There were quaint street lamps at every corner. Sandboxes and swings decorated each line of condominiums which were built exactly alike, but were somehow individualized with flower boxes, snow men, and decorations fashioned by each family.

Lars stopped the car and I got out. I looked around at the look-alike community. "You know," I said, "I'd probably walk into the wrong condominium at least once a week. It sort of forces you to look more carefully at the individuality of each house so you don't make a mistake."

Lars smiled. He and Birgitta led me to one of the condominiums and rang the bell. A cheerful female voice came from inside and soon a plump, rosy-cheeked woman opened the door and greeted us with a stream of Swedish.

"This is Turid," said Lars. "She says she's sorry she doesn't

speak English. She knows your movies and she is very happy you want to meet Ambres."

Turid ushered us into her living room which looked like a Swedish version of a small place in the San Fernando Valley: a low, modern couch, bookshelves, a Tiffany-style lamp hanging over a smooth wooden modern coffee table. There were people sitting around the table. Spreading green ivy spilled from vases on the tables.

"Sturé made all his own furniture," said Lars.

With Lars translating, Turid introduced me to her other friends as Shirley. She never mentioned my last name. After the initial pleasantries at her front door, it didn't seem to matter to her.

"Sturé is resting," she said. "He'll be out from the bedroom in a moment." She invited us to sit down and have some beer and cheese which was spread out on the handmade coffee table.

The three of us wolfed down some cheese and Swedish crackers. "Sturé and Turid are devoting their lives now to bringing about spiritual communication," said Lars. "But Turid is concerned that Sturé might be draining his energies with trance channeling, but they want to be helpful to as many people as possible."

"Why?" I asked. "I mean, does that mean that Sturé has completely given up his regular work as a carpenter?"

"Close to it."

"Well, where do they make enough money to live on?"

"People contribute what they feel is commensurate with what they learn from the channelings."

So here was this Swedish carpenter who suddenly found a spiritual voice speaking through him giving up his regular life and work to help people by providing himself as an instrument for communication from a spiritual entity, very much like Edgar Cayce. Was this similar to what had happened with Moses and Abraham and some of the ancient prophets spoken of in the Bible? Were the same patterns occurring today that had happened then—only in modern-day terms?

"Why do they do it, Lars?" I asked.

"Well, they don't know. They just feel they have to. They are aware that the world is deteriorating and they feel this is a way to provide spiritual knowledge to prevent that human course of action. I feel the same way, as a matter of fact. We listen to what Ambres says and it has changed the way we relate to our lives. I can make more positive and compassionate decisions when I know more about my purpose as a human being."

The other people talked quietly among themselves, eating cheese and drinking beer. Some discussed occurrences in their lives. Others discussed spiritual truths that they said they didn't quite understand.

I looked up. Sturé came quietly into the room. He was about five-foot-nine, solidly built with a stocky, sturdy walk and an even modulated voice. He seemed very shy, but his handshake was strong when Lars introduced us. He greeted me in Swedish. His face was extremely kind. He was about thirty-five. He stood around for a moment shyly greeting his other friends until Turid motioned that the two of them should sit. They sat side by side in hard-backed chairs with a glass of water on a table beside Turid.

"We must begin immediately," she apologized, "because we have others to see later."

She gently turned off the lights and lit a candle on the coffee table in the center of the room. Sturé sat quietly, seemingly preparing himself to relax.

"May we observe a few moments of silent meditation," asked Turid.

We all bowed our heads and waited until Sturé was in the proper trance state for Ambres to come through.

As I sat in the candlelit darkness, I wondered what Gerry would think if he saw me. He was intrusive, and I deliberately concentrated on the candle. I had never been much for doing anything communally, usually preferring to do my own thing in private and in my own way, at my own pace. But in so many of the books I

had been reading, it seemed that communal energy benefited everyone more than one's individual energy. Certainly any performer or speaker knows about audience energy. And anyone who has been in a live audience has felt and shared in that community of feeling. As a matter of fact, the books said a positive collective energy apparently was much stronger, more intense, and more beneficial and healing in *any* human endeavor, according to the spiritual point of view. Presently I became aware of a sense of unity with the others in the room.

About ten silent minutes passed. My tape recorder purred quietly beside me. Lars sat directly over the recorder. He reminded me again that the ancient Swedish would be difficult to translate quickly. He said he would try to keep up.

I looked over at Sturé. He sat quietly, breathing deeply but calmly. His eyes were shut. His hands rested unmoving on his stocky thighs. His brown curly hair was cut just above the ears. I was conscious of focusing on small detail. After about fifteen minutes, he began to quiver slightly . . . quiver as though an electrical charge was surging through him. Turid took his hand, almost as though she was grounding him with a physical touch. She smiled. Lars whispered into my ear.

"Because of the electromagnetic energy of Ambres' spiritual entity, Sturé needs Turid's earthbound energy to neutralize his body. That's why they need to work together."

Sturé's body suddenly became rigid and sat totally upright. His eyes opened. Then his head strained forward and cocked itself to one side. His whole body shook and when it stopped, he opened his mouth and said something in a guttural voice in Swedish. The voice didn't sound anything like the man I had just been introduced to. Lars leaned over to me and whispered, "Ambres is saying, 'Greetings' and he is happy we have gathered together. He is identifying himself and he is giving us a reading on the level of spiritual energy in the room."

I don't know what I thought. I wanted to stop Lars and ask how

such energy levels could be obtained by this Ambres, but before I could raise any questions, the session had already progressed into a dialogue between Ambres and the people who had come to learn from him.

Lars translated as quickly as he could. Then I realized that most of the people present were not interested in *how* it worked. They had already accepted the process. They were interested only in the "teachings" that Ambres was imparting. And from their questions it didn't seem they were interested in past-life information or energy levels either. They were asking Ambres questions about the beginning of Creation!

Lars tried to keep up with the translation. I tried to keep up with what was happening. In a swift but careful rhythm, Ambres talked. I say Ambres because it "felt" like Ambres. I felt certain that Sturé had nothing to do with it. He was only a kind of telephone through which some spiritual entity spoke. In fact, I could "feel" the personality, the humor, the ancient rhythm of the thoughts of this entity called Ambres. He gestured and laughed and made succinct and overt points with his own energy, not the energy of Sturé. At least, that's what it "felt" like to me. His back was rigid and formal, not at all like the casual body movement of the man I had observed a half hour before.

Lars translated in capsulized statements as Ambres described God as Intelligence. He described the first stirrings of God's thought and the creation of matter. He described the birth of worlds, and worlds within worlds; and universes, and universes within universes. He described God's love for his creations and his need to receive love reflected in "feeling." And he described God's need to create Life.

I could see what Lars meant about the limitations of language. I found myself identifying with how Ambres must have felt, saddled with the limitation of earth language!

About two hours passed. Lars continued to translate in generalized fashion. Ambres passed from the rise and fall of civiliza-

tions to the creation of the Great Pyramid, which appeared to have considerable significance and which he described as a "library in stone." I somehow felt I could visualize what he was saying. The others in the room asked questions in Swedish and Ambres acknowledged that he realized there were other "entities" present who spoke only "another tongue," but he said he was an ancient Swede and even if he could speak "other tongues," the "instrument" could not do so comfortably. It would drain too much energy from him because of the strain to form words in a language he knew nothing about.

Even with his monumental account of the beginning of Creation, this entity Ambres seemed to have an understanding of humor on a human level. I wondered how long ago *he* had been human, or if he *ever* had been, but the session raced on beyond my mundane questions. I could only feel that everyone present was more advanced than I. I sat back and tried to absorb what was happening.

Ambres-Sturé would get up and walk around the room with a hunched-over stride. He appeared to be nothing like the Sturé I had met. Sometimes he laughed deeply and made jokes to emphasize a point. He went to a drawing pad tacked up on the wall and drew diagrams and cosmic geometric designs and spirals to make his descriptions more graphic. He asked the group questions as though he was a master teacher conducting a class. The group was involved and excited, confused sometimes over a crucial point which he patiently explained again. A few times he scolded someone who obviously hadn't done his homework. Then he sat down next to Turid again.

"The instrument is losing his energy," said Ambres. "He must now revitalize."

He said he hoped he would have an encounter with us again. He said we should take care of each other. Then, he said a prayer in his ancient tongue giving thanks to God for the opportunity to serve.

Sturé trembled. The electrical charge known as Ambres seemed to leave his body. Turid quickly thrust water into her husband's hands. Sturé drank all of it. He slowly came around to his own consciousness and stood up.

I looked around not knowing what to think. The guests talked quietly among themselves, asked me if I understood enough of the Swedish to comprehend what was going on, and I said yes, not wanting to admit that the process itself would take me awhile to understand, much less the information. But they seemed to understand anyway and said once I found it acceptable, it would be beneficial for me.

Beneficial? It was enough to scramble my brains. I was just glad I had read the Cayce stuff before coming.

I walked over to Sturé.

"Thank you," I said. "I hope you're all right. I've never seen anything like this."

Sturé shook my hand as Lars translated. He seemed tired but calm. His eyes looked liquid and kind. He said he hoped I had learned something from Ambres, said he would like to talk to him someday himself, and gave a little shrug as though he didn't understand what was really going on either. I was struck by his direct simplicity. Turid put her arm around me.

"Ambres is a great teacher," she said. "I'm so glad you could hear him. Sturé needs to rest now."

She guided Lars and Birgitta and me to the door and said we could talk tomorrow if I wanted.

We said goodnight to everyone and left. Snow was falling outside. The snow man in the sandbox was a square bulk now, newly fashioned by fresh snow as the children of the neighborhood slept.

The three of us walked under the white sky to the car.

"What did you think?" asked Lars.

I wanted to say something profound.

"I guess I need time to think," I stalled.

"You know," I said, "I'm beginning to feel that I was somehow

guided to come here. There's too much happening to me lately to believe in accidents anymore. I think I was *supposed* to come to Stockholm."

Lars and Birgitta smiled and led me through the falling snow to the car. We didn't say anything to each other.

Then, as we drove back to Stockholm, each lost in our own thoughts, I began to wonder about the string of "coincidences" in my life. I was aware that I was beginning to feel some preordained plan, unfolding according to my own awareness and willingness to accept what I was ready for. As though the events and incidents were bound to happen if I let them. The timing was up to me, but the inevitability felt fixed and predestined. I was surprised at what I was thinking. I had never believed in such things. Yet the serried coincidences of my relationship with Gerry: its very nature, based on earthbound frustrations, political realities, and negative obstacles coincidental (that word again!) with my slow friendship and understanding of David with his spiritual point of view—all this was gently forcing on me an awareness of other dimensions.

I seemed to be a middle-ground observer of dual realities. And I felt I was gradually developing an understanding of both points of view which, as I thought about it, seemed to represent the dualities in life (something like what my father pointed out)—the grounded Earth reality and the Cosmic Spiritual reality. Maybe they were both supposed to be necessary for human happiness. It was becoming more and more clear to me that to call one point of view the only true reality was limited, prejudiced, and probably incorrect. Maybe all human beings were Mind, Body, and Spirit as the great ancients had tried to tell us. That was their legacy. Maybe I had to *re*learn it.

I said goodbye to Lars and Birgitta and said I'd be in touch.

Chapter 11

"There is a principle which is proof against all information, which is proof against all arguments, which cannot fail to keep a man in everlasting ignorance; that principle is contempt, prior to investigation."

—Herbert Spencer

When I walked into my hotel room, the telephone was ringing. I picked it up.

"Hi," said Gerry. "How are you?"

"Fine," I said.

"I'm sorry I'm a few days late."

"That's okay. I know you were busy."

"Yes."

"How are you feeling?"

"The snow on the trees is paradise."

"Yes," I said, "the countryside must be beautiful."

"My wife came from London."

I felt the breath go out of me. I didn't know what to say. I felt paralyzed. Had he known she was going to come? Had he *asked* her to come?

"Hello?" he said.

"Yes. I'm here."

"Well . . ." he said, "I'll be over later."

"Yes, sure. I'll be here."

I went into a tailspin. I felt sick and angry. My stomach felt as if it had a hole in it. I wondered what Edgar Cayce or Ambres would prescribe for this and tried to force my mind into a peaceful and

spiritual space. I couldn't. I decided they were full of crap when it came to living a reality on Earth. I managed to laugh at the vulgarity of my thought.

When Gerry came to me I was withdrawn. I couldn't communicate. We made love, but I was afraid. He said nothing—either about his wife's presence or my reaction. Neither did I.

He asked me if I thought his hair smelled of perfume. I said he knew I wasn't wearing any and hadn't for months.

When I opened the bathroom door to see if he needed anything, I saw his huge body crouched in the tub in an embryonic position, washing and looking as though he hadn't been born yet.

He was gone for the next two days and nights.

I wrote. I wrote everything I was feeling.

I wrote until my head spun. I relived everything that was happening. I wrote to understand it. I wrote to decide what to do. I tried to hang on to who I was, what I wanted, what I wanted to do with or without Gerry. I wrote to try to understand myself. I wrote about my life and my thoughts and my questions. I wrote for days.

Whenever Gerry called I told him I was writing. He said he was glad I was doing something. It made him feel less guilty about not being able to see me. I told him he needn't worry. I was one person who would always find something to do. Then I felt guilty that I was writing partly about him and not saying so.

On the sixth night he finished working at about nine-thirty, called, and said he wanted to come to me but felt he should go home to his wife. I said fine.

I wrote well into that night, and got up at six and began again. I never left my hotel room. I wrote what I was living and feeling, like an extended diary, a way of talking to myself.

He came the next night. We ate and talked. He ate kiwi fruit and melon. He wore a thin turquoise tie which was a gift from the small town he had visited the day before. His hair fell across his

forehead as he gestured with his hands cupped and scooping into the air. I made no move toward him at all.

I crossed the room to get him more tea. He reached out, stopped me, and pulled me to him. I stood still. Slowly and with delicate sweetness he kissed my eyes, my chin, my hair, and finally my lips. He encircled me with his arms. I left mine beside my body. He pressed himself against me. I stood still.

With a kind of sly certainty he led me into the bedroom. I didn't want to go. He was taking the initiative and I wasn't sure I wanted it. He lowered me onto the bed and kissed me long and deeply as though he was experimenting with his own right to take what he wanted. I responded but with no aggressiveness. He pulled my thick wool sweater off and felt my body underneath. His hands moved all over me.

He undid my slacks and pulled them off. His hands wound in and around and underneath me. He reached up and held my head and squeezed my hair.

"I love you," he said.

I said nothing.

"I said I love you."

I said nothing.

Then like a dam bursting, he cried, "I love you, I love you, I love you . . ."

We lay together until some kind of reality swam back into focus.

He sat up and looked over me and out of the window. His face looked a hundred years old, as though his mind had seeped through it and dripped down his cheeks. He looked down at me.

"What are you thinking about?" he asked. It was the first time he had inquired about what I was thinking.

"I'm thinking about how unreal all of this is," I said. "I've been in this room watching a tugboat going in circles breaking ice. I've watched six layers of snow fall over the curb downstairs. I've eaten Swedish crackers and butter and nothing else. I've written and written and written until my hand aches. I've become the furniture

and the rug and the cold air. And now you're here. You're here and it's so unreal to me."

"Maybe what we're doing is what's more real," he said.

"Yes," I said. "Maybe." I shook my head to shock myself back to normal. "So now," I said, "you have to return to your unreality."

He got up and headed for the shower. I remained lying on the bed. He turned around and ran back into the bedroom.

"I love you," he said.

I held him in my arms.

"Thank you," I said. "Thank you."

He beamed. His dark eyes glistened. He walked toward the shower again. Again he returned.

"I love you," he said.

"Yes," I said. "I love you too."

"But I still can't understand why. I still can't understand why you want me."

"Neither can I," I answered. "In fact, most of this I don't understand."

He shook his head.

"And more than anything else," he said, "I want to spend a whole night with you again."

"I think," I said, "it's because you can't have that right now."

"No, I know myself better than that."

He nodded seriously. He got up again. This time he made it to the shower. He returned wet and cold. I dried him off. He pulled me towards him and hugged me close.

I dried his hair with the hair dryer while he put on his shoes and socks.

When he was dressed we discussed his schedule for the next two days. He had meetings and press conferences.

I told him I had to get back to America soon. He said he couldn't see me the next day; it was crammed too full. I said fine, it didn't matter.

He put on his coat and fur gloves and walked to the door. Instead of proceeding through it as he usually did, he turned around and said, "And how's your writing coming?"

"Fine," I said. "Fine. I'm just not sure where I'm going with it."

He looked at me. "Maybe it should just fade away," he said. His words smacked the air. I didn't know what he meant, or maybe I did.

He winked at me and said, "*Ciao*," and closed the door behind him.

Deep confusion swept over me. Then it was followed by guilt . . . then a kind of double vision. I didn't know what was real again. I hated the feeling. To be unclear about the emotional horizon was the worst thing that could happen to me.

I started writing again—I had no one to talk to but myself. My self.

❄ Everything seemed to be feeling like an illusion. W*as* it an illusion? Was physical reality only what *I* thought it was anyway? A simple day in the life of anyone was just a series of acting scenes; acting what we *thought* we felt. Shakespeare had said it. Maybe all of life was a stage and we were merely actors on that stage playing out our roles. Was he talking about reincarnation when he wrote that? So, if today was acting, was yesterday an illusion? And tomorrow?

Maybe Gerry and our meetings and my work and our world wouldn't even be there tomorrow. Or, maybe what was driving me crazy was the pressure to define reality in physical terms. Perhaps the truth was that everything was real on every level because everything was relative and needed to be taken into account. Maybe we loved and laughed and worked and played in an unconscious effort to remind ourselves that we *must* have a *purpose*

beyond this reality. If *that* purpose was real, was each of us using someone else to bounce off so as to define our own purpose more clearly? Did we simply use others we loved to try out our own hidden potentials, our unseen capacities to get some definition of our selves? Were we looking for the source of our own meaning from another time? Or had we actually known each other before? Were Gerry and I really working out some relationship that had been unresolved in another life? If that was so, and if somehow we came to understand that, perhaps then we would no longer need one another. Was that the final joke? Maybe that was the profound reason for humor. Maybe all of life was a colossal cosmic joke because it would continue on its own course regardless of what we did or didn't do. Maybe we should just smile our way to the end, because maybe the end was only the beginning anyway. It might be true that the cycle would start all over again until we got it right. That really wasn't so bad. We'd certainly not need to fear death. If death never even happened, then life was a joke on us. So, we might as well smile through it while we worked our way through our purpose.

Gerry became more clear in my mind. As I wrote about him I understood things more objectively. I began to see his role in my life with more clarity. I wasn't so compulsively intense about either his or my confusion and I began to feel that whatever we meant in each other's lives had a reason, a purpose behind it. In the scheme of his life and in the scheme of mine, the purpose might not be so clear now, but it probably would be soon.

I wrote as though I were talking to myself. The hours melted into one another. I never left the hotel room. I began to wear the walls. I knew every circle of the tugboat doing its icy duty each day in the bay below my window by heart. I watched the days become longer with each successive snowstorm. And now, at the end of another week, the city below me lay carpeted in white, while a veil of new snow made it even whiter.

I walked through the snow. I must have walked five miles . . .

through the city and into the animal park, rolling knolls of white snow cream spreading all around me. The sun was sharp and crisp. I felt I could hear myself breathe in the silence miles ahead of myself. Three deer watched me as I walked by them ankle deep in snow, crunching softly. I held my head to the sun. Five white swans flew across it. A man walked by in the distance smoking a pipe.

Gerry hung silently in the air with me as I walked. He was like this air, this country, this environment. It was a pastel environment, not overtly splashed with color or accents. It was an environment that seemed to cover its intentions, as though its real meaning was hidden. It didn't reach out—it lay back almost waiting to be discovered, to be touched, to be walked through and understood. It wasn't exactly afraid of itself as one might think at first. No, it waited on itself instead; with its long, silent patience, those who were new to it might feel rejected and excluded from integrating into it. But that wouldn't be a legitimate response. That wouldn't be giving the detached stillness a chance to come out of itself.

And so maybe it was with people.

To feel emotionally starved because of the lack of overt clarity and discernible communication was to deny the inner richness of communicating with silence. Indeed, the silence could probably be even more full, and if I felt a victim of no communication, that was my problem because it probably wasn't true. I had been used to explosive communication in my life. What I was experiencing now was implosive communication. I had to find what was inside of me and so did Gerry.

I walked all day and came home just in time to see Gerry on Swedish television discussing Third World economic problems.

I had heard it all before but watched carefully anyway. He was assured and strong in the way he presented his proposed solutions. I was reading the *Herald Tribune*, waiting for his call, when I heard the hotel door open.

He looked as though he had run all the way. He was totally out of breath, his face frozen, his eyebrows and eyelashes sparkling with melting snow. I kissed him quickly. He was still on a "high," vivacious and anxious to know what I thought of his appearance on television. We talked about how he was learning to orchestrate his personality for TV. He ate two chocolate-filled biscuits and drank lukewarm tea. We talked about Jimmy Carter and China and the variety show I hoped to do from Peking. We talked about everything under the sun but what was concerning me most. I decided it was time to introduce Gerry to the things that had been happening to me—to us—the things I had been writing about (he had *not* asked).

"Gerry?" I said bravely.

"Hmm . . ."

"Are you curious about what I've been writing about?"

He looked surprised. "Yes," he said, "of course."

"It's about us," I went on, and seeing the look of carefully checked alarm on his face, "in a way, that is."

"In what way?"

"Look, a whole lot of strange things have been happening to me lately, at least since we met. There's been one coincidence after another throwing us together. There's the strength of the pull between us which is illogical in the circumstances. You and I know it is much more than just a physical thing, but *why?* All this time with you I've been having these pre-cognitive feelings and recognition feelings. Gerry, tell me honestly—do you feel that you have known me some place before?"

"Good God! I don't understand you. In any case, what difference would it make?"

"Well, maybe if we could figure out what we were before, we could sort out what we should be now."

He took a long breath. "Darling, you've been alone too long in this room . . ."

"No, dammit!" I was suddenly out of patience. "Don't patronize

me! I just want to *talk* about this. I'm not overwrought, I'm not nuts, and I'm not stupid. And there seems to be a whole lot more to this world than you're willing to acknowledge."

He gave a wry grin. "Well, that's probably true at any rate," he said. "What, specifically, are you thinking about?"

"Reincarnation, for one."

"I've no objection to reincarnation—it's fine for those who need it."

"Gerry, I'm not talking about starving peasants. There are a lot of people, all up and down the social and intellectual scale, and all through time, who believe in reincarnation. But specifically, I'm talking about *us*."

"Oh, for God's sake! If you're suggesting that we have actually lived some previous life together, Shirley, so *what*? What the hell difference would it make since we can't remember anyhow?"

"Well, it might make a difference if we could find out through channeling." I knew I was doing this all wrong.

"What the hell is channeling?"

"I mean," I swallowed, "talking with disembodied spirits through a channel—people do it all the time to find out all kinds of things."

Gerry looked aghast and then very concerned. "Shirley, have you been going to mediums?"

"You don't have to make it sound like a dirty word," I told him.

"No, no! Of course not, I didn't mean it that way." He took a deep breath. "You're right, we do have to talk about this. What, exactly, is it that you have been doing?"

Feeling guilty and defensive, and resenting it, I told him about Cat and Ambres, about Edgar Cayce, about the reading I had been doing. He listened in silence as I slowly wound down. Then he looked at me in what, I realized with surprise, was embarrassment.

"Gerry, what are you thinking?" I asked.

He shook his head. "I don't know what to say," he muttered. "I mean, you just can't be serious about this."

"Why not?"

"Well, my God, isn't it obvious? These mediums are psychos, or weird, dragging stuff up out of their own unconscious. Or else they're taking you. You surely don't believe they're actually communicating with *spirits*?"

"*They* aren't communicating. They're just channeling—they don't even remember what's been said."

"Whatever they're doing, it's utter rubbish. They do it for money, exploiting gullible people who want to be told some sugary nonsense about dead relatives or some other damned thing."

"Edgar Cayce took no money, the advice he gave was sound, and it didn't come from his unconscious because he had no medical training."

Gerry looked at me helplessly. "Why in the name of God do you have to get involved with this sort of thing?" he asked desperately.

"I'm just trying to find an explanation for us," I said, "or maybe just for me. I'm beginning to think I can't do it for us . . ."

"I should hope not! Look, darling [he so rarely used endearments, and that made twice in the same conversation—he must be really upset], you really mustn't go on with this business. I mean, it can't possibly gain you anything. Ninety percent of these people are charlatans and everyone knows it—all your friends are going to think you've gone soft in the head. And God knows what the public would think if it ever got out."

It was interesting that he was concerned with my public image. I suppose it was logical that he should be, being himself at all times very aware of the importance of his own. But he still had not considered in any way the possibilities of the world I was exploring: it was something completely outside his ken, he couldn't see it, he could not begin to acknowledge the possible validity of its existence.

"What d'you mean 'if it ever got out,' Gerry? This is what I've been writing about."

"You can't," he said flatly. "Not for publication."

"Why *not?*" His rigidity was pushing me into a false position, because in fact, at this point, I had no intention of publishing.

"Because every intellectual you've ever known, anybody with half a brain to use will tear you to pieces—" he stopped, floundering and unhappy.

I was amused at his bland assumption that *all* intelligent people would share his views and touched by his obvious distress for me. But his blanket rejection of all I was talking about seemed to preclude further discussion—if indeed, there had been any! Leaning forward, I murmured, "Oh, the hell with it," and kissed his nose. "It's warm," I said.

"What's warm?"

"Your nose. It was cold when you came in."

He fingered my earrings and swept back my hair. I knelt beside him. He lifted my face and, in the middle of a word, kissed me and stroked my eyes.

He lifted me onto him and when I raised the soft material of my negligee into the air and let it fall around our bodies, he watched the movement and made a soft noise. We never undressed. We made love just as we were leading our lives, the pleasure of it hidden from view.

I fell against him. He kissed my eyes and neck.

"You're leaving tomorrow?" he asked.

"Yes," I said, "I have to go."

"I love you more than I can say," he said.

I felt myself go into a sad limbo.

"When do you think we'll be able to spend a whole evening together again?" he asked.

"Well, it's January now," I said. "Do you figure by September when your election is over?"

He swept his arm up and, hiding his face behind it, stifled a cry under his breath.

"Well," I said, "let's wait and see."

"I have to get up now," he said. "Otherwise I'll be too melancholy to bear it. Where will you be?"

I told him I didn't know. I would be traveling.

He tried to get up, but stopped himself. He looked at our bodies and said, "This next move of yours may be impossible. We are one person, you know."

I smiled. He lifted me up and over him and stood up.

"That was an extremely complicated maneuver, wasn't it?"

"Not as complicated as we are."

When he toddled off to the bathroom with his trousers piled around his ankles, I couldn't believe he wanted to be Prime Minister of England.

When he returned I was still on the sofa. He looked down at me and said, "You're lovely. You're really lovely."

"When is your birthday?" I asked.

He said, "Tuesday, how did you know?"

I said I just had a feeling.

He said his deputy leader's birthday was on the same day and he would be extremely disappointed if Gerry didn't get back to England and help him celebrate it.

I said, "What about celebrating *your* birthday?"

He said, "That doesn't matter."

I grabbed his arms and shook them. "Doesn't matter? Gerry, *what about* your *birthday*!!" Then I stopped. I stopped in the middle of a thought.

He said, "Yes?"

I said, "Nothing."

I took some pictures of him with my Polaroid camera and flash. He submitted to it and then was curious to see how he looked. Slowly the image bled through in color.

"Oh," he said, "I look dreadful." Gently I shook his arm again. He raced to the hallway for his coat and fur gloves. He put my hotel room keys on the coffee table, picked up his briefcase, and with more aggressive speed than ever, he headed for the door. I stood still without following him. He opened the door and turned around to look at me as though he was burning whatever I looked like into his memory.

"You are really beautiful," he said, and then he was gone.

I ran to the door and locked it. When I walked back to the living room I saw he had forgotten his glasses.

I raced into the hallway and whistled. I heard him retrace his steps. As he retrieved his glasses from me he said, "When is your birthday?"

"April twenty-fourth," I said.

He nodded as if to say it was another date in the future he could look forward to. Then he said, "What do you think we have together?"

I sighed and ran my fingers over the hair in his eyes.

"I know," he said, "to get to the fruit on a tree, you have to go out on a limb."

He looked into my eyes and walked away. He didn't look back. I walked inside and closed the door.

I lit a cigarette and went to the bay window. Opening it, I blew smoke into the air watching it mingle with the steam of my breath in the winter air. Snow was falling thickly now.

I looked down into the street. He walked into the courtyard below. I whistled softly. He looked up and waved. His fur gloves and black coat were outlined sharply against the solid white background. Snow tumbled around him as he walked into the street looking for a cab. The street was empty. I felt him decide to walk. He looked up and waved again. I waved back and threw him a kiss, but he had already disappeared determinedly into the thick cold silent white Swedish night. ❧

Chapter 12

"The 'soul' is indeed a vague conception and the reality of the thing to which it refers cannot be demonstrated. But consciousness is the most evident of all (invisible) facts . . . The physiologists are very fond of comparing the network of our cerebral nerves with a telephone system but they overlook the significant fact that a telephone system does not function *until someone talks over it.* The brain does not create thought (Sir Julian Huxley has recently pointed out this fact); it is an instrument which thought finds useful."

—Joseph Wood Krutch
More Lives Than One

T he flight back to America was a strange one. I didn't really know who or what I had just left or who or what I was returning to. Something remarkable was underway in my life. But it had no name and eluded description. It spoke to something very ancient and yet I had the feeling it was the forerunner to what could be a new age of thought for me. The experience with Ambres had been fascinating but the questions I had asked Lars and Birgitta still bugged me. Pragmatic child of my time, I decided, for one thing at least, to check out the process of channeling.

In the weeks and months that followed, I read and investigated and checked. I asked questions and, wherever possible, I listened to tapes. I found there were a remarkable number of mediums, or trance channelers, functioning. With the exception of Edgar Cayce, almost no one spoke of these people by the name of the medium. The personality channeled was dominant, and among these there were a few whose reputations stood out above the rest, largely in terms of the clarity and cohesiveness of the messages channeled.

Like experts, or talents, in any field, some mediums were better than others. (I established also that, like any professionals, there were days when absolutely nothing would go right: in that case, some relied on past experience, some faked, and some said flat out that nothing was working and everybody would do better to go home).

But I was struck also by the variety and strength of personality demonstrated by the different entities who were channeled through. The rather hazy odor of solemnity that surrounds the phenomenon of channeling in the minds of most people (perhaps because their own mood in approaching the prospect of a discussion with a disembodied spirit would be somewhat somber?) seemed to be at odds with the reality. There was rich humor and occasional downright flippancy in some of the channeled personalities, for instance. Whoever, or whatever, these entities were, they conveyed enormous individuality of character and an aura, not so much of solemnity, as of experience.

Moreover, channeling was something that had been going on for some time and several famous people not only "believed" in it but had practiced it, including Abraham Lincoln, who used Carpenter (the medium actually lived in the White House with the President) for regular consultations, J. P. Morgan (who used Evangeline Adams), William Randolph Hearst—and many, many more from widely varying fields. The work of Sir Oliver Lodge and Mrs. Piper was of course well known. There seemed to have been almost a fashion for this kind of thing around the turn of the century, and not only channeling, but table-tapping, the use of the planchette, and the ouija board. No doubt it was entertaining, but equally clear was the fact that many worthy and serious people took channeling—and all that it implied—very seriously.

It was also clear that some could not handle the sheer volume of information being channeled through, much less the quality of its nature. The cosmos is a staggering concept: to relate each individual human to such vastness was often more than the listeners

could bear. And when it came to the particularities of extraterrestrial life, the structure of the atom, the cohesion of all matter, all thought—these were matters to which most people had not given very much attention. The entities communicating this information frequently appeared to have no idea of how much the party on the other end of the telephone, so to speak, could absorb.

In sum, it seemed as though there was an individual pace, or rhythm, which each person gradually developed in assimilating the mind-boggling floods of information that came through. When dealing with the mind and the emotions, concentrated force-feeding simply did not work. It even appeared to alienate a good many people.

I turned my attention to the more modern channelers and the entities who communicated through them.

Best known of the current channeled spiritual entities appeared to be a spiritual master known as D.K., channeled by Alice Bailey, and later by Benjamin Creme. Seth, channeled by Jane Roberts, was a particularly interesting case and one which presented more than one facet of the phenomenon of channeling.

Since 1963, when Mrs. Roberts was first approached by Seth, she and her husband (who, from the beginning, had taken notes on what Seth said) had accumulated a library of notes on the sessions. Some of this material has appeared in several published works, one actually dictated by Seth himself. What I found most interesting was the strong doubt evidenced by Mrs. Roberts in the early contacts with Seth (*The Seth Material*).

Having no previous contact with, nor interest or belief in, psychic phenomena, Mrs. Roberts was assailed one night while writing her own poetry by a torrent of words which demanded to be put down on paper. Scribbling furiously for hours, she eventually discovered herself writing the title of what she describes as "that odd batch of notes, *The Physical Universe as Idea Construction*." (These subsequently proved to be a synthesis of material that Seth would later develop). But at the time, knowing nothing

of Seth, Mrs. Roberts was made uneasy, astonished, and upset by both the event and the content of "her" writing.

In the weeks and months that followed, after Seth had virtually insisted on "coming through," she and her husband conducted many tests to prove, or disprove, the existence of Seth as a separate personality, or the disembodied entity he claimed to be. In fact, it took Seth a considerable time and some quite spectacular displays of special abilities to prove to Mrs. Roberts that he was not a part of her own subconscious!

Nevertheless, actual "proof" of channeling, that is, a physical presence on Earth acting as a channel of communication for another kind of presence on a different plane, was hard to establish in scientific terms. In the end, proof of the process came down to content: if a channel spoke in a foreign language, or displayed a talent (such as playing the piano) or practiced a professional skill (such as medicine) or conveyed information, let's say, from a distant place or about a particular event or person which the channel had no way of knowing, then it would appear that the foreign language, or the talent, or the skill, or the knowledge, had to be coming from another source.

(Over a period of time to follow I was to come across many instances of such "proof," but by then the process had become commonplace to me—not unimportant, but rather like the preparation of a good meal: one was grateful for a good cook but the meal was what counted.) In fact, even at the end of two or three months of intense reading and questioning I had decided that the process was of lesser relevance. At least one aspect of the channeled information I was reading about cropped up again and again and that related to past-life recall. I was probably more curious about this as it seemed I might learn something helpful about my relationship with Gerry, but what had taken my real attention in the vast volume of material available for study was the fact that so much of the message seemed to be universal—that is, entities channeling through a variety of people in many countries in differ-

ent languages were saying basically the same thing. Look into yourselves, explore yourselves, *you* are the Universe . . .

More and more, as I read and thought, the *message* forced me to reexamine motives, to rethink, or perhaps to think for the first time, about values and aspects of living I had heretofore simply accepted.

I had been used to living in a world where, by the very nature of the life we led, it was nearly impossible to get the time to look into yourself. Where just to stay alive, to say nothing of staying on top, seemed to require attitudes that were just the opposite . . . if you weren't carefully checking out the progress of your neighbor, you had the impression that it wouldn't be long before you'd be left behind yourself. If you were a successful person, you had to keep going in the rat race to stay there. If you were poor, you had to keep going to survive. There was never any time for just yourself, to do nothing, to enjoy a sunset, to listen to a bird sing, to watch a bee bumble, to hear what you were thinking, much less what anybody else was thinking.

Human contact seemed superficial, striving for meaningful goals, wanting deeper meaning but only talking around it. Competitive living left no time for what we were, who we could be, and what we could mean to each other. I had seen very few relationships with real and lasting meaning—my own included. They hadn't seemed able to survive our own scrutiny of them.

And instead of going deeper, we chose to respond to urges to be comfortable, to just accept the limits and restrictions imposed by safe superficiality, to be successful and well-attended creatures of comfort with protection and warmth and no challenges from what could be frighteningly new and unknown . . . no challenges from what more we could be or were, no challenge from what more we could understand, no challenge from how that might threaten us, and no recognition of what it could mean to end up alone.

Alone . . . that was the cold word. Everyone was afraid of being alone. Yet it didn't really matter who we lived with or slept with or

loved or married. In the final analysis, we were all alone—alone with ourselves—and that's where the rub came. So many relationships were failing because the people involved didn't know who *they* were, much less the person or people they were involved with.

But could that now be changing? Were people now beginning to search into their own depths as a kind of instinctive survival mechanism to offset the polarity of violence and disturbance that was clearly stalking the world? Were they finding the potential for unbridled joy in themselves—as Lars and Birgitta had described? It could be that thousands of people all over the world were involved with this mystery of whether or not there was a life beyond the physical, or in addition to it, rather, and hence necessarily, something we called a "soul." I found myself giving more and more credence to spiritual teaching, the helpfulness of meditation, the essential decency and rightness of the emotional message, and the boundless possibilities of metaphysical reality. If all energy was eternal and infinite, then our own unseen energy—thought, soul, mind, personality, whatever you wanted to call it—had to go somewhere. I was finding it increasingly difficult to believe this energy merely dissipated when the physical envelope decayed. And apparently a great many other people felt the same way. Was I rapidly being drawn into a groundswell of human realization? If Gerry represented the old, intellectual, rather cynically pragmatic approach to the meaning of life, it could be that that was why both of us found the relationship ultimately unsatisfying. I wanted to "be." He wanted to "do." I was beginning to think that each of us had only half the equation.

I wondered what other friends of mine would think of what I'd been reading and thinking. Anything of a spiritual nature would undoubtedly embarrass them, or make them laugh, given the kind of world we live in. But the psychics I was reading about were all saying the same thing. Rudolf Steiner, Leadbetter, Cayce, and so

many countless others—all claiming the fundamental existence of a Divine Will—an energy force from which everything else sprang. The same Divine Will was in all living things. We were part of it and it was part of us. The task was to find that divinity in ourselves and live by it.

And I wondered, if we indeed found life on other planets, would it too know what we knew, or would "they" have a clearer understanding? Science seemed virtually certain that there had to be life on other planets. The chances against its having developed were remote. And if there were, would that life have a different Divine Will or would it be the same? Was the energy force at the center of all the cosmos attending to life on other planets as well as life on our own?

The ancients said, "Study yourself, for in the self one may find the answers to all problems that may confront you. For the spirit of man, with all its attributes, physical and mental, is a portion of the whole great spirit. Hence the answers are all within the self. Your destiny and your karma depend on what your soul has done about what it has become aware of. And know that every soul will eventually meet itself. No problem can be run away from. Meet yourself now."

I thought that what the ancient seers said was no different from what modern psychologists said, or religions, or science, or Shakespeare for that matter. It was all the same: "Know yourself, have the courage to look, and it will set you free."

To know oneself perhaps it was necessary to simply be aware, to acknowledge one's own soul. To know the sum of the lifetimes that soul had experienced seemed outrageously impossible and maybe even irrelevant. But many people I knew did want this knowledge and moreover accepted the theory of re-embodiment as readily as they accepted the sun coming up each morning.

Eventually I was to learn that a very accomplished actor, and one with whom I had had wonderful professional experience and a

warm personal relationship, was certainly one of these people—
Peter Sellers. And an experience he lived through, which he con-
fided to me, helped to confirm his belief to himself that his soul was
in fact separate from his body.

I had made two pictures with Peter. One was called *Woman
Times Seven*, in which he played a supporting role as one of my
seven husbands, and the other was *Being There*, in which I played
a supporting role to the most brilliant acting job of his entire
career. Peter always *became* the characters he played, offscreen
as well as on. In my opinion he was a genius, but he suffered
personally from what he called a lack of knowledge of his own
identity. He said he knew the characters he played better than he
knew himself, that he felt he had *been* those characters at one time
in a way that could only be described as "having lived them in the
past."

One day toward the end of filming *Being There*, we talked
about it. We had returned from location in Asheville, North Caro-
lina, and were shooting some interiors on the Goldwyn lot in
Hollywood. When I arrived on the lot that morning, I was struck
with the feeling that something was wrong. I didn't know if it was
because memories of the films I had made there flooded back to
me—*Irma La Douce, Two for the Seesaw, Children's Hour*, and
The Apartment—or whether something was actually going on that
I'd learn about later.

Peter wasn't in great form that morning. Probably because he
was tired, I thought. He was working ten hours a day with a pace-
maker in his heart and he had never been a candidate for the
marathon. We sat together in the back of a mock-up limousine
waiting for the lighting to be set up.

Suddenly Peter clutched his chest and grabbed my arm. It
wasn't a huge overt lunge or anything. Actually, it was very insignificant as far as anyone else could tell, but I knew something was
really wrong. I casually called over the production manager and

whispered to him to have a doctor stand by. He nodded and went away. Peter went on talking about acting and parts and how he felt he *knew* all the characters he had played. In fact, he was quite specific about feeling that he "*was* each of those characters at one time or another."

At first I didn't realize what I was hearing, but as he continued, I understood he was talking about having lived those characters in some of his own past-life incarnations.

"Oh," I said casually, "you mean you feel you are drawing on those experiences and feelings that you actually remember living in other lifetimes?" I was very matter-of-fact. "That's probably why you are so good at acting. You just have better past-life recall on a creative level than most people have."

His eyes lit up as though he had finally found somebody he could talk to, to share this belief of his.

"I don't go into this with many people, you know," he said, "or they'll think I'm bonkers."

"Yes," I said, "I know. Neither do I. But there are probably more cosmic closet believers than we are aware of."

He seemed to relax a bit.

"So what was that pain you just had?" I asked.

"Oh, just a touch of indigestion, I guess."

"Well maybe," I said, "but maybe it would be good to talk about it."

He didn't seem to want to go into it immediately. He fumbled and talked about food and what was right and wrong for him to eat and what it was like living with "this goddamn toy contraption I have in my heart."

I listened. I knew he still hadn't gotten to what he wanted to say.

"This sound stage gives me the creeps," he said.

"Why?"

"Because."

"Because why?"

He wiped perspiration from his forehead and took a deep breath.

"Because," he said, "this is the sound stage where I died."

I tried not to overreact. I remembered reading in the papers what an awful brush with death he had had.

"Rex Kennamer saved my life," he said, "and I saw him do it."

"No kidding," I said. "How?"

Like a person recounting a scene that had happened to somebody else, he said:

"Well, I felt myself leave my body. I just floated out of my physical form and I saw them cart my body away to the hospital. I went with it. I was curious. I wondered what was wrong with me. I wasn't frightened or anything like that because I was fine; and it was my body that was in trouble. Then I saw Dr. Kennamer come. And he felt my pulse and saw that I was dead. He and some other people pushed down and up on my chest. In fact, they pummeled the shit out of me . . . literally, I believe. They did everything but jump up and down on me to get my heart beating again. Then I saw Rex shout at somebody and say there was no time to prepare me for heart surgery. He commanded somebody to carve me open right there on the spot. Rex took my heart out of my body and massaged the hell out of it. Did everything but toss it up in the air. I was so curious watching him. He just refused to accept that I was dead. Then I looked around myself and I saw an incredibly beautiful bright loving white light above me. I wanted to go to that white light more than anything. I've never wanted anything more. I knew there was love, real love, on the other side of the light which was attracting me so much. It was kind and loving and I remember thinking, 'That's God.' I tried to elevate myself toward it as Rex was working on my heart. But somehow I couldn't quite make it. Then I saw a hand reach through the light. I tried to touch it, to grab onto it, to clasp it so it could sweep me up and pull me through it. Then I heard Rex say below me, 'It's beating again. I'm

getting a heartbeat.' At the same moment a voice attached to the hand I wanted to touch so much said, 'It's not time. Go back and finish. It's not time.' The hand disappeared on the other side and I felt myself floating back into my body. I was bitterly disappointed. After that I don't remember anything until I regained consciousness back inside my body."

When Peter finished, I tried to continue to sound matter-of-fact. "Yes," I said, "I've read a lot of Elizabeth Kubler-Ross's stuff and she has so many documented accounts of so many people describing the same phenomenon when they were pronounced clinically dead. But apparently it wasn't time for them either, and they came back to tell about it."

Peter looked at me closely in that way he used to have of openly questioning whether he should go further. I tried not to press him but I didn't want him to stop talking about it either.

"You don't think I'm crazy?" he asked.

"No," I said, "of course not. I've heard about too many people describing the same phenomenon. They can't all be nuts. I think the important thing is to figure out what one comes back *for*." I said *"one"* instead of "you" because with Peter, if you pressed too hard on the personal stuff, you could lose him. As I have said, the identity of "Peter Sellers" completely eluded him. He had often said to reporters that he understood his characters to the core and many other mysteries of life besides, but Sellers? Nothing . . . he didn't have a clue.

Peter squirmed around in the mock-up.

"Are you all right?" I asked.

"Yes," he said, "but all of this . . . this set . . . that camera . . . these lights . . . this car . . . reminds me that I haven't yet understood just what you said. I don't know why I'm here! I don't know what I came back for this time! That's why I act like I do. I don't know. I can't figure out my purpose. What am I supposed to be doing?"

His eyes filled with tears. He began to whisper under his breath,

"I know. I'm a pain in the ass to so many people. And I know they think I'm crazy. But I'm crazy about the right things. I'm not sure they are."

He wiped his eyes with the sleeve of his immaculate costume in the character of Chauncey Gardiner. He blinked and sniffed as Chauncey would have.

"I know I have lived many times before," he said, "and that experience confirmed it to me, because in *this* lifetime I felt what it was for my soul to actually be *out* of my body. But ever since I came back, I don't know why, I don't know what it is I'm supposed to do, or what I came back for."

He took another deep breath, a long agonized sigh—still maintaining the persona of Chauncey Gardiner.

A few minutes later the camera crew was ready. Hal Ashby, the director, walked onto the set and we went into the scene as though nothing had happened. We were shooting our first scene in the picture on the last day of filming. Life was an illusion . . . just like the movies.

❀   About a year and a half later, I was sitting with some friends in my apartment in Malibu. I had been traveling and didn't know that Peter had had another heart attack.

We were chatting amiably when suddenly I jumped up from my chair.

"Peter," I said. "Something has happened to Peter Sellers."

When I said it, I could feel his presence. It was as though he was right there in my living room watching me say it.

I felt ridiculous. Of course, all conversation stopped.

Then the telephone rang.

I disguised my voice and said hello. It was a newspaper reporter. "I'd like to speak to Miss MacLaine," he said. "Well, actually I wanted to get her reaction."

"To what?" I said.

"Oh," he said. "If you haven't heard, I'm sorry, but her friend Peter Sellers just died."

I turned in toward the room. I could feel Peter watching me. I wanted to tell the reporter he was mistaken. I wanted to say, "Yes, you probably *think* he's dead, but he's really only left his latest body." I wanted to say, "Listen, he did the best work of his life in our movie, and he did it portraying one of the gentlest, sweetest souls that ever walked this earth. There was nothing else left to accomplish, he probably couldn't figure out what else he was hanging around for, so he must have gone for the white light . . . and besides, he really missed his mother."

But of course, I didn't. Though Peter would have loved it . . .

Instead I said, "Shirley isn't in. But I'll give her the message."

I turned away from the phone.

"What happened?" asked my friends.

I could feel Peter smile.

"Nothing," I said. "Some reporter was trying to tell me that Peter Sellers just died." ❧

Chapter 13

"Why should it be thought incredible that the same soul should inhabit in succession an indefinite number of mortal bodies . . . ? Even during this one life our bodies are perpetually changing, though by a process of decay and restoration which is so gradual that it escapes our notice. Every human being thus dwells successively in many bodies, even during one short life."

—Francis Bowen
"Christian Metempsychosis"

W hen I first got back to California from Sweden I had called Cat at The Ashram. I told her I had seen Ambres in Stockholm and that I wanted to talk with her. At the time I asked her to meet me for a mountain walk. In the undulating hills of Calabasas perhaps I could clear up my intentions. During our walk I told her about my experience with Ambres and that the whole thing was so puzzling that I had been writing about it to try to clear it up. Her blue eyes lit up like neon saucers and she clapped her hands.

"Great, Shirley!" she said. "Oh! That's great! You're going to write about being drawn into the spiritual dimension? You know, there are so many people who would love to read about what you're doing, and you know they're ready out there to read about this stuff. Really they are!"

This was going further than I had intended, but nevertheless I asked why she thought anyone would be interested.

"Because nothing else these days is working for them," she said. "So many sense that there is another way to lead their lives . . . and the spiritual path is about the only one they haven't tried."

We walked for a little while longer and then she said, "Would

you like to have a great spiritual channeling in English? I know a very well-respected trance medium here in California. He's busy channeling all the time but he's coming down from Santa Barbara to channel for some of the guests here at The Ashram. Maybe he could work in a session with you."

"Oh, really?" I said, marveling once again at how Cat was a catalyst in my life. "Have you had a session with him?"

"Oh, Shirley," she said, seeming to spread her arms and her radiant energy all over the mountain tops. "Yes! And you will love his light, and you will love the spiritual entities that speak through him!"

Cat always talked in exclamation points and had such a sunny nature I couldn't imagine her *not* loving anyone, disembodied or otherwise.

"Sure," I said, getting into the spirit of the thing as it were, "that would be fun. What do you think would happen?"

"Oh," she said, "several entities come through as a rule, and it's just as though they're right in the room with you."

"And what do I do?"

"Just ask anything you want. They can tell you about your past lives, or help with physical diagnosis and pain, or with diets that are good for your vibrations—anything you want . . ."

"Well," I said, "after hearing about the creation of the world from Ambres I'd like to hear something a little more personal."

"Besides," Cat was striding merrily along, "you need a good spiritual rest."

I wondered how on earth Cat could translate channeling into being spiritually restful. Well, maybe for her it was . . .

❦   Three months and a mini-library of books later I felt the time had come for me to do some personal channeling investigation. Through Cat I made an appointment with Kevin Ryerson, resolv-

ing at the same time that I would try to be noncommittal, bland and several other things I am not . . .

My doorbell in Malibu rang at six-forty-five the following evening. I opened it not knowing what to expect. Looking at me under a slouched beige hat was a young man, about twenty-nine years old, with direct, kind, deep blue eyes. He was wearing a beige suit to match the hat, a beige vest, and beige shoes and beige socks. He wore an overcoat (also beige) slung over one shoulder and smiled directly into my face. His smile was innocent and gentle. Ironically, he didn't seem to be aware of his amusingly theatrical garb. Looking at him made me want a huge slice of beige coconut cream pie.

"Hello?" he said. "I'm Kevin?" His tone went up at the end of the sentence as though he had just asked me a question. "I'm Kevin Ryerson." He gave the impression of being a little uncertain, yet relaxed somewhere way underneath.

"Yes, Kevin." I opened the door and ushered him in. "Please come in and sit down."

I watched him closely as he walked through the door, unaware that his beige coat was dangling nearly off his shoulder. He moved smoothly, though with a slouch, planting his heels down first as he walked.

"May I leave my vehicle where it is outside?" he asked.

"Your vehicle?" I said. "Oh, you mean your car. Yes, sure. It doesn't matter."

"Thank you," he said. "My lady may drop in to meet me. I'd like her to be able to directly recognize it."

"Your lady?"

"Yes," he said, "we were just recently wed and we had planned a celebration dinner later tonight depending on the time periods we would be occupying?"

I hesitated a moment not knowing how to react to his use of the English language. It sounded so affected. Combined with the way

he walked and the way he dressed, it made me wonder whether he could be taken seriously.

"Oh, sure," I said perfectly casually. "I don't know how long a session like this will take. You would very likely know better than I."

Kevin walked into my living room and sat down rather formally in one of my chairs.

"Yes," he said, "you direct your questions to the spiritual guides and they will determine the length of time required."

Kevin seemed strangely out of time, anachronistic. Or maybe I was just reading such an impression into his odd formality. Maybe that was what happened when you were with a trance medium.

I asked him if he would like a drink or a cup of coffee or something.

"No," he said, "alcohol inhibits my accuracy. But tea would be fine."

I fixed the tea, telling myself firmly not to confuse the message with the messenger.

"So, you've just recently gotten married?" I asked, making small talk and wanting to know what it was like to be living with a trance medium.

"Yes," he said, "I pretty well did in the bubble gum brigade before deciding to settle down."

I laughed out loud. He seemed to swing back and forth between the Knights of the Round Table and the rock generation.

"Hmm. And will you be having children do you think?" I asked.

"No," he said, "my lady and I would like to go out and change the world, but we can't afford a babysitter."

I served Kevin the tea.

"Are you familiar with trance channeling?" he asked.

"Well, slightly," I answered. I told him about Ambres in Sweden and about other people who had described their experiences to me. I said I was familiar with the Edgar Cayce material. Kevin said

modestly that he was an expert on Cayce and admired him very much. "A great soul," he said. "I have several Cayce books that are impossible to find. You're welcome to them."

We chatted on about Cayce and spiritual guidance and medical diagnosis through the phenomenon of trance channeling. We discussed Sir Oliver Lodge's research with the British Society for Psychical Research in England, and his experiments in contacting the soul of his dead son. We discussed the case of Mrs. Piper in Boston and how her information always checked out to be infallible.

Kevin talked in a relaxed way, appeared to be well read in metaphysical matters, articulate, and surprisingly humorous with his intelligent assessments of some of the circumstances he found himself in as a result of his psychic and metaphysical talents.

"I didn't know what was happening to me either when this all first started," he volunteered. "Spirit came through during one of my meditations. I didn't even know it. But someone ran and got a tape recorder and got the whole thing. When they played it back to me I freaked. I knew nothing about the medical information I had channeled through. I didn't know the voices that came through me either, and I certainly didn't make up the past-life information while fabricating a phony voice."

It was difficult for me to accept what he was saying at face value. Why should I believe that he couldn't or wouldn't fabricate strange voices and intricate stories about past lives? I thought of Ambres in Sweden. If I had understood or spoken Swedish I would have asked *him* more questions too. Well, I'll just keep listening, I thought. I folded my arms.

"I couldn't explain it in any rational way," Kevin continued. "I just knew that I must be channeling spiritual guides. My sister can do the same thing. And it always freaked out our parents who just plain didn't understand any of it. Then I began to read about other people who found themselves capable of the same thing—even kids eight and nine years old, channeling through languages they

didn't speak, and stuff like that. So I relaxed and just let it happen, and it's helped a lot of people."

I looked at Kevin, quietly sifting what he'd said through my mind, remembering all the other case histories I had read. He sipped his tea. He seemed so modest, so unpretentious, even though he was dressed as though he had come straight from Western Costume. I had always trusted what a friend of mine described as my built-in "bullshit detector"—that inbred sense of skepticism. But I decided against questioning him about his garb for fear of intimidating him.

I wondered what my ideal impression of a credible trance medium would be. Each individual was just that—an individual. What would a "typical" trance medium sound or look like? What would a "typical" psychiatrist or doctor or lawyer be like? Were there trance mediums who faked ninety percent of what they did, just as there were practitioners of other professions who made mistakes or were careless on "off" days or who really didn't give a damn *any* day of the week? Didn't one, in any case, have to judge pretty much by *results*? Was invisible reality something that could ever be proved?

And, for that matter, what *was* invisible reality? It was, quite simply, something one *believed* to be true. Praying to a deity called God was investing faith in an invisible reality: when a baseball player made the sign of the cross before stepping up to the plate, he was invoking a higher invisible reality; when a basketball player crossed himself before attempting a tie-breaking foul shot, no one in the bleachers laughed at him; there were supposed to be no atheists in foxholes, and the moving spectacle of loved ones praying to an invisible God in a hospital emergency room was all too familiar.

Millions of people spent every Sunday participating in the invisible reality of worshipping something they could not prove. None of this seemed to require skepticism in order to be credible. The invisible reality was accepted and had been for centuries. No one

questioned it. In fact, faith in an invisible reality was what reverence was all about.

"Well," said Kevin finally, "whatever one thinks of channeling invisible spiritual guides, it is an individual decision. People usually just 'know' whether it feels reasonable or not. I don't try to convince anyone. I just try to understand it and learn as I go along. I feel quite guided by my spiritual friends and continue to develop my metaphysical talents. You'll have to make up your own mind."

I thought about what he said, wondering if my having a session with him actually constituted believing in what he was saying. Was it a way of asking to be convinced? I found myself analyzing my own "open-mindedness" in a new light. Was open-mindedness an act of gullibility? I sipped my tea.

"So, are you religious, Kevin?" I asked.

He choked involuntarily on his tea. "Are you kidding? What church would have me? I'm treading on their territory. I say folks have God inside them. The Church says it has God inside of it. There's a phrase in the Bible which states that one should never countenance spiritual entities other than God. Most Christians go by that. But then the Bible says nothing about reincarnation either and it's quite well known that the Council of Nicea voted to strike the teaching of reincarnation from the Bible."

"How do you know that?" I asked.

"Well, most serious metaphysical students of the Bible know that. The Council of Nicea altered many of the interpretations of the Bible. The man Jesus studied for eighteen years in India before he returned to Jerusalem. He was studying the teaching of Buddha and became an adept yogi himself. He obviously had complete control over his body and understood that the body was only the house for a soul. Each soul has many mansions. Christ taught that a person's behavior would determine future events—as karma, as the Hindus say. What one sows, so shall he reap."

I didn't question these rather sweeping assumptions. I offered

Kevin a cookie. He seemed to like sugar. He ate it in two bites.

I thought about the similarity between the Cayce readings and Ambres and Buddha and the countless numbers of people who had been professing the same kind of belief.

"So," I said, "what's going to happen here?"

Kevin swallowed another cookie. "All right," he said, "right. Now . . . two, three, or maybe four spiritual entities use me to channel information. The first who usually comes through to greet people calls himself John. There are some of us who feel that he is the most highly evolved of all the disincarnate entities. He speaks in a biblical lingo that is sometimes hard to follow. If you prefer, or if John senses a difficulty in communication, another entity comes through. He calls himself Tom McPherson because his favorite incarnation was that of an Irish pickpocket a few hundred years ago. He can be very amusing. Lots of folks like working with him. Others find him too humorous to take seriously. Some folks prefer their spiritual guides to be solemn. Then there's Dr. Shangru, a Pakistani of a few hundred years ago, well-versed in medical matters, and Obidaya, whose favorite incarnation was that of a Jamaican who understands modern-day racial problems."

I felt my mind trying to turn off again. It sounded like a comic strip with a collection of unlikely characters. But wait a minute, I thought. This only bore out everything I had been reading. If these entities *are* entities from the "astral plane," then they would have individual personalities just as we in the body had.

"Wait a minute," I said. "Let me adjust. You say this Tom McPherson was an Irish pickpocket? Does that mean that was all he ever was?"

"No," said Kevin, "as I said before, it's just that his pickpocket personality was his favorite incarnation. He teaches from the vantage point of that lifetime."

"Oh," I said, "okay, why did he like being a pickpocket?"

"Ask him," Kevin replied. "But I think it's because of his sense of humor."

"Okay, so do you hear these entities when they speak through you?"

"No," he answered. "I am not aware of my conscious mind. But I can speak to them on the astral plane when I am sleeping if I want to. And I can feel them guiding me when I'm in a consciously aware state."

"Do you believe everyone has spiritual guides?" I asked.

Kevin looked surprised. "Why sure," he said, "that's what the soul does after it passes out of the body. Souls that have died, so to speak, help those who are still in the body. Why, that's what spiritual understanding is all about."

"What *is* what spiritual understanding is all about?"

Kevin sat up in his chair and leaned toward me. "Haven't you ever had the feeling that you were being guided to do something by a force you didn't understand?"

I thought of all the times in my life when I thought I was listening to my intuition which seemed to almost compel me to make a certain decision or meet a person or go to a place. I thought of my experiences in Africa with a force that seemed to protect me when I traveled alone, or the time in Bhutan in the Himalayas when I felt impelled to inquire and investigate what the lamas were doing as they sat meditating in their monasteries 18,000 feet high above the clouds. I had seemed to recognize some similar force way back then, nearly twenty-five years ago. That force had motivated my curiosity and my drive to question what I couldn't see.

"Yes," I said now to Kevin. "I must admit I've felt guided by some kind of force throughout my life. What does that mean?"

"It means," said Kevin, "that, along with your own intuitive certainty, you were being guided by your spiritual friends and guides and teachers. You might have defined it simply as a force but now I'm suggesting that you become more aware in your understanding of what was really going on."

I stood up. "What does it feel like to know that spiritual entities speak through you?"

"Sometimes," he said hesitatingly, "sometimes I'd like to be a gardener instead of the custodian of the garden. But maybe that's my karma. We all have our roles in life, don't we? Maybe mine is to be a human telephone."

Kevin suddenly looked so vulnerable sitting in his upright position with his tea cup balanced on his beige knee. I wondered what his life was like, what he did on Saturday nights, how he felt about politics. Had others who had gone through their spiritual questioning also gone through the same *personalization* of what they learned?

I didn't realize it then but Kevin Ryerson would come to be one of the telephones in my life. And, on this Friday night in Malibu, I was about to talk to some new friends . . . *Real or not, I once again was reminded that each person experiences his own reality,* and no one else can be the judge of what that reality really is. But it wasn't simply a matter of believing what one wanted to believe. It was more a question of taking care to refrain from being so skeptical that one automatically shut out challenging ideas and new perceptions. ❊

Chapter 14

"Every new-born being indeed comes fresh and blithe into the new existence, and enjoys it as a free gift: but . . . its fresh existence is paid for by . . . a worn-out existence which had perished, but which contained the indestructible seed out of which this new existence has arisen: they are one being. To show the bridge between the two would certainly be the solution of a great riddle."

—Arthur Schopenhauer
The World as Will and Idea

I lowered the lights in my living room. The ocean tumbled gently outside. I put the tape recorder on, and asked Kevin if he needed anything.

"No," he answered, "I think I'll be going out now."

"Okay," I said, "I'll be here."

"Right," said Kevin. "See you in a while then."

He leaned back, placed his hands over his chest and crossed them. He closed his eyes. I moved the tape recorder closer to him. Slowly he began to breathe deeply. I waited. He sat still for about three minutes and breathed even more deeply. Then very gently his head toppled forward onto his chest and a catch spluttered slightly in his throat. His head straightened up and cocked to one side. About thirty more seconds elapsed. Then he opened his mouth and his body shuddered. His breathing changed rhythm. Slowly his mouth transposed into a smooth smile. His eyebrows lifted, giving his facial expression one of momentary surprise. His hands moved to the arm rests. In a raspy whisper which didn't sound in Kevin's vocal range, I heard,

"Hail. I'm John. Greetings. Please identify yourself and state purpose of gathering."

I cleared my throat and shifted onto the floor next to Kevin's chair.

"Yes," I began, "my name is Shirley MacLaine. I am from Richmond, Virginia, in the United States, but I am speaking to you from Malibu, California. I am a performer who also writes, and I can't really say why I'm here."

"As such," said the Voice.

As such . . . I guessed that meant okay. I remembered Kevin had said one of the spiritual entities spoke in a biblical lingo.

"We are taken to find ye have investigations. We sense your vibrational condition as such and have familiarity with it."

There was a pause as though he was waiting for me to ask a question or say something. I didn't know where to begin.

"Yes," I said, "well, could you tell me please who 'we' might be?"

"As such," he said, "we are those who have known ye in lives past."

He startled me.

"You people have known me in past lives?"

"As such."

"Are you my spiritual guides then? Is that why I am here?"

"As such."

"Oh, I see," I said inaccurately. He went on.

"To understand yourself now you must understand that you are more than what you seem now. The sum of your talents, the sum of your feelings, are those which ye have experienced before . . . and all that ye are is part of the oneness of all. Is that to your understanding?"

I squirmed around on my carpet. Didn't everyone have certain talents, feelings, and thoughts which did not correspond to present life experience? "Excuse me," I said, "on what do you base your information either about me or anything cosmic?"

With barely a pause he said, "On that which ye would term the Akashic Records." He stopped as though I should be thoroughly

acquainted with his references. He seemed so distant, so pseudo-Biblical. I felt detached.

"Ye are taken to find that Akasha is that which ye might term the collective unconscious of mankind, stored in ethereal energy. This energy could be termed as the mind of God. Ye are taken to find that communication of said ideas is difficult given the limited dimension of language."

"Yes," I said, "I can see what you mean. And while we're at it, why do you speak the way you do?"

There was a pause. Then he said, "I will endeavor to bring my language more up to date, as you would term it." He went on immediately, "This stored energy called the Akashic Records is as vast scrolls housed in vast libraries. You, as an individual, would be thought of as a single scroll within the libraries, or as a single soul within the mind of God."

"Excuse me," I said. "Isn't what you are saying just a little too simple?"

"All truth is not so much simple as it is designed to be easily revealed."

"Well, if it's so easily revealed, why don't we know it?" I asked.

"Man refuses to accept that he is in possession of all truth and has been from the beginning of time and space. Man refuses to accept responsibility for himself. Man is the co-creator with God of the cosmos."

No, I thought, in the church we are taught that *God* created everything.

But "John" was plowing on.

"Only when man accepts that he is part of the truth he is seeking, are the truths themselves apparent."

"So you're saying that if I understand myself and where I come from, I will understand everything?"

"Correct," he said.

"Well," I said, "I've never really been sure there is such a thing as God until maybe lately. With what's going on in the world, why should anyone believe in God?"

"You are saying," he asked, "that you need proof of your own existence?"

"Well, I don't know what you mean. No, I'm sure I exist. Yes."

"You have a mind?"

"Of course."

"The mind is a reflection of the soul. The soul is a reflection of God. The soul and God are eternal and unto each other."

"So you mean if I'm to understand what this God thing is, I must know myself?"

"Correct," he said, "your soul is a metaphor for God."

"Huh? Wait a minute," I said. "I can't prove either one—soul or God. I don't mean to be disrespectful, but that's a tricky way of confirming that there's a soul."

"Tricks," he said, "are a game of mankind, not of God."

I felt strangely embarrassed.

"Well, I could become very arrogant if I really believed *I* was a metaphor for God."

"Never," he said, "never confuse the path you take with the truth itself."

I felt slightly shamed. I waited for him to say something else.

"Pause," he said, "another entity is desiring to speak."

"What?"

Kevin shifted his position in his chair. His arms rearranged themselves. His head swiveled to the other side. He covered his face for a moment and then crossed one leg over the other.

I got up on my knees trying to understand what was going on.

"Tip o' the hat to ya," said a completely new voice. "McPherson here. Tom McPherson. How are you doing out there?"

The accent was funny. I laughed out loud. Kevin cocked his

head as though *he* wasn't really doing it. The expression on his face made me feel he wondered why I found him so funny.

"My, my," said the McPherson voice. "I didn't expect a reaction like that quite so soon. It usually takes me a while to work up to that."

Kevin had said this McPherson character was amusing. I felt as though I could *feel* his personality coming through. It wasn't just the sound of the voice, it was almost the presence of a distinct new energy in the room. It was remarkable how he seemed so separate from Kevin. Being an actress, I had to hand it to Kevin. If he was acting, it was a superb transition.

"Is your whirring box going?" said McPherson.

"My what?"

"Your whirring box."

I looked down at my tape recorder.

"Oh that," I said. "Yes. Is it all right?"

"Oh, yes," he said, "of course. I just wanted to make certain you captured the details."

"The details?"

"Quite right," he said.

Kevin coughed. He cleared his throat and coughed again.

"Excuse me," I said, "but what's wrong with Kevin's throat?"

"Oh, nothing," said McPherson. "I'm just having a little difficulty adjusting to the vibrations of the instrument."

"Oh. You mean you try to adjust your energy vibrations with Kevin's energy vibrations?"

"Yes. Quite right. Over here we work with vibrational frequencies. Do you have any of your brew about?"

"My brew?"

"Yes, I believe there is an herbal brew about?"

"Oh, you mean tea?"

"Quite right."

"Why yes," I said. "Would you like some?"

"Very good."

"The cup is very small. Shall I put it in Kevin's hand? Will he be able to handle it?"

"Oh, yes," said McPherson.

I filled the cup and held it in front of Kevin. He made no move to lift his hand. His eyes remained closed.

"Just place it in the young man's hand. Thank you."

I lifted Kevin's right hand and slipped the cup into his palm.

"The cup is not so much small as it is tiny," said McPherson.

I laughed. I didn't like these little cups myself.

"Have you a mug about?" asked McPherson. "I believe you have glass mugs in your cupboard?"

I looked over to my kitchen. He was right. I did have glass mugs. Only I never served tea in them.

"I'm partial to mugs," said McPherson. "A bit of the old pub feeling. Helps me to think clearly."

I climbed from my knees, walked into the kitchen, and fetched the mug. I continued talking to McPherson as I went.

"So you really are an Irishman? Do all Irishmen think better with mugs?"

"Quite right," said McPherson to my back.

I returned and poured more tea into the mug and exchanged the cup.

"Well, it's not like the pub, but anyway," said McPherson.

Kevin raised the mug to his mouth and took a sip. His eyes were still closed. He swallowed the tea.

"Can you actually taste the tea?" I asked.

"Well, I sense it more than I taste it. I use the instrument's oral faculties to gain a sense of it."

He took another sip.

"If it was too hot, would you feel it or would Kevin feel it?" I asked.

"I would react to protect the instrument," said McPherson. "I wouldn't feel the pain, but there would be empathy on my part, yes."

"And if it was really hot, what would you do?" I asked.

"Probably use a better command of the instrument's system to deaden the pain."

There was a silence. I could feel McPherson waiting for me.

"May I call you Tom?" I asked.

"Very good."

"I hear you were a pickpocket," I said.

"Quite right. Although pickpocketing was more what you would term my 'cover trade.'"

"Your cover trade?"

"Quite right. Actually I was what you would term a diplomatic spy."

"A diplomatic spy? For whom?"

"For the English Crown, I'm sorry to say."

"You were a spy for England and you're Irish?"

"Quite right. I was Irish even though the name McPherson is Scottish. I took the name of McPherson to disguise my Irish identity as there was deeper prejudice against the Irish than the Scots in those days. Hasn't changed much either."

"Well, why were you spying for the English if they were so prejudiced against your people?"

"I like to think of myself as a freelance spy. The Crown simply hired me to lift important papers from Spanish diplomats. I was very good at that sort of thing. Therefore I call myself a pickpocket. It is more humorous for me."

I sipped some tea, trying to make heads out of tails and not getting very far.

"So, now you ply your trade more positively to help others down here, do you?"

"Quite right. Balance and karma and all that."

"Didn't you get points against you for being a pickpocket— diplomatic or otherwise?"

"Quite right. I am working off some of my karma now by being of service to you."

"I see." I was alternately amused and skeptical.

"Have you any more of your brew about?" asked Tom.

"Yes, certainly." I poured another mug of hot tea.

"Did you wish to make any other inquiries?" Tom asked.

Now I poured some tea for myself, considering what would be a productive line of approach.

"I was discussing the existence of the soul with someone the other night," I said, "using déjà vu as an example of previous existence. You know, when you feel you're in a place where you've been before but know you can't have been? Or you have that back-of-the-head feeling about an experience that it has all happened before?"

"Quite right."

"Well, some people were saying that cellular memory or ancestral memory (like some of the scientists are also saying) was really the explanation. They believed that we just inherit genetically the memory of things our ancestors might have experienced. Now, how would *you* debate the issue of the existence of the soul?"

There was a moment of silence.

"How would *you* do it?" he said, "now that you have had time to reflect?"

"Well, I guess I should have said that there are cases of people —say, in tribal societies in Africa—whose ancestors have never moved out of their environment. Yet they have memories of North America, India, etc."

"My goodness," said Tom, "that *is* a good argument. Then of course you also have heard of your telepathy and mind-out-of-body experiences. Many people in your time have spoken publicly of out-of-body experiences. They were actually experiencing their souls as separate from the physical envelope."

I remembered how many people indeed had described this experience when going through a close brush with death. Most described the same white light as Peter Sellers had, drawing them with a compelling sense of love and peace, while looking down at

their own dying body. Some did not want to return to the body. Many such experiences have been recorded in *Life After Life* by Dr. Raymond Moody. In my own acquaintance were a surprising number who had reported having the experience.

"And," Tom was continuing, "as for déjà vu being simply a form of cellular memory, there are many individuals who have had memory patterns of places their ancestors had never been."

"Yeah," I said, "that's what I said. But maybe some of *his* ancestors had been to Africa—like the Romans, for instance—and their cellular memory recorded their reactions and the offspring inherited those cellular memories."

"Possibly," said Tom, "except for one thing. Déjà vu also occurs in the modern context. For example, you may have déjà vu when you walk into a house that's only a few years old. That's hardly inherited cellular memory."

"What is it, then?"

"That is the result of the soul astrally projecting to the new house. Something like your experience in what you call the floating dream that you loved so much. You remember that experience?"

He stopped me in my tracks. I had never mentioned that to anyone.

"My goodness," I said, "how did you know that?"

"Oh, a bit of the old spiritual voo-doo, so to speak."

I needed a moment to adjust to what had just happened. Could this have been a predictable guess? Did he tell this to everyone he channeled for? I choked back a cough.

"Just give me a moment," I said.

"Quite right," he said, "one thing we have plenty of is time."

I felt confounded. Could it be that certain dreams were astral projections of the soul?

"Have you any more inquiries?" McPherson asked.

I collected myself.

"Well," I said, "why is there such resistance to the study of the

soul as a realistic fact? Why isn't as much time and money spent on researching the existence of the soul as there is on splitting the atom or nuclear energy?"

"Well, for one thing," he answered, "the material isn't available. The soul is not a material thing. Also the field of soul study has a tendency to have scorn and ridicule heaped upon it and professional reputations go down the tubes, so to speak, very easily."

"But *why* is it so scorned?"

"Because it is considered to be a ludicrous waste of time. Superstition and the like. Serious people who admit to such investigations are sometimes made to feel ridiculous. But as a friend of yours said recently, 'To get to the fruit on the tree one must go out on a limb.' "

I was silent—floored. He had used the same analogy as Gerry. I had been most careful never to even mention Gerry to anyone, much less what he said.

McPherson went on. "You must be patient with your Gerry. We are being patient with you."

I was struck dumb. How the hell could this guy know about us? He not only knew about Gerry, he knew what Gerry had said.

"Do we have a revelation here?" asked Tom.

"Oh God," I said.

"Quite right," he responded cheerfully.

I sipped more tea and tried to sort myself out. A few moments passed.

"Would you like to continue?" said Tom.

Jesus, I thought, this stuff could be real. There were so many questions I had to ask. "Okay," I said under my breath. Then, "Okay. Tell me, why is there such a gap between science and the Church?"

"Well," said Tom, "because science just lately (in cosmic terms, of course) feels it has rid itself of the shackles of religious superstition and is now enjoying its freedom and golden age. The attitude

is understandable. To research those domains of the Church which was its former jailer would only rebuild the power base of that old traditional persecutor."

"Is the soul under the dominion only of the Church?"

"Quite right. That is, it is considered so in the orthodox sense, yes. Actually, one's soul is, um, a highly personal matter, in a manner of speaking."

"But would proof of the soul's existence radically alter the attitude of science?"

"Yes, of course. But quite honestly, science feels there is no basis on which to inquire about the existence of the soul. Also, there isn't much money in that kind of research."

"You mean, if you research electricity you can turn it into an electric light? Or, if you research the atom you can turn it into a bomb?"

"Quite right."

"But if you research the soul there is no material profit in it?"

"Quite right. Could I have a bit more of your brew?"

I poured more tea. It was almost gone.

"So," I asked, "are there research groups who solely devote themselves to the soul?"

"You turned a nice one there," he said.

"I turned a nice one where?"

"*Solely* for the soul? Very good."

"Are you aware," I asked seriously, "that you are performing for me right now?"

"Quite frankly," he said, "I believe I am sensationally entertaining at all times. This is my natural nature. There's another: 'natural nature.' "

"You're quite a punster, aren't you?"

"No," he said. "I don't feel I'm being, so to speak, overly campy. No, it's all a natural extension of my personality."

I sat quietly for a while considering this outrageous tea party we

were having. I wondered if I was so gullible I was swallowing a whale. The tape recorder whirred in the silence.

"Well," I said.

"Quite right," said Tom.

"Well, I'd really like to know something more about my past lives. Would that be all right?"

"Very good," said Tom. "Has the instrument any alcohol in his system?"

"No," I said. "He said it inhibited trance channeling, so I don't think so."

"Very good then. One moment please. Would you remove the mug please?"

I got up, took the mug from Kevin's grasp, checked my tape recorder, and settled down again. ❈

Chapter 15

"In view of the endless duration of the immortal soul throughout the infinity of time . . . shall the soul remain forever attached to this point of world-space, our earth? Will it never participate in a closer contemplation of the remaining wonders of creation? Who knows but that the intention is for it to become acquainted at close range, some day, with those far distant globes of the cosmic system . . . which from this distance already provoke our curiosity?"

—Immanuel Kant
General History of Nature

A shudder went through Kevin. His head moved around until once again he had assumed the character of John.

"Hail," said the John voice. "You have inquiries as to your past lives?"

"Yes," I answered.

The telephone rang.

John reacted and cocked his head.

I waited.

I could feel John "adjust his vibrations," as McPherson had said. The telephone rang again. Again, I didn't answer.

"You will find," said John, "that to understand the soul within yourself today, you must also understand something of the previous civilizations you have known."

"Really?" I said inanely, feeling sort of ridiculous and nonplussed.

"Indeed," said John, "you were incarnate several times during the five-hundred-thousand-year period of the most highly evolved civilization ever known to man. It was what the Bible symbolized as the Garden of Eden. I would like you now to understand one

very important concept. The level of achievement in any civilization is judged by its spiritual evolvement. Technological advancement is important and attractive, but if it detains, detracts, or deters spiritual understanding, it bears the seeds of its own destruction. You are bearing witness to such a simple truth in your present civilization on Earth today. Your spiritual understanding is lagging at great lengths behind your technological knowledge and as a result, you are witnessing progressive insanity, depression, confusion of purpose, and total human inequality and despair."

"So where is the hope for us then? I mean, if we're going backward instead of forward, why are we living?"

"A good and important question," said John, "which brings us to the subject of karma yet again, and makes it necessary for you to grasp your basic identity and the understanding of the power of your free will to understand your divinity and partnership with God."

"Excuse me," I said, "but can I ask where religion fits into all this, please?"

"There is much that I am saying that your worldly religions would take exception to. Your religions teach religion—not spirituality. Religion has exploited man for the most part. Your world religions are on the right track basically, but they do *not* teach that every individual is fundamentally the creator and controller of his own destiny. They teach that *God* assumes such a role. What I am endeavoring to explain is that each individual is a co-creator with God. This does not sit well with your churches and religions because they prefer to have control over mankind, rather than help teach that mankind can only control itself through self-knowledge and through knowledge of its *past* and of its purpose in the present and future."

I was aware of how explosive such a concept would be. But didn't many people within the Church pursue self-knowledge? Weren't there many people who, while following the precepts of the Church, still searched restlessly for truth beyond precepts?

I looked out the window across the dark ocean. A fishing boat blinked its light in the darkness. I wondered how many of the great truths in life one might never be able to see or prove or confirm. It was unsettling and anxiety-arousing. Was the truth only truth when we could "prove" it? I couldn't cope with what I was thinking. I looked away from the window and back to Kevin and the "disembodied spiritual entity" he was channeling.

"So," I said anxiously, and finding myself slightly breathless, "so I lived way back in some ancient civilization?"

"Yes, several times," said John. "Twice as a male and once as a female."

I was quiet as one of the finer points of reincarnation hit home again. "Have we all experienced living as different sexes in order to be able to empathize with the opposite sex?"

"That is correct," said John. "Certainly. How else could mankind reach an understanding of itself and its identities without such diversified physical experiences?"

I leaned forward again. "Could that be a metaphysical explanation for homosexuality?" I asked. "I mean, maybe a soul makes a rocky transition from a female to a male body, for instance, and there is left over emotional residue and attraction from the previous incarnation?"

"As such," said John. "The sexual preference of such individuals plays an important part in the requirement for understanding that we are all basically the same because we have all experienced being both sexes; our souls, if you will, are basically androgynous."

"Androgynous?" I asked.

"Yes, high spiritual understanding knows no sexuality differences because the elements of both sexes are simultaneously present. The polarities are evenly opposed. Your ancient prophets and Christ figures such as Jesus and Buddha, et cetera, were not so much celibate as they were vibrating at an even and perfectly balanced frequency. Their yin and yang were so evenly distributed

that sexuality was of no interest to them because there was no conflict and therefore no tension. It was not a subject they needed to sublimate or repress. It simply didn't interest them because of their peaceful spiritual level of achievement."

"I'm not sure I'd be ready to trade."

John paused a moment. "We don't recommend the abstaining of sex," he said. "Definitely not. Sex in human terms is also a pathway to God if it is enjoyed spiritually as well as physically."

I looked at the tape recorder. "Excuse me," I said, "are we getting off the subject?"

"Yes," said John. "But sex is a fascinating subject, even for me."

I laughed. "And who are you?" I asked. "I mean, were you once in a physical body?"

"Oh yes," said John. "I have embodied many times as both male and female but recently have remained in astral form."

"I see," I said. I was curious but I really wanted to know about myself.

"So, who was I in my previous lives?"

"According to the Akashic Records, you were incarnate with a twin soul."

"Oh? What exactly is a twin soul?"

"That question takes a great deal of explanation which I will endeavor to accomplish later. For now, let me begin by explaining *soul mates*."

"Soul mates?" I asked. I had heard the term from time to time, usually in reference to people who said they had found their other half.

"Soul mates," John continued, "were actually created for one another at the beginning of time, or what you call at the moment of the Big Bang. They vibrate at exactly the same electromagnetic frequency because they are identical counterparts of one another. Twin souls are more common to find because they have experienced many lifetimes together in one form or another. But *soul*

mates were actually created at the beginning of time as pairs who belonged together . . . So you see, there is more to your Big Bang theory than you imagine . . . and quite romantic at that, wouldn't you say?"

I made some noncommittal noise.

"So let me begin there," said John, "where, as I said, we knew each other."

"Oh?"

"Yes, we were teacher and pupil. You were one of my brightest, and what you would term today, 'pet students.' "

I looked around my living room wishing I had someone to share this with. "So we knew each other?"

"Correct. It is no accident that you are here today. We believe you have matured to the understanding that there is no such thing as an accident?"

"Who's 'we' again?" I asked.

"Your spiritual guides, of whom I am one," said John.

"You mean, I was drawn here somehow by you and these guides?"

"That is correct," said John.

"How?"

"By your own need to explain your behavior and your questions and your search for the truth and by psychic guidance from those of us who feel you are ready for more of your own truth."

"Is that what is meant by Spiritual Guidance?"

"That is correct."

There was a pause as John the Voice seemed to be gathering his thoughts, or some kind of information, or both. Quite casually the Voice resumed and said:

"We have isolated your vibration during one of the lifetimes that you spent with an entity with whom you are also now involved. We believe this entity is living in your British Isles. Would that be correct?"

"Gerry?" I said with a rather high-pitched squeak. "Are you talking about Gerry?"

"As such. We have also isolated his vibration and find that the two of you were man and wife during one of your previous lifetimes."

"Oh, my God," I said, amused and flabbergasted. "Did we get along then? I mean, was communication better between us then than it is now?"

There was another pause.

"Your Gerry was equally devoted to his work then. And we must admit it was to the detriment of your union. However, he was doing important work involving cultural exchanges with the extraterrestrials who were endeavoring to be of help technologically and spiritually."

"*Extraterrestrials?*" John seemed to sense my astonishment. He replied more firmly than usual.

"As such. There were extraterrestrials visiting this planet then, as now."

"Oh, Jesus." I took a breath. "Well, could you tell me more about that? I mean, what are you really saying? Are you saying that we have had outer space visitations since the beginning of time?"

"That is correct. There are planets more advanced in knowledge than your Earth, just as your Earth is more advanced than some other planets."

I deliberately relaxed myself and breathed deeply. I supposed the logic of what he was saying held together in its own terms. But I wished I knew what questions to ask.

"Well," I said, floundering around in my own head. Maybe this was all an act, but what if it wasn't? I didn't want to waste an opportunity to learn something. "Well," I said again, "what kind of knowledge were these extraterrestrials bringing?"

John answered immediately. "The only important knowledge is

the spiritual knowledge of God within man. Every other knowledge flows from that."

"*Every* other knowledge?"

"That is correct. Your scientific knowledge, for example, depends on your understanding of vibrational frequencies and how they pertain to the universe. God is love—which is the highest vibrational frequency of all. In your physical world light is the highest and fastest speed frequency. But to beings who have more knowledge, more control, *thought* has a much higher frequency than light. Thought is part of God, just as thought is part of man. Therefore, when *thought is love* your frequencies are vibrating at the highest level of energy. That is what the extraterrestrials were teaching just as you of the Earth plane will someday teach it to others. Is this to your understanding?"

I didn't know how to answer.

I cleared my throat and tried to stretch my mind to understand. I couldn't personally relate to what John was saying in any specific or detailed and understandable way. The implications of what he was saying were so stunning that I couldn't really think of a good question. I wanted to get back to myself. *That* I could cope with.

"Excuse me, please," I said. "Could I just ask you about me? I'm having enough trouble just relating to that."

"Of course," said John. "You must proceed at your own pace."

"Okay," I said, relieved. "Thank you. So Gerry and I were man and wife. Does that mean we were twin souls?"

"No. But you were and are a twin soul of the entity you call David."

I stopped him. "You know about David, too?"

"That is correct. You had several lifetimes with the David entity during that early period, as well as many others down through the march of time."

Maybe that was why I felt so comfortable with David now.

But John was continuing. "Your David is a good teacher and you can trust him. But we feel that you already feel that. You must

learn to trust your feelings more and refrain from approaching so many issues in life from strictly an intellectual perspective. Intellect as a marvel is limited. Feelings are limitless. Trust your heart . . . or your intuition, as you term it."

Trust my intuition? Yes, I could see that as I thought back on my life I could fairly say that whenever I went against my intuition I got in trouble. "You're saying that if we all follow what is in our hearts we'll be fine?"

"No. Not necessarily. There are wrong, or hurtful, feelings to be overcome. But mankind, and all life, is basically good. You must learn to give it a chance. Life represents the thought of God and God is love."

Frankly, all this talk of "God" was embarrassing me. "Okay." I said, "but what do you call God?"

"God, or the God Force, of which all things are a part," said John, "is the Divine Energy that created the Universe and holds it together harmoniously."

"You would describe what's going on here as harmonious?"

"In the ultimate scheme of life, yes, it is harmonious in the sense that matters are balancing out. But you must understand the process of each soul's progress and reembodiment and purification to understand the harmony."

"Wait a minute," I said. "Isn't the Bible supposed to be the Word of God?"

"Yes, in the main it is. Although much of what exists in your Bible today has been reinterpreted."

"Reinterpreted by whom?"

"By various persons through time and through various languages. Ultimately, by the Church. It was to the advantage of the Church to 'protect the people' from the real truth."

"The real truth being what?"

"The real truth being the process of each soul's progression through the ages. The real truth being each soul's responsibility for its own behavior in the realization of its own divinity."

"You mean reincarnation?"

"That is correct. That is the word you use to term it. That is the carrying out of Cosmic Justice toward an ultimate harmony."

"Well, would the Church deny us that truth?"

"Yes, because such a truth would make the power and the authority of the Church unnecessary. Each person, that is, each entity, becomes responsible to itself for its conduct. It does not need a church. It does not need rituals, and stratifications, and cubbyholes to crawl into to get absolution issued by the Church. Let us say simply that the authorities in the Church desired to 'shelter' mankind from a truth they felt you were not prepared for."

"You mean in somewhat the same spirit that governments act today?"

"As such."

I stretched out on my carpet. I didn't know what to think, nor could I think of any more questions. Kevin sat impassively in the chair. The tea on the table was cold.

"Will there be any more inquiries then?" asked John.

I looked out at the blinking lights of the fishing boat.

I thought of some of the people I had talked to who found me naive and gullible for even considering the believability of disembodied spiritual masters speaking through a medium. How could I fall for such stuff, they said. I had always replied that I felt I was simply learning. I wasn't sure what it meant really but it somehow confirmed to me that there were more dimensions to the reality of life than one understood—in somewhat the same way that the dimensions of our own personalities and characters were a mystery to us until we began to explore those aspects which we were not familiar with and certainly were not aware of because we couldn't "see" them.

But why did *I* feel more comfortable than some others in allowing myself to explore dimensions of unprovable possibilities? I really didn't know. It just felt all right. That's all I could say. It didn't threaten me. It didn't upset my emotional investment in

what I was already sure was real: it did not seem to destroy my image of myself. This whole exploration simply seemed to be expanding what my perceptions of reality already were. So I wondered, then, why some of my friends, and Gerry in particular, found this pursuit of a new knowledge along spiritual paths, through mediums and reincarnation, so threatening in terms of my credibility. Why were they so worried for me? Out of love and protectiveness certainly. They didn't want to see me ridiculed—any more than I did. But it was more than that. They were also threatened themselves. Why? Why *not* ask questions seriously and delve into areas and possibilities that were not necessarily "provable"? What "real" harm could it do? Would it shatter the conditioned images they had of themselves? Would it confuse their own views of "reality"?

I turned over onto my knees.

"John," I said, "why do so many people find this phenomenon of trance channeling a disembodied master such as yourself through a human instrument so unacceptable?"

There was a slight pause.

"Because," he said, "they do not remember the experience of having been disembodied themselves. People think that life is the totality of everything they see. They believe that man himself is simply a body and a brain. But personality is more."

"How do you mean?"

"Personality is the intangible aspect of consciousness which is only lodged in the body for a brief period of cosmic time."

"But they don't believe that concept is real."

"Real?" asked John. "Is a thought not real? Yet how does one scientifically prove that? Thought is energy. Those who question the physical existence of a thought, or of thought energy, question with deep skepticism their own identities."

"Yes, but aren't questions good? I mean, absolute certainty in something creates egomania and corruptive power."

"That is correct. But it is worrisome when skepticism becomes

so profound and demoralizing that it restricts the potential of learning glorious truths which would be in their favor."

"But how can I convey to them that being open-minded is actually wise?"

"You do not have to do that. You who *are* open-minded simply say what *is* from your point of view. Give the skeptics the freedom to be skeptical. If you did not I would accuse you of being an enslaver. Give them the privilege of continuing their doubt. There will come a time when they too will want to know and they will be drawn to dimensions which are more true. They will seek a greater counsel when they are ready. If people insist upon remaining within their "logical" belief systems they are safe within their own perceived reality, and thus are safe within the position of power they hold, whatever that power might be. They will not change their perceptions and thus be required to change themselves or grow into an expanded awareness of themselves."

"But what about the security of one's ego?" I asked.

"Most people are suffering from *altered* egos. Altered by society, by the Church, and by education. Their true egos know the truth. I am as believable as anyone else. You cannot see me but there are many aspects of yourself that you cannot see either. People are searching for these aspects in themselves every day. But while they search they require that their worlds remain secure. To believe I am as real as they would be to deter them from their comfort zones—the zones they understand and can control. When you begin to understand more you are essentially understanding that there is so much more to understand that is beyond your grasp."

"No, but that isn't what people say to me. What they tell me is that the whole theory of reincarnation is too *tidy*. They say it is too simple-minded to be real."

"As I have said before to you: the truth *is* simple. It is man who insists on making it complicated. And man cannot just *learn* the truth as one would learn a lesson. He must *experience* aspects

of it in himself in order to go further. Learning and experiencing the truth of itself is a struggle. A struggle toward simple awareness. You must remember that the natural habitat of the human is not Earth; the natural habitat of human beings is the ether. Each individual already knows the Divine truth. They have simply complicated it and forgotten that they know it."

"But my intellectual friends say that believing one knows *the* truth is the ultimate act of arrogance."

"Each person knows his own truth. That is correct. But the only truth that matters is the truth of the relationship that one has with the source, or the God force. And *that* truth is limited when intellectual skepticism is applied to it. Because one does not need intellect to know God. In that respect, all individuals are equal. Your intellectuals seek to separate themselves from the masses in order to feel elite. They rely more on their intellect than they do on the God force within themselves. Many people, and not only intellectuals, are embarrassed to acknowledge the spark of Divinity within themselves. But the intellectual skeptics are more likely to be conflicted, confused and unhappy within themselves. All people seek peace. The path to inner peace is not through the intellect but through the inner heart. Within the inner heart one finds God, peace, and oneself. Intellectual skeptics avoid themselves. The *self*, however, knows the Divine truth because the self is itself Divine. Is this to your understanding?"

I sat up feeling that, yes, I did understand. None of this felt religious either. It just made sense. And I could not understand why some others I knew had to make such a big deal of it—either couldn't understand or didn't want to.

"Why are there wars, John? What causes people to want to conquer others?"

"Because those who feel the need to conquer do not understand the truth of themselves. However, if a closed-minded tyrant is exposed to inner knowingness, inner awareness, he soon loses the

intent of his conquest. He sees how vast *he* really is and does not need to secure his own immortality by conquering others. When the human mind experiences an expansion of dimensions on many levels it becomes more peaceful, more satisfied. The skeptic's view of higher knowledge of self is most limiting. Your dogmatic religions, for example, are most limiting for mankind because they demand unquestioned reverence for authority—an exterior authority. *You* are God. *You* know you are Divine. But you must continually remember your Divinity and, most important, *act* accordingly."

"John, you mentioned extraterrestrials before. I don't quite know what to think about that, but are they involved with the same struggle of inner knowingness?"

"That is correct," said John, "perhaps they are operating, at least some of them, on a higher level of awareness and a higher level of technology also. But they are not to be revered as Godlike. They are merely teachers. They have visited your Earth over the eons to bring knowledge and spiritual truth because they have found through the evolution of time that the spiritual understanding of the individual is the *only* understanding required for peace. All other knowledge stems from that."

"And the possible extraterrestrial references in the Bible were real? I mean in Ezekiel and all that?"

"That is correct. They appeared at that time on your Earth to bring higher knowledge of God and spiritual love. They always appear when they are most needed. They serve as a symbol of hope and higher understanding."

"Will I ever meet one?"

There was a pause. "We will speak of these matters again at another time. Think about what I have said and what you are willing to learn. Will that be all for now?"

My mind felt so stuffed I had to say yes. "Thank you, John," I said, "whoever you are. I just can't think of anything else right now. I have to absorb what you've said."

"Very well," said John. "Seek to be at peace with yourself and with God and his work, for you are part of that work. God bless you." ❊

> "Something unknown to our
> understanding is visiting the earth."
> —Dr. Mitrovan Zverev,
> Soviet scientist

❊ Kevin shuddered as though the vibration of John's spirit passed through his body and was gone. His hands lifted to his eyes and covered them. Then he rubbed them as though waking from a deep sleep.

"Hello?" he asked drowsily, trying to focus on the room around him. "Hello?"

I stood up and stretched and walked in a circle in front of him.

"Hello," I said, "I'm here."

"How did it go?" asked Kevin.

"My God," I said. "It was incredible. I just don't know what to think."

Kevin straightened up in the chair and then stood up. "Just do what feels right," he said. "Did what came through *feel* right? They've told me to just trust my feelings. There's nothing else you can do once you begin to ask these questions."

"But they were saying incredible stuff."

"Like what?"

"Oh, about previous lifetimes. A whole lot of stuff about people I know now that I'm supposed to have known in other lives. And John and McPherson as well."

"So?"

"Well, do you believe all that?"

"I believe what feels right."

"And does reincarnation feel right to you?" I asked.

"Well, it would have to, wouldn't it? I mean I am an instrument through which many spiritual entities speak, aren't I? So the existence of the soul in many dimensions makes sense to me. Otherwise that makes me either an actor or crazy. And as far as I know I'm neither."

I looked at Kevin closely.

"Yeah," I said hesitantly, "but John also said a lot of stuff about extraterrestrials having provided all kinds of spiritually advanced input for the human race. Do you believe that?"

He sat down. "Sure," he said, "why not? Not only are they mentioned all through the Bible, but they figure in one form or another in nearly every culture on Earth. So why wouldn't they exist? Besides, I know lots of people today who say they've seen them."

"Have you ever seen a UFO?" I asked.

"No," said Kevin, "I have not yet had that pleasure."

"But you believe it anyway?"

"Of course. It feels comfortable to me. And besides, who am I to argue with all the authorities who say there is a good chance they exist? I know there are a lot of people who say they don't, but there's no proof of that either."

Absently Kevin sipped what was left of some cold tea. Then he looked at the mug.

"Where did this come from?" he asked.

"McPherson. He said he needed an Irish-type mug to think more clearly."

"I was holding this mug?"

"Yeah."

"Interesting."

"Yeah."

"What time frame would it be right about now?" he asked.

"Good question," I said. I got it sorted out. "A little before ten."

"I'll be picking up my lady then." He walked toward my door.

"Well, could we get together again soon? I know how busy you are. But would it be possible to work me in?"

"Let me check with my lady and I'll be getting back to you."

I opened the door and thanked him.

With his low-slung slouch, he slid his beige western costume overcoat over his shoulders. He moved out and descended the stairs like a character in *The Lodger* (an old movie I had seen in my childhood).

I watched him walk to his "vehicle" on the street. As I looked after him, I wondered if trance mediums needed to be involuntarily theatrical in order to sustain an identity of their own.

I fell into bed. I couldn't sleep. My legs were vibrating with a strange almost magnetic energy from inside. I shifted my position. It didn't help. The energy continued to vibrate . . . I was almost afraid of it because it was so unfamiliar. I felt the same vibration in my fingertips and around my lips. It felt physical but at the same time I could feel the energy emanating from my mind somehow.

I tried to focus on small, familiar things—the softness of the breeze coming through my window off the Pacific, the slap of the waves, the walk I would take in the morning through the mountain of wildflowers. I went through some familiar choreography which I often did in order to fall asleep. I counted each step and movement to the music. I felt the meaning of the music in my mind. I stretched the muscles in my legs attempting to neutralize the magnetic stream of energy flaming inside. It was such a foreign energy, yet somehow positive. I pictured the pleasure of a hot fudge sundae dripping with thick, sweet chocolate over cold vanilla-bean ice cream.

I felt I needed somehow to ground myself in the here and now

on Earth. I laughed to myself. What the hell was going on? What was real? Had I in fact lived someplace with Gerry and with David five hundred thousand years ago? If I really believed this stuff there was no way I could continue walking around in this world the way I'd always done. It was bound to change my perceptions. Was that what happened to Walt Whitman and Pythagoras and Aristotle and Thoreau when they came to the conclusion that reincarnation was not only possible but probable? No wonder the people in Asia had a different concept of time than we in the West did. They grew up in the belief of the reembodiment of the soul from lifetime to lifetime. Jesus, I thought, maybe time and space are so relative they are not measurable. Maybe they both exist at the same time. Maybe the soul inside my body was telling me that *everything is real*. And if that was true, then reality had more dimensions than I had ever considered. Perhaps, as philosophers and even some scientists claimed, reality was only what one perceived it to be.

If that were the case, I could understand on a colossal scale what an added spiritual dimension could mean to the planet and all the human beings living on it. What a wonder, what a marvel that would be!

Everyone's perception of reality would be valid. If the soul's experience was all that mattered and one's physical existence was literally irrelevant because, from a cosmic perspective, there was no such thing as death, then every living second on Earth was precious precisely because it *did* relate to a grand overall design *which we had helped to create*, and precisely because every *atom* had a purpose, maybe the purpose of this particular collection of atoms writhing around here on the bed was to convey the message that we are part of the God-force that created all things—it is as much a part of us as we are of it.

In a ball of vibrating confusion, I rolled over and finally fell asleep. ❀

Chapter 16

"And whether I come to my own today or in ten thousand
    or ten million years,
I can cheerfully take it now, or with equal cheerfulness
    I can wait . . .
And as to you, Life, I reckon you are the leavings
    of many deaths,
(No doubt I have died myself ten thousand times before.)"

—Walt Whitman
Song of Myself

I slept until late the next day. I just could not get up. When I finally did I went to the Colony Market and got a double-dip peach frozen yogurt. Anything with peaches always helped.

On the way home I began to consider how my friends would react to what had happened. My thoughts flashed to my friend Bella Abzug. I had known and worked with her on the McGovern presidential campaign and we had become very close. She was tough, brilliant, compassionate, and pragmatic. I wondered what she'd think. I wondered if there would ever come a time when politicians could engage in their own spiritual search without seeming off the wall to voters.

As I opened the door the phone was ringing. It was Bella.

I told her all about what had happened in my session with Kevin. It took a long time and she didn't interrupt once. Finally I stopped.

"Let's get this straight," Bella said. "This Kevin told you you'd lived a previous life in an ancient civilization with someone you're in love with now?"

"No, not Kevin. Kevin was the channel. I talked with two entities, one called McPherson, the other called John."

"Yes, well," she said, "whoever. Listen, this Kevin character could be just making it up and acting."

"Oh, Bella. That's the first thing that occurred to me. And of course it *could* be true—but if he was he should be getting an Academy Award they haven't invented yet. I've been doing a helluva lot of reading on this business of channeling and I really don't believe I'm being taken in any way. I mean, this is something a lot of people are experiencing every day."

"Well," Bella considered, "not meaning to be funny—would you say you were having a religious experience?"

"God, *no!*"

"Then, what? Are you saying you believe in reincarnation?"

"Bella, I don't know. I really just don't know. The thing is it all seems to be about 'feeling,' not thinking. I *feel* that what those spiritual entities said could have really happened to me. In a way, it's *me* I'm listening to, not anyone else." As I spoke I had realized something. "And I can't stop now and just forget the whole thing. I've got to know more."

There was a long silence.

"My darling," she said finally. "I don't want you to be hurt. Just don't do anything dramatic or public about it, okay?" I said okay. "And call me." I said okay.

❋ An interesting and multi-dimensional period of my life now began for me. I can only describe it as a time of living on several levels. I went into rehearsals for a world tour with my live stage show. I danced, sang, acted, and made jokes with my company during the day while at night I pored over every book I could find to help me sort out my feelings and thoughts arising from the questions I found myself asking about life and purpose.

My bookshelves began to bulge with esoteric metaphysical material. I was glad that I had an office in my house in Malibu private

enough to shut the door and lock. I wasn't prepared to answer questions about the books I was reading.

There were reams of material on reincarnation alone. I read heavily in this area since it was a subject that interested me particularly. I was astonished to find, not only that reincarnation was an integrated part of most Eastern beliefs (which I already knew) but that hosts of notable thinkers from the West shared this view of the cosmic purpose of the soul, even though the Eastern beliefs were rooted in religion and the Western concepts seemed to grow more from philosophical roots. From Pythagoras to Plato to Socrates to Aristotle (even though he later denied reincarnation, splitting off from his Platonic master) on to Plutarch and down to the seventeenth century when a whole school of thinkers rose known as the Cambridge Platonists; from this followed many—John Milton, the poet Dryden, the statesman-intellectual Joseph Addison.

I hit the eighteenth century—the Age of Reason as it is called, thinking that here I would find rebuttal and skepticism. Skepticism indeed there was—but not of belief in the soul and a deity, rather there was a rejection of formalized religion and of authoritarian thought. There was in fact an explosion of new thinking and a ratification of the right to think. This was a time that saw Isaac Newton, Benjamin Franklin, Voltaire, the great German philosopher Immanuel Kant, Sir William Jones the brilliant Orientalist, and the Scottish historian and economist David Hume (the latter dedicated to reason, but acknowledging that if there was such a thing as an immortal soul then certainly, in logic, it had to exist both before and after death!) This was a time of the flowering of intellect—yet most of these extraordinary minds believed in the rebirth of the soul.

If I was overwhelmed I was rapidly discovering I had good company...

Many writers and poets, such as William Blake and Goethe, gave expression to their beliefs in their work. Goethe wrote of his beliefs in letters. Heinrich Heine, the German lyric poet and critic,

was, in fact, remarkably "image" conscious: *Who can tell what tailor now inherits the soul of a Plato, what dominie is heir to Caesar's spirit? . . . Perchance the soul of Genghis Khan now animates a reviewer who, without knowing it, daily slashes the soul of his faithful Bashirs and Kalmucks in the pages of a critical journal . . . (The North Sea)*

Closer to home, I read my way through reports on the American Transcendentalists—spearheaded by Emerson and Thoreau. These were men in revolt against conventional, authoritarian Western religion, as their forerunners—among them Kant, Schopenhauer, Carlyle, and Wordsworth—had been. Walt Whitman's *Leaves of Grass* is of course a paean to reincarnation. Malcolm Cowley said of Whitman. "The universe was an eternal becoming for Whitman, a process not a structure, and it had to be judged from the standpoint of eternity."

So all through the eighteenth and nineteenth centuries there were great men of letters, philosophers, and scientists; and musicians, artists, poets, historians, essayists—and politicians—all giving voice to a belief in reincarnation arrived at through a pragmatic examination of the wonder of life on this earth, often combined with study of the Orientalists. This included men like Thomas Edison, Camille Flammarion (the French astronomer), Gustaf Stomberg (Swedish-American astronomer and physicist), to name just a few.

What, I wondered, did the twentieth century have to say? I found immediately, and again, that there was an enormous body of writing on the subject. I could only begin to scratch the surface. Among the many writers were Henry Miller, Pearl Buck, Thomas Wolfe, Jack London, Mark Twain, Louisa May Alcott—the litany of names was endless. I was delighted to find such diverse characters as Lord Hugh Dowding (British Air Chief Marshal during World War II), Sir Arthur Conan Doyle, Ernest Seton Thompson (founder of the Boy Scouts of America!), Lloyd George (British politician) and—my God—Henry Ford, all in the same reincar-

national boat, as it were; also innumerable scientists, a whole school of modern art headed by Mondrian, Kandinsky, Klee, Malevich (Theosophists, one and all); and Herman Hesse, Rainer Maria Rilke, Robert Frost, John Masefield—to name, again, just a very few of the rich and distinguished roster of believers in the theory of reincarnation.

If the work of one man stood out from the rest, it was that of John Ellis McTaggart. At the age of twenty-five McTaggart had been acknowledged as the most distinguished dialectician and metaphysician since Hegel. C. D. Broad, who succeeded McTaggart as lecturer in the Moral Sciences at Trinity College, Cambridge, said that McTaggart was "in the front rank of the great historical philosophers [who might] quite fairly be compared with the *Enneads* of Plotinus, the *Ethics* of Spinoza, and the *Encyclopaedia* of Hegel."

Needless to say I was not familiar with any of these heady works. But I found what Mr. McTaggart himself had to say in his *Human Immortality and Pre-Existence* made a great deal of sense:

> Even the best men are not, when they die, in such a state of intellectual and moral perfection as would fit them to enter heaven immediately. . . . This is generally recognized, and one of two alternatives is commonly adopted to meet it. The first is that some tremendous improvement—an improvement out of all proportion to any which can ever be observed in life—takes place at the moment of death. . . . The other and more probable alternative is that the process of gradual improvement can go on in each of us after the death of our present bodies. . . . The absence of memory need not destroy the chance of an improvement spreading over many lives . . . a man who dies after acquiring knowledge—and all men acquire some—might enter his new life, deprived indeed of his knowledge, but not deprived of the

increased strength and delicacy of mind which he had gained in acquiring knowledge. And, if so, he will be wiser in the second life because of what has happened in the first . . . we cannot doubt that character may remain determined by an event which has been forgotten. I have forgotten the greater number of the good and evil acts which I have done in my present life. And yet each must have left a trace on my character. And so a man may carry over into his next life the dispositions and tendencies which he had gained by the moral contests of this life. . . .

There remains love. The problem here is more important, if, as I believe, it is in love, and in nothing else, that we find not only the supreme value of life, but also the supreme reality of life, and, indeed, of the universe. . . . Much has been forgotten in any friendship which has lasted for several years within the limits of a single life—many confidences, many services, many hours of happiness and sorrow. But they have not passed away without leaving their mark on the present. They contribute, though they are forgotten, to the present love which is not forgotten. In the same way, if the whole memory of the love of a life is swept away at death, its value is not lost if the same love is stronger in a new life because of what passed before.

If McTaggart's philosophy made sense to me, I found there were those who were concerned—as I was discovering of myself—with a *use* for past life recall: not just simply believing in it, but finding a purpose for it. In particular, psychologists had been using regressive hypnosis to uncover *past-life* traumas which were showing up in this life. A certain Dr. Helen Wambach had conducted a series of experiments, not in fact originally designed to assist patients, (although, in several instances, this was one of the results) but rather to establish the validity of past lives. In her book, *Reliving Past Lives*, she fully describes the genesis of her experiments,

how each of them was conducted, and the extraordinary results of her investigations into past-life recall of over one thousand subjects, each of whom made at least three "trips," each of whom was asked the same questions on each trip. The results, written down before they had discussed each trip with anyone else, were then correlated by time period, social strata, race, type of food eaten, clothing, architecture, and other cross-reference points.

This book, perhaps more than any other, left no doubt in my mind that we have indeed lived past lives. For me it became a matter of exploring further for myself—when I could take the time to do so. For I was still in the midst of my tour, accompanied by bags full of books . . .

I played Europe, Australia, Canada, Scandinavia, and America. I played in the theaters at night, and read and scanned, and skimmed and read during the day. I found I was meeting people who, over drinks and dinner after the show, professed hidden interests of their own in reincarnation and memory feelings that they couldn't define or explain. Some had had out-of-body experiences, some had done trance channeling themselves, some had had past-life recall that they were sure was real but were reluctant to discuss for fear of appearing weird.

I talked with Gerry from exotic parts of the world but it was difficult to discuss my growing interest in spiritual metaphysics on long distance lines, or indeed in any way at all. I wished that we could meet, but my schedule never fitted into his availability, and vice versa. With each stilted conversation I was aware of how deeply grounded in his politics he was, and also that my attitude toward his reluctance to express any interest in my concern for expanded consciousness was one of growing impatience. I found myself remembering that "John" had said I should allow people in my life to conduct their awareness capacity at their own pace: allow the skeptics their skepticism. In fact, I didn't necessarily believe *all* I was reading and learning—but I longed for someone I was really involved with to be interested in the possibilities of other

dimensions. Reality was a subjective truth and I knew my reality was expanding. I felt more aware and more able to cope with ideas of my own inner reality: and I sure as hell wanted to talk to someone about them.

The tour was a joy. The work was hard but rewarding, and some of the people I met along the way seemed quietly involved with their own search for deeper identity. Many told me that psychiatric help did not go deep enough: that there were events and traumas even earlier than the lifetime they found themselves in today. Many said they felt their childhood conditioning and experience did not explain some of their deep-seated fears and anxieties. I listened with guarded astonishment that there could be so *many* people thinking that way.

One episode in particular struck me as it was both coherent and touched off very unexpectedly. An old friend of mine from Ireland whom I hadn't seen for years described a recent trip he had taken to Japan; he said he was calmly strolling along a street in Kyoto when he spotted a Samurai outfit in the window of a Japanese antique shop. He stopped as though riveted and stared at the outfit that he "knew" had belonged to him. He said he remembered the sword, how the material had felt next to his skin and the way in which he swaggered as he wore it. As he stood staring at the ancient garments, scenes of battle flooded through his memory until he remembered having died wearing that uniform. He said he walked in to inquire about buying it but it was not for sale. As he related the story to me he said he was surprised that he felt free enough to actually express what he believed about having lived a lifetime in Japan. I nodded and listened, wondering when I myself would possibly begin to remember lifetimes that I may have had before.

And so for about three months I toured, talked to people, and read. I tried on new thoughts and new assumptions with each country I visited. I began to be more free in applying my new ideas to the life and work around me. I was selective with whom I

discussed what I was feeling, but more often than not I found this wasn't necessary.

I returned to Malibu for a rest and to reexamine my notes and try to sort out my thinking. I wasn't sure how to approach what was on my mind. When one first discovers new awarenesses it can be confusing. So I did a lot of walking on the beach, and sometimes, with one of my books, I would sit under a tree in the small park near the health food restaurant in Malibu.

One afternoon after carrot juice and a tofu burger, a friend of mine with whom I had had a deeply personal love affair happened by and found me under my tree. He was a writer and TV director from New York and he could be extremely caustic and cynically witty. I knew him well—in fact his quirky brilliance had been a major factor in keeping me interested in him for quite a number of years.

At first I felt a tap on the head which had usually been the way he said hello. I knew it was Mike right away. He was puffing on his pipe, casually clad in jeans, T-shirt and leather jacket. You could tell he was intelligent from this costume—the I'm-just-a-bum-who-doesn't-care look.

Without any preamble he said, "What's happening? Where have you been for the past year?"

"Oh, around," I said. "I've been on tour all over the world. Got back a few days ago."

"Ahh," said Mike, "still have that mystical wanderlust, eh?" He surprised me a bit with this insight. But he was continuing, "You've really combined your work with your wanderlust pretty well, haven't you? That's good. I could always tell when you wanted to get out and look around."

I sat up on my knees as he plopped down beside me. "Did you really always know that about me?" I asked, seeing an aspect to him that had not been evident to me when we were together.

"Sure," he said. "But I didn't want you to go, so I never mentioned it. Honest, eh?"

We sat for a moment and smiled at each other. "It's good to see you," he said, really meaning it, and immediately went on. "Something's on your mind. I hear you've been keeping to yourself a lot, except for some secret guy you keep making trips to Europe to see."

Oh, brother, I thought. Sometimes the world was too much of a golf ball.

But I laughed. So did Mike . . . not really expecting me to go into my love life.

"Tell me something, old friend," I said, "do you think I'm naive? I mean do you think I'm the kind of person who believes everything I'm told?"

Mike puffed on his pipe, suddenly serious, as though understanding (as he always had) that I was concerned about character traits in myself that I was unaware of.

"No," he answered, "I wouldn't say you were naive. You've got a really tough inquiring mind. But I do think you sometimes read good into things that isn't really there."

"What do you mean?"

"Well, for example, when you went to China you *wanted* the revolution there to be successful so I think you tended to overlook areas which were a problem. Of course I know you only saw what they wanted you to see so I can understand your positive assessment of what was happening there. But that's what I mean."

"Well, what did you mean a moment ago when you called me mystical?"

"Shirley, you always had an understanding somehow that sounded like Eastern philosophy to me. I don't know. I called it abstract for a while there but you seemed attracted to ideas that weren't exactly meat and potatoes. You know I always wanted to know who collected the garbage, and you wanted to know what was underneath the garbage collector's mind."

"Yeah," I said, going over other relationships I had had where I had heard the same complaint. "Is that a complaint, Mike?"

"No," he answered, "not at all. Its just the way you are. You always wanted to get underneath everything, looking for a deeper meaning. I admire that. It can drive a guy nuts but it made me look deeper too."

I smiled. He smiled. A pair of ex-lovers smiling about appreciating each other. Mike leaned over me and picked up my book.

"What's this?" he asked.

"Oh, just a book."

"On reincarnation?"

"Yeah."

"Oh."

"Yeah."

"Why?"

"I don't know." I swallowed, deciding whether or not to get into the discussion. "I think it might be true. And I'm just reading a lot about it."

Mike looked into my eyes. "So you've gone California, eh?"

"California?"

"Yeah. Everybody out here is into that stuff. Only California could elect a Governor Moonbeam, right?"

"I guess so," I answered tentatively. "But I've found it lots of other places too."

"Yeah? Where?"

"Oh, Mike. All over the world."

"For example?"

When Mike decided to interrogate, you felt like you were on trial.

"Well, on tour I talked with lots of people in Europe, Australia, Canada. Wherever."

"Yeah? What did they say?"

"They told stories. Sometimes they remembered real past-life experiences. Sometimes it was just a feeling they had—or sometimes the déjà vu thing."

"Yeah," he said, "I have proof that there is life *after* death."

"What do you mean?" I asked, pleasantly surprised that maybe we could have a dialogue here. "What proof?"

"The Congress of the United States," said Mike.

I laughed but my tummy turned over. Oh God, I thought, I might as well get the full treatment. "That's funny," I said.

"I'll tell you," he said, "I think we've got enough trouble in the world here and now. I'm not too interested in whether I was an Egyptian slave five thousand years ago."

Of course I found myself wondering why he came up with that particular image but I let it go. "Have you ever heard of trance channeling?" I asked.

"You mean that stuff Oliver Lodge wrote about at the turn of the century in England? He got in touch with his dead son or something?"

Mike floored me. I knew he read nearly everything there was to read but I couldn't imagine him haunting the occult bookstores.

"Yeah," I answered, "Lodge did a lot of psychical research which was never explained—other than the fact that it must have happened."

"So what have you got to do with that? Are you getting in touch with Chou En Lai through a medium?" Mike knew that I thought Chou En Lai was attractive and that I would probably have gone to any lengths to meet him!

"No," I answered, "not Chou. But maybe it's possible to get in touch with disembodied spiritual guides who were once in the body and are not any longer."

Mike leaned back on his elbow and chewed on his pipe. "You want to tell me about it?" he asked.

I took out a cigarette and lit it. Very carefully I outlined what had been happening. I told him about Ambres in Sweden, about John and McPherson and Kevin in California. I told him that many people were learning through trance channeling all over the world. And that I realized some mediums might be phony but that

did not rule out all of them. I told him about the past-life information I had heard about myself, along with the teachings of spiritual love and God and extraterrestrials having supposedly brought the same message. I told him how I had read and read about other people in the world, past and present, who also felt an affinity toward having lived before. I mentioned all the famous, intelligent, artistic, philosophic, scientific, and even religious leaders I could think of to whom reincarnation was an accepted part of their lives —and I was defensive enough to conclude my presentation by reminding Mike that I was in pretty good company.

He took his pipe from his teeth and sat up, hunched over.

"Shirl," he said, "I'm Mike, remember? I'm on *your* side, right?"

I said nothing. Just looked at him.

"I mean," he went on, "a person goes into a trance and another voice comes out of their mouth and you sit there and believe what you're hearing?"

I kept quiet.

"Look," he went on, "people would have to say what's happened to our Shirley? They tell you about past lives, they tell you about extraterrestrials, for God's sake! It's preposterous! You sound gullible and ridiculous. I don't like to see you put yourself in that position."

I sucked on my straw, making a grating sound on the bottom of the empty cup. "Who is 'people'?" I said. "That's why I asked *you* if you thought I was naive. You see, Mike, I don't feel naive, or gullible. I feel inquiring. I want to know. I feel that anything is possible—and why the hell not?"

"But do you *believe* it?"

"I don't know. I'm just about convinced on the matter of past lives, and hence reincarnation—just on empirical evidence. I'm in the middle of finding out a bunch of other new stuff. It's a process of considering new dimensions. It's a whole damn fascinating world that I'm not willing to throw out the window and I don't see

anything naive about that. I've always been open-minded, right?"

"Right."

"Well, I guess that's what I'm continuing to be. The only thing is right now I'm a bit confused about whether there is such a thing as actual 'reality.' I mean reality seems to be so relative."

"Wait a minute," Mike protested, "just hang in there a minute. When a Hollywood producer screws a writer out of his salary—that's *real*."

"Sure. It's real to *him*. Maybe it becomes real to his kids because for the first time in their lives they become conscious of want, or deprivation. But being screwed out of a house, car, TV set, clothing, warmth, food—all that is absolutely meaningless, not *real*, don't you see, to millions of people who have never, ever had those things. And it is just as *unreal* to a handful at the other extreme who have always had everything. So maybe it isn't the money part that's important. Maybe there's a lesson in that. Maybe life is about *lessons* and *that*'s reality."

"Well, what's the lesson in a man not being able to feed his kids?"

"I don't really know, Mike," I answered. "It didn't happen to me. But if it had I would try to figure it out rather than let it rest at being pissed off. I would try to find out *why* and not lay the whole thing on someone who had screwed me."

"Oh shit," he said. "Are you saying that you'll just sit back with all this God and love crap and allow yourself to be fucked over?"

Mike's eloquence was uplifting at times.

"No, I'm not saying that. I'm saying that perhaps I wouldn't actually be fucked over. Perhaps, what looks like fucked-overness is really something I needed to experience in order to understand myself better. Besides, that stuff goes on all the time anyway whether you allow it to happen or not. So I guess I'm saying if I decide not to allow it I'll have to go to war, right?"

"War?" asked Mike.

"Sure. You can extend this example to a worldwide scene of

haves and have-nots. It's the same dilemma. But if we never really actually die anyway, then life becomes a question of how we handle a situation of injustice rather than not allowing it to happen by violent means."

Mike leaned back against the tree. A cloud passed in front of the sun and a scream of seagulls took off as though they had made a collective decision to leave. "Do you realize," said Mike, "that every despot in the world has taken advantage of that kind of thinking and gone on to cause incomprehensible suffering? To support that philosophy is despicably self-righteous. I mean, to teach that everyone should turn the other cheek is an open invitation to tyranny. I believe in self-determination and revolution if some bastard is doing me wrong."

"So then you're agreeing with killing if *you* are the one who feels it is necessary?"

"If some guy is trying to kill me first, yeah."

"Okay," I said, "I understand that. That is certainly the usual way out. But I'm wondering if we ever really kill our enemies anyway. Regardless of what one's reason is for killing another person, I mean whether it's personal or because some government or maybe religious authority tells one to, if the law of cause and effect is in operation—and that *is* at the root of reincarnation—then what have you accomplished except to accumulate a lot of bad karma? If death, meaning oblivion, a final end, is not a reality, what's the point of killing? If we could 'prove,' as they say, that killing is *not* an answer, is ultimately self-defeating in a literal sense, maybe more than a few good minds would look for other solutions."

"It's a bit esoteric," Mike said. "I can see why you have to worry at it because that's the kind of mind you have. And I guess you're bound and determined to unravel the knot to your own satisfaction. But Shirl, what's it going to do to you?"

"How d'you mean?"

"Well, shit," he said, "people will wonder what's happened to

you. I mean they don't know you like I do, they'll think you've gone off the deep end with no paddles in the water."

Mike was genuinely concerned for me just as Bella was—even as Gerry had been. But why such concepts should be so personally threatening to Mike was another issue. Why he couldn't relate with open-mindedness instead of anxiety was of course what I was concerned about, and not just in Mike.

"But Mike," I said, "don't you find nearly everyone has wondered about this stuff in one way or another? Don't you think everyone has had something happen to them that they can't explain?"

"Sure they have. But they just leave it unexplained. Why do you feel you have to develop this elaborate set of beliefs in order to explain things that are probably better off left alone?"

I was defensive enough to feel somewhat exasperated. "Who *says* they are better off left alone? What's so good about the status quo that the world wants to preserve it as is? I'm looking for *better* answers, Mike. Part of it is just plain cussed curiosity I guess—I've always wanted to know why a rose was red, or a thought was strong. Surface explanations have never been enough for me so I suppose it is inevitable that I would carry my questioning all the way through—wherever it brings me out."

Mike took my hand and patted it. "Well, a lot of other folks couldn't leave well enough alone, like Louis Pasteur or Madame Curie. And look what they came up with. So who knows? But what bothers me is that what they did was *all* they did. They didn't have to depend on audiences not being alienated to make a living. I don't want that to happen to you."

"I don't think that'll happen, Mike. Anyway, it's the most meaningful thing in my life right now—to put it mildly. I just can't leave it alone. And when I go the limit with my identity or anyone else's identity I ultimately get to the fuller identity of what might have gone before this life. I mean I can see where you and I might have had a karmic relationship in a life before this one. I can see that we

were together this time around because there was stuff still left to work out from before."

"You mean maybe this conversation is part of working that out?"

"Could be."

"Well. But I can only handle this life. That gives me enough to think about. And I don't see how understanding any of what you're talking about will help me raise the bail for a friend of mine who got busted for coke."

Mike got up and stretched. "Be careful, Shirl. That's all, okay?"

"Okay."

"Wanna walk?"

"Sure."

We put our arms around each other and walked out from under the tree toward the mountains. Mike leaned over and whispered in my ear, "So tell me. In our last lifetime together did you make secret trips to Europe to see me?"

✸ That evening I felt really tired. I decided to take it real easy, maybe not do any writing that night. At the end of the day I sat out on my balcony and watched the wind play on gusts of sand as the sun set. The low glasslike tide reflected a glow of pink-orange. I wondered when the grunion were supposed to run and how they knew they were supposed to. I wondered if fish had souls.

A lone figure walked along the shallow rippling waves about a mile down the coast. I watched him. I always wondered what other people thought about when they walked at sunset. Some walked with purpose, some ambled and others walked as though they weren't walking at all—perhaps they were somewhere else. This lone figure walked as though he were looking for someone. He didn't look much out to sea but more at the direction of the build-

ings on their pilings. He was eating something, an apple. He carried a pair of sandals in his other hand and walked with a slumped left shoulder. I looked closer as he came nearer. He saw me looking at him from above and waved. It was David.

Oh my God, I thought. Now what? When he reached the front of my building he stopped, smiled, waved again and yelled up at me. ❀

Chapter 17

"I maintain that cosmic religious feeling is the strongest and noblest incitement to scientific research."

—Albert Einstein
The World As I See It

"Hi," he said. "It's beautiful down here."

I got up and leaned on the railing. David was wearing a sweater over a shirt and a pair of white gym socks hung from the back pocket of his slacks.

"How are you?" I called.

He threw his cigarette into the waves. "Come on down and walk," he yelled. "Let's walk up to the big rock. Then if you feel like it, we can have some dinner at Holiday House."

I straightened up from the railing.

"But bring a sweater," he yelled. "It'll be cold later."

I got the woolen sweater that had been around the world with me, the green one Gerry loved, and climbed down the wooden stairs leading to the sand, feeling that I was seeing David for the first time—and in some respects wishing I had never met him at all. I was feeling bruised from the encounter with Mike which I was far from having sorted through.

David looked at me hard when I joined him. "Are you okay?" he said.

"Okay, fine, just fine."

"I see," he said, as we began to walk into the sun. "So you've been thinking a lot, eh?"

"Haven't had time, really," I said noncommittally.

He lit a cigarette.

"You sure do smoke a lot," I commented. "Why d'you smoke so much if you're into this spiritual stuff and all squared away with yourself?"

"I don't know," he said. "I guess it helps to ground me. Otherwise I'd be out on Cloud Thirty-nine all the time. Wouldn't you smoke if you really got into it?"

"Smoke?" My voice was a little shrill. "I'd be inhaling giant redwoods if I really believed all I'm learning about."

"Yeah," he said, "it's scary at first, like everything new is, but after a while you learn to desensitize yourself. Smoking is one way to do it. Also, I'm addicted."

We walked a way in the cold sand. The sandpipers did their sundown minuet. I felt I was doing my own minuet with David. For a time I said nothing. Then I thought I might as well.

"I guess you know," I said, "that we're old friends and have been married before?"

"Yeah," he laughed, "I know."

"Who from?"

"Oh, around. We're lifetime partners or something, right?"

"Hmm."

He puffed on his cigarette and looked up into the sunset. He had a way of sounding so sure of things he was almost pompous.

"You know," I said, "I've been thinking. When the astronauts travel out there in space, are there spirits all around the space capsules?"

David laughed and coughed. "Well yeah," he said. "You could say that because the spirit world is everywhere, even around us right now. I mean the spiritual plane is invisible to us most of the time because our consciousness is too dense to see them, but we aren't invisible to them. And you can feel it sometimes, can't you? I mean, don't you really wonder sometimes where certain ideas and inspirations come from? Don't you sometimes feel you are

actually being guided by some invisible force? You know how so many of the great minds have talked about really feeling an invisible kind of inspirational force? Well, I think it's probably their spiritual guides as well as a kind of recall from a talent they experienced in a past lifetime. You can see it in child prodigies. I mean, Mozart was probably playing the piano at four because he was *remembering* how."

"David," I said, interrupting his dissertation, "what proof is there that all this stuff is true? I mean really. You can sound like an asshole spouting off these theories like it's fact and Santa Claus is real."

"Well, there's no question about it to me. I just feel it. I believe it. I know it. That's all. Of course there's no proof. So what? But the connection between the spiritual and physical planes is what's missing in the world today. To me, the soul is the missing link to life. I mean if everyone understood that their souls never really die, they wouldn't be so frightened, and they would understand *why* they're alive as well."

Every time David opened his mouth he delivered a spiritual sermon.

"So," I said, "what you're saying is that reincarnation is like show business. You just keep doing it until you get it right."

"Yeah." He had the good humor to laugh. "Something like that. You know," he continued, "I'm convinced that Christ was teaching the theory of reincarnation."

I wrapped my turtleneck sweater closer around my neck. Everything gave me chills these days. When David made one of his statements, he never gave it a buildup.

"Why do you think that?" I said, remembering what John had told me about the Bible.

David swished his feet in the water, breaking the mirrored reflection below us in the sand. "I've read a lot about the interpretations of Christ's teaching other than what appears in the Bible." He

looked into my face and hesitated. "You know that nothing is recorded in the Bible about Christ from the time he was about twelve until he began to really teach at about thirty years old. Right?"

"Yes," I said. "I had heard about that and I just figured he didn't have much to say until he got older."

"Well, no," said David, "a lot of people think that those eighteen missing years were spent traveling in and around India and Tibet and Persia and the Near East. There are all kinds of legends and stories about a man who sounds just like Christ. His description is matched everywhere and he said he was the Son of God and he corroborated the beliefs of the Hindus that reincarnation was in fact true. They say he became an adept yogi and mastered complete control over his body and the physical world around him. He evidently went around doing all those miracles that were recorded later in the Bible and tried to teach people that they could do the same things too if they got more in touch with their spiritual selves and their own potential power."

David did not know about my session with Kevin and John, nor that I had met a woman at The Ashram, a kind of protege of Sai Baba's (an avatar in India). She and her husband had written a book and done a documentary film on the missing years of Christ. Their names were Janet and Richard Bock and they had done extensive research on that period in Christ's life on Earth. They had compiled stacks of evidence researched by respected archeologists, theologians, students of Sanskrit and Hebrew writings, et cetera. All seemed to agree that Christ had indeed traveled extensively in India.

As we walked I told David about Janet and Richard and he said he had never met them but would love to compare the notes he had made when he spent two years in India researching the same thing. He said when Christ returned to Israel he taught what he had learned from the Indian masters, that is, the theory of reincarnation.

"But David," I said, "why aren't these teachings recorded in the Bible?"

"They are," he said. "The theory of reincarnation *is* recorded in the Bible. But the proper interpretations were struck from it during an Ecumenical Council meeting of the Catholic Church in Constantinople sometime around 553 A.D., called the Council of Nicea. The Council members voted to strike those teachings from the Bible in order to solidify Church control.

"The Church needed to be the sole authority where the destiny of man was concerned, but Christ taught that every human being was responsible for his or her own destiny—now and future. Christ said there was only one judge—God—and he was very opposed to the formation of a church of any kind, or any other kind of ceremonial religion that might enslave man's free will or his struggle for truth."

This confirmed what Kevin had said, but it seemed logical that anyone heavily into reincarnation would have read about that famous Council.

The sun began to set behind the waves now, sweeping a pink-purple slash across the clouds above the Pacific.

"Anyway," said David, "that's what I believe Christ was really doing and when the Church destroyed those teachings, it screwed up mankind from then on."

I didn't answer him. I thought that if the Church *had* been teaching that our souls were involved in a continual physical embodiment in order to work out Karmic Justice, I would have been interested in it from the time I was little. *That* would have made sense to me. It would have given me a *reason* to believe in the spiritual dimension of man, because *I* would have been responsible for my own destiny (and so would everyone else). It would be up to our own consciences, not up to the Church to judge our behavior. And it also would have explained all the suffering and horror in the world which all my life had rendered me helplessly incapable of understanding or altering. "Whatsoever a man

soweth, that shall he also reap," would have taken on a different meaning. And it would have given me a deep-rooted comfort that we did indeed live forever and eternally according to our actions and reactions as we went along. "Turn the other cheek" would have had new meaning also. In fact, it would have been more possible because we would have held our eternal priorities higher than our earthly problems.

The law of cause and effect was accepted in science as fundamental. Why wasn't that same law operable where human life was concerned? Laws were not always based on what we could see, and therefore prove. Morality, ethics, love—these were not visible, tangible things. But that didn't mean they were not there.

I was not an expert in science or any of the given fields of provable facts. But, I was slowly beginning to wonder why these fields mattered so much. I didn't see much value in physical proofs when it came to the struggle of understanding why we were alive. Such a struggle belonged to each individual personally and in the deepest sense. It didn't necessarily belong in the domain of "experts" of any variety. Maybe that's what was meant by "the meek shall inherit the earth." Perhaps the meek who didn't see any need to act "strong" were those who related to God and the goodness of life and *mankind*; and the Golden Rule *was* the first and last axiom to live by. Maybe all those who tended to complicate life out of fear were adding, not only to the karmic complexities of the earth itself, but also to the karmic complexities of their own lives.

David and I walked on in silence. We walked to the public beach about three miles up the coast where he had parked his car.

It was an old Dodge, green, and in the back seat was a stack of books tied with string. "I brought you some more books, plus a Bible. Just read and see what you think. Want to go eat?" Books? I needed more books?

We sat together in the restaurant above the sea. Whenever we talked, it was never small talk—never, "How was your day?" or

"Do you like Brahms?" It was always big talk, as though chat would have been a waste of time. It was unusual for me not to be personal where a man was concerned because the "personal conversation" was usually a lead up to what we both wanted from each other . . . either clues to character or indications of goals in life.

This was different. I wasn't interested in this man in that way. I was interested in what he had to say. I guess all people establish a set of unstated but understood rules of communication when they're together one on one. It's something you don't think about, but it's there and in operation until one of the two breaks what's established and attempts to go on to another level.

David didn't seem interested in breaking what was established either. It made me comfortable, and I instinctively knew that what we had was how it was going to be. Paradoxically, this created an atmosphere in which each encounter with this man who was partially responsible for my deeply questioning our perceptions of reality was a new experience for me.

So, even though we had a delicious Bordeaux wine and a really good beef Wellington, and even though there were candles on the table and we were deeply engrossed each in what the other was saying, and even though some of the other patrons wondered who it was I was with, I never felt inclined to relate to him on a man-woman level, and I didn't really care specifically how he came to believe what he believed. This process was usually an abstract evolution of thinking, anyway. At least, it had been in my case, prompted by a few specific moments that motivated me further. We talked instead about the *need* for faith and a feeling of purpose, about whether the human race had progressed by itself or with some kind of spiritual "guidance," and finally, about the wisdom of being open-minded about all new concepts.

David spoke of how open-mindedness was the mark of real intelligence to him because "only an open-minded person can embrace new ideas and grow."

"I went through a lot of confusion," he said, "when I first started making my spiritual connections. But whenever I felt sort of 'absurd' in the 'real' world around me, I'd stop myself and listen to what my own intuition was telling me was real. I had been conditioned to believe in what I could prove rather than what I could sense. But the more I listened to my own inner voice, the more I got in touch with myself. It finally all became so simple. And now, so many people are doing the same thing that *that* has become what is real."

David didn't seem to be reviewing his belief struggles as any kind of identifiable blueprint for me. It was more just simply what he'd been through. And when he talked, it was with that same calm dignity.

Then, somewhere near the end of the dinner, he asked, "Have you ever seen a UFO?"

I was a bit startled to hear such a question from him. It was one thing to hear "John" discuss God, spiritual truth and extraterrestrials in one breath, and quite another to have a personal friend apparently about to make the same connection.

"No," I said casually, "but I know a few people who have, including Jimmy Carter when he was Governor of Georgia. Carter never talked about it to me, but I saw the report he filed in the newspaper, and it seemed to be professional and unemotional, like most of the reports Jimmy Carter files."

"Right," said David. "What do you think they are?"

"God," I said, "I don't know. Maybe they're secret military weapons nobody will talk about, or maybe they're weather contraptions, or maybe they're hoaxes, or maybe they're from outer space. I don't know. What do you think?"

He sipped his coffee and cognac and wiped the edges of his mouth with his napkin. "I think," he said, "they are from outer space. I think the extraterrestrials in them are highly evolved spiritually. And I think they've been here for a long time."

"For God's sake!" I said. "What makes you think that?" I watched him as he swallowed another sip of coffee. I watched how his eyes blinked calmly over the candlelight. I watched for any expression that would indicate what he was getting at . . . why he should mention such a thing in relation to what we were talking about.

"Well, a lot of people have written about them."

"A lot of kooks have."

"And they're all over the Old Testament. There are all sorts of descriptions that sound like spacecraft to me, and to many others, of course." Again I was reminded of "John," and indeed of my own readings. But David was continuing, "I think Von Daniken is a little kooky, but I believe he's on the right track."

"You mean *Chariots of the Gods* Von Daniken?"

"Yes."

I could feel my "open mind" threatening to snap shut.

"Didn't he do time in a Swiss jail for passing bad checks?"

"Sure. But what's that got to do with what he uncovered? People are full of contradictions and what he did was wrong. He should have found another way to solve his problems because in the end he discredited himself. But not necessarily his work."

After the session with "John" I read all of Von Daniken's work —material that described his contention that many ancient ruins had in fact been constructed by highly advanced civilizations with extraterrestrial help: the Great Pyramid, Stonehenge, Machu Picchu in Peru, the airstrips on the Nazca Plains in Peru, etc.

He also contended that, for example, Ezekiel's descriptions of wheels of fire were spacecraft as well as the pillar of fire that guided Moses and the Israelites for forty years in the desert, culminating with the parting of the Red Sea.

I saw the film *Chariots of the Gods* which alluded to the presence of extraterrestrials all through human history, offering cave

drawings and monuments as proof of this contention. What had struck me as I watched the film was the reaction of the audience. They were riveted to the screen and when the film was over, no one got up to leave. They seemed genuinely entranced by the speculations yet unsure how to react. I listened carefully to people as they filed out of the theater. No one made sarcastic remarks or ridiculed the information. In fact, they weren't threatened or intimidated one way or the other. They just filed out silently thinking to themselves until someone mentioned a hamburger. I remember being more interested in their reaction to the film than I was in my own reaction to it.

And now, just as John had done, David tied in UFOs with spiritual intelligence. I listened and questioned him further.

"You mean," I asked, "that angels and chariots spitting fire and things like that in the Bible were really people from another world?"

"Yes, why wouldn't advanced alien beings try to teach us higher spiritual truth? Maybe the God-force is really scientific. I mean, Christ and Moses and some of those people were capable of producing physical miracles, as we call them, that our science can't explain. And too many people are reported to have seen those 'miracles' to allow them to be simply made-up myths. It's got to be that the gifted ones knew something we don't know."

I took a sip of David's brandy.

"Listen," I said, "how did you come to make the connection between the spiritual possibilities of man and outer space?"

"Because," he said, "it makes sense, doesn't it? I mean, there is so much unexplained superior intelligence in ancient history and so much of it relates to religion and spirituality, or at least to the question of God."

"Well, yes," I said, "but that intelligence could have been extremely advanced human civilizations right here on Earth which disappeared or vanished or did themselves in or something. Why

does superior intelligence have to come from some other world?"

"Well," he said, "I asked myself that too. But you see there wasn't just one example of superior intelligence. It happened all over the world and at different times. According to Plato and Aristotle and lots of other great minds, Atlantis *really* existed as an extremely advanced civilization. The Incas and the Mayans had as much astronomical and astrological knowledge as we have today, and maybe more. The Sumerians, who lived two thousand years before Christ, had highly developed mathematics and astronomy . . . I mean, I'll give you some more stuff to read, but it indicates to me that this Earth has been observed and helped and taught throughout its human history by beings that knew more than we do; who knew spiritual as well as scientific, astronomical, mathematical, and physical truths that we are only beginning to fathom."

The brandy was gone. And I felt my mind checking out.

"So, why couldn't humans have learned it themselves?"

David pressed on, downing the ice water which was left.

"Because there's too much evidence to indicate that humans had help from 'gods,' from people who were advanced in a *cosmic* sense. Too many of the writings of ancient cultures talk about the 'gods' who went to and from the stars in fiery flying machines bringing 'help and knowledge and promises of immortality.' So I said to myself—why not? No healthy-minded scientist today believes we are the only life in the universe—right?"

"Yes."

"Well, it's worth thinking about, isn't it? I mean, why not take it seriously? It makes sense. It's wild according to some accepted points of view, but it makes sense. Since you're into all this, you might as well go further. Sorry to be so relentless."

We paid the check (Dutch treat) and got up from our table. I was exhausted. By now my earthbound frustration with Gerry looked good. Relentless, David had called himself? *That* was a term usually applied to me. *I* was usually the relentless one with

whatever I wanted to figure out. Now somebody was out-relent-lessing me.

David gave me his stack of books and dropped me off at my beach apartment.

We had talked about life after death, life before birth, and now we were into life above life!

I thanked him and said goodnight. ❋

Chapter 18

"True fortitude of understanding consists in not letting what we know to be embarrassed by what we don't know."

—Ralph Waldo Emerson
The Skeptic

I had read concentratedly in the area of channeling and then on the subject of reincarnation, and always for my own spiritual guidance. I concentrated now on a new viewpoint—the possibility of extraterrestrial life and its connection to human life.

I read for days, until my eyes hurt.

A very brief synopsis follows of what I read. Much of this research was important to me in relation to what happened to me later. With respect to the Bible, I use its terminology—that is, angels, pillars of fire, and so on—because these are the words used by the ancients to describe phenomena in the terms understandable in their day.

In the book of Ezekiel in the Old Testament, Ezekiel described what the Earth looked like from great heights. He talked of what it was like to be lifted into a flying ship almost as though by a magnet. He described the back and forth movement of the vehicle as something fast as lightning. He referred to the commander of the craft as "The Lord."

Ezekiel encountered people and ships like that four different times over a period of nineteen years. He spoke of how peaceful the people from the ships were when they *made contact with humans,* going to great pains to avoid causing fear. There was no sign of "hostility or reckless attitudes." He said "The Lord" showed care and respect for him.

In the book of Exodus a vehicle that moved and led the Hebrews out of Egypt to the Red Sea was described as "a pillar of cloud by day and a pillar of fire by night." The pillar hovered over the waters and parted them enabling the Israelites to escape into the wilderness. The "pillar" that led the Israelites for forty years as they wandered in the wilderness gave religious guidance all during that period, and an "angel within" provided Moses with the Ten Commandments. "Angels" are all over the Bible—in fact, the Bible more than suggests that "angels" were missionaries from another world.

During that forty-year period the Israelites were without a source for food or sustenance. But the "pillar of fire" was in charge. The Lord said to Moses, "Behold, I will rain bread from heaven for you" (Exodus 16:4).

The "cloudy pillar" served as a beacon for Israel's journeys in the wilderness. "For throughout all their journeys the cloud of the Lord was upon the tabernacle by day, and fire was in it by night, in the sight of all of the house of Israel" (Exodus 40:38).

The book of Numbers is more specific. The cloudy pillar directed every move the Israelites made. When the cloud moved the people moved, when the cloud stopped the people rested and made another camp (Numbers 9:15–23).

Moses was in day-to-day contact with a being in the "cloudy pillar." The Lord spoke to the people one day saying "Hear my words; if there is a prophet among you, I, the Lord, make myself known to him in a vision, I speak with him in a dream. Not so with my servant Moses; he is entrusted with all my house. With him I speak mouth to mouth, clearly and not in dark speech; and he beholds the form of the Lord" (Numbers 12:6–8).

Until Exodus the Israelites didn't really have a religion. They believed in a kind of promise. But during a forty-year period of wandering in the wilderness, angels implanted the gospel and religion from another world—the Kingdom of Heaven.

A select group of people was instructed in a course of behavior

and ethics and worship . . . Moses, Abraham, Peter, St. Luke, Jacob, and so on. Jacob encountered angels on many occasions. Once he encountered so many he said, "This is God's Army" (Genesis 32:2). The teachings were very concerned that people on Earth learn the values of love, the Golden Rule, and belief in life everlasting.

In the book of Acts, Christ instructed his disciples to take the message of *his* world to all of *their* world.

In the New Testament Christ said: "You are from below, I am from above; You are of this world, I am not of this world" (John 8:23). He said he was in constant contact with beings from his world and he called them "angels." He said the angels were very concerned about the success of their message on Earth.

When I finished reading the Bible notations, I turned to David's other books.

On the Plains of Nazca in Peru there are what appear to be airstrips thousands of years old, and at the same location there are earth paintings of animals, birds, and a figure with a helmet similar in shape to those used by our modern day astronauts. The airstrips and drawings can only be seen from an airplane at a fairly high altitude.

The astrological calendar of Tiahuanaco in the City of Tiahuanaco, 13,000 feet high, symbolically recorded astrological knowledge based on the premise of a round Earth 27,000 years ago. The revolutions of the Earth in accordance with the sun, moon and other planets were all correct.

The Legend of Tiahuanaco told of a golden spaceship coming from the stars.

At Sacsahuaman lies a monument of rock 20,000 tons in weight which was extracted and transported from some distance away and then turned upside down.

Sand vitrifications had been found in the Gobi Desert and at old Iraqi archeological sites, resembling the vitrifications of sand produced by the atomic explosions in the Nevada desert in our times.

Cuneiform texts and tablets from Ur, one of the oldest writings of mankind, told of gods who rode in the heavens in "ships" or gods who came from the stars possessing terrible and powerful weapons and returning again to their stars.

The Eskimos talked of the first tribes brought to the north by gods with metal wings.

The oldest American Indian sages mentioned a thunderbird who introduced fire and fruit to them.

The Mayan legends spoke of how the "gods" were able to recognize everything: the universe, the four cardinal points of the compass, and the round shape of the Earth. The Mayan calendar was so highly developed that its calculations projected for sixty-four million years.

The religious legends of the pre-Inca people said that the stars were inhabited and that "gods" came down to them from the constellation of the Pleiades. Sumerian, Assyrian, Babylonian and Egyptian cuneiform inscriptions presented the same picture: "gods" came from the stars and went back to them; they traveled in fireships or boats of the air, and possessed terrifying and powerful weapons and promised immortality to individual people.

The ancient Indian epic, Mahahbarata, about 5000 years old, talked of flying machines, navigated at great heights over vast distances, that could travel forward, backward, upward, and downward at incredible speeds.

In the Tibetan books, *Tantyua* and *Kantyua*, there were constant mentions of flying machines in prehistory. These they called "pearls in the sky." Both books emphasized that the information was secret and not for the masses. Whole chapters in the Samarangava Sutradhara were devoted to describing airships whose tails spouted "fire" and "quicksilver."

Ancient peoples lifted hundreds of tons of stone from one place to another. The Egyptians brought their obelisk from Aswan, the architects of Stonehenge brought their stone blocks from southwest Wales and Marlborough, the stonemasons of Easter Island

(known to the natives as the Island of the Bird Man) brought their ready-made statues from quarries miles away.

And the Great Pyramid of Giza stood unexplained.

David's notes said that according to scientific and geological research today, the Great Pyramid is constructed on the exact geophysical land center of the Earth. In other words, if one were to spread the land masses of Earth out flat, the Pyramid would be in the exact epicenter. Its measurements correspond (using Pyramid inches) to the polar diameter and radius of the Earth and also accurately correspond to the measurements in time and movement of the equinoxes and the solar year. And that is only the beginning of the mathematical marvels *built into* the Pyramid of Cheops. Within the halls, rooms and passageways of the Pyramid, the measurements correspond in time to momentous historical events known to the civilizations of Earth, except that they were prophesied rather than simply recorded. The time frame of the great flood was prophesied accurately as well as the rise and fall of man's spiritual and worldly involvement; the birth of Christ and the crucifixion, the ruling of kingdoms by great leaders, outstanding wars between nations and the development of religious and moral movements among people. The two world wars were accurately prophesied in time as well as their respective post-war agreements. Again, I read that Christ's teachings about reincarnation were struck from the Bible during the Fifth Ecumenical Council meeting in Constantinople in the year 553 A.D. The *Catholic Encyclopedia* itself states, in regard to the Fifth Ecumenical Council meeting, that "anyone asserting the belief in the pre-existence of souls" would be anathema.

When I finished reading what David had given me I was exhausted. It was true that I had heard much of what I read in dribs and drabs throughout my life, but somehow having it compiled and organized in written form with respected and credible researchers and scientists and archeologists and theologians backing it up—it was different. The accumulation of evidence was too

powerful to take casually, much less dismiss. And it certainly wasn't possible for me to comfortably ignore.

I didn't know what I thought about it really. I only know I couldn't stop thinking about it.

I wondered why it was so new to me. Every now and then I'd see a scientist or someone like Carl Sagan allude to the "inevitability of extraterrestrial life in the cosmos" on television. But I hadn't seen anyone present all this overwhelming material at one time, which seemed to point to the need to take our extraterrestrial past more seriously—particularly in relation to spiritual understanding and the birth of monotheism.

I knew that whatever scientific argument one scientist might suggest was usually rejected by another. None of the "experts" seemed to agree on anything anyway. Perhaps this was why there had not been any really unified presentation, much less any unified approach of all the sciences to solving the problem.

And the same was true of the Church. I could just imagine some fundamentalist preacher expounding from his electronic pulpit on Sunday morning that Moses had been guided through the desert by a space craft.

I began to laugh. I sat on my balcony looking out at the minuet of the sandpipers and just laughed out loud. It was absurd. Everything was upside down.

One thing was for sure. As a child and adolescent and now as an adult living in the free land of American democracy, *I had not been educated to think beyond the perimeters of what my traditional teachers had wanted me to know.* Now I had to learn to think for myself. Maybe all of this was crazy, but Columbus wasn't the first person to say the world wasn't flat. And when you came to think of it, how arrogant of us to assume that we were the only rational, reasoning race in the universe.

Eventually David called.

"How're ya doing?" he asked.

"Oh, just sitting around with my head on crooked."

"Well, do you feel like taking a trip?"

Before I thought about it I said, "Sure. Where?"

"Peru."

"You mean the Andes?"

"Why not?"

"Why not? I have a couple of weeks. I don't care where I go. I just want to go somewhere."

"Meet me in Lima at the airport in two days."

"You're on." ❀

Chapter 19

"I am certain that I have been here as I am now a thousand times before, and I hope to return a thousand times. . . . Man is the dialogue between nature and God. On other planets this dialogue will doubtless be of a higher and profounder character. What is lacking is Self-Knowledge. After that the rest will follow."

—J. W. von Goethe
Memoirs of Johannes Falk

On the night flight to Peru it was like the old days when I took off whenever I wanted to—free and unencumbered. Spur-of-the-moment adventure—alone and traveling swiftly. I dropped contentedly to sleep.

When I woke up I was over Lima. Somewhere under the soup of smog there was a coastal city. It was worse than Los Angeles. I filled out my entrance card, declared the money I had brought with me and wondered what a South American military dictatorship would be like.

I disembarked at the Jorge Chavez Airport to a chilly morning and an open airport that was made out of cement. I hadn't told anyone where I was going. I hadn't wanted to. I just said I was leaving town on a trip. Most of my friends and my agent were used to that. There were many international travelers on board, not only returning Peruvians. Obviously Lima was a center for international business . . . mostly shady, illegal, and having nothing to do with helping the plight of the poor, I thought. There I was again: a rich bleeding-heart liberal. No one recognized me and when I produced my papers and passport it didn't make any impression. The customs, police, luggage carriers, airport authorities

. . . everyone . . . wore uniforms that looked like leftovers from the Keystone Cops. And the people acted that way too. I expected rigid Gestapo-like military behavior even though the government was supposed to be a left-wing military group. I didn't know anything about Peru. I only knew of the Inca civilization, the Nazca Plains, and the fact that most of Peru had mountains.

I had packed one fair-sized suitcase with warm- and cold-weather clothes . . . a pair of combat boots and lots of tapes and a tape recorder and note paper. Whatever was going to happen to me I wanted it down in writing.

Except for the fact that I didn't fill out one document in triplicate, nothing untoward happened as I passed through customs and waited for my suitcase on the other side. The sun had just come up to take the chill off the air when I looked over at the wall where people waited for arrivals. I didn't recognize anyone. The cement airport couldn't have been more depressing. The baggage carousel turned and down tumbled my suitcase. I picked it up along with my hand luggage and made my way to the street where I would look around some more and then decide whether to take a cab into town. I wasn't frightened.

I walked toward the front entrance of the airport and just as I saw a dilapidated cab that looked as though it might take me to the local Sheraton I felt someone take my suitcase out of my hand. Quickly I turned and looked into the face of David.

"Hi," he said. He had a woolen scarf wrapped around his neck and a combat jacket zipped up the front. He was tanned and smiling.

"Hi," I said, "you're Mr. Livingstone, I presume?"

"Anything you say, ma'am. Did you have a good trip?"

"It was okay."

"Welcome to the mountains I love very much. They have saved my life many times. They are peaceful."

I looked into his eyes, not needing to know any more than that.

"Come," he said, "don't mind my jalopy, but I couldn't get a Land Rover. That's the best way to travel in the mountains."

"The mountains?" I asked. "We're going right away to the Andes?"

"Sure. It would be hard to avoid. Peru *is* the Andes. But wait 'til you see them. They're different from the Himalayas but just as gorgeous."

He picked up both bags and led me to an old, red, rental Plymouth which was parked alongside a dirt road adjacent to the airport.

"Did you eat breakfast on the plane?"

"Yep."

"Okay. Then we'll stop and get some provisions before we head straight for Llocllapampa."

The pollution mixed with fog made me cough. I had thought of Lima as a sun-splashed resort city by the sea with perfect climate and people running around in South American muu-muus. This was dank, damp, dingy, and depressing.

David said there was a legend based on fact about Lima. When Pizarro invaded the Inca civilization, by way of a peace offering, the Incas directed Pizarro's armies to make their base camp here in what was now Lima. They proudly showed their conquering masters this territory during the months of January and February, which were the most exquisite months for weather locally and, indeed, anywhere in the world. But that was it. The rest of the year was dismal. As soon as the armies settled in, the weather changed. The Incas professed it to be an accident. But, of course, it never got any better and in no time most of Pizarro's armies had pneumonia.

"Hey, what about those Incas? How come they were so intelligent?" I asked.

"I guess they were easy to help," David said. "Primitive people don't fight miracles, they relax and figure somebody else knows better than they."

"Like who?"

He just winked.

"Oh," I said. "I forgot," and I pointed upward and patted my knee.

David lit up one of his Camels and asked if there was anything special I would be needing because where we were going if there was a kerosene lantern around we'd be lucky.

"I know you're used to roughing it," he said, "but this time there won't be any Sherpas or bearers or anybody to do anything for you except yourself." He suggested toilet paper, basic canned food, a hot water bottle, and anything to keep myself warm. He said there was no heat where we were going either.

I thought of the time I spent in a hut in the Himalayas when I was sure I would freeze to death. My only recourse had been to employ some sort of mind-over-matter technique, so I concentrated on the hottest thing I could think of—the sun. Shivering and chattering I lay down on a makeshift cot, closed my eyes and somewhere in the center of my mind I found my own orange sun. I concentrated as hard as I could and before long I felt perspiration drip from my midriff and finally I had the impression that daylight had come in my head. Every night for the two weeks I spent in the Himalayan snow I used that technique. Now it looked as though I might have to do it again and I was afraid I was out of practice.

The road leading into Lima was paved but clogged with smoke-spewing trucks and dirty cars. People nonchalantly walked around in gray overworn business suits and I wondered what offices they worked in so early in the morning.

"Lima is on the brink of revolution," said David. "The rate of inflation is climbing so rapidly that people find it impossible to live. It's awful. And as usual it's the poor who suffer most. Their salaries stay the same—the prices rise. Anyway—I'm not too interested in how the government here is screwing things up. It would just be a question of time anyway. And it's only symptomatic of what's happening with governments all over the world.

Right?" I nodded. "Now to a Peruvian supermarket for basics—okay?"

It felt strange to be in a new place and yet know at the same time that it's being new was not really why I was here.

The so-called supermarket was a little like a small New York privately owned market—not quite a delicatessen on First Avenue, maybe, but I had the feeling the proprietors could raise their prices whenever they felt like it. The meats and cheeses and breads and pastries were housed in glass-enclosed cases and a soft drink called Inca Cola seemed to be David's favorite staple. He bought a case of it and a bottle opener. He opened one bottle right there, shook the fizz out of it and drank it down.

"Between cigarettes and this delicious crap I guess you could say I'm not exactly a health resort."

Remembering my low blood sugar, I bought canned nuts, tuna fish, cheese, and a dozen eggs that I hoped I would be able to hard-boil somewhere. There were many Peruvian pastry delicacies but I couldn't eat them, and I found myself wondering what it would be like if I had a low blood sugar attack in the mountains.

David spoke fluent Spanish. I was surprised, but said nothing, and as he rattled on with the cashier, the shape of his face seemed almost to mold itself around the Peruvian words. He seemed to have the facility to *become* the nationality he was portraying.

"Ah, yes," he said as we left the store. "The world *is* a stage, isn't it, and we are all nothing but actors portraying the scenario."

"You have an advantage," I said. "You seem to know how the script is going to come out."

"Something like that," he answered, lifting his case of Inca Cola into the back seat. "Only you never can tell about those actors who haven't read the script." He winked and opened the door of the used car.

We never did drive through Lima. So I couldn't say what it was like. I knew there was a Sheraton Hotel in there somewhere and

the Museum of Natural History tracing the civilization of the Incas and even pre-Incas.

We drove northeast further out of town and toward the foothills of the Andes. David said he had been to Peru many times and that it was about three times the size of California and had, because of its varying terrain, three different climates. He said we were on our way to a city of about 100,000 inhabitants called Huancayo, located high in the Andes. We wouldn't be actually staying in Huancayo because it was too dusty and crowded. We would be staying along the way in a little place that barely existed at all except for the fact that there were mineral baths, some food, a place to sleep and the most incredible view of the heavens available on earth. He winked again when he described it and even though the weather on the outskirts of Lima was sunless and dismal I began to feel happy. Huancayo was 225 miles away—all uphill . . .

We stopped in a bazaar just outside the city where David suggested I buy a poncho made of alpaca wool. He said the very style of the poncho would come in handy because it would act as a blanket as well as a wrap. It was lovely and soft and an oatmeal color I loved. David said nothing about my Ralph Lauren leather coat and I was just as glad to cover it up. Along with the poncho I bought a neck scarf to match. The price of both items together was eighteen dollars. At the moment I was sweltering in my blue jeans, but I had traveled enough to know that where mountains were concerned nothing was warm enough when the sun went down.

The road, with native Indians draped in their own ponchos alongside, began to wind. About forty-three kilometers outside of Lima we passed a community called Chosica.

"People come to the lowlands looking for a new life and end up in a place like this," said David, shaking his head.

There was no grass, no trees, a few cactus, but for the most part

the land was barren: the hills surrounding were rock, sand and dust.

Advertisements for Inca Cola were splashed across billboards.

A truck carrying used box spring mattresses, with a picture of Che Guevara on the wheel flaps, passed us. "They admire him here," said David. "Because he died for his ideas."

The people along the road looked Tibetan.

Telephone wires leading to the top of the Andes crisscrossed overhead.

Tiny stalls sold fruit and ice cream and more Inca Cola.

A train transporting coal from above passed us going the other way on the tracks that ran beside the road.

About forty-five minutes outside of Lima the sun broke through the bruise-colored sky and it turned light turquoise. The air became fresher, the trees showed green and once again I was reminded of how badly contaminated our lives had become in big cities regardless of where we lived in the world. Even the smiles on people's faces were more pronounced. I felt happy and was unconcerned that I had no idea what to expect or what might happen to me.

Small communities sprang up with mountain Indians working the fields surrounding them. The higher we climbed the greener it got. We passed Cocachacra. We began to follow the beginning of a river.

"That's the Mantaro," said David. "Wait 'til you see it higher up."

A tunnel railroad wound around the cliffs which were getting steeper now. Burros appeared along the road. We passed a smelting factory.

"They smelt the coal they mine in the mountains," said David. "These are coal smelting communities. They live and die doing just that."

The community was called Rio Seco and behind it the soil was richer and blacker. The river bed began to grow greenery. Tea gardens were visible now underneath the volcanic hills.

The river began to tumble over rocks.

There were small square stones with flowers placed before them jutting out of the ground.

"Those are tombstones," said David. "Here in the Andes whenever a person dies in a car accident he is buried on the spot where the accident occurred."

Shrines of bright turquoise were placed in strategic positions.

We were at 5,000 feet now. I began to feel a bit sleepy. A woman in a pink striped serape carried water to her destination which David said must be Rio Seco, now two miles behind us.

We climbed higher.

Small valleys with grazing cattle were nestled in between the foothills and soon when the road became unpaved, dusty and filled with potholes, lumps and ruts, David suggested we stop at a roadside restaurant and have some rice and beans. We had been driving for an hour without stops and he said we had another five or six hours to go.

The restaurant looked like a Mexican luncheonette but the food could have been Peruvian gourmet as far as I was concerned. David ordered us some bottled water and we settled in to eat rice and beans, stuffed eggs with hot sauce, and cold boiled potatoes smothered with a kind of peanut mayonnaise. It was delicious. I began to breathe a little quicker. He noticed and took me in the back where an oxygen machine waited, fully equipped to assist any tourist who might suffer from altitude sickness. We were now at about 10,000 feet and since I had danced at a height of about 7,500 feet with no trouble I didn't think I would be bothered now. But I breathed some of the oxygen anyway and left the machine feeling I was flying.

At lunch we talked mostly of Peruvian customs, how he felt the left wing military government wouldn't last long and how Peru imported almost all of its gas and oil from the Middle East when it had a rich supply of its own right under the mountains. David was relaxed, happy that I was too, and seemed less intense than he had

been back in Los Angeles. He refused a drink offered by the owner, protesting the altitude and the necessity of keeping his wits for the long winding trip ahead of us. We didn't speak of anything personal, and soon we finished and left the restaurant. On the counter near the door were two jars. One bore the inscription, "Para Llorar," the other "Para Reir." Under them in English it said, "Does your woman love you?"

Back in the Plymouth again and passing a small mining village I noticed a sign saying that we were at 3,746 meters (or 11,238 feet) above sea level. So far I felt nothing really serious. If I did feel altitude nausea David said I could get more oxygen at a nearby mining center called Casapalca. But it wasn't necessary. The greenery disappeared from the mountains and only a red-orange clay earth remained. People pounded rocks alongside the road reminding me of what I had seen in the Himalayas. Many of them smoked. David said seventy per cent of the Peruvian people were Indians and to my eyes their features could have been Oriental or Mongolian. Their hair was blue-black and their eyes like black grapes swimming in suntanned leather faces. The women wore long thick black braids and starched white hats surrounded by black ribboned brims. Their dresses were thick brightly colored cottons.

Mining iron ore and other minerals seemed to be the work around which their lives revolved. Pyramids of mineral earth dotted the valleys where the Indians worked, using hand shovels to fill nearby pickup trucks.

"There is a wealth of minerals in these mountains," said David, "minerals that are not found anywhere else on earth."

He talked awhile about the geological shifts in the earth under the Andes and told me that all over Peru were buried civilizations thousands of years old just waiting to be excavated if the Peruvian government would allocate enough money for that purpose. "But they won't," he said. "They haven't got enough respect for the

past. That's why they will always be condemned to make the same mistakes in the future."

Now we passed a chalk mining community called Chicla. There was a white church and every other structure was painted turquoise. Even the buses passing us were turquoise. Maybe the people were painting the color of the sky.

More Peruvian Indians pounded rocks along the roadside. Just before we entered a railway tunnel the car sputtered and conked out.

"It's the lack of oxygen," said David. "There's not enough combustion. Don't worry, it'll start up again." And it did, just as a herd of llamas was led through the tunnel looking for all the world like a picture postcard you'd sign saying, "Wish you were here."

The smoke from our tailpipe was blue now. The contour of the mountains changed. They were more horizontal, less vertical. There was snow on their tops. Wildflowers grew and the higher the altitude the brighter their colors.

We passed more tombstones along the road, graced with purple wildflowers.

Passing through San Mateo I now saw eucalyptus and pine trees. Peruvian peasants dressed like Tibetans led herds of goats. The women wore iridescent crimson mixed with orange in their serapes.

There was a Catholic church in every community.

The mountain soil was a deep red now. Iron ore, David said. Clothes hung on lines in the hot sun which was getting hotter the higher we climbed. Two women, wearing white straw-brimmed hats, sat knitting with long strands of llama wool.

The road was rock now, not paved. A wild hairy pig walked between two dwellings with a Mobil Oil sign on one side and Coca-Cola on the other.

The road was dangerously narrow. David said it was not uncommon for a bus to topple over the edge.

Even though the hot sun was beating down, the men wore wool sweaters and wool skull caps as though their basic association with the mountains was cold. All day they gazed at the snowcapped mountains above.

We looked below us at the winding mountain road. And above us at about 20,000 feet on a mountain top waved the Peruvian flag.

The temperature was cooler now. The sunshine brilliant, the air pure and rarefied. Then at 15,806 feet above sea level we came to a sign.

A sign beside a railway crossing called Abra Anticona. It said: "PUNTO FERROVIARO MAS ALTO DEL MUNDO." In English: "Highest Railway Point in the World." Just adjacent to that sign was another one. It said: "EXISTEN LOS PLATILLOS VOLADORES CONTACTO CON OVNIS." In English: "Flying Saucers Do Exist. UFO Contact Point."

I looked over at David with raised eyebrows. He smiled. "Well," he said, "I'm not the only crazy one, am I?"

"What does that mean?" I asked.

"It means that people see lots of UFOs around here and it's common knowledge and no one is particularly disturbed by it."

I took a deep breath.

"Did we come here to see UFOs? Is that why I'm here?"

"Maybe."

"Oh. My. God."

"Yes," he said. "Exactly."

We drove on. The road became smoother, and now we were descending in altitude. The mountains were dotted with green again and there, running parallel to the road, was a magnificent copper-colored river.

"There's the Mantaro River," said David, "just like I wanted you to see it. Have you ever seen anything more beautiful? Out across the plain ahead is what we call the Mantaro River Valley."

The mountains were like undulating hills. The colors were a

mixture of yellows and oranges and falling purple shadows as the afternoon sun descended into what we in films called the Magic Hour.

Puffy whipped clouds hung motionless in the clear sky as I had my first glimpse of an Andean Shangri-La.

David pulled the Plymouth to the side of the road where two men beside an adobe building were patting square mud cakes together with their hands.

"This is it," he said. "This is Llocllapampa. This is where we're going to stay."

"Where?"

"There." He pointed to another adobe building across the street. Except for one other structure about seventy-five feet away there were no other buildings anywhere around.

"That's our hotel," said Paul. "C'mon, let's get out and stretch."

I couldn't believe what he said. There *was* no hotel. Three women with straw brooms pounded a pile of grain by the roadside while a rooster ran in and out of their skirts.

They smiled at us and waved at David. He spoke to them in Spanish and gestured to me as though he was introducing us. I nodded. He took our bags from the car and told me to follow him.

Through a wooden door separated in the middle so either the top or the bottom could be shut we entered a dirt patio inside the adobe building. There was a paved walkway which led to what turned out to be two rooms. They were next to each other but with no adjoining door. I opened the door to one of the rooms. Across the door was a piece of cotton material on a string. Inside the room was a dirt floor and a low-slung cot. Beside the cot was a crate of some kind which served as a bedside table. There was no electricity and no bathroom. There was a blanket on the bed and a gray-colored pillow . . . no sheets . . . no pillow cases . . .

I turned to David.

"You've got a great imagination."

He smiled. "Yep."

"Is this really it?"

"Yep. It's not much but It's Home," he said. "I'm right next door."

There were some nails hammered into the adobe wall.

"Your closet," he said. "You'd better unpack now if you're going to, because when the sun goes down you won't be able to see a thing."

"I see," I said reluctantly.

"I'll be back in a minute," he said and disappeared into his room, which had exactly the same decor as mine.

He pounded on the thin wall and said the Mantaro River would be our bathroom and he'd take me there in a minute but I should change into something warmer before we went for our first mineral water bath.

This was not science fiction. This was definitely out of one of my old lives. ❀

Chapter 20

"It is immediately apparent . . . that this sense-world, this seemingly real external universe, though it may be useful and valid in other respects, cannot be *the* external world, but only the self's projected picture of it. . . . The evidence of the senses cannot be accepted as evidence of the nature of ultimate reality."

—E. Underhill
Mysticism

I unzipped my suitcase that had been all over the world with me and hung up a sweater, my new poncho and a sun hat. I never forgot to take a sun hat with me wherever I went, because my face turned into a tomato after two hours in high-altitude sun. I left my underwear in the suitcase, wondering how I would ever wash it anyway, and I thanked God (or somebody) that I had just finished my period and wouldn't have to contend with that. I looked at my ring watch which somehow always made me feel secure. I pulled out my tapes, recording machine and note paper. Sketchily and quickly I jotted down what the place looked and felt like. With each passing moment of the setting sun I realized how really cold it was going to get.

David rapped on my door, handed me a towel and directed me to take my poncho and change into my combat boots for our first visit to the mineral baths.

Mineral baths in this cold? "Sure," he said. "At first it's murder but then just wait . . ."

We walked from the paved patio back onto the road. The surrounding mountains were splashed with purple shadows. Barnyard animals that I couldn't see gurgled and clucked at each other. A

mangy dog waddled up to us wagging her tail followed by three puppies. The men patting the earth squares were gone for the evening and right across the street from our "hotel" was an adobe building called FOOD. That meant the people inside would cook for us. Loudly through the door I heard a scratchy radio broadcasting a soccer game. Inside, Peruvian Indians laughed and cheered to themselves and then shuffled back and forth in between tables that had been set up for the evening. Soup steamed on a gas stove and an old Indian woman with no teeth asked if we'd like some. "No," David said to me. "Let's eat afterward. We'll get heartburn from the mineral baths if we eat now."

I wasn't particularly hungry anyway, but I asked if someone would boil some eggs for me just so I'd have some food on hand in case I needed it. David asked the Indian woman to take the eggs out of the Plymouth. She smiled and nodded.

He led me around toward the back of the building and using a flashlight from his back pocket we went down some stairs. They were steep, and in the fading light I was afraid I might trip. I might be in Shangri-La now but some day I'd have to go back to dancing. I heard water flowing below. Then spread out in the sunset before me was the glorious Mantaro River. It rushed over the mountain rocks and splashed against the over-hanging trees embedded in the high banks. There were level green knolls of grass leading down to the water where a few Indians hunched in their ponchos sat gazing at the sun settling behind the mountains. Even in the fading light I could see that the river was orange.

"Come," said David, leading me to what looked like an adobe enclosure covered with a tin roof. "It's not much to look at but wait 'til you feel it inside." He unbolted a crude wooden door, went in and from another pocket took a candle, lit it, and placed it on a wooden bench inside the enclosure. Next to the bench deep in the ground was a gurgling pool of sparkling water.

"This is one of the famous Andes mineral baths," he said.

I looked down into it. It wasn't just the candlelight that made it

sparkle. It seemed to be the water itself. A light film of steam hung over it. I knelt down on the earth floor and ran my hand through the water. To my surprise it felt warm and bubbly . . . bubbly and stinging and effervescent . . . like champagne.

"The minerals make it bubble," said David. "And it's great for aching bones and muscles. You'll see."

When I drew my hand out of the water it was freezing.

"I'm supposed to go all the way in that water and not freeze to death when I get out?" I asked, laughing.

"Well, for a few minutes it's cold as hell but after that you'll be warmer than if you didn't do it at all."

I stood up awkwardly. I wished I could go in with all my clothes on. Now how was this supposed to work? Was I supposed to peel off my clothes with him standing right there or what?

"You go ahead," said David. "I'll wait outside. Call me when you're ready."

Slowly I took off my poncho and hung it on one of five nails protruding from the wall. I wondered how many people had done the same thing in the candlelight. Then I took off my sweater and slacks. I wondered what they did after they got out of the water. I wondered how I could hang each garment so I could put them back on quickly when I was ready to leave. Down to my underpants and socks, I ripped them off quickly because by now I was shivering. The hell with it. I left everything in a little pile on the wooden bench wondering how it would look to David when he came back in.

The candlelight flickered against the cold stone walls. I stepped quickly to the bubbling pool of water in the ground and slowly I put my right leg in. I hoped I would find a bottom and I did. It was slightly slippery. Tangy bubbles settled onto my skin. I slid in all the way up to my neck. It felt as though I had just stepped into a giant deep dish pie of warm bubbling soda water. It felt wonderful.

The water was so buoyant I felt I was floating. In fact, it was difficult to firmly find the bottom. It felt as though I was walking in

the midst of the water, somehow upright. There was a square hole in the opposite wall where the water drained out to the river outside. Apparently this was a constantly fed pool from underground somewhere.

"Okay," I yelled to David, "I'm in now and it's great."

"Sure," he said, coming through the door, "wait 'til you feel it really go through your skin."

David turned around, pulled off his jacket, sweater, shirt, underpants and boots and socks in about five seconds and said, "Now *you* turn around." I did.

"Okay," he said.

I turned back around. He was standing under the water across the small pool from me.

I breathed deeply and tried to relax. "You'll have to bear with me awhile," I said. "This is all so sudden, and I know I've done a lot of things in my life, but I have a feeling that none of it was like this." I felt ridiculous.

"Yep, you're right."

"Yes," I breathed again. I didn't even want to ask what he meant.

"Look," he said, "swish your arms up and down like this in the water and feel how the bubbles stick to your skin."

I swirled my arms up and down and around and it was like two swizzle sticks going through freshly poured champagne. The swizzle was like self-generating heat. It wasn't the same as the sulphur baths in Japan. They were more mild and calm. These waters had zing and punch and a verve of their own.

David stood quietly with the candlelight flickering off the opposite wall. His blue eyes seemed lit themselves and small drops of water fell from his chin. I wondered what I looked like to him.

I couldn't think of what to say so I said, "Do you come here often?"

David laughed. "Yep," he said. He stared into the candle. "Want to try something?" he asked.

I thought, Oh shit, here it comes. "What do you mean?" I asked, looking around casually.

"See the light of that candle?" he asked.

"Yes," I answered.

"Okay, focus on the light real hard and take a deep breath."

"Take a deep breath?" I asked.

"Yes, take a deep breath."

I breathed deeply, almost choking on some spit. I had been taking deep breaths all day. "Can I just let my arms go?" I asked, wanting to appear as though I was willing to try anything.

"Sure. In this water they float. In fact, it would really be hard to sink in this water."

I thought, that's a relief. At least I wouldn't drown if worse came to worst. I let my arms go as though they were unattached, smiling in the candlelight. I felt them rise slightly beside me.

My God, I thought. Now he'll just leap across this pool and scoop me under my arms and because of this goddamn buoyancy I'll never get them down.

"Now just concentrate on the candle until you feel *you* are the candlelight."

Jesus, I thought. He must be kidding. Until I'*m* the candlelight? I can't even be *me* right now, whoever that was.

I stared at the flickering light. I tried not to blink. I took another deep breath. My heart was pounding. I was sure he could hear it reverberate through the water. I just stood there staring into the candle as he had suggested.

Quietly David said, "Hey, Shirl. What are you afraid of?"

"Me?" I asked.

"No," he said teasingly. "The woman standing behind you."

I felt really ridiculous now. I thought of all the guys who had said, "Hey, I just want to lie down with you and relax. I don't want to *do* anything."

"Hey," said David, "if that was on my mind all I'd have to do is suggest it, right?"

Jesus, he was direct.

I coughed. "Well," I said. "Well, I hesitate," I said.

"Well, you don't have to hesitate. I just want you to try something, and it isn't what you think. Besides, I don't even want to."

I felt myself get indignant. He didn't even want to?

"Why?" I asked. "Why not?"

"What do you mean, why not?" he asked. "That's not what we came here for. If you thought it was, you'll just have to be patient and give me time."

I laughed out loud, making an echo on the walls.

"Come on," he said, "concentrate on the candle and breathe deeply."

"Okay," I said, "I guess I might as well. After all, we've had a couple of lifetimes together, right?"

He laughed. "Right."

It was clear he thought I was a jerk.

I tried again to gaze freely at the candle.

"Okay, breathe deeply again," he gently directed me.

I tried to breathe deeply again.

"Okay," he said. "Now concentrate on the light of the candle as though it were the center of your own being. Make the candle *you*. Only think about the candle—nothing else."

I concentrated and breathed deeper. I guess I'll really have to do this, I thought. Besides, he's right. I'm a jerk and he's really nice. I felt my mind begin to relax. I concentrated with more relaxation. My eyelids felt a little bit heavy until I could tell that my eyes were half closed, but still the candle was visible.

I heard David's voice faintly in the background of my mind.

"That's good. Great, you're doing great."

I liked the sound of his voice above the water. It seemed to skip along with the bubbles. I felt my breathing slow down. Slowly, I was aware that my heartbeat was pulsating in rhythm with my breathing. Somehow the rhythm of the two seemed in sync. Time slowly slipped away until I became unaware of it. The candle

continued to flicker, but now it began to be the center of my mind. My whole body seemed to float too, not only my arms, but all of me. Slowly, slowly, I *became* the water and each tingling bubble was a component part of the water. It was a marvelous double feeling. I was totally conscious, aware of myself, yet part of every-thing around me. I remember being aware that every single bubble was a part of all of the water that surrounded me, almost as though the water wouldn't be what it was without each bubble doing its part to sustain the whole of it. I felt the cool sides of the walls housing the warm water pool even though I was lost somewhere in its midst. I felt shadows and flickers and a slight breeze. But mostly, I felt the inside of myself. I felt the involuntary reflex of my own breathing. It seemed to be a moving entity oblivious of my control. Then I felt the interconnection of my breathing with the pulse of the energy around me. The air itself seemed to pulsate. In fact, I *was* the air. I was the air, the water, the darkness, the walls, the bubbles, the candle, the wet rocks under the water, and even the sound of the rushing river outside. Then I felt my energy vi-brate to David. Since I was part of everything around me, that meant David too. At that moment I stopped myself. I could feel myself make a conscious decision not to go that far. Again my hesitation, my fear or whatever you want to call it, stopped me, and I stopped the flow of relaxation and the attempt to become "one" with everything.

"That's okay," I heard David say, "that was good. How was it for a first attempt at breathing meditation?"

I stretched my arms out of the water and asked what time it was.

"It doesn't matter about time," he said. "What matters is that you forget about it for a while. You *breathed*. You really breathed. Breathing is life. Don't you feel like you've had a rest?"

Yes, I did. Definitely. I asked him if I had been hypnotized.

"No, just a kind of self-relaxing expanded awareness," he said. "You can learn to rejuvenate like that instantaneously. Breathing

is an involuntary act, and if you can learn to regulate it, you will stay young longer."

Shit, I thought in a kind of dream, Elizabeth Arden should teach this in her beauty courses. I could hear David talking to me, but I was still spaced out from my own breath. He was talking about animals, and how the ones who lived the longest were the ones that breathed the least. Something about giant tortoises only breathing four times a minute and they live to be three hundred years old. I remember thinking if I had cold blood I'd only breathe four times a minute too. But I had warm blood and I was beginning to feel shivery.

"So, are you interested in living a long time, eh?" he asked.

I shook my head. I felt the champagne bubbles in my brain.

"Living a long time? I don't know. Are you?"

"Me?" he said.

"No," I said. "The man standing behind you."

He smiled. "Am I interested in living a long time?"

"Yeah."

"Yeah," he answered. "I am, but I don't think I will."

There was something in the way he said it that made me shiver. The shiver surprised me.

"Well, nobody could live long in this cold. I'm cold now. What do you say?"

"I say," he said, "let's get out of here."

He turned to face the flickering wall. I stepped slowly out of the water. My teeth clacked together as though they were false and my arms and hands shook so hard I could barely reach for the towel on the nail in the wall. Then as hard as I could I rubbed my arms, legs, feet and torso until I could feel the blood come to the surface and I actually began to tingle with a warm afterglow. My clothes felt cold next to my skin but soon my body heat reflected inside the wool of the sweater and socks.

"I feel wonderful now," I said. "That water is really something."

"Take the flashlight out of my pocket and wait for me outside," said David. "I'll be there as quick as I can get dry."

The cold mountain air must have registered somewhere around fifteen degrees, but it was fresh and clear. I walked around the side of the pool shelter and looked out over the river and the dark looming mountains above. Life was a novel, I thought to myself. Two months ago I never could have predicted in my wildest imagination that I would be here doing this. And I was really loving it. I was also learning that trusting the best instincts in myself had its virtues. You could actually space out on them.

I felt suddenly hungry and when those pangs came I knew I should eat immediately or my blood sugar would drop.

"Okay," said David, fully dressed, rubbing his hands together and smiling. "Let's go up and get some grub. They'll have hot milk waiting for us and some Indian stew made of meat and vegetables and mountain herbs."

He blew out the candle, stuffed it into his pocket and said we'd need it later in our rooms. He also suggested that I use the river for the bathroom now because later it would be much too cold to make the trek.

I squatted behind a rock and used some Kleenex I had stashed in my pocket. Climbing the cold stone stairs, I wondered how the cold would be when I tried to sleep.

"Don't worry about sleeping," said David, once again seeming to read my mind. "It'll all come in its own time."

If he had said that an hour before I would have assumed he meant something else.

The radio soccer game was on full blast when we walked into the FOOD building on the road above. Runny-nosed children scampered back and forth in between the tables that were set up for tourists who might be exploring the area and want to eat. One younger woman cooking had a child at her skirts and another strapped to her back. She wore the customary white starched hat

with the black ribboned brim even though it was night time.

David called for some hot milk and stew and we talked about food. I told him how much I loved "junk food" and he told me how bad it was to eat. I told him I knew that. I loved it anyway. He talked about how important it was to take care of the body because at the same time you'd be taking care of your spirit. He said it was just a question of chemistry. I said I wasn't very good at that either. He gave me a run down on food-combining and I said, yes, I had heard most of it before. As he talked, I reflected on how he had been all evening. He seemed compelled to teach me everything there was in as fast a time as possible. He was telling me I should relax, yet he himself was driven. He was criticizing my junk-food habits, but he had them too. Sometimes he sounded almost pompous and presumptuous. Sometimes he didn't seem to really be enjoying the life he said I should relax and enjoy more.

It was funny; I was hacking Gerry about letting himself go so he could know more who he was and David was doing the same thing with me. I wondered what Gerry would think if he could see me now. I thought of my theme song, "If They Could See Me Now." I wondered what the audience in Vegas would think if I came out and gave them a few jokes about spiritual discovery in the Andes. I really seemed to be two people—or ten people—I didn't know. Yet was I an actress because I was more closely in touch with some of the roles I had played in other lives?

The woman with the child on her back came to our table. She was carrying hot milk and stew. I scooped it up as though eating might go out of style.

It was delicious, spiced with mountain herbs I had never heard of. I sopped up the natural juices with the thick homemade heavy bread rolls. They reminded me of my happiest time as a child camping out in Virginia when the world and life seemed simple.

"Tomorrow," said David, "we'll take a long walk. I'll show you some of the territory, and you'll see for yourself why I love this place."

He led me across the road to our hotel. The stars were so close I felt that I could reach out and pluck them like plums. I could almost hear the surrounding mountains sway under them. The Andes were not like the Bhutanese Himalayas. They felt lower and more spread out. The environment wasn't as isolated, and because of the pervasive Peruvian Indian culture, I didn't feel as insignificant as I had high above the world with the Bhutanese lamas.

Our rooms smelled dank and dusty, and I wondered who else had slept there. There was a good five-degree drop in temperature when I walked inside. David handed me the candle, said he had another for himself, and said goodnight.

"By the way," he said, "just a little tip about sleeping in a cold climate—if you sleep with no clothes on under your poncho, you'll find it much warmer."

I couldn't understand. I was intending to put on everything I brought.

"No," he said, "the body generates its own aura heat. Try it. You'll see what I mean."

I said goodnight. I didn't want to hear any more from him. I took off my clothes under the poncho. I crawled in under the wool blanket on the cot and prayed (so to speak) that I would get warm. My feet were ice. I waited. Since the alpaca wool was soft, it felt nice. I waited some more. I felt I was watching my own pot boil. I calmed my mind and my chattering teeth as much as I could. I thought of my electric blanket by the ocean and how I had loved to sleep in a cold rainstorm with the windows wide open and the blanket turned up high. Right that minute, as I lay in the wilds of the Andes, that electric blanket was my favorite part of an advanced civilization. I thought of Gerry again. It was nice being without him. I thought of how impossible it would be for me to describe what I was up to, to him. I wondered where he was. I wondered if he was *really* seeing it. I thought of my show. Where were my gypsies tonight?—my dancers . . . at Joe Allen's having cheeseburgers and gossiping about how the big stars were not

nearly so all-around talented as they were? I thought of what it was to be a star when you really weren't all that sure you deserved it.

Soon I realized my muscles were relaxing from the warmth of the space between my body and the covers. It was the *space* that was warm, not the covers. I suddenly understood that most of what we didn't understand in our lives was what we couldn't *see*. The invisible truth was the truth that required the most struggle to find. *Seeing* wasn't believing—not at all. *Looking* was what it was more about.

With a kind of relaxed shiver I fell off to sleep, with only the sound of silence. Then somewhere behind the building I heard pigs snorting. ❅

Chapter 21

"No theory of physics that deals only with physics will ever explain physics. I believe that as we go on trying to understand the universe, we are at the same time trying to understand man. Today I think we are beginning to suspect that man is not a tiny cog that doesn't really make much difference to the running of the huge machine but rather that there is a much more intimate tie between man and the universe than we heretofore suspected. . . . the physical world is in some deep sense tied to the human being."

—Dr. John A. Wheeler

The sun rose over the mountains about five-thirty A.M. It didn't stream into my room because there were no windows but the contrast from the cold of the night was so pronounced I could feel the warmth of the first rays even through the walls. My poncho lay comfortably around me. I had been warm all night.

I stood in my bare feet on the cold earth floor and thought what contradictory logic it was getting dressed now when the sun was out, and undressed during the cold night. I knew the mountain air would be fresh and sharp and because of the altitude the sun would burn. I put on my California sun hat and walked outside. I could smell morning smoke from across the road and as I rounded the Plymouth I saw David sitting on a mud wall watching the men from the day before pat their square bricks into what would ultimately be the foundation of a house they were building.

"Good morning," he said. "How was it last night?"

"Just like you said. Nude meant warmth. I wouldn't have believed it but there it was."

"That's beginning to become a habit with you, isn't it?"

"What is?"

"You're finally believing because it *is*."

"Yeah, well. What's for breakfast?"

"They boiled your eggs for you. So all you need now is a bag and some salt. Let's get some hot milk and rolls."

We walked into the food room and the woman with the baby on her back smiled openly, with a kind of tacit understanding that the two-room love affair that David and I were conducting was just another strange North American custom.

"They don't ask personal questions around here," he said. "Anything we do is anything we do."

We sat next to a window and I saw the women from the evening before continue to pound their grain.

"They are separating the wheat from the chaff," said David with a wink. He certainly did wink a lot. "We'll have bread made from those very wheat kernels in a day or two."

In the morning light I could see that the tile roof on our adobe hotel was red and around the women were roosters with feathers of the same color.

David leaned back in his chair and watched me. I guess he had decided to grow a beard because he hadn't shaved and probably couldn't have if he wanted to. He really did have a handsome face.

"Did you sleep well, did you dream?" he asked.

"I can't remember. I was mostly pleased with being warm enough." I didn't feel like being analyzed.

We munched our rolls and hot milk and I peeled an egg and ate it. In a place like this a person didn't need much except maybe more of themselves.

"Can we go for a walk?" I asked.

"Sure. Great idea."

We stepped outside into the sunlight. The air felt thin and crisp against my face. My heart raced slightly with the altitude. I

stretched my arms out beside me and breathed and lifted my face into the sun.

I loved mountains more than any other part of the Earth. To me they had been through so much and seemed so patient and resigned and wisely silent. They represented every extreme I could think of—height, depth, bottom, top, grandeur, insignificance, struggle, attainment—everything. And regardless of what adversity befell a mountain it seemed to tower with its steadfast resilience when it was over, even if it erupted from inside itself.

"Let's walk down by the river," said David. "Want to brush your teeth?"

I had my toothbrush in my back pocket and as we walked down the stone stairs and passed the mineral pool bathhouse David ran ahead of me, skipping with his arms outstretched almost like a kid from kindergarten during recess. He skipped across the grassy river bank tilting his head from one side to another in sheer childish glee.

"I love it out here!!" I heard him yell to the river. "You river—you are rushing so fast—why? Where are you going that you have to be on time!"

I laughed with a kind of amazement and ran up to him. "I love the water," he said, "excuse me. Here, over here is another mineral pool for drinking, or tooth-brushing, or washing." He ran with great leaps to the water and knelt down, put his head under and came up laughing and sputtering in the sunlight. His salt-and-pepper hair dripped like a bowl around his face and he smiled with such playful abandon that I felt like a child too.

I knelt beside the pool and looked into it. Patches of white sulphur film swam on top. A slow current from beneath fed fresh running bubbles into the center.

David cupped his hands and drank. "You have to get used to the taste but it's sensational for the system; cleans out the impurities and settles your digestion."

I dug out my toothbrush, dipped it into the water and tasted it on my tongue. It was like medicinal salt.

"You're not sad today, are you?" I asked him.

"No, I'm never sad when I'm outside. It's too real here to be sad. Cities make me sad because people care too much about the wrong things. When you're in touch with this, you're in touch with people." He shook his wet hair into the air and sprawled out on his back with his head on his hands looking up at the sky.

I finished brushing my teeth, stood up, stretched in the sunlight and we began to walk.

I opened and shut my eyes blinking into the cloud-puffed brilliant blue sky. God, it was beautiful. And it was even more beautiful when I thought that beauty simply existed for the sake of itself. Beauty didn't need a reason and couldn't be explained. It just was. It didn't have anything to do with anyone else. It didn't need to be shared to be appreciated. Beauty was beauty. And it was necessary like food and water.

I felt David walking beside me relaxed and unassuming.

"Feel better?" he asked.

"Yeah, I feel good," I said, partially wondering at the same time what it would feel like to feel totally good, feel totally myself . . . to feel that I knew myself completely. I felt like a walking cliché. So what else was new? Wasn't everybody looking for the same feeling—to know themselves? Three blue birds sat on a tree limb looking down at me as we passed under them. They didn't even blink. Their audacity made me chuckle out loud.

The Mantaro River bubbled and rushed beside us. I picked up a tree branch and began to drag it behind me. I liked the feeling of having nothing to do but drag a tree branch.

"David?" I asked, breaking what I could feel was a reverie of his own, "do you think there is any such thing as human nature?"

He looked up and took a deep breath. "I don't think so. No," he said. "I think we humans are taught most everything we feel. I

think people can do and be and think anything . . . it depends on what we learn."

I dragged the branch behind me thinking of the time I had spent in China. It was that trip that had made me come to the same conclusion. The Chinese had acted brutally and cruelly with each other in their bitter past because that was the behavior of the times, the mode of the day, the attitude to be observed in order to sustain the pecking order of the class system.

But Mao had said the Chinese people were a blank piece of paper on which something beautiful could be written. He had believed that human nature was basically a question of education . . . you could educate people into observing behavior patterns that were more democratic, more fair, more kind. In fact, he had used a kind of militant sledgehammer approach in the education of fairness. People were forced to be fair through education and reeducation. They were all required to participate in the self-criticism sessions on every level. No one was excused from participation. It was a gigantic, monumental effort in group therapy directed toward changing the patterns of the past. And it seemed to work. Privacy and the right not to participate were not respected, but then the country was in such big trouble everyone realized they had to pull together. So to me, the overwhelming characteristic of the New China had been the people working together to change what they believed to be their basic natures.

Modern China now said a handful of chopsticks held together tightly was more unbreakable than one pair. And as they held together, they were allowing themselves to totally reevaluate the value system they had held sacred for centuries. They seemed to understand that they were revolutionizing the priorities that they had thought were immutable. And the big lesson to them seemed to be what they were learning about themselves.

I often thought about what it must be like to find out that you are not necessarily competitive or territorial or jealous or ma-

terialistic. Maybe the real human conflict wasn't about what we really believed we were or were not, but what we actually could be if we allowed ourselves the option of trusting the possibilities of our own spiritual potential. And if our own potential was to be more spiritual, then where did the new Chinese come in? I could find nothing spiritual in the New China. In fact, they seemed to ridicule spiritual concepts, almost afraid that spiritual notions would thwart their revolution.

I could see the Chinese revolution going the way of all modern day revolutions if they negated the need for the spiritual recognition of man. I was beginning to believe that what was wrong with all of us was our refusal to live with the knowledge that God—the word we use for a concept of incredibly complex spiritual energies —was the missing link that should be part of our daily lives.

Now Buckminster Fuller's theory about most of what transpires within the human activity of *reality* being utterly invisible, unsmellable, and untouchable began to make sense. He said that ninety-nine percent of reality could only be comprehended by man's metaphysical mind, guided by something he only sensed might be the truth. He said man *was* metaphysical mind. And the brain was only a place to store information. He said only man's metaphysical mind could communicate. The *brain* could not. That man was a self-contained microcommunicating system, and humanity was a macrocommunicating system. And that *all information of everything, including God,* was continually being broadcast and received through electromagnetic waves, only we weren't aware of it because we were only using one percent of our capacities to perceive the truth.

But what would help man to understand, not only what he came from, but where he was actually going? How could the State answer the deep, gnawing, longing questions of our origins and our purpose? How could the State be helpful in putting us more closely in touch with why we were alive when it was afraid that in doing so its power would be dissipated?

I could see why the communists had never gone into India. It would be impossible to sway the deep spirituality of the Indian people. They would never condone the State replacing their spiritual philosophy even if it meant eating better. Their spiritual beliefs were the oldest on earth. The Indians had been taught and conditioned to be in touch with their spiritual natures since Krishna walked the earth so that it was a part of everything they did or didn't do. A communist regime would have a tough time getting the Indian people to go along with the revolutionary materialism of Marx. Even Mahatma Gandhi couldn't get the cows out of the houses or off the streets because the Indians still believed in the transmigration of souls (which was the animal forerunner to reincarnation into human forms). Maybe they were even right about that for all we know.

It was astonishing to me how the unraveling of mystery worked. As long as there was one loose thread, it was possible to unravel the whole ball of wax. As long as the human race continued to be basically unhappy in its struggle to understand the Great Mystery, the impetus would be there to thwart all authority that stood in its path . . . whether it was the Church, the State, or the revolutionary society itself. No matter where we looked, the answer seemed to be in a force that was more knowing, more wise, more understanding, and more benevolent than we ourselves. And before we could understand that force, we would have to understand ourselves. We then became the Great Mystery. It wasn't, who is God? It was, who were *we*?

❋ David and I walked upstream along the rocky banks of the orange river. The early noon sun was hot and shimmering. I was perspiring under my poncho. I took it off and David carried it for me. My California sun hat suddenly seemed my most valuable possession. The rubber-soled combat boots were solid and heavy

against the jagged rocks. My feet were comfortable. When my feet were comfortable, *I* was comfortable.

I sat down on a rock and made some notes. David waded into the river.

Peruvian mountain people dotted the sides of the river either washing their clothes or lying on the ground—mostly in the sun. Their sense of time seemed slow and unhurried—almost careless —and their body movements corresponded. Sometimes they smiled as they ambled past us, but usually they just acknowledged our presence with a nod. David greeted them with his friendly Spanish. He never really seemed foreign anywhere.

"There's an outdoor sulphur pool not too far up the river," he called to me. "Do you want to wash your hair or something? It's great to take the baths in the sunlight."

It sounded great. I got up wondering if I would be able to recall the emotional carefreeness I felt here in the Andes. I wondered if I would be able to remember how close this was to supreme peace the next time I was caught in crosstown traffic in New York, or when the lights didn't work properly during a dramatic number in my show, or when my latest picture flopped at the box office. Or Gerry . . . would I let myself be rankled and frustrated over the human obstacle course that had become our relationship? Would I be able to understand his drawbacks, and see my own, with more perspective if I conjured up the image of a moment on the Mantaro River banks when the sun was hot and my thoughts soared?

I continued to trail my branch as we walked further upstream toward the sulphur pool. I heard sharp crystal birdcalls pierce the rarefied mountain air. I wondered if it would ever be possible to *see* music and *hear* the colors in a rainbow.

"What's on your mind?" asked David.

"Oh, I don't know," I said. "I was just wondering if there was some kind of technique a person could use to feel inner peace and happiness when all hell was breaking loose in their own little world."

David shrugged his eyebrows. "I don't know how it would work for you, but somebody once described a technique they used that they called 'The Golden Dream.' For example, if you are trying to fall asleep and your mind is bouncing around with all kinds of so-called problems that won't quit—here's what I do. I think of what would make me *at that moment* the happiest person in the world. I picture all of it in detail—what I would be wearing, who I would be with, what it would sound like, what kind of weather would be going on, what food I would be eating, what I would be touching . . . all that kind of stuff that would make me happy, in detail. Then I wait. I have the whole picture in my mind—created by my own will and fantasy, and it becomes so real that I *am* happy. I feel myself begin to relax and actually vibrate on a kind of even frequency, and in no time I'm off to sleep—or 'on the astral plane,' as I like to term it."

I listened, picturing myself doing what he said. It seemed very possible.

"So that's the Golden Dream, eh?" I said.

"Yes," said David. "Good title for a song."

"Yeah. Much better than 'The Impossible Dream.' "

"So," he went on, "when you concentrate on what would make you happy, you actually produce an electromagnetic frequency which operates internally and literally soothes you into a feeling of inner peace."

"So it's really just plain mind over matter, isn't it?"

"Sure," he said, "but I really think something more is involved. For me, I think it would be exhibiting faith to myself and faith in myself. In other words, if I have enough faith in something, particularly through concentration or meditation, or whatever you want to call it, then I am unconsciously giving off enough positive energy which could ultimately result in its attainment."

"Even if what you want is unrealistic?"

"Who knows if it's unrealistic?"

"You mean faith moves mountains?"

"Yeah, probably. I think the positive mind is limitless. So I guess that would include mountains. That's apparently something like what Christ was doing. Only it's more than just faith, or meditation, or concentration. He had the *knowledge* of how to do it."

"And where did the son-of-a-gun get that knowledge?"

"He said it was from God. But he also said He was the Son of God. So I think He was telling us that through God He had learned. That's what all the Indian avatars say too. They don't say *they* are the reasons they can materialize bread out of stones or cures out of disease. They say *God* gives them the power and the knowledge to carry out His works."

"You really are a believer, David. Aren't you?"

"I believe," said David, "that most of us don't really know ourselves well enough to know what we want. And by knowing ourselves better we would be better in touch with God, or the Creative Source."

I was huffing and puffing now as we trudged in the noon day heat. The altitude was getting to me.

David moved slightly ahead of me looking for a footpath that he knew led to the sulphur pool. I was ready for the buoyant water. I wanted to sit, and soak, and think about my dream which I was suddenly aware I was unaware of. I had no dream. I couldn't imagine what would make me *specifically* happy. I couldn't meditate on the details of the smells, the sights, the touch or the sounds of such a dream because I didn't know what my dream was.

He led me up the mountain to a path which ran parallel to the river. About half a mile further on we came to a wooden hut that housed the beginning of some stone stairs which led down into a niche inside the mountain. Walls of mountain rock loomed up around us as we descended the narrow stone stairs. At the bottom was a bubbling sulphur pool. Three old women waded in the bubbles wearing their starched hats and colorful native dresses. When they looked up and saw us they covered their faces and turned away.

"The mountain elders are very reserved up here," said David. "They have a thing about nudity and they need their privacy, so let's turn our backs when we reach bottom and I think they will quietly leave."

Across the pool on the other side a young man lay sprawled in the water with his legs over the rocks. He was completely dressed in blue jeans and a shirt.

"Is that his concession to the elders?" I asked David.

"Sure, otherwise he'd have to wait for them too. Besides, his clothes are no problem to him. A short walk home and they'll be dry."

David took out another hardboiled egg, peeled it and handed it to me. "It's not good to eat this before a sulphur bath, but anyway."

The old women waded out of the water and climbed the stairs nodding to us stoically as they left. The young boy stayed where he was. We walked to the edge of the water. White clumps of sulphur sparkled in the sunlight and gentle steam wafted above the water as the warmth met the mountain air. David put down my poncho and the bag of eggs.

I stretched in the sun and watched the young boy. He didn't make a move to leave, just stared into the water.

"Well, what should we do?" I asked. "Get undressed or what?"

"Hmmm. Let's see," said David. "Let's leave on our underwear. That'll make it easier for everybody."

I took off my slacks, socks and combat boots, leaving my blouse 'til last because I wasn't wearing a bra. Then with self-conscious flurry I whipped it off and walked into the water. The young boy continued to stare into the water, and David was busy getting undressed himself. Nobody really cared whether I was half nude or not.

The water was warm and tingly just as it had been the night before but the experience of feeling it in the sunlight now was incandescent. First of all the top of the water looked like dancing

silver. There was something about the way the sun played on the clusters of white sulphur that made the water look like silver liquid underneath. The rocks on the bottom were slippery with moss and algae but the buoyancy kept me upright. Somewhere near the center of the pool I found a comfortable rock to sit on and let myself in up to my neck. Now the reflection of the silver liquid nearly blinded me at eye level. I was happy I had my sunglasses and my hat. How ridiculous, I thought. Here I am engulfed in such ravishing natural beauty and I feel I have to protect myself from bad effects. I pumped my arms up and down under the water until my entire body was covered with sulphur mineral bubbles. They clung to my skin with a stringent kind of prickle, stinging ever so slightly but because of it, seeming to make my blood rush faster. I could feel the pool being fed from an underground source. The water rushed gently to the surface in a warm stream. The surface of the pool was warm from the mountain sunlight. And the temperature of my body fell somewhere in between. David stepped into the pool. He wore jockey shorts. He had muscular straight legs, except that his left one looked as though it might have been broken and reset. It was unnoticeable in street clothes. His torso was trim but not particularly muscular and his shoulders were narrow rather than broad. He didn't look like a man who worked out with weights but he did look in good shape.

He smiled slightly as though he knew I was checking him out but he said nothing as he waded in and knelt up to his neck. He breathed deeply and shut his eyes in pleasure at the tingly warmth of the water in the mountain air.

The young boy didn't move. He seemed in a trance. The liquid silver could probably do that to a person. I asked David.

"Yeah, it can," he said. "That's why it's so relaxing. The mountain people use the waters as much for their spirits as their bodies. It's just too bad they won't take off their clothes."

As the water began to take effect slowly, I realized I was getting

heartburn. It began as a small knot somewhere in my upper chest region and spread.

"It's just the sulphur and minerals bringing out digestive defects," said David. "That's why it's better not to eat before. But it doesn't do any harm. Just makes you aware that your digestion is upset."

He retired to the opposite side of the sulphur pool to think and meditate. He sat quietly on the underwater rocks and gazed serenely into the water at eye level. I lifted my closed eyes to the sun. Heavenly, I thought. I looked over at David. His eyes weren't blinking and his face was expressionless. A fly crawled across the bridge of his nose. He looked totally at peace, and as if he just weren't there. I watched him for a long time. The boy with the blue jeans left. The three old women waited at the top of the stairs.

I drifted over and put my sun hat on a dry rock. Then I dunked my hair into the water and rinsed it. I could feel the sulphur make my hair soft. In and out of the water I lifted my head, leaning backward. I felt so exhilarated, filled with elation. I remembered how I wished I could rush into the sea giving myself up totally to it. But just rushing my body into the water wouldn't have been enough. I needed to plunge my head and face under in order to feel that I was free of reluctance . . . that's what I wanted to be . . . free of reluctance . . . reluctance about everything . . . it didn't matter. I wanted to feel totally open and embracing as though there was nothing to be suspicious about. I looked over at David again. That's the way his face looked . . . completely oblivious to anything negative . . . serene. He looked as though he could have been part of the water . . . he *was* the water—only his form was human.

I wondered how long David would meditate in the bubbling water. He hadn't moved. Carbonated bubbles clung to his unmoving arms under the surface of the water. I wished I could go under

the way he seemed to be doing. I wondered what might be going on inside of him as he sat so peacefully inert.

I wondered if his soul could leave his body if he wanted it to. I wondered whether he was his soul or whether he was his body. No . . . the body died . . . the soul's energy lived eternally. So, that must mean we are our souls—the body only houses the soul.

David opened his eyes slowly. He blinked up at the sun and wiped his chin.

"Jesus," he said, "I was meditating! How long have I been under?"

I said I didn't know, maybe over an hour. Time didn't matter anyway. In fact, it probably didn't exist.

David laughed and nodded. "What's on your mind?" he asked.

Oh God, I thought, how could I condense everything into words? "I don't know," I said, "just thinking and wondering. Wondering if a baby is born knowing everything and if little by little it forgets."

"Yeah," said David. "Being in the body can be a drag. I have a much better time out there," he pointed to the sky and gently moved an arm through it. "Come on," he said, "let's go for a walk. I have something to tell you, but I don't know how. Sometimes it's easier to think when you're moving."

He climbed out of the water.

One old woman waited at the top of the stairs for us to leave.

We dressed quickly in the warm sun. David stopped, handed me a peeled egg and said, "Take it easy with yourself. Have patience. It will all be fine."

We climbed the stairs, said goodbye to the woman, apologizing for the amount of time we had spent in the water, and began to walk back along the orange water of the Mantaro River.

David walked ahead of me and stretched out his arms. He lifted his face up to the sun and sighed. "Oh," he said, "I hope you can begin to feel some of the happiness and inner peace just waiting to be touched inside you."

I was taken aback by the direct personal quality of what he said. "All of this stuff *is* personal," he said, sensing my reaction, "because what we're missing is ourselves. You're beginning to put the pieces of yourself together."

I lifted my face upward to the sun and thought of the few times I could honestly say I had experienced a sheer and complete feeling of happiness. Most of the time I had aborted the feeling by reminding myself of the negatives that persisted either during that moment or in my life in general. Like right this moment. The hot sun on my face filled me with unabashed pleasure until I remembered that I could get sunburned if it lasted too long. I laughed at myself. So what if I got a red nose and it peeled later? So what?

David began to skip. He certainly loved to skip. I skipped with him. Our knapsacks bounced on our shoulders and our knees buckled under us when we skidded on pebbles. I found myself laughing with him. I laughed and laughed and the moment I felt a twinge of negative thought, I drove it from my mind with a mental sweep. Quick flashes of Gerry, the pictures I had made . . . Hollywood, Hawaii, New York . . . the world . . . dancing people I knew, people I wished I didn't know . . . and when the darting flashes turned negative, I would overwhelm them with that same inner light that I experienced in the Himalayas. What was it I had read? First we are in the light, next the light is in us, and finally we and the light become one.

Past the small streams that emptied into the Mantaro, we skipped and walked and skipped again. Blue birds and sparrows darted in and out of tree branches. A hand-woven swinging bridge swayed under us when we crossed back and forth across the river. Time passed but time stood still. I could honestly say I felt happy. Now I could honestly say I didn't care what time it was. Time wasn't feeling. It wasn't action. It was only time. If only I could keep the negative thoughts of my other world—my real world— out of my head.

We raced into Llocllapampa perspiring and exhausted, put our

knapsacks in our rooms and in the afternoon light we sat in the "eating" hall and had warm milk and cold rolls. Outside, the woman with the child on her back pounded wheat from chaff while three men from the village chewed coca leaves and packed dirt and straw into square blocks for what would be their new home. ❋

Chapter 22

"I cannot believe for a moment that life in the first instance originated on this insignificant little ball which we call the earth. . . . The particles which combined to evolve living creatures on this planet of ours probably came from some other body elsewhere in the universe."

—Thomas A. Edison
The Diary and Sundry Observations

N ext day the morning was crisp and for some reason seemed hopeful and new. I looked at my ring watch. It was my favorite piece of jewelry. I had been around the world with that ring watch. It said 9:00 A.M., July tenth. I wondered how the weather was in London. I visualized it somehow. I saw rain and murky streets and people dripping with umbrellas. I saw Gerry coming out of a subway walking toward Parliament. I wondered if my visualization was real or fantasy.

I put on my combat boots, slacks, blouse and sweater and walked outside.

Across the street David was sitting on the stone wall.

"I thought we'd go into Ataura," he said, "but first let's get you some more eggs. Not much of a gourmet menu up here, is it?" He winked and did a hitch step as he disappeared into the restaurant.

The lady with no teeth and the baby came out with a basket of vegetables which she took to our car.

"We're taking her too," said David, handing me some hot milk and two peeled eggs. "She needs to sell her vegetables and doesn't often get a lift."

She smiled with toothless delight and got into the back seat. I wished I could get her fitted for some real-world dentures.

The morning light across the Andes was different from the Himalayas. The shadows fell with broader strokes and were more horizontal because the mountains were more spread out. The mountains looked more like humped plains.

Golden slashes of wheat waved gently in the morning breeze. Sheep and cows and llamas ambled lazily together on the roadside interspersed every so often with toddling babies whose mothers carried other children in orange-pink pouches on their backs.

I ate my eggs. David spoke in Spanish to the woman who sat in the back seat. He translated for me. She was talking about wild flowers that could be ground up into a paste, heated and placed on the sinuses to relieve pressure. She said there was a medical use for every herb in the hills and we could buy them all in Ataura. Her baby slept so soundly it looked like dead weight in her lap.

I lifted my arm and hand across the back of the seat. The woman saw my ring watch. She touched it and her hands were warm. She said something in Spanish. David said, "She wants your ring. She thinks it's beautiful and wants it."

Immediately I felt my mind clutch. Would I give my favorite piece of jewelry and my connection to the real world (because it was a watch) to this lady that I didn't know? I watched David watch me.

The woman took my finger in her hand and removed the ring watch. I didn't resist. She clutched it in her hand, then looked up at the sun.

"What would make her happy?" I asked David. "Ask her, would you please? What would make her really happy?"

He did. She answered, "Rings and things."

I said, "That would make you happier than happiness?"

"Oh, yes," she said with conviction, "because it would mean my family was comfortable." She turned the ring over on her finger posing her hand out in front of her and smiling. "What is that?" she asked next, pointing to our box of Kleenex. "Is it like toilet paper?"

I handed it to her, first demonstrating how the pop-up box worked. She seized the box and turned it over and over examining each edge. Then slowly she pulled out the first tissue. When the tissue under it replaced it she seemed startled. But she didn't make a game out of it; she conserved the tissues. She folded her hands across her baby on her lap and looked at the ring watch. I didn't say anything. I watched the scenery, feeling ashamed that I was afraid she would keep it. Why couldn't I just sweepingly say, "It's yours. I can get another one later." But I couldn't. It represented personal attachments and memories. But it wasn't just the ring watch. It was any "thing" that I had had a personal experience with. The monetary value of the "thing" had nothing to do with it. It was the emotional attachment. It was almost as though "the things" were extensions of an investment in love. Those "things" were always there when I wanted them. They never went away. They were permanent. All I had to do was reach out and touch them and they were there. I could depend on them. They made me feel safe because behind them were the people whose love I wanted the most. Was that then the basis for greed? Was it mostly a manifestation of the need for human love that we somehow never got enough of? Was a security blanket or a teddy bear the beginning of the acquisitionary replacement of love? I gazed out at the morning feeling David feel me thinking. Up ahead of us, looming into the white clouds, were high mountains covered with ice and snow.

"Those are the Huaytapallana Ice Peaks," said David.

I looked out at them. They seemed above the real world—white and graceful and stark. I wondered what the weather was like on the mountains. I wondered if Shangri-La lay beyond. I wondered what it would be like to try to get there on foot.

"Have you been to the Ice Peaks?" asked the woman.

"No," I answered. "Have you?"

"Oh, no," she said. "But many people have seen the flying discs that come from behind the peaks. Do you have flying discs in your mountains in the United States?"

I turned around in my seat and looked into her eyes. They were innocent and casual.

"Yes," I said. "I guess so. But I've never seen one."

"They leave marks when they land," she said. "And if you come too close they get frightened and go away. They come out at night, when it's too cold for us to watch them. Lots of them go back and forth across the sky."

I took a piece of Kleenex out of the box and blew my nose.

"What are they, do you think?" I asked.

"I have no opinion. I only listen," she said.

"Well, what are they doing?"

"Scientists come here to look at them. And they say we are nothing compared to those discs."

"What do you think the discs are doing?"

"They come from Venus."

"From Venus?"

"Yes, the scientists told us. They said they were studying our planet."

"Are you afraid of them?" I asked.

"No. A friend of mine saw one land and he walked over to it. But just when he got up to it it flew away. He thought the people were afraid of him."

"Why?"

"Because he is bigger than they are."

I waited for her to say more. She didn't. She just looked out of the window. It wasn't that she didn't want to talk. She just wasn't much interested in the subject and had apparently exhausted its possibilities. Or perhaps she was just being polite in satisfying a stranger's curiosity. In any case, she held the baby's head and embarked on an animated conversation about the sale of her vegetables and how prices were getting so high. She said she had heard that we used some chemical medicine to grow our vegetables bigger and wondered how she could get some.

We drove on over the spreading terrain. I tried to absorb what

the woman had said. The sun was directly above the Ice Peaks now, making them glisten.

At an intersection three policemen stopped us and asked David where we were going and why. They peered in at us. Seeing that foreigners were driving they cautioned us about the riots in Huancayo (where we were not going) and waved us on.

More people appeared along the roadside the closer we got to town. Every now and then we'd see a man dressed in a black western suit.

"They are in mourning when they're dressed like that," said David.

The woman talked about her children. She said she had five of them. She said she didn't want any more so she and her husband stopped having sex. When I mentioned birth control methods she had trouble understanding and had no knowledge at all about her own body. She was young, in her thirties, and so were her friends, who were all having the same problem. None of her friends had sex anymore either, in an effort to keep their families from expanding.

More women with magenta-striped pouches on their backs appeared walking toward Ataura. They wore their customary white wide-brimmed hats and skirts with white piqué petticoats, looking as though they were costumed extras in a movie being shot on location. There were dogs everywhere, and as we entered the town the first thing I heard was a Neil Sedaka record playing on a juke box. We parked the car and got out to walk. The woman walked away with my ring watch and her baby. I stared after her. David watched me.

The street bazaars sold everything from bedding to freshly ground coffee and old records. The sun was hot now but in the shade of the buildings it was cool. Pictures of Christ with a candle underneath hung in every shop. People sipped a sweet corn cola called Maiz as they ambled about. Dogs scampered through the fresh fruits and vegetables. Laid out on the streets in the sun for

sale were rope, shoes, plastic tubs, beans, peas, and colored materials. Young boys rented comic books to read. A woman braided
rope she had just bought.

An old man dressed in a pair of beat-up slacks, sneakers, a
brown felt hat with a flower over his left ear and a gray tattered
sweater stood next to a restaurant juke box. He moved gently, but
out of rhythm, trying to keep time to an Elvis Presley record. An
empty Inca Cola bottle protruded from his back pocket as he
shuffled over to someone in the restaurant and begged for food
which he immediately dumped into his brown felt hat. Eating soup
at a table across from him sat a man who was clearly drunk,
shouting obscenities at the wall.

Down the street young people waited for a movie theater to
open. *The Ten Commandments* was on the bill and a turquoise
wrought-iron gate separated the people from the box office.

Our lady caught up with us and directed us to the herb stall.
Laid out on a blanket were small piles of herbs which she said
would cure most any ailment a person could have. Tara for
asthma, valeriana for the nervous system, *Hircampuri* for the liver,
digestion, diabetes, bile and heartburn. I took some of that to
make tea and there was a tree bark called *Sangredanada* which
was good for ulcers. I should have bought that too.

Three women sat on a curb. One was nursing a baby with her
hand in the lap of a friend, while the third petted a dog gnawing on
a bone between them. A man rubbed powdered sulphur on the
brim of his white hat to make it stiff. Beside him was some cheese
made of boiled milk called *quesillo*.

Inside a flower market, a fairyland display of gladiolas, daisies,
Spanish carnations, rooster's crests, chrysanthemums and jonquils
dazzled my eyes. Children, eating Peruvian popcorn made with
sugar, walked among the flowers.

Our lady took her vegetables off to sell. She still had my ring
watch. I tried not to notice. I knew I would see her later. David
and I walked until we were hungry. We sat in an indoor-outdoor

restaurant having rice and beans topped with onions and a hot sauce called *rocoto* which must be the spiciest condiment devised by man.

"Do you like it here?" I asked David.

"Yes," he said, "it's real. The people have no pretensions. They are what they are. They're simple."

"Maybe when people are comfortable," I said, "they hurt each other more. Maybe we should all stay poor and struggling."

"No," he said, "I don't think so. That would negate progress and the drive for a better life. No, the answer is something like my credo. Do you want to hear it?"

"Sure."

He cleared his throat and, as though he was reciting at graduation class, he said, "Work hard. Don't lie. And try not to hurt anyone. That's it. That's how I live. I remind myself of that three-pronged philosophy every day. I've educated myself not to forget it."

"Do you get depressed and lonely?"

"Sure."

"How do you keep going?"

"I guess you could say that happiness is knowing what you believe in."

"But the lack of self-doubt is what makes some people self-righteous and dangerous."

"Yes, but a person who is self-righteous wants everyone else to think as they do."

I thought about that for a moment.

"Do you think I do that?"

"What?"

"Want things my way?"

David put down his fork. "From what I pick up about you, I would have to say yes."

I felt as though he had slapped me. My eyes welled with tears.

"What's wrong?" he said.

I tried to hold the tears back, but I couldn't. I could feel them run down my cheeks and David's soft blue eyes looking through to my insides. And at the same time, I was flooded with insight.

David reached over and mashed a tear on my chin. "That one traveled a long way down," he said. "It's the same journey we all have to travel before we realize who we are." He paused. "Is that what's going wrong with you and your friend?" he asked.

I tried to talk clearly. "My friend?"

"Yes," said David, "there must be some man you're involved with that you're going off to meet in strange places all the time."

"You mean like I'm doing with you?"

"Well, yes," he said.

"I guess what you said about me is fair, and I guess our problems are inevitable. I want him to *look* at what he's doing and he won't. Not really. I guess I do want him to see things my way. If only he would *really* look, he'd find his own way. But he won't. It's frightening to him. And I guess I have to accept that. If he *wants* to ignore the truth of himself, I guess I must allow him that privilege, mustn't I? He has the right, I guess."

David reached across the table and took my hand.

"You, on the other hand," he said, "have a mind like an oil drill. You're one of those people who may hassle others but you'll also get to yourself. You *have* the self-courage or whatever you want to call it to take a good honest look and you will be ruthless with yourself once you see what you're doing. In fact you shouldn't be too ruthless. As I've said before—be patient with yourself."

Why did gentleness make me cry?

"C'mon," said David. "I went through the same thing, you know. You have to, to get to where you want to be."

"Where do I want to be?" I spluttered.

"Where you live, don't you? Where you deeply and basically live is what you are trying to reach, isn't it? Isn't that how it feels?"

"It feels like everything I've lived has been a sham, a glossy eight-by-ten. And it turns out that most everything I lived and believed was a myth."

"Like what?"

"Well, I thought when I died that was the end. I believed that what I saw was what there was. I believed there was nothing more and nothing less than here and now and that was all I had to deal with. I believed that the life the human race led was real and physical. Now I find we've been playing parts in some spiritual play, with an ongoing script. So when I start thinking about how I've played my part, I'm not too happy."

"Well, we all feel that way, don't we? Besides, what are you worried about? You'll get to play another part after this and another one after that. In fact you'll keep on playing parts until you finally get it right!"

I laughed and sputtered and ate some more beans and hot sauce.

"This hot sauce is the worst," I said. "It makes me cry."

"Well, life is like hot sauce. As soon as you start enjoying it, it makes you cry. It's *accepting* the combinations that is the key. And you can't accept any of that stuff until you accept yourself. And to accept yourself you have to know yourself. To know yourself is the deepest knowledge of all. Christ said it: 'Know thyself.' And then be true to it. Because *you* are a microcosm of the cosmos."

I leaned back and sighed. My legs were stiff from sitting. I needed to stand up and stretch and walk.

David paid the check and we went outside. People were packing up their wares to be ready for sundown. In the mountains the sun dictated all commerce, activity and behavior.

We walked around for a while. David had some Inca Cola at a candy stand and I had a tangerine. The lady with the vegetables and my ring watch had disappeared, either hitching a ride from someone else or staying in town.

David and I got in the car and started back to Llocllapampa.

The early evening light was clear and purplish blue. The stretched plains outside of Ataura were dotted with people trudging home for the night. Dogs barked in the distance and a baby or two cried. David was quiet as he drove. I thought about the truth of what he had said. That I wanted life my way, and on my terms. That whoever I was involved with should look as closely at themselves as I was trying to look at myself. He hadn't said it as an accusation, but more that I would have to admit it if I wanted to move on. He had implied also that my strident compulsion to insist that others analyze themselves was not altogether unfair because it forced a degree of progress in them, but I should respect their inability or reluctance to do that if they didn't want to.

I, in fact, was having a problem looking at the truth myself, so why couldn't I respect the fact that others might experience the same pain? Gerry really must have gone through hell; loving me and caring so much about what I thought, but at the same time feeling it impossible to look at himself in a light that he knew would please me. He had often told me he felt so inadequate in living up to my expectations. I could see what he meant. No man could live with that kind of challenge. He had to be his own man, not the man I wanted him to be. And, if it wasn't enough, it wasn't enough.

The sun was completely gone now. Life in the mountains revolved around the sun. I felt my stomach settle into a kind of an easy place. When it was easy, I was easy.

David seemed to be mesmerized by the road. He stared straight ahead saying nothing. Then he turned to me.

"Shirl?" he said. "There's something I need to tell you. About a girl called Mayan."

"Sure," I said quietly. "Whatever you want."

He drove on for a moment or two. Then he said, "Ask me some questions so I can lead into it, okay?"

"Okay," I said, liking the game. "Let's see. Did you have a love affair with her?"

"Well, yes," he said, "but it wasn't what you'd call a regular type love affair. It was more like a cosmic love affair."

I chuckled to myself thinking that all love affairs seemed cosmic when you were having them.

"Well," I said, "I can understand that. What did she do? I mean did she have a profession?"

David lit up one of his cigarettes and opened the window to breathe deeper. "Well, actually she's a geologist. She was up here on a mining expedition."

"Here? Oh, I see. So you had your love affair up here in the sulphur baths and along the banks of the bubbling Mantaro?" I realized how sarcastic I must be sounding but I really did it so David would feel comfortable with the teasing.

He didn't react. "No," he said, "I was up here with two other guys just bumming around when I met her."

"Oh, a mountain pickup?" I said, going too far.

He still did not react. "Well, no," he said. "It wasn't like that. I was out walking alone one morning and she came driving along this very road in an old Pontiac. She stopped and got out. When I first saw her I thought she was the most beautiful woman I had ever seen. She seemed almost translucent. I mean her skin was shining. I didn't notice what she was wearing—jeans, probably—but the way she moved was like flowing. And I remember I couldn't take my eyes off her face. I don't know. It was the whole effect. It just knocked me for a loop, and yet I felt perfectly and wonderfully peaceful. *At peace.*"

As David described his feelings I noticed that his face relaxed. All the muscular tension that was usually operating with quick awareness in him dropped away. He sounded as though he had been instantly hypnotized.

"What else did she look like?" I asked.

"Small," he said. "Real small and petite, with long thick black hair, this marvelous very white transparent skin, and dark dark almost almond-shaped eyes. Not Oriental eyes, I mean not with

those lids, but with a tilt, a slant to them. She walked over to me, almost as though she knew I'd be there. We began to walk together. And the strange thing, although it didn't seem so at the time, is that we didn't say anything to each other. It was as though we didn't need to. I had never experienced anything like that before and I didn't give it much mind. I felt almost that she knew what I was thinking anyway."

David stopped, remembering.

"Yeah," he continued, shaking his head with memories. "Yeah, so after a while I thought I should say *something*. So I asked her what she was doing up here, and she said she was with her people doing some geological studies in the mountains. I asked her what people. She said she'd tell me later. That sounded okay. I asked her where she was from. She said she'd tell me that later, too. So I didn't ask her anything else. Then she began to ask me all about myself. But for some reason I can't explain I felt there was no need for her to do that."

"How do you mean?" I asked, feeling that David was in some other world as he recalled this extraordinary meeting.

"Well," he said hesitantly, "you know that feeling you sometimes get when you meet someone new that they really know you and understand you? Well, it was like that. I felt that she really seemed to know all about me and she was just kind of giving me time to get used to the idea."

David looked ahead, thinking to himself.

"And you?" I asked. "Did you feel that you knew her?"

I thought he was going to tell me that he was feeling he had known her in another life or something.

"No, not really." He hesitated. "So then," he continued, "well, we walked together, and soon she began to talk about all kinds of stuff . . . the world, governments, different attitudes in different countries, God, languages. I mean it was Greek to me. I wasn't into any of this stuff at the time, you understand."

"So it was quite a time ago?"

"Yeah. Long time. I was beginning to think she was some kind of international spy only I couldn't figure out who for. She talked about the negative energy of some of our world leaders and how people needed to believe in themselves, that the most important relationship was between each soul and God. I asked if she was a Jesus freak. She laughed and said in a way she was a lot freakier than that but that if we had really understood what Christ was talking about no one would call it freakish. She talked and talked. We had dinner, and she talked. I loved talking and listening and being with her but I just didn't know what to make of most of what she said. After awhile I asked her where she was staying. But she wouldn't tell me. I didn't press it. Soon she smiled and said she had to leave but that I'd see her again. She showed up the next day and found me. We went for another all day walk and she talked more. Always important stuff. I couldn't figure out what was going on and told her so. She said she'd tell me when the time came, but if I felt I was learning from her I should just relax and learn.

"I took a walk in and around these hills every day. And every day she found me, regardless of where I walked. We talked about so many things. Then one day, we were sitting by the river and she began to talk, very specifically, about the human soul and what it was. Before I met Mayan I couldn't have cared less whether there was life after death or whether God was alive and well and living in Orange County. And souls? . . . Jesus. But I listened to her and after awhile I realized she sounded as though she was giving me some sort of important scientific information. She said I should write it down because she said I was capable of absorbing it and one day I would pass it on to the right person who would see that it was noticed . . . maybe that person is you."

"Me?" I asked, startled. I was thoroughly absorbed in his story about this Mayan and didn't see myself as a part of it at all.

"Well, maybe. She said I should record everything she was teaching me, which I did, and she said I should commit it all to paper so I could look at it and show it to others."

"Oh, did you write it down?"

"Yes. Would you like to read it?"

"Well, sure. But I think I'm still missing the point. Why didn't you give me that stuff about her along with all the other reading material you gave me?"

"Well, because of who she is."

"Who she is? What do you mean?"

David actually blushed. Then he clammed up. "Ask me some more questions," he said. He sounded a bit strained.

This was more than a simple tale of boy-meets-girl in the mountains. This was some kind of therapy.

"Okay," I said. "Mayan. That's an exotic name. Where is she from?"

David choked on his cigarette. "You mean what country or what city?"

"Well, yeah." I couldn't understand the problem. "I mean, from the way you described her she sounded very exotic. Might she have been from Polynesia?"

"No. Further than that."

"Further—what do you mean, further east? Is she from Japan or China or something?"

"No, not further east, further up."

"Further up?" I was beginning to sound like the straight man in a vaudeville act.

"Yes, further up and further out."

"David," I said, "now you're the one who's far out. What's going on here? What are you talking about? *Tell me.* This is a stupid game. You've had enough lead-in—just tell me. Where could she be from that's so hard to say? Another planet?"

David turned around and took both hands off the wheel and held them in the air. "You got it!" he said. "You guessed it. You're right."

"What, for God's sake?"

"What you just said."

"That Mayan was from another planet?"

"Yes, yes, yes, yes! That's what I found so hard to tell you. It's true though. I swear to God, it's true. And she proved it to me several times over, which I'll tell you about."

I felt myself shut my mouth. I took one of David's cigarettes from the pack and lit it and inhaled. I opened the window on my side and blew the smoke into the night air. Then, holding the cigarette, I scrunched down into the seat and put my feet on the dashboard and smoked. I remember in detail every move I made because the thing that was mind-boggling to me was that I felt he was sincere. I know it must sound crazy, but I actually felt that he was not nuts or hallucinating or making it up.

We drove on quietly. I didn't say anything. Neither did David. The night was clear and dry and cold. The stars hung like zircons in the sky. I looked up. Had I really heard him say what he said? He was a man I trusted. He had been so much a part of my growing spiritual understanding. I at least believed he believed what he had said. In fact I'd heard about quite a few people who claimed to have had contact with extraterrestrials but I had never been in the position of having to evaluate their sincerity. I left that up to interested scientists or psychologists.

But now it seemed I would have to make some kind of judgment about a friend. I stared at the crystal stars and remembered the Christmas telescope I had received as a child after months of begging. I remembered the nights I had gazed through the telescope into the heavens, feeling somehow that I belonged there. Wasn't that everyone's haunting desire? Were the heavens a fundamental reminder that we as humans belonged to the magic network of the cosmos? That we were all an integral piece of a gigantic universal puzzle which was not so clear to us yet because of our limited three-dimensional consciousness? Did David and others like him desire to understand so fervently that they actually believed they had

"contact" with a piece of the cosmic puzzle? I smoked my cigarette and then breathed deeply, aware of the contradiction that I desired pure air at the same time that I was polluting my own lungs.

Llocllapampa was dark and peaceful when we arrived. Next to our "hotel" some piglets truffled around in an old rubber tire enjoying mush grain which was their dinner, while their mother looked on patiently.

The woman with the child had not returned. Her mother had cooked a kidney stew in wine sauce for the evening meal. The hot thick rolls were freshly baked and sweet churned butter spilled around the edges. Two kerosene lamps hung from a coat hanger on a beam above us giving light to our table. The radio blared with the soccer game as the family's young children walked in and around our table watching us eat. The older woman used a gas stove to cook on, which was fueled by a propane pipe on the side of the road. The stove and sink and refrigerator were up against one wall of the restaurant and barely had any light over them.

"Beautiful night tonight," the older woman said to David. "It would be a good night for the astronomers."

David stretched his arms over his head and sighed. Then quite casually he asked her in Spanish, "Have you ever seen a UFO?"

"Oh yes," she said, "many. And my uncle has seen them fly right into Lake Titicaca and disappear. He was frightened at first because he thought maybe he was going loco." She pointed to her head. "But then several of his friends told him they had seen the same thing. He felt better."

David sighed deeply again as though he were relieved at what she said. She went to the stove and dished out some stew for us. I followed her.

"What do you think they are?" I said, feeling like one of thousands of tourists who must have asked the same question.

She put the stew on the table for us. "Extraterrestrial aliens," she said. "Everyone knows that."

"Do you think they're friendly?" I asked.

"I don't know. I think so," she said. "They live high in the mountains and they fly their discs way under the mountains so that no one can find them."

She brought us some hot rolls to go with the stew and asked if we had enjoyed Ataura. I nodded and smiled. But she didn't seem particularly interested in pursuing the preposterous nature of her previous subject of conversation: like our friend in the car, the extraterrestrials in her landscape were unimportant, a curiosity that did not affect her life. Daily living, making ends meet, had a lot more significance for her.

Now, having observed the conversational amenities, she simply set our table and went about her after-dinner chores.

I looked at David across the steaming stew. I wasn't hungry.

"That's the way they all act up here," he said apologetically. "They're just used to it. They wonder why people like us are so intrigued. They laugh about the astronomers who come to study and wait. They say the discs will never come out when *they* are here. They say the disc people like to be alone, and that's the way the mountain people treat them. The mountain people don't know why they're here, except a lot of them say they are mining minerals in the mountains."

"And they're not afraid of them?"

"Don't seem to be. They say they've never hurt anybody, in fact, they say they run away."

"And lots of people have seen them?"

"Shirley," said David, "everyone I've talked to up here has a flying-disc story. *Every single one.*"

I looked into his eyes. They were calm and I would have to say relieved.

"David," I said, "where can I find your Mayan?"

He looked at me and let his shoulders drop away as though a big load had been removed from his back.

"I can't *find* Mayan," he said quietly. "I miss her terribly and keep coming back here hoping she'll turn up. She changed my life.

Everything I think now is because of what I learned from her. She is the reason I found such peace in myself. And I want to impart it all to you."

I looked out the window of the building called FOOD into the dark night of the Andes mountains.

"David," I said, "whatever I could say about what I've suddenly found myself involved in here would be truly—to coin a cliché—a masterpiece of understatement."

I got up from the table. We walked under the low-slung gateway to our "hotel."

"But thanks, David," I said, "thanks for trusting me and for telling me about it."

His hand squeezed gently on my shoulder. In the dark his voice caught in his throat.

"G'night," he said. "Don't let the bedbugs bite."

I kissed him on the cheek and went into my dark and dank sleeping room and fell asleep immediately because I was frankly a little bit frightened to stay awake and think about what was going on. ❀

Chapter 23

"Looking at the matter from the most rigidly scientific point of view, the assumption that, amidst the myriads of worlds scattered through endless space, there can be no intelligence, as much greater than man's as his is greater than a blackbeetle's, no being endowed with powers of influencing the course of nature as much greater than his, as his is greater than a snail's, seems to me not merely baseless, but impertinent. Without stepping beyond the analogy of that which is known, it is easy to people the cosmos with entities, in ascending scale until we reach something practically indistinguishable from omnipotence, omnipresence, and omniscience."

—Thomas H. Huxley
Essays Upon Some Controverted
Questions

The next morning I stepped into the sunlight refreshed as though I had slept for a week.

David was waiting. He had some of our famous hot milk and rolls for me and we drank and ate as we began to walk.

I looked out across the mountainous plains toward the Ice Peaks on the horizon. "So what else hides up there besides all the UFOs the locals chat about?" I asked, gently choking on a roll.

David laughed. "Well, since you ask—Mayan said the valleys in between the peaks are unreachable by land. That's why it's safe for them. When she first described it to me it sounded like *Lost Horizon.*"

"David," I said, "umm—did Mayan say exactly where she was from?"

"Sure. The Pleiades."

"Well. Did you ever question her claim that she was an extraterrestrial?"

David laughed and spit out part of his roll.

"Are you kidding? I thought I had gotten ahold of some bad pot. Or she had. Of course I didn't believe her. In fact, after she told me I was openly hostile to her. Then one day very early in the morning, sunrise, as a matter of fact—long before anyone else was up—she instructed me to go to the base of one of the foothills over there and watch the top of a specific peak. I did. And you know what I saw?"

"What?" I wasn't sure I wanted to know.

"I looked up into the sky and exactly over that peak came one of those flying discs I had heard the peasants talk about. I thought I would crap. From then on she had no problem with me. But I have to tell you she scolded me for forcing her to use the 'seeing is believing' technique. She said I should have been more intelligent and open-minded."

"You mean gullible like me?"

"Well," he answered, "I told you in the beginning—real intelligence is being open-minded. That doesn't make you a fool."

"No?" (Why did I feel like one?)

David glanced at me. "No," he said very firmly. "Listen, Shirl. What's happening to you *is* mind-blowing. Just the way it was with me. And it's happening awfully fast. There's no way to really say these things without going all the way. That's why it seems so heavy. Look, there's a lot of outside proof of unidentified spacecraft—I mean from sources like the Air Force, radar tracking stations, literally hundreds of *multiple* sightings, that is, people who've seen them at the same time and place and *with* others—so we can go along with that, right?"

"Right."

"Okay. If there are UFOs, somebody's got to be controlling them—in person, or by remote. And if not Earth people—and everyone seems agreed these craft do things our technology does not know about—then it's got to be extraterrestrials."

He peered at me to see how I was taking this. "It's a pity every-one needs their own private proof," he went on, "because from what Mayan told me, the extraterrestrials are *superior* because they understand the process of the *spiritual* domain of life. She says science, really highly advanced science, and spiritual under-standing, are the same thing. Even Einstein was saying that. So, if you've gone as far as you have with the spiritual stuff, why not try to make the connection with higher technology? If it doesn't feel right, forget about it."

Forget about it? My God, who in hell could forget this kind of thing?

David saw me thinking . . . "open-minded" as he would say.

"Look," he said, "you don't have a problem with the reincarna-tion stuff, do you?"

"No," I said, "not really. Not after all I've read on the subject and experienced myself. I mean, when I play a role, I put on the emotional cloak of another person. So, I can see that the soul might do the same thing every time it re-embodies."

I was reminded of the many, many actors and actresses I had met who expressed bewilderment at where they got their inspiration when confronted with roles entirely alien to anything they had personally experienced: many times we based feelings we were supposed to act out on events in our own lives, but more often than not we were asked to dredge up feelings and reactions that we had never been familiar with, and as far as we knew, were outside our frame of reference. Yet the miracle of inspiration carried us to some deeper understanding, and when we were especially good, there was a faint resonance under our consciousness that reminded us that we had in fact emotionally been there before.

Maybe actors really were in effect the spiritual re-enactors of the soul's experience. Maybe that's why it felt familiar to me.

My mind drifted again to those haunting summer nights lolling on the hot grass with my telescope. It was as though I *remembered*

the "feelings" I had had when I was looking at the stars. They felt familiar. It was as simple as that. Was I remembering an acquaintance with the knowledge of life there? Had I, or for that matter, had everyone on Earth today experienced the familiarity with "helpers" from other celestial places during our long struggle through the traumas of time? John and McPherson and Ambres had said as much. But who were *they*? Shit, I thought, it's perfectly straightforward—they are disembodied spirits who believe the world has always been visited by extraterrestrials. David is an embodied spirit who believes the same . . . My mind leapt to the Bible and I wondered if Ezekiel and Moses, for example, had been in the same circumstances centuries ago that David believed he found himself in with his Mayan today? It was easier then, I thought. Wonders and marvels were practically an everyday affair—*everybody* believed in such things then. Oh God, I thought—just like the folks around here . . .

I asked David if we could just sit in the sun for awhile. We found a grassy spot nestled in the mountain rocks and stretched out. We breathed deeply for a few minutes and lay down looking up at the sky.

I tried to put everything out of my mind and just "be." I felt David do the same. Birds chirped and the river water gurgled and splashed. A small black dog ambled by, left his signature on a bush, and trotted happily away.

About half an hour must have gone by. We didn't speak. It was nice to feel peaceful. Then I heard David say something. His voice was slurred and sleepy. Or maybe it was I who was sleepy.

I looked over at him. "What?" I asked.

He sighed, turned over on his side, and looked at me. "Want to talk about Mayan?" he asked. "Because she had a lot to say about you."

"About *me*?" I felt foolish. "Look, David. I don't know any Mayan. I mean, she's *your* problem."

David grinned. "Oh, she's no problem—although she may have created a couple for you."

"What do you mean?"

"Well, that's why we need to talk about her."

I thought a moment. "Okay if I record this?"

"Sure."

I took out my tape recorder and pushed the record button. If this was really happening, I wanted to be able to prove it to somebody. I checked the moving tape and proceeded. "Well," I said, "now what's this all about, David?"

"In the first place, do you remember a guy coming to your door—oh, maybe ten years ago, with three stones from the Masai chieftain you knew so well?"

My memory raced backward. Yes, I remembered someone ringing my doorbell in Encino about two years after my African trip, sometime in the mid-sixties. He didn't identify himself. He made no impression on me at all, but he handed me three colored stones which he said were magic amulets for health, wisdom, and security. The Masai chieftain had met him on safari and had asked if he was from America. He had said yes, and the chieftain then had asked him if he knew me. He said no, but he had heard of me. The chieftain had simply said, "Will you give these to her?" And the guy said yes, somehow he would.

Then it struck me.

"How the hell do you know about that guy?"

"Oh, it was me," David said.

"*You?*" My voice rose to a strangled squeak.

"Yes. Now calm down, Shirl. As a matter of fact, I didn't know myself at the time what it was all about. All I knew was the man gave me the stones for you and asked me to deliver them. I simply thought 'far out'—and did it."

"And then what?" I said belligerently, feeling somehow invaded.

"Well, a good deal later, Mayan told me about it. I mean what it

meant. She said I had been directed to you because we'd known each other in previous lives, and some day you'd want proof of it."

"Well, why all the goddamn secrecy? Why couldn't you tell me who you were all this time?" And even as I asked I knew the answer.

"You weren't ready, were you? The whole point was to deliver the stones—even before *either* of us knew what it was about. Then Mayan had to convince me. And now I have to convince you . . ."

"I guess," I said slowly, "if proof is needed, it makes sense. But what's the point? What does it all mean?"

"What it comes down to, Shirley, is that you're to be a teacher. Like me. But on a much wider scale."

"A wider scale?"

"Yes."

"What do you mean? I'm no teacher. I haven't got the patience. I'm a learner."

"Yes, but you like to write, don't you?"

Oh my God, I thought. Am I *supposed* to write a book about all of this? Did I subconsciously plan to do that? Was that why I took my tape recorder with me everywhere and wrote notes at the end of every day?

"She thought that with your particular mental bent you could write a very entertaining, informative account of your personal excursion into these matters and maybe teach people at the same time."

Jesus, I thought, did this make sense? My other two books had been a personal account of my travels and thoughts through Africa, India, Bhutan, America, politics, show business, and China —was I now supposed to write an account of my past lives, God, and extraterrestrials?!? I laughed at the logical absurdity of it.

"Who would believe it if I wrote for publication about all this?" I asked.

"You'd be surprised," he said. "There are more people out there doing this than you realize. Everyone is motivated by a desire to know the truth. *Everyone.*"

"The truth? *What* truth?"

"The simple truth," he said, "of knowing yourself. And to know yourself is to know God."

"You mean *that* is the Big Truth?"

"That's it. The point, Shirley, is that it *is* simple. God is simplicity. *Man* is complexity. Man has made himself complex. But he yearns toward understanding, toward the truth behind that complexity. And those who begin to understand it, *desire* to share their understanding."

"But that would be only *my* understanding. That wouldn't necessarily be the truth."

"No," David said, "there is only one truth, and that is God. You can help others understand God through themselves by sharing the account of how you understand God through *yourself.*"

I felt a kind of clutch in my stomach and in my heart. It was true that I loved to share my adventures with my writing. But to say I would now write about how *I found God* was ridiculous to me. I wasn't even sure I believed in this thing called God. I was interested in people. The idea of having had past lives interested me because it offered an explanation of who I was today.

"David," I said, "look, my own personal identity and how I came to be who I am is something I feel comfortable with, but I can't say I *believe* in God."

"That's right," he said. "You don't *believe* in God. You *know* God. Belief implies acceptance of something unknown. You have simply forgotten what you already know."

I sat in the sunlit silence, my mind battering at itself. I had forgotten what I already knew.

David seemed to sense my flash of fear because he continued, "You certainly picked the wrong line of work if you are afraid of public humiliation, didn't you?"

He caught me off guard.

"What do you mean?" I asked.

"Well," he said, "you set yourself up for a fall every time you walk out on the stage or act in a film, don't you?"

I hadn't quite thought of it that way, but he was right. I had terrible stage fright and it wasn't based on whether I'd be good or not, it was based on what the people would think of me. There was a big difference.

"Did it ever occur to you," he went on, "that you chose a public profession so you would *overcome* your fear of humiliation?"

I had often thought the same thing, but never really admitted it to myself. I longed for anonymity, wanted to be the fly on the wall, was much more interested in asking questions than being asked, and whenever I was involved with the public exposure of my profession, I couldn't wait for it to be over so I could become a recluse again and go away somewhere and think and write.

Yet, I kept on being a public personality as though I was slowly, little by little, trying to squeeze the fear out of myself. And it had gotten better recently too. In fact, the more I learned about my internal self the less self-conscious I was of what others might think. I had always longed for the feeling of being carefree and totally unconcerned with what others thought of me. In fact, I think I had orchestrated a public personality so distinct in that regard that people really did believe I didn't give a damn what anybody else thought. I remembered telling my press agent once that I wanted to appear totally free-spirited.

So I said to David, "Do you think I *planned* to become a so-called 'free-spirited' public personality so I could get away with writing what you and Mayan have been talking about?"

"Maybe," he said. "Maybe that's the karma you chose for yourself. Why don't you just put it on the back burner for now?"

On the back burner? I was trying to stop my mind from lurching over itself. I felt as though I was grasping way beyond what I could understand. It was a feeling of groping in a darkness with only the

help of clichés as lanterns to light the way . . . phrases like inner knowingness, higher consciousness, high vibrations, inner peace, enlightenment, et cetera, et cetera, et cetera. I was feeling none of those things. Instead, I was feeling set up. Was David setting me up to write about all of this?"

"David," I shouted. "For God's sake, you say this Mayan is an *extraterrestrial*? Well, okay. Jesus, if you want to believe it, that's your affair—but I think the whole thing sounds like a tub of shit!" It was more than I could stand.

I was suddenly overcome with suspicion, feeling absurd that I was directing honest questions, as though the discussion was credible at all, to a person who claimed to have had a relationship with an extraterrestrial. It was just suddenly too damn much. I felt more than a little hostile. In fact, I wanted to be even more than harsh. Write about this stuff? I couldn't even think about it anymore. I felt my brain would explode. I had reached my limit of open-mindedness.

David continued to sit peacefully. Then he rolled over on his stomach, apparently unconcerned and uninvolved with what was transpiring. I could feel my pulse accelerate and I began to calculate how long it would take for me to get down from the mountains and onto a plane back to the sane world I understood.

My mind and hostility raced on as though I was having an inner dialogue with myself over my own stupid open-mindedness and the awful truth that I might be one of those suckers born every minute as P.T. Barnum would say.

David breathed calmly.

"David!" My voice was harsh. "Are you there or not?"

"I am here," he answered immediately. His voice was soft, with an annoyingly patient tone.

"Well?" I said loudly and defensively.

He raised up on an elbow. "Well, what, Shirley? You seem to have accepted the idea of reincarnation, you are at least partly convinced that there are UFOs and hence something that flies

them. Now what can possibly make you think the human race has an exclusive on life in the cosmos?"

I didn't know what to think. I began to feel physically uncomfortable. My skin itched. The sun was suffocating. *I did not want to be there.*

Finally David said, "Try to be calm. Breathe deeply and concentrate on that. I know it's a struggle. I went through the same process. What you're suffering from is overload. Overload with everything. Just proceed at your own pace, and try to proceed peacefully. You'll make more progress that way."

"Progress?" I screamed at him. "You are upsetting everything mankind believes in, replacing it instead with some kind of outrageous metaphysical twilight zone mumbo jumbo, and *this* you call progress?"

"It's funny," he said. "They think *our* priorities are mumbo jumbo. *We* are still in the Dark Ages. Certainly the behavior of the human race would seem to bear me out. The fact is, we are still basically rather primitive."

"Well okay," I said, "all *right*. I know that, goddammit. But man is probably only animalistic anyway. That explains why we act the way we do. So why do you espouse all these ideas that we are better than we are?"

"Ah," he said, not in an I-told-you-so manner, but more as if *I* had proved his point. "That's the rub, isn't it? You are upset because *I* believe in you more than you do. And that challenges you to improve beyond what you believe you are capable of."

My God, I thought. That's what I had been doing to Gerry. I snorted out a breath that turned into a chuckle at the way I brought my cosmic outrage down to a personal example.

"Feeling better?" David asked. "I know that when you understand, you understand quickly."

"Oh shit," I said. "I don't know. I don't know what you're talking about."

"Yes, you do," he said gently.

I got up and began to pace around David. I wanted to nudge him with my foot. No—I wanted to kick him.

"Don't be afraid," he said. "Remember you are on the right path or you wouldn't be here."

That made me laugh. Oh Christ, I thought.

"It's all only a question of time anyway," he went on. "But as you can see, just looking around at the world—time is running out. It's a struggle, I know. But that's life."

I laughed again.

"And remember you have already been through this struggle in many lifetimes. So relax. You can do it again."

I knelt back down on the ground beside him.

"But if I've been through this so-called spiritual struggle before, why am I going through it again?"

"Because," he said, "there are other aspects of your soul's progression you need to work out. Patience and tolerance, for example. It's not enough to intellectually understand the spiritual aspect of man. You have to *live* it. Understand?"

"What do you mean? Like Jesus Christ or somebody?"

"Right. He worked out his soul's progression to near perfection. Others can too. That, in fact, was Christ's message: all people can accomplish what he accomplished—know your potential, that's all it takes."

"What about these extraterrestrials of yours? Are they doing it too? Do they *need* to?"

"Certainly," he answered. "Every living soul in the cosmos needs to. *That* is the purpose of life. That's all they are trying to teach . . . know your complete potential. The extraterrestrials are still learning about themselves too. But the spiritual aspect of ourselves is what is missing on Earth."

I looked up into the sun. My skin had stopped itching and once again the sun rays felt good. I sighed to myself and looked over at my tape recorder. It was nearly to the end of the sixty-minute tape.

"Mayan always says," David's voice was a murmur, "love God, love your neighbor, love yourself, and love God's work for you are part of that work. Remember that. And something else. She told me not to forget to tell you one thing. She said that in order to get to the fruit of the tree you have to go out on a limb."

He stopped. I shut off the tape recorder and passed out on my back.

But I have that tape. I have listened to it again and again and heard David repeat the very words that McPherson and Gerry both used. ❊

"The UFO phenomenon is a challenge to mankind. It is the duty of scientists to take up this challenge, to disclose the nature of the UFO and to establish the scientific truth."

—Dr. Felix Zigel,
Moscow Institute of Aviation

❊ I lay there for a long time. Then I felt David move. I turned over and looked at him. He opened his eyes all the way and shielded them from the sun. A tear dribbled from one eye. He looked as though he had just woken from a deep sleep.

He sighed heavily and stretched. "Christ," he said, "I was out. I'm sorry, but I felt so peaceful in the sun I let myself go way under."

He churned his arms in the air and brushed his eyes again. "It's so warm and beautiful."

I just looked at him.

"What's on your mind?" he said, wiping perspiration from his chin. "How long have you been lying there like that?"

"About an hour," I said. "And I have something to say."

Some quality in the tone of my voice must have caught him. He sat up. So did I.

"This is unbelievable," I said. "I feel like a horse's ass. The hell with open-minded intelligence. I think I must be a first-class gullible jerk."

David looked at me with sadness. "You mean about Mayan," he said.

"I mean about the whole damn thing!" I said, almost in tears with outrage, exasperation and a much deeper feeling—of fear that my rage was mistaken . . .

"I know," he said. "Jesus, do I know. I went through all of that too. But then after awhile I just couldn't ignore that what she said 'felt' right. You know what I mean? I mean I know you can make fun of feelings and everything. But when you come right down to it 'feelings' *are* everything. I mean even scientists have to have a 'feeling' about something before they set out to prove it. I just 'felt' that she was telling the truth."

I sat staring at him with my arms dangling onto the grass. Then I stood up and looked down at him.

"David," I said, "how do you know you weren't just projecting some need you felt deep in your subconscious and it manifested in your believing what this person named Mayan said about herself? Maybe you *needed* to believe it—so she picked that up and just told you what you wanted to believe."

David looked at me, astonished.

"But I *didn't want* to believe it," he said. "I told you. It took two trips back here and months of talking to her before I was even civil to her when she tried to tell me about this stuff. I hated what she was saying. I mean, she said she nearly gave up on me. She said I was almost too hostile to tolerate. And she was right. She upset all my beliefs and even my sanity for awhile. I liked my fast cars, and fast women and my life in the fast lane. The last thing I wanted

was to give that stuff up and become spiritual. I wasn't even unhappy. I wasn't looking for anything. But after awhile I had to
admit that what she was saying made sense."

"What made sense, being a person from the Pleiades?"

"Well no," he answered. "Not that. Her spiritual message made
sense. All of her teachings and explanations of the reincarnation of
life and cosmic laws and justice. *That's* what made sense. I
couldn't run away from it."

I watched him closely. He seemed to be so genuine.

"I don't want to convince you of anything, Shirley," he said.
"What you believe is up to you. I just feel you should seriously
consider the possibility of what I am saying. It doesn't make any
difference to my life one way or the other. I already know what I
believe."

I stood with my arms unmoving against my sides.

Another antique-yellow colored train came through the mountains. I wanted to jump into the freshly mined cargo of coal and
dunk myself until I was black with its residue. *That* would be real.
I wanted to dance to every Peruvian juke box I heard. *That* would
be real. I also wanted to skip on top of the orange bubbles of the
Mantaro, unconcerned that I might sink. I wanted to march to the
Huaytapallana Ice Peaks and project myself over them so I could
see for myself what was on the other side.

I got up and started to walk. David stayed where he was.

I walked for the rest of the day alone. My thoughts clanged
together like thick new chains . . . full of confusion, fear, sadness,
and hurt. Then I would experience bewildering eruptions of joy.
What was going on, what was happening to me?

❊ Was David only believing what he needed to believe? I
thought back to California. Did Kevin Ryerson and Cat need to
believe in spiritual entities? Were Sturé and Turid and Lars and

Birgitta so agonized in their lives that they all needed to believe that this incarnate spiritual entity really guided them? Certainly they did not seem agonized, and David had never met any of these people, yet they were all thinking the same thing—from the reality of Karmic cosmic justice to the existence of extraterrestrial spirituality. ❋

Chapter 24

"Take our own bodies. I believe they are composed of myriads and myriads of infinitesimally small individuals, each in itself a unit of life, and that these units work in squads—or swarms, as I prefer to call them—and that these infinitesimally small units live forever. When we 'die' these swarms of units, like a swarm of bees, so to speak, betake themselves elsewhere, and go on functioning in some other form or environment."

—Thomas Edison
The Diary and
Sundry Observations of
Thomas Alva Edison

I went off by myself the next morning, rambling and thinking—or not really thinking, just letting all the new experiences wash through me without trying to sort things out. Absorbing really new thinking, getting a new view, a totally different set of perspectives on life, is a process that takes and needs time—just time—to percolate through. We are so accustomed to the things we have grown up with that we don't even remember the necessary silent times, the shut-out-the-world times, the solitary times of one's growing up. And maybe one always needed some solitude. I sure as hell did right then.

It was late afternoon before I got back to David. "Let's get to the sulphur baths," I said.

"Sure."

As we headed that way David reached into his pocket and handed me a bracelet of what looked like silver. It was just like the one he wore all the time. "Mayan gave me this," he said. "I want you to have it. Wear it on your wrist all the time you are here. It will help make things more clear."

I put it on wondering what he meant.

"What's it made out of?" I asked.

"Oh," he said, "I don't know. It's hard to say. But it works."

"What do you mean? It makes what work?" I couldn't understand what he was talking about.

"Well, when I wear mine, I feel my thoughts are somehow more amplified so that I think with more clarity."

"How come?"

"I don't know exactly," he said. "It's something to do with what she calls the third force."

"Mayan gave you the bracelets?" I asked.

"Yes. Let's get on down to the bathhouse. I can think better there and I'll try to tell you what she told me."

"Okay."

The temperature was beginning to chill as we made our way to the pool house through the afternoon light; the sky was so clear and crisp that I could see the moon hovering in the daylight like a gigantic heavy gray ball. I felt my head vibrate. Some of my confusion lifted. The sky was real. The chill was penetrating. The moon was actual. Of those facts, there was no question.

David carried a candle and I carried my tape recorder. At night, my soft woolen poncho meant as much to me as my hat did during the day. I thought of immersing myself in the lukewarm sulphur water. Already my muscular aches were subsiding. The "waters" were helpful; that was also a fact. Hanging our clothes on the nails of the musty-smelling walls, we quickly undressed and inched our way under the water. It bubbled around us almost like a language. Maybe that was how water talked. Churning our arms around us, we touched the mossy rocks underneath with our feet, and again I was pleasantly surprised at how buoyant the bubbling water was. I felt I couldn't sink if I wanted to. I wondered if I'd be water-logged before this adventure ended.

The bathhouse was dim. David struck a match, lit the candle, turned it upside down to drip wax onto the earth floor above us

and placed the candle securely in the drippings as they dried on the cold stone.

"Relax a little," he said, "you're wound up tight as a drum. I have to tell you more of what Mayan taught me. It's a mind-blower." As though my mind hadn't already been blown enough.

I reached over to the tape recorder and turned it on.

"First," said David, "let's review your high school chemistry and the makeup of the atom."

"I didn't take chemistry," I said. "I always knew I wanted to be in show business, so it didn't seem useful."

"All right—no problem. You know that the proton is the positive charge of energy and the electron is the negative."

"Yes."

"And you know that each of these charges carries energy equally balanced."

"Yes."

"And that the negative and the positive attract each other and the alike charges repel each other."

"Yes."

"You know that the electrons rotate around the protons constantly and at great speeds. In fact, the electrons and neutrons rotate around the protons in relatively the same way that the Earth and other planets in our system revolve around the sun. In other words, this atom is a miniature planetary system."

"Yes, I remember reading that. Quite exciting, I think, that the atom is a microcosm of a planetary system. It makes you wonder if the whole universe isn't in one drop of water."

David's face lit up. But he didn't stop.

"Now," he said, "there is a force at work that acts as the cohesive element enabling that miniature planetary system to rotate. This energy is what Mayan called a Divine Force—a force that is the organizer of all matter in the cosmos. It organizes the atom.

Everything in creation is made up of atoms—trees, sand, water, whiskers on kittens, planets, galaxies—everything. Everything that is physical is made out of atoms. You might say this Force is the ultimate Source, the thinking element of nature."

"Wait a minute," I said, "hold it. A *thinking* element?"

He stopped a minute and looked into the candlelight. Then he said, "Look, Shirley, let me tell you that later, okay? Just listen for now and if it doesn't make sense, forget it."

"Okay," I said. "You brought it up. Take your time. So this Source is the 'thinking' element of nature. Then what?"

"Okay," he said, "now let me break down the components of the atom. You understand that one simple atom is made up of protons, neutrons and electrons, right?"

"Right."

"And for the moment, you understand that this Source is the cohesive glue that holds the electrons and protons and neutrons together?"

"Well, if you say so," I said. "You mean it is a kind of ocean in which everything floats?"

"Good, yes," said David, "that ocean holds the atoms together, the planets together, the galaxies together and the Universe together—together in harmony."

"This is what Mayan told you?" I asked, beginning to feel a strange stirring in my head.

David nodded. "Bear with me."

"Okay." I swallowed.

"Okay." David went on. "The Source, or 'ocean,' as you call it, is made up of balancing and contrasting polarities."

"Polarities?" I asked.

"Yes," said David. "Polarities of positive and negative, yin and yang, or as scientists refer to it today, 'quarks.'"

"I've heard of that," I said.

"I'm not surprised. Some of our scientists suspect this energy is

there but they can't measure it because it is not molecular. They say there's an energy that fills interatomic space, but they don't know what it is. Even *they* call it the cohesive element of the atom, which they term as 'gluon.' They know it is not matter, but rather units of energy."

"Well, specifically, what is it you are getting at?"

"Mayan says it is this subatomic energy that makes up the Source. Therefore the Source, that form of energy, is not molecular. Now I'm going to tell you the hard part to understand, but the part that is the most important. This energy is the energy that makes up the soul. Our bodies are made out of atoms; our souls are made of this Source energy."

I could feel a nervous perspiration begin to seep out of my scalp. Could the soul be made of an energy force as real as the physical? Was that why the soul lived infinitely? My mind tumbled over and over. David's words rescued me.

"Our science doesn't recognize the existence of the soul, so it can't recognize the scientific makeup of the Source. If and when science does get to establishing the Source, it will be acknowledging spirituality as a physical reality."

"*Why?* David, can't you see what a colossal assumption that is? I mean, who *says* this Source, if it exists, is necessarily the soul force? It could be anything—part of a fourth dimension, or space, or time—anything at all. And it seems to me to make damn little difference, at this point, whether we know for a fact, or don't know, what the soul is made of. I mean, if we have to take its basic existence on faith—and we do, there isn't any *proof*—then what's the point of breaking down its components—why the hell not take its composition on faith? Why even ask any questions about the mechanics of the thing? Mechanics only have meaning because they can be proved. The soul can't be *proved*, and so as far as I'm concerned, it doesn't need to be. But don't try and sell me mechanics on faith."

David chuckled. "Mayan said that that's what's wrong with our science. It doesn't allow for the existence of forces that seem to dwell in the simple spiritual realm. That's why they don't really know what electricity *is*—they know it exists only because it has physical results."

"But you really believe the soul is a *physical* force?"

"Yes, exactly. But it is a significantly different *kind* of force from the physical atomic and molecular forces that comprise the body. It is a subatomic force, the intelligent energy that organizes life. It is part of every cell, it is part of DNA, it is in us, and of us, and the whole of it—everywhere—is what we call 'God.' "

I was perspiring now and feeling dizzy. No matter how I protested it, I can only say that this sounded real to me. I don't know why. I can't explain it. I felt I was *remembering* something somewhere way underneath my mind in a place I had never touched. What David reported Mayan as saying triggered *recognition* in me, like suddenly coming into focus on something familiar that you've been staring at without seeing. I felt what he was saying was true because I had known it somewhere, sometime, before. Not the structure of it, so much, as the sure knowledge of a meaningful awareness that exists outside of, or rather *in addition to,* and as a part of, the life we know.

"You see?" he said gently. "This is it. This Source fills and organizes all life. It is the beginning and the end; the Alpha and the Omega. It is the God of Creation. And it is very much in Us."

I stared at him. I couldn't talk. There really was nothing to say.

I thought how arrogant it was to imagine God as a human, with a physical form like ours, created in our own image. No wonder we negated the spirit. Even our religious concepts of the soul were based mostly on physical images. And science couldn't admit the possibility that a spiritual form might actually exist.

"So you see," said David, "when Christ said God is everywhere, in a sense he was being literal—what he meant was this life-guiding spiritual energy is everywhere. Life, then, is the combination of the molecular structure which is physical matter, and the Source which is spiritual energy. The physical form dies. The spiritual energy lives forever."

I clutched my arms around my midriff. Then I wiped the perspiration from my scalp and clutched myself again. I said out loud: "Energy cannot be created or destroyed, just transformed," as though I was reciting high school physics.

"Right," said David. "All is energy. But science only deals in what it can see and prove. Molecular properties are easier to find than energy units. And the soul is an accumulation of energy units. It has its own free will and when its accompanying body dies, it simply individualizes itself until it makes its karmic decision as to what new form will house it. Hence what we call reincarnation. Hence life after death. Hence the life before birth."

I was silent. I wanted to think. I wanted not to think. I wanted, above all, to rest. I breathed deeply. A kind of bile rose to my throat. I stared at the flickering candle. My head felt light. I physically felt a kind of tunnel open in my mind. It grew like a cavern of clear space that was open and free of jumble. It didn't feel like thought. It felt actually physical. The flame of the candle slowly melted into the space in my mind. Once again I felt myself *become* the flame. I had no arms, no legs, no body, no physical form. I became the space in my mind. I felt myself flow into the space, fill it, and float off, rising out of my body until I began to soar. I was aware that my body remained in the water. I looked down and saw it. David stood next to it. My spirit or mind or soul, or whatever it was, climbed higher into space. Right through the ceiling of the pool house and upward over the twilight river I literally felt I was flying . . . no, flying wasn't the right word . . . it was more gentle than that . . . wafting seemed to describe it best . . . wafting higher

and higher until I could see the mountains and the landscape below me and I recognized what I had seen during the day.

And attached to my spirit was a thin, thin silver cord that remained stretched though attached to my body in the pool of water. I wasn't in a dream. No, I was conscious of everything, it seemed. I was even conscious that I didn't want to soar too high. I was conscious that I didn't want to soar too far away from my body. I definitely felt connected. What was certain to me was that I felt two forms . . . my body form below and my spirit form that soared. I was in two places at once, and I accepted it completely. I was aware, as I soared, of vibrational energy around me. I couldn't see it, but I felt a new sense of "sensing" it. It felt like a new dimension of perception, somehow, that had nothing to do with hearing or seeing or smelling or tasting or touching. I couldn't describe it to myself. I knew it was there—physically—yet I knew my body was below me.

Was this what all those people interviewed by Elizabeth Kubler-Ross had experienced? Had my spiritual energy separated itself from the physical form? Was I floating *as* my soul? I was consciously aware of my questions as I soared freely above the Earth. I was so conscious of what I felt that in those moments I understood how irrelevant my physical body was. I was experiencing the separation, I guess. Experiencing the two entities—and very much more besides.

I watched the silver cord attached to my body. I had read about the silver cord in metaphysical literature. It glistened in the air. It felt limitless in length . . . totally elastic, always attached to my body. My sight came from some kind of spiritual eye. It wasn't like seeing with real eyes. I soared higher and wondered how far the cord would stretch without snapping. The moment I thought about hesitation, my soaring stopped. I stopped my flight, consciously, in space. I didn't want to go any higher. As it was I could see the curvature of the Earth, and darkness on the other side of the globe. The space surrounding my spirit was soothing and gentle and pure.

I began to perceive waves of energy connections and undulating thought energy patterns. The silver cord wasn't taut or stretched. It only floated gently.

I directed myself downward, back to my body. Slowly I descended. Slowly . . . down, down . . . gently through the space I wafted back to earth. The energy vibrations subsided . . . the rolling sensation of the undulating thought waves disappeared above me and with a soft fusion of contact that felt like a puff, I melded back into my body. My body felt comfortable, familiar, but it also felt restricting and cumbersome and limiting . . . I was glad to be back, but knew that I would want to go out again.

The silver cord melded into the flickering candlelight and I shook myself free of the concentration and looked over at David who was smiling.

I didn't really understand what had happened. I tried to explain it to David.

"I know," he said. "See how realization is a physical act?" he said. "What you *realized* was your soul and your soul left your body. That's all." But he was clearly delighted.

"You mean I was astrally projecting just then?" I asked.

"Sure," he said. "I was doing that this morning right here while you were off walking. I take trips all over the place. I save on fuel costs," he grinned. "In the astral world you can go anywhere you feel like, meet all kinds of other souls too. It's just that when you return to your body and wake up you often don't remember where you've been. Something like dreaming."

"So is that what happens when you die; your soul just rises out of your body and floats and soars into the astral world?"

"Sure," said David, "except you're only dead if your silver cord snaps. The cord snaps and breaks off when the body can no longer sustain the life force. It's really very simple. I can't tell you specifically how it is to die, but I can tell you that the principle is the same as astral projection, only there's no body to return to."

I began to shiver slightly in the water. I wanted more hot milk . . . something familiar. I couldn't go back to a warm cozy room or bask in a really hot soapy tub. I could only keep going forward regardless of how uncomfortable it might be.

"I guess I should get out of this water," I said, feeling my teeth begin to chatter.

"Okay," said David. "Let's go get some milk and food."

I rubbed my skin hard until it tingled and whipped on my clothes like a quick change artist. Outside David hugged me hard as though I had graduated or something.

All my perceptions were upside down . . . that is all of my worldly, conditioned, perceptions were topsy-turvy. My new perceptions were becoming more clearly simple. What I had experienced had a dreamlike quality to it but it wasn't a dream. It was more like a new dimension.

A cloak of calm settled over me as we had our hot milk and stew with the woman with no teeth and her children. The soccer game from Lima blared loudly on a shortwave radio interspersed with reports of widespread riots in Huancayo about an hour further into the mountains. The announcer said they were "inflation" riots. People were throwing rocks and debris into shop windows protesting the high cost of living. Even here in the Andes people couldn't afford to live because their wages couldn't accommodate the prices. David said there would probably be a change in government soon, whether by coup or otherwise, but it probably wouldn't matter anyway because it would be the same problem all over again.

When we walked outside to cross the highway to our "hotel," it was dark. We stumbled over some large rocks. David said the protestors used the line of boulders as a technique to prevent traffic from making it to Huancayo where its 100,000 residents were already subject to a curfew after nine o'clock. The rocks prevented government troops from rushing to the rescue too.

I had a kerosene lamp which gave off a kind of gaseous, smelly heat. But at least there was some warmth as I walked into my room and collapsed on the bed. The cold earth floor smelled musty and when I wrapped myself in my poncho, I wondered how open I would be to learning if I were more comfortable. Was it necessary to live with basic discomfort in order to learn basics?

"Okay," said David, "have a good sleep. Relax. Maybe I'll see you on the astral plane!" He winked and quietly left.

I stared into the silver fragment of the kerosene lamp until my eyes hurt. I lay on the makeshift cot—listening to the silence of the rocky mountains. I could hear the pigs snorting outside.

My brain swirled and leapt and crawled around inside itself. I was exhausted. I wanted to leave myself. Did I want to run and hide and forget everything I had experienced up here? I had been a grabber at life, wanting to feel, touch, experience everything I possibly could. I couldn't imagine not being avidly involved in the daily scrabble. Yet did I really want my old life back, the familiar agony of searching for purpose and reason, my fears, jealousies, struggles in driving toward whatever was true in reality? Did I long to have back again everything that had made me unhappy, or ecstatic, simply because it was familiar? Would I ever be able to relax again in the belief that life and reality were simply what I could see, touch and hear? That death was death and simply the *end*? Did I want to go back to the "safe" feeling that without proof, nothing was worthy of faith?

I heard a soft tap on the wall separating my room from David's.

"Relax, Shirley," David whispered loudly with a laugh in his voice. "I can feel your brain and it's keeping me awake."

I laughed too. "You got me into this," I said, staring at the gray slab wall beside my head. "Now you say I'm keeping you awake . . ."

"Try to sleep. You need it."

"Sure. How? How do I fall asleep when I know I'm going to live a million years? I'm not sure I've even liked this much."

"Concentrate."

"On what?"

"On your golden dream, remember?"

"Yes, I remember."

Only I didn't. I couldn't think of anything I could call my golden dream. And *that* was harder than anything. ❀

Chapter 25

"... now our whole life, from birth unto death, with all its dreams, is it not in its turn also a dream, which we take as the real life, the reality of which we do not doubt only because we do not know of the other more real life? Our life is but one of the dreams of that more real life, and so it is endlessly, until the very last one, the very real life—the life of God."

—Leo Tolstoy
Letters

I spent the next few days walking and thinking. Sometimes David came with me, sometimes not. Sometimes I wanted to go home, back to America, back to the familiarity of my old world with its fast-paced involvement, its clanking relationships, its unrealistic romance, all the rushing with no seeming purpose—the events, the news, the arts, movies, hits, flops, sweat, hard work, black humor, competition, new fashions, profits, color TV, and success. I missed it all. I was used to it. I had survived in its colorful confusion, and I missed it. But I didn't want to be unfulfilled in it anymore either. I watched the woman with no teeth wash her clothes by stamping on them with her feet. They came out clean. The clothes, I mean. (Probably the feet, too.) That's what I wanted to do with my life . . . stamp on it until it came out clean. *Could* I go back to my old world now? Would I be two people? Was I more than one person anyway? I stopped and laughed right there. That was the whole lesson, wasn't it? I was all the people I had ever lived. I had probably been through versions of this brain drain more than a few times before.

David watched me go through the emotional pull with calm understanding.

"I had to do the same thing," he said one day, sitting on a rock staring into a mountain daisy. "Just know yourself, remember? And in yourself is the universe."

One night after stew in the FOOD building, he asked if I wanted to watch the sky for a while. The food made us warm and gave us a feeling of reinforcement against the cold.

"Let's try it," he said. "If it's too cold, we'll go inside. Straw is warm if we bury ourselves deep enough."

So, using a shovel belonging to one of the coca-chewing workmen, we dug a fairly deep rectangular hole in the soft earth just behind our "hotel." Then we piled mounds of straw into it. We lay on top of the straw and piled even more on top around us. It seemed warm enough to relax. If I thought I was warm, I was warm.

David gazed up into the sky. He had a kind of longing expression on his face.

I lay in the straw wondering how I would feel about Peru when I left it. I had a curious habit of getting homesick for every country I had ever been in—even the Soviet Union which I didn't like very much. Some spark in me was always touched when I went to a new place and I was usually haunted by it when I left. I wondered how many countries I had lived in in my other lives. I didn't understand why I couldn't remember.

The stars above us looked two feet over our heads. I shivered a little but the grandeur made the chill ridiculous. David lay quietly beside me. We looked into the sky for about an hour.

Then I looked over at him.

"I'm glad I came," I said. "Thank you."

Soon after that we fell asleep. If the space discs came out it was irrelevant to both of us. We needed rest. We woke up with the sunrise and walked in the dawn shadows for about two hours. We didn't talk much. And later, when we ate our rolls and hot milk, our conversation was about how reassuring it was that no one or nothing ever dies. In the afternoon, we walked some more . . . up

and down the sides of mountains and along the Mantaro River. We bought Mantaro yogurt along the road. We skipped and ran. We waded in the cold river and splashed with the orange water. I felt totally and completely in the present, and when I took a nap in the late afternoon sun, stretched out on the hot grass, my mind and heart felt as though gentle waves of liquid velvet undulated over and around me.

I began to feel (rather than to think about) a new way of looking at life and myself. I felt as though I was giving up an old self. A self that had believed that guilt, jealousy, materialism, sexual hangups, and doubt were part of being human. I had once come to terms with the permanence of those emotions, felt reasonably resigned to them, and now I was having to undo the resignation and venture into a new kind of life-thought that required that I not only work out the negatives, but that if I didn't I would have to pay for avoiding it with my own karma later on. Since my life would apparently not be over when I died, I was stuck with it right smack into eternity. So I might as well get started now. Such a concept had been alien to anything I ever imagined. I thought about my life and relationships back home.

I remembered Gerry's sudden revelation one day when he said that I had romanticized him to such an extent that he couldn't possibly live up to it. It was my way of programming the relationship so that it couldn't possibly work. Romantic notions did that. They made life impossible to live—realistically or otherwise, because romantic notions were impossible to sustain.

I found myself thinking of Gerry in a different way. I looked at him in a more objective light. Much more realistically and from *his* point of view.

David and I talked about it, although I never identified Gerry. But David helped me with understanding my own feelings. As we talked, it slowly dawned on me that I had always used my loving, protective, cocoon relationships with men *to hold myself back*. To keep from being really free and expansive, I had woven a web of

soothing safety around myself and the man in my life. The *us*, therefore, had been more important to me than *me*. I was protecting myself from my own potential in the name of love.

David and I walked miles every day across the plains of wheat and along the Mantaro River banks. We sat and watched sunups and sundowns. When my conflict got me down, I talked it over with him and he reminded me to examine the reasons for it, my conditioning, my contradictions and that the choice of breaking through to a new freedom and learning process was mine.

Sitting in a relaxed sunlit mood on a hill somewhere, or in the bubbly sulphur water, he came back again and again to his talks with Mayan.

In one session, she had spoken of the need for all women to believe in themselves as women, the need to be secure in that. "Women have the right, even with the independence already achieved in the United States, to be even more independent and free," she said. "No society can function democratically until women are considered equal on every basis, *particularly to themselves*. And you will never attain such a thing other than through your own self-effort. In fact," she said, "nothing is worth having, except that which is won by 'self-effort.' The souls of human beings, particularly women, are chained to the earth through the comforts of home and land and limited love, and until you learn to break those chains for higher knowledge, you will continue to suffer."

She had reminded David that women are cleverer than men —which he repeated with a straight face. He sure took Mayan seriously.

In another session, Mayan had described science as the handmaiden of God. But she said that science had so advanced technology on Earth that it had outstripped our ability to cope with it to the point where technology had become totally life-threatening; that we actually needed to dismantle our nuclear fission plants and concentrate research resources on solving the problems of danger-

ous technological wastes of all kinds. Even technology, she said, is not a bad thing—it is how you use it and what you use it for: as an example she had cited the sun as a limitless source of energy which we should learn to store and utilize. Then science, through technology, would serve both man and Earth.

Mayan continually emphasized that in all of the cosmos, nothing was valued as highly as one living soul, and in the value of one living soul lay the value of the entire cosmos. She said that humankind follows a spiral projection upward, that although it may appear we are not progressing, that is in fact not true. With each rebirth and afterlife reflection, humankind finds itself on a higher plane, whether we realize it or not. And, she said, with each individual soul's progression, the machinery and the movement of the entire cosmos is affected, because each individual soul is *that* important.

She said that man has a habit of reducing his understanding to the perceptions of his own mind, that it is difficult for us to break through our own frames of reference and allow our imaginations to take quantum leaps into other dimensions, transcending the limits imposed on us by lifetimes of structured thinking.

❀ We had been in the Andes now for two-and-a-half weeks. It seemed two-and-a-half years. To say my point of view had been altered was obvious. I could feel it in everything I thought. I felt as though my own potential was opening up. Now, I thought, if I could only hang on to it when I returned to earth! And I wondered whether my new point of view would also change my life.

We took side trips to Ataura every few days for tape batteries, paper, pens, and just to see crowds of people. We didn't see any rioting, but police were everywhere. When I shopped in the small, dusty food markets, the fruit and vegetables were not fresh and the prices were outrageous. Fifty-nine cents for an apple. Small tape

recorders were $450.00 and prices for other electrical hardware appliances would have been exorbitant even for a thriving economy: no wonder there were incipient rebels all over the place. Prices were astronomical and salaries low. There were few Americans visible, mostly college students on treks through the Andes.

At the Sunday fair in Ataura people came from hundreds of miles away to sell wares that included everything from antique Victrolas to goats. We ate rice and beans, and I didn't care whether the onions sprinkled on top gave me heartburn or not. We continued to hear people in shops and restaurants talk about UFOs. David translated and it seemed that each person had had some kind of UFO experience, describing cigar-shaped craft out of which flew discs, or just discs alone.

Nearly everyone had a story about the Huaytapallana Ice Peaks. Either they seemed on fire at certain times "with the sky lighting up," or formations of craft were seen above them. There didn't seem to be much fear running through the related experiences, only awe. And everyone who had seen a UFO believed the craft belonged to beings from outer space.

We were sitting in the heartburn cafe on my last day in the Andes. I was scheduled to leave for New York from Lima at six o'clock the next morning. Looking out at the Ice Peaks, David got up, plucked a daisy from the vase on the table, put it behind his ear, and went to buy a Spanish newspaper. I saw his face drop when he read the headlines.

"There's been a big blackout in New York City," he said, "and lots of people went 'free shopping.' "

"Free shopping?" I asked.

"Looting," he said.

"My God," I said, "was anybody hurt or killed or anything?"

He read on. "No," he said, "the system just broke down. Like it does everywhere. Now there'll be a big clamor for more law and order and racism will be a big thing again, I guess, because most of the people who went on the shopping spree weren't white."

My mind flashed to my friend Bella Abzug. She would be gearing up her campaign for mayor right about now. I wondered if she'd win or whether she should have stayed in the House of Representatives. She lost the Senate race by half a percentage point and most people believed she was the front runner for mayor.

I told David what I was thinking and how I loved Bella and how I hoped she'd be effective if she won.

"I like her too," he said. "You always know where you stand with Bella. I guess I could say the people who don't like Bella are the people I don't like."

I nodded, thinking of her strong personality and of how I might help her in her campaign if I were in New York.

"God, I wonder if Bella will really win," I said. "I wonder if the Liberal wing of the Democratic party in New York will fragment itself again, or whether they'll really let her win this time."

David chewed on his daisy. "Want to ask someone?" he asked.

"What do you mean?"

"Well, there's a woman up here who's a famous psychic. She's been uncanny with me. Let's go ask her about Bella."

"What the hell," I said. "I might as well know what I'm getting into when I go back to New York."

✹ David drove to a house on the edge of town nestled into the side of the mountains. It was modest and white stucco. There were wild flowers growing against the walls.

A young girl answered the door and welcomed David as though she knew him. He explained that we'd like to see her mother. She nodded and said her mother had been working on her Sanskrit texts all morning.

"Sanskrit?" I asked. "What is a Peruvian woman in the Andes doing with Sanskrit?"

"She doesn't understand either," said David. "She's never had

any education in Sanskrit, doesn't consciously know how to read it or write it, but she goes into a trance and the automatic writing starts to flow through her fingers. Something like the way Mohammed wrote the Koran, except that he was illiterate."

"You mean," I asked, "that some kind of inner voice inspires her to write down stuff she doesn't know anything about?"

"Yes," said David. "She says she has no control over it. It commands her at all sorts of odd hours. So she finds herself, even in the dark, writing long passages of spiritual teachings in a language that she doesn't recognize."

"Have these passages been verified?" I asked.

"Oh sure," he said, "she's known to be one of the world's renowned experts on Sanskrit, but nobody understands how. Historians and language scholars on Sanskrit from all over the world have verified that what she is writing is real. She says she doesn't want to understand it as long as it helps people."

We waited in a clean and Spartan hallway for Maria.

When she appeared, I was struck by how plain and middle-class Peruvian she looked. A print dress clung to her broad hips and she waddled as she walked in scuffed shoes with thick heels run down on the outside. Her face was open and friendly and her hair bore the remnants of an old permanent.

She greeted David with an embrace and, holding my arm, ushered us into her well-kept living room with a glass-topped coffee table and furniture from Sears and Roebuck, Lima branch.

She spoke only Spanish which David translated.

"How can I be of help?" she asked.

David looked at me. "Do you want to ask her about Bella?"

"Sure."

I ran through the background on Bella once more and he translated to Maria.

She reached out her hand and said, "Could I please hold something that you wear all the time?"

"Why?" I asked.

"Because," she said, "I need to touch your energy vibrations."

I reached up and took off my diamond heart necklace that I wore during the filming of *The Turning Point* and had worn ever since.

Maria fondled the necklace in her right hand and closed her eyes and seemed to "feel" its vibrations.

"You are a good friend of the woman in question," she said.

I nodded.

"And she is in a competition to win a position of leadership in your New York City." She was making statements rather than asking me.

I nodded again.

Maria's eyes opened.

"No," she said, "I don't see her winning this competition. I see instead a man with a bald head and long fingers."

I looked over at David in confusion. I didn't know who she could be talking about. She clearly knew nothing about New York politics and was operating on some other kind of imagery.

"Are you sure?" I asked. "There must be some mistake. I don't know who you are describing, and I know the people who have declared their candidacy. So, something doesn't fit."

"This person has not declared himself yet," she responded.

I felt a drop of perspiration trickle down my midriff and changed the subject.

I asked her about the movies I might make. She answered by saying I had already made a good one which would win awards and was beautiful because it revolved around the world of the ballet (*The Turning Point* had not yet been released).

I sat quietly for a moment.

"I also see a man standing by a window," she said. "He gazes into white snow and understands that it is impossible for you to be together."

I blinked and coughed softly to myself.

"He has thought a great deal about it, but cannot see his way clear to be with you. I hope you understand what I refer to."

I didn't want to talk anymore about myself.

"What about Bella?" I asked.

Maria looked over at me with sad, round eyes.

"Your woman will not win," she said. "She won't even be in the running. A bald man with long fingers whom no one has yet considered will be victorious."

I stood up with Maria. She obviously had other things to do. I thanked her. She was warm and sad. She hooked my necklace around my neck for me and said she would be happy to see me again if I wanted. She embraced us and we left.

I was upset with what she had said—mostly because she had seemed so sure.

"How could she be so definite?" I asked David as we headed toward the car, a slight drizzle of rain falling, slowly making the mountain town a mass of mud.

"I don't know," he answered. "Just wait and see. Maybe she's wrong. But I have to admit that's rare." He shivered a little and gestured toward the car. I walked with him, unable to think of much to say. He started the car and we headed for Llocllapampa. David was silent and I respected my reluctance to break into his thoughts, but I wondered again about the string of "coincidence" which had marked the growth of the very special and dear relationship we shared. Every word he spoke now took on hidden meaning. *Why* had he come along in the first place? He had absolutely nothing to gain from knowing me—in fact, ten years ago he had come and gone as a stranger, leaving the Masai stones with me to remind us both, it seems, that that was not a simple accident.

I thought of all I had learned because of him . . . the adventurous wonder of his Mayan, whoever she was . . . the world of the spirit she and he had introduced me to . . . their reminders that the big mysteries of life were there to solve if we would only look

. . . of the books David had suggested I read . . . of the dozens of people here to whom UFOs were commonplace. I tried to piece it all together: the sessions with Ambres, with McPherson and John, worlds apart but saying the same thing . . . the continual connections of God and spirit and love and karma and other worlds and Cosmic Justice and basic kindness and spiritual enlightenment and Jesus and flying machines and the Golden Rule and advanced civilizations and "gods" who came in chariots of fire and people throughout human history who had performed unexplained miracles.

Was it all beginning to make sense? Perhaps humans *were* a part of an overall cosmic plan that had been in effect for thousands and thousands of years? Could it even be that people who claimed to have had trips in spacecraft were telling the truth—even though their stories ended up in the *National Enquirer*? No, that would really be too much . . . But what was I going to do about all this? Would anybody believe me if I were to write about it? Was that why David had come into my life? He had said I would be able to risk humiliation if I really believed what I had learned. But then he said my credibility wouldn't be damaged if people believed I was sincere. Well, I was. But I had this horrible jellylike feeling about *what* it was I was sincere about . . .

On toward Llocllapampa we drove. I thought about packing my suitcase quickly so we could enjoy the sunset before leaving for Lima. But when we got there, a Peruvian man dressed in a uniform was waiting outside our hotel. David turned to me and said, "A friend of mine will drive you down the mountain. He doesn't speak English, but he's reliable. You'll make your plane for New York. I'm going to stay here for a while."

My stomach fell to my feet. I wanted to cry. "Wait a minute," I said, "just like that? I'm leaving and you're staying here? I want to talk some more. Why are you staying?"

He looked at me. "I don't have to get back. You do. That's all. Just think about everything that's happened over the last few

weeks. Absorb it slowly. It's just the beginning for you. You need time alone now. I would think you'd better get back to your real life just to ground yourself. You have your notes and your tapes and a million books to read and investigations to investigate. Do it. You've thought a lot and learned a lot. Now it's better for you to be on your own."

The tears welled in my eyes. I didn't know what to say. He reached over and took my hand. "Look at that sky," he said. "Is that freedom or is that freedom? Now go on and pack."

I eased myself into my cold dark room for the last time. As I stuffed my clothes and tapes and notes into my suitcase, I longed for another mineral bath. I wouldn't hear the pigs snorting in the mountain silence that night. I wouldn't brush my teeth in the orange river in the morning. I wouldn't walk in the mountain afternoon again. I wouldn't be with David anymore. I hadn't really speculated about the future at all, and suddenly it was in my lap.

❋ When I finished packing, I walked out into the setting sun. The lady with no teeth was waiting at the Plymouth with my ring watch. I looked at David: he shrugged and smiled. I took the watch, put it in the palm of her hand and closed her fingers over it. I nodded and smiled over her voluble delight and turned back to David.

Very gently he pinched my chin and kind of waggled it a bit. I grabbed his hand in both of mine and held on hard. "Am I supposed to go now? Just like that? Just *leave*?"

"Yes." Holding my hand he walked me to my side of the Plymouth. I looked around at the purple-hued mountains. With one arm he hugged my shoulders as he opened the car door. "We'll see each other again. I promise. Trust me. Remember we've been together through many lives, right?"

I scratched the back of my neck and tried not to cry. I climbed

in as his friend put my suitcase in the back seat. David slammed the door and leaned in to me.

"I love you," he said. "And remember nothing is more important than love."

I felt an unbearable ache in my throat. I could hardly speak for fear of losing complete control. "Yes," I choked. "I don't understand but I love you too."

"Good," he said. "Now go get 'em. That's all . . . it's simple. Be yourself, don't be afraid, and love the world."

His friend turned on the ignition and stepped on the gas. We pulled away from the town that wasn't a town. I didn't look back, but I could feel David waving, his left shoulder slumped as he stood watching us go.   ❋

"... what marvellous deepening of emotional power may be gained with the recognition of the idea of pre-existence ... we learn that we have been living in a hemisphere only, that we have been thinking half-thoughts, that we need a new faith to join past with future over the great parallel of the present, and so to round out our emotional world to a perfect sphere."

—Lafcadio Hearn
Kokoro

❋   The man driving said something in Spanish and I nodded and smiled and was relieved I couldn't talk to him.

I tried to ease the ache in my throat by drinking in the familiar countryside. Down the Andes we wound, past the mining towns, past the herds of llamas, past the women dressed in wide-brimmed white starched hats, past the UFO signpost at the railway crossing.

The air became dustier, less rarefied, thicker, easier to breathe but not as heady. The sun fell behind the mountains behind us. Chugging up the other side of the steep winding roads we passed empty trucks that would be full of coal and iron ore and rock when they descended again a day later.

My mind tumbled with images: bubbling sulphur water, hot languid mountain grass, the orange river, the peasant mountain people chewing coke leaves for energy, confusing talks with David in the sunlight. I dozed.

I woke with a jolt at a break in the road. Night had fallen completely now and the Peruvian stars glistened like chunks of low-flying crystal. My Peruvian driver drove stolidly on.

Driving into Lima was like entering a backward world. I tried not to look. Squatters' huts lined the roadside. People walked aimlessly. Factories spewed dirty smoke into the already filthy night air. Clouds hung over the city, wet and thick and putrid, obscuring the glistening beauty of the other world above.

I felt a chill and put on my Ralph Lauren butter-leather coat to prepare for New York. The man stopped in front of Varig Airlines and helped me with my suitcase. I thanked him and thought better than to give him money. We shook hands and he smiled and drove off in the old jalopy that had been like a home in the mountains.

I checked in and went right to the plane. Two hours out of Lima, at an altitude of 35,000 feet, I saw an electrical storm on the horizon that looked as though the Kingdom of Heaven was clashing against itself. The lightning splashed the sky pure white like blazing daylight for as far as I could see. The colossal power of the electricity made me cower in my seat feeling as insignificant as a flea. Nothing seemed to be as powerful as nature. Except, according to David, and Mayan, and John, and Ambres, and McPherson, and Cat, and Cayce, and—I now realized—many, many others, nothing was as powerful as the *collective* human mind, that infinitely elastic web of strength called human consciousness, and represented by the communal energy people re-

ferred to as their souls. It seemed to me that there were endless worlds for me to explore. And I *wanted* to, I really wanted to know.

Maybe one could never physically prove whether the soul existed or not. I wasn't sure that that even mattered. Perhaps reality was only what one believed it to be anyway. That would make all perceived realities real. Maybe that was the lesson I was learning —learning *to think with unlimitedness* . . . to believe that anything is possible . . . to believe that one can do anything, soar anywhere, *become everything*. Maybe one human soul *was everything*. And such a reality was up to each of us to relearn.

Maybe the tragedy of the human race was that we had forgotten we were each Divine. And if we re-realized that, we could dispel fear from our lives. In dispelling fear, we could dispel hate. And much more. With the fear we would rid ourselves of greed and war and killing. Fear was the root and circle around which our lives revolved—fear of failure, fear of pain, fear of humiliation, fear of loneliness, of being unloved, of ourselves, fear of death, ultimately fear of fear. Fear itself was insidious, infectious, seeping in from one point of unreality to permeate all our lives. Perhaps our belief in death was the gravest unreality of all. If we could truly know that we never really died, that we always got another chance, that no pain, no humiliation, no loss, was ever final, total and forever, maybe we could understand that there was nothing to fear. It could be that human beings were using their talent for complexity as an excuse to avoid the responsibility for being what we really understood we were from the beginning—basically part of what we called "God," and without limitation, masters of our own divine potential.

I sat quietly tense, held in place by the seat-belt—man's answer to the electrical storm exploding around us. The airplane shook and bobbed violently in the stupefying display of dazzling, raw, natural power visible from every window. What was night outside had become a thunderously electrified daylight, flash after blazing

flash revealing clouds and colors and an astral terrain of currents and rains whirling and raging around our small craft. No one spoke. No one screamed. As far as I could tell, no one cried. We had no choice. It was moments like this, I thought, that forced one to think and stretch one's awareness beyond what we had been taught. It was moments like this, maybe too few and far between, that acted as a catalyst for our understanding a little better the internal control of which we were really capable. No one in the airplane could fight the storm. No one could overcome it. No one could really even understand it. It just *was*. And this elemental crisis had brought us all together, sharing without a word having been spoken.

I determined to relax, beginning with my feet. Then I worked my way up, through ankles, legs, arms, hands, solar plexus, and chest. It worked. I began to feel I was part of the bobbing, creaking plane. My breathing came more evenly. My heart stopped beating so fast. The perspiration on my midriff and forehead cooled. Then I stopped and realized I had controlled my fear by using the mind to control the body . . . a positive mind insisting on not being afraid. And what was controlling my mind? I can only say it was my soul. My soul knew it was going to be all right, no matter what happened to the body. My soul—my own, subconscious, individualized piece of the universal energy—believed it was a part of everything, even of the crashing, tumultuous storm outside. My soul knew it would survive, that it was eternal, that it was ongoing and unlimited in its understanding that this, too, was part of the adventure we call life.

At peace and exhausted, I fell asleep. ❀

Chapter 26

"This day before dawn I ascended a hill and look'd at the
crowded heaven.
And I said to my spirit, When we become the enfolders of those
orbs, and the pleasure and knowledge of everything
in them, shall we be fill'd and satisfied then?
And my spirit said, No, we but level that lift to pass and
continue beyond.
You are also asking me questions and I hear you,
I answer that I cannot answer, you must find out for yourself."

—Walt Whitman
Song of Myself

When I arrived in New York I met with Bella immediately. It was her birthday and her campaign staff threw a fundraising party at Studio 54.

Bella knew I had been in Peru, and I told her I had been meditating in a hut in the Andes. She had read my books and believed I was capable of any kind of weird adventure. In any case, it was not the time for a talk together. I told her I had had a good rest in my mud hut and she laughed, rolling her eyes, and then plunged into her campaign strategy just to return to a familiar kind of insanity.

I watched intently, waiting for something that would confirm or deny what Maria in the Andes had said. Bella's losing campaign for the mayoralty of New York is now history. She never even made it to the runoffs. Ed Koch, that tall, balding fellow with the long fingers, won, hands down.

I wished I had asked Maria more questions.

❋   With the accumulation of the events that led up to my trip to Peru and the events in Peru itself, I began to lead a life beneath the life that was obvious to most of my friends. I made my films, danced and sang in my television specials, and toured with my live show. I was still reasonably active in the women's movement, politics and human rights, but I found that I really preferred to travel and think.

The relationship with Gerry cooled, and ended. With my new perspectives, it did indeed feel like something from another life . . .

I loved traveling because it helped me gain a more accurate and objective view of the world as well as of myself. I went all over Europe, Scandinavia, Southeast Asia, Japan, Australia, Canada, Mexico, and to many cities in America.

And the more I traveled, the more I learned about the spiritual dimensions of life that I was growing to understand. My own convictions were taking shape and being confirmed wherever I went.

I found that the theory of the progression of souls through the process of reincarnation had become part of new age thought systems, not only in California, but all over the Western world. Over casual conversations it would come out. And whenever I pursued it more seriously, I found that people were thirsty to compare notes on their feelings about past-life recall and spiritual consciousness. They usually concluded by saying it was good to have a serious dialogue on such theories with someone who didn't believe they were crazy. Some of the people were just regular citizens in their respective countries. But others held high-level positions of influence in political and journalistic circles. The latter were careful to hold their beliefs close to their vests and felt saddened by the need to do so.

Yet I did not want to be talking to myself, as it were. I wanted and needed opposition, criticism, questioning. I searched for it first

in my reading and found the strongest skeptics were among those with the most serious beliefs. I don't know why it surprised me. People to whom spirituality and higher consciousness are truly important most particularly do *not* want to be taken in by fakes, charlatans, self-deluded prophets, or parlor mystics. I found that searching experiments had been conducted, sometimes over periods of many years, and certainly in all areas of psychic phenomena.

The literature on the whole subject was vast—almost overwhelming—dating back to the ancient Sumerian cuneiform tablets, and down the centuries through Egyptian records, the Greek oracles, Hindu scriptures, the Druidic tradition, Essene literature, the records of secret societies such as the Free Masons, and many more; all the way to the writings of Carl Jung and even more recent parapsychological investigations. The quest, and the point of view, was always to recognize the potential for expanded consciousness in man in order to enable him to live more fully and peacefully *with and through* his spiritual dimension.

Along with my reading, I questioned many different kinds of people about their beliefs. Time and again the strongest prejudice I encountered was firmly entrenched in the minds of those who thought of themselves as intellectual pragmatists. These were people who had a kind of knee-jerk reaction to mere words like psychic, astral, spiritual dimension, and could not get beyond a conditioned reflex.

After a while, I began to see that there was another kind of rejection of spiritual values, a rejection which was a real need in certain people. They had come to terms with this world just as it is, accepting the wonder and joy that life on earth offers, accepting as well the horror, pain, and agony. Courageously, such people embraced the whole, willing and eager to go the limit, but always within the compass that this life is all there is. A whole additional dimension which might—or might not—be crucial to their ills and joys was just the additional straw they could not, did not, want to

cope with. Again, it was a view I could well understand. Enough is enough, after all. And yet . . .

And yet everywhere I went, I continually encountered a deep need for spirituality and expanded consciousness, a need for people to come together, to share their energies in *something* that worked. I found people had had experiences similar to mine: people involved with trance channeling, past life recall, growing spiritual awareness, and even contact with UFOs. I found spiritual communities, such as Findhorn, were springing up all over the world. I visited and stayed at several.

I wondered whether coming into the Aquarian Age (as the astrologers and astronomers called it) also meant that we were coming into an age of Love and Light. Those were the two words most often used to characterize the feelings attached to the new age discoveries. Some of the world's leaders spoke in spiritual terms—Pierre Trudeau urged a "conspiracy of love" for humanity. Zbigniew Brzezinski spoke of an "increasing yearning for something spiritual" in a world of technology where materialism had proven unsatisfying. The spiritual urge, then, knew no politics, as I supposed it never had. Nor was the urge to transcend the material plane of existence new, either.

I went back and read more about the American transcendentalist movement. Some of the people involved in that movement were Ralph Waldo Emerson, Henry Thoreau, Bronson Alcott (father to Louisa M., of *Little Women* fame) and dozens of others. They had been rebels against over-intellectualism and the linear custom of believing only what one could see or prove. They found this both limiting and ultimately wasteful since within these bounds man's full potential could never be developed. They believed that the real essentials were invisible, untouchable—*but not unreal.*

In fact, interestingly enough, even the American Revolution itself was conceived and initiated by men whose belief in the spiritual world was an integrated part of their lives. As I reread some

of that period of American history, I realized how much we had forgotten, how *metaphysically* bold those revolutionaries had been. Our forefathers—Thomas Jefferson, Thomas Paine, John Adams, Benjamin Franklin, George Washington—all were transcendentalists.

The significance of their beliefs emerged all over the Great Seal of America, on the reverse of which the legend reads, "A New Order of Ages Begins," along with the third eye which also appears at the top of the Great Pyramid of Giza on the dollar bill! All of this symbolism was designated by our transcendentalist founders at the birth of the United States.

I began to read more about these men and realized how deeply they threatened the older orders of the time with their new thinking. The transcendentalists drew not only from Quaker and Puritan traditions, but also from German and Greek philosophers, as well as from Eastern religions. When they were accused of having contempt for history, they replied that humankind should be liberated from history. They believed that all observation was relative. They saw *through* their eyes, not *with* their eyes.

All pointed out that *inner reform must precede social reform.* Continually they emphasized the need for personal transformation, but as the American Revolution moved into the Industrial Revolution, the transcendentalists found themselves increasingly isolated and misunderstood. Technology and machines were on the minds of Americans.

They came to be known as occultists and began to operate more within their own circles. By the end of the nineteenth century, the worst fears of our founding fathers had been realized. We were now fully on the path of materialism—our spiritual heritage overwhelmed by industrialization, history books barely mentioning our mystical beginnings.

But the spiritual support system of our revolutionary forefathers had taken hold in art and in literature.

William Blake, for example, considered the American and

French revolutions as only the first steps toward a worldwide spiritual revolution.

Just as Blake had been influenced by the German mystic and writer and philosopher Jacob Boehme and by Emanuel Swedenborg, Blake now influenced writers and artists and politicians for years to come: Nathaniel Hawthorne, Emily Dickinson, Herman Melville, John Dewey, Thoreau, Gandhi, Martin Luther King—all deeply believed in metaphysical dimensions that would ultimately explain the mystery of life.

I read and read and talked more and more freely to people about my experiences in spiritual search. Many others seemed to be searching also for a balance between their inner lives and their outer lives. Many of them attended spiritual channelings, seeking answers from the "other side."

Studio executives, bank presidents, journalists, actors and actresses, musicians, writers, househusbands and housewives attended the spiritual channelings that I had been introduced to. No one questioned the validity of the process anymore. They only wrestled with the information they received—past-life information, psychological information, dietary information, medical and scientific information: information about Atlantis, Lemuria, the creation of the cosmos, extraterrestrials . . . everything one could think of to ask. The spiritual entities (not in the body) became their friends and confidants. People discussed their personalities, their humor, their understanding, as if they were physically present.

As I talked with the hundreds who came to these sessions, I realized they were more comfortable and open with each other than with those in their lives who had not recognized the need for spirituality. This was not a religious feeling. Not at all. It was simply that to be without spiritual awareness was like being without arms and legs. Some had skeptical questions when they found the going rough. But all of the people I talked to just kept going. They told me about the predictions that had been channeled that had come to pass. They told me how some of the past-life informa-

tion had altered their perspectives on their present lives. They told me how vacant the lives of friends seemed to be who did not share their search—to whom they could not speak in spiritual terms.

They were not at all close-mouthed when I questioned them, but all said they found it difficult to relate to others who did not understand. They went about their daily lives with the knowledge and support that they had each other, but mostly they derived great happiness and joy from the fact that they were getting more in touch with their own spiritual selves. Some of their relationships and long friendships eventually foundered because their spiritual beliefs and values could not be shared and they could not abide the cynical and intellectual limitations of the past. Some said they found it necessary to lead two lives—for fear of threatening those they loved.

At the same time science was having its own struggle. I read in *The New York Times* that scientists had been forced to come around to the "big bang" theory of the creation of the universe. It looked as though the theologians had been right after all. The Bible had called the shot and the scientists were having to admit it. The universe had been created by a colossal explosion all at once, "in one moment of time," about twenty billion years ago. The astronomical and scientific and biblical accounts of Genesis all concided now, much to the dismay of most scientists, who found it "irritating," to say the least. The universe was expanding in some places as fast as one hundred million miles an hour. That meant *there had been a beginning.*

So the question the scientists posed was, "What came before the beginning?" They were concluding now that, "There must have been a Divine Will constituting nature from nothingness."

So perhaps a theological explanation might hold an answer. Scientists had been able to trace the origins of humanity on the planet, the chemical ingredients of life itself, the formation of stars out of primal mists: but now they had hit a solid barrier. An article (by the scientist Robert Jastrow, Director of NASA's Goddard

Institute for Space Studies) said, "For the scientist who has lived by his faith in the power of reason, the story ends like a bad dream. He has scaled the mountains of ignorance, he is about to conquer the highest peak; as he pulls himself over the final rock, he is greeted by a band of theologians who have been sitting there for centuries."

✿ It seemed as though the whole world was rushing toward a confrontation with itself. In the last hundred years we had progressed farther and faster than in all the time preceding, most particularly in the areas of technology, matched only by the various scientific disciplines, fairly bursting with new discoveries. And this rapid growth was very much ongoing. People now living remembered a wholly different world, one they had experienced in their childhood, when life moved at the pace it took to walk to your neighbor's for company; while others, now living, had been raised in the age of television and telephone communication, a computer-wise generation to whom reading was difficult and writing awkward.

The energy packed into this period by the acceleration of discovery on all fronts had altered time. We were experiencing a form of time dilation, the kind of adrenaline-induced, stretched-out feeling that occurs in a moment of sharp crisis: but this dilation, this crisis, was on a massive scale, confronting us daily in every aspect of our lives. No wonder that more and more people were turning to the dimension of the spirit, seeking a wholeness that had been lost in the maelstrom of energy vibrating through their lives. The more intense their living became, the more they needed to control those energies.

Now, it seemed to me, this search, this sense of spiritual dimension, this turning to a source for inner strength was inevitable, a process of humanity catching up with itself, an acceleration of

spiritual discovery beginning to match the energy of discovery in other areas. More, spiritual discovery seemed to me an essential component if we were not to become disoriented by the other energies we were releasing. We needed that centered calm, the inward certainty that relaxes and concentrates our vitality so that we can direct our own energies, not have them merely react with an adrenal response to outside stimuli.

As my spiritual interests and experiences increased, I wrote more and more about it. At first, this was mainly for myself. It helped me to clarify what I thought, and besides, I have always liked to write about what I was up to. What I had always liked now had an added dimension. My whole life was beginning to light up for me, but sometimes I'd wonder how readers would respond to what I was putting down on paper if I were ever to put it into a book. (By now, I needed no spiritual guides to inform me on the likely reactions of many intellectuals I know—of all those without even the leaven of personal friendship to soften their views. Nor could I really hold it against them. But I was sick and tired of dead-end philosophy—and I didn't want to give up on the human race.)

✳ As for myself in the here and now, I had arrived at some kind of crossroads. I still had to deal with my private fear of writing about this material from the new point of view of belief. So what could a person do when confronted—although it had been a gradual confrontation—with understanding that the life they had led up to that point was only *part* of the truth? I never had been one to shut off about anything. I wasn't about to do so now. As far as going public was concerned, I had gone public on politics, on women's rights, on social change, on war and on what I believed to be injustice. I *was public*. That was my character. I was not used to holding back what interested me or what I believed in. I had thought a lot about that during every phase of my life. I had grown

up in public. I had made my mistakes in public. I had been right and wrong in public. I had laughed and cried in public, been in love in public, written in public, apologized in public, and now, I thought, I suppose I will have to say what I think about human and extraterrestrial spirituality in public. Well, so be it.

I talked it over with Bella, as I had a tendency to do about things that counted. I had long since told her everything that had happened in Peru. She knew that I was continuing to pursue my new concepts; that I was working with channelers, healers, and meditation; reading classics; visiting psychic centers and the like; and trying to expand and raise my own conscious awareness of dimensions that might be presently beyond our understanding.

Now I tried to explain that the political solutions she was involved in seemed to be resulting in the same failures they had in the past, and that maybe it was time for all of us in the world to take a look at life from another perspective. We were sitting in an all-night restaurant in Manhattan after having seen yet another movie that exploited violence and fear.

"We can't go on like this," I said. "We're all scared and frightened. We can blow the planet apart any day. Life in any case seems to be falling apart around us, and the only solutions we can come up with are more law and order and more military spending."

"So?" she said, with one of her penetrating looks. "So? What's your solution?"

"Well," I hesitated. "Well, look. For starters, I think we have all become slaves to our own fear. We keep *expecting* that we'll run into bad trouble to the point where we almost get a sense of satisfaction when things do turn to crap."

Bella put her hands in her lap and stared at her midnight salad. "Yeah, well," she said, "so things turn to crap. That's what politicians have to deal with."

"Could it be that they're so busy coping with the mess that they don't take the time to figure out how to turn it off?"

Bella shrugged. "This isn't something you can argue from gen-

eralities. You've had enough to do with politics to know that. So what is it you're getting at?"

"Fear, Bella. Fear. Fear of death; fear of self-made holocaust; fear of the future, or fear that we won't have one because we are literally, for the first time in history, capable of destroying the world; fear of much smaller things like losing our jobs, or our families, or the regard of friends and neighbors . . ."

"Now, wait a minute. Being afraid is perfectly natural—in some situations it's downright healthy. Mankind wouldn't have got where it has without fear."

"Okay, right. But by the same token, mankind wouldn't have got where it has if it had always let fear dictate its actions. I'm not saying it's wrong to be afraid, but that it's dangerous to let fear control our lives. Plus the very important fact that, to me now, most of these fears are unnecessary."

"How come?"

"Well, frankly Bella, to me, being certain about the actual existence of the soul, I mean as a reality, has made all the difference. It's not something I came to easily. But that's where I am now, so I believe that everyone has, or rather *is*, a soul, of divine origin, and one that has lived many times before and will live again."

"Oh," she said, twisting her hands, "we should just sit back and leave it all to cosmic design or something?"

"No," I said. "I wouldn't put it that way. I guess that it is really a question of tending to one's own self and the people we come in contact with as kindly and tolerantly as possible, knowing that what we put out will come back. I guess I'm saying that each of us has to start with ourselves, because that's all that we can really control in the first place."

"Does that mean you're opting out of involvement in politics, the women's liberation movement and everything?"

"No way. On the contrary. If anything, I'm going to be even more concerned and involved."

"So, what's different then?"

"What's different is how I *feel* about it. I'm looking at the whole thing from a new perspective, one that doesn't include fear. Fear is what has turned us all off, alienated us from ourselves and from each other. So many people are indifferent, apathetic—my God, you know yourself what a struggle it is to get the voting population to the polls. A helluva lot of people are simply too afraid to care, or believe that it wouldn't make any difference if they did. They don't realize that it is *themselves* they don't *dare* care about; it's *themselves* they're opting out on. Instead, they bitch about what the other guy is doing. It always comes back to the individual. Yet they're the ones who, out of fear, shut themselves off. All other life, on earth anyway, flourishes with 'feelings.' Feeling, *caring*, has become our most precious missing dimension. As far as I'm concerned, non-believers in spirituality, the soul, reincarnation, whatever, can start right there, by letting their imaginations help them to care; and if they never got any further, the world would still be a better place. But what I myself really believe is that if each of us could rid ourselves of fear by honestly understanding our own spirituality, by acknowledging it and achieving a higher awareness, that the ripple effect would be astonishing."

"I don't know what you mean. Give me an example," said Bella. "I mean, with the world going the way it is, *who* is an example of that?"

I thought a moment, and almost involuntarily I said, "Anwar Sadat, for one, or Martin Luther King, or Buddha, or Christ, or Mother Teresa, or Gandhi. All these people personally believed in a higher cosmic design which enabled them to take up a positive belief in human potential. They emphasized the positive. Also, Thomas Jefferson, Thoreau, Voltaire—and a lot more."

"Yeah," said Bella. "But what are you saying they believed in?"

"A kind of higher harmony; that they were part of a larger design that was not related only to *this* life experience."

"Are you saying that they all believed in reincarnation?"

I sipped my red wine, remembering all that I had read on the founding fathers of the American revolution; their involvement with mystical sects and teachings, and the existence of the soul.

"Not necessarily," I said. "But Jefferson and Washington and Ben Franklin—in fact, most of the men who signed the Bill of Rights and drew up the Constitution, said they wanted to form a new republic based on spiritual values. And those values they believed in went all the way back to the beliefs of Hindu scriptures and Egyptian mysticism. That's why they put the pyramid on the dollar bill—in fact, the dollar and the Great Seal are full of spiritual symbols that link way back to long before the revolution. And all those pre-Christian beliefs had to do with reincarnation."

"Show me the research," said Bella.

"Of course I will. I just mention it because they were our original politicians, yet none of the people in politics these days seem to even know the origins of their democracy. I can see that they're distracted because everything is in such a mess, but if some of them did acquaint themselves with what our forefathers actually intended, if they could identify with the early principles, that might influence how they vote now and what priorities they find most important. They might even manage to stop the destructive course we're on."

Bella lit a cigarette and tossed the match into an ashtray. "So you believe that humans fit into a larger plan than most of us think we do. Our ideas and beliefs are off the mark and that's why we've screwed up the world so badly?"

"Right. Except it's not 'most of us.' Most of the world's people do believe in reincarnation, in a larger plan. It's Westerners who leave out the important part."

"And that important part is what?"

"The pre-existence of the soul—the fact that we have lived many times and will live many more as the laws of cause and effect work themselves out."

Bella considered awhile, pulled on the cigarette, blew out a deep breath. "Listen," she said, "I was educated in the orthodox Jewish tradition and a deep belief in a spiritual being is not foreign to me." I had never heard her say that before. "But," she went on, "believing in the soul is one thing. Believing in reincarnation of the soul is another. You might be right in what you can sense and what you believe, but I can't go along with it. I'll tell you one thing though—I wish I could."

I felt tears well up in my eyes. "Why, Bella?"

"Because," she said slowly, "then I could believe that everything was going to turn out okay, even if I did nothing about it. I wouldn't have to fight so hard to make things better. Maybe I need the challenge. But, my darling, if people like me didn't fight to do our part it just might not turn out well. You see?"

I blew my nose. "I guess so," I said. "Yes, I see. It could be that all of us have our own roles to play, but the challenge would be there anyway, I think. Or maybe this time around, it's necessary to you to perceive it that way. I know that *I* must have been many different people in many different times. That's why I feel so at home in so many places in the world. I usually feel I've been there before. And I'm just learning to trust these feelings that my intellect might say were ridiculous. The point is, if all this happened to me, then it has to have happened to others. In some strange way we may all know each other. How many times have you met someone and had an instant recognition of what we even call 'a kindred spirit'?"

"Well, yeah." Bella sounded careful. "And you are saying that, from your point of view, you believe that we are all part of each other—and also part of a larger design?"

"Right. That's where disincarnate beings come in. If I lived many lifetimes, then what was I doing between each lifetime? I mean, where was I? If my soul energy went to spend a while in the ether, as the mystical texts suggest, then what would be the difference between me in-between lifetimes and Tom McPherson now

who says he is an entity speaking through Kevin? I mean, maybe there are all kinds of dimensions of reality of which the earth plane is only one."

Bella looked at me searchingly. "What I'm trying to understand," she said, "is how you got into all of this. How did all this happen? I know you and all those other famous and intelligent people who believe as you do weren't bananas. So what is going on?"

I leaned back in my chair. "I don't know, Bellitchka. Maybe life is a cosmic joke on us. We take it all so seriously. We try to legislate morality instead of living it, and go around judging everybody who thinks differently than we do when maybe there is no such thing as one reality. Maybe everything is real—earth plane, astral plane, plain plane, I don't know. I just know that from what I have learned, felt, and read, I can't ignore it. And why should I? Some of the greatest minds this planet has ever seen believed in what I'm just beginning to understand. So I'm going to go on investigating, not only because I'm just plain curious but because it's also making me happy."

Bella smiled. "Okay, that I can go along with. So tell me what difference all this is really making in your life. That's what I'm concerned about."

I thought a bit, trying to find the words that would reassure my friend. Finally I said, "Bella, it's strange, but *knowing* that there is a law of cause and effect in operation makes me very aware of how precious every single moment of every single day can be."

"How does that work?" she questioned.

"Nothing—literally nothing—is insignificant. Every thought, every gesture, everything I say and do, has an energy attached to it which is hopefully positive. In the back of my head I am constantly aware that harmony does exist, I mean, as a real energy, a resource I can draw on. I am aware that everything has a reason for happening. Also, I know that whatever good I can do, whatever fun I can share, whatever contribution I make, even if it's to say 'Good morning!' to someone, will, somewhere, sometime, come

back to me. It's not a matter of making Brownie points. It just feels a whole hell of a lot better in *me*. It gives me a kind of feeling of living in a universal *now*. Every *now* second becomes important. In fact, I think I might be seeing in a—what—a *whole* way, that the past, present and future are interdependent, are really what amounts to the same thing."

"And you're not going to opt out and go away and meditate in a hut?"

I laughed. "No, I promise you, no. I had to stay away while I searched out this stuff. It *has* taken me years to get to this point. But now, well—it's an added dimension, a tremendous joy, a well of energy for me. It means I can be more fully involved than before. But now I don't see life as a battlefield. On the contrary, I believe it can be a paradise, and what's more, we should *expect* it to be. That is reality to me now. Dwelling on the negative simply contributes to its power."

"But my darling, the negative exists. It has to be dealt with, doesn't it?"

"Sure. What I'm saying is that a lot of it exists because we make it so. We *need* to believe in a positive reality right here on earth because the believing will help to make *it* so. That's the real power we have for change. Look, Bella. Use nature as a guidepost. There's no morality or judgment in nature. Sure, animals kill—for food, not because they hate, not for 'sport.' I don't see nature judging our destruction of it. It just disappears if we destroy it. But it comes back again, doesn't it? Maybe in another form? So the real lesson in all of this is that life is eternal regardless of how mindlessly we behave. And I believe that souls, invisible entities, are a part of the cyclical harmony of nature. None of it ever dies; it just changes form. If you want to think of it that way, it could be that *this* is science, not mysticism."

The waitress came with the check.

"Well," said Bella, "I guess you were never able to do anything by halves, were you?"

"Nope. I guess not. And I guess that what I'm really getting at is to be whole. For the first time in my life I'm beginning to understand what being whole really means. Particularly when it involves the recognition of everything you've *ever* been, which leads you to the realization of whom you are now. I don't worry about the past and I don't worry about the future. I think, act, live for the present, which the past created, and which is creating the future. It's like Krishnamurti says—each person is a universe. If you know yourself, you know everything."

"Oh my God," said Bella. "Is that the way you get to be a Senator?"

"I don't know. Is being a Senator better than being you?"

"Are you judging me, Madame Nature?"

I took her hand and patted it. "Sorry. I'm still learning . . ."

❀ We walked out together into the clear Manhattan night. I looked up and searched the stars above us as we strolled together, hand in hand. Neither of us talked. We walked for a few blocks before Bella decided to hail a cab.

"Well, my darling," she said, "maybe there is a way to avoid disaster for the world . . ."

"Hey, Bella," I said, "do you know the etymology of the word 'disaster'?"

"Jesus," she said, "now what?"

"Well, it comes from the Latin word *disastrum* and the Greek word *disastrato*. Broken down, *dis* is defined as 'torn away from or apart from,' and *astrato* means 'the stars.' Therfore a person who is 'disastrato' has been separated from the heavenly bodies or, torn from the stars. He then experiences what the Latin language describes as *disastro*—a disaster."

Bella looked up into the sky, then back at me, and blinked. "I can't deal with it," she said. "Just so long as it's right for you." She

kissed me and I watched her climb into a cab and barrel down Second Avenue.

I walked back to my apartment, looking up until I found the North Star, the Big Dipper, and then the Little Dipper. Then I looked for the Pleiades, the Seven Sisters. I remembered reading about the Pleiades in the Book of Job. I remembered the Pleiadean connections in the research I had done that seemed to indicate a relationship with the Great Pyramid, the Incas, the Mayans, the Greeks, the American Indians, and the East Indians. I stopped again to look up to the Pleiades cluster and tried to imagine, in terms I could understand, how far away those stars really were. Scientists said it was impossible to cross such distances, that one would die of old age before getting there. But wasn't thought faster than the speed of light? Would it ever be possible to travel by the projection of one's own thought? Could thought control and propel physical matter? Maybe that, in the end, would be the connection between the spiritual mind and technology—making the discovery that the power of the spiritual mind is the highest power of all. Learning to work with it would develop an even higher technology. In other words, if we learned to raise our spiritual thought, perhaps we could locate our bodies wherever we desired them to be.

I walked on toward my apartment, thinking of all the human beings who had been so much a part of my new way of thinking. I thought of Bella and what she meant to me with her combustible, challenging personality, so consistently and determinedly intent on making the world a better place.

I thought of Mike and his good-hearted skepticism, of Gerry and his humanitarian political solutions, of Kevin and his shining pure faith, of Cat and Anne Marie and my friends in Sweden who had helped show me another world of reality. Then I thought of David and wondered if I would ever see him again.

Watching the crosstown bus chug to a stop at the corner of my apartment building, I saw a taxi careen around in front of it,

372 · *Shirley MacLaine*

running the red light. And I laughed at the insane, sweet chaos that is Manhattan.

I took a final look at the stars, went upstairs, and found the stones that David had delivered to me from the Masai tribesman years before: stones which I had had set in a pyramidal shape, long before that held any significance for me, long before David meant anything to me or I even knew who he was. I cradled the pyramidal shape in my hand.

Then I sat down and began to draft a book. I wrote until five o'clock the next morning.

Maybe one day I would take a trip to the Pleiades and see what was on the other side. Would it be as full of wonder as the inner journey I was just beginning? ❀

ABOUT THE AUTHOR

SHIRLEY MACLAINE was born and raised in Virginia. She began her career as a Broadway dancer and singer, and made the transition to featured performer when, as an understudy, she took over for Carol Haney in *The Pajama Game*. Soon after, she found herself making movies and television specials. She won five Emmy Awards or her specials and was nominated for five Academy Awards.

She traveled extensively on her own all over the world. Her experiences in Africa, India, the Far East, and in the Hollywood film community formed the basis for her first book, *"Don't Fall Off the Mountain,"* which became a national bestseller and has been translated into eight languages. Soon Ms. MacLaine's career expanded to include political involvement. She was a delegate from California to the 1968 and 1972 Democratic Conventions, and served as co-chairwoman with Bella Abzug for women's issues during George McGovern's presidential campaign. In 1973 she was invited by the Peoples' Republic of China to lead the first American women's delegation to that country to study and film what she saw. The result was a documentary of her visit called *The Other Half of the Sky*, which she wrote, produced, and co-directed, and which was also nominated for an Academy Award. Her second book, *You Can Get There From Here*, described her personal evolution during and after that time spent in China, and also became a bestseller.